Volume II

Intermediate Accounting

17th Edition

DONALD E. KIESO PhD, CPA
Northern Illinois University
DeKalb, Illinois

JERRY J. WEYGANDT PhD, CPA
University of Wisconsin—Madison
Madison, Wisconsin

TERRY D. WARFIELD, PhD
University of Wisconsin—Madison
Madison, Wisconsin

WILEY

DEDICATED TO

Our wives,
Donna, Enid, and Mary, for their love,
support, and encouragement

DIRECTOR AND VICE PRESIDENT	Michael McDonald
SENIOR ACQUISITIONS EDITOR	Emily Marcoux
PRODUCT DESIGNER	Lindsey Myers
EDITORIAL SUPERVISOR	Terry Ann Tatro
SENIOR CONTENT MANAGER	Dorothy Sinclair
SENIOR PRODUCTION EDITOR	Elena Saccaro
DIRECTOR OF MARKETING	Karolina Honsa Zarychta
MARKETING MANAGER	Jenny Geiler
SENIOR DESIGNER	Wendy Lai
EDITORIAL ASSISTANT	Kirsten Loose
COVER IMAGE	© andersphoto/Shutterstock

This book was set in STIX Two Text by Aptara®, Inc. and printed and bound by Quad Graphics/Versailles. The cover was printed by Quad Graphics/Versailles.

Founded in 1807, John Wiley & Sons, Inc. has been a valued source of knowledge and understanding for more than 200 years, helping people around the world meet their needs and fulfill their aspirations. Our company is built on a foundation of principles that include responsibility to the communities we serve and where we live and work. In 2008, we launched a Corporate Citizenship Initiative, a global effort to address the environmental, social, economic, and ethical challenges we face in our business. Among the issues we are addressing are carbon impact, paper specifications and procurement, ethical conduct within our business and among our vendors, and community and charitable support. For more information, please visit our website: www.wiley.com/go/citizenship.

To order books or for customer service, please call 1-800-CALL WILEY (225-5945).

ISBN-13 978-1-119613763

The inside back cover will contain printing identification and country of origin if omitted from this page. In addition, if the ISBN on the back cover differs from the ISBN on this page, the one on the back cover is correct.

Printed in the United States of America

V10011431_062019

Brief Contents

From the Authors

Through many editions, this text has continued to reflect the constant changes taking place in the GAAP environment. This edition continues this tradition, which has become even more significant as the financial reporting environment is exploding with major change. Here are three areas of major importance that are now incorporated extensively into this edition of the text.

> "If this text helps you appreciate the challenges, worth, and limitations of financial reporting, if it encourages you to evaluate critically and understand financial accounting concepts and practice, and if it prepares you for advanced study, professional examinations, and the successful and ethical pursuit of your career in accounting or business in a global economy, then we will have attained our objectives."

CONVERGENCE OF GAAP AND IFRS One of the most important innovations shaping our capital markets was the idea of GAAP. It might be said that it would be even better if we had one common set of accounting rules for the whole world, which would make it easier for international investors to compare the financial results of companies from different countries. Fortunately, GAAP and international accounting standards have converged to result in a number of common standards between GAAP and **International Financial Reporting Standards (IFRS)**. And you have the chance to be on the ground floor as we develop for you the similarities and differences in the two systems that ultimately will be one.

A FAIR VALUE MOVEMENT The FASB believes that fair value information is more relevant to users than historical cost. As a result, there is more information that is being reported on this basis, and even more will occur in the future. The financial press is full of articles discussing how financial institutions must fair value their assets, which has led to massive losses during the financial crisis. In addition, additional insight into the reliability related to fair values is being addressed and disclosed to help investors make important capital allocation decisions. We devote a considerable amount of material that discusses and illustrates fair value concepts in this edition, including its relevance to three major accounting standards updates: revenue, leases, and financial instruments.

A NEW WAY OF LOOKING AT GENERALLY ACCEPTED ACCOUNTING PRINCIPLES (GAAP) Learning GAAP used to be a daunting task, as it is comprised of many standards that vary in form, completeness, and structure. Fortunately, the profession has developed the Financial Accounting Standards Board Codification (often referred to as the Codification). This Codification provides in one place all the GAAP related to a given topic. This textbook is the first to incorporate this Codification—it will make learning GAAP easier and more interesting!

Intermediate Accounting is the market-leading text in providing the tools needed to understand what GAAP is and how it is applied in practice. With this Seventeenth Edition, we strive to continue to provide the material needed to understand this subject area. The text is comprehensive and up-to-date. We also include proven pedagogical tools, designed to help you learn more effectively and to answer the changing needs of this course.

We are excited about *Intermediate Accounting*, Seventeenth Edition. We believe it meets an important objective of providing useful information to educators and students interested in learning about both GAAP and IFRS. Suggestions and comments from users of this text will be appreciated. Please feel free to e-mail any one of us.

Donald E. Kieso
Somonauk, Illinois

Jerry J. Weygandt
Madison, Wisconsin

Terry D. Warfield
Madison, Wisconsin

About the Authors

Don **Kieso**

DONALD E. KIESO, PhD, CPA, received his bachelor's degree from Aurora University and his doctorate in accounting from the University of Illinois. He has served as chairman of the Department of Accountancy and is currently the KPMG Emeritus Professor of Accountancy at Northern Illinois University. He has public accounting experience with Price Waterhouse & Co. (San Francisco and Chicago) and Arthur Andersen & Co. (Chicago) and research experience with the Research Division of the American Institute of Certified Public Accountants (New York). He has done postdoctorate work as a Visiting Scholar at the University of California at Berkeley and is a recipient of NIU's Teaching Excellence Award and four Golden Apple Teaching Awards. Professor Kieso is the author of other accounting and business books and is a member of the American Accounting Association, the American Institute of Certified Public Accountants, and the Illinois CPA Society. He has served as a member of the Board of Directors of the Illinois CPA Society, then AACSB's Accounting Accreditation Committees, the State of Illinois Comptroller's Commission, as Secretary-Treasurer of the Federation of Schools of Accountancy, and as Secretary-Treasurer of the American Accounting Association. Professor Kieso is currently serving on the Board of Trustees and Executive Committee of Aurora University, as a member of the Board of Directors of Kishwaukee Community Hospital, and as Treasurer and Director of Valley West Community Hospital. From 1989 to 1993, he served as a charter member of the National Accounting Education Change Commission. He is the recipient of the Outstanding Accounting Educator Award from the Illinois CPA Society, the FSA's Joseph A. Silvoso Award of Merit, the NIU Foundation's Humanitarian Award for Service to Higher Education, a Distinguished Service Award from the Illinois CPA Society, and in 2003 an honorary doctorate from Aurora University.

Jerry **Weygandt**

JERRY J. WEYGANDT, PhD, CPA, is the Arthur Andersen Alumni Emeritus Professor of Accounting at the University of Wisconsin—Madison. He holds a Ph.D. in accounting from the University of Illinois. Articles by Professor Weygandt have appeared in the *Accounting Review, Journal of Accounting Research, Accounting Horizons, Journal of Accountancy,* and other academic and professional journals. These articles have examined such financial reporting issues as accounting for price-level adjustments, pensions, convertible securities, stock option contracts, and interim reports. Professor Weygandt is author of other accounting and financial reporting books and is a member of the American Accounting Association, the American Institute of Certified Public Accountants, and the Wisconsin Society of Certified Public Accountants. He has served on numerous committees of the American Accounting Association and as a member of the editorial board of the Accounting Review; he also has served as President and Secretary-Treasurer of the American Accounting Association. In addition, he has been actively involved with the American Institute of Certified Public Accountants and has been a member of the Accounting Standards Executive Committee (AcSEC) of that organization. He has served on the FASB task force that examined the reporting issues related to accounting for income taxes and served as a trustee of the Financial Accounting Foundation. Professor Weygandt has received the Chancellor's Award for Excellence in Teaching and the Beta Gamma Sigma Dean's Teaching Award. He is on the board of directors of M & I Bank of Southern Wisconsin. He is the recipient of the Wisconsin Institute of CPA's Outstanding Educator's Award and the Lifetime Achievement Award. In 2001, he received the American Accounting Association's Outstanding Educator Award.

Terry **Warfield**

TERRY D. WARFIELD, PhD, is the PwC Professor in Accounting at the University of Wisconsin—Madison. He received a B.S. and M.B.A. from Indiana University and a Ph.D. in accounting from the University of Iowa. Professor Warfield's area of expertise is financial reporting, and prior to his academic career, he worked for five years in the banking industry. He served as the Academic Accounting Fellow in the Office of the Chief Accountant at the U.S. Securities and Exchange Commission in Washington, D.C. from 1995–1996. Professor Warfield's primary research interests concern financial accounting standards and disclosure policies. He has published scholarly articles in *The Accounting Review, Journal of Accounting and Economics, Research in Accounting Regulation, and Accounting Horizons*, and he has served on the editorial boards of *The Accounting Review, Accounting Horizons*, and *Issues in Accounting Education*. He has served as president of the Financial Accounting and Reporting Section, the Financial Accounting Standards Committee of the American Accounting Association (Chair 1995–1996), and on the AAA-FASB Research Conference Committee. He also served on the Financial Accounting Standards Advisory Council of the Financial Accounting Standards Board and as a trustee of the Financial Accounting Foundation. Professor Warfield has received teaching awards at both the University of Iowa and the University of Wisconsin, and he was named to the Teaching Academy at the University of Wisconsin in 1995. Professor Warfield has developed and published several case studies based on his research for use in accounting classes. These cases have been selected for the AICPA Professor-Practitioner Case Development Program and have been published in *Issues in Accounting Education*.

New to This Edition

Content Changes by Chapter

Chapter 1: Financial Accounting and Accounting Standards

- Generally updated for content and recent developments.

Chapter 2: Conceptual Framework for Financial Reporting

- New footnote detailing most recent FASB updates related to disclosures.
- Completely updated *IFRS Insights* section for the most recent information concerning the IASB and FASB conceptual statements.

Chapter 3: The Accounting Information System

- New section on the chart of accounts, as well as increased explanation and graphics of the recording process.
- Updated opening story on economic crime to reflect latest data and trends.
- New "What Do the Numbers Mean?" (WDNM) box on blockchain.
- New Analytics in Action activity on collecting financial data from a variety of sources.

Chapter 4: Income Statement and Related Information

- New WDNM box on how and why companies use earnings management to misrepresent company performance.
- Updated information about joint FASB-IASB project on financial statement presentation (currently on hold).
- Updated Evolving Issue box on most recent information concerning non-GAAP reporting.

Chapter 5: Balance Sheet and Statement of Cash Flows

- Rewrote "Additional Information" section for most recent FASB updates and recommendations on note disclosures regarding accounting policies, contractual situations, contingencies, and fair value.
- New Analytics in Action activity on ratio analysis for companies in the Dow Jones average.

Chapter 6: Accounting and the Time Value of Money

- New Analytics in Action activity on analyzing business alternatives, with consideration of time value of money concepts.

Chapter 7: Cash and Receivables

- New opening story, discussing current effect of the Tax Cuts and Jobs Act of 2017 in terms of amounts of company cash parked overseas.
- New Evolving Issue, on what companies should include as part of cash and cash equivalents on the balance sheet, such as cryptocurrencies.
- Updated discussion of allowance method for uncollectible accounts per latest FASB standards (i.e., net amount expected to be collected instead of net realizable value).
- New Analytics in Action activity on estimating the allowance for doubtful accounts and conducting financial analysis of the collectibility of accounts receivable.

Chapter 8: Valuation of Inventories: A Cost-Basis Approach

- Generally updated for content and recent developments.

Chapter 9: Inventories: Additional Valuation Issues

- New WDNM boxes on (1) corporate barter to handle problem inventory and (2) importance of identifying markdown method (cost versus retail) used by retailers.
- New Analytics in Action activity on analyzing inventory balances for possible impairment.

Chapter 10: Acquisition and Disposition of Property, Plant, and Equipment

- Moved contributions discussion as a new appendix, expanding its discussion per recent FASB guidance.
- New WDNM box on importance for companies to effectively manage capital spending.

Chapter 11: Depreciation, Impairments, and Depletion

- Updated opening story on technical and environmental issues affecting recognition of impaired assets.
- Updated footnote 15 to include the financial impacts of the most recent legislation, Tax Cuts and Jobs Act of 2017.
- New WDNM box on how changes in tax depreciation rules related to bonus depreciation.
- New Analytics in Action activity on analyzing company information related to depreciation and impairment of property, plant, and equipment.

Chapter 12: Intangible Assets

- Updated discussion of goodwill impairment test per recent FASB.
- New WDNM box on how goodwill impairments reported by companies can signal their future cash flows.
- New Analytics in Action activity on analyzing goodwill for companies in the Dow Jones average.

Chapter 13: Current Liabilities and Contingencies

- New WDNM boxes on (1) advantages of increased employee benefits over wage growth and (2) how Penn Central Railroad provides example of need for rules for liabilities expected to be refinanced.
- Updated Refinancing Criteria section for short-term obligations expected to be refinanced due to latest proposed FASB Accounting Standards Update.
- New Analytics in Action activity on analyzing current liabilities as part of a valid analysis of liquidity.
- New case illustration on determining whether a lawsuit liability should be recognized.

Chapter 14: Long-Term Liabilities

- New WDNM box on why some companies are issuing 100-year and even longer-duration bonds.

Chapter 15: Stockholders' Equity

- Generally updated for content and recent developments.
- New Analytics in Action activity on analyzing ROE using the DuPont method.

Chapter 16: Dilutive Securities and Earnings per Share

- New discussion and illustrations on stock compensation costs.

Chapter 17: Investments

- New opening story on how new FASB standard on reporting loans at amortized cost and equity investments at fair value is resulting in wins for banks and losses for companies.
- Updated discussion of impairments for receivables, available-for-sale and held-to-maturity debt investments, and equity investments.
- Deleted dated WDNM box on disclosure of equity investments.

Chapter 18: Revenue Recognition

- Generally updated for content and recent developments.

Chapter 19: Accounting for Income Taxes

- Chapter updated throughout to reflect the Tax Cuts and Jobs Act of 2017, including a new opening story that discusses its most important provisions.
- Loss carrybacks now discussed in a new Appendix 19B.
- New WDNM box on impact of a lower corporate tax rate.

Chapter 20: Accounting for Pensions and Postretirement Benefits

- Moved up last part of the continuing pension expense worksheet example earlier in the chapter, for improved continuity.
- Completely updated section on the reporting and disclosure requirements for pensions, now discussed in four categories: (1) assets and liabilities, (2) net income, (3) comprehensive income, and (4) notes to the financial statements.

Chapter 21: Accounting for Leases

- Chapter consists of Updated Chapter 21 available with Kieso 16e.
- Opening story updated per most recent information on impact of new lease standard on companies' balance sheets.

Chapter 22: Accounting Changes and Error Analysis

- New WDNM box on how substantial depreciation-related changes might affect financial information.
- Completely updated discussion of converting to the equity method in Appendix 22A, given the recent FASB standard.

Chapter 23: Statement of Cash Flows

- Expanded WDNM boxes to include recent FASB rule for classifying operating cash flows.

Chapter 24: Full Disclosure in Financial Reporting

- New discussion of FASB Disclosure Framework project on improving the effectiveness of disclosures in financial statements, which has resulted in a new concepts statement in August 2018.
- New discussion of recent controversy regarding "short-termism" of interim reporting.
- Moved "Errors, Fraud, and Illegal Acts" section later in chapter under "Fraudulent Reporting" for improved presentation of topics.

Improved Digital Assets

Intermediate Accounting is completely integrated with WileyPLUS, featuring a suite of teaching and learning resources developed under the close review of the authors. Driven by the same basic beliefs as the text, WileyPLUS allows students to create a personalized study plan, assess their progress along the way, and access the content and resources needed to master the material. Features of the WileyPLUS course include the following:

- **NEW Integrated CPA Exam Test Prep:** Each chapter in the text now includes additional content from Wiley CPAexcel, which is designed to help students pass the CPA exam efficiently. Integrated within WileyPLUS, this new content includes CPA exam video lessons, CPA exam practice questions, and assignable task-based simulations (TBSs), which are the primary form of assessment used by the American Institute of Certified Public Accountants (AICPA) to assess mastery of the content at the analysis and evaluation cognitive level.
- **NEW Data Analytics:** Analytics in Action activities include corresponding data sets and assignments in WileyPLUS. These resources further prepare and enhance data analytics skills that students will need in their future accounting careers. *Intermediate Accounting* also includes a "Data Analytics and Accounting" module within WileyPLUS that contains seven interactive lessons with industry-validated content to prepare students for the evolving workforce, video tutorials of real-world data analytics applications, and a case study using Excel that allows students to manipulate and think critically about data.
- **NEW Solution Walkthrough Videos:** The library of solution walkthrough videos has been expanded with the addition of approximately 15 new videos. Question-usage data helped determine which assessment content to highlight, ensuring that this student-favorite resource is available for the most frequently assigned content.
- **Accessible Lecture PowerPoints:** PowerPoints are a hallmark of many lectures as well as an important study tool for students. In addition to the fully accessible WileyPLUS course, we have also improved the lecture PowerPoints to be accessible, including high-quality alt text and screen-reader capabilities.

Proven Pedagogical Framework

This edition continues to provide numerous key learning aids to help you master the text material and prepare you for a successful career in accounting.

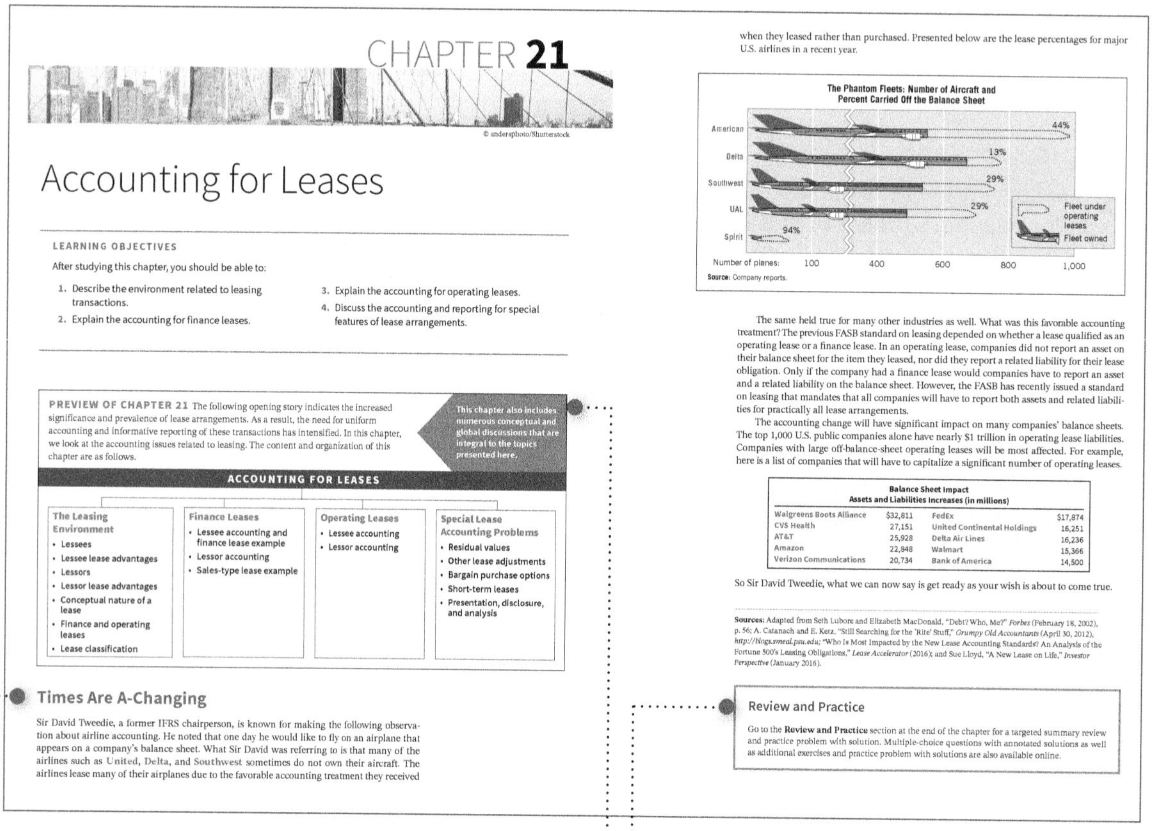

CHAPTER 21

© andersphoto/Shutterstock

Accounting for Leases

LEARNING OBJECTIVES

After studying this chapter, you should be able to:

1. Describe the environment related to leasing transactions.
2. Explain the accounting for finance leases.
3. Explain the accounting for operating leases.
4. Discuss the accounting and reporting for special features of lease arrangements.

PREVIEW OF CHAPTER 21 The following opening story indicates the increased significance and prevalence of lease arrangements. As a result, the need for uniform accounting and informative reporting of these transactions has intensified. In this chapter, we look at the accounting issues related to leasing. The content and organization of this chapter are as follows.

This chapter also includes numerous conceptual and global discussions that are integral to the topics presented here.

ACCOUNTING FOR LEASES

The Leasing Environment	Finance Leases	Operating Leases	Special Lease Accounting Problems
• Lessees • Lessee lease advantages • Lessors • Lessor lease advantages • Conceptual nature of a lease • Finance and operating leases • Lease classification	• Lessee accounting and finance lease example • Lessor accounting • Sales-type lease example	• Lessee accounting • Lessor accounting	• Residual values • Other lease adjustments • Bargain purchase options • Short-term leases • Presentation, disclosure, and analysis

Times Are A-Changing

Sir David Tweedie, a former IFRS chairperson, is known for making the following observation about airline accounting. He noted that one day he would like to fly on an airplane that appears on a company's balance sheet. What Sir David was referring to is that many of the airlines such as United, Delta, and Southwest sometimes do not own their aircraft. The airlines lease many of their airplanes due to the favorable accounting treatment they received when they leased rather than purchased. Presented below are the lease percentages for major U.S. airlines in a recent year.

The Phantom Fleets: Number of Aircraft and Percent Carried Off the Balance Sheet

American 44%
Delta 13%
Southwest 29%
UAL 29%
Spirit 94%
Fleet under operating leases
Fleet owned
Number of planes: 100 400 600 800 1,000
Source: Company reports.

The same held true for many other industries as well. What was this favorable accounting treatment? The previous FASB standard on leasing depended on whether a lease qualified as an operating lease or a finance lease. In an operating lease, companies did not report an asset on their balance sheet for the item they leased, nor did they report a related liability for their lease obligation. Only if the company had a finance lease would companies have to report an asset and a related liability on the balance sheet. However, the FASB has recently issued a standard on leasing that mandates that all companies will have to report both assets and related liabilities for practically all lease arrangements.

The accounting change will have significant impact on many companies' balance sheets. The top 1,000 U.S. public companies alone have nearly $1 trillion in operating lease liabilities. Companies with large off-balance-sheet operating leases will be most affected. For example, here is a list of companies that will have to capitalize a significant number of operating leases.

Balance Sheet Impact
Assets and Liabilities Increases (in millions)

Walgreens Boots Alliance	$32,811	FedEx	$17,874
CVS Health	27,151	United Continental Holdings	16,251
AT&T	25,928	Delta Air Lines	16,236
Amazon	22,848	Walmart	15,366
Verizon Communications	20,734	Bank of America	14,500

So Sir David Tweedie, what we can now say is get ready as your wish is about to come true.

Sources: Adapted from Seth Lubore and Elizabeth MacDonald, "Debt? Who, Me?" *Forbes* (February 18, 2002), p. 56; A. Catanach and E. Ketz, "Still Searching for the 'Rite' Stuff," *Grumpy Old Accountants* (April 30, 2012), *http://blogs.smeal.psu.edu;* "Who Is Most Impacted by the New Lease Accounting Standards? An Analysis of the Fortune 500's Leasing Obligations," *Lease Accelerator* (2016); and Sue Lloyd, "A New Lease on Life," *Investor Perspective* (January 2016).

Review and Practice

Go to the **Review and Practice** section at the end of the chapter for a targeted summary review and practice problem with solution. Multiple-choice questions with annotated solutions as well as additional exercises and practice problem with solutions are also available online.

Chapter Opener Vignettes

The Chapter Opener Vignettes provide an engaging introduction as well as place the content of the chapter's topics in context in terms of recent accounting, economic, and political developments.

Review and Practice

The Review and Practice section, placed after the text discussion, offers students the opportunity to assess their understanding of the chapter's topics before tackling homework assignments.

Chapter Preview

The Chapter Preview summarizes the major issues discussed in the chapter, and provides students with a visual outline of the key topics.

NEW MORE Illustration Walk-Throughs

These unique illustrations include mini-cases so that students can immediately understand how to apply the accounting concepts and procedures to specific situations.

ILLUSTRATION 21.3
Variable Lease Payments

INCLUDING VARIABLE LEASE PAYMENTS

Facts: On January 1, 2020, Jose Company leases an airplane for 6 years. The annual lease payments are $1,000,000 per year, payable at the beginning of each year (annuity-due basis). In addition, the lease agreement specifies that the lease payment increases by $30,000 every year.

***Question:* What are the lease payments in 2021?**

Solution: On January 1, 2021, the lease payment is $1,030,000 ($1,000,000 + $30,000), which is considered a variable payment. Given that the amount of the variable payment is known from year to year (the rate is set at commencement of the lease and in substance fixed), such variable payments are included in calculating the present value of the lease liability.

ILLUSTRATION 21.4
Variable Lease Payments

EXPENSING VARIABLE LEASE PAYMENTS

Facts: Assume the same information as in Illustration 21.3, except that the lease payments are adjusted each year by a change in the Consumer Price Index (CPI).

***Question:* If the CPI is 100 at January 1, 2020, and increases to 104 on January 1, 2021, what is the payment on January 1, 2021?**

Solution: The variable payment on January 1, 2021, is $1,040,000 ($1,000,000 × 1.04). Because the amount of the variable payment from year to year is not known at the lease commencement date, this payment is not included in determining the present value of the lease liability. This additional payment ($40,000) is recognized as an expense in the period it is incurred. Similarly, when lease payments vary with a performance measure (e.g., sales at a store location, asset usage), the variable amounts will be expensed in the period incurred.

Lerch records this loss as follows.

Loss on Impairment	40,000,000	
Patents		40,000,000

After recognizing the impairment, the reduced carrying amount of the patents is its new cost basis (see Underlying Concepts). Lerch should amortize the patent's new cost over its remaining useful life or legal life, whichever is shorter. Even if shale-oil prices increase in subsequent periods and the value of the patent increases, Lerch **may not recognize restoration of the previously recognized impairment loss.**

Underlying Concepts

The basic attributes of intangibles, their uncertainty as to future benefits, and their uniqueness have discouraged valuation in excess of cost.

Underlying Concepts

The Underlying Concepts highlight and explain major conceptual topics in the chapter.

Global View

Global Views provide students with specific examples of how global companies (and countries) implement key accounting regulations. They also provide examples of how and where IFRS differs from GAAP.

Two difficulties arise in accounting for R&D expenditures: (1) identifying the costs associated with particular activities, projects, or achievements, and (2) determining the magnitude of the future benefits and length of time over which such benefits may be realized. Because of these latter uncertainties, the FASB has simplified the accounting practice in this area. **Companies must expense all research and development costs when incurred** (see Global View). [14]

Global View

IFRS requires the capitalization of certain development expenditures. This conflicts with GAAP.

What Do the Numbers Mean? **Not So Fast**

As an illustration of the importance of the control criteria, consider the case of computer leasing companies, which at one time bought IBM equipment, leased the equipment to their customers, and removed the leased assets from their balance sheets. In leasing the assets, the computer lessors stated that they would substitute new IBM equipment if obsolescence occurred (a sales return provision). However, when IBM introduced a new computer line, IBM refused to sell it to the computer leasing companies. As a result, a number of the lessors could not meet their contracts with their customers and had to take back the old equipment. Thus, control had not been fully transferred and the computer leasing companies therefore had to reinstate the assets they had taken off the books. Such a case demonstrates one reason why the lessor classification tests must be aligned with those for revenue recognition.

What Do the Numbers Mean?

The "What Do the Numbers Mean?" boxes further students' understanding of key concepts with practical, real-world examples.

Evolving Issue

The Evolving Issue feature introduces and discusses a current topic in the accounting industry in which the profession may be encountering controversy or nearing resolution. The feature shows how the key standard-setting organizations make decisions to adjust to the changing global business environment.

Evolving Issue **Recognition of R&D and Internally Generated Intangibles**

The requirement that companies expense immediately all R&D costs (as well as start-up costs) incurred internally is a practical solution. It ensures consistency in practice and uniformity among companies. But the practice of immediately writing off expenditures made in the expectation of benefiting future periods is conceptually incorrect.

Proponents of immediate expensing contend that from an income statement standpoint, long-run application of this standard frequently makes little difference. They argue that because of the ongoing nature of most companies' R&D activities, the amount of R&D cost charged to expense each accounting period is about the same, whether there is immediate expensing or capitalization and subsequent amortization.

Others criticize this practice. They believe that the balance sheet should report an intangible asset related to expenditures that have future benefit. To preclude capitalization of all R&D expenditures removes from the balance sheet what may be a company's most valuable asset.

Indeed, research findings indicate that capitalizing R&D costs may be helpful to investors. For example, one study showed a significant relationship between R&D outlays and subsequent benefits in the form of increased productivity, earnings, and shareholder value for R&D-intensive companies. Another study found that there was a significant decline in earnings' usefulness for companies that were forced to switch from capitalizing to expensing R&D costs, and that the decline appears to persist over time.

The current accounting for R&D and other internally generated intangible assets represents one of the many trade-offs made among relevance, faithful representation, and cost-benefit considerations. The FASB and IASB have completed some limited-scope projects on the accounting for intangible assets, and the Boards have contemplated a project on the accounting for identifiable intangible assets (i.e., excluding goodwill). Such a project would address concerns that the current accounting requirements lead to inconsistent treatments for some types of intangible assets depending on how they arise.

Sources for research studies: Baruch Lev and Theodore Sougiannis, "The Capitalization, Amortization, and Value-Relevance of R&D," *Journal of Accounting and Economics* (February 1996); and Martha L. Loudder and Bruce K. Behn, "Alternative Income Determination Rules and Earnings Usefulness: The Case of R&D Costs," *Contemporary Accounting Research* (Fall 1995). See also the recent critique of the accounting for intangible assets in Baruch Lev and Feng Gu, *The End of Accounting* (Hoboken, NJ: John Wiley & Sons, 2016).

End-of-Chapter Pedagogy

Review and Practice

Review and Practice section includes Key Terms Review, Learning Objectives Review, and a Practice Problem with Solution. In addition, multiple-choice questions with solutions, review exercises with solutions, and a full glossary of all key terms are available online.

Review and Practice

Key Terms Review

amortization 12-4
bargain purchase 12-14
business combination 12-4(n)
copyright 12-8
development activities 12-19
fair value test 12-15
franchise 12-8
goodwill 12-11
impairment 12-14
indefinite-life intangibles 12-4
intangible assets 12-3
license (permit) 12-9
limited (finite)-life intangibles 12-4
master valuation approach 12-13
organizational costs 12-21
patent 12-9
recoverability test 12-14
research activities 12-19
research and development (R&D) costs 12-19
start-up costs 12-21
trademark, trade name 12-6

Learning Objectives Review

1 **Discuss the characteristics, valuation, and amortization of intangible assets.**

Intangible assets have two main characteristics: (1) they lack physical existence, and (2) they are not financial instruments. In most

3 **Explain the accounting issues for recording goodwill.**

Unlike receivables, inventories, and patents that a company can sell or exchange individually in the marketplace, goodwill can be identified only with the company as a whole. **Goodwill is a "going con-**

Practice Problem

Sky Co., organized in 2020, provided you with the following information.

1. Purchased a license for $20,000 on July 1, 2020. The license gives Sky exclusive rights to sell its services in the tri-state region and will expire on July 1, 2028.
2. Purchased a patent on January 2, 2021, for $40,000. It is estimated to have a 5-year life.
3. Costs incurred to develop an exclusive Internet connection process as of June 1, 2021, were $45,000. The process has an indefinite life.

Practice Problem

The Practice Problem offers students a comprehensive exercise, incorporating many of the chapter's topics, followed by a detailed, step-by-step solution.

Using Your Judgment

The Using Your Judgment section provides students with real-world homework problems including (1) a financial reporting problem, (2) a comparative analysis case, (3) financial statement analysis cases, and (4) an accounting, analysis, and principles problem.

Using Your Judgment

Financial Reporting Problem

The Procter & Gamble Company (P&G)

The financial statements of P&G are presented in Appendix B. The company's complete annual report, including the notes to the financial statements, is available online.

Comparative Analysis Case

The Coca-Cola Company and PepsiCo, Inc.

The financial statements of Coca-Cola and PepsiCo are presented in Appendices C and D, respectively. The companies' complete annual reports, including the notes to the financial statements, are available online.

Instructions

Use the companies' financial information to answer the following questions.

a. 1. What amounts for intangible assets were reported in their respective balance sheets by Coca-Cola and PepsiCo at year-end 2017?

Data Analytics **NEW**

Analytics in Action activities discuss how data analytics are used for specific accounting situations as well as offer hands-on experience so that students understand the power and value of analytical tools.

Analytics in Action

Accounting software systems collect vast amounts of data about the economic events experienced by a company and about the parties with whom the company engages, such as suppliers and customers. Business decision-makers take advantage of this wealth of information by using data analytics, which often employs both software and statistics, to draw inferences and make more informed business decisions. As both data access and analytical software improve, the use of data analytics to support decisions is becoming increasingly common at virtually all types of companies.

For example, consider goodwill, which has been rising briskly since 2011, to a total of $3.408 trillion among all corporate filers in 2015. The bad news is that impairments have plummeted further during this same period, from a low of $34.66 billion in 2013 to $83.02 billion in 2015 (see *http://www.radicalcompliance.com/2016/05/04/impairments-hinting-at-bigger-problems-ahead/*). So are goodwill impairments more likely as goodwill balances rise? Business decision-makers would definitely want to investigate this trend further using data analytics.

Instructions Go to WileyPLUS for a data analytics exercise focusing on goodwill for companies in the Dow Jones average.

Bridge to the Profession

This section includes FASB Codification References, Codification Exercises, and a Codification Research Case, all designed to refer students to the relevant FASB literature for key concepts in the text and provide assessment of their understanding.

Bridge to the Profession

FASB Codification References

[1] FASB ASC 350-10-05. [Predecessor literature: "Goodwill and Other Intangible Assets," *Statement of Financial Accounting Standards No. 142* (Norwalk, Conn.: FASB, 2001).]

[2] FASB ASC 350-30-35. [Predecessor literature: "Goodwill and Other Intangible Assets," *Statement of Financial Accounting Standards No. 142* (Norwalk, Conn.: FASB, 2001), par. 11.]

[15] FASB ASC Master Glossary. [Predecessor literature: "Accounting for Research and Development Costs," *Statement of Financial Accounting Standards No. 2* (Stamford, Conn.: FASB, 1974), par. 8.]

[16] FASB ASC 805-10. [Predecessor literature: "Business Combinations," *Statement of Financial Accounting Standards No. 141–Revised* (Norwalk, Conn.: FASB, 2007), par. E11.]

[17] FASB ASC 730-10-25-2. [Predecessor literature: "Accounting for Research and Development Costs," *Statement of Financial*

IFRS Insights

IFRS Insights offer students a detailed discussion and assessment material (including IFRS Self-Test Questions, IFRS Concepts and Application, and an International Financial Reporting Problem) of international accounting standards at the end of each chapter.

IFRS Insights

LEARNING OBJECTIVE 6

Compare the accounting for intangible assets under GAAP and IFRS.

There are some significant differences between IFRS and GAAP in the accounting for both intangible assets and impairments. IFRS related to intangible assets is presented in *IAS 38* ("Intangible Assets"). IFRS related to impairments is found in *IAS 36* ("Impairment of Assets").

Acknowledgments

Intermediate Accounting has benefited greatly from the input of focus group participants, manuscript reviewers, those who have sent comments by letter or e-mail, ancillary authors, and proofers. We greatly appreciate the constructive suggestions and innovative ideas of reviewers and the creativity and accuracy of the ancillary authors and checkers.

Prior Edition Reviewers

We greatly appreciate the over 400 reviewers who have assisted with the prior editions of Intermediate Accounting. *These instructors have been invaluable in the development and continued improvement of our text.*

Seventeenth Edition

Maggie Atkinson
Stark State College

Michael Bitter
Stetson University

Stephen Brown
University of Maryland

Sudheer Kumar Chella
Hurix

Timothy Coville
St. John's University

Bill Davenport
CPA

Charmaine Felder
Brandman University

Kristen Fuhremann
Wisconsin School of Business

Liz Grant
Northern Illinois University

Vicki Greshik
University of Jamestown

Michael Gurevitz
Montgomery College

Coby Harmon
University of California–Santa Barbara

James Hay
Wilson College

Michelle Hodgen-Smith

Gun-Ho Joh
San Diego State University

Katie Landgraf
University of Hawaii—West Oahu

Jim Leisenring
FASB

Lisa Ludlum
Western Illinois University

Dan Lynch
Wisconsin School of Business

David Massaglia
Bemidji State University

Monica McElhaney
Bellevue University

Cynthia Mille
University of Kentucky

Allison Moreno
Texas Tech University

Kingsley Olibe
Kansas State University

Pete Poznanski
Cleveland State University

Gregory Prescott
University of South Alabama

Ada Rodriguez
Lehman College

Mark Ross
Western Kentucky University

David Scott
Purdue University

Paula Thomas
Middle Tennessee State University

Bruce Wampler
Louisiana State University Shreveport

Jeff Wang
San Diego State University

Dave Weber
University of Connecticut

Donna Whitten
Purdue University Northwest

Melanie Yonn

Allie Zimmerman
Northern Illinois University

In addition, we thank the following colleagues who contributed to several of the unique features of this edition.

Codification Cases

Katie Adler
Deloitte LLP, Chicago

Jack Cathey
University of North Carolina—Charlotte

Erik Frederickson
Madison, Wisconsin

Danielle Griffin
KPMG, Chicago

Jason Hart
Deloitte LLP, Milwaukee

Frank Heflin
University of Georgia

Mike Katte
SC Johnson, Racine, WI

Kelly Krieg
Ernst & Young, Milwaukee

Jeremy Kunicki
Walgreens

Courtney Meier
Deloitte LLP, Milwaukee

Andrew Prewitt
KPMG, Chicago

Jeff Seymour
KPMG, Minneapolis

Matt Sullivan
Northwestern Mutual

Matt Tutaj
Deloitte LLP, Chicago

Jen Vaughn
PricewaterhouseCoopers, Chicago

Erin Viel
PricewaterhouseCoopers, Milwaukee

Ancillary Authors, Contributors, Proofers, and Accuracy Checkers

Ellen Bartely
St. Joseph's University (NYC)

LuAnn Bean
Florida Institute of Technology

Jack Borke
University of Wisconsin—Platteville

Melodi Bunting
Edgewood College

Bea Chiang
The College of New Jersey

Susetta Emery
York College of Pennsylvania

Jim Emig
Villanova University

Larry Falcetto
Emporia State University

Kim Hurt
Central Community College

Derek Jackson
St. Mary's University of Minnesota

Mark Kohlbeck
Florida Atlantic University

Cynthia Lovick
Austin Community College

Kirk Lynch
Sandhills Community College

Anthony Masino
East Tennessee University

Jill Misuraca
University of Tampa

Barb Muller
Arizona State University

Alison Parker
Camosun College

Yvonne Phang
Borough of Manhattan Community College

Tim Potsaid
Madison, Wisconsin

Laura Prosser
Blackhills State University

Mark Riley
Northern Illinois University

Alice Sineath
University of Maryland University College

Lynn Stallworth
Appalachian State University

Sheila Viel
University of Wisconsin—Milwaukee

Dick Wasson
Southwestern College

Suzanne Wright
Pennsylvania State University

Lori Zaher
Bucks County Community College

Advisory Board

We gratefully acknowledge the following members of the Intermediate Accounting Advisory Board for their advice and assistance with this edition.

Barbara Durham
University of Central Florida

Pamela Graybeal
University of Central Florida

Jeffery Hales
Georgia Institute of Technology

Melissa Larson
Brigham Young University—Provo

Ming Lu
Santa Monica College

Linda Matuszewski
Northern Illinois University

Kevin Rich
Marquette University

Angela Spencer
Oklahoma State University—Stillwater

Practicing Accountants and Business Executives

From the fields of corporate and public accounting, we owe thanks to the following practitioners for their technical advice and for consenting to interviews.

Sue Cosper
FASB

Tracy Golden
Deloitte LLP

John Gribble
PricewaterhouseCoopers (retired)

Darien Griffin
S.C. Johnson & Son

Michael Lehman
Sun Microsystems, Inc.

Michele Lippert
Evoke.com

Sue McGrath
Vision Capital Management

David Miniken
Sweeney Conrad

Robert Sack
University of Virginia

Clare Schulte
Deloitte LLP

Willie Sutton
Mutual Community Savings Bank, Durham, NC

Lynn Turner
former SEC Chief Accountant

Rachel Woods
PricewaterhouseCoopers

Finally, we appreciate the exemplary support and professional commitment given us by the development, marketing, production, and editorial staffs of John Wiley & Sons, including the following: Michael McDonald, Emily Marcoux, Lindsey Myers, Elena Saccaro, and Wendy Lai. Thanks, too, to Denise Showers and the staff at Aptara®, Inc. for their work on the text, and the staff at Lumina Datamatics for their work on the solutions manual.

We also appreciate the cooperation of the American Institute of Certified Public Accountants and the Financial Accounting Standards Board in permitting us to quote from their pronouncements. We also acknowledge permission from the American Institute of Certified Public Accountants, the Institute of Management Accountants, and the Institute of Internal Auditors to adapt and use material from the Uniform CPA Examinations, the CMA Examinations, and the CIA Examinations, respectively.

Suggestions and comments from users of this text will be appreciated. Please feel free to e-mail any one of us.

Donald E. Kieso
Somonauk, Illinois

Jerry J. Weygandt
Madison, Wisconsin

Terry D. Warfield
Madison, Wisconsin

Table of Contents

20 Accounting for Pensions and Postretirement Benefits 20-1

21 Accounting for Leases 21-1

22 Accounting Changes and Error Analysis 22-1

23 Statement of Cash Flows 23-1

24 Full Disclosure in Financial Reporting 24-1

CHAPTER **15**

© andersphoto/Shutterstock

Stockholders' Equity

LEARNING OBJECTIVES

After studying this chapter, you should be able to:

1. Describe the corporate form and the issuance of shares of stock.
2. Describe the accounting and reporting for reacquisition of shares.
3. Explain the accounting and reporting issues related to dividends.
4. Indicate how to present and analyze stockholders' equity.

PREVIEW OF CHAPTER 15 As the following opening story indicates, the growth of global equity capital markets indicates that equity investors around the world need useful information. In this chapter, we explain the accounting issues related to the stockholders' equity of a corporation. The content and organization of the chapter are as follows.

This chapter also includes numerous conceptual and global discussions that are integral to the topics presented here.

STOCKHOLDERS' EQUITY

Corporate Capital
- Corporate form
- Components of equity
- Issuance of stock
- Preferred stock

Reacquisition of Shares
- Purchase
- Sale
- Retirement

Dividend Policy
- Financial condition and dividend distributions
- Types of dividends
- Stock dividends and stock splits

Presentation and Analysis
- Presentation
- Analysis

It's a Global Market

As mentioned in prior chapters, we are moving toward one set of global financial reporting standards and one "common language" for financial information. This change will probably lead to more consolidation of our capital markets. To understand how quickly the global financial world is changing, let's examine a few trends occurring on stock exchanges around the world.

In 2007, the New York Stock Exchange (NYSE) merged with Paris-based Euronext, creating the world's first transatlantic stock exchange. **NYSE Euronext** is the world's largest exchange group, now with more than 8,000 listed issuers representing over one-third of global equity trading. Similarly, NASDAQ, the world's largest electronic stock market, merged with **OMX**, the Nordic stock market operator. This electronic exchange operates in 29 countries, on six continents, and has over 3,000 listed issuers, with a market value of approximately $8.5 trillion. (Further exchange consolidation may be in the offing, with **IntercontinentalExchange** and international exchanges in Asia exploring mergers with NYSE Euronext.)

Another reason behind the movement to international financial reporting standards can be found in recent initial public offerings (IPOs). For example, total global IPO listings, as well as by region percentages, were as follows.

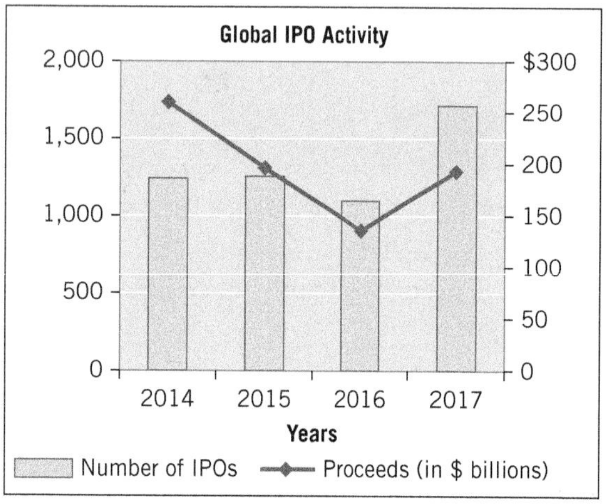

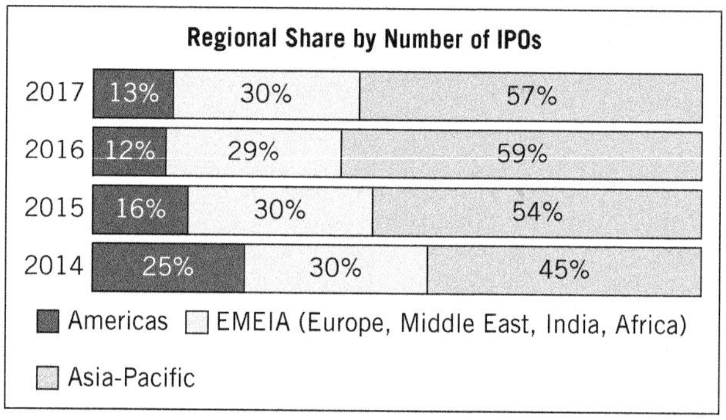

As indicated, global stock listings have been on the rise, and listings in Asia-Pacific continue to be the biggest share of IPOs.

Finally, globalization has been an enormous boon for some of the biggest names in corporate America. And that is what investors are saying as well. As shown in the adjacent chart, approximately 59 percent of the energy sector's revenue came from abroad in 2016. Information technology followed closely at 57 percent.

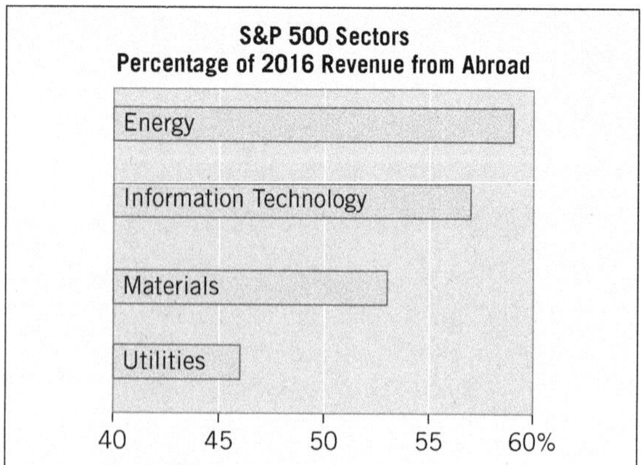

Source: S&P Dow Jones Indices.

Large companies that had significant foreign sales are **Wal-Mart Stores, Inc.** 24.49 percent, **Microsoft Corporation** 52.44 percent, **Ford Motor Company** 38.45 percent, and **The Coca-Cola Company** 52.47 percent. Foreign exposure allows U.S.-based companies to capitalize on rapid growth in emerging markets like China, India, and Latin America, and earn much stronger profits than if they were totally dependent on the U.S. economy. As one analyst noted, "[Returns for companies] . . . in the S&P 500 continue to outgrow the U.S. economy. Earnings power is decoupled from U.S. GDP."

Sources: R. Newman, "Why U.S. Companies Aren't So American Anymore," *http://money.usnews.com* (June 30, 2011); *EY Global IPO Trends: Q1 2018*, EYGM Limited (2018); and H. Silverblatt, "S&P 500 2016: Global Sales," *S&P Dow Jones Indices* (July 2017).

Review and Practice

Go to the **Review and Practice** section at the end of the chapter for a targeted summary review and practice problem with solution. Multiple-choice questions with annotated solutions as well as additional exercises and practice problem with solutions are also available online.

Corporate Capital

LEARNING OBJECTIVE 1

Describe the corporate form and the issuance of shares of stock.

Of the three **primary forms of business organization**—the proprietorship, the partnership, and the corporation—the corporate form dominates. The corporation is by far the leader in terms of the aggregate amount of resources controlled, goods and services produced, and people employed. All of the "Fortune 500" largest industrial firms are corporations. Although the corporate form has a number of advantages (as well as disadvantages) over the other two forms, its principal advantage is its facility for attracting and accumulating large amounts of capital.

Corporate Form

The special characteristics of the corporate form that affect accounting include:

1. Influence of state corporate law.
2. Use of the capital stock or share system.
3. Development of a variety of ownership interests.

State Corporate Law

Anyone who wishes to establish a corporation must submit **articles of incorporation** to the state in which incorporation is desired. After fulfilling requirements, the state issues a corporation charter, thereby recognizing the company as a legal entity subject to state law. Regardless of the number of states in which a corporation has operating divisions, it is incorporated in only one state.

It is to the company's advantage to incorporate in a state whose laws favor the corporate form of business organization. For example, consider that nearly half of all public corporations in the United States are incorporated in Delaware. Why Delaware? The state has a favorable tax and regulatory environment, resulting in Delaware being home to more corporations—public and private—than people.[1]

Each state has its own business incorporation act. The accounting for stockholders' equity follows the provisions of these acts. In many cases, states have adopted the principles contained in the Model Business Corporate Act prepared by the American Bar Association. State laws are complex and vary both in their provisions and in their definitions of certain terms. Some laws fail to define technical terms. As a result, terms often mean one thing in one state and another thing in a different state. These problems may be further compounded because legal authorities often interpret the effects and restrictions of the laws differently.

What Do the Numbers Mean? 1209 North Orange Street

Nothing about 1209 North Orange Street hints at the secrets inside. It's a humdrum office building, a low-slung affair with a faded awning and a view of a parking garage. Hardly worth a second glance, if even a first one. But behind its doors is one of the most remarkable corporate collections in the world: 1209 North Orange, you see, is the legal address of no fewer than 285,000 separate businesses.

Its occupants, on paper, include giants like **American Airlines**, **Apple**, **Bank of America**, **Berkshire Hathaway**, **Cargill**, **Coca-Cola**, **Ford**, **General Electric**, **Google**, **JPMorgan Chase**, and **Wal-Mart**. These companies do business across the nation and around the world. Here at 1209 North Orange, they simply have a dropbox.

[1]L. Wayne, "How Delaware Thrives as a Corporate Tax Haven," *The New York Times* (June 30, 2012).

What brings these marquee names to 1209 North Orange, and to other Delaware addresses, also attracts less-upstanding corporate citizens. For instance, 1209 North Orange was, until recently, a business address of Timothy S. Durham, known as "the Midwest Madoff." Recently, Durham was found guilty of bilking 5,000 mostly middle-class and elderly investors out of $207 million. It was also an address of Stanko Subotic, a Serbian businessman and convicted smuggler—just one of many Eastern Europeans drawn to the state.

Big corporations, small-time businesses, rogues, scoundrels, and worse—all have turned up at Delaware addresses in hopes of minimizing taxes, skirting regulations, plying friendly courts, or, when needed, covering their tracks. Federal authorities worry that, in addition to the legitimate businesses flocking here, drug-traffickers, embezzlers, and money-launderers are increasingly heading to Delaware, too. It's easy to set up shell companies here, no questions asked.

Today, Delaware regularly tops lists of domestic and foreign tax havens because it allows companies to lower their taxes in another state—for instance, the state in which they actually do business or have their headquarters—by shifting royalties and similar revenues to holding companies in Delaware, where they are not taxed. In tax circles, the arrangement is known as "the Delaware loophole." Over the last decade, the Delaware loophole has enabled corporations to reduce the taxes paid to other states by an estimated $9.5 billion.

However, recently some companies are concerned that the environment in Delaware has become more hostile. Among their gripes: a growing tide of shareholder litigation, for which some feel that the state has not done enough to curb. Only time will tell if these developments have soured companies on Delaware as an incorporation target. Yet in the past two years, approximately 85 percent of the companies that went public incorporated in Delaware.

Sources: L. Wayne, "How Delaware Thrives as a Corporate Tax Haven," *The New York Times* (June 30, 2012); and L. Hoffman, "Dole and Other Companies Sour on Delaware as a Corporate Haven," *Wall Street Journal* (August 8, 2015).

Capital Stock or Share System

Stockholders' equity in a corporation generally consists of a large number of units or shares. Within a given class of stock, each share exactly equals every other share. The number of shares possessed determines each owner's interest. If a company has one class of stock divided into 1,000 shares, a person who owns 500 shares controls one-half of the ownership interest. One holding 10 shares has a one-hundredth interest.

Each share of stock has certain rights and privileges. Only by special contract can a company restrict these rights and privileges at the time it issues the shares. Owners must examine the articles of incorporation, stock certificates, and the provisions of the state law to ascertain such restrictions on or variations from the standard rights and privileges (see Global View). In the absence of restrictive provisions, each share carries the following rights:

Global View

In the United States, stockholders are treated equally as far as access to financial information. That is not always the case in other countries. For example, in Mexico, foreign investors as well as minority investors often have difficulty obtaining financial data. These restrictions are rooted in the habits of companies that, for many years, were tightly controlled by a few stockholders and managers.

1. To share proportionately in profits and losses.
2. To share proportionately in management (the right to vote for directors).
3. To share proportionately in corporate assets upon liquidation.
4. To share proportionately in any new issues of stock of the same class—called the **preemptive right**.[2]

The first three rights are self-explanatory. The last right is used to protect each stockholder's proportional interest in the company. **The preemptive right protects an existing stockholder from involuntary dilution of ownership interest.** Without this right, stockholders might find their interest reduced by the issuance of additional stock without their knowledge and at prices unfavorable to them. However, many corporations have eliminated the preemptive right. Why? Because this right makes it inconvenient for corporations to issue large amounts of additional stock, as they frequently do in acquiring other companies.

The share system easily allows one individual to transfer an interest in a company to another investor. For example, individuals owning shares in Google **may sell them to others at any time and at any price without obtaining the consent of the company or other stockholders**. Each share is personal property of the owner, who may dispose of it at will. Google simply maintains a list or subsidiary ledger of stockholders as a guide to dividend payments, issuance of stock rights, voting proxies, and the like. Because owners freely and frequently transfer shares, Google must revise the subsidiary ledger of stockholders periodically, generally in advance of every dividend payment or stockholders' meeting.

[2]This privilege is referred to as a **stock right** or **warrant**. The warrants issued in these situations are of short duration, unlike the warrants issued with other securities.

In addition, the major stock exchanges require ownership controls that the typical corporation finds uneconomic to provide. Thus, corporations often use **registrars and transfer agents** who specialize in providing services for recording and transferring stock. The Uniform Stock Transfer Act and the Uniform Commercial Code govern the negotiability of stock certificates.

Variety of Ownership Interests

In every corporation, one class of stock must represent the basic ownership interest. That class is called common stock. **Common stock** is the residual corporate interest that bears the ultimate risks of loss and receives the benefits of success. Common stockholders are not guaranteed dividends or assets upon dissolution. But common stockholders generally control the management of the corporation and tend to profit most if the company is successful. In the event that a corporation has only one authorized issue of capital stock, that issue is by definition common stock, whether so designated in the charter or not.

In an effort to broaden investor appeal, corporations may offer two or more classes of stock, each with different rights or privileges. As indicated in the preceding section, each share of stock of a given issue has the same inherent rights as other shares of the same issue. By special stock contracts between the corporation and its stockholders, however, the stockholder may sacrifice certain of these rights in return for other special rights or privileges. Thus, special classes of stock, usually called **preferred stock**, are created. In return for any special preference, the preferred stockholder always sacrifices some of the inherent rights of common stock ownership.

A common type of preference is to give the preferred stockholders a priority claim on earnings. The corporation thus assures them a dividend, usually at a stated rate, before it distributes any amount to the common stockholders. In return for this preference, the preferred stockholders may sacrifice their right to a voice in management or their right to share in profits beyond the stated rate (see **Global View**).

Global View

The U.S. and British systems of corporate governance and finance depend to a large extent on equity financing and the widely dispersed ownership of shares traded in highly liquid markets. The German and Japanese systems have relied more on debt financing, interlocking stock ownership, and banker/director and worker/shareholder rights.

Components of Stockholders' Equity

Owners' equity in a corporation is defined as stockholders' equity, shareholders' equity, or corporate capital. The following four categories normally appear as part of stockholders' equity:

1. Capital stock.
2. Additional paid-in capital.
3. Retained earnings.
4. Accumulated other comprehensive income.

The first two categories, capital stock and additional paid-in capital, constitute contributed (paid-in) capital. **Contributed (paid-in) capital** is the total amount paid in on capital stock—the amount provided by stockholders to the corporation for use in the business. Contributed capital includes items such as the par value of all outstanding stock and premiums less discounts on issuance.

Earned capital is the capital that develops from profitable operations. It consists of all undistributed income that remains invested in the company. **Retained earnings** represents the earned capital of the company. **Accumulated other comprehensive income** reflects the aggregate amount of the other comprehensive income items. It includes such items as unrealized gains and losses on available-for-sale debt investments and unrealized gains and losses on certain derivative transactions.[3]

Stockholders' equity is the difference between the assets and the liabilities of the company. That is, the owners' or stockholders' interest in a company like **The Walt Disney Company** is a **residual interest.**[4] **Stockholders' (owners') equity** represents the

[3]Chapter 17 contains an expanded discussion of accumulated other comprehensive income. Many companies report noncontrolling interests and treasury stock as part of the equity section. Chapter 5 also highlights the presentation of noncontrolling interests. The accounting and reporting for treasury stock is discussed later in this chapter.

[4]"Elements of Financial Statements," *Statement of Financial Accounting Concepts No. 6* (Stamford, Conn.: FASB, 1985), par. 60.

cumulative net contributions by stockholders plus retained earnings. As a residual interest, stockholders' equity has no existence apart from the assets and liabilities of Disney—stockholders' equity equals net assets. Stockholders' equity is not a claim to specific assets but a claim against a portion of the total assets. Its amount is not specified or fixed; it depends on Disney's profitability. Stockholders' equity grows if the company is profitable. It shrinks, or may disappear entirely, if Disney loses money.

Issuance of Stock

In issuing stock, companies follow these procedures. First, the state must authorize the stock, generally in a certificate of incorporation or charter. Next, the corporation offers shares for sale, entering into contracts to sell stock. Then, after receiving amounts for the stock, the corporation issues shares. The corporation generally makes no entry in the general ledger accounts when it receives its stock authorization from the state of incorporation.

We discuss the accounting problems involved in the issuance of stock under the following topics.

1. Accounting for par value stock.
2. Accounting for no-par stock.
3. Accounting for stock issued in combination with other securities (lump-sum sales).
4. Accounting for stock issued in noncash transactions.
5. Accounting for costs of issuing stock.

Par Value Stock

The par value of a stock has no relationship to its fair value. At present, the par value associated with most capital stock issuances is very low. For example, **PepsiCo**'s par value is 1⅔¢, **Kellogg**'s is $0.25, and **Hershey**'s is $1. Such values contrast dramatically with the situation in the early 1900s, when practically all stock issued had a par value of $100. Low par values help companies avoid the contingent liability associated with stock sold below par.[5]

To show the required information for issuance of par value stock, corporations maintain accounts for each class of stock as follows.

1. ***Preferred Stock or Common Stock.*** Together, these two stock accounts reflect the par value of the corporation's issued shares. The company credits these accounts when it originally issues the shares. It makes no additional entries in these accounts unless it issues additional shares or retires them.
2. ***Paid-in Capital in Excess of Par (also called Additional Paid-in Capital).*** The **Paid-in Capital in Excess of Par** account indicates any excess over par value paid in by stockholders in return for the shares issued to them. Once paid in, the excess over par becomes a part of the corporation's additional paid-in capital. The individual stockholder has no greater claim on the excess paid in than all other holders of the same class of shares.

No-Par Stock

Many states permit the issuance of capital stock without par value, called **no-par stock**. The reasons for issuance of no-par stock are twofold. First, issuance of no-par stock **avoids the contingent liability** (see footnote 5) that might occur if the corporation issued par value stock at a discount. Second, some confusion exists over the relationship (or rather the absence of a relationship) between the par value and fair value. If shares have no-par value, **the questionable treatment of using par value as a basis for fair value never arises.**

[5]Companies rarely, if ever, issue stock at a value below par value. If issuing stock below par, the company records the discount as a debit to Additional Paid-in Capital. In addition, the corporation may call on the original purchaser or the current holder of the shares issued below par to pay in the amount of the discount to prevent creditors from sustaining a loss upon liquidation of the corporation.

This is particularly advantageous whenever issuing stock for property items such as intangible or tangible fixed assets.

A major disadvantage of no-par stock is that some states levy a high tax on these issues. In addition, in some states the total issue price for no-par stock may be considered legal capital, which could reduce the flexibility in paying dividends.

Corporations sell no-par shares, like par value shares, for whatever price they will bring. However, unlike par value shares, corporations issue them without a premium or a discount. The exact amount received represents the credit to common or preferred stock. For example, Video Electronics Corporation is organized with authorized common stock of 10,000 shares without par value. Video Electronics makes only a memorandum entry for the authorization, inasmuch as no amount is involved. If Video Electronics then issues 500 shares for cash at $10 per share, it makes the following entry.

Cash	5,000	
Common Stock (no-par value)		5,000

If it issues another 500 shares for $11 per share, Video Electronics makes this entry:

Cash	5,500	
Common Stock (no-par value)		5,500

True no-par stock should be carried in the accounts at issue price without any additional paid-in capital or discount reported. But some states require that no-par stock have a **stated value**. The stated value is a minimum value below which a company cannot issue it. Thus, instead of being no-par stock, such stated-value stock becomes, in effect, stock with a very low par value. It thus is open to all the criticism and abuses that first encouraged the development of no-par stock.[6]

If no-par stock has a stated value of $5 per share but sells for $11, all such amounts in excess of $5 are recorded as additional paid-in capital, which in many states is fully or partially available for dividends. Thus, no-par value stock with a low stated value permits a new corporation to commence its operations with additional paid-in capital that may exceed its stated capital. For example, if a company issued 1,000 of the shares with a $5 stated value at $15 per share for cash, it makes the following entry.

Cash	15,000	
Common Stock		5,000
Paid-in Capital in Excess of Stated Value—Common Stock		10,000

Most corporations account for no-par stock with a stated value as if it were par value stock with par equal to the stated value.

Stock Issued with Other Securities (Lump-Sum Sales)

Generally, corporations sell classes of stock separately from one another. The reason to do so is to track the proceeds relative to each class, as well as relative to each lot. Occasionally, a corporation issues two or more classes of securities for a single payment or lump sum (e.g., in the acquisition of another company). The accounting problem in such **lump-sum sales** is how to allocate the proceeds among the several classes of securities. Companies use one of two methods of allocation: (1) the proportional method and (2) the incremental method.

Proportional Method If the fair value or other sound basis for determining relative value is available for each class of security, **the company allocates the lump sum received among the classes of securities on a proportional basis.** For instance, assume a company issues 1,000 shares of $10 stated value common stock having a market price of $20 a share, and 1,000 shares of $10 par value preferred stock having a market price of $12 a share, for a lump sum of $30,000. **Illustration 15.1** shows how the company allocates the $30,000 to the two classes of stock.

[6]*Accounting Trends and Techniques* indicated that of its 500 surveyed companies, there were just 40 no-par issues; 3 of the no-par issues were shown at their stated (assigned) values.

ILLUSTRATION 15.1

Allocation in Lump-Sum Securities Issuance—Proportional Method

Fair value of common (1,000 × $20) =		$20,000
Fair value of preferred (1,000 × $12) =		12,000
Aggregate fair value		$32,000
Allocated to common:	$\frac{\$20,000}{\$32,000} \times \$30,000 =$	$18,750
Allocated to preferred:	$\frac{\$12,000}{\$32,000} \times \$30,000 =$	$11,250
Total allocation		$30,000

Incremental Method In instances where a company cannot determine the fair value of all classes of securities, it may use the incremental method. It uses the fair value of the securities as a basis for those classes that it knows, and allocates the remainder of the lump sum to the class for which it does not know the fair value. For instance, if a company issues 1,000 shares of $10 stated value common stock having a fair value of $20, and 1,000 shares of $10 par value preferred stock having no established fair value, for a lump sum of $30,000, it allocates the $30,000 to the two classes as shown in Illustration 15.2.

ILLUSTRATION 15.2

Allocation in Lump-Sum Securities Issuance—Incremental Method

Lump-sum receipt	$30,000
Allocated to common (1,000 × $20)	(20,000)
Balance allocated to preferred	$10,000

If a company cannot determine fair value for any of the classes of stock involved in a lump-sum exchange, it may need to use other approaches. It may rely on an expert's appraisal. Or, if the company knows that one or more of the classes of securities issued will have a determinable fair value in the near future, it may use a best estimate basis with the intent to adjust later, upon establishment of the future fair value.

Stock Issued in Noncash Transactions

Accounting for the issuance of shares of stock for property or services involves an issue of valuation. **The general rule is: Companies should record stock issued for services or property other than cash at either the fair value of the stock issued or the fair value of the noncash consideration received, whichever is more clearly determinable.**

If a company can readily determine both, and the transaction results from an arm's-length exchange, there will probably be little difference in their fair values. In such cases, the basis for valuing the exchange should not matter.

If a company cannot readily determine either the fair value of the stock it issues or the property or services it receives, it should employ an appropriate valuation technique. Depending on available data, the valuation may be based on market transactions involving comparable assets or the use of discounted expected future cash flows. Companies should avoid the use of the book, par, or stated values as a basis of valuation for these transactions.

A company may exchange unissued stock or treasury stock (issued shares that it has reacquired but not retired) for property or services. If it uses treasury shares, the cost of the treasury shares **should not** be considered the decisive factor in establishing the fair value of the property or services. Instead, it should use the fair value of the treasury stock, if known, to value the property or services. Otherwise, if it does not know the fair value of the treasury stock, it should use the fair value of the property or services received, if determinable.

The transactions shown in Illustration 15.3 indicate the procedure for recording the issuance of 10,000 shares of $10 par value common stock for a patent for Marlowe Company, in various circumstances.

ILLUSTRATION 15.3

Common Stock Issuance

Marlowe cannot readily determine the fair value of the patent, but it knows the fair value of the stock is $140,000.

Patents	140,000	
Common Stock (10,000 shares × $10 per share)		100,000
Paid-in Capital in Excess of Par—Common Stock		40,000

Marlowe cannot readily determine the fair value of the stock, but it determines the fair value of the patent is $150,000.

Patents	150,000	
Common Stock (10,000 shares × $10 per share)		100,000
Paid-in Capital in Excess of Par—Common Stock		50,000

Marlowe cannot readily determine the fair value of the stock nor the fair value of the patent. An independent consultant values the patent at $125,000 based on discounted expected cash flows.

Patents	125,000	
Common Stock (10,000 shares × $10 share)		100,000
Paid-in Capital in Excess of Par—Common Stock		25,000

In corporate law, the board of directors has the power to set the value of noncash transactions. However, boards sometimes abuse this power. The issuance of stock for property or services has resulted in cases of overstated corporate capital through intentional overvaluation of the property or services received. The overvaluation of the stockholders' equity resulting from inflated asset values creates **watered stock**. The corporation should eliminate the "water" by simply writing down the overvalued assets.

If, as a result of the issuance of stock for property or services, a corporation undervalues the recorded assets, it creates **secret reserves**. An understated corporate structure (secret reserve) may also result from other methods: excessive depreciation or amortization charges, expensing capital expenditures, excessive write-downs of inventories or receivables, or any other understatement of assets or overstatement of liabilities. An example of a liability overstatement is an excessive provision for estimated product warranties that ultimately results in an understatement of owners' equity, thereby creating a secret reserve.

Costs of Issuing Stock

When a company like **Walgreens** issues common stock, it should report direct costs incurred to sell stock, such as underwriting costs, accounting and legal fees, printing costs, and taxes, as a reduction of the amounts paid in. Walgreens therefore debits issue costs to Paid-in Capital in Excess of Par—Common Stock because they are unrelated to corporate operations. In effect, **issue costs are a cost of financing**. As such, issue costs should reduce the proceeds received from the sale of the stock.

Walgreens should expense management salaries and other indirect costs related to the stock issue because it is difficult to establish a relationship between these costs and the sale proceeds. In addition, Walgreens expenses recurring costs, primarily registrar and transfer agents' fees, as incurred.

What Do the Numbers Mean? The Case of the Disappearing Receivable

Sometimes companies issue stock but may not receive cash in return. As a result, a company records a receivable.

Controversy existed regarding the presentation of this receivable on the balance sheet. Some argued that the company should report the receivable as an asset similar to other receivables. Others argued that the company should report the receivable as a deduction from stockholders' equity (similar to the treatment of treasury stock). The SEC settled this issue: It requires companies to use the contra equity approach because the risk of collection in this type of transaction is often very high.

This accounting issue surfaced in **Enron**'s accounting. Starting in early 2000, Enron issued shares of its common stock to four "special-purpose entities" in exchange for which it received a note receivable. Enron then increased its assets (by recording a receivable) and stockholders' equity, a move the company later called an accounting error. As a result of this accounting treatment, Enron overstated assets and stockholders' equity by $172 million in its 2000 audited financial statements and by $828 million in its unaudited 2001 statements. This $1 billion overstatement was 8.5 percent of Enron's reported stockholders' equity at that time.

As Lynn Turner, a former chief accountant of the SEC, noted, "It is a basic accounting principle that you don't record equity until you get cash, and a note doesn't count as cash." Situations like this led investors, creditors, and suppliers to lose faith in the credibility of Enron, which eventually caused its bankruptcy.

Source: Adapted from Jonathan Weil, "Basic Accounting Tripped Up Enron—Financial Statements Didn't Add Up—Auditors Overlook a Simple Rule," *Wall Street Journal* (November 11, 2001), p. C1.

Preferred Stock

As noted earlier, **preferred stock** is a special class of shares that possesses certain preferences or features not possessed by the common stock.[7] The following features are those most often associated with preferred stock issues.

1. Preference as to dividends.
2. Preference as to assets in the event of liquidation.
3. Convertible into common stock.
4. Callable at the option of the corporation.
5. Nonvoting.

The features that distinguish preferred from common stock may be of a more restrictive and negative nature than preferences. For example, the preferred stock may be nonvoting, noncumulative, and nonparticipating.

Companies usually issue preferred stock with a par value, expressing the dividend preference as a **percentage of the par value**. Thus, holders of 8 percent preferred stock with a $100 par value are entitled to an annual dividend of $8 per share. This stock is commonly referred to as 8 percent preferred stock. In the case of no-par preferred stock, a corporation expresses a dividend preference as a **specific dollar amount** per share, for example, $7 per share. This stock is commonly referred to as $7 preferred stock.

A preference as to dividends does not assure the payment of dividends. It merely assures that **the corporation must pay the stated dividend rate or amount applicable to the preferred stock before paying any dividends on the common stock**.

A company often issues preferred stock (instead of debt) because of a high debt-to-equity ratio. In other instances, it issues preferred stock through private placements with other corporations at a lower-than-market dividend rate because the acquiring corporation receives largely tax-free dividends (owing to the IRS's 70 percent or 80 percent dividends received deduction).

Features of Preferred Stock

A corporation may attach whatever preferences or restrictions, in whatever combination it desires, to a preferred stock issue, as long as it does not specifically violate its state incorporation law. Also, it may issue more than one class of preferred stock. We discuss the most common features attributed to preferred stock next.

Cumulative Preferred Stock **Cumulative preferred stock** requires that if a corporation fails to pay a dividend in any year, it must make it up in a later year before paying any dividends to common stockholders. If the directors fail to declare a dividend at the normal date for dividend action, the dividend is said to have been "passed." Any passed dividend on cumulative preferred stock constitutes a **dividend in arrears**. Because no liability exists until the board of directors declares a dividend, a corporation does not record a dividend in arrears as a liability but discloses it in a note to the financial statements. A corporation seldom issues noncumulative preferred stock because a passed dividend is lost forever to the preferred stockholder. As a result, this stock issue would be less marketable.

[7] *Accounting Trends and Techniques* reported that of its 500 surveyed companies, 35 had preferred stock outstanding.

Participating Preferred Stock Holders of **participating preferred stock** share ratably with the common stockholders in any profit distributions beyond the prescribed rate. That is, 5 percent preferred stock, if fully participating, will receive not only its 5 percent return, but also dividends at the same rates as those paid to common stockholders if paying amounts in excess of 5 percent of par or stated value to common stockholders. Note that participating preferred stock may be only partially participating. Although seldom used, examples of companies that have issued participating preferred stock are **LTV Corporation**, **Southern California Edison**, and **Allied Products Corporation**.

Convertible Preferred Stock **Convertible preferred stock** allows stockholders, at their option, to exchange preferred shares for common stock at a predetermined ratio. The convertible preferred stockholder not only enjoys a preferred claim on dividends but also has the option of converting into a common stockholder with unlimited participation in earnings.

Callable Preferred Stock **Callable preferred stock** permits the corporation at its option to call or redeem the outstanding preferred shares at specified future dates and at stipulated prices. Many preferred issues are callable. The corporation usually sets the call or redemption price slightly above the original issuance price and commonly states it in terms related to the par value. The callable feature permits the corporation to use the capital obtained through the issuance of such stock until the need has passed or it is no longer advantageous.

The existence of a call price or prices tends to set a ceiling on the market price of the preferred shares unless they are convertible into common stock. When a corporation redeems preferred stock, it must pay any dividends in arrears.

Redeemable Preferred Stock Recently, more and more issuances of preferred stock have features that make the security more like debt (legal obligation to pay) than an equity instrument. For example, **redeemable preferred stock** has a mandatory redemption period or a redemption feature that the issuer cannot control.

Previously, public companies were not permitted to report these debt-like preferred stock issues in equity, but they were not required to report them as a liability either. There were concerns about classification of these debt-like securities, which may have been reported as equity or in the "mezzanine" section of balance sheets between debt and equity. There also was diversity in practice as to how dividends on these securities were reported. The FASB now requires debt-like securities, such as redeemable preferred stock, to be classified as liabilities and be measured and accounted for similar to liabilities. [1] (See the FASB Codification References near the end of the chapter.)

Accounting for and Reporting Preferred Stock

The accounting for preferred stock at issuance is similar to that for common stock. A corporation allocates proceeds between the par value of the preferred stock and additional paid-in capital. To illustrate, assume that Bishop Co. issues 10,000 shares of $10 par value preferred stock for $12 cash per share. Bishop records the issuance as follows.

Cash	120,000	
Preferred Stock		100,000
Paid-in Capital in Excess of Par—Preferred Stock		20,000

Thus, Bishop maintains separate accounts for these different classes of shares.

In contrast to convertible bonds (recorded as a liability on the date of issue), corporations consider convertible preferred stock as a part of stockholders' equity. In addition, when exercising the conversion option on convertible preferred stock, there is no theoretical justification for recognition of a gain or loss. A company recognizes no gain or loss when dealing with stockholders in their capacity as business owners. Instead, the company **employs the book value method**: debit Preferred Stock, along with any related Paid-in Capital in Excess of Par—Preferred Stock, and credit Common Stock and Paid-in Capital in Excess of Par—Common Stock (if an excess exists).

Preferred stock generally has no maturity date. Therefore, no legal obligation exists to pay the preferred stockholder. As a result, companies classify preferred stock as part of stockholders' equity. Companies generally report preferred stock at par value as the first item in the stockholders' equity section. They report any excess over par value as part of additional paid-in capital. They also consider dividends on preferred stock as a distribution of income and not an expense. Companies must disclose the pertinent rights of the preferred stock outstanding. [2]

What Do the Numbers Mean? A Class (B) Act

Some companies grant preferences to different shareholders by issuing different classes of common stock. For example, ownership of **Dow Jones & Co.** was controlled by family members who owned Class B shares, which carry super voting powers. The same is true for the Ford family's control of **Ford Motor Co.** Class B shares are often criticized for protecting owners' interest at the expense of shareholder return. These shares often can determine if a takeover deal gets done, or not. Here are some notable companies with two-tiered shares in which the Class A shares have one vote and the Class B shares have 10 votes.

Companies with Two-Tiered Shares	
1-800-Flowers.com	Ralph Lauren
Dick's Sporting Goods	Skechers
Domino's Pizza	Under Amour
Expedia	Tootsie Roll
Go Pro	Box

Source: The list derives from Council of Institutional Investors analysis of Fact Set Shark Repellent data, *https://www.cii.org/dualclass_stock*.

For family-controlled companies, issuing newer classes of lower or nonvoting stock effectively creates currency for acquisitions, increases liquidity, or puts a public value on the company without diluting the family's voting control. This was one of the main reasons **Facebook** gave when it created a dual-class share structure. In that IPO, Facebook founder Mark Zuckerberg owns only 16 percent of the company's shares but still holds nearly 60 percent of Facebook's voting rights.

Google has gone even further and created a Class C stock that gives its owners zero votes. That sounds bad. In practice, however, the nonvoting shares won't be so different from holders of Google's Class A shares, which get one vote apiece. Both groups are dominated by holders of the only shares that matter: Class B shares with 10 votes each. Most of those are owned by Google's founders, Larry Page and Sergey Brin.

Yet Page and Brin aren't satisfied with the 55.7 percent majority of votes that they control. As Google issues less-potent Class A shares—to compensate employees or to finance acquisitions—the company's founders have seen their voting power diluted. But now that the company is issuing the neutered Class C shares, Page and Brin are free to create as many shares as they like without giving up an iota of their grip on Google's direction.

Sources: Adapted from Andy Serwer, "Dual-Listed Companies Aren't Fair or Balanced," *Fortune* (September 20, 2004), p. 83; Alex Halperin, "A Class (B) Act," *Businessweek* (May 28, 2007), p. 12; The Big Number, "20 Companies That Went Public in 2011 with Two or More Classes of Stock," *Wall Street Journal* (February 8, 2012), p. B5; MoneyWatch, "Facebook's IPO by the Important Numbers," *www.cbsnews.com* (May 17, 2012); and N. Summers, "Why Google Is Issuing a New Kind of Toothless Stock," *Businessweek* (April 3, 2014).

Reacquisition of Shares

LEARNING OBJECTIVE 2

Describe the accounting and reporting for reacquisition of shares.

Companies often buy back their own shares. In fact, share buybacks now exceed dividends as a form of distribution to stockholders. For example, oil producer **ConocoPhillips**, healthcare-products giant **Johnson & Johnson**, and discount retailer **Wal-Mart Stores, Inc.** have ambitious buyback plans. As shown in **Illustration 15.4**, companies in the S&P 500 stock index are estimated to buy back $650 billion of their own shares in 2018.

Corporations purchase their outstanding stock for several reasons:

1. ***To provide tax-efficient distributions of excess cash to shareholders.*** Capital gain rates on sales of stock to the company by the stockholders have been approximately half

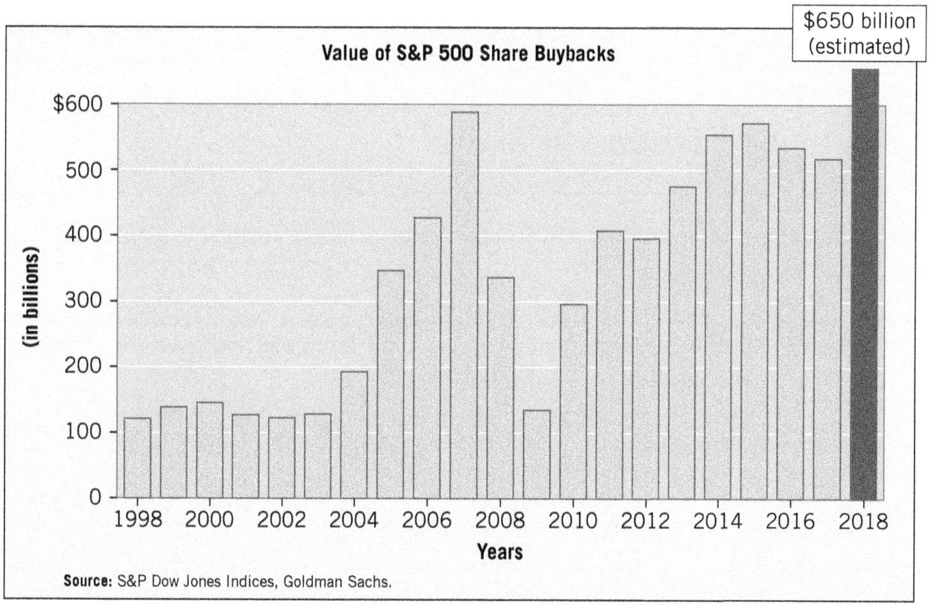

ILLUSTRATION 15.4
Share Buybacks 1998—2018

the ordinary tax rate for many investors. This advantage has been somewhat diminished by recent changes in the tax law related to dividends.

2. ***To increase earnings per share and return on equity.*** Reducing both shares outstanding and stockholders' equity often enhances certain performance ratios. However, strategies to hype performance measures might increase performance in the short-run, but these tactics add no real long-term value.
3. ***To provide stock for employee stock compensation contracts or to meet potential merger needs.*** Honeywell Inc. reported that it would use part of its purchase of one million common shares for employee stock compensation contracts. Other companies acquire shares to have them available for business acquisitions.
4. ***To thwart takeover attempts or to reduce the number of stockholders.*** By reducing the number of shares held by the public, existing owners and managements bar "outsiders" from gaining control or significant influence. When Ted Turner attempted to acquire CBS, CBS started a substantial buyback of its stock. Companies may also use stock purchases to eliminate dissident stockholders.
5. ***To make a market in the stock.*** As one company executive noted, "Our company is trying to establish a floor for the stock." Purchasing stock in the marketplace creates a demand. This may stabilize the stock price or, in fact, increase it.

Some publicly held corporations have chosen to "go private," that is, to eliminate public (outside) ownership entirely by purchasing all of their outstanding stock. Companies often accomplish such a procedure through a **leveraged buyout (LBO)**, in which the company borrows money to finance the stock repurchases.

After reacquiring shares, a company may either retire them or hold them in the treasury for reissue. If not retired, such shares are referred to as **treasury stock** (**treasury shares**). Technically, treasury stock is a corporation's own stock, reacquired after having been issued and fully paid.

Treasury stock is not an asset. When a company purchases treasury stock, a reduction occurs in both assets and stockholders' equity. It is inappropriate to imply that a corporation can own a part of itself. A corporation may sell treasury stock to obtain funds, but that does not make treasury stock a balance sheet asset. When a corporation buys back some of its own outstanding stock, it has not acquired an asset; it reduces net assets (see Underlying Concepts).

Underlying Concepts

As we indicated in Chapter 2, an asset should have probable future economic benefits. Treasury stock simply reduces common stock outstanding.

The possession of treasury stock does not give the corporation the right to vote, to exercise preemptive rights as a stockholder, to receive cash dividends, or to receive assets upon corporate liquidation. **Treasury stock is essentially the same as unissued capital stock.** No one advocates classifying unissued capital stock as an asset in the balance sheet.[8]

Purchase of Treasury Stock

Companies use two general methods of handling treasury stock in the accounts: the cost method and the par value method. Both methods are generally acceptable. The cost method enjoys more widespread use.[9]

- The **cost method** results in debiting the Treasury Stock account for the reacquisition cost and in reporting this account as a deduction from the total paid-in capital **and** retained earnings on the balance sheet.
- The **par (stated) value method** records all transactions in treasury shares at their par value and reports the treasury stock as a deduction from capital stock only.

No matter which method a company uses, most states consider the cost of the treasury shares acquired as a restriction on retained earnings.

Companies generally use the cost method to account for treasury stock. This method derives its name from the fact that a company maintains the Treasury Stock account at the cost of the shares purchased.[10] Under the cost method, the company debits the Treasury Stock account for the cost of the shares acquired. Upon reissuance of the shares, it credits the account for this same cost. The original price received for the stock does not affect the entries to record the acquisition and reissuance of the treasury stock.

To illustrate, assume that Pacific Company issued 100,000 shares of $1 par value common stock at a price of $10 per share. In addition, it has retained earnings of $300,000. Illustration 15.5 shows the stockholders' equity section on December 31, 2019, before purchase of treasury stock.

ILLUSTRATION 15.5

Stockholders' Equity with No Treasury Stock

Stockholders' equity	
Paid-in capital	
Common stock, $1 par value, 100,000 shares issued and outstanding	$ 100,000
Additional paid-in capital	900,000
Total paid-in capital	1,000,000
Retained earnings	300,000
Total stockholders' equity	$1,300,000

On January 20, 2020, Pacific acquires 10,000 shares of its stock at $11 per share. Pacific records the reacquisition as follows.

January 20, 2020		
Treasury Stock	110,000	
Cash		110,000

Note that Pacific debited Treasury Stock for the cost of the shares purchased. The original paid-in capital account, Common Stock, is not affected because the number of issued shares does not change. The same is true for the Paid-in Capital in Excess of Par—Common Stock account. Pacific deducts treasury stock from total paid-in capital and retained earnings in the stockholders' equity section.

Illustration 15.6 shows the stockholders' equity section for Pacific after purchase of the treasury stock.

[8]The possible justification for classifying these shares as assets is that the company will use them to liquidate a specific liability that appears on the balance sheet. *Accounting Trends and Techniques* reported that out of 500 companies surveyed, 341 disclosed treasury stock, but none classified it as an asset.

[9]*Accounting Trends and Techniques* indicated that of its selected list of 500 companies, of the 341 companies with treasury stock, all carried common stock in treasury at cost. Only one company carried preferred stock in treasury.

[10]If making numerous acquisitions of blocks of treasury shares at different prices, a company may use inventory costing methods—such as specific identification, average-cost, or FIFO—to identify the cost at date of reissuance.

ILLUSTRATION 15.6
Stockholders' Equity with Treasury Stock

Stockholders' equity	
Paid-in capital	
Common stock, $1 par value, 100,000 shares issued and 90,000 outstanding	$ 100,000
Additional paid-in capital	900,000
Total paid-in capital	1,000,000
Retained earnings	300,000
Total paid-in capital and retained earnings	1,300,000
Less: Cost of treasury stock (10,000 shares)	110,000
Total stockholders' equity	$1,190,000

Pacific subtracts the cost of the treasury stock from the total of common stock, additional paid-in capital, and retained earnings. It therefore reduces stockholders' equity. Many states require a corporation to restrict retained earnings for the cost of treasury stock purchased. The restriction keeps intact the corporation's legal capital that it temporarily holds as treasury stock. When the corporation sells the treasury stock, it lifts the restriction.

Pacific discloses both the number of shares issued (100,000) and the number in the treasury (10,000). The difference is the number of shares of stock outstanding (90,000). The term **outstanding stock** means the number of shares of issued stock that stockholders own.

Sale of Treasury Stock

Companies usually reissue or retire treasury stock. When selling treasury shares, the accounting for the sale depends on the price. If the selling price of the treasury stock equals its cost, the company records the sale of the shares by debiting Cash and crediting Treasury Stock. In cases where the selling price of the treasury stock is not equal to cost, then accounting for treasury stock sold **above cost** differs from the accounting for treasury stock sold **below cost**. However, the sale of treasury stock either above or below cost increases both total assets and stockholders' equity.

Sale of Treasury Stock Above Cost

When the selling price of shares of treasury stock exceeds its cost, a company credits the difference to Paid-in Capital from Treasury Stock. To illustrate, assume that Pacific acquired 10,000 shares of its treasury stock at $11 per share. It now sells 1,000 shares at $15 per share on March 10. Pacific records the entry as follows.

March 10, 2020		
Cash	15,000	
Treasury Stock		11,000
Paid-in Capital from Treasury Stock		4,000

There are two reasons why Pacific does not credit $4,000 to Gain on Sale of Treasury Stock. (1) Gains on sales occur when selling **assets**; treasury stock is not an asset. (2) A gain or loss should not be recognized from stock transactions with its own stockholders. Thus, Pacific should not include paid-in capital arising from the sale of treasury stock in the measurement of net income. Instead, it lists paid-in capital from treasury stock separately on the balance sheet, as a part of paid-in capital.

Sale of Treasury Stock Below Cost

When a corporation sells treasury stock below its cost, it usually debits the excess of the cost over selling price to Paid-in Capital from Treasury Stock. Thus, if Pacific sells an additional 1,000 shares of treasury stock on March 21 at $8 per share, it records the sale as follows.

March 21, 2020		
Cash	8,000	
Paid-in Capital from Treasury Stock	3,000	
Treasury Stock		11,000

We can make several observations based on the two sale entries (sale above cost and sale below cost). (1) Pacific credits Treasury Stock at cost in each entry. (2) Pacific uses Paid-in Capital from Treasury Stock for the difference between the cost and the resale price of the shares. (3) Neither entry affects the original paid-in capital account, Common Stock.

After eliminating the credit balance in Paid-in Capital from Treasury Stock, the corporation debits any additional excess of cost over selling price to Retained Earnings. To illustrate, assume that Pacific sells an additional 1,000 shares at $8 per share on April 10. Illustration 15.7 shows the balance in the Paid-in Capital from Treasury Stock account (before the April 10 sale).

ILLUSTRATION 15.7

Treasury Stock Transactions in Paid-in Capital Account

Paid-in Capital from Treasury Stock			
Mar. 21	3,000	Mar. 10	4,000
		Balance	1,000

In this case, Pacific debits $1,000 of the excess to Paid-in Capital from Treasury Stock. It debits the remainder to Retained Earnings. The entry is:

April 10, 2020		
Cash	8,000	
Paid-in Capital from Treasury Stock	1,000	
Retained Earnings	2,000	
Treasury Stock		11,000

Retiring Treasury Stock

The board of directors may approve the retirement of treasury shares. This decision results in cancellation of the treasury stock and a reduction in the number of shares of issued stock. Retired treasury shares have the status of authorized and unissued shares. The accounting effects are similar to the sale of treasury stock except that corporations debit the **paid-in capital accounts applicable to the retired shares** instead of cash. For example, if a corporation originally sells the shares at par, it debits Common Stock for the par value per share. If it originally sells the shares at $3 above par value, it also debits Paid-in Capital in Excess of Par—Common Stock for $3 per share at retirement.

What Do the Numbers Mean? Buybacks—Good or Bad?

As indicated in Illustration 15.4, companies have ramped up repurchases of their own stock. Providing a look into the individual companies engaged in share buybacks shown in Illustration 15.4, here is what the top companies in the S&P 500 spent repurchasing shares in fiscal 2017.

Company	Fiscal 2017 Buybacks ($ billion)
Apple	$33.0
Amazon	0.0
Alphabet	4.8
Microsoft	10.3
Facebook	2.1
Berkshire Hathaway	0.0
JP Morgan Chase	15.4
Exxon/Mobil	0.5
Johnson & Johnson	6.4
Bank of America	12.8

Is this good or bad news for investors? Maybe neither. While it might appear that companies are getting better at timing their purchases (when prices are falling), they also buy shares for reasons that go beyond giving a boost to shareholders—everything from mergers and acquisitions to eliminating the impact of equity compensation.

The conventional wisdom is that companies that buy back shares believe their shares are undervalued. Thus, analysts view the buyback announcement as an important piece of inside information about future company prospects. On the other hand, buybacks can actually hurt businesses and their shareholders over the long run. For example, drug-makers Merck, Pfizer, and Amgen spent heavily on stock repurchases, possibly at the expense of research and development. And whether the buyback is a good thing appears to depend a lot on why the company did the buyback and what the repurchased shares were used for.

Sources: Adapted from W. Lazonick, "The Buyback Boondoggle," *BusinessWeek* (August 24, 2009); B. Levisohn, "Beware All Those Buybacks," *Wall Street Journal* (September 29–30, 2012), p. B9; and A. Bary, "Why the Buyback Boom Is Bullish for Investors," *Barron's* (May 12, 2018).

Dividend Policy

LEARNING OBJECTIVE 3

Explain the accounting and reporting issues related to dividends.

Dividend payouts can be important signals to the market. The practice of paying dividends declined sharply in the 1980s and 1990s as companies focused on growth and plowed profits back into the business. A resurgence in dividend payouts is due in large part to the dividend tax cut of 2003, which reduced the rate of tax on dividends to 15 percent (quite a bit lower than the ordinary income rate charged in the past). In addition, investors who were burned by accounting scandals in recent years began demanding higher payouts in the form of dividends. Why? A dividend check provides proof that at least some portion of a company's profits is genuine.[11] As one analyst noted, "Companies with the ability to grow dividends over time tend to be durable businesses with strong cash flow and relatively predictable earnings. . . . So you're more likely to get a return on your investment year in and year out."

Determining the proper amount of dividends to pay is a difficult financial management decision. Companies paying dividends are extremely reluctant to reduce or eliminate their dividend. They fear that the securities market might negatively view this action. As a consequence, dividend-paying companies will make every effort to continue to do so. In addition, the type of shareholder the company has (taxable or nontaxable, retail investor or institutional investor) plays a large role in determining dividend policy.

Very few companies pay dividends in amounts equal to their legally available retained earnings. The major reasons are as follows.

1. To maintain agreements (bond covenants) with specific creditors, to retain all or a portion of the earnings, in the form of assets, to build up additional protection against possible loss.
2. To meet state corporation requirements, that earnings equivalent to the cost of treasury shares purchased be restricted against dividend declarations.
3. To retain assets that would otherwise be paid out as dividends, to finance growth or expansion. This is sometimes called internal financing, reinvesting earnings, or "plowing" the profits back into the business.
4. To smooth out dividend payments from year to year by accumulating earnings in good years and using such accumulated earnings as a basis for dividends in bad years.
5. To build up a cushion or buffer against possible losses or errors in the calculation of profits.

The reasons above are self-explanatory except for the second. The laws of some states require that the corporation restrict its legal capital from distribution to stockholders, to protect against loss for creditors.[12] The applicable state law determines the legality of a dividend.

Financial Condition and Dividend Distributions

Effective management of a company requires attention to more than the legality of dividend distributions. Management must also consider economic conditions, most importantly, liquidity. Assume an extreme situation as shown in **Illustration 15.8**.

[11]The share of U.S. and European companies expected to increase dividends in 2018 is forecast to reach its highest level in at least a decade—a boost for investors facing resurgent stock volatility, rising interest rates, and geopolitical risk. Among big listed companies in the United States and Europe, about 71 percent and 83 percent, respectively, are expected to increase dividends in 2018, the highest share in at least a decade, according to research by **JPMorgan**. See J. Sindreu, "Firms Poised to Jack Up Dividends," *Wall Street Journal* (April 19, 2018).

[12]If the corporation buys its own outstanding stock, it reduces its legal capital and distributes assets to stockholders. If permitted, the corporation could, by purchasing treasury stock at any price desired, return to the stockholders their investments and leave creditors with little or no protection against loss.

ILLUSTRATION 15.8

Balance Sheet, Showing a Lack of Liquidity

Balance Sheet			
Plant assets	$500,000	Capital stock	$400,000
	$500,000	Retained earnings	100,000
			$500,000

The depicted company has a retained earnings credit balance. Unless restricted, it can declare a dividend of $100,000. But because all its assets are plant assets used in operations, payment of a cash dividend of $100,000 would require the sale of plant assets or borrowing.

Even if a balance sheet shows current assets, as in **Illustration 15.9**, the question remains as to whether the company needs its cash for other purposes.

ILLUSTRATION 15.9

Balance Sheet, Showing Cash but Minimal Working Capital

Balance Sheet				
Cash	$100,000	Current liabilities		$ 60,000
Plant assets	460,000	Capital stock	$400,000	
	$560,000	Retained earnings	100,000	500,000
				$560,000

The existence of current liabilities strongly implies that the company needs some of the cash to meet current debts as they mature. In addition, day-to-day cash requirements for payrolls and other expenditures not included in current liabilities also require cash.

Thus, before declaring a dividend, management must consider **availability of funds to pay the dividend**. A company should not pay a dividend unless both the present and future financial position warrant the distribution.

The SEC encourages companies to disclose their dividend policy in their annual report, especially those that (1) have earnings but fail to pay dividends, or (2) do not expect to pay dividends in the foreseeable future. In addition, the SEC encourages companies that consistently pay dividends to indicate whether they intend to continue this practice in the future.

Types of Dividends

Companies generally base dividend distributions either on accumulated profits (that is, retained earnings) or on some other capital item such as additional paid-in capital. Dividends are of the following types.

1. Cash dividends.
2. Property dividends (dividends in kind).
3. Liquidating dividends.

Although commonly paid in cash, companies occasionally pay dividends in stock or some other asset.[13] **All dividends, except for stock dividends, reduce the total stockholders' equity in the corporation.** When declaring a stock dividend, the corporation does not pay out assets or incur a liability. It issues additional shares of stock to each stockholder and nothing more.

The natural expectation of any stockholder who receives a dividend is that the corporation has operated successfully. As a result, he or she is receiving a share of its profits. A company should disclose a **liquidating dividend**—that is, a dividend not based on retained earnings—to the stockholders so that they will not misunderstand its source.

[13]*Accounting Trends and Techniques* reported that of its 500 surveyed companies, 343 paid a cash dividend on common stock, 33 paid a cash dividend on preferred stock, 2 issued stock dividends, and 1 issued or paid dividends in kind. Some companies declare more than one type of dividend in a given year.

Cash Dividends

The board of directors votes on the declaration of **cash dividends**. Upon approval of the resolution, the board declares a dividend. Before paying it, however, the company must prepare a current list of stockholders. For this reason, there is usually a time lag between declaration and payment. For example, the board of directors might approve a resolution at the January 10 (**date of declaration**) meeting and declare it payable February 5 (**date of payment**) to all stockholders of record January 25 (**date of record**).[14] In this example, the period from January 10 to January 25 gives time for the company to complete and register any transfers in process. The time from January 25 to February 5 provides an opportunity for the transfer agent or accounting department, depending on who does this work, to prepare a list of stockholders as of January 25 and to prepare and mail dividend checks.

A declared cash dividend is a liability. Because payment is generally required very soon, it is usually a current liability. To illustrate, Roadway Freight Corp. on June 10 declared a cash dividend of 50 cents a share on 1.8 million shares payable July 16 to all stockholders of record June 24. The entries for declaration and payment of a cash dividend are presented in **Illustration 15.10**.

ILLUSTRATION 15.10

Cash Dividend Entries

At date of declaration (June 10)		
Retained Earnings (Cash Dividends Declared)	900,000	
Dividends Payable		900,000
At date of record (June 24)		
No entry		
At date of payment (July 16)		
Dividends Payable	900,000	
Cash		900,000

To set up a ledger account that shows the amount of dividends declared during the year, Roadway Freight might debit Cash Dividends Declared instead of Retained Earnings at the time of declaration. It then closes this account to Retained Earnings at year-end.

A company may declare dividends either as a certain percentage of par, such as a 6 percent dividend on preferred stock, or as an amount per share, such as 60 cents per share on no-par common stock. In the first case, the rate multiplied by the par value of outstanding shares equals the total dividend. In the second, the dividend equals the amount per share multiplied by the number of shares outstanding. **Companies do not declare or pay cash dividends on treasury stock.**

Dividend policies vary among corporations. Some companies, such as **JP Morgan Chase**, **Clorox Co.**, and **Tootsie Roll Industries**, take pride in a long, unbroken string of quarterly dividend payments. They would lower or pass the dividend only if forced to do so by a sustained decline in earnings or a critical shortage of cash.

"Growth" companies, on the other hand, pay little or no cash dividends because their policy is to expand as rapidly as internal and external financing permit. For example, **Questcor Pharmaceuticals Inc.** has never paid cash dividends to its common stockholders. These investors hope that the price of their shares will appreciate in value. The investors will then realize a profit when they sell their shares. Many companies focus more on increasing share price, stock repurchase programs, and corporate earnings than on dividend payout.

Property Dividends

Dividends payable in assets of the corporation other than cash are called **property dividends** or **dividends in kind**. Property dividends may be merchandise, real estate, or investments,

[14]Theoretically, the ex-dividend date is the day after the date of record. However, to allow time for transfer of the shares, the stock exchanges generally advance the ex-dividend date two to four days. Therefore, the party who owns the stock on the day prior to the expressed ex-dividend date receives the dividends. The party who buys the stock on and after the ex-dividend date does not receive the dividend. Between the declaration date and the ex-dividend date, the market price of the stock includes the dividend.

or whatever form the board of directors designates. **Ranchers Exploration and Development Corp.** reported one year that it would pay a fourth-quarter dividend in gold bars instead of cash. Because of the obvious difficulties of divisibility of units and delivery to stockholders, the usual property dividend is in the form of securities of other companies that the distributing corporation holds as an investment.

For example, after ruling that **DuPont**'s 23 percent stock interest in **General Motors** (GM) violated antitrust laws, the Supreme Court ordered DuPont to divest itself of the GM stock within 10 years. The stock represented 63 million shares of GM's 281 million shares then outstanding. DuPont could not sell the shares in one block of 63 million. Further, it could not sell 6 million shares annually for the next 10 years without severely depressing the value of the GM stock. DuPont solved its problem by declaring a property dividend and distributing the GM shares as a dividend to its own stockholders.

When declaring a property dividend, the corporation should **restate at fair value the property it will distribute, recognizing any gain or loss** as the difference between the property's fair value and carrying value at date of declaration. The corporation may then record the declared dividend as a debit to Retained Earnings (or Property Dividends Declared) and a credit to Property Dividends Payable, at an amount equal to the fair value of the distributed property. Upon distribution of the dividend, the corporation debits Property Dividends Payable and credits the account containing the distributed asset (restated at fair value).

For example, Trendler, Inc. transferred to stockholders some of its equity investments costing $1,250,000 by declaring a property dividend on December 28, 2019, to be distributed on January 30, 2020, to stockholders of record on January 15, 2020. At the date of declaration, the securities have a fair value of $2,000,000. Trendler makes the entries shown in **Illustration 15.11**.

ILLUSTRATION 15.11

Property Dividend Entries

At date of declaration (December 28, 2019)		
Equity Investments	750,000	
Unrealized Holding Gain or Loss—Income ($2,000,000 – $1,250,000)		750,000
Retained Earnings (Property Dividends Declared)	2,000,000	
Property Dividends Payable		2,000,000
At date of distribution (January 30, 2020)		
Property Dividends Payable	2,000,000	
Equity Investments		2,000,000

Liquidating Dividends

Some corporations use paid-in capital as a basis for dividends. Without proper disclosure of this fact, stockholders may erroneously believe the corporation has been operating at a profit. To avoid this type of deception, intentional or unintentional, a clear statement of the source of every dividend should accompany the dividend check.

Dividends based on other than retained earnings are sometimes described as **liquidating dividends**. This term implies that such dividends are a return of the stockholder's investment rather than of profits. In other words, **any dividend not based on earnings reduces corporate paid-in capital and to that extent, it is a liquidating dividend**. Companies in the extractive industries may pay dividends equal to the total of accumulated income and depletion. The portion of these dividends in excess of accumulated income represents a return of part of the stockholder's investment.

For example, McChesney Mines Inc. issued a "dividend" to its common stockholders of $1,200,000. The cash dividend announcement noted that stockholders should consider $900,000 as income and the remainder a return of capital. McChesney Mines records the dividend as shown in **Illustration 15.12**.

In some cases, management simply decides to cease business and declares a liquidating dividend. In these cases, liquidation may take place over a number of years to ensure an

ILLUSTRATION 15.12
Liquidating Dividend Entries

At date of declaration		
Retained Earnings	900,000	
Paid-in Capital in Excess of Par—Common Stock	300,000	
Dividends Payable		1,200,000
At date of payment		
Dividends Payable	1,200,000	
Cash		1,200,000

orderly and fair sale of assets. For example, when Overseas National Airways dissolved, it agreed to pay a liquidating dividend to its stockholders over a period of years equivalent to $8.60 per share. Each liquidating dividend payment in such cases reduces paid-in capital.

Stock Dividends and Stock Splits

Stock Dividends

If management wishes to "capitalize" part of the earnings (i.e., reclassify amounts from earned to contributed capital) and thus retain earnings in the business on a permanent basis, it may issue a stock dividend. In this case, **the company distributes no assets**. Each stockholder maintains exactly the same proportionate interest in the corporation and the same total book value after the company issues the stock dividend. Of course, the book value per share is lower because each stockholder holds more shares.

A stock dividend therefore is the issuance by a corporation of its own stock to its stockholders on a pro rata basis, without receiving any consideration. In recording a stock dividend, some believe that the company should transfer the **par value of the stock issued** as a dividend from retained earnings to capital stock. Others believe that it should transfer the **fair value of the stock issued**—its market value at the declaration date—from retained earnings to capital stock and additional paid-in capital.

Underlying Concepts

By requiring fair value, the intent was to punish companies that used stock dividends. This approach violates the neutrality concept (that is, that standards-setting should be even-handed).

The fair value position was adopted, at least in part, in order to influence the stock dividend policies of corporations. Evidently in 1941, both the New York Stock Exchange and many in the accounting profession regarded periodic stock dividends as objectionable. They believed that the term dividend when used with a distribution of additional stock was misleading because investors' net assets did not increase as a result of this "dividend." As a result, these groups decided to make it more difficult for corporations to sustain a series of such stock dividends out of their accumulated earnings, by requiring the use of fair value when it substantially exceeded book value (see Underlying Concepts).[15]

When the stock dividend is less than 20–25 percent of the common shares outstanding at the time of the dividend declaration, the company is therefore required to transfer the **fair value** of the stock issued from retained earnings. Stock dividends of less than 20–25 percent are often referred to as small (ordinary) stock dividends. This method of handling stock dividends is justified on the grounds that "many recipients of stock dividends look upon them as distributions of corporate earnings and usually in an amount equivalent to the fair value of the additional shares received." [3] We consider this argument unconvincing. It is generally agreed that stock dividends are not income to the recipients. Therefore, sound accounting should not recommend procedures simply because some recipients think they are income.[16]

To illustrate a small stock dividend, assume that Vine Corporation has outstanding 1,000 shares of $100 par value common stock and retained earnings of $50,000. If Vine declares a

[15]This was perhaps the earliest instance of "economic consequences" affecting an accounting pronouncement. The Committee on Accounting Procedure described its action as required by "proper accounting and corporate policy." See Stephen A. Zeff, "The Rise of 'Economic Consequences'," *The Journal of Accountancy* (December 1978), pp. 53–66.

[16]One study concluded that *small* stock dividends do not always produce significant amounts of extra value on the date after issuance (ex date) and that *large* stock dividends almost always fail to generate extra value on the ex-dividend date. Taylor W. Foster III and Don Vickrey, "The Information Content of Stock Dividend Announcements," *The Accounting Review*, Vol. LIII, No. 2 (April 1978), pp. 360–370.

10 percent stock dividend, it issues 100 additional shares to current stockholders. If the fair value of the stock at the time of the stock dividend is $130 per share, the entry is:

At date of declaration		
Retained Earnings (100 × $130)	13,000	
Common Stock Dividend Distributable (100 × $100)		10,000
Paid-in Capital in Excess of Par—Common Stock		3,000

Note that the stock dividend does not affect any asset or liability. **The entry merely reflects a reclassification of stockholders' equity.** If Vine prepares a balance sheet between the dates of declaration and distribution, it should show the common stock dividend distributable in the stockholders' equity section as an addition to common stock (whereas it shows cash or property dividends payable as current liabilities).

When issuing the stock, the entry is:

At date of distribution		
Common Stock Dividend Distributable	10,000	
Common Stock		10,000

No matter what the fair value is at the time of the stock dividend, each stockholder retains the same proportionate interest in the corporation.

Some state statutes specifically prohibit the issuance of stock dividends on treasury stock. In those states that permit treasury shares to participate in the distribution accompanying a stock dividend or stock split, the planned use of the treasury shares influences corporate practice. For example, if a corporation issues treasury shares in connection with employee stock options, the treasury shares may participate in the distribution because the corporation usually adjusts the number of shares under option for any stock dividends or splits. But no useful purpose is served by issuing additional shares to the treasury stock without a specific purpose, since they are essentially equivalent to authorized but unissued shares.

To continue with our example of the effect of the small stock dividend, note in **Illustration 15.13** that the stock dividend does not change the total stockholders' equity. Also, it does not change the proportion of the total shares outstanding held by each stockholder.

ILLUSTRATION 15.13

Effects of a Small (10%) Stock Dividend

Before dividend	
Common stock, 1,000 shares at $100 par	$100,000
Retained earnings	50,000
Total stockholders' equity	$150,000
Stockholders' interests:	
A. 400 shares, 40% interest, book value	$ 60,000
B. 500 shares, 50% interest, book value	75,000
C. 100 shares, 10% interest, book value	15,000
	$150,000
After declaration but before distribution of 10% stock dividend	
If fair value ($130) is used as basis for entry:	
Common stock, 1,000 shares at $100 par	$100,000
Common stock distributable, 100 shares at $100 par	10,000
Paid-in capital in excess of par—common stock	3,000
Retained earnings ($50,000 – $13,000)	37,000
Total stockholders' equity	$150,000
After declaration and distribution of 10% stock dividend	
If fair value ($130) is used as basis for entry:	
Common stock, 1,100 shares at $100 par	$110,000
Paid-in capital in excess of par—common stock	3,000
Retained earnings ($50,000 – $13,000)	37,000
Total stockholders' equity	$150,000
Stockholders' interest:	
A. 440 shares, 40% interest, book value	$ 60,000
B. 550 shares, 50% interest, book value	75,000
C. 110 shares, 10% interest, book value	15,000
	$150,000

Stock Splits

If a company has undistributed earnings over several years and accumulates a sizable balance in retained earnings, the market value of its outstanding shares likely increases. Stock issued at prices less than $50 a share can easily attain a market price in excess of $200 a share. The higher the market price of a stock, however, the less readily some investors can purchase it.

The managements of many corporations believe that better public relations depend on wider ownership of the corporation's stock. They therefore target a market price sufficiently low to be within range of the majority of potential investors. To reduce the market price of shares, they use the common device of a **stock split**. For example, after its stock price increased by 25-fold, **Qualcomm Inc.** split its stock 4-for-1. Qualcomm's stock had risen above $500 per share. The split led analysts to reduce their target to $250, which it could better meet with wider distribution of shares at lower trading prices.[17]

From an accounting standpoint, Qualcomm **records no entry for a stock split**. However, it enters a memorandum note to indicate the changed par value of the shares and the increased number of shares. **Illustration 15.14** shows the lack of change in stockholders' equity for a 2-for-1 stock split on 1,000 shares of $100 par value stock with the par being halved upon issuance of the additional shares.

ILLUSTRATION 15.14
Effects of a Stock Split

Stockholders' Equity Before 2-for-1 Split		Stockholders' Equity After 2-for-1 Split	
Common stock, 1,000 shares at $100 par	$100,000	Common stock, 2,000 shares at $50 par	$100,000
Retained earnings	50,000	Retained earnings	50,000
	$150,000		$150,000

What Do the Numbers Mean? Splitsville

Guessing which companies might be next to split their shares is a hobby of investors. When companies' per share prices get high, some look to lower their per share prices to make them more attractive to individual investors. It's a bit of an old-fashioned development, but one that investors are still conditioned to monitor. There's no question that stocks with the highest per share prices would be the logical place to consider for possible splits.

On the other hand, certain large companies are taking a different approach. The godfather of the no-split camp is **Berkshire Hathaway**'s chairman Warren Buffett. Berkshire's Class A shares were recently selling in excess of $250,000 per share. Buffett said he didn't want to split the shares for people who found such a move a good reason for buying the stock. His point—people who buy for non-value reasons are likely to sell for non-value reasons. The table in the next column lists some companies that in 2018 have split their stock.

Company	Ratio
TrovaGene (TROV)	1-12
Gevo (GEVO)	1-20
Reshape Lifesciences (RSLS)	1-15
Horizon Bancorp (IN) (HBNC)	3-2
Trex (TREX)	2-1
Arch Capital Group (ACGL)	3-1

Some companies are considering reverse stock splits in which, say, five shares are consolidated into one. Thus, a stock previously trading at $5 per share would be part of an unsplit share trading at $25. Unsplitting might thus avoid some of the negative consequences of a low trading price. The downside to this strategy is that analysts might view reverse splits as additional bad news about the direction of the stock price. For example, **Webvan**, a failed Internet grocer, did a 1-for-25 reverse split just before it entered bankruptcy. And struggling **Tenet Healthcare** executed a 1-for-4 reverse split in combination with a debt restructuring, in order to get its stock price into a more favorable trading range.

Sources: M. Murphy, "Tenet CFO Says Reverse Split Could Help Land New Business," *Wall Street Journal* (October 2, 2012); M. Krantz, "Starbucks Splits Stock. Who's Next?" *USA TODAY* (March 18, 2015); and Erik Holm and Ben Eisen, "Amazon's Brush with $1,000 Signals the Death of the Stock Split," *Wall Street Journal* (May 26, 2017). Split data found at *https://www.marketbeat.com/stock-splits/*.

[17]Another classic case is **Coca-Cola**. Coca-Cola had split its stock 11 times. If it had not done all of these splits, one of Coke's original shares would be worth $10.3 *million*. See S. Jakab, "Coca-Cola's Currency Is Its Resilience," *Wall Street Journal* (July 16, 2012).

Stock Split and Stock Dividend Differentiated

From a legal standpoint, a stock split differs from a stock dividend. How? A stock split increases the number of shares outstanding and decreases the par or stated value per share. **A stock dividend, although it increases the number of shares outstanding, does not decrease the par value; thus, it increases the total par value of outstanding shares.**

As discussed, the reasons for issuing a stock dividend are numerous and varied. Stock dividends can be primarily a publicity gesture **because many consider stock dividends as dividends**. Another reason is that the corporation may simply wish to retain profits in the business by capitalizing a part of retained earnings. In such a situation, it makes a transfer on declaration of a stock dividend from earned capital to contributed capital.

A corporation may also use a stock dividend, like a stock split, to increase the marketability of the stock, although marketability is often a secondary consideration. If the stock dividend is large, it has the same effect on market price as a stock split. **Whenever corporations issue additional shares for the purpose of reducing the unit market price, then the distribution more closely resembles a stock split than a stock dividend. This effect usually results only if the number of shares issued is more than 20–25 percent of the number of shares previously outstanding.** [4] A stock dividend of more than 20–25 percent of the number of shares previously outstanding is called a **large stock dividend**.[18] Such a distribution should not be called a stock dividend but instead "a split-up effected in the form of a dividend" or "stock split-up."

Also, since a split-up effected in the form of a dividend does not alter the par value per share, companies generally are required to transfer the par value amount from retained earnings. In other words, companies transfer from retained earnings to capital stock **the par value of the stock issued**, as opposed to a transfer of the market price of the shares issued as in the case of a small stock dividend.[19] For example, **Brown Group, Inc.** at one time authorized a 2-for-1 split, effected in the form of a stock dividend. As a result of this authorization, it distributed approximately 10.5 million shares, and transferred more than $39 million representing the par value of the shares issued from Retained Earnings to the Common Stock account.

To illustrate a large stock dividend (stock split-up effected in the form of a dividend), Rockland Steel, Inc. declared a 30 percent stock dividend on November 20, distributable December 29 to stockholders of record December 12. At the date of declaration, 1,000,000 shares, par value $10, are outstanding and with a fair value of $200 per share. The entries are shown in **Illustration 15.15**.

ILLUSTRATION 15.15

Stock Dividend Entries

At date of declaration (November 20)		
Retained Earnings	3,000,000	
Common Stock Dividend Distributable		3,000,000
Computation: 1,000,000 shares × .30 = 300,000	300,000 Additional shares × $10 Par value = $3,000,000	
At date of distribution (December 29)		
Common Stock Dividend Distributable	3,000,000	
Common Stock		3,000,000

Illustration 15.16 summarizes and compares the effects in the balance sheet and related items of various types of dividends and stock splits.

[18]The SEC has added more precision to the 20–25 percent rule. Specifically, the SEC indicates that companies should consider distributions of 25 percent or more as a "split-up effected in the form of a dividend." Companies should account for distributions of less than 25 percent as a stock dividend. The SEC more precisely defined GAAP here. As a result, public companies follow the SEC rule.

[19]Often, a company records a split-up effected in the form of a dividend as a debit to Paid-in Capital instead of Retained Earnings to indicate that this transaction should affect only paid-in capital accounts. No reduction of retained earnings is required except as indicated by legal requirements. *For homework purposes, assume that the debit is to Retained Earnings.* See, for example, Taylor W. Foster III and Edmund Scribner, "Accounting for Stock Dividends and Stock Splits: Corrections to Textbook Coverage," *Issues in Accounting Education* (February 1998).

Effect on:	Declaration of Cash Dividend	Payment of Cash Dividend	Declaration and Distribution of Small Stock Dividend	Declaration and Distribution of Large Stock Dividend	Stock Split
Retained earnings	Decrease	-0-	Decrease[a]	Decrease[b]	-0-
Capital stock	-0-	-0-	Increase[b]	Increase[b]	-0-
Additional paid-in capital	-0-	-0-	Increase[c]	-0-	-0-
Total stockholders' equity	Decrease	-0-	-0-	-0-	-0-
Working capital	Decrease	-0-	-0-	-0-	-0-
Total assets	-0-	Decrease	-0-	-0-	-0-
Number of shares outstanding	-0-	-0-	Increase	Increase	Increase

[a]Market price of shares. [b]Par or stated value of shares. [c]Excess of market price over par.

ILLUSTRATION 15.16

Effects of Dividends and Stock Splits on Financial Statement Elements

Presentation and Analysis of Stockholders' Equity

LEARNING OBJECTIVE 4

Indicate how to present and analyze stockholders' equity.

Presentation

Balance Sheet

Illustration 15.17 shows a comprehensive stockholders' equity section from the balance sheet of Frost Company that includes most of the equity items we discussed in this chapter.

ILLUSTRATION 15.17

Comprehensive Stockholders' Equity Presentation

Frost Company
Stockholders' Equity
December 31, 2020

Capital stock		
Preferred stock, $100 par value, 7% cumulative, 100,000 shares authorized, 30,000 shares issued and outstanding		$ 3,000,000
Common stock, no-par, stated value $10 per share, 500,000 shares authorized, 400,000 shares issued		4,000,000
Common stock dividend distributable, 20,000 shares		200,000
Total capital stock		7,200,000
Additional paid-in capital[20]		
Excess over par—preferred	$150,000	
Excess over stated value—common	840,000	990,000
Total paid-in capital		8,190,000
Retained earnings		4,360,000
Total paid-in capital and retained earnings		12,550,000
Less: Cost of treasury stock (2,000 shares, common)		190,000
Accumulated other comprehensive loss[21]		360,000
Total stockholders' equity		$12,000,000

[20]*Accounting Trends and Techniques* reported that of its 500 surveyed companies, 465 had additional paid-in capital.

[21]Companies may include a number of items in "Accumulated other comprehensive income (loss)." *Accounting Trends and Techniques* reported that of its 500 surveyed companies, 407 reported cumulative translation adjustments, 386 reported defined benefit postretirement plan adjustments (discussed in Chapter 20), 286 reported changes in the fair value of derivatives (discussed in Appendix 17A), and 218 reported unrealized losses/gains on certain investments (discussed in Chapter 17). A number of companies had more than one item.

Frost should disclose the pertinent rights and privileges of the various securities outstanding. For example, companies must disclose all of the following: dividend and liquidation preferences, participation rights, call prices and dates, conversion or exercise prices and pertinent dates, sinking fund requirements, unusual voting rights, and significant terms of contracts to issue additional shares. Liquidation preferences should be disclosed in the equity section of the balance sheet, rather than in the notes to the financial statements, to emphasize the possible effect of this restriction on future cash flows. [5]

Disclosure of Restrictions on Retained Earnings

Many corporations restrict retained earnings or dividends, without any formal journal entries. Such restrictions are **best disclosed by note**. Parenthetical notations are sometimes used, but restrictions imposed by bond indentures and loan agreements commonly require an extended explanation. Notes provide a medium for more complete explanations and free the financial statements from abbreviated notations. The note disclosure should reveal the source of the restriction, pertinent provisions, and the amount of retained earnings subject to restriction, or the amount not restricted.

Restrictions may be based on the retention of a certain retained earnings balance, the ability to maintain certain working capital requirements, additional borrowing, and other considerations. The example from the annual report of Alberto-Culver Company in Illustration 15.18 shows a note disclosing potential restrictions on retained earnings and dividends.

ILLUSTRATION 15.18

Disclosure of Restrictions on Retained Earnings and Dividends

Alberto-Culver Company

Note 3 (in part): The $200 million revolving credit facility, the term note, and the receivables agreement impose restrictions on such items as total debt, working capital, dividend payments, treasury stock purchases, and interest expense. At year-end, the company was in compliance with these arrangements, and $220 million of consolidated retained earnings was not restricted as to the payment of dividends.

Statement of Stockholders' Equity

The statement of stockholders' equity is frequently presented in the following basic format.

1. Balance at the beginning of the period.
2. Additions.
3. Deductions.
4. Balance at the end of the period.

Companies must disclose changes in the separate accounts comprising stockholders' equity, to make the financial statements sufficiently informative. Such changes may be disclosed in separate statements or in the basic financial statements or notes thereto.[22]

A **columnar format** for the presentation of changes in stockholders' equity items in published annual reports is gaining in popularity. An example is ConAgra Foods' statement of common stockholders' equity, shown in Illustration 15.19.

[22]*Accounting Trends and Techniques* reported that of the 500 companies surveyed, 486 presented statements of stockholders' equity, 4 presented separate statements of retained earnings only, 1 presented combined statements of income and retained earnings, and 9 presented changes in equity items in the notes only.

ILLUSTRATION 15.19 **Columnar Format for Statement of Common Stockholders' Equity**

ConAgra Foods, Inc. and Subsidiaries

For the Fiscal Year Ended May 2017

(Dollars in millions except per share amounts)	Common Shares	Common Stock	Additional Paid-in Capital	Retained Earnings	Accumulated Other Comprehensive Income (Loss)	Treasury Stock	Noncontrolling Interests	Total Equity
Balance at May 29, 2016	567.9	$2,839.7	$1,136.3	$3,218.3	$(344.5)	$(3,136.2)	$81.2	$ 3,794.8
Adoption of ASU 2019-9				(3.9)				(3.9)
Stock option and incentive plans			36.4	(1.3)		81.3		116.4
Spinoff of Lamb Weston				783.3	13.6			796.9
Currency translation adjustment					(16.6)		3.2	(13.4)
Repurchase of common shares						(1,000.0)		(1,000.0)
Unrealized gain on securities					0.3			0.3
Derivative adjustment, net of reclassification adjustments					(0.7)			(0.7)
Activities of noncontrolling interests			(0.8)				2.6	1.8
Pension and postretirement healthcare benefits					135.0			135.0
Dividends declared on common stock; $1.00 per share				(388.7)				(388.7)
Net (loss) income attributable to ConAgra Foods, Inc.				639.3				639.3
Balance at May 28, 2017	567.9	$2,839.7	$1,171.9	$4,247.0	$(212.9)	$(4,054.9)	$87.0	$ 4,077.8

Analysis

Analysts use stockholders' equity ratios to evaluate a company's profitability and long-term solvency. We discuss and illustrate the following three ratios below.

1. Return on common stockholders' equity.
2. Payout ratio.
3. Book value per share.

Return on Common Stockholders' Equity

The **return on common stockholders' equity**, often referred to as **return on equity (ROE)**, measures profitability from the common stockholders' viewpoint. This ratio shows how many dollars of net income the company earned for each dollar invested by the owners. Return on equity also helps investors judge the worthiness of a stock when the overall market is not doing well. For example, **Best Buy** shares at one time dropped nearly 40 percent. But a review of its return on equity during this period and since shows a steady return of 20 to 22 percent while the overall market ROE declined from 16 percent to 8 percent. More importantly, Best Buy and other stocks, such as **3M** and **Procter & Gamble**, recovered their lost market value, while other stocks with less robust ROEs stayed in the doldrums.

Return on equity equals net income less preferred dividends, divided by average common stockholders' equity. For example, assume that Gerber's Inc. had net income of $360,000, declared and paid preferred dividends of $54,000, and average common stock holders' equity of $2,550,000. **Illustration 15.20** shows how to compute Gerber's ratio.

$$\text{Return on Common Stockholders' Equity} = \frac{\text{Net Income} - \text{Preferred Dividends}}{\text{Average Common Stockholders' Equity}}$$

$$= \frac{\$360{,}000 - \$54{,}000}{\$2{,}550{,}000}$$

$$= 12\%$$

ILLUSTRATION 15.20

Computation of Return on Common Stockholders' Equity

As shown in Illustration 15.20, when preferred stock is present, income available to common stockholders equals net income less preferred dividends. Similarly, the amount of common stock equity used in this ratio equals **total stockholders' equity less the par value of preferred stock**.

A company can improve its return on common stockholders' equity through the prudent use of debt or preferred stock financing. **Trading on the equity** describes the practice of using borrowed money or issuing preferred stock in hopes of obtaining a higher rate of return on the money used. Shareholders win if return on the assets is higher than the cost of financing these assets. When this happens, the return on common stockholders' equity will exceed the return on total assets. In short, the company is "trading on the equity at a gain." In this situation, the money obtained from bondholders or preferred stockholders earns enough to pay the interest or preferred dividends and leaves a profit for the common stockholders. On the other hand, if the cost of the financing is higher than the rate earned on the assets, the company is trading on equity at a loss and stockholders lose.

Payout Ratio

Another ratio of interest to investors, the **payout ratio**, is the ratio of cash dividends to net income. If preferred stock is outstanding, this ratio equals cash dividends paid to common stockholders, divided by net income available to common stockholders. For example, assume that Troy Co. has cash dividends of $100,000 and net income of $500,000, and no preferred stock outstanding. **Illustration 15.21** shows the payout ratio computation.

ILLUSTRATION 15.21

Computation of Payout Ratio

$$\text{Payout Ratio} = \frac{\text{Cash Dividends}}{\text{Net Income}}$$

$$= \frac{\$100{,}000}{\$500{,}000}$$

$$= 20\%$$

ExxonMobil at one time had a payout ratio of 35.5 percent, **Apple** 28.1 percent, and **General Electric** 59.2 percent, at a time when the average payout ratio for the S&P 500 was 32.2 percent.[23]

Book Value per Share

A much-used basis for evaluating net worth is found in the book value or equity value per share of stock. **Book value per share** of stock is the amount each share would receive if the company were liquidated **on the basis of amounts reported on the balance sheet**. However, the figure loses much of its relevance if the valuations on the balance sheet fail to approximate fair value of the assets. Book value per share equals common stockholders' equity divided by outstanding common shares. Assume that Chen Corporation's common stockholders' equity is $1,000,000 and it has 100,000 shares of common stock outstanding. **Illustration 15.22** shows its book value per share computation.

ILLUSTRATION 15.22

Computation of Book Value per Share

$$\text{Book Value per Share} = \frac{\text{Common Stockholders' Equity}}{\text{Outstanding Shares}}$$

$$= \frac{\$1{,}000{,}000}{100{,}000}$$

$$= \$10 \text{ per share}$$

[23]In computing ratios like return on common stockholders' equity or the payout ratio, do not subtract the noncontrolling interest from common stockholders' equity or net income.

APPENDIX 15A

Dividend Preferences and Book Value per Share

Dividend Preferences

LEARNING OBJECTIVE *5

Explain the different types of preferred stock dividends and their effect on book value per share.

Illustrations 15A.1 to 15A.4 indicate the **effects** of various **dividend preferences** on dividend distributions to common and preferred stockholders. Assume that in 2020, Mason Company is to distribute $50,000 as cash dividends, its outstanding common stock has a par value of $400,000, and its 6 percent preferred stock has a par value of $100,000. Mason would distribute dividends to each class, employing the assumptions given, as follows.

1. If the preferred stock is noncumulative and nonparticipating:

	Preferred	Common	Total
6% of $100,000	$6,000		$ 6,000
The remainder to common		$44,000	44,000
Totals	$6,000	$44,000	$50,000

ILLUSTRATION 15A.1

Dividend Distribution, Noncumulative and Nonparticipating Preferred

2. If the preferred stock is cumulative and nonparticipating, and Mason Company did not pay dividends on the preferred stock in the preceding two years:

	Preferred	Common	Total
Dividends in arrears, 6% of $100,000 for 2 years	$12,000		$12,000
Current year's dividend, 6% of $100,000	6,000		6,000
The remainder to common		$32,000	32,000
Totals	$18,000	$32,000	$50,000

ILLUSTRATION 15A.2

Dividend Distribution, Cumulative and Nonparticipating Preferred, with Dividends in Arrears

3. If the preferred stock is noncumulative and is fully participating:[24]

[24]When preferred stock is participating, there may be different agreements as to how the participation feature is to be executed. However, in the absence of any specific agreement the following procedure is recommended:

a. After the preferred stock is assigned its current year's dividend, the common stock will receive a "like" percentage of par value outstanding. In example (3) shown in Illustration 15A.3, this amounts to 6 percent of $400,000.

b. In example (3), shown in Illustration 15A.3, the remainder of the declared dividend is $20,000. We divide this amount by total par value ($500,000) to find the rate of participation to be applied to each class of stock. In this case, the rate of participation is 4 percent ($20,000 ÷ $500,000), which we then multiply by the par value of each class of stock to determine the amount of participation.

ILLUSTRATION 15A.3

Dividend Distribution, Noncumulative and Fully Participating Preferred

	Preferred	Common	Total
Current year's dividend, 6%	$ 6,000	$24,000	$30,000
Participating dividend of 4%	4,000	16,000	20,000
Totals	$10,000	$40,000	$50,000

The participating dividend was determined as follows.

Current year's dividend:		
Preferred, 6% of $100,000 =	$ 6,000	
Common, 6% of $400,000 =	24,000	$ 30,000
Amount available for participation ($50,000 − $30,000)		$ 20,000
Par value of stock that is to participate ($100,000 + $400,000)		$500,000
Rate of participation ($20,000 ÷ $500,000)		4%
Participating dividend:		
Preferred, 4% of $100,000		$ 4,000
Common, 4% of $400,000		16,000
		$ 20,000

4. If the preferred stock is cumulative and is fully participating, and Mason Company did not pay dividends on the preferred stock in the preceding two years:

ILLUSTRATION 15A.4

Dividend Distribution, Cumulative and Fully Participating Preferred, with Dividends in Arrears

	Preferred	Common	Total
Dividends in arrears, 6% of $100,000 for 2 years	$12,000		$12,000
Current year's dividend, 6%	6,000	$24,000	30,000
Participating dividend, 1.6% ($8,000 ÷ $500,000)	1,600	6,400	8,000
Totals	$19,600	$30,400	$50,000

Book Value per Share

Book value per share in its simplest form is computed as net assets divided by outstanding common shares at the end of the year. The computation of book value per share becomes more complicated if a company has preferred stock in its capital structure. For example, if preferred dividends are in arrears, if the preferred stock is participating, or if preferred stock has a redemption or liquidating value higher than its carrying amount, the company must allocate retained earnings between the preferred and common stockholders in computing book value.

To illustrate, assume that the situation shown in **Illustration 15A.5** exists.

ILLUSTRATION 15A.5

Computation of Book Value per Share—No Dividends in Arrears

Stockholders' equity	Preferred	Common
Preferred stock, 5%	$300,000	
Common stock		$400,000
Excess of issue price over par of common stock		37,500
Retained earnings		162,582
Totals	$300,000	$600,082
Common shares outstanding		4,000
Book value per share		$150.02

The situation in Illustration 15A.5 assumes that no preferred dividends are in arrears and that the preferred is not participating. Now assume that the same facts exist except that the 5 percent preferred is cumulative, participating up to 8 percent, and that dividends for three years before the current year are in arrears. **Illustration 15A.6** shows how to compute the book value of the common stock, assuming that no action has yet been taken concerning dividends for the current year.

ILLUSTRATION 15A.6

Computation of Book Value per Share—with Dividends in Arrears

Stockholders' equity	Preferred	Common
Preferred stock, 5%	$300,000	
Common stock		$400,000
Excess of issue price over par of common stock		37,500
Retained earnings:		
Dividends in arrears (3 years at 5% a year)	45,000	
Current year requirement at 5%	15,000	20,000
Participating—additional 3%	9,000	12,000
Remainder to common		61,582
Totals	$369,000	$531,082
Shares outstanding		4,000
Book value per share		$132.77

In connection with the book value computation, the analyst must know how to handle the following items: the number of authorized and unissued shares; the number of treasury shares on hand; any commitments with respect to the issuance of unissued shares or the reissuance of treasury shares; and the relative rights and privileges of the various types of stock authorized. As an example, if the liquidating value of the preferred stock is higher than its carrying amount, the liquidating amount should be used in the book value computation.

Review and Practice

Key Terms Review

accumulated other comprehensive income 15-5
Additional Paid-in Capital 15-6
book value per share 15-28
callable preferred stock 15-11
cash dividends 15-19
common stock 15-5
contributed (paid-in) capital 15-5
convertible preferred stock 15-11
cost method 15-14
cumulative preferred stock 15-10
dividend in arrears 15-10
earned capital 15-5
large stock dividend 15-24
leveraged buyout (LBO) 15-13
liquidating dividends 15-18, 15-20
lump-sum sales 15-7
no-par stock 15-6
outstanding stock 15-15
Paid-in Capital in Excess of Par 15-6
par (stated) value method 15-14
participating preferred stock 15-11
payout ratio 15-28
preemptive right 15-4
preferred stock 15-5, 15-10
property dividends 15-19
redeemable preferred stock 15-11
residual interest 15-5
retained earnings 15-5
return on common stockholders' equity 15-27
secret reserves 15-9
small (ordinary) stock dividends 15-21
stated value 15-7
statement of stockholders' equity 15-26
stock dividends 15-21
stockholders' (owners') equity 15-5
stock split 15-23
trading on the equity 15-28
treasury stock 15-13
watered stock 15-9

Learning Objectives Review

1 Describe the corporate form and the issuance of shares of stock.

Among the **specific characteristics of the corporate form** that affect accounting are the (1) influence of state corporate law, (2) use of the capital stock or share system, and (3) development of a variety of ownership interests. In the absence of restrictive provisions, each share of stock carries the right to share proportionately in (1) profits and losses, (2) management (the right to vote for directors), (3) corporate assets upon liquidation, and (4) any new issues of stock of the same class (called the preemptive right).

Stockholders' or owners' equity is classified into two categories: contributed capital and earned capital. Contributed capital (paid-in capital) describes the total amount paid in on capital stock. Put another way, it is the amount that stockholders invested in the corporation for use in the business. Contributed capital includes items such as the par value of all outstanding capital stock and premiums less any discounts on issuance. Earned capital is the capital that develops if the business operates profitably; it consists of all undistributed income that remains invested in the company (retained earnings and accumulated other comprehensive income).

Accounts are kept for the following **different types of stock.** *Par value stock:* (a) preferred stock or common stock, (b) paid-in capital in excess of par or additional paid-in capital, and (c) discount on stock. *No-par stock:* common stock or common stock and additional paid-in capital, if stated value used.

Stock issued in combination with other securities (lump-sum sales): The two methods of allocation available are (a) the proportional method and (b) the incremental method. **Stock issued in noncash transactions:** When issuing stock for services or property other than cash, the company should record the property or services at either the fair value of the stock issued, or the fair value of the noncash consideration received, whichever is more clearly determinable.

Preferred stock is a special class of shares that possesses certain preferences or features not possessed by the common stock. The features that are most often associated with preferred stock issues are (1) preference as to dividends, (2) preference as to assets in the event of liquidation, (3) convertible into common stock, (4) callable at the option of the corporation, and (5) nonvoting. At issuance, the accounting for preferred stock is similar to that for common stock. When convertible preferred stock is converted, a company uses the book value method. It debits Preferred Stock, along with any related Paid-in Capital in Excess of Par—Preferred Stock and credits Common Stock and Paid-in Capital in Excess of Par—Common Stock (if an excess exists).

2 Describe the accounting and reporting for reacquisition of shares.

The cost method is generally used in accounting for treasury stock. This method derives its name from the fact that a company maintains the Treasury Stock account at the cost of the shares purchased. Under the cost method, a company debits the Treasury Stock account for the cost of the shares acquired and credits it for this same cost upon reissuance. The price received for the stock when originally issued does not affect the entries to record the acquisition and reissuance of the treasury stock.

3 Explain the accounting and reporting issues related to dividends.

The state incorporation laws normally provide information concerning the legal restrictions related to the payment of dividends. Corporations rarely pay dividends in an amount equal to the legal limit. This is due, in part, to the fact that companies use assets represented by undistributed earnings to finance future operations of the business. If a company is considering declaring a dividend, it must ask two preliminary questions. (1) Is the condition of the corporation such that the dividend is **legally permissible**? (2) Is the condition of the corporation such that a dividend is **economically sound**?

Dividends are of the following types: (1) cash dividends, (2) property dividends, (3) liquidating dividends (dividends based on other than retained earnings), and (4) stock dividends (the issuance by a corporation of its own stock to its stockholders on a pro rata basis, but without receiving consideration).

Generally accepted accounting principles require that the accounting for **small stock dividends** (less than 20–25 percent) rely on the fair value of the stock issued. When declaring a common stock dividend, a company debits Retained Earnings at the fair value of the stock it distributes. The entry includes a credit to Common Stock Dividend Distributable at par value times the number of shares, with any excess credited to Paid-in Capital in Excess of Par—Common Stock. If the number of shares issued exceeds 20–25 percent of the shares outstanding **(large stock dividend)**, it debits Retained Earnings at par value and credits Common Stock Distributable—there is no additional paid-in capital.

A **stock dividend** is a capitalization of retained earnings that reduces retained earnings and increases certain contributed capital accounts. The par value per share and total stockholders' equity remain unchanged with a stock dividend, and all stockholders retain their same proportionate share of ownership. A **stock split** results in an increase or decrease in the number of shares outstanding, with a corresponding decrease or increase in the par or stated value per share. No accounting entry is required for a stock split.

4 Indicate how to present and analyze stockholders' equity.

The stockholders' equity section of a balance sheet includes capital stock, additional paid-in capital, and retained earnings. A company might also present additional items such as treasury stock and accumulated other comprehensive income. Companies often provide a statement of stockholders' equity. Common ratios that use stockholders' equity amounts are **return on common stockholders' equity**, **payout ratio**, and **book value per share**.

*5 Explain the different types of preferred stock dividends and their effect on book value per share.

The dividend preferences of preferred stock affect the dividends paid to stockholders. Preferred stock can be (1) cumulative or noncumulative, and (2) fully participating, partially participating, or nonparticipating. If preferred dividends are in arrears, if the preferred stock is participating, or if preferred stock has a redemption or liquidation value higher than its carrying amount, allocate retained earnings between preferred and common stockholders in computing book value per share.

Enhanced Review and Practice

Go online for multiple-choice questions with solutions, review exercises with solutions, and a full glossary of all key terms.

Practice Problem

D'Ouville Company was formed on July 1, 2017. It was authorized to issue 500,000 shares of $10 par value common stock and 100,000 shares of 4%, $25 par value, cumulative and nonparticipating preferred stock. D'Ouville Company has a July 1–June 30 fiscal year. The following information relates to the stockholders' equity accounts of D'Ouville Company.

Common Stock: Prior to the 2019–2020 fiscal year, D'Ouville Company had 110,000 shares of outstanding common stock issued as follows.

1. 95,000 shares were issued for cash on July 1, 2017, at $31 per share.
2. On July 24, 2017, 5,000 shares were exchanged for a plot of land which cost the seller $70,000 in 2011 and had an estimated fair value of $220,000 on July 24, 2017.
3. 10,000 shares were issued on March 1, 2019, for $42 per share.

During the 2019–2020 fiscal year, the following transactions regarding common stock took place.

November 30, 2019	D'Ouville purchased 2,000 shares of its own stock on the open market at $39 per share. D'Ouville uses the cost method for treasury stock.
December 15, 2019	D'Ouville declared a 5% stock dividend for stockholders of record on January 15, 2020, to be issued on January 31, 2020. D'Ouville was having a liquidity problem and could not afford a cash dividend at the time. D'Ouville's common stock was selling at $52 per share on December 15, 2019.
June 20, 2020	D'Ouville sold 500 shares of its own common stock that it had purchased on November 30, 2019, for $21,000.

Preferred Stock: D'Ouville issued 100,000 shares of preferred stock at $44 per share on July 1, 2018.

Cash Dividends: D'Ouville has followed a schedule of declaring cash dividends in December and June, with payment being made to stockholders of record in the following month. The cash dividends which have been declared since inception of the company through June 30, 2020, are shown below.

Declaration Date	Common Stock	Preferred Stock
12/15/18	$0.30 per share	$0.50 per share
6/15/19	$0.30 per share	$0.50 per share
12/15/19	—	$0.50 per share

No cash dividends were declared during June 2020 due to the company's liquidity problems.

Retained Earnings: As of June 30, 2019, D'Ouville retained earnings account had a balance of $550,000. For the fiscal year ending June 30, 2020, D'Ouville reported net income of $120,000.

Instructions

Prepare the stockholders' equity section of the balance sheet, including appropriate notes, for D'Ouville Company as of June 30, 2020, as it should appear in its annual report to the shareholders.

Solution

D'Ouville Company
Stockholders' Equity
June 30, 2020

Capital stock	
4% preferred stock, $25 par value, cumulative and nonparticipating, 100,000 shares authorized, 100,000 shares issued and outstanding—Note A	$2,500,000
Common stock, $10 par value, 500,000 shares authorized, 115,400 shares issued, with 1,500 shares held in the treasury	1,154,000

(continued)

Additional paid-in capital		
On preferred stock	$1,900,000	
On common stock	2,711,800*	
On treasury stock	1,500	4,613,300
Total paid-in capital		8,267,300
Retained earnings		339,200**
Total paid-in capital and retained earnings		8,606,500
Less: Treasury stock, 1,500 shares at cost		58,500
Total stockholders' equity		$8,548,000

Note A: D'Ouville Company is in arrears on the preferred stock in the amount of $100,000.

*Premium on Common Stock:

Issue of 95,000 shares × ($31 – $10)	$1,995,000
Issue of 5,000 shares for plot of land ($220,000 – $50,000)	170,000
10,000 shares issued (3/1/19) [10,000 × ($42 – $10)]	320,000
5,400 shares as dividend [5,400 × ($52 – $10)]	226,800
	$ 2,711,800

**Retained Earnings:

Beginning balance	+ Income	– Stock dividend	– Preferred dividend	= Ret. earnings, ending balance
$550,000	+ $120,000	– $280,800***	– $50,000	= $339,200

***[(108,000 × .05) × $52]

WileyPLUS

Exercises, Problems, Problem Solution Walkthrough Videos, and many more assessment tools and resources are available for practice in WileyPLUS.

Note: All asterisked Questions, Exercises, and Problems relate to material in the appendix to the chapter.

Questions

1. In the absence of restrictive provisions, what are the basic rights of stockholders of a corporation?

2. Why is a preemptive right important?

3. Distinguish between common and preferred stock.

4. Why is the distinction between paid-in capital and retained earnings important?

5. Explain each of the following terms: authorized capital stock, unissued capital stock, issued capital stock, outstanding capital stock, and treasury stock.

6. What is meant by par value, and what is its significance to stockholders?

7. Describe the accounting for the issuance for cash of no-par value common stock at a price in excess of the stated value of the common stock.

8. Explain the difference between the proportional method and the incremental method of allocating the proceeds of lump-sum sales of capital stock.

9. What are the different bases for stock valuation when assets other than cash are received for issued shares of stock?

10. Explain how underwriting costs and accounting and legal fees associated with the issuance of stock should be recorded.

11. What features or rights may alter the character of preferred stock?

12. Dagwood Inc. recently noted that its 4% preferred stock and 4% participating preferred stock, which are both cumulative, have priority as to dividends up to 4% of their par value. Its participating preferred stock participates equally with the common stock in any dividends in excess of 4%. What is meant by the term participating? Cumulative?

13. Where in the financial statements is preferred stock normally reported?

14. For what reasons might a corporation purchase its own stock?

15. Discuss the propriety of showing:

   a. Treasury stock as an asset.

   b. "Gain" or "loss" on sale of treasury stock as additions to or deductions from income.

   c. Dividends received on treasury stock as income.

16. List possible sources of additional paid-in capital.

17. Satchel Inc. purchases 10,000 shares of its own previously issued $10 par common stock for $290,000. Assuming the shares are held in the treasury with intent to reissue, what effect does this transaction have on (a) net income, (b) total assets, (c) total paid-in capital, and (d) total stockholders' equity?

18. Indicate how each of the following accounts should be classified in the stockholders' equity section.

a. Common Stock.

b. Retained Earnings.

c. Paid-in Capital in Excess of Par—Common Stock.

d. Treasury Stock.

e. Paid-in Capital from Treasury Stock.

f. Paid-in Capital in Excess of Stated Value—Common Stock.

g. Preferred Stock.

19. What factors influence the dividend policy of a company?

20. What are the principal considerations of a board of directors in making decisions involving dividend declarations? Discuss briefly.

21. Dividends are sometimes said to have been paid "out of retained earnings." What is the error, if any, in that statement?

22. Distinguish among: cash dividends, property dividends, liquidating dividends, and stock dividends.

23. Describe the accounting entry for a stock dividend, if any. Describe the accounting entry for a stock split, if any.

24. Stock splits and stock dividends may be used by a corporation to change the number of shares of its stock outstanding.

a. What is meant by a stock split effected in the form of a dividend?

b. From an accounting viewpoint, explain how the stock split effected in the form of a dividend differs from an ordinary stock dividend.

c. How should a stock dividend that has been declared but not yet issued be classified in a balance sheet? Why?

25. The following comment appeared in the notes of Colorado Corporation's annual report: "Such distributions, representing proceeds from the sale of Sarazan, Inc., were paid in the form of partial liquidating dividends and were in lieu of a portion of the Company's ordinary cash dividends." How would a partial liquidating dividend be accounted for in the financial records?

26. This comment appeared in the annual report of MacCloud Inc.: "The Company could pay cash or property dividends on the Class A common stock without paying cash or property dividends on the Class B common stock. But if the Company pays any cash or property dividends on the Class B common stock, it would be required to pay at least the same dividend on the Class A common stock." How is a property dividend accounted for in the financial records?

27. For what reasons might a company restrict a portion of its retained earnings?

28. How are restrictions of retained earnings reported?

*29. McNabb Corp. had $100,000 of 7%, $20 par value preferred stock and 12,000 shares of $25 par value common stock outstanding throughout 2020.

a. Assuming that total dividends declared in 2020 were $64,000, and that the preferred stock is not cumulative but is fully participating, common stockholders should receive 2020 dividends of what amount?

b. Assuming that total dividends declared in 2020 were $64,000, and that the preferred stock is fully participating and cumulative with preferred dividends in arrears for 2019, preferred stockholders should receive 2020 dividends totaling what amount?

c. Assuming that total dividends declared in 2020 were $30,000, that the preferred stock is cumulative, nonparticipating, and was issued on January 1, 2019, and that $5,000 of preferred dividends were declared and paid in 2019, the common stockholders should receive 2020 dividends totaling what amount?

Brief Exercises

BE15.1 (LO 1) Buttercup Corporation issued 300 shares of $10 par value common stock for $4,500. Prepare Buttercup's journal entry.

BE15.2 (LO 1) Swarten Corporation issued 600 shares of no-par common stock for $8,200. Prepare Swarten's journal entry if (a) the stock has no stated value, and (b) the stock has a stated value of $2 per share.

BE15.3 (LO 1, 2) Wilco Corporation has the following account balances at December 31, 2020.

Common stock, $5 par value	$ 510,000
Treasury stock	90,000
Retained earnings	2,340,000
Paid-in capital in excess of par—common stock	1,320,000

Prepare Wilco's December 31, 2020, stockholders' equity section.

BE15.4 (LO 1) Ravonette Corporation issued 300 shares of $10 par value common stock and 100 shares of $50 par value preferred stock for a lump sum of $13,500. The common stock has a market price of $20 per share, and the preferred stock has a market price of $90 per share. Prepare the journal entry to record the issuance.

BE15.5 (LO 1) On February 1, 2020, Buffalo Corporation issued 3,000 shares of its $5 par value common stock for land worth $31,000. Prepare the February 1, 2020, journal entry.

BE15.6 (LO 1) Moonwalker Corporation issued 2,000 shares of its $10 par value common stock for $60,000. Moonwalker also incurred $1,500 of costs associated with issuing the stock. Prepare Moonwalker's journal entry to record the issuance of the company's stock.

BE15.7 **(LO 1)** Hinges Corporation issued 500 shares of $100 par value preferred stock for $61,500. Prepare Hinges's journal entry.

BE15.8 **(LO 2)** Sprinkle Inc. has outstanding 10,000 shares of $10 par value common stock. On July 1, 2020, Sprinkle reacquired 100 shares at $87 per share. On September 1, Sprinkle reissued 60 shares at $90 per share. On November 1, Sprinkle reissued 40 shares at $83 per share. Prepare Sprinkle's journal entries to record these transactions using the cost method.

BE15.9 **(LO 2)** Arantxa Corporation has outstanding 20,000 shares of $5 par value common stock. On August 1, 2020, Arantxa reacquired 200 shares at $80 per share. On November 1, Arantxa reissued the 200 shares at $70 per share. Arantxa had no previous treasury stock transactions. Prepare Arantxa's journal entries to record these transactions using the cost method.

BE15.10 **(LO 3)** Woolford Inc. declared a cash dividend of $1.00 per share on its 2 million outstanding shares. The dividend was declared on August 1, payable on September 9 to all stockholders of record on August 15. Prepare all journal entries necessary on those three dates.

BE15.11 **(LO 3)** Cole Inc. owns shares of Marlin Corporation stock. At December 31, 2020, the securities were carried in Cole's accounting records at their cost of $875,000, which equals their fair value. On September 21, 2021, when the fair value of the securities was $1,200,000, Cole declared a property dividend whereby the Marlin securities are to be distributed on October 23, 2021, to stockholders of record on October 8, 2021. Prepare all journal entries necessary on those three dates.

BE15.12 **(LO 3)** Graves Mining Company declared, on April 20, a dividend of $500,000 payable on June 1. Of this amount, $125,000 is a return of capital. Prepare the April 20 and June 1 entries for Graves.

BE15.13 **(LO 3)** Green Day Corporation has outstanding 400,000 shares of $10 par value common stock. The corporation declares a 5% stock dividend when the fair value of the stock is $65 per share. Prepare the journal entries for Green Day Corporation for both the date of declaration and the date of distribution.

BE15.14 **(LO 3)** Use the information from BE15.13, but assume Green Day Corporation declared a 100% stock dividend rather than a 5% stock dividend. Prepare the journal entries for both the date of declaration and the date of distribution.

*BE15.15 **(LO 5)** Nottebart Corporation has outstanding 10,000 shares of $100 par value, 6% preferred stock and 60,000 shares of $10 par value common stock. The preferred stock was issued in January 2020, and no dividends were declared in 2020 or 2021. In 2022, Nottebart declares a cash dividend of $300,000. How will the dividend be shared by common and preferred stockholders if the preferred is (a) noncumulative and (b) cumulative?

Exercises

E15.1 **(LO 1)** Excel **(Recording the Issuances of Common Stock)** During its first year of operations, Collin Raye Corporation had the following transactions pertaining to its common stock.

Jan. 10	Issued 80,000 shares for cash at $6 per share.
Mar. 1	Issued 5,000 shares to attorneys in payment of a bill for $35,000 for services rendered in helping the company to incorporate.
July 1	Issued 30,000 shares for cash at $8 per share.
Sept. 1	Issued 60,000 shares for cash at $10 per share.

Instructions

a. Prepare the journal entries for these transactions, assuming that the common stock has a par value of $5 per share.

b. Prepare the journal entries for these transactions, assuming that the common stock is no-par with a stated value of $3 per share.

E15.2 **(LO 1)** **(Recording the Issuance of Common and Preferred Stock)** Kathleen Battle Corporation was organized on January 1, 2020. It is authorized to issue 10,000 shares of 8%, $100 par value preferred stock, and 500,000 shares of no-par common stock with a stated value of $1 per share. The following stock transactions were completed during the first year.

Jan. 10	Issued 80,000 shares of common stock for cash at $5 per share.
Mar. 1	Issued 5,000 shares of preferred stock for cash at $108 per share.
Apr. 1	Issued 24,000 shares of common stock for land. The asking price of the land was $90,000; the fair value of the land was $80,000.
May 1	Issued 80,000 shares of common stock for cash at $7 per share.
Aug. 1	Issued 10,000 shares of common stock to attorneys in payment of their bill of $50,000 for services rendered in helping the company organize.
Sept. 1	Issued 10,000 shares of common stock for cash at $9 per share.
Nov. 1	Issued 1,000 shares of preferred stock for cash at $112 per share.

Instructions

Prepare the journal entries to record the above transactions.

E15.3 **(LO 1, 2)** **(Stock Issued for Land)** Twenty-five thousand shares reacquired by Elixir Corporation for $53 per share were exchanged for undeveloped land that has an appraised value of $1,700,000. At the time of the exchange, the common stock was trading at $62 per share on an organized exchange.

Instructions

a. Prepare the journal entry to record the acquisition of land assuming that the purchase of the stock was originally recorded using the cost method.

b. Briefly identify the possible alternatives (including those that are totally unacceptable) for quantifying the cost of the land and briefly support your choice.

E15.4 **(LO 1)** **(Lump-Sum Sale of Stock with Bonds)** Faith Evans Corporation is a regional company which is an SEC registrant. The corporation's securities are thinly traded on NASDAQ. Faith Evans Corp. has issued 10,000 units. Each unit consists of a $500 par, 12% subordinated debenture and 10 shares of $5 par common stock. The units were sold to outside investors for cash at $880 per unit. Prior to this sale, the 2-week ask price of common stock was $40 per share. Twelve percent is a reasonable market yield for the debentures, and therefore the par value of the bonds is equal to the fair value.

Instructions

a. Prepare the journal entry to record Evans' transaction, under the following conditions.

  1. Employing the incremental method.

  2. Employing the proportional method, assuming the recent price quote on the common stock reflects fair value.

b. Briefly explain which method is, in your opinion, the better method.

E15.5 **(LO 1)** **(Lump-Sum Sales of Stock with Preferred Stock)** Dave Matthew Inc. issues 500 shares of $10 par value common stock and 100 shares of $100 par value preferred stock for a lump sum of $100,000.

Instructions

a. Prepare the journal entry for the issuance when the market price of the common shares is $165 each and market price of the preferred is $230 each. (Round to nearest dollar.)

b. Prepare the journal entry for the issuance when only the market price of the common stock is known and it is $170 per share.

E15.6 **(LO 1, 2)** **(Stock Issuances and Repurchase)** Lindsey Hunter Corporation is authorized to issue 50,000 shares of $5 par value common stock. During 2020, Lindsey Hunter took part in the following selected transactions.

1. Issued 5,000 shares of stock at $45 per share, less costs related to the issuance of the stock totaling $7,000.

2. Issued 1,000 shares of stock for land appraised at $50,000. The stock was actively traded on a national stock exchange at approximately $46 per share on the date of issuance.

3. Purchased 500 shares of treasury stock at $43 per share. The treasury shares purchased were issued in 2016 at $40 per share.

Instructions

a. Prepare the journal entry to record item 1.

b. Prepare the journal entry to record item 2.

c. Prepare the journal entry to record item 3 using the cost method.

E15.7 (LO 2) (Effect of Treasury Stock Transactions on Financials) Joe Dumars Company has outstanding 40,000 shares of $5 par common stock which had been issued at $30 per share. Joe Dumars then entered into the following transactions.

1. Purchased 5,000 treasury shares at $45 per share.
2. Resold 2,000 of the treasury shares at $49 per share.
3. Resold 500 of the treasury shares at $40 per share.

Instructions

Use the following code to indicate the effect each of the three transactions has on the financial statement categories listed in the table below, assuming Joe Dumars Company uses the cost method (I = Increase; D = Decrease; NE = No effect).

#	Assets	Liabilities	Stockholders' Equity	Paid-in Capital	Retained Earnings	Net Income
1						
2						
3						

E15.8 (LO 1, 2) (Correcting Entries for Equity Transactions) Pistons Inc. recently hired a new accountant with extensive experience in accounting for partnerships. Because of the pressure of the new job, the accountant was unable to review what he had learned earlier about corporation accounting. During the first month, he made the following entries for the corporation's capital stock.

May 2	Cash	192,000	
	Capital Stock		192,000
	(Issued 12,000 shares of $5 par value common stock at $16 per share)		
10	Cash	600,000	
	Capital Stock		600,000
	(Issued 10,000 shares of $30 par value preferred stock at $60 per share)		
15	Capital Stock	15,000	
	Cash		15,000
	(Purchased 1,000 shares of common stock for the treasury at $15 per share)		
31	Cash	8,500	
	Capital Stock		5,000
	Gain on Sale of Stock		3,500
	(Sold 500 shares of treasury stock at $17 per share)		

Instructions

On the basis of the explanation for each entry, prepare the entries that should have been made for the capital stock transactions.

E15.9 (LO 1, 3) (Preferred Stock Entries and Dividends) Otis Thorpe Corporation has 10,000 shares of $100 par value, 8%, preferred stock and 50,000 shares of $10 par value common stock outstanding at December 31, 2020.

Instructions

Answer the questions in each of the following independent situations.

a. If the preferred stock is cumulative and dividends were last paid on the preferred stock on December 31, 2017, (1) what are the dividends in arrears on December 31, 2020, and (2) how should these dividends be reported?

b. If the preferred stock is convertible into seven shares of $10 par value common stock and 4,000 shares are converted, what entry is required for the conversion assuming the preferred stock was issued at par value?

c. If the preferred stock was issued at $107 per share, how should the preferred stock be reported in the stockholders' equity section?

E15.10 (LO 2, 4) (Analysis of Equity Data and Equity Section Preparation) For a recent 2-year period, the balance sheet of Santana Dotson Company showed the following stockholders' equity data at December 31 (in millions).

	2020	2019
Additional paid-in capital	$ 931	$ 817
Common stock	545	540
Retained earnings	7,167	5,226
Treasury stock	1,564	918
Total stockholders' equity	$7,079	$5,665
Common stock shares issued	218	216
Common stock shares authorized	500	500
Treasury stock shares	34	27

Instructions

a. Answer the following questions.

1. What is the par value of the common stock?
2. What is the cost per share of treasury stock at December 31, 2020, and at December 31, 2019?

b. Prepare the stockholders' equity section at December 31, 2020.

E15.11 **(LO 3, 4)** **(Equity Items on the Balance Sheet)** The following are selected transactions that may affect stockholders' equity.

1. Recorded accrued interest earned on a note receivable.
2. Declared a cash dividend.
3. Declared and distributed a stock split.
4. Approved a retained earnings restriction.
5. Recorded the expiration of insurance coverage that was previously recorded as prepaid insurance.
6. Paid the cash dividend declared in item 2 above.
7. Recorded accrued interest expense on a note payable.
8. Declared a stock dividend.
9. Distributed the stock dividend declared in item 8.

Instructions

In the following table, indicate the effect each of the nine transactions has on the financial statement elements listed. Use the following code: I = Increase, D = Decrease, NE = No effect.

Item	Assets	Liabilities	Stockholders' Equity	Paid-in Capital	Retained Earnings	Net Income

E15.12 **(LO 3)** **(Cash Dividend and Liquidating Dividend)** Lotoya Davis Corporation has 10 million shares of common stock issued and outstanding. On June 1, the board of directors voted an 80 cents per share cash dividend to stockholders of record as of June 14, payable June 30.

Instructions

a. Prepare the journal entry for each of the dates above assuming the dividend represents a distribution of earnings.

b. How would the entry differ if the dividend were a liquidating dividend?

E15.13 **(LO 3)** **(Stock Split and Stock Dividend)** The common stock of Alexander Hamilton Inc. is currently selling at $120 per share. The directors wish to reduce the share price and increase share volume prior to a new issue. The per share par value is $10; book value is $70 per share. Nine million shares are issued and outstanding.

Instructions

Prepare the necessary journal entries assuming the following.

a. The board votes a 2-for-1 stock split.

b. The board votes a 100% stock dividend.

c. Briefly discuss the accounting and securities market differences between these two methods of increasing the number of shares outstanding.

E15.14 **(LO 3)** **(Entries for Stock Dividends and Stock Splits)** The stockholders' equity accounts of G.K. Chesterton Company have the following balances on December 31, 2020.

Common stock, $10 par, 300,000 shares issued and outstanding	$3,000,000
Paid-in capital in excess of par—common stock	1,200,000
Retained earnings	5,600,000

Shares of G.K. Chesterton Company stock are currently selling on the Midwest Stock Exchange at $37.

Instructions

Prepare the appropriate journal entries for each of the following cases.

a. A stock dividend of 5% is declared and issued.

b. A stock dividend of 100% is declared and issued.

c. A 2-for-1 stock split is declared and issued.

E15.15 **(LO 3)** Excel **(Dividend Entries)** The following data were taken from the balance sheet accounts of Masefield Corporation on December 31, 2019.

Current assets	$540,000
Debt investments (trading)	624,000
Common stock (par value $10)	500,000
Paid-in capital in excess of par	150,000
Retained earnings	840,000

Instructions

Prepare the required journal entries for the following unrelated items.

a. A 5% stock dividend is declared and distributed at a time when the market price per share is $39.

b. The par value of the common stock is reduced to $2 with a 5-for-1 stock split.

c. A dividend is declared January 5, 2020, and paid January 25, 2020, in bonds held as an investment. The bonds have a book value of $100,000 and a fair value of $135,000.

E15.16 **(LO 4)** **(Computation of Retained Earnings)** The following information has been taken from the ledger accounts of Isaac Stern Corporation.

Total income since incorporation	$317,000
Total cash dividends paid	60,000
Total value of stock dividends distributed	30,000
Gains on treasury stock transactions	18,000
Unamortized discount on bonds payable	32,000

Instructions

Determine the current balance of retained earnings.

E15.17 **(LO 4)** **(Stockholders' Equity Section)** Bruno Corporation's post-closing trial balance at December 31, 2020, is shown as follows.

Bruno Corporation
Post-Closing Trial Balance
December 31, 2020

	Dr.	Cr.
Accounts payable		$ 310,000
Accounts receivable	$ 480,000	
Accumulated depreciation—buildings		185,000
Additional paid-in capital in excess		
of par—common		1,300,000
From treasury stock		160,000

	Dr.	Cr.
Allowance for doubtful accounts		30,000
Bonds payable		300,000
Buildings	1,450,000	
Cash	190,000	
Common stock ($1 par)		200,000
Dividends payable (preferred stock—cash)		4,000
Inventory	560,000	
Land	400,000	
Preferred stock ($50 par)		500,000
Prepaid expenses	40,000	
Retained earnings		301,000
Treasury stock (common at cost)	170,000	
Totals	$3,290,000	$3,290,000

At December 31, 2020, Bruno had the following number of common and preferred shares.

	Common	Preferred
Authorized	600,000	60,000
Issued	200,000	10,000
Outstanding	190,000	10,000

The dividends on preferred stock are $4 cumulative. In addition, the preferred stock has a preference in liquidation of $50 per share.

Instructions

Prepare the stockholders' equity section of Bruno's balance sheet at December 31, 2020.

(AICPA adapted)

E15.18 (LO 1, 2, 3, 4) Groupwork (Dividends and Stockholders' Equity Section) Anne Cleves Company reported the following amounts in the stockholders' equity section of its December 31, 2019, balance sheet.

Preferred stock, 10%, $100 par (10,000 shares authorized, 2,000 shares issued)	$200,000
Common stock, $5 par (100,000 shares authorized, 20,000 shares issued)	100,000
Additional paid-in capital	125,000
Retained earnings	450,000
Total	$875,000

During 2020, Cleves took part in the following transactions concerning stockholders' equity.

1. Paid the annual 2019 $10 per share dividend on preferred stock and a $2 per share dividend on common stock. These dividends had been declared on December 31, 2019.
2. Purchased 1,700 shares of its own outstanding common stock for $40 per share. Cleves uses the cost method.
3. Reissued 700 treasury shares for land valued at $30,000.
4. Issued 500 shares of preferred stock at $105 per share.
5. Declared a 10% stock dividend on the outstanding common stock when the stock is selling for $45 per share.
6. Issued the stock dividend.
7. Declared the annual 2020 $10 per share dividend on preferred stock and the $2 per share dividend on common stock. These dividends are payable in 2021.

Instructions

a. Prepare journal entries to record the transactions described above.

b. Prepare the December 31, 2020, stockholders' equity section. Assume 2020 net income was $330,000.

E15.19 (LO 4) (Comparison of Alternative Forms of Financing) Shown below is the liabilities and stockholders' equity section of the balance sheet for Jana Kingston Company and Mary Ann Benson Company. Each has assets totaling $4,200,000.

Jana Kingston Co.		Mary Ann Benson Co.	
Current liabilities	$ 300,000	Current liabilities	$ 600,000
Long-term debt, 10%	1,200,000	Common stock ($20 par)	2,900,000
Common stock ($20 par)	2,000,000	Retained earnings (Cash dividends, $328,000)	700,000
Retained earnings (Cash dividends, $220,000)	700,000		
	$4,200,000		$4,200,000

For the year, each company has earned the same income before interest and taxes.

	Jana Kingston Co.	Mary Ann Benson Co.
Income before interest and taxes	$1,200,000	$1,200,000
Interest expense	120,000	–0–
	1,080,000	1,200,000
Income taxes (20%)	216,000	240,000
Net income	$ 864,000	$ 960,000

At year-end, the market price of Kingston's stock was $101 per share, and Benson's was $63.50.

Instructions

a. Which company is more profitable in terms of return on total assets?

b. Which company is more profitable in terms of return on common stockholders' equity?

c. Which company has the greater net income per share of stock? Neither company issued or reacquired shares during the year.

d. From the point of view of net income, is it advantageous to the stockholders of Jana Kingston Co. to have the long-term debt outstanding? Why?

e. What is the book value per share for each company?

E15.20 **(LO 4)** **(Trading on the Equity Analysis)** Presented below is information from the annual report of Emporia Plastics, Inc.

Operating income	$ 532,150
Bond interest expense	135,000
	397,150
Income taxes	183,432
Net income	$ 213,718
Bonds payable	$1,000,000
Common stock	875,000
Retained earnings	375,000

Instructions

a. Compute the return on common stockholders' equity and the rate of interest paid on bonds. (Assume balances for debt and equity accounts approximate averages for the year.)

b. Is Emporia Plastics, Inc. trading on the equity successfully? Explain.

*E15.21 **(LO 5)** **(Preferred Dividends)** The outstanding capital stock of Edna Millay Corporation consists of 2,000 shares of $100 par value, 8% preferred, and 5,000 shares of $50 par value common.

Instructions

Assuming that the company has retained earnings of $90,000, all of which is to be paid out in dividends, and that preferred dividends were not paid during the 2 years preceding the current year, state how much each class of stock should receive under each of the following conditions.

a. The preferred stock is noncumulative and nonparticipating.

b. The preferred stock is cumulative and nonparticipating.

c. The preferred stock is cumulative and participating. (Round dividend rate percentages to four decimal places.)

*E15.22 **(LO 5)** **(Preferred Dividends)** Matt Schmidt Company's ledger shows the following balances on December 31, 2020.

7% Preferred stock—$10 par value, outstanding 20,000 shares	$ 200,000
Common stock—$100 par value, outstanding 30,000 shares	3,000,000
Retained earnings	630,000

Instructions

Assuming that the directors decide to declare total dividends in the amount of $366,000, determine how much each class of stock should receive under each of the conditions stated below. One year's dividends are in arrears on the preferred stock.

a. The preferred stock is cumulative and fully participating.

b. The preferred stock is noncumulative and nonparticipating.

c. The preferred stock is noncumulative and is participating in distributions in excess of a 10% dividend rate on the common stock.

*E15.23 **(LO 5)** **(Preferred Stock Dividends)** Cajun Company has outstanding 2,500 shares of $100 par, 6% preferred stock and 15,000 shares of $10 par value common. The following schedule shows the amount of dividends paid out over the last 4 years.

Instructions

Allocate the dividends to each type of stock under assumptions (a) and (b). Express your answers in per share amounts using the format shown below.

		Assumptions			
		(a) Preferred, Noncumulative, and Nonparticipating		(b) Preferred, Cumulative, and Fully Participating	
Year	Paid-Out	Preferred	Common	Preferred	Common
2018	$13,000				
2019	$26,000				
2020	$57,000				
2021	$76,000				

*E15.24 **(LO 5)** **(Computation of Book Value per Share)** Morgan Sondgeroth Inc. began operations in January 2018 and reported the following results for each of its 3 years of operations.

2018	$260,000 net loss	2019	$40,000 net loss	2020	$800,000 net income

At December 31, 2020, Morgan Sondgeroth Inc. capital accounts were as follows.

8% cumulative preferred stock, par value $100; authorized, issued, and outstanding 5,000 shares	$500,000
Common stock, par value $1.00; authorized 1,000,000 shares; issued and outstanding 750,000 shares	$750,000

Morgan Sondgeroth Inc. has never paid a cash or stock dividend. There has been no change in the capital accounts since Sondgeroth began operations. The state law permits dividends only from retained earnings.

Instructions

a. Compute the book value of the common stock at December 31, 2020.

b. Compute the book value of the common stock at December 31, 2020, assuming that the preferred stock has a liquidating value of $106 per share.

Problems

P15.1 **(LO 1, 2, 3, 4)** Excel Groupwork **(Equity Transactions and Statement Preparation)** On January 5, 2020, Phelps Corporation received a charter granting the right to issue 5,000 shares of $100 par value, 8% cumulative and nonparticipating preferred stock, and 50,000 shares of $10 par value common stock. It then completed these transactions.

Jan. 11	Issued 20,000 shares of common stock at $16 per share.
Feb. 1	Issued to Sanchez Corp. 4,000 shares of preferred stock for the following assets: equipment with a fair value of $50,000; a factory building with a fair value of $160,000; and land with an appraised value of $270,000.

July 29	Purchased 1,800 shares of common stock at $17 per share. (Use cost method.)
Aug. 10	Sold the 1,800 treasury shares at $14 per share.
Dec. 31	Declared a $0.25 per share cash dividend on the common stock and declared the preferred dividend.
Dec. 31	Closed the Income Summary account. There was a $175,700 net income.

Instructions

a. Record the journal entries for the transactions listed above.

b. Prepare the stockholders' equity section of Phelps Corporation's balance sheet as of December 31, 2020.

P15.2 **(LO 2, 4)** **(Treasury Stock Transactions and Presentation)** Clemson Company had the following stockholders' equity as of January 1, 2020.

Common stock, $5 par value, 20,000 shares issued	$100,000
Paid-in capital in excess of par—common stock	300,000
Retained earnings	320,000
Total stockholders' equity	$720,000

During 2020, the following transactions occurred.

Feb. 1	Clemson repurchased 2,000 shares of treasury stock at a price of $19 per share.
Mar. 1	800 shares of treasury stock repurchased above were reissued at $17 per share.
Mar. 18	500 shares of treasury stock repurchased above were reissued at $14 per share.
Apr. 22	600 shares of treasury stock repurchased above were reissued at $20 per share.

Instructions

a. Prepare the journal entries to record the treasury stock transactions in 2020, assuming Clemson uses the cost method.

b. Prepare the stockholders' equity section as of April 30, 2020. Net income for the first 4 months of 2020 was $130,000.

P15.3 **(LO 1, 2, 3, 4)** **(Equity Transactions and Statement Preparation)** Hatch Company has two classes of capital stock outstanding: 8%, $20 par preferred and $5 par common. At December 31, 2020, the following accounts were included in stockholders' equity.

Preferred Stock, 150,000 shares	$ 3,000,000
Common Stock, 2,000,000 shares	10,000,000
Paid-in Capital in Excess of Par—Preferred Stock	200,000
Paid-in Capital in Excess of Par—Common Stock	27,000,000
Retained Earnings	4,500,000

The following transactions affected stockholders' equity during 2021.

Jan. 1	30,000 shares of preferred stock issued at $22 per share.
Feb. 1	50,000 shares of common stock issued at $20 per share.
June 1	2-for-1 stock split (par value reduced to $2.50).
July 1	30,000 shares of common treasury stock purchased at $10 per share. Hatch uses the cost method.
Sept. 15	10,000 shares of treasury stock reissued at $11 per share.
Dec. 31	The preferred dividend is declared, and a common dividend of 50¢ per share is declared.
Dec. 31	Net income is $2,100,000.

Instructions

Prepare the stockholders' equity section for Hatch Company at December 31, 2021. Show all supporting computations.

P15.4 **(LO 1)** **(Stock Transactions—Lump Sum)** Seles Corporation's charter authorized issuance of 100,000 shares of $10 par value common stock and 50,000 shares of $50 preferred stock. The following transactions involving the issuance of shares of stock were completed. Each transaction is independent of the others.

1. Issued a $10,000, 9% bond payable at par and gave as a bonus one share of preferred stock, which at that time was selling for $106 a share.
2. Issued 500 shares of common stock for equipment. The equipment had been appraised at $7,100; the seller's book value was $6,200. The most recent market price of the common stock is $16 a share.

3. Issued 375 shares of common and 100 shares of preferred for a lump sum amounting to $10,800. The common had been selling at $14 and the preferred at $65.
4. Issued 200 shares of common and 50 shares of preferred for equipment. The common had a fair value of $16 per share; the equipment has a fair value of $6,500.

Instructions

Record the transactions listed above in journal entry form.

P15.5 **(LO 2)** **Excel** **(Treasury Stock—Cost Method)** Before Gordon Corporation engages in the following treasury stock transactions, its general ledger reflects, among others, the following account balances (par value of its stock is $30 per share).

Paid-in Capital in Excess of Par—Common Stock	Common Stock	Retained Earnings
$99,000	$270,000	$80,000

Instructions

Record the treasury stock transactions (given below) under the cost method of handling treasury stock; use the FIFO method for purchase-sale purposes.

a. Bought 380 shares of treasury stock at $40 per share.
b. Bought 300 shares of treasury stock at $45 per share.
c. Sold 350 shares of treasury stock at $42 per share.
d. Sold 110 shares of treasury stock at $38 per share.

P15.6 **(LO 2, 3, 4)** **Groupwork** **(Treasury Stock—Cost Method—Equity Section Preparation)** Washington Company has the following stockholders' equity accounts at December 31, 2020.

Common Stock ($100 par value, authorized 8,000 shares)	$480,000
Retained Earnings	294,000

Instructions

a. Prepare entries in journal form to record the following transactions, which took place during 2021.
   1. 280 shares of outstanding stock were purchased at $97 per share. (These are to be accounted for using the cost method.)
   2. A $20 per share cash dividend was declared.
   3. The dividend declared in (2) above was paid.
   4. The treasury shares purchased in (1) above were resold at $102 per share.
   5. 500 shares of outstanding stock were purchased at $105 per share.
   6. 350 of the shares purchased in (5) above were resold at $96 per share.
b. Prepare the stockholders' equity section of Washington Company's balance sheet after giving effect to these transactions, assuming that the net income for 2021 was $94,000. State law requires restriction of retained earnings for the amount of treasury stock.

P15.7 **(LO 3)** **(Cash Dividend Entries)** The books of Conchita Corporation carried the following account balances as of December 31, 2020.

Cash	$ 195,000
Preferred Stock (6% cumulative, nonparticipating, $50 par)	300,000
Common Stock (no-par value, 300,000 shares issued)	1,500,000
Paid-in Capital in Excess of Par—Preferred Stock	150,000
Treasury Stock (common 2,800 shares at cost)	33,600
Retained Earnings	105,000

The company decided not to pay any dividends in 2020.

The board of directors, at their annual meeting on December 21, 2021, declared the following: "The current year dividends shall be 6% on the preferred and $.30 per share on the common. The dividends in arrears shall be paid by issuing 1,500 shares of treasury stock." At the date of declaration, the preferred is selling at $80 per share, and the common at $12 per share. Net income for 2021 is estimated at $77,000.

Instructions

a. Prepare the journal entries required for the dividend declaration and payment, assuming that they occur simultaneously.

b. Could Conchita Corporation give the preferred stockholders 2 years' dividends and common stockholders a 30 cents per share dividend, all in cash?

P15.8 (LO 3) Groupwork (Dividends and Splits) Myers Company provides you with the following condensed balance sheet information.

Assets		Liabilities and Stockholders' Equity		
Current assets	$ 40,000	Current and long-term liabilities		$100,000
Equity investments	60,000	Stockholders' equity		
Equipment (net)	250,000	Common stock ($5 par)	$ 20,000	
Intangibles	60,000	Paid-in capital in excess of par	110,000	
Total assets	$410,000	Retained earnings	180,000	310,000
		Total liabilities and stockholders' equity		$410,000

Instructions

For each of the following transactions, indicate the dollar impact (if any) on the following five items: (1) total assets, (2) common stock, (3) paid-in capital in excess of par, (4) retained earnings, and (5) stockholders' equity. (Each situation is independent.)

a. Myers declares and pays a $0.50 per share cash dividend.

b. Myers declares and issues a 10% stock dividend when the market price of the stock is $14 per share.

c. Myers declares and issues a 30% stock dividend when the market price of the stock is $15 per share.

d. Myers declares and distributes a property dividend. Myers gives one share of its equity investment (ABC stock) for every two shares of Myers Company stock held. Myers owns 10,000 shares of ABC. ABC is selling for $10 per share on the date the property dividend is declared.

e. Myers declares a 2-for-1 stock split and issues new shares.

P15.9 (LO 1, 2, 3, 4) (Stockholders' Equity Section of Balance Sheet) The following is a summary of all relevant transactions of Vicario Corporation since it was organized in 2020.

In 2020, 15,000 shares were authorized and 7,000 shares of common stock ($50 par value) were issued at a price of $57. In 2021, 1,000 shares were issued as a stock dividend when the stock was selling for $60. Three hundred shares of common stock were bought in 2022 at a cost of $64 per share. These 300 shares are still in the company treasury.

In 2021, 10,000 preferred shares were authorized and the company issued 5,000 of them ($100 par value) at $113. Some of the preferred stock was reacquired by the company and later reissued for $4,700 more than it cost the company.

The corporation has earned a total of $610,000 in net income after income taxes and paid out a total of $312,600 in cash dividends since incorporation.

Instructions

Prepare the stockholders' equity section of the balance sheet in proper form for Vicario Corporation as of December 31, 2022. Account for treasury stock using the cost method.

P15.10 (LO 3) Writing (Stock Dividends and Stock Split) Oregon Inc. $10 par common stock is selling for $110 per share. Four million shares are currently issued and outstanding. The board of directors wishes to stimulate interest in Oregon common stock before a forthcoming stock issue but does not wish to distribute capital at this time. The board also believes that too many adjustments to the stockholders' equity section, especially retained earnings, might discourage potential investors.

The board has considered three options for stimulating interest in the stock:

1. A 20% stock dividend.
2. A 100% stock dividend.
3. A 2-for-1 stock split.

Instructions

Acting as financial advisor to the board, you have been asked to report briefly on each option and, considering the board's wishes, make a recommendation. Discuss the effects of each of the foregoing options.

P15.11 (LO 3, 4) (Stock and Cash Dividends) Earnhart Corporation has outstanding 3,000,000 shares of common stock with a par value of $10 each. The balance in its Retained Earnings account at January 1, 2020, was $24,000,000, and it then had Paid-in Capital in Excess of Par—Common Stock of $5,000,000. During 2020, the company's net income was $4,700,000. A cash dividend of $0.60 a share was declared on May 5, 2020, and was paid June 30, 2020, and a 6% stock dividend was declared on

November 30, 2020, and distributed to stockholders of record at the close of business on December 31, 2020. You have been asked to advise on the proper accounting treatment of the stock dividend.

The existing stock of the company is quoted on a national stock exchange. The market price of the stock has been as follows.

October 31, 2020	$31
November 30, 2020	$34
December 31, 2020	$38

Instructions

a. Prepare the journal entry to record the declaration and payment of the cash dividend.

b. Prepare the journal entry to record the declaration and distribution of the stock dividend.

c. Prepare the stockholders' equity section (including schedules of retained earnings and additional paid-in capital) of the balance sheet of Earnhart Corporation for the year 2020 on the basis of the foregoing information. Draft a note to the financial statements setting forth the basis of the accounting for the stock dividend, and add separately appropriate comments or explanations regarding the basis chosen.

P15.12 **(LO 1, 2, 3, 4)** **(Analysis and Classification of Equity Transactions)** Penn Company was formed on July 1, 2018. It was authorized to issue 300,000 shares of $10 par value common stock and 100,000 shares of 8% $25 par value, cumulative and nonparticipating preferred stock. Penn Company has a July 1–June 30 fiscal year.

The following information relates to the stockholders' equity accounts of Penn Company.

Common Stock

Prior to the 2020–2021 fiscal year, Penn Company had 110,000 shares of outstanding common stock issued as follows.

1. 85,000 shares were issued for cash on July 1, 2018, at $31 per share.
2. On July 24, 2018, 5,000 shares were exchanged for a plot of land which cost the seller $70,000 in 2012 and had a fair value (based on recent land sales) of $220,000 on July 24, 2018.
3. 20,000 shares were issued on March 1, 2019, for $42 per share.

During the 2020–2021 fiscal year, the following transactions regarding common stock took place.

November 30, 2020	Penn purchased 2,000 shares of its own stock on the open market at $39 per share. Penn uses the cost method for treasury stock.
December 15, 2020	Penn declared a 5% stock dividend for stockholders of record on January 15, 2021, to be issued on January 31, 2021. Penn was having a liquidity problem and could not afford a cash dividend at the time. Penn's common stock was selling at $52 per share on December 15, 2020.
June 20, 2021	Penn sold 500 shares of its own common stock that it had purchased on November 30, 2020, for $21,000.

Preferred Stock

Penn issued 40,000 shares of preferred stock at $44 per share on July 1, 2019.

Cash Dividends

Penn has followed a schedule of declaring cash dividends in December and June, with payment being made to stockholders of record in the following month. The cash dividends which have been declared since inception of the company through June 30, 2021, are shown below.

Declaration Date	Common Stock	Preferred Stock
12/15/19	$0.30 per share	$1.00 per share
6/15/20	$0.30 per share	$1.00 per share
12/15/20	—	$1.00 per share

No cash dividends were declared during June 2021 due to the company's liquidity problems.

Retained Earnings

As of June 30, 2020, Penn's retained earnings account had a balance of $690,000. For the fiscal year ending June 30, 2021, Penn reported net income of $40,000.

Instructions

Prepare the stockholders' equity section of the balance sheet, including appropriate notes, for Penn Company as of June 30, 2021, as it should appear in its annual report to the shareholders.

(CMA adapted)

Concepts for Analysis

CA15.1 **(LO 1)** **(Preemptive Rights and Dilution of Ownership)** Wallace Computer Company is a small, closely held corporation. Eighty percent of the stock is held by Derek Wallace, president. Of the remainder, 10% is held by members of his family and 10% by Kathy Baker, a former officer who is now retired. The balance sheet of the company at June 30, 2020, was substantially as shown below.

Assets		Liabilities and Stockholders' Equity	
Cash	$ 22,000	Current liabilities	$ 50,000
Other	450,000	Common stock	250,000
	$472,000	Retained earnings	172,000
			$472,000

Additional authorized common stock of $300,000 par value had never been issued. To strengthen the cash position of the company, Wallace issued common stock with a par value of $100,000 to himself at par for cash. At the next stockholders' meeting, Baker objected and claimed that her interests had been injured.

Instructions

a. Which stockholder's right was ignored in the issue of shares to Derek Wallace?

b. How may the damage to Baker's interests be repaired most simply?

c. If Derek Wallace offered Baker a personal cash settlement and they agreed to employ you as an impartial arbitrator to determine the amount, what settlement would you propose? Present your calculations with sufficient explanation to satisfy both parties.

CA15.2 **(LO 1)** **(Issuance of Stock for Land)** Martin Corporation is planning to issue 3,000 shares of its own $10 par value common stock for two acres of land to be used as a building site.

Instructions

a. What general rule should be applied to determine the amount at which the land should be recorded?

b. Under what circumstances should this transaction be recorded at the fair value of the land?

c. Under what circumstances should this transaction be recorded at the fair value of the stock issued?

d. Assume Martin intentionally records this transaction at an amount greater than the fair value of the land and the stock. Discuss this situation.

CA15.3 **(LO 1, 2, 3)** Writing **(Conceptual Issues—Equity)** Statements of Financial Accounting Concepts set forth financial accounting and reporting objectives and fundamentals that will be used by the Financial Accounting Standards Board in developing standards. *Concepts Statement No. 6* defines various elements of financial statements.

Instructions

Answer the following questions based on *SFAC No. 6*.

a. Define and discuss the term "equity."

b. What transactions or events change owners' equity?

c. Define "investments by owners" and provide examples of this type of transaction. What financial statement element other than equity is typically affected by owner investments?

d. Define "distributions to owners" and provide examples of this type of transaction. What financial statement element other than equity is typically affected by distributions?

e. What are examples of changes within owners' equity that do not change the total amount of owners' equity?

CA15.4 **(LO 3)** **(Stock Dividends and Splits)** The directors of Merchant Corporation are considering the issuance of a stock dividend. They have asked you to discuss the proposed action by answering the following questions.

Instructions

a. What is a stock dividend? How is a stock dividend distinguished from a stock split (1) from a legal standpoint, and (2) from an accounting standpoint?

b. For what reasons does a corporation usually declare a stock dividend? A stock split?

c. Discuss the amount, if any, of retained earnings to be capitalized in connection with a stock dividend.

(AICPA adapted)

CA15.5 **(LO 3)** **(Stock Dividends)** Kulikowski Inc., a client, is considering the authorization of a 10% common stock dividend to common stockholders. The financial vice president of Kulikowski wishes to discuss the accounting implications of such an authorization with you before the next meeting of the board of directors.

Instructions

a. The first topic the vice president wishes to discuss is the nature of the stock dividend to the recipient. Discuss the case against considering the stock dividend as income to the recipient.

b. The other topic for discussion is the propriety of issuing the stock dividend to all "stockholders of record" or to "stockholders of record exclusive of shares held in the name of the corporation as treasury stock." Discuss the case against issuing stock dividends on treasury shares.

(AICPA adapted)

CA15.6 **(LO 3)** **(Stock Dividend, Cash Dividend, and Treasury Stock)** Mask Company has 30,000 shares of $10 par value common stock authorized and 20,000 shares issued and outstanding. On August 15, 2020, Mask purchased 1,000 shares of treasury stock for $18 per share. Mask uses the cost method to account for treasury stock. On September 14, 2020, Mask sold 500 shares of the treasury stock for $20 per share.

In October 2020, Mask declared and distributed 1,950 shares as a stock dividend from unissued shares when the market price of the common stock was $21 per share.

On December 20, 2020, Mask declared a $1 per share cash dividend, payable on January 10, 2021, to shareholders of record on December 31, 2020.

Instructions

a. How should Mask account for the purchase and sale of the treasury stock, and how should the treasury stock be presented in the balance sheet at December 31, 2020?

b. How should Mask account for the stock dividend, and how would it affect the stockholders' equity at December 31, 2020? Why?

c. How should Mask account for the cash dividend, and how would it affect the balance sheet at December 31, 2020? Why?

(AICPA adapted)

CA15.7 **(LO 2)** Ethics **(Treasury Stock—Ethics)** Lois Kenseth, president of Sycamore Corporation, is concerned about several large stockholders who have been very vocal lately in their criticisms of her leadership. She thinks they might mount a campaign to have her removed as the corporation's CEO. She decides that buying them out by purchasing their shares could eliminate them as opponents, and she is confident they would accept a "good" offer. Kenseth knows the corporation's cash position is decent, so it has the cash to complete the transaction. She also knows the purchase of these shares will increase earnings per share, which should make other investors quite happy. (Earnings per share is calculated by dividing net income available for the common shareholders by the weighted-average number of shares outstanding. Therefore, if the number of shares outstanding is decreased by purchasing treasury shares, earnings per share increases.)

Instructions

Answer the following questions.

a. Who are the stakeholders in this situation?

b. What are the ethical issues involved?

c. Should Kenseth authorize the transaction?

Using Your Judgment

Financial Reporting Problem

The Procter & Gamble Company (P&G)

The financial statements of P&G are presented in Appendix B. The company's complete annual report, including the notes to the financial statements, is available online.

Instructions

Refer to P&G's financial statements and the accompanying notes to answer the following questions.

a. What is the par or stated value of P&G's preferred stock?

b. What is the par or stated value of P&G's common stock?

c. What percentage of P&G's authorized common stock was issued at June 30, 2017?

d. How many shares of common stock were outstanding at June 30, 2017, and June 30, 2016?

e. What was the dollar amount effect of the cash dividends on P&G's stockholders' equity?

f. What is P&G's return on common stockholders' equity for 2017 and 2016?

g. What is P&G's payout ratio for 2017 and 2016?

h. What was the market price range (high/low) of P&G's common stock during the quarter ended June 30, 2017?

Comparative Analysis Case

The Coca-Cola Company and PepsiCo, Inc.

The financial statements of **Coca-Cola** and **PepsiCo** are presented in Appendices C and D, respectively. The companies' complete annual reports, including the notes to the financial statements, are available online. Stock price data can be found in the company's annual 10K, filed at the SEC.

Instructions

Use the companies' financial information to answer the following questions.

a. What is the par or stated value of Coca-Cola's and PepsiCo's common or capital stock?

b. What percentage of authorized shares was issued by Coca-Cola at December 31, 2017, and by PepsiCo at December 31, 2017?

c. How many shares are held as treasury stock by Coca-Cola at December 31, 2017, and by PepsiCo at December 31, 2017?

d. How many Coca-Cola common shares are outstanding at December 31, 2017? How many PepsiCo shares of capital stock are outstanding at December 31, 2017?

e. What amounts of cash dividends per share were declared by Coca-Cola and PepsiCo in 2017? What were the dollar amount effects of the cash dividends on each company's stockholders' equity?

f. What are Coca-Cola's and PepsiCo's return on common/capital stockholders' equity for 2017? Which company gets the higher return on the equity of its shareholders?

g. What are Coca-Cola's and PepsiCo's payout ratios for 2017?

Financial Statement Analysis Cases

Case 1: Kellogg Company

Kellogg Company is the world's leading producer of ready-to-eat cereal products. In recent years, the company has taken numerous steps aimed at improving its profitability and earnings per share. Presented below are some basic facts for Kellogg.

(in millions)	Current Year	Prior Year
Net sales	$14,792	$14,580
Net income	1,807	632
Total assets	15,474	15,153
Total liabilities	11,867	12,302
Common stock, $0.25 par value	105	105
Capital in excess of par value	626	678
Retained earnings	6,749	6,689
Treasury stock, at cost	2,999	3,470
Number of shares outstanding (in millions)	363	358

Instructions

a. What are some of the reasons that management purchases its own stock?

b. Explain how earnings per share might be affected by treasury stock transactions.

c. Calculate the debt to assets ratio for the current year and the prior year, and discuss the implications of the change.

Case 2: Wiebold, Inc.

The following note related to stockholders' equity was reported in **Wiebold, Inc.**'s annual report.

> On February 1, the Board of Directors declared a 3-for-2 stock split, distributed on February 22 to shareholders of record on February 10. Accordingly, all numbers of common shares, except unissued shares and treasury shares, and all per share data have been restated to reflect this stock split.
>
> On the basis of amounts declared and paid, the annualized quarterly dividends per share were \$0.80 in the current year and \$0.75 in the prior year.

Instructions

a. What is the significance of the date of record and the date of distribution?

b. Why might Wiebold have declared a 3-for-2 for stock split?

c. What impact does Wiebold's stock split have on (1) total stockholders' equity, (2) total par value, (3) outstanding shares, and (4) book value per share?

Accounting, Analysis, and Principles

On January 1, 2020, Agassi Corporation had the following stockholders' equity accounts.

Common Stock (\$10 par value, 60,000 shares issued and outstanding)	\$600,000
Paid-in Capital in Excess of Par—Common Stock	500,000
Retained Earnings	620,000

During 2020, the following transactions occurred.

Jan. 15	Declared and paid a \$1.05 cash dividend per share to stockholders.
Apr. 15	Declared and paid a 10% stock dividend. The market price of the stock was \$14 per share.
May 15	Reacquired 2,000 common shares at a market price of \$15 per share.
Nov. 15	Reissued 1,000 shares held in treasury at a price of \$18 per share.
Dec. 31	Determined that net income for the year was \$370,000.

Accounting

Journalize the above transactions. (Include entries to close net income to Retained Earnings.) Determine the ending balances for Paid-in Capital, Retained Earnings, and Stockholders' Equity.

Analysis

Calculate the payout ratio and the return on common stockholders' equity.

Principles

R. Federer is examining Agassi's financial statements and wonders whether the "gains" or "losses" on Agassi's treasury stock transactions should be included in income for the year. Briefly explain whether, and the conceptual reasons why, gains or losses on treasury stock transactions should be recorded in income.

Analytics in Action

Accounting software systems collect vast amounts of data about the economic events experienced by a company and about the parties with whom the company engages, such as suppliers and customers. Business decision-makers take advantage of this wealth of information by using data analytics, which often employs both software and statistics, to draw inferences and make more informed business decisions. As both data access and analytical software improve, the use of data analytics to support decisions is becoming increasingly common at virtually all types of companies.

Equity investors and other analysts use the return on equity (ROE) ratio to assess the profitability of an investment in a company's stock. To gain a better insight into the factors that drive ROE, many analysts decompose ROE into profitability, asset turnover, and leverage components (referred to as the **DuPont** method).

Instructions Go to WileyPLUS for a data analytics exercise focusing on analysis of ROE, using the DuPont method.

Bridge to the Profession

FASB Codification References

[1] FASB ASC 480-10-05. [Predecessor literature: "Accounting for Certain Financial Instruments with Characteristics of Both Liabilities and Equity," *Statement of Financial Accounting Standards No. 150* (Norwalk Conn.: FASB, 2003).]

[2] FASB ASC 505-10-50-3. [Predecessor literature: "Disclosure of Information about Capital Structure," *Statement of Financial Accounting Standards No. 129* (Norwalk, Conn.: FASB, 1997).]

[3] FASB ASC 505-20-05-2. [Predecessor literature: American Institute of Certified Public Accountants, *Accounting Research and Terminology Bulletins, No. 43* (New York: AICPA, 1961), Ch. 7, par. 10.]

[4] FASB ASC 505-20-25-3. [Predecessor literature: American Institute of Certified Public Accountants, *Accounting Research and Terminology Bulletins, No. 43* (New York: AICPA, 1961), par. 13.]

[5] FASB ASC 505-10-50-3. [Predecessor literature: "Disclosure of Information about Capital Structure," *Statement of Financial Accounting Standards No. 129* (Norwalk, Conn.: FASB, February 1997), par. 4.]

Codification Exercises

If your school has a subscription to the FASB Codification, log in and prepare responses to the following. Provide Codification references for your responses.

CE15.1 Access the glossary ("Master Glossary") to answer the following.

a. What is a "convertible security"?

b. What is a "stock dividend"?

c. What is a "stock split"?

d. What are "participation rights"?

CE15.2 At what percentage point can the issuance of additional shares still qualify as a stock dividend, as opposed to a stock split?

CE15.3 A company plans to issue shares and wants to know the SEC's stance on the accounting treatment for the costs of issuing stock. Can these costs be deferred, or must they be expensed immediately?

CE15.4 If a company chooses to purchase its own shares and then either (1) retires the repurchased shares and issues additional shares, or (2) resells the repurchased shares, can a gain or loss be recognized by the company? Why or why not?

Codification Research Case

Recall from Chapter 13 that Hincapie Co. (a specialty bike-accessory manufacturer) is expecting growth in sales of some products targeted to the low-price market. Hincapie is contemplating a preferred stock issue to help finance this expansion in operations. The company is leaning toward participating preferred stock because ownership will not be diluted, but the investors will get an extra dividend if the company does well. The company management wants to be certain that its reporting of this transaction is transparent to its current shareholders and wants you to research the disclosure requirements related to its capital structure.

Instructions

If your school has a subscription to the FASB Codification, log in and prepare responses to the following. Provide Codification references for your responses.

a. Identify the authoritative literature that addresses disclosure of information about capital structure.

b. Find definitions of the following:

1. Securities.

2. Participation rights.

3. Preferred stock.

c. What information about securities must companies disclose? Discuss how Hincapie should report the proposed preferred stock issue.

Additional Professional Resources

Go to WileyPLUS for other career-readiness resources, such as career coaching, internship opportunities, and CPAexcel prep.

IFRS Insights

LEARNING OBJECTIVE 6

Compare the accounting procedures for stockholders' equity under GAAP and IFRS.

The primary IFRS related to stockholders' equity are *IAS 1* ("Presentation of Financial Statements"), *IAS 32* ("Financial Instruments: Presentation"), and *IAS 39* ("Financial Instruments: Recognition and Measurement").

Relevant Facts

Following are the key similarities and differences between GAAP and IFRS related to stockholders' equity.

Similarities

- The accounting for the issuance of shares and purchase of treasury stock are similar under both IFRS and GAAP.
- The accounting for declaration and payment of dividends and the accounting for stock splits are similar under both IFRS and GAAP.

Differences

- Major differences relate to terminology used, introduction of concepts such as revaluation surplus, and presentation of stockholders' equity information.
- Many countries have different investor groups than the United States. For example, in Germany, financial institutions like banks are not only the major creditors but often are the largest shareholders as well. In the United States and the United Kingdom, many companies rely on substantial investment from private investors.
- The accounting for treasury share retirements differs between IFRS and GAAP. Under GAAP, a company has three options: (1) charge the excess of the cost of treasury shares over par value to retained earnings, (2) allocate the difference between paid-in capital and retained earnings, or (3) charge the entire amount to paid-in capital. Under IFRS, the excess may have to be charged to paid-in capital, depending on the original transaction related to the issuance of the shares.
- The statement of changes in equity is usually referred to as the statement of stockholders' equity (or shareholders' equity) under GAAP.
- Both IFRS and GAAP use the term retained earnings. However, IFRS relies on the term "reserve" as a dumping ground for other types of equity transactions, such as other comprehensive income items as well as various types of unusual transactions related to convertible debt and share option contracts. GAAP relies on the account Accumulated Other Comprehensive Income (Loss). We also use this account in the discussion below, as it appears this account is gaining prominence within the IFRS literature.
- Under IFRS, it is common to report "revaluation surplus" related to increases or decreases in items such as property, plant, and equipment; mineral resources; and intangible assets. The term surplus is generally not used in GAAP. In addition, unrealized gains on the above items are not reported in the financial statements under GAAP.

About the Numbers

Equity

Equity is the residual interest in the assets of the company after deducting all liabilities. Equity is often referred to as shareholders' equity, stockholders' equity, or corporate capital. Equity is often subclassified on the statement of financial position (balance sheet) into the following categories (as discussed in Chapter 5).

1. Share capital.
2. Share premium.
3. Retained earnings.
4. Accumulated other comprehensive income.
5. Treasury shares.
6. Non-controlling interest (minority interest).

Such classifications help financial statement users to better understand the legal or other restrictions related to the ability of the company to pay dividends or otherwise use its equity for certain defined purposes. Companies often make a distinction between contributed capital (paid-in capital) and earned capital. **Contributed capital (paid-in capital)** is the total amount paid in on capital shares—the amount provided by shareholders to the corporation for use in the business. Contributed capital includes items such as the par value of all outstanding shares and premiums less discounts on issuance. **Earned capital** is the capital that develops from profitable operations. It consists of all undistributed income that remains invested in the company. **Retained earnings** represents the earned capital of the company.

As indicated above, equity is a **residual interest** and therefore its value is derived from the amount of the corporations' assets and liabilities. Only in unusual cases will a company's equity equal the total fair value of its shares. For example, **BMW** recently had total equity of €20,265 million and a market capitalization of €21,160 million. BMW's equity represents the net contributions from shareholders (from both majority and minority shareholders) plus retained earnings and accumulated other comprehensive income. As a residual interest, its equity has no existence apart from the assets and liabilities of BMW—equity equals net assets. Equity is not a claim to specific assets but a claim against a portion of the total assets. Its amount is not specified or fixed; it depends on BMW's profitability. Equity grows if it is profitable. It shrinks, or may disappear entirely, if BMW loses money.

Issuance of Ordinary Shares Under IFRS, the accounting for share issuances is similar to GAAP. The primary difference is the account titles. GAAP uses an account, Common Stock, for the par value of shares, while IFRS uses an account labeled Share Capital. What about no-par shares? In some countries, as in the United States, the total issue price for no-par shares may be considered legal capital, which could reduce the flexibility in paying dividends. Corporations sell no-par shares, like par value shares, for whatever price they will bring. However, unlike par value shares, corporations issue them without a premium or a discount. The exact amount received represents the credit to ordinary or preference shares.

For example, Video Electronics is organized with 10,000 ordinary shares authorized without par value. Video Electronics makes only a memorandum entry for the authorization, inasmuch as no amount is involved. If Video Electronics then issues 500 shares for cash at $10 per share, it makes the following entry.

Cash	5,000	
Share Capital—Ordinary		5,000

If it issues another 500 shares for $11 per share, Video Electronics makes this entry.

Cash	5,500	
Share Capital—Ordinary		5,500

True no-par shares should be carried in the accounts at issue price without any share premium reported. But some countries require that no-par shares have a **stated value**. The stated value is a minimum value below which a company cannot issue shares. Thus, instead of being no-par shares, such stated-value shares become, in effect, shares with a very low par value. It thus is open to all the criticism and abuses that first encouraged the development of no-par shares.

If no-par shares have a stated value of $5 per share but sell for $11, all such amounts in excess of $5 are recorded as share premium, which in many jurisdictions is fully or partially available for dividends. Thus, no-par value shares, with a low stated value, permit a new corporation to commence its operations with share premium that may exceed its stated capital. For example, if a company issued 1,000 of the shares with a $5 stated value at $15 per share for cash, it makes the following entry.

Cash	15,000	
Share Capital—Ordinary		5,000
Share Premium—Ordinary		10,000

Most corporations account for no-par shares with a stated value as if they were par value shares with par equal to the stated value.

Accounting for and Reporting Preference Shares

The accounting for preference shares at issuance is similar to that for ordinary shares. A corporation allocates proceeds between the par value of the preference shares and share premium. To illustrate, assume that Bishop Co. issues 10,000 shares of $10 par value preference shares for $12 cash per share. Bishop records the issuance as follows.

Cash	120,000	
Share Capital—Preference		100,000
Share Premium—Preference		20,000

Thus, Bishop maintains separate accounts for these different classes of shares. Corporations consider convertible preference shares as a part of equity. In addition, when exercising convertible preference shares, there is no theoretical justification for recognition of a gain or loss. A company recognizes no gain or loss when dealing with shareholders in their capacity as business owners. Instead, the company **employs the book value method**: debit Share Capital—Preference, along with any related Share Premium—Preference; credit Share Capital—Ordinary and Share Premium—Ordinary (if an excess exists).

Preference shares generally have no maturity date. Therefore, no legal obligation exists to pay the preference shareholder. As a result, companies classify preference shares as part of equity. Companies generally report preference shares at par value as the first item in the equity section. They report any excess over par value as part of share premium. They also consider dividends on preference shares as a distribution of income and not an expense. Companies must disclose the pertinent rights of the preference shares outstanding.

Presentation of Equity

Statement of Financial Position Illustration IFRS15.1 shows a comprehensive equity section from the statement of financial position of Frost Company that includes the equity items we discussed previously.

ILLUSTRATION IFRS15.1

Comprehensive Equity Presentation

Frost Company
Equity
December 31, 2020

Share capital—preference, $100 par value, 7% cumulative, 100,000 shares authorized, 30,000 shares issued and outstanding	$3,000,000	
Share capital—ordinary, no-par, stated value $10 per share, 500,000 shares authorized, 400,000 shares issued	4,000,000	
Ordinary share dividend distributable	200,000	$ 7,200,000
Share premium—preference	150,000	
Share premium—ordinary	840,000	990,000
Retained earnings		4,360,000
Treasury shares (2,000 ordinary shares)		(190,000)
Accumulated other comprehensive loss		(360,000)
Total equity		$12,000,000

Frost should disclose the pertinent rights and privileges of the various securities outstanding. For example, companies must disclose all of the following: dividend and liquidation preferences, participation rights, call prices and dates, conversion or exercise prices and pertinent dates, sinking fund requirements, unusual voting rights, and significant terms of contracts to issue additional shares. Liquidation preferences should be disclosed in the equity section of the statement of financial position, rather than in the notes to the financial statements, to emphasize the possible effect of this restriction on future cash flows.

Presentation of Statement of Changes in Equity Companies are also required to present a statement of changes in equity. The statement of changes in equity includes the following.

1. Total comprehensive income for the period, showing separately the total amounts attributable to owners of the parent and to non-controlling interests.
2. For each component of equity, the effects of retrospective application or retrospective restatement.
3. For each component of equity, a reconciliation between the carrying amount at the beginning and the end of the period, separately disclosing changes resulting from:
   a. Profit or loss;
   b. Each item of other comprehensive income; and
   c. Transactions with owners in their capacity as owners, showing separately contributions by and distributions to owners and changes in ownership interests in subsidiaries that do not result in a loss of control.

A typical statement of changes in equity is shown in Illustration IFRS15.2.

ILLUSTRATION IFRS15.2 Statement of Changes in Equity

	Share Capital	Retained Earnings	Unrealized Holding Gain (Loss) on Non-Trading Equity Investments	Unrealized Holding Gain (Loss) on Property, Plant, and Equipment	Total
Balance—December 31, 2020	$600,000	$120,000	$22,000	$15,000	$ 757,000
Issue of Ordinary Shares	200,000				200,000
Total Comprehensive Income		70,000	11,000	8,000	89,000
Dividends		(20,000)			(20,000)
Balance—December 31, 2021	$800,000	$170,000	$33,000	$23,000	$1,026,000

In addition, companies are required to present, either in the statement of changes in equity or in the notes, the amount of dividends recognized as distributions to owners during the period and the related amount per share.

On the Horizon

As indicated in earlier discussions, the IASB and the FASB are currently working on projects related to financial statement presentation. An important part of these studies is to determine whether certain line items, subtotals, and totals should be clearly defined and required to be displayed in the financial statements. For example, it is likely that the statement of changes in equity and its presentation will be examined closely. In addition, the options of how to present other comprehensive income under GAAP will change in any converged standard.

IFRS Self-Test Questions

1. Which of the following does **not** represent a pair of GAAP/IFRS-comparable terms?
    - **a.** Additional paid-in capital/Share premium.
    - **b.** Treasury stock/Repurchase reserve.
    - **c.** Common stock/Share capital—ordinary.
    - **d.** Preferred stock/Preference shares.

2. Under IFRS, the amount of capital received in excess of par value would be credited to:
    - **a.** Retained Earnings.
    - **b.** Contributed Capital.
    - **c.** Share Premium.
    - **d.** Par value is not used under IFRS.

3. The term *reserves* is used under IFRS with reference to all of the following **except**:
    - **a.** gains and losses on revaluation of property, plant, and equipment.
    - **b.** capital received in excess of the par value of issued shares.
    - **c.** retained earnings.
    - **d.** fair value differences.

4. Which of the following is **false**?
    - **a.** Under GAAP, companies cannot record gains on transactions involving their own shares.
    - **b.** Under IFRS, companies cannot record gains on transactions involving their own shares.
    - **c.** Under IFRS, the statement of stockholders' equity is a required statement.
    - **d.** Under IFRS, a company records a revaluation surplus when it experiences an increase in the price of its common stock.

5. Under IFRS, a purchase by a company of its own shares results in:
    - **a.** an increase in treasury shares.
    - **b.** a decrease in assets.
    - **c.** a decrease in equity.
    - **d.** All of the above.

IFRS Concepts and Application

IFRS15.1 Where can authoritative IFRS guidance related to stockholders' equity be found?

IFRS15.2 Briefly describe some of the similarities and differences between GAAP and IFRS with respect to the accounting for stockholders' equity.

IFRS15.3 Briefly discuss the implications of the financial statement presentation project for the reporting of stockholders' equity.

IFRS15.4 Mary Tokar is comparing a GAAP-based company to a company that uses IFRS. Both companies report available-for-sale debt investments. The IFRS company reports unrealized losses on these investments under the heading "Reserves" in its equity section. However, Mary can find no similar heading in the GAAP-based company financial statements. Can Mary conclude that the GAAP-based company has no unrealized gains or losses on its available-for-sale debt investments? Explain.

IFRS15.5 Explain each of the following terms: authorized ordinary shares, unissued ordinary shares, issued ordinary shares, outstanding ordinary shares, and treasury shares.

IFRS15.6 Indicate how each of the following accounts should be classified in the equity section.

- **a.** Share Capital—Ordinary.
- **b.** Retained Earnings.
- **c.** Share Premium—Ordinary.
- **d.** Treasury Shares.
- **e.** Share Premium—Treasury.
- **f.** Share Capital—Preference.
- **g.** Accumulated Other Comprehensive Income.

IFRS15.7 Kaymer Corporation issued 300 shares of $10 par value ordinary shares for $4,500. Prepare Kaymer's journal entry.

IFRS15.8 Wilco Corporation has the following account balances at December 31, 2020.

Share capital—ordinary, $5 par value	$ 510,000
Treasury shares	90,000
Retained earnings	2,340,000
Share premium—ordinary	1,320,000

Instructions

Prepare Wilco's December 31, 2020, equity section.

IFRS15.9 Ravonette Corporation issued 300 shares of $10 par value ordinary shares and 100 shares of $50 par value preference shares for a lump sum of $13,500. The ordinary shares have a market price of $20 per share, and the preference shares have a market price of $90 per share.

Instructions

Prepare the journal entry to record the issuance.

IFRS15.10 Weisberg Corporation has 10,000 shares of $100 par value, 6%, preference shares and 50,000 ordinary shares of $10 par value outstanding at December 31, 2020.

Instructions

Answer the questions in each of the following independent situations.

a. If the preference shares are cumulative and dividends were last paid on the preference shares on December 31, 2017, what are the dividends in arrears that should be reported on the December 31, 2020, statement of financial position? How should these dividends be reported?

b. If the preference shares are convertible into seven shares of $10 par value ordinary shares and 3,000 shares are converted, what entry is required for the conversion, assuming the preference shares were issued at par value?

c. If the preference shares were issued at $107 per share, how should the preference shares be reported in the equity section?

IFRS15.11 Teller Corporation's post-closing trial balance at December 31, 2020, was as follows.

Teller Corporation
Post-Closing Trial Balance
December 31, 2020

	Dr.	Cr.
Accounts payable		$ 310,000
Accounts receivable	$ 480,000	
Accumulated depreciation—building and equipment		185,000
Allowance for doubtful accounts		30,000
Bonds payable		700,000
Building and equipment	1,450,000	
Cash	190,000	
Dividends payable on preference shares—cash		4,000
Inventories	560,000	
Land	400,000	
Prepaid expenses	40,000	
Retained earnings		201,000
Share capital—ordinary ($1 par value)		200,000
Share capital—preference ($50 par value)		500,000
Share premium—ordinary		1,000,000
Share premium—treasury		160,000
Treasury shares—ordinary at cost	170,000	
Totals	$3,290,000	$3,290,000

At December 31, 2020, Teller had the following number of ordinary and preference shares.

	Ordinary	Preference
Authorized	600,000	60,000
Issued	200,000	10,000
Outstanding	190,000	10,000

The dividends on preference shares are $4 cumulative. In addition, the preference shares have a preference in liquidation of $50 per share.

Instructions

Prepare the equity section of Teller's statement of financial position at December 31, 2020.

Professional Research

IFRS15.12 Hincapie Co. (a specialty bike-accessory manufacturer) is expecting growth in sales of some products targeted to the low-price market. Hincapie is contemplating a preference share issue to help finance this expansion in operations. The company is leaning toward preference shares because ownership will not be diluted, but the investors will get an extra dividend if the company does well. The company management wants to be certain that its reporting of this transaction is transparent to its current shareholders and wants you to research the disclosure requirements related to its capital structure.

Instructions

Access the IFRS authoritative literature at the IASB website. (Click on the IFRS tab and then register for free eIFRS access if necessary.) When you have accessed the documents, you can use the search tool in your Internet browser to respond to the following questions. (Provide paragraph citations.)

a. Identify the authoritative literature that addresses disclosure of information about capital structure.

b. What information about share capital must companies disclose? Discuss how Hincapie should report the proposed preference share issue.

International Financial Reporting Problem

Marks and Spencer plc (M&S)

IFRS15.13 The financial statements of **M&S** are presented in Appendix E. The company's complete annual report, including the notes to the financial statements, is available online.

Instructions

Refer to M&S's financial statements and the accompanying notes to answer the following questions.

a. What is the par or stated value of M&S's preference shares?

b. What is the par or stated value of M&S's ordinary shares?

c. What percentage of M&S's authorized ordinary shares was issued at 1 April 2017?

d. What was the pound amount effect of the cash dividends on M&S's equity?

e. What is M&S's return on ordinary share equity for 2017 and 2016?

f. What is M&S's payout ratio for 2017 and 2016?

Answers to IFRS Self-Test Questions

1. b **2.** c **3.** b **4.** d **5.** d

CHAPTER **16**

© andersphoto/Shutterstock

Dilutive Securities and Earnings per Share

LEARNING OBJECTIVES

After studying this chapter, you should be able to:

1. Describe the accounting for the issuance, conversion, and retirement of convertible securities.
2. Contrast the accounting for stock warrants with stock warrants issued with other securities.
3. Describe the accounting and reporting for stock compensation plans.
4. Compute basic earnings per share.
5. Compute diluted earnings per share.

PREVIEW OF CHAPTER 16 As the following opening story indicates, companies are rethinking the use of various forms of stock-based compensation. The purpose of this chapter is to discuss the proper accounting for stock-based compensation. In addition, the chapter examines issues related to other types of financial instruments, such as convertible securities, warrants, and contingent shares, including their effects on reporting earnings per share. The content and organization of the chapter are as follows.

This chapter also includes numerous conceptual and global discussions that are integral to the topics presented here.

DILUTIVE SECURITIES AND EARNINGS PER SHARE

Dilutive Securities
- Debt and equity
- Convertible debt
- Convertible preferred stock

Stock Warrants
- Warrants and other securities
- Stock rights

Stock Compensation Plans
- Measurement
- Recognition
- Restricted stock
- Employee stock-purchase plans
- Disclosure of compensation plans

Basic Earnings per Share
- Simple structure
- Comprehensive example

Diluted Earnings per Share
- Convertible securities
- Options and warrants
- Contingent issues
- Antidilution
- Presentation and disclosure

Kicking the Habit

Some habits die hard. Take stock options—called by some "the crack cocaine of incentives." Stock options are a form of compensation that gives key employees the choice to purchase shares at a given (usually lower-than-market) price. For many years, companies were hooked on these products. Why? The combination of a hot equity market and favorable accounting treatment made stock options the incentive of choice. They were compensation with no expense to the companies that granted them, and they were popular with key employees, so companies granted them with abandon. However, the accounting rules that took effect in 2005 required expensing the fair value of stock options when granted. This new treatment has made it easier for companies to kick this habit.

As shown in the following chart, for both large companies and high-tech companies, a shift has occurred in the use of stock options versus restricted stock. In fact, starting in 2006 (at the time of a new standard on stock compensation), both types of companies started switching to restricted-stock plans. As a spokesperson at one company commented, "Once you begin expensing options, the attractiveness significantly drops."

	Large Companies		High-Tech Companies	
	2016	2013	2016	2013
Types of equity awards granted—by number of units (median)				
Stock options	54%	74%	67%	76%
Restricted stock	46	26	33	24
Types of equity awards granted—by value of awards (median)				
Stock options	22	48	44	55
Restricted stock	78	52	56	45

These stock-based awards in most cases are reserved for the key officers of a company. When coupled with other forms of compensation, these pay elements often lead to compensation levels that are quite high. To provide additional information on these levels of compensation, Congress passed the Dodd-Frank Act (2010), resulting in SEC rules requiring companies to disclose:

- The median of the annual total compensation of all employees of the company, except the CEO.
- The annual total compensation of its CEO.
- The ratio of the two amounts.

Often referred to as the "pay ratio rule," the purpose of this disclosure is to inform investors of the magnitude of a company's CEO pay package in relationship to the overall pay package of its employees. Some believe that this requirement does not go far enough because it shows only the CEO's pay in relation to a median pay of its employees (two data points) without consideration of the allocations of pay amounts within the organization. Others contend that this information may be helpful to the board of directors in evaluating pay packages related to key executives.

For the largest 100 companies, these pay ratios are considerably higher. For example, one study had an estimate of 235-to-1 for large companies, whereas for smaller companies such as in the Russell 3000 index, the ratio is approximately 72-to-1. In some cases, the ratio is quite high because certain companies employ large groups of retail, temporary, or foreign workers whose wages are quite low. Two examples are **Manpower Group** (2,483-to-1) or retailer **Kohl's** 1,264-to-1. Conversely, Warren Buffett, one of the richest individuals in the world and the CEO of **Berkshire Hathaway**, only takes a salary of $100,000 plus costs related to security. Berkshire Hathaway's ratio is just 1.87-to-1.

Sources: Louis Lavelle, "Kicking the Stock-Options Habit," *Businessweek Online* (February 16, 2005); J. Ciesielski, "S&P 500 Executive Pay: The Bread Keeps Rising," *The Analyst's Accounting Observer* (June 25, 2012); "Stock Compensation: 2017 Assumptions and Disclosure Study," PricewaterhouseCoopers (July 2017); J. Ciesielski, "2016 S&P 500 Executive Pay: Why and How Much It Matters to Shareholders," *The Analyst's Accounting Observer*, Volume 26, No. 9 (August 25, 2017); and *https://www.thecorporatecounsel.net/blog/2017/07/survey-results-pay-ratio-readiness.html.*

Review and Practice

Go to the **Review and Practice** section at the end of the chapter for a targeted summary review and practice problem with solution. Multiple-choice questions with annotated solutions as well as additional exercises and practice problem with solutions are also available online.

Dilutive Securities

LEARNING OBJECTIVE 1

Describe the accounting for the issuance, conversion, and retirement of convertible securities.

Debt and Equity

Many of the controversies related to the accounting for financial instruments such as stock options, convertible securities, and preferred stock relate to whether companies should report these instruments as a liability or as equity. For example, companies should classify nonredeemable common shares as equity because the issuer has no **obligation** to pay dividends or repurchase the stock. Declaration of dividends is at the issuer's discretion, as is the decision to repurchase the stock. Similarly, preferred stock that is not redeemable does not require the issuer to pay dividends or repurchase the stock. Thus, nonredeemable common or preferred stock lacks an important characteristic of a liability—an obligation to pay the holder of the common or preferred stock at some point in the future.

However the classification is not as clear-cut for other financial instruments. For example, in Chapter 15 we discussed the accounting for mandatorily redeemable preferred stock. Companies originally classified this security as part of equity. The SEC then prohibited equity classification, and most companies classified these securities between debt and equity on the balance sheet in a separate section often referred to as the "mezzanine section." The FASB now requires companies to report these types of securities as a liability.[1] [1] (See the FASB Codification References near the end of the chapter.)

In this chapter, we discuss securities that have characteristics of *both* debt and equity. For example, a convertible bond has both debt and equity characteristics. Should a company classify this security as debt, as equity, or as part debt and part equity? In addition, how should a company compute earnings per share if it has convertible bonds and other convertible securities in its capital structure? Convertible securities as well as options, warrants, and other securities are often called **dilutive securities** because upon exercise they may reduce (dilute) earnings per share.

Accounting for Convertible Debt

Convertible bonds can be changed into other corporate securities during some specified period of time after issuance. A convertible bond combines the benefits of a bond with the privilege of exchanging it for stock at the holder's option. Investors who purchase it desire the security of a bond holding (guaranteed interest and principal) plus the added option of conversion if the value of the stock appreciates significantly.

Corporations issue convertible securities for two main reasons. One is to raise equity capital without giving up more ownership control than necessary. To illustrate, assume a company wants to raise $1 million; its common stock is selling at $45 a share. To raise the $1 million, the company would have to sell 22,222 shares (ignoring issue costs). By selling 1,000 bonds at $1,000 par, each

[1] The FASB (and IASB) have studied the accounting for financial instruments with characteristics of both debt and equity. At one time, the Boards proposed a definition of equity that is far more restrictive than current practice. Under the proposed "basic ownership approach," only common stock is classified as equity. All other instruments (e.g., preferred stock, options, and convertible debt) are classified as liabilities. Instruments classified as liabilities are measured at fair value, and changes are reported in income. Adoption of a narrow definition provides fewer opportunities to structure instruments and arrangements to achieve a desired accounting treatment.

The FASB has a project on distinguishing liabilities from equity (including convertible debt) with the objective of improving understandability and reducing complexity (without loss of information for users). Go to the FASB website (click on Projects and then Technical Agenda) for more details.

convertible into 20 shares of common stock, the company could raise $1 million by committing only 20,000 shares of its common stock.

A second reason to issue convertibles is to obtain debt financing at cheaper rates. Many companies could issue debt only at high interest rates unless they attach a convertible covenant. The conversion privilege entices the investor to accept a lower interest rate than would normally be the case on a straight debt issue. For example, **Amazon.com** at one time issued convertible bonds that pay interest at an effective yield of 4.75 percent. This rate was much lower than Amazon would have had to pay by issuing straight debt. For this lower interest rate, the investor receives the right to buy Amazon's common stock at a fixed price until the bond's maturity.[2]

As indicated earlier, the accounting for convertible debt involves reporting issues at the time of (1) issuance, (2) conversion, and (3) retirement.

At Time of Issuance

The method for recording convertible bonds **at the date of issue follows the method used to record straight debt issues**. None of the proceeds are recorded as equity (see Global View). Companies amortize to the maturity date any discount or premium that results from the issuance of convertible bonds. Why this treatment? Because it is difficult to predict when, if at all, conversion will occur. However, the accounting for convertible debt as a straight debt issue is controversial; we discuss it more fully later in the chapter.

> **Global View**
>
> IFRS requires that the issuer of convertible debt record the liability and equity components separately.

At Time of Conversion

If converting bonds into other securities, a company uses the **book value method** to record the conversion. The book value method records the securities exchanged for the bond at the carrying amount (book value) of the bond.

To illustrate, assume that Hilton, Inc. has a $1,000 bond that is convertible into 10 shares of common stock (par value $10). At the time of conversion, the unamortized premium is $50. Hilton records the conversion of the bonds as follows.

Bonds Payable	1,000	
Premium on Bonds Payable	50	
Common Stock (10 × $10)		100
Paid-in Capital in Excess of Par—Common Stock		950

Support for the book value approach is based on the argument that an agreement was established at the date of the issuance either to pay a stated amount of cash at maturity or to issue a stated number of shares of equity securities. Therefore, when the debtholder converts the debt to equity in accordance with the preexisting contract terms, the issuing company recognizes no gain or loss upon conversion.

Induced Conversions

Sometimes the issuer wishes to encourage prompt conversion of its convertible debt to equity securities in order to reduce interest costs or to improve its debt to equity ratio. Thus, the issuer may offer some form of additional consideration (such as cash or common stock), called a "sweetener," to **induce conversion**. The issuing company reports the sweetener as an expense of the current period. Its amount is the fair value of the additional securities or other consideration given.

[2]As with any investment, a buyer has to be careful. For example, **Wherehouse Entertainment Inc.**, which had 6¼ percent convertibles outstanding, was taken private in a leveraged buyout. As a result, the convertible was suddenly as risky as a junk bond of a highly leveraged company with a coupon of only 6¼ percent. As one holder of the convertibles noted, "What's even worse is that the company will be so loaded down with debt that it probably won't have enough cash flow to make its interest payments. And the convertible debt we hold is subordinated to the rest of Wherehouse's debt." These types of situations make convertibles less attractive and lead to the introduction of take-over protection covenants in some convertible bond offerings. Or, sometimes convertibles are permitted to be called at par, and therefore the conversion premium may be lost.

Assume that Helloid, Inc. has outstanding $1,000,000 par value convertible debentures convertible into 100,000 shares of $1 par value common stock. Helloid wishes to reduce its annual interest cost. To do so, Helloid agrees to pay the holders of its convertible debentures an additional $80,000 if they will convert. Assuming conversion occurs, Helloid makes the following entry.

Debt Conversion Expense	80,000	
Bonds Payable	1,000,000	
Common Stock (100,000 × $1)		100,000
Paid-in Capital in Excess of Par—Common Stock		900,000
Cash		80,000

Helloid records the additional $80,000 as **an expense of the current period** and not as a reduction of equity.

Some argue that the cost of a conversion inducement is a cost of obtaining equity capital. As a result, they contend, companies should recognize the cost of conversion as a cost of (a reduction of) the equity capital acquired, and not as an expense. However, the FASB indicated that when an issuer makes an additional payment to encourage conversion, the payment is for a service (bondholders converting at a given time) and should be reported as an expense.

Retirement of Convertible Debt

As indicated earlier, the method for recording the **issuance** of convertible bonds follows that used in recording straight debt issues. Specifically this means that issuing companies should not attribute any portion of the proceeds to the conversion feature, nor should it credit a paid-in capital account.

Although some raise theoretical objections to this approach, to be consistent, companies need to recognize a gain or loss on **retiring convertible debt in the same way that they recognize a gain or loss on retiring nonconvertible debt**. For this reason, companies should report differences between the cash acquisition price of debt and its carrying amount **in current income as a gain or loss**.

Convertible Preferred Stock

Convertible preferred stock includes an option for the holder to convert preferred shares into a fixed number of common shares. The major difference between accounting for a convertible bond and convertible preferred stock at the date of issue is their classification. Convertible bonds are considered liabilities, whereas convertible preferreds (unless mandatory redemption exists) are considered part of stockholders' equity.

In addition, when stockholders exercise convertible preferred stock, there is no theoretical justification for recognizing a gain or loss. A company does not recognize a gain or loss when it deals with stockholders in their capacity as business owners. Therefore, companies do not recognize a gain or loss when stockholders exercise convertible preferred stock.

In accounting for the exercise of convertible preferred stock, a company uses the **book value method**. It debits Preferred Stock, along with any related Paid-in Capital in Excess of Par—Preferred Stock, and it credits Common Stock and Paid-in Capital in Excess of Par—Common Stock (if an excess exists). The treatment differs when the par value of the common stock issued **exceeds** the book value of the preferred stock. In that case, the company usually debits Retained Earnings for the difference.

To illustrate, assume Host Enterprises issued 1,000 shares of common stock (par value $2) upon conversion of 1,000 shares of preferred stock (par value $1) that was originally issued for a $200 premium. The entry would be:

Convertible Preferred Stock (1,000 × $1)	1,000	
Paid-in Capital in Excess of Par—Preferred Stock	200	
Retained Earnings	800	
Common Stock (1,000 × $2)		2,000

The rationale for the debit to Retained Earnings is that Host has offered the preferred stockholders an **additional return** to facilitate their conversion to common stock. In this example, Host charges the additional return to retained earnings. Many states, however, require that this charge simply reduce additional paid-in capital from other sources.

What Do the Numbers Mean? How Low Can You Go?

What do Tesla Motors Inc., Twitter Inc., Etsy, Inc., Red Hat Inc., and Priceline Group Inc. all have in common? They are part of the wave of U.S. companies who have raised capital in the convertible bond market. And quite a wave it is. As indicated in the following chart, convertible bond issuances are on an upward trend with over $20 billion issued in the first two quarters of 2018.

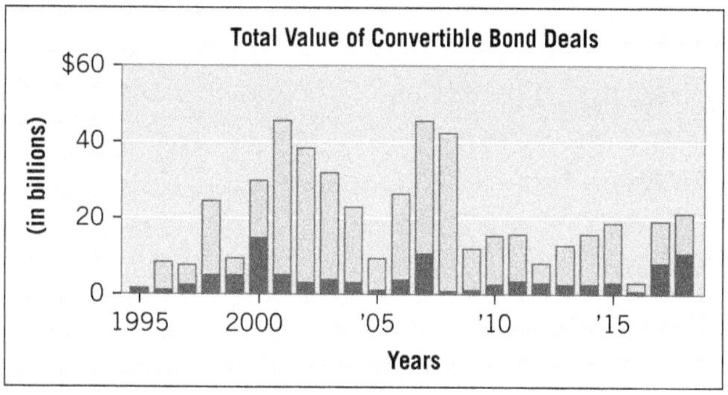

These bonds are popular with issuing companies and investors. As we have discussed, companies like them because they allow them to raise money at rates lower than those on ordinary bonds. Investors like them because, at a time of low interest rates, they can book extra profit if the issuer's stock price rises. However, depending on the features of the bond and the stock value, some unusual results may be observed.

Consider the convertible bonds issued by STMicroelectronics (STM). STM's 10-year bonds have a zero coupon and are convertible into STM common stock at an exercise price of $33.43. When issued, the bonds sold at an effective yield of *minus 0.05* percent. That's right—a negative yield. How could this happen? When STM issued the bonds, investors thought the options to convert were so valuable that they were willing to take zero interest payments and invest an amount *in excess of* the maturity value of the bonds.

In essence, the investors are paying interest to STM, and STM records interest revenue. Why would investors do this? If the stock price rises, as many thought it would for STM and many tech companies at that time, these bond investors could convert and get a big gain in the stock.

Investors did get some additional protection in the deal: They can redeem the $1,000 bonds after three years and receive $975 (and after five and seven years, for lower amounts) if it looks like the bonds will never convert. In the end, STM has issued bonds with a significant equity component. And because the entire bond issue is classified as debt, STM records negative interest expense.

Sources: STM Financial Reports. See also Floyd Norris, "Legal but Absurd: They Borrow a Billion and Report a Profit," *The New York Times* (August 8, 2003), p. C1; M. Cherney, "Convertible Bonds Take Off in Low-Yield Era," *Wall Street Journal* (October 5, 2014); and M. Farrell, "Bull Market in Tech-Company Convertible Debt Rages On," *Wall Street Journal* (May 25, 2018).

Stock Warrants

LEARNING OBJECTIVE 2

Contrast the accounting for stock warrants with stock warrants issued with other securities.

Warrants are certificates entitling the holder to acquire shares of stock at a certain price within a stated period. This option is similar to the conversion privilege in a convertible bond. Warrants, if exercised, become common stock and usually have a dilutive effect (reduce earnings per share) similar to that of the conversion of convertible securities. However, a substantial difference between convertible securities and stock warrants is that upon exercise of the warrants, the holder has to pay a certain amount of money to obtain the shares.

The issuance of warrants or options to buy additional shares normally arises under three situations:

1. When issuing different types of securities, such as bonds or preferred stock, companies often include warrants **to make the security more attractive**—by providing an "equity kicker."
2. Upon the issuance of additional common stock, existing stockholders have a **preemptive right to purchase common stock** first. Companies may issue warrants to evidence that right.

3. Companies give warrants, often referred to as *stock options*, **to executives and employees** as a form of **compensation**.

The problems in accounting for stock warrants are complex and present many difficulties—some of which remain unresolved. The following sections address the accounting for stock warrants in the three situations listed above.

Stock Warrants Issued with Other Securities

Warrants issued with other securities are basically long-term options to buy common stock at a fixed price. Generally the life of warrants is five years, occasionally 10 years; very occasionally, a company may offer perpetual warrants.

A warrant works like this. **Tenneco, Inc.** offered a unit comprising one share of stock and one detachable warrant. As its name implies, the **detachable stock warrant** can be detached (separated) from the stock and traded as a separate security. The Tenneco warrant in this example is exercisable at $24.25 per share and good for five years. The unit (share of stock plus detachable warrant) sold for 22.75 ($22.75). Since the price of the common stock the day before the sale was 19.88 ($19.88), the difference suggests a price of 2.87 ($2.87) for the warrant.

The investor pays for the warrant in order to receive the right to buy the stock, at a fixed price of $24.25, sometime in the future. It would not be profitable at present for the purchaser to exercise the warrant and buy the stock, because the price of the stock was much below the exercise price.[3] But if, for example, the price of the stock rises to $30, the investor gains $2.88 ($30 – $24.25 – $2.87) on an investment of $2.87, a 100 percent increase! If the price never rises, the investor loses the full $2.87 per warrant.[4]

A company should allocate the proceeds from the sale of debt with detachable stock warrants **between the two securities.**[5] The profession takes the position that two separable instruments are involved, that is, (1) a bond and (2) a warrant giving the holder the right to purchase common stock at a certain price. Companies can trade detachable warrants separately from the debt. This allows the determination of a fair value. The two methods of allocation available are:

1. The proportional method.
2. The incremental method.

Proportional Method

At one time, **AT&T** issued bonds with detachable five-year warrants to buy one share of common stock (par value $5) at $25. At the time, a share of AT&T stock was selling for approximately $50. These warrants enabled AT&T to price its bond offering at par with an 8¾ percent yield (quite a bit lower than prevailing rates at that time). To account for the proceeds from this offering, AT&T would place a value on the two securities: (1) the value of the bonds without the warrants, and (2) the value of the warrants. The **proportional method** then allocates the proceeds using the proportion of the two amounts, based on fair values.

For example, assume that AT&T's bonds (par $1,000) sold for 99 without the warrants soon after their issue. The market price of the warrants at that time was $30. (Prior to sale the warrants will not have a fair value.) The allocation relies on an estimate of fair value, generally as established by an investment banker, or on the relative fair value of the bonds and the warrants soon after the company issues and trades them. The price paid for 10,000, $1,000 bonds with the warrants attached was par, or $10,000,000. **Illustration 16.1** shows the proportional allocation of the bond proceeds between the bonds and warrants.

[3]Later in this discussion, we will show that the value of the warrant is normally determined on the basis of a relative fair value approach because of the difficulty of imputing a warrant value in any other manner.

[4]From the example, it is apparent that buying warrants can be an "all or nothing" proposition.

[5]A detachable warrant means that the warrant can sell separately from the bond. GAAP makes a distinction between detachable and nondetachable warrants because companies must sell nondetachable warrants with the security as a complete package. Thus, no allocation is permitted. [2]

ILLUSTRATION 16.1

Proportional Allocation of Proceeds between Bonds and Warrants

Fair value of bonds (without warrants) ($10,000,000 × .99)		$ 9,900,000
Fair value of warrants (10,000 × $30)		300,000
Aggregate fair value		$10,200,000
Allocated to bonds:	$\frac{\$9,900,000}{\$10,200,000} \times \$10,000,000 =$ $ 9,705,882	
Allocated to warrants:	$\frac{\$300,000}{\$10,200,000} \times \$10,000,000 =$ $ 294,118	
Total allocation	$10,000,000	

In this situation, the bonds sell at a discount. AT&T records the sale as follows.

Cash	9,705,882	
Discount on Bonds Payable	294,118	
Bonds Payable		10,000,000

In addition, AT&T sells warrants that it credits to paid-in capital. It makes the following entry.

Cash	294,118	
Paid-in Capital—Stock Warrants		294,118

AT&T may combine the entries if desired. Here, we show them separately, to indicate that the purchaser of the bond is buying not only a bond but also a possible future claim on common stock in the form of the stock warrant.

Assuming investors exercise all 10,000 warrants (one warrant per one share of stock), AT&T makes the following entry.

Cash (10,000 × $25)	250,000	
Paid-in Capital—Stock Warrants	294,118	
Common Stock (10,000 × $5)		50,000
Paid-in Capital in Excess of Par—Common Stock		494,118

What if investors fail to exercise the warrants? In that case, AT&T debits Paid-in Capital—Stock Warrants for $294,118 and credits Paid-in Capital—Expired Stock Warrants for a like amount. The additional paid-in capital reverts to the former stockholders.

Incremental Method

In instances where a company cannot determine the fair value of either the warrants or the bonds, it applies the **incremental method** used in lump-sum security purchases (as explained in Chapter 15). That is, the company uses the security for which it *can* determine the fair value. It allocates the remainder of the purchase price to the security for which it does not know the fair value.

For example, assume that the fair value of the AT&T warrants is $300,000, but the company cannot determine the fair value of the bonds without the warrants. **Illustration 16.2** shows the amount allocated to the warrants and the stock in this case.

ILLUSTRATION 16.2

Incremental Allocation of Proceeds between Bonds and Warrants

Lump-sum receipt	$10,000,000
Allocated to the warrants	(300,000)
Balance allocated to bonds	$ 9,700,000

Conceptual Questions

The question arises whether the allocation of value to the warrants is consistent with the handling of convertible debt, in which companies allocate no value to the conversion privilege. The FASB stated that the features of a convertible security are **inseparable** in the sense that choices are mutually exclusive. The holder either converts the bonds or redeems them for cash, but cannot do both. No basis, therefore, exists for recognizing the conversion value in the accounts.

The Board, however, indicated that the issuance of bonds with **detachable warrants** involves *two* securities, one a debt security, which will remain outstanding until maturity, and the other a warrant to purchase common stock. At the time of issuance, separable instruments exist. The existence of two instruments therefore justifies separate treatment. **Nondetachable warrants**, however, **do not require an allocation of the proceeds between the bonds and the warrants**. Similar to the accounting for convertible bonds, companies record the entire proceeds from nondetachable warrants as debt (see **Underlying Concepts**).[6]

Underlying Concepts

Reporting a convertible bond solely as debt is not representationally faithful. However, the cost constraint is used to justify the failure to allocate between debt and equity.

Rights to Subscribe to Additional Shares

If the directors of a corporation decide to issue new shares of stock, the old stockholders generally have the right (**preemptive privilege**) to purchase newly issued shares in proportion to their holdings. This privilege, referred to as a **stock right**, saves existing stockholders from suffering a dilution of voting rights without their consent. Also, it may allow them to purchase stock somewhat below its fair value. Unlike the warrants issued with other securities, the warrants issued for stock rights are of short duration.

The certificate representing the stock right states the number of shares the holder of the right may purchase. Each share of stock owned ordinarily gives the owner one stock right. The certificate also states the price at which the new shares may be purchased. The price is normally less than the current market price of such shares, which gives the rights a value in themselves. From the time they are issued until they expire, holders of stock rights may purchase and sell them like any other security.

Companies make only a memorandum entry when they issue rights to existing stockholders. This entry indicates the number of rights issued to existing stockholders in order to ensure that the company has additional unissued stock registered for issuance in case the rights are exercised. Companies make no formal entry at this time because they have not yet issued stock nor received cash.

If holders exercise the stock rights, a cash payment of some type usually is involved. If the company receives cash equal to the par value, it makes an entry crediting Common Stock at par value. If the company receives cash in excess of par value, it credits Paid-in Capital in Excess of Par—Common Stock. If it receives cash less than par value, a debit to Paid-in Capital in Excess of Par—Common Stock is appropriate.

What Do the Numbers Mean? Is That All Debt?

Many argue that the conversion feature of a convertible bond is not significantly different in nature from the call represented by a warrant. The question is whether, although the legal forms differ, sufficient similarities of substance exist to support the same accounting treatment. Some contend that inseparability *per se* is an insufficient basis for restricting allocation between identifiable components of a transaction.

Examples of allocation between assets of value in a single transaction *do* exist, such as allocation of values in basket purchases and separation of principal and interest in capitalizing long-term leases. Critics of the current accounting for convertibles say that to deny recognition of value to the conversion feature merely looks to the form of the instrument and does not deal with the substance of the transaction. In an exposure draft on this subject, the FASB indicates that companies should separate the debt and equity components of securities such as convertible debt or bonds issued with nondetachable warrants (see footnotes 1 and 6).

[6]GAAP requires that for convertible debt that can be settled in cash, companies should account for the liability and equity components separately. In deliberations of the debt/equity project (see footnote 1), the FASB has proposed that all convertible bonds be separated into liability and equity components. [3] Academic research indicates that estimates of the debt and equity components of convertible bonds are subject to considerable measurement error. See Mary Barth, Wayne Landsman, and Richard Rendleman, Jr., "Option Pricing–Based Bond Value Estimates and a Fundamental Components Approach to Account for Corporate Debt," *The Accounting Review* (January 1998). This and other challenges explain in part the extended time needed to develop new standards in this area.

We agree with this position. In both situations (convertible debt and debt issued with warrants, whether detachable or not), the investor has made a payment to the company for an equity feature—the right to acquire an equity instrument in the future. The only real distinction between them is that the additional payment made when the equity instrument is formally acquired takes different forms. The warrant holder pays additional cash to the issuing company; the convertible debt holder pays for stock by forgoing the receipt of interest from conversion date until maturity date and by forgoing the receipt of the maturity value itself. Thus, the difference is one of method or form of payment only, rather than one of substance. However, until the profession officially reverses its stand with respect to accounting for convertible debt, companies will continue to report convertible debt and bonds issued with nondetachable warrants solely as debt.

Stock Compensation Plans

LEARNING OBJECTIVE 3

Describe the accounting and reporting for stock compensation plans.

Effective compensation programs do the following:

1. Base compensation on employee and company performance.
2. Motivate employees to high levels of performance.
3. Help retain executives and allow for recruitment of new talent.
4. Maximize the employee's after-tax benefit and minimize the employer's after-tax cost.
5. Use performance criteria over which the employee has control.

Straight cash-compensation plans (salary and perhaps a bonus), though important, are oriented to the short run. Many companies recognize that they need a longer-term compensation plan in addition to the cash component.

Long-term compensation plans attempt to develop company loyalty among key employees by giving them "a piece of the action"—that is, an equity interest. These plans, generally referred to as **stock-based compensation plans**, come in many forms. For example, a **stock option** gives key employees the option to purchase common stock at a given price over an extended period of time. Essentially, these plans provide the employee with the opportunity to receive stock if the performance of the company (by whatever measure) is satisfactory. Typical performance measures focus on long-term improvements that are readily measurable and that benefit the company as a whole, such as increases in earnings per share, revenues, stock price, or market share.

Stock-based compensation is the largest single component for executive officers' pay for companies that comprise the S&P 500 (the largest companies in the United States). As shown in **Illustration 16.3**, the stock compensation of these executives far exceeds regular cash compensation (salary and bonuses).

ILLUSTRATION 16.3

Total Executive Pay by Form

($ in millions)	2016	% of Total	2015	% of Total	Change
Salary	$ 1,983.7	11.2%	$ 1,972.4	11.9%	0.6%
Bonus	522.7	2.9	515.3	3.1	1.4
Salary and bonus	$ 2,506.4	14.1%	$ 2,487.7	14.9%	0.8%
Stock awards	$ 8,249.3	46.5%	$ 7.319.1	44.0%	12.7%
Option awards	2,267.4	12.8	2,371.0	14.2	−4.4
Equity instrument pay	$10,516.7	59.3%	$ 9,690.1	58.2%	8.5%
Non-equity incentives	$ 2,948.5	16.6%	$ 2,959.5	17.8%	−0.4%
Pension/deferred pay	897.7	5.1	671.6	4.0	33.7
Other	854.3	4.8	832.1	5.0	2.7
Total	$17,723.6	100.0%	$16,641.1	100.0%	6.5%

Sources: S&P 500 companies; J. Ciesielski, "2016 S&P 500 Executive Pay: Why and How Much It Matters to Shareholders," *The Analyst's Accounting Observer*, Volume 26, No. 9 (August 25, 2017).

Salaries and bonuses comprise only 14.1 percent of total compensation, whereas stock compensation is 59.3 percent of total compensation. Interestingly, the remaining 26.6 percent are primarily non-equity incentives and pension and deferred payments. These compensation amounts are particularly high when you compare the level of compensation to a company's pretax income. For example, **Illustration 16.4** shows the relationship of the top five officers' total pay in relationship to pretax income for five different industries.

ILLUSTRATION 16.4 Top Five Company Officers' Total Pay vs. Pretax Income

($ in millions)	Number of Firms	Total Pay 2016	Total Pay 2015	Pretax Income 2016	Pretax Income 2015	% of Pretax Income 2016	% of Pretax Income 2015
Real estate	31	$ 770.3	$ 754.4	$ 23,703.9	$ 17,619.8	3.2%	4.3%
Utilities	27	713.8	625.7	27,567.5	36,253.0	2.6	1.7
Materials	25	679.5	678.8	27,030.3	26,411.6	2.5	2.6
Consumer discretionary	77	3,221.3	2,756.6	164,423.9	155,627.0	2.0	1.8
Industrials	63	1,934.1	1,919.6	132,333.5	141,372.5	1.5	1.4
Health care	54	1,827.9	1,918.2	131,924.6	122,718.1	1.4	1.6
Information technology	61	2,483.7	2,439.0	221,970.5	232,275.3	1.1	1.1
Consumer staples	34	1,447.6	1,168.5	148,347.9	130,620.0	1.0	0.9
Financials	63	2,394.2	2,230.2	284,754.1	293,858.1	0.8	0.8
Telecom	4	178.6	168.6	42,660.0	50,531.0	0.4	0.3
Energy	31	997.5	969.4	(31,835.3)	(80,089.5)	NM	NM
	470	$16,648.4	$15,629.1	$1,172,880.8	$1,127,196.9	1.4	1.4

Sources: S&P 500 companies; J. Ciesielski, "2016 S&P 500 Executive Pay: Why and How Much It Matters to Shareholders," *The Analyst's Accounting Observer*, Volume 26, No. 9 (August 25, 2017).

As indicated by the above levels of compensation, compensation costs related to key executives is significant. Indeed, the pay of the five key executives for S&P 500 companies accounted for nearly 1.5 percent of the companies' pretax income, with executives in the real estate industry leading the way at 3.2 percent. Specific examples of companies' pay amounts to pretax income are **Under Armour** 6.3 percent, **Netflix** 25 percent, and **Caterpillar** and **Estee Lauder** 5.7 percent. As a result, even with the required expensing of stock options and other stock award plans (like restricted-stock awards), companies continue to use these plans as the primary component to compensate key personnel.

Measurement—Stock Compensation

Suppose that as an employee for Hurdle Inc., you receive options to purchase 10,000 shares of the firm's common stock as part of your compensation. The date you receive the options is referred to as the **grant date**. The options are good for 10 years. The market price and the exercise price for the stock are both $20 at the grant date. **What is the value of the compensation you just received?**

Some believe that what you have received has no value. They reason that because the difference between the market price and the exercise price is zero, no compensation results. Others argue these options do have value. If the stock price goes above $20 any time in the next 10 years and you exercise the options, you may earn substantial compensation. For example, if at the end of the fourth year, the market price of the stock is $30 and you exercise your options, you earn $100,000 [10,000 options × ($30 – $20)], ignoring income taxes.

The question for Hurdle is how to report the granting of these options. One approach measures compensation cost by the excess of the market price of the stock over its exercise price at the grant date. This approach is referred to as the **intrinsic-value method**. It measures what the holder would receive today if the option was immediately exercised. That intrinsic value **is the difference between the market price of the stock and the exercise price of the options at the grant date**. Using the intrinsic-value method, Hurdle would not recognize any compensation expense related to your options because at the grant date the market price equaled the exercise price. (In the preceding paragraph, those who answered that the options had no value were looking at the question from the intrinsic-value approach.)

The second way to look at the question of how to report the granting of these options bases the cost of employee stock options on the **fair value** of the stock options granted. Under this **fair value method**, companies use acceptable option-pricing models to value the options at the date of grant. These models take into account the many factors that determine an option's underlying value.[7]

GAAP requires that companies recognize compensation cost using the fair value method (see **Global View**). [4] The FASB position is that companies should base the accounting for the cost of employee services on the fair value of compensation paid. This amount is presumed to be a measure of the value of the services received. The concept of fair value therefore applies to stock options as well as restricted-stock plans.

> **Global View**
>
> IFRS follows the same model as GAAP for recognizing share-based compensation.

Many in corporate America resisted the fair value method. Many small high-technology companies were especially vocal in their opposition, arguing that only through offering stock options can they attract top professional management. They contended that recognizing large amounts of compensation expense under these plans places them at a competitive disadvantage against larger companies that can withstand higher compensation charges. As one high-tech executive stated, "If your goal is to attack fat-cat executive compensation in multi-billion dollar firms, then please do so! But not at the expense of the people who are 'running lean and mean,' trying to build businesses and creating jobs in the process."

The stock-option saga is a classic example of the difficulty the FASB faces in issuing new accounting guidance. Many powerful interests aligned against the Board. Even some who initially appeared to support the Board's actions later reversed themselves. These efforts undermine the authority of the FASB, which in turn damages confidence in our financial reporting system.

Transparent financial reporting—including recognition of stock-based expense—should not be criticized because companies will report lower income. We may not like what the financial statements say, but we are always better off when the statements are representationally faithful to the underlying economic substance of transactions (see **Underlying Concepts**).

> **Underlying Concepts**
>
> The stock-option controversy involves economic-consequence issues. The FASB believes companies should follow the neutrality concept. Others disagree, noting that factors other than accounting theory should be considered.

What Do the Numbers Mean? What's the Debate About?

A look at the history of accounting for stock options indicates that the FASB faced considerable opposition when it proposed the fair value method for accounting for stock options. This is not surprising, given that the fair value method results in greater compensation costs relative to the intrinsic-value model. **Merrill Lynch** estimated that if all S&P 500 companies were to expense options, reported profits would fall by as much as 10 percent. Nevertheless, some companies, such as **Coca-Cola**, **General Electric**, **Wachovia**, and **Bank One**, decided to use the fair value method.

You might think investors would punish companies that decided to expense stock options. After all, most of corporate America has been battling for years to avoid having to expense them, worried that accounting for those perks would destroy earnings. Yet, for this small band of big-name companies that voluntarily made the switch to expensing, investors for the most part showered them with love. As shown in the following table, with a few exceptions, the stock prices of the "expensers," from **Cinergy** to **The Washington Post**, outpaced the market after they announced the change.

	Estimated EPS		% Change Since Announcement
Company	Without Options	With Options Expensed	Company Stock Price
Cinergy	$ 2.80	$ 2.77	22.4%
The Washington Post	20.48	20.10	16.4
Computer Associates	−0.46	−0.62	11.1
Fannie Mae	6.15	6.02	6.7
Bank One	2.77	2.61	2.6
General Motors	5.84	5.45	2.6
Procter & Gamble	3.57	3.35	−2.3
Coca-Cola	1.79	1.70	−6.2
General Electric	1.65	1.61	−6.2
Amazon.com	0.04	−0.99	−11.4

Sources: Merril Lynch; company reports.

[7]These factors include the volatility of the underlying stock, the expected life of the options, the risk-free rate during the option life, and expected dividends during the option life.

So what's the fuss? As the CFO of Coca-Cola stated, "There is no doubt that stock options are compensation. If they weren't, none of us would want them." It is puzzling why some companies continued to fight implementation of the expensing rule. Indeed, the market's general positive reaction to the expensing of stock options provides a good case study supporting the value that investors place on transparent accounting and earnings.

Sources: David Stires, "A Little Honesty Goes a Long Way," *Fortune* (September 2, 2002), p. 186; and Troy Wolverton, "Foes of Expensing Welcome FASB Delay," *TheStreet.com* (October 15, 2004).

Recognition—Stock Compensation

Stock-option plans involve two main accounting issues:

1. How to determine compensation expense.
2. Over what periods to allocate compensation expense.

Determining Expense

Under the fair value method, companies compute total compensation expense based on the fair value of the options expected to vest on the date they grant the options to the employee(s) (i.e., the **grant date**).[8] Public companies estimate fair value by using an option-pricing model, with some adjustments for the unique factors of employee stock options. No adjustments occur after the grant date in response to subsequent changes in the stock price—either up or down.

Allocating Compensation Expense

In general, a company recognizes compensation expense in the periods in which its employees perform the service—the **service period**. Unless otherwise specified, the service period is the vesting period—the time between the grant date and the vesting date. Thus, the company determines total compensation cost at the grant date and allocates it to the periods benefited by its employees' services.

Stock Compensation Example

An example will help show the accounting for a stock-option plan. Assume that on November 1, 2019, the stockholders of Chen Company approve a plan that grants the company's five executives options to purchase 2,000 shares each of the company's $1 par value common stock. The company grants the options on January 1, 2020. The executives may exercise the options at any time within the next 10 years. The option price per share is $60, and the market price of the stock at the date of grant is $70 per share.

Under the fair value method, the company computes total compensation expense by applying an acceptable fair value option-pricing model (such as the Black-Scholes option-pricing model). To keep this illustration simple, we assume that the fair value option-pricing model determines Chen's total compensation expense to be $220,000.

Basic Entries Under the fair value method, a company recognizes the value of the options as an expense in the periods in which the employee performs services. In the case of Chen Company, assume that the expected period of benefit is two years, starting with the grant date. Chen would record the transactions related to this option contract as shown in **Illustration 16.5**.

[8] "To vest" means "to earn the rights to." An employee's award becomes vested at the date that the employee's right to receive or retain shares of stock or cash under the award is no longer contingent on remaining in the service of the employer.

ILLUSTRATION 16.5
Option Contract Entries

At date of grant (January 1, 2020)		
No entry.		
To record compensation expense for 2020 (December 31, 2020)		
Compensation Expense	110,000	
Paid-in Capital—Stock Options ($220,000 ÷ 2)		110,000
To record compensation expense for 2021 (December 31, 2021)		
Compensation Expense	110,000	
Paid-in Capital—Stock Options		110,000

As indicated, Chen allocates compensation expense evenly over the two-year service period.

Exercise If Chen's executives exercise 2,000 of the 10,000 options (20 percent of the options) on June 1, 2023 (three years and five months after date of grant), the company records the following journal entry.

June 1, 2023		
Cash (2,000 × $60)	120,000	
Paid-in Capital—Stock Options (.20 × $220,000)	44,000	
Common Stock (2,000 × $1.00)		2,000
Paid-in Capital in Excess of Par—Common Stock		162,000

Expiration If Chen's executives fail to exercise the remaining stock options before their expiration date, the company transfers the balance in the Paid-in Capital—Stock Options account to a more properly titled paid-in capital account, such as Paid-in Capital—Expired Stock Options. Chen records this transaction at the date of expiration as follows.

January 1, 2030 (expiration date)		
Paid-in Capital—Stock Options	176,000	
Paid-in Capital—Expired Stock Options (.80 × $220,000)		176,000

Adjustment An unexercised stock option does not nullify the need to record the costs of services received from executives and attributable to the stock option plan. Under GAAP, a company therefore does not adjust compensation expense upon expiration of the options.

However, if an employee forfeits a stock option because **the employee fails to satisfy a service requirement** (e.g., leaves employment), the company should adjust the estimate of compensation expense recorded in the current period (as a change in estimate). A company records this change in estimate by debiting Paid-in Capital—Stock Options and crediting Compensation Expense for the amount of cumulative compensation expense recorded to date (thus decreasing compensation expense in the period of forfeiture).

Restricted Stock

As indicated earlier, many companies also use restricted stock (in some cases, replacing options altogether) to compensate employees. **Restricted-stock plans** transfer shares of stock to employees, subject to an agreement that the shares cannot be sold, transferred, or pledged until vesting occurs. Similar to stock options, these shares are subject to forfeiture if the conditions for vesting are not met.[9]

Major advantages of restricted-stock plans are:

1. ***Restricted stock never becomes completely worthless.*** In contrast, if the stock price does not exceed the exercise price for a stock option, the options are worthless. The restricted stock, however, still has value.

[9]Most companies base vesting on future service for a period of generally three to five years. Vesting may also be conditioned on some performance target such as revenue, net income, cash flows, or some combination of these three factors. The employee also collects dividends on the restricted stock, and these dividends generally must be repaid if forfeiture occurs.

2. ***Restricted stock generally results in less dilution to existing stockholders.*** Restricted-stock awards are usually one-half to one-third the size of stock options. For example, if a company issues stock options on 1,000 shares, an equivalent restricted-stock offering might be 333 to 500 shares. The reason for the difference is that at the end of the vesting period, the restricted stock will have value, whereas the stock options may not. As a result, fewer shares are involved in restricted-stock plans, and therefore less dilution results if the stock price rises.
3. ***Restricted stock better aligns the employee incentives with the companies' incentives.*** The holder of restricted stock is essentially a stockholder and should be more interested in the long-term objectives of the company. In contrast, the recipients of stock options often have a short-run focus which leads to taking risks to hype the stock price for short-term gain to the detriment of the long-term.[10]

The accounting for restricted stock follows the same general principles as accounting for stock options at the date of grant. That is, the company determines the fair value of the restricted stock at the date of grant (usually the fair value of a share of stock) and then expenses that amount over the service period. Subsequent changes in the fair value of the stock are ignored for purposes of computing compensation expense.

Restricted Stock Example

Assume that on January 1, 2020, Ogden Company issues 1,000 shares of restricted stock to its CEO, Christie DeGeorge. Ogden's stock has a fair value of $20 per share on January 1, 2020. Additional information is as follows.

1. The service period related to the restricted stock is five years.
2. Vesting occurs if DeGeorge stays with the company for a five-year period.
3. The par value of the stock is $1 per share.

Ogden makes the following entry on the grant date (January 1, 2020).

Unearned Compensation	20,000	
Common Stock (1,000 × $1)		1,000
Paid-in Capital in Excess of Par—Common Stock (1,000 × $19)		19,000

The credits to Common Stock and Paid-in Capital in Excess of Par—Common Stock indicate that Ogden has issued shares of stock. The debit to Unearned Compensation (often referred to as Deferred Compensation Expense) identifies the total compensation expense the company will recognize over the five-year period. **Unearned Compensation represents the cost of services yet to be performed, which is not an asset.** Consequently, the company reports Unearned Compensation in stockholders' equity in the balance sheet, as a contra equity account (similar to the reporting of treasury stock at cost).

At December 31, 2020, Ogden records compensation expense of $4,000 (1,000 shares × $20 × .20) as follows.

Compensation Expense	4,000	
Unearned Compensation		4,000

Ogden records compensation expense of $4,000 for each of the next four years (2021, 2022, 2023, and 2024).

What happens if DeGeorge leaves the company before the five years has elapsed? In this situation, DeGeorge forfeits her rights to the stock, and Ogden reverses the compensation expense already recorded.

[10]One important rationale for moving away from options to restricted stock is summarized by Bill Gates of **Microsoft**: "When you win [with options], you win the lottery. And when you don't win, you still want it. I can imagine an employee going home at night and considering two wildly different possibilities with his compensation program. Either he can buy six summer homes or no summer homes. Either he can send his kids to college 50 times, or no times. The variation is huge; much greater than most employees have an appetite for. And so as soon as they saw that options could go both ways, we proposed an economic equivalent. So what we do now is give shares, not options." See *http://www.mystockoptions.com/pdfs/Restricted%20Stock.pdf.*

For example, assume that DeGeorge leaves on February 3, 2022 (before any expense has been recorded during 2022). The entry to record this forfeiture is as follows.

Common Stock (1,000 × $1)	1,000	
Paid-in Capital in Excess of Par—Common Stock	19,000	
Compensation Expense ($4,000 × 2)		8,000
Unearned Compensation		12,000

In this situation, Ogden reverses the compensation expense of $8,000 recorded through 2021. In addition, the company debits Common Stock and Paid-in Capital in Excess of Par—Common Stock, reflecting DeGeorge's forfeiture. It credits the balance of Unearned Compensation since none remains when DeGeorge leaves Ogden.

This accounting is similar to accounting for stock options when employees do not fulfill vesting requirements. Recall that once compensation expense is recorded for stock options, it is not reversed. The only exception is if the employee does not fulfill the vesting requirement, by leaving the company before vesting occurs.

In Ogden's restricted-stock plan, vesting never occurred because DeGeorge left the company before she met the service requirement. Because DeGeorge was never vested, she had to forfeit her shares. Therefore, the company must reverse compensation expense recorded to date.[11]

Employee Stock-Purchase Plans

Employee stock-purchase plans (ESPPs) generally permit all employees to purchase stock at a discounted price for a short period of time. The company often uses such plans to secure equity capital or to induce widespread ownership of its common stock among employees. These plans are considered compensatory unless they satisfy **all three** conditions presented below.

1. Substantially all full-time employees may participate on an equitable basis.
2. The discount from market is small. That is, the discount does not exceed the per share amount of costs avoided by not having to raise cash in a public offering. If the amount of the discount is 5 percent or less, no compensation needs to be recorded.
3. The plan offers no substantive option feature.

For example, Masthead Company's stock-purchase plan allowed employees who met minimal employment qualifications to purchase its stock at a 5 percent reduction from market price for a short period of time. The reduction from market price is not considered compensatory. Why? Because the per share amount of the costs avoided by not having to raise the cash in a public offering equals 5 percent.

Companies that offer their employees a compensatory ESPP should record the compensation expense over the service life of the employees (see Global View). It will be difficult for some companies to claim that their ESPPs are non-compensatory (and therefore not record compensation expense) unless they change their discount policy which in the past often was 15 percent. If they change their discount policy to 5 percent, participation in these plans will undoubtedly be lower. As a result, it is likely that some companies will not offer these plans.

Global View

IFRS requires that any discount from the market price in employee stock-purchase plans be recorded as compensation expense.

Disclosure of Compensation Plans

Companies must fully disclose the status of their compensation plans at the end of the periods presented. To meet these objectives, companies must make extensive disclosures. Specifically, a company with one or more share-based payment arrangements must disclose information that enables users of the financial statements to understand:

1. The nature and terms of such arrangements that existed during the period and the potential effects of those arrangements on shareholders.

[11]There are numerous variations on restricted-stock plans, including restricted-stock units (for which the shares are issued at the end of the vesting period) and restricted-stock plans with performance targets, such as EPS or stock price growth.

2. The effect on the income statement of compensation cost arising from share-based payment arrangements.
3. The method of estimating the fair value of the goods or services received, or the fair value of the equity instruments granted (or offered to grant), during the period.
4. The cash flow effects resulting from share-based payment arrangements.

Illustration 16.6 presents the type of information disclosed for compensation plans.

ILLUSTRATION 16.6

Stock-Option Plan Disclosure

Stock-Option Plan

The Company has a share-based compensation plan. The compensation cost that has been charged against income for the plan was $29.4 million, and $28.7 million for 2020 and 2019, respectively.

The Company's 2020 Employee Share-Option Plan (the Plan), which is shareholder-approved, permits the grant of share options and shares to its employees for up to 8 million shares of common stock. The Company believes that such awards better align the interests of its employees with those of its shareholders. Option awards are generally granted with an exercise price equal to the market price of the Company's stock at the date of grant; those option awards generally vest based on 5 years of continuous service and have 10-year contractual terms. Share awards generally vest over five years. Certain option and share awards provide for accelerated vesting if there is a change in control (as defined by the Plan).

— Description of plan

The fair value of each option award is estimated on the date of grant using an option valuation model based on the assumptions noted in the following table.

	2020	2019
Expected volatility	25%–40%	24%–38%
Weighted-average volatility	33%	30%
Expected dividends	1.5%	1.5%
Expected term (in years)	5.3–7.8	5.5–8.0
Risk-free rate	6.3%–11.2%	6.0%–10.0%

— Valuation model assumptions

A summary of option activity under the Plan as of December 31, 2020, and changes during the year then ended are presented below.

Options	Shares (000)	Weighted-Average Exercise Price	Weighted-Average Remaining Contractual Term	Aggregate Intrinsic Value ($000)
Outstanding at January 1, 2020	4,660	42		
Granted	950	60		
Exercised	(800)	36		
Forfeited or expired	(80)	59		
Outstanding at December 31, 2020	4,730	47	6.5	85,140
Exercisable at December 31, 2020	3,159	41	4.0	75,816

The weighted-average grant-date fair value of options granted during the years 2020 and 2019 was $19.57 and $17.46, respectively. The total intrinsic value of options exercised during the years ended December 31, 2020 and 2019, was $25.2 million, and $20.9 million, respectively.

— Option plan activity and balances

As of December 31, 2020, there was $25.9 million of total unrecognized compensation cost related to nonvested share-based compensation arrangements granted under the Plan. That cost is expected to be recognized over a weighted-average period of 4.9 years. The total fair value of shares vested during the years ended December 31, 2020 and 2019, was $22.8 million and $21 million, respectively.

— Option expense

Restricted-Stock Awards

The Company also has a restricted-stock plan. The Plan is intended to retain and motivate the Company's Chief Executive Officer over the term of the award and to bring his total compensation package closer to median levels for Chief Executive Officers of comparable companies. The fair value of grants during the year was $1,889,000, or $35.68 per share, equivalent to 92% of the market price of a share of the Company's Common Stock on the date the award was granted.

Restricted-stock activity for the year ended 2020 is as follows.

	Shares	Price
Outstanding at December 31, 2019	57,990	—
Granted	149,000	$12.68
Vested	(19,330)	—
Forfeited	—	—
Outstanding at December 31, 2020	187,660	

— Restricted-stock plan details

Required expense recognition of compensation related to stock options and restricted stock represents a significant improvement in financial reporting. By leaving stock-based compensation expense out of income, reported income is biased. Biased reporting not only raises concerns about the credibility of companies' reports, but also of financial reporting in general. Even good companies get tainted by the biased reporting of a few "bad apples." If we write standards to achieve some social, economic, or public policy goal, financial reporting loses its credibility.

Basic Earnings per Share

LEARNING OBJECTIVE 4

Compute basic earnings per share.

As indicated earlier, stockholders and potential investors widely use earnings per share in evaluating the profitability of a company. As a result, much attention is given to earnings per share by the financial press. **Earnings per share** indicates the income earned by each share of common stock. Thus, **companies report earnings per share only for common stock.** For example, if Oscar Co. has net income of $300,000 and a weighted average of 100,000 shares of common stock outstanding for the year, earnings per share is $3 ($300,000 ÷ 100,000). Because of the importance of earnings per share information, most companies must report this information on the face of the income statement.[12] [5] The exception, due to cost-benefit considerations, is nonpublic companies.[13] Generally, companies report earnings per share information below net income in the income statement. **Illustration 16.7** shows Oscar Co.'s income statement presentation of earnings per share.

ILLUSTRATION 16.7

Income Statement Presentation of EPS

Net income	$300,000
Earnings per share	$3.00

When the income statement contains intermediate components of income (such as discontinued operations), companies should disclose earnings per share for each component. The presentation in **Illustration 16.8** is representative.

ILLUSTRATION 16.8

Income Statement Presentation of EPS Components

Earnings per share:	
Income from continuing operations	$4.00
Loss from discontinued operations, net of tax	0.60
Net income	$3.40

These disclosures enable the user of the financial statements to recognize the effects on EPS of income from continuing operations, as distinguished from income or loss from discontinued operations.[14]

[12]For articles on the usefulness of reported EPS data and the application of the qualitative characteristics of accounting information to EPS data, see Lola W. Dudley, "A Critical Look at EPS," *Journal of Accountancy* (August 1985), pp. 102–111; and R. Jennings, M.J. LeClere, and R.B. Thompson, "Evidence on the Usefulness of Alternative Earnings per Share Measures," *Financial Analysts Journal*, Vol. 53, No. 6 (1997), pp. 24–33.

[13]A nonpublic enterprise is an enterprise (1) whose debt or equity securities are not traded in a public market on a foreign or domestic stock exchange or in the over-the-counter market (including securities quoted locally or regionally), or (2) that is not required to file financial statements with the SEC. An enterprise is not considered a nonpublic enterprise when its financial statements are issued in preparation for the sale of any class of securities in a public market.

[14]Companies should present, either on the face of the income statement or in the notes to the financial statements, per share amounts for discontinued operations.

Earnings per Share—Simple Capital Structure

A corporation's capital structure is simple if it consists only of common stock or includes no **potential common stock** that upon conversion or exercise could dilute earnings per common share. A capital structure is complex if it includes securities that could have a dilutive effect on earnings per common share.

The computation of earnings per share for a simple capital structure involves two items (other than net income)—(1) preferred stock dividends and (2) weighted-average number of shares outstanding.

Preferred Stock Dividends

As we indicated earlier, earnings per share relates to earnings per *common share*. When a company has both common and preferred stock outstanding, **it subtracts the current-year preferred stock dividend from net income to arrive at** income available to common stockholders. Illustration 16.9 shows the formula for computing earnings per share.

$$\text{Earnings per Share} = \frac{\text{Net Income} - \text{Preferred Dividends}}{\text{Weighted-Average Common Shares Outstanding}}$$

ILLUSTRATION 16.9
Formula for Computing Earnings per Share

In reporting earnings per share information, a company must calculate income available to common stockholders. To do so, the company subtracts dividends on preferred stock from each of the intermediate components of income (income from continuing operations) and finally from net income. If a company declares dividends on preferred stock and a net loss occurs, **the company adds the preferred dividend to the loss** (thus increasing the amount of the loss) for purposes of computing the loss per share.

If the preferred stock is cumulative and the company has net income but declares no dividend in the current year, it subtracts **an amount equal to the dividend that it should have declared for the current year only**. If the stock is cumulative and the company reports a net loss, but declares no dividend in the current year, it **adds** an amount equal to the dividend to the net loss. The company should have included dividends in arrears for previous years in the previous years' computations (see Global View).

Global View

The FASB and the IASB have worked on a project to improve EPS accounting by simplifying the computational guidance and thereby increasing the comparability of EPS data on an international basis.

Weighted-Average Number of Shares Outstanding

In all computations of earnings per share, the weighted-average number of shares outstanding during the period constitutes the basis for the per share amounts reported. Shares issued or purchased during the period affect the amount outstanding. Companies must **weight the shares by the fraction of the period they are outstanding**. The rationale for this approach is to find the equivalent number of whole shares outstanding for the year.

To illustrate, assume that Franks Inc. has changes in its common stock shares outstanding for the period as shown in Illustration 16.10.

Date	Share Changes	Shares Outstanding
January 1	Beginning balance	90,000
April 1	Issued 30,000 shares for cash	30,000
		120,000
July 1	Purchased 39,000 shares	(39,000)
		81,000
November 1	Issued 60,000 shares for cash	60,000
December 31	Ending balance	141,000

ILLUSTRATION 16.10
Shares Outstanding, Ending Balance—Franks Inc.

Franks computes the weighted-average number of shares outstanding as shown in Illustration 16.11.

ILLUSTRATION 16.11

Weighted-Average Number of Shares Outstanding

Dates Outstanding	(A) Shares Outstanding	(B) Fraction of Year	(C) Weighted Shares (A × B)
Jan. 1–Apr. 1	90,000	3/12	22,500
Apr. 1–July 1	120,000	3/12	30,000
July 1–Nov. 1	81,000	4/12	27,000
Nov. 1–Dec. 31	141,000	2/12	23,500
Weighted-average number of shares outstanding			103,000

As Illustration 16.11 shows, 90,000 shares were outstanding for three months, which is equivalent to 22,500 whole shares for the entire year. Because Franks issued additional shares on April 1, it must weight these shares for the time outstanding. When the company purchased 39,000 shares on July 1, it reduced the shares outstanding. Therefore, from July 1 to November 1, only 81,000 shares were outstanding, which is equivalent to 27,000 shares. The issuance of 60,000 shares increases shares outstanding for the last two months of the year. Franks then makes a new computation to determine the proper weighted shares outstanding.

Stock Dividends and Stock Splits When **stock dividends** or **stock splits** occur, companies need to restate the shares outstanding before the stock dividend or split, in order to compute the weighted-average number of shares. For example, assume that Vijay Corporation had 100,000 shares outstanding on January 1 and issued a 25 percent stock dividend on June 30. For purposes of computing a weighted-average for the current year, it assumes the additional 25,000 shares outstanding as a result of the stock dividend to be **outstanding since the beginning of the year**. Thus, the weighted-average for the year for Vijay is 125,000 shares.

Companies restate the issuance of a stock dividend or stock split, but not the issuance or repurchase of stock for cash. Why? Because stock splits and stock dividends do not increase or decrease the net assets of the company. The company merely issues additional shares of stock. Because of the added shares, it must restate the weighted-average shares. Restating allows valid comparisons of earnings per share between periods before and after the stock split or stock dividend. Conversely, the issuance or purchase of stock for cash **changes the amount of net assets**. As a result, the company either earns more or less in the future as a result of this change in net assets. Stated another way, **a stock dividend or split does not change the shareholders' total investment**—it only increases (unless it is a reverse stock split) the number of common shares representing this investment.

To illustrate how a stock dividend affects the computation of the weighted-average number of shares outstanding, assume that Sabrina Company has the changes in its common stock shares during the year as shown in **Illustration 16.12**.

ILLUSTRATION 16.12

Shares Outstanding, Ending Balance—Sabrina Company

Date	Share Changes	Shares Outstanding
January 1	Beginning balance	100,000
March 1	Issued 20,000 shares for cash	20,000
		120,000
June 1	60,000 additional shares (50% stock dividend)	60,000
		180,000
November 1	Issued 30,000 shares for cash	30,000
December 31	Ending balance	210,000

Sabrina computes the weighted-average number of shares outstanding as shown in **Illustration 16.13**.

Dates Outstanding	(A) Shares Outstanding	(B) Restatement	(C) Fraction of Year	(D) Weighted Shares (A × B × C)
Jan. 1–Mar. 1	100,000	1.50	2/12	25,000
Mar. 1–June 1	120,000	1.50	3/12	45,000
June 1–Nov. 1	180,000		5/12	75,000
Nov. 1–Dec. 31	210,000		2/12	35,000
Weighted-average number of shares outstanding				180,000

ILLUSTRATION 16.13

Weighted-Average Number of Shares Outstanding—Stock Issue and Stock Dividend

Sabrina must restate the shares outstanding prior to the stock dividend. The company adjusts the shares outstanding from January 1 to June 1 for the stock dividend, so that it now states these shares on the same basis as shares issued subsequent to the stock dividend. Sabrina does not restate shares issued after the stock dividend because they are on the new basis. The stock dividend simply restates existing shares. **The same type of treatment applies to a stock split.**

If a stock dividend or stock split occurs after the end of the year but before issuing the financial statements, a company must restate the weighted-average number of shares outstanding for the year (and any other years presented in comparative form). For example, assume that Hendricks Company computes its weighted-average number of shares as 100,000 for the year ended December 31, 2020. On January 15, 2021, before issuing the financial statements, the company splits its stock 3 for 1. In this case, the weighted-average number of shares used in computing earnings per share for 2020 is now 300,000 shares. If providing earnings per share information for 2019 as comparative information, Hendricks must also adjust it for the stock split.

Comprehensive Example

Let's study a comprehensive illustration for a simple capital structure. Darin Corporation has income from continuing items of $580,000 and a gain on discontinued operations, net of tax, of $240,000. In addition, it has declared preferred dividends of $1 per share on 100,000 shares of preferred stock outstanding. Illustration 16.14 shows the changes in Darin's common stock shares outstanding during 2020.

Date	Share Changes	Shares Outstanding
January 1	Beginning balance	180,000
May 1	Purchased 30,000 treasury shares	(30,000)
		150,000
July 1	300,000 additional shares (3-for-1 stock split)	300,000
		450,000
December 31	Issued 50,000 shares for cash	50,000
December 31	Ending balance	500,000

ILLUSTRATION 16.14

Shares Outstanding, Ending Balance—Darin Corp.

To compute the earnings per share information, Darin determines the weighted-average number of shares outstanding as shown in Illustration 16.15.

Dates Outstanding	(A) Shares Outstanding	(B) Restatement	(C) Fraction of Year	(D) Weighted Shares (A × B × C)
Jan. 1–May 1	180,000	3	4/12	180,000
May 1–July 1	150,000	3	2/12	75,000
July 1–Dec. 31	450,000		6/12	225,000
Weighted-average number of shares outstanding				480,000

ILLUSTRATION 16.15

Weighted-Average Number of Shares Outstanding

In computing the weighted-average number of shares, the company ignores the shares sold on December 31, 2020, because they have not been outstanding during the year. Darin then divides the weighted-average number of shares into income from continuing operations and net income to determine earnings per share. It subtracts its preferred dividends of $100,000 from income from continuing operations ($580,000) to arrive at income from continuing operations available to common stockholders of $480,000 ($580,000 – $100,000).

Deducting the preferred dividends from the income from continuing operations also reduces net income without affecting the gain on discontinued operations. The final amount is referred to as **income available to common stockholders**, as shown in Illustration 16.16.

ILLUSTRATION 16.16

Computation of Income Available to Common Stockholders

	(A) Income Information	(B) Weighted Shares	(C) Earnings per Share (A ÷ B)
Income from continuing operations available to common stockholders	$480,000*	480,000	$1.00
Gain on discontinued operations, net of tax	240,000	480,000	0.50
Income available to common stockholders	$720,000	480,000	$1.50

*$580,000 – $100,000

Darin must disclose the per share amount for the discontinued operations (net of tax) either on the face of the income statement or in the notes to the financial statements. Illustration 16.17 shows the income and per share information reported on the face of Darin's income statement.

ILLUSTRATION 16.17

Earnings per Share, with Discontinued Operations

Income from continuing operations	$580,000
Gain on discontinued operations, net of tax	240,000
Net income	$820,000
Earnings per share:	
Income from continuing operations	$1.00
Discontinued operations, net of tax	0.50
Net income	$1.50

Diluted Earnings per Share

LEARNING OBJECTIVE 5

Compute diluted earnings per share.

The EPS discussion to this point applies to basic EPS for a simple capital structure. One problem with a **basic EPS** computation is that it fails to recognize the potential impact of a corporation's dilutive securities. As discussed at the beginning of the chapter, dilutive securities are securities that can be converted to common stock.[15] Upon conversion or exercise by the holder, the dilutive securities reduce (dilute) earnings per share. This adverse effect on EPS can be significant and, more importantly, *unexpected* unless financial statements call attention to their potential dilutive effect.

As indicated earlier, a complex capital structure exists when a corporation has convertible securities, options, warrants, or other rights that upon conversion or exercise could dilute earnings per share. When a company has a complex capital structure, **it generally reports both basic and diluted earnings per share**.

[15]Issuance of these types of securities is typical in mergers and compensation plans.

Computing **diluted EPS** is similar to computing basic EPS. The difference is that diluted EPS includes the effect of all potentially dilutive common shares that were outstanding during the period. The formula in **Illustration 16.18** shows the relationship between basic EPS and diluted EPS.

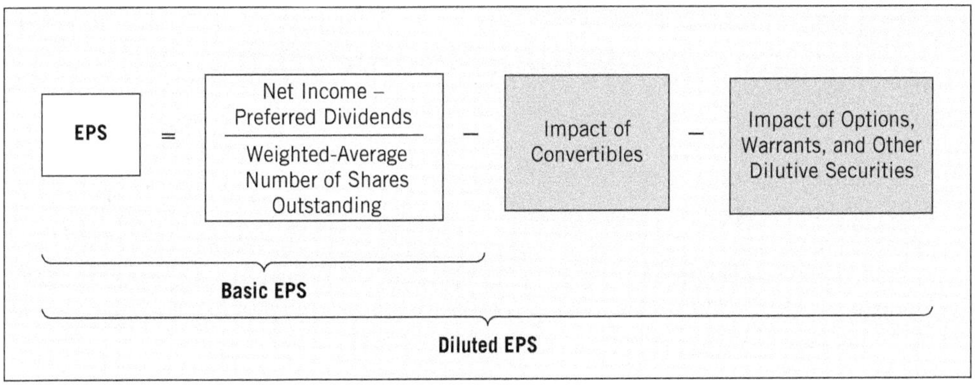

ILLUSTRATION 16.18
Relationship Between Basic and Diluted EPS

Some securities are antidilutive. **Antidilutive securities** are securities that upon conversion or exercise **increase** earnings per share (or reduce the loss per share). Companies with complex capital structures will not report diluted EPS if the securities in their capital structure are antidilutive. The purpose of presenting both basic and diluted EPS is to inform financial statement users of situations that will likely occur (basic EPS) and also to provide "worst case" dilutive situations (dilutive EPS). If the securities are antidilutive, the likelihood of conversion or exercise is considered remote. Thus, companies that have only antidilutive securities must report only the basic EPS number (see **Global View**). We illustrated the computation of basic EPS in the prior section. In the following sections, we address the effects of convertible and other dilutive securities on EPS calculations.

Global View

The provisions in GAAP are substantially the same as those in *International Accounting Standard No. 33*, "Earnings per Share," issued by the IASB.

Diluted EPS—Convertible Securities

At conversion, companies exchange convertible securities for common stock. Companies measure the dilutive effects of potential conversion on EPS using the **if-converted method**. This method for a convertible bond assumes (1) the conversion of the convertible securities at the beginning of the period (or at the time of issuance of the security, if issued during the period), and (2) the elimination of related interest, net of tax. Thus, the additional shares assumed issued increase the **denominator**—the weighted-average number of shares outstanding. The amount of interest expense, net of tax associated with those potential common shares, increases the **numerator**—net income.

Comprehensive Example—If-Converted Method

As an example, Mayfield Corporation has net income of $210,000 for the year and a weighted-average number of common shares outstanding during the period of 100,000 shares. The basic earnings per share is therefore $2.10 ($210,000 ÷ 100,000). The company has two convertible debenture bond issues outstanding. One is a 6 percent issue sold at 100 (total $1,000,000) in a prior year and convertible into 30,000 common shares. The other is a 10 percent issue sold at 100 (total $1,000,000) on April 1 of the current year and convertible into 36,000 common shares. The tax rate is 20 percent.

As **Illustration 16.19** shows, to determine the numerator for diluted earnings per share, Mayfield adds back the interest on the if-converted securities, less the related tax effect.

Net income for the year	$210,000
Add: Adjustment for interest (net of tax)	
6% debentures ($60,000 × [1 – 0.20])	48,000
10% debentures ($100,000 × 9/12 × [1 – 0.20])	60,000
Adjusted net income	$318,000

ILLUSTRATION 16.19
Computation of Adjusted Net Income

Because the if-converted method assumes conversion as of the beginning of the year, Mayfield assumes that it pays no interest on the convertible bonds during the year. The interest on the 6 percent convertibles is $60,000 for the year ($1,000,000 × .06). The increased tax expense is $12,000 ($60,000 × 0.20). The interest added back net of taxes is $48,000 [$60,000 – $12,000, or simply $60,000 × (1 – 0.20)].

Continuing with the information in Illustration 16.19, because Mayfield issues 10 percent convertibles subsequent to the beginning of the year, it weights the shares. In other words, it considers these shares to have been outstanding from April 1 to the end of the year. As a result, the interest adjustment to the numerator for these bonds reflects the interest for only nine months. Thus, the interest added back on the 10 percent convertible is $60,000 [$1,000,000 × .10 × 9/12 year × (1 – 0.20)]. The final item in Illustration 16.19 shows the adjusted net income. This amount becomes the numerator for Mayfield's computation of diluted earnings per share.

Mayfield then calculates the weighted-average number of shares outstanding, as shown in Illustration 16.20. This number of shares becomes the denominator for Mayfield's computation of diluted earnings per share.

ILLUSTRATION 16.20

Computation of Weighted-Average Number of Shares

Weighted-average number of shares outstanding	100,000
Add: Shares assumed to be issued:	
6% debentures (as of beginning of year)	30,000
10% debentures (as of date of issue, April 1; 9/12 × 36,000)	27,000
Weighted-average number of shares adjusted for dilutive securities	157,000

In its income statement, Mayfield reports basic and diluted earnings per share.[16] Illustration 16.21 shows this dual presentation.

ILLUSTRATION 16.20

Earnings per Share Disclosure

Net income for the year	$210,000
Earnings per Share (Note X)	
Basic earnings per share ($210,000 ÷ 100,000)	$2.10
Diluted earnings per share ($318,000 ÷ 157,000)	$2.03

Other Factors

The example above assumed that Mayfield sold its bonds at the face amount. If it instead sold the bonds at a premium or discount, the company must adjust the interest expense each period to account for this occurrence. Therefore, the interest expense reported on the income statement is the amount of interest expense, net of tax, added back to net income. (It is not the interest paid in cash during the period.)

In addition, the conversion rate on a dilutive security may change during the period in which the security is outstanding. For the diluted EPS computation in such a situation, the **company uses the most dilutive conversion rate available**. For example, assume that a company issued a convertible bond on January 1, 2019, with a conversion rate of 10 common shares for each bond starting January 1, 2021. Beginning January 1, 2024, the conversion rate is 12 common shares for each bond, and beginning January 1, 2028, it is 15 common shares for each bond. In computing diluted EPS in 2019, the company uses the conversion rate of 15 shares to one bond.

[16]Conversion of bonds is dilutive because EPS with conversion ($2.03) is less than basic EPS ($2.10). See Appendix 16B for a comprehensive evaluation of antidilution with multiple securities.

A final issue relates to preferred stock. For example, assume that Mayfield's 6 percent convertible debentures were instead 6 percent convertible *preferred stock*. In that case, Mayfield considers the convertible preferred as potential common shares. Thus, it includes them in its diluted EPS calculations as shares outstanding. The company does not subtract preferred dividends from net income in computing the numerator. Why not? Because for purposes of computing EPS, it assumes conversion of the convertible preferreds to outstanding common stock. The company uses net income as the numerator—it computes **no tax effect** because preferred dividends generally are not tax-deductible.

Diluted EPS—Options and Warrants

A company includes in diluted earnings per share stock options and warrants outstanding (whether or not presently exercisable), unless they are antidilutive. Companies use the **treasury-stock method** to include options and warrants and their equivalents in EPS computations.

The treasury-stock method assumes that the options or warrants are exercised at the beginning of the year (or date of issue if later), and that the company uses those proceeds to purchase common stock for the treasury. If the exercise price is lower than the market price of the stock, then the proceeds from exercise are insufficient to buy back all the shares. The company then adds the incremental shares remaining to the weighted-average number of shares outstanding for purposes of computing diluted earnings per share.

For example, if the exercise price of a warrant is $5 and the market price of the stock is $15, the treasury-stock method increases the shares outstanding. Exercise of the warrant results in one additional share outstanding, but the $5 received for the one share issued is insufficient to purchase one share in the market at $15. The company needs to exercise three warrants (and issue three additional shares) to produce enough money ($15) to acquire one share in the market. Thus, a net increase of two shares outstanding results.

To see this computation using larger numbers, assume 1,500 options outstanding at an exercise price of $30 for a common share and a common stock market price per share of $50. Through application of the treasury-stock method, the company would have 600 incremental shares outstanding, computed as shown in **Illustration 16.22**.[17]

ILLUSTRATION 16.22
Computation of Incremental Shares

Proceeds from exercise of 1,500 options (1,500 × $30)	$45,000
Shares issued upon exercise of options	1,500
Treasury shares purchasable with proceeds ($45,000 ÷ $50)	(900)
Incremental shares outstanding (potential common shares)	600

Thus, if the exercise price of the option or warrant is **lower** than the market price of the stock, dilution occurs. An exercise price of the option or warrant **higher** than the market price of the stock reduces common shares. In this case, the options or warrants are **antidilutive** because their assumed exercise leads to an increase in earnings per share.

For both options and warrants, exercise is assumed only if the average market price of the stock exceeds the exercise price during the reported period.[18] As a practical matter, a simple average of the weekly or monthly prices is adequate, so long as the prices do not fluctuate significantly.

[17]The incremental number of shares may be more simply computed:

$$\frac{\text{Market price} - \text{Option price}}{\text{Market price}} \times \text{Number of options} = \text{Number of shares}$$

$$\frac{\$50 - \$30}{\$50} \times 1{,}500 \text{ option} = 600 \text{ shares}$$

[18]Options and warrants have essentially the same assumptions and computational problems, although the warrants may allow or require the tendering of some other security, such as debt, in lieu of cash upon exercise. In such situations, the accounting becomes quite complex and is beyond the scope of this text.

Comprehensive Example—Treasury-Stock Method

To illustrate application of the treasury-stock method, assume that Kubitz Industries, Inc. has net income for the period of $220,000. The average number of shares outstanding for the period was 100,000 shares. Hence, basic EPS—ignoring all dilutive securities—is $2.20. The average number of shares related to options outstanding (although not exercisable at this time), at an option price of $20 per share, is 5,000 shares. The average market price of the common stock during the year was $28. **Illustration 16.23** shows the computation of EPS using the treasury-stock method.

ILLUSTRATION 16.23

Computation of Earnings per Share—Treasury-Stock Method

	Basic Earnings per Share	Diluted Earnings per Share
Average number of shares related to options outstanding Option price per share		5,000 × $20
Proceeds upon exercise of options		$100,000
Average market price of common stock		$28
Treasury shares that could be repurchased with proceeds ($100,000 ÷ $28)		3,571
Excess of shares under option over the treasury shares that could be repurchased (5,000 – 3,571)—potential common incremental shares		1,429
Average number of common shares outstanding	100,000	100,000
Total average number of common shares outstanding and potential common shares	100,000 (A)	101,429 (C)
Net income for the year	$220,000 (B)	$220,000 (D)
Earnings per share	$2.20 (B ÷ A)	$2.17 (D ÷ C)

Contingent Issue Agreement

In business combinations, the acquirer may promise to issue additional shares—referred to as **contingent shares**—under certain conditions. Sometimes the company issues these contingent shares as a result of a **passage-of-time condition** or upon the attainment of a **certain earnings or market price level**. If this passage-of-time condition occurs during the current year, or if the company meets the earnings or market price **by the end of the year**, the company considers the contingent shares as outstanding for the computation of diluted earnings per share.[19]

For example, assume that Watts Corporation purchased Cardoza Company and agreed to give Cardoza's stockholders 20,000 additional shares in 2023 if Cardoza's net income in 2022 is $90,000. In 2021, Cardoza's net income is $100,000. Because Cardoza has already attained the 2022 stipulated earnings of $90,000, in computing diluted earnings per share for 2021, Watts would include the 20,000 contingent shares in the shares-outstanding computation.

Antidilution Revisited

In computing diluted EPS, a company must consider the aggregate of all dilutive securities. But first it must determine which potentially dilutive securities are in fact individually dilutive and which are antidilutive. **A company should exclude any security that is antidilutive**, nor can the company use such a security to offset dilutive securities.

[19]In addition to contingent issuances of stock, other situations that might lead to dilution are the issuance of participating securities and two-class common shares. The reporting of these types of securities in EPS computations is beyond the scope of this text.

Recall that including antidilutive securities in earnings per share computations increases earnings per share (or reduces net loss per share). With options or warrants, whenever the exercise price exceeds the market price, the security is antidilutive. Convertible debt is antidilutive if the addition to income of the interest (net of tax) causes a greater percentage increase in income (numerator) than conversion of the bonds causes a percentage increase in common and potentially dilutive shares (denominator). In other words, convertible debt is antidilutive if conversion of the security causes common stock earnings to increase by a greater amount per additional common share than earnings per share was before the conversion.

To illustrate, assume that Martin Corporation has a 6 percent, $1,000,000 debt issue that is convertible into 10,000 common shares. Net income for the year is $210,000, the weighted-average number of common shares outstanding is 100,000 shares, and the tax rate is 20 percent. In this case, assumed conversion of the debt into common stock at the beginning of the year requires adjustments of net income and the weighted-average number of shares outstanding as shown in **Illustration 16.24**.

ILLUSTRATION 16.24
Test for Antidilution

Net income for the year	$210,000	Average number of shares outstanding	100,000
Add: Adjustment for interest (net of tax) on 6% debentures $60,000 × (1 − 0.20)	48,000	Add: Shares issued upon assumed conversion of debt	10,000
Adjusted net income	$258,000	Average number of common and potential common shares outstanding	110,000

Basic EPS = $210,000 ÷ 100,000 = $2.10
Diluted EPS = $258,000 ÷ 110,000 = $2.35 = **Antidilutive**

As a shortcut, Martin can also identify the convertible debt as antidilutive by comparing the EPS resulting from conversion, $4.80 ($48,000 additional earnings ÷ 10,000 additional shares), with EPS before inclusion of the convertible debt, $2.10.

Companies should ignore antidilutive securities in all calculations and in computing diluted earnings per share. This approach is reasonable. The profession's intent was to inform the investor of the possible dilution that might occur in reported earnings per share and not to be concerned with securities that, if converted or exercised, would result in an increase in earnings per share. Appendix 16B to this chapter provides an extended example of how companies consider antidilution in a complex situation with multiple securities.

EPS Presentation and Disclosure

Illustration 16.25 shows how a company with a complex capital structure would present its EPS information.

ILLUSTRATION 16.25
EPS Presentation—Complex Capital Structure

Earnings per common share	
Basic earnings per share	$3.30
Diluted earnings per share	$2.70

When the earnings of a period include discontinued operations, a company should show per share amounts (where applicable) for the following: income from continuing operations, discontinued operations, and net income. Companies that report a discontinued operation should present per share amounts **for this line item** either on the face of the income statement or in the notes to the financial statements. **Illustration 16.26** shows a presentation reporting discontinued operations.

ILLUSTRATION 16.26

EPS Presentation, with Discontinued Operations

Basic earnings per share	
Income from continuing operations	$3.80
Discontinued operations (loss)	(0.80)
Net income	$3.00
Diluted earnings per share	
Income from continuing operations	$3.35
Discontinued operations (loss)	(0.65)
Net income	$2.70

A company must show earnings per share amounts for all periods presented. Also, the company should restate all prior period earnings per share amounts presented for stock dividends and stock splits. If it reports diluted EPS data for at least one period, the company should report such data for all periods presented, even if it is the same as basic EPS. When a company restates results of operations of a prior period as a result of an error or a change in accounting principle, it should also restate the earnings per share data shown for the prior periods. Complex capital structures and dual presentation of earnings per share require the following additional disclosures in note form.

1. Description of pertinent rights and privileges of the various securities outstanding.
2. A reconciliation of the numerators and denominators of the basic and diluted per share computations, including individual income and share amount effects of all securities that affect EPS.
3. The effect given preferred dividends in determining income available to common stockholders in computing basic EPS.
4. Securities that could potentially dilute basic EPS in the future that were excluded in the computation because they would be antidilutive.
5. Effect of conversions subsequent to year-end, but before issuing statements.

Illustration 16.27 presents the reconciliation and the related disclosure to meet the requirements of this standard.[20] [6]

ILLUSTRATION 16.27

Reconciliation for Basic and Diluted EPS

	For the Year Ended 2020		
	Income (Numerator)	Shares (Denominator)	Per Share Amount
Income from continuing operations	$ 7,500,000		
Less: Preferred stock dividends	45,000		
Basic EPS	7,455,000	3,991,666	$1.87
Warrants		30,768	
Convertible preferred stock	45,000	308,333	
4% convertible bonds (net of tax)	60,000	50,000	
Diluted EPS	$7,560,000	4,380,767	$1.73

Stock options to purchase 1,000,000 shares of common stock at $85 per share were outstanding during the second half of 2020 but were not included in the computation of diluted EPS because the options' exercise price was greater than the average market price of the common shares. The options were still outstanding at the end of year 2020 and expire on June 30, 2030.

[20]Note that GAAP has specific disclosure requirements regarding stock-based compensation plans and earnings per share disclosures as well. The earnings per share effects of noncontrolling interest (discussed in Chapter 4) should also be presented, with the amounts of income from continuing operations and discontinued operations (if present), attributable to the controlling interest disclosed. However, only the net income attributable to the controlling interest should be used in computing earnings per share.

Summary of EPS Computation

As you can see, computation of earnings per share is a complex issue. It is a controversial area because many securities, although technically not common stock, have many of its basic characteristics. Indeed, some companies have issued these other securities rather than common stock in order to avoid an adverse dilutive effect on earnings per share. Illustrations 16.28 and 16.29 display the elementary points of calculating earnings per share in a simple capital structure and in a complex capital structure.

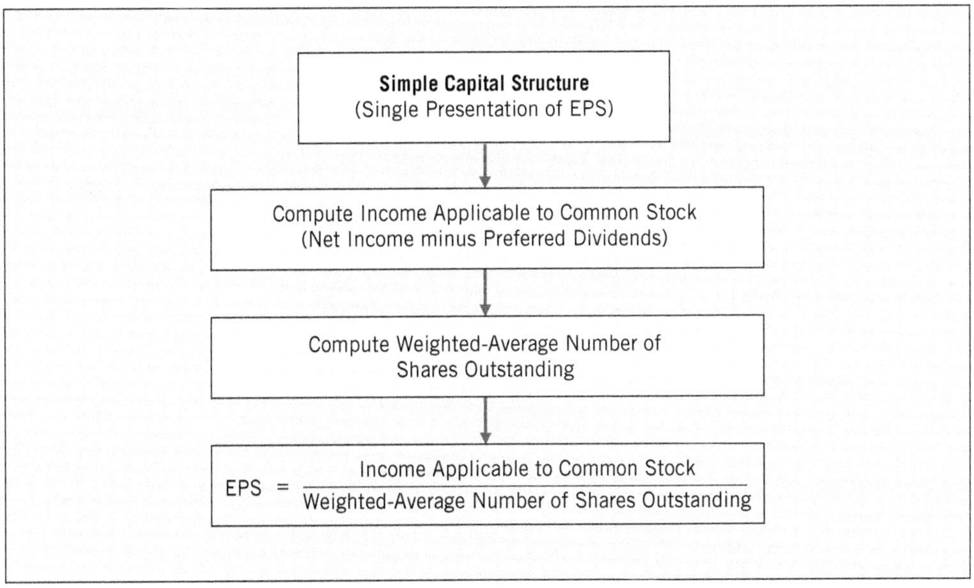

ILLUSTRATION 16.28
Calculating EPS, Simple Capital Structure

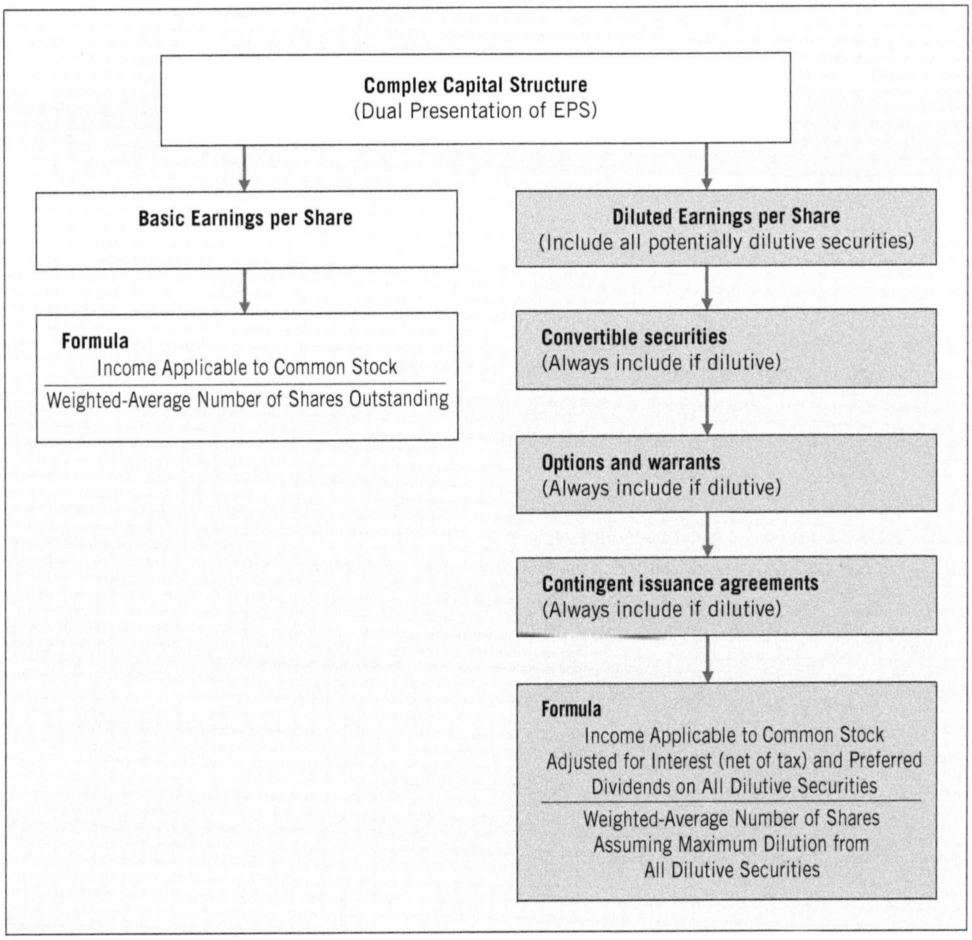

ILLUSTRATION 16.29
Calculating EPS, Complex Capital Structure

What Do the Numbers Mean? Pro Forma EPS Confusion

As discussed in Chapter 4, many companies are reporting pro forma (non-GAAP) EPS numbers along with GAAP-based EPS numbers in the financial information provided to investors. Pro forma earnings generally exceed GAAP earnings because the non-GAAP numbers exclude such items as restructuring charges, impairments of assets, R&D expenditures, and stock compensation expense. In some industries such as high-tech, the major item excluded is stock compensation expense. The following table lists some examples.

	EPS		Stock-Based Compensation (in billions)	
Company	GAAP	Non-GAAP	2014	2015
Google	$22.70	$28.35	$4.2	$4.4
Facebook	1.01	2.00	1.8	3.2
Amazon.com	0.37	4.14	1.5	2.0
Cisco Systems	1.79	2.17	1.3	1.4
Qualcomm	3.64	4.79	1.1	1.1
Oracle	2.23	2.75	0.8	0.9
Twitter	−0.90	0.34	0.6	0.8

Sources: FactSet; Thomson Reuters; company reports (Credit Suisse, Wedbush Securities, Piper Jaffray, Cantor Fitzgerald).

Google is a classic example. As indicated by one analyst, Google at one time paid out huge, share-laden compensation packages totaling more than $300 million to three key executives. Only a small amount of this compensation will be reported in the non-GAAP income measures.

Another case of possibly misleading reporting is social gaming company **Zynga**. It reported so much stock-compensation expense ($600 million) that it overwhelmed its operating profit; these expenses took operating profit negative to the tune of $406 million. The accounting? Zynga "window dressed" the expense by encouraging Wall Street analysts to use a non-GAAP accounting figure—"adjusted earnings before interest, taxes, depreciation and amortization"—that ignores the stock compensation.

LinkedIn and **Groupon** also use non-GAAP metrics that exclude stock compensation. LinkedIn's $30 million stock-compensation expense roughly halved its operating profit, while Groupon's $94 million took operating profit $203 million into the red. Wall Street analysts tend to go along with the accounting hocus-pocus, as it allows them to justify higher valuations for stocks. Investors should remember, however, that employee equity awards are real costs.

As discussed in Chapter 4, SEC Regulation G requires companies to provide a clear reconciliation between pro forma and GAAP information. And this applies to EPS measures as well. This reconciliation is especially important, given the spike in pro forma reporting by companies adding back employee stock-option expense.

Sources: M. Moran, A. J. Cohen, and K. Shaustyuk, "Stock Option Expensing: The Battle Has Been Won; Now Comes the Aftermath," *Portfolio Strategy/Accounting*, Goldman Sachs (March 17, 2005); R. Winkler, "Stock and Awe at Facebook and Zynga," *Wall Street Journal* (February 16, 2012); and A. Bary, "How Much Do Silicon Valley Firms Really Earn?" *Barron's* (June 27, 2015).

APPENDIX 16A Accounting for Stock-Appreciation Rights

LEARNING OBJECTIVE *6

Explain the accounting for stock-appreciation rights plans.

A major disadvantage of many stock-option plans is that an executive must pay income tax on the difference between the market price of the stock and the option price at the **date of exercise**. This feature of stock-option plans (those referred to as **nonqualified**) can be a financial hardship for an executive who wishes to keep the stock (rather than sell it immediately) because he or she would have to pay not only income tax but the option price as well. In another type of plan (an **incentive plan**), the executive pays no taxes at exercise but may need to borrow to finance the exercise price, which leads to related interest cost.

One solution to this problem was the creation of **stock-appreciation rights (SARs)**. In this type of plan, the company gives an executive the right to receive compensation equal to the share appreciation. **Share appreciation** is the excess of the market price of the stock at the date of exercise over a pre-established price. The company may pay the share appreciation in cash, shares, or a combination of both.

The major advantage of SARs is that the executive often does not have to make a cash outlay at the date of exercise, but receives a payment for the share appreciation. Unlike shares acquired under a stock-option plan, the company does not issue the shares that constitute the basis for computing the appreciation in a SARs plan. Rather, the company simply awards the executive cash or stock having a fair value equivalent to the appreciation. The accounting for stock-appreciation rights depends on whether the company classifies the rights as equity or as a liability.

SARs—Share-Based Equity Awards

Companies classify SARs as **equity awards** if at the date of exercise, the holder receives shares of stock from the company upon exercise. In essence, SARs are essentially equivalent to a stock option. The major difference relates to the form of payment. With the stock option, the holder pays the exercise price and then receives the stock. In an equity SAR, the holder receives shares in an amount equal to the **share-price appreciation** (the difference between the market price and the pre-established price). The accounting for SARs when they are equity awards follows the accounting used for stock options. At the date of grant, the company determines a fair value for the SAR and then allocates this amount to compensation expense over the service period of the employees.

SARs—Share-Based Liability Awards

Companies classify SARs as liability awards if at the date of exercise, the holder receives a cash payment. In this case the holder is not receiving additional shares of stock but a cash payment equal to the amount of share-price appreciation. The company's compensation expense therefore changes as the value of the liability changes.

A company uses the following approach to record share-based liability awards:

1. Measure the fair value of the award at the grant date and accrue compensation over the service period.
2. Remeasure the fair value each reporting period, until the award is settled. Adjust the compensation cost each period for changes in fair value prorated for the portion of the service period completed.
3. Once the service period is completed, determine compensation expense each subsequent period by reporting the full change in market price as an adjustment to compensation expense.

For liability awards, the company estimates the fair value of the SARs, using an option-pricing model. The company then allocates this total estimated compensation cost over the service period, recording expense (or a decrease in expense if fair value declines) in each period. At the end of each period, total compensation expense reported to date should equal the percentage of the total service period that has elapsed, multiplied by the total estimated compensation cost.

For example, assume that the service period is 20 percent complete and total estimated compensation is \$100,000. The company reports cumulative compensation expense to date of \$20,000 (\$100,000 × 0.20).

The method of allocating compensation expense is called the **percentage approach**. In this method, in the first year of, say, a four-year plan, the company charges one-fourth of the estimated cost to date. In the second year, it charges off two-fourths, or 50 percent, of the estimated cost to date, less the amount already recognized in the first year. In the third year, it charges off three-fourths of the estimated cost to date, less the amount recognized previously. In the fourth year, it charges off the remaining compensation expense.

A special problem arises when the exercise date is later than the service period. In the previous example, if the stock-appreciation rights were not exercised at the end of four years, in the fifth year the company would have to account for the difference in the market price and the pre-established price. In this case, the company adjusts compensation expense whenever a change in the market price of the stock **occurs in subsequent reporting periods, until the rights expire or are exercised, whichever comes first**.

Increases or decreases in the fair value of the SAR between the date of grant and the exercise date, therefore, result in a change in the measure of compensation. Some periods will have credits to compensation expense if the fair value decreases from one period to the next. The credit to compensation expense, however, cannot exceed previously recognized compensation expense. In other words, **cumulative compensation expense cannot be negative.**

Stock-Appreciation Rights Example

Assume that American Hotels, Inc. establishes a stock-appreciation rights plan on January 1, 2020. The plan entitles executives to receive cash at the date of exercise for the difference between the market price of the stock and the pre-established price of $10 on 10,000 SARs. The fair value of the SARs on December 31, 2020, is $3, and the service period runs for two years (2020–2021). **Illustration 16A.1** indicates the amount of compensation expense to be recorded each period, assuming that the executives hold the SARs for three years, at which time they exercise the rights.

ILLUSTRATION 16A.1 Compensation Expense, Stock-Appreciation Rights

Stock-Appreciation Rights
Schedule of Compensation Expense

(1) Date	(2) Fair Value	(3) Cumulative Compensation Recognizable[a]	(4) Percentage Accrued[b]	(5) Cumulative Compensation Accrued to Date	Expense 2020	Expense 2021	Expense 2022
12/31/20	$3	$30,000	50%	$ 15,000	$15,000		
				55,000		$55,000	
12/31/21	7	70,000	100%	70,000			
				(20,000)			$(20,000)
12/31/22	5	50,000	100%	$ 50,000			

[a]Cumulative compensation for unexercised SARs to be allocated to periods of service.
[b]The percentage accrued is based upon a two-year service period (2020–2021).

In 2020, American Hotels records compensation expense of $15,000 because 50 percent of the $30,000 total compensation cost estimated at December 31, 2020, is allocable to 2020. In 2021, the fair value increased to $7 per right ($70,000 total). The company recorded additional compensation expense of $55,000 ($70,000 minus $15,000).

The executives held the SARs through 2022, during which time the fair value declined to $5 (and the obligation to the executives equals $50,000). American Hotels recognizes the decrease by recording a $20,000 credit to compensation expense and a debit to Liability under Stock-Appreciation Plan. Note that after the service period ends, since the rights are still outstanding, the company adjusts the rights to market at December 31, 2022. Any such credit to compensation expense cannot exceed previous charges to expense attributable to that plan.

As the company records the compensation expense each period, the corresponding credit is to a liability account, because the company will pay the stock appreciation in cash. American Hotels records compensation expense in the first year as follows.

Compensation Expense	15,000	
Liability under Stock-Appreciation Plan		15,000

The company makes a similar entry in 2021 to credit the liability account for $55,000. In 2022, when it records negative compensation expense, American would debit the account for $20,000. The entry to record the negative compensation expense is as follows.

Liability under Stock-Appreciation Plan	20,000	
Compensation Expense		20,000

At December 31, 2022, the executives receive $50,000 (which equals the market price of the shares less the pre-established price). American would remove the liability with the following entry.

Liability under Stock-Appreciation Plan	50,000	
Cash		50,000

Compensation expense can increase or decrease substantially from one period to the next. The reason is that compensation expense is remeasured each year, which can lead to large swings in compensation expense.

APPENDIX 16B Comprehensive Earnings per Share Example

LEARNING OBJECTIVE *7

Compute earnings per share in a complex situation.

This appendix illustrates the method of computing dilution when many securities are involved. Illustration 16B.1 presents the section of the balance sheet of Webster Corporation for analysis. Assumptions related to the capital structure follow the balance sheet.

ILLUSTRATION 16B.1

Balance Sheet for Comprehensive Illustration

Webster Corporation
Balance Sheet (partial)
At December 31, 2020

Long-term debt	
Notes payable, 14%	$ 1,000,000
8% convertible bonds payable	2,500,000
10% convertible bonds payable	2,500,000
Total long-term debt	$ 6,000,000
Stockholders' equity	
7% cumulative, convertible preferred stock, par value $100, 100,000 shares authorized, 25,000 shares issued and outstanding	$ 2,500,000
Common stock, par value $1, 5,000,000 shares authorized, 500,000 shares issued and outstanding	500,000
Additional paid-in capital	2,000,000
Retained earnings	9,000,000
Total stockholders' equity	$14,000,000

Notes and Assumptions
December 31, 2020

1. Options were granted in July 2018 to purchase 50,000 shares of common stock at $20 per share. The average market price of Webster's common stock during 2020 was $30 per share. All options are still outstanding at the end of 2020.
2. Both the 8 percent and 10 percent convertible bonds were issued in 2019 at face value. Each convertible bond is convertible into 40 shares of common stock. (Each bond has a face value of $1,000.)
3. The 7 percent cumulative, convertible preferred stock was issued at the beginning of 2020 at par. Each share of preferred is convertible into two shares of common stock.
4. The average income tax rate is 20 percent.
5. The 500,000 shares of common stock were outstanding during the entire year.
6. Preferred dividends were not declared in 2020.
7. Net income was $1,750,000 in 2020.
8. No bonds or preferred stock were converted during 2020.

The computation of basic earnings per share for 2020 starts with the amount based upon the weighted-average number of shares outstanding, as shown in Illustration 16B.2.

ILLUSTRATION 16B.2

Computation of Earnings per Share—Simple Capital Structure

Net income	$1,750,000
Less: 7% cumulative, convertible preferred stock dividend requirements (.07 × $2,500,000)	175,000
Income applicable to common stockholders	$1,575,000
Weighted-average number of shares outstanding	500,000
Earnings per common share ($1,575,000 ÷ 500,000)	$3.15

Note the following points concerning this calculation.

1. When preferred stock is cumulative, the company subtracts the preferred dividend to arrive at income applicable to common stock, whether the dividend is declared or not.
2. The company must compute earnings per share of $3.15 as a starting point, because it is the per share amount that is subject to reduction due to the existence of convertible securities and options.

Diluted Earnings per Share

The steps for computing diluted earnings per share are:

1. Determine, for each dilutive security, the per share effect assuming exercise/conversion.
2. Rank the results from Step 1 from smallest to largest earnings effect per share. That is, rank the results from most dilutive to least dilutive.
3. Beginning with the earnings per share based upon the weighted-average number of shares outstanding ($3.15), recalculate earnings per share by adding the smallest per share effects from Step 2. If the results from this recalculation are less than $3.15, proceed to the next smallest per share effect and recalculate earnings per share. Continue this process so long as each recalculated earnings per share is smaller than the previous amount. The process will end either because there are no more securities to test or a particular security maintains or increases earnings per share (is antidilutive).

We'll now apply the three steps to Webster Corporation. (Note that net income and income available to common stockholders are not the same if preferred dividends are declared or cumulative.) Webster Corporation has four securities that could reduce EPS: options, 8 percent convertible bonds, 10 percent convertible bonds, and the convertible preferred stock.

The first step in the computation of diluted earnings per share is to determine a per share effect for each potentially dilutive security. Illustrations 16B.3 through 16B.6 show these computations.

ILLUSTRATION 16B.3

Per Share Effect of Options (Treasury-Stock Method), Diluted Earnings per Share

Number of shares under option	50,000
Option price per share	× $20
Proceeds upon assumed exercise of options	$1,000,000
Average 2020 market price of common	$30
Treasury shares that could be acquired with proceeds ($1,000,000 ÷ $30)	33,333
Excess of shares under option over treasury shares that could be repurchased (50,000 − 33,333)	16,667
Per share effect:	
$\frac{\text{Incremental Numerator Effect}}{\text{Incremental Denominator Effect}} = \frac{\text{None}}{\text{16,667 shares}} =$	$0

Interest expense for year (.08 × \$2,500,000)	\$200,000
Income tax reduction due to interest (.20 × \$200,000)	40,000
Interest expense avoided (net of tax)	\$160,000
Number of common shares issued assuming conversion of bonds (2,500 bonds × 40 shares)	100,000
Per share effect:	
Incremental Numerator Effect / Incremental Denominator Effect = \$160,000 / 100,000 shares =	\$1.60

ILLUSTRATION 16B.4

Per Share Effect of 8% Bonds (If-Converted Method), Diluted Earnings per Share

Interest expense for year (.10 × \$2,500,000)	\$250,000
Income tax reduction due to interest (.20 × \$250,000)	50,000
Interest expense avoided (net of tax)	\$200,000
Number of common shares issued assuming conversion of bonds (2,500 bonds × 40 shares)	100,000
Per share effect:	
Incremental Numerator Effect / Incremental Denominator Effect = \$200,000 / 100,000 shares =	\$2.00

ILLUSTRATION 16B.5

Per Share Effect of 10% Bonds (If-Converted Method), Diluted Earnings per Share

Dividend requirement on cumulative preferred (25,000 shares × \$7)	\$175,000
Income tax effect (dividends not a tax deduction)	none
Dividend requirement avoided (\$2,500,000 × .07)	\$175,000
Number of common shares issued assuming conversion of preferred (2 × 25,000 shares)	50,000
Per share effect:	
Incremental Numerator Effect / Incremental Denominator Effect = \$175,000 / 50,000 shares =	\$3.50

ILLUSTRATION 16B.6

Per Share Effect of 7% Convertible Preferred (If-Converted Method), Diluted Earnings per Share

Illustration 16B.7 shows the ranking of all four potentially dilutive securities.

	Effect per Share
1. Options	\$ 0
2. 8% convertible bonds	1.60
3. 10% convertible bonds	2.00
4. 7% convertible preferred	3.50

ILLUSTRATION 16B.7

Ranking of per Share Effects (Smallest to Largest), Diluted Earnings per Share

The next step is to determine earnings per share giving effect to the ranking in Illustration 16B.7. Starting with the earnings per share of \$3.15 computed previously, add the incremental effects of the options to the original calculation, as shown in **Illustration 16B.8**.

Options

Income applicable to common stockholders	\$1,575,000
Add: Incremental numerator effect of options	none
Total	\$1,575,000
Weighted-average number of shares outstanding	500,000
Add: Incremental denominator effect of options (Illustration 16B.3)	16,667
Total	516,667
Recomputed earnings per share (\$1,575,000 ÷ 516,667 shares)	\$3.05

ILLUSTRATION 16B.8

Recomputation of EPS Using Incremental Effect of Options

Since the recomputed earnings per share is reduced (from $3.15 to $3.05), the effect of the options is dilutive. Again, we could have anticipated this effect because the average market price ($30) exceeded the option price ($20).

Assuming that Webster converts the 8 percent bonds, recomputed earnings per share is as shown in **Illustration 16B.9**.

ILLUSTRATION 16B.9

Recomputation of EPS Using Incremental Effect of 8% Convertible Bonds

8% Convertible Bonds	
Numerator from previous calculation	$1,575,000
Add: Interest expense avoided (net of tax)	160,000
Total	$1,735,000
Denominator from previous calculation (shares)	516,667
Add: Number of common shares assumed issued upon conversion of bonds	100,000
Total	616,667
Recomputed earnings per share ($1,735,000 ÷ 616,667 shares)	$2.81

Since the recomputed earnings per share is reduced (from $3.05 to $2.81), the effect of the 8 percent bonds is dilutive.

Next, assuming Webster converts the 10 percent bonds, the company recomputes earnings per share as shown in **Illustration 16B.10**.

ILLUSTRATION 16B.10

Recomputation of EPS Using Incremental Effect of 10% Convertible Bonds

10% Convertible Bonds	
Numerator from previous calculation	$1,735,000
Add: Interest expense avoided (net of tax)	200,000
Total	$1,935,000
Denominator from previous calculation (shares)	616,667
Add: Number of common shares assumed issued upon conversion of bonds	100,000
Total	716,667
Recomputed earnings per share ($1,935,000 ÷ 716,667 shares)	$2.70

Since the recomputed earnings per share is reduced (from $2.81 to $2.70), the effect of the 10 percent convertible bonds is dilutive.

The final step is the recomputation that includes the 7 percent preferred stock. This is shown in **Illustration 16B.11**.

ILLUSTRATION 16B.11

Recomputation of EPS Using Incremental Effect of 7% Convertible Preferred

7% Convertible Preferred	
Numerator from previous calculation	$1,935,000
Add: Dividend requirement avoided	175,000
Total	$2,110,000
Denominator from previous calculation (shares)	716,667
Add: Number of common shares assumed issued upon conversion of preferred	50,000
Total	766,667
Recomputed earnings per share ($2,110,000 ÷ 766,667 shares)	$2.75

Since the recomputed earnings per share is not reduced, the effect of the 7 percent convertible preferred is not dilutive. Diluted earnings per share is $2.70. The per share effects of the preferred are not used in the computation.

Finally, **Illustration 16B.12** shows Webster Corporation's disclosure of earnings per share on its income statement.

Net income	$1,750,000
Basic earnings per common share (Note X)	$3.15
Diluted earnings per common share	$2.70

ILLUSTRATION 16B.12

Income Statement Presentation, EPS

A company uses income from continuing operations (adjusted for preferred dividends) to determine whether potential common stock is dilutive or antidilutive. Some refer to this measure as the **control number**. To illustrate, assume that Barton Company provides the information shown in **Illustration 16B.13**.

Income from continuing operations	$2,400,000
Loss from discontinued operations	3,600,000
Net loss	$1,200,000
Weighted-average number of shares outstanding	1,000,000
Potential common stock	200,000

ILLUSTRATION 16B.13

Barton Company Data

Barton reports basic and dilutive earnings per share as shown in **Illustration 16B.14**.

Basic earnings per share	
Income from continuing operations ($2,400,000 ÷ 1,000,000)	$2.40
Loss from discontinued operations ($3,600,000 ÷ 1,000,000)	3.60
Net loss	$1.20
Diluted earnings per share	
Income from continuing operations ($2,400,000 ÷ 1,200,000)	$2.00
Loss from discontinued operations ($3,600,000 ÷ 1,200,000)	3.00
Net loss	$1.00

ILLUSTRATION 16B.14

Basic and Diluted EPS

As Illustration 16B.14 shows, basic earnings per share from continuing operations is higher than the diluted earnings per share from continuing operations. The reason: The diluted earnings per share from continuing operations includes an additional 200,000 shares of potential common stock in its denominator.

Companies use income from continuing operations as the control number because many of them show income from continuing operations (or a similar line item above net income if it appears on the income statement) but report a final net loss due to a loss on discontinued operations. If a company uses final net loss as the control number, basic and diluted earnings per share would be the same because the potential common shares are antidilutive.[21]

[21]If a company reports a loss from continuing operations, basic and diluted earnings per share will be the same because potential common stock will be antidilutive, even if the company reports final net income. The FASB believes that comparability of EPS information will be improved by using income from continuing operations as the control number.

Review and Practice

Key Terms Review

Learning Objectives Review

1 Describe the accounting for the issuance, conversion, and retirement of convertible securities.

The method for **recording convertible bonds at the date of issuance follows that used to record straight debt issues**. Companies amortize any discount or premium that results from the issuance of convertible bonds, assuming the bonds will be held to maturity. If companies **convert bonds into other securities**, the principal accounting problem is to determine the amount at which to record the securities exchanged for the bonds. The book value method is considered GAAP. The **retirement of convertible debt** is considered a debt retirement, and the difference between the carrying amount of the retired convertible debt and the cash paid should result in a gain or loss.

When convertible preferred stock is converted, a company uses the book value method. It debits Preferred Stock, along with any related Paid-in Capital in Excess of Par—Preferred Stock, and credits Common Stock and Paid-in Capital in Excess of Par—Common Stock (if an excess exists).

2 Contrast the accounting for stock warrants with stock warrants issued with other securities.

Stock warrants: Companies should allocate the proceeds from the sale of debt with detachable warrants between the two securities. Warrants that are detachable can be traded separately from the debt, and therefore companies can determine their fair value. Two methods of allocation are available: the proportional method and the incremental method. Nondetachable warrants do not require an allocation of the proceeds between the bonds and the warrants; companies record the entire proceeds as debt. **Stock rights**: No entry is required when a company issues rights to existing stockholders. The company needs only to make a memorandum entry to indicate the number of rights issued to existing stockholders and to ensure that the company has additional unissued stock registered for issuance in case the stockholders exercise the rights.

3 Describe the accounting and reporting for stock compensation plans.

Companies must use the **fair value approach** to account for stock-based compensation. Under this approach, a company computes total compensation expense based on the fair value of the options that it expects to vest on the grant date. Companies recognize compensation expense in the periods in which the employee performs the services. Restricted-stock plans follow the same general accounting principles as those for stock options. Companies estimate total compensation cost at the grant date based on the fair value of the restricted stock; they expense that cost over the service period. If vesting does not occur, companies reverse the compensation expense.

When first proposed, there was considerable opposition to the recognition provisions contained in the fair value approach. The reason: that approach could result in substantial, previously unrecognized compensation expense. Corporate America, particularly the high-technology sector, vocally opposed the proposed standard. They believed that the standard would place them at a competitive disadvantage with larger companies that can withstand higher compensation charges. Offsetting such opposition is the need for greater transparency in financial reporting, on which our capital markets depend.

4 Compute basic earnings per share.

When a company has both common and preferred stock outstanding, it subtracts the current-year preferred stock dividend from net income to arrive at income available to common stockholders. The formula for computing earnings per share is **net income less preferred stock dividends, divided by the weighted-average common shares outstanding**.

5 Compute diluted earnings per share.

A complex capital structure requires a dual presentation of earnings per share, each with equal prominence on the face of the income statement. These two presentations are referred to as basic earnings per share and diluted earnings per share. Basic earnings per share relies on the number of weighted-average common shares outstanding (i.e., equivalent to EPS for a simple capital structure). Diluted earnings per share indicates the dilution of earnings per share that will occur if all potential issuances of common stock that would reduce earnings per share takes place. Companies with complex capital structures should exclude antidilutive securities when computing earnings per share.

*6 Explain the accounting for stock-appreciation rights plans.

The accounting for stock-appreciation rights depends on whether the rights are classified as equity- or liability-based. If equity-based, the accounting is similar to that used for stock options. If liability-based, companies remeasure compensation expense each period and allocate it over the service period using the percentage approach.

*7 Compute earnings per share in a complex situation.

For diluted EPS, make the following computations. (1) For each potentially dilutive security, determine the per share effect assuming exercise/conversion. (2) Rank the results from most dilutive to least dilutive. (3) Recalculate EPS starting with the most dilutive, and continue adding securities until EPS does not change or becomes larger.

Enhanced Review and Practice

Go online for multiple-choice questions with solutions, review exercises with solutions, and a full glossary of all key terms.

Practice Problem

On January 1, 2019, Scutaro Company issued 10-year, $200,000 face value, 6% bonds at par (payable annually on January 1). Each $1,000 bond is convertible into 30 shares of Scutaro $2 par value common stock. The company has had 10,000 shares of common stock (and no preferred stock) outstanding throughout its life. None of the bonds have been converted as of the end of 2020.

Scutaro also has adopted a stock-option plan that granted options to key executives to purchase 4,000 shares of the company's common stock. The options were granted on January 2, 2019, and were exercisable 2 years after the date of grant if the grantee was still an employee of the company (the service period is 2 years). The options expired 6 years from the date of grant. The option price was set at $4, and the fair value option-pricing model determines the total compensation expense to be $18,000. All of the options were exercised during the year 2021: 3,000 on January 3 when the market price was $6, and 1,000 on May 1 when the market price was $7 a share. (Ignore all tax effects.)

Instructions

a. Prepare the journal entry Scutaro would have made on January 1, 2019, to record the issuance of the bonds.

b. Prepare the journal entry to record interest expense and compensation expense in 2020.

c. Scutaro's net income in 2020 was $30,000 and was $27,000 in 2019. Compute basic and diluted earnings per share for Scutaro for 2020 and 2019. Scutaro's average stock price was $4.40 in 2019 and $5 in 2020.

d. Assume that 75 percent of the holders of Scutaro's convertible bonds convert their bonds to stock on June 30, 2021, when Scutaro's stock is trading at $8 per share. Scutaro pays $2 per bond to induce bondholders to convert. Prepare the journal entry to record the conversion.

Solution

a. Under GAAP, proceeds from the issuance of convertible debt are recorded entirely as debt.

Cash	200,000	
Bonds Payable		200,000

b. **December 31, 2020**

Interest Expense	12,000	
Interest Payable		12,000
[To record interest expense for 2020 ($200,000 × .06)]		
Compensation Expense	9,000	
Paid-in Capital—Stock Options		9,000
[To record compensation expense for 2020 (1/2 × $18,000)]		

c.

Basic EPS	**2020**	**2019**
Net income (a)	$30,000	$27,000
Outstanding shares (b)	10,000	10,000
Basic EPS (a ÷ b)	$ 3.00	$ 2.70
Diluted EPS		
Net income	$30,000	$27,000
Add: Interest savings ($200,000 × .06)	12,000	12,000
Adjusted net income (a)	$42,000	$39,000

(continued)

	2020	2019
Outstanding shares	10,000	10,000
Shares upon conversion (200 × 30)	6,000	6,000
Options (treasury-stock method)	800*	364*
Total shares for diluted EPS (b)	16,800	16,364
Diluted EPS (a ÷ b)	$ 2.50	$ 2.38

*Treasury-stock method:

	2020		2019	
Cash proceeds	($4 × 4,000)	$16,000		$16,000
Shares repurchased	($16,000 ÷ $5)	3,200	($16,000 ÷ $4.40)	3,636
Net shares issued	(4,000 − 3,200)	800	(4,000 − 3,636)	364

d.

Bond Conversion Expense**	300	
Bonds Payable	150,000	
Common Stock*		9,000
Paid-in Capital in Excess of Par—Common Stock*		141,000
Cash		300

*$200,000 × .75 = $150,000 of bonds converted
$150,000 ÷ $1,000 per bond = 150 bonds
150 bonds × 30 shares per bond = 4,500 new shares issued
4,500 shares × $2 par value = $9,000 increase in common stock account
$150,000 − $9,000 = $141,000 increase in paid-in capital account
**150 bonds × $2 per bond = $300 bond conversion expense

WileyPLUS

Exercises, Problems, Problem Solution Walkthrough Videos, and many more assessment tools and resources are available for practice in WileyPLUS.

Note: All asterisked Questions, Exercises, and Problems relate to material in the appendices to the chapter.

Questions

1. What is meant by a dilutive security?

2. Briefly explain why corporations issue convertible securities.

3. Discuss the similarities and the differences between convertible debt and debt issued with stock warrants.

4. Bridgewater Corp. offered holders of its 1,000 convertible bonds a premium of $160 per bond to induce conversion into shares of its common stock. Upon conversion of all the bonds, Bridgewater Corp. recorded the $160,000 premium as a reduction of paid-in capital. Comment on Bridgewater's treatment of the $160,000 "sweetener."

5. Explain how the conversion feature of convertible debt has a value (a) to the issuer and (b) to the purchaser.

6. What are the arguments for giving separate accounting recognition to the conversion feature of debentures?

7. Four years after issue, debentures with a face value of $1,000,000 and book value of $960,000 are tendered for conversion into 80,000 shares of common stock immediately after an interest payment date. At that time, the market price of the debentures is 104, and the common stock is selling at $14 per share (par value $10). The company records the conversion as follows.

Bonds Payable	1,000,000	
Discount on Bonds Payable		40,000
Common Stock		800,000
Paid-in Capital in Excess of Par—Common Stock		160,000

Discuss the propriety of this accounting treatment.

8. On July 1, 2020, Roberts Corporation issued $3,000,000 of 9% bonds payable in 20 years. The bonds include detachable warrants giving the bondholder the right to purchase for $30 one share of $1 par value common stock at any time during the next 10 years. The bonds were sold for $3,000,000. The value of the warrants at the time of issuance was $100,000. Prepare the journal entry to record this transaction.

9. What are stock rights? How does the issuing company account for them?

10. Briefly explain the accounting requirements for stock compensation plans under GAAP.

11. Cordero Corporation has an employee stock-purchase plan which permits all full-time employees to purchase 10 shares of common stock on the third anniversary of their employment and an additional 15 shares

on each subsequent anniversary date. The purchase price is set at the market price on the date purchased and no commission is charged. Discuss whether this plan would be considered compensatory.

12. What date or event does the profession believe should be used in determining the value of a stock option? What arguments support this position?

13. Over what period of time should compensation cost be allocated?

14. How is compensation expense computed using the fair value approach?

15. What are the advantages of using restricted stock to compensate employees?

16. At December 31, 2020, Reid Company had 600,000 shares of common stock issued and outstanding, 400,000 of which had been issued and outstanding throughout the year and 200,000 of which were issued on October 1, 2020. Net income for 2020 was $2,000,000, and dividends declared on preferred stock were $400,000. Compute Reid's earnings per common share. (Round to the nearest penny.)

17. What effect do stock dividends or stock splits have on the computation of the weighted-average number of shares outstanding?

18. Define the following terms.

a. Basic earnings per share.

b. Potentially dilutive security.

c. Diluted earnings per share.

d. Complex capital structure.

e. Potential common stock.

19. What are the computational guidelines for determining whether a convertible security is to be reported as part of diluted earnings per share?

20. Discuss why options and warrants may be considered potentially dilutive common shares for the computation of diluted earnings per share.

21. Explain how convertible securities are determined to be potentially dilutive common shares and how those convertible securities that are not considered to be potentially dilutive common shares enter into the determination of earnings per share data.

22. Explain the treasury-stock method as it applies to options and warrants in computing dilutive earnings per share data.

23. Earnings per share can affect market prices of common stock. Can market prices affect earnings per share? Explain.

24. What is meant by the term antidilution? Give an example.

25. What type of earnings per share presentation is required in a complex capital structure?

*26. How is antidilution determined when multiple securities are involved?

Brief Exercises

BE16.1 **(LO 1)** Archer Inc. issued $4,000,000 par value, 7% convertible bonds at 99 for cash. If the bonds had not included the conversion feature, they would have sold for 95. Prepare the journal entry to record the issuance of the bonds.

BE16.2 **(LO 1)** Petrenko Corporation has outstanding 2,000 $1,000 bonds, each convertible into 50 shares of $10 par value common stock. The bonds are converted on December 31, 2020, when the unamortized discount is $30,000 and the market price of the stock is $21 per share. Record the conversion using the book value approach.

BE16.3 **(LO 1)** Pechstein Corporation issued 2,000 shares of $10 par value common stock upon conversion of 1,000 shares of $50 par value preferred stock. The preferred stock was originally issued at $60 per share. The common stock is trading at $26 per share at the time of conversion. Record the conversion of the preferred stock.

BE16.4 **(LO 2)** Eisler Corporation issued 2,000 $1,000 bonds at 101. Each bond was issued with one detachable stock warrant. After issuance, the bonds were selling in the market at 98, and the warrants had a market price of $40. Use the proportional method to record the issuance of the bonds and warrants.

BE16.5 **(LO 2)** McIntyre Corporation issued 2,000 $1,000 bonds at 101. Each bond was issued with one detachable stock warrant. After issuance, the bonds were selling separately at 98. The market price of the warrants without the bonds cannot be determined. Use the incremental method to record the issuance of the bonds and warrants.

BE16.6 **(LO 3)** On January 1, 2020, Barwood Corporation granted 5,000 options to executives. Each option entitles the holder to purchase one share of Barwood's $5 par value common stock at $50 per share at any time during the next 5 years. The market price of the stock is $65 per share on the date of grant. The fair value of the options at the grant date is $150,000. The period of benefit is 2 years. Prepare Barwood's journal entries for January 1, 2020, and December 31, 2020 and 2021.

BE16.7 **(LO 3)** Refer to the data for Barwood Corporation in BE16.6. Repeat the requirements assuming that instead of options, Barwood granted 2,000 shares of restricted stock.

BE16.8 **(LO 3)** On January 1, 2020 (the date of grant), Lutz Corporation issues 2,000 shares of restricted stock to its executives. The fair value of these shares is $75,000, and their par value is $10,000. The stock is forfeited if the executives do not complete 3 years of employment with the company. Prepare the journal entry (if any) on January 1, 2020, and on December 31, 2020, assuming the service period is 3 years.

BE16.9 **(LO 4)** Kalin Corporation had 2020 net income of $1,000,000. During 2020, Kalin paid a dividend of $2 per share on 100,000 shares of preferred stock. During 2020, Kalin had outstanding 250,000 shares of common stock. Compute Kalin's 2020 earnings per share.

BE16.10 **(LO 4)** Douglas Corporation had 120,000 shares of stock outstanding on January 1, 2020. On May 1, 2020, Douglas issued 60,000 shares. On July 1, Douglas purchased 10,000 treasury shares, which were reissued on October 1. Compute Douglas's weighted-average number of shares outstanding for 2020.

BE16.11 **(LO 4)** Tomba Corporation had 300,000 shares of common stock outstanding on January 1, 2020. On May 1, Tomba issued 30,000 shares. (a) Compute the weighted-average number of shares outstanding if the 30,000 shares were issued for cash. (b) Compute the weighted-average number of shares outstanding if the 30,000 shares were issued in a stock dividend.

BE16.12 **(LO 4)** The 2020 income statement of Wasmeier Corporation showed net income of $480,000 and a loss from discontinued operations of $120,000. Wasmeier had 100,000 shares of common stock outstanding all year. Prepare Wasmeier's income statement presentation of earnings per share.

BE16.13 **(LO 5)** Rockland Corporation earned net income of $300,000 in 2020 and had 100,000 shares of common stock outstanding throughout the year. Also outstanding all year was $800,000 of 9% bonds, which are convertible into 16,000 shares of common. Rockland's tax rate is 20%. Compute Rockland's 2020 diluted earnings per share.

BE16.14 **(LO 5)** DiCenta Corporation reported net income of $270,000 in 2020 and had 50,000 shares of common stock outstanding throughout the year. Also outstanding all year were 5,000 shares of cumulative preferred stock, each convertible into 2 shares of common. The preferred stock pays an annual dividend of $5 per share. DiCenta's tax rate is 20%. Compute DiCenta's 2020 diluted earnings per share.

BE16.15 **(LO 5)** Bedard Corporation reported net income of $300,000 in 2020 and had 200,000 shares of common stock outstanding throughout the year. Also outstanding all year were 45,000 options to purchase common stock at $10 per share. The average market price of the stock during the year was $15. Compute diluted earnings per share.

*BE16.16 **(LO 6)** Ferraro, Inc. established a stock-appreciation rights (SARs) program on January 1, 2020, which entitles executives to receive cash at the date of exercise for the difference between the market price of the stock and the pre-established price of $20 on 5,000 SARs. The required service period is 2 years. The fair value of the SARs are determined to be $4 on December 31, 2020, and $9 on December 31, 2021. Compute Ferraro's compensation expense for 2020 and 2021.

Exercises

E16.1 **(LO 1, 2)** Excel **(Issuance and Conversion of Bonds)** For each of the unrelated transactions described below, present the entry(ies) required to record each transaction.

1. Grand Corp. issued $20,000,000 par value 10% convertible bonds at 99. If the bonds had not been convertible, the company's investment banker estimates they would have been sold at 95.
2. Hoosier Company issued $20,000,000 par value 10% bonds at 98. One detachable stock purchase warrant was issued with each $100 par value bond. At the time of issuance, the warrants were selling for $4.
3. Suppose Sepracor, Inc. called its convertible debt in 2020. Assume the following related to the transaction. The 11%, $10,000,000 par value bonds were converted into 1,000,000 shares of $1 par value common stock on July 1, 2020. On July 1, there was $55,000 of unamortized discount applicable to the bonds, and the company paid an additional $75,000 to the bondholders to induce conversion of all the bonds. The company records the conversion using the book value method.

E16.2 **(LO 1)** **(Conversion of Bonds)** Aubrey Inc. issued $4,000,000 of 10%, 10-year convertible bonds on June 1, 2020, at 98 plus accrued interest. The bonds were dated April 1, 2020, with interest payable April 1 and October 1. Bond discount is amortized semiannually on a straight-line basis.

On April 1, 2021, $1,500,000 of these bonds were converted into 30,000 shares of $20 par value common stock. Accrued interest was paid in cash at the time of conversion.

Instructions

a. Prepare the entry to record the interest expense at October 1, 2020. Assume that accrued interest payable was credited when the bonds were issued. (Round to nearest dollar.)

b. Prepare the entry(ies) to record the conversion on April 1, 2021. (Book value method is used.) Assume that the entry to record amortization of the bond discount and interest payment has been made.

E16.3 **(LO 1)** **(Conversion of Bonds)** Vargo Company has bonds payable outstanding in the amount of $500,000, and the Premium on Bonds Payable account has a balance of $7,500. Each $1,000 bond is convertible into 20 shares of preferred stock of par value of $50 per share. All bonds are converted into preferred stock.

Instructions

Assuming that the book value method was used, what entry would be made?

E16.4 **(LO 1)** **(Conversion of Bonds)** On January 1, 2019, when its $30 par value common stock was selling for $80 per share, Plato Corp. issued $10,000,000 of 8% convertible debentures due in 20 years. The conversion option allowed the holder of each $1,000 bond to convert the bond into five shares of the corporation's common stock. The debentures were issued for $10,800,000. The present value of the bond payments at the time of issuance was $8,500,000, and the corporation believes the difference between the present value and the amount paid is attributable to the conversion feature. On January 1, 2020, the corporation's $30 par value common stock was split 2 for 1, and the conversion rate for the bonds was adjusted accordingly. On January 1, 2021, when the corporation's $15 par value common stock was selling for $135 per share, holders of 30% of the convertible debentures exercised their conversion options. The corporation uses the straight-line method for amortizing any bond discounts or premiums.

Instructions

a. Prepare in general journal form the entry to record the original issuance of the convertible debentures.

b. Prepare in general journal form the entry to record the exercise of the conversion option, using the book value method. Show supporting computations in good form.

E16.5 **(LO 1)** **(Conversion of Bonds)** The December 31, 2020, balance sheet of Kepler Corp. is as follows.

10% callable, convertible bonds payable (semiannual interest dates April 30 and October 31; convertible into 6 shares of $25 par value common stock per $1,000 of bond principal; maturity date April 30, 2026)	$500,000	
Discount on bonds payable	10,240	$489,760

On March 5, 2021, Kepler Corp. called all of the bonds as of April 30 for the principal plus interest through April 30. By April 30, all bondholders had exercised their conversion to common stock as of the interest payment date. Consequently, on April 30, Kepler Corp. paid the semiannual interest and issued shares of common stock for the bonds. The discount is amortized on a straight-line basis. Kepler uses the book value method.

Instructions

Prepare the entry(ies) to record the interest expense and conversion on April 30, 2021. Reversing entries were made on January 1, 2021. (Round to the nearest dollar.)

E16.6 **(LO 1)** **(Conversion of Bonds)** On January 1, 2020, Gottlieb Corporation issued $4,000,000 of 10-year, 8% convertible debentures at 102. Interest is to be paid semiannually on June 30 and December 31. Each $1,000 debenture can be converted into eight shares of Gottlieb Corporation $100 par value common stock after December 31, 2021.

On January 1, 2022, $400,000 of debentures are converted into common stock, which is then selling at $110. An additional $400,000 of debentures are converted on March 31, 2022. The market price of the common stock is then $115. Accrued interest at March 31 will be paid on the next interest date.

Bond premium is amortized on a straight-line basis.

Instructions

Make the necessary journal entries for:

a. December 31, 2021.

b. January 1, 2022.

c. March 31, 2022.

d. June 30, 2022.

Record the conversions using the book value method.

E16.7 **(LO 2)** **(Issuance of Bonds with Warrants)** Illiad Inc. has decided to raise additional capital by issuing $170,000 face value of bonds with a coupon rate of 10%. In discussions with investment bankers, it was determined that to help the sale of the bonds, detachable stock warrants should be issued at the rate of one warrant for each $100 bond sold. The value of the bonds without the warrants is considered to be $136,000, and the value of the warrants in the market is $24,000. The bonds sold in the market at issuance for $152,000.

Instructions

a. What entry should be made at the time of the issuance of the bonds and warrants?

b. If the warrants were nondetachable, would the entries be different? Discuss.

E16.8 **(LO 2)** **(Issuance of Bonds with Detachable Warrants)** On September 1, 2020, Sands Company sold at 104 (plus accrued interest) 4,000 of its 9%, 10-year, $1,000 face value, nonconvertible bonds with detachable stock warrants. Each bond carried two detachable warrants. Each warrant was for one share of common stock at a specified option price of $15 per share. Shortly after issuance, the warrants were quoted on the market for $3 each. No fair value can be determined for the Sands Company bonds. Interest is payable on December 1 and June 1.

Instructions

Prepare in general journal format the entry to record the issuance of the bonds.

(AICPA adapted)

E16.9 **(LO 2)** **(Issuance of Bonds with Stock Warrants)** On May 1, 2020, Friendly Company issued 2,000 $1,000 bonds at 102. Each bond was issued with one detachable stock warrant. Shortly after issuance, the bonds were selling at 98, but the fair value of the warrants cannot be determined.

Instructions

a. Prepare the entry to record the issuance of the bonds and warrants.

b. Assume the same facts as part (a), except that the warrants had a fair value of $30. Prepare the entry to record the issuance of the bonds and warrants.

E16.10 **(LO 3)** **(Issuance and Exercise of Stock Options)** On November 1, 2020, Columbo Company adopted a stock-option plan that granted options to key executives to purchase 30,000 shares of the company's $10 par value common stock. The options were granted on January 2, 2021, and were exercisable 2 years after the date of grant if the grantee was still an employee of the company. The options expired 6 years from date of grant. The option price was set at $40, and the fair value option-pricing model determines the total compensation expense to be $450,000.

All of the options were exercised during the year 2023: 20,000 on January 3 when the market price was $67, and 10,000 on May 1 when the market price was $77 a share.

Instructions

Prepare journal entries relating to the stock option plan for the years 2021, 2022, and 2023. Assume that the employee performs services equally in 2021 and 2022.

E16.11 **(LO 3)** **(Issuance, Exercise, and Termination of Stock Options)** On January 1, 2021, Titania Inc. granted stock options to officers and key employees for the purchase of 20,000 shares of the company's $10 par common stock at $25 per share. The options were exercisable within a 5-year period beginning January 1, 2023, by grantees still in the employ of the company, and expiring December 31, 2027. The service period for this award is 2 years. Assume that the fair value option-pricing model determines total compensation expense to be $350,000.

On April 1, 2022, 2,000 options were terminated when the employees resigned from the company. The market price of the common stock was $35 per share on this date.

On March 31, 2023, 12,000 options were exercised when the market price of the common stock was $40 per share.

Instructions

Prepare journal entries to record issuance of the stock options, termination of the stock options, exercise of the stock options, and charges to compensation expense, for the years ended December 31, 2021, 2022, and 2023.

E16.12 **(LO 3)** **(Issuance, Exercise, and Termination of Stock Options)** On January 1, 2019, Nichols Corporation granted 10,000 options to key executives. Each option allows the executive to purchase one share of Nichols' $5 par value common stock at a price of $20 per share. The options were exercisable within a 2-year period beginning January 1, 2021, if the grantee is still employed by the company at the time of the exercise. On the grant date, Nichols' stock was trading at $25 per share, and a fair value option-pricing model determines total compensation to be $400,000.

On May 1, 2021, 8,000 options were exercised when the market price of Nichols' stock was $30 per share. The remaining options lapsed in 2023 because executives decided not to exercise their options.

Instructions

Prepare the necessary journal entries related to the stock option plan for the years 2019 through 2023.

E16.13 (LO 3) (Accounting for Restricted Stock) Derrick Company issues 4,000 shares of restricted stock to its CFO, Dane Yaping, on January 1, 2020. The stock has a fair value of $120,000 on this date. The service period related to this restricted stock is 4 years. Vesting occurs if Yaping stays with the company for 4 years. The par value of the stock is $5. At December 31, 2021, the fair value of the stock is $145,000.

Instructions

a. Prepare the journal entries to record the restricted stock on January 1, 2020 (the date of grant), and December 31, 2021.

b. On March 4, 2022, Yaping leaves the company. Prepare the journal entry (if any) to account for this forfeiture.

E16.14 (LO 3) (Accounting for Restricted Stock) Tweedie Company issues 10,000 shares of restricted stock to its CFO, Mary Tokar, on January 1, 2020. The stock has a fair value of $500,000 on this date. The service period related to this restricted stock is 5 years. Vesting occurs if Tokar stays with the company until December 31, 2024. The par value of the stock is $10. At December 31, 2020, the fair value of the stock is $450,000.

Instructions

a. Prepare the journal entries to record the restricted stock on January 1, 2020 (the date of grant), and December 31, 2021.

b. On July 25, 2024, Tokar leaves the company. Prepare the journal entry (if any) to account for this forfeiture.

E16.15 (LO 4) Excel (Weighted-Average Number of Shares) Newton Inc. uses a calendar year for financial reporting. The company is authorized to issue 9,000,000 shares of $10 par common stock. At no time has Newton issued any potentially dilutive securities. Listed below is a summary of Newton's common stock activities.

1. Number of common shares issued and outstanding at December 31, 2018	2,000,000
2. Shares issued as a result of a 10% stock dividend on September 30, 2019	200,000
3. Shares issued for cash on March 31, 2020	2,000,000
Number of common shares issued and outstanding at December 31, 2020	4,200,000
4. A 2-for-1 stock split of Newton's common stock took place on March 31, 2021	

Instructions

a. Compute the weighted-average number of common shares used in computing earnings per common share for 2019 on the 2020 comparative income statement.

b. Compute the weighted-average number of common shares used in computing earnings per common share for 2020 on the 2020 comparative income statement.

c. Compute the weighted-average number of common shares to be used in computing earnings per common share for 2020 on the 2021 comparative income statement.

d. Compute the weighted-average number of common shares to be used in computing earnings per common share for 2021 on the 2021 comparative income statement.

(CMA adapted)

E16.16 (LO 4) (EPS: Simple Capital Structure) On January 1, 2021, Wilke Corp. had 480,000 shares of common stock outstanding. During 2021, it had the following transactions that affected the common stock account.

February 1	Issued 120,000 shares
March 1	Issued a 10% stock dividend
May 1	Acquired 100,000 shares of treasury stock
June 1	Issued a 3-for-1 stock split
October 1	Reissued 60,000 shares of treasury stock

Instructions

a. Determine the weighted-average number of shares outstanding as of December 31, 2021.

b. Assume that Wilke Corp. earned net income of $3,456,000 during 2021. In addition, it had 100,000 shares of 9%, $100 par nonconvertible, noncumulative preferred stock outstanding for the entire year. Because of liquidity considerations, however, the company did not declare and pay a preferred dividend in 2021. Compute earnings per share for 2021, using the weighted-average number of shares determined in part (a).

c. Assume the same facts as in part (b), except that the preferred stock was cumulative. Compute earnings per share for 2021.

d. Assume the same facts as in part (b), except that net income included a loss from discontinued operations of $432,000 (net of tax). Compute earnings per share for 2021.

E16.17 (LO 4) (EPS: Simple Capital Structure) Ace Company had 200,000 shares of common stock outstanding on December 31, 2021. During the year 2022, the company issued 8,000 shares on May 1 and retired 14,000 shares on October 31. For the year 2022, Ace Company reported net income of $249,690 after a loss from discontinued operations of $40,600 (net of tax).

Instructions

What earnings per share data should be reported at the bottom of its income statement?

E16.18 (LO 4) (EPS: Simple Capital Structure) Flagstad Inc. presented the following data.

Net income	$2,500,000
Preferred stock: 50,000 shares outstanding, $100 par, 8% cumulative, not convertible	5,000,000
Common stock: Shares outstanding 1/1	750,000
Issued for cash, 5/1	300,000
Acquired treasury stock for cash, 8/1	150,000
2-for-1 stock split, 10/1	

Instructions

Compute earnings per share.

E16.19 (LO 4) (EPS: Simple Capital Structure) A portion of the combined statement of income and retained earnings of Seminole Inc. for the current year follows.

Income from continuing operations		$15,000,000
Loss from discontinued operations, net of applicable income tax (Note 1)		1,340,000
Net income		13,660,000
Retained earnings at the beginning of the year		83,250,000
		96,910,000
Dividends declared:		
On preferred stock—$6.00 per share	$ 300,000	
On common stock—$1.75 per share	14,875,000	15,175,000
Retained earnings at the end of the year		$81,735,000

Note 1. During the year, Seminole Inc. suffered a major loss from discontinued operations of $1,340,000 after applicable income tax reduction of $1,200,000.

At the end of the current year, Seminole Inc. has outstanding 8,500,000 shares of $10 par common stock and 50,000 shares of 6% preferred. On April 1 of the current year, Seminole Inc. issued 1,000,000 shares of common stock for $32 per share to help finance the loss from discontinued operations.

Instructions

Compute the earnings per share on common stock for the current year as it should be reported to stockholders.

E16.20 (LO 4) (EPS: Simple Capital Structure) On January 1, 2020, Lennon Industries had stock outstanding as follows.

6% Cumulative preferred stock, $100 par value, issued and outstanding 10,000 shares	$1,000,000
Common stock, $10 par value, issued and outstanding 200,000 shares	2,000,000

To acquire the net assets of three smaller companies, Lennon authorized the issuance of an additional 160,000 common shares. The acquisitions took place as shown below.

Date of Acquisition	Shares Issued
Company A April 1, 2020	50,000
Company B July 1, 2020	80,000
Company C October 1, 2020	30,000

On May 14, 2020, Lennon realized a $90,000 (before taxes) gain on discontinued operations. On December 31, 2020, Lennon recorded income of $300,000 from continuing operations.

Instructions

Assuming a 20% tax rate, compute the earnings per share data that should appear on the financial statements of Lennon Industries as of December 31, 2020.

E16.21 (LO 4) (EPS: Simple Capital Structure) At January 1, 2020, Langley Company's outstanding shares included the following.

280,000 shares of $50 par value, 7% cumulative preferred stock
900,000 shares of $1 par value common stock

Net income for 2020 was $2,530,000. No cash dividends were declared or paid during 2020. On February 15, 2021, however, all preferred dividends in arrears were paid, together with a 5% stock dividend on common shares. There were no dividends in arrears prior to 2020.

On April 1, 2020, 450,000 shares of common stock were sold for $10 per share, and on October 1, 2020, 110,000 shares of common stock were purchased for $20 per share and held as treasury stock.

Instructions

Compute earnings per share for 2020. Assume that financial statements for 2020 were issued in March 2021.

E16.22 (LO 5) (EPS with Convertible Bonds, Various Situations) In 2019, Chirac Enterprises issued, at par, 60 $1,000, 8% bonds, each convertible into 100 shares of common stock. Chirac had revenues of $17,500 and expenses other than interest and taxes of $8,400 for 2020. (Assume that the tax rate is 20%.) Throughout 2020, 2,000 shares of common stock were outstanding; none of the bonds was converted or redeemed.

Instructions

a. Compute diluted earnings per share for 2020.

b. Assume the same facts as those assumed for part (a), except that the 60 bonds were issued on September 1, 2020 (rather than in 2019), and none have been converted or redeemed. Compute diluted earnings per share for 2020.

c. Assume the same facts as assumed for part (a), except that 20 of the 60 bonds were actually converted on July 1, 2020. Compute diluted earnings per share for 2020.

E16.23 (LO 5) (EPS with Convertible Bonds) On June 1, 2018, Andre Company and Agassi Company merged to form Lancaster Inc. A total of 800,000 shares were issued to complete the merger. The new corporation reports on a calendar-year basis.

On April 1, 2020, the company issued an additional 400,000 shares of stock for cash. All 1,200,000 shares were outstanding on December 31, 2020.

Lancaster Inc. also issued $600,000 of 20-year, 8% convertible bonds at par on July 1, 2020. Each $1,000 bond converts to 40 shares of common at any interest date. None of the bonds have been converted to date.

Lancaster Inc. is preparing its annual report for the fiscal year ending December 31, 2020. The annual report will show earnings per share figures based upon a reported after-tax net income of $1,540,000. (The tax rate is 20%.)

Instructions

Determine the following for 2020.

a. The number of shares to be used for calculating:

  1. Basic earnings per share.

  2. Diluted earnings per share.

b. The earnings figures to be used for calculating:

  1. Basic earnings per share.

  2. Diluted earnings per share.

(CMA adapted)

E16.24 (LO 5) (EPS with Convertible Bonds and Preferred Stock) The Simon Corporation issued 10-year, $5,000,000 par, 7% callable convertible subordinated debentures on January 2, 2020. The bonds have a par value of $1,000, with interest payable annually. The current conversion ratio is 14:1, and in 2 years it will increase to 18:1. At the date of issue, the bonds were sold at 98. Bond discount is amortized on a straight-line basis. Simon's effective tax was 20%. Net income in 2020 was $9,500,000, and the company had 2,000,000 shares outstanding during the entire year.

Instructions

a. Prepare a schedule to compute both basic and diluted earnings per share.

b. Discuss how the schedule would differ if the security was convertible preferred stock.

E16.25 (LO 5) (EPS with Convertible Bonds and Preferred Stock) On January 1, 2020, Crocker Company issued 10-year, $2,000,000 face value, 6% bonds, at par. Each $1,000 bond is convertible into 15 shares of Crocker common stock. Crocker's net income in 2020 was $400,000, and its tax rate was 20%. The company had 100,000 shares of common stock outstanding throughout 2020. None of the bonds were converted in 2020.

Instructions

a. Compute diluted earnings per share for 2020.

b. Compute diluted earnings per share for 2020, assuming the same facts as above, except that $1,000,000 of 6% convertible preferred stock was issued instead of the bonds. Each $100 preferred share is convertible into 5 shares of Crocker common stock.

E16.26 **(LO 5)** **(EPS with Options, Various Situations)** Venzuela Company's net income for 2020 is $50,000. The only potentially dilutive securities outstanding were 1,000 options issued during 2019, each exercisable for one share at $6. None has been exercised, and 10,000 shares of common were outstanding during 2020. The average market price of Venzuela's stock during 2020 was $20.

Instructions

a. Compute diluted earnings per share. (Round to nearest cent.)

b. Assume the same facts as those assumed for part (a), except that the 1,000 options were issued on October 1, 2020 (rather than in 2019). The average market price during the last 3 months of 2020 was $20.

E16.27 **(LO 5)** **(EPS with Contingent Issuance Agreement)** Winsor Inc. recently purchased Holiday Corp., a large midwestern home painting corporation. One of the terms of the merger was that if Holiday's income for 2020 was $110,000 or more, 10,000 additional shares would be issued to Holiday's stockholders in 2021. Holiday's income for 2019 was $120,000.

Instructions

a. Would the contingent shares have to be considered in Winsor's 2019 earnings per share computations?

b. Assume the same facts, except that the 10,000 shares are contingent on Holiday's achieving a net income of $130,000 in 2020. Would the contingent shares have to be considered in Winsor's earnings per share computations for 2019?

E16.28 **(LO 5)** **(EPS with Warrants)** Howat Corporation earned $360,000 during a period when it had an average of 100,000 shares of common stock outstanding. The common stock sold at an average market price of $15 per share during the period. Also outstanding were 15,000 warrants that could be exercised to purchase one share of common stock for $10 for each warrant exercised.

Instructions

a. Are the warrants dilutive?

b. Compute basic earnings per share.

c. Compute diluted earnings per share.

*E16.29 **(LO 6)** **(Stock-Appreciation Rights)** On December 31, 2016, Beckford Company issues 150,000 stock-appreciation rights to its officers entitling them to receive cash for the difference between the market price of its stock and a pre-established price of $10. The fair value of the SARs is estimated to be $4 per SAR on December 31, 2017; $1 on December 31, 2018; $10 on December 31, 2019; and $9 on December 31, 2020. The service period is 4 years, and the exercise period is 7 years.

Instructions

a. Prepare a schedule that shows the amount of compensation expense allocable to each year affected by the stock-appreciation rights plan.

b. Prepare the entry at December 31, 2020, to record compensation expense, if any, in 2020.

c. Prepare the entry on December 31, 2020, assuming that all 150,000 SARs are exercised.

*E16.30 **(LO 6)** **(Stock-Appreciation Rights)** Capulet Company establishes a stock-appreciation rights program that entitles its new president Ben Davis to receive cash for the difference between the market price of the stock and a pre-established price of $30 (also market price) on December 31, 2016, on 30,000 SARs. The date of grant is December 31, 2016, and the required employment (service) period is 4 years. President Davis exercises all of the SARs in 2022. The fair value of the SARs is estimated to be $6 per SAR on December 31, 2017; $9 on December 31, 2018; $15 on December 31, 2019; $6 on December 31, 2020; and $18 on December 31, 2021.

Instructions

a. Prepare a 5-year (2017–2021) schedule of compensation expense pertaining to the 30,000 SARs granted president Davis.

b. Prepare the journal entry for compensation expense in 2017, 2020, and 2021 relative to the 30,000 SARs.

Problems

P16.1 (LO 1, 2, 3) Groupwork (Entries for Various Dilutive Securities) The stockholders' equity section of Martino Inc. at the beginning of the current year appears below.

Common stock, $10 par value, authorized 1,000,000 shares, 300,000 shares issued and outstanding	$3,000,000
Paid-in capital in excess of par—common stock	600,000
Retained earnings	570,000

During the current year, the following transactions occurred.

1. The company issued to the stockholders 100,000 rights. Ten rights are needed to buy one share of stock at $32. The rights were void after 30 days. The market price of the stock at this time was $34 per share.
2. The company sold to the public a $200,000, 10% bond issue at 104. The company also issued with each $100 bond one detachable stock purchase warrant, which provided for the purchase of common stock at $30 per share. Shortly after issuance, similar bonds without warrants were selling at 96 and the warrants at $8.
3. All but 5,000 of the rights issued in (1) were exercised in 30 days.
4. At the end of the year, 80% of the warrants in (2) had been exercised, and the remaining were outstanding and in good standing.
5. During the current year, the company granted stock options for 10,000 shares of common stock to company executives. The company, using a fair value option-pricing model, determines that each option is worth $10. The option price is $30. The options were to expire at year-end and were considered compensation for the current year.
6. All but 1,000 shares related to the stock-option plan were exercised by year-end. The expiration resulted because one of the executives failed to fulfill an obligation related to the employment contract.

Instructions

a. Prepare general journal entries for the current year to record the transactions listed above.

b. Prepare the stockholders' equity section of the balance sheet at the end of the current year. Assume that retained earnings at the end of the current year is $750,000.

P16.2 (LO 1) Excel (Entries for Conversion, Amortization, and Interest of Bonds) Volker Inc. issued $2,500,000 of convertible 10-year bonds on July 1, 2020. The bonds provide for 12% interest payable semiannually on January 1 and July 1. The discount in connection with the issue was $54,000, which is being amortized monthly on a straight-line basis.

The bonds are convertible after one year into 8 shares of Volker Inc.'s $100 par value common stock for each $1,000 of bonds.

On August 1, 2021, $250,000 of bonds were turned in for conversion into common stock. Interest has been accrued monthly and paid as due. At the time of conversion, any accrued interest on bonds being converted is paid in cash.

Instructions

Prepare the journal entries to record the conversion, amortization, and interest in connection with the bonds as of the following dates. (Round to the nearest dollar.)

a. August 1, 2021. (Assume the book value method is used.)

b. August 31, 2021.

c. December 31, 2021, including closing entries for end-of-year.

(AICPA adapted)

P16.3 (LO 3) Excel (Stock-Option Plan) Berg Company adopted a stock-option plan on November 30, 2019, that provided that 70,000 shares of $5 par value stock be designated as available for the granting of options to officers of the corporation at a price of $9 a share. The market price was $12 a share on November 30, 2020.

On January 2, 2020, options to purchase 28,000 shares were granted to president Tom Winter—15,000 for services to be rendered in 2020 and 13,000 for services to be rendered in 2021. Also on that date, options to purchase 14,000 shares were granted to vice president Michelle Bennett—7,000 for services to be rendered in 2020 and 7,000 for services to be rendered in 2021. The market price of the stock was $14 a share on January 2, 2020. The options were exercisable for a period of one year following the year in which the services were rendered. The fair value of the options on the grant date was $4 per option.

In 2021, neither the president nor the vice president exercised their options because the market price of the stock was below the exercise price. The market price of the stock was $8 a share on December 31, 2021, when the options for 2020 services lapsed.

On December 31, 2022, both president Winter and vice president Bennett exercised their options for 13,000 and 7,000 shares, respectively, when the market price was $16 a share.

Instructions

Prepare the necessary journal entries in 2019 when the stock-option plan was adopted, in 2020 when options were granted, in 2021 when options lapsed, and in 2022 when options were exercised.

P16.4 (LO 3) (Stock-Based Compensation) Assume that Amazon.com has a stock-option plan for top management. Each stock option represents the right to purchase a share of Amazon $1 par value common stock in the future at a price equal to the fair value of the stock at the date of the grant. Amazon has 5,000 stock options outstanding, which were granted at the beginning of 2020. The following data relate to the option grant.

Exercise price for options	$40
Market price at grant date (January 1, 2020)	$40
Fair value of options at grant date (January 1, 2020)	$6
Service period	5 years

Instructions

a. Prepare the journal entry(ies) for the first year of the stock-option plan.

b. Prepare the journal entry(ies) for the first year of the plan assuming that, rather than options, 700 shares of restricted stock were granted at the beginning of 2020.

c. Now assume that the market price of Amazon stock on the grant date was $45 per share. Repeat the requirements for (a) and (b).

d. Amazon would like to implement an employee stock-purchase plan for rank-and-file employees, but it would like to avoid recording expense related to this plan. Which of the following provisions must be in place for the plan to avoid recording compensation expense?

1. Substantially all employees may participate.
2. The discount from market is small (less than 5%).
3. The plan offers no substantive option feature.
4. There is no preferred stock outstanding.

P16.5 (LO 5) Groupwork (EPS with Complex Capital Structure) Amy Dyken, controller at Fitzgerald Pharmaceutical Industries, a public company, is currently preparing the calculation for basic and diluted earnings per share and the related disclosure for Fitzgerald's financial statements. Below is selected financial information for the fiscal year ended June 30, 2020.

Fitzgerald Pharmaceutical Industries
Selected Balance Sheet Information
June 30, 2020

Long-term debt	
Notes payable, 10%	$ 1,000,000
8% convertible bonds payable	5,000,000
10% bonds payable	6,000,000
Total long-term debt	$12,000,000
Shareholders' equity	
Preferred stock, 6% cumulative, $50 par value, 100,000 shares authorized, 25,000 shares issued and outstanding	$ 1,250,000
Common stock, $1 par, 10,000,000 shares authorized, 1,000,000 shares issued and outstanding	1,000,000
Additional paid-in capital	4,000,000
Retained earnings	6,000,000
Total shareholders' equity	$12,250,000

The following transactions have also occurred at Fitzgerald.

1. Options were granted on July 1, 2019, to purchase 200,000 shares at $15 per share. Although no options were exercised during fiscal year 2020, the average price per common share during fiscal year 2020 was $20 per share.

2. Each bond was issued at face value. The 8% convertible bonds will convert into common stock at 50 shares per $1,000 bond. The bonds are exercisable after 5 years and were issued in fiscal year 2019.
3. The preferred stock was issued in 2019.
4. There are no preferred dividends in arrears; however, preferred dividends were not declared in fiscal year 2020.
5. The 1,000,000 shares of common stock were outstanding for the entire 2020 fiscal year.
6. Net income for fiscal year 2020 was $1,500,000, and the average income tax rate is 20%.

Instructions

For the fiscal year ended June 30, 2020, calculate the following for Fitzgerald Pharmaceutical Industries.

a. Basic earnings per share.

b. Diluted earnings per share.

P16.6 **(LO 4)** **(Basic EPS: Two-Year Presentation)** Melton Corporation is preparing the comparative financial statements for the annual report to its shareholders for fiscal years ended May 31, 2020, and May 31, 2021. The income from operations for the fiscal year ended May 31, 2020, was $1,800,000 and income from continuing operations for the fiscal year ended May 31, 2021, was $2,500,000. In both years, the company incurred a 10% interest expense on $2,400,000 of debt, an obligation that requires interest-only payments for 5 years. The company experienced a loss from discontinued operations of $600,000 on February 2021. The company uses a 20% effective tax rate for income taxes.

The capital structure of Melton Corporation on June 1, 2019, consisted of 1 million shares of common stock outstanding and 20,000 shares of $50 par value, 6%, cumulative preferred stock. There were no preferred dividends in arrears, and the company had not issued any convertible securities, options, or warrants.

On October 1, 2019, Melton sold an additional 500,000 shares of the common stock at $20 per share. Melton distributed a 20% stock dividend on the common shares outstanding on January 1, 2020. On December 1, 2020, Melton was able to sell an additional 800,000 shares of the common stock at $22 per share. These were the only common stock transactions that occurred during the two fiscal years.

Instructions

a. Identify whether the capital structure at Melton Corporation is a simple or complex capital structure, and explain why.

b. Determine the weighted-average number of shares that Melton Corporation would use in calculating earnings per share for the fiscal year ended:

   1. May 31, 2020.
   2. May 31, 2021.

c. Prepare, in good form, a comparative income statement, beginning with income from operations, for Melton Corporation for the fiscal years ended May 31, 2020, and May 31, 2021. This statement will be included in Melton's annual report and should display the appropriate earnings per share presentations.

(CMA adapted)

P16.7 **(LO 4, 5)** **Groupwork** **(Computation of Basic and Diluted EPS)** Charles Austin of the controller's office of Thompson Corporation was given the assignment of determining the basic and diluted earnings per share values for the year ending December 31, 2021. Austin has compiled the information listed below.

1. The company is authorized to issue 8,000,000 shares of $10 par value common stock. As of December 31, 2020, 2,000,000 shares had been issued and were outstanding.
2. The per share market prices of the common stock on selected dates were as follows.

	Price per Share
July 1, 2020	$20.00
January 1, 2021	21.00
April 1, 2021	25.00
July 1, 2021	11.00
August 1, 2021	10.50
November 1, 2021	9.00
December 31, 2021	10.00

3. A total of 700,000 shares of an authorized 1,200,000 shares of convertible preferred stock had been issued on July 1, 2020. The stock was issued at its par value of $25, and it has a cumulative dividend of $3 per share. The stock is convertible into common stock at the rate of one share of convertible

preferred for one share of common. The rate of conversion is to be automatically adjusted for stock splits and stock dividends. Dividends are paid quarterly on September 30, December 31, March 31, and June 30.

4. Thompson Corporation is subject to a 20% income tax rate.
5. The after-tax net income for the year ended December 31, 2021, was $11,550,000.

The following specific activities took place during 2021.

1. January 1—A 5% common stock dividend was issued. The dividend had been declared on December 1, 2020, to all stockholders of record on December 29, 2020.
2. April 1—A total of 400,000 shares of the $3 convertible preferred stock was converted into common stock. The company issued new common stock and retired the preferred stock. This was the only conversion of the preferred stock during 2021.
3. July 1—A 2-for-1 split of the common stock became effective on this date. The board of directors had authorized the split on June 1.
4. August 1—A total of 300,000 shares of common stock were issued to acquire a factory building.
5. November 1—A total of 24,000 shares of common stock were purchased on the open market at $9 per share. These shares were to be held as treasury stock and were still in the treasury as of December 31, 2021.
6. Common stock cash dividends—Cash dividends to common stockholders were declared and paid as follows.

   April 15—$0.30 per share
   October 15—$0.20 per share

7. Preferred stock cash dividends—Cash dividends to preferred stockholders were declared and paid as scheduled.

Instructions

a. Determine the number of shares used to compute basic earnings per share for the year ended December 31, 2021.

b. Determine the number of shares used to compute diluted earnings per share for the year ended December 31, 2021.

c. Compute the adjusted net income to be used as the numerator in the basic earnings per share calculation for the year ended December 31, 2021.

P16.8 (LO 5) (Computation of Basic and Diluted EPS) The information below pertains to Barkley Company for 2021.

Net income for the year	$1,200,000
7% convertible bonds issued at par ($1,000 per bond); each bond is convertible into 30 shares of common stock	2,000,000
6% convertible, cumulative preferred stock, $100 par value; each share is convertible into 3 shares of common stock	4,000,000
Common stock, $10 par value	6,000,000
Tax rate for 2021	20%
Average market price of common stock	$25 per share

There were no changes during 2021 in the number of common shares, preferred shares, or convertible bonds outstanding. There is no treasury stock. The company also has common stock options (granted in a prior year) to purchase 75,000 shares of common stock at $20 per share.

Instructions

a. Compute basic earnings per share for 2021.

b. Compute diluted earnings per share for 2021.

P16.9 (LO 4) (EPS with Stock Dividend and Discontinued Operations) Christina Corporation is preparing the comparative financial statements to be included in the annual report to stockholders. Christina employs a fiscal year ending May 31.

Income from operations before income taxes for Christina was $1,400,000 and $660,000, respectively, for fiscal years ended May 31, 2021 and 2020. Christina experienced a loss from discontinued operations of $400,000 on March 3, 2021. A 20% combined income tax rate pertains to any and all of Christina Corporation's profits, gains, and losses.

Christina's capital structure consists of preferred stock and common stock. The company has not issued any convertible securities or warrants and there are no outstanding stock options.

Christina issued 40,000 shares of $100 par value, 6% cumulative preferred stock in 2017. All of this stock is outstanding, and no preferred dividends are in arrears.

There were 1,000,000 shares of $1 par common stock outstanding on June 1, 2019. On September 1, 2019, Christina sold an additional 400,000 shares of the common stock at $17 per share. Christina distributed a 20% stock dividend on the common shares outstanding on December 1, 2020. These were the only common stock transactions during the past 2 fiscal years.

Instructions

a. Determine the weighted-average number of common shares that would be used in computing earnings per share on the current comparative income statement for:

1. The year ended May 31, 2020.
2. The year ended May 31, 2021.

b. Starting with income from operations before income taxes, prepare a comparative income statement for the years ended May 31, 2021 and 2020. The statement will be part of Christina Corporation's annual report to stockholders and should include appropriate earnings per share presentation.

c. The capital structure of a corporation is the result of its past financing decisions. Furthermore, the earnings per share data presented on a corporation's financial statements is dependent upon the capital structure.

1. Explain why Christina Corporation is considered to have a simple capital structure.
2. Describe how earnings per share data would be presented for a corporation that has a complex capital structure.

(CMA adapted)

Concepts for Analysis

CA16.1 **(LO 2) (Warrants Issued with Bonds and Convertible Bonds)** Incurring long-term debt with an arrangement whereby lenders receive an option to buy common stock during all or a portion of the time the debt is outstanding is a frequent corporate financing practice. In some situations, the result is achieved through the issuance of convertible bonds; in others, the debt instruments and the warrants to buy stock are separate.

Instructions

a. 1. Describe the differences that exist in current accounting for original proceeds of the issuance of convertible bonds and of debt instruments with separate warrants to purchase common stock.

2. Discuss the underlying rationale for the differences described in (a)(1) above.
3. Summarize the arguments that have been presented in favor of accounting for convertible bonds in the same manner as accounting for debt with separate warrants.

b. At the start of the year, Huish Company issued $18,000,000 of 12% bonds along with detachable warrants to buy 1,200,000 shares of its $10 par value common stock at $18 per share. The bonds mature over the next 10 years, starting one year from date of issuance, with annual maturities of $1,800,000. At the time, Huish had 9,600,000 shares of common stock outstanding. The company received $20,040,000 for the bonds and the warrants. For Huish Company, 12% was a relatively low borrowing rate. If offered alone, at this time, the bonds would have sold in the market at a 22% discount. Prepare the journal entry (or entries) for the issuance of the bonds and warrants for the cash consideration received.

(AICPA adapted)

CA16.2 **(LO 3) Ethics (Ethical Issues—Compensation Plan)** The executive officers of Rouse Corporation have a performance-based compensation plan. The performance criteria of this plan is linked to growth in earnings per share. When annual EPS growth is 12%, the Rouse executives earn 100% of the shares; if growth is 16%, they earn 125%. If EPS growth is lower than 8%, the executives receive no additional compensation.

In 2020, Joan Devers, the controller of Rouse, reviews year-end estimates of bad debt expense and warranty expense. She calculates the EPS growth at 15%. Kurt Adkins, a member of the executive group, remarks over lunch one day that the estimate of bad debt expense might be decreased, increasing EPS growth to 16.1%. Devers is not sure she should do this because she believes that the current estimate of bad debts is sound. On the other hand, she recognizes that a great deal of subjectivity is involved in the computation.

Instructions

Answer the following questions.

a. What, if any, is the ethical dilemma for Devers?

b. Should Devers's knowledge of the compensation plan be a factor that influences her estimate?

c. How should Devers respond to Adkins's request?

CA16.3 **(LO 2, 3)** Writing **(Stock Warrants—Various Types)** For various reasons a corporation may issue warrants to purchase shares of its common stock at specified prices that, depending on the circumstances, may be less than, equal to, or greater than the current market price. For example, warrants may be issued:

1. To existing stockholders on a pro rata basis.

2. To certain key employees under an incentive stock-option plan.

3. To purchasers of the corporation's bonds.

Instructions

For each of the three examples of how stock warrants are used:

a. Explain why they are used.

b. Discuss the significance of the price (or prices) at which the warrants are issued (or granted) in relation to (1) the current market price of the company's stock, and (2) the length of time over which they can be exercised.

c. Describe the information that should be disclosed in financial statements, or notes thereto, that are prepared when stock warrants are outstanding in the hands of the three groups listed above.

(AICPA adapted)

CA16.4 **(LO 3)** Writing **(Stock Compensation Plans)** The following two items appeared on the Internet concerning the GAAP requirement to expense stock options.

> *WASHINGTON, D.C.—February 17, 2005* Congressman David Dreier (R–CA), Chairman of the House Rules Committee, and Congresswoman Anna Eshoo (D–CA) reintroduced legislation today that will preserve broad-based employee stock option plans and give investors critical information they need to understand how employee stock options impact the value of their shares.
>
> "Last year, the U.S. House of Representatives overwhelmingly voted for legislation that would have ensured the continued ability of innovative companies to offer stock options to rank-and-file employees," Dreier stated. "Both the Financial Accounting Standards Board (FASB) and the Securities and Exchange Commission (SEC) continue to ignore our calls to address legitimate concerns about the impact of FASB's new standard on workers' ability to have an ownership stake in the New Economy, and its failure to address the real need of shareholders: accurate and meaningful information about a company's use of stock options."
>
> "In December 2004, FASB issued a stock option expensing standard that will render a huge blow to the 21st century economy," Dreier said. "Their action and the SEC's apparent lack of concern for protecting shareholders, requires us to once again take a firm stand on the side of investors and economic growth. Giving investors the ability to understand how stock options impact the value of their shares is critical. And equally important is preserving the ability of companies to use this innovative tool to attract talented employees."
>
> *"Here We Go Again!" by Jack Ciesielski* (2/21/2005, *http://www.accountingobserver.com/blog/2005/02/here-we-go-again)* On February 17, Congressman David Dreier (R–CA), and Congresswoman Anna Eshoo (D–CA), officially entered Silicon Valley's bid to gum up the launch of honest reporting of stock option compensation: They co-sponsored a bill to "preserve broad-based employee stock option plans and give investors critical information they need to understand how employee stock options impact the value of their shares." You know what "critical information" they mean: stuff like the stock compensation for the top five officers in a company, with a rigged value set as close to zero as possible. Investors *crave* this kind of information. Other ways the good Congresspersons want to "help" investors: The bill "also requires the SEC to study the effectiveness of those disclosures over three years, during which time, no new accounting standard related to the treatment of stock options could be recognized. Finally, the bill requires the Secretary of Commerce to conduct a study and report to Congress on the impact of broad-based employee stock option plans on expanding employee corporate ownership, skilled worker recruitment and retention, research and innovation, economic growth, and international competitiveness."

It's the old "four corners" basketball strategy: stall, stall, stall. In the meantime, hope for regime change at your opponent, the FASB.

Instructions

a. What are the major recommendations of the stock-based compensation pronouncement?

b. How do the provisions of GAAP in this area differ from the bill introduced by members of Congress (Dreier and Eshoo), which would require expensing for options issued to only the top five officers in a company? Which approach do you think would result in more useful information? (Focus on comparability.)

c. The bill in Congress urges the FASB to develop a rule that preserves "the ability of companies to use this innovative tool to attract talented employees." Write a response to these Congress-people explaining the importance of neutrality in financial accounting and reporting.

CA16.5 **(LO 4, 5)** **(EPS: Preferred Dividends, Options, and Convertible Debt)** "Earnings per share" (EPS) is the most featured, single financial statistic about modern corporations. Daily published quotations of stock prices have recently been expanded to include for many securities a "times earnings" figure that is based on EPS. Stock analysts often focus their discussions on the EPS of the corporations they study.

Instructions

a. Explain how dividends or dividend requirements on any class of preferred stock that may be outstanding affect the computation of EPS.

b. One of the technical procedures applicable in EPS computations is the "treasury-stock method." Briefly describe the circumstances under which it might be appropriate to apply the treasury-stock method.

c. Convertible debentures are considered potentially dilutive common shares. Explain how convertible debentures are handled for purposes of EPS computations.

(AICPA adapted)

CA16.6 **(LO 4, 5)** **Writing** **(EPS, Antidilution)** Brad Dolan, a stockholder of Rhode Corporation, has asked you, the firm's accountant, to explain why his stock warrants were not included in diluted EPS. In order to explain this situation, you must briefly explain what dilutive securities are, why they are included in the EPS calculation, and why some securities are antidilutive and thus not included in this calculation.

Rhode Corporation earned $228,000 during the period, when it had an average of 100,000 shares of common stock outstanding. The common stock sold at an average market price of $25 per share during the period. Also outstanding were 30,000 warrants that could be exercised to purchase one share of common stock at $30 per warrant.

Instructions

Write Mr. Dolan a 1–1.5-page letter explaining why the warrants are not included in the calculation.

Using Your Judgment

Financial Reporting Problem

The Procter & Gamble Company (P&G)

The financial statements of P&G are presented in Appendix B. The company's complete annual report, including the notes to the financial statements, is available online.

Instructions

Refer to P&G's financial statements and accompanying notes to answer the following questions.

a. Under P&G's stock-based compensation plan, stock options are granted annually to key managers and directors.

1. How many options were granted during 2017 under the plan?
2. How many options were exercisable at June 30, 2017?
3. How many options were exercised in 2017, and what was the average price of those exercised?
4. What is the total stock-based compensation expense for stock options and the total compensation expense for restricted stock, restricted stock units (RSUs), and performance stock units (PSUs) for 2017, 2016, and 2015?
5. To what accounts are the proceeds from these option exercises credited?
6. What was the number of outstanding options at June 30, 2017, and at what average exercise price?

b. What number of diluted weighted-average common shares outstanding was used by P&G in computing earnings per share for 2017, 2016, and 2015? What was P&G's diluted earnings per share in 2017, 2016, and 2015?

c. What other stock-based compensation plans does P&G have?

Comparative Analysis Case

The Coca-Cola Company and PepsiCo, Inc.

The financial statements of **Coca-Cola** and **PepsiCo** are presented in Appendices C and D, respectively. The companies' complete annual reports, including the notes to the financial statements, are available online.

Instructions

Use the companies' financial information to answer the following questions.

a. What employee stock-option compensation plans are offered by Coca-Cola and PepsiCo?

b. How many options are outstanding at year-end 2017 for both Coca-Cola and PepsiCo?

c. How many options were granted by Coca-Cola and PepsiCo to officers and employees during 2017?

d. How many options were exercised during 2017?

e. What was the average exercise price for Coca-Cola and PepsiCo employees at December 31, 2017?

f. What was the diluted net income per share for Coca-Cola and PepsiCo for 2017, 2016, and 2015?

Financial Statement Analysis Case

Ragatz, Inc.

Ragatz, Inc., a drug company, reported the following information. The company prepares its financial statements in accordance with GAAP.

	2020 (,000)
Current liabilities	$ 554,114
Convertible subordinated debt	648,020
Total liabilities	1,228,313
Stockholders' equity	176,413
Net income	58,333

Analysts attempting to compare Ragatz to drug companies that issue debt with detachable warrants may face a challenge due to differences in accounting for convertible debt.

Instructions

a. Compute the following ratios for Ragatz, Inc. (Assume that year-end balances approximate annual averages.)

1. Return on assets.
2. Return on common stock equity.
3. Debt to assets ratio.

b. Briefly discuss the operating performance and financial position of Ragatz. Industry averages for these ratios in 2020 were ROA 3.5%, return on equity 16%, and debt to assets 75%. Based on this analysis, would you make an investment in the company's 5% convertible bonds? Explain.

c. Assume you want to compare Ragatz to an IFRS company like **Merck** (which issues nonconvertible debt with detachable warrants). Assuming that the fair value of the equity component of Ragatz's convertible bonds is $150,000, how would you adjust the analysis above to make valid comparisons between Ragatz and Merck?

Accounting, Analysis, and Principles

On January 1, 2019, Garner issued 10-year, $200,000 face value, 6% bonds at par. Each $1,000 bond is convertible into 30 shares of Garner $2 par value common stock. The company has had 10,000 shares of common stock (and no preferred stock) outstanding throughout its life. None of the bonds have been converted as of the end of 2020. (Ignore all tax effects.)

Accounting

a. Prepare the journal entry Garner would have made on January 1, 2019, to record the issuance of the bonds.

b. Garner's net income in 2020 was $30,000 and was $27,000 in 2019. Compute basic and diluted earnings per share for Garner for 2020 and 2019.

c. Assume that 75% of the holders of Garner's convertible bonds convert their bonds to stock on June 30, 2021, when Garner's stock is trading at $32 per share. Garner pays $50 per bond to induce bondholders to convert. Prepare the journal entry to record the conversion.

Analysis

Show how Garner will report income and EPS for 2020 and 2019. Briefly discuss the importance of GAAP for EPS to analysts evaluating companies based on price-earnings ratios. Consider comparisons for a company over time, as well as comparisons between companies at a point in time.

Principles

In order to converge GAAP and IFRS, the FASB is considering whether the equity element of a convertible bond should be reported as equity. Describe how the journal entry you made in part (a) above would differ under IFRS. In terms of the accounting principles discussed in Chapter 2, what does IFRS for convertible debt accomplish that GAAP potentially sacrifices? What does GAAP for convertible debt accomplish that IFRS potentially sacrifices?

Bridge to the Profession

FASB Codification References

[1] FASB ASC 480-10-25. [Predecessor literature: "Accounting for Certain Financial Instruments with Characteristics of Both Liabilities and Equity," *Statement of Financial Accounting Standards No. 150* (Norwalk, Conn.: FASB, 2003), par. 23.]

[2] FASB ASC 470-20-25-1 to 2. [Predecessor literature: "Accounting for Convertible Debt and Debt Issued with Stock Purchase Warrants," *Opinions of the Accounting Principles Board No. 14* (New York, NY: AICPA, 1973).]

[3] FASB ASC 470-20-30. [Predecessor literature: "Accounting for Convertible Debt Instruments that May Be Settled in Cash Upon Conversion," *FASB Staff Position No. 14-1* (Norwalk, Conn.: FASB, 2008).]

[4] FASB ASC 718-10-10. [Predecessor literature: "Accounting for Stock-Based Compensation," *Statement of Financial Accounting Standards No. 123* (Norwalk, Conn.: FASB, 1995); and "Share-Based Payment," *Statement of Financial Accounting Standard No. 123(R)* (Norwalk, Conn.: FASB, 2004).]

[5] FASB ASC 260-10-45-2. [Predecessor literature: "Earnings per Share," *Statement of Financial Accounting Standards No. 128* (Norwalk, Conn.: FASB, 1997).]

[6] FASB ASC 260-10-50. [Predecessor literature: "Earnings per Share," *Statement of Financial Accounting Standards No. 128*, (Norwalk, Conn.: FASB, 1997.)]

Codification Exercises

If your school has a subscription to the FASB Codification, log in and prepare responses to the following. Provide Codification references for your responses.

CE16.1 Access the glossary ("Master Glossary") to answer the following.

a. What is the definition of "basic earnings per share"?

b. What is "dilution"?

c. What is a "warrant"?

d. What is a "grant date"?

CE16.2 For how many periods must a company present EPS data?

CE16.3 For each period that an income statement is presented, what must a company disclose about its EPS?

CE16.4 If a company's outstanding shares are increased through a stock dividend or a stock split, how would that alter the presentation of its EPS data?

Codification Research Case

Richardson Company is contemplating the establishment of a share-based compensation plan to provide long-run incentives for its top management. However, members of the compensation committee of the board of directors have voiced some concerns about adopting these plans, based on news accounts related to a recent accounting standard in this area. They would like you to conduct some research on this recent standard so they can be better informed about the accounting for these plans.

Instructions

If your school has a subscription to the FASB Codification, log in and prepare responses to the following. Provide Codification references for your responses.

a. Identify the authoritative literature that addresses the accounting for share-based payment compensation plans.

b. Briefly discuss the objectives for the accounting for stock compensation. What is the role of fair value measurement?

c. The Richardson Company board is also considering an employee share-purchase plan, but the Board does not want to record expense related to the plan. What criteria must be met to avoid recording expense on an employee stock-purchase plan?

Additional Professional Resources

Go to WileyPLUS for other career-readiness resources, such as career coaching, internship opportunities, and CPAexcel prep.

IFRS Insights

LEARNING OBJECTIVE 8

Compare the accounting for dilutive securities and earnings per share under GAAP and IFRS.

The primary IFRS related to financial instruments, including dilutive securities, is *IAS 39*, "Financial Instruments: Recognition and Measurement." The accounting for various forms of stock-based compensation under IFRS is found in *IFRS 2*, "Share-Based Payment." This standard was recently amended, resulting in significant convergence between IFRS and GAAP in this area. The IFRS addressing accounting and reporting for earnings per share computations is *IAS 33*, "Earnings per Share."

Relevant Facts

Following are the key similarities and differences between GAAP and IFRS related to dilutive securities and earnings per share.

Similarities

- IFRS and GAAP follow the same model for recognizing stock-based compensation: The fair value of shares and options awarded to employees is recognized over the period to which the employees' services relate.
- Although the calculation of basic and diluted earnings per share is similar between IFRS and GAAP, the Boards have worked to resolve the few minor differences in EPS reporting. One proposal in the FASB project concerns contracts that can be settled in either cash or shares. IFRS requires that share settlement must be used, while GAAP gives companies a choice. If the FASB adopts the IFRS approach, GAAP and IFRS would be converged in this regard.

Differences

- A significant difference between IFRS and GAAP is the accounting for securities with characteristics of debt and equity, such as convertible debt. Under GAAP, all of the proceeds of convertible debt are recorded as long-term debt. Under IFRS, convertible bonds are "bifurcated"—separated into the equity component (the value of the conversion option) of the bond issue and the debt component.
- Related to employee share-purchase plans, under IFRS, all employee share-purchase plans are deemed to be compensatory; that is, compensation expense is recorded for the amount of the discount. Under GAAP, these plans are often considered noncompensatory and therefore no compensation is recorded. Certain conditions must exist before a plan can be considered noncompensatory—the most important being that the discount generally cannot exceed 5 percent.
- Modification of a share option results in the recognition of any incremental fair value under both IFRS and GAAP. However, if the modification leads to a reduction, IFRS does not permit the reduction but GAAP does.
- Other EPS differences relate to (1) the treasury-stock method and how the proceeds from extinguishment of a liability should be accounted for, and (2) how to compute the weighted average of contingently issuable shares.

About the Numbers

Accounting for Convertible Debt

Convertible debt is accounted for as a **compound instrument** because it contains both a liability and an equity component. IFRS requires that compound instruments be separated into their liability and equity components for purposes of accounting. Companies use the **"with-and-without" method** to value compound instruments. **Illustration IFRS16.1** identifies the components used in the with-and-without method.

ILLUSTRATION IFRS16.1

Convertible Debt Components

Fair value of convertible debt at date of issuance (with both debt and equity components)	−	Fair value of liability component at date of issuance, based on present value of cash flows	=	Equity component at date of issuance (without the debt component)

As indicated, the equity component is the residual amount after subtracting the liability component. IFRS does not permit companies to assign a value to the equity amount first and then determine the liability component. To do so would be inconsistent with the definition of equity, which is considered a residual amount. To implement the with-and-without approach, companies do the following.

1. First, the company determines the total fair value of the convertible debt *with* both the liability and equity component. **This is straightforward, as this amount is the proceeds received upon issuance.**
2. The company then determines the liability component by computing the net present value of all contractual future cash flows discounted at the market rate of interest. This market rate is the rate the company would pay on similar nonconvertible debt.
3. In the final step, the company subtracts the liability component estimated in the second step from the fair value of the convertible debt (issue proceeds) to arrive at the equity component. That is, the equity component is the fair value of the convertible debt *without* the liability component.

Accounting at Time of Issuance To illustrate the accounting for convertible debt, assume that **Roche Group** issues 2,000 convertible bonds at the beginning of 2019. The bonds have a four-year term with a stated rate of interest of 6 percent, and are issued at par with a face value of $1,000 per bond (the total proceeds received from issuance of the bonds are $2,000,000). Interest is payable annually at December 31. Each bond is convertible into 250 ordinary shares with a par value of $1. The market rate of interest on similar nonconvertible debt is 9 percent. The time diagram in **Illustration IFRS16.2** depicts both the interest and principal cash flows.

ILLUSTRATION IFRS16.2

Time Diagram for Convertible Bond

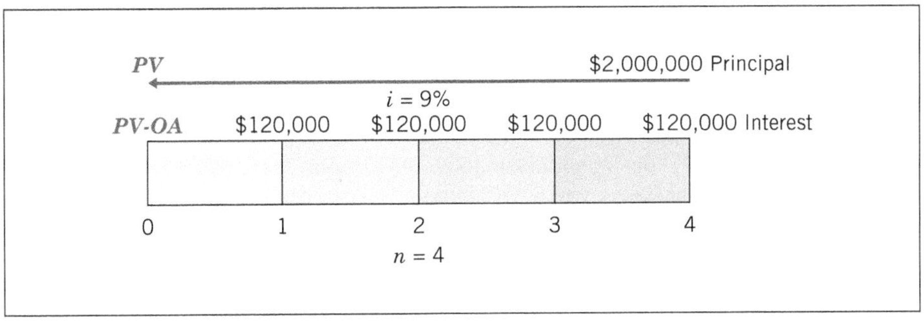

The liability component of the convertible debt is computed as shown in **Illustration IFRS16.3**.

ILLUSTRATION IFRS16.3

Fair Value of Liability Component of Convertible Bond

Present value of principal: $2,000,000 × .70843 (Table 6.2; $n = 4$, $i = 9\%$)	$1,416,860
Present value of the interest payments: $120,000 × 3.23972 (Table 6.4; $n = 4$, $i = 9\%$)	388,766
Present value of the liability component	$1,805,626

The equity component of Roche's convertible debt is then computed as shown in **Illustration IFRS16.4**.

ILLUSTRATION IFRS16.4

Equity Component of Convertible Bond

Fair value of convertible debt at date of issuance	$2,000,000
Less: Fair value of liability component at date of issuance	1,805,626
Fair value of equity component at date of issuance	$ 194,374

The journal entry to record this transaction is as follows.

Cash	2,000,000	
Bonds Payable		1,805,626
Share Premium—Conversion Equity		194,374

The liability component of Roche's convertible debt issue is recorded as Bonds Payable. As shown in Chapter 14, the amount of the discount relative to the face value of the bond is amortized at each reporting period so at maturity, the Bonds Payable account is reported at $2,000,000 (face value). The equity component of the convertible bond is recorded in the Share Premium—Conversion Equity account and is reported in the equity section of the statement of financial position. Because this amount is considered part of contributed capital, it does not change over the life of the convertible. **Transaction costs related to the liability and equity components are allocated in proportion to the proceeds received from the two components.** *For purposes of homework, use the Share Premium—Conversion Equity account to record the equity component.* **In practice, there may be considerable variation in the accounts used to record this component.**

Settlement of Convertible Bonds We illustrate four settlement situations: (1) repurchase at maturity, (2) conversion at maturity, (3) conversion before maturity, and (4) repurchase before maturity.

Repurchase at Maturity If the bonds are not converted at maturity, Roche makes the following entry to pay off the convertible debtholders.

Bonds Payable	2,000,000	
Cash		2,000,000
(To record the purchase of bonds at maturity)		

Because the carrying value of the bonds equals the face value, there is no gain or loss on repurchase at maturity. The amount originally allocated to equity of $194,374 either remains in the Share Premium—Conversion Equity account or is transferred to Share Premium—Ordinary.

Conversion of Bonds at Maturity If the bonds are converted at maturity, Roche makes the following entry.

Share Premium—Conversion Equity	194,374	
Bonds Payable	2,000,000	
Share Capital—Ordinary		500,000
Share Premium—Ordinary		1,694,374
(To record the conversion of bonds at maturity)		

As indicated, Roche records a credit to Share Capital—Ordinary for $500,000 (2,000 bonds × 250 shares × $1 par) and the remainder to Share Premium—Ordinary for $1,694,374. There is no gain or loss on conversion at maturity. The original amount allocated to equity ($194,374) is transferred to the Share Premium—Ordinary account. As a result, Roche's equity has increased by a total of $2,000,000 through issuance and conversion of the convertible bonds. This accounting approach is often referred to as the **book value method** in that the carrying amount (book value) of the bond and related conversion equity determines the amount in the ordinary equity accounts.

Conversion of Bonds Before Maturity What happens if bonds are converted before maturity? To understand the accounting, we again use the Roche Group example. A schedule of bond amortization related to Roche's convertible bonds is shown in Illustration IFRS16.5.

ILLUSTRATION IFRS16.5

Convertible Bond Amortization Schedule

Schedule of Bond Amortization
Effective-Interest Method
6% Bond Discounted at 9%

Date	Cash Paid	Interest Expense (9%)	Discount Amortized	Carrying Amount of Bonds
1/1/19				$1,805,626
12/31/19	$120,000	$162,506	$42,506	1,848,132
12/31/20	120,000	166,332	46,332	1,894,464
12/31/21	120,000	170,502	50,502	1,944,966
12/31/22	120,000	175,034*	55,034	2,000,000

*$13 difference due to rounding.

Assuming that Roche converts its bonds into ordinary shares on December 31, 2020, Roche debits the Bonds Payable account for its carrying value of $1,894,464 (see Illustration IFRS16.5). In addition, Roche credits Share Capital—Ordinary for $500,000 (2,000 × 250 × $1) and credits Share Premium—Ordinary for $1,588,838. The entry to record this conversion is as follows.

Share Premium—Conversion Equity	194,374	
Bonds Payable	1,894,464	
Share Capital—Ordinary		500,000
Share Premium—Ordinary		1,588,838
(To record the conversion of bonds before maturity)		

There is no gain or loss on conversion before maturity: The original amount allocated to equity ($194,374) is transferred to the Share Premium—Ordinary account.

Repurchase Before Maturity In some cases, companies decide to repurchase the convertible debt before maturity. The approach used for allocating the amount paid upon repurchase follows the approach used when the convertible bond was originally issued. That is, Roche determines the fair value of the liability component of the convertible bonds at December 31, 2020, and then subtracts this amount from the fair value of the convertible bond issue (including the equity component) to arrive at the value for the equity. After this allocation is completed:

1. The difference between the consideration allocated to the liability component and the carrying amount of the liability is recognized as a gain or loss, and
2. The amount of consideration relating to the equity component is recognized (as a reduction) in equity.

To illustrate, instead of converting the bonds on December 31, 2020, assume that Roche repurchases the convertible bonds from the bondholders. Pertinent information related to this conversion is as follows.

- Fair value of the convertible debt (including both liability and equity components), based on market prices at December 31, 2020, is $1,965,000.
- The fair value of the liability component is $1,904,900. This amount is based on computing the present value of a nonconvertible bond with a two-year term (which corresponds to the shortened time to maturity of the repurchased bonds).

We first determine the gain or loss on the liability component, as computed in Illustration IFRS16.6.

ILLUSTRATION IFRS16.6

Gain or Loss on Debt Repurchase

Present value of liability component at December 31, 2020 (given above)	$ 1,904,900
Carrying value of liability component at December 31, 2020 (per Illustration IFRS16.5)	(1,894,464)
Loss on repurchase	$ 10,436

Roche has a loss on this repurchase because the value of the debt extinguished is greater than its carrying amount. To determine any adjustment to equity, we compute the value of the equity as shown in Illustration IFRS16.7.

ILLUSTRATION IFRS16.7

Equity Adjustment on Repurchase of Convertible Bonds

Fair value of convertible debt at December 31, 2020 (**with equity component**)	$1,965,000
Less: Fair value of liability component at December 31, 2020 (similar 2-year nonconvertible debt)	1,904,900
Fair value of equity component at December 31, 2020 (**without debt component**)	$ 60,100

Roche makes the following compound journal entry to record the entire repurchase transaction.

Bonds Payable	1,894,464	
Share Premium—Conversion Equity	60,100	
Loss on Repurchase	10,436	
Cash		1,965,000
(To record the repurchase of convertible bonds)		

In summary, the repurchase results in a loss related to the liability component and a reduction in Share Premium—Conversion Equity. The remaining balance in Share Premium—Conversion Equity of $134,274 ($194,374 – $60,100) is often transferred to Share Premium—Ordinary upon the repurchase.

Employee Share-Purchase Plans

Employee share-purchase plans (ESPPs) generally permit all employees to purchase shares at a discounted price for a short period of time. The company often uses such plans to secure equity capital or to induce widespread ownership of its ordinary shares among employees. **These plans are considered compensatory and should be recorded as expense over the service period.**

To illustrate, assume that Masthead Company offers all its 1,000 employees the opportunity to participate in an employee share-purchase plan. Under the terms of the plan, the employees are entitled to purchase 100 ordinary shares (par value $1 per share) at a 20 percent discount. The purchase price must be paid immediately upon acceptance of the offer. In total, 800 employees accept the offer, and each employee purchases on average 80 shares. That is, the employees purchase a total of 64,000 shares. The weighted-average market price of the shares at the purchase date is $30 per share, and the weighted-average purchase price is $24 per share. The entry to record this transaction is as follows.

Cash (64,000 × $24)	1,536,000	
Compensation Expense [64,000 × ($30 − $24)]	384,000	
Share Capital—Ordinary (64,000 × $1)		64,000
Share Premium—Ordinary		1,856,000
(Issue shares in an employee share-purchase plan)		

The IASB indicates that there is no reason to treat broad-based employee share plans differently from other employee share plans. Some have argued that because these plans are used to raise capital, they should not be compensatory. However, IFRS requires recording expense for these arrangements. The Board notes that because these arrangements are available only to employees, it is sufficient to conclude that the benefits provided represent employee compensation.

On the Horizon

As discussed in the chapter, the FASB is working on a standard that will likely converge to IFRS in the accounting for convertible debt. Similar to the FASB, the IASB is examining the classification of hybrid securities; the IASB is also examining *Financial Instruments with Characteristics of Equity.* While GAAP and IFRS are similar as to the presentation of EPS, the Boards have worked together to resolve remaining differences related to earnings per share computations.

IFRS Self-Test Questions

1. All of the following are key similarities between GAAP and IFRS with respect to accounting for dilutive securities and EPS **except**:

   a. the model for recognizing stock-based compensation.

   b. the calculation of basic and diluted EPS.

   c. the accounting for convertible debt.

   d. the accounting for modifications of share options, when the value increases.

2. Which of the following statements is **correct**?

   a. IFRS separates the proceeds of a convertible bond between debt and equity by determining the fair value of the debt component before the equity component.

   b. Both IFRS and GAAP assume that when there is choice of settlement of an option for cash or shares, share settlement is assumed.

   c. IFRS separates the proceeds of a convertible bond between debt and equity, based on relative fair values.

   d. Both GAAP and IFRS separate the proceeds of convertible bonds between debt and equity.

3. Under IFRS, convertible bonds:

   a. are separated into the bond component and the expense component.

   b. are separated into debt and equity components.

   c. are separated into their components based on relative fair values.

   d. All of the above.

4. Mae Jong Corp. issues $1,000,000 of 10% bonds payable which may be converted into 10,000 shares of $2 par value ordinary shares. The market rate of interest on similar bonds is 12%. Interest is payable annually on December 31, and the bonds were issued for total proceeds of $1,000,000. In accounting for these bonds, Mae Jong Corp. will:

   a. first assign a value to the equity component, then determine the liability component.

   b. assign no value to the equity component since the conversion privilege is not separable from the bond.

   c. first assign a value to the liability component based on the face amount of the bond.

   d. use the "with-and-without" method to value the compound instrument.

5. Anazazi Co. offers all its 10,000 employees the opportunity to participate in an employee share-purchase plan. Under the terms of the plan, the employees are entitled to purchase 100 ordinary shares (par value $1 per share) at a 20% discount. The purchase price must be paid immediately upon acceptance of the offer. In total, 8,500 employees accept the offer, and each employee purchases on average 80 shares at $22 per share (market price $27.50). Under IFRS, Anazazi Co. will record:

   a. no compensation since the plan is used to raise capital, not compensate employees.

   b. compensation expense of $5,500,000.

   c. compensation expense of $18,700,000.

   d. compensation expense of $3,740,000.

IFRS Concepts and Application

IFRS16.1 Where can authoritative IFRS be found related to dilutive securities, stock-based compensation, and earnings per share?

IFRS16.2 Briefly describe some of the similarities and differences between GAAP and IFRS with respect to the accounting for dilutive securities, stock-based compensation, and earnings per share.

IFRS16.3 Norman Co., a fast-growing golf equipment company, uses GAAP. It is considering the issuance of convertible bonds. The bonds mature in 10 years, have a face value of $400,000, and pay interest annually at a rate of 4%. The equity component of the bond issue has a fair value of $35,000. Greg Shark is curious as to the difference in accounting for these bonds if the company were to use IFRS. (a) Prepare the entry to record issuance of the bonds at par under GAAP. (b) Repeat the requirement for part (a), assuming application of IFRS to the bond issuance. (c) Which approach provides the better accounting? Explain.

IFRS16.4 Briefly discuss the convergence efforts that are under way by the IASB and FASB in the area of dilutive securities and earnings per share.

IFRS16.5 Explain how the conversion feature of convertible debt has a value (a) to the issuer and (b) to the purchaser.

IFRS16.6 What are the arguments for giving separate accounting recognition to the conversion feature of debentures?

IFRS16.7 Four years after issue, debentures with a face value of $1,000,000 and book value of $960,000 are tendered for conversion into 80,000 ordinary shares immediately after an interest payment date. At that time, the market price of the debentures is 104, and the ordinary shares are selling at $14 per share (par value $10). At date of issue, the company recorded Share Premium—Conversion Equity of $50,000. The company records the conversion as follows.

Bonds Payable	960,000	
Share Premium—Conversion Equity	50,000	
Share Capital—Ordinary		800,000
Share Premium—Ordinary		210,000

Discuss the propriety of this accounting treatment.

IFRS16.8 Cordero Corporation has an employee share-purchase plan which permits all full-time employees to purchase 10 ordinary shares on the third anniversary of their employment and an additional 15 shares on each subsequent anniversary date. The purchase price is set at the market price on the date purchased less a 10% discount. How is this discount accounted for by Cordero?

IFRS16.9 Archer Company issued $4,000,000 par value, 7% convertible bonds at 99 for cash. The net present value of the debt without the conversion feature is $3,800,000. Prepare the journal entry to record the issuance of the convertible bonds.

IFRS16.10 Petrenko Corporation has outstanding 2,000 $1,000 bonds, each convertible into 50 shares of $10 par value ordinary shares. The bonds are converted on December 31, 2020. The bonds payable has a carrying value of $1,950,000 and conversion equity of $20,000. Record the conversion using the book value method.

IFRS16.11 Angela Corporation issues 2,000 convertible bonds at January 1, 2019. The bonds have a 3-year life, and are issued at par with a face value of $1,000 per bond, giving total proceeds of $2,000,000. Interest is payable annually at 6%. Each bond is convertible into 250 ordinary shares (par value of $1). When the bonds are issued, the market rate of interest for similar debt without the conversion option is 8%.

Instructions

a. Compute the liability and equity component of the convertible bond on January 1, 2019.

b. Prepare the journal entry to record the issuance of the convertible bond on January 1, 2019.

c. Prepare the journal entry to record the repurchase of the convertible bond for cash at January 1, 2022, its maturity date.

IFRS16.12 Assume the same information in IFRS16.11, except that Angela Corporation converts its convertible bonds on January 1, 2020.

Instructions

a. Compute the carrying value of the bond payable on January 1, 2020.

b. Prepare the journal entry to record the conversion on January 1, 2020.

c. Assume that the bonds were repurchased on January 1, 2020, for $1,940,000 cash instead of being converted. The net present value of the liability component of the convertible bonds on January 1, 2020, is $1,900,000. Prepare the journal entry to record the repurchase on January 1, 2020.

IFRS16.13 Assume that Sarazan Company has a share-option plan for top management. Each share option represents the right to purchase a $1 par value ordinary share in the future at a price equal to the fair value of the shares at the date of the grant. Sarazan has 5,000 share options outstanding, which were granted at the beginning of 2020. The following data relate to the option grant.

Exercise price for options	$40
Market price at grant date (January 1, 2020)	$40
Fair value of options at grant date (January 1, 2020)	$6
Service period	5 years

Instructions

a. Prepare the journal entry(ies) for the first year of the share-option plan.

b. Prepare the journal entry(ies) for the first year of the plan assuming that, rather than options, 700 shares of restricted shares were granted at the beginning of 2020.

c. Now assume that the market price of Sarazan shares on the grant date was $45 per share. Repeat the requirements for (a) and (b).

d. Sarazan would like to implement an employee share-purchase plan for rank-and-file employees, but it would like to avoid recording expense related to this plan. Explain how employee share-purchase plans are recorded.

Professional Research

IFRS16.14 Richardson Company is contemplating the establishment of a share-based compensation plan to provide long-run incentives for its top management. However, members of the compensation committee of the board of directors have voiced some concerns about adopting these plans, based on news accounts related to a recent accounting standard in this area. They would like you to conduct some research on this recent standard so they can be better informed about the accounting for these plans.

Instructions

Access the IFRS authoritative literature at the IASB website. (Click on the IFRS tab and then register for free eIFRS access if necessary.) When you have accessed the documents, you can use the search tool in your Internet browser to respond to the following questions. (Provide paragraph citations.)

a. Identify the authoritative literature that addresses the accounting for share-based payment compensation plans.

b. Briefly discuss the objectives for the accounting for share-based compensation. What is the role of fair value measurement?

c. The Richardson Company board is also considering an employee share-purchase plan, but the Board does not want to record expense related to the plan. What are the IFRS requirements for the accounting for an employee share-purchase plan?

International Financial Reporting Problem

Marks and Spencer plc (M&S)

IFRS16.15 The financial statements of M&S are presented in Appendix E. The company's complete annual report, including the notes to the financial statements, is available online.

Instructions

Refer to M&S's financial statements and the accompanying notes to answer the following questions.

a. Under M&S's share-based compensation plan, share options are granted annually to key managers and directors.

1. What is M&S's accounting policies related to share-based payments?
2. How many options were granted during 2017 under the plan?
3. How many options were exercisable at 1 April 2017?
4. How many options were exercised in 2017, and what was the average price of those exercised?
5. To what accounts are the proceeds from these option exercises credited?
6. What was the number of outstanding options at 1 April 2017, and at what average exercise price?

b. What number of diluted weighted-average shares outstanding was used by M&S in computing earnings per share for 2017 and 2016?

c. What was M&S's diluted earnings per share in 2017 and 2016?

Answers to IFRS Self-Test Questions

1. c **2.** a **3.** b **4.** d **5.** d

CHAPTER **17**

© andersphoto/Shutterstock

Investments

LEARNING OBJECTIVES

After studying this chapter, you should be able to:

1. Describe the accounting for investments in debt securities.
2. Describe the accounting for investments in equity securities.
3. Explain the equity and consolidation methods of accounting.
4. Evaluate other major issues related to investments in debt and equity securities.

PREVIEW OF CHAPTER 17 As indicated in the following opening story, the accounting for financial assets is highly controversial. How to measure, recognize, and disclose this information is being debated and discussed extensively. In this chapter, we address the accounting for debt and equity investments. Appendices to this chapter discuss the accounting for derivative instruments and fair value disclosures. The content and organization of this chapter are as follows.

This chapter also includes numerous conceptual and global discussions that are integral to the topics presented here.

INVESTMENTS

Investments in Debt Securities
- Debt investment classifications
- Held-to-maturity securities
- Available-for-sale securities
- Trading securities

Investments in Equity Securities
- Holdings of less than 20%
- Holdings between 20% and 50%
- Holdings of more than 50%

Other Financial Reporting Issues
- Fair value option
- Impairment of value
- Reclassification adjustments
- Transfers related to debt securities
- Summary

Winners and Losers

Valuing financial assets such as loans, derivatives, and other debt investments as well as equity investments is a challenge. The fundamental question is: Should financial instruments be valued at amortized cost, fair value, or some other measure(s)? As one writer noted, the opinion that fair value accounting weakens financial and economic stability has persisted among many companies, regulators, and politicians. On the other hand, investors and others believe that fair value is the right answer because it is more transparent information. Ok, so what to do?

Recently, the FASB issued a new standard in this area. This new standard lets companies report loans at amortized cost. This decision means that banks will continue to value loans as they do today. The continued use of amortized cost for these debt securities is a big victory for the banking industry, which argued that the fair value approach would hurt lending and provide unnecessary volatility in the financial statements.

However, the FASB took a different approach with respect to equity investments. It now requires that most equity investments should be reported at fair value. And some companies are not happy with this new requirement. For example, Warren Buffett's **Berkshire Hathaway** posted a $1.14 billion first quarter loss in 2018 because of $6.2 billion losses on equity investments that the company must now count in income as a result of the new standard. These losses resulted because of the following equity investments: shares of **Wells Fargo** lost 13.6 percent during the quarter, **Coca-Cola** shares lost 5.3 percent, and **American Express** was down 6.1 percent.

Buffett was not happy to have to report these losses, indicating that this new measurement distorts Berkshire's earnings. Specifically, "these investment gains and losses are often meaningless in terms of understanding our reported results or evaluating our periodic economic performance." He went on to note: "If you look at the figure of operating earnings—which we look at—we actually earned a record amount in any quarter we've ever had."

At the same time, other companies benefited from the change in accounting for equity investments. For example, **Alphabet** (Google's parent) reported a $3 billion gain as a result of equity investments in **Uber Technologies** and other hot technology companies that are closely held.

Sources: "Financial Instruments—Overall Recognition and Measurement of Financial Assets and Financial Liabilities," *Accounting Standards Update No. 2016-1* (Norwalk, Conn.: FASB, 2016); and M. Rapoport, "Warren Buffett's New Target: Rule That Cut $6.2 Billion from Berkshire Earnings," *Wall Street Journal* (May 7, 2018).

Review and Practice

Go to the **Review and Practice** section at the end of the chapter for a targeted summary review and practice problem with solution. Multiple-choice questions with annotated solutions as well as additional exercises and practice problem with solutions are also available online.

Investments in Debt Securities

LEARNING OBJECTIVE 1

Describe the accounting for investments in debt securities.

In Chapter 7, we discussed two types of financial assets—cash and receivables (primarily short-term). In this chapter, we discuss two other financial assets—debt investments and stock investments.[1] Companies have different motivations for investing in debt or equity securities issued by other companies. **One motivation is to earn a high rate of return.** For example, companies like **Coca-Cola** and **PepsiCo** can receive interest revenue from a debt investment or dividend revenue from an equity investment. In addition, they can realize capital gains on both types of securities. **Another motivation for investing (in equity securities) is to secure certain operating or financing arrangements with another company.** For example, Coca-Cola and PepsiCo are able to exercise some control over bottler companies based on their significant (but not controlling) equity investments.

[1] A financial asset is an asset whose value comes from a contractual claim to cash flows. Examples of financial assets (in addition to cash and receivables) are equity investments in another company (e.g., common or preferred stock) or a contractual right to receive cash from another party (e.g., loans and bonds). In contrast, the value of physical assets such as land and buildings comes from their use in the business and is not from a contractual claim.

To provide useful information, companies account for investments based on the type of security (debt or equity) and their intent with respect to the investment. As indicated in **Illustration 17.1**, we organize our study of investments by type of security. Within this section, we explain the accounting for investments in debt. We address equity securities later in the chapter.

ILLUSTRATION 17.1
Summary of Investment Accounting Approaches

Type of Security	Management Intent	Valuation Approach
Debt	No plans to sell	Amortized cost
	Plan to sell	Fair value
Equity	Plan to sell	Fair value
	Exercise some control	Equity method

Debt Investment Classifications

Debt securities represent a creditor relationship with another entity. Debt securities include U.S. government securities, municipal securities, corporate bonds, convertible debt, and commercial paper. Trade accounts receivable and loans receivable are not debt securities because they do not meet the definition of a security.[2]

Companies group investments in debt securities into three separate categories for accounting and reporting purposes (see **Global View**):

Global View

Under IFRS, debt investments are classified as either held-for-collection or trading.

- **Held-to-maturity**: Debt securities that the company has the positive intent and ability to hold to maturity.
- **Trading**: Debt securities bought and held primarily for sale in the near term to generate income on short-term price differences.
- **Available-for-sale**: Debt securities not classified as held-to-maturity or trading securities.

Illustration 17.2 identifies these categories, along with the accounting and reporting treatments required for each.

ILLUSTRATION 17.2
Accounting for Debt Securities by Category

Category	Valuation	Unrealized Holding Gains or Losses	Other Income Effects
Held-to-maturity	Amortized cost	Not recognized	Interest when earned; gains and losses from sale.
Trading securities	Fair value	Recognized in net income	Interest when earned; gains and losses from sale.
Available-for-sale	Fair value	Recognized as other comprehensive income and as separate component of stockholders' equity	Interest when earned; gains and losses from sale.

Global View

Under IFRS, held-for-collection debt investments are valued at amortized cost; all other investments are measured at fair value.

Amortized cost is the acquisition cost adjusted for the amortization of discount or premium, if appropriate. **Fair value** is the price that would be received to sell an asset or paid to transfer a liability in an orderly transaction between market participants at the measurement date (see **Global View**). [2]

[2]A **security** is a share, participation, or other interest in property or in an enterprise of the issuer or an obligation of the issuer that has the following three characteristics. (1) It either is represented by an instrument issued in bearer or registered form or, if not represented by an instrument, is registered in books maintained to record transfers by or on behalf of the issuer. (2) It is commonly traded on securities exchanges or markets or, when represented by an instrument, is commonly recognized in any area in which it is issued or dealt in as a medium for investment. (3) It either is one of a class or series or by its terms is divisible into a class or series of shares, participations, interests, or obligations. [1] (See the FASB Codification Reference near the end of the chapter.)

Held-to-Maturity Securities (Amortized Cost)

Only debt securities can be classified as held-to-maturity. By definition, equity securities have no maturity date. A company like Starbucks should classify a debt security as **held-to-maturity** only if it has **both (1) the positive intent** and **(2) the ability to hold those securities to maturity**. It should not classify a debt security as held-to-maturity if it intends to hold the security for an indefinite period of time. Likewise, if Starbucks anticipates that a sale may be necessary due to changes in interest rates, foreign currency risk, liquidity needs, or other asset-liability management reasons, it should not classify the security as held-to-maturity.[3]

Companies account for held-to-maturity securities **at amortized cost**, not fair value. If management intends to hold certain investment securities to maturity and has no plans to sell them, fair values (selling prices) are not relevant for measuring and evaluating the cash flows associated with these securities. Finally, because companies do not adjust held-to-maturity securities to fair value, these securities do not increase the volatility of either reported earnings or reported capital as do trading securities and available-for-sale securities.

To illustrate the accounting for held-to-maturity debt securities, assume that Robinson Company purchased $100,000 of 8 percent bonds of Evermaster Corporation on January 1, 2019, at a discount, paying $92,278. The bonds mature January 1, 2024, and yield 10%. Interest is payable each July 1 and January 1. Robinson records the investment as follows.

Calculator Solution for Bond Price

	Inputs	Answer
N	10	
I	5	
PV	?	−92,278
PMT	4,000	
FV	100,000	

January 1, 2019		
Debt Investments	92,278	
Cash		92,278

Robinson uses a Debt Investments account to indicate the type of security purchased.[4]

As indicated in Chapter 14, companies must amortize a premium or discount using the **effective-interest method** unless some other method—such as the straight-line method—yields a similar result (see **Underlying Concepts**). They apply the effective-interest method to bond investments in a way similar to that for bonds payable. To compute interest revenue, companies compute the effective-interest rate or yield at the time of investment and apply that rate to the beginning carrying amount (book value) for each interest period. The investment carrying amount is increased by the amortized discount or decreased by the amortized premium in each period.

Underlying Concepts

The use of some simpler method that yields results similar to the effective-interest method is an application of the materiality concept.

Illustration 17.3 shows the effect of the discount amortization on the interest revenue that Robinson records each period for its investment in Evermaster bonds.

Robinson records the receipt of the first semiannual interest payment on July 1, 2019 (using the data in Illustration 17.3), as follows.

July 1, 2019		
Cash	4,000	
Debt Investments	614	
Interest Revenue		4,614

[3]The FASB defines situations where, even though a company sells a security before maturity, it has constructively held the security to maturity, and thus does not violate the held-to-maturity requirement. These include selling a security close enough to maturity (such as three months) so that interest rate risk is no longer an important pricing factor.

However, companies must be extremely careful with debt securities held to maturity. If a company prematurely sells a debt security in this category, the sale may "taint" the entire held-to-maturity portfolio. That is, a management's statement regarding "intent" is no longer credible. Therefore, the company may have to reclassify the securities. This could lead to unfortunate consequences. An interesting by-product of this situation is that companies that wish to retire their debt securities early are finding it difficult to do so. The holder will not sell because the securities are classified as held-to-maturity.

[4]Companies generally record investments acquired at par, at a discount, or at a premium in the accounts at cost, including brokerage and other fees but excluding the accrued interest. They generally do not record investments at maturity value. The use of a separate discount or premium account as a valuation account is acceptable procedure for investments, but in practice companies do not widely use it.

ILLUSTRATION 17.3

Schedule of Interest Revenue and Bond Discount Amortization—Effective-Interest Method

8% Bonds Purchased to Yield 10%

Date	Cash Received	Interest Revenue	Bond Discount Amortization	Carrying Amount of Bonds
1/1/19				$ 92,278
7/1/19	$ 4,000[a]	$ 4,614[b]	$ 614[c]	92,892[d]
1/1/20	4,000	4,645	645	93,537
7/1/20	4,000	4,677	677	94,214
1/1/21	4,000	4,711	711	94,925
7/1/21	4,000	4,746	746	95,671
1/1/22	4,000	4,783	783	96,454
7/1/22	4,000	4,823	823	97,277
1/1/23	4,000	4,864	864	98,141
7/1/23	4,000	4,907	907	99,048
1/1/24	4,000	4,952	952	100,000
	$40,000	$47,722	$7,722	

[a]$4,000 = $100,000 × .08 × 6/12
[b]$4,614 = $92,278 × .10 × 6/12
[c]$614 = $4,614 − $4,000
[d]$92,892 = $92,278 + $614

Because Robinson is on a calendar-year basis, it accrues interest and amortizes the discount at December 31, 2019, as follows.

December 31, 2019		
Interest Receivable	4,000	
Debt Investments	645	
Interest Revenue		4,645

Again, Illustration 17.3 shows the interest and amortization amounts.

Robinson reports its investment in Evermaster bonds in its December 31, 2019, financial statements as shown in Illustration 17.4.

ILLUSTRATION 17.4

Reporting of Held-to-Maturity Securities

Balance Sheet	
Current assets	
Interest receivable	$ 4,000
Long-term investments	
Debt investments (held-to-maturity)	$93,537
Income Statement	
Other revenues and gains	
Interest revenue ($4,614 + $4,645)	$ 9,259

Sometimes, a company sells a held-to-maturity debt security so close to its maturity date that a change in the market interest rate would not significantly affect the security's fair value. Such a sale may be considered a sale at maturity and would not call into question the company's original intent to hold the investment to maturity. Let's assume, as an example, that Robinson Company sells its investment in Evermaster bonds on November 1, 2023, at 99¾ plus accrued interest. The discount amortization from July 1, 2023, to November 1, 2023, is $635 (4/6 × $952). Robinson records this discount amortization as follows.

November 1, 2023		
Debt Investments	635	
Interest Revenue		635

Illustration 17.5 shows the computation of the realized gain on the sale.

ILLUSTRATION 17.5

Computation of Gain on Sale of Bonds

Selling price of bonds (exclusive of accrued interest)		$99,750
Less: Book value of bonds on November 1, 2023:		
Amortized cost, July 1, 2023	$99,048	
Add: Discount amortized for the period July 1, 2023, to November 1, 2023	635	99,683
Gain on sale of bonds		$ 67

Robinson records the sale of the bonds as:

November 1, 2023		
Cash	102,417	
Interest Revenue (4/6 × $4,000)		2,667
Debt Investments		99,683
Gain on Sale of Investments		67

The credit to Interest Revenue represents accrued interest for four months, for which the purchaser pays cash. The debit to Cash represents the selling price of the bonds plus accrued interest ($99,750 + $2,667). The credit to Debt Investments represents the book value of the bonds on the date of sale. The credit to Gain on Sale of Investments represents the excess of the selling price over the book value of the bonds.

Available-for-Sale Securities (Fair Value Through Other Comprehensive Income)

Underlying Concepts

Recognizing unrealized gains and losses is an application of the concept of comprehensive income.

Companies like Amazon.com report **available-for-sale** debt securities at fair value. It records the unrealized gains and losses related to changes in the fair value of available-for-sale debt securities in an unrealized holding gain or loss account. Amazon reports these unrealized gains and losses in other comprehensive income for the period (see Underlying Concepts). Other comprehensive income is then added to (subtracted from) accumulated other comprehensive income, which is shown as a separate component of stockholders' equity until realized. Thus, **companies report available-for-sale securities at fair value on the balance sheet but do not report changes in fair value as part of net income until after selling the security**. This approach reduces the volatility of net income.

Example: Single Security

Calculator Solution for Bond Price

	Inputs	Answer
N	10	
I	4	
PV	?	−108,111
PMT	5,000	
FV	100,000	

To illustrate the accounting for available-for-sale securities, assume that Graff Corporation purchases $100,000, 10 percent, five-year bonds on January 1, 2019, with interest payable on July 1 and January 1. The bonds sell for $108,111, which results in a bond premium of $8,111 and an effective-interest rate of 8 percent.

Graff records the purchase of the bonds as follows.

January 1, 2019		
Debt Investments	108,111	
Cash		108,111

Illustration 17.6 discloses the effect of the premium amortization on the interest revenue Graff records each period using the effective-interest method.

The entry to record interest revenue on July 1, 2019, is as follows.

July 1, 2019		
Cash	5,000	
Debt Investments		676
Interest Revenue		4,324

10% Bonds Purchased to Yield 8%				
Date	Cash Received	Interest Revenue	Bond Premium Amortization	Carrying Amount of Bonds
1/1/19				$108,111
7/1/19	$ 5,000[a]	$ 4,324[b]	$ 676[c]	107,435[d]
1/1/20	5,000	4,297	703	106,732
7/1/20	5,000	4,269	731	106,001
1/1/21	5,000	4,240	760	105,241
7/1/21	5,000	4,210	790	104,451
1/1/22	5,000	4,178	822	103,629
7/1/22	5,000	4,145	855	102,774
1/1/23	5,000	4,111	889	101,885
7/1/23	5,000	4,075	925	100,960
1/1/24	5,000	4,040	960	100,000
	$50,000	$41,889	$8,111	

[a]$5,000 = $100,000 × .10 × 6/12
[b]$4,324 = $108,111 × .08 × 6/12
[c]$676 = $5,000 − $4,324
[d]$107,435 = $108,111 − $676

ILLUSTRATION 17.6

Schedule of Interest Revenue and Bond Premium Amortization—Effective-Interest Method

At December 31, 2019, Graff makes the following entry to recognize interest revenue.

December 31, 2019		
Interest Receivable	5,000	
Debt Investments		703
Interest Revenue		4,297

As a result, Graff reports interest revenue for 2019 of $8,621 ($4,324 + $4,297).

To apply the fair value method to these debt investments, assume that at year-end the fair value of the bonds is $105,000 and that the carrying amount of the investments is $106,732. Comparing this fair value with the carrying amount (amortized cost) of the bonds at December 31, 2019, Graff recognizes an unrealized holding loss of $1,732 ($106,732 − $105,000). It reports this loss as other comprehensive income. Graff makes the following entry.

December 31, 2019		
Unrealized Holding Gain or Loss—Equity	1,732	
Fair Value Adjustment		1,732

Graff uses a valuation account instead of crediting the Debt Investments account. The use of the **Fair Value Adjustment**[5] account enables the company to maintain a record of its amortized cost (see **Underlying Concepts**). Because the adjustment account has a credit balance in this case, Graff subtracts it from the balance of the Debt Investments account to determine fair value. Graff reports this fair value amount on the balance sheet. At each reporting date, Graff reports the bonds at fair value with an adjustment to the Unrealized Holding Gain or Loss—Equity account.

Underlying Concepts

Companies report some debt securities at fair value not only because the information is relevant but also because it is representationally faithful.

Example: Portfolio of Securities

To illustrate the accounting for a portfolio of securities, assume that Webb Corporation has two debt securities classified as available-for-sale. **Illustration 17.7** identifies the amortized cost, fair value, and the amount of the unrealized gain or loss.

[5]Various account titles might be used instead of Fair Value Adjustment, such as Fair Value Allowance or Valuation Allowance for Debt Investments. *For homework problems, use the account title Fair Value Adjustment.*

ILLUSTRATION 17.7

Computation of Fair Value Adjustment—Available-for-Sale Securities (2020)

Available-for-Sale Debt Security Portfolio
December 31, 2020

Investments	Amortized Cost	Fair Value	Unrealized Gain (Loss)
Watson Corporation 8% bonds	$ 93,537	$103,600	$10,063
Anacomp Corporation 10% bonds	200,000	180,400	(19,600)
Total of portfolio	$293,537	$284,000	(9,537)
Previous fair value adjustment balance			-0-
Fair value adjustment—Cr.			$ (9,537)

The fair value of Webb's available-for-sale portfolio totals $284,000. The gross unrealized gains are $10,063, and the gross unrealized losses are $19,600, resulting in a net unrealized loss of $9,537. That is, the fair value of available-for-sale securities is $9,537 lower than its amortized cost. Webb makes an adjusting entry to a valuation allowance to record the decrease in value and to record the loss as follows.

December 31, 2020		
Unrealized Holding Gain or Loss—Equity	9,537	
Fair Value Adjustment		9,537

Webb reports the unrealized holding loss of $9,537 as other comprehensive income and a reduction of stockholders' equity. Recall that companies exclude from net income any unrealized holding gains and losses related to available-for-sale securities.

Sale of Available-for-Sale Securities

If a company sells bonds carried as investments in available-for-sale securities before the maturity date, it must make entries to remove from the Debt Investments account the amortized cost of bonds sold. To illustrate, assume that Webb Corporation sold the Watson bonds (from Illustration 17.7) on July 1, 2021, for $90,000, at which time it had an amortized cost of $94,214. **Illustration 17.8** shows the computation of the realized loss.

ILLUSTRATION 17.8

Computation of Loss on Sale of Bonds

Amortized cost (Watson bonds)	$94,214
Less: Selling price of bonds	90,000
Loss on sale of bonds	$ 4,214

Webb records the sale of the Watson bonds as follows.

July 1, 2021		
Cash	90,000	
Loss on Sale of Investments	4,214	
Debt Investments		94,214

Webb reports this realized loss in the "Other expenses and losses" section of the income statement.[6] Assuming no other purchases and sales of bonds in 2021, Webb on December 31, 2021, prepares the information shown in **Illustration 17.9**.

[6]On the date of sale, any unrealized gains or losses on the sold security is not adjusted in accumulated other comprehensive income. This adjustment occurs at year-end when the entire portfolio is evaluated for fair value adjustment.

ILLUSTRATION 17.9

Computation of Fair Value Adjustment—Available-for-Sale (2021)

Available-for-Sale Debt Security Portfolio
December 31, 2021

Investments	Amortized Cost	Fair Value	Unrealized Gain (Loss)
Anacomp Corporation 10% bonds (total portfolio)	$200,000	$195,000	$(5,000)
Previous fair value adjustment balance—Cr.			(9,537)
Fair value adjustment—Dr.			$ 4,537

Webb has an unrealized holding loss of $5,000. However, the Fair Value Adjustment account already has a credit balance of $9,537. To reduce the adjustment account balance to $5,000, Webb debits it for $4,537, as follows.

December 31, 2021

Fair Value Adjustment	4,537	
Unrealized Holding Gain or Loss—Equity		4,537

Financial Statement Presentation

Webb's December 31, 2021, balance sheet and the 2021 income statement include the items and amounts shown in **Illustration 17.10** (the Anacomp bonds are long-term investments but are not intended to be held to maturity).

ILLUSTRATION 17.10

Reporting of Available-for-Sale Securities

Balance Sheet	
Current assets	
Interest receivable	$ xxx
Investments	
Debt investments (available-for-sale)	$195,000
Stockholders' equity	
Accumulated other comprehensive loss	$ 5,000
Income Statement	
Other revenues and gains	
Interest revenue	$ xxx
Other expenses and losses	
Loss on sale of investments	$ 4,214

Some favor including the unrealized holding gain or loss in net income rather than showing it as other comprehensive income.[7] However, some companies, particularly financial institutions, note that recognizing gains and losses on assets, but not liabilities, introduces substantial volatility in net income. They argue that hedges often exist between assets and liabilities so that gains in assets are offset by losses in liabilities, and vice versa. In short, to recognize gains and losses only on the asset side is unfair and not representative of the economic activities of the company.

This argument convinced the FASB. As a result, companies **do not include in net income** these unrealized gains and losses. [3] However, even this approach solves only some of the problems because **volatility of capital** still results. This is of concern to financial institutions because regulators restrict financial institutions' operations based on their level of capital. However, companies can still manage their net income by engaging in **gains trading** (i.e., selling the winners and holding the losers).

[7]In Chapter 4, we discussed the concept of, and reporting for, other comprehensive income.

Trading Securities (Fair Value Through Net Income)

Companies hold **trading securities** with the intention of selling them in a short period of time. "Trading" in this context means frequent buying and selling. Companies thus use trading securities to generate profits from short-term differences in price. Companies generally hold these securities for less than three months, some for merely days or hours.

Companies report trading securities at fair value, with unrealized holding gains and losses reported as part of net income. Similar to held-to-maturity or available-for-sale investments, companies are required to amortize any discount or premium. A **holding gain or loss** is the net change in the fair value of a security from one period to another, exclusive of dividend or interest revenue recognized but not received. In short, the FASB says to adjust the trading securities to fair value, at each reporting date. In addition, companies report the change in value as part of net income, not other comprehensive income.

For example, assume that on December 31, 2020, Western Publishing Corporation determined its trading securities portfolio to be as shown in **Illustration 17.11**. (Assume that 2020 is the first year that Western Publishing held trading securities.) At the date of acquisition, Western Publishing recorded these trading securities at cost, including brokerage commissions and taxes, in the account entitled Debt Investments. This is the first valuation of this recently purchased portfolio.

ILLUSTRATION 17.11

Computation of Fair Value Adjustment—Trading Securities Portfolio (2020)

Trading Debt Security Portfolio
December 31, 2020

Investments	Amortized Cost	Fair Value	Unrealized Gain (Loss)
Burlington Northern 6% bonds	$ 43,860	$ 51,500	$ 7,640
GM Corporation 7% bonds	184,230	175,200	(9,030)
Time Warner 8% bonds	86,360	91,500	5,140
Total of portfolio	$314,450	$318,200	3,750
Previous fair value adjustment balance			-0-
Fair value adjustment—Dr.			$ 3,750

The total cost of Western Publishing's trading portfolio is $314,450. The gross unrealized gains are $12,780 ($7,640 + $5,140), and the gross unrealized losses are $9,030, resulting in a net unrealized gain of $3,750. The fair value of trading securities is $3,750 greater than its cost.

At December 31, Western Publishing makes an adjusting entry to the Fair Value Adjustment account, to record both the increase in value and the unrealized holding gain.

December 31, 2020		
Fair Value Adjustment	3,750	
Unrealized Holding Gain or Loss—Income		3,750

Because the Fair Value Adjustment account balance is a debit, Western Publishing adds it to the cost of the Debt Investments account to arrive at a fair value for the trading securities. Western Publishing reports this fair value amount on the balance sheet.

As with other debt investments, when a trading investment is sold, the Debt Investments account is reduced by the amount of the amortized cost of the bonds. Any realized gain or loss is recorded in the "Other revenues and gains" or the "Other expenses and losses" section of the income statement. The Unrealized Holding Gain or Loss—Income account is reported in the income statement under "Other revenues and gains" or "Other expenses or losses." The Fair Value Adjustment account is then adjusted at year-end for the unrealized gains or losses on the remaining securities in the trading investment portfolio.

When securities are actively traded, the FASB believes that the investments should be reported at fair value on the balance sheet. In addition, changes in fair value (unrealized gains and losses) should be reported in income. Such reporting on trading securities provides more relevant information to existing and prospective stockholders.

What Do the Numbers Mean? **To Have and to Hold**

Wall Street is a romantic place these days. Recently, many banks, especially big ones, entered into long-term relationships with their securities portfolios, promising that hundreds of billions of dollars of assets will be "held-to-maturity." As a result, the banks may appear to have higher book values and be better capitalized in the eyes of regulators even if the value of these securities declines.

In fact, many banks, especially the large ones, have recently shifted their debt investments portfolios into the "held-to-maturity" category from trading or available-for-sale. For example, in a recent 18-month period, banks have moved $293 billion of their investments to the held-to-maturity category. That means that about $640 billion, or one in five dollars in the banks' portfolios, cannot be sold easily, as shown in the chart to the right.

Why the shift? One major reason is that banks recognize when securities are classified as held-to-maturity, they are carried at their original cost, typically face value. As you have learned, declines in market values hit neither book value nor earnings. Their value is written down only if they are considered to be permanently impaired. If long-term interest rates are expected to rise (which appears to be the consensus today), then bond prices will drop. And if bond prices drop, banks that hold trading or available-for-sale securities will have their earnings and capital drop. As a result, the shift to held-to-maturity portfolios provides protection from this level of volatility.

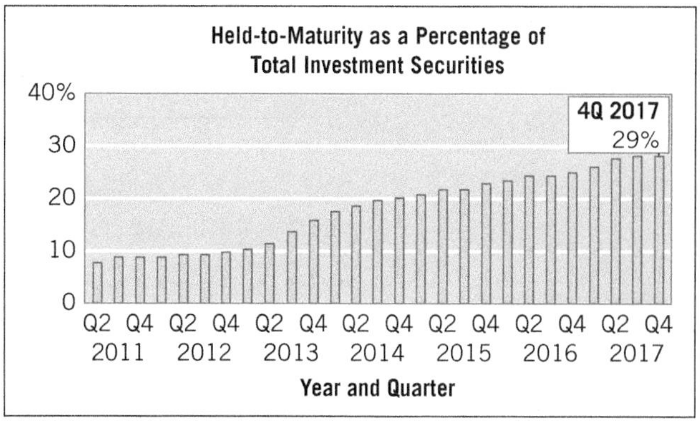

But banks should be careful. For example, if the bank has liquidity problems, it may have to sell these held-to-maturity securities for a large loss at inopportune times. And given the financial crisis of 2008, the process of trying to hype capital and maintain less volatile earnings may backfire if investors believe that shenanigans are taking place in the financial institution area.

Sources: John Carney, "Accounting Trick Can Help Banks Dodge Some Capital Pain," *Wall Street Journal* (March 28, 2014); and Michael Rapoport, "Banks Shift Bond Portfolios," *Wall Street Journal* (March 23, 2015).

Investments in Equity Securities

LEARNING OBJECTIVE 2

Describe the accounting for investments in equity securities.

Equity securities represent ownership interests such as common, preferred, or other capital stock. They also include rights to acquire or dispose of ownership interests at an agreed-upon or determinable price, such as in warrants, rights, and call or put options. Companies do not treat convertible debt securities as equity securities. Nor do they treat as equity securities redeemable preferred stock (which must be redeemed for common stock or cash). The cost of equity securities includes the purchase price of the security plus broker's commissions and other fees incidental to the purchase.

The degree to which one corporation (**investor**) acquires an interest in the common stock of another corporation (**investee**) generally determines the accounting treatment for the investment subsequent to acquisition. The classification of such investments depends on the percentage of the investee voting stock that is held by the investor:

1. Holdings of less than 20 percent (**fair value method**)—investor has passive interest.
2. Holdings between 20 percent and 50 percent (**equity method**)—investor has significant influence.
3. Holdings of more than 50 percent (**consolidated statements**)—investor has controlling interest.

Illustration 17.12 lists these levels of interest or influence and the corresponding valuation and reporting method that companies must apply to the investment.

ILLUSTRATION 17.12

Levels of Influence Determine Accounting Methods

Percentage of Ownership	0% ◄──► 20%	◄──► 50%	◄──► 100%
Level of Influence	Little or None	Significant	Control
Valuation Method	Fair Value Method	Equity Method	Consolidation

The accounting and reporting for equity securities therefore depend on the level of influence and the type of security involved, as shown in Illustration 17.13.

ILLUSTRATION 17.13

Accounting and Reporting for Equity Securities by Category

Category	Valuation	Unrealized Holding Gains or Losses	Other Income Effects
Holdings less than 20%	Fair value*	Recognized in net income	Dividends declared; gains and losses from sale
Holdings between 20% and 50%	Equity	Not recognized	Proportionate share of investee's net income
Holdings more than 50%	Consolidation	Not recognized	Not applicable

*Companies report equity holdings of less than 20% at fair value and record unrealized gains and losses through net income. The only exception would be for practicability reasons for determining fair value.

Holdings of Less Than 20%

When an investor has an interest of less than 20 percent, it is presumed that the investor has little or no influence over the investee. In such cases, if market prices are available subsequent to acquisition, the company values and reports the investment using the **fair value method**. Because equity securities have no maturity date, companies cannot classify them as held-to-maturity.

In some cases, companies can use a practicability exception when measuring equity securities that do not have a readily determinable fair value, often referred to as nonmarketable equity securities. If the practicability exception is elected, companies record investments at cost, less impairment. Companies recognize dividends when received and generally recognize gains and losses when selling the securities.[8]

Illustration

Upon acquisition, companies record equity securities at cost.[9] To illustrate, assume that on November 3, 2020, Republic Corporation purchased common stock of three companies, each investment representing less than a 20 percent interest.

	Cost
Northwest Industries, Inc.	$259,700
Campbell Soup Co.	317,500
St. Regis Pulp Co.	141,350
Total cost	$718,550

[8]A company is encouraged to adjust for observable price changes subsequent to recording the investment at cost if it can determine prices in orderly transactions for identical investments or from similar investments of the same issuer.

[9]Companies should record equity securities acquired in **exchange for noncash consideration** (property or services) at (1) the fair value of the consideration given, or (2) the fair value of the security received, whichever is more clearly determinable. Accounting for numerous purchases of securities requires the preservation of information regarding the cost of individual purchases, as well as the dates of purchases and sales. If specific identification is not possible, companies may use average-cost for multiple purchases of the same class of security. The **first-in, first-out method (FIFO)** of assigning costs to investments at the time of sale is also acceptable and normally employed.

Republic records these investments as follows.

November 3, 2020		
Equity Investments	718,550	
Cash		718,550

On December 6, 2020, Republic receives a cash dividend of $4,200 on its investment in the common stock of Campbell Soup Co. It records the cash dividend as follows.

December 6, 2020		
Cash	4,200	
Dividend Revenue		4,200

All three of the investee companies reported net income for the year, but only Campbell Soup declared and paid a dividend to Republic. But recall that when an investor owns less than 20 percent of the common stock of another corporation, it is presumed that the investor has relatively little influence on the investee. As a result, **net income of the investee is not a proper basis for recognizing income from the investment by the investor**. Why? Because the increased net assets resulting from profitable operations may be permanently retained for use in the investee's business. Therefore, **the investor recognizes net income only when the investee declares cash dividends.**

At December 31, 2020, Republic's equity security portfolio has the cost and fair value shown in **Illustration 17.14**.

ILLUSTRATION 17.14

Computation of Fair Value Adjustment—Equity Security Portfolio (2020)

Equity Security Portfolio
December 31, 2020

Investments	Cost	Fair Value	Unrealized Gain (Loss)
Northwest Industries, Inc.	$259,700	$275,000	$ 15,300
Campbell Soup Co.	317,500	304,000	(13,500)
St. Regis Pulp Co.	141,350	104,000	(37,350)
Total of portfolio	$718,550	$683,000	(35,550)
Previous fair value adjustment balance			-0-
Fair value adjustment—Cr.			$(35,550)

For Republic's equity securities portfolio, the gross unrealized gains are $15,300, and the gross unrealized losses are $50,850 ($13,500 + $37,350), resulting in a net unrealized loss of $35,550. That is, the fair value of the equity securities portfolio is below cost by $35,550.

Republic records the net unrealized gains and losses related to changes in the fair value of **equity** securities in an Unrealized Holding Gain or Loss—Income account. In this case, Republic prepares an adjusting entry debiting the Unrealized Holding Gain or Loss—Income account and crediting the Fair Value Adjustment account to record the decrease in fair value and to record the loss as follows.

December 31, 2020		
Unrealized Holding Gain or Loss—Income	35,550	
Fair Value Adjustment		35,550

On January 23, 2021, Republic sold all of its Northwest Industries, Inc. common stock receiving net proceeds of $287,220. **Illustration 17.15** shows the computation of the realized gain on the sale.

ILLUSTRATION 17.15

Computation of Gain on Sale of Stock

Net proceeds from sale	$287,220
Cost of **Northwest** shares	259,700
Gain on sale of stock	$ 27,520

Republic records the sale as follows.

January 23, 2021		
Cash	287,220	
Equity Investments		259,700
Gain on Sale of Investments		27,520

In addition, assume that on February 10, 2021, Republic purchased 20,000 shares of Continental Trucking at a market price of $12.75 per share plus brokerage commissions of $1,850 (total cost, $256,850).

Illustration 17.16 lists Republic's portfolio of equity securities as of December 31, 2021.

ILLUSTRATION 17.16

Computation of Fair Value Adjustment—Equity Security Portfolio (2021)

Equity Security Portfolio
December 31, 2021

Investments	Cost	Fair Value	Unrealized Gain (Loss)
Continental Trucking	$256,850	$278,350	$ 21,500
Campbell Soup Co.	317,500	362,550	45,050
St. Regis Pulp Co.	141,350	139,050	(2,300)
Total of portfolio	$715,700	$779,950	64,250
Previous fair value adjustment balance—Cr.			(35,550)
Fair value adjustment—Dr.			$ 99,800

At December 31, 2021, the fair value of Republic's equity securities portfolio exceeds cost by $64,250 (unrealized gain). The Fair Value Adjustment account had a credit balance of $35,550 at December 31, 2021. To adjust its December 31, 2021, equity portfolio to fair value, the company debits the Fair Value Adjustment account for $99,800 ($35,550 + $64,250). Republic records this adjustment as follows.

December 31, 2021		
Fair Value Adjustment	99,800	
Unrealized Holding Gain or Loss—Income		99,800

Holdings Between 20% and 50% (Equity Method)

LEARNING OBJECTIVE 3

Explain the equity and consolidation methods of accounting.

An investor corporation may hold an interest of less than 50 percent in an investee corporation and thus not possess legal control. However, an investment in voting stock of less than 50 percent can still give the investor the ability to exercise significant influence over the operating and financial policies of an investee. [4] For example, Siemens AG owns 34 percent of Areva (which constructs power plants). Areva is very important to Siemens because the power industry is a key customer for its generators and other power-related products. Thus, Siemens has a significant (but not controlling) ownership stake in a power plant construction company, which helps Siemens push its products into the market. Significant influence may be indicated in several ways. Examples include representation on the board of directors, participation in policy-making processes, material intercompany transactions, interchange of managerial personnel, or technological dependency.

Another important consideration is the extent of ownership by an investor in relation to the concentration of other shareholdings. To achieve a reasonable degree of uniformity in application of the "significant influence" criterion, the profession concluded that an investment (direct or indirect) of 20 percent or more of the voting stock of an investee should lead to a presumption, that in the absence of evidence to the contrary, an investor has the ability to exercise significant influence over an investee.[10]

In instances of "significant influence" (generally an investment of 20 percent or more), the investor must account for the investment using the **equity method**.

Comparison of Equity Method to Fair Value

Under the **equity method**, the investor and the investee acknowledge a substantive economic relationship. The company originally records the investment at the cost of the shares acquired but subsequently adjusts the amount each period for changes in the investee's net assets. That is, **the investor's proportionate share of the earnings (losses) of the investee periodically increases (decreases) the investment's carrying amount. All cash dividends received by the investor from the investee also decrease the investment's carrying amount.** The equity method recognizes that investee's earnings increase investee's net assets, and that investee's losses and dividends decrease these net assets.

To illustrate the equity method and compare it with the fair value method, assume that Maxi Company purchases a 20 percent interest in Mini Company. To apply the fair value method in this example, assume that Maxi does not have the ability to exercise significant influence. Where this example applies the equity method, assume that the 20 percent interest permits Maxi to exercise significant influence. Illustration 17.17 shows the entries.

ILLUSTRATION 17.17 Comparison of Fair Value Method and Equity Method

Entries by Maxi Company

Fair Value Method			**Equity Method**		
On January 2, 2020, Maxi Company acquired 48,000 shares (20% of Mini Company common stock) at a cost of $10 a share.					
Equity Investments	480,000		Equity Investments	480,000	
Cash		480,000	Cash		480,000
For the year 2020, Mini Company reported net income of $200,000; Maxi Company's share is 20%, or $40,000.					
No entry			Equity Investments	40,000	
			Investment Income		40,000
At December 31, 2020, the 48,000 shares of Mini Company have a fair value (market price) of $12 a share, or $576,000.					
Fair Value Adjustment	96,000		No entry		
Unrealized Holding Gain or Loss—Income		96,000			
On January 28, 2021, Mini Company announced and paid a cash dividend of $100,000; Maxi Company received 20%, or $20,000.					
Cash	20,000		Cash	20,000	
Dividend Revenue		20,000	Equity Investments		20,000
For the year 2021, Mini reported a net loss of $50,000; Maxi Company's share is 20%, or $10,000.					
No entry			Investment Loss	10,000	
			Equity Investments		10,000
At December 31, 2021, the Mini Company 48,000 shares have a fair value (market price) of $11 a share, or $528,000.					
Unrealized Holding Gain or Loss—Income	48,000		No entry		
Fair Value Adjustment		48,000			

[10] Cases in which an investment of 20 percent or more might not enable an investor to exercise significant influence include (1) the investee opposes the investor's acquisition of its stock, (2) the investor and investee sign an agreement under which the investor surrenders significant shareholder rights, (3) the investor's ownership share does not result in "significant influence" because majority ownership of the investee is concentrated among a small group of shareholders who operate the investee without regard to the views of the investor, and (4) the investor tries and fails to obtain representation on the investee's board of directors. [5]

Note that under the fair value method, Maxi reports as revenue only the cash dividends received from Mini. **The earning of net income by Mini (the investee) is not considered a proper basis for recognition of income from the investment by Maxi (the investor).** Why? Mini may permanently retain in the business any increased net assets resulting from its profitable operation. Therefore, Maxi only recognizes revenue when it receives dividends from Mini.

Under the equity method, Maxi reports as revenue its share of the net income reported by Mini. Maxi records the cash dividends received from Mini as a decrease in the investment carrying value. As a result, Maxi records its share of the net income of Mini in the year when it is recognized. With significant influence, Maxi can ensure that Mini will pay dividends, if desired, on any net asset increases resulting from net income. To wait until receiving a dividend ignores the fact that Maxi is better off if the investee has earned income (see Global View).

> **Global View**
> IFRS has similar accounting rules for significant influence equity investments.

Using dividends as a basis for recognizing income poses an additional problem. For example, assume that the investee reports a net loss. However, the investor exerts influence to force a dividend payment from the investee. In this case, the investor reports income, even though the investee is experiencing a loss. **In other words, using dividends as a basis for recognizing income fails to report properly the economics of the situation.**

For some companies, equity accounting can be a real pain to the bottom line. For example, Amazon.com, the pioneer of Internet retailing, at one time struggled to turn a profit. Furthermore, some of Amazon's equity investments had resulted in Amazon's earnings performance going from bad to worse. At one time, Amazon disclosed equity stakes in such companies as Altera International, Basis Technology, Drugstore.com, and Eziba.com. These equity investees reported losses that made Amazon's already bad bottom line even worse, accounting for up to 22 percent of its reported loss in one year alone.

Investee Losses Exceed Carrying Amount

If an investor's share of the investee's losses exceeds the carrying amount of the investment, should the investor recognize additional losses? Ordinarily, the investor should discontinue applying the equity method and not recognize additional losses.

If the investor's potential loss is not limited to the amount of its original investment (by guarantee of the investee's obligations or other commitment to provide further financial support) or if imminent return to profitable operations by the investee appears to be assured, the investor should recognize additional losses. [6]

Holdings of More Than 50% (Consolidation)

When one corporation acquires a voting interest of more than 50 percent in another corporation, it is said to have a **controlling interest**. In such a relationship, the investor corporation is referred to as the **parent** and the investee corporation as the **subsidiary**. Companies present the investment in the common stock of the subsidiary as a long-term investment on the separate financial statements of the parent.

When the parent treats the investment as a subsidiary, the parent generally prepares **consolidated financial statements**. Consolidated financial statements treat the parent and subsidiary corporations as a single economic entity. (Advanced accounting courses extensively discuss the subject of when and how to prepare consolidated financial statements.) Whether or not consolidated financial statements are prepared, the parent company generally accounts for the investment in the subsidiary **using the equity method** as explained in the previous section of this chapter (see Global View).

> **Global View**
> In contrast to U.S. firms, financial statements of non-U.S. companies often include both consolidated (group) statements and parent company financial statements.

What Do the Numbers Mean? Who's in Control Here?

Lenovo Group owns a significant percentage (45 percent) of the shares of Beijing Lenovo Parasaga Information Technology Co. (which develops and distributes computer software). Beijing Lenovo is important to Lenovo because it develops and sells the software that is used with Lenovo computers. In return, Beijing Lenovo depends on Lenovo to provide the products that make its software and services valuable, as well as perform significant customer and market support. Indeed, it can be said that to some extent Lenovo controls Beijing Lenovo, which would likely not exist without the support of Lenovo.

As you have learned, because a company like Lenovo owns less than 50 percent of the shares, it does not consolidate Beijing Lenovo but instead accounts for its investment using the **equity method**. Under the equity method, Lenovo reports a single income item for its profits from Beijing Lenovo and only the net amount of its investment in the statement of financial position. Equity method accounting gives Lenovo a pristine statement of financial position and income statement, by separating the assets and liabilities and the profit margins of the related companies from its laptop-computer businesses.

Some are critical of equity method accounting. They argue that some investees, like Beijing Lenovo, should be consolidated. The FASB has issued rules to consider other factors, in addition to voting interests, when determining whether an entity should be consolidated. The FASB has tightened up consolidation rules, so that companies will be more likely to consolidate more of their 20–50-percent-owned investments. Consolidation of entities, such as Beijing Lenovo, is warranted if Lenovo effectively controls its equity method investments.

Other Financial Reporting Issues

LEARNING OBJECTIVE 4

Evaluate other major issues related to investments in debt and equity securities.

Fair Value Option

As indicated in earlier chapters, companies have the option to report most financial instruments at **fair value, with all gains and losses related to changes in fair value reported in the income statement**. This option is applied on an instrument-by-instrument basis. The fair value option is generally available only at the time a company first purchases the financial asset or incurs a financial liability. If a company chooses to use the fair value option, it must measure this instrument at fair value until the company no longer has ownership.

For example, assume that **Abbott Laboratories** purchased debt securities in 2020 that it classified as held-to-maturity. Abbott does not choose to report this security using the fair value option. In 2021, Abbott buys another held-to-maturity debt security. Abbott decides to report this security using the fair value option. Once it chooses the fair value option for the security bought in 2021, the decision is irrevocable (may not be changed). In addition, Abbott does not have the option to value the held-to-maturity security purchased in 2020 at fair value in 2021 or in subsequent periods.

Many support the use of the fair value option as a step closer to total fair value reporting for financial instruments. They believe this treatment leads to an improvement in financial reporting. Others argue that the fair value option is confusing. A company can choose from period to period whether to use the fair value option for any new investment in a financial instrument. By permitting an instrument-by-instrument approach, companies are able to report some financial instruments at fair value but not others. To illustrate the accounting issues related to the fair value option, we discuss two different situations.

Available-for-Sale Debt Securities Illustration

Available-for-sale debt securities are presently reported at fair value, with any unrealized gains and losses recorded as part of other comprehensive income. Assume that Hardy Company purchases bonds in Fielder Company during 2020 that it classifies as available-for-sale. At December 31, 2020, the cost of this security is $100,000; its fair value at December 31, 2020, is $125,000. If Hardy chooses the fair value option to account for the Fielder Company stock, it makes the following entry at December 31, 2020.

Debt Investments	25,000	
Unrealized Holding Gain or Loss—Income		25,000

In this situation, Hardy uses the Debt Investments account to record the change in fair value at December 31. It does not use a Fair Value Adjustment account because the accounting for a fair value option is on an investment-by-investment basis rather than on a portfolio basis. **Because Hardy selected the fair value option, the unrealized gain or loss is recorded as part of net income.** Hardy must continue to use the fair value option to record this investment until it no longer has ownership of the security.

Equity Method Investments Illustration

Companies may also use the fair value option for investments that otherwise follow the equity method of accounting. To illustrate, assume that Durham Company holds a 28 percent stake in Suppan Inc. Durham purchased the investment in 2020 for $930,000. At December 31, 2020, the fair value of the investment is $900,000. Durham elects to report the investment in Suppan using the fair value option. The entry to record this investment is as follows.

Unrealized Holding Gain or Loss—Income	30,000	
Equity Investments		30,000

In contrast to equity method accounting, if the fair value option is chosen, Durham does not report its pro rata share of the income or loss from Suppan. In addition, any dividend payments are credited to Dividend Revenue and therefore do not reduce the Equity Investments account.

One major advantage of using the fair value option for this type of investment is that it addresses confusion about the equity method of accounting. In other words, what exactly does the one-line consolidation related to the equity method of accounting on the balance sheet tell investors? Many believe it does not provide information about liquidity or solvency, nor does it provide an indication of the worth of the company (see Global View).

Global View

IFRS does not allow the use of the fair value option for equity method investments.

Evolving Issue Fair Value Controversy

As discussed in the opening story, the reporting of investment securities is controversial. Some believe that all securities should be reported at fair value with the unrealized gain or loss reported in net income. Others believe the unrealized gain or loss should be reported in other comprehensive income. A third group believes all debt securities should be stated at amortized cost, and still others favor the present approach. Here are some of the major unresolved issues:

- ***Measurement based on intent.*** Companies classify debt securities as held-to-maturity, available-for-sale, or trading. As a result, companies can report three identical debt securities in three different ways in the financial statements. Some argue such treatment is confusing. Furthermore, the held-to-maturity category relies on intent, a subjective evaluation. What is not subjective is the fair value of the debt instrument. In other words, the three classifications are subjective, resulting in arbitrary classifications.
- ***Gains trading.*** Companies can classify certain debt securities as held-to-maturity and therefore report them at amortized cost. Companies can classify other debt securities as available-for-sale and report them at fair value, with the unrealized gain or loss reported as other comprehensive income. In either case, a company can become involved in "gains trading" (also referred to as "cherry picking," "snacking," or "sell the best and keep the rest"). In **gains trading**, companies sell their "winners," reporting the gains in income, and hold on to the losers.
- ***Liabilities not fairly valued.*** Many argue that if companies report investment securities at fair value, they also should report liabilities at fair value. Why? By recognizing changes in value on only one side of the balance sheet (the asset side), a high degree of volatility can occur in the income and stockholders' equity amounts. Further, financial institutions are involved in asset and liability management (not just asset management). Viewing only one side may lead managers to make uneconomic decisions as a result of the accounting. The fair value option may address this concern to some extent. However, there is debate on the usefulness of fair value estimates for liabilities.

Impairment of Value

Receivables

As indicated in Chapter 7 for receivables, companies use the current expected credit loss (CECL) model to measure impairment of receivables. To recognize the impairment, an entry is made to increase Bad Debt Expense and credit Allowance for Doubtful Accounts for the amount of the impairment. When it is probable that a company will be unable to collect all amounts due under the terms of the transaction, the receivable is permanently written off by a debit to Allowance for Doubtful Accounts and a credit to Accounts Receivable.

Debt Investments: Held-to-Maturity

The rules for debt investments (debt securities and loans) reported at **amortized cost** follow the same approach as discussed in Chapter 7. That is, companies should use the CECL model to record the impairment of debt investments similar to receivables. To illustrate, assume that Strickler Company holds held-to-maturity bond securities with a par value and amortized cost of $1 million. The fair value of these securities is $800,000. In evaluating the securities, Strickler now determines that it is probable that it will not collect all amounts due. In this case, it records a debit to Allowance for Doubtful Accounts of $200,000. Strickler includes this amount in income and records the impairment as follows.

Allowance for Doubtful Accounts	200,000	
Debt Investments		200,000

The new cost basis of the investment in debt securities is $800,000 and will not change unless additional impairment occurs.

Debt Investments: Available-for-Sale

Companies holding available-for-sale debt investments follow a different approach in accounting for impairments than the current expected credit loss (CECL) model. The reason is that the CECL model is designed to estimate credit losses over the contractual term of the debt investment, such as is the case with held-to-maturity debt investments. However, if companies hold available-for-sale debt investments, they may choose to sell the securities before the contractual term ends. Thus, companies have two choices with available-for-sale securities. They may realize the value of these securities either (1) through collection of the cash flows or (2) by sale of the securities.

As a result, the amount of credit losses that can be realized on available-for-sale debt securities is limited to the amount that the fair value is less than amortized cost. In other words, if the credit loss exceeds the amount that the fair value is below amortized cost of these securities, the company can sell the securities and thereby avoid the higher credit loss. To illustrate, assume Acular Company has an available-for-sale security with an amortized cost of $100,000; its fair value is $90,000, and its expected credit losses on this security is $15,000. In this case, Acular would sell the security and have a loss of only $10,000 rather than hold the security and have a loss of $15,000.[11]

Illustration 17.18 provides data for an impairment analysis for available-for-sale impairment guidelines for Alexander Company.

ILLUSTRATION 17.18

Impairment Analysis, Available-for-Sale Investments

Facts	Situation A	Situation B	Situation C
Amortized cost	$1,000,000	$1,000,000	$1,000,000
Fair value	1,100,000	960,000	860,000
Expected credit loss	110,000	110,000	110,000
Expected credit loss recognized in net income	-0-	40,000	110,000
Unrealized Holding Gain or (Loss)—Equity	100,000	-0-	30,000

- ***Situation A.*** Alexander does not recognize an impairment loss because the fair value of $1,100,000 is higher than the amortized cost of $1,000,000. The entry Alexander makes is to record an unrealized holding gain of $100,000 ($1,100,000 – $1,000,000) in other comprehensive income.

[11] In our earlier discussion related to available-for-sale investments, we assumed that these securities did not have any credit losses associated with them. As a result, unrealized gains and losses were reported in other comprehensive income. If available-for-sale investments have credit losses, they must be analyzed on an individual basis. These securities therefore cannot be combined with other available-for-sale securities to determine whether credit losses have occurred.

Fair Value Adjustment	100,000	
Unrealized Holding Gain or Loss—Equity		100,000

In this situation, Alexander does not recognize any impairment even though it has an expected credit loss of $110,000 because the fair value of its security is above its amortized cost.[12]

- ***Situation B.*** Alexander recognizes an impairment loss of $40,000 ($1,000,000 – $960,000) even though the expected credit loss is $110,000. In other words, Alexander's impairment loss is limited to the amount that fair value is less than amortized cost. Alexander makes the following entry to record this loss.

Bad Debt Expense	40,000	
Allowance for Doubtful Accounts		40,000

The Allowance for Doubtful Accounts account is reported on the balance sheet as an adjustment to the carrying value of the available-for-sale debt investments. An allowance account is used because subsequent to recording an impairment, events or economic conditions may change such that the extent of the impairment loss decreases (e.g., due to an improvement in the debtor's credit rating). In this situation, for available-for-sale investments, some or all of the previously recognized impairment loss is reversed with a debit to the allowance account (which increases the carrying value of the investment) and a credit to Bad Debt Expense. The reversal of impairment losses must not result in a carrying amount of the investment that exceeds the amortized cost that would have been reported had the impairment not been recognized.

- ***Situation C.*** Alexander recognizes an impairment loss of $110,000 and an unrealized holding loss through other comprehensive income of $30,000. In other words, Alexander separates the total loss of $140,000 ($1,000,000 – $860,000) into the following two components.

1. The credit loss or the amount representing the decrease in cash flows expected to be collected of $110,000.
2. The noncredit-related factors, such as changes in interest rates, market volatility, and liquidity concerns, of $30,000.

Alexander makes the following entry to record this transaction.

Bad Debt Expense	110,000	
Unrealized Holding Gain or Loss—Equity	30,000	
Allowance for Impaired Debt Investments		110,000
Fair Value Adjustment		30,000

In summary, companies recognize credit losses on an available-for-sale security when the security's fair value is less than amortized cost. For held-to-maturity securities, a company can still report a credit loss even when fair value is higher than amortized cost.

Equity Investments

The accounting for impairments related to equity securities with holdings of less than 20 percent, **which are recorded at fair value with unrealized gains and losses through net income**, is straightforward. That is, if fair value is less than cost, the decline in value is reported through net income. As a consequence, it is not necessary to write off the individual stock investment unless a permanent impairment occurs. This same treatment applies to trading debt investments.

Illustration 17.19 provides a summary of the guidelines related to impairments.

[12]Such an adjustment—an unrealized gain—is more likely in a decreasing-rate environment. The inverse is true in an increasing-rate environment.

Asset Measurement Basis	Impairment Model
Loans, receivables, and debt securities measured at amortized cost.	Expected losses recognized in net income.
Debt securities measured at fair value with gains and losses recorded in other comprehensive income (available-for-sale).	No expected credit losses recognized if fair value is greater than or equal to amortized cost. If fair value is less than amortized cost, the expected credit loss is recognized in net income. Credit losses are limited to the difference between fair value and amortized cost.
Debt and equity securities measured at fair value with gains and losses recorded in net income (trading).	Impairment measured as the difference between the lower of amortized cost or fair value (debt securities) or lower of cost or fair value (equity securities).

ILLUSTRATION 17.19
Impairment Model Summary

Reclassification Adjustments

As we indicated in Chapter 4, companies may display the components of other comprehensive income in one of two ways: (1) in a combined statement of income and comprehensive income, or (2) in a separate statement of comprehensive income that begins with net income.

Reporting Issues

Single-Period Example To provide a single-period example of the reporting of investment securities and related gain or loss on available-for-sale debt securities, assume that on January 1, 2020, Hinges Co. had cash and common stock of $50,000.[13] At that date, the company had no other asset, liability, or equity balance. On January 2, Hinges purchased for cash $50,000 of debt securities classified as available-for-sale. On June 30, Hinges sold part of the available-for-sale security debt portfolio, realizing a gain as shown in Illustration 17.20.

Fair value of securities sold	$22,000
Less: Cost of securities sold	20,000
Realized gain	$ 2,000

ILLUSTRATION 17.20
Computation of Realized Gain

Hinges did not purchase or sell any other securities during 2020. It received $3,000 in interest during the year. At December 31, 2020, the remaining portfolio is as shown in Illustration 17.21.

Fair value of portfolio	$34,000
Less: Cost of portfolio	30,000
Unrealized gain	$ 4,000

ILLUSTRATION 17.21
Computation of Unrealized Gain

Illustration 17.22 shows the company's income statement for 2020.

Hinges Co.
Income Statement
For the Year Ended December 31, 2020

Interest revenue	$3,000
Realized gains on investment in securities	2,000
Net income	$5,000

ILLUSTRATION 17.22
Income Statement

[13]We adapted this example from Dennis R. Beresford, L. Todd Johnson, and Cheri L. Reither, "Is a Second Income Statement Needed?" *Journal of Accountancy* (April 1996), p. 71.

The company reports its change in the unrealized holding gain in a statement of comprehensive income as shown in Illustration 17.23.

ILLUSTRATION 17.23
Statement of Comprehensive Income

Hinges Co.
Statement of Comprehensive Income
For the Year Ended December 31, 2020

Net income (includes realized gain of $2,000)	$5,000
Other comprehensive income:	
Unrealized holding gain	4,000
Comprehensive income	$9,000

Illustration 17.24 shows its statement of stockholders' equity.

ILLUSTRATION 17.24
Statement of Stockholders' Equity

Hinges Co.
Statement of Stockholders' Equity
For the Year Ended December 31, 2020

	Common Stock	Retained Earnings	Accumulated Other Comprehensive Income	Total
Beginning balance	$50,000	$ -0-	$ -0-	$50,000
Add: Net income		5,000		5,000
Other comprehensive income			4,000	4,000
Ending balance	$50,000	$5,000	$4,000	$59,000

The comparative balance sheet is shown in Illustration 17.25.

ILLUSTRATION 17.25
Comparative Balance Sheet

Hinges Co.
Comparative Balance Sheet

	1/1/20	12/31/20
Assets		
Cash	$50,000	$25,000
Debt investments		34,000
Total assets	$50,000	$59,000
Stockholders' equity		
Common stock	$50,000	$50,000
Retained earnings		5,000
Accumulated other comprehensive income		4,000
Total stockholders' equity	$50,000	$59,000

This example indicates how an unrealized gain or loss on available-for-sale debt securities affects all the financial statements. Note that a company must disclose the components that comprise accumulated other comprehensive income.

Multi-Period Example When a company sells securities during the year, double-counting of the realized gains or losses in comprehensive income can occur. This double-counting results when a company reports unrealized gains or losses in other comprehensive income in a *prior period* and reports these gains or losses as part of net income in the *current period*.

To ensure that gains and losses are not counted twice when a sale occurs, a **reclassification adjustment** is necessary. To illustrate, assume that Open Company has the two available-for-sale debt securities in its portfolio at the end of 2020 (its first year of operations) shown in Illustration 17.26.

ILLUSTRATION 17.26

Available-for-Sale Security Portfolio (2020)

Investments	Amortized Cost	Fair Value	Unrealized Holding Gain (Loss)
Lehman Inc. bonds 6%	$ 80,000	$105,000	$25,000
Woods Co. bonds 7%	120,000	135,000	15,000
Total of portfolio	$200,000	$240,000	40,000
Previous fair value adjustment balance			-0-
Fair value adjustment—Dr.			$40,000

The entry to record the unrealized holding gain in 2020 is as follows.

December 31, 2020

Fair Value Adjustment	40,000	
Unrealized Holding Gain or Loss—Equity		40,000

If Open Company reports net income in 2020 of $350,000, it presents a statement of comprehensive income as shown in **Illustration 17.27**.

ILLUSTRATION 17.27

Statement of Comprehensive Income (2020)

Open Company
Statement of Comprehensive Income
For the Year Ended December 31, 2020

Net income	$350,000
Other comprehensive income	
Unrealized holding gain	40,000
Comprehensive income	$390,000

At December 31, 2020, Open Company reports on its balance sheet debt investments of $240,000 (cost $200,000 plus fair value adjustment of $40,000) and accumulated other comprehensive income in stockholders' equity of $40,000. The entry to transfer the unrealized holding gain—equity to accumulated other comprehensive income is as follows.

December 31, 2020 (Closing Entry)

Unrealized Holding Gain or Loss—Equity	40,000	
Accumulated Other Comprehensive Income		40,000

On August, 10, 2021, Open Company sells its Lehman Inc. bonds for $105,000 and realizes a gain on the sale of $25,000 ($105,000 – $80,000). The journal entry to record this transaction is as follows.

August 10, 2021

Cash	105,000	
Debt Investments		80,000
Gain on Sale of Investments		25,000

At the end of 2021, the fair value of the Woods Co. bonds increased an additional $20,000 ($155,000 – $135,000), to $155,000. **Illustration 17.28** shows the computation of the change in the Fair Value Adjustment account (based on only the Woods Co. investment as the Lehman bonds have been sold).

ILLUSTRATION 17.28

Available-for-Sale Security Portfolio (2021)

Investments	Cost	Fair Value	Unrealized Holding Gain (Loss)
Woods Co. bonds 7%	$120,000	$155,000	$35,000
Previous fair value adjustment balance—Dr.			(40,000)
Fair value adjustment—Cr.			$ (5,000)

The entry to record the unrealized holding gain or loss in 2021 is as follows.

December 31, 2021		
Unrealized Holding Gain or Loss—Equity	5,000	
Fair Value Adjustment		5,000

If we assume that Open Company reports net income of $720,000 in 2021, including the realized sale on the Lehman bonds, its statement of comprehensive income is presented as shown in Illustration 17.29.

ILLUSTRATION 17.29

Statement of Comprehensive Income (2021)

Open Company
Statement of Comprehensive Income
For the Year Ended December 31, 2021

Net income (includes $25,000 realized gain on Lehman bonds)	$720,000
Other comprehensive income	
Unrealized holding loss	(5,000)
Comprehensive income	$715,000

At December 31, 2021, Open Company reports on its balance sheet debt investments of $155,000 (cost $120,000 plus a fair value adjustment of $35,000) and accumulated other comprehensive income in stockholders' equity of $35,000 ($40,000 – $5,000). The entry to transfer the unrealized holding loss—equity to accumulated other comprehensive income is as follows.

December 31, 2021 (Closing Entry)		
Accumulated Other Comprehensive Income	5,000	
Unrealized Holding Gain or Loss—Equity		5,000

In 2020, Open included the unrealized gain on the Lehman Co. bonds in comprehensive income. In 2021, Open sold the bonds. It reported the realized gain ($25,000) in net income, which increased comprehensive income again. To avoid double-counting this gain, Open makes a **reclassification adjustment** to eliminate the realized gain from the computation of comprehensive income in 2021.

This reclassification adjustment may be made in the income statement, in accumulated other comprehensive income or in a note to the financial statements. The FASB prefers to show the reclassification amount in accumulated other comprehensive income in the notes to the financial statements. For Open Company, this presentation is as shown in Illustration 17.30.

ILLUSTRATION 17.30

Note Disclosure of Reclassification Adjustments

Open Company
Notes to Financial Statements
Changes in Accumulated Other Comprehensive Income

Beginning balance, January 1, 2021		$40,000
Current-period other comprehensive income ($155,000 – $135,000)	$ 20,000	
Amount reclassified from accumulated other comprehensive income	(25,000)	
Unrealized holding loss		(5,000)
Ending balance, December 31, 2021		$35,000

Transfers Related to Debt Securities

Companies account for transfers between any of the categories at fair value. Thus, if a company transfers available-for-sale debt securities to held-to-maturity investments, it records the new investments (held-to-maturity) at the date of transfer at **fair value** in the new category. Similarly, if it transfers held-to-maturity investments to available-for-sale debt investments, it records the new investments (available-for-sale) at **fair value**. This **fair value** rule assures that a company cannot omit recognition of fair value simply by transferring securities to the held-to-maturity category. Illustration 17.31 summarizes the accounting treatment for transfers.

ILLUSTRATION 17.31 Accounting for Transfers

Type of Transfer	Measurement Basis	Impact of Transfer on Stockholders' Equity*	Impact of Transfer on Net Income*
Transfer from trading to available-for-sale	Security transferred at fair value at the date of transfer, which is the new cost basis of the security.	The unrealized gain or loss at the date of transfer increases or decreases stockholders' equity.	The unrealized gain or loss at the date of transfer is recognized in income.
Transfer from available-for-sale to trading	Security transferred at fair value at the date of transfer, which is the new cost basis of the security.	The unrealized gain or loss at the date of transfer increases or decreases stockholders' equity.	The unrealized gain or loss at the date of transfer is recognized in income.
Transfer from held-to-maturity to available-for-sale**	Security transferred at fair value at the date of transfer.	The separate component of stockholders' equity is increased or decreased by the unrealized gain or loss at the date of transfer.	None.
Transfer from available-for-sale to held-to-maturity	Security transferred at fair value at the date of transfer.	The unrealized gain or loss at the date of transfer carried as a separate component of stockholders' equity is amortized over the remaining life of the security.	None.

*Assumes that adjusting entries to report changes in fair value for the current period are not yet recorded.
**According to GAAP, these types of transfers should be rare.

Summary of Reporting Treatment of Securities

Illustration 17.32 summarizes the major debt and equity securities and their reporting treatment.[14]

ILLUSTRATION 17.32 Summary of Treatment of Major Debt and Equity Securities

Classification*	Valuation Approach and Balance Sheet Reporting	Income Effects
Debt Classifications		
Trading	Fair value. Current assets.	Interest is recognized as revenue. Unrealized holding gains and losses are recognized in income.
Available-for-sale	Fair value. Current or noncurrent assets.	Interest is recognized as revenue. Unrealized holding gains and losses are not recognized in income but in other comprehensive income.
Held-to-maturity	Amortized cost. Current or noncurrent assets.	Interest is recognized as revenue.
Equity Classifications		
Holdings less 20%	Fair value. Current or noncurrent assets.	Dividends are recognized as revenue. Unrealized gains and losses are included in income.
Holdings between 20% and 50%	Equity method. Investments originally recorded at cost with periodic adjustment for the investor's share of the investee's income or loss, and decreased by all dividends received from the investee, subsequent to the date of the investment.	Revenue is recognized to the extent of the investee's income or loss.
Holdings more than 50%	Consolidation of financial statements.	Parent and subsidiary company income or loss combined.
Nonmarketable	Cost.	Dividends are recognized as revenue.

*Companies have the option to report financial instruments at fair value with all gains and losses related to changes in fair value reported in the income statement. If a company chooses to use the fair option for some of its financial instruments, these assets or liabilities should be reported separately from other financial instruments that use a different valuation basis.

[14]Not surprisingly, the disclosure requirements for investments and other financial assets and liabilities are extensive. We provide an expanded discussion with examples of these disclosure requirements in Appendix 17B.

What Do the Numbers Mean? So You Think It Is Easy?

Millions of Americans own a piece of some of the hottest private technology companies through their mutual funds. The managers of these mutual funds face a difficult task—how to assign a current value to these securities every day so investors can better understand the value of their holdings. It appears that no one is quite sure what those investments are actually worth. Take **Uber Technologies**, the ride-hailing king, whose stock on June 30, 2015, was valued by BlackRock Global Allocation Fund at $40.02 a share, Vanguard U.S. Growth Fund at $39.64 a share, and Fidelity Contrafund Investments at $33.32 a share. The graphs below show similar examples for **Cloudera** and **Dropbox**, and illustrate again how values of these private technology companies can deviate among investment funds.

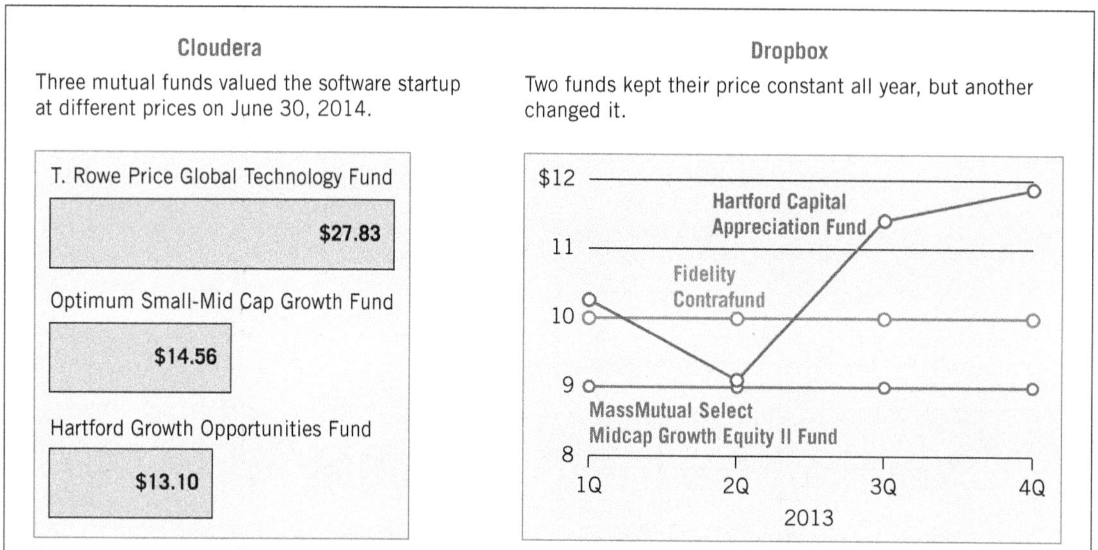

Sources: Morningstar; *Wall Street Journal*; the mutual funds.

Some experts say the rising popularity of investing in private technology stocks is hazardous simply because the shares are hard to sell, lack a broad secondary market, and could react wildly if the overall market drops. So what to do? Everyone seems to agree that determining the worth of these investments is a time-consuming process that must be monitored. For investors, it is important to understand the composition of the mutual fund they purchase. The amount of hard-to-sell shares is an indicator of how easily mutual fund investors would be able to recover their investment.

Sources: K. Grind, "SEC Takes Closer Look at Startup Valuations," *Wall Street Journal* (November 18, 2015); and K. Grind, "Mutual Funds Flail at Valuing Hot Startups Like Uber," *Wall Street Journal* (October 29, 2015).

APPENDIX 17A Accounting for Derivative Instruments

LEARNING OBJECTIVE *5

Describe the uses of and accounting for derivatives.

Until the early 1970s, most financial managers worked in a cozy, if unthrilling, world. Since then, constant change caused by volatile markets, new technology, and deregulation has increased the risks to businesses. In response, the financial community developed products to manage these risks.

These products—called **derivative financial instruments** or simply **derivatives**—are useful for managing risk. Companies use the fair values or cash flows of these instruments to offset the changes in fair values or cash flows of the at-risk assets. The development of powerful computing and communication technology has aided the growth in derivative use. This technology provides new ways to analyze information about markets as well as the power to process high volumes of payments.

Defining Derivatives

In order to understand derivatives, consider the following examples.

- ***Example 1—Forward Contract.*** Assume that a company like **Dell** believes that the price of **Google**'s stock will increase substantially in the next 3 months. Unfortunately, it does not have the cash resources to purchase the stock today. Dell therefore enters into a contract with a broker for delivery of 10,000 shares of Google stock in 3 months at the price of $110 per share.

  Dell has entered into a **forward contract**, a type of derivative. As a result of the contract, Dell **has received the right** to receive 10,000 shares of Google stock in 3 months. Further, it **has an obligation** to pay $110 per share at that time. What is the benefit of this derivative contract? Dell can buy Google stock today and take delivery (and make payment) in 3 months. If the price goes up, as it expects, Dell profits. If the price goes down, Dell loses.
- ***Example 2—Option Contract.*** Now suppose that Dell needs 2 weeks to decide whether to purchase Google stock. It therefore enters into a different type of contract, one that gives it the right to purchase Google stock at its current price any time within the next 2 weeks. As part of the contract, the broker charges $3,000 for holding the contract open for 2 weeks at a set price.

  Dell has now entered into an **option contract**, another type of derivative. As a result of this contract, **it has received the right but not the obligation** to purchase this stock. If the price of the Google stock increases in the next 2 weeks, Dell exercises its option. In this case, the cost of the stock is the price of the stock stated in the contract, plus the cost of the option contract. If the price does not increase, Dell does not exercise the contract but still incurs the cost for the option.

The forward contract and the option contract both involve a future delivery of stock. The value of the contract relies on the underlying asset—the Google stock. Thus, these financial instruments are known as derivatives because they **derive their value from** values of other assets (e.g., stocks, bonds, or commodities). Or, put another way, their value relates to a market-determined indicator (e.g., stock price, interest rates, or the Standard and Poor's 500 stock composite index).

In this appendix, we discuss the accounting for three different types of derivatives:

1. Financial forwards or financial futures.
2. Options.
3. Swaps.

Who Uses Derivatives, and Why?

Whether to protect for changes in interest rates, the weather, stock prices, oil prices, or foreign currencies, derivative contracts help to smooth the fluctuations caused by various types of risks. A company that wants to ensure against certain types of business risks often uses derivative contracts to achieve this objective.[15]

Producers and Consumers

To illustrate, assume that Heartland Ag is a large producer of potatoes for the consumer market. The present price for potatoes is excellent. Unfortunately, Heartland needs two months

[15]Derivatives are traded on many exchanges throughout the world. In addition, many derivative contracts (primarily interest rate swaps) are privately negotiated.

to harvest its potatoes and deliver them to the market. Because Heartland expects the price of potatoes to drop in the coming months, it signs a forward contract. It agrees to sell its potatoes today at the current market price for delivery in 2 months.

Who would buy this contract? Suppose on the other side of the contract is **McDonald's Corporation**. McDonald's wants to have potatoes (for French fries) in 2 months and believes that prices will increase. McDonald's is therefore agreeable to accepting delivery in 2 months at current prices. It knows that it will need potatoes in 2 months and that it can make an acceptable profit at this price level.

In this situation, if the price of potatoes increases before delivery, Heartland loses and McDonald's wins. Conversely, if the price decreases, Heartland wins and McDonald's loses. However, the objective is not to gamble on the outcome. Regardless of which way the price moves, both Heartland and McDonald's have received a price at which they obtain an acceptable profit. In this case, although Heartland is a **producer** and McDonald's is a **consumer**, both companies are **hedgers**. They both **hedge their positions** to ensure an acceptable financial result.

Commodity prices are volatile. They depend on weather, crop production, and general economic conditions. For the producer and the consumer to plan effectively, it makes good sense to lock in specific future revenues or costs in order to run their businesses successfully.

Speculators and Arbitrageurs

In some cases, instead of McDonald's taking a position in the forward contract, a speculator may purchase the contract from Heartland. The **speculator** bets that the price of potatoes will rise, thereby increasing the value of the forward contract. The speculator, who may be in the market for only a few hours, will then sell the forward contract to another speculator or to a company like McDonald's.

Arbitrageurs also use derivatives. These market players attempt to exploit inefficiencies in markets. They seek to lock in profits by simultaneously entering into transactions in two or more markets. For example, an arbitrageur might trade in a futures contract. At the same time, the arbitrageur will also trade in the commodity underlying the futures contract, hoping to achieve small price gains on the difference between the two. Markets rely on speculators and arbitrageurs to keep the market liquid on a daily basis.

In these illustrations, we explained why Heartland (the producer) and McDonald's (the consumer) would become involved in a derivative contract. Consider other types of situations that companies face.

1. Airlines, like **Delta**, **Southwest**, and **United**, are affected by changes in the price of jet fuel.
2. Financial institutions, such as **Citigroup**, **Bankers Trust**, and **BMO Harris**, are involved in borrowing and lending funds that are affected by changes in interest rates.
3. Multinational corporations, like **Cisco Systems**, **Coca-Cola**, and **General Electric**, are subject to changes in foreign exchange rates.

In fact, most corporations are involved in some form of derivatives transactions. Companies give these reasons (in their annual reports) as to why they use derivatives:

1. **ExxonMobil** uses derivatives to hedge its exposure to fluctuations in interest rates, foreign currency exchange rates, and hydrocarbon prices.
2. **Caterpillar** uses derivatives to manage foreign currency exchange rates, interest rates, and commodity price exposure.
3. **Johnson & Johnson** uses derivatives to manage the impact of interest rate and foreign exchange rate changes on earnings and cash flows.

Many corporations use derivatives extensively and successfully. However, derivatives can be dangerous. All parties involved must understand the risks and rewards associated with these contracts.[16]

[16]There are some well-publicized examples of companies that have suffered considerable losses using derivatives. For example, companies such as **Fannie Mae** (U.S.), **Enron** (U.S.), **Showa Shell Sekiyu** (Japan), **Metallgesellschaft** (Germany), **Procter & Gamble** (U.S.), and **Air Products & Chemicals** (U.S.) incurred significant losses from investments in derivative instruments.

Basic Principles in Accounting for Derivatives

The FASB concluded that derivatives such as forwards and options are assets and liabilities. It also concluded that companies should report them in the balance sheet **at fair value**.[17] The Board believes that fair value will provide statement users the best information about derivatives. Relying on some other basis of valuation for derivatives, such as historical cost, does not make sense. Why? Because many derivatives have a historical cost of zero. Furthermore, the markets for derivatives, and the assets upon which derivatives' values rely, are well developed. As a result, the Board believes that companies can determine reliable fair value amounts for derivatives.[18]

On the income statement, a company should recognize any unrealized gain or loss in income, if it uses the derivative for speculation purposes. If using the derivative for hedging purposes, the accounting for any gain or loss depends on the type of hedge used. We discuss the accounting for hedged transactions later in the appendix.

In summary, companies follow these guidelines in accounting for derivatives.

1. Recognize derivatives in the financial statements as assets and liabilities.
2. Report derivatives at fair value.
3. Recognize gains and losses resulting from speculation in derivatives immediately in income.
4. Report gains and losses resulting from hedge transactions differently, depending on the type of hedge.

Example of Derivative Financial Instrument—Speculation

To illustrate the measurement and reporting of a derivative for speculative purposes, we examine a derivative whose value depends on the market price of Laredo Inc. common stock. A company can realize a gain from the increase in the value of the Laredo shares with the use of a derivative, such as a call option.[19] A **call option** gives the holder the right, but not the obligation, to buy shares at a preset price. This price is often referred to as the **strike price** or the **exercise price**.

For example, assume a company enters into a call option contract with Baird Investment Co., which gives it the option to purchase Laredo stock at $100 per share.[20] If the price of Laredo stock increases above $100, the company can exercise this option and purchase the shares for $100 per share. If Laredo's stock never increases above $100 per share, the call option is worthless.

[17] GAAP covers accounting and reporting for all derivative instruments, whether financial or not. In this appendix, we place greater focus on derivative financial instruments because of their widespread use in practice. [7]

[18] As discussed in earlier chapters, fair value is defined as "the price that would be received to sell an asset or paid to transfer a liability in an orderly transaction between market participants at the measurement date." Fair value is therefore a market-based measure. As discussed in Chapter 2, the FASB has also developed a fair value hierarchy, which indicates the priority of valuation techniques to use to determine fair value. *Level 1* fair value measures are based on observable inputs that reflect quoted prices for identical assets or liabilities in active markets. *Level 2* measures are based on inputs other than quoted prices included in Level 1 but that can be corroborated with observable data. *Level 3* fair values are based on unobservable inputs (for example, a company's own data or assumptions). Thus, Level 1 is the most reliable because it is based on quoted prices, like a closing stock price in the *Wall Street Journal*. Level 2 is the next most reliable and would rely on evaluating similar assets or liabilities in active markets. For Level 3 (the least reliable), much judgment is needed, based on the best information available, to arrive at a relevant and reliable fair value measurement. [8]

[19] Investors can use a different type of option contract—a **put option**—to realize a gain if anticipating a decline in the Laredo stock value. A put option gives the holder the option to sell shares at a preset price. Thus, a put option **increases** in value when the underlying asset **decreases** in value.

[20] Baird Investment Co. is referred to as the **counterparty**. Counterparties frequently are investment bankers or other companies that hold inventories of financial instruments.

Accounting Entries

To illustrate the accounting for a call option, assume that the company purchases a call option contract on January 2, 2020, when Laredo shares are trading at $100 per share. The contract gives it the option to purchase 1,000 shares (referred to as the **notional amount**) of Laredo stock at an option price of $100 per share. The option expires on April 30, 2020. The company purchases the call option for $400 and makes the following entry.

	January 2, 2020	
Call Option	400	
Cash		400

This payment is referred to as the **option premium**. It is generally much less than the cost of purchasing the shares directly. The option premium consists of two amounts: (1) intrinsic value and (2) time value. Illustration 17A.1 shows the formula to compute the option premium.

ILLUSTRATION 17A.1
Option Premium Formula

Option Premium = Intrinsic Value + Time Value

Intrinsic value is the difference between the market price and the preset strike price at any point in time. It represents the amount realized by the option holder, if exercising the option immediately. On January 2, 2020, the intrinsic value is zero because the market price equals the preset strike price.

Time value refers to the option's value over and above its intrinsic value. Time value reflects the possibility that the option has a fair value greater than zero. How? Because there is some expectation that the price of Laredo shares will increase above the strike price during the option term. As indicated, the time value for the option is $400.[21]

The following additional data are available with respect to the call option.

Date	Market Price of Laredo Shares	Time Value of Call Option
March 31, 2020	$120 per share	$100
April 16, 2020	115 per share	60

As indicated, on March 31, 2020, the price of Laredo shares increases to $120 per share. The intrinsic value of the call option contract is now $20,000. That is, the company can exercise the call option and purchase 1,000 shares from Baird Investment for $100 per share. It can then sell the shares in the market for $120 per share. This gives the company a gain of $20,000 ($120,000 – $100,000) on the option contract.[22] It records the increase in the intrinsic value of the option as follows.

	March 31, 2020	
Call Option	20,000	
Unrealized Holding Gain or Loss—Income		20,000

A market appraisal indicates that the time value of the option at March 31, 2020, is $100.[23] The company records this change in value of the option as follows.

[21]This cost is estimated using option-pricing models, such as the Black-Scholes equation. The volatility of the underlying stock, the expected life of the option, the risk-free rate of interest, and expected dividends on the underlying stock during the option term affect the Black-Scholes fair value estimate.

[22]In practice, investors generally do not have to actually buy and sell the Laredo shares to settle the option and realize the gain. This is referred to as the **net settlement feature of option contracts**.

[23]The decline in value reflects both the decreased likelihood that the Laredo shares will continue to increase in value over the option period and the shorter time to maturity of the option contract.

March 31, 2020

Unrealized Holding Gain or Loss—Income	300	
Call Option ($400 – $100)		300

At March 31, 2020, the company reports the call option in its balance sheet at fair value of $20,100.[24] The unrealized holding gain increases net income for the period. The loss on the time value of the option decreases net income.

On April 16, 2020, the company settles the option before it expires. To properly record the settlement, it updates the value of the option for the decrease in the intrinsic value of $5,000 [($120 – $115) × 1,000] as follows.

April 16, 2020

Unrealized Holding Gain or Loss—Income	5,000	
Call Option		5,000

The decrease in the time value of the option of $40 ($100 – $60) is recorded as follows.

April 16, 2020

Unrealized Holding Gain or Loss—Income	40	
Call Option		40

Thus, at the time of the settlement, the call option's carrying value is as follows.

Call Option

January 2, 2020	400	March 31, 2020	300
March 31, 2020	20,000	April 16, 2020	5,000
		April 16, 2020	40
Balance, April 16, 2020	15,060		

The company records the settlement of the option contract with Baird as follows.

April 16, 2020

Cash	15,000	
Loss on Settlement of Call Option	60	
Call Option		15,060

Illustration 17A.2 summarizes the effects of the call option contract on net income.

Date	Transaction	Income (Loss) Effect
March 31, 2020	Net increase in value of call option ($20,000 – $300)	$19,700
April 16, 2020	Decrease in value of call option ($5,000 + $40)	(5,040)
April 16, 2020	Settle call option	(60)
	Total net income	$14,600

ILLUSTRATION 17A.2
Effect on Income—Derivative Financial Instrument

The accounting summarized in Illustration 17A.2 is in accord with GAAP. That is, because the call option meets the definition of an asset, the company records it in the balance sheet on March 31, 2020. Furthermore, it reports the call option at fair value, with any gains or losses reported in income.

Differences Between Traditional and Derivative Financial Instruments

How does a traditional financial instrument differ from a derivative one? A derivative financial instrument has the following three basic characteristics. [9]

[24]As indicated earlier, the total value of the option at any point in time equals the intrinsic value plus the time value.

1. ***The instrument has (1) one or more underlyings and (2) an identified payment provision.*** An underlying is a specified interest rate, security price, commodity price, index of prices or rates, or other market-related variable. The interaction of the underlying, with the face amount or the number of units specified in the derivative contract (the notional amounts), determines payment. For example, the value of the call option increased in value when the value of the Laredo stock increased. In this case, the underlying is the stock price. To arrive at the payment provision, multiply the change in the stock price by the number of shares (notional amount).
2. ***The instrument requires little or no investment at the inception of the contract.*** To illustrate, the company paid a small premium to purchase the call option—an amount much less than if purchasing the Laredo shares as a direct investment.
3. ***The instrument requires or permits net settlement.*** As indicated in the call option example, the company could realize a profit on the call option without taking possession of the shares. This **net settlement** feature reduces the transaction costs associated with derivatives.

Illustration 17A.3 summarizes the differences between traditional and derivative financial instruments. Here, we use a trading security for the traditional financial instrument and a call option as an example of a derivative one.

ILLUSTRATION 17A.3

Features of Traditional and Derivative Financial Instruments

Feature	Traditional Financial Instrument (Trading Security)	Derivative Financial Instrument (Call Option)
Payment provision	Stock price times the number of shares.	Change in stock price (underlying) times number of shares (notional amount).
Initial investment	Investor pays full cost.	Initial investment is much less than full cost.
Settlement	Deliver stock to receive cash.	Receive cash equivalent, based on changes in stock price times the number of shares.

Derivatives Used for Hedging

LEARNING OBJECTIVE *6

Explain the accounting for hedges.

Flexibility in use and the low-cost features of derivatives relative to traditional financial instruments explain the popularity of derivatives. An additional use for derivatives is in risk management. For example, companies such as Coca-Cola, ExxonMobil, and General Electric borrow and lend substantial amounts in credit markets. In doing so, they are exposed to significant **interest rate risk**. That is, they face substantial risk that the fair values or cash flows of interest-sensitive assets or liabilities will change if interest rates increase or decrease. These same companies also have significant international operations. As such, they are also exposed to **exchange rate risk**—the risk that changes in foreign currency exchange rates will negatively impact the profitability of their international businesses.

Companies can use derivatives to offset the negative impacts of changes in interest rates or foreign currency exchange rates. This use of derivatives is referred to as hedging. GAAP established accounting and reporting standards for derivative financial instruments used in hedging activities. The FASB allows special accounting for two types of hedges—fair value and cash flow hedges.[25]

[25]GAAP also addresses the accounting for certain foreign currency hedging transactions. In general, these transactions are special cases of the two hedges we discuss here. [10] Understanding of foreign currency hedging transactions requires knowledge related to consolidation of multinational entities, which is beyond the scope of this text.

What Do the Numbers Mean? Risky Business

As shown in the following graph, use of derivatives has grown substantially in recent years. In fact, nearly *$550 trillion* (in notional amounts) in derivative contracts were in play at the end of 2017. The primary players in the market for derivatives are large companies and various financial institutions, which continue to find new uses for derivatives for speculation and risk management.

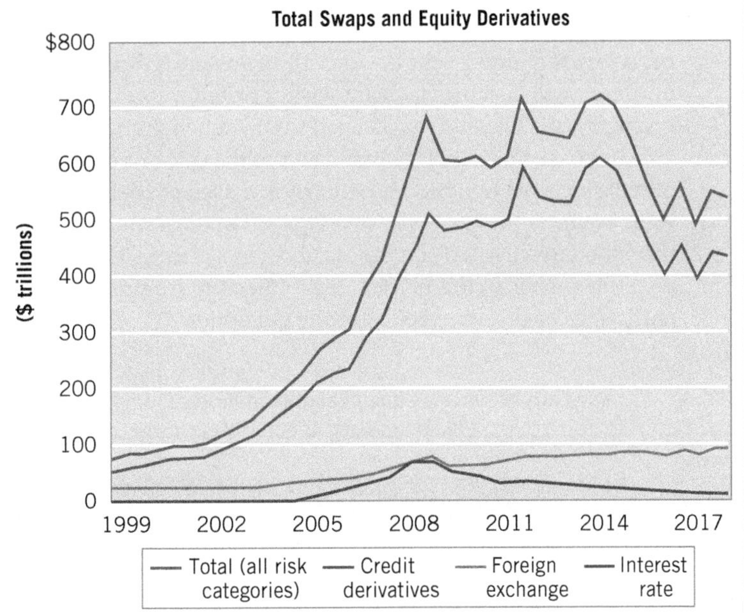

Sources: Data from International Swaps and Derivatives Association Market Survey (2017); *https://www.bis.org/statistics/about_derivatives_stats.htm.*

Financial engineers continue to develop new uses for derivatives, many times through the use of increasingly complex webs of transactions, spanning a number of markets. As new uses for derivatives appear, the financial system as a whole can be dramatically affected. As a result, some market-watchers are concerned about the risk that a crisis in one company or sector could bring the entire financial system to its knees.

This was the case recently when credit default swaps were used to facilitate the sales of mortgage-backed securities (MBS). However, when the real estate market went south, the MBS defaulted, exposing large international financial institutions, like **Barclays**, **AIG**, and **Bank of America**, to massive losses. The losses were so widespread that government bailouts were required to prevent international securities markets from collapsing. In response, market regulators are proposing new rules to mitigate risks to broader markets from derivatives trading.

Source: P. Eavis, "Bill on Derivatives Overhaul Is Long Overdue," *Wall Street Journal* (April 14, 2010).

Fair Value Hedge

In a **fair value hedge**, a company uses a derivative to hedge (offset) the exposure to changes in the fair value of a recognized asset or liability or of an unrecognized commitment. In a perfectly hedged position, the gain or loss on the fair value of the derivative equals and offsets that of the hedged asset or liability.

To illustrate a fair value hedge, assume that on December 1, 2020, Hayward Tire Fabricators, Inc. holds an inventory of 1,000 tractor tires, with a cost of $200 per tire. Hayward has been building an inventory of tractor tires in anticipation of demand for these tires in the upcoming spring planting season. Hayward records the inventory on its balance sheet at $200,000 (1,000 × $200), using lower-of-FIFO-cost-or-net realizable value.

Illustration 17A.4 indicates how Hayward reports the tire inventory in its balance sheet at December 31, 2020, assuming none of the tires have been sold.

ILLUSTRATION 17A.4

Balance Sheet Presentation of Inventory

Hayward Tire Fabricators, Inc. Balance Sheet (partial) December 31, 2020	
Current assets	
Inventory	$200,000

Hayward could benefit from an increase in the price of tires (based on realized gross profit on tire sales). But until it sells the tires, the company is exposed to the risk that the value of the tire inventory will decline. Hayward wishes to hedge its exposure to fair value declines for its tire inventory (the inventory is pledged as collateral for one of its bank loans).

To hedge this risk, Hayward locks in the value of its tire inventory on January 2, 2021, by purchasing a put option to sell rubber at a fixed price. Hayward designates the option as a fair value hedge of the tire inventory. This put option (which expires in two years) gives Hayward the option to sell 4,000 pounds of rubber at a price of $50 per pound, which is the current spot price for rubber in the market. Since the exercise price equals the current market price, no entry is necessary at inception of the put option.[26]

January 2, 2021

No entry required. A memorandum indicates the signing of the put option contract and its designation as a fair value hedge for the tire inventory.

At March 31, 2021, the fair value of the inventory has declined by 10 percent. Hayward records the following entry for the tire inventory.

March 31, 2021		
Unrealized Holding Gain or Loss—Income ($200,000 × .10)	20,000	
Allowance to Reduce Inventory to Fair Value		20,000

Note that upon designation of the hedge, the accounting for the inventory fair value change deviates from regular GAAP.[27] That is, Hayward records an unrealized holding loss in income, even though it has not yet sold the inventory. **If Hayward had not followed this accounting, a mismatch of gains and losses in the income statement would result.** Thus, special accounting for the hedged item (in this case, the tire inventory) is necessary in a fair value hedge.

The following journal entry records the increase in value of the put option to sell rubber, assuming that the spot price for rubber declined by 10 percent.

March 31, 2021		
Put Option	20,000	
Unrealized Holding Gain or Loss—Income		20,000

The decline in the spot price of rubber results in an increase in the fair value of the put option. That is, Hayward could realize a gain on the put option, by purchasing 4,000 pounds of rubber in the open market for $45 (.90 × $50), and then exercise the put option, selling the rubber for $50 per pound. This results in a gain to Hayward of $20,000 (4,000 pounds × $5).[28]

Illustration 17A.5 indicates how Hayward reports the amounts related to the Inventory and the put option.

[26] To simplify the example, we assume no premium is paid for the option. A put option on rubber is a good candidate for this hedge because the rubber raw material is the primary driver of fair value changes on tires.

[27] The accounting for inventory is discussed in Chapters 8 and 9. In this example, the inventory is not subject to a lower-of-cost-or-net realizable value assessment.

[28] In practice, Hayward generally does not have to actually buy and sell the rubber in the commodity market to realize this gain. Rather, unless the counterparty wants to hold the rubber, Hayward can "close out" the contract by having the counterparty pay it $20,000 in cash. This is an example of the net settlement feature of derivatives.

ILLUSTRATION 17A.5

Balance Sheet Presentation of Fair Value Hedge

Hayward Tire Fabricators, Inc.
Balance Sheet (partial)
March 31, 2021

Current assets	
Inventory (net of the allowance of $20,000)	$180,000
Put option	20,000

As indicated, the increase in fair value on the option offsets or hedges the decline in value of Hayward's tire inventory. By using fair value accounting for both the inventory and the put option, the financial statements reflect the underlying substance of Hayward's net exposure to the risks of holding the inventory. That is, the balance sheet reports the amount that Hayward would receive for the inventory and the put option contract if Hayward sold and settled them, respectively.

Illustration 17A.6 indicates the reporting of the effects of the hedging transaction on income for the year ended December 31, 2021.

ILLUSTRATION 17A.6

Income Statement Presentation of Fair Value Hedge

Hayward Tire Fabricators, Inc.
Income Statement (partial)
For the Quarter Ended March 31, 2021

Other income	
Unrealized holding gain—put option	$20,000
Unrealized holding loss—inventory	(20,000)

The income statement indicates that the gain on the put option offsets the loss on the inventory.[29] The reporting for these financial instruments, even when they reflect a hedging relationship, illustrates why the FASB argues that fair value accounting provides the most relevant information about financial instruments, including derivatives.

Cash Flow Hedge

Companies use cash flow hedges to hedge exposures to **cash flow risk**, which results from the variability in cash flows. The FASB allows special accounting for cash flow hedges. Generally, companies measure and report derivatives at fair value on the balance sheet. They report gains and losses directly in net income. However, companies account for derivatives used in cash flow hedges at fair value on the balance sheet, but they **record gains or losses in equity, as part of other comprehensive income.**

To illustrate, assume that in September 2020, Allied Can Co. anticipates purchasing 1,000 metric tons of aluminum in January 2021. Concerned that prices for aluminum will increase in the next few months, Allied wants to hedge the risk that it might pay higher prices for inventory in January 2021. As a result, Allied enters into an aluminum futures contract.

A futures contract gives the holder the right and the obligation to purchase an asset at a preset price for a specified period of time.[30] In this case, the aluminum futures contract gives Allied the right and the obligation to purchase 1,000 metric tons of aluminum for $1,550 per ton. This contract price is good until the contract expires in January 2021. The underlying for this derivative is the price of aluminum. If the price of aluminum rises above $1,550, the value

[29]Note that the fair value changes in the option contract will not offset *increases* in the value of the Hayward inventory. Should the price of rubber increase above $50 per pound, Hayward would have no incentive to exercise the put option.

[30]A **futures contract** is a firm contractual agreement between a buyer and seller for a specified asset on a fixed date in the future which also trades on an exchange. The contract also has a standard specification so both parties know exactly what is being traded. A **forward** is similar but is not traded on an exchange and does not have standardized conditions.

of the futures contract to Allied increases. Why? Because Allied will be able to purchase the aluminum at the lower price of $1,550 per ton.[31]

Allied enters into the futures contract on September 1, 2020. Assume that the price to be paid today for inventory to be delivered in January—the **spot price**—equals the contract price. With the two prices equal, the futures contract has no value. Therefore, no entry is necessary.

September 2020

No entry required. A memorandum indicates the signing of the futures contract.

At December 31, 2020, the price for January delivery of aluminum increases to $1,575 per metric ton. Allied makes the following entry to record the increase in the value of the futures contract.

December 31, 2020		
Futures Contract	25,000	
Unrealized Holding Gain or Loss—Equity [($1,575 − $1,550) × 1,000 tons]		25,000

Allied reports the futures contract in the balance sheet as a current asset. It reports the gain on the futures contract as part of other comprehensive income.

Since Allied has not yet purchased and sold the inventory, this gain arises from an **anticipated transaction**. In this type of transaction, **a company accumulates in equity gains or losses on the futures contract as part of other comprehensive income until the period in which it sells the inventory, thereby affecting earnings.**

In January 2021, Allied purchases 1,000 metric tons of aluminum for $1,575 and makes the following entry.[32]

January 2021		
Aluminum Inventory	1,575,000	
Cash ($1,575 × 1,000 tons)		1,575,000

At the same time, Allied makes final settlement on the futures contract. It records the following entry.

January 2021		
Cash	25,000	
Futures Contract ($1,575,000 − $1,550,000)		25,000

Through use of the futures contract derivative, Allied fixes the cost of its inventory. The $25,000 futures contract settlement offsets the amount paid to purchase the inventory at the prevailing market price of $1,575,000. The result: net cash outflow of $1,550 per metric ton, as desired. As **Illustration 17A.7** shows, Allied has therefore effectively hedged the cash flow for the purchase of inventory.

ILLUSTRATION 17A.7 Effect of Hedge on Cash Flows

Anticipated Cash Flows		Actual Cash Flows	
Wish to fix cash paid for inventory at $1,550,000	=	Actual cash paid	$1,575,000
		Less: Cash received on futures contract	(25,000)
		Final cash paid	$1,550,000

[31]As with the earlier call option example, the actual aluminum does not have to be exchanged. Rather, the parties to the futures contract settle by paying the cash difference between the futures price and the price of aluminum on each settlement date.

[32]In practice, futures contracts are settled on a daily basis. For our purposes, we show only one settlement for the entire amount.

There are no income effects at this point. Allied accumulates in equity the gain on the futures contract as part of other comprehensive income until the period when it sells the inventory, affecting earnings through cost of goods sold.

For example, assume that Allied processes the aluminum into finished goods (cans). The total cost of the cans (including the aluminum purchases in January 2021) is $1,700,000. Allied sells the cans in July 2021 for $2,000,000, and records this sale as follows.

July 2021		
Cash	2,000,000	
Sales Revenue		2,000,000
Cost of Goods Sold	1,700,000	
Inventory (cans)		1,700,000

Since the effect of the anticipated transaction has now affected earnings, Allied makes the following entry related to the hedging transaction.

July 2021		
Unrealized Holding Gain or Loss—Equity	25,000	
Cost of Goods Sold		25,000

The gain on the futures contract, which Allied reported as part of other comprehensive income, now reduces cost of goods sold. As a result, the cost of aluminum included in the overall cost of goods sold is $1,550,000. The futures contract has worked as planned. Allied has managed the cash paid for aluminum inventory and the amount of cost of goods sold.

Other Reporting Issues

LEARNING OBJECTIVE *7

Identify special reporting issues related to derivative financial instruments that cause unique accounting problems.

The preceding examples illustrate the basic reporting issues related to the accounting for derivatives. Next, we discuss the following additional issues:

1. The accounting for embedded derivatives.
2. Qualifying hedge criteria.

Embedded Derivatives

As we indicated at the beginning of this appendix, rapid innovation in the development of complex financial instruments drove efforts toward unifying and improving the accounting standards for derivatives. In recent years, this innovation has led to the development of **hybrid securities**. These securities have characteristics of both debt and equity. They often combine traditional and derivative financial instruments.

For example, a convertible bond (discussed in Chapter 16) is a hybrid instrument. It consists of two parts: (1) a debt security, referred to as the **host security**, combined with (2) an option to convert the bond to shares of common stock, the **embedded derivative**.

To provide consistency in accounting for similar derivatives, a company must account for embedded derivatives similarly to other derivatives. Therefore, to account for an embedded derivative, a company **should separate it from the host security** and then account for it using the accounting for derivatives. This separation process is referred to as **bifurcation**.[33]

[33] A company can also designate such a derivative as a hedging instrument. The company would apply the hedge accounting provisions outlined earlier in the chapter.

Thus, a company investing in a convertible bond must separate the stock option component of the instrument. It then accounts for the derivative (the stock option) at fair value and the host instrument (the debt) according to GAAP, as if there were no embedded derivative.[34]

Qualifying Hedge Criteria

> **Global View**
> IFRS qualifying hedge criteria are similar to those used in GAAP.

The FASB identified certain criteria that hedging transactions must meet before requiring the special accounting for hedges (see Global View). The FASB designed these criteria to ensure the use of hedge accounting in a consistent manner across different hedge transactions. The general criteria relate to the following areas.

1. ***Documentation, risk management, and designation.*** At inception of the hedge, there must be formal documentation of the hedging relationship, the company's risk management objective, and the strategy for undertaking the hedge. Designation refers to identifying the hedging instrument, the hedged item or transaction, the nature of the risk being hedged, and how the hedging instrument will offset changes in the fair value or cash flows attributable to the hedged risk.

   The FASB decided that documentation and designation are critical to the implementation of the special accounting for hedges. Without these requirements, companies might try to apply the hedge accounting provisions retroactively, only in response to negative changes in market conditions, to offset the negative impact of a transaction on the financial statements. Allowing special hedge accounting in such a setting could mask the speculative nature of the original transaction.

2. ***Effectiveness of the hedging relationship.*** At inception and on an ongoing basis, the hedging relationship should be highly effective in achieving offsetting changes in fair value or cash flows. Companies must assess effectiveness whenever preparing financial statements.

   The general guideline for effectiveness is that the fair values or cash flows of the hedging instrument (the derivative) and the hedged item exhibit a high degree of correlation. In practice, high effectiveness is assumed when the correlation is close to one (e.g., within plus or minus 10%). In our earlier hedging examples (put option and the futures contract on aluminum inventory), the fair values and cash flows are perfectly correlated. That is, when the cash payment for the inventory purchase increased, it offset, dollar for dollar, the cash received on the futures contract.

   If the effectiveness criterion is not met, either at inception or because of changes following inception of the hedging relationship, the FASB no longer allows special hedge accounting. The company should then account for the derivative as a free-standing derivative.[35]

3. ***Effect on reported earnings of changes in fair values or cash flows.*** A change in the fair value of a hedged item or variation in the cash flow of a hedged forecasted transaction must have the potential to change the amount recognized in reported earnings.[36] There is no need for special hedge accounting if a company accounts for both the hedging instrument and the hedged item at fair value under existing GAAP. In this case, earnings will properly reflect the offsetting gains and losses.

---

[34]The issuer of the convertible bonds would not bifurcate the option component of the convertible bonds payable. GAAP explicitly precludes embedded derivative accounting for an embedded derivative that is indexed to a company's own common stock. If the conversion feature was tied to **another company's** stock, then the derivative would be bifurcated.

[35]That is, the accounting for the part of a derivative that is not effective in a hedge is at fair value, with gains and losses recorded in income.

[36]GAAP gives companies the option to measure most types of financial instruments—from equity investments to debt issued by the company—at fair value. Changes in fair value are recognized in net income each reporting period. Thus, GAAP provides companies with the opportunity to hedge their financial instruments without the complexity inherent in applying hedge accounting provisions. For example, if the fair value option is used, bifurcation of an embedded derivative is not required. [11]

For example, special accounting is not needed for a fair value hedge of a trading security, because a company accounts for both the investment and the derivative at fair value on the balance sheet with gains or losses reported in earnings. Thus, "special" hedge accounting is necessary only when there is a mismatch of the accounting effects for the hedging instrument and the hedged item under GAAP.[37]

Summary of Derivatives Accounting

Illustration 17A.8 summarizes the accounting provisions for derivatives and hedging transactions.

ILLUSTRATION 17A.8

Summary of Derivative Accounting under GAAP

Derivative Use	Accounting for Derivative	Accounting for Hedged Item	Common Example
Speculation	At fair value with unrealized holding gains and losses recorded in income.	Not applicable.	Call or put option on an equity security.
Hedging			
Fair value	At fair value with holding gains and losses recorded in income.	At fair value with gains and losses recorded in income.	Put option to hedge inventory.
Cash flow	At fair value with unrealized holding gains and losses from the hedge recorded in other comprehensive income, and reclassified in income when the hedged transaction's cash flows affect earnings.	Use other generally accepted accounting principles for the hedged item.	Use of a futures contract to hedge a forecasted purchase of inventory.

As indicated, the general accounting for derivatives relies on fair values. GAAP also establishes special accounting guidance when companies use derivatives **for hedging purposes**. For example, when a company uses a put option to hedge price changes in inventory in a fair value hedge (see the Hayward example earlier), it records unrealized gains on the investment in earnings, which is not GAAP for inventory without such a hedge. This special accounting is justified in order to accurately report the nature of the hedging relationship in the balance sheet (recording both the put option and the inventory at fair value) and in the income statement (reporting offsetting gains and losses in the same period).

Special accounting also is used for cash flow hedges. Companies account for derivatives used in qualifying cash flow hedges at fair value on the balance sheet, but record unrealized holding gains or losses in other comprehensive income until selling or settling the hedged item. In a cash flow hedge, a company continues to record the hedged item at its historical cost.

Disclosure requirements for derivatives are complex. Recent pronouncements on fair value information and financial instruments provide a helpful disclosure framework for reporting derivative instruments. Appendix 17B illustrates many of these disclosures, except for discussion of hedging issues. In general, companies that have derivatives are required to disclose the objectives for holding or issuing those instruments (speculation or hedging), the hedging context (fair value or cash flow), and the strategies for achieving risk-management objectives.

[37]An important criterion specific to cash flow hedges is that the forecasted transaction in a cash flow hedge "is likely to occur." A company should support this probability (defined as significantly greater than the term "more likely than not") by observable facts such as frequency of similar past transactions and its financial and operational ability to carry out the transaction.

Comprehensive Hedge Accounting Example

To provide a comprehensive example of hedge accounting, we examine the use of an interest rate swap. First, let's consider how swaps work and why companies use them.

Options and futures trade on organized securities exchanges. Because of this, options and futures have standardized terms. Although that standardization makes the trading easier, it limits the flexibility needed to tailor contracts to specific circumstances. In addition, most types of derivatives have relatively short time horizons, thereby excluding their use for reducing long-term risk exposure.

As a result, many corporations instead turn to the swap, a very popular type of derivative. A **swap** is a transaction between two parties in which the first party promises to make a payment to the second party. Similarly, the second party promises to make a simultaneous payment to the first party.

The most common type of swap is the **interest rate swap**. In this type, one party makes payments based on a fixed or floating rate, and the second party does just the opposite. In most cases, large money-center banks bring together the two parties. These banks handle the flow of payments between the parties, as shown in **Illustration 17A.9**.

ILLUSTRATION 17A.9 **Swap Transaction**

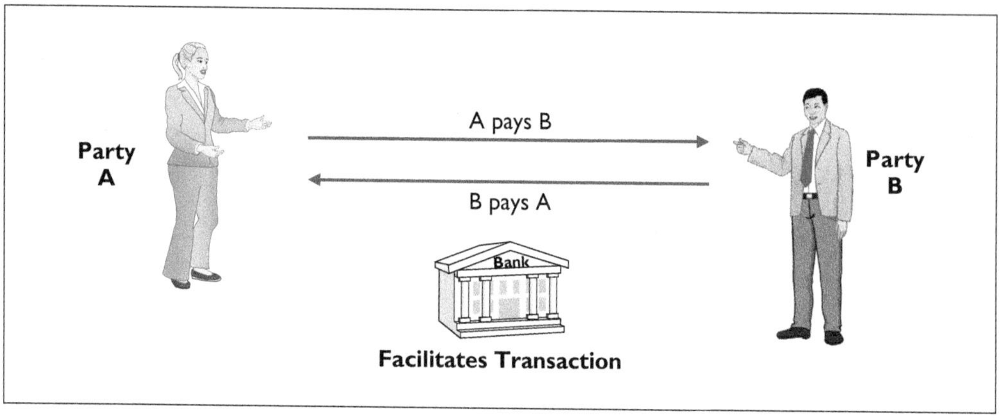

Fair Value Hedge

To illustrate the use of a swap in a fair value hedge, assume that Jones Company issues $1,000,000 of five-year, 8 percent bonds on January 2, 2020. Jones records this transaction as follows.

	January 2, 2020	
Cash	1,000,000	
Bonds Payable		1,000,000

Jones offered a fixed interest rate to appeal to investors. But Jones is concerned that if market interest rates decline, the fair value of the liability will increase. The company will then suffer an economic loss.[38] To protect against the risk of loss, Jones hedges the risk of a decline in interest rates by entering into a five-year interest rate swap contract. Jones agrees to the following terms:

1. Jones will receive fixed payments at 8 percent (based on the $1,000,000 amount).
2. Jones will pay variable rates, based on the market rate in effect for the life of the swap contract. The variable rate at the inception of the contract is 6.8 percent.

As **Illustration 17A.10** shows, this swap allows Jones to change the interest on the bonds payable from a fixed rate to a variable rate.

[38]This economic loss arises because Jones is locked into the 8 percent interest payments even if rates decline.

ILLUSTRATION 17A.10 Interest Rate Swap

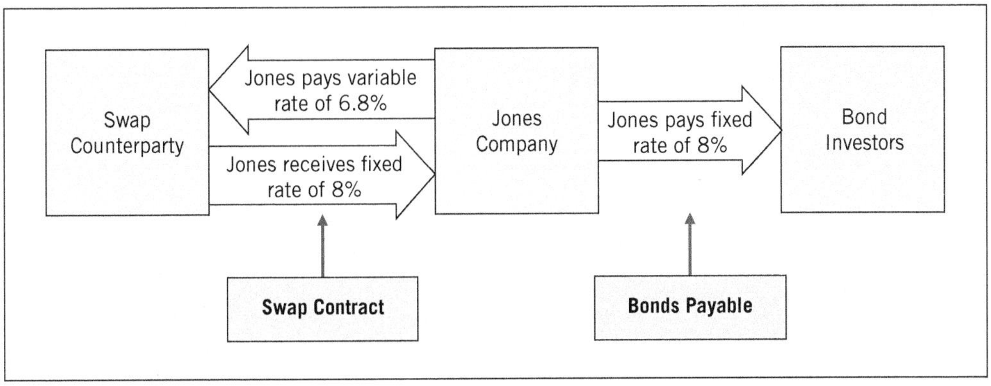

The settlement dates for the swap correspond to the interest payment dates on the debt (December 31). On each interest payment (settlement) date, Jones and the counterparty compute the difference between current market interest rates and the fixed rate of 8 percent, and determine the value of the swap.[39] If interest rates decline, the value of the swap contract to Jones increases (Jones has a gain), while at the same time Jones's fixed-rate debt obligation increases (Jones has an economic loss).

The swap is an effective risk-management tool in this setting. Its value relates to the same underlying (interest rates) that will affect the value of the fixed-rate bond payable. Thus, if the value of the swap goes up, it offsets the loss related to the debt obligation.

Assuming that Jones enters into the swap on January 2, 2020 (the same date as the issuance of the debt), the swap at this time has no value. Therefore, no entry is necessary.

January 2, 2020

No entry required. A memorandum indicates the signing of the swap contract.

At the end of 2020, Jones makes the interest payment on the bonds. It records this transaction as follows.

December 31, 2020

Interest Expense	80,000	
Cash (.08 × $1,000,000)		80,000

At the end of 2020, market interest rates have declined substantially. Therefore, the value of the swap contract increases. Recall (see Illustration 17A.9) that in the swap, Jones receives a fixed rate of 8 percent, or $80,000 ($1,000,000 × .08), and pays a variable rate (6.8%), or $68,000. Jones therefore receives $12,000 ($80,000 − $68,000) as a settlement payment on the swap contract on the first interest payment date. Jones records this transaction as follows.

December 31, 2020

Cash	12,000	
Interest Expense		12,000

In addition, a market appraisal indicates that the value of the interest rate swap has increased $40,000. Jones records this increase in value as follows.[40]

December 31, 2020

Swap Contract	40,000	
Unrealized Holding Gain or Loss—Income		40,000

Jones reports this swap contract in the balance sheet. It reports the gain on the hedging transaction in the income statement. Because interest rates have declined, the company records a loss and a related increase in its liability as follows.

[39]The underlying for an interest rate swap is some index of market interest rates. The most commonly used index is the London Interbank Offer Rate, or LIBOR. In this example, we assume the LIBOR is 6.8 percent.

[40]Theoretically, this fair value change reflects the present value of expected future differences in variable and fixed interest rates.

December 31, 2020		
Unrealized Holding Gain or Loss—Income	40,000	
Bonds Payable		40,000

Jones reports the loss on the hedging activity in net income. It adjusts bonds payable in the balance sheet to fair value (which deviates from normal accounting at amortized cost).

Financial Statement Presentation of an Interest Rate Swap

Illustration 17A.11 indicates how Jones reports the asset and liability related to this hedging transaction on the balance sheet.

ILLUSTRATION 17A.11
Balance Sheet Presentation of Fair Value Hedge

Jones Company
Balance Sheet (partial)
December 31, 2020

Current assets	
Swap contract	$40,000
Long-term liabilities	
Bonds payable	$1,040,000

The effect on Jones's balance sheet is the addition of the swap asset and an increase in the carrying value of the bonds payable. Illustration 17A.12 indicates how Jones reports the effects of this swap transaction in the income statement.

ILLUSTRATION 17A.12
Income Statement Presentation of Fair Value Hedge

Jones Company
Income Statement (partial)
For the Year Ended December 31, 2020

Interest expense ($80,000 – $12,000)		$68,000
Other income		
Unrealized holding gain—swap contract	$40,000	
Unrealized holding loss—bonds payable	(40,000)	
Net gain (loss)		-0-

On the income statement, Jones reports interest expense of $68,000. Jones has effectively changed the debt's interest rate from fixed to variable. That is, by receiving a fixed rate and paying a variable rate on the swap, the company converts the fixed rate on the bond payable to variable. This results in an effective-interest rate of 6.8 percent in 2020.[41] Also, the gain on the swap offsets the loss related to the debt obligation. Therefore, the net gain or loss on the hedging activity is zero.

Illustration 17A.13 shows the overall impact of the swap transaction on the financial statements.

ILLUSTRATION 17A.13
Impact on Financial Statements of Fair Value Hedge

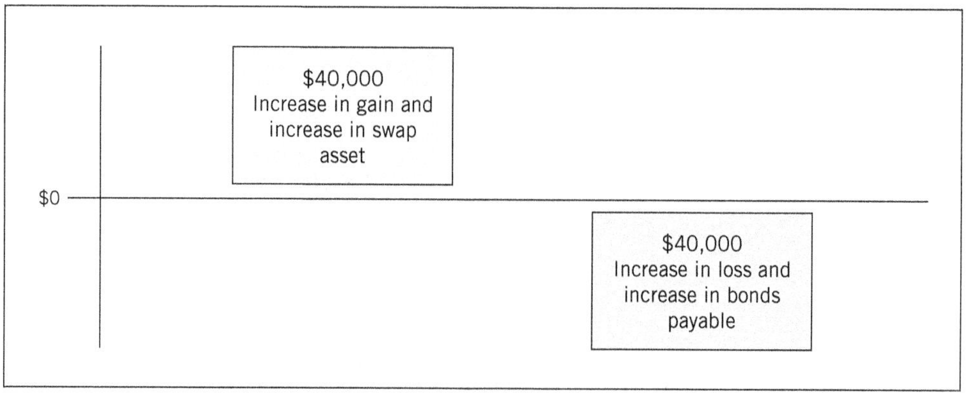

[41]Jones will apply similar accounting and measurement at future interest payment dates. Thus, if interest rates increase, Jones will continue to receive 8 percent on the swap (records a loss) but will also be locked into the fixed payments to the bondholders at an 8 percent rate (records a gain).

In summary, to account for fair value hedges (as illustrated in the Jones example) **record the derivative at its fair value in the balance sheet, and record any gains and losses in income**. Thus, the gain on the swap offsets or hedges the loss on the bond payable, due to the decline in interest rates (see **Global View**).

By adjusting the hedged item (the bond payable in the Jones case) to fair value, with the gain or loss recorded in earnings, the accounting for the Jones bond payable deviates from amortized cost. This special accounting is justified in order to report accurately the nature of the hedging relationship between the swap and the bond payable in the balance sheet (both the swap and the debt obligation are recorded at fair value) and in the income statement (offsetting gains and losses are reported in the same period).[42]

Global View

International accounting for hedges (*IFRS 9*) is similar to the provisions of GAAP.

Controversy and Concluding Remarks

Companies need rules to properly measure and report derivatives in financial statements. However, some argue that reporting derivatives at fair value results in unrealized gains and losses that are difficult to interpret. Others raise concerns about the complexity and cost of implementing GAAP in this area.

However, we believe that the long-term benefits of reporting derivatives at fair value far outweigh any implementation costs. As the volume and complexity of derivatives and hedging transactions continue to grow, so does the risk that investors and creditors will be exposed to unexpected losses arising from derivative transactions. Statement readers must have comprehensive information concerning many derivative financial instruments and the effects of hedging transactions using derivatives.

APPENDIX 17B Fair Value Disclosures

LEARNING OBJECTIVE *8

Describe required fair value disclosures.

As indicated in the chapter, the FASB believes that fair value information is relevant for making effective business decisions. However, others express concern about fair value measurements for two reasons: (1) the lack of reliability related to the fair value measurement in certain cases, and (2) the ability to manipulate fair value measurements to achieve financial results inconsistent with the underlying economics of the situation.

The Board recognizes these concerns and has attempted to develop a sound conceptual basis for measuring and reporting fair value information. In addition, it has placed emphasis on developing guidelines for reporting fair value information for financial instruments because many of these instruments have relatively active markets for which valuations can be reliably determined. The purpose of this appendix is to explain the disclosure requirements for financial instruments related to fair value information.

[42]An interest rate swap can also be used in a cash flow hedge. A common setting is the cash flow risk inherent in having variable rate debt as part of a company's debt structure. In this situation, the variable debt issuer can hedge the cash flow risk by entering into a swap contract to receive variable rate cash flows but pay fixed rate. The cash received on the swap contract will offset the variable cash flows to be paid on the debt obligation.

Disclosure of Fair Value Information: Financial Instruments

One requirement related to fair value disclosure is that both the cost and the fair value of all financial instruments be reported in the notes to the financial statements. [12] This enables readers of the financial statements to understand the fair value of the company's financial instruments and the potential gains and losses that might occur in the future as a result of these instruments.

The Board also decided that companies should disclose information that enables users to determine the extent of usage of fair value and the inputs used to implement fair value measurement. Two reasons for additional disclosure beyond the simple itemization of fair values are:

1. ***Differing levels of reliability exist in the measurement of fair value information.*** It therefore is important to understand the varying risks involved in measurement. It is difficult to incorporate these levels of uncertainty into the financial statements. Disclosure provides a framework for addressing the qualitative aspects related to risk and measurement.
2. ***Changes in the fair value of financial instruments are reported differently in the financial statements, depending on the type of financial instrument involved and whether the fair value option is employed.*** Note disclosure provides an opportunity to explain more precisely the impact that changes in the value of financial instruments have on financial results. In assessing the inputs, the Board recognizes that the reliability of the fair value measurement is of extreme importance. Many financial instruments are traded in active markets, and their valuation is not difficult. Other instruments are complex/illiquid, and their valuation is difficult.

To highlight these levels of reliability in valuation, the FASB established a fair value hierarchy. As discussed in Chapter 2, this hierarchy identifies three broad levels—1, 2, and 3—related to the measurement of fair values. Level 1 is the most reliable measurement because fair value is based on quoted prices in active markets *for identical assets or liabilities*. Level 2 is less reliable; it is not based on quoted market prices for identical assets and liabilities but instead may be based on *similar assets or liabilities*. Level 3 is least reliable; it uses unobservable inputs that reflect the company's assumption as to the value of the financial instrument.

Illustration 17B.1 is an example of a fair value note disclosure for Sabathia Company. It includes both the fair value amounts and the reliability level. (A similar disclosure would be presented for liabilities.)

ILLUSTRATION 17B.1

Example of Fair Value Hierarchy

Sabathia Company
Notes to the Financial Statements

($ in 000s)	Fair Value Measurements at Reporting Data Using			
Description	Fair Value 12/31/20	Quoted Prices in Active Markets for Identical Assets (Level 1)	Significant Other Observable Inputs (Level 2)	Significant Unobservable Inputs (Level 3)
Trading securities	$115	$105	$10	
Available-for-sale securities	75	75		
Derivatives	60	25	15	$20
Venture capital investments	10			10
Total	$260	$205	$25	$30

For assets and liabilities measured at fair value and classified as Level 3, a reconciliation of Level 3 changes for the period is required. In addition, companies should report an analysis of how Level 3 changes in fair value affect total gains and losses and their impact on net income. **Illustration 17B.2** is an example of this disclosure.

ILLUSTRATION 17B.2

Reconciliation of Level 3 Inputs

Sabathia Company
Notes to the Financial Statements

($ in 000s)	Fair Value Measurements Using Significant Unobservable Inputs (Level 3)		
	Derivatives	Venture Capital Investments	Total
Beginning balance	$14	$11	$25
Total gains or losses (realized/unrealized)			
Included in earnings (or changes in net assets)	11	(3)	8
Included in other comprehensive income	4		4
Purchases, issuances, and settlements	(7)	2	(5)
Transfers in and/or out of Level 3	(2)		(2)
Ending balance	$20	$10	$30
The amount of total gains or losses for the period included in earnings (or changes in net assets) attributable to the change in unrealized gains or losses relating to assets still held at the reporting date	$7	$2	$9

Gains and losses (realized and unrealized) included in earnings (or changes in net assets) for the period (above) are reported in trading revenues and in other revenues as follows.

	Trading Revenues	Other Revenues
Total gains or losses included in earnings (or changes in net assets) for the period (as shown in the table above)	$11	$(3)
Change in unrealized gains or losses relating to assets still held at reporting date	$7	$2

Sabathia Company's disclosure provides to the user of the financial statements an understanding of the following:

1. The carrying amount and the fair value of the company's financial instruments segregated by level of reliability. Thus, the reader of the financial statements has a basis for judging what credence should be given to the fair value amounts.
2. For Level 3 financial instruments, a reconciliation of the balance from the beginning to the end of the period. This reconciliation enables the reader to understand the composition of the change. It is important because these calculations are most affected by subjective estimates and could be subject to manipulation.
3. The impact of changes in fair value on the net assets of the company from one period to the next.

For companies that choose to use the fair value option for some or all of their financial instruments [13], they are permitted to incorporate the entire guidelines related to fair value measurement into one master schedule, or they can provide in a separate schedule information related solely to the fair value option.

Finally, companies must provide the following (with special emphasis on Level 3 measurements):

1. Quantitative information about significant unobservable inputs used for all Level 3 measurements.
2. A qualitative discussion about the sensitivity of recurring Level 3 measurements to changes in the unobservable inputs disclosed, including interrelationships between inputs.
3. Any transfers between Levels 1 and 2 of the fair value hierarchy.
4. Information about nonfinancial assets measured at fair value at amounts that differ from the assets' highest and best use.

5. The proper hierarchy classification for items that are not recognized on the balance sheet but are disclosed in the notes to the financial statements.

A typical disclosure related to Level 3 fair value measurements is presented in **Illustration 17B.3**.

ILLUSTRATION 17B.3 Quantitative Information about Level 3 Fair Value Measurements

($ in millions)	Fair Value at 12/31/2020	Valuation Technique(s)	Unobservable Input	Range (Weighted-Average)
Residential mortgage-backed securities	125	Discounted cash flow	Constant prepayment rate Probability of default Loss severity	3.5%–5.5% (4.5%) 5%–50% (10%) 40%–100% (60%)
Collateralized debt obligations	35	Consensus pricing	Offered quotes Comparability adjustments (%)	20–45 −10%–+15% (+5%)
Direct venture capital investments: Healthcare	53	Discounted cash flow	Weighted-average cost of capital Long-term revenue growth rate Long-term pretax operating margin Discount for lack of marketability[a] Control premium[a]	7%–16% (12.1%) 2%–5% (4.2%) 3%–20% (10.3%) 5%–20% (17%) 10%–30% (20%)
		Market-comparable companies	EBITDA multiple[b] Revenue multiple[b] Discount for lack of marketability[a] Control premium[a]	6.5–12 (9.5) 1.0–3.0 (2.0) 5%–20% (10%) 10%–20% (12%)
Credit contracts	38	Option model	Annualized volatility of credit[c] Counterparty credit risk[d] Own credit risk[d]	10%–20% 0.5–3.5% 0.3–2.0%

[a]Represents amounts used when the reporting entity has determined that market participants would take into account these premiums and discounts when pricing the investments.
[b]Represents amounts used when the reporting entity has determined that market participants would use such multiples when pricing the investments.
[c]Represents the range of the volatility curves used in the valuation analysis that the reporting entity has determined market participants would use when pricing the contracts.
[d]Represents the range of the credit default swap spread curves used in the valuation analysis that the reporting entity has determined market participants would use when pricing the contracts.

(*Note:* For liabilities, a similar table should be presented.)

Disclosure of Fair Values: Impaired Assets or Liabilities

In addition to financial instruments, companies often have assets or liabilities that are remeasured on a nonrecurring basis due to impairment. In this case, the fair value hierarchy can highlight the reliability of the measurement, coupled with the related gain or loss for the period. **Illustration 17B.4** highlights this disclosure for McClung Company.

ILLUSTRATION 17B.4
Disclosure of Fair Value, with Impairment

McClung Company
Notes to the Financial Statements

($ in millions)		Fair Value Measurements Using		
Description	Year Ended 12/31/20	Quoted Prices in Active Markets for Identical Assets (Level 1)	Significant Other Observable Inputs (Level 2)	Significant Unobservable Inputs (Level 3)
Long-lived assets held and used	$75	—	$75	—
Goodwill	30	—	—	$30
Long-lived assets held for sale	26	—	26	—

(continued)

ILLUSTRATION 17B.4

(continued)

Long-lived assets held and used with a carrying amount of $100 million were written down to their fair value of $75 million, resulting in an impairment charge of $25 million, which was included in earnings for the period.

Goodwill with a carrying amount of $65 million was written down, resulting in an impairment charge of $35 million, which was included in earnings for the period.

In accordance with the provisions of the Impairment or Disposal of Long-Lived Assets Subsections of FASB Codification Subtopic 360-10, long-lived assets held for sale with a carrying amount of $35 million were written down to their fair value of $26 million, less cost to sell of $6 million (or $20 million), resulting in a loss of $15 million, which was included in earnings for the period.

Conclusion

With recent joint FASB and IASB standard-setting efforts, we now have convergence with respect to fair value measurement, both in terms of the definition and measurement guidelines when fair value is the measurement approach in GAAP and IFRS. In addition, GAAP and IFRS have similar fair value disclosure requirements, as illustrated in this appendix. As the former chair of the IASB noted, this "marks the completion of a major convergence project and is a fundamentally important element of our joint response to the global crisis. The result is clearer and more consistent guidance on measuring fair value, where its use is already required."[43]

[43]The FASB continues to evaluate standards to improve existing disclosure requirements related to fair value measurement. For example, in its recent Accounting Standards Update (ASU 2016-01), the FASB requires separate presentation of financial assets and financial liabilities by measurement category and form of financial asset (e.g., securities or loans and receivables) on the balance sheet or in the accompanying notes to the financial statements.

Review and Practice

Key Terms Review

amortized cost 17-3
*anticipated transaction 17-36
*arbitrageurs 17-28
available-for-sale securities 17-3
*bifurcation 17-37
*call option 17-29
*cash flow hedge 17-35
consolidated financial statements 17-16
controlling interest 17-16
*counterparty 17-29(*n*)
debt securities 17-3
*derivative financial instruments, derivatives 17-26
*designation 17-38
*documentation 17-38
effective-interest method 17-4
*embedded derivative 17-37
equity method 17-15
equity securities 17-11
exchange for noncash consideration 17-12(*n*)
fair value 17-3
Fair Value Adjustment 17-7
*fair value hedge 17-33
fair value method 17-12
*forward contract 17-27
*futures contract 17-35
gains trading 17-9
*hedging 17-32
held-to-maturity securities 17-3
*highly effective 17-38
holding gain or loss 17-10
*host security 17-37
*hybrid security 17-37
*interest rate swap 17-40
*intrinsic value 17-30
investee 17-11
investor 17-11
*net settlements 17-30(*n*)
*notional amount 17-30
*option contract 17-27
*option premium 17-30
parent 17-16
*put option 17-29(*n*)
reclassification adjustment 17-22
*risk management 17-38
security 17-3(*n*)
significant influence 17-14
*speculators 17-28
*spot price 17-36
*strike (exercise) price 17-29
subsidiary 17-16
*swap 17-40
*time value 17-30
trading securities 17-3
*underlying 17-32

Learning Objectives Review

1 Describe the accounting for investments in debt securities.

(1) Carry and report *held-to-maturity debt securities* at amortized cost. (2) Value *trading debt securities* for reporting purposes at fair value, with unrealized holding gains or losses included in net income. (3) Value *available-for-sale debt securities* for reporting purposes at fair value, with unrealized holding gains or losses reported as other comprehensive income and as a separate component of stockholders' equity.

2 Describe the accounting for investments in equity securities.

The degree to which one corporation (investor) acquires an interest in the common stock of another corporation (investee) generally determines the accounting treatment for the investment. Long-term investments by one corporation in the common stock of another can be classified according to the percentage of the voting stock of the investee held by the investor.

3 Explain the equity and consolidation methods of accounting.

Under the **equity method**, the investor and the investee acknowledge a substantive economic relationship. The company originally records the investment at cost but subsequently adjusts the amount each period for changes in the net assets of the investee. That is, the investor's proportionate share of the earnings (losses) of the investee periodically increases (decreases) the investment's carrying amount. All dividends received by the investor from the investee decrease the investment's carrying amount. Under the **fair value method**, a company reports the equity investment at fair value each reporting period irrespective of the investee's earnings or dividends paid to it. A company applies the equity method to investment holdings between 20 percent and 50 percent of ownership. It applies the fair value method to holdings below 20 percent. Equity investments with holdings greater than 50 percent are accounted for using consolidation procedures.

4 Evaluate other major issues related to investments in debt and equity securities.

Fair Value Option. Companies have the option to report most financial instruments at fair value, with all gains and losses related to changes in fair value reported in the income statement. This option is applied on an instrument-by-instrument basis. The fair value option is generally available only at the time a company first purchases the financial asset or incurs a financial liability. If a company chooses to use the fair value option, it must measure this instrument at fair value until the company no longer has ownership.

Impairments. Refer to Illustration 17.19 for a summary of the guidelines related to impairments.

Reclassifications. A company needs a reclassification adjustment when it reports realized gains or losses as part of net income but also shows the amounts as part of other comprehensive income in the current or in previous periods. Companies should report unrealized holding gains or losses related to available-for-sale securities in other comprehensive income and the aggregate balance as accumulated comprehensive income on the balance sheet.

Transfers. Transfers of securities between categories of investments should be accounted for at fair value, with unrealized holding gains or losses treated in accordance with the nature of the transfer.

*5 Describe the uses of and accounting for derivatives.

Any company or individual that wants to ensure against different types of business risks may use derivative contracts to achieve this objective. In general, these transactions involve some type of hedge. Speculators also use derivatives, attempting to find an enhanced return. Speculators are very important to the derivatives market because they keep it liquid on a daily basis. Arbitrageurs attempt to exploit inefficiencies in various derivative contracts. A company primarily uses derivatives for purposes of hedging its exposure to fluctuations in interest rates, foreign currency exchange rates, and commodity prices.

Companies should recognize derivatives in the financial statements as assets and liabilities, and report them at fair value. Companies should recognize gains and losses resulting from speculation immediately in income. They report gains and losses resulting from hedge transactions in different ways, depending on the type of hedge.

Companies report derivative financial instruments in the balance sheet and record them at fair value. Except for derivatives used in cash flow hedges, companies record realized and unrealized gains and losses on derivative financial instruments in income.

*6 Explain the accounting for hedges.

Fair Value Hedges. A company records the derivative used in a qualifying fair value hedge at its fair value in the balance sheet, recording any gains and losses in income. In addition, the company also accounts for the item being hedged with the derivative at fair value. By adjusting the hedged item to fair value, with the gain or loss recorded in earnings, the accounting for the hedged item may deviate from GAAP in the absence of a hedge relationship. This special accounting is justified in order to report accurately the nature of the hedging relationship between the derivative hedging instruments and the hedged item. A company reports both in the balance sheet, reporting offsetting gains and losses in income in the same period.

Cash Flow Hedge. Companies account for derivatives used in qualifying cash flow hedges at fair value on the balance sheet, but record gains or losses in equity as part of other comprehensive income. Companies accumulate these gains or losses, and reclassify them in income when the hedged transaction's cash flows affect earnings. Accounting is according to GAAP for the hedged item.

*7 Identify special reporting issues related to derivative financial instruments that cause unique accounting problems.

A company should separate a derivative that is embedded in a hybrid security from the host security and account for it using the accounting for derivatives. This separation process is referred to as **bifurcation**. Special hedge accounting is allowed only for hedging relationships that meet certain criteria. The main criteria are as follows. (1) There is formal documentation of the hedging relationship, the company's risk-management objective, and the strategy for undertaking the hedge, and the company designates the derivative as either a cash flow or fair value hedge. (2) The company expects the hedging relationship to be highly effective in achieving offsetting changes in fair value or cash flows. (3) "Special" hedge accounting is necessary only when there is a mismatch of the accounting effects for the hedging instrument and the hedged item under GAAP.

*8 Describe required fair value disclosures.

The FASB has developed required fair value disclosures in response to concerns about the reliability of fair value measures. Disclosure elements include fair value amounts and reliability levels as well as impaired assets or liabilities.

Enhanced Review and Practice

Go online for multiple-choice questions with solutions, review exercises with solutions, and a full glossary of all key terms.

Practice Problem

Rogers Corporation carries an account in its general ledger called Investments, which contained the following debits for investment purchases and no credits.

Feb. 1, 2020	Jordy Company common stock, $100 par, 200 shares	$ 37,400
April 1	U.S. government bonds, 5%, due April 1, 2030, interest payable April 1 and October 1, 100 bonds at $1,000 each	100,000
July 1	Driver Company 6% bonds, par $50,000, dated March 1, 2016, purchased at par plus accrued interest, interest payable annually on March 1, due March 1, 2040	51,000

Instructions

a. Prepare entries necessary to classify the amounts into proper accounts, assuming that all the bonds are classified as available-for-sale.

b. Prepare the entry to record the accrued interest on December 31, 2020.

c. The fair values of the securities on December 31, 2020, were:

Jordy Company common stock	$ 33,800 (1% of total shares)
U.S. government bonds	124,700
Driver Company bonds	58,600

What entry or entries, if any, would you recommend be made?

d. The U.S. government bonds were sold on July 1, 2021, for $119,200 plus accrued interest. Give the proper entry.

e. Now assume Rogers' investment in Jordy Company represents 30% of Jordy's shares. Prepare the 2020 entries for the investment in Jordy stock. In 2020, Jordy declared and paid dividends of $9,000 (on September 30) and reported net income of $30,000.

Solution

a.	Equity Investments	37,400	
	Debt Investments (available-for-sale) ($100,000 + $50,000)	150,000	
	Interest Revenue ($50,000 × .06 × 4/12)	1,000	
	Investments		188,400

December 31, 2020

b.	Interest Receivable	3,750	
	Interest Revenue		3,750*

*($100,000 × .05 × 3/12 = $1,250; $50,000 × .06 × 10/12 = $2,500; $1,250 + $2,500 = $3,750)

c.	Fair Value Adjustment	33,300	
	Unrealized Holding Gain or Loss—Equity		33,300

Available-for-Sale Portfolio
December 31, 2020

Securities	Cost	Fair Value	Unrealized Gain (Loss)
U.S. government bonds	$100,000	$124,700	$24,700
Driver Company bonds	50,000	58,600	8,600
Total	$150,000	$183,300	33,300
Previous fair value adjustment balance			0
Fair value adjustment—Dr.			$33,300

Unrealized Holding Loss—Income	3,600	
Fair Value Adjustment ($37,400 – $33,800)		3,600

d.

July 1, 2021

Cash ($119,200 + $1,250)	120,450	
Debt Investments (available-for-sale)		100,000
Interest Revenue ($100,000 × .05 × 3/12)		1,250
Gain on Sale of Investments		19,200

e.

February 1, 2020

Equity Investments (Jordy Company)	37,400	
Cash		37,400

September 30, 2020

Cash	2,700	
Equity Investments (Jordy Company) (.30 × $9,000)		2,700

December 31, 2020

Equity Investments (Jordy Company)	9,000	
Investment Income (.30 × $30,000)		9,000

WileyPLUS

Brief Exercises, Exercises, Problems, Problem Solution Walkthrough Videos, and many more learning and assessment tools and resources are available for practice in WileyPLUS.

Note: All asterisked Questions, Exercises, and Problems relate to material in the appendices to the chapter.

Questions

1. Distinguish between a debt security and an equity security.

2. What purpose does the variety in bond features (types and characteristics) serve?

3. What is the cost of a long-term investment in bonds?

4. Identify and explain the three types of classifications for investments in debt securities.

5. When should a debt security be classified as held-to-maturity?

6. Explain how trading debt securities are accounted for and reported.

7. At what amount should trading, available-for-sale, and held-to-maturity debt securities be reported on the balance sheet?

8. On July 1, 2020, Wheeler Company purchased $4,000,000 of Duggen Company's 8% bonds, due on July 1, 2027. The bonds, which pay interest semiannually on January 1 and July 1, were purchased for $3,500,000 to yield 10%. Determine the amount of interest revenue Wheeler should report on its income statement for the year ended December 31, 2020.

9. If the bonds in Question 8 are classified as available-for-sale and they have a fair value at December 31, 2020, of $3,604,000, prepare the journal entry (if any) at December 31, 2020, to record this transaction.

10. Indicate how unrealized holding gains and losses should be reported for debt investments classified as trading, available-for-sale, and held-to-maturity.

11. (a) Assuming no Fair Value Adjustment account balance at the beginning of the year, prepare the adjusting entry at the end of the year if Laura Company's available-for-sale debt securities have a fair value $60,000 below cost. (b) Assume the same information as part (a), except that Laura Company has a debit balance in its Fair Value Adjustment account of $10,000 at the beginning of the year. Prepare the adjusting entry at year-end.

12. Identify and explain the different types of classifications for investments in equity securities.

13. Why are held-to-maturity investments applicable only to debt securities?

14. Hayes Company sold 10,000 shares of Kenyon Co. common stock for $27.50 per share, incurring $1,770 in brokerage commissions. These securities originally cost $260,000. Prepare the entry to record the sale of these securities.

15. Distinguish between the accounting treatment for marketable versus nonmarketable equity securities.

16. What constitutes "significant influence" when an investor's financial interest is below the 50% level?

17. Explain how the investment account is affected by investee activities under the equity method.

18. Your classmate Kate believes that the equity method is applied with a strict application of the "20%" rule. Do you agree? Explain.

19. Hiram Co. uses the equity method to account for investments in common stock. What accounting should be made for dividends received from these investments subsequent to the date of investment?

20. Raleigh Corp. has an investment with a carrying value (equity method) on its books of $170,000 representing a 30% interest in Borg Company, which suffered a $620,000 loss this year. How should Raleigh Corp. handle its proportionate share of Borg's loss?

21. Where on the asset side of the balance sheet are debt investments classified as trading securities, available-for-sale securities, and held-to-maturity securities reported? Explain.

22. Explain why reclassification adjustments are necessary.

23. Briefly discuss how a transfer of securities from the available-for-sale category to the trading category affects stockholders' equity and income.

24. Explain how to account for the impairment of a held-to-maturity debt security.

25. Explain how to account for the impairment of an available-for-sale debt investment.

26. What is the GAAP definition of fair value?

27. What is the fair value option?

28. Franklin Corp. has a debt investment that it has held for several years. When it purchased the debt investment, Franklin classified and accounted for it as available-for-sale. Can Franklin use the fair value option for this investment? Explain.

*29. What is meant by the term "underlying" as it relates to derivative financial instruments?

*30. What are the main distinctions between a traditional financial instrument and a derivative financial instrument?

*31. What is the purpose of a fair value hedge?

*32. In what situation will the unrealized holding gain or loss on inventory be reported in income?

*33. Why might a company become involved in an interest rate swap contract to receive fixed interest payments and pay variable?

*34. What is the purpose of a cash flow hedge?

*35. Where are gains and losses related to cash flow hedges involving anticipated transactions reported?

*36. What are hybrid securities? Give an example of a hybrid security.

Brief Exercises

BE17.1 **(LO 1)** Garfield Company purchased, on January 1, 2020, as a held-to-maturity investment, $80,000 of the 9%, 5-year bonds of Chester Corporation for $74,086, which provides an 11% return. Prepare Garfield's journal entries for (a) the purchase of the investment, and (b) the receipt of annual interest and discount amortization. Assume effective-interest amortization is used.

BE17.2 **(LO 1)** Use the information from BE17.1 but assume the bonds are purchased as an available-for-sale security. Prepare Garfield's journal entries for (a) the purchase of the investment, (b) the receipt of annual interest and discount amortization, and (c) the year-end fair value adjustment. (Assume a zero balance in the Fair Value Adjustment account.) The bonds have a year-end fair value of $75,500.

BE17.3 **(LO 1)** Carow Corporation purchased on January 1, 2020, as a held-to-maturity investment, $60,000 of the 8%, 5-year bonds of Harrison, Inc. for $65,118, which provides a 6% return. The bonds pay interest semiannually. Prepare Carow's journal entries for (a) the purchase of the investment, and (b) the receipt of semiannual interest and premium amortization. Assume effective-interest amortization is used.

BE17.4 **(LO 1)** Hendricks Corporation purchased trading investment bonds for $50,000 at par. At December 31, Hendricks received annual interest of $2,000, and the fair value of the bonds was $47,400. Prepare Hendricks' journal entries for (a) the purchase of the investment, (b) the interest received, and (c) the fair value adjustment. (Assume a zero balance in the Fair Value Adjustment account.)

BE17.5 **(LO 2)** Fairbanks Corporation purchased 400 shares of Sherman Inc. common stock for $13,200 (Fairbanks does not have significant influence). During the year, Sherman paid a cash dividend of $3.25 per share. At year-end, Sherman stock was selling for $34.50 per share. Prepare Fairbanks' journal entries to record (a) the purchase of the investment, (b) the dividends received, and (c) the fair value adjustment. (Assume a zero balance in the Fair Value Adjustment account.)

BE17.6 **(LO 2)** Use the information from BE17.5 but assume the stock is nonmarketable. Prepare Fairbanks' journal entries to record (a) the purchase of the investment, (b) the dividends received, and (c) the fair value adjustment, if any.

BE17.7 (LO 3) Zoop Corporation purchased for $300,000 a 30% interest in Murphy, Inc. This investment enables Zoop to exert significant influence over Murphy. During the year, Murphy earned net income of $180,000 and paid dividends of $60,000. Prepare Zoop's journal entries related to this investment.

BE17.8 (LO 2) Cleveland Company has a stock portfolio valued at $4,000. Its cost was $3,300. If the Fair Value Adjustment account has a debit balance of $200, prepare the journal entry at year-end.

BE17.9 (LO 2, 4) The following information relates to Moran Co. for the year ended December 31, 2020: net income $1,245.7 million; unrealized holding loss of $10.9 million related to available-for-sale debt securities during the year; accumulated other comprehensive income of $57.2 million on December 31, 2019. Assuming no other changes in accumulated other comprehensive income, determine (a) other comprehensive income for 2020, (b) comprehensive income for 2020, and (c) accumulated other comprehensive income at December 31, 2020.

BE17.10 (LO 4) Hillsborough Co. has a held-to-maturity investment in the bonds of Schuyler Corp. with a carrying value of $70,000. Hillsborough determined that due to poor economic prospects for Schuyler, the bonds have decreased in value to $60,000. It is determined that this loss in value is uncollectible. Prepare the journal entry, if any, to record the reduction in value.

BE17.11 (LO 4) Presented below are two independent cases related to available-for-sale debt investments.

	Case 1	Case 2
Amortized cost	$40,000	$100,000
Fair value	30,000	110,000
Expected credit losses	25,000	92,000

For each case, determine the amount of impairment loss, if any.

BE17.12 (LO 4) Stave Company invests $10,000,000 in 5% fixed rate corporate bonds on January 1, 2020. All the bonds are classified as available-for-sale and are purchased at par. At year-end, market interest rates have declined, and the fair value of the bonds is now $10,600,000. Interest is paid on January 1. Prepare journal entries for Stave Company to (a) record the transactions related to these bonds in 2020, assuming Stave does not elect the fair option; and (b) record the transactions related to these bonds in 2020, assuming that Stave Company elects the fair value option to account for these bonds.

BE17.13 (LO 4) Michek Company loans Sarasota Company $2,000,000 at 6% for 3 years on January 1, 2020. Michek intends to hold this loan to maturity and has the financial ability to do so. The fair value of the loan at the end of each reporting period is as follows.

December 31, 2020	$2,050,000
December 31, 2021	2,020,000
December 31, 2022	2,000,000

Prepare the journal entry(ies) at December 31, 2020, and December 31, 2022, for Michek related to these bonds, assuming (a) it does not use the fair value option, and (b) it uses the fair value option. Interest is paid on January 1.

Exercises

E17.1 (LO 1, 2) (Investment Classifications) For the following investments, identify whether they are:

1. Trading debt securities.
2. Available-for-sale debt securities.
3. Held-to-maturity debt securities.
4. None of the above.

Each case is independent of the other.

a. A bond that will mature in 4 years was bought 1 month ago when the price dropped. As soon as the value increases, which is expected next month, it will be sold.

b. 10% of the outstanding stock of Farm-Co was purchased. The company is planning on eventually getting a total of 30% of its outstanding stock.

c. Bonds were purchased in December of this year. The bonds are expected to be sold in January of next year.

d. Bonds that will mature in 5 years are purchased. The company would like to hold them until they mature, but money has been tight recently and they may need to be sold.

e. Preferred stock was purchased for its constant dividend. The company is planning to hold the preferred stock for a long time.

f. A bond that matures in 10 years was purchased. The company has committed the money for an expansion project planned 10 years from now.

E17.2 **(LO 1)** Excel **(Entries for Held-to-Maturity Securities)** On January 1, 2020, Dagwood Company purchased at par 6% bonds having a maturity value of $300,000. They are dated January 1, 2020, and mature January 1, 2025, with interest received on January 1 of each year. The bonds are classified in the held-to-maturity category.

Instructions

a. Prepare the journal entry at the date of the bond purchase.

b. Prepare the journal entry to record the interest revenue on December 31, 2020.

c. Prepare the journal entry to record the interest received on January 1, 2021.

E17.3 **(LO 1)** **(Entries for Held-to-Maturity Securities)** On January 1, 2020, Hi and Lois Company purchased 12% bonds having a maturity value of $300,000 for $322,744.44. The bonds provide the bondholders with a 10% yield. They are dated January 1, 2020, and mature January 1, 2025, with interest received on January 1 of each year. Hi and Lois Company uses the effective-interest method to allocate unamortized discount or premium. The bonds are classified in the held-to-maturity category.

Instructions

a. Prepare the journal entry at the date of the bond purchase.

b. Prepare a bond amortization schedule.

c. Prepare the journal entry to record the interest revenue and the amortization at December 31, 2020.

d. Prepare the journal entry to record the interest revenue and the amortization at December 31, 2021.

E17.4 **(LO 1)** **(Entries for Available-for-Sale Securities)** Assume the same information as in E17.3 except that the securities are classified as available-for-sale. The fair value of the bonds at December 31 of each year-end is as follows.

2020	$320,500	2023	$310,000
2021	$309,000	2024	$300,000
2022	$308,000		

Instructions

a. Prepare the journal entry at the date of the bond purchase.

b. Prepare the journal entries to record the interest revenue and recognition of fair value for 2020.

c. Prepare the journal entry to record the recognition of fair value for 2021.

E17.5 **(LO 1)** Excel **(Effective-Interest versus Straight-Line Bond Amortization)** On January 1, 2020, Phantom Company acquires $200,000 of Spiderman Products, Inc., 9% bonds at a price of $185,589. Interest is received on January 1 of each year, and the bonds mature on January 1, 2023. The investment will provide Phantom Company a 12% yield. The bonds are classified as held-to-maturity.

Instructions

a. Prepare a 3-year schedule of interest revenue and bond discount amortization, applying the straight-line method.

b. Prepare a 3-year schedule of interest revenue and bond discount amortization, applying the effective-interest method.

c. Prepare the journal entry for the interest revenue and discount amortization under the straight-line method at December 31, 2021.

d. Prepare the journal entry for the interest revenue and discount amortization under the effective-interest method at December 31, 2021.

E17.6 **(LO 2)** **(Entries for Equity Securities)** The following information is available for Barkley Company at December 31, 2020, regarding its investments.

Securities	Cost	Fair Value
3,000 shares of Myers Corporation common stock	$40,000	$48,000
1,000 shares of Cole Incorporated preferred stock	25,000	22,000
	$65,000	$70,000

Instructions

a. Prepare the adjusting entry (if any) for 2020, assuming no balance in the Fair Value Adjustment account at January 1, 2020. Neither of Barkley's investments result in significant influence.

b. Discuss how the amounts reported in the financial statements are affected by the entries in (a).

E17.7 (LO 2) **(Equity Securities Entries)** On December 21, 2020, Bucky Katt Company provided you with the following information regarding its equity investments.

	December 31, 2020		
Investments	Cost	Fair Value	Unrealized Gain (Loss)
Clemson Corp. stock	$20,000	$19,000	$(1,000)
Colorado Co. stock	10,000	9,000	(1,000)
Buffaloes Co. stock	20,000	20,600	600
Total of portfolio	$50,000	$48,600	(1,400)
Previous fair value adjustment balance			–0–
Fair value adjustment—Cr.			$(1,400)

During 2021, Colorado Co. stock was sold for $9,400. The fair value of the stock on December 31, 2021, was Clemson Corp. stock—$19,100; Buffaloes Co. stock—$20,500. None of the equity investments result in significant influence.

Instructions

a. Prepare the adjusting journal entry needed on December 31, 2020.

b. Prepare the journal entry to record the sale of the Colorado Co. stock during 2021.

c. Prepare the adjusting journal entry needed on December 31, 2021.

E17.8 (LO 2) **(Equity Securities Entries and Reporting)** Satchel Corporation purchases equity securities costing $73,000. At December 31, the fair value of the portfolio is $65,000.

Instructions

Prepare the adjusting entry to report the securities properly, assuming that the investments purchased represent less than a 5% interest in the other companies. Indicate the statement presentation of the accounts in your entry.

E17.9 (LO 1) **(Available-for-Sale Debt Securities Entries and Financial Statement Presentation)** At December 31, 2020, the available-for-sale debt portfolio for Steffi Graf, Inc. is as follows.

Security	Cost	Fair Value	Unrealized Gain (Loss)
A	$17,500	$15,000	($2,500)
B	12,500	14,000	1,500
C	23,000	25,500	2,500
Total	$53,000	$54,500	1,500
Previous fair value adjustment balance—Dr.			400
Fair value adjustment—Dr.			$1,100

On January 20, 2021, Steffi Graf, Inc. sold security A for $15,100. The sale proceeds are net of brokerage fees.

Instructions

a. Prepare the adjusting entry at December 31, 2020, to report the portfolio at fair value.

b. Show the balance sheet presentation of the investment-related accounts at December 31, 2020. (Ignore notes presentation.)

c. Prepare the journal entry for the 2021 sale of security A.

E17.10 (LO 4) **(Comprehensive Income Disclosure)** Assume the same information as E17.9 and that Steffi Graf, Inc. reports net income in 2020 of $120,000 and in 2021 of $140,000. Total holding gains (including any realized holding gain or loss) equal $40,000 in 2021.

Instructions

a. Prepare a statement of comprehensive income for 2020, starting with net income.

b. Prepare a statement of comprehensive income for 2021, starting with net income.

E17.11 **(LO 2) (Equity Securities Entries)** Aranda Corporation made the following cash purchases of securities during 2020, which is the first year in which Aranda invested in securities.

1. On January 15, purchased 10,000 shares of Sanchez Company's common stock at $33.50 per share plus commission $1,980.
2. On April 1, purchased 5,000 shares of Vicario Co.'s common stock at $52.00 per share plus commission $3,370.
3. On September 10, purchased 7,000 shares of WTA Co.'s preferred stock at $26.50 per share plus commission $4,910.

On May 20, 2020, Aranda sold 4,000 shares of Sanchez Company's common stock at a market price of $35 per share less brokerage commissions, taxes, and fees of $3,850. The year-end fair values per share were Sanchez $30, Vicario $55, and WTA $28. In addition, the chief accountant of Aranda told you that the corporation plans to hold these securities for the long-term but may sell them in order to earn profits from appreciation in prices. The equity method of accounting is not appropriate for these stock purchases.

Instructions

a. Prepare the journal entries to record the above three security purchases.

b. Prepare the journal entry for the security sale on May 20.

c. Compute the unrealized gains or losses and prepare the adjusting entries for Aranda on December 31, 2020.

E17.12 **(LO 2, 3) (Journal Entries for Fair Value and Equity Methods)** The following are independent situations.

Situation 1: Conchita Cosmetics acquired 10% of the 200,000 shares of common stock of Martinez Fashion at a total cost of $13 per share on March 18, 2020. On June 30, Martinez declared and paid $75,000 cash dividends to all stockholders. On December 31, Martinez reported net income of $122,000 for the year. At December 31, the market price of Martinez Fashion was $15 per share.

Situation 2: Monica, Inc. obtained significant influence over Seles Corporation by buying 30% of Seles's 30,000 outstanding shares of common stock at a total cost of $9 per share on January 1, 2020. On June 15, Seles declared and paid cash dividends of $36,000 to all stockholders. On December 31, Seles reported a net income of $85,000 for the year.

Instructions

Prepare all necessary journal entries in 2020 for both situations.

E17.13 **(LO 3) (Equity Method)** Parent Co. invested $1,000,000 in Sub Co. for 25% of its outstanding stock. Sub Co. pays out 40% of net income in dividends each year.

Instructions

Use the information in the following T-account for the investment in Sub to answer the following questions.

Investment in Sub Co.	
1,000,000	
110,000	
	44,000

a. How much was Parent Co.'s share of Sub Co.'s net income for the year?

b. What was Sub Co.'s total net income for the year?

c. What was Sub Co.'s total dividends for the year?

d. How much was Parent Co.'s share of Sub Co.'s dividends for the year?

E17.14 **(LO 2) (Equity Investment)** Oregon Co. had purchased 200 shares of Washington Co. for $40 each this year (Oregon Co. does not have significant influence). Oregon Co. sold 100 shares of Washington Co. stock for $45 each. At year-end, the price per share of the Washington Co. stock had dropped to $35.

Instructions

Prepare the journal entries for these transactions and any year-end adjustments.

E17.15 **(LO 2) (Equity Investments)** Kenseth Company has the following securities in its portfolio on December 31, 2020. None of these investments are accounted for under the equity method.

Investments	Cost	Fair Value
1,500 shares of Gordon, Inc., common	$ 73,500	$ 69,000
5,000 shares of Wallace Corp., common	180,000	175,000
400 shares of Martin, Inc., preferred	60,000	61,600
	$313,500	$305,600

All of the securities were purchased in 2020.

In 2021, Kenseth completed the following securities transactions.

March 1 Sold the 1,500 shares of Gordon, Inc., common, @ $45 less fees of $1,200.
April 1 Bought 700 shares of Earnhart Corp., common, @ $75 plus fees of $1,300.

Kenseth's portfolio of equity securities appeared as follows on December 31, 2021.

Investments	Cost	Fair Value
5,000 shares of Wallace Corp., common	$180,000	$175,000
700 shares of Earnhart Corp., common	53,800	50,400
400 shares of Martin, Inc., preferred	60,000	58,000
	$293,800	$283,400

Instructions

Prepare the general journal entries for Kenseth Company for:

a. The 2020 adjusting entry.

b. The sale of the Gordon stock.

c. The purchase of the Earnhart stock.

d. The 2021 adjusting entry for the portfolio.

E17.16 **(LO 2, 3)** **(Fair Value and Equity Method Compared)** Jaycie Phelps Inc. acquired 20% of the outstanding common stock of Theresa Kulikowski Inc. on December 31, 2020. The purchase price was $1,200,000 for 50,000 shares. Kulikowski Inc. declared and paid an $0.85 per share cash dividend on June 30 and on December 31, 2021. Kulikowski reported net income of $730,000 for 2021. The fair value of Kulikowski's stock was $27 per share at December 31, 2021.

Instructions

a. Prepare the journal entries for Jaycie Phelps Inc. for 2020 and 2021, assuming that Phelps cannot exercise significant influence over Kulikowski.

b. Prepare the journal entries for Jaycie Phelps Inc. for 2020 and 2021, assuming that Phelps can exercise significant influence over Kulikowski.

c. At what amount is the investment in securities reported on the balance sheet under each of these methods at December 31, 2021? What is the total net income reported in 2021 under each of these methods?

E17.17 **(LO 3)** **(Equity Method)** On January 1, 2020, Pennington Corporation purchased 30% of the common shares of Edwards Company for $180,000. During the year, Edwards earned net income of $80,000 and paid dividends of $20,000.

Instructions

Prepare the entries for Pennington to record the purchase and any additional entries related to this investment in Edwards Company in 2020.

E17.18 **(LO 4)** **(Impairment of Debt Securities)** Hagar Corporation has municipal bonds classified as a held-to-maturity at December 31, 2020. These bonds have a par value of $800,000, an amortized cost of $800,000, and a fair value of $720,000. The company believes that impairment accounting is now appropriate for these bonds.

Instructions

a. Prepare the journal entry to recognize the impairment.

b. What is the new cost basis of the municipal bonds? Given that the maturity value of the bonds is $800,000, should Hagar Corporation amortize the difference between the carrying amount and the maturity value over the life of the bonds?

c. At December 31, 2021, the fair value of the municipal bonds is $760,000. Prepare the entry (if any) to record this information.

E17.19 **(LO 2, 4)** **(Fair Value Measurement)** Presented below is information related to the purchases of common stock by Lilly Company during 2020.

	Cost (at purchase date)	Fair Value (at December 31)
Investment in Arroyo Company stock	$100,000	$ 80,000
Investment in Lee Corporation stock	250,000	300,000
Investment in Woods Inc. stock	180,000	190,000
Total	$530,000	$570,000

Instructions

(Assume a zero balance for any Fair Value Adjustment account.)

a. What entry would Lilly make at December 31, 2020, to record the investment in Arroyo Company stock if it chooses to report this security using the fair value option?

b. What entry(ies) would Lilly make at December 31, 2020, to record the investments in the Lee and Woods corporations, assuming that Lilly did not select the fair value option for these investments?

E17.20 **(LO 2, 4)** **(Fair Value Measurement Issues)** Assume the same information as in E17.19 for Lilly Company. In addition, assume that the investment in the Woods Inc. stock was sold during 2021 for $195,000. At December 31, 2021, the following information relates to its two remaining investments of common stock.

	Cost (at purchase date)	Fair Value (at December 31)
Investment in Arroyo Company stock	$100,000	$140,000
Investment in Lee Corporation stock	250,000	310,000
Total	$350,000	$450,000

Net income before any security gains and losses for 2021 was $905,000.

Instructions

a. Compute the amount of net income or net loss that Lilly should report for 2021, taking into consideration Lilly's security transactions for 2021.

b. Prepare the journal entry to record unrealized gain or loss related to the investment in Arroyo Company stock at December 31, 2021.

E17.21 **(LO 1, 2, 4)** **(Fair Value Option)** Presented below is selected information related to the financial instruments of Dawson Company at December 31, 2020. This is Dawson Company's first year of operations.

	Carrying Amount	Fair Value (at December 31)
Investment in debt securities (intent is to hold to maturity)	$ 40,000	$ 41,000
Investment in Chen Company stock	800,000	910,000
Bonds payable	220,000	195,000

Instructions

a. Dawson elects to use the fair value option for these investments. Assuming that Dawson's net income is $100,000 in 2020 before reporting any securities gains or losses, determine Dawson's net income for 2020. Assume that the difference between the carrying value and fair value is due to credit deterioration.

b. Record the journal entry, if any, necessary at December 31, 2020, to record the fair value option for the bonds payable.

E17.22 **(LO 4)** **(Impairment)** Elaina Company has the following investments as of December 31, 2020:

Investments in common stock of Laser Company	$1,500,000
Investment in debt securities of FourSquare Company	$3,300,000

In both investments, the carrying value and the fair value of these two investments are the same at December 31, 2020. Elaina's stock investments does not result in significant influence on the operations of Laser Company. Elaina's debt investment is considered held-to-maturity. At December 31, 2021, the shares in Laser Company are valued at $1,100,000; the debt investment securities of FourSquare are valued at $2,500,000 and are considered impaired.

Instructions

a. Prepare the journal entry to record the impairment of the debt securities at December 31, 2021.

b. Assuming the fair value of the Laser shares is $1,400,000 and the value of its debt investment is $2,950,000, what entries, if any, should be recorded in 2022 related to impairment?

c. Assume that the debt investment in FourSquare Company was available-for-sale and the expected credit loss was $900,000. Prepare the journal entry to record this impairment on December 31, 2021.

E17.23 **(LO 4)** **(Impairment)** Morley Company in its first year of operations provides the following information related to one of its available-for-sale debt securities at December 31, 2020.

Amortized cost	$50,000
Fair value	40,000
Expected credit loss	12,000

a. What is the amount of the credit loss that Morley should report on this available-for-sale security at December 31, 2020?

b. Prepare the journal entry to record the credit loss, if any (and any other adjustment needed), at December 31, 2020.

c. Assume that the fair value of the available-for-sale security is $53,000 at December 31, 2020, instead of $40,000. What is the amount of the credit loss that Morley should report at December 31, 2020?

d. Assume the same information as for part (c). Prepare the journal entry to record the credit loss, if necessary (and any other adjustment needed), at December 31, 2020.

*E17.24 **(LO 5)** **(Derivative Transaction)** On January 2, 2020, Jones Company purchases a call option for $300 on Merchant common stock. The call option gives Jones the option to buy 1,000 shares of Merchant at a strike price of $50 per share. The market price of a Merchant share is $50 on January 2, 2020 (the intrinsic value is therefore $0). On March 31, 2020, the market price for Merchant stock is $53 per share, and the time value of the option is $200.

Instructions

a. Prepare the journal entry to record the purchase of the call option on January 2, 2020.

b. Prepare the journal entry(ies) to recognize the change in the fair value of the call option as of March 31, 2020.

c. What was the effect on net income of entering into the derivative transaction for the period January 2 to March 31, 2020?

*E17.25 **(LO 6)** **(Fair Value Hedge)** On January 2, 2020, MacCloud Co. issued a 4-year, $100,000 note at 6% fixed interest, interest payable semiannually. MacCloud now wants to change the note to a variable-rate note.

As a result, on January 2, 2020, MacCloud Co. enters into an interest rate swap where it agrees to receive 6% fixed and pay LIBOR of 5.7% for the first 6 months on $100,000. At each 6-month period, the variable rate will be reset. The variable rate is reset to 6.7% on June 30, 2020.

Instructions

a. Compute the net interest expense to be reported for this note and related swap transaction as of June 30, 2020.

b. Compute the net interest expense to be reported for this note and related swap transaction as of December 31, 2020.

*E17.26 **(LO 6)** **(Cash Flow Hedge)** On January 2, 2020, Parton Company issues a 5-year, $10,000,000 note at LIBOR, with interest paid annually. The variable rate is reset at the end of each year. The LIBOR rate for the first year is 5.8%.

Parton Company decides it prefers fixed-rate financing and wants to lock in a rate of 6%. As a result, Parton enters into an interest rate swap to pay 6% fixed and receive LIBOR based on $10 million. The variable rate is reset to 6.6% on January 2, 2021.

Instructions

a. Compute the net interest expense to be reported for this note and related swap transactions as of December 31, 2020.

b. Compute the net interest expense to be reported for this note and related swap transactions as of December 31, 2021.

*E17.27 **(LO 6)** **(Fair Value Hedge)** Sarazan Company issues a 4-year, 7.5% fixed-rate interest only, nonprepayable $1,000,000 note payable on December 31, 2019. It decides to change the interest rate from a fixed rate to variable rate and enters into a swap agreement with M&S Corp. The swap agreement specifies that Sarazan will receive a fixed rate at 7.5% and pay variable with settlement dates that match the interest payments on the debt. Assume that interest rates have declined during 2020 and that Sarazan received $13,000 as an adjustment to interest expense for the settlement at December 31, 2020. The loss related to the debt (due to interest rate changes) was $48,000. The value of the swap contract increased $48,000.

Instructions

a. Prepare the journal entry to record the payment of interest expense on December 31, 2020.

b. Prepare the journal entry to record the receipt of the swap settlement on December 31, 2020.

c. Prepare the journal entry to record the change in the fair value of the swap contract on December 31, 2020.

d. Prepare the journal entry to record the change in the fair value of the debt on December 31, 2020.

*E17.28 **(LO 5) (Call Option)** On August 15, 2019, Outkast Co. invested idle cash by purchasing a call option on Counting Crows Inc. common shares for $360. The notional value of the call option is 400 shares, and the option price is $40. The option expires on January 31, 2020. The following data are available with respect to the call option.

Date	Market Price of Counting Crows Shares	Time Value of Call Option
September 30, 2019	$48 per share	$180
December 31, 2019	46 per share	65
January 15, 2020	47 per share	30

Instructions

Prepare the journal entries for Outkast for the following dates.

a. Investment in call option on Counting Crows shares on August 15, 2019.

b. September 30, 2019—Outkast prepares financial statements.

c. December 31, 2019—Outkast prepares financial statements.

d. January 15, 2020—Outkast settles the call option on the Counting Crows shares.

*E17.29 **(LO 6) (Cash Flow Hedge)** Hart Golf Co. uses titanium in the production of its specialty drivers. Hart anticipates that it will need to purchase 200 ounces of titanium in November 2020, for clubs that will be sold in advance of the spring and summer of 2021. However, if the price of titanium increases, this will increase the cost to produce the clubs, which will result in lower profit margins.

To hedge the risk of increased titanium prices, on May 1, 2020, Hart enters into a titanium futures contract and designates this futures contract as a cash flow hedge of the anticipated titanium purchase. The notional amount of the contract is 200 ounces, and the terms of the contract give Hart the right and obligation to purchase titanium at a price of $500 per ounce. The price will be good until the contract expires on November 30, 2020.

Assume the following data with respect to the price of the futures contract and the titanium inventory purchase.

Date	Spot Price for November Delivery
May 1, 2020	$500 per ounce
June 30, 2020	520 per ounce
September 30, 2020	525 per ounce

Instructions

Present the journal entries for the following dates/transactions.

a. May 1, 2020—Inception of futures contract, no premium paid.

b. June 30, 2020—Hart prepares financial statements.

c. September 30, 2020—Hart prepares financial statements.

d. October 5, 2020—Hart purchases 200 ounces of titanium at $525 per ounce and settles the futures contract.

e. December 15, 2020—Hart sells clubs containing titanium purchased in October 2020 for $250,000. The cost of the finished goods inventory is $140,000.

f. Indicate the amount(s) reported in the income statement related to the futures contract and the inventory transactions on December 31, 2020.

Problems

P17.1 (LO 1) (Debt Securities) Presented below is an amortization schedule related to Spangler Company's 5-year, $100,000 bond with a 7% interest rate and a 5% yield, purchased on December 31, 2018, for $108,660.

Date	Cash Received	Interest Revenue	Bond Premium Amortization	Carrying Amount of Bonds
12/31/18				$108,660
12/31/19	$7,000	$5,433	$1,567	107,093
12/31/20	7,000	5,354	1,646	105,447
12/31/21	7,000	5,272	1,728	103,719
12/31/22	7,000	5,186	1,814	101,905
12/31/23	7,000	5,095	1,905	100,000

The following schedule presents a comparison of the amortized cost and fair value of the bonds at year-end.

	12/31/19	12/31/20	12/31/21	12/31/22	12/31/23
Amortized cost	$107,093	$105,447	$103,719	$101,905	$100,000
Fair value	106,500	107,500	105,650	103,000	100,000

Instructions

a. Prepare the journal entry to record the purchase of these bonds on December 31, 2018, assuming the bonds are classified as held-to-maturity securities.

b. Prepare the journal entry(ies) related to the held-to-maturity bonds for 2019.

c. Prepare the journal entry(ies) related to the held-to-maturity bonds for 2021.

d. Prepare the journal entry(ies) to record the purchase of these bonds, assuming they are classified as available-for-sale.

e. Prepare the journal entry(ies) related to the available-for-sale bonds for 2019.

f. Prepare the journal entry(ies) related to the available-for-sale bonds for 2021.

P17.2 (LO 1) (Available-for-Sale Debt Securities) On January 1, 2020, Novotna Company purchased $400,000, 8% bonds of Aguirre Co. for $369,114. The bonds were purchased to yield 10% interest. Interest is payable semiannually on July 1 and January 1. The bonds mature on January 1, 2025. Novotna Company uses the effective-interest method to amortize discount or premium. On January 1, 2022, Novotna Company sold the bonds for $370,726 after receiving interest to meet its liquidity needs.

Instructions

a. Prepare the journal entry to record the purchase of bonds on January 1. Assume that the bonds are classified as available-for-sale.

b. Prepare the amortization schedule for the bonds.

c. Prepare the journal entries to record the semiannual interest on July 1, 2020, and December 31, 2020.

d. If the fair value of Aguirre bonds is $372,726 on December 31, 2021, prepare the necessary adjusting entry. (Assume the fair value adjustment balance on December 31, 2020, is a debit of $3,375.)

e. Prepare the journal entry to record the sale of the bonds on January 1, 2022.

P17.3 (LO 1, 2) (Debt and Equity Investments) Cardinal Paz Corp. carries an account in its general ledger called Investments, which contained debits for investment purchases, and no credits, with the following descriptions.

Feb. 1, 2020	Sharapova Company common stock, $100 par, 200 shares	$ 37,400
April 1	U.S. government bonds, 11%, due April 1, 2030, interest payable April 1 and October 1, 110 bonds of $1,000 par each	110,000
July 1	McGrath Company 12% bonds, par $50,000, dated March 1, 2020, purchased at 104 plus accrued interest, interest payable annually on March 1, due March 1, 2040	54,000

Instructions

(Round all computations to the nearest dollar.)

a. Prepare entries necessary to classify the amounts into proper accounts, assuming that the debt securities are classified as available-for-sale.

b. Prepare the entry to record the accrued interest and the amortization of premium on December 31, 2020, using the straight-line method.

c. The fair values of the investments on December 31, 2020, were:

Sharapova Company common stock	$ 31,800
U.S. government bonds	124,700
McGrath Company bonds	58,600

What entry or entries, if any, would you recommend be made?

d. The U.S. government bonds were sold on July 1, 2021, for $119,200 plus accrued interest. Give the proper entry.

P17.4 **(LO 1)** **(Debt Investments)** Presented below is information taken from a bond investment amortization schedule with related fair values provided. These bonds are classified as available-for-sale.

	12/31/20	12/31/21	12/31/22
Amortized cost	$491,150	$519,442	$550,000
Fair value	497,000	509,000	550,000

Instructions

a. Indicate whether the bonds were purchased at a discount or at a premium.

b. Prepare the adjusting entry to record the bonds at fair value at December 31, 2020. The Fair Value Adjustment account has a debit balance of $1,000 prior to adjustment.

c. Prepare the adjusting entry to record the bonds at fair value at December 31, 2021.

P17.5 **(LO 2)** Excel **(Equity Securities Entries and Disclosures)** Parnevik Company has the following securities in its investment portfolio on December 31, 2020 (all securities were purchased in 2020): (1) 3,000 shares of Anderson Co. common stock which cost $58,500, (2) 10,000 shares of Munter Ltd. common stock which cost $580,000, and (3) 6,000 shares of King Company preferred stock which cost $255,000. The Fair Value Adjustment account shows a credit of $10,100 at the end of 2020.

In 2021, Parnevik completed the following securities transactions.

1. On January 15, sold 3,000 shares of Anderson's common stock at $22 per share less fees of $2,150.
2. On April 17, purchased 1,000 shares of Castle's common stock at $33.50 per share plus fees of $1,980.

On December 31, 2021, the market prices per share of these securities were Munter $61, King $40, and Castle $29. In addition, the accounting supervisor of Parnevik told you that, even though all these securities have readily determinable fair values, Parnevik will not actively trade these securities because the top management intends to hold them for more than one year.

Instructions

a. Prepare the entry for the security sale on January 15, 2021.

b. Prepare the journal entry to record the security purchase on April 17, 2021.

c. Compute the unrealized gains or losses and prepare the adjusting entry for Parnevik on December 31, 2021.

d. How should the unrealized gains or losses be reported on Parnevik's income statement and balance sheet?

P17.6 **(LO 2)** **(Equity Securities Entries)** McElroy Company has the following portfolio of investment securities at September 30, 2020, its most recent reporting date.

Investment Securities	Cost	Fair Value
Horton, Inc. common (5,000 shares)	$215,000	$200,000
Monty, Inc. preferred (3,500 shares)	133,000	140,000
Oakwood Corp. common (1,000 shares)	180,000	179,000

On October 10, 2020, the Horton shares were sold at a price of $54 per share. In addition, 3,000 shares of Patriot common stock were acquired at $54.50 per share on November 2, 2020. The December 31, 2020, fair values were Monty $106,000, Patriot $132,000, and Oakwood $193,000.

Instructions

Prepare the journal entries to record the sale, purchase, and adjusting entries related to the equity securities in the last quarter of 2020.

P17.7 (LO 1) (Available-for-Sale and Held-to-Maturity Debt Securities Entries) The following information relates to the debt securities investments of Wildcat Company.

1. On February 1, the company purchased 10% bonds of Gibbons Co. having a par value of $300,000 at 100 plus accrued interest. Interest is payable April 1 and October 1.
2. On April 1, semiannual interest is received.
3. On July 1, 9% bonds of Sampson, Inc. were purchased. These bonds with a par value of $200,000 were purchased at 100 plus accrued interest. Interest dates are June 1 and December 1.
4. On September 1, bonds with a par value of $60,000, purchased on February 1, are sold at 99 plus accrued interest.
5. On October 1, semiannual interest is received.
6. On December 1, semiannual interest is received.
7. On December 31, the fair value of the bonds purchased February 1 and July 1 are 95 and 93, respectively.

Instructions

a. Prepare any journal entries you consider necessary, including year-end entries (December 31), assuming these are available-for-sale securities.

b. If Wildcat classified these as held-to-maturity investments, explain how the journal entries would differ from those in part (a).

P17.8 (LO 2, 3) (Fair Value and Equity Methods) Brooks Corp. is a medium-sized corporation specializing in quarrying stone for building construction. The company has long dominated the market, at one time achieving a 70% market penetration. During prosperous years, the company's profits, coupled with a conservative dividend policy, resulted in funds available for outside investment. Over the years, Brooks has had a policy of investing idle cash in equity securities. In particular, Brooks has made periodic investments in the company's principal vendor of mining equipment, Norton Industries. Although the firm currently owns 12% of the outstanding common stock of Norton Industries, Brooks does not have significant influence over the operations of Norton Industries.

Cheryl Thomas has recently joined Brooks as assistant controller, and her first assignment is to prepare the 2020 year-end adjusting entries for the accounts that are valued by the "fair value" rule for financial reporting purposes. Thomas has gathered the following information about Brooks' pertinent accounts.

1. Brooks has equity securities related to Delaney Motors and Patrick Electric. During 2020, Brooks purchased 100,000 shares of Delaney Motors for $1,400,000; these shares currently have a fair value of $1,600,000. Brooks' investment in Patrick Electric has not been profitable; the company acquired 50,000 shares of Patrick in April 2020 at $20 per share, a purchase that currently has a value of $720,000.
2. Prior to 2020, Brooks invested $22,500,000 in Norton Industries and has not changed its holdings this year. This investment in Norton Industries was valued at $21,500,000 on December 31, 2019. Brooks' 12% ownership of Norton Industries has a current fair value of $22,225,000 on December 2020.

Instructions

a. Prepare the appropriate adjusting entries for Brooks as of December 31, 2020, to reflect the application of the "fair value" rule for the securities described above.

b. For the securities presented above, describe how the results of the valuation adjustments made in (a) would be reflected in the body of Brooks' 2020 financial statements.

c. Prepare the entries for the Norton investment, assuming that Brooks owns 25% of Norton's shares. Norton reported income of $500,000 in 2020 and paid cash dividends of $100,000.

P17.9 (LO 2, 4) (Gain on Sale of Investments and Comprehensive Income) On January 1, 2020, Acker Inc. had the following balance sheet.

Acker Inc.
Balance Sheet
As of January 1, 2020

Assets		Equity	
Cash	$ 50,000	Common stock	$260,000
Debt investments (available-for-sale)	240,000	Accumulated other comprehensive income	30,000
Total	$290,000	Total	$290,000

The accumulated other comprehensive income related to unrealized holding gains on available-for-sale debt securities. The fair value of Acker Inc.'s available-for-sale debt securities at December 31, 2020, was $190,000; its cost was $140,000. No securities were purchased during the year. Acker Inc.'s income statement for 2020 was as follows. (Ignore income taxes.)

Acker Inc.
Income Statement
For the Year Ended December 31, 2020

Dividend revenue	$ 5,000
Gain on sale of investments	30,000
Net income	$35,000

Instructions

(Assume all transactions during the year were for cash.)

a. Prepare the journal entry to record the sale of the available-for-sale debt securities in 2020.

b. Prepare the journal entry to record the Unrealized Holding Gain or Loss for 2020.

c. Prepare a statement of comprehensive income for 2020.

d. Prepare a balance sheet as of December 31, 2020.

P17.10 **(LO 2)** Excel **(Equity Investments)** Castleman Holdings, Inc. had the following equity investment portfolio at January 1, 2020.

Evers Company	1,000 shares @ $15 each	$15,000
Rogers Company	900 shares @ $20 each	18,000
Chance Company	500 shares @ $9 each	4,500
Equity investments @ cost		37,500
Fair value adjustment		(7,500)
Equity investments @ fair value		$30,000

During 2020, the following transactions took place.

1. On March 1, Rogers Company paid a $2 per share dividend.
2. On April 30, Castleman Holdings, Inc. sold 300 shares of Chance Company for $11 per share.
3. On May 15, Castleman Holdings, Inc. purchased 100 more shares of Evers Company stock at $16 per share.
4. At December 31, 2020, the stocks had the following price per share values: Evers $17, Rogers $19, and Chance $8.

During 2021, the following transactions took place.

5. On February 1, Castleman Holdings, Inc. sold the remaining Chance shares for $8 per share.
6. On March 1, Rogers Company paid a $2 per share dividend.
7. On December 21, Evers Company declared a cash dividend of $3 per share to be paid in the next month.
8. At December 31, 2021, the stocks had the following price per share values: Evers $19 and Rogers $21.

Instructions

a. Prepare journal entries for each of the above transactions.

b. Prepare a partial balance sheet showing the investment-related amounts to be reported at December 31, 2020 and 2021.

P17.11 **(LO 2, 4)** **(Equity Securities—Statement Presentation)** Fernandez Corp. invested its excess cash in securities during 2020. As of December 31, 2020, the securities portfolio consisted of the following common stocks.

Security	Quantity	Cost	Fair Value
Lindsay Jones, Inc.	1,000 shares	$ 15,000	$ 21,000
Poley Corp.	2,000 shares	40,000	42,000
Arnold Aircraft	2,000 shares	72,000	60,000
	Totals	$127,000	$123,000

Instructions

a. What should be reported on Fernandez's December 31, 2020, balance sheet relative to these securities? What should be reported on Fernandez's 2020 income statement?

On December 31, 2021, Fernandez's securities portfolio consisted of the following common stocks.

Security	Quantity	Cost	Fair Value
Lindsay Jones, Inc.	1,000 shares	$ 15,000	$20,000
Lindsay Jones, Inc.	2,000 shares	33,000	40,000
Duff Company	1,000 shares	16,000	12,000
Arnold Aircraft	2,000 shares	72,000	22,000
	Totals	$136,000	$94,000

During the year 2021, Fernandez Corp. sold 2,000 shares of Poley Corp. for $38,200 and purchased 2,000 more shares of Lindsay Jones, Inc. and 1,000 shares of Duff Company.

b. What should be reported on Fernandez's December 31, 2021, balance sheet? What should be reported on Fernandez's 2021 income statement?

On December 31, 2022, Fernandez's securities portfolio consisted of the following common stocks.

Security	Quantity	Cost	Fair Value
Arnold Aircraft	2,000 shares	$72,000	$82,000
Duff Company	500 shares	8,000	6,000
	Totals	$80,000	$88,000

During the year 2022, Fernandez Corp. sold 3,000 shares of Lindsay Jones, Inc. for $39,900 and 500 shares of Duff Company at a loss of $2,700.

c. What should be reported on the face of Fernandez's December 31, 2022, balance sheet? What should be reported on Fernandez's 2022 income statement?

*P17.12 **(LO 5)** Excel **(Derivative Financial Instrument)** The treasurer of Miller Co. has read on the Internet that the stock price of Wade Inc. is about to take off. In order to profit from this potential development, Miller Co. purchased a call option on Wade common shares on July 7, 2020, for $240. The call option is for 200 shares (notional value), and the strike price is $70. (The market price of a share of Wade stock on that date is $70.) The option expires on January 31, 2021. The following data are available with respect to the call option.

Date	Market Price of Wade Shares	Time Value of Call Option
September 30, 2020	$77 per share	$180
December 31, 2020	75 per share	65
January 4, 2021	76 per share	30

Instructions

Prepare the journal entries for Miller Co. for the following dates.

a. July 7, 2020—Investment in call option on Wade shares.

b. September 30, 2020—Miller prepares financial statements.

c. December 31, 2020—Miller prepares financial statements.

d. January 4, 2021—Miller settles the call option on the Wade shares.

*P17.13 **(LO 5)** **(Derivative Financial Instrument)** Johnstone Co. purchased a put option on Ewing common shares on July 7, 2020, for $240. The put option is for 200 shares, and the strike price is $70. (The market price of a share of Ewing stock on that date is $70.) The option expires on January 31, 2021. The following data are available with respect to the put option.

Date	Market Price of Ewing Shares	Time Value of Put Option
September 30, 2020	$77 per share	$125
December 31, 2020	75 per share	50
January 31, 2021	78 per share	0

Instructions

Prepare the journal entries for Johnstone Co. for the following dates.

a. July 7, 2020—Investment in put option on Ewing shares.

b. September 30, 2020—Johnstone prepares financial statements.

c. December 31, 2020—Johnstone prepares financial statements.

d. January 31, 2021—Put option expires.

*P17.14 **(LO 5)** **(Free-Standing Derivative)** Warren Co. purchased a put option on Echo common shares on January 7, 2020, for $360. The put option is for 400 shares, and the strike price is $85 (which equals the price of an Echo share on the purchase date). The option expires on July 31, 2020. The following data are available with respect to the put option.

Date	Market Price of Echo Shares	Time Value of Put Option
March 31, 2020	$80 per share	$200
June 30, 2020	82 per share	90
July 6, 2020	77 per share	25

Instructions

Prepare the journal entries for Warren Co. for the following dates.

a. January 7, 2020—Investment in put option on Echo shares.

b. March 31, 2020—Warren prepares financial statements.

c. June 30, 2020—Warren prepares financial statements.

d. July 6, 2020—Warren settles the put option on the Echo shares.

*P17.15 **(LO 6)** Excel **(Fair Value Hedge Interest Rate Swap)** On December 31, 2020, Mercantile Corp. had a $10,000,000, 8% fixed-rate note outstanding, payable in 2 years. It decides to enter into a 2-year swap with Chicago First Bank to convert the fixed-rate debt to variable-rate debt. The terms of the swap indicate that Mercantile will receive interest at a fixed rate of 8% and will pay a variable rate equal to the 6-month LIBOR rate, based on the $10,000,000 amount. The LIBOR rate on December 31, 2020, is 7%. The LIBOR rate will be reset every 6 months and will be used to determine the variable rate to be paid for the following 6-month period.

Mercantile Corp. designates the swap as a fair value hedge. Assume that the hedging relationship meets all the conditions necessary for hedge accounting. The 6-month LIBOR rate and the swap and debt fair values are as follows.

Date	6-Month LIBOR Rate	Swap Fair Value	Debt Fair Value
December 31, 2020	7.0%	—	$10,000,000
June 30, 2021	7.5%	(200,000)	9,800,000
December 31, 2021	6.0%	60,000	10,060,000

Instructions

a. Present the journal entries to record the following transactions.
   1. The entry, if any, to record the swap on December 31, 2020.
   2. The entry to record the semiannual debt interest payment on June 30, 2021.
   3. The entry to record the settlement of the semiannual swap amount receivables at 8%, less amount payable at LIBOR, 7%.
   4. The entry to record the change in the fair value of the debt on June 30, 2021.
   5. The entry to record the change in the fair value of the swap at June 30, 2021.

b. Indicate the amount(s) reported on the balance sheet and income statement related to the debt and swap on December 31, 2020.

c. Indicate the amount(s) reported on the balance sheet and income statement related to the debt and swap on June 30, 2021.

d. Indicate the amount(s) reported on the balance sheet and income statement related to the debt and swap on December 31, 2021.

*P17.16 **(LO 6)** **(Cash Flow Hedge)** LEW Jewelry Co. uses gold in the manufacture of its products. LEW anticipates that it will need to purchase 500 ounces of gold in October 2020, for jewelry that will be shipped for the holiday shopping season. However, if the price of gold increases, LEW's cost to produce its jewelry will increase, which would reduce its profit margins.

To hedge the risk of increased gold prices, on April 1, 2020, LEW enters into a gold futures contract and designates this futures contract as a cash flow hedge of the anticipated gold purchase. The notional amount of the contract is 500 ounces, and the terms of the contract give LEW the right and the obligation to purchase gold at a price of $300 per ounce. The price will be good until the contract expires on October 31, 2020.

Assume the following data with respect to the price of the futures contract and the gold inventory purchase:

Date	Spot Price for October Delivery
April 1, 2020	$300 per ounce
June 30, 2020	310 per ounce
September 30, 2020	315 per ounce

Instructions

Prepare the journal entries for the following transactions.

a. April 1, 2020—Inception of the futures contract, no premium paid.

b. June 30, 2020—LEW Co. prepares financial statements.

c. September 30, 2020—LEW Co. prepares financial statements.

d. October 10, 2020—LEW Co. purchases 500 ounces of gold at $315 per ounce and settles the futures contract.

e. December 20, 2020—LEW sells jewelry containing gold purchased in October 2020 for $350,000. The cost of the finished goods inventory is $200,000.

f. Indicate the amount(s) reported on the balance sheet and income statement related to the futures contract on June 30, 2020.

g. Indicate the amount(s) reported in the income statement related to the futures contract and the inventory transactions on December 31, 2020.

*P17.17 **(LO 6)** **(Fair Value Hedge)** On October 15, 2020, Oil Products Co. purchased 4,000 barrels of fuel oil with a cost of $240,000 ($60 per barrel). Oil Products is holding this inventory in anticipation of the winter 2021 heating season. Oil Products accounts for its inventory at the lower-of-FIFO-cost-or-net realizable value. To hedge against potential declines in the value of the inventory, Oil Products also purchased a put option on the fuel oil. Oil Products paid an option premium of $300 for the put option, which gives Oil Products the option to sell 4,000 barrels of fuel oil at a strike price of $60 per gallon. The option expires on March 1, 2021. The following data are available with respect to the values of the fuel of inventory and the put option.

Date	Market Price of Fuel Oil	Time Value of Put Option
October 31, 2020	$58 per gallon	$175
November 30, 2020	57 per gallon	105
December 31, 2020	54 per gallon	40

Instructions

a. Prepare the journal entries of Oil Products for the following dates.
   1. October 15, 2020—Oil Products purchases fuel oil and the put option on fuel oil.
   2. October 31, 2020—Oil Products prepares financial statements.
   3. November 30, 2020—Oil Products prepares financial statements.
   4. December 31, 2020—Oil Products prepares financial statements.

b. Indicate the amount(s) reported on the balance sheet and income statement related to the fuel oil inventory and the put option on November 30, 2020.

c. Indicate the amount(s) reported on the balance sheet and income statement related to the fuel oil and the put option on December 31, 2020.

Concepts for Analysis

CA17.1 **(LO 1)** **(Issues Raised About Investment Securities)** You have just started work for Warren Co. as part of the controller's group involved in current financial reporting problems. Jane Henshaw, controller for Warren, is interested in your accounting background because the company has experienced a series of financial reporting surprises over the last few years. Recently, the controller has learned from the company's auditors that there is authoritative literature that may apply to its investment in securities. She assumes that you are familiar with this pronouncement and asks how the following situations should be reported in the financial statements.

Situation 1: Trading debt securities in the current assets section have a fair value that is $4,200 lower than cost.

Situation 2: A trading debt security whose fair value is currently less than cost is transferred to the available-for-sale category.

Situation 3: An available-for-sale debt security whose fair value is currently less than cost is classified as noncurrent but is to be reclassified as current.

Situation 4: The company's portfolio of held-to-maturity debt securities consists of the bonds of one company. At the end of the prior year, the fair value of the security was 50% of original cost, and this reduction in fair value was reported as an impairment. However, at the end of the current year, the fair value of the security had appreciated to twice the original cost.

Situation 5: The company has purchased some equity securities that it plans to hold for less than a year. The fair value of the securities is $7,700 below its cost.

Instructions

What is the effect upon carrying value and earnings for each of the situations above? Assume that these situations are unrelated.

CA17.2 **(LO 2)** **(Equity Securities)** Lexington Co. has the following securities outstanding on December 31, 2020 (its first year of operations).

	Cost	Fair Value
Greenspan Corp. stock	$20,000	$19,000
Summerset Company stock	9,500	8,800
Tinkers Company stock	20,000	20,600
	$49,500	$48,400

During 2021, Summerset Company stock was sold for $9,200, the difference between the $9,200 and the "fair value" of $8,800 being recorded as a "Gain on Sale of Investments." The market price of the stock on December 31, 2021, was Greenspan Corp. stock $19,900; Tinkers Company stock $20,500.

Instructions

a. What justification is there for valuing equity securities at fair value and reporting the unrealized gain or loss as part of net income?

b. How should Lexington Co. report this information in its financial statements at December 31, 2020? Explain.

c. Did Lexington Co. properly account for the sale of the Summerset Company stock? Explain.

d. Are there any additional entries necessary for Lexington Co. at December 31, 2021, to reflect the facts on the financial statements in accordance with generally accepted accounting principles? Explain.

(AICPA adapted)

CA17.3 **(LO 1)** **(Financial Statement Effect of Securities)** Presented below are three unrelated situations involving equity securities.

Situation 1: A debt security, whose fair value is currently less than cost, is classified as available-for-sale but is to be reclassified as trading.

Situation 2: A noncurrent held-to-maturity portfolio with an aggregate fair value in excess of cost includes one particular debt security whose fair value has declined to less than one-half of the original cost. The decline in value is considered to be permanent.

Situation 3: The portfolio of trading debt securities has a cost in excess of fair value of $13,500. The available-for-sale debt portfolio has a fair value in excess of cost of $28,600.

Instructions

What is the effect upon carrying value and earnings for each of the situations above?

CA17.4 **(LO 3)** **(Investment Accounted for Under the Equity Method)** On July 1, 2021, Fontaine Company purchased for cash 40% of the outstanding common stock of Knoblett Company. Both Fontaine Company and Knoblett Company have a December 31 year-end. Knoblett Company, whose common stock is actively traded in the over-the-counter market, reported its total net income for the year to Fontaine Company and also paid cash dividends on November 15, 2021, to Fontaine Company and its other stockholders.

Instructions

How should Fontaine Company report the above facts in its December 31, 2021, balance sheet and its income statement for the year then ended? Discuss the rationale for your answer.

(AICPA adapted)

CA17.5 **(LO 3)** Writing **(Equity Investment)** On July 1, 2020, Selig Company purchased for cash 30% of the outstanding common stock of Spoor Corporation. Both Selig and Spoor have a December 31 year-end. Spoor Corporation, whose common stock is actively traded on the NASDAQ exchange, paid a cash dividend on November 15, 2020, to Selig Company and its other stockholders. It also reported its total net income for the year of $920,000 to Selig Company.

Instructions

Prepare a one-page memorandum of instructions on how Selig Company should report the above facts in its December 31, 2020, balance sheet and its 2020 income statement. In your memo, identify and describe the method of valuation you recommend. Provide rationale where you can. Address your memo to the chief accountant at Selig Company.

CA17.6 **(LO 4)** Ethics **(Fair Value)** Addison Manufacturing holds a large portfolio of debt securities as an investment. The fair value of the portfolio is greater than its original cost, even though some debt securities have decreased in value. Sam Beresford, the financial vice president, and Angie Nielson, the controller, are near year-end in the process of classifying for the first time this securities portfolio in accordance with GAAP. Beresford wants to classify those securities that have increased in value during the period as trading securities in order to increase net income this year. He wants to classify all the securities that have decreased in value as held-to-maturity.

Nielson disagrees. She wants to classify those debt securities that have decreased in value as trading securities and those that have increased in value as held-to-maturity. She contends that the company is having a good earnings year and that recognizing the losses will help to smooth the income this year. As a result, the company will have built-in gains for future periods when the company may not be as profitable.

Instructions

Answer the following questions.

a. Will classifying the portfolio as each proposes actually have the effect on earnings that each says it will?

b. Is there anything unethical in what each of them proposes? Who are the stakeholders affected by their proposals?

c. Assume that Beresford and Nielson properly classify the entire portfolio into trading, available-for-sale, and held-to-maturity categories. But then each proposes to sell just before year-end the securities with gains or with losses, as the case may be, to accomplish their effect on earnings. Is this unethical?

Using Your Judgment

Financial Reporting Problem

The Procter & Gamble Company (P&G)

The financial statements of P&G are presented in Appendix B. The company's complete annual report, including the notes to the financial statements, is available online.

Instructions

Refer to P&G's financial statements and the accompanying notes to answer the following questions.

a. What investments does P&G report in 2017, and how are these investments accounted for in its financial statements?

b. How are P&G's investments valued? How does P&G determine fair value?

c. How does P&G use derivative financial instruments?

Comparative Analysis Case

The Coca-Cola Company and PepsiCo, Inc.

The financial statements of Coca-Cola and PepsiCo are presented in Appendices C and D, respectively. The companies' complete annual reports, including the notes to the financial statements, are available online.

Instructions

Use the companies' financial information to answer the following questions.

a. Based on the information contained in these financial statements, determine each of the following for each company.

1. Cash used in (for) investing activities during 2017 (from the statement of cash flows).
2. What was the total other comprehensive income for the year 2017?
3. What was the unrealized gains or losses reported as part of other comprehensive income?

b. Identify from Coca-Cola's December 31, 2017, balance sheet the investments it reported as being accounted for under the equity method.

c. In Note 3, what is Coca-Cola's policy regarding its cost method investments?

Financial Statement Analysis Case

Union Planters

Union Planters is a Tennessee bank holding company (that is, a corporation that owns banks). (Union Planters is now part of **Regions Bank**.) Union Planters manages $32 billion in assets, the largest of which is its loan portfolio of $19 billion. In addition to its loan portfolio, however, like other banks it has significant debt investments. The nature of these investments varies from short-term to long-term. As a consequence, consistent with the requirements of accounting rules, Union Planters reports its investments in two different categories—trading and available-for-sale. The following facts were found in a recent Union Planters' annual report.

(all dollars in millions)	Amortized Cost	Gross Unrealized Gains	Gross Unrealized Losses	Fair Value
Trading account assets	$ 275	—	—	$ 275
Securities available for sale	8,209	$108	$15	8,302
Net income				224
Net securities gains (losses)				(9)

Instructions

a. Why do you suppose Union Planters purchases investments, rather than simply making loans? Why does it purchase investments that vary in nature both in terms of their maturities and in type (debt versus stock)?

b. How must Union Planters account for its investments in each of the two categories?

c. In what ways does classifying investments into two different categories assist investors in evaluating the profitability of a company like Union Planters?

d. Suppose that the management of Union Planters was not happy with its net income for the year. What step could it have taken with its investment portfolio that would have definitely increased reported profit? How much could it have increased reported profit? Why do you suppose it chose not to do this?

Accounting, Analysis, and Principles

Instar Company has several investments in the securities of other companies. The following information regarding these investments is available at December 31, 2020.

1. Instar holds bonds issued by Dorsel Corp. The bonds have an amortized cost of $320,000 and their fair value at December 31, 2020, is $400,000. Instar intends to hold the bonds until they mature on December 31, 2028.
2. Instar has invested idle cash in the equity securities of several publicly traded companies. Instar intends to sell these securities during the first quarter of 2021, when it will need the cash to acquire seasonal inventory. These equity securities have a cost basis of $800,000 and a fair value of $920,000 at December 31, 2020.
3. Instar has an ownership stake in one of the companies that supplies Instar with various components Instar uses in its products. Instar owns 6% of the common stock of the supplier, does not have any representation on the supplier's board of directors, does not exchange any personnel with the supplier, and does not consult with the supplier on any of the supplier's operating, financial, or strategic decisions. The cost basis of the investment in the supplier is $1,200,000 and the fair value of the investment at December 31, 2020, is $1,550,000. Instar does not intend to sell the investment in the foreseeable future. The supplier reported net income of $80,000 for 2020 and paid no dividends.
4. Instar purchased 25% of the stock of Slobbaer Co. for $900,000. Instar has significant influence over the operating activities of Slobbaer Co. During 2020, Slobbaer Co. reported net income of $300,000 and paid a dividend of $100,000.

Accounting

a. Determine how each of the investments described above should be classified and accounted far.

b. Prepare any December 31, 2020, journal entries needed for Instar relating to Instar's various investments in other companies. Assume 2020 is Instar's first year of operations.

Analysis

What is the effect on Instar's 2020 net income (as reported on Instar's income statement) of Instar's investments in other companies?

Principles

Briefly explain the different rationales for the different accounting and reporting rules for different types of investments in the securities of other companies.

Bridge to the Profession

FASB Codification References

[1] FASB ASC Glossary. [Predecessor literature: "Accounting for Certain Investments in Debt and Equity Securities," *Statement of Financial Accounting Standards No. 115* (Norwalk, Conn.: FASB, 1993), par. 137.]

[2] FASB ASC 820-10-20. [Predecessor literature: "Fair Value Measurement," *Statement of Financial Accounting Standards No. 157* (Norwalk, Conn.: FASB, September 2006).]

[3] FASB ASC 220. [Predecessor literature: "Reporting Comprehensive Income," *Statement of Financial Accounting Standards No. 130* (Norwalk, Conn.: FASB, 1997).]

[4] FASB ASC 323-10-15. [Predecessor literature: "The Equity Method of Accounting for Investments in Common Stock," *Opinions of the Accounting Principles Board No. 18* (New York: AICPA, 1971), par. 17.]

[5] FASB ASC 323-10-15-10. [Predecessor literature: "Criteria for Applying the Equity Method of Accounting for Investments in Common Stock," *Interpretations of the Financial Accounting Standards Board No. 35* (Stamford, Conn.: FASB, 1981).]

[6] FASB ASC 323-10-35. [Predecessor literature: "The Equity Method of Accounting for Investments in Common Stock," *Opinions of the Accounting Principles Board No. 18* (New York: AICPA, 1971), par. 19(i).]

[7] FASB ASC 815-10-05. [Predecessor literature: "Accounting for Derivative Instruments and Hedging Activities," *Statement of Financial Accounting Standards No. 133* (Stamford, Conn.: FASB, 1998).]

[8] FASB ASC 820-10. [Predecessor literature: "Fair Value Measurement," *Statement of Financial Accounting Standards No. 157* (Norwalk, Conn.: FASB, September 2006).]

[9] FASB ASC 815-10-05-4. [Predecessor literature: "Accounting for Derivative Instruments and Hedging Activities," *Statement of Financial Accounting Standards No. 133* (Stamford, Conn.: FASB, 1998), par. 249.]

[10] FASB ASC 815-10-05-4. [Predecessor literature: "Accounting for Derivative Instruments and Hedging Activities," *Statement of Financial Accounting Standards No. 133* (Stamford, Conn.: FASB, 1998).]

[11] FASB ASC 825-10-25-1. [Predecessor literature: "The Fair Value Option for Financial Assets and Liabilities, Including an Amendment of FASB Statement No. 115," *Statement of Financial Accounting Standards No. 159* (Norwalk, Conn.: FASB, February 2007).]

[12] FASB ASC 820-10. [Predecessor literature: "Fair Value Measurement," *Statement of Financial Accounting Standards No. 157* (Norwalk, Conn.: FASB, September 2006).]

[13] FASB ASC 825-10-25-1. [Predecessor literature: "The Fair Value Option for Financial Assets and Liabilities, Including an Amendment of FASB Statement No. 115," *Statement of Financial Accounting Standards No. 159* (Norwalk, Conn.: FASB, February 2007).]

Codification Exercises

If your school has a subscription to the FASB Codification, log in and prepare responses to the following. Provide Codification references for your responses.

CE17.1 Access the glossary ("Master Glossary") to answer the following.

a. What are trading securities?

b. What is the definition of "holding gain or loss"?

c. What is a cash flow hedge?

d. What is a fair value hedge?

CE17.2 What guidance does the SEC give for disclosures regarding accounting policies used for derivatives?

CE17.3 When would an investor discontinue applying the equity method in an investment? Are there any exceptions to this rule?

CE17.4 For balance sheet purposes, can the fair value of a derivative in a loss position be netted against the fair value of a derivative in a gain position?

Codification Research Case

Your client, Cascade Company, is planning to invest some of its excess cash in 5-year revenue bonds issued by the county and in the stock of one of its suppliers, Teton Co. Teton's shares trade on the over-the-counter market. The company would like you to conduct some research on the accounting for these investments.

Instructions

If your school has a subscription to the FASB Codification, log in and prepare responses to the following. Provide Codification references for your responses.

a. Since the Teton shares do not trade on one of the large stock markets, Cascade argues that the fair value of this investment is not readily available. According to the authoritative literature, when is the fair value of a security "readily determinable"?

b. To avoid volatility in their financial statements due to fair value adjustments, Cascade debated whether the bond investment could be classified as held-to-maturity; Cascade is pretty sure it will hold the bonds for 5 years. How close to maturity could Cascade sell an investment and still classify it as held-to-maturity?

c. What disclosures must be made for any sale or transfer from securities classified as held-to-maturity?

Additional Professional Resources

Go to WileyPLUS for other career-readiness resources, such as career coaching, internship opportunities, and CPAexcel prep.

IFRS Insights

LEARNING OBJECTIVE 9

Compare the accounting for investments under GAAP and IFRS.

The accounting for investments is discussed in *IAS 27* ("Consolidated and Separate Financial Statements"), *IAS 28* ("Accounting for Investments in Associates"), *IAS 39* ("Financial Instruments: Recognition and Measurement"), and *IFRS 9* ("Financial Instruments"). Until recently, when the IASB issued *IFRS 9*, the accounting and reporting for investments under IFRS and GAAP were for the most part very similar. However, *IFRS 9* introduces new investment classifications and increases the situations when investments are accounted for at fair value, with gains and losses recorded in income.

Relevant Facts

Following are the key similarities and differences between GAAP and IFRS related to investments.

Similarities

- GAAP and IFRS use similar classifications for financial assets: cash, loans and receivables, investments, and derivatives.
- Both IFRS and GAAP require that financial assets be sorted into specific categories for measurement and classification purposes.
- Held-to-maturity (GAAP) and held-for-collection (IFRS) investments are accounted for at amortized cost. Gains and losses on some investments are reported in other comprehensive income.
- Amortized cost or fair value is used depending upon the classification of the financial instrument.
- The definitions of amortized cost and fair value are the same.
- Both GAAP and IFRS use the same test to determine whether the equity method of accounting should be used, that is, significant influence with a general guideline of over 20 percent ownership.
- GAAP and IFRS are similar in the accounting for the fair value option. That is, the option to use the fair value method must be made at initial recognition, the selection is irrevocable, and gains and losses are reported as part of income.

Differences

- While GAAP classifies debt investments as trading, available-for-sale, and held-to-maturity, IFRS classifies debt investments as held-for-collection (debt investments) and trading.
- GAAP requires that all changes in fair value for **all equity securities** be reported as part of income. IFRS requires that changes in fair value for **non-trading equity securities** be reported as part of other comprehensive income.

- While the measurement of impairments is similar under GAAP and IFRS, GAAP does not permit the reversal of an impairment charge related to held-to-maturity debt investments and equity investments. IFRS allows reversals of impairments of held-for-collection investments.
- While GAAP and IFRS are similar in the accounting for the fair value option, one difference is that GAAP permits the fair value option for equity method investments; IFRS does not.

About the Numbers

Accounting for Financial Assets

A **financial asset** is cash, an equity investment of another company (e.g., ordinary or preference shares), or a contractual right to receive cash from another party (e.g., loans, receivables, and bonds). The accounting for cash is relatively straightforward and is discussed in Chapter 7. The accounting and reporting for equity and debt investments, as discussed in the opening story, is extremely contentious, particularly in light of the credit crisis in the latter part of 2008.

IFRS requires that companies determine how to measure their financial assets based on two criteria:

- The company's business model for managing its financial assets; and
- The contractual cash flow characteristics of the financial asset.

If a company has (1) a business model whose objective is to hold assets in order to collect contractual cash flows and (2) the contractual terms of the financial asset provides specified dates to cash flows that are solely payments of principal and interest on the principal amount outstanding, then the company should use amortized cost.

For example, assume that **Mitsubishi** purchases a bond investment that it intends to hold to maturity. Its business model for this type of investment is to collect interest and then principal at maturity. The payment dates for the interest rate and principal are stated on the bond. In this case, Mitsubishi accounts for the investment at amortized cost. If, on the other hand, Mitsubishi purchased the bonds as part of a trading strategy to speculate on interest rate changes (a trading investment), then the debt investment is reported at fair value. As a result, only debt investments such as receivables, loans, and bond investments that meet the two criteria above are recorded at amortized cost. All other debt investments are recorded and reported at fair value.

Equity investments are generally recorded and reported at fair value. Equity investments do not have a fixed interest or principal payment schedule and therefore cannot be accounted for at amortized cost. In summary, companies account for investments based on the type of security, as indicated in **Illustration IFRS17.1**.

ILLUSTRATION IFRS17.1
Summary of Investment Accounting Approaches

Type of Investment	Assessment of Accounting Criteria	Valuation Approach
Debt	Meets business model (held-for-collection) and contractual cash flow tests.	Amortized cost
	Does not meet the business model test (not held-for-collection).	Fair value
Equity	Does not meet contractual cash flow test.	Fair value
	Exercises some control.	Equity method

Debt Investments

Debt Investments—Amortized Cost Only debt investments can be measured at amortized cost. If a company like **Carrefour** makes an investment in the bonds of **Nokia**, it will receive contractual cash flows of interest over the life of the bonds and repayment of the principal at maturity. If it is Carrefour's strategy to hold this investment in order to receive these cash flows over the life of the bond, it has a held-for-collection strategy and it will measure the investment at amortized cost.[44]

[44]Classification as held-for-collection does not mean the security must be held to maturity. For example, a company may sell an investment before maturity if (1) the security does not meet the company's investment strategy (e.g., the company has a policy to invest in only AAA-rated bonds but the bond investment has a decline in its credit rating), (2) a company changes its strategy to invest only in securities within a certain maturity range, or (3) the company needs to sell a security to fund certain capital expenditures. However, if a company begins trading held-for-collection investments on a regular basis, it should assess whether such trading is consistent with the held-for-collection classification.

Example: Debt Investment at Amortized Cost. To illustrate the accounting for a debt investment at amortized cost, assume that Robinson Company purchased $100,000 of 8 percent bonds of Evermaster Corporation on January 1, 2020, at a discount, paying $92,278. The bonds mature January 1, 2025, and yield 10 percent; interest is payable each July 1 and January 1. Robinson records the investment as follows.

January 1, 2020

Debt Investments	92,278	
Cash		92,278

As indicated in Chapter 14, companies must amortize premiums or discounts using the **effective-interest method**. They apply the effective-interest method to bond investments in a way similar to that for bonds payable. To compute interest revenue, companies compute the effective-interest rate or yield at the time of investment and apply that rate to the beginning carrying amount (book value) for each interest period. The investment carrying amount is increased by the amortized discount or decreased by the amortized premium in each period.

Illustration IFRS17.2 shows the effect of the discount amortization on the interest revenue that Robinson records each period for its investment in Evermaster bonds.

ILLUSTRATION IFRS17.2

Schedule of Interest Revenue and Bond Discount Amortization—Effective-Interest Method

8% Bonds Purchased to Yield 10%

Date	Cash Received	Interest Revenue	Bond Discount Amortization	Carrying Amount of Bonds
1/1/20				$ 92,278
7/1/20	$ 4,000[a]	$ 4,614[b]	$ 614[c]	92,892[d]
1/1/21	4,000	4,645	645	93,537
7/1/21	4,000	4,677	677	94,214
1/1/22	4,000	4,711	711	94,925
7/1/22	4,000	4,746	746	95,671
1/1/23	4,000	4,783	783	96,454
7/1/23	4,000	4,823	823	97,277
1/1/24	4,000	4,864	864	98,141
7/1/24	4,000	4,907	907	99,048
1/1/25	4,000	4,952	952	100,000
	$40,000	$47,722	$7,722	

[a]$4,000 = $100,000 × .08 × 6/12
[b]$4,614 = $92,278 × .10 × 6/12
[c]$614 = $4,614 − $4,000
[d]$92,892 = $92,278 + $614

Robinson records the receipt of the first semiannual interest payment on July 1, 2020 (using the data in Illustration IFRS17.2), as follows.

July 1, 2020

Cash	4,000	
Debt Investments	614	
Interest Revenue		4,614

Because Robinson is on a calendar-year basis, it accrues interest and amortizes the discount at December 31, 2020, as follows.

December 31, 2020

Interest Receivable	4,000	
Debt Investments	645	
Interest Revenue		4,645

Again, Illustration IFRS17.2 shows the interest and amortization amounts. Thus, the accounting for held-for-collection investments in IFRS is the same as held-to-maturity investments under GAAP.

Debt Investments—Fair Value In some cases, companies both manage and evaluate investment performance on a fair value basis. In these situations, these investments are managed and evaluated based on a documented risk-management or investment strategy based on fair value information. For example, some companies often hold debt investments with the intention of selling them in a short period of time.

These debt investments are often referred to as **trading investments** because companies frequently buy and sell these investments to generate profits in short-term differences in price.

Companies that account for and report debt investments at fair value follow the same accounting entries as debt investments held-for-collection during the reporting period. That is, they are recorded at amortized cost. However, **at each reporting date, companies adjust the amortized cost to fair value, with any unrealized holding gain or loss reported as part of net income (fair value method)**. An **unrealized holding gain or loss** is the net change in the fair value of a debt investment from one period to another.

Example: Debt Investment at Fair Value. To illustrate the accounting for debt investments using the fair value approach, assume the same information as in our previous illustration for Robinson Company. Recall that Robinson Company purchased $100,000 of 8 percent bonds of Evermaster Corporation on January 1, 2020, at a discount, paying $92,278.[45] The bonds mature January 1, 2025, and yield 10 percent; interest is payable each July 1 and January 1.

The journal entries in 2020 are exactly the same as those for amortized cost. These entries are as follows.

January 1, 2020		
Debt Investments	92,278	
Cash		92,278
July 1, 2020		
Cash	4,000	
Debt Investments	614	
Interest Revenue		4,614
December 31, 2020		
Interest Receivable	4,000	
Debt Investments	645	
Interest Revenue		4,645

Again, Illustration IFRS17.2 shows the interest and amortization amounts. If the debt investment is held-for-collection, no further entries are necessary. To apply the fair value approach, Robinson determines that, due to a decrease in interest rates, the fair value of the debt investment increased to $95,000 at December 31, 2020. Comparing the fair value with the carrying amount of these bonds at December 31, 2020, Robinson has an unrealized holding gain of $1,463, as shown in **Illustration IFRS17.3**.

ILLUSTRATION IFRS17.3

Computation of Unrealized Gain on Fair Value Debt Investment (2020)

Fair value at December 31, 2020	$95,000
Amortized cost at December 31, 2020 (per Illustration IFRS17.2)	93,537
Unrealized holding gain or (loss)	$ 1,463

Robinson therefore makes the following entry to record the adjustment of the debt investment to fair value at December 31, 2020.

Fair Value Adjustment	1,463	
Unrealized Holding Gain or Loss—Income		1,463

Robinson uses a valuation account (**Fair Value Adjustment**) instead of debiting Debt Investments to record the investment at fair value. The use of the Fair Value Adjustment account enables Robinson to maintain a record at amortized cost in the accounts. Because the valuation account has a debit balance, in this case the fair value of Robinson's debt investment is higher than its amortized cost.

The Unrealized Holding Gain or Loss—Income account is reported in the other income and expense section of the income statement as part of net income. This account is closed to net income each period. The Fair Value Adjustment account is not closed each period and is simply adjusted each period to its proper valuation. The Fair Value Adjustment balance is not shown on the statement of financial position but is simply used to restate the debt investment account to fair value.

[45]Companies may incur brokerage and transaction costs in purchasing securities. For investments accounted for at fair value (both debt and equity), IFRS requires that these costs be recorded in net income as other income and expense and not as an adjustment to the carrying value of the investment.

Robinson reports its investment in Evermaster bonds in its December 31, 2020, financial statements as shown in **Illustration IFRS17.4**.

ILLUSTRATION IFRS17.4

Financial Statement Presentation of Debt Investments at Fair Value

Statement of Financial Position	
Current assets	
Interest receivable	$ 4,000
Debt investments (trading)	95,000
Income Statement	
Other income and expense	
Interest revenue ($4,614 + $4,645)	$ 9,259
Unrealized holding gain or (loss)	1,463

As you can see from this example, the accounting for trading debt investments under IFRS is the same as GAAP.

Equity Investments

As in GAAP, under IFRS, the degree to which one corporation (**investor**) acquires an interest in the shares of another corporation (**investee**) generally determines the accounting treatment for the investment subsequent to acquisition. To review, the classification of such investments depends on the percentage of the investee voting shares that is held by the investor:

1. Holdings of less than 20 percent (**fair value method**)—investor has passive interest.
2. Holdings between 20 percent and 50 percent (**equity method**)—investor has significant influence.
3. Holdings of more than 50 percent (**consolidated statements**)—investor has controlling interest.

The accounting and reporting for equity investments therefore depend on the level of influence and the type of security involved, as shown in **Illustration IFRS17.5**.

ILLUSTRATION IFRS17.5

Accounting and Reporting for Equity Investments by Category

Category	Valuation	Unrealized Holding Gains or Losses	Other Income Effects
Holdings less than 20%			
1. Trading	Fair value	Recognized in net income	Dividends declared; gains and losses from sale.
2. Non-Trading	Fair value	Recognized in "Other comprehensive income" (OCI) and as separate component of equity	Dividends declared; gains and losses from sale.
Holdings between 20% and 50%	Equity	Not recognized	Proportionate share of investee's net income.
Holdings more than 50%	Consolidation	Not recognized	Not applicable.

Equity Investments at Fair Value When an investor has an interest of less than 20 percent, it is presumed that the investor has little or no influence over the investee. As indicated in Illustration IFRS17.5, there are two classifications for holdings less than 20 percent. Under IFRS, the presumption is that equity investments are held-for-trading. That is, companies hold these securities to profit from price changes. As with debt investments that are held for trading, the general accounting and reporting rule for these investments is to value the securities at fair value and record unrealized gains and losses in net income (**fair value method**).[46]

[46]Fair value at initial recognition is the transaction price (exclusive of brokerage and other transaction costs). Subsequent fair value measurements should be based on market prices, if available. For non-traded investments, a valuation technique based on discounted expected cash flows can be used to develop a fair value estimate. While IFRS requires that all equity investments be measured at fair value, in certain limited cases, cost may be an appropriate estimate of fair value for an equity investment.

However, some equity investments are held for purposes other than trading. For example, a company may be required to hold an equity investment in order to sell its products in a particular area. In this situation, the recording of unrealized gains and losses in income, as is required for trading investments, is not indicative of the company's performance with respect to this investment. As a result, IFRS allows companies to classify some equity investments as non-trading. **Non-trading equity investments** are recorded at fair value on the statement of financial position, with unrealized gains and losses reported in other comprehensive income.

Example: Equity Investment (Income). Upon acquisition, companies record equity investments at fair value. To illustrate, assume that on November 3, 2020, Republic Corporation purchased ordinary shares of three companies, each investment representing less than a 20 percent interest.

	Cost
Burberry	$259,700
Nestlé	317,500
St. Regis Pulp Co.	141,350
Total cost	$718,550

Republic records these investments as follows.

November 3, 2020		
Equity Investments	718,550	
Cash		718,550

On December 6, 2020, Republic receives a cash dividend of $4,200 on its investment in the ordinary shares of Nestlé. It records the cash dividend as follows.

December 6, 2020		
Cash	4,200	
Dividend Revenue		4,200

All three of the investee companies reported net income for the year, but only Nestlé declared and paid a dividend to Republic. But, recall that when an investor owns less than 20 percent of the shares of another corporation, it is presumed that the investor has relatively little influence on the investee. As a result, **net income of the investee is not a proper basis for recognizing income from the investment by the investor**. Why? Because the increased net assets resulting from profitable operations may be permanently retained for use in the investee's business. Therefore, **the investor recognizes net income only when the investee declares cash dividends.**

At December 31, 2020, Republic's equity investment portfolio has the carrying value and fair value shown in Illustration IFRS17.6.

ILLUSTRATION IFRS17.6

Computation of Fair Value Adjustment—Equity Investment Portfolio (2020)

Equity Investment Portfolio
December 31, 2020

Investments	Carrying Value	Fair Value	Unrealized Gain (Loss)
Burberry	$259,700	$275,000	$ 15,300
Nestlé	317,500	304,000	(13,500)
St. Regis Pulp Co.	141,350	104,000	(37,350)
Total of portfolio	$718,550	$683,000	(35,550)
Previous fair value adjustment balance			-0-
Fair value adjustment—Cr.			$(35,550)

For Republic's equity investment portfolio, the gross unrealized gains are $15,300, and the gross unrealized losses are $50,850 ($13,500 + $37,350), resulting in a net unrealized loss of $35,550. The fair value of the equity investment portfolio is below cost by $35,550.

As with **debt** investments, Republic records the net unrealized gains and losses related to changes in the fair value of **equity** investments in an Unrealized Holding Gain or Loss—Income account. Republic reports this amount as other income and expense. In this case, Republic prepares an adjusting entry debiting the Unrealized Holding Gain or Loss—Income account and crediting the Fair Value Adjustment account to record the decrease in fair value and to record the loss as follows.

December 31, 2020		
Unrealized Holding Gain or Loss—Income	35,550	
Fair Value Adjustment		35,550

On January 23, 2021, Republic sold all of its Burberry ordinary shares, receiving $287,220. Illustration IFRS17.7 shows the computation of the realized gain on the sale.

ILLUSTRATION IFRS17.7

Computation of Gain on Sale of Burberry Shares

Net proceeds from sale	$287,220
Cost of **Burberry** shares	259,700
Gain on sale of shares	$ 27,520

Republic records the sale as follows.

January 23, 2021		
Cash	287,220	
Equity Investments		259,700
Gain on Sale of Equity Investment		27,520

As indicated in this example, the fair value method accounting for trading equity investments under IFRS is the same as GAAP for trading equity investments.

Example: Equity Investments (OCI). The accounting entries to record non-trading equity investments are the same as for trading equity investments, except for recording the unrealized holding gain or loss. For non-trading equity investments, companies **report the unrealized holding gain or loss as other comprehensive income (OCI)**. Thus, the account titled Unrealized Holding Gain or Loss—Equity is used.

To illustrate, assume that on December 10, 2020, Republic Corporation purchased $20,750 of 1,000 ordinary shares of Hawthorne Company for $20.75 per share (which represents less than a 20 percent interest). Hawthorne is a distributor for Republic products in certain locales, the laws of which require a minimum level of share ownership of a company in that region. The investment in Hawthorne meets this regulatory requirement. As a result, Republic accounts for this investment at fair value, with unrealized gains and losses recorded in OCI.[47] Republic records this investment as follows.

December 10, 2020		
Equity Investments	20,750	
Cash		20,750

On December 27, 2020, Republic receives a cash dividend of $450 on its investment in the ordinary shares of Hawthorne Company. It records the cash dividend as follows.

December 27, 2020		
Cash	450	
Dividend Revenue		450

Similar to the accounting for trading investments, when an investor owns less than 20 percent of the ordinary shares of another corporation, it is presumed that the investor has relatively little influence on the investee. Therefore, **the investor earns income when the investee declares cash dividends**.

At December 31, 2020, Republic's investment in Hawthorne has the carrying value and fair value shown in Illustration IFRS17.8.

[47]The classification of an equity investment as non-trading is irrevocable. This approach is designed to provide some discipline to the application of the non-trading classification, which allows unrealized gains and losses to bypass net income.

ILLUSTRATION IFRS17.8
Computation of Fair Value Adjustment—Non-Trading Equity Investment (2020)

Non-Trading Equity Investment	Carrying Value	Fair Value	Unrealized Gain (Loss)
Hawthorne Company	$20,750	$24,000	$3,250
Previous fair value adjustment balance			0
Fair value adjustment (Dr.)			$3,250

For Republic's non-trading investment, the unrealized gain is $3,250. That is, the fair value of the Hawthorne investment exceeds cost by $3,250. Because Republic has classified this investment as non-trading, Republic records the unrealized gains and losses related to changes in the fair value of this non-trading **equity** investment in an Unrealized Holding Gain or Loss—Equity account. Republic reports this amount as **a part of other comprehensive income and as a component of accumulated other comprehensive income (reported in equity) until realized**. In this case, Republic prepares an adjusting entry crediting the Unrealized Holding Gain or Loss—Equity account and debiting the Fair Value Adjustment account to record the decrease in fair value and to record the loss as follows.

December 31, 2020		
Fair Value Adjustment	3,250	
Unrealized Holding Gain or Loss—Equity		3,250

Republic reports its equity investments in its December 31, 2020, financial statements as shown in **Illustration IFRS17.9**.

ILLUSTRATION IFRS17.9
Financial Statement Presentation of Equity Investments at Fair Value (2020)

Statement of Financial Position	
Investments	
Equity investments (non-trading)	$24,000
Equity	
Accumulated other comprehensive gain	$ 3,250
Statement of Comprehensive Income	
Other income and expense	
Dividend revenue	$ 450
Other comprehensive income	
Unrealized holding gain	$ 3,250

During 2021, sales of Republic products through Hawthorne as a distributor did not meet management's goals. As a result, Republic withdrew from these markets and on December 20, 2021, Republic sold all of its Hawthorne Company ordinary shares, receiving net proceeds of $22,500. **Illustration IFRS17.10** shows the computation of the realized gain on the sale.

ILLUSTRATION IFRS17.10
Computation of Gain on Sale of Shares

Net proceeds from sale	$22,500
Cost of Hawthorne shares	20,750
Gain on sale of shares	$ 1,750

Republic records the sale as follows.

December 20, 2021		
Cash	22,500	
Equity Investments		20,750
Gain on Sale of Equity Investment		1,750

Because Republic no longer holds any equity investments, it makes the following entry to eliminate the Fair Value Adjustment account.

December 31, 2021		
Unrealized Holding Gain or Loss—Equity	3,250	
Fair Value Adjustment		3,250

In summary, the accounting for non-trading equity investments deviates from the general provisions for equity investments. The IASB noted that while fair value provides the most useful information about investments in equity investments, recording unrealized gains or losses in other comprehensive income is more representative for non-trading equity investments.

Impairments

A company should evaluate every held-for-collection investment, at each reporting date, to determine if it has suffered **impairment**—a loss in value such that the fair value of the investment is below its carrying value.[48] For example, if an investee experiences a bankruptcy or a significant liquidity crisis, the investor may suffer a permanent loss. **If the company determines that an investment is impaired, it writes down the amortized cost basis of the individual security to reflect this loss in value.** The company accounts for the write-down as a realized loss, and it includes the amount in net income.

For debt investments, a company uses the impairment test to determine whether "it is probable that the investor will be unable to collect all amounts due according to the contractual terms." If an investment is impaired, the company should measure the loss due to the **impairment**. This impairment loss is calculated as the difference between the carrying amount plus accrued interest and the expected future cash flows discounted at the investment's historical effective-interest rate.

Example: Impairment Loss At December 31, 2019, Mayhew Company has a debt investment in Bellovary Inc., purchased at par for $200,000. The investment has a term of four years, with annual interest payments at 10 percent, paid at the end of each year (the historical effective-interest rate is 10 percent). This debt investment is classified as held-for-collection. Unfortunately, Bellovary is experiencing significant financial difficulty and indicates that it will be unable to make all payments according to the contractual terms. Mayhew uses the present value method for measuring the required impairment loss. Illustration IFRS17.11 shows the cash flow schedule prepared for this analysis.

ILLUSTRATION IFRS17.11

Investment Cash Flows

Dec. 31	Contractual Cash Flows	Expected Cash Flows	Loss of Cash Flows
2020	$ 20,000	$ 16,000	$ 4,000
2021	20,000	16,000	4,000
2022	20,000	16,000	4,000
2023	220,000	216,000	4,000
Total cash flows	$280,000	$264,000	$16,000

As indicated, the expected cash flows of $264,000 are less than the contractual cash flows of $280,000. The amount of the impairment to be recorded equals the difference between the recorded investment of $200,000 and the present value of the expected cash flows, as shown in Illustration IFRS17.12.

ILLUSTRATION IFRS17.12

Computation of Impairment Loss

Recorded investment		$200,000
Less: Present value of $200,000 due in 4 years at 10% (Table 6.2); FV($PVF_{4,10\%}$); ($200,000 × .68301)	$136,602	
Present value of $16,000 interest receivable annually for 4 years at 10% (Table 6.4); R($PVF\text{-}OA_{4,10\%}$); ($16,000 × 3.16986)	50,718	187,320
Loss on impairment		$ 12,680

The loss due to the impairment is $12,680. Why isn't it $16,000 ($280,000 – $264,000)? A loss of $12,680 is recorded because Mayhew must measure the loss at a present value amount, not at an undiscounted amount. Mayhew recognizes an impairment loss of $12,680 by debiting Loss on Impairment for the expected loss. At the same time, it reduces the overall value of the investment. The journal entry to record the loss is therefore as follows.

Loss on Impairment	12,680	
Debt Investments		12,680

[48]Note that impairments tests are conducted only for debt investments that are held-for-collection (which are accounted for at amortized cost). Other debt and equity investments are measured at fair value each period; thus, an impairment test is not needed.

Recovery of Impairment Loss Subsequent to recording an impairment, events or economic conditions may change such that the extent of the impairment loss decreases (e.g., due to an improvement in the debtor's credit rating). In this situation, some or all of the previously recognized impairment loss shall be reversed with a debit to the Debt Investments account and a credit to Recovery of Impairment Loss. Similar to the accounting for impairments of receivables shown in Chapter 7, the reversal of impairment losses shall not result in a carrying amount of the investment that exceeds the amortized cost that would have been reported had the impairment not been recognized.

On the Horizon

At one time, both the FASB and IASB indicated that they believe that all financial instruments should be reported at fair value and that changes in fair value should be reported as part of net income. Through recent standards in this area, the Boards continue to move toward that goal. GAAP and IFRS are substantially converged, except for non-trading equity investments.

IFRS Self-Test Questions

1. All of the following are key similarities between GAAP and IFRS with respect to accounting for investments **except**:
   - **a.** IFRS and GAAP require the same accounting for equity securities.
   - **b.** IFRS and GAAP apply the equity method to significant influence equity investments.
   - **c.** IFRS and GAAP have a fair value option for financial instruments.
   - **d.** the accounting for impairment of investments is similar, although IFRS allows recovery of impairment losses.

2. Which of the following statements is **correct**?
   - **a.** IFRS permits the fair value option for the equity method of accounting.
   - **b.** GAAP permits recovery of impairment losses.
   - **c.** Under IFRS, non-trading equity investments are accounted for at amortized cost.
   - **d.** IFRS and GAAP both have a trading investment classification.

3. IFRS requires companies to measure their financial assets at fair value **except** when based on:
   - **a.** whether the equity method of accounting is used.
   - **b.** whether the financial asset is a debt investment.
   - **c.** whether the financial asset is an equity investment.
   - **d.** whether an investment is classified as trading.

4. Select the investment accounting approach with the correct valuation approach:

	Not Held-for-Collection	Held-for-Collection
a.	Amortized cost	Amortized cost
b.	Fair value	Fair value
c.	Fair value	Amortized cost
d.	Amortized cost	Fair value

5. Under IFRS, a company:
   - **a.** should evaluate only equity investments for impairment.
   - **b.** accounts for an impairment as an unrealized loss, and includes it as a part of other comprehensive income and as a component of other accumulated comprehensive income until realized.
   - **c.** calculates the impairment loss on debt investments as the difference between the carrying amount plus accrued interest and the expected future cash flows discounted at the investment's historical effective-interest rate.
   - **d.** All of the above.

IFRS Concepts and Application

IFRS17.1 Where can authoritative IFRS be found related to investments?

IFRS17.2 Briefly describe some of the similarities and differences between GAAP and IFRS with respect to the accounting for investments.

IFRS17.3 Describe the two criteria for determining the valuation of financial assets.

IFRS17.4 Which types of investments are valued at amortized cost? Explain the rationale for this accounting.

IFRS17.5 Lady Gaga Co. recently made an investment in the bonds issued by Chili Peppers Inc. Lady Gaga's business model for this investment is to profit from trading in response to changes in market interest rates. How should this investment be classified by Lady Gaga? Explain.

IFRS17.6 Consider the bond investment by Lady Gaga in IFRS17.5. Discuss the accounting for this investment if Lady Gaga's business model is to hold the investment to collect interest while outstanding and to receive the principal at maturity.

IFRS17.7 Indicate how unrealized holding gains and losses should be reported for investments classified as trading and held-for-collection.

IFRS17.8 Ramirez Company has a held-for-collection investment in the 6%, 20-year bonds of Soto Company. The investment was originally purchased for $1,200,000 in 2019. Early in 2020, Ramirez recorded an impairment of $300,000 on the Soto investment, due to Soto's financial distress. In 2021, Soto returned to profitability and the Soto investment was no longer impaired. What entry does Ramirez make in 2021 under (a) GAAP and (b) IFRS?

IFRS17.9 Carow Corporation purchased, as a held-for-collection investment, $60,000 of the 8%, 5-year bonds of Harrison, Inc. for $65,118, which provides a 6% return. The bonds pay interest semiannually. Prepare Carow's journal entries for (a) the purchase of the investment, and (b) the receipt of semiannual interest and premium amortization.

IFRS17.10 Fairbanks Corporation purchased 400 ordinary shares of Sherman Inc. as a trading investment for $13,200. During the year, Sherman paid a cash dividend of $3.25 per share. At year-end, Sherman shares were selling for $34.50 per share. Prepare Fairbanks' journal entries to record (a) the purchase of the investment, (b) the dividends received, and (c) the fair value adjustment.

IFRS17.11 Use the information from IFRS17.10 but assume the shares were purchased to meet a non-trading regulatory requirement. Prepare Fairbanks' journal entries to record (a) the purchase of the investment, (b) the dividends received, and (c) the fair value adjustment.

IFRS17.12 On January 1, 2020, Roosevelt Company purchased 12% bonds, having a maturity value of $500,000, for $537,907.40. The bonds provide the bondholders with a 10% yield. They are dated January 1, 2020, and mature January 1, 2025, with interest received January 1 of each year. Roosevelt's business model is to hold these bonds to collect contractual cash flows.

Instructions

a. Prepare the journal entry at the date of the bond purchase.

b. Prepare a bond amortization schedule.

c. Prepare the journal entry to record the interest revenue and the amortization for 2020.

d. Prepare the journal entry to record the interest revenue and the amortization for 2021.

IFRS17.13 Assume the same information as in IFRS17.12 except that Roosevelt has an active trading strategy for these bonds. The fair value of the bonds at December 31 of each year-end is as follows.

2020	$534,200	2023	$517,000
2021	$515,000	2024	$500,000
2022	$513,000		

Instructions

a. Prepare the journal entry at the date of the bond purchase.

b. Prepare the journal entries to record the interest revenue and recognition of fair value for 2020.

c. Prepare the journal entry to record the recognition of fair value for 2021.

IFRS17.14 On December 21, 2020, Zurich Company provided you with the following information regarding its trading investments.

December 31, 2020

Investments (Trading)	Cost	Fair Value	Unrealized Gain (Loss)
Stargate Corp. shares	$20,000	$19,000	$(1,000)
Carolina Co. shares	10,000	9,000	(1,000)
Vectorman Co. shares	20,000	20,600	600
Total of portfolio	$50,000	$48,600	$(1,400)
Previous fair value adjustment balance			-0-
Fair value adjustment—Cr.			$(1,400)

During 2021, Carolina Co. shares were sold for $9,500. The fair value of the shares on December 31, 2021, was Stargate Corp. shares—$19,300; Vectorman Co. shares—$20,500.

Instructions

a. Prepare the adjusting journal entry needed on December 31, 2020.

b. Prepare the journal entry to record the sale of the Carolina Co. shares during 2021.

c. Prepare the adjusting journal entry needed on December 31, 2021.

IFRS17.15 Komissarov Company has a debt investment in the bonds issued by Keune Inc. The bonds were purchased at par for $400,000 and, at the end of 2020, have a remaining life of 3 years with annual interest payments at 10%, paid at the end of each year. This debt investment is classified as held-for-collection. Keune is facing a tough economic environment and informs all of its investors that it will be unable to make all payments according to the contractual terms. The controller of Komissarov has prepared the following revised expected cash flow forecast for this bond investment.

Dec. 31	Expected Cash Flows
2021	$ 35,000
2022	35,000
2023	385,000
Total cash flows	$455,000

Instructions

a. Determine the impairment loss for Komissarov at December 31, 2020.

b. Prepare the entry to record the impairment loss for Komissarov at December 31, 2020.

c. On January 15, 2021, Keune receives a major capital infusion from a private equity investor. It informs Komissarov that the bonds now will be paid according to the contractual terms. Briefly describe how Komissarov would account for the bond investment in light of this new information.

Professional Research

IFRS17.16 Your client, Cascade Company, is planning to invest some of its excess cash in 5-year revenue bonds issued by the county and in the shares of one of its suppliers, Teton Co. Teton's shares trade on the over-the-counter market. Cascade plans to classify these investments as trading. The company would like you to conduct some research on the accounting for these investments.

Instructions

Access the IFRS authoritative literature at the IASB website. (Click on the IFRS tab and then register for free eIFRS access if necessary.) When you have accessed the documents, you can use the search tool in your Internet browser to respond to the following questions. (Provide paragraph citations.)

a. Since the Teton shares do not trade on one of the large securities exchanges, Cascade argues that the fair value of this investment is not readily available. According to the authoritative literature, when is the fair value of a security "readily determinable"?

b. To avoid volatility in their financial statements due to fair value adjustments, Cascade debated whether the bond investment could be classified as held-for-collection; Cascade is pretty sure it will hold the bonds for 5 years. What criteria must be met for Cascade to classify it as held-for-collection?

International Financial Reporting Problem

Marks and Spencer plc (M&S)

IFRS17.17 The financial statements of M&S are presented in Appendix E. The company's complete annual report, including the notes to the financial statements, is available online.

Instructions

Refer to M&S's financial statements and the accompanying notes to answer the following questions.

a. What investments does M&S report in 2017, and where are these investments reported in its financial statements?

b. How are M&S's investments valued? How does M&S determine fair value?

c. How does M&S use derivative financial instruments?

Answers to IFRS Self-Test Questions

1. a **2.** d **3.** a **4.** c **5.** c

CHAPTER 18

© andersphoto/Shutterstock

Revenue Recognition

LEARNING OBJECTIVES

After studying this chapter, you should be able to:

1. Discuss the fundamental concepts related to revenue recognition and measurement.
2. Explain and apply the five-step revenue recognition process.
3. Apply the five-step process to major revenue recognition issues.
4. Describe presentation and disclosure regarding revenue.

PREVIEW OF CHAPTER 18 As the following opening story indicates, the issue of when revenue should be recognized is complex. The many methods of marketing products and services make it difficult to develop guidelines that will apply to all situations. This chapter provides you with general guidelines used in most business transactions. The content and organization of the chapter are as follows.

This chapter also includes numerous conceptual discussions. Because of the converged FASB/IASB standard on revenue recognition, there is no *IFRS Insights* in this chapter.

REVENUE RECOGNITION

Fundamentals of Revenue Recognition
- Background
- New revenue recognition standard
- Overview of five-step process: Boeing example
- Extended example of five-step process: BEAN

The Five-Step Process Revisited
- Identifying the contract with customers
- Identifying separate performance obligations
- Determining the transaction price
- Allocating the transaction price
- Satisfying performance obligations

Revenue Recognition Issues
- Sales returns and allowances
- Repurchase agreements
- Bill-and-hold arrangements
- Principal-agent relationships
- Consignments
- Warranties
- Nonrefundable upfront fees

Presentation and Disclosure
- Presentation
- Disclosure

It's Back

A number of years after passage, the accounting world continues to be preoccupied with the Sarbanes-Oxley Act of 2002 (SOX). Unfortunately, SOX did not solve one of the classic accounting issues—how to properly account for revenue. In fact, revenue recognition practices are the most prevalent reason for accounting restatements. A number of revenue recognition issues relate to possible fraudulent behavior by company executives and employees.

As a result of such revenue recognition problems, the SEC has increased its enforcement actions in this area. In some of these cases, companies made significant adjustments to previously issued financial statements. As Lynn Turner, a former chief accountant of the SEC, indicated, "When people cross over the boundaries of legitimate reporting, the Commission will take appropriate action to ensure the fairness and integrity that investors need and depend on every day."

Consider some SEC actions:

- The SEC charged the former co-chairman and CEO of **Qwest Communications International Inc.** and eight other former Qwest officers and employees with fraud and other violations of the federal securities laws. Three of these people fraudulently characterized nonrecurring revenue from one-time sales as revenue from recurring data and Internet services. The SEC release notes that internal correspondence likened Qwest's dependence on these transactions to fill the gap between actual and projected revenue to an addiction.
- The SEC filed a complaint against three former senior officers of **iGo Corp.**, alleging that the defendants collectively caused iGo to improperly recognize revenue on consignment sales and products that were not shipped or that were shipped after the end of a fiscal quarter.
- The SEC filed a complaint against the former CEO and chairman of **Homestore Inc.** and its former executive vice president of business development, alleging that they engaged in a fraudulent scheme to overstate advertising and subscription revenues. The scheme involved a complex structure of "round-trip" transactions using various third-party companies that, in essence, allowed Homestore to recognize its own cash as revenue.
- The SEC claims that **Lantronix** deliberately sent excessive product to distributors and granted them generous return rights and extended payment terms. In addition, as part of its alleged channel stuffing and to prevent product returns, Lantronix loaned funds to a third party to purchase Lantronix products from one of its distributors. The third party later returned the products. The SEC also asserted that Lantronix engaged in other improper revenue recognition practices, including shipping without a purchase order and recognizing revenue on a contingent sale.
- The SEC issued an order finding that a subsidiary of **Alere Inc.** improperly inflated revenues by prematurely recording sales for products that were still being stored at warehouses or otherwise not yet delivered to customers. The SEC also cited Alere for engaging in similar improper revenue recognition practices at several other subsidiaries.

Revenue numbers are attracting more attention from investors these days. In a recent survey, financial executives noted that the revenue recognition process is increasingly more complex to manage, more prone to error, and more material to financial statements compared to any other area in financial reporting. The report went on to note that revenue recognition is a top fraud risk and that regardless of the accounting rules followed (GAAP or IFRS), the risk of errors and inaccuracies in revenue reporting is significant.

In response, the FASB and IASB issued a new standard on revenue recognition to improve the reporting of revenue transactions. This new standard provides a set of guidelines to follow in determining when revenue should be reported and how it should be measured. The new standard is comprehensive and applies to all companies. As a result, comparability and consistency in reporting revenue should be enhanced. After studying this chapter, you should have a good understanding of the new revenue recognition concepts.

Sources: Cheryl de Mesa Graziano, "Revenue Recognition: A Perennial Problem," *Financial Executive* (July 14, 2005), *www.fei.org/mag/articles/7-2005_revenue.cfm;* S. Taub, "SEC Accuses Ex-CFO of Channel Stuffing," *CFO.com* (September 30, 2006); *www.softrax.com/resources/pdf/intlriskrevreporting* and *Accounting Standards Update No. 2014-09, Revenue from Contracts with Customers (Topic 606)* (Norwalk, Conn.: FASB, May 2014); and "Medical Manufacturer Settles Accounting Fraud Charges," *SEC Press Release* (September 28, 2017).

Review and Practice

Go to the **Review and Practice** section at the end of the chapter for a targeted summary review and practice problem with solution. Multiple-choice questions with annotated solutions as well as additional exercises and practice problem with solutions are also available online.

Fundamentals of Revenue Recognition

LEARNING OBJECTIVE 1

Discuss the fundamental concepts related to revenue recognition and measurement.

Background

Revenue is one of, if not the most, important measures of financial performance that a company reports. Revenue provides insights into a company's past and future performance and is a significant driver of other performance measures, such as EBITDA, net income, and earnings per share. Therefore, establishing robust guidelines for recognizing revenue is a standard-setting priority.

Most revenue transactions pose few problems for revenue recognition. That is, most companies initiate and complete transactions at the same time. However, not all transactions are that simple. For example, consider a cell phone contract between a company such as **Verizon** and a customer. Verizon often provides a customer with a package that may include a handset, free minutes of talk time, data downloads, and text messaging service. In addition, some providers will bundle that with a fixed-line broadband service. At the same time, the customer may pay for these services in a variety of ways, possibly receiving a discount on the handset and then paying higher prices for connection fees and so forth. In some cases, depending on the package purchased, the company may provide free upgrades in subsequent periods. How, then, should Verizon report the various pieces of this sale? The answer is not obvious.

Both the FASB and the IASB indicated that the state of reporting for revenue was unsatisfactory. IFRS was criticized because it lacked guidance in a number of areas. For example, IFRS had one general standard on revenue recognition—*IAS 18*—plus some limited guidance related to certain minor topics. In contrast, GAAP had numerous standards related to revenue recognition (by some counts, well over 100), but many believed the standards were often inconsistent with one another. Thus, the accounting for revenue provided a most fitting contrast of the principles-based (IFRS) and rules-based (GAAP) approaches.[1]

Recently, the FASB and IASB issued a converged standard on revenue recognition entitled *Revenue from Contracts with Customers* (see **Global View**). [1] (See the FASB Codification References near the end of the chapter.) To address the inconsistencies and weaknesses of the previous approaches, a comprehensive revenue recognition standard now applies to a wide range of transactions and industries. The Boards believe this new standard will improve GAAP and IFRS by:

Global View

The converged revenue recognition standard represents a significant milestone in the FASB/IASB convergence project.

a. Providing a more robust framework for addressing revenue recognition issues.

b. Improving comparability of revenue recognition practices across entities, industries, jurisdictions, and capital markets.

c. Simplifying the preparation of financial statements by reducing the number of requirements to which companies must refer.

d. Requiring enhanced disclosures to help financial statement users better understand the amount, timing, and uncertainty of revenue that is recognized. [2]

[1]See, for example, "Preliminary Views on Revenue Recognition in Contracts with Customers," *IASB/FASB Discussion Paper* (December 19, 2008). Some noted that GAAP has so many standards that at times they are inconsistent with each other in applying basic principles. In addition, even with the many standards, no comprehensive guidance was provided for service transactions. Conversely, IFRS lacked guidance in certain fundamental areas such as multiple-deliverable arrangements. In addition, there were inconsistencies in applying revenue recognition principles to long-term contracts versus other elements of revenue recognition.

New Revenue Recognition Standard

The new standard, *Revenue from Contracts with Customers*, adopts an **asset-liability approach** as the basis for revenue recognition. The asset-liability approach recognizes and measures revenue based on changes in assets and liabilities. The Boards decided that focusing on (a) the recognition and measurement of assets and liabilities and (b) changes in those assets or liabilities over the life of the contract brings more discipline to the measurement of revenue, compared to the "earned and realized" criteria in prior standards.

Under the asset-liability approach, companies account for revenue based on the asset or liability arising from contracts with customers. Companies analyze contracts with customers because contracts initiate revenue transactions. Contracts indicate the terms of the transaction, provide the measurement of the consideration, and specify the promises that must be met by each party (see **Underlying Concepts**).

> **Underlying Concepts**
>
> The asset-liability approach is consistent with the conceptual framework approach to recognition.

Illustration 18.1 shows the key concepts related to this new standard on revenue recognition. The new standard first identifies the key objective of revenue recognition, followed by a five-step process that companies should use to ensure that revenue is measured and reported correctly.

ILLUSTRATION 18.1

Key Concepts of Revenue Recognition

Key Objective

Recognize revenue to depict the transfer of goods or services to customers in an amount that reflects the consideration that the company receives, or expects to receive, in exchange for these goods or services.

Five-Step Process for Revenue Recognition

1. Identify the contract with customers.
2. Identify the separate performance obligations in the contract.
3. Determine the transaction price.
4. Allocate the transaction price to the separate performance obligations.
5. Recognize revenue when each performance obligation is satisfied.

Revenue Recognition Principle

Recognize revenue in the accounting period when the performance obligation is satisfied.

The culmination of the process is the **revenue recognition principle**, which states that revenue is recognized when the performance obligation is satisfied. We examine all steps in more detail in the following section.

Overview of the Five-Step Process: Boeing Example

Assume that **Boeing Corporation** signs a contract to sell airplanes to **Delta Air Lines** for $100 million. **Illustration 18.2** shows the five steps that Boeing follows to recognize revenue.

As indicated, Step 5 is when Boeing recognizes revenue related to the sale of the airplanes to Delta. At this point, Boeing delivers the airplanes to Delta and satisfies its performance obligation. In essence, a change in control from Boeing to Delta occurs. Delta now controls the assets because it has the ability to direct the use of and obtain substantially all the remaining benefits from the airplanes. Control also includes Delta's ability to prevent other companies from directing the use of, or receiving the benefits from, the airplanes.

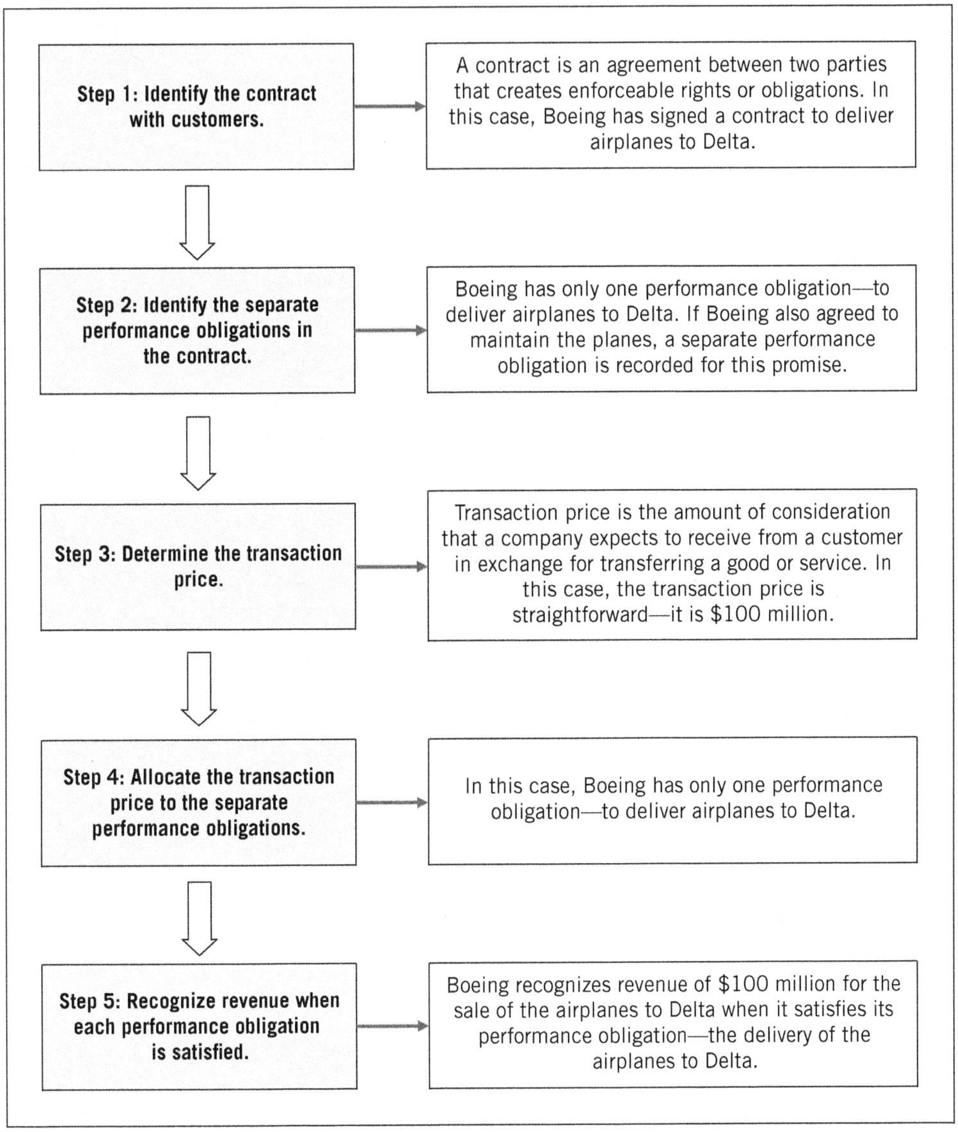

ILLUSTRATION 18.2

Five Steps of Revenue Recognition

Extended Example of the Five-Step Process: BEAN

To provide another application of the basic principles of the five-step revenue recognition model, we use a coffee and wine business called BEAN. BEAN is located in the Midwest and serves gourmet coffee, espresso, lattes, teas, and smoothies. It also sells pastries, coffee beans, other food products, wine, and beer.

Identifying the Contract with Customers—Step 1

Assume that Tyler Angler orders a large cup of black coffee costing $3 from BEAN. Tyler gives $3 to a BEAN barista, who pours the coffee into a large cup and gives it to Tyler.

Question: How much revenue should BEAN recognize on this transaction?

Step 1 We first must determine whether a valid contract exists between BEAN and Tyler. Here are the components of a valid contract and how it affects BEAN and Tyler.

1. ***The contract has commercial substance:*** Tyler gives cash for the coffee.
2. ***The parties have approved the contract:*** Tyler agrees to purchase the coffee and BEAN agrees to sell it.
3. ***Identification of the rights of the parties is established:*** Tyler has the right to the coffee and BEAN has the right to receive $3.
4. ***Payment terms are identified:*** Tyler agrees to pay $3 for the coffee.
5. ***It is probable that the consideration will be collected:*** BEAN received $3 before it delivered the coffee. [3][2]

From this information, it appears that BEAN and Tyler have a valid contract with one another.

Step 2 The next step is to identify BEAN's performance obligation(s), if any. The answer is straightforward—BEAN has a performance obligation to provide a large cup of coffee to Tyler. BEAN has no other performance obligation for any other good or service.

Step 3 BEAN must determine the transaction price related to the sale of the coffee. The price of the coffee is $3, and no discounts or other adjustments are available. Therefore, the transaction price is $3.

Step 4 BEAN must allocate the transaction price to all performance obligations. Given that BEAN has only one performance obligation, no allocation is necessary.

Step 5 Revenue is recognized when the performance obligation is satisfied. BEAN satisfies its performance obligation when Tyler obtains control of the coffee. The following conditions are indicators that control of the coffee has passed to Tyler:

a. BEAN has the right to payment for the coffee.
b. BEAN has transferred legal title to the coffee.
c. BEAN has transferred physical possession of the coffee.
d. Tyler has significant risks (e.g., he might spill the coffee) and rewards of ownership (he gets to drink the coffee).
e. Tyler has accepted the asset.

Solution: BEAN should recognize $3 in revenue from this transaction when Tyler receives the coffee.

Identifying Separate Performance Obligations—Step 2

The following day, Tyler orders another large cup of coffee for $3 and also purchases two bagels at a price of $5. The barista provides these products and Tyler pays $8.

Question: How much revenue should BEAN recognize on the purchase of these two items?

Step 1 A valid contract exists as it meets the five conditions necessary for a contract to be enforceable as discussed in the previous example.

Step 2 BEAN must determine whether the sale of the coffee and the sale of the two bagels involve one or two performance obligations. In the previous transaction between BEAN and Tyler, this determination was straightforward because BEAN provided a single distinct product (a large cup of coffee) and therefore only one performance obligation existed. However, an arrangement to purchase coffee and bagels may have more than one performance obligation. Multiple performance obligations exist when the following two conditions are satisfied:

1. BEAN must provide a distinct product or service. In other words, BEAN must be able to sell the coffee and the bagels separately from one another.
2. BEAN's products are distinct within the contract. In other words, if the performance obligation is not highly dependent on, or interrelated with, other promises in the contract, then each performance obligation should be accounted for separately. Conversely, if each of these products is interdependent and interrelated, these products are combined and reported as one performance obligation. [4]

[2]BEAN disregards revenue guidance for a contract that is wholly unperformed and for which each party can unilaterally terminate the contract without compensation.

The large cup of coffee and the two bagels appear to be distinct from one another and are not highly dependent or interrelated. That is, BEAN can sell the coffee and the two bagels separately, and Tyler benefits separately from the coffee and the bagels.

BEAN should therefore record two performance obligations—one for the sale of the coffee and one for the sale of the bagels.

Step 3 The transaction price is $8 ($3 + $5).

Step 4 BEAN has two performance obligations: to provide (1) a large cup of coffee and (2) the two bagels. Each of these obligations is distinct and not interrelated (and priced separately); no allocation of the transaction price is necessary. That is, the coffee sale is recorded at $3 and the sale of the bagels is priced at $5.

Step 5 BEAN has satisfied both performance obligations when the coffee and bagels are given to Tyler (control of the product has passed to the customer).

Solution: BEAN should recognize $8 ($3 + $5) of revenue when Tyler receives the coffee and bagels.

Determining the Transaction Price—Step 3

BEAN decides to provide an additional incentive to its customers to shop at its store. BEAN roasts its own coffee beans and sells the beans wholesale to grocery stores, restaurants, and other commercial companies. In addition, it sells the coffee beans at its retail location. BEAN is interested in stimulating sales of its Smoke Jumper coffee beans on Tuesdays, a slow business day for the store. Normally, these beans sell for $10 for a 12-ounce bag, but BEAN decides to cut the price by $1 when customers buy them on Tuesdays (the discounted price is now $9 per bag). Tyler has come to the store on a Tuesday, decides to purchase a bag of Smoke Jumper beans, and pays BEAN $9.

***Question:* How much revenue should BEAN recognize on this transaction?**

Step 1 As in our previous examples, with the sale of a large cup of coffee or the sale of a large cup of coffee and two bagels, a valid contract exists. The same is true for the sale of Smoke Jumper beans as well.

Step 2 The identification of the performance obligation is straightforward. BEAN has a performance obligation to provide a bag of Smoke Jumper coffee beans to Tyler. BEAN has no other performance obligation to provide a product or service.

Step 3 The transaction price for a bag of Smoke Jumper beans sold to Tyler is $9, not $10. The transaction price is the amount that a company expects to receive from a customer in exchange for transferring goods and services. **[5]** The transaction price in a contract is often easily determined because the customer agrees to pay a fixed amount to the company over a short period of time. In other contracts, companies must consider adjustments such as when they make payments or provide some other consideration to their customers (e.g., a coupon) as part of a revenue arrangement.[3]

Step 4 BEAN allocates the transaction price to the performance obligations. Given that there is only one performance obligation, no allocation is necessary.

Step 5 BEAN has satisfied the performance obligation as control of the product has passed to Tyler.

Solution: BEAN should recognize $9 of revenue when Tyler receives the Smoke Jumper coffee beans.

Allocating the Transaction Price to Separate Performance Obligations—Step 4

For revenue arrangements with multiple performance obligations, BEAN might be required to allocate the transaction price to more than one performance obligation in the contract. If an allocation is needed, the transaction price is allocated to the various performance obligations

[3]We provide expanded discussion and examples of variation in transaction price, including variable consideration, later in the chapter.

based on their relative standalone selling prices. If this information is not available, companies should use their best estimate of what the good or service might sell for as a standalone unit. [6]

BEAN wants to provide even more incentive for customers to buy its coffee beans, as well as purchase a cup of coffee. BEAN therefore offers customers a $2 discount on the purchase of a large cup of coffee when they buy a bag of its premium Motor Moka beans (which normally sell for $12) at the same time. Tyler decides this offer is too good to pass up and buys a bag of Motor Moka beans for $12 and a large cup of coffee for $1. As indicated earlier, a large cup of coffee normally retails for $3 at BEAN.

***Question:* How much revenue should BEAN recognize on the purchase of these two items?**

Step 1 In our previous situations, valid contracts have existed. The same is also true for the sale of a bag of Motor Moka beans and the large cup of coffee.

Step 2 The bag of Motor Moka beans and the large cup of coffee are distinct from one another and are not highly dependent on or highly interrelated with the other. BEAN can sell a bag of the Motor Moka beans and a large cup of coffee separately. Furthermore, Tyler benefits separately from both the large cup of coffee and the Motor Moka coffee beans.

Step 3 BEAN's transaction price is $13 ($12 for the bag of Motor Moka beans and $1 for the large cup of coffee).

Step 4 BEAN allocates the transaction price to the two performance obligations based on their relative standalone selling prices. The standalone selling price of a bag of Motor Moka beans is $12 and the large cup of coffee is $3. The allocation of the transaction price of $13 is as follows.

Product	Standalone Selling Price	Percentage		Allocated Amount
Motor Moka beans (one bag)	$12	80%	($12 ÷ $15)	$10.40 ($13 × .80)
Large cup of coffee	3	20	($3 ÷ $15)	2.60 ($13 × .20)
Total	$15	100%		$13.00

As indicated, the total transaction price ($13) is allocated $10.40 to the bag of Motor Moka beans and $2.60 to the large cup of coffee.

Step 5 BEAN has satisfied both performance obligations as control of the bag of Motor Moka beans and the large cup of coffee has passed to Tyler.

Solution: BEAN should recognize revenue of $13, comprised of revenue from the sale of the Motor Moka beans at $10.40 and the sale of the large cup of coffee at $2.60.

Recognizing Revenue When (or as) Each Performance Obligation Is Satisfied—Step 5

As indicted in the examples presented, BEAN satisfied its performance obligation(s) when Tyler obtained control of the product(s). Change in control is the deciding factor in determining when a performance obligation is satisfied. A customer controls the product or service when the customer has the ability to direct the use of and obtain substantially all the remaining benefits from the product. Control also includes Tyler's ability to prevent other companies from directing the use of, or receiving benefits from, the coffee or coffee beans. As discussed earlier, the indicators that Tyler has obtained control are as follows:

a. BEAN has the right to payment for the coffee.

b. BEAN has transferred legal title to the coffee.

c. BEAN has transferred physical possession of the coffee.

d. Tyler has significant risks and rewards of ownership.

e. Tyler has accepted the asset.[4]

[4]While in the BEAN example recognition occurred at a point in time, in certain cases, companies satisfy performance obligations over a period of time. We address the criteria for determining point-in-time versus over-time recognition later in the chapter.

The Five-Step Process Revisited

LEARNING OBJECTIVE 2

Explain and apply the five-step revenue recognition process.

The **Boeing** and BEAN examples provide a basic understanding of the five-step process used to recognize revenue. We now discuss more technical issues related to the implementation of these five steps.

Identifying the Contract with Customers—Step 1

A **contract** is an agreement between two or more parties that creates enforceable rights or obligations. Contracts can be written, oral, or implied from customary business practice (such as the BEAN contract with Tyler). Revenue is recognized only when a valid contract exists. On entering into a contract with a customer, a company obtains rights to receive consideration from the customer and assumes obligations to transfer goods or services to the customer (performance obligations). The combination of those rights and performance obligations gives rise to an (net) asset or (net) liability.

In some cases, there are multiple contracts related to an arrangement; accounting for each contract may or may not occur, depending upon the circumstances. These situations often develop when not only a product is provided but some type of service is performed as well. To be valid, a contract must meet the five conditions illustrated in the BEAN example. If the contract is wholly unperformed and each party can unilaterally terminate the contract without compensation, then revenue should not be recognized until one or both of the parties have performed. A basic contract in which these issues are discussed is presented in **Illustration 18.3**.

ILLUSTRATION 18.3
Basic Revenue Transaction

Contracts and Recognition

Facts: On March 1, 2020, Margo Company enters into a contract to transfer a product to Soon Yoon on July 31, 2020. The contract is structured such that Soon Yoon is required to pay the full contract price of $5,000 on August 31, 2020. The cost of the goods transferred is $3,000. Either party can unilaterally terminate the contract without compensation. Margo delivers the product to Soon Yoon on July 31, 2020.

***Question:* What journal entries should Margo Company make in regards to this contract in 2020?**

Solution: No entry is required on March 1, 2020, because neither party has performed on the contract. On July 31, 2020, Margo delivers the product and therefore should recognize revenue on that date as it satisfies its performance obligation by delivering the product to Soon Yoon.

The journal entry to record the sale and related cost of goods sold is as follows.

July 31, 2020

Accounts Receivable	5,000	
Sales Revenue		5,000
Cost of Goods Sold	3,000	
Inventory		3,000

After receiving the cash payment on August 31, 2020, Margo makes the following entry.

August 31, 2020

Cash	5,000	
Accounts Receivable		5,000

A key feature of the revenue arrangement is that the contract between the two parties is not recorded (does not result in a journal entry) until one or both of the parties *perform under the contract.* **Until performance occurs, no net asset or net liability exists.**[5]

Identifying Separate Performance Obligations—Step 2

A **performance obligation** is a promise to provide a product or service to a customer. This promise may be explicit, implicit, or possibly based on customary business practice. To determine whether a performance obligation exists, the company must provide a distinct product or service to the customer.

A product or service is distinct when a customer is able to benefit from a good or service on its own or together with other readily available resources. This situation typically occurs when the company can sell a good or service on a standalone basis (can be sold separately). For example, BEAN provided a good (a large cup of coffee) on a standalone basis to Tyler. Tyler benefited from this cup of coffee by consuming it.

To determine whether a company has to account for multiple performance obligations, the company's promise to sell the good or service to the customer must be separately identifiable from other promises within the contract (that is, the good or service must be distinct within the contract). In other words, the **objective is to determine whether the nature of a company's promise is to transfer individual goods and services to the customer or to transfer a combined item (or items) for which individual goods or services are inputs**.

For example, when BEAN sold Tyler a large cup of coffee and two bagels, two performance obligations occurred. In that case, the large cup of coffee had a standalone selling price and the two bagels had a standalone selling price—even though the two promises may be part of one contract.

Conversely, assume that BEAN sold a large latte (comprised of coffee and milk) to Tyler. In this case, BEAN sold two distinct products (coffee and milk), but these two goods are not distinct within the contract. That is, the coffee and milk in the latte are highly interdependent or interrelated within the contract. As a result, the products are combined and reported as one performance obligation.

To illustrate another situation, assume that **General Motors** sells an automobile to Marquart Auto Dealers at a price that includes six months of telematics services such as navigation and remote diagnostics. These telematics services are regularly sold on a standalone basis by General Motors for a monthly fee. After the six-month period, the consumer can renew these services on a fee basis with General Motors. The question is whether General Motors sold one or two products. If we look at General Motors' objective, it appears that it is to sell two goods, the automobile and the telematic services. **Both are distinct (they can be sold separately) and are not interdependent.**

As another example, SoftTech Inc. licenses customer-relationship software to Lopez Company. In addition to providing the software itself, SoftTech promises to perform consulting services by extensively customizing the software to Lopez's information technology environment, for total consideration of $600,000. In this case, the objective of SoftTech appears to be to transfer a combined product and service for which individual goods and services are inputs. In other words, SoftTech is providing a significant service by integrating the goods and services (the license and the consulting service) into one combined item for which Lopez

[5]Recall a valid contract exists when (1) the contract has commercial substance, (2) the parties have approved the contract, (3) the contract identifies the rights of the parties, (4) payment terms are identified, and (5) it is probable that the consideration will be collected. The FASB included this last criterion (which acts like a collectibility threshold) because the Board concluded that the assessment of a customer's credit risk was important to determine whether a contract is valid. That is, under the revenue standard (and discussed later in the chapter), collectibility is not a consideration for determining whether revenue is recognized. However, collectibility may be a consideration in assessing whether parties to the contract are committed to perform. In determining whether it is probable that a company will collect the amount of consideration to which it is entitled, the company assesses both the customer's ability and intent to pay as amounts become due. [7]

has contracted. In addition, the software is significantly customized by SoftTech in accordance with specifications negotiated by Lopez. As a result, **the license and the consulting services are distinct but interdependent, and therefore should be accounted for as one performance obligation.**[6]

Determining the Transaction Price—Step 3

The **transaction price** is the amount of consideration that a company expects to receive from a customer in exchange for transferring goods and services. The transaction price in a contract is often easily determined because the customer agrees to pay a fixed amount to the company over a short period of time. In other contracts, companies must consider the following factors. [8]

- Variable consideration.
- Time value of money.
- Noncash consideration.
- Consideration paid or payable to the customer.

Variable Consideration

In some cases, the price of a good or service is dependent on future events. These future events might include price increases, volume discounts, rebates, credits, performance bonuses, or royalties. In these cases, the company estimates the amount of variable consideration it will receive from the contract to determine the amount of revenue to recognize. Companies use either the **expected value,** which is a probability-weighted amount, or the **most likely amount** in a range of possible amounts to estimate variable consideration (see Underlying Concepts). Companies select among these two methods based on which approach better predicts the amount of consideration to which a company is entitled. [9] Illustration 18.4 highlights the issues to be considered in selecting the appropriate method.

Underlying Concepts

The expected value approach is also illustrated in Chapter 6 to determine the liability for warranties.

ILLUSTRATION 18.4
Estimating Variable Consideration

Expected Value: Probability-weighted amount in a range of possible consideration amounts.	**Most Likely Amount:** The single most likely amount in a range of possible consideration outcomes.
• May be appropriate if a company has a large number of contracts with similar characteristics. • Can be based on a limited number of discrete outcomes and probabilities.	• May be appropriate if the contract has only two possible outcomes.

Illustration 18.5 provides an application of the two estimation methods.

ILLUSTRATION 18.5
Transaction Price—Variable Consideration

Estimating Variable Consideration

Facts: Peabody Construction Company enters into a contract with a customer to build a warehouse for $100,000, with a performance bonus of $50,000 that will be paid based on the timing of completion. The amount of the performance bonus decreases by 10% per week for every week beyond the agreed-upon completion date. The contract requirements are similar to contracts that Peabody has performed previously, and management believes that such experience is predictive for this contract. Management estimates that there is a 60% probability that the contract will be completed by the agreed-upon completion date, a 30% probability that it will be completed 1 week late, and only a 10% probability that it will be completed 2 weeks late.

(continued)

[6]In practice, determining whether multiple performance obligations exist can be complex. *For homework purposes, you need to determine the objective of the transaction.* If the objective is to transfer individual goods or services, then account for these performance obligations separately. As discussed, indicators that help to understand whether performance obligations should be accounted for separately are (1) the performance obligations have a standalone selling price and (2) the goods or services are not highly interdependent or interrelated.

ILLUSTRATION 18.5
(continued)

Question: How should Peabody account for this revenue arrangement?

Solution: The transaction price should include management's estimate of the amount of consideration to which Peabody will be entitled. Management has concluded that the **probability-weighted method** is the most predictive approach for estimating the variable consideration in this situation:

On time: 60% chance of $150,000 [$100,000 + ($50,000 × 1.0)] =	$ 90,000
1 week late: 30% chance of $145,000 [$100,000 + ($50,000 × .90)] =	43,500
2 weeks late: 10% chance of $140,000 [$100,000 + ($50,000 × .80)] =	14,000
	$147,500

Thus, the total transaction price is $147,500 based on the probability-weighted estimate. Management should update its estimate at each reporting date. Using a most likely outcome approach may be more predictive if a performance bonus is binary (Peabody either will or will not earn the performance bonus), such that Peabody earns either the $50,000 bonus for completion on the agreed-upon date or nothing for completion after the agreed-upon date. In this scenario, if management believes that Peabody will meet the deadline and estimates the consideration using the **most likely outcome**, the total transaction price would be $150,000 (the outcome with 60% probability).

A word of caution—a company only **allocates variable consideration if it is reasonably assured that it will be entitled to that amount**. Companies therefore may only recognize variable consideration if (1) they have experience with similar contracts and are able to estimate the cumulative amount of revenue, and (2) based on experience, it is highly probable that there will not be a significant reversal of revenue previously recognized.[7] If these criteria are not met, revenue recognition is constrained. **[11]** **Illustration 18.6** provides an example of how the revenue constraint works.

ILLUSTRATION 18.6
Transaction Price—Revenue Constraint

Revenue Constraint

Facts: On January 1, Shera Company enters into a contract with Hornung Inc. to perform asset-management services for 1 year. Shera receives a quarterly management fee based on a percentage of Hornung's assets under management at the end of each quarter. In addition, Shera receives a performance-based incentive fee of 20% of the fund's return in excess of the return of an observable index at the end of the year.

Shera accounts for the contract as a single performance obligation to perform investment-management services for 1 year because the services are interdependent and interrelated. To recognize revenue for satisfying the performance obligation over time, Shera selects an output method of measuring progress toward complete satisfaction of the performance obligation. Shera has had a number of these types of contracts with customers in the past.

Question: At what point should Shera recognize the management fee and the performance-based incentive fee related to Hornung?

Solution: Shera should record the management fee each quarter as it performs the management of the fund. However, Shera should not record the incentive fee until the end of the year. Although Shera has experience with similar contracts, that experience is not predictive of the outcome of the current contract because the amount of consideration is highly susceptible to volatility in the market. In addition, the incentive fee has a large number and high variability of possible consideration amounts. Thus, revenue related to the incentive fee is constrained (not recognized) until the incentive fee is known at the end of the year.

[7]Conditions such as one of the following would indicate that the revenue is constrained (or not recognized):

1. The amount of consideration is highly susceptible to factors outside the company's influence. Factors include volatility in a market, the judgment of third parties, weather conditions, and a high risk of obsolescence of the promised good or service.
2. The uncertainty about the amount of consideration is not expected to be resolved for a long period of time.
3. The company's experience (or other evidence) with similar types of performance obligations is limited.
4. The contract has a large number and broad range of possible consideration amounts. **[10]**

Time Value of Money

Timing of payment to the company sometimes does not match the transfer of the goods or services to the customer. In most situations, companies receive consideration after the product is provided or the service performed. In essence, the company provides financing for the customer.

Companies account for the time value of money if the contract **involves a significant financing component**. When a sales transaction involves a significant financing component (i.e., interest is accrued on consideration to be paid over time), the fair value should be determined by discounting the payment using an imputed interest rate. The imputed interest rate is the more clearly determinable of either (1) the prevailing rate for a similar instrument of an issuer with a similar credit rating, or (2) a rate of interest that discounts the nominal amount of the instrument to the current sales price of the goods or services. The company will report the effects of the financing as interest revenue. Illustration 18.7 provides an example of a financing transaction.

ILLUSTRATION 18.7

Transaction Price—Extended Payment Terms

Extended Payment Terms

Facts: On July 1, 2020, SEK Company sold goods to Grant Company for $900,000 in exchange for a 4-year, zero-interest-bearing note with a face amount of $1,416,163. The goods have an inventory cost on SEK's books of $590,000. SEK uses the perpetual inventory method.

***Questions:* (a) How much revenue should SEK Company record on July 1, 2020? (b) How much revenue should it report related to this transaction on December 31, 2020?**

Solution:

(a) SEK should record revenue of $900,000 on July 1, 2020, which is the fair value of the inventory in this case.

(b) SEK is also financing this purchase and records interest revenue on the note over the 4-year period. In this case, the interest rate is imputed and is determined to be 12%. SEK records interest revenue of $54,000 ($.12 \times {}^6/_{12} \times \$900,000$) at December 31, 2020.

The entry to record SEK's sale to Grant Company is as follows.

July 1, 2020		
Notes Receivable	1,416,163	
Discount on Notes Receivable		516,163
Sales Revenue		900,000
Cost of Goods Sold	590,000	
Inventory		590,000

SEK makes the following entry to record (accrue) interest revenue at the end of the year.

December 31, 2020		
Discount on Notes Receivable	54,000	
Interest Revenue ($.12 \times {}^6/_{12} \times \$900,000$)		54,000

As a practical expedient, companies are not required to reflect the time value of money to determine the transaction price if the time period for payment is less than a year. [12]

Noncash Consideration

Companies sometimes receive consideration in the form of goods, services, or other noncash consideration. When these situations occur, **companies generally recognize revenue on the basis of the fair value of what is received.** For example, assume that Raylin Company receives common stock of Monroe Company in payment for consulting services. In that case, Raylin Company recognizes revenue in the amount of the fair value of the common stock received. If Raylin cannot determine this amount, then it should estimate the selling price of the services performed and recognize this amount as revenue.

In addition, companies sometimes receive contributions (e.g., donations and gifts). A contribution is often some type of asset (e.g., securities, land, buildings, or use of facilities) but it could be the forgiveness of debt. In these cases, companies recognize revenue for the fair value of the consideration received. Similarly, customers sometimes contribute goods or services, such as equipment or labor, as consideration for goods provided or services performed. This consideration should be recognized as revenue based on the fair value of the consideration received (see Chapter 10).

Consideration Paid or Payable to Customers

Companies often make payments to their customers as part of a revenue arrangement. Consideration paid or payable may include discounts, volume rebates, coupons, free products, or services. In general, these elements reduce the consideration received and the revenue to be recognized. Illustration 18.8 provides an example of this type of transaction.

ILLUSTRATION 18.8

Transaction Price—Volume Discount

Volume Discount

Facts: Sansung Company offers its customers a 3% volume discount if they purchase at least $2 million of its product during the calendar year. On March 31, 2020, Sansung has made sales of $700,000 to Artic Co. In the previous 2 years, Sansung sold over $3,000,000 to Artic in the period April 1 to December 31. Assume that Sansung prepares financial statements quarterly.

***Question:* How much revenue should Sansung recognize for the first 3 months of 2020?**

Solution: In this case, Sansung should reduce its revenue by $21,000 ($700,000 × .03) because it is probable that it will provide this rebate. Revenue is therefore $679,000 ($700,000 − $21,000). To not recognize this volume discount overstates Sansung's revenue for the first 3 months of 2020. In other words, the appropriate revenue to be recognized is $679,000, not $700,000.

Given these facts, Sansung makes the following entry on March 31, 2020, to recognize revenue.

Accounts Receivable	679,000	
Sales Revenue		679,000

Assuming that Sansung's customer **meets the discount threshold**, Sansung makes the following entry to record collection of accounts receivable.

Cash	679,000	
Accounts Receivable		679,000

If Sansung's customer **fails to meet the discount threshold**, Sansung makes the following entry to record collection of accounts receivable.

Cash	700,000	
Accounts Receivable		679,000
Sales Discounts Forfeited		21,000

As indicated in Chapter 7, Sales Discounts Forfeited is reported in the "Other revenues and gains" section of the income statement.

In many cases, companies provide cash discounts to customers for a short period of time (often referred to as prompt settlement discounts). For example, assume that terms are payment due in 60 days, but if payment is made within five days, a two percent discount is given (referred to as 2/5, net 60). These prompt settlement discounts should reduce revenues, if material. In most cases, companies record the revenue at full price (gross) and record a sales discount if payment is made within the discount period.

Allocating the Transaction Price to Separate Performance Obligations—Step 4

Companies often have to allocate the transaction price to more than one performance obligation in a contract. If an allocation is needed, the transaction price allocated to the various performance obligations is based on their relative fair values. The best measure of fair value is what the company could sell the good or service for on a standalone basis, referred to as the **standalone selling price**. If this information is not available, companies should use their best estimate of what the good or service might sell for as a standalone unit. **Illustration 18.9** summarizes the approaches that companies follow (in preferred order of use).

ILLUSTRATION 18.9

Transaction Price—Allocation

Allocation Approach	Implementation
Adjusted market assessment approach	Evaluate the market in which the company sells goods or services and estimate the price that customers in that market are willing to pay for those goods or services. That approach also might include referring to prices from the company's competitors for similar goods or services and adjusting those prices as necessary to reflect the company's costs and margins.
Expected cost plus a margin approach	Forecast expected costs of satisfying a performance obligation and then add an appropriate margin for that good or service.
Residual approach	If the standalone selling price of a good or service is highly variable or uncertain, then a company may estimate the standalone selling price by reference to the total transaction price less the sum of the observable standalone selling prices of other goods or services promised in the contract.[8]

To illustrate, Travis Company enters into a contract with a customer to sell Products A, B, and C in exchange for $100,000. Travis Company regularly sells Product A separately, and therefore the standalone selling price is directly observable at $50,000. The standalone selling price of Product B is estimated using the adjusted market assessment approach and is determined to be $30,000. Travis Company decides to use the residual approach to value Product C as it has confidence that Products A and B are valued correctly. The selling price for the products is allocated as shown in **Illustration 18.10**.

ILLUSTRATION 18.10

Residual Value Allocation

Product	Price	Rationale
A	$ 50,000	Directly observable using standalone selling price.
B	30,000	Directly observable using adjusted market assessment approach.
C	20,000	[$100,000 − ($50,000 + $30,000)]; using the residual approach given reliability of the two above measurements.
Total transaction price	$100,000	

Illustrations 18.11 and **18.12** are additional examples of the measurement issues involved in allocating the transaction price.

[8]A selling price is highly variable when a company sells the same good or service to different customers (at or near the same time) for a broad range of amounts. A selling price is uncertain when a company has not yet established a price for a good or service and the good or service has not previously been sold. [13]

ILLUSTRATION 18.11

Allocation—Multiple Performance Obligations

Multiple Performance Obligations—Example 1

Facts: Lonnie Company enters into a contract to build, run, and maintain a highly complex piece of electronic equipment for a period of 5 years, commencing upon delivery of the equipment. There is a fixed fee for each of the build, run, and maintenance deliverables, and any progress payments made are nonrefundable. It is determined that the transaction price must be allocated to the three performance obligations: building, running, and maintaining the equipment. There is verifiable evidence of the selling price for the building and maintenance but not for running the equipment.

***Question:* What procedure should Lonnie Company use to allocate the transaction price to the three performance obligations?**

Solution: The performance obligations relate to building the equipment, running the equipment, and maintaining the equipment. As indicated, Lonnie can determine verifiable standalone selling prices for the equipment and the maintenance agreements. The company then can make a best estimate of the selling price for running the equipment, using the adjusted market assessment approach or expected cost plus a margin approach. Lonnie next applies the proportional standalone selling price method at the inception of the transaction to determine the proper allocation to each performance obligation. Once the allocation is performed, Lonnie recognizes revenue independently for each performance obligation using regular revenue recognition criteria.

If, on the other hand, Lonnie is unable to estimate the standalone selling price for running the equipment because such an estimate is highly variable or uncertain, Lonnie may use a residual approach. In this case, Lonnie uses the standalone selling prices of the equipment and maintenance agreements and subtracts these prices from the total transaction price to arrive at a residual value for running the equipment.

ILLUSTRATION 18.12

Multiple Performance Obligations—Product, Installation, and Service

Multiple Performance Obligations—Example 2

Facts: Handler Company is an established manufacturer of equipment used in the construction industry. Handler's products range from small to large individual pieces of automated machinery to complex systems containing numerous components. Unit selling prices range from $600,000 to $4,000,000 and are quoted inclusive of installation and training. The installation process does not involve changes to the features of the equipment and does not require proprietary information about the equipment in order for the installed equipment to perform to specifications. Handler has the following arrangement with Chai Company.

- Chai purchases equipment from Handler for a price of $2,000,000 and chooses Handler to do the installation. Handler charges the same price for the equipment irrespective of whether it does the installation or not. (Some companies do the installation themselves because they either prefer their own employees to do the work or because of relationships with other customers.) The installation service included in the arrangement is estimated to have a standalone selling price of $20,000.
- The standalone selling price of the training sessions is estimated at $50,000. Other companies can also perform these training services.
- Chai is obligated to pay Handler the $2,000,000 upon the delivery and installation of the equipment.
- Handler delivers the equipment on September 1, 2020, and completes the installation of the equipment on November 1, 2020 (transfer of control is complete after installation). Training related to the equipment starts once the installation is completed and lasts for 1 year. The equipment has a useful life of 10 years.

***Questions:* (a) What are the performance obligations for purposes of accounting for the sale of the equipment? (b) If there is more than one performance obligation, how should the payment of $2,000,000 be allocated to various components?**

Solution:

(a) Handler's primary objective is to sell equipment. The other services (installation and training) can be performed by other parties if necessary. As a result, the equipment, installation, and training are three separate products or services. Each of these items has a standalone selling price and is not interdependent.

(b) The total revenue of $2,000,000 should be allocated to the three components based on their relative standalone selling prices. In this case, the standalone selling price of the equipment is $2,000,000, the installation fee is $20,000, and the training is $50,000. The total standalone selling price therefore is $2,070,000 ($2,000,000 + $20,000 + $50,000). The allocation is as follows.

Equipment	$1,932,367	[($2,000,000 ÷ $2,070,000) × $2,000,000]
Installation	19,324	[($20,000 ÷ $2,070,000) × $2,000,000]
Training	48,309	[($50,000 ÷ $2,070,000) × $2,000,000]
	$2,000,000	

(*continued*)

ILLUSTRATION 18.12
(continued)

Handler makes the following entry on November 1, 2020, to record both sales revenue and service revenue on the installation, as well as unearned service revenue.

November 1, 2020

Cash	2,000,000	
Service Revenue (installation)		19,324
Unearned Service Revenue		48,309
Sales Revenue		1,932,367

Assuming the cost of the equipment is $1,500,000, the entry to record cost of goods sold is as follows.

November 1, 2020

Cost of Goods Sold	1,500,000	
Inventory		1,500,000

As indicated by these entries, Handler recognizes revenue from the sale of the equipment once the installation is completed on November 1, 2020. In addition, it recognizes revenue for the installation fee because these services have been performed.

Handler recognizes the training revenues on a straight-line basis starting on November 1, 2020, or $4,026 ($48,309 ÷ 12) per month for 1 year (unless a more appropriate method such as the percentage-of-completion method—discussed in the next section—is warranted). The journal entry to recognize the training revenue for 2 months in 2020 is as follows.

December 31, 2020

Unearned Service Revenue	8,052	
Service Revenue (training) ($4,026 × 2)		8,052

Therefore, Handler recognizes revenue at December 31, 2020, in the amount of $1,959,743 ($1,932,367 + $19,324 + $8,052). Handler makes the following journal entry to recognize the remaining training revenue in 2021, assuming adjusting entries are made at year-end.

December 31, 2021

Unearned Service Revenue	40,257	
Service Revenue (training) ($48,309 – $8,052)		40,257

Recognizing Revenue When (or as) Each Performance Obligation Is Satisfied—Step 5

A company satisfies its performance obligation when the customer obtains control of the good or service. As indicated in the Handler example (in Illustration 18.12) and the BEAN example, the concept of change in control is the deciding factor in determining when a performance obligation is satisfied. The customer controls the product or service when it has the ability to direct the use of and obtain substantially all the remaining benefits from the asset or service. Control also includes the customer's ability to prevent other companies from directing the use of, or receiving the benefits, from the asset or service. Illustration 18.13 summarizes the indicators that the customer has obtained control. [14]

ILLUSTRATION 18.13
Change in Control Indicators

1. The company has a right to payment for the asset.
2. The company has transferred legal title to the asset.
3. The company has transferred physical possession of the asset.
4. The customer has significant risks and rewards of ownership.
5. The customer has accepted the asset.

This is a list of indicators, not requirements or criteria. Not all of the indicators need to be met for management to conclude that control has transferred and revenue can be recognized. Management must use judgment to determine whether the factors collectively indicate that the customer has obtained control. This assessment should be focused primarily on the customer's perspective.

Companies satisfy performance obligations either at a point in time or over a period of time. Companies recognize revenue over a period of time if one of the following three criteria is met.

1. The customer receives and consumes the benefits as the seller performs.
2. The customer controls the asset as it is created or enhanced (e.g., a builder constructs a building on a customer's property).
3. The company does not have an alternative use for the asset created or enhanced (e.g., an aircraft manufacturer builds specialty jets to a customer's specifications) and either (a) the customer receives benefits as the company performs and therefore the task would not need to be re-performed, or (b) the company has a right to payment and this right is enforceable.

Illustration 18.14 provides an example of the point in time when revenue should be recognized.

ILLUSTRATION 18.14

Satisfying a Performance Obligation

Timing of Revenue Recognition

Facts: Gomez Software Company enters into a contract with Hurly Company to develop and install customer relationship management (CRM) software. Progress payments are made upon completion of each stage of the contract. If the contract is terminated, then the partly completed CRM software passes to Hurly Company. Gomez Software is prohibited from redirecting the software to another customer.

***Question:* At what point should Gomez Software Company recognize revenue related to its contract with Hurly Company?**

Solution: Gomez Software does not create an asset with an alternative use because it is prohibited from redirecting the software to another customer. In addition, Gomez Software is entitled to payments for performance to date and expects to complete the project. Therefore, Gomez Software concludes that the contract meets the criteria for recognizing revenue over time.

A company recognizes revenue from a performance obligation over time by measuring the progress toward completion. The method selected for measuring progress should depict the transfer of control from the company to the customer. **For many service arrangements, revenue is recognized on a straight-line basis because the performance obligation is being satisfied ratably over the contract period.** In other settings (e.g., long-term construction contracts), companies use various methods to determine the extent of progress toward completion. The most common are the cost-to-cost and units-of-delivery methods. The objective of all these methods is to measure the extent of progress in terms of costs, units, or value added. Companies identify the various measures (costs incurred, labor hours worked, tons produced, floors completed, etc.) and classify them as input or output measures.

Input measures (e.g., costs incurred and labor hours worked) are efforts devoted to a contract. Output measures (with units of delivery measured as tons produced, floors of a building completed, miles of a highway completed, etc.) track results. Neither is universally applicable to all long-term projects. Their use requires the exercise of judgment and careful tailoring to the circumstances.

The most popular input measure used to determine the progress toward completion is the cost-to-cost basis. Under this basis, a company measures the percentage of completion by comparing costs incurred to date with the most recent estimate of the total costs required to complete the contract. The percentage-of-completion method is discussed more fully in Appendix 18A, which examines the accounting for long-term contracts.

Summary

Illustration 18.15 provides a summary of the five-step revenue recognition process.

ILLUSTRATION 18.15 **Summary of the Five-Step Revenue Recognition Process**

Step in Process	Description	Implementation
1. Identify the contract with customers.	A contract is an agreement that creates enforceable rights or obligations.	A company applies the revenue guidance to contracts with customers.
2. Identify the separate performance obligations in the contract.	A performance obligation is a promise in a contract to provide a product or service to a customer. A performance obligation exists if the customer can benefit from the good or service on its own or together with other readily available resources.	A contract may be comprised of multiple performance obligations. The accounting for multiple performance obligations is based on evaluation of whether the product or service is distinct within the contract. If each of the goods or services is distinct, but is interdependent and interrelated, these goods and services are combined and reported as one performance obligation.
3. Determine the transaction price.	The transaction price is the amount of consideration that a company expects to receive from a customer in exchange for transferring goods and services.	In determining the transaction price, companies must consider the following factors: (1) variable consideration, (2) time value of money, (3) noncash consideration, and (4) consideration paid or payable to customer.
4. Allocate the transaction price to the separate performance obligations.	If more than one performance obligation exists, allocate the transaction price based on relative fair values.	The best measure of fair value is what the good or service could be sold for on a standalone basis (standalone selling price). Estimates of standalone selling price can be based on (1) adjusted market assessment, (2) expected cost plus a margin approach, or (3) a residual approach.
5. Recognize revenue when each performance obligation is satisfied.	A company satisfies its performance obligation when the customer obtains control of the good or service.	Companies satisfy performance obligations either at a point in time or over a period of time. Companies recognize revenue over a period of time if one of the following criteria is met: (1) the customer receives and consumes the benefits as the seller performs, (2) the customer controls the asset as it is created, or (3) the company does not have an alternative use for the asset.

Accounting for Revenue Recognition Issues

LEARNING OBJECTIVE 3

Apply the five-step process to major revenue recognition issues.

This section addresses revenue recognition issues found in practice. Most of these issues relate to determining the transaction price (Step 3) and evaluating when control of the product or service passes to the customer (Step 5). The revenue recognition principle and the concept of control are illustrated for the following situations.

- Sales returns and allowances.
- Repurchase agreements.
- Bill and hold.
- Principal-agent relationships.
- Consignments.
- Warranties.
- Nonrefundable upfront fees.

Sales Returns and Allowances

Sales returns and allowances are very common for many companies that sell goods to customers. For example, assume that Fafco Solar sells solar panels to customers on account. Fafco grants customers the right of return for these panels for various reasons (e.g., dissatisfaction with the product). Customers may receive any combination of the following.

1. A full or partial refund of any consideration paid.
2. A credit that can be applied against amounts owed, or that will be owed, to the seller.
3. Another product in exchange.

To account for these sales returns and allowances, Fafco should recognize the following:

a. Revenue for the transferred solar panels in the amount of consideration to which Fafco is reasonably assured to be entitled (considering the products to be returned or allowance granted).
b. An asset (and corresponding adjustment to cost of goods sold) for the goods returned from customers.

Credit Sales with Returns and Allowances

To illustrate the accounting for a return situation in more detail, assume that on January 12, 2020, Venden Company sells 100 cameras for $100 each on **account** to Amaya Inc. Venden allows Amaya to return any unused cameras within 45 days of purchase. The cost of each product is $60. Venden estimates that:

1. Three products will be returned.
2. The cost of recovering the products will be immaterial.
3. The returned products are expected to be resold at a profit.

On January 24, Amaya returns two of the cameras because they were the wrong color. On January 31, Venden prepares financial statements and determines that it is likely that only one more camera will be returned. Venden makes the following entries related to these transactions.

To record the sale of the cameras and related cost of goods sold on January 12, 2020		
Accounts Receivable	10,000	
Sales Revenue (100 × $100)		10,000
Cost of Goods Sold	6,000	
Inventory (100 × $60)		6,000
To record the return of the two cameras on January 24, 2020		
Sales Returns and Allowances	200	
Accounts Receivable (2 × $100)		200
Returned Inventory	120	
Cost of Goods Sold (2 × $60)		120

The Sales Returns and Allowances account is a contra-account to Sales Revenue. The Returned Inventory account is used to separate returned inventory from regular inventory.

On January 31, 2020, Venden prepares financial statements. As indicated earlier, Venden originally estimated that the most likely outcome was that three cameras would be returned. Venden believes the original estimate is correct and makes the following adjusting entries to account for expected returns at January 31, 2020.

To record expected sales returns on January 31, 2020		
Sales Returns and Allowances	100	
Allowance for Sales Returns and Allowances (1 × $100)		100
To record the expected return of the one camera and related reduction in Cost of Goods Sold		
Estimated Inventory Returns	60	
Cost of Goods Sold (1 × $60)		60

The Allowance for Sales Returns and Allowances account is a contra-account to Accounts Receivable. The Estimated Inventory Returns account will generally be added to the Returned Inventory account at the end of the reporting period.[9]

For the month of January, Venden's income statement reports the information presented in **Illustration 18.16**.

ILLUSTRATION 18.16
Income Statement Reporting

Sales revenue (100 × $100)	$10,000
Less: Sales returns and allowances ($200 + $100)	300
Net sales	9,700
Cost of goods sold (97 × $60)	5,820
Gross profit	$ 3,880

As a result, at the end of the reporting period, the net sales reflects the amount that Venden expects to be entitled to collect.

Venden reports the following information in the balance sheet as of January 31, 2020, as shown in **Illustration 18.17**.

ILLUSTRATION 18.17
Balance Sheet Reporting

Accounts receivable ($10,000 − $200)	$9,800
Less: Allowance for sales returns and allowances	100
Accounts receivable (net)	$9,700
Returned inventory (including estimated) (3 × $60)	$ 180

Cash Sales with Returns and Allowances

Assume now that Venden sold the cameras to Amaya **for cash** instead of on account. In this situation, Venden makes the following entries related to these transactions.

To record the sale of the cameras and related cost of goods sold on January 12, 2020		
Cash	10,000	
Sales Revenue (100 × $100)		10,000
Cost of Goods Sold	6,000	
Inventory (100 × $60)		6,000

Assuming that Venden did not pay cash at the time of the return of the two cameras to Amaya on January 24, 2020, the entries to record the return of the two cameras and related cost of goods sold are as follows.

[9]As indicated, at the date of sale, both sales revenue and accounts receivable are recorded at their gross amounts without consideration of sales returns and allowances. Then, at the end of the reporting period, adjusting entries are made, resulting in both sales revenues and accounts receivable being reported at net amounts and which reflect actual and estimated returns and allowances. As discussed in Chapter 7, most companies follow this adjusting entry approach because estimating net sales at the date of sale is often difficult and time-consuming. In addition, recording accounts receivables net at the sale date may lead to a lack of correspondence between the control account and the subsidiary ledger related to accounts receivable. By waiting to make the necessary adjusting entries at the end of the reporting period, information related to actual sales returns and allowances is available, and a company still achieves the FASB's objective of reflecting accounts receivable and sales revenue at the amount the company is entitled to receive (and inventories and cost of goods sold at cost).

To record the return of two cameras on January 24, 2020		
Sales Returns and Allowances	200	
Accounts Payable (2 × $100)		200
Returned Inventory	120	
Cost of Goods Sold (2 × $60)		120

Venden records an accounts payable to Amaya to recognize that it owes Amaya for the return of two cameras. As indicated earlier, the Sales Returns and Allowances account is a contra-revenue account. The Returned Inventory account is used to separate returned inventory from regular inventory.

On January 31, 2020, Venden prepares financial statements. As indicated earlier, Venden estimates that the most likely outcome is that one more camera will be returned. Venden therefore makes the following adjusting entries.

To record expected sales returns on January 31, 2020		
Sales Returns and Allowances	100	
Accounts Payable (1 × $100)		100
To record the expected return of the one camera and related Cost of Goods Sold		
Estimated Inventory Returns	60	
Cost of Goods Sold (1 × $60)		60

At January 31, 2020, Venden records an accounts payable to recognize its estimated additional liability to Amaya for expected future returns. The Estimated Inventory Returns account will generally be added to the Returned Inventory account at the end of the reporting period to identify returned and estimated inventory returns.

Illustration 18.18 presents the information related to these sales that will be reported on Venden's income statement for the month of January.

ILLUSTRATION 18.18

Income Statement Reporting Sales Returns and Allowances

Sales revenue (100 × $100)	$10,000
Less: Sales returns and allowances (3 × $100)	300
Net sales	9,700
Cost of goods sold (97 × $60)	5,820
Gross profit	$ 3,880

On Venden's balance sheet as of January 31, 2020, the information shown in Illustration 18.19 is reported.

ILLUSTRATION 18.19

Balance Sheet Reporting Sales Returns and Allowances

Cash (assuming no cash payments to date to Amaya)	$10,000
Returned inventory (including estimated) (3 × $60)	180
Accounts payable ($200 + $100)	300

Companies record the returned asset in a separate account from inventory to provide transparency. The carrying value of the returned asset is subject to impairment testing, separate from the inventory. If a company is unable to estimate the level of returns with any reliability, it should not report any revenue until the returns become predictive.

Repurchase Agreements

In some cases, companies enter into **repurchase agreements**, which allow them to transfer an asset to a customer but have an unconditional (forward) obligation or unconditional right (call option) to repurchase the asset at a later date. In these situations, the question is whether the company sold the asset.[10] Generally, companies report these transactions as a financing (borrowing). That is, if the company has a forward obligation or call option to repurchase the asset for an amount **greater than or equal to its selling price,** then the transaction is a financing transaction by the company.[11] **Illustration 18.20** examines the issues related to a repurchase agreement.

ILLUSTRATION 18.20

Recognition—Repurchase Agreement

Repurchase Agreement

Facts: Morgan Inc., an equipment dealer, sells equipment on January 1, 2020, to Lane Company for $100,000. It agrees to repurchase this equipment (an unconditional obligation) from Lane Company on December 31, 2021, for a price of $121,000.

***Question:* Should Morgan Inc. record a sale for this transaction?**

Solution: For a sale and repurchase agreement, the terms of the agreement need to be analyzed to determine whether Morgan Inc. has transferred control to the customer, Lane Company. As indicated earlier, control of an asset refers to the ability to direct the use of and obtain substantially all the benefits from the asset. Control also includes the ability to prevent other companies from directing the use of and receiving the benefit from a good or service. In this case, Morgan Inc. continues to have control of the asset because it has agreed to repurchase the asset at an amount greater than the selling price. Therefore, this agreement is a financing transaction and not a sale. Thus, the asset is not removed from the books of Morgan Inc.

Assuming that an interest rate of 10% is imputed from the agreement, Morgan Inc. makes the following entries to record this agreement. Morgan Inc. records the financing on January 1, 2020, as follows.

January 1, 2020

Cash	100,000	
Liability to Lane Company		100,000

Morgan Inc. records interest on December 31, 2020, as follows.

December 31, 2020

Interest Expense	10,000	
Liability to Lane Company ($100,000 × .10)		10,000

Morgan Inc. records interest and retirement of its liability to Lane Company as follows.

December 31, 2021

Interest Expense	11,000	
Liability to Lane Company ($110,000 × .10)		11,000
Liability to Lane Company	121,000	
Cash ($100,000 + $10,000 + $11,000)		121,000

Rather than Morgan Inc. having a forward or call option to repurchase the asset, assume that Lane Company **has the option** to require Morgan Inc. to repurchase the asset at December 31, 2021. This option is a put option; that is, Lane Company has the option to put the asset back to Morgan Inc. In this situation, Lane Company has control of the asset as it can keep the equipment or sell it to Morgan Inc. or to some other third party. The value of a put option increases when the value of the underlying asset (in this case, the equipment) decreases. In determining how to account for this transaction, Morgan Inc. has to determine whether Lane Company will have an economic incentive to exercise this put option at the end of 2021.

Specifically, Lane Company has a significant economic incentive to exercise its put option if the value of the equipment declines. In this case, the transaction is generally reported as a financing transaction as shown in Illustration 18.20. That is, Lane Company will return (put)

[10]Beyond financing motivations, a company may transfer inventory to another party on a short-term basis to avoid inventory taxes. If the counterparty is able to use the inventory during the transfer period, the transaction may more appropriately be accounted for as a rental agreement.

[11]If the repurchase price is less than the selling price, then the transaction is accounted for as a lease. [15] The accounting for leases is discussed in Chapter 21.

the equipment back to Morgan Inc. if the repurchase price exceeds the fair value of the equipment. For example, if the repurchase price of the equipment is $150,000 but its fair value is $125,000, Lane Company is better off returning the equipment to Morgan Inc.

Conversely, if Lane Company does not have a significant economic incentive to exercise its put option, then the transaction should be reported as a sale of a product with a right of return.

Bill-and-Hold Arrangements

A **bill-and-hold arrangement** is a contract under which an entity bills a customer for a product but the entity retains physical possession of the product until it is transferred to the customer at a point in time in the future. Bill-and-hold sales result when the buyer is not yet ready to take delivery but does take title and accepts billing. For example, a customer may request a company to enter into such an arrangement because of (1) lack of available space for the product, (2) delays in its production schedule, or (3) more than sufficient inventory in its distribution channel. **[16]** **Illustration 18.21** provides an example of a bill-and-hold arrangement.

ILLUSTRATION 18.21

Recognition—Bill and Hold

Bill and Hold

Facts: Butler Company sells $450,000 (cost $280,000) of fireplaces on March 1, 2020, to a local coffee shop, Baristo, which is planning to expand its locations around the city. Under the agreement, Baristo asks Butler to retain these fireplaces in its warehouses until the new coffee shops that will house the fireplaces are ready. Title passes to Baristo at the time the agreement is signed.

***Question:* When should Butler recognize the revenue from this bill-and-hold arrangement?**

Solution: When to recognize revenue in a bill-and-hold arrangement depends on the circumstances. Butler determines when it has satisfied its performance obligation to transfer a product by evaluating when Baristo obtains control of that product. For Baristo to have obtained control of a product in a bill-and-hold arrangement, it must meet all of the conditions for change in control plus all of the following criteria:

(a) The reason for the bill-and-hold arrangement must be substantive.
(b) The product must be identified separately as belonging to Baristo.
(c) The product currently must be ready for physical transfer to Baristo.
(d) Butler cannot have the ability to use the product or to direct it to another customer.

In this case, assuming that the above criteria were met in the contract, revenue recognition should be permitted at the time the contract is signed. Butler has transferred control to Baristo; that is, Butler has a right to payment for the fireplaces and legal title has transferred.

Butler makes the following entry to record the bill-and-hold sale and related cost of goods sold.

March 1, 2020

Accounts Receivable	450,000	
Sales Revenue		450,000
Cost of Goods Sold	280,000	
Inventory		280,000

Principal-Agent Relationships

In a **principal-agent relationship**, the principal's performance obligation is to provide goods or perform services for a customer. The agent's performance obligation is to arrange for the principal to provide these goods or services to a customer. Examples of principal-agent relationships are as follows.

- Preferred Travel Company (agent) facilitates the booking of cruise excursions by finding customers for Regency Cruise Company (principal).
- **Priceline** (agent) facilitates the sale of various services such as car rentals for **Hertz** (principal).

In these types of situations, amounts collected on behalf of the principal are not revenue of the agent. Instead, revenue for the agent is the amount of the commission it receives (usually a percentage of total revenue). **Illustration 18.22** provides an example of the issues related to principal-agent relationships.

ILLUSTRATION 18.22

Recognition—Principal-Agent Relationship

Principal-Agent Relationship

Facts: Fly-Away Travel sells airplane tickets for British Airways (BA) to various customers.

***Question:* What are the performance obligations in this situation and how should revenue be recognized for both the principal and agent?**

Solution: The principal in this case is BA and the agent is Fly-Away Travel. Because BA has the performance obligation to provide air transportation to the customer, it is the principal. Fly-Away Travel facilitates the sale of the airline ticket to the customer in exchange for a fee or commission. Its performance obligation is to arrange for BA to provide air transportation to the customer.

Although Fly-Away collects the full airfare from the customer, it then remits this amount to BA less the commission. Fly-Away therefore should not record the full amount of the fare as revenue on its books—to do so overstates revenue. Its revenue is the commission, not the full price. Control of performing the air transportation is with BA, not Fly-Away Travel.

Some might argue that there is no harm in letting Fly-Away record revenue for the full price of the ticket and then charging the cost of the ticket against the revenue (often referred to as the **gross method** of recognizing revenue). Others note that this approach overstates the agent's revenue and is misleading. The revenue received is the commission for providing the travel services, not the full fare price (often referred to as the **net approach**). The profession believes the net approach is the correct method for recognizing revenue in a principal-agent relationship. As a result, the FASB has developed specific criteria to determine when a principal-agent relationship exists.[12] An important feature in deciding whether Fly-Away is acting as an agent is whether the amount it earns is predetermined, being either a fixed fee per transaction or a stated percentage of the amount billed to the customer.

Consignments

A common principal-agent relationship involves consignments. In these cases, manufacturers (or wholesalers) deliver goods but retain title to the goods until they are sold. This specialized method of marketing certain types of products makes use of an agreement known as a **consignment**. Under this arrangement, the **consignor** (manufacturer or wholesaler) ships merchandise to the **consignee** (dealer), who is to act as an agent for the consignor in selling the merchandise. Both consignor and consignee are interested in selling—the former to make a profit or develop a market, the latter to make a commission on the sale.

The consignee accepts the merchandise and agrees to exercise due diligence in caring for and selling it. The consignee remits to the consignor cash received from customers, after deducting a sales commission and any chargeable expenses. In consignment sales, the consignor uses a modified version of the point-of-sale basis of revenue recognition. That is, the consignor recognizes revenue only after receiving notification of the sale.

[12]Indicators that the company's performance obligation is to arrange for the providing of goods or the performing of services by another party (i.e., the company is an agent and should recognize revenue in the net amount) include the following: (a) the other party is primarily responsible for fulfilling the contract; (b) the company does not have inventory risk before or after the customer order, during shipping, or on return; (c) the company does not have latitude in establishing prices for the other party's goods or services and, hence, the benefit that the company can receive from those goods or services is constrained; (d) the company's consideration is in the form of a commission; and (e) the company does not have customer credit risk for the amount receivable in exchange for the other party's goods or services. [17]

The consignor carries the merchandise as inventory throughout the consignment, separately classified as Inventory (consignments). **The consignee does not record the merchandise as an asset on its books.** Upon sale of the merchandise, the consignee has **a liability for the net amount due the consignor**. The consignor periodically receives from the consignee a report called **account sales** that shows the merchandise received, merchandise sold, expenses chargeable to the consignment, and the cash remitted. Revenue is then recognized by the consignor. Analysis of a consignment arrangement is provided in **Illustration 18.23**.

ILLUSTRATION 18.23

Recognition—Sales on Consignment

Sales on Consignment

Facts: Nelba Manufacturing Co. ships merchandise costing $36,000 on consignment to Best Value Stores. Nelba pays $3,750 of freight costs, and Best Value pays $2,250 for local advertising costs that are reimbursable from Nelba. By the end of the period, Best Value has sold two-thirds of the consigned merchandise for $40,000 cash. Best Value notifies Nelba of the sales, retains a 10% commission, and remits the cash due Nelba.

***Question:* What are the journal entries that the consignor (Nelba) and the consignee (Best Value) make to record this transaction?**

Solution:

Nelba Mfg. Co. (Consignor)			Best Value Stores (Consignee)		
Shipment of consigned merchandise					
Inventory (consignments)	36,000		No entry (record memo of merchandise received).		
Finished Goods Inventory		36,000			
Payment of freight costs by consignor					
Inventory (consignments)	3,750		No entry.		
Cash		3,750			
Payment of advertising by consignee					
No entry until notified.			Receivable from Consignor	2,250	
			Cash		2,250
Sales of consigned merchandise					
No entry until notified.			Cash	40,000	
			Payable to Consignor		40,000
Notification of sales and expenses and remittance of amount due					
Cash	33,750		Payable to Consignor	40,000	
Advertising Expense	2,250		Receivable from Consignor		2,250
Commission Expense	4,000		Commission Revenue		4,000
Revenue from Consignment Sales		40,000	Cash		33,750
Adjustment of inventory on consignment for cost of sales					
Cost of Goods Sold	26,500		No entry.		
Inventory (consignments) [2/3 ($36,000 + $3,750) = $26,500]		26,500			

Under the consignment arrangement, the consignor accepts the risk that the merchandise might not sell and relieves the consignee of the need to commit part of its working capital to inventory. Consignors use a variety of systems and account titles to record consignments, but they all share the common goal of postponing the recognition of revenue until it is known that a sale to a third party has occurred. **Consignees only recognize commission revenue.**

What Do the Numbers Mean? Grossed Out

As you learned in Chapter 4, many corporate executives obsess over the bottom line. However, analysts on the outside look at the big picture, which includes examination of both the top line and the important subtotals in the income statement, such as gross profit. Not too long ago, the top line caused some concern, with nearly all companies in the S&P 500 reporting a 2 percent decline in the bottom line while the top line saw revenue decline by 1 percent. This was troubling because it was the first decline in revenues since we crawled out of the recession following the financial crisis.

What about income subtotals like gross margin? These metrics too have been under pressure. There is concern that struggling companies may employ a number of manipulations to mask the impact of gross margin declines on the bottom line. In fact, **Rite Aid** prepares an income statement that omits the gross margin subtotal. Rite Aid has used a number of suspect accounting adjustments related to tax allowances and inventory gains to offset its weak gross margin.

Or, consider the classic case of **Priceline.com**. In one quarter, Priceline reported that it earned $152 million in revenues. But, that included the full amount customers paid for tickets, hotel rooms, and rental cars. Traditional travel agencies call that amount "gross bookings," not revenues. And, much like regular travel agencies, Priceline keeps only a small portion of gross bookings—namely, the spread between the customers' payments and the price the company paid for the merchandise. The rest, which Priceline calls "product costs," it pays to the airlines and hotels that supply the tickets and rooms.

However, Priceline's product costs came to $134 million, leaving Priceline just $18 million of what it calls "gross profit" and what most other companies would call revenues. And that's before all of Priceline's other costs—like advertising and salaries—which netted out to a loss of $102 million. The difference isn't academic. Priceline shares traded at about 23 times its reported revenues but at a mind-boggling 214 times its "gross profit." This and other aggressive recognition practices explain the stricter revenue recognition guidance, indicating that if a company performs as an agent or broker without assuming the risks and rewards of ownership of the goods, the company should report sales on a net (fee) basis.

Sources: Jeremy Kahn, "Presto Chango! Sales Are Huge," *Fortune* (March 20, 2000), p. 44; A. Catanach and E. Ketz, "RITE AID: Is Management Selling Drugs or Using Them?" *Grumpy Old Accountants* (August 22, 2011); and S. Jakab, "Weak Revenue Is New Worry for Investors," *Wall Street Journal* (November 25, 2012).

Warranties

As discussed in Chapter 13, companies often provide one of two types of **warranties** to customers:

1. Warranties that the product **meets agreed-upon specifications in the contract at the time the product is sold**. This type of warranty is included in the sales price of a company's product and is often referred to as an **assurance-type warranty**.
2. Warranties that provide an **additional service beyond the assurance-type warranty**. This warranty is not included in the sales price of the product and is referred to as a **service-type warranty**. As a consequence, it is recorded as a separate performance obligation.

Companies do not record a separate performance obligation for assurance-type warranties. This type of warranty is nothing more than a quality guarantee that the good or service is free from defects at the point of sale. In this case, the sale of the product and the related assurance warranty are one performance obligation as they are interdependent of and interrelated with each other. The objective for companies that issue an assurance warranty is to provide a combined item (product and a warranty).

These types of obligations should be expensed in the period the goods are provided or services performed. In addition, the company should record a warranty liability. The estimated amount of the liability includes all the costs that the company is expected to incur after sale due to the correction of defects or deficiencies required under the warranty provisions.

In addition, companies sometimes provide customers with an option to purchase a warranty separately. In most cases, these extended warranties provide the customer a service beyond fixing defects that existed at the time of sale. For example, when you purchase a TV, you are entitled to the company's warranty. You will also undoubtedly be offered an extended warranty on the product at an additional cost. These service-type warranties represent a **separate service and are an additional performance obligation**. The service-type warranty is sold separately and therefore has a standalone selling price. In this case, the objective of the company is to sell an additional service to customers. As a result, companies should allocate a portion of the transaction price to this performance obligation, if provided. The company recognizes revenue in the period that the service-type warranty is in effect. **Illustration 18.24** presents an example of both an assurance-type and a service-type warranty.

ILLUSTRATION 18.24

Recognition—Performance Obligations and Warranties

Warranties

Facts: Maverick Company sold 1,000 Rollomatics on October 1, 2020, at total price of $6,000,000, with a warranty guarantee that the product was free of defects. The cost of the Rollomatics is $4,000,000. The term of this assurance warranty is 2 years, which Maverick estimates will cost $80,000. In addition, Maverick sold extended warranties related to 400 Rollomatics for 3 years beyond the 2-year period for $18,000. On November 22, 2020, Maverick incurred labor costs of $3,000 and part costs of $25,000 related to the assurance warranties. Maverick prepares financial statements on December 31, 2020. It estimates that its future assurance warranty costs will total $44,000 at December 31, 2020.

***Question:* What are the journal entries that Maverick Company should make in 2020 related to the sale of the Rollomatics and the assurance and extended warranties?**

Solution: Maverick makes the following entries in 2020 related to Rollomatics sold with warranties.

October 1, 2020

To record the sale of the Rollomatics and the related extended warranties:

Cash ($6,000,000 + $18,000)	6,018,000	
Sales Revenue		6,000,000
Unearned Warranty Revenue		18,000

To record the cost of goods sold and reduce the inventory of Rollomatics:

Cost of Goods Sold	4,000,000	
Inventory		4,000,000

November 22, 2020

To record the warranty costs incurred:

Warranty Expense	28,000	
Salaries and Wages Payable		3,000
Inventory (parts)		25,000

December 31, 2020

To record the adjusting entry related to its assurance warranty at the end of the year:

Warranty Expense	44,000	
Warranty Liability		44,000

Maverick Company makes an adjusting entry on December 31, 2020, to record a liability for the expected warranty costs related to the sale of the Rollomatics. When actual warranty costs are incurred in 2021, the Warranty Liability account is reduced.

In most cases, Unearned Warranty Revenue (related to the service-type warranty) is recognized on a straight-line basis as Warranty Revenue over the three-year period to which it applies. Revenue related to the extended warranty is not recognized until the warranty becomes effective on October 1, 2022. If financial statements are prepared on December 31, 2022, Maverick makes the following entry to recognize revenue:

Unearned Warranty Revenue	1,500	
Warranty Revenue [($18,000 ÷ 36) × 3]		1,500

Similar to that illustrated in Chapter 13, Maverick Company reduces the Warranty Liability account over the warranty period as the actual warranty costs are incurred.[13] The company

[13]As with the accounting for sales returns and allowances, the entries shown here reflect a gross (as opposed to net) treatment of the warranty obligation. That is, at the date of sale, Maverick recorded sales with an assurance warranty at the gross amount, without adjustment for expected warranty costs (sometimes referred to as the expense warranty approach). Then at the end of the accounting period when financial statements are prepared, Maverick prepares adjusting entries to record a liability for any remaining estimated warranty expenses (after accounting for actual warranty expenditures). Companies generally do not use the net method because it requires additional analysis and bookkeeping to adjust the warranty liability for unused warranty claims.

also recognizes revenue related to the service-type warranty over the three-year period that extends beyond the assurance warranty period (two years). In most cases, the unearned warranty revenue is recognized on a straight-line basis. The costs associated with the service-type warranty are expensed as incurred.

Nonrefundable Upfront Fees

Companies sometimes receive payments (**upfront fees**) from customers before they deliver a product or perform a service. Upfront payments generally relate to the initiation, activation, or setup of a good or service to be provided or performed in the future. In most cases, these upfront payments are nonrefundable. Examples include fees paid for membership in a health club or buying club, and activation fees for phone, Internet, or cable.

Companies must determine whether these nonrefundable advance payments are for products or services in the current period. In most situations, these payments are for future delivery of products and services and should therefore not be recorded as revenue at the time of payment. In some cases, the upfront fee is viewed similar to a renewal option for future products and services at a reduced price. An example would be a health club where once the initiation fee is paid, no additional fee is necessary upon renewal. **Illustration 18.25** provides an example of an upfront fee payment.

ILLUSTRATION 18.25

Transaction Price—Upfront Fee Considerations

Upfront Fee Considerations

Facts: Erica Felise signs a 1-year contract with Bigelow Health Club. The terms of the contract are that Erica is required to pay a nonrefundable initiation fee of $200 and a membership fee of $50 per month. Bigelow determines that its customers, on average, renew their annual membership two times before terminating their membership.

***Question:* What is the amount of revenue Bigelow Health Club should recognize in the first year?**

Solution: In this case, the membership fee arrangement may be viewed as a single performance obligation (similar services are provided in all periods). That is, Bigelow is providing a discounted price in the second and third years for the same services, and this should be reflected in the revenue recognized in those periods. Bigelow determines the total transaction price to be $2,000—the upfront fee of $200 and the three years of monthly fees of $1,800 ($50 × 36)—and allocates it over the three years. In this case, Bigelow would report revenue of $55.56 ($2,000 ÷ 36) each month for three years. *Unless otherwise instructed, use this approach for homework problems.*[14]

Summary

Illustration 18.26 provides a summary of the additional issues related to transfer of control and revenue recognition.

[14] The initiation fee might be viewed as a separate performance obligation (it provides a renewal option at a lower price than normally charged, perhaps with different services). In this situation, in the first period, Bigelow would report revenue of $600 ($50 × 12). The initiation fee would then be allocated to years two and three ($100 in each year) unless forfeited earlier.

ILLUSTRATION 18.26 Summary—Other Revenue Recognition Issues

Issue	Description	Implementation
Sales returns and allowances	Return of product by customer (e.g., due to dissatisfaction with the product) in exchange for refunds, a credit against amounts owed or that will be owed, and/or another product in exchange.	Seller may recognize (a) an adjustment to revenue for products expected to be returned, and (b) an asset (and corresponding adjustment to cost of goods sold) for the goods returned from customers.
Repurchase agreements	Seller has an obligation or right to repurchase the asset at a later date.	Generally, if the company has an obligation or right to repurchase the asset for an amount greater than its selling price, then the transaction is a financing transaction.
Bill-and-hold	Result when the buyer is not yet ready to take delivery but does take title and accept billing.	Revenue is recognized depending on when the customer obtains control of that product.
Principal-agent	Arrangement in which the principal's performance obligation is to provide goods or perform services for a customer. The agent's performance obligation is to arrange for the principal to provide these goods or services to a customer.	Amounts collected on behalf of the principal are not revenue of the agent. Instead, revenue for the agent is the amount of the commission it receives. The principal recognizes revenue when the goods or services are sold to a third-party customer.
Consignments	A principal-agent relationship in which the consignor (manufacturer or wholesaler) ships merchandise to the consignee (dealer), who is to act as an agent for the consignor in selling the merchandise.	The consignor recognizes revenue only after receiving notification of the sale and the cash remittance from the consignee (consignor carries the merchandise as inventory throughout the consignment). The consignee records commission revenue (usually some percentage of the selling price).
Warranties	Warranties can be assurance-type (product meets agreed-upon specifications) or service-type (provides additional service beyond the assurance-type warranty).	A separate performance obligation is not recorded for assurance-type warranties (considered part of the product). Service-type warranties are recorded as a separate performance obligation. Companies should allocate a portion of the transaction price to service type-warranties, when present.
Nonrefundable upfront fees	Upfront payments generally relate to initiation, activation, or setup activities for a good or service to be delivered in the future.	The upfront payment should be allocated over the periods benefited.

Presentation and Disclosure

LEARNING OBJECTIVE 4

Describe presentation and disclosure regarding revenue.

Presentation

As discussed earlier, companies use an asset-liability approach to recognize revenue. For example, when **General Mills** delivers cereal to **Whole Foods Market** (satisfying its performance obligation), it has a right to consideration from Whole Foods and therefore has a contract asset. If, on the other hand, Whole Foods Market performs first, by prepaying for this cereal, General Mills has a contract liability. Companies must present these contract assets and contract liabilities on their balance sheets.

Contract Assets and Liabilities

Contract assets are of two types: (1) unconditional rights to receive consideration because the company has satisfied its performance obligation with a customer, and (2) conditional rights to receive consideration because the company has satisfied one performance obligation but must satisfy another performance obligation in the contract before it can bill the customer. Companies should report unconditional rights to receive consideration as a receivable on the balance sheet. Conditional rights on the balance sheet should be reported separately as contract assets. Illustration 18.27 provides an example of the accounting and reporting for a contract asset.

ILLUSTRATION 18.27

Contract Asset Recognition and Presentation

Contract Asset

Facts: On January 1, 2020, Finn Company enters into a contract to transfer Product A and Product B to Obermine Co. for $100,000. The contract specifies that payment of Product A will not occur until Product B is also delivered. In other words, payment will not occur until both Product A and Product B are transferred to Obermine. Finn determines that standalone selling prices are $30,000 for Product A and $70,000 for Product B. Finn delivers Product A to Obermine on February 1, 2020. On March 1, 2020, Finn delivers Product B to Obermine.

***Question:* What journal entries should Finn Company make in regards to this contract in 2020?**

Solution: No entry is required on January 1, 2020, because neither party has performed on the contract. On February 1, 2020, Finn records the following entry.

February 1, 2020

Contract Asset	30,000	
Sales Revenue		30,000

On February 1, Finn has satisfied its performance obligation and therefore reports revenue of $30,000. However, it does not record an accounts receivable at this point because it does not have an unconditional right to receive the $100,000 unless it also transfers Product B to Obermine. In other words, a contract asset occurs generally when a company must satisfy another performance obligation before it is entitled to bill the customer. When Finn transfers Product B on March 1, 2020, it makes the following entry.

March 1, 2020

Accounts Receivable	100,000	
Contract Asset		30,000
Sales Revenue		70,000

As indicated above, a **contract liability** is a company's obligation to transfer goods or services to a customer for which the company has received consideration from the customer. A contract liability is generally referred to as Unearned Sales Revenue, Unearned Service Revenue, or another appropriate account title. Illustration 18.28 provides an example of the recognition and presentation of a contract liability.

ILLUSTRATION 18.28

Contract Liability Recognition and Presentation

Contract Liability

Facts: On March 1, 2020, Henly Company enters into a contract to transfer a product to Propel Inc. on July 31, 2020. It is agreed that Propel will pay the full price of $10,000 in advance on April 15, 2020. Henly delivers the product on July 31, 2020. The cost of the product is $7,500.

***Question:* What journal entries are required in 2020?**

Solution: No entry is required on March 1, 2020, because neither party has performed on the contract. On receiving the cash on April 15, 2020, Henly records the following entry.

April 15, 2020

Cash	10,000	
Unearned Sales Revenue		10,000

(continued)

ILLUSTRATION 18.28
(continued)

On satisfying the performance obligation on July 31, 2020, Henly records the following entry to record the sale.

July 31, 2020

Unearned Sales Revenue	10,000	
Sales Revenue		10,000

In addition, Henly records cost of goods sold as follows.

Cost of Goods Sold	7,500	
Inventory		7,500

Companies are not required to use the terms "contract assets" and "contract liabilities" on the balance sheet. For example, contract liabilities are performance obligations and therefore more descriptive titles (as noted earlier) such as unearned service revenue, unearned sales revenue, repurchase liability, and return liability may be used where appropriate. For contract assets, it is important that financial statement users can differentiate between unconditional and conditional rights through appropriate account presentation.

Contract Modifications

Companies sometimes change the contract terms while it is ongoing; this is referred to as a **contract modification**. When a contract modification occurs, companies determine whether a new contract (and performance obligations) results or whether it is a modification of the existing contract.

Separate Performance Obligation A company accounts for a contract modification as a new contract if **both** of the following conditions are satisfied:

- The promised **goods or services are distinct** (i.e., the company sells them separately and they are not interdependent with other goods and services), and
- The company has the right to receive an amount of **consideration that reflects the standalone selling price** of the promised goods or services. [18]

For example, Crandall Co. has a contract to sell 100 products to a customer for $10,000 ($100 per product) at various points in time over a six-month period. After 60 products have been delivered, Crandall modifies the contract by promising to deliver 20 more products for an additional $1,900, or $95 per product (which is the standalone selling price of the products at the time of the contract modification). Crandall regularly sells the products separately. In this situation, the contract modification for the additional 20 products is, in effect, a **new and separate contract** because it meets both of the conditions above. That is, it does not affect the accounting for the original contract.

Given a new contract, Crandall recognizes an additional $4,000 [(100 units − 60 units) × $100] related to the original contract terms and $1,900 (20 units × $95) related to the new products. Total revenue after the modification is therefore $5,900 ($4,000 + $1,900).

Prospective Modification What if Crandall Co. determines that the additional products are not a separate performance obligation? This might arise if the new products are not priced at the proper standalone selling price or if they are not distinct. In this situation, companies generally account for the modification using a prospective approach.

Under the prospective approach, Crandall should account for the effect of the change in the period of change as well as future periods if the change affects both. Crandall should not change previously reported results. Thus, for Crandall, the amount recognized as revenue for each of the remaining products would be a blended price of $98.33, computed as shown in Illustration 18.29.

ILLUSTRATION 18.29
Revenue Under Prospective Modification

Consideration for products not yet delivered under original contract ($100 × 40)	$4,000
Consideration for products to be delivered under the contract modification ($95 × 20)	1,900
Total remaining revenue	$5,900

Revenue per remaining unit ($5,900 ÷ 60) = $98.33

Therefore, under the prospective approach, this computation differs from that in the separate performance obligation approach in that revenue on the remaining units is recognized at the blended price. Total revenue after the modification is therefore $5,900 (60 units × $98.33). **Illustration 18.30** shows the revenue reported under the two contract modification approaches for Crandall Co.

ILLUSTRATION 18.30
Comparison of Contract Modification Approaches

	Revenue Recognized Prior to Modification	Revenue Recognized After Modification	Total Revenue Recognized
Separate performance obligation	$6,000	$5,900	$11,900
No separate performance obligation—prospectively	$6,000	$5,900	$11,900

As indicated, whether a modification is treated as a separate performance obligation or prospectively, the same amount of revenue is recognized before and after the modification. However, under the prospective approach, a blended price ($98.33) is used for sales in the periods after the modification.[15]

Costs to Fulfill a Contract

Companies may also report assets associated with fulfillment costs related to a revenue arrangement. Companies divide fulfillment costs (contract acquisition costs) into two categories:

1. Those that give rise to an asset.
2. Those that are expensed as incurred.

Companies recognize an asset for the incremental costs if these costs are incurred to obtain a contract with a customer. In other words, incremental costs are those that a company would not incur if the contract had not been obtained (e.g., selling commissions). Additional examples that give rise to an asset are as follows.

a. Direct labor, direct materials, and allocation of costs that relate directly to the contract (e.g., costs of contract management and supervision, insurance, and depreciation of tools and equipment).

b. Costs that generate or enhance resources of the company that will be used in satisfying performance obligations in the future. Such costs include intangible design or engineering costs that will continue to give rise to benefits in the future.

Other costs that are expensed as incurred include general and administrative costs (unless those costs are explicitly chargeable to the customer under the contract) as well as costs of wasted materials, labor, or other resources to fulfill the contract that were not reflected in the price of the contract. That is, **companies only capitalize costs that are direct, incremental, and recoverable** (assuming that the contract period is more than one year). **Illustration 18.31** provides an example of costs capitalized to fulfill a contract.

As a practical expedient, a company recognizes the incremental costs of obtaining a contract as an expense when incurred if the amortization period of the asset that the company otherwise would have recognized is one year or less.

[15]Another approach to account for a contract modification is to report the information in a cumulative catch-up manner. In other words, assuming that these new products are part of the original contract, companies adjust the revenue account to reflect the cumulative effect for periods prior to when the modification occurred. An example of a catch-up situation is a long-term construction contract, which is discussed in more detail in Appendix 18A. Use of the prospective approach avoids the complexity of opening up the accounting for previously satisfied performance obligations. However, it ignores any adjustments to revenue that have already been recognized. [19] *For homework purposes, unless instructed otherwise, use the prospective approach for modifications that do not result in a separate performance obligation.* Expanded discussion of the prospective and cumulative catch-up (retrospective) approaches to accounting changes is provided in Chapter 22.

ILLUSTRATION 18.31

Recognition—Contract Costs

Contract Costs

Facts: Rock Integrators enters into a contract to operate Dello Company's information technology data center for 5 years. Rock Integrators incurs selling commission costs of $10,000 to obtain the contract. Before performing the services, Rock Integrators designs and builds a technology platform that interfaces with Dello's systems. That platform is not transferred to Dello. Dello promises to pay a fixed fee of $20,000 per month. Rock Integrators incurs the following additional costs: design services for the platform $40,000, hardware for the platform $120,000, software $90,000, and testing of data center $100,000.

***Question:* What are Rock Integrators' costs for fulfilling the contract to Dello Company?**

Solution: The $10,000 selling commission cost related to obtaining the contract is recognized as an asset. The design services cost of $40,000 and the hardware for the platform of $120,000 are also capitalized. As the technology platform is independent of the contract, the pattern of amortization of this platform may not be related to the terms of the contract. The testing costs are expensed as incurred; in general, these costs are not recoverable.

Collectibility

As indicated earlier, if it is probable that the transaction price will not be collected, this is an indication that the parties are not committed to their obligations. As a result, one of the criteria for the existence of a contract is not met and therefore revenue is not recognized.

Any time a company sells a product or performs a service on account, a collectibility issue occurs. **Collectibility** refers to a customer's credit risk, that is, the risk that a customer will be unable to pay the amount of consideration in accordance with the contract. Under the revenue guidance—as long as a contract exists (it is probable that the customer will pay)—the amount recognized as revenue is not adjusted for customer credit risk.

Thus, companies report the revenue gross (without consideration of credit risk) and then present an allowance for any impairment due to bad debts (recognized initially and subsequently in accordance with the respective bad debt guidance). An impairment related to bad debts is reported as an operating expense in the income statement. As a result, whether a company will get paid for satisfying a performance obligation is not a consideration in determining revenue recognition. **[20]**

Disclosure

The disclosure requirements for revenue recognition are designed to help financial statement users understand the nature, amount, timing, and uncertainty of revenue and cash flows arising from contracts with customers. To achieve that objective, companies disclose qualitative and quantitative information about all of the following:

- ***Contracts with customers.*** These disclosures include the disaggregation of revenue, presentation of opening and closing balances in contract assets and contract liabilities, and significant information related to their performance obligations.
- ***Significant judgments.*** These disclosures include judgments and changes in these judgments that affect the determination of the transaction price, the allocation of the transaction price, and the determination of the timing of revenue.
- ***Assets recognized from costs incurred to fulfill a contract.*** These disclosures include the closing balances of assets recognized to obtain or fulfill a contract, the amount of amortization recognized, and the method used for amortization.

To implement these requirements and meet the disclosure objectives, companies provide a range of disclosures, as summarized in **Illustration 18.32**. **[21]**[16]

[16]See *PricewaterhouseCoopers Dataline 2013–2014.*

ILLUSTRATION 18.32 Revenue Disclosures

Disclosure Type	Requirements
Disaggregation of revenue	Disclose disaggregated revenue information in categories that depict how the nature, amount, timing, and uncertainty of revenue and cash flows are affected by economic factors. Reconcile disaggregated revenue to revenue for reportable segments.
Reconciliation of contract balances	Disclose opening and closing balances of contract assets (e.g., unbilled receivables) and liabilities (e.g., deferred revenue) and provide a qualitative description of significant changes in these amounts. Disclose the amount of revenue recognized in the current period relating to performance obligations satisfied in a prior period (e.g., from contracts with variable consideration). Disclose the opening and closing balances of trade receivables if not presented elsewhere.
Remaining performance obligations	Disclose the amount of the transaction price allocated to remaining performance obligations not subject to significant revenue reversal. Provide a narrative discussion of potential additional revenue in constrained arrangements.
Costs to obtain or fulfill contracts	Disclose the closing balances of capitalized costs to obtain and fulfill a contract and the amount of amortization in the period. Disclose the method used to determine amortization for each reporting period.
Other qualitative disclosures	Disclose significant judgments and changes in judgments that affect the amount and timing of revenue from contracts with customers. Disclose how management determines the minimum amount of revenue not subject to the variable consideration constraint.

Evolving Issue Revenue: "It's Like an Octopus"

As you have learned in this chapter, the revenue recognition standard provides a comprehensive and general framework for recognizing revenue and should result in improvements in the reporting of revenue. However, these new rules reflect significant change relative to the prior revenue guidance. As one senior accountant noted, "Revenue touches everything . . . It's like an octopus . . . It has tentacles all over the income statement." The new rules—to be adopted by most companies in 2018—are expected to create implementation challenges, especially for companies that:

- Currently recognize revenue using industry-specific guidance.
- Have customer contracts with diverse terms and conditions.
- Have arrangements with goods or services delivered over long periods.
- Have systems or processes that do not easily provide new data requirements.

Among the companies that are likely to experience significant changes are those in the telecommunications, aerospace, construction, asset management, real estate, and software industries.

In the months after issuance of the new guidance, the FASB and IASB issued documents that addressed common questions posed by these industries. In addition, the Boards created a joint transition resource group that is responsible for informing the FASB and IASB about interpretive issues that could arise as companies, institutions, and other organizations implement the revenue recognition standard. The transition group is comprised of specialists representing financial statement preparers, auditors, regulators, users, and other stakeholders, as well as members of the FASB and IASB.

The resource group solicits, analyzes, and discusses stakeholder issues that apply to common transactions that could reasonably create diversity in practice. In addition to providing a forum to discuss the application of the requirements, the transition group provides information that will help the Boards determine what, if any, action will be needed to resolve that diversity. The group itself will not issue guidance.

As noted by Russ Golden, chairman of the FASB:

> "Effective implementation of the revenue recognition standard is critical to its success in providing financial statement users with the information they need to make the right decisions about how to allocate their capital. The Boards are committed to ensuring a smooth transition to the new standard, and the transition resource group is an important tool for determining any areas that will need additional guidance before the standard becomes effective."

Thus, change is necessary to achieve improvements in revenue recognition accounting. Hopefully, the extended transition period and expanded support by the transition group will make the change a bit less painful.

Sources: *Executive Accounting Update:* "Changes to Revenue Recognition," KPMG (January 22, 2014); *Defining Issues No. 14-9*: "Implementing the Forthcoming Revenue Recognition Standard," KPMG (February 2014); and E. Chasen, "Revenue Recognition Accounting Changes Could Have Long Tentacles," *Wall Street Journal* (November 16, 2015).

APPENDIX **18A**

Long-Term Construction Contracts

LEARNING OBJECTIVE *5

Apply the percentage-of-completion method for long-term contracts.

Revenue Recognition over Time

For the most part, companies recognize revenue at the point of sale because that is when the performance obligation is satisfied. However, as indicated in the chapter, under certain circumstances companies recognize revenue over time. The most notable context in which revenue is recognized over time is long-term construction contract accounting.

Long-term contracts frequently provide that the seller (builder) may bill the purchaser at intervals, as it reaches various points in the project. Examples of long-term contracts are construction-type contracts, development of military and commercial aircraft, weapons-delivery systems, and space exploration hardware. When the project consists of separable units, such as a group of buildings or miles of roadway, contract provisions may provide for delivery in installments. In that case, the seller would bill the buyer and transfer title at stated stages of completion, such as the completion of each building unit or every 10 miles of road. The accounting records should record sales when installments are "delivered."

A company satisfies a performance obligation and recognizes revenue over time if at least one of the following three criteria is met: [22]

1. The customer simultaneously receives and consumes the benefits of the seller's performance as the seller performs.
2. The company's performance creates or enhances an asset (for example, work in process) that the customer controls as the asset is created or enhanced; or
3. The company's performance does not create an asset with an alternative use. For example, the asset cannot be used by another customer. In addition to this alternative use element, at least *one* of the following criteria must be met:
   a. Another company would not need to substantially re-perform the work the company has completed to date if that other company were to fulfill the remaining obligation to the customer.
   b. The company has a right to payment for its performance completed to date, and it expects to fulfill the contract as promised.[17]

Therefore, if criterion 1, 2, or 3 is met, then a company recognizes revenue over time *if* **it can reasonably estimate its progress toward satisfaction of the performance obligations**. That is, it recognizes revenues and gross profits each period based upon the progress of the construction—referred to as the **percentage-of-completion method**. The company accumulates construction costs plus gross profit recognized to date in an inventory account (Construction in Process), and it accumulates progress billings in a contra inventory account (Billings on Construction in Process).

[17]The right to payment for performance completed to date does not need to be for a fixed amount. However, the company must be entitled to an amount that would compensate the company for performance completed to date (even if the customer can terminate the contract for reasons other than the company's failure to perform as promised). Compensation for performance completed to date includes payment that approximates the selling price of the goods or services transferred to date (for example, recovery of the company's costs plus a reasonable profit margin).

The rationale for using percentage-of-completion accounting is that under most of these contracts the buyer and seller have enforceable rights. The buyer has the legal right to require specific performance on the contract. The seller has the right to require progress payments that provide evidence of the buyer's ownership interest. As a result, a continuous sale occurs as the work progresses. Companies should recognize revenue according to that progression.

Alternatively, if the criteria for recognition over time are not met (e.g., the company does not have a right to payment for work completed to date), the company recognizes revenues and gross profit at a point in time, that is, when the contract is completed. This approach is referred to as the **completed-contract method**.[18] The company accumulates construction costs in an inventory account (Construction in Process), and it accumulates progress billings in a contra inventory account (Billings on Construction in Process).

Percentage-of-Completion Method

The **percentage-of-completion method** recognizes revenues, costs, and gross profit as a company makes progress toward completion on a long-term contract. To defer recognition of these items until completion of the entire contract is to misrepresent the efforts (costs) and accomplishments (revenues) of the accounting periods during the contract. In order to apply the percentage-of-completion method, a company must have some basis or standard for measuring the progress toward completion at particular interim dates.

Measuring the Progress Toward Completion

As one practicing accountant wrote, "The big problem in applying the percentage-of-completion method . . . has to do with the ability to make reasonably accurate estimates of completion and the final gross profit." Companies use various methods to determine the **extent of progress toward completion**. The most common are the *cost-to-cost* and *units-of-delivery* methods.

As indicated in the chapter, the objective of all these methods is to measure the extent of progress in terms of costs, units, or value added. Companies identify the various measures (costs incurred, labor hours worked, tons produced, floors completed, etc.) and classify them as input or output measures. **Input measures** (costs incurred, labor hours worked) are efforts devoted to a contract. **Output measures** (with units of delivery measured as tons produced, floors of a building completed, miles of a highway completed) track results. Neither measure is universally applicable to all long-term projects. Their use requires the exercise of judgment and careful tailoring to the circumstances.

Both input and output measures have disadvantages. The input measure is based on an established relationship between a unit of input and productivity. If inefficiencies cause the productivity relationship to change, inaccurate measurements result. Another potential problem is front-end loading, in which significant upfront costs result in higher estimates of completion. To avoid this problem, companies should disregard some early-stage construction costs—for example, costs of uninstalled materials or costs of subcontracts not yet performed—if they do not relate to contract performance.

Similarly, output measures can produce inaccurate results if the units used are not comparable in time, effort, or cost to complete. For example, using floors (stories) completed can be deceiving. Completing the first floor of an eight-story building may require more than one-eighth the total cost because of the substructure and foundation construction.

The most popular input measure used to determine the progress toward completion is the **cost-to-cost basis**. Under this basis, a company like **Halliburton** measures the percentage of completion by comparing costs incurred to date with the most recent estimate of the total costs required to complete the contract. **Illustration 18A.1** shows the formula for the cost-to-cost basis.

[18]*Accounting Trends and Techniques* reports that of the 83 of its 500 sample companies that referred to long-term construction contracts, 75 used the percentage-of-completion method and 8 used the completed-contract method. In some circumstances (e.g., in the early stages of a contract), a company may not be able to reasonably measure the outcome of a performance obligation, but it expects to recover the costs incurred in satisfying the performance obligation. In these situations, companies recognize revenue only to the extent of the costs incurred until such time that they can reasonably measure the outcome of the performance obligation. This is referred to as the **cost-recovery method.** [23]

ILLUSTRATION 18A.1

Formula for Percentage-of-Completion, Cost-to-Cost Basis

$$\frac{\text{Costs Incurred to Date}}{\text{Most Recent Estimate of Total Costs}} = \text{Percent Complete}$$

Once Halliburton knows the percentage that costs incurred bear to total estimated costs, it applies that percentage to the total revenue or the estimated total gross profit on the contract. The resulting amount is the revenue or the gross profit to be recognized to date. Illustration 18A.2 shows this computation.

ILLUSTRATION 18A.2

Formula for Total Revenue (or Gross Profit) to Be Recognized to Date

Percent Complete	×	Estimated Total Revenue (or Gross Profit)	=	Revenue (or Gross Profit) to Be Recognized to Date

To find the amounts of revenue and gross profit recognized each period, Halliburton subtracts total revenue or gross profit recognized in prior periods, as shown in Illustration 18A.3.

ILLUSTRATION 18A.3

Formula for Amount of Current-Period Revenue (or Gross Profit) Cost-to-Cost Basis

Revenue (or Gross Profit) to Be Recognized to Date	−	Revenue (or Gross Profit) Recognized in Prior Periods	=	Current-Period Revenue (or Gross Profit)

Because **the cost-to-cost method is widely used** (without excluding other bases for measuring progress toward completion), we have adopted it for use in our examples.

Example of Percentage-of-Completion Method—Cost-to-Cost Basis

To illustrate the percentage-of-completion method, assume that Hardhat Construction Company has a contract to construct a $4,500,000 bridge at an estimated cost of $4,000,000. The contract is to start in July 2020, and the bridge is to be completed in October 2022. The following data pertain to the construction period. (Note that by the end of 2021, Hardhat has revised the estimated total cost from $4,000,000 to $4,050,000.)

	2020	2021	2022
Costs to date	$1,000,000	$2,916,000	$4,050,000
Estimated costs to complete	3,000,000	1,134,000	—
Progress billings during the year	900,000	2,400,000	1,200,000
Cash collected during the year	750,000	1,750,000	2,000,000

Hardhat would compute the percent complete as shown in Illustration 18A.4.

ILLUSTRATION 18A.4

Application of Percentage-of-Completion Method, Cost-to-Cost Basis

	2020	2021	2022
Contract price	$4,500,000	$4,500,000	$4,500,000
Less estimated cost:			
Costs to date	1,000,000	2,916,000	4,050,000
Estimated costs to complete	3,000,000	1,134,000	—
Estimated total costs	4,000,000	4,050,000	4,050,000
Estimated total gross profit	$ 500,000	$ 450,000	$ 450,000
Percent complete	25%	72%	100%
	$\left(\frac{\$1,000,000}{\$4,000,000}\right)$	$\left(\frac{\$2,916,000}{\$4,050,000}\right)$	$\left(\frac{\$4,050,000}{\$4,050,000}\right)$

On the basis of the data above, Hardhat would make the entries shown in Illustration 18A.5 to record (1) the costs of construction, (2) progress billings, and (3) collections. These entries appear as summaries of the many transactions that would be entered individually as they occur during the year.

ILLUSTRATION 18A.5
Journal Entries—Percentage-of-Completion Method, Cost-to-Cost Basis

	2020		2021		2022	
To record costs of construction:						
Construction in Process	1,000,000		1,916,000		1,134,000	
Materials, Cash, Payables, etc.		1,000,000		1,916,000		1,134,000
To record progress billings:						
Accounts Receivable	900,000		2,400,000		1,200,000	
Billings on Construction in Process		900,000		2,400,000		1,200,000
To record collections:						
Cash	750,000		1,750,000		2,000,000	
Accounts Receivable		750,000		1,750,000		2,000,000

In this example, the costs incurred to date are a measure of the extent of progress toward completion. To determine this, Hardhat evaluates the costs incurred to date as a proportion of the estimated total costs to be incurred on the project. The estimated revenue and gross profit that Hardhat will recognize for each year are calculated as shown in **Illustration 18A.6**.

ILLUSTRATION 18A.6
Percentage-of-Completion Revenue, Costs, and Gross Profit by Year

	To Date	Recognized in Prior Years	Recognized in Current Year
2020			
Revenues ($4,500,000 × .25)	$1,125,000		$1,125,000
Costs	1,000,000		1,000,000
Gross profit	$ 125,000		$ 125,000
2021			
Revenues ($4,500,000 × .72)	$3,240,000	$1,125,000	$2,115,000
Costs	2,916,000	1,000,000	1,916,000
Gross profit	$ 324,000	$ 125,000	$ 199,000
2022			
Revenues ($4,500,000 × 1.00)	$4,500,000	$3,240,000	$1,260,000
Costs	4,050,000	2,916,000	1,134,000
Gross profit	$ 450,000	$ 324,000	$ 126,000

Illustration 18A.7 shows Hardhat's entries to recognize revenue and gross profit each year and to record completion and final approval of the contract.

ILLUSTRATION 18A.7
Journal Entries to Recognize Revenue and Gross Profit and to Record Contract Completion—Percentage-of-Completion Method, Cost-to-Cost Basis

	2020		2021		2022	
To recognize revenue and gross profit:						
Construction in Process (gross profit)	125,000		199,000		126,000	
Construction Expenses	1,000,000		1,916,000		1,134,000	
Revenue from Long-Term Contracts		1,125,000		2,115,000		1,260,000
To record completion of the contract:						
Billings on Construction in Process					4,500,000	
Construction in Process						4,500,000

Note that **Hardhat debits gross profit (as computed in Illustration 18A.6) to Construction in Process**. Similarly, it credits Revenue from Long-Term Contracts for the amounts computed. Hardhat then debits the difference between the amounts recognized each year for revenue and gross profit to a nominal account, Construction Expenses (similar to Cost of Goods Sold in a manufacturing company). It reports that amount in the income statement as the actual cost of construction incurred in that period. For example, in 2020 Hardhat uses the actual costs of $1,000,000 to compute both the gross profit of $125,000 and the percent complete (25 percent).

Hardhat continues to accumulate costs in the Construction in Process account, in order to maintain a record of total costs incurred (plus recognized gross profit) to date. Although theoretically a series of "sales" takes place using the percentage-of-completion method, the selling company cannot remove the inventory cost until the construction is completed and transferred to the new owner. Hardhat's Construction in Process account for the bridge would include the summarized entries shown in **Illustration 18A.8** over the term of the construction project.

ILLUSTRATION 18A.8

Content of Construction in Process Account—Percentage-of-Completion Method

Construction in Process				
2020 construction costs	$1,000,000	12/31/22	To close completed project	$4,500,000
2020 recognized gross profit	125,000			
2021 construction costs	1,916,000			
2021 recognized gross profit	199,000			
2022 construction costs	1,134,000			
2022 recognized gross profit	126,000			
Total	$4,500,000	Total		$4,500,000

Recall that the Hardhat Construction Company example contained a **change in estimated costs**: In the second year, 2021, it increased the estimated total costs from $4,000,000 to $4,050,000. The change in estimate is accounted for in a **cumulative catch-up manner**, as indicated in the chapter. This is done by first adjusting the percent completed to the new estimate of total costs. Next, Hardhat deducts the amount of revenues and gross profit recognized in prior periods from revenues and gross profit computed for progress to date. That is, it accounts for the change in estimate in the period of change. That way, the balance sheet at the end of the period of change and the accounting in subsequent periods are as they would have been if the revised estimate had been the original estimate.

Financial Statement Presentation—Percentage-of-Completion

Generally, when a company records a receivable from a sale, it reduces the Inventory account. Under the percentage-of-completion method, however, the company continues to carry both the receivable and the inventory. Subtracting the balance in the **Billings account** from Construction in Process avoids double-counting the inventory. During the life of the contract, Hardhat reports in the balance sheet the difference between the Construction in Process and the Billings on Construction in Process accounts. If that amount is a debit, Hardhat reports it **as a current asset**; if it is a credit, it reports it **as a current liability**.

At times, the costs incurred plus the gross profit recognized to date (the balance in Construction in Process) exceed the billings. In that case, Hardhat reports this excess as a current asset entitled "Costs and recognized profit in excess of billings." Hardhat can at any time calculate the unbilled portion of revenue recognized to date by subtracting the billings to date from the revenue recognized to date, as illustrated for 2020 for Hardhat Construction in **Illustration 18A.9**.

ILLUSTRATION 18A.9

Computation of Unbilled Contract Price at 12/31/20

Contract revenue recognized to date: $\$4{,}500{,}000 \times \frac{\$1{,}000{,}000}{\$4{,}000{,}000}$	$1,125,000
Billings to date	(900,000)
Unbilled revenue	$ 225,000

At other times, the billings exceed costs incurred and gross profit to date. In that case, Hardhat reports this excess as a current liability entitled "Billings in excess of costs and recognized profit."

What happens, as is usually the case, when companies have more than one project going at a time? When a company has a number of projects, costs exceed billings on some contracts and billings exceed costs on others. In such a case, the company segregates the contracts. The asset side includes only those contracts on which costs and recognized profit exceed billings. The liability side includes only those on which billings exceed costs and recognized profit. Separate disclosures of the dollar volume of billings and costs are preferable to a summary presentation of the net difference.

Using data from the bridge example, Hardhat Construction Company would report the status and results of its long-term construction activities in 2020 under the percentage-of-completion method as shown in **Illustration 18A.10**.

ILLUSTRATION 18A.10
Financial Statement Presentation—Percentage-of-Completion Method (2020)

Hardhat Construction Company

Income Statement (from Illustration 18A.6)		2020
Revenue from long-term contracts		$1,125,000
Costs of construction		1,000,000
Gross profit		$ 125,000

Balance Sheet (12/31)		2020
Current assets		
Accounts receivable ($900,000 – $750,000)		$ 150,000
Inventory		
Construction in process	$1,125,000	
Less: Billings	900,000	
Costs and recognized profit in excess of billings		225,000

Illustration 18A.11 shows its financial statement presentation in 2021.

ILLUSTRATION 18A.11
Financial Statement Presentation—Percentage-of-Completion Method (2021)

Hardhat Construction Company

Income Statement (from Illustration 18A.6)		2021
Revenue from long-term contracts		$2,115,000
Costs of construction		1,916,000
Gross profit		$ 199,000

Balance Sheet (12/31)		
Current assets		
Accounts receivable ($150,000 + $2,400,000 – $1,750,000)		$ 800,000
Current liabilities		
Billings	$3,300,000	
Less: Construction in process	3,240,000	
Billings in excess of costs and recognized profit		60,000

In 2022, as shown in **Illustration 18A.12**, Hardhat's financial statements only include an income statement because the bridge project was completed and settled.

ILLUSTRATION 18A.12
Financial Statement Presentation—Percentage-of-Completion Method (2022)

Hardhat Construction Company

Income Statement (from Illustration 18A.6)	2022
Revenue from long-term contracts	$1,260,000
Costs of construction	1,134,000
Gross profit	$ 126,000

In addition, Illustration 18A.13 shows the information that Hardhat should disclose in each year.

ILLUSTRATION 18A.13

Percentage-of-Completion Method Note Disclosure

Note 1. Summary of significant accounting policies.
Long-Term Construction Contracts. The company recognizes revenues and reports profits from long-term construction contracts, its principal business, under the percentage-of-completion method of accounting. These contracts generally extend for periods in excess of one year. The amounts of revenues and profits recognized each year are based on the ratio of costs incurred to the total estimated costs. Costs included in construction in process include direct materials, direct labor, and project-related overhead. Corporate general and administrative expenses are charged to the periods as incurred and are not allocated to construction contracts.

Completed-Contract Method

LEARNING OBJECTIVE *6

Apply the completed-contract method for long-term contracts.

Under the completed-contract method, companies recognize revenue and gross profit only at point of sale—that is, when the contract is completed. Under this method, companies accumulate costs of long-term contracts in process, but they make no interim charges or credits to income statement accounts for revenues, costs, or gross profit.

The principal advantage of the completed-contract method is that reported revenue reflects final results rather than *estimates* of unperformed work. Its major disadvantage is that it does not reflect current performance when the period of a contract extends into more than one accounting period. Although operations may be fairly uniform during the period of the contract, the company will not report revenue until the year of completion, creating a distortion of earnings.

Under the completed-contract method, the company would make the same **annual entries** to record costs of construction, progress billings, and collections from customers as those illustrated under the percentage-of-completion method (see Illustration 18A.5). The significant difference is that the company **would not make entries to recognize revenue and gross profit**.

For example, under the completed-contract method for the bridge project previously illustrated, Hardhat Construction Company would make the following entries in 2022 to recognize revenue and costs and to close out the inventory and billing accounts.

Billings on Construction in Process	4,500,000	
Revenue from Long-Term Contracts		4,500,000
Costs of Construction	4,050,000	
Construction in Process		4,050,000

Illustration 18A.14 compares the amount of gross profit that Hardhat Construction Company would recognize for the bridge project under the two revenue recognition methods.

ILLUSTRATION 18A.14

Comparison of Gross Profit Recognized under Different Methods

	Percentage-of-Completion	Completed-Contract
2020	$125,000	$ 0
2021	199,000	0
2022	126,000	450,000

Under the completed-contract method, Hardhat Construction would report its long-term construction activities as shown in Illustration 18A.15.

ILLUSTRATION 18A.15

Financial Statement Presentation—Completed-Contract Method

Hardhat Construction Company		2020	2021	2022
Income Statement				
Revenue from long-term contracts		—	—	$4,500,000
Costs of construction		—	—	4,050,000
Gross profit		—	—	$ 450,000
Balance Sheet (12/31)				
Current assets				
Accounts receivable		$150,000	$800,000	$ -0-
Inventory				
Construction in process	$1,000,000			
Less: Billings	900,000			
Costs in excess of billings		100,000		-0-
Current liabilities				
Billings ($3,300,000) in excess of costs ($2,916,000)			384,000	-0-

Note 1. Summary of significant accounting policies.
Long-Term Construction Contracts. The company recognizes revenues and reports profits from long-term construction contracts, its principal business, under the completed-contract method. These contracts generally extend for periods in excess of one year. Contract costs and billings are accumulated during the periods of construction, but no revenues or profits are recognized until completion of the contract. Costs included in construction in process include direct material, direct labor, and project-related overhead. Corporate general and administrative expenses are charged to the periods as incurred.

Long-Term Contract Losses

LEARNING OBJECTIVE *7

Identify the proper accounting for losses on long-term contracts.

Two types of losses can become evident under long-term contracts:

1. ***Loss in the current period on a profitable contract.*** This condition arises when, during construction, there is a significant increase in the estimated total contract costs but the increase does not eliminate all profit on the contract. Under the percentage-of-completion method only, the estimated cost increase requires a current-period adjustment of excess gross profit recognized on the project in prior periods. The company records this adjustment as a loss in the current period because it is a change in accounting estimate (discussed in Chapter 22).
2. ***Loss on an unprofitable contract.*** Cost estimates at the end of the current period may indicate that a loss will result on completion of the *entire* contract. Under both the percentage-of-completion and the completed-contract methods, the company must recognize in the current period the entire expected contract loss.

The treatment described for unprofitable contracts is consistent with the accounting custom of anticipating foreseeable losses to avoid overstatement of current and future income (conservatism). [24]

Loss in Current Period

To illustrate a loss in the current period on a contract expected to be profitable upon completion, we'll continue with the Hardhat Construction Company bridge project. Assume that on December 31, 2021, Hardhat estimates the costs to complete the bridge contract at $1,468,962 instead of $1,134,000. Assuming all other data are the same as before, Hardhat would compute the percent complete and recognize the loss as shown in Illustration 18A.16. Compare these computations with those for 2021 in Illustration 18A.4. The "percent complete" has dropped, from 72 percent to 66½ percent, due to the increase in estimated future costs to complete the contract.

ILLUSTRATION 18A.16

Computation of Recognizable Loss, 2021—Loss in Current Period

Cost to date (12/31/21)	$2,916,000
Estimated costs to complete (revised)	1,468,962
Estimated total costs	$4,384,962
Percent complete ($2,916,000 ÷ $4,384,962)	66½%
Revenue recognized in 2021 ($4,500,000 × .665) − $1,125,000	$1,867,500
Costs incurred in 2021	1,916,000
Loss recognized in 2021	$ (48,500)

The 2021 loss of $48,500 is a cumulative adjustment of the "excessive" gross profit recognized on the contract in 2020. Instead of restating the prior period, the company absorbs the prior period misstatement entirely in the current period. In this illustration, the adjustment was large enough to result in recognition of a loss.

Hardhat Construction would record the loss in 2021 as follows.

Construction Expenses	1,916,000	
Construction in Process (loss)		48,500
Revenue from Long-Term Contracts		1,867,500

Hardhat will report the loss of $48,500 on the 2021 income statement as the difference between the reported revenue of $1,867,500 and the costs of $1,916,000.[19] **Under the completed-contract method, the company does not recognize a loss in 2021.** Why not? Because the company still expects the contract **to result in a profit**, to be recognized in the year of completion.

Loss on an Unprofitable Contract

To illustrate the accounting for an **overall loss on a long-term contract**, assume that at December 31, 2021, Hardhat Construction Company estimates the costs to complete the bridge contract at $1,640,250 instead of $1,134,000. Revised estimates for the bridge contract are as follows.

	2020 Original Estimates	2021 Revised Estimates
Contract price	$4,500,000	$4,500,000
Estimated total cost	4,000,000	4,556,250*
Estimated gross profit	$ 500,000	
Estimated loss		$ (56,250)

*($2,916,000 + $1,640,250)

Under the percentage-of-completion method, Hardhat recognized $125,000 of gross profit in 2020 (see Illustration 18A.6). This amount must be offset in 2021 because it is no longer expected to be realized. In addition, since losses must be recognized as soon as estimable, the company must recognize the total estimated loss of $56,250 in 2021. Therefore, Hardhat must recognize a total loss of $181,250 ($125,000 + $56,250) in 2021.

[19]In 2022, Hardhat Construction will recognize the remaining 33½ percent of the revenue ($1,507,500), with costs of $1,468,962 as expected, and will report a gross profit of $38,538. The total gross profit over the three years of the contract would be $115,038 [$125,000 (2020) − $48,500 (2021) + $38,538 (2022)]. This amount is the difference between the total contract revenue of $4,500,000 and the total contract costs of $4,384,962.

Illustration 18A.17 shows Hardhat's computation of the revenue to be recognized in 2021.

ILLUSTRATION 18A.17

Computation of Revenue Recognizable, 2021—Unprofitable Contract

Revenue recognized in 2021:		
Contract price		$4,500,000
Percent complete		× .64*
Revenue recognizable to date		2,880,000
Less: Revenue recognized prior to 2021		1,125,000
Revenue recognized in 2021		$1,755,000
*Cost to date (12/31/21)	$2,916,000	
Estimated cost to complete	1,640,250	
Estimated total costs	$4,556,250	
Percent complete: $2,916,000 ÷ $4,556,250 = 64%		

To compute the construction costs to be expensed in 2021, Hardhat adds the total loss to be recognized in 2021 ($125,000 + $56,250) to the revenue to be recognized in 2021. Illustration 18A.18 shows this computation.

ILLUSTRATION 18A.18

Computation of Construction Expense, 2021—Unprofitable Contract

Revenue recognized in 2021 (computed above)		$1,755,000
Total loss recognized in 2021:		
Reversal of 2020 gross profit	$125,000	
Total estimated loss on the contract	56,250	181,250
Construction cost expensed in 2021		$1,936,250

Hardhat Construction would record the long-term contract revenues, expenses, and loss in 2021 as follows.

Construction Expenses	1,936,250	
Construction in Process (loss)		181,250
Revenue from Long-Term Contracts		1,755,000

At the end of 2021, Construction in Process has a balance of $2,859,750 as shown in Illustration 18A.19.[20]

ILLUSTRATION 18A.19

Content of Construction in Process Account at End of 2021—Unprofitable Contract

Construction in Process			
2020 Construction costs	1,000,000		
2020 Recognized gross profit	125,000		
2021 Construction costs	1,916,000	2021 Recognized loss	181,250
Balance	**2,859,750**		

Under the completed-contract method, Hardhat also would recognize the contract loss of $56,250 through the following entry in 2021 (the year in which the loss first became evident).

Loss from Long-Term Contracts	56,250	
Construction in Process (loss)		56,250

Just as the Billings account balance cannot exceed the contract price, neither can the balance in Construction in Process exceed the contract price. In circumstances where the Construction in Process balance exceeds the billings, the company can deduct the recognized loss from such accumulated costs on the balance sheet. That is, under both the percentage-of-completion and the completed-contract methods, the provision for the loss (the credit) may be combined

[20]If the costs in 2022 are $1,640,250 as projected, at the end of 2022 the Construction in Process account will have a balance of $1,640,250 + $2,859,750, or $4,500,000, equal to the contract price. When the company matches the revenue remaining to be recognized in 2022 of $1,620,000 [$4,500,000 (total contract price) − $1,125,000 (2020) − $1,755,000 (2021)] with the construction expense to be recognized in 2022 of $1,620,000 [total costs of $4,556,250 less the total costs recognized in prior years of $2,936,250 (2020, $1,000,000; 2021, $1,936,250)], a zero profit results. Thus, the total loss has been recognized in 2021, the year in which it first became evident.

with Construction in Process, thereby reducing the inventory balance. In those circumstances, however (as in the 2021 example above), where the billings exceed the accumulated costs, Hardhat must report separately on the balance sheet, as a current liability, the amount of the estimated loss. That is, under both the percentage-of-completion and the completed-contract methods, Hardhat would take the $56,250 loss, as estimated in 2021, from the Construction in Process account and report it separately as a current liability titled "Estimated liability from long-term contracts."

APPENDIX 18B Revenue Recognition for Franchises

LEARNING OBJECTIVE *8

Explain revenue recognition for franchises.

In this appendix, we cover a common yet unique type of business transaction—franchises. As indicated throughout this chapter, companies recognize revenue when performance obligations in a revenue arrangement are satisfied. Franchises represent a challenging area because a variety of performance obligations may exist in a given franchise agreement. As a result, companies must carefully analyze franchise agreements to identify the separate performance obligations, determine when performance obligations are satisfied, and, therefore, when revenue should be recognized.[21]

Four types of franchising arrangements have evolved: (1) manufacturer-retailer, (2) manufacturer-wholesaler, (3) service sponsor-retailer, and (4) wholesaler-retailer. The fastest-growing category of franchising, and the one that has given rise to accounting challenges, is the third category, **service sponsor-retailer**. Included in this category are such industries and businesses as:

- Soft ice cream/frozen yogurt stores (**Tastee Freez, TCBY, Dairy Queen**).
- Food drive-ins (**McDonald's, KFC, Burger King**).
- Restaurants (**TGI Friday's, Pizza Hut, Denny's**).
- Motels (**Holiday Inn, Marriott, Best Western**).
- Auto rentals (**Avis, Hertz, National**).
- Others (**H & R Block, Meineke Mufflers, 7-Eleven Stores, Kelly Services**).

Franchise companies derive their revenue from one or both of two sources: (1) from the sale of initial franchises and related assets or services, and (2) from continuing fees based on the operations of franchises. The franchisor (the party who grants business rights under the franchise) normally provides the franchisee (the party who operates the franchised business) with the following services.

1. Assistance in site selection: (a) analyzing location and (b) negotiating lease.
2. Evaluation of potential income.
3. Supervision of construction activity: (a) obtaining financing, (b) designing building, and (c) supervising contractor while building.
4. Assistance in the acquisition of signs, fixtures, and equipment.

[21]Franchises are an example of a license or similar rights to use intellectual property. In such arrangements, a company grants a customer the right to use, but not own, intellectual property of the company. Other examples of intellectual property include (1) software and technology; (2) motion pictures, music, and other forms of media and entertainment; and (3) patents, trademarks, and copyrights. Generally, revenue is recognized in these situations when the customer obtains control of the rights. In some cases, a license is a promise to provide a right, which transfers to the customer at a point in time. In other cases, a license is a promise to provide access to an entity's intellectual property, which transfers benefits to the customer over time. [25]

5. Bookkeeping and advisory services: (a) setting up franchisee's records; (b) advising on income, real estate, and other taxes; and (c) advising on local regulations of the franchisee's business.
6. Employee and management training.
7. Quality control.
8. Advertising and promotion.

In the past, it was standard practice for franchisors to recognize the entire franchise fee at the date of sale, whether the fee was received then or was collectible over a long period of time. Frequently, franchisors recorded the entire amount as revenue in the year of sale, even though many of the services were yet to be performed and uncertainty existed regarding the collection of the entire fee. (In effect, the franchisors were counting their fried chickens before they were hatched.) However, a **franchise agreement** may provide for refunds to the franchisee if certain conditions are not met, and franchise fee profit can be reduced sharply by future costs of obligations and services to be rendered by the franchisor.

Franchise Accounting

As indicated, the performance obligations in a franchise arrangement relate to the right to open a business, use of the trade name or other intellectual property of the franchisor, and continuing services, such as marketing help, training, and in some cases supplying inventory and inventory management. Franchisors commonly charge an initial franchise fee as well as continuing franchise fees. The **initial franchise fee** is payment for establishing the franchise relationship and providing some initial services. **Continuing franchise fees** are received in return for the continuing rights granted by the franchise agreement and for providing such services as management training, advertising and promotion, legal assistance, and other support. **Illustration 18B.1** provides an example of a franchise arrangement.

ILLUSTRATION 18B.1
Recognition—Franchise Arrangement

Franchise

Facts: Tum's Pizza Inc. enters into a franchise agreement on December 31, 2020, giving Food Fight Corp. the right to operate as a franchisee of Tum's Pizza for 5 years. Tum's charges Food Fight an initial franchise fee of $50,000 for the right to operate as a franchisee. Of this amount, $20,000 is payable when Food Fight signs the agreement, and the note balance is payable in five annual payments of $6,000 each on December 31. As part of the arrangement, Tum's helps locate the site, negotiate the lease or purchase of the site, supervise the construction activity, and provide employee training and the equipment necessary to be a distributor of its products. Similar training services and equipment are sold separately.

Food Fight also promises to pay ongoing royalty payments of 1% of its annual sales (payable each January 31 of the following year) and is obliged to purchase products from Tum's at its current standalone selling prices at the time of purchase. The credit rating of Food Fight indicates that money can be borrowed at 8%. The present value of an ordinary annuity of five annual receipts of $6,000 each discounted at 8% is $23,957. The discount of $6,043 represents the interest revenue to be accrued by Tum's over the payment period.

***Question:* What are the performance obligations in this arrangement and the point in time at which the performance obligations for Tum's are satisfied and revenue is recognized?**

Solution: To identify the performance obligations, Tum's must determine whether the promised rights, site selection and construction services, training services, and equipment are distinct.

- Rights to the trade name, market area, and proprietary know-how for 5 years are not individually distinct because each one is not sold separately and cannot be used with other goods or services that are readily available to the franchisee. Therefore, those combined rights give rise to a single performance obligation. Tum's satisfies the performance obligation to grant those rights at the point in time when Food Fight obtains control of the rights. That is, once Food Fight begins operating the store, Tum's has no further obligation with respect to these rights.

(continued)

ILLUSTRATION 18B.1
(continued)

- Training services and equipment are distinct because similar services and equipment are sold separately. Tum's satisfies those performance obligations when it transfers the services and equipment to Food Fight.
- Tum's cannot recognize revenue for the royalty payments because it is not reasonably assured to be entitled to those sales-based royalty amounts. That is, these payments represent variable consideration. Therefore, Tum's recognizes revenue for the royalties when (or as) the uncertainty is resolved.

Tum's promise to stand ready to provide products to the franchisee in the future at standalone selling prices is not accounted for as a separate performance obligation in the contract because it does not provide Food Fight with a material right. Thus, revenue from those sales is recorded in the future when the sales are made.

To illustrate the accounting for this franchise, consider the following values for allocation of the transaction price at December 31, 2020.

Rights to the trade name, market area, and proprietary know-how	$20,000
Training services	9,957
Equipment (cost of $10,000)	14,000
Total transaction price	$43,957

Training is completed in January 2021, the equipment is installed in January 2021, and Food Fight holds a grand opening on February 2, 2021. The entries for the Tum's franchise arrangement are summarized in **Illustration 18B.2**.

ILLUSTRATION 18B.2
Franchise Entries—Inception and Commencement of Operations

Tum's signs the agreement and receives upfront payment and note on December 31, 2020		
Cash	20,000	
Notes Receivable ($50,000 – $20,000)	30,000	
Discount on Notes Receivable		6,043
Unearned Franchise Revenue		20,000
Unearned Service Revenue (training)		9,957
Unearned Sales Revenue (equipment)		14,000
Franchise opens; Tum's satisfies the performance obligations related to the franchise rights, training, and equipment (that is, Tum's has no further obligations related to these elements of the franchise) on February 2, 2021		
Unearned Franchise Revenue	20,000	
Franchise Revenue		20,000
Unearned Service Revenue (training)	9,957	
Service Revenue (training)		9,957
Unearned Sales Revenue (equipment)	14,000	
Sales Revenue		14,000
Cost of Goods Sold	10,000	
Inventory		10,000

As indicated, when Food Fight begins operations, Tum's satisfies the performance obligations related to the franchise rights, training, and equipment under the franchise agreement. That is, Tum's has no further obligations related to these elements of the franchise.

During 2021, Food Fight does well, recording $525,000 of sales in its first year of operations. The entries for Tum's related to the first year of operations of the franchise are summarized in **Illustration 18B.3**.

ILLUSTRATION 18B.3

Franchise Entries—First Year of Franchise Operations

To record continuing franchise fees on December 31, 2021		
Accounts Receivable ($525,000 × .01)	5,250	
Franchise Revenue		5,250
To record payment received and interest revenue on note on December 31, 2021		
Cash	6,000	
Notes Receivable		6,000
Discount on Notes Receivable ($23,957 × .08)	1,917	
Interest Revenue		1,917

Tum's will make similar entries in subsequent years of the franchise agreement.

Recognition of Franchise Rights Revenue over Time

In the franchise example presented in Illustration 18B.1, Tum's transferred control of the franchise rights at a point in time—that is, when the franchisee began operations and could benefit from control of the rights—with no further involvement by Tum's. In other situations, depending on the economic substance of the rights, the franchisor may be providing **access to the right** rather than transferring control of the franchise rights. In this case, **the franchise revenue is recognized over time**, rather than at a point in time. The franchise arrangement presented in **Illustration 18B.4** provides an example of a franchise agreement with revenue recognized over time.

ILLUSTRATION 18B.4

Revenue Recognition over Time—Franchise

Franchise Revenue over Time

Facts: Tech Solvers Corp. is a franchisor in the emerging technology consulting service business. Tech Solvers' stores provide a range of computing services (hardware/software installation, repairs, data backup, device syncing, and network solutions) on popular Apple and PC devices. Each franchise agreement gives a franchisee the right to open a Tech Solvers store and sell Tech Solvers' products and services in the area for 5 years. Under the contract, Tech Solvers also provides the franchisee with a number of services to support and enhance the franchise brand, including (a) advising and consulting on the operations of the store; (b) communicating new hardware and software developments, and service techniques; (c) providing business and training manuals; and (d) advertising programs and training. As an almost entirely service operation (all parts and other supplies are purchased as needed by customers), Tech Solvers provides few upfront services to franchisees. Instead, the franchisee recruits service technicians, who are given Tech Solvers' training materials (online manuals and tutorials), which are updated for technology changes, on a monthly basis at a minimum.

Tech Solvers enters into a franchise agreement on December 15, 2020, giving a franchisee the rights to operate a Tech Solvers franchise in eastern Indiana for 5 years. Tech Solvers charges an initial franchise fee of $5,000 for the right to operate as a franchisee, payable upon signing the contract. Tech Solvers also receives ongoing royalty payments of 7% of the franchisee's annual sales (payable each January 15 of the following year). The franchise began operations in January 2021 and recognized $85,000 of revenue in 2021.

***Question:* What are the performance obligations in this arrangement and the point in time at which the performance obligations will be satisfied and revenue will be recognized?**

Solution: To identify the performance obligations, Tech Solvers must determine whether the promised rights and the ongoing franchisee technology support and training services are distinct.

- Rights to the trade name, market area, and proprietary know-how for 5 years are not individually distinct because each one is not sold separately and cannot be used with other goods or services that are readily available to the franchisee. In addition, these licensed rights have a close connection with the underlying Tech Solvers' intellectual property (its ability to keep its service and training materials up-to-date).

(continued)

ILLUSTRATION 18B.4
(continued)

Therefore, those combined rights and the ongoing training materials are a single performance obligation. Tech Solvers satisfies the performance obligation over time. That is, once the franchisee begins operating a Tech Solvers franchise, Tech Solvers is providing access to the rights and must continue to perform updates and services.

- Tech Solvers cannot recognize revenue for the royalty payments because it is not reasonably assured to be entitled to those revenue-based royalty amounts. That is, these payments represent variable consideration. Therefore, Tech Solvers recognizes revenue for the royalties when (or as) the uncertainty is resolved.

The entries for Tech Solvers related to the franchise are summarized in **Illustration 18B.5**.

ILLUSTRATION 18B.5
Franchise Entries—Revenue Recognized over Time

Franchise agreement signed and receipt of upfront payment and note on December 15, 2020		
Cash	5,000	
Unearned Franchise Revenue		5,000
Franchise begins operations in January 2021 and records $85,000 of revenue for the year ended December 31, 2021 on December 31, 2021		
Unearned Franchise Revenue	1,000	
Franchise Revenue ($5,000 ÷ 5)		1,000
Accounts Receivable	5,950	
Franchise Revenue ($85,000 × .07)		5,950
To record payment received from franchisee on January 15, 2022		
Cash	5,950	
Accounts Receivable		5,950

As indicated, Tech Solvers satisfies the performance obligation related to the franchise rights and training materials over time (in this case, on a straight-line basis). Continuing franchise fees are recognized when uncertainty related to the variable consideration is resolved.

In summary, analysis of the characteristics of the Tech Solvers franchise indicates that it does not reflect a right that is transferred at a point in time. That is, Tech Solvers has a continuing obligation to provide updated materials and ongoing support, suggesting the control of the right has not been transferred to the franchisee. Thus, revenue from the franchise rights is recognized over time.

Review and Practice

Key Terms Review

Learning Objectives Review

1 Discuss the fundamental concepts related to revenue recognition and measurement.

Most revenue transactions pose few problems for revenue recognition. This is because, in many cases, the transaction is initiated and completed at the same time. Increasing complexity of business and revenue arrangements have resulted in revenue recognition practices being identified as the most prevalent reasons for accounting restatements. A number of the revenue recognition issues relate to possible fraudulent behavior by company executives and employees, but are also due to sometimes incomplete and inconsistent accounting guidelines for revenue recognition. A recent standard provides a set of guidelines to follow in determining when revenue should be reported and how it should be measured. The standard is comprehensive and applies to all companies. As a result, comparability and consistency in reporting revenue should be enhanced.

The five steps in the revenue recognition process are (1) identify the contract with customers, (2) identify the separate performance obligations in the contract, (3) determine the transaction price, (4) allocate the transaction price to the separate performance obligations, and (5) recognize revenue when each performance obligation is satisfied.

2 Explain and apply the five-step revenue recognition process.

1. **Identify the contract with customers.** A contract is an agreement that creates enforceable rights or obligations. A company applies the revenue guidance to contracts with customers.
2. **Identify the separate performance obligations in the contract.** A performance obligation is a promise in a contract to provide a product or service to a customer. A contract may be comprised of multiple performance obligations. The accounting for multiple performance obligations is based on evaluation of whether the product or service is distinct within the contract. If each of the goods or services is distinct, but is interdependent and interrelated, these goods and services are combined and reported as one performance obligation.
3. **Determine the transaction price.** The transaction price is the amount of consideration that a company expects to receive from a customer in exchange for transferring goods and services. In determining the transaction price, companies must consider the following factors: (1) variable consideration, (2) time value of money, (3) noncash consideration, and (4) consideration paid or payable to a customer.
4. **Allocate the transaction price to the separate performance obligations.** If more than one performance obligation exists in a contract, allocate the transaction price based on relative standalone selling prices. Estimates of standalone selling price can be based on (1) adjusted market assessment, (2) expected cost plus a margin approach, or (3) a residual approach.
5. **Recognize revenue when the company satisfies its performance obligation.** A company satisfies its performance obligation when the customer obtains control of the good or service. Companies satisfy performance obligations either at a point in time or over a period of time. Companies recognize revenue over a period of time if one of the following criteria is met: (1) the customer receives and consumes the benefits as the seller performs, (2) the customer controls the asset as it is created, or (3) the company does not have an alternative use for the asset.

3 Apply the five-step process to major revenue recognition issues.

Refer to Illustration 18.26 for a summary of the accounting for (a) sales returns and allowances, (b) repurchase agreements, (c) bill-and-hold sales, (d) principal-agent relationships, (e) consignments, (f) warranties, and (g) nonrefundable upfront fees.

4 Describe presentation and disclosure regarding revenue.

Under the asset-liability approach to recognize revenue, companies present contract assets and contract liabilities on their balance sheets. Contract assets are rights to receive consideration. A contract liability is a company's obligation to transfer goods or services to a customer for which the company has received consideration from the customer. Companies must determine if new performance obligations are created by a contract modification and may also report assets associated with fulfillment costs and contract acquisition costs related to a revenue arrangement. Companies disclose qualitative and quantitative information about (a) contracts with customers with disaggregation of revenue, presentation of opening and closing balances in contract assets and contract liabilities, and significant information related to their performance obligations; (b) significant judgments that affect the determination of the transaction price, the allocation of the transaction price, and the determination of the timing of revenue; and (c) assets recognized from costs incurred to fulfill a contract.

*5 Apply the percentage-of-completion method for long-term contracts.

To apply the percentage-of-completion method to long-term contracts, a company must have some basis for measuring the progress toward completion at particular interim dates. One of the most popular input measures used to determine the progress toward completion is the cost-to-cost basis. Using this basis, a company measures the percentage of completion by comparing costs incurred to date with the most recent estimate of the total costs to complete the contract. The company applies that percentage to the total revenue or the estimated total gross profit on the contract to arrive at the amount of revenue or gross profit to be recognized to date.

*6 Apply the completed-contract method for long-term contracts.

Under the completed-contract method, companies recognize revenue and gross profit only at a point in time—that is, when the company completes the contract. The company accumulates costs of long-term contracts in process and current billings. It makes no interim charges or credits to income statement accounts for revenues, costs, and gross profit. The annual journal entries to record costs of construction, progress billings, and collections from customers would be identical to those for the percentage-of-completion method—with the significant exclusion of the recognition of revenue and gross profit.

***7 Identify the proper accounting for losses on long-term contracts.**

Two types of losses can become evident under long-term contracts. (1) *Loss in current period on a profitable contract:* Under the percentage-of-completion method only, the estimated cost increase requires a current-period adjustment of excess gross profit recognized on the project in prior periods. The company records this adjustment as a loss in the current period because it is a change in accounting estimate. (2) *Loss on an unprofitable contract:* Under both the percentage-of-completion and the completed-contract methods, the company must recognize the entire expected contract loss in the current period.

***8 Explain revenue recognition for franchises.**

In a franchise arrangement, the franchisor satisfies its performance obligation for a franchise license when control of the franchise rights is transferred, generally when the franchisee begins operations of the franchise. In situations where the franchisor provides *access to the rights* rather than transferring control of the franchise rights, the franchise rights' revenue is recognized over time rather than at a point in time. Franchisors recognize continuing franchise fees over time (as uncertainty related to the variable consideration is resolved).

Enhanced Review and Practice

Go online for multiple-choice questions with solutions, review exercises with solutions, and a full glossary of all key terms.

Practice Problem

Outback Industries manufactures emergency power equipment. Its most popular generator is a model called the E-Booster, which has a retail price of $1,500 and costs Outback $740 to manufacture. It sells the E-Booster on a standalone basis directly to businesses, as well as provides installation services. Outback also distributes the E-Booster through a consignment agreement with **Home Depot**. Income data for Outback's first quarter of 2020 from operations other than the E-Booster generator are as follows.

Revenues	$6,500,000
Expenses	4,350,000

Outback has the following information related to four E-Booster revenue arrangements during the first quarter of 2020.

1. Outback entered into an arrangement with the Grocers Co-op in eastern Minnesota to deliver E-Boosters for the meat lockers in the grocers' stores. Outback provides a 5% volume discount for E-Boosters purchased by Grocers Co-op if at least $450,000 of E-Boosters are purchased during 2020. By March 31, 2020, Outback has made sales of $360,000 ($1,500 × 240 generators) to Grocers Co-op. Based on prior experience with this promotion in two neighboring states, the discount threshold is met for the year if more than one-half of the target had been met by mid-year.
2. On January 1, 2020, Outback sells 20 E-Boosters to Nick's Liquors. Nick's signs a 6-month note due in 6 months at an annual interest rate of 12%. Outback allows Nick's to return any E-Boosters that it cannot use within 120 days and receive a full refund. Based on prior experience, Outback estimates that three units will be returned (using the most likely outcome approach). Outback's costs to recover the products will be immaterial, and the returned generators are expected to be resold at a profit. No E-Boosters have been returned as of March 31, 2020, and Outback still estimates that three units will be returned in the future.
3. Outback sells 30 E-Boosters to a community bank in the Florida Keys to provide uninterrupted power for bank branches with ATMs for a total contract price of $50,000. In addition to the E-Boosters, Outback also provides installation at a standalone selling price of $200 per E-Booster; the cost to Outback to install is $150 per E-Booster. The E-Boosters are delivered and installed on March 1, 2020, and full payment is made to Outback.
4. Outback ships 300 E-Boosters to Home Depot on consignment. By March 31, 2020, Home Depot has sold three-fourths of the consigned merchandise at the listed price of $1,500 per unit. Home Depot notifies Outback of the sales, retains an 8% commission, and remits the cash due to Outback.

Instructions

a. Determine net income for Outback Industries for the first quarter of 2020. (Ignore taxes.)

b. In reviewing the credit history of Nick's Liquors, Outback has some concerns about the collectibility of the full amount due on the note. Briefly discuss how collectibility of the note affects revenue recognition and income measurement for Outback.

Solution

a. The amount of revenue and expense recognized on each of the arrangements is as follows.

1. Sales revenue [.95 × ($1,500 × 240)]		$342,000	
Cost of goods sold ($740 × 240)		177,600	
Gross profit (income effect of this arrangement)			$164,400
2. Sales revenue (20 × $1,500)		30,000	
Less: Estimated returns (3 × $1,500)		4,500	
Net sales		25,500	
Cost of goods sold (17 × $740)		12,580	
Gross profit		12,920	
Interest revenue ($30,000 × .12 × 3/12)		900	
Net income on this arrangement			13,820

3. The total transaction price of $50,000 is allocated between the equipment and installation. The transaction price for the equipment and installation is allocated based on relative standalone selling prices:

Equipment: $44,118 = ($45,000 ÷ $51,000*) × $50,000
Installation: $5,882 = ($6,000 ÷ $51,000) × $50,000

*$45,000 + $6,000

Sales revenue	$44,118		
Cost of goods sold (30 × $740)	22,200		
Gross profit		21,918	
Installation revenue	5,882		
Installation expense (30 × $150)	4,500		
Net profit		1,382	
Net income on this arrangement			23,300
4. Sales revenue (225* × $1,500)		337,500	
Cost of goods sold (225* × $740)		166,500	
Gross profit		171,000	
Commission expense ($337,500 × .08)		27,000	
Net income on this arrangement			144,000
Net income on E-Booster			$345,520

*300 × 3/4

Outback Industries' net income for the quarter: $6,500,000 – $4,350,000 + $345,520 = $2,495,520.

b. Whether a company will get paid for satisfying a performance obligation is not a consideration in determining revenue recognition. That is, the amount recognized is not adjusted for customer credit risk. If significant doubt exists at contract inception about collectibility, Outback reports the revenue gross and then presents an allowance for any impairment due to bad debts, which will reduce net income and which is reported as an operating expense in the income statement.

WileyPLUS

Exercises, Problems, Problem Solution Walkthrough Videos, and many more assessment tools and resources are available for practice in WileyPLUS.

Note: All asterisked Questions, Exercises, and Problems relate to material in the appendices to the chapter.

Questions

1. Explain the current environment regarding revenue recognition.

2. What was viewed as a major criticism of GAAP as it relates to revenue recognition?

3. Describe the revenue recognition principle.

4. Identify the five steps in the revenue recognition process.

5. Describe the critical factor in evaluating whether a performance obligation is satisfied.

6. When is revenue recognized in the following situations? (a) Revenue from selling products, (b) revenue from services performed, (c) revenue from permitting others to use company assets, and (d) revenue from disposing of assets other than products.

7. Explain the importance of a contract in the revenue recognition process.

8. On October 10, 2020, Executor Co. entered into a contract with Belisle Inc. to transfer Executor's specialty products (sales value of

$10,000, cost of $6,500) on December 15, 2020. Belisle agrees to make a payment of $5,000 upon delivery and signs a promissory note to pay the remaining balance on January 15, 2021. What entries does Executor make in 2020 on this contract? Ignore time value of money considerations.

9. What is a performance obligation? Under what conditions does a performance obligation exist?

10. When must multiple performance obligations in a revenue arrangement be accounted for separately?

11. Engelhart Implements Inc. sells tractors to area farmers. The price for each tractor includes GPS positioning service for 9 months (which facilitates field settings for planting and harvesting equipment). The GPS service is regularly sold on a standalone basis by Engelhart for a monthly fee. After the 9-month period, the consumer can renew the service on a fee basis. Does Engelhart have one or multiple performance obligations? Explain.

12. What is the transaction price? What additional factors related to the transaction price must be considered in determining the transaction price?

13. What are some examples of variable consideration? What are the two approaches for estimating variable consideration?

14. Allee Corp. is evaluating a revenue arrangement to determine proper revenue recognition. The contract is for construction of 10 speedboats for a contract price of $400,000. The customer needs the boats in its showrooms by February 1, 2021, for the boat purchase season; the customer provides a bonus payment of $21,000 if all boats are delivered by the February 1 deadline. The bonus is reduced by $7,000 each week that the boats are delivered after the deadline until no bonus is paid if the boats are delivered after February 15, 2021. Allee frequently includes such bonus terms in it contracts and thus has good historical data for estimating the probabilities of completion at different dates. It estimates an equal probability (25%) for each full delivery outcome. What approach should Allee use to determine the transaction price for this contract? Explain.

15. Refer to the information in Question 14. Assume that Allee has limited experience with a construction project on the same scale as the 10 speedboats. How does this affect the accounting for the variable consideration?

16. In measuring the transaction price, explain the accounting for (a) time value of money, and (b) noncash consideration.

17. What is the proper accounting for volume discounts on sales of products?

18. On what basis should the transaction price be allocated to various performance obligations? Identify the approaches for allocating the transaction price.

19. Fuhremann Co. is a full-service manufacturer of surveillance equipment. Customers can purchase any combination of equipment, installation services, and training as part of Fuhremann's security services. Thus, each of these performance obligations are separate with individual standalone selling prices. Laplante Inc. purchased cameras, installation, and training at a total price of $80,000. Estimated standalone selling prices of the equipment, installation, and training are $90,000, $7,000, and $3,000, respectively. How should the transaction price be allocated to the equipment, installation, and training?

20. When does a company satisfy a performance obligation? Identify the indicators of satisfaction of a performance obligation.

21. Under what conditions does a company recognize revenue over a period of time?

22. How do companies recognize revenue from a performance obligation over time?

23. Explain the accounting for sales with right of return.

24. What are the reporting issues in a sale with a repurchase agreement?

25. Explain a bill-and-hold sale. When is revenue recognized in these situations?

26. Explain a principal-agent relationship and its significance to revenue recognition.

27. What is the nature of a sale on consignment?

28. What are the two types of warranties? Explain the accounting for each type.

29. Campus Cellular provides cell phones and 1 year of cell service to students for an upfront, nonrefundable fee of $300 and a usage fee of $5 per month. Students may renew the service without paying another upfront fee for each year they are on campus (on average, students renew their service one time). What amount of revenue should Campus Cellular recognize in the first year of the contract?

30. Describe the conditions when contract assets and liabilities are recognized and presented in financial statements.

31. Explain the accounting for contract modifications.

32. Explain the reporting for (a) costs to fulfill a contract and (b) collectibility.

33. What qualitative and quantitative disclosures are required related to revenue recognition?

*34. What are the two basic methods of accounting for long-term construction contracts? Indicate the circumstances that determine when one or the other of these methods should be used.

*35. For what reasons should the percentage-of-completion method be used over the completed-contract method whenever possible?

*36. What methods are used in practice to determine the extent of progress toward completion? Identify some "input measures" and some "output measures" that might be used to determine the extent of progress.

*37. What are the two types of losses that can become evident in accounting for long-term contracts? What is the nature of each type of loss? How is each type accounted for?

*38. Why in franchise arrangements may it be improper to recognize the entire franchise fee as revenue at the date of sale?

*39. How should a franchisor account for continuing franchise fees and routine sales of equipment and supplies to franchisees?

Brief Exercises

BE18.1 (LO 1) Leno Computers manufactures tablet computers for sale to retailers such as Fallon Electronics. Recently, Leno sold and delivered 200 tablet computers to Fallon for $20,000 on January 5, 2020. Fallon has agreed to pay for the 200 tablet computers within 30 days. Fallon has a good credit rating and should have no difficulty in making payment to Leno. (a) Explain whether a valid contract exists between

Leno Computers and Fallon Electronics. (b) Assuming that Leno Computers has not yet delivered the tablet computers to Fallon Electronics, what might cause a valid contract not to exist between Leno and Fallon?

BE18.2 **(LO 1)** On May 10, 2020, Cosmo Co. enters into a contract to deliver a product to Greig Inc. on June 15, 2020. Greig agrees to pay the full contract price of $2,000 on July 15, 2020. The cost of the goods is $1,300. Cosmo delivers the product to Greig on June 15, 2020, and receives payment on July 15, 2020. Prepare the journal entries for Cosmo related to this contract. Either party may terminate the contract without compensation until one of the parties performs.

BE18.3 **(LO 2)** Hillside Company enters into a contract with Sanchez Inc. to provide a software license and 3 years of customer support. The customer-support services require specialized knowledge that only Hillside Company's employees can perform. How many performance obligations are in the contract?

BE18.4 **(LO 2)** Destin Company signs a contract to manufacture a new 3D printer for $80,000. The contract includes installation which costs $4,000 and a maintenance agreement over the life of the printer at a cost of $10,000. The printer cannot be operated without the installation. Destin Company as well as other companies could provide the installation and maintenance agreement. What are Destin Company's performance obligations in this contract?

BE18.5 **(LO 2)** Ismail Construction enters into a contract to design and build a hospital. Ismail is responsible for the overall management of the project and identifies various goods and services to be provided, including engineering, site clearance, foundation, procurement, construction of the structure, piping and wiring, installation of equipment, and finishing. Does Ismail have a single performance obligation to the customer in this revenue arrangement? Explain.

BE18.6 **(LO 2)** Nair Corp. enters into a contract with a customer to build an apartment building for $1,000,000. The customer hopes to rent apartments at the beginning of the school year and provides a performance bonus of $150,000 to be paid if the building is ready for rental beginning August 1, 2021. The bonus is reduced by $50,000 each week that completion is delayed. Nair commonly includes these completion bonuses in its contracts and, based on prior experience, estimates the following completion outcomes:

Completed by	Probability
August 1, 2021	70%
August 8, 2021	20
August 15, 2021	5
After August 15, 2021	5

Determine the transaction price for this contract.

BE18.7 **(LO 2)** Referring to the revenue arrangement in BE18.6, determine the transaction price for the contract, assuming (a) Nair is only able to estimate whether the building can be completed by August 1, 2021, or not (Nair estimates that there is a 70% chance that the building will be completed by August 1, 2021), and (b) Nair has limited information with which to develop a reliable estimate of completion by the August 1, 2021, deadline.

BE18.8 **(LO 2)** Presented below are three revenue recognition situations.

a. Groupo sells goods to MTN for $1,000,000, payment due at delivery.

b. Groupo sells goods on account to Grifols for $800,000, payment due in 30 days.

c. Groupo sells goods to Magnus for $500,000, payment due in two installments, the first installment payable in 18 months and the second payment due 6 months later. The present value of the future payments is $464,000.

Indicate the transaction price for each of these situations and when revenue will be recognized.

BE18.9 **(LO 2)** On January 2, 2020, Adani Inc. sells goods to Geo Company in exchange for a zero-interest-bearing note with face value of $11,000, with payment due in 12 months. The fair value of the goods at the date of sale is $10,000 (cost $6,000). Prepare the journal entry to record this transaction on January 2, 2020. How much total revenue should be recognized in 2020?

BE18.10 **(LO 2)** On March 1, 2020, Parnevik Company sold goods to Goosen Inc. for $660,000 in exchange for a 5-year, zero-interest-bearing note in the face amount of $1,062,937 (an inputed rate of 10%). The goods have an inventory cost on Parnevik's books of $400,000. Prepare the journal entries for Parnevik on (a) March 1, 2020, and (b) December 31, 2020.

BE18.11 **(LO 2, 3)** Telephone Sellers Inc. sells prepaid telephone cards to customers. Telephone Sellers then pays the telecommunications company, TeleExpress, for the actual use of its telephone lines related to the prepaid telephone cards. Assume that Telephone Sellers sells $4,000 of prepaid cards in January 2020. It then pays TeleExpress based on usage, which turns out to be 50% in February, 30%

in March, and 20% in April. The total payment by Telephone Sellers for TeleExpress lines over the 3 months is $3,000. Indicate how much income Telephone Sellers should recognize in January, February, March, and April.

BE18.12 **(LO 2, 3)** Manual Company sells goods to Nolan Company during 2020. It offers Nolan the following rebates based on total sales to Nolan. If total sales to Nolan are 10,000 units, it will grant a rebate of 2%. If it sells up to 20,000 units, it will grant a rebate of 4%. If it sells up to 30,000 units, it will grant a rebate of 6%. In the first quarter of the year, Manual sells 11,000 units to Nolan at a sales price of $110,000. Manual, based on past experience, has sold over 40,000 units to Nolan, and these sales normally take place in the third quarter of the year. What amount of revenue should Manual report for the sale of the 11,000 units in the first quarter of the year?

BE18.13 **(LO 3)** On July 10, 2020, Amodt Music sold CDs to retailers on account and recorded sales revenue of $700,000 (cost $560,000). Amodt grants the right to return CDs that do not sell in 3 months following delivery. Past experience indicates that the normal return rate is 15%. By October 11, 2020, retailers returned CDs to Amodt and were granted credit of $78,000. Prepare Amodt's journal entries to record (a) the sale on July 10, 2020, and (b) $78,000 of returns on October 11, 2020, and on October 31, 2020. Assume that Amodt prepares financial statement on October 31, 2020.

BE18.14 **(LO 3)** Kristin Company sells 300 units of its products for $20 each to Logan Inc. for cash. Kristin allows Logan to return any unused product within 30 days and receive a full refund. The cost of each product is $12. To determine the transaction price, Kristin decides that the approach that is most predictive of the amount of consideration to which it will be entitled is the probability-weighted amount. Using the probability-weighted amount, Kristin estimates that (1) 10 products will be returned and (2) the returned products are expected to be resold at a profit. Indicate the amount of (a) net sales, (b) estimated liability for refunds, and (c) cost of goods sold that Kristen should report in its financial statements (assume that none of the products have been returned at the financial statement date).

BE18.15 **(LO 3)** On June 1, 2020, Mills Company sells $200,000 of shelving units to a local retailer, ShopBarb, which is planning to expand its stores in the area. Under the agreement, ShopBarb asks Mills to retain the shelving units at its factory until the new stores are ready for installation. Title passes to ShopBarb at the time the agreement is signed. The shelving units are delivered to the stores on September 1, 2020, and ShopBarb pays in full. Prepare the journal entries for this bill-and-hold arrangement (assuming that conditions for recognizing the sale as a bill-and-hold sale have been met) for Mills on June 1 and September 1, 2020. The cost of the shelving units to Mills is $110,000.

BE18.16 **(LO 3)** Travel Inc. sells tickets for a Caribbean cruise on ShipAway Cruise Lines to Carmel Company employees. The total cruise package price to Carmel Company employees is $70,000. Travel Inc. receives a commission of 6% of the total price. Travel Inc. therefore remits $65,800 to ShipAway. Prepare the journal entry to record (1) the receipt of payment of $70,000 from employees for the cruise packages and (2) the remittance and revenue recognized by Travel Inc. on this transaction.

BE18.17 **(LO 3)** Jansen Corporation shipped $20,000 of merchandise on consignment to Gooch Company. Jansen paid freight costs of $2,000. Gooch Company paid $500 for local advertising, which is reimbursable from Jansen. By year-end, 60% of the merchandise had been sold for $21,500. Gooch notified Jansen, retained a 10% commission, and remitted the cash due to Jansen. Prepare Jansen's journal entry when the cash is received.

BE18.18 **(LO 3)** Talarczyk Company sold 10,000 Super-Spreaders on December 31, 2020, at a total price of $1,000,000, with a warranty guarantee that the product was free of any defects. The cost of the spreaders sold is $550,000. The assurance warranties extend for a 2-year period and are estimated to cost $40,000. Talarczyk also sold extended warranties (service-type warranties) related to 2,000 spreaders for 2 years beyond the 2-year period for $12,000. Given this information, determine the amounts to report for the following at December 31, 2020: sales revenue, warranty expense, unearned warranty revenue, warranty liability, and cash.

BE18.19 **(LO 4)** On May 1, 2020, Mount Company enters into a contract to transfer a product to Eric Company on September 30, 2020. It is agreed that Eric will pay the full price of $25,000 in advance on June 15, 2020. Eric pays on June 15, 2020, and Mount delivers the product on September 30, 2020. Prepare the journal entries required for Mount in 2020.

BE18.20 **(LO 3)** Nate Beggs signs a 1-year contract with BlueBox Video. The terms of the contract are that Nate is required to pay a nonrefundable initiation fee of $100. No annual membership fee is charged in the first year. After the first year, membership can be renewed by paying an annual membership fee of $5 per month. BlueBox determines that its customers, on average, renew their annual membership three times after the first year before terminating their membership. What amount of revenue should BlueBox recognize in its first year?

BE18.21 (LO 4) Stengel Co. enters into a 3-year contract to perform maintenance service for Laplante Inc. Laplante promises to pay $100,000 at the beginning of each year (the standalone selling price of the service at contract inception is $100,000 per year). At the end of the second year, the contract is modified and the fee for the third year of service, which reflects a reduced menu of maintenance services to be performed at Laplante locations, is reduced to $80,000 (the standalone selling price of the services at the beginning of the third year is $80,000 per year). Briefly describe the accounting for this contract modification.

***BE18.22 (LO 5)** Turner, Inc. began work on a $7,000,000 contract in 2020 to construct an office building. During 2020, Turner, Inc. incurred costs of $1,700,000, billed its customers for $1,200,000, and collected $960,000. At December 31, 2020, the estimated additional costs to complete the project total $3,300,000. Prepare Turner's 2020 journal entries using the percentage-of-completion method.

***BE18.23 (LO 6)** Guillen, Inc. began work on a $7,000,000 contract in 2020 to construct an office building. Guillen uses the completed-contract method. At December 31, 2020, the balances in certain accounts were Construction in Process $1,715,000, Accounts Receivable $240,000, and Billings on Construction in Process $1,000,000. Indicate how these accounts would be reported in Guillen's December 31, 2020, balance sheet.

***BE18.24 (LO 7)** Archer Construction Company began work on a $420,000 construction contract in 2020. During 2020, Archer incurred costs of $278,000, billed its customer for $215,000, and collected $175,000. At December 31, 2020, the estimated additional costs to complete the project total $162,000. Prepare Archer's journal entry to record profit or loss, if any, using (a) the percentage-of-completion method and (b) the completed-contract method.

***BE18.25 (LO 8)** Frozen Delight, Inc. charges an initial franchise fee of $75,000 for the right to operate as a franchisee of Frozen Delight. Of this amount, $25,000 is collected immediately. The remainder is collected in four equal annual installments of $12,500 each. These installments have a present value of $41,402. As part of the total franchise fee, Frozen Delight also provides training (with a fair value of $2,000) to help franchisees get the store ready to open. The franchise agreement is signed on April 1, 2020, training is completed, and the store opens on July 1, 2020. Prepare the journal entries required by Frozen Delight on April 1 and July 1, 2020.

Exercises

E18.1 (LO 1) (Fundamentals of Revenue Recognition) Presented below are five different situations. Provide an answer to each of these questions.

1. The Kawaski Jeep dealership sells both new and used Jeeps. Some of the Jeeps are used for demonstration purposes; after 6 months, these Jeeps are then sold as used vehicles. Should Kawaski Jeep record these sales of used Jeeps as revenue or as a gain?
2. One of the main indicators of whether control has passed to the customer is whether revenue has been earned. Is this statement correct?
3. One of the five steps in determining whether revenue should be recognized is whether the sale has been realized. Do you agree?
4. One of the criteria that contracts must meet to apply the revenue standard is that collectibility of the sales price must be reasonably possible. Is this correct?
5. Many believe the distinction between revenue and gains is important in the financial statements. Given that both revenues and gains increase net income, why is the distinction important?

E18.2 (LO 1) (Fundamentals of Revenue Recognition) Respond to the questions related to the following statements.

1. A wholly unperformed contract is one in which the company has neither transferred the promised goods or services to the customer nor received, or become entitled to receive, any consideration. Why are these contracts not recorded in the accounts?
2. Performance obligations are the unit of account for purposes of applying the revenue recognition standard and therefore determine when and how revenue is recognized. Is this statement correct?
3. Elaina Company contracts with a customer and provides the customer with an option to purchase additional goods for free or at a discount. Should Elaina Company account for this option?

4. The transaction price is generally not adjusted to reflect the customer's credit risk, meaning the risk that the customer will not pay the amount to which the entity is entitled to under the contract. Comment on this statement.

E18.3 **(LO 1, 2)** **(Existence of a Contract)** On May 1, 2020, Richardson Inc. entered into a contract to deliver one of its specialty mowers to Kickapoo Landscaping Co. The contract requires Kickapoo to pay the contract price of $900 in advance on May 15, 2020. Kickapoo pays Richardson on May 15, 2020, and Richardson delivers the mower (with cost of $575) on May 31, 2020.

Instructions

a. Prepare the journal entry on May 1, 2020, for Richardson.

b. Prepare the journal entry on May 15, 2020, for Richardson.

c. Prepare the journal entry on May 31, 2020, for Richardson.

E18.4 **(LO 2)** **(Determine Transaction Price)** Jupiter Company sells goods to Danone Inc. by accepting a note receivable on January 2, 2020. The goods have a sales price of $610,000 (cost of $500,000). The terms are net 30. If Danone pays within 5 days, however, it receives a cash discount of $10,000. Past history indicates that the cash discount will be taken. On January 28, 2020, Danone makes payment to Jupiter for the full sales price.

Instructions

a. Prepare the journal entry(ies) to record the sale and related cost of goods sold for Jupiter Company on January 2, 2020, and the payment on January 28, 2020. Assume that Jupiter Company records the January 2, 2020, transaction using the net method.

b. Prepare the journal entry(ies) to record the sale and related cost of goods sold for Jupiter Company on January 2, 2020, and the payment on January 28, 2020. Assume that Jupiter Company records the January 2, 2020, transaction using the gross method.

E18.5 **(LO 2)** **(Determine Transaction Price)** Jeff Heun, president of Concrete Always, agrees to construct a concrete cart path at Dakota Golf Club. Concrete Always enters into a contract with Dakota to construct the path for $200,000. In addition, as part of the contract, a performance bonus of $40,000 will be paid based on the timing of completion. The performance bonus will be paid fully if completed by the agreed-upon date. The performance bonus decreases by $10,000 per week for every week beyond the agreed-upon completion date. Jeff has been involved in a number of contracts that had performance bonuses as part of the agreement in the past. As a result, he is fairly confident that he will receive a good portion of the performance bonus. Jeff estimates, given the constraints of his schedule related to other jobs , that there is 55% probability that he will complete the project on time, a 30% probability that he will be 1 week late, and a 15% probability that he will be 2 weeks late.

Instructions

a. Determine the transaction price that Concrete Always should compute for this agreement.

b. Assume that Jeff Heun has reviewed his work schedule and decided that it makes sense to complete this project on time. Assuming that he now believes that the probability for completing the project on time is 90% and otherwise it will be finished 1 week late, determine the transaction price.

E18.6 **(LO 2)** **(Determine Transaction Price)** Bill Amends, owner of Real Estate Inc., buys and sells commercial properties. Recently, he sold land for $3,000,000 to the Blackhawk Group, a developer that plans to build a new shopping mall. In addition to the $3,000,000 sales price, Blackhawk Group agrees to pay Real Estate Inc. 1% of the retail sales of the mall for 10 years. Blackhawk estimates that retail sales in a typical mall project is $1,000,000 a year. Given the substantial increase in online sales that are occurring in the retail market, Bill had originally indicated that he would prefer a higher price for the land instead of the 1% royalty arrangement and suggested a price of $3,250,000. However, Blackhawk would not agree to those terms.

Instructions

What is the transaction price for the land and related royalty payment that Real Estate Inc. should record?

E18.7 **(LO 2)** **(Determine Transaction Price)** Blair Biotech enters into a licensing agreement with Pang Pharmaceutical for a drug under development. Blair will receive a payment of $10,000,000 if the drug receives regulatory approval. Based on prior experience in the drug-approval process, Blair determines it is 90% likely that the drug will gain approval and a 10% chance of denial.

Instructions

a. Determine the transaction price of the arrangement for Blair Biotech.

b. Assuming that regulatory approval was granted on December 20, 2020, and that Blair received the payment from Pang on January 15, 2021, prepare the journal entries for Blair. The license meets the criteria for point-in-time revenue recognition.

E18.8 **(LO 2, 3)** **(Determine Transaction Price)** Aaron's Agency sells an insurance policy offered by Capital Insurance Company for a commission of $100 on January 2, 2020. In addition, Aaron will receive an additional commission of $10 each year for as long as the policyholder does not cancel the policy. After selling the policy, Aaron does not have any remaining performance obligations. Based on Aaron's significant experience with these types of policies, it estimates that policyholders on average renew the policy for 4.5 years. It has no evidence to suggest that previous policyholder behavior will change.

Instructions

a. Determine the transaction price of the arrangement for Aaron, assuming 100 policies are sold.

b. Determine the revenue that Aaron will recognize in 2020.

E18.9 **(LO 2, 3)** **(Determine Transaction Price)** Taylor Marina has 300 available slips that rent for $800 per season. Payments must be made in full by the start of the boating season, April 1, 2021. The boating season ends October 31, and the marina has a December 31 year-end. Slips for future seasons may be reserved if paid for by December 31, 2021. Under a new policy, if payment for 2022 season slips is made by December 31, 2021, a 5% discount is allowed. If payment for 2023 season slips is made by December 31, 2021, renters get a 20% discount (this promotion hopefully will provide cash flow for major dock repairs).

On December 31, 2020, all 300 slips for the 2021 season were rented at full price. On December 31, 2021, 200 slips were reserved and paid for the 2022 boating season, and 60 slips were reserved and paid for the 2023 boating season.

Instructions

a. Prepare the appropriate journal entries for December 31, 2020, and December 31, 2021.

b. Assume the marina operator is unsophisticated in business. Explain the managerial significance of the above accounting to this person.

E18.10 **(LO 2, 3)** **(Allocate Transaction Price)** Geraths Windows manufactures and sells custom storm windows for three-season porches. Geraths also provides installation service for the windows. The installation process does not involve changes in the windows, so this service can be performed by other vendors. Geraths enters into the following contract on July 1, 2020, with a local homeowner. The customer purchases windows for a price of $2,400 and chooses Geraths to do the installation. Geraths charges the same price for the windows irrespective of whether it does the installation or not. The installation service is estimated to have a standalone selling price of $600. The customer pays Geraths $2,000 (which equals the standalone selling price of the windows, which have a cost of $1,100) upon delivery and the remaining balance upon installation of the windows. The windows are delivered on September 1, 2020, Geraths completes installation on October 15, 2020, and the customer pays the balance due. Prepare the journal entries for Geraths in 2020. (Round amounts to nearest dollar.)

E18.11 **(LO 2, 3)** **(Allocate Transaction Price)** Refer to the revenue arrangement in E18.10. Repeat the requirements, assuming (a) Geraths estimates the standalone selling price of the installation based on an estimated cost of $400 plus a margin of 20% on cost, and (b) given uncertainty of finding skilled labor, Geraths is unable to develop a reliable estimate for the standalone selling price of the installation. (Round amounts to nearest dollar.)

E18.12 **(LO 3)** **(Allocate Transaction Price)** Shaw Company sells goods that cost $300,000 to Ricard Company for $410,000 on January 2, 2020. The sales price includes an installation fee, which has a standalone selling price of $40,000. The standalone selling price of the goods is $370,000. The installation is considered a separate performance obligation and is expected to take 6 months to complete.

Instructions

a. Prepare the journal entries (if any) to record the sale on January 2, 2020.

b. Shaw prepares an income statement for the first quarter of 2020, ending on March 31, 2020 (installation was completed on June 18, 2020). How much revenue should Shaw recognize related to its sale to Ricard?

E18.13 **(LO 3)** **(Allocate Transaction Price)** Crankshaft Company manufactures equipment. Crankshaft's products range from simple automated machinery to complex systems containing numerous components. Unit selling prices range from $200,000 to $1,500,000 and are quoted inclusive of installation. The installation process does not involve changes to the features of the equipment and does not require proprietary information about the equipment in order for the installed equipment to perform to specifications. Crankshaft has the following arrangement with Winkerbean Inc.

- Winkerbean purchases equipment from Crankshaft for a price of $1,000,000 and contracts with Crankshaft to install the equipment. Crankshaft charges the same price for the equipment irrespective of whether it does the installation or not. Using market data, Crankshaft determines installation service is estimated to have a standalone selling price of $50,000. The cost of the equipment is $600,000.
- Winkerbean is obligated to pay Crankshaft the $1,000,000 upon the delivery and installation of the equipment.

Crankshaft delivers the equipment on June 1, 2020, and completes the installation of the equipment on September 30, 2020. The equipment has a useful life of 10 years. Assume that the equipment and the installation are two distinct performance obligations which should be accounted for separately.

Instructions

a. How should the transaction price of $1,000,000 be allocated among the service obligations?

b. Prepare the journal entries for Crankshaft for this revenue arrangement on June 1, 2020 and September 30, 2020, assuming Crankshaft receives payment when installation is completed.

E18.14 **(LO 3)** **(Allocate Transaction Price)** Refer to the revenue arrangement in E18.13.

Instructions

Repeat requirements (a) and (b) assuming Crankshaft does not have market data with which to determine the standalone selling price of the installation services. As a result, an expected cost plus margin approach is used. The cost of installation is $36,000; Crankshaft prices these services with a 25% margin relative to cost.

E18.15 **(LO 3)** **(Allocate Transaction Price)** Appliance Center is an experienced home appliance dealer. Appliance Center also offers a number of services for the home appliances that it sells. Assume that Appliance Center sells ovens on a standalone basis. Appliance Center also sells installation services and maintenance services for ovens. However, Appliance Center does not offer installation or maintenance services to customers who buy ovens from other vendors. Pricing for ovens is as follows.

Oven only	$ 800
Oven with installation service	850
Oven with maintenance services	975
Oven with installation and maintenance services	1,000

In each instance in which maintenance services are provided, the maintenance service is separately priced within the arrangement at $175. Additionally, the incremental amount charged by Appliance Center for installation approximates the amount charged by independent third parties. Ovens are sold subject to a general right of return. If a customer purchases an oven with installation and/or maintenance services, in the event Appliance Center does not complete the service satisfactorily, the customer is only entitled to a refund of the portion of the fee that exceeds $800.

Instructions

a. Assume that a customer purchases an oven with both installation and maintenance services for $1,000. Based on its experience, Appliance Center believes that it is probable that the installation of the equipment will be performed satisfactorily to the customer. Assume that the maintenance services are priced separately (i.e., the three components are distinct). Identify the separate performance obligations related to the Appliance Center revenue arrangement.

b. Indicate the amount of revenue that should be allocated to the oven, the installation, and to the maintenance contract.

E18.16 **(LO 3)** Excel **(Sales with Returns)** On March 10, 2020, Steele Company sold to Barr Hardware 200 tool sets at a price of $50 each (cost $30 per set) with terms of n/60, f.o.b. shipping point. Steele allows Barr to return any unused tool sets within 60 days of purchase. Steele estimates that (1) 10 sets will be returned, (2) the cost of recovering the products will be immaterial, and (3) the returned tools sets can be resold at a profit. On March 25, 2020, Barr returned six tool sets and received a credit to its account.

Instructions

a. Prepare journal entries for Steele to record (1) the sale on March 10, 2020, (2) the return on March 25, 2020, and (c) any adjusting entries required on March 31, 2020 (when Steele prepares financial statements). Steele believes the original estimate of returns is correct.

b. Indicate the income statement and balance sheet reporting by Steele at March 31, 2020, of the information related to the Barr sales transaction.

E18.17 **(LO 3)** Excel **(Sales with Returns)** Refer to the revenue arrangement in E18.16. Assume that instead of selling the tool sets on credit, that Steele sold them for cash.

Instructions

a. Prepare journal entries for Steele to record (1) the sale on March 10, 2020, (2) the return on March 25, 2020, and (c) any adjusting entries required on March 31, 2020 (when Steele prepares financial statements). Steele believes the original estimate of returns is correct.

b. Indicate the income statement and balance sheet reporting by Steele at March 31, 2020, of the information related to the Barr sale.

E18.18 **(LO 3)** Excel **(Sales with Allowances)** On October 2, 2020, Laplante Company sold $6,000 of its elite camping gear (with a cost of $3,600) to Lynch Outfitters. As part of the sales agreement, Laplante includes a provision that if Lynch is dissatisfied with the product, Laplante will grant an allowance on the sales price or agree to take the product back (although returns are rare, given the long-term relationship between Laplante and Lynch). Lynch expects total allowances to Lynch to be $800. On October 16, 2020, Laplante grants an allowance of $400 to Lynch because the color for some of the items delivered was a bit different than what appeared in the catalog.

Instructions

a. Prepare journal entries for Laplante to record (1) the sale on October 2, 2020, (2) the granting of the allowance on October 16, 2020, and, (c) any adjusting required on October 31, 2020 (when Laplante prepares financial statements). Laplante now estimates additional allowances of $250 will be granted to Lynch in the future.

b. Indicate the income statement and balance sheet reporting by Laplante at October 31, 2020, of the information related to the Lynch transaction.

E18.19 **(LO 3)** Excel **(Sales with Returns)** On June 3, 2020, Hunt Company sold to Ann Mount merchandise having a sales price of $8,000 (cost $6,000) with terms of n/60, f.o.b. shipping point. Hunt estimates that merchandise with a sales value of $800 will be returned. An invoice totaling $120 was received by Mount on June 8 from Olympic Transport Service for the freight cost. Upon receipt of the goods, on June 8, Mount returned to Hunt $300 of merchandise containing flaws. Hunt estimates the returned items are expected to be resold at a profit. The freight on the returned merchandise was $24, paid by Hunt on June 8. On July 16, the company received a check for the balance due from Mount.

Instructions

Prepare journal entries for Hunt Company to record all the events in June and July.

E18.20 **(LO 3)** **(Sales with Returns)** Organic Growth Company is presently testing a number of new agricultural seed planters that it has recently developed. To stimulate interest, it has decided to grant to five of its largest customers the unconditional right of return to these products if not fully satisfied. The right of return extends for 4 months. Organic Growth estimates returns of 20%. Organic Growth sells these planters on account for $1,500,000 (cost $750,000) on January 2, 2020. Customers are required to pay the full amount due by March 15, 2020.

Instructions

a. Prepare the journal entry for Organic Growth at January 2, 2020.

b. Assume that one customer returns planters on March 1, 2020, due to unsatisfactory performance. Prepare the journal entry to record this transaction, assuming this customer purchased $100,000 of planters from Organic Growth.

c. Assume Organic Growth prepares financial statements quarterly. Prepare the necessary entries (if any) to adjust Organic Growth's financial results for the above transactions on March 31, 2020, assuming remaining expected returns of $200,000.

E18.21 (LO 3) **(Sales with Returns)** Uddin Publishing Co. publishes college textbooks that are sold to bookstores on the following terms. Each title has a fixed wholesale price, terms f.o.b. shipping point, and payment is due 60 days after shipment. The retailer may return a maximum of 30% of an order at the retailer's expense. Sales are made only to retailers who have good credit ratings. Past experience indicates that the normal return rate is 12%. The costs of recovery are expected to be immaterial, and the textbooks are expected to be resold at a profit.

Instructions

a. Identify the revenue recognition criteria that Uddin could employ concerning textbook sales.

b. Briefly discuss the reasoning for your answers in (a) above.

c. On July 1, 2020, Uddin shipped books invoiced at $15,000,000 (cost $12,000,000). Prepare the journal entry to record this transaction.

d. On October 3, 2020, $1.5 million of the invoiced July sales were returned according to the return policy, and the remaining $13.5 million was paid. Prepare the journal entries for the return and payment.

e. Assume Uddin prepares financial statements on October 31, 2020, the close of the fiscal year. No other returns are anticipated. Indicate the amounts reported on the income statement and balance related to the above transactions.

E18.22 (LO 3) **(Sales with Repurchase)** Cramer Corp. sells idle machinery to Enyart Company on July 1, 2020, for $40,000. Cramer agrees to repurchase this equipment from Enyart on June 30, 2021, for a price of $42,400 (an imputed interest rate of 6%).

Instructions

a. Prepare the journal entry for Cramer for the transfer of the asset to Enyart on July 1, 2020.

b. Prepare any other necessary journal entries for Cramer in 2020.

c. Prepare the journal entry for Cramer when the machinery is repurchased on June 30, 2021.

E18.23 (LO 3) **(Repurchase Agreement)** Zagat Inc. enters into an agreement on March 1, 2020, to sell Werner Metal Company aluminum ingots. As part of the agreement, Zagat also agrees to repurchase the ingots on May 1, 2020, at the original sales price of $200,000 plus 2%.

Instructions

a. Prepare Zagat's journal entry necessary on March 1, 2020.

b. Prepare Zagat's journal entry for the repurchase of the ingots on May 1, 2020.

E18.24 (LO 3) **(Bill and Hold)** Wood-Mode Company is involved in the design, manufacture, and installation of various types of wood products for large construction projects. Wood-Mode recently completed a large contract for Stadium Inc., which consisted of building 35 different types of concession counters for a new soccer arena under construction. The terms of the contract are that upon completion of the counters, Stadium would pay $2,000,000. Unfortunately, due to the depressed economy, the completion of the new soccer arena is now delayed. Stadium has therefore asked Wood-Mode to hold the counters for 2 months at its manufacturing plant until the arena is completed. Stadium acknowledges in writing that it ordered the counters and that they now have ownership. The time that Wood-Mode Company must hold the counters is totally dependent on when the arena is completed. Because Wood-Mode has not received additional progress payments for the counters due to the delay, Stadium has provided a deposit of $300,000.

Instructions

a. Explain this type of revenue recognition transaction.

b. What factors should be considered in determining when to recognize revenue in this transaction?

c. Prepare the journal entry(ies) that Wood-Mode should make, assuming it signed a valid sales contract to sell the counters and received at the time the $300,000 deposit.

E18.25 (LO 3) **(Consignment Sales)** On May 3, 2020, Eisler Company consigned 80 freezers, costing $500 each, to Remmers Company. The cost of shipping the freezers amounted to $840 and was paid by Eisler Company. On December 30, 2020, a report was received from the consignee, indicating that 40 freezers had been sold for $750 each. Remittance was made by the consignee for the amount due after deducting a commission of 6%, advertising of $200, and total installation costs of $320 on the freezers sold.

Instructions

a. Compute the inventory value of the units unsold in the hands of the consignee.

b. Compute the profit for the consignor for the units sold.

c. Compute the amount of cash that will be remitted by the consignee.

E18.26 **(LO 3) (Warranty Arrangement)** On January 2, 2020, Grando Company sells production equipment to Fargo Inc. for $50,000. Grando includes a 2-year assurance warranty service with the sale of all its equipment. The customer receives and pays for the equipment on January 2, 2020. During 2020, Grando incurs costs related to warranties of $900. At December 31, 2020, Grando estimates that $650 of warranty costs will be incurred in the second year of the warranty.

Instructions

a. Prepare the journal entry to record this transaction on January 2, 2020, and on December 31, 2020 (assuming financial statements are prepared on December 31, 2020).

b. Repeat the requirements for (a), assuming that in addition to the assurance warranty, Grando sold an extended warranty (service-type warranty) for an additional 2 years (2022–2023) for $800.

E18.27 **(LO 3) (Warranties)** Celic Inc. manufactures and sells computers that include an assurance-type warranty for the first 90 days. Celic offers an optional extended coverage plan under which it will repair or replace any defective part for 3 years from the expiration of the assurance-type warranty. Because the optional extended coverage plan is sold separately, Celic determines that the 3 years of extended coverage represents a separate performance obligation. The total transaction price for the sale of a computer and the extended warranty is $3,600 on October 1, 2020, and Celic determines the standalone selling price of each is $3,200 and $400, respectively. Further, Celic estimates, based on historical experience, it will incur $200 in costs to repair defects that arise within the 90-day coverage period for the assurance-type warranty. The cost of the equipment is $1,440. Assume that the $200 in costs to repair defects in the computers occurred on October 25, 2020.

Instructions

a. Prepare the journal entry(ies) to record the October transactions related to sale of the computers.

b. Briefly describe the accounting for the service-type warranty after the 90-day assurance-type warranty period.

E18.28 **(LO 4) (Existence of a Contract)** On January 1, 2020, Gordon Co. enters into a contract to sell a customer a wiring base and shelving unit that sits on the base in exchange for $3,000. The contract requires delivery of the base first but states that payment for the base will not be made until the shelving unit is delivered. Gordon identifies two performance obligations and allocates $1,200 of the transaction price to the wiring base and the remainder to the shelving unit. The cost of the wiring base is $700; the shelves have a cost of $320.

Instructions

a. Prepare the journal entry on January 1, 2020, for Gordon.

b. Prepare the journal entry on February 5, 2020, for Gordon when the wiring base is delivered to the customer.

c. Prepare the journal entry on February 25, 2020, for Gordon when the shelving unit is delivered to the customer and Gordon receives full payment.

E18.29 **(LO 4) (Contract Modification)** In September 2020, Gaertner Corp. commits to selling 150 of its iPhone-compatible docking stations to Better Buy Co. for $15,000 ($100 per product). The stations are delivered to Better Buy over the next 6 months. After 90 stations are delivered, the contract is modified and Gaertner promises to deliver an additional 45 products for an additional $4,275 ($95 per station). All sales are cash on delivery.

Instructions

a. Prepare the journal entry for Gaertner for the sale of the first 90 stations. The cost of each station is $54.

b. Prepare the journal entry for the sale of 10 more stations after the contract modification, assuming that the price for the additional stations reflects the standalone selling price at the time of the contract modification. In addition, the additional stations are distinct from the original products as Gaertner regularly sells the products separately.

c. Prepare the journal entry for the sale of 10 more stations (as in (b)), assuming that the pricing for the additional products *does not* reflect the standalone selling price of the additional products and the prospective method is used.

E18.30 **(LO 4)** **(Contract Modification)** Tyler Financial Services performs bookkeeping and tax-reporting services to startup companies in the Oconomowoc area. On January 1, 2020, Tyler entered into a 3-year service contract with Walleye Tech. Walleye promises to pay $10,000 at the beginning of each year, which at contract inception is the standalone selling price for these services. At the end of the second year, the contract is modified and the fee for the third year of services is reduced to $8,000. In addition, Walleye agrees to pay an additional $20,000 at the beginning of the third year to cover the contract for 3 additional years (i.e., 4 years remain after the modification). The extended contract services are similar to those provided in the first 2 years of the contract.

Instructions

a. Prepare the journal entries for Tyler in 2020 and 2021 related to this service contract.

b. Prepare the journal entries for Tyler in 2022 related to the modified service contract, assuming a prospective approach.

c. Repeat the requirements for part (b), assuming Tyler and Walleye agree on a revised set of services (fewer bookkeeping services but more tax services) in the extended contract period and the modification results in a separate performance obligation.

E18.31 **(LO 4)** **(Contract Costs)** Rex's Reclaimers entered into a contract with Dan's Demolition to manage the processing of recycled materials on Dan's various demolition projects. Services for the 3-year contract include collecting, sorting, and transporting reclaimed materials to recycling centers or contractors who will reuse them. Rex's incurs selling commission costs of $2,000 to obtain the contract. Before performing the services, Rex's also designs and builds receptacles and loading equipment that interfaces with Dan's demolition equipment at a cost of $27,000. These receptacles and equipment are retained by Rex's and can be used for other projects. Dan's promises to pay a fixed fee of $12,000 per year, payable every 6 months for the services under the contract. Rex's incurs the following costs: design services for the receptacles to interface with Dan's equipment $3,000, loading equipment controllers $6,000, and special testing and OSHA inspection fees $2,000 (some of Dan's projects are on government property).

Instructions

a. Determine the costs that should be capitalized as part of Rex's Reclaimers revenue arrangement with Dan's Demolition.

b. Dan's also expects to incur general and administrative costs related to this contract, as well as costs of wasted materials and labor that likely cannot be factored into the contract price. Can these costs be capitalized? Explain.

E18.32 **(LO 4)** **(Contract Costs, Collectibility)** Refer to the information in E18.31.

Instructions

a. Does the accounting for capitalized costs change if the contract is for 1 year rather than 3 years? Explain.

b. Dan's Demolition is a startup company; as a result, there is more than insignificant uncertainty about Dan's ability to make the 6-month payments on time. Does this uncertainty affect the amount of revenue to be recognized under the contract? Explain.

*E18.33 **(LO 5, 6)** **(Recognition of Profit on Long-Term Contracts)** During 2020, Nilsen Company started a construction job with a contract price of $1,600,000. The job was completed in 2022. The following information is available.

	2020	2021	2022
Costs incurred to date	$400,000	$825,000	$1,070,000
Estimated costs to complete	600,000	275,000	–0–
Billings to date	300,000	900,000	1,600,000
Collections to date	270,000	810,000	1,425,000

Instructions

a. Compute the amount of gross profit to be recognized each year, assuming the percentage-of-completion method is used.

b. Prepare all necessary journal entries for 2021.

c. Compute the amount of gross profit to be recognized each year, assuming the completed-contract method is used.

***E18.34 (LO 5) (Analysis of Percentage-of-Completion Financial Statements)** In 2020, Steinrotter Construction Corp. began construction work under a 3-year contract. The contract price was $1,000,000. Steinrotter uses the percentage-of-completion method for financial accounting purposes. The income to be recognized each year is based on the proportion of cost incurred to total estimated costs for completing the contract. The financial statement presentations relating to this contract at December 31, 2020, are shown below.

Balance Sheet		
Accounts receivable		$18,000
Construction in process	$65,000	
Less: Billings	61,500	
Costs and recognized profit in excess of billings		3,500
Income Statement		
Income (before tax) on the contract recognized in 2020		$19,500

Instructions

a. How much cash was collected in 2020 on this contract?

b. What was the initial estimated total income before tax on this contract?

(AICPA adapted)

***E18.35 (LO 5) Excel (Gross Profit on Uncompleted Contract)** On April 1, 2020, Dougherty Inc. entered into a cost plus fixed fee contract to construct an electric generator for Altom Corporation. At the contract date, Dougherty estimated that it would take 2 years to complete the project at a cost of $2,000,000. The fixed fee stipulated in the contract is $450,000. Dougherty appropriately accounts for this contract under the percentage-of-completion method. During 2020, Dougherty incurred costs of $800,000 related to the project. The estimated cost at December 31, 2020, to complete the contract is $1,200,000. Altom was billed $600,000 under the contract.

Instructions

Prepare a schedule to compute the amount of gross profit to be recognized by Dougherty under the contract for the year ended December 31, 2020. Show supporting computations in good form.

(AICPA adapted)

***E18.36 (LO 5, 6) (Recognition of Revenue on Long-Term Contract and Entries)** Hamilton Construction Company uses the percentage-of-completion method of accounting. In 2020, Hamilton began work under contract #E2-D2, which provided for a contract price of $2,200,000. Other details follow:

	2020	2021
Costs incurred during the year	$640,000	$1,425,000
Estimated costs to complete, as of December 31	960,000	–0–
Billings during the year	420,000	1,680,000
Collections during the year	350,000	1,500,000

Instructions

a. What portion of the total contract price would be recognized as revenue in 2020? In 2021?

b. Assuming the same facts as those above except that Hamilton uses the completed-contract method of accounting, what portion of the total contract price would be recognized as revenue in 2021?

c. Prepare a complete set of journal entries for 2020 (using the percentage-of-completion method).

***E18.37 (LO 5, 6) (Recognition of Profit and Balance Sheet Amounts for Long-Term Contracts)** Yanmei Construction Company began operations on January 1, 2020. During the year, Yanmei Construction entered into a contract with Lundquist Corp. to construct a manufacturing facility. At that time, Yanmei estimated that it would take 5 years to complete the facility at a total cost of $4,500,000. The total contract price for construction of the facility is $6,000,000. During the year, Yanmei incurred $1,185,800 in construction costs related to the construction project. The estimated cost to complete the contract is $4,204,200. Lundquist Corp. was billed and paid 25% of the contract price.

Instructions

Prepare schedules to compute the amount of gross profit to be recognized for the year ended December 31, 2020, and the amount to be shown as "costs and recognized profit in excess of billings" or "billings in excess of costs and recognized profit" at December 31, 2020, under each of the following methods. Show supporting computations in good form.

a. Completed-contract method.

b. Percentage-of-completion method.

(AICPA adapted)

*E18.38 **(LO 8)** **(Franchise Entries)** Pacific Crossburgers Inc. charges an initial franchise fee of $70,000. Upon the signing of the agreement (which covers 3 years), a payment of $28,000 is due. Thereafter, three annual payments of $14,000 are required. The credit rating of the franchisee is such that it would have to pay interest at 10% to borrow money. The franchise agreement is signed on May 1, 2020, and the franchise commences operation on July 1, 2020.

Instructions

Prepare the journal entries in 2020 for the franchisor under the following assumptions. (Round to the nearest dollar.)

a. No future services are required by the franchisor once the franchise starts operations.

b. The franchisor has substantial services to perform, once the franchise begins operations, to maintain the value of the franchise.

c. The total franchise fee includes training services (with a value of $2,400) for the period leading up to the franchise opening and for 2 months following opening.

*E18.39 **(LO 8)** **(Franchise Fee, Initial Down Payment)** On January 1, 2020, Lesley Benjamin signed an agreement, covering 5 years, to operate as a franchisee of Campbell Inc. for an initial franchise fee of $50,000. The amount of $10,000 was paid when the agreement was signed, and the balance is payable in five annual payments of $8,000 each, beginning January 1, 2021. The agreement provides that the down payment is nonrefundable and that no future services are required of the franchisor once the franchise commences operations on April 1, 2020. Lesley Benjamin's credit rating indicates that she can borrow money at 11% for a loan of this type.

Instructions

a. Prepare journal entries for Campbell for 2020-related revenue for this franchise arrangement.

b. Prepare journal entries for Campbell for 2020-related revenue for this franchise arrangement, assuming that in addition to the franchise rights, Campbell also provides 1 year of operational consulting and training services, beginning on the signing date. These services have a value of $3,600.

c. Repeat the requirements for part (a), assuming that Campbell must provide services to Benjamin throughout the franchise period to maintain the franchise value.

Problems

P18.1 **(LO 2, 3)** **(Allocate Transaction Price, Upfront Fees)** Tablet Tailors sells tablet PCs combined with Internet service, which permits the tablet to connect to the Internet anywhere and set up a Wi-Fi hot spot. It offers two bundles with the following terms.

1. Tablet Bundle A sells a tablet with 3 years of Internet service. The price for the tablet and a 3-year Internet connection service contract is $500. The standalone selling price of the tablet is $250 (the cost to Tablet Tailors is $175). Tablet Tailors sells the Internet access service independently for an upfront payment of $300. On January 2, 2020, Tablet Tailors signed 100 contracts, receiving a total of $50,000 in cash.
2. Tablet Bundle B includes the tablet and Internet service plus a service plan for the tablet PC (for any repairs or upgrades to the tablet or the Internet connections) during the 3-year contract period.

That product bundle sells for $600. Tablet Tailors provides the 3-year tablet service plan as a separate product with a standalone selling price of $150. Tablet Tailors signed 200 contracts for Tablet Bundle B on July 1, 2020, receiving a total of $120,000 in cash.

Instructions

a. Prepare any journal entries to record the revenue arrangement for Tablet Bundle A on January 2, 2020, and December 31, 2020.

b. Prepare any journal entries to record the revenue arrangement for Tablet Bundle B on July 1, 2020, and December 31, 2020.

c. Repeat the requirements for part (a), assuming that Tablet Tailors has no reliable data with which to estimate the standalone selling price for the Internet service.

P18.2 **(LO 2, 3, 4) (Allocate Transaction Price, Modification of Contract)** Refer to the Tablet Bundle A revenue arrangement in P18.1. In response to competitive pressure for Internet access for Tablet Bundle A, after 2 years of the 3-year contract, Tablet Tailors offers a modified contract and extension incentive. The extended contract services are similar to those provided in the first 2 years of the contract. Signing the extension and paying $90 (which equals the standalone selling of the revised Internet service package) extends access for 2 more years of Internet connection. Forty Tablet Bundle A customers sign up for this offer.

Instructions

a. Prepare the journal entries when the contract is signed on January 2, 2022, for the 40 extended contracts. Assume the modification does not result in a separate performance obligation.

b. Prepare the journal entries on December 31, 2022, for the 40 extended contracts (the first year of the revised 3-year contract).

P18.3 **(LO 2, 3, 4) (Allocate Transaction Price, Discounts, Time Value)** Grill Master Company sells total outdoor grilling solutions, providing gas and charcoal grills, accessories, and installation services for custom patio grilling stations.

Instructions

Respond to the requirements related to the following independent revenue arrangements for Grill Master products and services.

a. Grill Master offers contract GM205, which is comprised of a free-standing gas grill for small patio use plus installation to a customer's gas line for a total price $800. On a standalone basis, the grill sells for $700 (cost $425), and Grill Master estimates that the standalone selling price of the installation service (based on cost-plus estimation) is $150. (The selling of the grill and the installation services should be considered two performance obligations.) Grill Master signed 10 GM205 contracts on April 20, 2020, and customers paid the contract price in cash. The grills were delivered and installed on May 15, 2020. Prepare journal entries for Grill Master for GM205 in April and May 2020.

b. The State of Kentucky is planning major renovations in its parks during 2020 and enters into a contract with Grill Master to purchase 400 durable, easy maintenance, standard charcoal grills during 2020. The grills are priced at $200 each (with a cost of $160 each), and Grill Master provides a 6% volume discount if Kentucky purchases at least 300 grills during 2020. On April 17, 2020, Grill Master delivered and received payment for 280 grills. Based on prior experience with the State of Kentucky renovation projects, the delivery of this many grills makes it certain that Kentucky will meet the discount threshold. Prepare the journal entries for Grill Master for grills sold on April 17, 2020. Assume the company records sales transaction net.

c. Grill Master sells its specialty combination gas/wood-fired grills to local restaurants. Each grill is sold for $1,000 (cost $550) on credit with terms 3/30, net/90. Prepare the journal entries for the sale of 20 grills on September 1, 2020, and upon payment, assuming the customer paid on (1) September 25, 2020, and (2) October 15, 2020. Assume the company records sales net.

d. On October 1, 2020, Grill Master sold one of its super deluxe combination gas/charcoal grills to a local builder. The builder plans to install it in one of its "Parade of Homes" houses. Grill Master accepted a 3-year, zero-interest-bearing note with face amount of $5,324. The grill has an inventory cost of $2,700. An interest rate of 10% is an appropriate market rate of interest for this customer. Prepare the journal entries on October 1, 2020, and December 31, 2020.

P18.4 (LO 2, 3, 4) (Allocate Transaction Price, Discounts, Time Value) Economy Appliance Co. manufactures low-price, no-frills appliances that are in great demand for rental units. Pricing and cost information on Economy's main products are as follows.

Item	Standalone Selling Price (Cost)
Refrigerator	$500 ($260)
Range	560 (275)
Stackable washer/dryer unit	700 (400)

Customers can contract to purchase either individually at the stated prices or a three-item bundle with a price of $1,800. The bundle price includes delivery and installation. Economy also provides installation (not a separate performance obligation).

Instructions

Respond to the requirements related to the following independent revenue arrangements for Economy Appliance Co.

a. On June 1, 2020, Economy sold 100 washer/dryer units without installation to Laplante Rentals for $70,000. Laplante is a newer customer and is unsure how this product will work in its older rental units. Economy offers a 60-day return privilege and estimates, based on prior experience with sales on this product, 4% of the units will be returned. Prepare the journal entries for the sale and related cost of goods sold on June 1, 2020.

b. YellowCard Property Managers operates upscale student apartment buildings. On May 1, 2020, Economy signs a contract with YellowCard for 300 appliance bundles to be delivered and installed in one of its new buildings. YellowCard pays 20% cash at contract signing and will pay the balance upon installation no later than August 1, 2020. Prepare journal entries for Economy on (1) May 1, 2020, and (2) August 1, 2020, when all appliances are installed.

c. Refer to the arrangement in part (b). It would help YellowCard secure lease agreements with students if the installation of the appliance bundles can be completed by July 1, 2020. YellowCard offers a 10% bonus payment if Economy can complete installation by July 1, 2020. Economy estimates its chances of meeting the bonus deadline to be 90%, based on a number of prior contracts of similar scale. Repeat the requirement for part (b), given this bonus provision. Assume installation is completed by July 1, 2020.

d. Epic Rentals would like to take advantage of the bundle price for its 400-unit project; on February 1, 2020, Economy signs a contract with Epic for 400 bundles. Under the agreement, Economy will hold the appliance bundles in its warehouses until the new rental units are ready for installation. Epic pays 10% cash at contract signing. On April 1, 2020, Economy completes manufacture of the appliances in the Epic bundle order and places them in the warehouse. Economy and Epic have documented the warehouse arrangement and identified the units designated for Epic. The units are ready to ship, and Economy may not sell these units to other customers. Prepare journal entries for Economy on (1) February 1, 2020, and (2) April 1, 2020.

P18.5 (LO 2, 3, 4) (Allocate Transaction Price, Returns, and Consignments) Ritt Ranch & Farm is a distributor of ranch and farm equipment. Its products range from small tools, power equipment for trench-digging and fencing, grain dryers, and barn winches. Most products are sold direct via its company catalog and Internet site. However, given some of its specialty products, select farm implement stores carry Ritt's products. Pricing and cost information on three of Ritt's most popular products are as follows.

Item	Standalone Selling Price (Cost)
Mini-trencher	$ 3,600 ($2,000)
Power fence hole auger	1,200 (800)
Grain/hay dryer	14,000 (11,000)

Instructions

Respond to the requirements related to the following independent revenue arrangements for Ritt Ranch & Farm.

a. On January 1, 2020, Ritt sells 40 augers to Mills Farm & Fleet for $48,000. Mills signs a 6-month note at an annual interest rate of 12%. Ritt allows Mills to return any auger that it cannot use within 60 days and receive a full refund. Based on prior experience, Ritt estimates that 5% of units sold to customers like Mills will be returned (using the most likely outcome approach). Ritt's costs to recover the products will be immaterial, and the returned augers are expected to be resold at a profit. Prepare the journal entry for Ritt on January 1, 2020.

b. On August 10, 2020, Ritt sells 16 mini-trenchers to a farm co-op in western Minnesota on account. Ritt provides a 4% volume discount on the mini-trenchers if the co-op has a 15% increase in purchases from Ritt compared to the prior year. Given the slowdown in the farm economy, sales to the co-op have been flat, and it is highly uncertain that the benchmark will be met. Prepare the journal entry for Ritt on August 10, 2020.

c. Ritt sells three grain/hay dryers to a local farmer at a total contract price of $45,200. In addition to the dryers, Ritt provides installation, which has a standalone selling price of $1,000 per unit installed. The contract payment also includes a $1,200 maintenance plan for the dryers for 3 years after installation. Ritt signs the contract on June 20, 2020, and receives a 20% down payment from the farmer. The dryers are delivered and installed on October 1, 2020, and full payment is made to Ritt. Prepare the journal entries for Ritt in 2020 related to this arrangement.

d. On April 25, 2020, Ritt ships 100 augers to Farm Depot, a farm supply dealer in Nebraska, on consignment. By June 30, 2020, Farm Depot has sold 60 of the consigned augers at the listed price of $1,200 per unit. Farm Depot notifies Ritt of the sales, retains a 10% commission, and remits the cash due Ritt. Prepare the journal entries for Ritt and Farm Depot for the consignment arrangement.

P18.6 **(LO 3)** **(Warranty, Customer Loyalty Program)** Hale Hardware takes pride as the "shop around the corner" that can compete with the big-box home improvement stores by providing good service from knowledgeable sales associates (many of whom are retired local handymen). Hale has developed the following two revenue arrangements to enhance its relationships with customers and increase its bottom line.

1. Hale sells a specialty portable winch that is popular with many of the local customers for use at their lake homes (putting docks in and out, launching boats, etc.). The Hale winch is a standard manufacture winch that Hale modifies so the winch can be used for a variety of tasks. Hale sold 70 of these winches during 2020 at a total price of $21,000, with a warranty guarantee that the product was free of any defects. The cost of winches sold is $16,000. The assurance warranties extend for a 3-year period with an estimated cost of $2,100. In addition, Hale sold extended warranties related to 20 Hale winches for 2 years beyond the 3-year period for $400 each.
2. To bolster its already strong customer base, Hale implemented a customer loyalty program that rewards a customer with 1 loyalty point for every $10 of purchases on a select group of Hale products. Each point is redeemable for a $1 discount on any purchases of Hale merchandise in the following 2 years. During 2020, customers purchased select group products for $100,000 (all products are sold to provide a 45% gross profit) and earned 10,000 points redeemable for future purchases. The standalone selling price of the purchased products is $100,000. Based on prior experience with incentives programs like this, Hale expects 9,500 points to be redeemed related to these sales (Hale appropriately uses this experience to estimate the value of future consideration related to bonus points).

Instructions

a. Identify the separate performance obligations in the Hale warranty and bonus point programs, and briefly explain the point in time when the performance obligations are satisfied.

b. Prepare the journal entries for Hale related to the sales of Hale winches with warranties.

c. Prepare the journal entries for the bonus point sales for Hale in 2020.

d. How much additional sales revenue is recognized by Hale in 2021, assuming 4,500 bonus points are redeemed?

P18.7 **(LO 3)** **(Customer Loyalty Program)** Martz Inc. has a customer loyalty program that rewards a customer with 1 customer loyalty point for every $10 of purchases. Each point is redeemable for a $3 discount on any future purchases. On July 2, 2020, customers purchase products for $300,000 (with a cost of $171,000) and earn 30,000 points redeemable for future purchases. Martz expects 25,000 points to be redeemed. Martz estimates a standalone selling price of $2.50 per point (or $75,000 total) on the basis of the likelihood of redemption. The points provide a material right to customers that they would not receive without entering into a contract. As a result, Martz concludes that the points are a separate performance obligation.

Instructions

a. Determine the transaction price for the product and the customer loyalty points.

b. Prepare the journal entries to record the sale of the product and related points on July 2, 2020.

c. At the end of the first reporting period (July 31, 2020), 10,000 loyalty points are redeemed. Martz continues to expect 25,000 loyalty points to be redeemed in total. Determine the amount of loyalty point revenue to be recognized at July 31, 2020.

P18.8 (LO 2, 3) **(Time Value, Gift Cards, Discounts)** Presented below are two independent revenue arrangements for Colbert Company.

Instructions

Respond to the requirements related to each revenue arrangement.

a. Colbert sells 3D printer systems. Recently, Colbert provided a special promotion of zero-interest financing for 2 years on any new 3D printer system. Assume that Colbert sells Lyle Cartright a 3D system, receiving a $5,000 zero-interest-bearing note on January 1, 2020. The cost of the 3D printer system is $4,000. Colbert imputes a 6% interest rate on this zero-interest note transaction. Prepare the journal entry to record the sale on January 1, 2020, and compute the total amount of revenue to be recognized in 2020.

b. Colbert sells 20 nonrefundable $100 gift cards for 3D printer paper on March 1, 2020. The paper has a standalone selling price of $100 (cost $80). The gift cards expiration date is June 30, 2020. Colbert estimates that customers will not redeem 10% of these gift cards. The pattern of redemption is as follows.

	Redemption Total
March 31	50%
April 30	80
June 30	85

Prepare the 2020 journal entries related to the gift cards at March 1, March 31, April 30, and June 30.

*P18.9 (LO 5, 6) Excel **(Recognition of Profit on Long-Term Contract)** Shanahan Construction Company has entered into a contract beginning January 1, 2020, to build a parking complex. It has been estimated that the complex will cost $600,000 and will take 3 years to construct. The complex will be billed to the purchasing company at $900,000. The following data pertain to the construction period.

	2020	2021	2022
Costs to date	$270,000	$450,000	$610,000
Estimated costs to complete	330,000	150,000	–0–
Progress billings to date	270,000	550,000	900,000
Cash collected to date	240,000	500,000	900,000

Instructions

a. Using the percentage-of-completion method, compute the estimated gross profit that would be recognized during each year of the construction period.

b. Using the completed-contract method, compute the estimated gross profit that would be recognized during each year of the construction period.

*P18.10 (LO 5, 6, 7) **(Long-Term Contract with Interim Loss)** On March 1, 2020, Pechstein Construction Company contracted to construct a factory building for Fabrik Manufacturing Inc. for a total contract price of $8,400,000. The building was completed by October 31, 2022. The annual contract costs incurred, estimated costs to complete the contract, and accumulated billings to Fabrik for 2020, 2021, and 2022 are given below.

	2020	2021	2022
Contract costs incurred during the year	$2,880,000	$2,230,000	$2,190,000
Estimated costs to complete the contract at 12/31	3,520,000	2,190,000	–0–
Billings to Fabrik during the year	3,200,000	3,500,000	1,700,000

Instructions

a. Using the percentage-of-completion method, prepare schedules to compute the profit or loss to be recognized as a result of this contract for the years ended December 31, 2020, 2021, and 2022. (Ignore income taxes.)

b. Using the completed-contract method, prepare schedules to compute the profit or loss to be recognized as a result of this contract for the years ended December 31, 2020, 2021, and 2022. (Ignore incomes taxes.)

*P18.11 (LO 5, 6, 7) Excel (Long-Term Contract with an Overall Loss) On July 1, 2020, Torvill Construction Company Inc. contracted to build an office building for Gumbel Corp. for a total contract price of $1,900,000. On July 1, Torvill estimated that it would take between 2 and 3 years to complete the building. On December 31, 2022, the building was deemed substantially completed. Following are accumulated contract costs incurred, estimated costs to complete the contract, and accumulated billings to Gumbel for 2020, 2021, and 2022.

	At 12/31/20	At 12/31/21	At 12/31/22
Contract costs incurred to date	$ 300,000	$1,200,000	$2,100,000
Estimated costs to complete the contract	1,200,000	800,000	–0–
Billings to Gumbel	300,000	1,100,000	1,850,000

Instructions

a. Using the percentage-of-completion method, prepare schedules to compute the profit or loss to be recognized as a result of this contract for the years ended December 31, 2020, 2021, and 2022. (Ignore income taxes.)

b. Using the completed-contract method, prepare schedules to compute the profit or loss to be recognized as a result of this contract for the years ended December 31, 2020, 2021, and 2022. (Ignore income taxes.)

*P18.12 (LO 8) (Franchise Revenue) Amigos Burrito Inc. sells franchises to independent operators throughout the northwestern part of the United States. The contract with the franchisee includes the following provisions.

1. The franchisee is charged an initial fee of $120,000. Of this amount, $20,000 is payable when the agreement is signed, and a $100,000 zero-interest-bearing note is payable with a $20,000 payment at the end of each of the 5 subsequent years. The present value of an ordinary annuity of five annual receipts of $20,000, each discounted at 10%, is $75,816.
2. All of the initial franchise fee collected by Amigos is to be refunded and the remaining obligation canceled if, for any reason, the franchisee fails to open his or her franchise.
3. In return for the initial franchise fee, Amigos agrees to (a) assist the franchisee in selecting the location for the business, (b) negotiate the lease for the land, (c) obtain financing and assist with building design, (d) supervise construction, (e) establish accounting and tax records, and (f) provide expert advice over a 5-year period relating to such matters as employee and management training, quality control, and promotion. This continuing involvement by Amigos helps maintain the brand value of the franchise.
4. In addition to the initial franchise fee, the franchisee is required to pay to Amigos a monthly fee of 2% of sales for menu planning, recipe innovations, and the privilege of purchasing ingredients from Amigos at or below prevailing market prices.

Management of Amigos Burrito estimates that the value of the services rendered to the franchisee at the time the contract is signed amounts to at least $20,000. All franchisees to date have opened their locations at the scheduled time, and none have defaulted on any of the notes receivable. The credit ratings of all franchisees would entitle them to borrow at the current interest rate of 10%.

Instructions

a. Discuss the alternatives that Amigos Burrito Inc. might use to account for the franchise fees.

b. Prepare the journal entries for the initial and continuing franchise fees, assuming:
   1. Franchise agreement is signed on January 5, 2020.
   2. Amigos completes franchise startup tasks and the franchise opens on July 1, 2020.
   3. The franchisee records $260,000 in sales in the first 6 months of operations and remits the monthly franchise fee on December 31, 2020.

c. Briefly describe the accounting for unearned franchise fees, assuming that Amigos has little or no involvement with the franchisee related to expert advice on employee and management training, quality control, and promotion, once the franchise opens.

Concepts for Analysis

CA18.1 (LO 2, 3) **(Five-Step Revenue Process)** Revenue is recognized based on a five-step process that is applied to a company's revenue arrangements.

Instructions

a. Briefly describe the five-step process.

b. Explain the importance of contracts when analyzing revenue arrangements.

c. How are fair value measurement concepts applied in implementation of the five-step process?

d. How does the five-step process reflect application of the definitions of assets and liabilities?

CA18.2 (LO 1, 2, 3) **(Satisfying Performance Obligations)** Judy Schaeffer is getting up to speed on the new guidance on revenue recognition. She is trying to understand the revenue recognition principle as it relates to the five-step revenue recognition process.

Instructions

a. Describe the revenue recognition principle.

b. Briefly discuss how the revenue recognition principle relates to the definitions of assets and liabilities. What is the importance of control?

c. Judy recalls that previous revenue recognition guidance required that revenue not be recognized unless the revenue was realized or realizable (also referred to as collectibility). Is collectibility a consideration in the recognition of revenue? Explain.

CA18.3 (LO 1, 2, 3) **(Recognition of Revenue—Theory)** Revenue is usually recognized at the point of sale (a point in time). Under special circumstances, however, bases other than the point of sale are used for the timing of revenue recognition.

Instructions

a. Why is the point of sale usually used as the basis for the timing of revenue recognition?

b. Disregarding the special circumstances when bases other than the point of sale are used, discuss the merits of each of the following objections to the point-of-sale basis of revenue recognition:

1. It is too conservative because revenue is earned throughout the entire process of production.
2. It is not conservative enough because accounts receivable do not represent disposable funds, sales returns and allowances may be made, and collection and bad debt expenses may be incurred in a later period.

c. Revenue may also be recognized over time. Give an example of the circumstances in which revenue is recognized over time and accounting merits of its use instead of the point-of-sale basis.

(AICPA adapted)

CA18.4 (LO 1, 2, 3) **(Recognition of Revenue—Theory)** Revenue is recognized for accounting purposes when a performance obligation is satisfied. In some situations, revenue is recognized over time as the fair values of assets and liabilities change. In other situations, however, accountants have developed guidelines for recognizing revenue at the point of sale.

Instructions

(Ignore income taxes.)

a. Explain and justify why revenue is often recognized at time of sale.

b. Explain in what situations it would be appropriate to recognize revenue over time.

CA18.5 (LO 2, 3) **(Discounts)** Fahey Company sells Stairmasters to a retailer, Physical Fitness, Inc., for $2,000,000. Fahey has a history of providing price concessions on this product if the retailer has difficulty selling the Stairmasters to customers. Fahey has experience with sales like these in the past and estimates that the maximum amount of price concessions is $300,000.

Instructions

a. Determine the amount of revenue that Fahey should recognize for the sale of Stairmasters to Physical Fitness, Inc.

b. According to GAAP, in some situations, the amount of revenue recognized may be constrained. Explain how the accounting for the Stairmasters sales might be affected by the revenue constraint due to variable consideration or returns.

c. Some believe that revenue recognition should be constrained by collectibility. Is such a view consistent with GAAP? Explain.

CA18.6 **(LO 1, 2, 3)** **(Recognition of Revenue from Subscriptions)** *Cutting Edge* is a monthly magazine that has been on the market for 18 months. It currently has a circulation of 1.4 million copies. Negotiations are underway to obtain a bank loan in order to update the magazine's facilities. *Cutting Edge* is producing close to capacity and expects to grow at an average of 20% per year over the next 3 years.

After reviewing the financial statements of *Cutting Edge*, Andy Rich, the bank loan officer, had indicated that a loan could be offered to *Cutting Edge* only if it could increase its current ratio and decrease its debt to equity ratio to a specified level. Jonathan Embry, the marketing manager of *Cutting Edge*, has devised a plan to meet these requirements. Embry indicates that an advertising campaign can be initiated to immediately increase circulation. The potential customers would be contacted after the purchase of another magazine's mailing list. The campaign would include:

1. An offer to subscribe to *Cutting Edge* at three-fourths the normal price.
2. A special offer to all new subscribers to receive the most current world atlas whenever requested at a guaranteed price of $2.
3. An unconditional guarantee that any subscriber will receive a full refund if dissatisfied with the magazine.

Although the offer of a full refund is risky, Embry claims that few people will ask for a refund after receiving half of their subscription issues. Embry notes that other magazine companies have tried this sales promotion technique and experienced great success. Their average cancellation rate was 25%. On average, each company increased its initial circulation threefold and in the long run increased circulation to twice that which existed before the promotion. In addition, 60% of the new subscribers are expected to take advantage of the atlas premium. Embry feels confident that the increased subscriptions from the advertising campaign will increase the current ratio and decrease the debt to equity ratio.

You are the controller of *Cutting Edge* and must give your opinion of the proposed plan.

Instructions

a. When should revenue from the new subscriptions be recognized?

b. How would you classify the estimated sales returns stemming from the unconditional guarantee?

c. How should the atlas premium be recorded? Is the estimated premium claims a liability? Explain.

d. Does the proposed plan achieve the goals of increasing the current ratio and decreasing the debt to equity ratio?

CA18.7 **(LO 2, 3)** **(Recognition of Revenue—Bonus Points)** Griseta & Dubel Inc. was formed early this year to sell merchandise credits to merchants, who distribute the credits free to their customers. For example, customers can earn additional credits based on the dollars they spend with a merchant (e.g., airlines and hotels). Accounts for accumulating the credits and catalogs illustrating the merchandise for which the credits may be exchanged are maintained online. Centers with inventories of merchandise premiums have been established for redemption of the credits. Merchants may not return unused credits to Griseta & Dubel.

The following schedule expresses Griseta & Dubel's expectations as to the percentages of a normal month's activity that will be attained. For this purpose, a "normal month's activity" is defined as the level of operations expected when expansion of activities ceases or tapers off to a stable rate. The company expects that this level will be attained in the third year and that sales of credits will average $6,000,000 per month throughout the third year.

Month	Actual Credit Sales Percent	Merchandise Premium Purchases Percent	Credit Redemptions Percent
6th	30%	40%	10%
12th	60	60	45
18th	80	80	70
24th	90	90	80
30th	100	100	95

Griseta & Dubel plans to adopt an annual closing date at the end of each 12 months of operation.

Instructions

a. Discuss the factors to be considered in determining when revenue should be recognized.

b. Apply the revenue recognition factors to the Griseta & Dubel Inc. revenue arrangement.

c. Provide balance sheet accounts that should be used and indicate how each should be classified.

(AICPA adapted)

CA18.8 **(LO 2, 3)** Ethics **(Revenue Recognition—Membership Fees)** Midwest Health Club (MHC) offers 1-year memberships. Membership fees are due in full at the beginning of the individual membership period. As an incentive to new customers, MHC advertised that any customers not satisfied for any reason could receive a refund of the remaining portion of unused membership fees. As a result of this policy, Richard Nies, corporate controller, recognized revenue ratably over the life of the membership. MHC is in the process of preparing its year-end financial statements. Rachel Avery, MHC's treasurer, is concerned about the company's lackluster performance this year. She reviews the financial statements Nies prepared and tells Nies to recognize membership revenue when the fees are received.

Instructions

Answer the following questions.

a. What are the ethical issues involved?

b. What should Nies do?

*CA18.9 **(LO5)** Writing **(Long-Term Contract—Percentage-of-Completion)** Widjaja Company is accounting for a long-term construction contract using the percentage-of-completion method. It is a 4-year contract that is currently in its second year. The latest estimates of total contract costs indicate that the contract will be completed at a profit to Widjaja Company.

Instructions

a. What theoretical justification is there for Widjaja Company's use of the percentage-of-completion method?

b. How would progress billings be accounted for? Include in your discussion the classification of progress billings in Widjaja Company financial statements.

c. How would the income recognized in the second year of the 4-year contract be determined using the cost-to-cost method of determining percentage of completion?

d. What would be the effect on earnings per share in the second year of the 4-year contract of using the percentage-of-completion method instead of the completed-contract method? Discuss.

(AICPA adapted)

Using Your Judgment

As the new revenue recognition guidance is not yet implemented, note that the financial statements and notes for ***Procter & Gamble, Coca-Cola, PepsiCo,*** *and* ***Westinghouse*** *reflect revenue recognition under prior standards.*

Financial Reporting Problem

The Procter & Gamble Company (P&G)

The financial statements of P&G are presented in Appendix B. The company's complete annual report, including the notes to the financial statements, is available online.

Instructions

Refer to P&G's financial statements and the accompanying notes to answer the following questions.

a. What were P&G's net sales for 2017?

b. What was the percentage of increase or decrease in P&G's net sales from 2016 to 2017? From 2015 to 2016? From 2015 to 2017?

c. In its notes to the financial statements, what criteria does P&G use to recognize revenue?

d. How does P&G account for trade promotions? Does the accounting conform to accrual accounting concepts? Explain.

Comparative Analysis Case

The Coca-Cola Company and PepsiCo, Inc.

The financial statements of **Coca-Cola** and **PepsiCo** are presented in Appendices C and D, respectively. The companies' complete annual reports, including the notes to the financial statements, are available online.

Instructions

Use the companies' financial information to answer the following questions.

a. What were Coca-Cola's and PepsiCo's net revenues (sales) for the year 2017? Which company increased its revenue more (dollars and percentage) from 2016 to 2017?

b. Are the revenue recognition policies of Coca-Cola and PepsiCo similar? Explain.

c. In which foreign countries (geographic areas) did Coca-Cola and PepsiCo experience significant revenues in 2017? Compare the amounts of foreign revenues to U.S. revenues for both Coca-Cola and PepsiCo.

Financial Statement Analysis Case

Westinghouse Electric Corporation

The following note appears in the "Summary of Significant Accounting Policies" section of the Annual Report of **Westinghouse Electric Corporation.**

Note 1 (in part): Revenue Recognition. Sales are primarily recorded as products are shipped and services are rendered. The percentage-of-completion method of accounting is used for nuclear steam supply system orders with delivery schedules generally in excess of five years and for certain construction projects where this method of accounting is consistent with industry practice.

WFSI revenues are generally recognized on the accrual method. When accounts become delinquent for more than two payment periods, usually 60 days, income is recognized only as payments are received. Such delinquent accounts for which no payments are received in the current month, and other accounts on which income is not being recognized because the receipt of either principal or interest is questionable, are classified as nonearning receivables.

Instructions

a. Identify the revenue recognition methods used by Westinghouse Electric as discussed in its note on significant accounting policies.

b. Under what conditions are the revenue recognition methods identified in the first paragraph of Westinghouse's note above acceptable?

c. From the information provided in the second paragraph of Westinghouse's note, identify the type of operation being described and defend the acceptability of the revenue recognition method.

Accounting, Analysis, and Principles

Diversified Industries manufactures sump-pumps. Its most popular product is called the Super Soaker, which has a retail price of $1,200 and costs $540 to manufacture. It sells the Super Soaker on a standalone basis directly to businesses. Diversified also provides installation services for these commercial customers, who want an emergency pumping capability (with regular and back-up generator power) at their businesses. Diversified also distributes the Super Soaker through a consignment agreement with Menards. Income data for the first quarter of 2020 from operations other than the Super Soaker are as follows.

Revenues	$9,500,000
Expenses	7,750,000

Diversified has the following information related to two Super Soaker revenue arrangements during the first quarter of 2020.

1. Diversified sells 30 Super Soakers to businesses in flood-prone areas for a total contract price of $54,600. In addition to the pumps, Diversified also provides installation (at a cost of $150 per pump). On a standalone basis, the fair value of this service is $200 per unit installed. The contract payment also includes a $10 per month service plan for the pumps for 3 years after installation (Diversified's cost to provide this service is $7 per month). The Super Soakers are delivered and installed on March 1, 2020, and full payment is made to Diversified. Any discount is applied to the pump/installation bundle.

2. Diversified ships 300 Super Soakers to Menards on consignment. By March 31, 2020, Menards has sold two-thirds of the consigned merchandise at the listed price of $1,200 per unit. Menards notifies Diversified of the sales, retains a 5% commission, and remits the cash due Diversified.

Accounting

Determine Diversified Industries' 2020 first-quarter net income. (Ignore taxes.)

Analysis

Determine free cash flow (see Chapter 5) for Diversified Industries for the first quarter of 2020. In the first quarter, Diversified had depreciation expense of $175,000 and a net increase in working capital (change in accounts receivable and accounts payable) of $250,000. In the first quarter, capital expenditures were $500,000; Diversified paid dividends of $120,000.

Principles

Explain how the five-step revenue recognition process, when applied to Diversified's two revenue arrangements, reflects the concept of control in the definition of an asset and trade-offs between relevance and faithful representation.

Bridge to the Profession

FASB Codification References

[1] FASB ASC 606. [Predecessor literature: None.]
[2] FASB Accounting Standards Update No. 2014-09, *Revenue from Contracts with Customers* (Topic 606) (May 2014), Summary.
[3] FASB ASC 606-10-25-1 to 4. [Predecessor literature: None.]
[4] FASB ASC 606-10-25-15. [Predecessor literature: None.]
[5] FASB ASC 606-10-32-2 to 4. [Predecessor literature: None.]
[6] FASB ASC 606-10-32-31 to 35. [Predecessor literature: None.]
[7] FASB ASC 606-10-25-1 (e). [Predecessor literature: None.]
[8] FASB ASC 606-10-32-2 to 4. [Predecessor literature: None.]
[9] FASB ASC 606-10-32-5 to 9. [Predecessor literature: None.]
[10] FASB ASC 606-10-32-12. [Predecessor literature: None.]
[11] FASB ASC 606-10-32-11. [Predecessor literature: None.]
[12] FASB ASC 606-10-32-18. [Predecessor literature: None.]
[13] FASB ASC 606-10-32-12. [Predecessor literature: None.]
[14] FASB Accounting Standards Update No. 2014-09, *Revenue from Contracts with Customers* (Topic 606) (May 2014), pp. 5–6.
[15] FASB ASC 606-10-55-72. [Predecessor literature: None.]
[16] FASB ASC 606-10-25-30 and 606-10-55-408. [Predecessor literature: None.]
[17] FASB ASC 606-10-55-38 to 39. [Predecessor literature: None.]
[18] FASB ASC 606-10-25-12. [Predecessor literature: None.]
[19] FASB ASC 606-10-25-13. [Predecessor literature: None.]
[20] FASB Accounting Standards Update No. 2014-09, *Revenue from Contracts with Customers* (Topic 606) (May 2014), par. BC261.
[21] FASB ASC 606-10-50-1 to 21. [Predecessor literature: None.]
[22] FASB ASC 606-10-25-27 to 29. [Predecessor literature: None.]
[23] FASB ASC 606-10-25-27. [Predecessor literature: None.]
[24] FASB ASC 450 *(Contingencies)*.
[25] FASB ASC 606-10-55-54 to 64. [Predecessor literature: None.]

Codification Exercises

If your school has a subscription to the FASB Codification, log in and prepare responses to the following. Provide Codification references for your responses.

CE18.1 Access the glossary ("Master Glossary") to answer the following.

a. What is the definition of a customer?

b. What is a performance obligation?

c. How is standalone selling price defined?

d. What is a transaction price?

CE18.2 Briefly explain the conditions when a contract modification shall be accounted for as a separate performance obligation.

CE18.3 Describe the accounting for refund liabilities.

CE18.4 What procedures are followed in the allocation of a discount?

Codification Research Case

Employees at your company disagree about the accounting for sales returns. The sales manager believes that granting more generous return provisions can give the company a competitive edge and increase sales revenue. The controller cautions that, depending on the terms granted, loose return provisions might lead to non-GAAP revenue recognition. The company CFO would like you to research the issue to provide an authoritative answer.

Instructions

If your school has a subscription to the FASB Codification, log in and prepare responses to the following. Provide Codification references for your responses. (Provide paragraph citations.)

a. What is the authoritative literature addressing revenue recognition when right of return exists?

b. What is meant by "right of return"? "Bill and hold"?

c. Describe the accounting when there is a right of return.

d. When goods are sold on a bill-and-hold basis, what conditions must be met to recognize revenue upon receipt of the order?

Additional Professional Resources

Go to WileyPLUS for other career-readiness resources, such as career coaching, internship opportunities, and CPAexcel prep.

CHAPTER 19

Accounting for Income Taxes

LEARNING OBJECTIVES

After studying this chapter, you should be able to:

1. Describe the fundamentals of accounting for income taxes.
2. Identify additional issues in accounting for income taxes.
3. Explain the accounting for loss carryforwards.
4. Describe the presentation of deferred income taxes in financial statements.

PREVIEW OF CHAPTER 19 As the following opening story indicates, changes in the tax code can lead to significant accounting adjustments. Therefore, it is important that companies present financial information to the investment community that provides a clear picture of present and potential tax obligations and tax benefits. In this chapter, we discuss the basic guidelines that companies must follow in reporting income taxes. The content and organization of the chapter are as follows.

This chapter also includes numerous conceptual and global discussions that are integral to the topics presented here.

ACCOUNTING FOR INCOME TAXES

Fundamentals of Accounting for Income Taxes
- Future taxable amounts and deferred taxes
- Future deductible amounts and deferred taxes
- Valuation allowance

Additional Considerations
- Income statement presentation
- Specific differences
- Tax rate considerations

Accounting for Net Operating Losses
- Loss carryforward
- Loss carryforward example

Financial Statement Presentation
- Balance sheet
- Note disclosure
- Income statement
- Asset-liability method

Taxes Are A-Changing

Corporate America received an early holiday present in 2017 in the form of the Tax Cuts and Jobs Act (TCJA). Here are some of the important provisions relevant to the accounting for income taxes.

- ***Decreased corporate tax rate.*** The most far-reaching change in the TCJA is the change in the corporate tax rate, which moves from a graduated rate of up to 35 percent to a flat rate of 21 percent. To illustrate, more than half of the combined net-income growth reported by the largest 200 companies for the first quarter of 2018 stem from a decline in companies' effective tax rates. As an example, JPMorgan plans to invest $20 billion to expand growth across its businesses due to the change in tax law. As shown in the

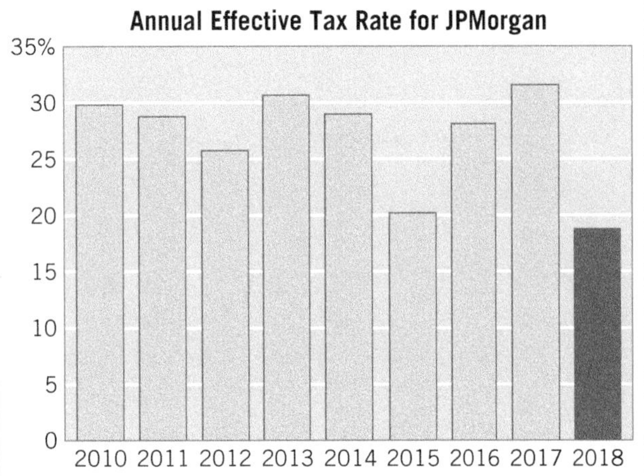

Note: Rate of 2018 is based on bank's estimate.
Source: JPMorgan.

adjacent chart, in 2018 its effective tax rate has dropped substantially, which should save JPMorgan $3.6 billion in taxes.

- ***Remeasurement of deferred tax assets and deferred tax liabilities.*** Deferred tax assets are past tax deductions and credits that companies can use to defray future tax bills. However, when tax rates are lowered, these deferred tax assets are no longer as valuable. As an example, **Citigroup** has a very large deferred asset balance for which the company has to take a $19 billion write-off. On the other hand, deferred tax liabilities are amounts that the company will have to pay to the government in the future. If tax rates are lower, the companies have a smaller liability. Fortunately for many companies, deferred tax liabilities are generally greater than deferred tax assets. The dollar amount of the deferred tax liabilities for calendar year-end companies at the end of 2016 was nearly twice the dollar amount of deferred tax assets. That's a net benefit for corporate America—one-time gains that will effectively transfer a liability into equity.
- ***Carryforward of net operating losses.*** When a company suffers a net operating loss (NOL), it can generally offset this loss against future income. In the past, companies could use these present losses to offset taxable income in the previous two years. The company filed amended tax returns (reducing taxable income) and received tax refunds from the government. No more—under new rules, NOLs cannot be carried back to any previous years. That means no more consolation prizes for money-losers. However, under the TCJA, NOLs can be carried forward indefinitely.
- ***Bonus depreciation and interest.*** Using bonus depreciation, companies may record tax deprecation at a higher rate compared to GAAP depreciation. Under the TCJA, that write-off can be up to 100 percent in order to write off the total cost of new and used qualifying property. One bit of bad news for highly leveraged companies is the TCJA limit on the deduction for interest expense to 30 percent of positive "adjusted taxable income" (calculated similarly to earnings before interest, taxes, depreciation, and amortization). However, if a company cannot completely use its interest expense deduction in a year, it may carry it forward indefinitely (which may create a deferred tax asset for interest expense, similar to NOLs).

In summary, the TCJA made significant changes in corporate tax rules. And while the FASB made no changes in GAAP (except for a very narrow update of accounting rules for deferred tax effects recorded on other comprehensive income), the TCJA changes could result in significant remeasurement of deferred tax assets and liabilities, and may change firms' plans for capital spending and financing for years to come. Read on to learn more about the accounting for taxes.

Source: Adapted from J. Ciesielski, "The Tax Cuts & Jobs Act: What Analysts Need to Know," *The Analyst's Accounting Observer*, Volume 27, No. 2 (February 14, 2018). See also E. Glazer, "How JPMorgan Will Spend a Big Chunk of Its Tax Windfall," *Wall Street Journal* (January 23, 2018).

Review and Practice

Go to the **Review and Practice** section at the end of the chapter for a targeted summary review and practice problem with solution. Multiple-choice questions with annotated solutions as well as additional exercises and practice problem with solutions are also available online.

Fundamentals of Accounting for Income Taxes

LEARNING OBJECTIVE 1

Describe the fundamentals of accounting for income taxes.

Up to this point, you have learned the basic guidelines that corporations use to report information to investors and creditors. Corporations also must file income tax returns following the guidelines developed by the Internal Revenue Service (IRS). Because GAAP and tax regulations differ in a number of ways, so frequently do pretax financial income and taxable income. Consequently, the amount that a company reports as tax expense will differ from the amount of taxes payable to the IRS. Illustration 19.1 highlights these differences.

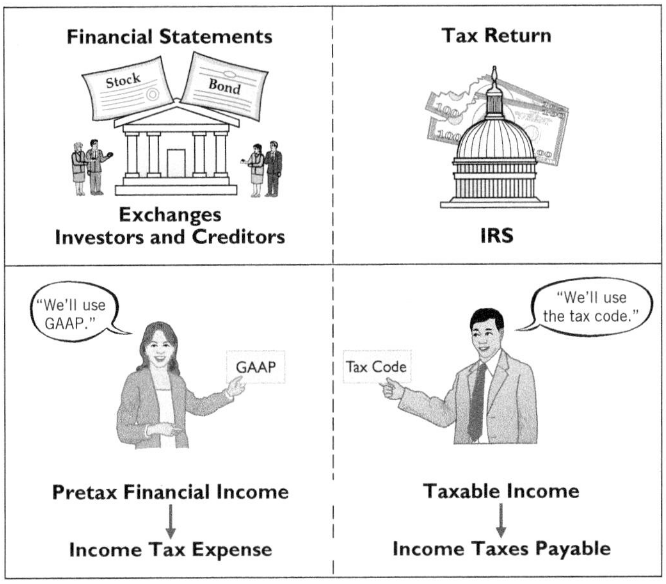

ILLUSTRATION 19.1
Fundamental Differences Between Financial and Tax Reporting

Pretax financial income is a **financial reporting** term. It also is often referred to as income before taxes, income for financial reporting purposes, or income for book purposes. Companies determine pretax financial income according to GAAP. They measure it with the objective of providing useful information to investors and creditors.

Taxable income (income for tax purposes) is a **tax accounting** term. It indicates the amount used to compute income taxes payable. Companies determine taxable income according to the Internal Revenue Code (the tax code). Income taxes provide money to support government operations.

To illustrate how differences in GAAP and IRS rules affect financial reporting and taxable income, assume that Chelsea Inc. reported revenues of $130,000 and expenses of $60,000 in each of its first three years of operations. Illustration 19.2 shows the (partial) income statement over these three years.

ILLUSTRATION 19.2
Financial Reporting Income

Chelsea Inc.
GAAP Reporting

	2020	2021	2022	Total
Revenues	$130,000	$130,000	$130,000	
Expenses	60,000	60,000	60,000	
Pretax financial income	$ 70,000	$ 70,000	$ 70,000	$210,000
Income tax expense (20%)	$ 14,000	$ 14,000	$ 14,000	$ 42,000

For tax purposes (following the tax code), Chelsea reported the same expenses to the IRS in each of the years. But, as Illustration 19.3 shows, Chelsea reported taxable revenues of $100,000 in 2020, $150,000 in 2021, and $140,000 in 2022.

ILLUSTRATION 19.3
Tax Reporting Income

Chelsea Inc.
Tax Reporting

	2020	2021	2022	Total
Revenues	$100,000	$150,000	$140,000	
Expenses	60,000	60,000	60,000	
Taxable income	$ 40,000	$ 90,000	$ 80,000	$210,000
Income taxes payable (20%)	$ 8,000	$ 18,000	$ 16,000	$ 42,000

Income tax expense and income taxes payable differed over the three years but were equal **in total**, as Illustration 19.4 shows.

ILLUSTRATION 19.4
Comparison of Income Tax Expense to Income Taxes Payable

Chelsea Inc.
Income Tax Expense and Income Taxes Payable

	2020	2021	2022	Total
Income tax expense	$14,000	$14,000	$14,000	$42,000
Income taxes payable	8,000	18,000	16,000	42,000
Difference	$ 6,000	$ (4,000)	$ (2,000)	$ -0-

The differences between income tax expense and income taxes payable in this example arise for a simple reason. For financial reporting, companies use the full accrual method to report revenues. For tax purposes, they use a modified cash basis. As a result, Chelsea reports pretax financial income of $70,000 and income tax expense of $14,000 for each of the three years. However, taxable income fluctuates. For example, in 2020 taxable income is only $40,000, so Chelsea owes just $8,000 to the IRS that year. Chelsea classifies the income taxes payable as a current liability on the balance sheet.

As Illustration 19.4 indicates, for Chelsea the $6,000 ($14,000 − $8,000) difference between income tax expense and income taxes payable in 2020 reflects taxes that it will pay in future periods. This $6,000 difference is often referred to as a **deferred tax amount**. In this case, it is a **deferred tax liability**. In cases where taxes will be lower in the future, Chelsea records a **deferred tax asset**. We explain the measurement and accounting for deferred tax liabilities and assets in the following two sections.[1]

Future Taxable Amounts and Deferred Taxes

The example summarized in Illustration 19.4 shows how income taxes payable can differ from income tax expense. This can happen when there are temporary differences between

[1]Determining the amount of tax to pay the IRS is a costly exercise for both individuals and companies. Individuals and businesses must pay not only the taxes owed but also the costs of their own time spent filing and complying with the tax code, including (1) the tax collection costs of the IRS, and (2) the tax compliance outlays that individuals and businesses pay to help them file their taxes. One recent study found that compliance with the federal income tax cost the economy over $230 billion annually. Another study noted how big the tax compliance industry has become. According to the research, the tax compliance industry employs more people than all the workers at **Wal-Mart**, **UPS**, **McDonald's**, **IBM**, and **Citigroup** combined. While it was hoped that the TCJA (2017) might reduce complexity—with a postcard-size tax return for some individual taxpayers—some complexity remains. See Michael Tasselmyer, "A Complex Problem: The Compliance Burdens of the Tax Code," National Taxpayers Union Foundation (April 8, 2015); A. El-Sibaie, "Tax Compliance Burden Could Cost America as Much as 1.2 Percent of Its GDP," *https://taxfoundation.org/tax-compliance-cost/* (February 21, 2018); and J. Tankersley, "The New Tax Form Is Postcard-Size, but More Complicated Than Ever," *The New York Times* (June 25, 2018).

the amounts reported for tax purposes and those reported for book purposes (see **Global View**). A **temporary difference** is the difference between the tax basis of an asset or liability and its reported (carrying or book) amount in the financial statements, which will result in taxable amounts or deductible amounts in future years. **Taxable amounts** increase taxable income in future years. **Deductible amounts** decrease taxable income in future years.

In Chelsea's situation, the only difference between the book basis and tax basis of the assets and liabilities relates to accounts receivable that arose from revenue recognized for book purposes. **Illustration 19.5** indicates that Chelsea reports accounts receivable at $30,000 in the December 31, 2020, GAAP-basis balance sheet. However, the receivables have a zero tax basis.

Global View

In some countries, taxable income equals pretax financial income. As a consequence, accounting for differences between tax and book income is insignificant.

ILLUSTRATION 19.5

Temporary Difference, Sales Revenue

Per Books	12/31/20	Per Tax Return	12/31/20
Accounts receivable	$30,000	Accounts receivable	$-0-

What will happen to the $30,000 temporary difference that originated in 2020 for Chelsea? Assuming that Chelsea expects to collect $20,000 of the receivables in 2021 and $10,000 in 2022, this collection results in future taxable amounts of $20,000 in 2021 and $10,000 in 2022. These future taxable amounts will cause taxable income to exceed pretax financial income in both 2021 and 2022.

An assumption inherent in a company's GAAP balance sheet is that companies recover and settle the assets and liabilities at their reported amounts (carrying amounts). This assumption creates a requirement under accrual accounting to recognize **currently** the deferred tax consequences of temporary differences. That is, companies recognize the amount of income taxes that are payable (or refundable) when they recover and settle the reported amounts of the assets and liabilities, respectively. **Illustration 19.6** shows the reversal of the temporary difference described in Illustration 19.5 and the resulting taxable amounts in future periods.

ILLUSTRATION 19.6

Reversal of Temporary Difference, Chelsea Inc.

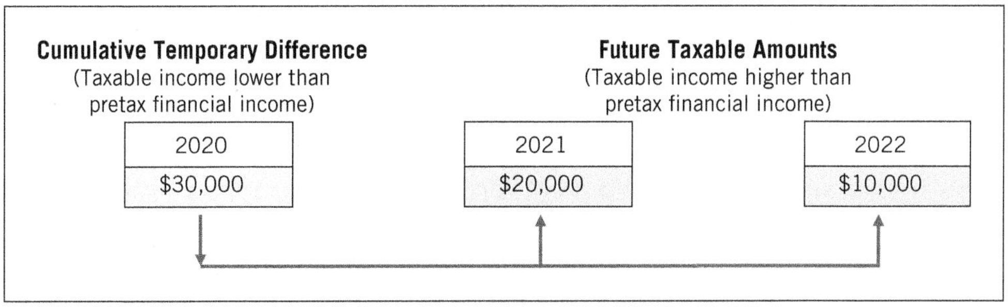

Chelsea assumes that it will collect the accounts receivable and report the $30,000 collection as taxable revenues in future tax returns. A payment of income tax in both 2021 and 2022 will occur. Chelsea should therefore record in its books in 2020 the deferred tax consequences of the revenue and related receivables reflected in the 2020 financial statements. Chelsea does this by recording a deferred tax liability.

Deferred Tax Liability

A **deferred tax liability** is the deferred tax consequences attributable to taxable temporary differences. In other words, **a deferred tax liability represents the increase in taxes payable in future years as a result of taxable temporary differences existing at the end of the current year.**

Recall from the Chelsea example that income taxes payable is $8,000 ($40,000 × .20) in 2020 (Illustration 19.4). In addition, a temporary difference exists at year-end because Chelsea reports the revenue and related accounts receivable differently for book and tax purposes. The book basis of accounts receivable is $30,000, and the tax basis is zero. Thus, the total deferred tax liability at the end of 2020 is $6,000, computed as shown in **Illustration 19.7**.

ILLUSTRATION 19.7

Computation of Deferred Tax Liability, End of 2020

Book basis of accounts receivable	$30,000
Tax basis of accounts receivable	-0-
Cumulative temporary difference at the end of 2020	30,000
Tax rate	20%
Deferred tax liability at the end of 2020	$ 6,000

Companies may also compute the deferred tax liability by preparing a schedule that indicates the future taxable amounts due to existing temporary differences. Such a schedule, as shown in **Illustration 19.8**, is particularly useful when the computations become more complex.

ILLUSTRATION 19.8

Schedule of Future Taxable Amounts

	Future Years		
	2021	2022	Total
Future taxable amounts	$20,000	$10,000	$30,000
Tax rate	20%	20%	
Deferred tax liability at the end of 2020	$ 4,000	$ 2,000	$ 6,000

Because it is the first year of operations for Chelsea, there is no deferred tax liability at the beginning of the year. Chelsea computes the income tax expense for 2020 as shown in **Illustration 19.9**.

ILLUSTRATION 19.9

Computation of Income Tax Expense, 2020

Deferred tax liability at end of 2020	$ 6,000
Deferred tax liability at beginning of 2020	-0-
Deferred tax expense for 2020	6,000
Current tax expense for 2020 (income taxes payable)	8,000
Income tax expense (total) for 2020	$14,000

This computation indicates that income tax expense has two components—**current tax expense** (the amount of income taxes payable for the period) and **deferred tax expense**. Deferred tax expense is the increase in the deferred tax liability balance from the beginning to the end of the accounting period.

Companies credit taxes due and payable to Income Taxes Payable, and credit the increase in deferred taxes to Deferred Tax Liability. They then debit the sum of those two items to Income Tax Expense. For Chelsea, it makes the following entry at the end of 2020.

Income Tax Expense	14,000	
Income Taxes Payable		8,000
Deferred Tax Liability		6,000

At the end of 2021 (the second year), the difference between the book basis and the tax basis of the accounts receivable is $10,000. Chelsea multiplies this difference by the applicable tax rate to arrive at the deferred tax liability of $2,000 ($10,000 × .20), which it reports at the end of 2021. Income taxes payable for 2021 is $18,000 (Illustration 19.3), and the income tax expense for 2021 is as shown in **Illustration 19.10**.

ILLUSTRATION 19.10

Computation of Income Tax Expense, 2021

Deferred tax liability at end of 2021	$ 2,000
Deferred tax liability at beginning of 2021	6,000
Deferred tax expense (benefit) for 2021	(4,000)
Current tax expense for 2021 (income taxes payable)	18,000
Income tax expense (total) for 2021	$14,000

Chelsea records income tax expense, the change in the deferred tax liability, and income taxes payable for 2021 as follows.

Income Tax Expense	14,000	
Deferred Tax Liability	4,000	
Income Taxes Payable		18,000

At the end of 2022 (the third and final year), the difference between the book basis and the tax basis of the receivable is zero. Income taxes payable for 2022 is $16,000 (Illustration 19.3), and the income tax expense for 2022 is $14,000 as shown in **Illustration 19.11**.

ILLUSTRATION 19.11

Computation of Income Tax Expense, 2022

Deferred tax liability at end of 2022	$ -0-
Deferred tax liability at beginning of 2022	2,000
Deferred tax expense (benefit) for 2022	(2,000)
Current tax expense for 2022 (income taxes payable)	16,000
Income tax expense (total) for 2022	$14,000

Chelsea records the income tax expense, the change in deferred tax liability, and income taxes payable for 2022 as follows.

Income Tax Expense	14,000	
Deferred Tax Liability	2,000	
Income Taxes Payable		16,000

The Deferred Tax Liability account appears as follows at the end of 2022.

ILLUSTRATION 19.12

Deferred Tax Liability Account after Reversals

Deferred Tax Liability			
2021	4,000	2020	6,000
2022	2,000		

As indicated the Deferred Tax Liability account has a zero balance at the end of 2022.

Financial Statement Effects

Chelsea reports the information on its balance sheets for 2020–2022 as shown in **Illustration 19.13**.

ILLUSTRATION 19.13

Balance Sheet Presentation, Deferred Tax Liabilities

Year-End	Income Taxes Payable	Deferred Tax Liability
2020	$ 8,000	$6,000
2021	18,000	2,000
2022	16,000	–0–

Income taxes payable is reported as a current liability, and the deferred tax liability is reported as a noncurrent liability.[2]

On its income statement, Chelsea reports the information as shown in **Illustration 19.14**, from information taken from Illustration 19.2.

ILLUSTRATION 19.14

Income Statement Presentation, Income Tax Expense

For the Year Ended	2020	2021	2022
Income before income taxes	$70,000	$70,000	$70,000
Income tax expense	14,000	14,000	14,000
Net income	$56,000	$56,000	$56,000

[2]As a result of a recent Accounting Standards Update (*FASB ASU 2015-17*), all deferred tax assets and liabilities are classified as noncurrent. [1] (See the FASB Codification References near the end of the chapter.) Expanded discussion of this provision is provided later in the chapter.

Companies also are required to show the components of income tax expense either in the income statement or in the notes to the financial statements. For example, if Chelsea reported this information in the income statement for 2020, the presentation is as shown in Illustration 19.15.

ILLUSTRATION 19.15

Components of Income Tax Expense

Income Statement (partial)

Income before income taxes		$70,000
Income tax expense		
Current	$8,000	
Deferred	6,000	14,000
Net income		$56,000

What Do the Numbers Mean? "Real Liabilities"

Some analysts dismiss deferred tax liabilities when assessing the financial strength of a company. But the FASB indicates that the deferred tax liability meets the definition of a liability established in *Statement of Financial Accounting Concepts No. 6,* "Elements of Financial Statements" because:

1. ***It results from a past transaction.*** In the Chelsea example, the company performed services for customers and recognized revenue in 2020 for financial reporting purposes but deferred it for tax purposes.
2. ***It is a present obligation.*** Taxable income in future periods will exceed pretax financial income as a result of this temporary difference. Thus, a present obligation exists.
3. ***It represents a future sacrifice.*** Taxable income and taxes due in future periods will result from past events. The payment of these taxes when they come due is the future sacrifice.

A set of studies indicates that deferred taxes do provide incremental information about future tax payments and that the market views deferred tax assets and liabilities similarly to other assets and liabilities.

Sources: B. Ayers, "Deferred Tax Accounting Under *SFAS No. 109*: An Empirical Investigation of Its Incremental Value-Relevance Relative to *APB No. 11*," *The Accounting Review* (April 1998); and R. Laux, "The Association Between Deferred Tax Assets and Liabilities and Future Tax Payments," *The Accounting Review* (February 2013).

Future Deductible Amounts and Deferred Taxes

Assume that during 2020, Cunningham Inc. estimated its warranty costs related to the sale of microwave ovens to be $500,000, paid evenly over the next two years. For book purposes, in 2020 Cunningham reported warranty expense and a related estimated liability for warranties of $500,000 in its financial statements. For tax purposes, **the warranty tax deduction is not allowed until paid**. Therefore, Cunningham recognizes no warranty liability on a tax-basis balance sheet. Illustration 19.16 shows the balance sheet difference at the end of 2020.

ILLUSTRATION 19.16

Temporary Difference, Warranty Liability

Per Books	12/31/20	Per Tax Return	12/31/20
Estimated liability for warranties	$500,000	Estimated liability for warranties	$-0-

When Cunningham pays the warranty liability, it reports an expense (deductible amount) for tax purposes. Because of this temporary difference, Cunningham should recognize in 2020 the tax benefits (positive tax consequences) for the tax deductions that will result from the future settlement of the liability. Cunningham reports this future tax benefit in the December 31, 2020, balance sheet as a **deferred tax asset**.

We can think about this situation another way. Deductible amounts occur in future tax returns. These **future deductible amounts** cause taxable income to be less than pretax financial income in the future as a result of an existing temporary difference. Cunningham's temporary difference originates (arises) in one period (2020) and reverses over two periods (2021 and 2022). Illustration 19.17 diagrams this situation.

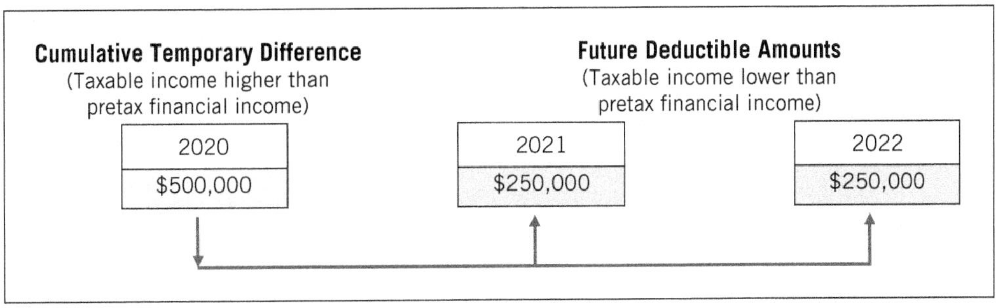

ILLUSTRATION 19.17

Reversal of Temporary Difference, Cunningham Inc.

Deferred Tax Asset

A **deferred tax asset** is the deferred tax consequence attributable to deductible temporary differences. In other words, a **deferred tax asset represents the increase in taxes refundable (or saved) in future years as a result of deductible temporary differences existing at the end of the current year.**

To illustrate, assume that Hunt Company has revenues of $900,000 for both 2020 and 2021. It also has operating expenses of $400,000 for each of these years. In addition, Hunt accrues a loss and related liability of $50,000 for financial reporting purposes because of pending litigation. Hunt cannot deduct this amount for tax purposes until it pays the liability, expected in 2021. As a result, a deductible amount will occur in 2021 when Hunt settles the liability, causing taxable income to be lower than pretax financial information. **Illustration 19.18** shows the GAAP and tax reporting over the two years.

ILLUSTRATION 19.18

GAAP and Tax Reporting, Hunt Company

GAAP Reporting	2020	2021
Revenues	$900,000	$900,000
Expenses (operating)	400,000	400,000
Litigation loss	50,000	–0–
Pretax financial income	$450,000	$500,000
Tax rate	20%	20%
Income tax expense	$ 90,000	$100,000

Tax Reporting	2020	2021
Revenues	$900,000	$900,000
Expenses (operating)	400,000	400,000
Litigation loss	–0–	50,000
Taxable income	$500,000	$450,000
Tax rate	20%	20%
Income taxes payable	$100,000	$ 90,000

Illustration 19.19 shows the computation of the deferred tax asset at the end of 2020 (assuming a 20 percent tax rate).

ILLUSTRATION 19.19

Computation of Deferred Tax Asset, End of 2020

Book basis of litigation liability	$50,000
Tax basis of litigation liability	–0–
Cumulative temporary difference at the end of 2020	50,000
Tax rate	20%
Deferred tax asset at the end of 2020	$10,000

In this case, Hunt records a deferred tax asset of $10,000 at the end of 2020 because it represents taxes that will be saved in future periods as a result of a deductible temporary difference existing at the end of 2020.

Hunt can also compute the deferred tax asset by preparing a schedule that indicates the future deductible amounts due to deductible temporary differences. **Illustration 19.20** shows this schedule.

ILLUSTRATION 19.20
Schedule of Future Deductible Amounts

	Future Years
Future deductible amounts	$50,000
Tax rate	20%
Deferred tax asset at the end of 2020	$10,000

Assuming that 2020 is Hunt's first year of operations and income taxes payable is $100,000, Hunt computes its income tax expense as shown in **Illustration 19.21**.

ILLUSTRATION 19.21
Computation of Income Tax Expense, 2020

Deferred tax asset at end of 2020	$ 10,000
Deferred tax asset at beginning of 2020	–0–
Deferred tax expense (benefit) for 2020	(10,000)
Current tax expense for 2020 (income taxes payable)	100,000
Income tax expense (total) for 2020	$ 90,000

The **deferred tax benefit** results from the increase in the deferred tax asset from the beginning to the end of the accounting period (similar to the Chelsea example earlier). The deferred tax benefit is a negative component of income tax expense. The total income tax expense of $90,000 on the income statement for 2020 thus consists of two elements—current tax expense of $100,000 and a deferred tax benefit of $10,000. Hunt makes the following journal entry at the end of 2020 to record income tax expense, deferred income taxes, and income taxes payable.

Income Tax Expense	90,000	
Deferred Tax Asset	10,000	
Income Taxes Payable		100,000

At the end of 2021 (the second year), the difference between the book value and the tax basis of the litigation liability is zero. Therefore, there is no deferred tax asset at this date. Assuming that income taxes payable for 2021 is $90,000, Hunt computes income tax expense for 2021 as shown in **Illustration 19.22**.

ILLUSTRATION 19.22
Computation of Income Tax Expense, 2021

Deferred tax asset at the end of 2021	$ –0–
Deferred tax asset at the beginning of 2021	10,000
Deferred tax expense (benefit) for 2021	10,000
Current tax expense for 2021 (income taxes payable)	90,000
Income tax expense (total) for 2021	$100,000

The company records income taxes for 2021 as follows.

Income Tax Expense	100,000	
Deferred Tax Asset		10,000
Income Taxes Payable		90,000

The total income tax expense of $100,000 on the income statement for 2021 thus consists of two elements—current tax expense of $90,000 and deferred tax expense of $10,000.

Financial Statement Effects

Hunt Company reports the following information on its balance sheets for 2020 and 2021 as shown in **Illustration 19.23**.

ILLUSTRATION 19.23
Balance Sheet Presentation, Deferred Tax Asset

Year-End	Income Taxes Payable	Deferred Tax Asset
2020	$100,000	$10,000
2021	90,000	–0–

Income taxes payable is reported as a current liability, and the deferred tax asset is reported as a noncurrent asset. On its income statement, Hunt Company reports the information as shown in Illustration 19.24.

ILLUSTRATION 19.24

Income Statement Presentation, Deferred Tax Asset

Hunt Company
Income Statement
For the Year Ending December 31, 2020

Revenues		$900,000
Expenses (operating)		400,000
Litigation loss		50,000
Income before income taxes		450,000
Income tax expense		
Current	$100,000	
Deferred	10,000	90,000
Net income		$360,000

As illustrated, Hunt reports both the current portion (the amount of income taxes payable for the period) and the deferred portion of the income tax expense. In this case, the deferred amount is subtracted from the current portion to arrive at the proper income tax expense.

Illustration 19.25 shows the Deferred Tax Asset account at the end of 2021.

ILLUSTRATION 19.25

Deferred Tax Asset Account after Reversals

Deferred Tax Asset

2020	10,000	2021	10,000

What Do the Numbers Mean? "Real Assets"

A key issue in accounting for income taxes is whether a company should recognize a deferred tax asset in the financial records. Based on the conceptual definition of an asset, a deferred tax asset meets the three main conditions for an item to be recognized as an asset:

1. ***It results from a past transaction.*** In the Hunt example, the accrual of the loss contingency is the past event that gives rise to a future deductible temporary difference.
2. ***It gives rise to a probable benefit in the future.*** Taxable income exceeds pretax financial income in the current year (2020). However, in the next year the exact opposite occurs. That is, taxable income is lower than pretax financial income. Because this deductible temporary difference reduces taxes payable in the future, a probable future benefit exists at the end of the current period.
3. ***The entity controls access to the benefits.*** Hunt can obtain the benefit of existing deductible temporary differences by reducing its taxes payable in the future. Hunt has the exclusive right to that benefit and can control others' access to it.

Market analysts' reactions to the **write-off** of deferred tax assets also supports their treatment as assets. When Twitter reported that it was writing off its net U.S deferred assets, analysts believed that Twitter was signaling that it would not realize the future benefits of these tax deductions. Thus, Twitter should write down these assets like other assets.

Sources: J. Weil and S. Liesman, "Stock Gurus Disregard Most Big Write-Offs but They Often Hold Vital Clues to Outlook," *Wall Street Journal Online* (December 31, 2001); and V. Fleisher, "Why Twitter May Have to Pay Income Taxes One Day," *The New York Times* (November 6, 2013).

Deferred Tax Asset—Valuation Allowance

Companies recognize a deferred tax asset for all deductible temporary differences. However, a company should reduce a deferred tax asset by a valuation allowance if, based on available evidence, **it is more likely than not** that it **will not realize** some portion or all of the deferred tax asset. "More likely than not" means a level of likelihood of at least slightly more than 50 percent.

Assume that Jensen Co. has a deductible temporary difference of $1,000,000 at the end of its first year of operations. Its tax rate is 20 percent, which means it records a deferred tax asset of

$200,000 ($1,000,000 × .20). Assuming $900,000 of income taxes payable, Jensen records income tax expense, the deferred tax asset, and income taxes payable as follows.

Income Tax Expense	700,000	
Deferred Tax Asset	200,000	
Income Taxes Payable		900,000

After careful review of all available evidence, Jensen determines that it is more likely than not that it will not realize $80,000 of this deferred tax asset. Jensen records this reduction in asset value as follows.

Income Tax Expense	80,000	
Allowance to Reduce Deferred Tax Asset to Expected Realizable Value		80,000

This journal entry increases income tax expense in the current period because Jensen does not expect to realize a favorable tax benefit for a portion of the deductible temporary difference. Jensen **simultaneously establishes a valuation allowance to recognize the reduction in the carrying amount of the deferred tax asset**. This valuation account is a contra account. Jensen reports it on the financial statements as shown in Illustration 19.26.

ILLUSTRATION 19.26

Balance Sheet Presentation of Valuation Allowance Account

Deferred tax asset	$200,000
Less: Allowance to reduce deferred tax asset to expected realizable value	80,000
Deferred tax asset (net)	$120,000

Jensen then evaluates this allowance account at the end of each accounting period. Jensen determines that it is more likely than not that it will not realize $50,000 of the deferred tax asset. Therefore, Jensen makes the following entry to adjust the valuation allowance at 2021.

Allowance to Reduce Deferred Tax Asset to Expected Realizable Value ($80,000 – $50,000)	30,000	
Income Tax Expense		30,000

Jensen should consider all available evidence, both positive and negative, to determine whether, based on the weight of available evidence, it needs a valuation allowance. For example, if Jensen has been experiencing a series of loss years, it reasonably assumes that these losses will continue. Therefore, Jensen will lose the benefit of the future deductible amounts. We discuss the use of a valuation account under other conditions later in the chapter.

Additional Considerations

LEARNING OBJECTIVE 2

Identify additional issues in accounting for income taxes.

Income Statement Presentation

Circumstances dictate whether a company should add or subtract the change in deferred income taxes to or from income taxes payable in computing income tax expense. For example, a company adds an increase in a deferred tax liability to income taxes payable. On the other hand, it subtracts an increase in a deferred tax asset from income taxes payable. The formula in Illustration 19.27 is used to compute income tax expense (benefit).

ILLUSTRATION 19.27

Formula to Compute Income Tax Expense

Income Taxes Payable or Refundable	±	**Change in Deferred Income Taxes**	=	**Total Income Tax Expense or Benefit**

In the income statement or in the notes to the financial statements, a company should disclose the significant components of income tax expense attributable to continuing operations. Given the information related to Chelsea in Illustrations 19.2 to 19.4, Chelsea reports its income statement as shown in Illustration 19.28.

ILLUSTRATION 19.28

Income Statement Presentation of Income Tax Expense

Chelsea Inc.
Income Statement
For the Year Ending December 31, 2020

Revenues		$130,000
Expenses		60,000
Income before income taxes		70,000
Income tax expense		
Current	$8,000	
Deferred	6,000	14,000
Net income		$ 56,000

As illustrated, Chelsea reports both the current portion (amount of income taxes payable for the period) and the deferred portion of income tax expense. Another option is to simply report the total income tax expense on the income statement and then indicate in the notes to the financial statements the current and deferred portions. Income tax expense is often referred to as "Provision for income taxes." Using this terminology, the current provision is $8,000, and the provision for deferred taxes is $6,000.

Specific Differences

Numerous items create differences between pretax financial income and taxable income. For purposes of accounting recognition, these differences are (1) temporary and (2) permanent.

Temporary Differences

Taxable temporary differences are temporary differences that will result in taxable amounts in future years when the related assets are recovered. **Deductible temporary differences** are temporary differences that will result in deductible amounts in future years, when the related book liabilities are settled. As discussed earlier, taxable temporary differences give rise to recording deferred tax liabilities. Deductible temporary differences give rise to recording deferred tax assets. Illustration 19.29 provides examples of temporary differences.

ILLUSTRATION 19.29 **Examples of Temporary Differences**

Revenues or gains are taxable after they are recognized in financial income.

An asset (e.g., accounts receivable or investment) may be recognized for revenues or gains that will result in **taxable amounts in future years (deferred tax liability)** when the asset is recovered. Examples:

1. Sales accounted for on the accrual basis for financial reporting purposes and on the installment (cash) basis for tax purposes.
2. Contracts accounted for under the percentage-of-completion method for financial reporting purposes and a portion of related gross profit deferred for tax purposes.
3. Investments accounted for under the equity method for financial reporting purposes and under the cost method for tax purposes.
4. Gain on involuntary conversion of a nonmonetary asset which is recognized for financial reporting purposes but deferred for tax purposes.
5. Unrealized holding gains for financial reporting purposes (including use of the fair value option), but deferred for tax purposes.

Expenses or losses are deductible after they are recognized in financial income.

A liability (or contra asset) may be recognized for expenses or losses that will result in **deductible amounts in future years (deferred tax asset)** when the liability is settled. Examples:

1. Product warranty liabilities.
2. Estimated liabilities related to discontinued operations or restructurings.
3. Litigation accruals.
4. Bad debt expense recognized using the allowance method for financial reporting purposes; direct write-off method used for tax purposes.
5. Stock-based compensation expense.
6. Unrealized holding losses for financial reporting purposes (including use of the fair value option) but deferred for tax purposes.

(continued)

ILLUSTRATION 19.29 *(continued)*

Revenues or gains are taxable before they are recognized in financial income.

A liability may be recognized for an advance payment for goods or services to be provided in future years. For tax purposes, the advance payment is included in taxable income upon the receipt of cash. Future sacrifices to provide goods or services (or future refunds to those who cancel their orders) that settle the liability will result in **deductible amounts in future years (deferred tax asset).** Examples:

1. Subscriptions received in advance.
2. Advance rental receipts.
3. Sales and leasebacks for financial reporting purposes (income deferral) but reported as sales for tax purposes.
4. Prepaid contracts and royalties received in advance.

Expenses or losses are deductible before they are recognized in financial income.

The cost of an asset may have been deducted for tax purposes faster than it was expensed for financial reporting purposes. Amounts received upon future recovery of the amount of the asset for financial reporting (through use or sale) will exceed the remaining tax basis of the asset and thereby result in **taxable amounts in future years (deferred tax liability).** Examples:

1. Depreciable property, depletable resources, and intangibles.
2. Deductible pension funding exceeding expense.
3. Prepaid expenses that are deducted on the tax return in the period paid.

Determining a company's temporary differences may prove difficult. A company should prepare a balance sheet for tax purposes that it can compare with its GAAP balance sheet. Many of the differences between the two balance sheets are temporary differences.

Originating and Reversing Aspects of Temporary Differences An **originating temporary difference** is the initial difference between the book basis and the tax basis of an asset or liability, regardless of whether the tax basis of the asset or liability exceeds or is exceeded by the book basis of the asset or liability. A **reversing difference**, on the other hand, occurs when eliminating a temporary difference that originated in prior periods and then removing the related tax effect from the deferred tax account.

For example, assume that Sharp Co. has tax depreciation in excess of book depreciation of \$4,000 in 2018, 2019, and 2020. Further, it has an excess of book depreciation over tax depreciation of \$6,000 in 2021 and 2022 for the same asset. Assuming a tax rate of 15 percent for all years involved, the Deferred Tax Liability account is as shown in Illustration 19.30.

ILLUSTRATION 19.30

Tax Effects of Originating and Reversing Differences

	Deferred Tax Liability				
Tax effects of reversing differences	2021	900	2018	600	Tax effects of originating differences
	2022	900	2019	600	
			2020	600	

Global View

If companies switch to IFRS, the impact on tax accounting methods will require consideration. For example, in cases in which GAAP and tax rules are the same, what happens if IFRS is different from GAAP? Should the tax method change to IFRS? And what might happen at the state level, due to changes in the financial reporting rules?

The originating differences for Sharp in each of the first three years are \$4,000. The related tax effect of each originating difference is \$600 (\$4,000 × .15). The reversing differences in 2021 and 2022 are each \$6,000. The related tax effect of each is \$900 (\$6,000 × .15).

Permanent Differences

Some differences between taxable income and pretax financial income are permanent. **Permanent differences** result from items that (1) enter into pretax financial income but **never** into taxable income, or (2) enter into taxable income but **never** into pretax financial income.

Congress has enacted a variety of tax law provisions to attain certain political, economic, and social objectives. Some of these provisions exclude certain revenues from taxation, limit the deductibility of certain expenses, and permit the deduction of certain other expenses in excess of costs incurred. A corporation that has tax-free income, nondeductible expenses, or allowable deductions in excess of cost has an effective tax rate that differs from its statutory (regular) tax rate (see Global View).

Since permanent differences affect only the period in which they occur, they do not give rise to future taxable or deductible amounts. As a result, **companies recognize no deferred tax consequences.** Illustration 19.31 shows examples of permanent differences.

ILLUSTRATION 19.31

Examples of Permanent Differences

Items are recognized for financial reporting purposes but not for tax purposes.

Examples:

1. Interest received on state and municipal obligations.
2. Expenses incurred in obtaining tax-exempt income.
3. Proceeds from life insurance carried by the company on key officers or employees.
4. Premiums paid for life insurance carried by the company on key officers or employees (company is beneficiary).
5. Fines and expenses resulting from a violation of law.

Items are recognized for tax purposes but not for financial reporting purposes.

Examples:

1. "Percentage depletion" of natural resources in excess of their cost.
2. The deduction for dividends received from U.S. corporations, generally 70% or 80%.

Examples of Temporary and Permanent Differences

To illustrate the computations used when both temporary and permanent differences exist, assume that Bio-Tech Company reports pretax financial income of $200,000 in each of the years 2018, 2019, and 2020. The company is subject to a 20 percent tax rate and has the following differences between pretax financial income and taxable income.

1. Bio-Tech reports gross profit of $18,000 from an installment sale in 2018. For tax purposes, it will recognize revenue over an 18-month period at a constant amount of $1,000 per month beginning January 1, 2019. It recognizes the entire amount for book purposes in 2018.
2. It pays life insurance premiums for its key officers of $5,000 in 2019 and 2020. Although not tax-deductible, Bio-Tech expenses the premiums for book purposes.

The installment sale is a temporary difference, whereas the life insurance premium is a permanent difference. Illustration 19.32 shows the reconciliation of Bio-Tech's pretax financial income to taxable income and the computation of income taxes payable.

ILLUSTRATION 19.32

Reconciliation and Computation of Income Taxes Payable

	2018	2019	2020
Pretax financial income	$200,000	$200,000	$200,000
Permanent difference			
Nondeductible expense		5,000	5,000
Temporary difference			
Installment sale	(18,000)	12,000	6,000
Taxable income	182,000	217,000	211,000
Tax rate	20%	20%	20%
Income taxes payable	$ 36,400	$ 43,400	$ 42,200

Note that Bio-Tech **deducts** the installment-sales gross profit from pretax financial income to arrive at taxable income. The reason: Pretax financial income includes the installment-sales gross profit; taxable income does not. Conversely, it **adds** the $5,000 insurance premium to pretax financial income to arrive at taxable income. The reason: Pretax financial income records an expense for this premium, but for tax purposes the premium is not deductible. As a result, pretax financial income is lower than taxable income. Therefore, the life insurance premium must be added back to pretax financial income to reconcile to taxable income.

Bio-Tech records income taxes for 2018, 2019, and 2020 as follows.

December 31, 2018

Income Tax Expense ($36,400 + $3,600)	40,000	
Deferred Tax Liability ($18,000 × .20)		3,600
Income Taxes Payable ($182,000 × .20)		36,400

(continued)

December 31, 2019		
Income Tax Expense ($43,400 – $2,400)	41,000	
Deferred Tax Liability ($12,000 × .20)	2,400	
Income Taxes Payable ($217,000 × .20)		43,400
December 31, 2020		
Income Tax Expense ($42,200 – $1,200)	41,000	
Deferred Tax Liability ($6,000 × .20)	1,200	
Income Taxes Payable ($211,000 × .20)		42,200

Bio-Tech has one temporary difference, which originates in 2018 and reverses in 2019 and 2020. It recognizes a deferred tax liability at the end of 2018 because the temporary difference causes future taxable amounts. As the temporary difference reverses, Bio-Tech reduces the deferred tax liability. There is no deferred tax amount associated with the difference caused by the nondeductible insurance expense because it is a permanent difference.

Although an enacted tax rate of 20 percent applies for all three years, the effective rate differs from the enacted rate in 2019 and 2020. Bio-Tech computes the **effective tax rate** by dividing total income tax expense for the period by pretax financial income. The effective rate is 20 percent for 2018 ($40,000 ÷ $200,000 = 20%) and 20.5 percent for 2019 and 2020 ($41,000 ÷ $200,000 = 20.5%).

Tax Rate Considerations

In our previous illustrations, the enacted tax rate did not change from one year to the next. Thus, to compute the deferred income tax amount to report on the balance sheet, a company simply multiplies the cumulative temporary difference by the current tax rate. Using Bio-Tech as an example, it multiplies the cumulative temporary difference of $18,000 by the enacted tax rate, 20 percent in this case, to arrive at a deferred tax liability of $3,600 ($18,000 × .20) at the end of 2018.

Future Tax Rates

What happens if tax rates are expected to change in the future? In this case, a company should use the **enacted tax rate** expected to apply. Therefore, a company must consider presently enacted changes in the tax rate that become effective for a particular future year(s) when determining the tax rate to apply to existing temporary differences. For example, assume that Warlen Co. at the end of 2017 has the following cumulative temporary difference of $300,000, computed as shown in **Illustration 19.33**.

ILLUSTRATION 19.33

Computation of Cumulative Temporary Difference

Book basis of depreciable assets	$1,000,000
Tax basis of depreciable assets	700,000
Cumulative temporary difference	$ 300,000

Furthermore, assume that the $300,000 will reverse and result in taxable amounts in the future, with the enacted tax rates shown in **Illustration 19.34**.

ILLUSTRATION 19.34

Deferred Tax Liability Based on Future Rates

	2018	2019	2020	2021	2022	Total
Future taxable amounts	$80,000	$70,000	$60,000	$50,000	$40,000	$300,000
Tax rate	20%	20%	18%	15%	15%	
Deferred tax liability	$16,000	$14,000	$10,800	$ 7,500	$ 6,000	$ 54,300

The total deferred tax liability at the end of 2017 is $54,300. Warlen may only use tax rates other than the current rate when the future tax rates have been enacted, as is the case in this example. **If new rates are not yet enacted for future years, Warlen should use the current rate.**[3]

What Do the Numbers Mean? Global Tax Rates

If you are concerned about your tax rate and the taxes you pay, you might want to consider moving to Switzerland, which has a personal tax rate of anywhere from zero percent to 18 percent. You don't want to move to Denmark though. Yes, the people of Denmark are regularly voted to be the happiest people on Earth but it's uncertain how many of these polls take place at tax time. The government in Denmark charges income tax rates ranging from zero percent to 52 percent. So, taxes are a major item to many individuals, wherever they reside.

Taxes are also a big deal to corporations. For example, the Organisation for Economic Co-operation and Development (OECD) is an international organization of 30 countries that accepts the principles of a free-market economy. Most OECD members are high-income economies and are regarded as developed countries. However, companies in the OECD can be subject to significant tax levies, as indicated in the following list of the ten highest corporate income tax rates for the OECD countries in 2014 and 2018.

	2014	2018	Percent Change
France	33.3%	33.3%	0.0%
Japan	35.6	30.9	−13.2
Australia	30.0	30.0	0.0
Germany	29.6	30.0	1.4
Belgium	33.9	29.0	−14.5
New Zealand	28.0	28.0	0.0
Canada	26.5	26.5	0.0
Luxembourg	29.2	26.0	−11.0
Spain	30.0	25.0	−16.7
United States	40.0	21.0	−47.5
OECD average	25.0	23.5	−5.9

As indicated, over the past four years, tax rates in the OECD have been on the decline. Only Germany had an increase in tax rates over this period. With the recent tax law, the United States fell from the highest rate in 2014 to the lowest on this list. Indeed, corporate tax rates have been dropping around the world as countries attempt to encourage capital investment, which in turn spurs international tax competition. Even lower on the tax rate spectrum are Iceland and Ireland, with tax rates of 20 percent and 12.5 percent, respectively.

On the other hand, with slowing global economic growth, there is concern that governments will target increases in corporate tax rates as a source of revenues to address budget shortfalls. In addition, further expansion of value-added taxes (VAT) is being considered a tax charged on the consumption of goods and services, which is much more stable than the corporate tax. If these tax proposals result in changes in the tax rates applied to future deductible and taxable amounts, be prepared for significant remeasurement of deferred tax assets and liabilities.

Source: The rates reported reflect the base corporate rate in effect in 2017. Effective rates paid may vary depending on country-specific additional levies for such items as unemployment and local taxes, and, in the case of Japan, earthquake damage assessments. Effective rates may be lower due to credits for investments and capital gains. See *https://home.kpmg.com/xx/en/home/services/tax/tax-tools-and-resources/tax-rates-online.html.*

Revision of Future Tax Rates

When a change in the tax rate is enacted, companies should record its effect on the existing deferred income tax accounts immediately. **A company reports the effect as an adjustment to income tax expense in the period of the change.**

Assume that on December 10, 2020, a new income tax act is signed into law that lowers the corporate tax rate from 40 percent to 20 percent, effective January 1, 2022. If Hostel Co. has one temporary difference at the beginning of 2020 related to $3 million of excess tax depreciation, then it has a Deferred Tax Liability account with a balance of $1,200,000 ($3,000,000 × .40) at January 1, 2020. If taxable amounts related to this difference are scheduled to occur equally in 2021, 2022, and 2023, the deferred tax liability at the end of 2020 is $1,100,000, computed as shown in Illustration 19.35.

	2021	2022	2023	Total
Future taxable amounts	$1,000,000	$1,000,000	$1,000,000	$3,000,000
Tax rate	40%	20%	20%	
Deferred tax liability	$ 400,000	$ 200,000	$ 200,000	$ 800,000

ILLUSTRATION 19.35
Schedule of Future Taxable Amounts and Related Tax Rates

[3]As indicated in the opening story, the Tax Cuts and Jobs Act of 2017 (TCJA) enacted a flat corporate federal tax rate of 21 percent. The tax rate for an individual company may be higher or lower than 21 percent, depending on state and international taxes, as well as various provisions in the tax code, which usually reduce the rate. Prior to the TCJA, the Internal Revenue Service (IRS) and other taxing jurisdictions taxed income on a graduated tax basis. For example, the IRS taxed the first $50,000 of taxable income at 15 percent, the next $25,000 at 25 percent, with higher incremental levels of income at rates as high as 39 percent. As a result, in computing deferred income taxes, companies for which graduated tax rates were a significant factor had to determine and then use the average tax rate.

Hostel, therefore, recognizes the decrease of $400,000 ($1,200,000 – $800,000) at the end of 2020 in the deferred tax liability as follows.

Deferred Tax Liability	400,000	
Income Tax Expense		400,000

Corporate tax rates do not change often. Therefore, companies usually employ the current rate. However, state and foreign tax rates change more frequently, and they require adjustments in deferred income taxes accordingly.

What Do the Numbers Mean? Lower Tax Rate—Good or Bad?

Tax rate changes nearly always will substantially impact income numbers and the reporting of deferred income taxes on the balance sheet. As a result, you can expect to hear an economic-consequences argument every time that Congress decides to change the tax rates. For example, when Congress raised the corporate rate from 34 percent to 35 percent in 1993, companies took an additional "hit" to earnings if they were in a deferred tax liability position. What if tax rates decline? Depending on a company's deferred tax position, a change in tax rates can have a positive or negative effect on net income. As indicated in the opening story, the most recent tax rate change from 35 percent to 21 percent resulted in serious losses for companies with significant deferred tax asset balances, as indicated in the following list.

Company ($ millions)	Net Deferred Tax Assets	2017 Profit Hit
Citigroup	$49,690	$15,005
General Motors	35,320	7,300
Bank of America	28,371	8,747
IBM	10,990	2,380
Hewlett Packard	8,394	1,347

Source: 2017 annual reports.

The news is not all bad. A number of companies are in deferred tax liability positions in the period leading up to the tax rate cut. The table in the adjacent column shows the sector distribution of deferred tax assets and liabilities for December year-end firms at the end of the year before the tax act was enacted, with the table sorted in decreasing order by the ratio of deferred tax liabilities to deferred tax assets.

($ in billions)	No. of Firms	Deferred Tax Assets	Deferred Tax Liabilities	DTLs ÷ DTAs
Utilities	28	$ 53.6	$ 232.3	4.3
Telecom services	3	16.7	66.1	4.0
Consumer staples	16	20.1	72.8	3.6
Real estate	32	1.6	4.4	2.8
Health care	46	55.0	126.3	2.3
Energy	31	94.4	169.9	1.8
Industrials	55	82.4	147.7	1.8
Consumer discretionary	47	81.1	116.7	1.4
Materials	22	24.8	34.2	1.4
Financials	64	273.4	271.1	1.0
Information technology	28	43.9	32.8	0.7
	372	$747.0	$1,274.2	1.7

Asset-heavy utilities, which generate plenty of accelerated depreciation-driven deferred tax liabilities, rank highest. Similarly, asset-heavy telecom services are close behind. These companies will report a positive income effect when these liabilities are remeasured at the lower tax rate. Not so for the information technology sector—like **IBM** and **HP** in the list above. Tech companies show significantly lower deferred tax liabilities than deferred tax assets. One reason is that unlike utilities and telecoms, the information technology sector is not capital-intensive and will not generate much in the way of accelerated depreciation, which in turn is a major driver of deferred tax liabilities. So the effect of a tax rate change could be good or bad—it depends on your deferred tax asset/liability position.

Sources: F. McKenna, "They May Be Able to Make It Up in Future Years by Paying Less, but First Some of Them Will Have to Take a Big Hit," *Marketwatch* (December 28, 2017); and J. Ciesielski, "The Tax Cuts & Jobs Act: What Analysts Need To Know," *The Analyst's Accounting Observer*, Volume 27, No. 2 (February 14, 2018).

Accounting for Net Operating Losses

LEARNING OBJECTIVE 3

Explain the accounting for loss carryforwards.

Every management hopes its company will be profitable. But hopes and profits may not materialize. For a start-up company, it is common to accumulate operating losses while expanding its customer base but before realizing economies of scale. For an established company, a major event such as a labor strike, rapidly changing regulatory and competitive forces, a disaster such as 9/11, or a general economic recession such as that experienced in the wake of the financial crisis can cause expenses to exceed revenues—a net operating loss.

A **net operating loss (NOL)** occurs for tax purposes in a year when tax-deductible expenses exceed taxable revenues. An inequitable tax burden would result if companies were taxed during profitable periods without receiving any tax relief during periods of net operating losses. Under certain circumstances, therefore, the federal tax laws permit taxpayers to use the losses of one year to offset the profits of other years.

Companies accomplish this income-averaging provision through the **carryforward of net operating losses**. Under this provision, a company pays no income taxes for a year in which it incurs a net operating loss. In addition, it can reduce future taxes payable as discussed on the following pages.

Loss Carryforward

Through use of a **loss carryforward**, a company may carry the net operating loss forward indefinitely to offset future taxable income and reduce taxes payable in future years.[4] **Illustration 19.36** shows this approach.

ILLUSTRATION 19.36

Loss Carryforward Procedure

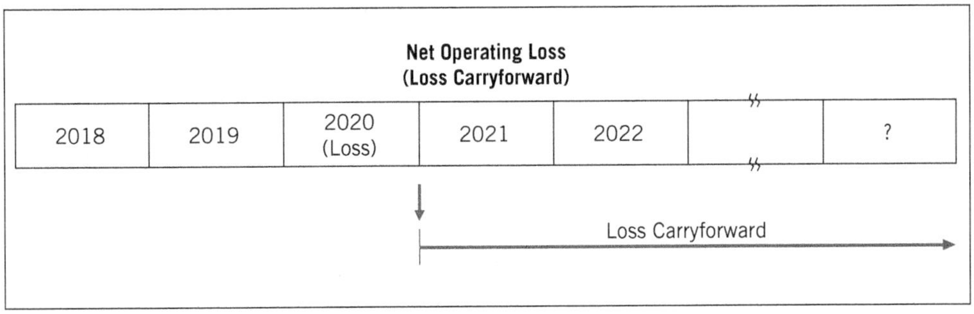

Operating losses can be substantial. For example, **Yahoo!** at one time had net operating losses of approximately $5.4 billion. That amount translates into tax savings of $1.4 billion if Yahoo! is able to generate taxable income in the future.

Loss Carryforward Example

Because companies use carryforwards to offset future taxable income, the **tax effect of a loss carryforward** represents **future tax savings**. However, realization of a future tax benefit depends on future earnings, an uncertain prospect.

The key accounting issue is whether there should be different requirements for recognition of a deferred tax asset for (a) deductible temporary differences and (b) operating loss carryforwards. The FASB's position is that in substance these items are the same—both are tax-deductible amounts in future years. As a result, the Board concluded that there **should not be different requirements** for recognition of a deferred tax asset from deductible temporary differences and operating loss carryforwards.[5]

Carryforward without Valuation Allowance

To illustrate the accounting procedures for a net operating loss carryforward, assume that Groh Inc. has no temporary or permanent differences. Groh experiences the net operating

[4] The length of carryforward periods has varied. The carryforward period has increased from seven years to 20 years over a period of time. As mentioned in the opening story, the indefinite carryforward period was enacted as part of the Tax Cuts and Jobs Act of 2017 (TCJA). The TCJA also eliminated carryback provisions, which permitted companies to carry back NOLs against prior taxable income and get a tax refund. We discuss the accounting for carrybacks in Appendix 19B.

[5] This requirement is controversial because many believe it is inappropriate to recognize deferred tax assets except when assured beyond a reasonable doubt. Others argue that companies should never recognize deferred tax assets for loss carryforwards until realizing the income in the future.

loss of $200,000 in 2020 and takes advantage of the carryforward provision. In 2020, the company records the tax effect of the $200,000 loss carryforward as a deferred tax asset of $40,000 ($200,000 × .20), assuming that the enacted future tax rate is 20 percent. Groh records the benefit of the carryforward in 2020 as follows.

Deferred Tax Asset	40,000	
Income Tax Expense (Loss Carryforward)		40,000

Groh establishes a Deferred Tax Asset account for the benefits of future tax savings. The account credited [Income Tax Expense (Loss Carryforward)] is a contra income tax expense item, which Groh presents on the 2020 income statement shown in Illustration 19.37. The $40,000 is the **deferred tax benefit** for 2020, which results from an increase in the deferred tax asset.

ILLUSTRATION 19.37

Recognition of the Benefit of the Loss Carryforward in the Loss Year

Groh Inc.
Income Statement (partial) for 2020

Operating loss before income taxes	$(200,000)
Income tax benefit	
Deferred	40,000*
Net loss	$(160,000)

*Carryforward ($200,000 × .20)

For 2021, assume that Groh returns to profitable operations and has taxable income of $250,000 (prior to adjustment for the NOL carryforward), subject to a 20 percent tax rate. Groh then realizes the benefits of the carryforward for tax purposes in 2021, which it recognized for accounting purposes in 2020. Groh computes the income taxes payable for 2021 as shown in Illustration 19.38.

ILLUSTRATION 19.38

Computation of Income Taxes Payable with Realized Loss Carryforward

Taxable income prior to loss carryforward	$ 250,000
Loss carryforward deduction	(200,000)
Taxable income for 2021	50,000
Tax rate	20%
Income taxes payable for 2021	$ 10,000

Groh records income taxes in 2021 as follows.

Income Tax Expense	50,000	
Deferred Tax Asset		40,000
Income Taxes Payable		10,000

The benefits of the NOL carryforward, realized in 2021, reduce the Deferred Tax Asset account to zero.

The 2021 income statement that appears in Illustration 19.39 does **not report** the tax effects of the loss carryforward because Groh had reported both previously.

ILLUSTRATION 19.39

Presentation of the Benefit of Loss Carryforward Realized in 2021, Recognized in 2020

Groh Inc.
Income Statement (partial) for 2021

Income before income taxes		$250,000
Income tax expense		
Current	$10,000	
Deferred	40,000	50,000
Net income		$200,000

Carryforward with Valuation Allowance

Let us return to the Groh example. Assume that it is more likely than not that Groh will *not* realize the entire NOL carryforward in future years. In this situation, Groh records a

Deferred Tax Asset of $40,000 ($200,000 × .20) for the potential benefits related to the loss carryforward, and an allowance to reduce the deferred tax asset by the same amount. Groh makes the following journal entries in 2020.

To recognize benefit of loss carryforward		
Deferred Tax Asset	40,000	
Income Tax Expense (Loss Carryforward)		40,000
To record allowance amount		
Income Tax Expense (Allowance)	40,000	
Allowance to Reduce Deferred Tax Asset to Expected Realizable Value		40,000

The latter entry indicates that because positive evidence of sufficient quality and quantity is unavailable to counteract the negative evidence, Groh needs a valuation allowance.

Illustration 19.40 shows Groh's 2020 income statement presentation.

ILLUSTRATION 19.40

Recognition of Benefit of Loss Carryforward Only

Groh Inc.
Income Statement (partial) for 2020

Operating loss before income taxes	$(200,000)
Income tax expense	
Deferred	-0-*
Net loss	$(200,000)

*Allowance ($40,000) – Carryforward ($40,000)

In 2021, assuming that Groh has taxable income of $250,000 (before considering the carryforward) subject to a tax rate of 20 percent, it realizes the deferred tax asset. It thus no longer needs the allowance. Groh records the following entries.

To record current and deferred income taxes		
Income Tax Expense	50,000	
Deferred Tax Asset		40,000
Income Taxes Payable		10,000
To eliminate allowance and recognize loss carryforward		
Allowance to Reduce Deferred Tax Asset to Expected Realizable Value	40,000	
Income Tax Expense (Allowance)		40,000

Groh reports the $40,000 Income Tax Expense (Loss Carryforward) on the 2021 income statement. The company did not recognize it in 2020 because it was more likely than not that it would not be realized. Assuming that Groh derives the income for 2021 from continuing operations, it prepares the income statement as shown in **Illustration 19.41**.

ILLUSTRATION 19.41

Recognition of Benefit of Loss Carryforward When Realized

Groh Inc.
Income Statement (partial) for 2021

Income before income taxes		$250,000
Income tax expense		
Current	$ 10,000	
Deferred	-0-*	10,000
Net income		$240,000

*Loss carryforward ($40,000) – Allowance ($40,000)

Another method is to report only one line for total income tax expense of $10,000 on the face of the income statement and disclose the components of income tax expense in the notes to the financial statements.

Valuation Allowance Revisited

A company should consider all positive and negative information in determining whether it needs a valuation allowance. Whether the company will realize a deferred tax asset depends on whether sufficient taxable income exists or will exist within the carryforward period available under tax law. Illustration 19.42 shows possible sources of taxable income that may be available under the tax law to realize a tax benefit for deductible temporary differences and carryforwards.[6]

ILLUSTRATION 19.42

Possible Sources of Taxable Income

Taxable Income Sources

a. Future reversals of existing taxable temporary differences.

b. Future taxable income exclusive of reversing temporary differences and carryforwards.

c. **Tax-planning strategies** that would, if necessary, be implemented to:
(1) Accelerate taxable amounts to utilize expiring carryforwards.
(2) Change the character of taxable or deductible amounts from ordinary income or loss to capital gain or loss.
(3) Switch from tax-exempt to taxable investments. [2]

If any one of these sources is sufficient to support a conclusion that a valuation allowance is unnecessary, a company need not consider other sources.

Forming a conclusion that a valuation allowance is not needed is difficult when there is negative evidence such as cumulative losses in recent years. Companies may also cite positive evidence indicating that a valuation allowance is not needed. Illustration 19.43 presents examples (not prerequisites) of evidence to consider when determining the need for a valuation allowance.

ILLUSTRATION 19.43

Evidence to Consider in Evaluating the Need for a Valuation Account

Negative Evidence

a. A history of operating loss or tax credit carryforwards expiring unused.

b. Losses expected in early future years (by a presently profitable entity).

c. Unsettled circumstances that, if unfavorably resolved, would adversely affect future operations and profit levels on a continuing basis in future years.

d. A carryforward period that is so brief that it would limit realization of tax benefits if (1) a significant deductible temporary difference is expected to reverse in a single year or (2) the enterprise operates in a traditionally cyclical business.

Positive Evidence

a. Existing contracts or firm sales backlog that will produce more than enough taxable income to realize the deferred tax asset based on existing sale prices and cost structures.

b. An excess of appreciated asset value over the tax basis of the entity's net assets in an amount sufficient to realize the deferred tax asset.

c. A strong earnings history exclusive of the loss that created the future deductible amount (tax loss carryforward or deductible temporary difference) coupled with evidence indicating that the loss is an aberration rather than a continuing condition (for example, the result of an unusual or infrequent item, or both). [3]

[6]Companies implement a tax-planning strategy to realize a tax benefit for an operating loss or tax credit carryforward before it expires. Companies consider tax-planning strategies when assessing the need for and amount of a valuation allowance for deferred tax assets.

The use of a valuation allowance provides a company with an opportunity to manage its earnings. As one accounting expert notes, "The 'more likely than not' provision is perhaps the most judgmental clause in accounting." Some companies may set up a valuation account and then use it to increase income as needed. Others may take the income immediately to increase capital or to offset large negative charges to income (see **Global View**).

> **Global View**
>
> Under IFRS (*IAS 12*), a company may not recognize a deferred tax asset unless realization is "probable." However, "probable" is not defined in the standard, leading to diversity in the recognition of deferred tax assets.

What Do the Numbers Mean? **NOLs: Good News or Bad?**

Here are some net operating loss numbers reported by several notable companies.

NOLs ($ in millions)

Company	Income (Loss)	Operating Loss Carryforward	Tax Deferred (Tax Asset)
Delta Air Lines	$3,577	$1,440	$6,134
Goodyear	365	1,515	2,344
Kodak	94	307	1,066
General Mills	1,701.1	109.5	1,205.2

All of these companies are using the carryforward provisions of the tax code for their NOLs. For many of them, the NOL is an amount far exceeding their reported profits. (Carryforwards can be claimed indefinitely into the future.) In some cases, management expects the tax rates in the future to be higher. This difference in expected rates provides a bigger tax benefit if the losses are carried forward and matched against future income.

Is there a downside? To realize the benefits of carryforwards, a company must have future taxable income in order to claim the NOL deductions. As we learned, if it is more likely than not that a company will not have taxable income, it must record a valuation allowance (and increased tax expense). As the data above indicate, recording a valuation allowance to reflect the uncertainty of realizing the tax benefits has merit.

A good example is **Sony Corp.**, which announced a $3.2 billion net loss, blaming a $4.4 billion write-off on a certain portion of deferred tax assets in Japan, in what would be the company's third straight year of red ink. The write-off was an admission that the March 2011 earthquake and tsunami shattered its expectations for a robust current fiscal year. Like other Japanese auto and electronics makers, Sony faced uncertainties because its recovery prospects were partially dependent on parts and materials suppliers, many of which were also affected by the quake. Thus, the post-quake outlook put Sony in a position where it had to set aside reserves of ¥360 billion on certain deferred tax assets due to uncertainty about future taxable income.

Sources: Company annual reports; and J. Osawa, "Sony Expects Hefty Loss: Electronics Giant Reverses Prediction for Full-Year Profit, Blaming Earthquake," *Wall Street Journal* (May 24, 2011).

Financial Statement Presentation

LEARNING OBJECTIVE 4

Describe the presentation of deferred income taxes in financial statements.

Balance Sheet

Income taxes payable and income tax refund receivable are reported as a current liability and current asset, respectively, on the balance sheet. In addition, companies often make estimated payments to taxing authorities quarterly; these payments are reported as prepaid income taxes in the current assets section. Companies are generally permitted to offset any balances in income taxes payable against related income tax refund receivable or prepaid income taxes balances.

Deferred tax accounts are also reported as assets and liabilities. Companies should classify deferred tax accounts as a net noncurrent amount on the balance sheet. That is, deferred tax assets and deferred tax liabilities are separately recognized and measured and then offset on the balance sheet. The net deferred tax asset or net deferred tax liability is therefore reported in the noncurrent section of the balance sheet.

To illustrate, assume that Scott Company has four deferred tax items at December 31, 2020, as shown in the following table.

	Amount	
Temporary Difference	(Asset)	Liability
1. Rent collected in advance: recognized when a performance obligation is satisfied for accounting purposes and when received for tax purposes.	$(42,000)	
2. Use of straight-line depreciation for accounting purposes and accelerated depreciation for tax purposes.		$ 214,000
3. Recognition of income on installment sales at the time of sale for accounting purposes and during period of collection for tax purposes.		45,000
4. Warranty liabilities: recognized at time of sale for accounting purposes and at time paid for tax purposes.	(12,000)	
Totals	$(54,000)	$ 259,000
Net liability		$ 205,000

As indicated, Scott Company has total deferred tax assets of $54,000 and total deferred tax liabilities of $259,000. Scott therefore reports a deferred tax liability of $205,000 ($259,000 – $54,000) in the noncurrent section of the balance sheet.

Some argue that the use of the noncurrent section for classification of deferred taxes on the balance sheet is incorrect. That is, the classification should be based on when the temporary difference reverses. For example, a temporary difference that reverses in the next period should be classified as current rather than noncurrent. The FASB recognizes that classifying all deferred tax items as noncurrent is conceptually deficient. However, it notes that determining when a temporary difference reverses is often difficult (such as with a loss carryforward). In addition, the scheduling of the reversals to determine current versus noncurrent is complex and costly, and provides limited usefulness to the financial statement reader. As a result, the Board decided to classify all deferred taxes as noncurrent.

Note Disclosure

Companies are required to disclose the total of all deferred tax liabilities, the total of all deferred assets, and the total valuation allowance in the notes to the financial statements. In addition, companies should disclose (1) any change during the year in the total valuation allowance, and (2) the types of temporary differences or carryforwards that give rise to significant portions of deferred tax liabilities and assets. For example, **PepsiCo** reported the information shown in **Illustration 19.44** related to its deferred tax assets, deferred tax liabilities, and valuation allowance account.

This disclosure of gross deferred tax assets, deferred tax liabilities, and changes in the valuation allowance helps users make better predictions of future cash flows. Examination of the deferred portion of income tax expense provides information as to whether taxes payable are likely to be higher or lower in the future. In PepsiCo's case, analysts expect future taxable amounts and higher tax payments, primarily from lower depreciation and amortization in the future. PepsiCo expects future deductible amounts and lower tax payments due to deductions for carryforwards, employee benefits, and state taxes. These deferred tax items indicate that actual tax payments for PepsiCo will be higher than the tax expense reported on the income statement in the future.[7]

[7]See R. P. Weber and J. E. Wheeler, "Using Income Tax Disclosures to Explore Significant Economic Transactions," *Accounting Horizons* (September 1992), for a discussion of how analysts use deferred tax disclosures to assess the quality of earnings and to predict future cash flows.

ILLUSTRATION 19.44

PepsiCo Tax Note

PepsiCo
(in millions)

Deferred tax liabilities and assets are comprised of the following:

	2017	2016
Deferred tax liabilities		
Debt guarantee of wholly-owned subsidiary	**$ 578**	$ 839
Property, plant and equipment	**1,397**	1,967
Intangible assets other than nondeductible goodwill	**3,169**	4,124
Other	**50**	245
Gross deferred tax liabilities	**5,194**	7,175
Deferred tax assets		
Net carryforwards	**1,400**	1,255
Stock-based compensation	**107**	219
Retiree medical benefits	**198**	316
Other employee-related benefits	**338**	614
Pension benefits	**22**	419
Deductible state tax and interest benefits	**157**	189
Other	**893**	839
Gross deferred tax assets	**3,115**	3,851
Valuation allowances	**(1,163)**	(1,110)
Deferred tax assets, net	**1,952**	2,741
Net deferred tax liabilities	**$3,242**	$4,434

A summary of our valuation allowance activity is as follows:

	2017	2016	2015
Balance, beginning of year	**$1,110**	$1,136	$1,230
(Benefit)/provision	**33**	13	(26)
Other (deductions)/additions	**20**	(39)	(68)
Balance, end of year	**$1,163**	$1,110	$1,136

What Do the Numbers Mean? Imagination at Work

Here's one thing you can say that's true about U.S. corporate taxes: The statutory rate in effect before the recent tax act (35 percent at the federal level, around 40 percent when you average in state rates) was the highest on earth. Here's another thing you can say that's true about U.S. corporate taxes: The average effective tax rate is less—sometimes much less—than the statutory rate.

How do they do it? Take **Apple**, for example. It uses a tax structure known as the "Double Irish with a Dutch Sandwich," which reduces taxes by routing profits through Irish subsidiaries and the Netherlands and then to the Caribbean. As a result of using this tactic, Apple paid cash taxes of $3.3 billion around the world on its reported profits of $34.2 billion in a recent year, a tax rate of just 9.8 percent. **Google** used the same strategy to reduce its overseas tax rate to 2.4 percent, the lowest of the top five U.S. technology companies by market capitalization, according to regulatory filings in six countries.

General Electric (GE) is generally viewed as the most skilled at reducing its tax burden. GE uses a maze of shelters, tax credits, and subsidiaries to pay far less than the stated tax rate. In a recent year, it reported worldwide profits of $14.2 billion, and said $5.1 billion of the total came from its operations in the United States. Its American tax bill? Zero. In fact, GE claimed a tax benefit of $3.2 billion. GE's giant tax department is viewed by some as the world's best tax law firm. Indeed, the company's slogan, "Imagination at Work," fits this department well. The team includes former officials not just from the Treasury, but also from the IRS and virtually all the tax-writing committees in Congress.

The strategies employed by Apple, Google, and GE, as well as changes in tax laws that encouraged some businesses and professionals to file as individuals, have pushed down the corporate share of the nation's tax receipts from 30 percent of all federal revenue in the mid-1950s to a much lower rate today. As many as two-thirds of U.S. and foreign corporations paid no federal income taxes from 1998–2005. Many citizens and public-interest groups cite corporate avoidance of income taxes as a reason for more tax reform.

There is ongoing debate as to whether the recently enacted tax reform with lower tax rates will lead to less-aggressive tax structuring in order to reduce corporate taxes. The lower rate—much closer to the rate in other countries—will certainly reduce the incentive to locate business headquarters and some intangible assets overseas (as Apple and Google did) because the tax savings will not be as large. However, other tax dodges, like those employed by GE tax engineers, are still in place. So the tax department at GE will still be busy trying to lower GE's effective tax rate below the 21 percent maximum.

Sources: D. Kocieniewski, "G.E.'s Strategies Let It Avoid Taxes Altogether," *The New York Times* (March 24, 2011); J. Fox, "Why Some Multinationals Pay Such Low Taxes," *HBR Blog Network* (March 27, 2012); Robert W. Wood, "Forget Inversions, These 20 Huge, Profitable Companies Already Pay Zero Tax," *Forbes* (August 15, 2014); and R. Rubin, "U.S. Tax Revamp Weakens Case for Companies to Shift Profit Overseas," *Wall Street Journal* (April 29, 2018).

Income Statement

Companies are required to report income before income taxes and income tax expense on the income statement. Illustration 19.45 shows the amounts that PepsiCo reported related to tax expense.

ILLUSTRATION 19.45
Tax Expense Disclosures

PepsiCo
(in millions)

	2017	2016	2015
Income before income taxes	$9,602	$8,553	$7,442
Provision for income taxes	4,694	2,174	1,941
Net income	4,908	6,379	5,501

Income tax expense (or benefit) generally equals the sum of income taxes payable (or refundable) and the change in the deferred tax expense or benefit. The formula in Illustration 19.46 is used to compute income tax expense (benefit).

ILLUSTRATION 19.46
Formula to Compute Income Tax Expense or Benefit

Income Taxes Payable or Refundable ± **Change in Deferred Income Taxes** = **Total Income Tax Expense or Benefit**

As indicated, the total deferred tax expense (or benefit) equals the sum of the changes in the deferred tax assets, deferred tax liabilities, and the valuation allowance for the year. For example, a company adds an increase in a deferred tax liability to income taxes payable. On the other hand, it subtracts an increase in a deferred tax asset from income taxes payable.

PepsiCo provided the disclosure shown in Illustration 19.47 in the notes to the financial statements providing additional explanation related to income before income taxes and deferred income taxes.

ILLUSTRATION 19.47
Components of Income Tax Expense

PepsiCo
(in millions)

The components of income before income taxes are as follows:

	2017	2016	2015
U.S.	$3,452	$2,630	$2,879
Foreign	6,150	5,923	4,563
	$9,602	$8,553	$7,442

The provision for income taxes consisted of the following:

		2017	2016	2015
Current:	U.S. Federal	$4,925	$1,219	$1,143
	Foreign	724	824	773
	State	136	77	65
		5,785	2,120	1,981
Deferred:	U.S. Federal	(1,159)	109	(14)
	Foreign	(9)	(33)	(32)
	State	77	(22)	6
		(1,091)	54	(40)
		$4,694	$2,174	$1,941

Although companies generally report only the change in the deferred portion on the income statement, it is important to recognize that the change can involve many of the following items:

1. Current tax expense or benefit.
2. Deferred tax expense or benefit, exclusive of other components listed below.

3. Government grants (if recognized as a reduction of income tax expense).
4. The benefits of operating loss carryforwards (resulting in a reduction of income tax expense).
5. Tax expense that results from allocating tax benefits either directly to paid-in capital or to reduce goodwill or other noncurrent intangible assets of an acquired entity.
6. Adjustments of a deferred tax liability or asset for enacted changes in tax laws or rates or a change in the tax status of a company.
7. Adjustments of the beginning-of-the-year balance of a valuation allowance because of a change in circumstances that causes a change in judgment about the realizability of the related deferred tax asset in future years.

In the notes, companies must also reconcile (using percentages or dollar amounts) income tax expense attributable to continuing operations with the amount that results from applying domestic or federal statutory tax rates to pretax income from continuing operations. Companies should disclose the estimated amount and the nature of significant reconciling items. Illustration 19.48 presents an example from the 2017 annual report of PepsiCo.

ILLUSTRATION 19.48

Tax Rate Reconciliation

PepsiCo

A reconciliation of the U.S. Federal statutory tax rate to our annual tax rate is as follows:

	2017	2016	2015
U.S. Federal statutory tax rate	**35.0%**	35.0%	35.0%
State income tax, net of U.S. Federal tax benefit	**0.9**	0.4	0.6
Lower taxes on foreign results	**(9.4)**	(8.0)	(10.5)
Impact of Venezuela impairment charges	—	—	6.4
Provisional one-time mandatory transition tax—TCJ Act	**41.4**	—	—
Provisional remeasurement of deferred taxes—TCJ Act	**(15.9)**	—	—
Tax settlements	**—**	—	(3.1)
Other, net	**(3.1)**	(2.0)	(2.3)
Annual tax rate	**48.9%**	25.4%	26.1%

This disclosure helps users assess the quality of earnings. Many investors seeking to assess the quality of a company's earnings are interested in the reconciliation of pretax financial income to taxable income. Analysts carefully examine earnings that are enhanced by a favorable tax effect, particularly if the tax effect is non-recurring.

For example, the tax rate reconciliation schedule indicates that PepsiCo's tax rate is approximately 14 percent higher than its statutory rate in 2017. The reason for this difference is primarily due to one-time adjustments for the recent enactment of the Tax Cuts and Jobs Act (remeasuring deferred taxes and taxes on foreign earnings). As indicated, in prior years Pepsi's tax rate was lower than the statutory rate. In 2018 and beyond, this is likely to be the case but beginning with a statutory rate of 21 percent.

Companies should also disclose the nature of their tax loss carryforward. PepsiCo, for example, provides the information shown in Illustration 19.49.

ILLUSTRATION 19.49

Disclosure of Carryforwards and Allowances

PepsiCo

Carryforwards and Allowances (partial)

Operating loss carryforwards totaling $12.6 billion at year-end 2017 are being carried forward in a number of foreign and state jurisdictions where we are permitted to use tax operating losses from prior periods to reduce future taxable income. These operating losses may be carried forward indefinitely. We establish valuation allowances for our deferred tax assets if, based on the available evidence, it is more likely than not that some portion or all of the deferred tax assets will not be realized.

This disclosure helps users predict future cash flows for operating loss carryforwards. From this disclosure, analysts determine the amount of income that the company may recognize in the future on which it will pay no income tax. For example, the PepsiCo disclosure in Illustration 19.49 indicates that PepsiCo has $12.6 billion in net operating loss carryforwards that it can use to reduce future taxes. However, the valuation allowance indicates that $1,163 million (see Illustration 19.44) of deferred tax assets may not be realized in the future.

Loss carryforwards can be valuable to a potential acquirer. For example, as mentioned earlier, **Yahoo!** has a substantial net operating loss carryforward. A potential acquirer would find Yahoo! more valuable as a result of these carryforwards. That is, the acquirer may be able to use these carryforwards to shield future income. However the acquiring company has to be careful because the structure of the deal may lead to a situation where the deductions will be severely limited.

Much the same issue arises in companies emerging from bankruptcy. In many cases, these companies have large NOLs but the value of the losses may be limited. This is because any gains related to the cancellation of liabilities in bankruptcy must be offset against the NOLs. For example, when **Kmart Holding Corp.** emerged from bankruptcy, it disclosed NOL carryforwards approximating $3.8 billion. At the same time, Kmart disclosed cancellation of debt gains that reduced the value of the NOL carryforward. These reductions soured the merger between Kmart and **Sears Roebuck** because the cancellation of the indebtedness gains reduced the value of the Kmart carryforwards to the merged company by $3.74 billion.[8]

Evolving Issue Uncertain Tax Positions

Whenever there is a contingency, companies determine if the contingency is **probable** and can be reasonably estimated. If both of these criteria are met, the company records the contingency in the financial statements. These guidelines also apply to uncertain tax positions. **Uncertain tax positions** are tax positions for which the tax authorities may disallow a deduction in whole or in part. Uncertain tax positions often arise when a company takes an aggressive approach in its tax planning. Examples are instances in which the tax law is unclear or the company may believe that the risk of audit is low. Uncertain tax positions give rise to tax benefits either by reducing income tax expense or related payables or by increasing an income tax refund receivable or deferred tax asset.

Unfortunately, companies have not applied these provisions consistently in accounting and reporting of uncertain tax positions. Some companies have not recognized a tax benefit unless it is probable that the benefit will be realized and can be reasonably estimated. Other companies have used a lower threshold, such as that found in the existing authoritative literature. As we have learned, the lower threshold—described as **"more likely than not"**—means that the company believes it has at least a 51 percent chance that the uncertain tax position will pass muster with the taxing authorities. Thus, there has been diversity in practice concerning the accounting and reporting of uncertain tax positions.

As a result, the FASB has issued rules for companies to follow to determine whether it is "more likely than not" that tax positions will be sustained upon audit. [4] If the probability is more than 50 percent, companies may reduce their liability or increase their assets. If the probability is less than 50 percent, companies may not record the tax benefit. In determining "more likely than not," companies must assume that they will be audited by the tax authorities. If the recognition threshold is passed, companies must then estimate the amount to record as an adjustment to their tax assets and liabilities. (This estimation process is complex and is beyond the scope of this text.)

Companies will experience varying financial statement effects upon adoption of these rules. Those with a history of conservative tax strategies may have their tax liabilities decrease or their tax assets increase. For example, **PepsiCo** recorded a $7 million increase to retained earnings upon adoption of the guidelines. Others that followed more aggressive tax planning may have to increase their liabilities or reduce their assets, with a resulting negative effect on net income.

The Asset-Liability Method

The FASB believes that the **asset-liability method** (sometimes referred to as the **liability approach**) is the most consistent method for accounting for income taxes. One objective of this approach is to recognize the amount of taxes payable or refundable for the current year.

[8]The IRS frowns on acquisitions done solely to obtain operating loss carryforwards. If it determines that the merger is solely tax-motivated, the IRS disallows the deductions. But because it is very difficult to determine whether a merger is or is not tax-motivated, the "purchase of operating loss carryforwards" continues.

A second objective is to recognize **deferred tax liabilities and assets** for the **future tax consequences** of events that have been recognized in the financial statements or tax returns.

To implement the objectives, companies apply some basic principles in accounting for income taxes at the date of the financial statements, as listed in Illustration 19.50. [5]

ILLUSTRATION 19.50

Basic Principles of the Asset-Liability Method

Basic Principles

a. A current tax liability or asset is recognized for the estimated taxes payable or refundable on the tax return for the current year.
b. A deferred tax liability or asset is recognized for the estimated future tax effects attributable to temporary differences and carryforwards.
c. The measurement of current and deferred tax liabilities and assets is based on provisions of the enacted tax law; the effects of future changes in tax laws or rates are not anticipated.
d. The measurement of deferred tax assets is reduced, if necessary, by the amount of any tax benefits that, based on available evidence, are not expected to be realized.

Illustration 19.51 diagrams the procedures for implementing the asset-liability method.

ILLUSTRATION 19.51

Procedures for Computing and Reporting Deferred Income Taxes

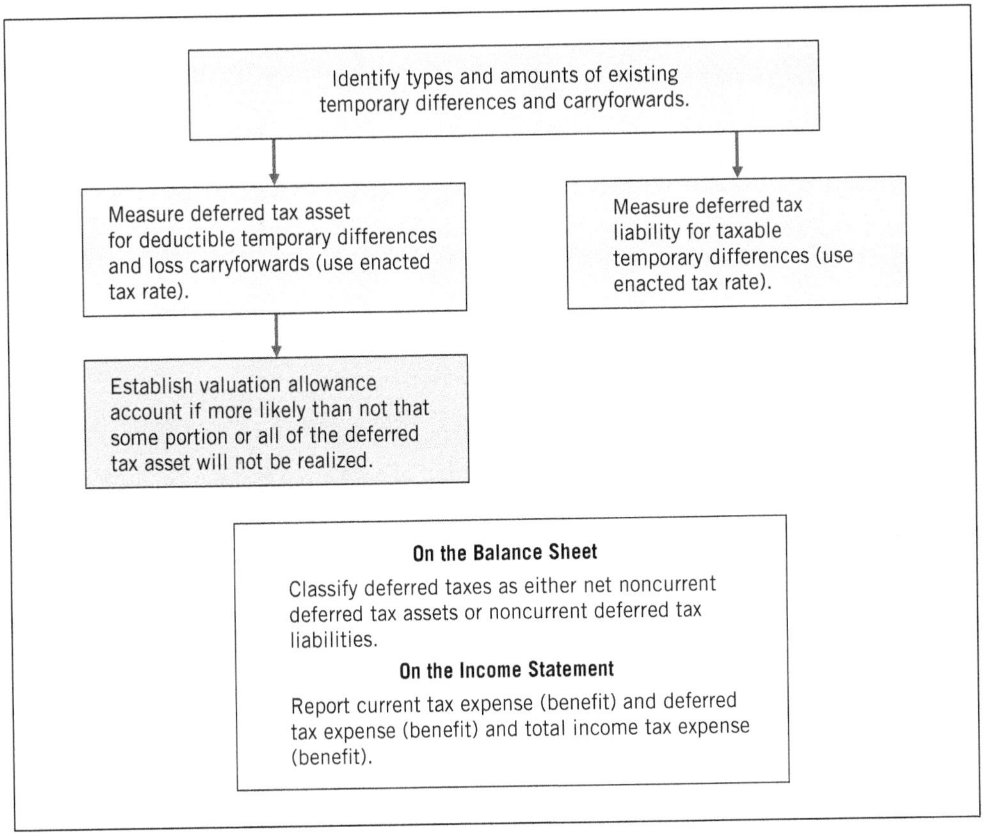

As an aid to understanding deferred income taxes, we provide the following glossary (see Global View).

Global View

IFRS on income taxes is based on the same principles as GAAP—comprehensive recognition of deferred tax assets and liabilities.

Key Deferred Income Tax Terms

Carryforwards. Deductions or credits that cannot be utilized on the tax return during a year and that may be carried forward to reduce taxable income or taxes payable in a future year. An **operating loss carryforward** is an excess of tax deductions over gross income in a year. A **tax credit carryforward** is the amount by which tax credits available for utilization exceed statutory limitations.

Current Tax Expense (Benefit). The amount of income taxes paid or payable (or refundable) for a year as determined by applying the provisions of the enacted tax law to the taxable income or excess of deductions over revenues for that year.

Deductible Temporary Difference. Temporary differences that result in deductible amounts in future years when recovering or settling the related asset or liability, respectively.

Deferred Tax Asset. The deferred tax consequences attributable to deductible temporary differences and carryforwards.

Deferred Tax Consequences. The future effects on income taxes as measured by the enacted tax rate and provisions of the enacted tax law resulting from temporary differences and carryforwards at the end of the current year.

Deferred Tax Expense (Benefit). The change during the year in a company's deferred tax liabilities and assets.

Deferred Tax Liability. The deferred tax consequences attributable to taxable temporary differences.

Income Taxes. Domestic and foreign federal (national), state, and local (including franchise) taxes based on income.

Income Taxes Currently Payable (Refundable). Refer to current tax expense (benefit).

Income Tax Expense (Benefit). The sum of current tax expense (benefit) and deferred tax expense (benefit).

Taxable Income. The excess of taxable revenues over tax-deductible expenses and exemptions for the year as defined by the governmental taxing authority.

Taxable Temporary Difference. Temporary differences that result in taxable amounts in future years when recovering or settling the related asset or liability, respectively.

Tax-Planning Strategy. An action that meets certain criteria and that a company implements to realize a tax benefit for an operating loss or tax credit carryforward. Companies consider tax-planning strategies when assessing the need for and amount of a valuation allowance for deferred tax assets.

Temporary Difference. A difference between the tax basis of an asset or liability and its reported amount in the financial statements that will result in taxable or deductible amounts in future years when recovering or settling the reported amount of the asset or liability, respectively.

Valuation Allowance. The portion of a deferred tax asset for which it is more likely than not that a company will not realize a tax benefit.

APPENDIX 19A Comprehensive Example of Interperiod Tax Allocation

LEARNING OBJECTIVE *5

Apply the concepts and procedures of interperiod tax allocation.

This appendix presents a comprehensive illustration of a deferred income tax problem with several temporary and permanent differences. The example follows one company through two complete years (2019 and 2020). **Study it carefully.** It should help you understand the concepts and procedures presented in the chapter.

First Year—2019

Allman Company, which began operations at the beginning of 2019, produces various products on a contract basis. Each contract generates a gross profit of $80,000. Some of Allman's contracts provide for the customer to pay on an installment basis. Under these contracts, Allman collects one-fifth of the contract revenue evenly over the current year and in each of the following four years. For financial reporting purposes, the company recognizes gross profit in the year of completion (accrual basis); for tax purposes, Allman recognizes gross profit in the year cash is collected (installment basis).

Presented below is information related to Allman's operations for 2019.

1. In 2019, the company completed seven contracts that allow for the customer to pay on an installment basis. Allman recognized the related gross profit of $560,000 for financial reporting purposes. It reported only $112,000 of gross profit on installment sales on the 2019 tax return. The company expects future collections on the related installment receivables to result in taxable amounts of $112,000 in each of the next four years.
2. At the beginning of 2019, Allman Company purchased depreciable assets with a cost of $540,000. For financial reporting purposes, Allman depreciates these assets using the

straight-line method over a six-year service life. For tax purposes, the assets fall in the five-year recovery class, and Allman uses the MACRS system. The depreciation schedules for both financial reporting and tax purposes are as follows.

Year	Depreciation for Financial Reporting Purposes	Depreciation for Tax Purposes	Difference
2019	$ 90,000	$108,000	$(18,000)
2020	90,000	172,800	(82,800)
2021	90,000	103,680	(13,680)
2022	90,000	62,208	27,792
2023	90,000	62,208	27,792
2024	90,000	31,104	58,896
	$540,000	$540,000	$ -0-

3. The company warrants its product for two years from the date of completion of a contract. During 2019, the product warranty liability accrued for financial reporting purposes was $200,000, and the amount paid for the satisfaction of warranty liability was $44,000. Allman expects to settle the remaining $156,000 by expenditures of $56,000 in 2020 and $100,000 in 2021.
4. In 2019, nontaxable municipal bond interest revenue was $28,000.
5. During 2019, nondeductible fines and penalties of $26,000 were paid.
6. Pretax financial income for 2019 amounts to $412,000.
7. Tax rates enacted before the end of 2019 were:

2019	30%
2020 and later years	20%

8. The accounting period is the calendar year.
9. The company is expected to have taxable income in all future years.

Taxable Income and Income Taxes Payable—2019

The first step is to determine Allman Company's income taxes payable for 2019 by calculating its taxable income. Illustration 19A.1 shows this computation.

ILLUSTRATION 19A.1

Computation of Taxable Income, 2019

Pretax financial income for 2019	$412,000
Permanent differences:	
Nontaxable revenue—municipal bond interest	(28,000)
Nondeductible expenses—fines and penalties	26,000
Temporary differences:	
Excess gross profit per books ($560,000 – $112,000)	(448,000)
Excess depreciation per tax ($108,000 – $90,000)	(18,000)
Excess warranty expense per books ($200,000 – $44,000)	156,000
Taxable income for 2019	$100,000

Allman computes income taxes payable on taxable income for $100,000 as shown in Illustration 19A.2.

ILLUSTRATION 19A.2

Computation of Income Taxes Payable, End of 2019

Taxable income for 2019	$100,000
Tax rate	30%
Income taxes payable (current tax expense) for 2019	$ 30,000

Computing Deferred Income Taxes—End of 2019

The schedule in Illustration 19A.3 summarizes the temporary differences and the resulting future taxable and deductible amounts.

ILLUSTRATION 19A.3

Schedule of Future Taxable and Deductible Amounts, End of 2019

	Future Years					
	2020	2021	2022	2023	2024	Total
Future taxable (deductible) amounts:						
Installment sales	$112,000	$112,000	$112,000	$112,000		$448,000
Depreciation	(82,800)	(13,680)	27,792	27,792	$58,896	18,000
Warranty costs	(56,000)	(100,000)				(156,000)

Allman computes the amounts of deferred income taxes to be reported at the end of 2019 as shown in **Illustration 19A.4**.

ILLUSTRATION 19A.4

Computation of Deferred Income Taxes, End of 2019

Temporary Difference	Future Taxable (Deductible) Amounts	Tax Rate	Deferred Tax (Asset)	Deferred Tax Liability
Installment sales	$448,000	20%		$89,600
Depreciation	18,000	20		3,600
Warranty costs	(156,000)	20	$(31,200)	
Totals	$310,000		$(31,200)	$93,200*

*Because only a single tax rate is involved in all relevant years, these totals can be reconciled: $310,000 × .20 = ($31,200) + $93,200.

A temporary difference is caused by the use of the accrual basis for financial reporting purposes and the installment method for tax purposes. This temporary difference will result in future taxable amounts and hence a deferred tax liability. Because of the installment contracts completed in 2019, a temporary difference of $448,000 originates that will reverse in equal amounts over the next four years. The company expects to have taxable income in all future years, and there is only one enacted tax rate applicable to all future years. Allman uses that rate (20 percent) to compute the entire deferred tax liability resulting from this temporary difference.

The temporary difference caused by different depreciation policies for books and for tax purposes originates over three years and then reverses over three years. This difference will cause deductible amounts in 2020 and 2021 and taxable amounts in 2022, 2023, and 2024. These amounts sum to a net future taxable amount of $18,000 (which is the cumulative temporary difference at the end of 2019). Because the company expects to have taxable income in all future years and because there is only one tax rate enacted for all of the relevant future years, Allman applies that rate to the net future taxable amount to determine the related net deferred tax liability.

The third temporary difference is caused by different methods of accounting for warranties. This difference will result in deductible amounts in each of the two future years it takes to reverse. Because the company expects to report a positive income on all future tax returns and because there is only one tax rate enacted for each of the relevant future years, Allman uses the 20 percent rate to calculate the resulting deferred tax asset.

Deferred Tax Expense (Benefit) and the Journal Entry to Record Income Taxes—2019

To determine the deferred tax expense (benefit), we need to compare the beginning and ending balances of the deferred income tax accounts. **Illustration 19A.5** shows that computation.

ILLUSTRATION 19A.5

Computation of Deferred Tax Expense (Benefit), 2019

Deferred tax asset at the end of 2019	$ 31,200
Deferred tax asset at the beginning of 2019	–0–
Deferred tax expense (benefit)	$(31,200)
Deferred tax liability at the end of 2019	$ 93,200
Deferred tax liability at the beginning of 2019	–0–
Deferred tax expense (benefit)	$ 93,200

The $31,200 increase in the deferred tax asset causes a deferred tax benefit to be reported in the income statement. The $93,200 increase in the deferred tax liability during 2019 results in a deferred tax expense. As Illustration 19A.6 shows, these two amounts **net** to a deferred tax expense of $62,000 for 2019.

ILLUSTRATION 19A.6

Computation of Net Deferred Tax Expense, 2019

Deferred tax expense (benefit)	$(31,200)
Deferred tax expense (benefit)	93,200
Net deferred tax expense for 2019	$ 62,000

Allman then computes the total income tax expense as shown in Illustration 19A.7.

ILLUSTRATION 19A.7

Computation of Total Income Tax Expense, 2019

Current tax expense for 2019	$30,000
Deferred tax expense for 2019	62,000
Income tax expense (total) for 2019	$92,000

Allman records income taxes payable, deferred income taxes, and income tax expense as follows.

Income Tax Expense	92,000	
Deferred Tax Asset	31,200	
Income Taxes Payable		30,000
Deferred Tax Liability		93,200

Financial Statement Presentation—2019

Companies should classify deferred tax assets and liabilities as noncurrent on the balance sheet. Multiple categories of deferred taxes are classified into a net noncurrent amount. Illustration 19A.8 shows the classification of Allman's deferred tax accounts at the end of 2019.

ILLUSTRATION 19A.8

Classification of Deferred Tax Accounts, End of 2019

	Resulting Deferred Tax	
Temporary Difference	(Asset)	Liability
Installment sales		$89,600
Depreciation		3,600
Warranty costs	$(31,200)	
Totals	$(31,200)	$93,200

Thus, Allman reports a net noncurrent deferred tax liability of $62,000 ($93,200 – $31,200). The balance sheet at the end of 2019 reports the amounts shown in Illustration 19A.9.

ILLUSTRATION 19A.9

Balance Sheet Presentation of Deferred Taxes, 2019

Current liabilities	
Income taxes payable	$30,000
Long-term liabilities	
Deferred tax liability ($93,200 – $31,200)	$62,000

Illustration 19A.10 shown Allman's income statement for 2019.

ILLUSTRATION 19A.10

Income Statement Presentation of Income Tax Expense, 2019

Income before income taxes		$412,000
Income tax expense		
Current	$30,000	
Deferred	62,000	92,000
Net income		$320,000

Second Year—2020

1. During 2020, Allman collected $112,000 from customers for the receivables arising from contracts completed in 2019. The company expects recovery of the remaining receivables to result in taxable amounts of $112,000 in each of the following three years.
2. In 2020, the company completed four new contracts that allow for the customer to pay on an installment basis. These installment sales created new installment receivables. Future collections of these receivables will result in reporting gross profit of $64,000 for tax purposes in each of the next four years.
3. During 2020, Allman continued to depreciate the assets acquired in 2019 according to the depreciation schedules presented earlier. Thus, depreciation amounted to $90,000 for financial reporting purposes and $172,800 for tax purposes.
4. An analysis at the end of 2020, of the product warranty liability account, showed the following details.

Balance of liability at beginning of 2020	$156,000
Expense for 2020 income statement purposes	180,000
Amount paid for contracts completed in 2019	(56,000)
Amount paid for contracts completed in 2020	(50,000)
Balance of liability at end of 2020	$230,000

The balance of the liability is expected to require expenditures in the future as follows.

$100,000 in 2021 due to 2019 contracts
$ 50,000 in 2021 due to 2020 contracts
$ 80,000 in 2022 due to 2020 contracts
$230,000

5. During 2020, nontaxable municipal bond interest revenue was $24,000.
6. Allman accrued a loss of $172,000 for financial reporting purposes because of pending litigation. This amount is not tax-deductible until the period the loss is realized, which the company estimates to be 2028.
7. Pretax financial income for 2020 amounts to $504,800.
8. The enacted tax rates still in effect are:

2019	30%
2020 and later years	20%

Taxable Income and Income Taxes Payable—2020

Allman computes taxable income for 2020 as shown in Illustration 19A.11.

ILLUSTRATION 19A.11

Computation of Taxable Income, 2020

Pretax financial income for 2020	$504,800
Permanent difference:	
Nontaxable revenue—municipal bond interest	(24,000)
Reversing temporary differences:	
Collection on 2019 installment sales	112,000
Payments on warranties from 2019 contracts	(56,000)
Originating temporary differences:	
Excess gross profit per books—2020 contracts	(256,000)
Excess depreciation per tax	(82,800)
Excess warranty expense per books—2020 contracts	130,000
Loss accrual per books	172,000
Taxable income for 2020	$500,000

Income taxes payable for 2020 are as shown in Illustration 19A.12.

Taxable income for 2020	$500,000
Tax rate	20%
Income taxes payable (current tax expense) for 2020	$100,000

ILLUSTRATION 19A.12
Computation of Income Taxes Payable, End of 2020

Computing Deferred Income Taxes—End of 2020

The schedule in Illustration 19A.13 summarizes the temporary differences existing at the end of 2020 and the resulting future taxable and deductible amounts.

ILLUSTRATION 19A.13 Schedule of Future Taxable and Deductible Amounts, End of 2020

	Future Years					
	2021	2022	2023	2024	2028	Total
Future taxable (deductible) amounts:						
Installment sales—2019	$112,000	$112,000	$112,000			$336,000
Installment sales—2020	64,000	64,000	64,000	$64,000		256,000
Depreciation	(13,680)	27,792	27,792	58,896		100,800
Warranty costs	(150,000)	(80,000)				(230,000)
Loss accrual					$(172,000)	(172,000)

Allman computes the amounts of deferred income taxes to be reported at the end of 2020 as shown in Illustration 19A.14.

Temporary Difference	Future Taxable (Deductible) Amounts	Tax Rate	Deferred Tax (Asset)	Deferred Tax Liability
Installment sales	$592,000*	20%		$118,400
Depreciation	100,800	20		20,160
Warranty costs	(230,000)	20	$(46,000)	
Loss accrual	(172,000)	20	(34,400)	
Totals	$290,800		$(80,400)**	$138,560**

*Cumulative temporary difference = $336,000 + $256,000
**Because of a flat tax rate, these totals can be reconciled: $290,800 × .20 = $(80,400) + $138,560

ILLUSTRATION 19A.14
Computation of Deferred Income Taxes, End of 2020

Deferred Tax Expense (Benefit) and the Journal Entry to Record Income Taxes—2020

To determine the deferred tax expense (benefit), Allman must compare the beginning and ending balances of the deferred income tax accounts, as shown in Illustration 19A.15.

Deferred tax asset at the end of 2020	$ 80,400
Deferred tax asset at the beginning of 2020	31,200
Deferred tax expense (benefit)	$ (49,200)
Deferred tax liability at the end of 2020	$138,560
Deferred tax liability at the beginning of 2020	93,200
Deferred tax expense (benefit)	$ 45,360

ILLUSTRATION 19A.15
Computation of Deferred Tax Expense (Benefit) 2020

The deferred tax expense (benefit) and the total income tax expense for 2020 are, therefore, as shown in Illustration 19A.16.

ILLUSTRATION 19A.16

Computation of Total Income Tax Expense, 2020

Deferred tax expense (benefit)	$ (49,200)
Deferred tax expense (benefit)	45,360
Deferred tax benefit for 2020	(3,840)
Current tax expense for 2020	100,000
Income tax expense (total) for 2020	$ 96,160

The deferred tax expense of $45,360 and the deferred tax benefit of $49,200 net to a deferred tax benefit of $3,840 for 2020.

Allman records income taxes for 2020 with the following journal entry.

Income Tax Expense	96,160	
Deferred Tax Asset	49,200	
Income Taxes Payable		100,000
Deferred Tax Liability		45,360

Financial Statement Presentation—2020

Illustration 19A.17 shows the classification of Allman's deferred tax accounts at the end of 2020.

ILLUSTRATION 19A.17

Classification of Deferred Tax Accounts, End of 2020

	Resulting Deferred Tax	
Temporary Difference	(Asset)	Liability
Installment sales		$118,400
Depreciation		20,160
Warranty costs	$(46,000)	
Loss accrual	(34,400)	
Totals	$(80,400)	$138,560

Allman's balance sheet at the end of 2020 reports the amounts shown in Illustration 19A.18.

ILLUSTRATION 19A.18

Balance Sheet Presentation of Deferred Taxes, End of 2020

Current liabilities	
Income taxes payable	$100,000
Noncurrent liabilities	
Deferred tax liability ($138,560 – $80,400)	$58,160

Illustration 19A.19 shows the income statement for 2020.

ILLUSTRATION 19A.19

Income Statement Presentation of Income Tax Expense, 2020

Income before income taxes		$504,800
Income tax expense		
Current	$100,000	
Deferred	3,840	96,160
Net income		$408,640

APPENDIX 19B Accounting for Net Operating Loss Carrybacks

LEARNING OBJECTIVE *6

Explain the accounting for loss carrybacks.

As discussed in the opening story, the Tax Cuts and Jobs Act of 2017 (TCJA) permits the carryforward of current net operating losses to offset future taxable income. Prior rules for net operating losses permitted net operating losses to be carried back for two years and carried forward for 20 years. Under the TCJA, companies have indefinite carryforward periods. However, the TCJA eliminated carryback provisions for NOLs. The carryback provision was sort of a reprieve for money-losing companies that generated an NOL. That is, by carrying the NOL back to two profitable years on amended tax returns, net-loss companies could free up some cash in the year of the loss. In this appendix, we present the accounting for loss carrybacks as future tax laws may reinstitute carryback provisions.

Loss Carryback

Through use of a **loss carryback**, a company may carry the net operating loss back two years and receive refunds for income taxes paid in those years. The company must apply the loss to the earlier year first and then to the second year. It may **carry forward** any loss remaining after the two-year carryback to offset future taxable income.[9] **Illustration 19B.1** diagrams the loss carryback procedure, assuming a loss in 2020.

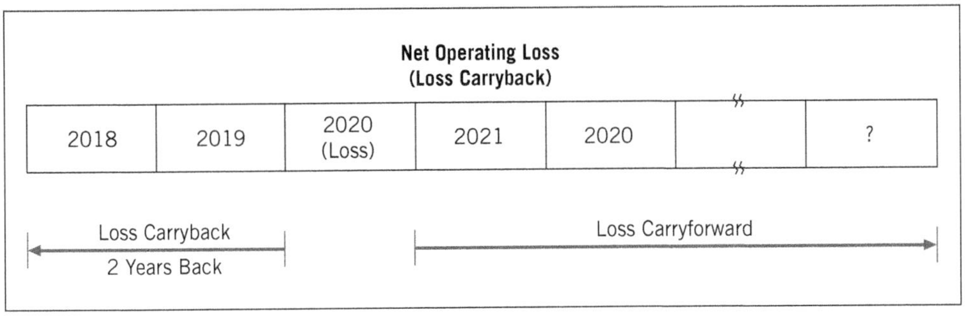

ILLUSTRATION 19B.1
Loss Carryback Procedure

Loss Carryback Example

To illustrate the accounting procedures for a net operating loss carryback, assume that Groh Inc. has no temporary or permanent differences. Groh experiences the following.

Year	Taxable Income or Loss	Tax Rate	Tax Paid
2017	$ 50,000	20%	$10,000
2018	100,000	15%	15,000
2019	200,000	25%	50,000
2020	(500,000)	—	-0-

In 2020, Groh incurs a net operating loss that it decides to carry back. Generally, Groh must apply the carryback first to the **second year preceding the loss year**. Therefore, it carries the loss back first to 2018. Then, Groh carries back any unused loss to 2019. Accordingly, Groh files amended tax returns for 2018 and 2019, receiving refunds for the $65,000 ($15,000 + $50,000) of taxes paid in those years.

For accounting as well as tax purposes, the $65,000 represents the **tax effect (tax benefit)** of the loss carryback. Groh should recognize this tax effect in 2020, the loss year. Since the tax loss gives rise to a refund that is both measurable and currently realizable, Groh should recognize the associated tax benefit in this loss period.

[9]As with carryforwards, carryback periods have varied over time. Indeed, as part of the Economic Recovery Act of 2009, Congress enacted a temporary extension of the carryback period from two to five years for operating losses incurred in 2008 and 2009 (during the financial crisis). It is estimated that the companies in the S&P 500 reaped a refund of $5 billion due to this change. See D. Zion, A. Varshney, and C. Cornett, "Spinning Losses into Gold," *Equity Research—Accounting and Tax*, Credit Suisse (November 12, 2009).

Groh makes the following journal entry for 2020.

Income Tax Refund Receivable	65,000	
Income Tax Expense (Loss Carryback)		65,000

Groh reports the account debited, **Income Tax Refund Receivable,** on the balance sheet as a current asset at December 31, 2020. It reports the account credited on the income statement for 2020 as shown in **Illustration 19B.2.**

ILLUSTRATION 19B.2

Recognition of the Benefit of the Loss Carryback in the Loss Year

Groh Inc.
Income Statement (partial) for 2020

Operating loss before income taxes	$(500,000)
Income tax benefit	
Income tax expense (loss carryback)	65,000
Net loss	$(435,000)

Since the $500,000 net operating loss for 2020 exceeds the $300,000 total taxable income from the two preceding years, Groh carries forward the remaining $200,000 loss.

Loss Carryback with Carryforward

If a carryback fails to fully absorb a net operating loss (as in the Groh example) or if the company decides not to carry the loss back, then it can carry forward the loss. To illustrate, return to the Groh example from the preceding section. In 2020, the company records the tax effect of the $200,000 loss carryforward as a deferred tax asset of $50,000 ($200,000 × .25), assuming that the enacted future tax rate is 25 percent. Groh records the benefits of the carryback and the carryforward in 2020 as follows.

To recognize benefit of loss carryback		
Income Tax Refund Receivable	65,000	
Income Tax Expense (Loss Carryback)		65,000
To recognize benefit of loss carryforward		
Deferred Tax Asset	50,000	
Income Tax Expense (Loss Carryforward)		50,000

Groh realizes the income tax refund receivable of $65,000 immediately as a refund of taxes paid in the past. It establishes a Deferred Tax Asset account for the benefits of future tax savings. The two accounts credited are contra income tax expense items, which Groh presents on the 2020 income statement shown in **Illustration 19B.3.**

ILLUSTRATION 19B.3

Recognition of the Benefit of the Loss Carryback and Carryforward in the Loss Year

Groh Inc.
Income Statement (partial) for 2020

Operating loss before income taxes		$(500,000)
Income tax benefit		
Income tax expense (loss carryback)	$65,000	
Income tax expense (loss carryforward)	50,000	115,000
Net loss		$(385,000)

The **current tax benefit** of $65,000 is the income tax refundable for the year. As shown earlier, Groh determines this amount by applying the carryback provisions of the tax law to the taxable loss for 2020. The $50,000 is the **deferred tax benefit** for the year, which results from an increase in the deferred tax asset, as discussed in the chapter.

Review and Practice

Key Terms Review

Learning Objectives Review

1 Describe the fundamentals of accounting for income taxes.

Companies compute pretax financial income (or income for book purposes) in accordance with generally accepted accounting principles. They compute taxable income (or income for tax purposes) in accordance with prescribed tax regulations. Because tax regulations and GAAP differ in many ways, so frequently do pretax financial income and taxable income. Differences may exist, for example, in the timing of revenue recognition and the timing of expense recognition.

Deferred tax liability. Revenue recognized for book purposes in the period earned but deferred and reported as revenue for tax purposes when collected results in future taxable amounts. The future taxable amounts will occur in the periods the company recovers the receivable and reports the collections as revenue for tax purposes. This results in a deferred tax liability.

Deferred tax asset. An accrued warranty expense that a company pays for and deducts for tax purposes, in a period later than the period in which it incurs and recognizes it for book purposes, results in future deductible amounts. The future deductible amounts will occur in the periods during which the company settles the related liability for book purposes. This results in a deferred tax asset.

Valuation allowance. A deferred tax asset should be reduced by a valuation allowance if, based on all available evidence, it is more likely than not (a level of likelihood that is at least slightly more than 50 percent) that it will not realize some portion or all of the deferred tax asset. The company should carefully consider all available evidence, both positive and negative, to determine whether, based on the weight of available evidence, it needs a valuation allowance.

2 Identify additional issues in accounting for income taxes.

Significant components of income tax expense should be disclosed in the income statement or in the notes to the financial statements. The most commonly encountered components are the current expense (or benefit) and the deferred expense (or benefit).

Examples of temporary differences are (1) revenues or gains that are taxable after recognition in financial income, (2) expenses or losses that are deductible after recognition in financial income, (3) revenues or gains that are taxable before recognition in financial income, and (4) expenses or losses that are deductible before recognition in financial income.

Examples of permanent differences are (1) items recognized for financial reporting purposes but not for tax purposes, and (2) items recognized for tax purposes but not for financial reporting purposes.

Companies may use tax rates other than the current rate only after enactment of the future tax rates. When a change in the tax rate is enacted, a company should immediately recognize its effect on the deferred income tax accounts. The company reports the effects as an adjustment to income tax expense in the period of the change.

3 Explain the accounting for loss carryforwards.

A company may carry a net operating loss forward indefinitely. A valuation allowance may be established for the deferred tax asset that arises from the carryforward, depending on uncertainty about future taxable income.

4 Describe the presentation of deferred income taxes in financial statements.

Companies report deferred tax accounts on the balance sheet as assets and liabilities. These deferred tax accounts are classified as a net noncurrent amount.

Companies apply the following basic principles in accounting for income taxes at the date of the financial statements. (1) Recognize a current tax liability or asset for the estimated taxes payable or refundable on the tax return for the current year. (2) Recognize a deferred tax liability or asset for the estimated future tax effects attributable to temporary differences and carryforwards using the enacted tax rate. (3) Base the measurement of current and deferred tax liabilities and assets on provisions of the enacted tax law.

(4) Reduce the measurement of deferred tax assets, if necessary, by the amount of any tax benefits that, based on available evidence, companies do not expect to realize.

***5 Apply the concepts and procedures of interperiod tax allocation.**

Accounting for deferred taxes involves the following steps. (1) Calculate taxable income and income taxes payable for the year. (2) Compute deferred income taxes at the end of the year. (3) Determine deferred tax expense (benefit) and make the journal entry to record income taxes. (4) Classify the net deferred tax asset or liability as noncurrent in the financial statements.

***6 Explain the accounting for loss carrybacks.**

When permitted by law, a company may carry a net operating loss back two years and receive refunds for taxes paid in those years. Any loss remaining after the two-year carryback may be carried forward to offset future taxable income.

Enhanced Review and Practice

Go online for multiple-choice questions with solutions, review exercises with solutions, and a full glossary of all key terms.

Practice Problem

Johnny Bravo Company began operations in 2020 and has provided the following information.

1. Pretax financial income for 2020 is $100,000.
2. The tax rate enacted for 2020 and future years is 20%.
3. Differences between the 2020 income statement and tax return are listed below.
   a. Warranty expense accrued for financial reporting purposes amounts to $5,000. Warranty deductions per the tax return amount to $2,000.
   b. Gross profit on construction contracts using the percentage-of-completion method for books amounts to $92,000. Gross profit on construction contracts for tax purposes amounts to $62,000.
   c. Depreciation of property, plant, and equipment for financial reporting purposes amounts to $60,000. Depreciation of these assets amounts to $80,000 for the tax return.
   d. A $3,500 fine paid for violation of pollution laws was deducted in computing pretax financial income.
   e. Interest revenue earned on an investment in tax-exempt municipal bonds amounts to $1,400.
4. Taxable income is expected for the next few years.

Instructions

a. Compute taxable income for 2020.

b. Compute the deferred taxes at December 31, 2020, that relate to the temporary differences described above.

c. Prepare the journal entry to record income tax expense, deferred taxes, and income taxes payable for 2020.

d. Draft the income tax expense section of the income statement, beginning with "Income before income taxes."

e. Assume that in 2021 Johnny Bravo reported a pretax operating loss of $44,900. There were no other temporary or permanent differences in tax and book income for 2021. Prepare the journal entry to record income tax expense for 2021. Johnny Bravo expects to return to profitability in 2022.

Solution

a.

Pretax financial income	$100,000
Permanent differences	
Fine for pollution	3,500
Tax-exempt interest	(1,400)
Originating temporary differences	
Excess warranty expense per books ($5,000 – $2,000)	3,000
Excess construction profits per books ($92,000 – $62,000)	(30,000)
Excess depreciation per tax ($80,000 – $60,000)	(20,000)
Taxable income	$ 55,100

b.

Temporary Difference	Future Taxable (Deductible) Amounts	Tax Rate	Deferred Tax (Asset)	Deferred Tax Liability
Warranty costs	$(3,000)	20%	$(600)	
Construction contracts	30,000	20		$ 6,000
Depreciation	20,000	20		4,000
Totals	$47,000		$(600)	$10,000

c.

Income Tax Expense	20,420	
Deferred Tax Asset	600	
Deferred Tax Liability		10,000
Income Taxes Payable		11,020

Taxable income for 2020 [from part (a)]	$55,100
Tax rate	20%
Income taxes payable for 2020	$11,020
Deferred tax liability at the end of 2020 [from part (b)]	$10,000
Deferred tax liability at the beginning of 2020	-0-
Deferred tax expense for 2020	$10,000
Deferred tax asset at the end of 2020 [from part (b)]	$ 600
Deferred tax asset at the beginning of 2020	-0-
Deferred tax benefit for 2020	$ (600)

d.

Income before income taxes		$100,000
Income tax expense		
Current	$11,020	
Deferred ($10,000 – $600)	9,400	20,420
Net income		$ 79,580

e.

2021

Deferred Tax Asset*	8,980	
Income Tax Expense (Loss Carryforward)		8,980

*Carryforward ($44,900 × .20 = $8,980 deferred tax asset)

No valuation allowance is needed since Johnny Bravo is expected to return to profitability in 2022. This is positive evidence that the deferred tax asset will be realized.

WileyPLUS

Exercises, Problems, Problem Solution Walkthrough Videos, and many more assessment tools and resources are available for practice in WileyPLUS.

Note: All asterisked Questions, Exercises, and Problems relate to material in the appendices to the chapter.

Questions

1. Explain the difference between pretax financial income and taxable income.

2. What are the two objectives of accounting for income taxes?

3. Explain the meaning of a temporary difference as it relates to deferred tax computations, and give three examples.

4. Differentiate between an originating temporary difference and a reversing difference.

5. The book basis of depreciable assets for Erwin Co. is $900,000, and the tax basis is $700,000 at the end of 2021. The enacted tax rate is 17% for all periods. Determine the amount of deferred taxes to be reported on the balance sheet at the end of 2021.

6. Roth Inc. has a deferred tax liability of $68,000 at the beginning of 2021. At the end of 2021, it reports accounts receivable on the books at $90,000 and the tax basis at zero (its only temporary difference). If the enacted tax rate is 17% for all periods, and income taxes payable for the period is $230,000, determine the amount of total income tax expense to report for 2021.

7. What is the difference between a future taxable amount and a future deductible amount? When is it appropriate to record a valuation account for a deferred tax asset?

8. Pretax financial income for Lake Inc. is $300,000, and its taxable income is $100,000 for 2021. Its only temporary difference at the end of the period relates to a $70,000 difference due to excess depreciation for tax purposes. If the tax rate is 20% for all periods, compute the amount of income tax expense to report in 2021. No deferred income taxes existed at the beginning of the year.

9. Feagler Company's current income taxes payable related to its taxable income for 2020 is $460,000. In addition, Feagler's deferred tax asset decreased $20,000 during 2020. What is Feagler's income tax expense for 2020?

10. Lee Company's current income taxes payable related to its taxable income for 2020 is $320,000. In addition, Lee's deferred tax liability increased $40,000 and its deferred tax asset increased $10,000 during 2020. What is Lee's income tax expense for 2020?

11. How are deferred tax assets and deferred tax liabilities reported on the balance sheet?

12. Interest on municipal bonds is referred to as a permanent difference when determining the proper amount to report for deferred taxes. Explain the meaning of permanent differences, and give two other examples.

13. At the end of the year, Falabella Co. has pretax financial income of $550,000. Included in the $550,000 is $70,000 interest income on municipal bonds, $25,000 fine for dumping hazardous waste, and depreciation of $60,000. Depreciation for tax purposes is $45,000. Compute income taxes payable, assuming the tax rate is 30% for all periods.

14. Addison Co. has one temporary difference at the beginning of 2020 of $500,000. The deferred tax liability established for this amount is $150,000, based on a tax rate of 30%. The temporary difference will provide the following taxable amounts: $100,000 in 2021, $200,000 in 2022, and $200,000 in 2023. If a new tax rate for 2023 of 20% is enacted into law at the end of 2020, what is the journal entry necessary in 2020 (if any) to adjust deferred taxes?

15. What are some of the reasons that the components of income tax expense should be disclosed and a reconciliation between the effective tax rate and the statutory tax rate be provided?

16. Describe a "loss carryforward." Discuss the uncertainty when it arises.

17. What is the possible treatment for tax purposes of a net operating loss? What is the proper treatment of a net operating loss for financial reporting purposes?

18. What controversy relates to the accounting for net operating loss carryforwards?

19. What is an uncertain tax position, and what are the general guidelines for accounting for uncertain tax positions?

Brief Exercises

BE19.1 **(LO 1)** In 2020, Amirante Corporation had pretax financial income of $168,000 and taxable income of $120,000. The difference is due to the use of different depreciation methods for tax and accounting purposes. The effective tax rate is 20%. Compute the amount to be reported as income taxes payable at December 31, 2020.

BE19.2 **(LO 1)** Oxford Corporation began operations in 2020 and reported pretax financial income of $225,000 for the year. Oxford's tax depreciation exceeded its book depreciation by $40,000. Oxford's tax rate for 2020 and years thereafter is 30%. In its December 31, 2020, balance sheet, what amount of deferred tax liability should be reported?

BE19.3 **(LO 1, 2)** Using the information from BE19.2, assume this is the only difference between Oxford's pretax financial income and taxable income. Prepare the journal entry to record the income tax expense, deferred income taxes, and income taxes payable, and show how the deferred tax liability will be classified on the December 31, 2020, balance sheet.

BE19.4 **(LO 1, 2)** At December 31, 2020, Appaloosa Corporation had a deferred tax liability of $25,000. At December 31, 2021, the deferred tax liability is $42,000. The corporation's 2021 current tax expense is $48,000. What amount should Appaloosa report as total 2021 income tax expense?

BE19.5 **(LO 1, 2)** At December 31, 2020, Suffolk Corporation had an estimated warranty liability of $105,000 for accounting purposes and $0 for tax purposes. (The warranty costs are not deductible until paid.) The effective tax rate is 20%. Compute the amount Suffolk should report as a deferred tax asset at December 31, 2020.

BE19.6 **(LO 1, 2)** At December 31, 2020, Percheron Inc. had a deferred tax asset of $30,000. At December 31, 2021, the deferred tax asset is $59,000. The corporation's 2021 current tax expense is $61,000. What amount should Percheron report as total 2021 income tax expense?

BE19.7 **(LO 1, 2)** At December 31, 2020, Hillyard Corporation has a deferred tax asset of $200,000. After a careful review of all available evidence, it is determined that it is more likely than not that $60,000 of this deferred tax asset will not be realized. Prepare the necessary journal entry.

BE19.8 **(LO 1, 2)** Mitchell Corporation had income before income taxes of $195,000 in 2020. Mitchell's current income tax expense is $24,000, and deferred income tax expense is $15,000. Prepare Mitchell's 2020 income statement, beginning with "Income before income taxes."

BE19.9 **(LO 1, 2)** Shetland Inc. had pretax financial income of $154,000 in 2020. Included in the computation of that amount is insurance expense of $4,000 which is not deductible for tax purposes. In addition, depreciation for tax purposes exceeds accounting depreciation by $10,000. Prepare Shetland's journal entry to record 2020 taxes, assuming a tax rate of 25%.

BE19.10 **(LO 1, 2)** Clydesdale Corporation has a cumulative temporary difference related to depreciation of $580,000 at December 31, 2020. This difference will reverse as follows: 2021, $42,000; 2022, $244,000; and 2023, $294,000. Enacted tax rates are 17% for 2021 and 2022, and 20% for 2023. Compute the amount Clydesdale should report as a deferred tax liability at December 31, 2020.

BE19.11 **(LO 2)** At December 31, 2020, Fell Corporation had a deferred tax liability of $340,000, resulting from future taxable amounts of $2,000,000 and an enacted tax rate of 17%. In May 2021, a new income tax act is signed into law that raises the tax rate to 20% for 2021 and future years. Prepare the journal entry for Fell to adjust the deferred tax liability.

BE19.12 **(LO 3)** Rode Inc. incurred a net operating loss of $500,000 in 2020. The tax rate for all years is 20%. Prepare the journal entries to record the benefits of the loss carryforward. Rode expects to return to profitability in 2021.

BE19.13 **(LO 3)** Use the information for Rode Inc. given in BE19.12. Assume that it is more likely than not that the entire net operating loss carryforward will not be realized in future years. Prepare all the journal entries necessary at the end of 2020.

BE19.14 **(LO 4)** Youngman Corporation has temporary differences at December 31, 2020, that result in the following deferred taxes.

Deferred tax liability related to depreciation difference	$38,000
Deferred tax asset related to warranty liability	62,000
Deferred tax liability related to revenue recognition	96,000
Deferred tax asset related to litigation accruals	27,000

Indicate how these balances would be presented in Youngman's December 31, 2020, balance sheet.

*BE19.15 **(LO 6)** Nolan Corporation had the following tax information.

Year	Taxable Income	Tax Rate	Taxes Paid
2018	$300,000	35%	$105,000
2019	325,000	30	97,500
2020	400,000	30	120,000

In 2021, Nolan suffered a net operating loss of $480,000, which it elected to carryback. The 2021 enacted tax rate is 29%. Prepare Nolan's entry to record the effect of the loss carryback.

*BE19.16 **(LO 6)** Sylvie Inc. incurred a net operating loss of $500,000 in 2020. Combined income for 2018 and 2019 was $350,000. The tax rate for all years is 20%. Sylvie elects the carryback option. Prepare the journal entries to record the benefits of the loss carryback and the loss carryforward. Sylvie expects to return to profitability in 2021.

Exercises

E19.1 **(LO 1, 2)** Excel **(One Temporary Difference, Future Taxable Amounts, One Rate, No Beginning Deferred Taxes)** South Carolina Corporation has one temporary difference at the end of 2020 that will reverse and cause taxable amounts of $55,000 in 2021, $60,000 in 2022, and $65,000 in 2023. South Carolina's pretax financial income for 2020 is $300,000, and the tax rate is 30% for all years. There are no deferred taxes at the beginning of 2020.

Instructions

a. Compute taxable income and income taxes payable for 2020.

b. Prepare the journal entry to record income tax expense, deferred income taxes, and income taxes payable for 2020.

c. Prepare the income tax expense section of the income statement for 2020, beginning with the line "Income before income taxes."

E19.2 (LO 1, 2) (Two Differences, No Beginning Deferred Taxes, Tracked through 2 Years) The following information is available for Wenger Corporation for 2019 (its first year of operations).

1. Excess of tax depreciation over book depreciation, $40,000. This $40,000 difference will reverse equally over the years 2020–2023.
2. Deferral, for book purposes, of $20,000 of rent received in advance. The rent will be recognized in 2020.
3. Pretax financial income, $300,000.
4. Tax rate for all years, 20%.

Instructions

a. Compute taxable income for 2019.

b. Prepare the journal entry to record income tax expense, deferred income taxes, and income taxes payable for 2019.

c. Prepare the journal entry to record income tax expense, deferred income taxes, and income taxes payable for 2020, assuming taxable income of $325,000.

E19.3 (LO 1, 2) Excel (One Temporary Difference, Future Taxable Amounts, One Rate, Beginning Deferred Taxes) Bandung Corporation began 2020 with a $46,000 balance in the Deferred Tax Liability account. At the end of 2020, the related cumulative temporary difference amounts to $350,000, and it will reverse evenly over the next 2 years. Pretax accounting income for 2020 is $525,000, the tax rate for all years is 20%, and taxable income for 2020 is $405,000.

Instructions

a. Compute income taxes payable for 2020.

b. Prepare the journal entry to record income tax expense, deferred income taxes, and income taxes payable for 2020.

c. Prepare the income tax expense section of the income statement for 2020 beginning with the line "Income before income taxes."

E19.4 (LO 1, 2) (Three Differences, Compute Taxable Income, Entry for Taxes) Zurich Company reports pretax financial income of $70,000 for 2020. The following items cause taxable income to be different than pretax financial income.

1. Depreciation on the tax return is greater than depreciation on the income statement by $16,000.
2. Rent collected on the tax return is greater than rent recognized on the income statement by $22,000.
3. Fines for pollution appear as an expense of $11,000 on the income statement.

Zurich's tax rate is 30% for all years, and the company expects to report taxable income in all future years. There are no deferred taxes at the beginning of 2020.

Instructions

a. Compute taxable income and income taxes payable for 2020.

b. Prepare the journal entry to record income tax expense, deferred income taxes, and income taxes payable for 2020.

c. Prepare the income tax expense section of the income statement for 2020, beginning with the line "Income before income taxes."

d. Compute the effective income tax rate for 2020.

E19.5 (LO 1, 2) (Two Temporary Differences, One Rate, Beginning Deferred Taxes) The following facts relate to Krung Thep Corporation.

1. Deferred tax liability, January 1, 2020, $20,000.
2. Deferred tax asset, January 1, 2020, $0.
3. Taxable income for 2020, $95,000.
4. Pretax financial income for 2020, $200,000.
5. Cumulative temporary difference at December 31, 2020, giving rise to future taxable amounts, $240,000.
6. Cumulative temporary difference at December 31, 2020, giving rise to future deductible amounts, $35,000.
7. Tax rate for all years, 20%.
8. The company is expected to operate profitably in the future.

Instructions

a. Compute income taxes payable for 2020.

b. Prepare the journal entry to record income tax expense, deferred income taxes, and income taxes payable for 2020.

c. Prepare the income tax expense section of the income statement for 2020, beginning with the line "Income before income taxes."

E19.6 **(LO 1, 2)** **(Identify Temporary or Permanent Differences)** Listed below are items that are commonly accounted for differently for financial reporting purposes than they are for tax purposes.

Instructions

For each item below, indicate whether it involves:

1. A temporary difference that will result in future deductible amounts and, therefore, will usually give rise to a deferred income tax asset.
2. A temporary difference that will result in future taxable amounts and, therefore, will usually give rise to a deferred income tax liability.
3. A permanent difference.

Use the appropriate number to indicate your answer for each.

a. _____ The MACRS depreciation system is used for tax purposes, and the straight-line depreciation method is used for financial reporting purposes for some plant assets.

b. _____ A landlord collects some rents in advance. Rents received are taxable in the period when they are received.

c. _____ Expenses are incurred in obtaining tax-exempt income.

d. _____ Costs of guarantees and warranties are estimated and accrued for financial reporting purposes.

e. _____ Installment sales of investments are accounted for by the accrual method for financial reporting purposes and the installment method for tax purposes.

f. _____ For some assets, straight-line depreciation is used for both financial reporting purposes and tax purposes, but the assets' lives are shorter for tax purposes.

g. _____ Interest is received on an investment in tax-exempt municipal obligations.

h. _____ Proceeds are received from a life insurance company because of the death of a key officer. (The company carries a policy on key officers.)

i. _____ The tax return reports a deduction for 80% of the dividends received from U.S. corporations. The cost method is used in accounting for the related investments for financial reporting purposes.

j. _____ Estimated losses on pending lawsuits and claims are accrued for books. These losses are tax-deductible in the period(s) when the related liabilities are settled.

k. _____ Expenses on stock options are accrued for financial reporting purposes.

E19.7 **(LO 1, 2)** **(Terminology, Relationships, Computations, Entries)**

Instructions

Complete the following statements by filling in the blanks.

a. In a period in which a taxable temporary difference reverses, the reversal will cause taxable income to be _____ (less than, greater than) pretax financial income.

b. If a $38,000 balance in Deferred Tax Asset was computed by use of a 20% rate, the underlying cumulative temporary difference amounts to $_____.

c. Deferred taxes _____ (are, are not) recorded to account for permanent differences.

d. If a taxable temporary difference originates in 2020, it will cause taxable income for 2020 to be _____ (less than, greater than) pretax financial income for 2020.

e. If total tax expense is $50,000 and deferred tax expense is $65,000, then the current portion of the expense computation is referred to as current tax _____ (expense, benefit) of $_____.

f. If a corporation's tax return shows taxable income of $100,000 for Year 2 and a tax rate of 20%, how much will appear on the December 31, Year 2, balance sheet for "Income taxes payable" if the company has made estimated tax payments of $18,250 for Year 2? $_____.

g. An increase in the Deferred Tax Liability account on the balance sheet is recorded by a _____ (debit, credit) to the Income Tax Expense account.

h. An income statement that reports current tax expense of $82,000 and deferred tax benefit of $23,000 will report total income tax expense of $______.

i. A valuation account is needed whenever it is judged to be ______ that a portion of a deferred tax asset ______ (will be, will not be) realized.

j. If the tax return shows total taxes due for the period of $75,000 but the income statement shows total income tax expense of $55,000, the difference of $20,000 is referred to as deferred tax ______ (expense, benefit).

E19.8 **(LO 1, 2) (Two Temporary Differences, One Rate, 3 Years)** Button Company has the following two temporary differences between its income tax expense and income taxes payable.

	2020	2021	2022
Pretax financial income	$840,000	$910,000	$945,000
Excess depreciation expense on tax return	(30,000)	(40,000)	(10,000)
Excess warranty expense in financial income	20,000	10,000	8,000
Taxable income	$830,000	$880,000	$943,000

The income tax rate for all years is 20%.

Instructions

a. Assuming there were no temporary differences prior to 2020, prepare the journal entry to record income tax expense, deferred income taxes, and income taxes payable for 2020, 2021, and 2022.

b. Indicate how deferred taxes will be reported on the 2022 balance sheet. Button's product warranty is for 12 months.

c. Prepare the income tax expense section of the income statement for 2022, beginning with the line "Pretax financial income."

E19.9 **(LO 4) (Three Differences, Classify Deferred Taxes)** At December 31, 2019, Belmont Company had a net deferred tax liability of $375,000. An explanation of the items that compose this balance is as follows.

Temporary Differences	Resulting Balances in Deferred Taxes
1. Excess of tax depreciation over book depreciation	$200,000
2. Accrual, for book purposes, of estimated loss contingency from pending lawsuit that is expected to be settled in 2020. The loss will be deducted on the tax return when paid.	(50,000)
3. Accrual method used for book purposes and installment method used for tax purposes for an isolated installment sale of an investment.	225,000
	$375,000

In analyzing the temporary differences, you find that $30,000 of the depreciation temporary difference will reverse in 2020, and $120,000 of the temporary difference due to the installment sale will reverse in 2020. The tax rate for all years is 20%.

Instructions

Indicate the manner in which deferred taxes should be presented on Belmont Company's December 31, 2019, balance sheet.

E19.10 **(LO 1, 2) (Two Temporary Differences, One Rate, Beginning Deferred Taxes, Compute Pretax Financial Income)** The following facts relate to Duncan Corporation.

1. Deferred tax liability, January 1, 2020, $30,000.
2. Deferred tax asset, January 1, 2020, $10,000.
3. Taxable income for 2020, $105,000.
4. Cumulative temporary difference at December 31, 2020, giving rise to future taxable amounts, $230,000.
5. Cumulative temporary difference at December 31, 2020, giving rise to future deductible amounts, $95,000.
6. Tax rate for all years, 20%. No permanent differences exist.
7. The company is expected to operate profitably in the future.

Instructions

a. Compute the amount of pretax financial income for 2020.

b. Prepare the journal entry to record income tax expense, deferred income taxes, and income taxes payable for 2020.

c. Prepare the income tax expense section of the income statement for 2020, beginning with the line "Income before income taxes."

d. Compute the effective tax rate for 2020.

E19.11 **(LO 1, 2) (One Difference, Multiple Rates, Effect of Beginning Balance versus No Beginning Deferred Taxes)** At the end of 2019, Lucretia McEvil Company has $180,000 of cumulative temporary differences that will result in reporting the following future taxable amounts.

2020	$ 60,000
2021	50,000
2022	40,000
2023	30,000
	$180,000

Tax rates enacted as of the beginning of 2018 are:

2018 and 2019	40%
2020 and 2021	30%
2022 and later	25%

McEvil's taxable income for 2019 is $320,000. Taxable income is expected in all future years.

Instructions

a. Prepare the journal entry for McEvil to record income taxes payable, deferred income taxes, and income tax expense for 2019, assuming that there were no deferred taxes at the end of 2018.

b. Prepare the journal entry for McEvil to record income taxes payable, deferred income taxes, and income tax expense for 2019, assuming that there was a balance of $22,000 in a Deferred Tax Liability account at the end of 2018.

E19.12 **(LO 1, 2) (Deferred Tax Asset with and without Valuation Account)** Jennifer Capriati Corp. has a deferred tax asset account with a balance of $75,000 at the end of 2019 due to a single cumulative temporary difference of $375,000. At the end of 2020, this same temporary difference has increased to a cumulative amount of $450,000. Taxable income for 2020 is $820,000. The tax rate is 20% for all years. No valuation account related to the deferred tax asset is in existence at the end of 2019.

Instructions

a. Record income tax expense, deferred income taxes, and income taxes payable for 2020, assuming that it is more likely than not that the deferred tax asset will be realized.

b. Assuming that it is more likely than not that $15,000 of the deferred tax asset will not be realized, prepare the journal entry at the end of 2020 to record the valuation account.

E19.13 **(LO 1, 2) (Deferred Tax Asset with Previous Valuation Account)** Assume the same information as E19.12, except that at the end of 2019, Jennifer Capriati Corp. had a valuation account related to its deferred tax asset of $22,500.

Instructions

a. Record income tax expense, deferred income taxes, and income taxes payable for 2020, assuming that it is more likely than not that the deferred tax asset will be realized in full.

b. Record income tax expense, deferred income taxes, and income taxes payable for 2020, assuming that it is more likely than not that none of the deferred tax asset will be realized.

E19.14 **(LO 1, 2, 4) (Deferred Tax Liability, Change in Tax Rate, Prepare Section of Income Statement)** Novotna Inc.'s only temporary difference at the beginning and end of 2019 is caused by a $3 million deferred gain for tax purposes for an installment sale of a plant asset, and the related receivable (only one-half of which is classified as a current asset) is due in equal installments in 2020 and 2021. The related deferred tax liability at the beginning of the year is $900,000. In the third quarter of 2019, a new tax rate of 20% is enacted into law and is scheduled to become effective for 2021. Taxable income for 2019 is $5,000,000, and taxable income is expected in all future years.

Instructions

a. Determine the amount reported as a deferred tax liability at the end of 2019. Indicate proper classification(s).

b. Prepare the journal entry (if any) necessary to adjust the deferred tax liability when the new tax rate is enacted into law.

c. Draft the income tax expense portion of the income statement for 2019. Begin with the line "Income before income taxes." Assume no permanent differences exist.

E19.15 (LO 1, 2) (Two Temporary Differences, Tracked through 3 Years, Multiple Rates) Taxable income and pretax financial income would be identical for Huber Co. except for its treatments of gross profit on installment sales and estimated costs of warranties. The following income computations have been prepared.

Taxable Income	2019	2020	2021
Excess of revenues over expenses (excluding two temporary differences)	$160,000	$210,000	$90,000
Installment gross profit collected	8,000	8,000	8,000
Expenditures for warranties	(5,000)	(5,000)	(5,000)
Taxable income	$163,000	$213,000	$93,000

Pretax Financial Income	2019	2020	2021
Excess of revenues over expenses (excluding two temporary differences)	$160,000	$210,000	$90,000
Installment gross profit recognized	24,000	–0–	–0–
Estimated cost of warranties	(15,000)	–0–	–0–
Income before taxes	$169,000	$210,000	$90,000

The tax rates in effect are 2019, 20%; 2020 and 2021, 25%. All tax rates were enacted into law on January 1, 2019. No deferred income taxes existed at the beginning of 2019. Taxable income is expected in all future years.

Instructions

Prepare the journal entry to record income tax expense, deferred income taxes, and income taxes payable for 2019, 2020, and 2021.

E19.16 (LO 1, 2) (Three Differences, Multiple Rates, Future Taxable Income) During 2020, Kate Holmes Co.'s first year of operations, the company reports pretax financial income at $250,000. Holmes's enacted tax rate is 45% for 2020 and 20% for all later years. Holmes expects to have taxable income in each of the next 5 years. The effects on future tax returns of temporary differences existing at December 31, 2020, are summarized as follows.

	Future Years					
	2021	2022	2023	2024	2025	Total
Future taxable (deductible) amounts:						
Installment sales	$32,000	$32,000	$32,000			$ 96,000
Depreciation	6,000	6,000	6,000	$6,000	$6,000	30,000
Unearned rent	(50,000)	(50,000)				(100,000)

Instructions

a. Complete the schedule below to compute deferred taxes at December 31, 2020.

b. Compute taxable income for 2020.

c. Prepare the journal entry to record income taxes payable, deferred taxes, and income tax expense for 2020.

Temporary Difference	Future Taxable (Deductible) Amounts	Tax Rate	December 31, 2020 Deferred Tax (Asset)	Liability
Installment sales	$ 96,000			
Depreciation	30,000			
Unearned rent	$(100,000)			
Totals	$			

E19.17 (LO 1, 2) (Two Differences, One Rate, Beginning Deferred Balance, Compute Pretax Financial Income) Andy McDowell Co. establishes a $100 million liability at the end of 2020 for the estimated site-cleanup costs at two of its manufacturing facilities. All related closing costs will be paid and deducted on the tax return in 2021. Also, at the end of 2020, the company has $50 million of temporary differences due to excess depreciation for tax purposes, $7 million of which will reverse in 2021.

The enacted tax rate for all years is 20%, and the company pays taxes of $32 million on $160 million of taxable income in 2020. McDowell expects to have taxable income in 2021.

Instructions

a. Determine the deferred taxes to be reported at the end of 2020.

b. Indicate how the deferred taxes computed in (a) are to be reported on the balance sheet.

c. Assuming that the only deferred tax account at the beginning of 2020 was a deferred tax liability of $5,000,000, draft the income tax expense portion of the income statement for 2020, beginning with the line "Income before income taxes." (*Hint:* You must first compute (1) the amount of temporary difference underlying the beginning $5,000,000 deferred tax liability, then (2) the amount of temporary differences originating or reversing during the year, and then (3) the amount of pretax financial income.)

E19.18 (LO 1, 2) (Two Differences, No Beginning Deferred Taxes, Multiple Rates) Teri Hatcher Inc., in its first year of operations, has the following differences between the book basis and tax basis of its assets and liabilities at the end of 2019.

	Book Basis	Tax Basis
Equipment (net)	$400,000	$340,000
Estimated warranty liability	$200,000	$ -0-

It is estimated that the warranty liability will be settled in 2020. The difference in equipment (net) will result in taxable amounts of $20,000 in 2020, $30,000 in 2021, and $10,000 in 2022. The company has taxable income of $520,000 in 2019. As of the beginning of 2019, the enacted tax rate is 34% for 2019–2021, and 30% for 2022. Hatcher expects to report taxable income through 2022.

Instructions

a. Prepare the journal entry to record income tax expense, deferred income taxes, and income taxes payable for 2019.

b. Indicate how deferred income taxes will be reported on the balance sheet at the end of 2019.

E19.19 (LO 1, 2, 4) (Two Temporary Differences, Multiple Rates, Future Taxable Income) Nadal Inc. has two temporary differences at the end of 2019. The first difference stems from installment sales, and the second one results from the accrual of a loss contingency. Nadal's accounting department has developed a schedule of future taxable and deductible amounts related to these temporary differences as follows.

	2020	2021	2022	2023
Taxable amounts	$40,000	$50,000	$60,000	$80,000
Deductible amounts		(15,000)	(19,000)	
	$40,000	$35,000	$41,000	$80,000

As of the beginning of 2019, the enacted tax rate is 34% for 2019 and 2020, and 20% for 2021–2024. At the beginning of 2019, the company had no deferred income taxes on its balance sheet. Taxable income for 2019 is $500,000. Taxable income is expected in all future years.

Instructions

a. Prepare the journal entry to record income tax expense, deferred income taxes, and income taxes payable for 2019.

b. Indicate how deferred income taxes would be classified on the balance sheet at the end of 2019.

E19.20 (LO 1, 2, 4) (Two Differences, One Rate, First Year) The differences between the book basis and tax basis of the assets and liabilities of Castle Corporation at the end of 2019 are presented below.

	Book Basis	Tax Basis
Accounts receivable	$50,000	$-0-
Litigation liability	30,000	-0-

It is estimated that the litigation liability will be settled in 2020. The difference in accounts receivable will result in taxable amounts of $30,000 in 2020 and $20,000 in 2021. The company has taxable income of $350,000 in 2019 and is expected to have taxable income in each of the following 2 years. Its enacted tax rate is 34% for all years. This is the company's first year of operations. The operating cycle of the business is 2 years.

Instructions

a. Prepare the journal entry to record income tax expense, deferred income taxes, and income taxes payable for 2019.

b. Indicate how deferred income taxes will be reported on the balance sheet at the end of 2019.

E19.21 **(LO 3)** **(Carryforward of NOL, No Valuation Account, No Temporary Differences)** The pretax financial income (or loss) figures for Jenny Spangler Company are as follows.

2017	$ 80,000
2018	(160,000)
2019	(380,000)
2020	120,000
2021	100,000

Pretax financial income (or loss) and taxable income (loss) were the same for all years involved. Assume a 25% tax rate for 2015 and 2016, and a 20% tax rate for the remaining years.

Instructions

Prepare the journal entries for the years 2017 to 2021 to record income tax expense and the effects of the net operating loss carryforwards. All income and losses relate to normal operations. (In recording the benefits of a loss carryforward, assume that no valuation account is deemed necessary.)

E19.22 **(LO 3)** **(Two NOLs, No Temporary Differences, No Valuation Account, Entries and Income Statement)** Felicia Rashad Corporation has pretax financial income (or loss) from 2015 through 2021 as follows.

	Income (Loss)	Tax Rate
2015	$ 48,000	25%
2016	(150,000)	20
2017	90,000	20
2018	30,000	20
2019	105,000	20
2020	(60,000)	25
2021	130,000	25

Pretax financial income (loss) and taxable income (loss) were the same for all years since Rashad has been in business. In recording the benefits of a loss carryforward, assume that it is more likely than not that the related benefits will be realized.

Instructions

a. What entry(ies) for income taxes should be recorded for 2016?

b. Indicate what the income tax expense portion of the income statement for 2016 should look like. Assume all income (loss) relates to continuing operations.

c. What entry for income taxes should be recorded in 2017?

d. How should the income tax expense section of the income statement for 2017 appear?

e. What entry for income taxes should be recorded in 2020?

f. How should the income tax expense section of the income statement for 2020 appear?

E19.23 **(LO 3)** **(NOL Carryforward, Valuation Account versus No Valuation Account)** Spamela Hamderson Inc. reports the following pretax income (loss) for both financial reporting purposes and tax purposes.

Year	Pretax Income (Loss)	Tax Rate
2018	$120,000	17%
2019	90,000	17
2020	(280,000)	19
2021	300,000	19

The tax rates listed were all enacted by the beginning of 2018.

Instructions

a. Prepare the journal entries for the years 2018–2021 to record income tax expense (benefit) and income taxes payable (refundable) and the tax effects of the loss carryforward, assuming that at the end of 2020 the benefits of the loss carryforward are judged more likely than not to be realized in the future.

b. Using the assumption in (a), prepare the income tax section of the 2020 income statement beginning with the line "Operating loss before income taxes."

c. Prepare the journal entries for 2020 and 2021, assuming that based on the weight of available evidence, it is more likely than not that one-fourth of the benefits of the loss carryforward will not be realized.

d. Using the assumption in (c), prepare the income tax section of the 2020 income statement beginning with the line "Operating loss before income taxes."

E19.24 **(LO 3)** **(NOL Carryforward, Valuation Account Needed)** Beilman Inc. reports the following pretax income (loss) for both book and tax purposes.

Year	Pretax Income (Loss)	Tax Rate
2018	$120,000	20%
2019	90,000	20
2020	(280,000)	25
2021	120,000	25

The tax rates listed were all enacted by the beginning of 2018.

Instructions

a. Prepare the journal entries for years 2018–2021 to record income tax expense (benefit) and income taxes payable (refundable), and the tax effects of the loss carryforward, assuming that based on the weight of available evidence, it is more likely than not that one-half of the benefits of the loss carryforward will not be realized.

b. Prepare the income tax section of the 2020 income statement beginning with the line "Operating loss before income taxes."

c. Prepare the income tax section of the 2021 income statement beginning with the line "Income before income taxes."

E19.25 **(LO 3)** **(NOL Carryforward, Valuation Account Needed)** Meyer reported the following pretax financial income (loss) for the years 2020–2022.

2020	$120,000
2021	(150,000)
2022	180,000

Pretax financial income (loss) and taxable income (loss) were the same for all years involved. The enacted tax rate was 20% for 2020–2022.

Instructions

a. Prepare the journal entries for the years 2020–2022 to record income tax expense, income taxes payable, and the tax effects of the loss carryforward, assuming that based on the weight of available evidence, it is more likely than not that one-fifth of the benefits of the loss carryforward will not be realized.

b. Prepare the income tax section of the 2021 income statement beginning with the line "Income (loss) before income taxes."

*E19.26 **(LO 6)** **(Carryback and Carryforward of NOL, No Valuation Account, No Temporary Differences)** The pretax financial income (or loss) figures for Dan Lynch Company are as follows.

2015	$160,000
2016	250,000
2017	80,000
2018	(160,000)
2019	(380,000)
2020	120,000
2021	100,000

Pretax financial income (or loss) and taxable income (loss) were the same for all years involved. Assume a 45% tax rate for 2015 and 2016, and a 20% tax rate for the remaining years.

Instructions

Prepare the journal entries for the years 2017 to 2021 to record income tax expense and the effects of the net operating loss carrybacks and carryforwards assuming Dan Lynch Company uses the carryback provision. All income and losses relate to normal operations. (In recording the benefits of a loss carryforward, assume that no valuation account is deemed necessary.)

*E19.27 (LO 6) **(NOL Carryback and Carryforward, Valuation Account Needed)** Wangerin Company reported the following pretax financial income (loss) for the years 2018–2022.

2018	$240,000
2019	350,000
2020	120,000
2021	(570,000)
2022	180,000

Pretax financial income (loss) and taxable income (loss) were the same for all years involved. The enacted tax rate was 34% for 2018 and 2019, and 20% for 2020–2022. Assume the carryback provision is used first for net operating losses.

Instructions

a. Prepare the journal entries for the years 2020–2022 to record income tax expense, income taxes payable (refundable), and the tax effects of the loss carryback and loss carryforward, assuming no valuation allowance is needed.

b. Prepare the income tax section of the 2021 income statement beginning with the line "Income (loss) before income taxes."

Problems

P19.1 (LO 1, 2, 4) Excel **(Three Differences, No Beginning Deferred Taxes, Multiple Rates)** The following information is available for Remmers Corporation for 2020.

1. Depreciation reported on the tax return exceeded depreciation reported on the income statement by $120,000. This difference will reverse in equal amounts of $30,000 over the years 2021–2024.
2. Interest received on municipal bonds was $10,000.
3. Rent collected in advance on January 1, 2020, totaled $60,000 for a 3-year period. Of this amount, $40,000 was reported as unearned at December 31, 2020, for book purposes.
4. The tax rates are 20% for 2020 and 17% for 2021 and subsequent years.
5. Income taxes of $160,000 are due per the tax return for 2020.
6. No deferred taxes existed at the beginning of 2020.

Instructions

a. Compute taxable income for 2020.

b. Compute pretax financial income for 2020.

c. Prepare the journal entries to record income tax expense, deferred income taxes, and income taxes payable for 2020 and 2021. Assume taxable income was $480,000 in 2021.

d. Prepare the income tax expense section of the income statement for 2020, beginning with "Income before income taxes."

P19.2 (LO 1, 2) **(One Temporary Difference, Tracked for 4 Years, One Permanent Difference, Change in Rate)** The pretax financial income of Truttman Company differs from its taxable income throughout each of 4 years as follows.

Year	Pretax Financial Income	Taxable Income	Tax Rate
2020	$290,000	$180,000	35%
2021	320,000	225,000	20
2022	350,000	260,000	20
2023	420,000	560,000	20

Pretax financial income for each year includes a nondeductible expense of $30,000 (never deductible for tax purposes). The remainder of the difference between pretax financial income and taxable income in each period is due to one depreciation temporary difference. No deferred income taxes existed at the beginning of 2020.

Instructions

a. Prepare journal entries to record income taxes in all 4 years. Assume that the change in the tax rate to 20% was not enacted until the beginning of 2021.

b. Prepare the income statement for 2021, beginning with Income before income taxes.

P19.3 **(LO 1, 2, 4)** **(Second Year of Depreciation Difference, Two Differences, Single Rate, Discontinued Operation)** The following information has been obtained for Gocker Corporation.

1. Prior to 2020, taxable income and pretax financial income were identical.
2. Pretax financial income is $1,700,000 in 2020 and $1,400,000 in 2021.
3. On January 1, 2020, equipment costing $1,200,000 is purchased. It is to be depreciated on a straight-line basis over 5 years for tax purposes and over 8 years for financial reporting purposes. (*Hint:* Use the half-year convention for tax purposes, as discussed in Appendix 11A.)
4. Interest of $60,000 was earned on tax-exempt municipal obligations in 2021.
5. Included in 2021 pretax financial income is a gain on discontinued operations of $200,000, which is fully taxable.
6. The tax rate is 20% for all periods.
7. Taxable income is expected in all future years.

Instructions

a. Compute taxable income and income taxes payable for 2021.

b. Prepare the journal entry to record 2021 income tax expense, income taxes payable, and deferred taxes.

c. Prepare the bottom portion of Gocker's 2021 income statement, beginning with "Income from continuing operations before income taxes."

d. Indicate how deferred income taxes should be presented on the December 31, 2021, balance sheet.

P19.4 **(LO 1, 2, 4)** **(Permanent and Temporary Differences, One Rate)** The accounting records of Shinault Inc. show the following data for 2020 (its first year of operations).

1. Life insurance expense on officers was $9,000.
2. Equipment was acquired in early January for $300,000. Straight-line depreciation over a 5-year life is used, with no salvage value. For tax purposes, Shinault used a 30% rate to calculate depreciation.
3. Interest revenue on State of New York bonds totaled $4,000.
4. Product warranties were estimated to be $50,000 in 2020. Actual repair and labor costs related to the warranties in 2020 were $10,000. The remainder is estimated to be paid evenly in 2021 and 2022.
5. Gross profit on an accrual basis was $100,000. For tax purposes, $75,000 was recorded on the installment-sales method.
6. Fines incurred for pollution violations were $4,200.
7. Pretax financial income was $750,000. The tax rate is 30%.

Instructions

a. Prepare a schedule starting with pretax financial income in 2020 and ending with taxable income in 2020.

b. Prepare the journal entry for 2020 to record income taxes payable, income tax expense, and deferred income taxes.

P19.5 **(LO 3)** Excel Groupwork **(NOL without Valuation Account)** Jennings Inc. reported the following pretax income (loss) and related tax rates during the years 2019–2022.

	Pretax Income (Loss)	Tax Rate
2019	80,000	40%
2020	(180,000)	40%
2021	200,000	20%
2022	100,000	20%

Pretax financial income (loss) and taxable income (loss) were the same for all years since Jennings began business. The tax rates from 2019–2022 were enacted in 2019.

Instructions

a. Prepare the journal entries for the years 2020–2022 to record income taxes payable (refundable), income tax expense (benefit), and the tax effects of the loss carryforward. Assume that Jennings expects to realize the benefits of any loss carryforward in the year that immediately follows the loss year.

b. Indicate the effect the 2020 entry(ies) has on the December 31, 2020, balance sheet.

c. Prepare the portion of the income statement, starting with "Operating loss before income taxes," for 2020.

d. Prepare the portion of the income statement, starting with "Income before income taxes," for 2021.

P19.6 **(LO 1, 4) (Two Differences, Two Rates, Future Income Expected)** Presented below are two independent situations related to future taxable and deductible amounts resulting from temporary differences existing at December 31, 2020.

1. Mooney Co. has developed the following schedule of future taxable and deductible amounts.

	2021	2022	2023	2024	2025
Taxable amounts	$300	$300	$300	$ 300	$300
Deductible amount	—	—	—	(1,600)	—

2. Roesch Co. has the following schedule of future taxable and deductible amounts.

	2021	2022	2023	2024
Taxable amounts	$300	$300	$ 300	$300
Deductible amount	—	—	(2,300)	—

Both Mooney Co. and Roesch Co. have taxable income of $4,000 in 2020 and expect to have taxable income in all future years. The tax rates enacted as of the beginning of 2020 are 30% for 2020–2023 and 35% for years thereafter. All of the underlying temporary differences relate to noncurrent assets and liabilities.

Instructions

For each of these two situations, compute the net amount of deferred income taxes to be reported at the end of 2020, and indicate how it should be classified on the balance sheet.

P19.7 **(LO 1, 2, 4) Groupwork (One Temporary Difference, Tracked 3 Years, Change in Rates, Income Statement Presentation)** Crosley Corp. sold an investment on an installment basis. The total gain of $60,000 was reported for financial reporting purposes in the period of sale. The company qualifies to use the installment-sales method for tax purposes. The installment period is 3 years; one-third of the sale price is collected in the period of sale. The tax rate was 40% in 2020, and 20% in 2021 and 2022. The 20% tax rate was not enacted in law until 2021. The accounting and tax data for the 3 years is shown below.

	Financial Accounting	Tax Return
2020 (40% tax rate)		
Income before temporary difference	$ 70,000	$70,000
Temporary difference	60,000	20,000
Income	$130,000	$90,000
2021 (20% tax rate)		
Income before temporary difference	$ 70,000	$70,000
Temporary difference	-0-	20,000
Income	$ 70,000	$90,000
2022 (20% tax rate)		
Income before temporary difference	$ 70,000	$70,000
Temporary difference	-0-	20,000
Income	$ 70,000	$90,000

Instructions

a. Prepare the journal entries to record the income tax expense, deferred income taxes, and the income taxes payable at the end of each year. No deferred income taxes existed at the beginning of 2020.

b. Explain how the deferred taxes will appear on the balance sheet at the end of each year.

c. Draft the income tax expense section of the income statement for each year, beginning with "Income before income taxes."

P19.8 (LO 1, 2, 4) (Two Differences, 2 Years, Compute Taxable Income and Pretax Financial Income) The following information was disclosed during the audit of Elbert Inc.

1.

Year	Amount Due per Tax Return
2020	$130,000
2021	104,000

2. On January 1, 2020, equipment costing $600,000 is purchased. For financial reporting purposes, the company uses straight-line depreciation over a 5-year life. For tax purposes, the company uses the elective straight-line method over a 5-year life. (*Hint:* For tax purposes, the half-year convention as discussed in Appendix 11A must be used.)
3. In January 2021, $225,000 is collected in advance rental of a building for a 3-year period. The entire $225,000 is reported as taxable income in 2021, but $150,000 of the $225,000 is reported as unearned revenue in 2021 for financial reporting purposes. The remaining amount of unearned revenue is to be recognized equally in 2022 and 2023.
4. The tax rate is 20% in 2020 and all subsequent periods. (*Hint:* To find taxable income in 2020 and 2021, the related income taxes payable amounts will have to be "grossed up.")
5. No temporary differences existed at the end of 2019. Elbert expects to report taxable income in each of the next 5 years.

Instructions

a. Determine the amount to report for deferred income taxes at the end of 2020, and indicate how it should be classified on the balance sheet.

b. Prepare the journal entry to record income taxes for 2020.

c. Draft the income tax section of the income statement for 2020, beginning with "Income before income taxes." (*Hint:* You must compute taxable income and then combine that with changes in cumulative temporary differences to arrive at pretax financial income.)

d. Determine the deferred income taxes at the end of 2021, and indicate how they should be classified on the balance sheet.

e. Prepare the journal entry to record income taxes for 2021.

f. Draft the income tax section of the income statement for 2021, beginning with "Income before income taxes."

P19.9 (LO 1, 2, 4) Groupwork (Five Differences, Compute Taxable Income and Deferred Taxes, Draft Income Statement) Wise Company began operations at the beginning of 2021. The following information pertains to this company.

1. Pretax financial income for 2021 is $100,000.
2. The tax rate enacted for 2021 and future years is 20%.
3. Differences between the 2021 income statement and tax return are listed below:
   a. Warranty expense accrued for financial reporting purposes amounts to $7,000. Warranty deductions per the tax return amount to $2,000.
   b. Gross profit on construction contracts using the percentage-of-completion method per books amounts to $92,000. Gross profit on construction contracts for tax purposes amounts to $67,000.
   c. Depreciation of property, plant, and equipment for financial reporting purposes amounts to $60,000. Depreciation of these assets amounts to $80,000 for the tax return.
   d. A $3,500 fine paid for violation of pollution laws was deducted in computing pretax financial income.
   e. Interest revenue recognized on an investment in tax-exempt municipal bonds amounts to $1,500.
4. Taxable income is expected for the next few years. (Assume (a) is short-term in nature; assume (b) and (c) are long-term in nature.)

Instructions

a. Compute taxable income for 2021.

b. Compute the deferred taxes at December 31, 2021, that relate to the temporary differences described above. Clearly label them as deferred tax asset or liability.

c. Prepare the journal entry to record income tax expense, deferred taxes, and income taxes payable for 2021.

d. Draft the income tax expense section of the income statement, beginning with "Income before income taxes."

Concepts for Analysis

CA19.1 (LO 1) Writing (Objectives and Principles for Accounting for Income Taxes) The amount of income taxes due to the government for a period of time is rarely the amount reported on the income statement for that period as income tax expense.

Instructions

a. Explain the objectives of accounting for income taxes in general-purpose financial statements.

b. Explain the basic principles that are applied in accounting for income taxes at the date of the financial statements to meet the objectives discussed in (a).

c. List the steps in the annual computation of deferred tax liabilities and assets.

CA19.2 (LO 1) Writing (Basic Accounting for Temporary Differences) Dexter Company appropriately uses the asset-liability method to record deferred income taxes. Dexter reports depreciation expense for certain machinery purchased this year using the modified accelerated cost recovery system (MACRS) for income tax purposes and the straight-line basis for financial reporting purposes. The tax deduction is the larger amount this year.

Dexter received rent revenues in advance this year. These revenues are included in this year's taxable income. However, for financial reporting purposes, these revenues are reported as unearned revenues, a current liability.

Instructions

a. What are the principles of the asset-liability approach?

b. How would Dexter account for the temporary differences?

c. How should Dexter classify the deferred tax consequences of the temporary differences on its balance sheet?

CA19.3 (LO 1, 2) (Identify Temporary Differences and Classification Criteria) The asset-liability approach for recording deferred income taxes is an integral part of generally accepted accounting principles.

Instructions

a. Indicate whether each of the following independent situations should be treated as a temporary difference or as a permanent difference, and explain why.

1. Estimated warranty costs (covering a 3-year warranty) are expensed for financial reporting purposes at the time of sale but deducted for income tax purposes when paid.
2. Depreciation for book and income tax purposes differs because of different bases of carrying the related property, which was acquired in a trade-in. The different bases are a result of different rules used for book and tax purposes to compute the basis of property acquired in a trade-in.
3. A company properly uses the equity method to account for its 30% investment in another company. The investee pays dividends that are about 10% of its annual earnings.
4. A company reports a gain on an involuntary conversion of a nonmonetary asset to a monetary asset. The company elects to replace the property within the statutory period using the total proceeds so the gain is not reported on the current year's tax return.

b. Discuss the nature of the deferred income tax accounts and the manner in which these accounts are to be reported on the balance sheet.

CA19.4 (LO 1, 2) (Accounting and Classification of Deferred Income Taxes)

Part A: This year, Gumowski Company has each of the following items in its income statement.

1. Gross profits on installment sales.
2. Revenues on long-term construction contracts.
3. Estimated costs of product warranty contracts.
4. Premiums on officers' life insurance policies with Gumowski as beneficiary.

Instructions

a. Indicate where deferred income taxes are reported in the financial statements.

b. Specify when deferred income taxes would need to be recognized for each of the items above, and indicate the rationale for such recognition.

Part B: Gumowski Company's president has heard that deferred income taxes can be classified in different ways in the balance sheet.

Instructions

Identify the conditions under which deferred income taxes would be classified as a noncurrent item in the balance sheet. What justification exists for such classification?

(AICPA adapted)

CA19.5 (LO 1, 2) (Explain Computation of Deferred Tax Liability for Multiple Tax Rates) At December 31, 2020, Higley Corporation has one temporary difference which will reverse and cause taxable amounts in 2021. In 2020, a new tax act set taxes equal to 35% for 2020, 30% for 2021, and 20% for 2022 and years thereafter.

Instructions

Explain what circumstances would call for Higley to compute its deferred tax liability at the end of 2020 by multiplying the cumulative temporary difference by:

a. 35%.

b. 30%.

c. 20%.

CA19.6 (LO 1, 2, 3) (Explain Future Taxable and Deductible Amounts, How Carryforward Affects Deferred Taxes) Maria Rodriquez and Lynette Kingston are discussing accounting for income taxes. They are currently studying a schedule of taxable and deductible amounts that will arise in the future as a result of existing temporary differences. The schedule is as follows.

		Future Years			
	2020	2021	2022	2023	2024
Taxable income	$850,000				
Taxable amounts		$375,000	$375,000	$375,000	$375,000
Deductible amounts				(2,400,000)	
Enacted tax rate	50%	45%	40%	35%	30%

Instructions

a. Explain the concept of future taxable amounts and future deductible amounts as illustrated in the schedule.

b. How does the carryforward provision affect the reporting of deferred tax assets and deferred tax liabilities?

CA19.7 (LO 1, 2) Ethics (Deferred Taxes, Income Effects) Stephanie Delaney, CPA, is the newly hired director of corporate taxation for Acme Incorporated, which is a publicly traded corporation. Ms. Delaney's first job with Acme was the review of the company's accounting practices on deferred income taxes. In doing her review, she noted differences between tax and book depreciation methods that permitted Acme to realize a sizable deferred tax liability on its balance sheet. As a result, Acme paid very little in income taxes at that time.

Delaney also discovered that Acme has an explicit policy of selling off plant assets before they reversed in the deferred tax liability account. This policy, coupled with the rapid expansion of its plant asset base, allowed Acme to "defer" all income taxes payable for several years, even though it always has reported positive earnings and an increasing EPS. Delaney checked with the legal department and found the policy to be legal, but she's uncomfortable with the ethics of it.

Instructions

Answer the following questions.

a. Why would Acme have an explicit policy of selling plant assets before the temporary differences reversed in the deferred tax liability account?

b. What are the ethical implications of Acme's "deferral" of income taxes?

c. Who could be harmed by Acme's ability to "defer" income taxes payable for several years, despite positive earnings?

d. In a situation such as this, what are Ms. Delaney's professional responsibilities as a CPA?

Using Your Judgment

Financial Reporting Problem

The Procter & Gamble Company (P&G)

The financial statements of P&G are presented in Appendix B. The company's complete annual report, including the notes to the financial statements, is available online.

Instructions

Refer to P&G's financial statements and the accompanying notes to answer the following questions.

a. What amounts relative to income taxes does P&G report in its:

1. 2017 income statement?
2. June 30, 2017, balance sheet?
3. 2017 statement of cash flows?

b. P&G's income taxes in 2015, 2016, and 2017 were computed at what effective tax rates? (See the notes to the financial statements.)

c. How much of P&G's 2017 total income taxes was current tax expense, and how much was deferred tax expense?

d. What did P&G report as the significant components (the details) of its June 30, 2017, deferred tax assets and liabilities?

Comparative Analysis Case

The Coca-Cola Company and PepsiCo, Inc.

The financial statements of **Coca-Cola** and **PepsiCo** are presented in Appendices C and D, respectively. The companies' complete annual reports, including the notes to the financial statements, are available online.

Instructions

Use the companies' financial information to answer the following questions.

a. What are the amounts of Coca-Cola's and PepsiCo's provision for income taxes for the year 2017? Of each company's 2017 provision for income taxes, what portion is current expense and what portion is deferred expense ?

b. What amount of cash was paid in 2017 for income taxes by Coca-Cola and by PepsiCo?

c. What was the U.S. federal statutory tax rate in 2017? What was the effective tax rate in 2017 for Coca-Cola and PepsiCo? Why might their effective tax rates differ?

d. For year-end 2017, what amounts were reported by Coca-Cola and PepsiCo as (1) gross deferred tax assets and (2) gross deferred tax liabilities?

e. Do either Coca-Cola or PepsiCo disclose any net operating loss carrybacks and/or carryforwards at year-end 2017? What are the amounts, and when do the carryforwards expire?

Financial Statement Analysis Case

Homestake Mining Company

Homestake Mining Company is a 120-year-old international gold mining company with substantial gold mining operations and exploration in the United States, Canada, and Australia. At year-end, Homestake reported the following items related to income taxes (thousands of dollars).

Total current taxes	$ 26,349
Total deferred taxes	(39,436)
Total income and mining taxes (the provision for taxes per its income statement)	$(13,087)
Deferred tax liabilities	$303,050
Deferred tax assets, net of valuation allowance of $207,175	95,275
Net deferred tax liability	$207,775

Note 6: The classification of deferred tax assets and liabilities is based on the related asset or liability creating the deferred tax. Deferred taxes not related to a specific asset or liability are classified based on the estimated period of reversal.

Tax loss carryforwards (U.S., Canada, Australia, and Chile)	$71,151
Tax credit carryforwards	$12,007

Instructions

a. What is the significance of Homestake's disclosure of "Current taxes" of $26,349 and "Deferred taxes" of $(39,436)?

b. Explain the concept behind Homestake's disclosure of gross deferred tax liabilities (future taxable amounts) and gross deferred tax assets (future deductible amounts).

c. Homestake reported tax loss carryforwards of $71,151 and tax credit carryforwards of $12,007. How do the carryforward provisions affect the reporting of deferred tax assets and deferred tax liabilities?

Accounting, Analysis, and Principles

DeJohn Company, which began operations at the beginning of 2018, produces various products on a contract basis. Each contract generates a gross profit of $80,000. Some of DeJohn's contracts provide for the customer to pay on an installment basis. Under these contracts, DeJohn collects one-fifth of the contract revenue in each of the following four years. For financial reporting purposes, the company recognizes gross profit in the year of completion (accrual basis). For tax purposes, DeJohn recognizes gross profit in the year cash is collected (installment basis).

Presented below is information related to DeJohn's operations for 2020:

1. In 2020, the company completed seven contracts that allow for the customer to pay on an installment basis. DeJohn recognized the related gross profit of $560,000 for financial reporting purposes. It reported only $112,000 of gross profit on installment sales on the 2020 tax return. The company expects future collections on the related installment receivables to result in taxable amounts of $112,000 in each of the next four years.
2. In 2020, nontaxable municipal bond interest revenue was $28,000.
3. During 2020, nondeductible fines and penalties of $26,000 were paid.
4. Pretax financial income for 2020 amounts to $500,000.
5. Tax rates (enacted before the end of 2020) are 30% for 2020 and 20% for 2021 and later.
6. The accounting period is the calendar year.
7. The company is expected to have taxable income in all future years.
8. The company has no deferred tax assets or liabilities at the end of 2019.

Accounting

Prepare the journal entry to record income taxes for 2020.

Analysis

Classify deferred income taxes on the balance sheet at December 31, 2020, and indicate, starting with the line "Income before income taxes," how income taxes are reported on the income statement. What is DeJohn's effective tax rate?

Principles

Explain how the conceptual framework is used as a basis for determining the proper accounting for deferred income taxes.

Bridge to the Profession

FASB Codification References

[1] FASB ASC 740-10-45-4. [Predecessor literature: "Accounting for Income Taxes," *Statement of Financial Accounting Standard No. 109* (Norwalk, Conn.: FASB, 1992)].

[2] FASB ASC 740-10-30-18. [Predecessor literature: "Accounting for Income Taxes," *Statement of Financial Accounting Standards No. 109* (Norwalk, Conn.: FASB, 1992).]

[3] FASB ASC 740-10-30-21 & 22. [Predecessor literature: "Accounting for Income Taxes," *Statement of Financial Accounting Standards No. 109* (Norwalk, Conn.: FASB, 1992), paras. 23 and 24.]

[4] FASB ASC 740-10-25-6. [Predecessor literature: "Accounting for Uncertainty in Income Taxes," *FASB Interpretation No. 48* (Norwalk, Conn.: FASB, 2006).]

[5] FASB ASC 740-10-05. [Predecessor literature: "Accounting for Income Taxes," *Statement of Financial Accounting Standards No. 109* (Norwalk, Conn.: FASB, 1992), paras. 6 and 8.]

Codification Exercises

If your school has a subscription to the FASB Codification, log in and prepare responses to the following. Provide Codification references for your responses.

CE19.1 Access the glossary ("Master Glossary") to answer the following.

a. What is a deferred tax asset?

b. What is taxable income?

c. What is the definition of valuation allowance?

d. What is a deferred tax liability?

CE19.2 What are the two basic requirements applied to the measurement of current and deferred income taxes at the date of the financial statements?

CE19.3 A company wishes to conduct business in a foreign country that attracts businesses by granting "holidays" from income taxes for a certain period of time. Would the company have to disclose this "holiday" to the SEC? If so, what information must be disclosed?

CE19.4 When is a company allowed to initially recognize the financial statement effects of a tax position?

Codification Research Case

Kleckner Company started operations in 2016. Although it has grown steadily, the company reported accumulated operating losses of $450,000 in its first four years in business. In the most recent year (2020), Kleckner appears to have turned the corner and reported modest taxable income of $30,000. In addition to a deferred tax asset related to its net operating loss, Kleckner has recorded a deferred tax asset related to product warranties and a deferred tax liability related to accelerated depreciation.

Given its past operating results, Kleckner has established a full valuation allowance for its deferred tax assets. However, given its improved performance, Kleckner management wonders whether the company can now reduce or eliminate the valuation allowance. They would like you to conduct some research on the accounting for its valuation allowance.

Instructions

If your school has a subscription to the FASB Codification, log in and prepare responses to the following. Provide Codification references for your responses.

a. Briefly explain to Kleckner management the importance of future taxable income as it relates to the valuation allowance for deferred tax assets.

b. What are the sources of income that may be relied upon to remove the need for a valuation allowance?

c. What are tax-planning strategies? From the information provided, does it appear that Kleckner could employ a tax-planning strategy to support reducing its valuation allowance?

Additional Professional Resources

Go to WileyPLUS for other career-readiness resources, such as career coaching, internship opportunities, and CPAexcel prep.

IFRS Insights

LEARNING OBJECTIVE 7

Compare the accounting for income taxes under GAAP and IFRS.

The accounting for income taxes in IFRS is covered in *IAS 12* ("Income Taxes"), which is based on an asset-liability approach to measurement of deferred taxes.

Relevant Facts

Following are the key similarities and differences between GAAP and IFRS related to accounting for taxes.

Similarities

- Similar to GAAP, IFRS uses the asset and liability approach for recording deferred taxes.
- The classification of deferred taxes under both IFRS and GAAP is always non-current.

Differences

- Under IFRS, an affirmative judgment approach is used, by which a deferred tax asset is recognized up to the amount that is probable to be realized. GAAP uses an impairment approach. In this approach, the deferred tax asset is recognized in full. It is then reduced by a valuation account if it is more likely than not that all or a portion of the deferred tax asset will not be realized.
- IFRS uses the enacted tax rate or substantially enacted tax rate. ("Substantially enacted" means virtually certain.) For GAAP, the enacted tax rate must be used.
- The tax effects related to certain items are reported in equity under IFRS. That is not the case under GAAP, which charges or credits the tax effects to income.
- GAAP requires companies to assess the likelihood of uncertain tax positions being sustainable upon audit. Potential liabilities must be accrued and disclosed if the position is "more likely than not" to be disallowed. Under IFRS, all potential liabilities must be recognized. With respect to measurement, IFRS uses an expected-value approach to measure the tax liability, which differs from GAAP.

About the Numbers

Deferred Tax Asset (Non-Recognition)

Under IFRS, companies recognize a deferred tax asset for all deductible temporary differences. However, based on available evidence, a company should reduce a deferred tax asset if it is probable that it **will not realize** some portion or all of the deferred tax asset. "**Probable**" means a level of likelihood of at least slightly more than 50 percent.

Assume that Jensen Co. has a deductible temporary difference of $1,000,000 at the end of its first year of operations. Its tax rate is 40 percent, which means it records a deferred tax asset of $400,000 ($1,000,000 × .40). Assuming $900,000 of income taxes payable, Jensen records income tax expense, the deferred tax asset, and income taxes payable as follows.

Income Tax Expense	500,000	
Deferred Tax Asset	400,000	
Income Taxes Payable		900,000

After careful review of all available evidence, Jensen determines that it is probable that it will not realize $100,000 of this deferred tax asset. Jensen records this reduction in asset value as follows.

Income Tax Expense	100,000	
Deferred Tax Asset		100,000

This journal entry increases income tax expense in the current period because Jensen does not expect to realize a favorable tax benefit for a portion of the deductible temporary difference. Jensen **simultaneously recognizes a reduction in the carrying amount of the deferred tax asset**. Jensen then reports a deferred tax asset of $300,000 ($400,000 – $100,000) in its statement of financial position.

Jensen evaluates the deferred tax asset account at the end of each accounting period. If, at the end of the next period, it expects to realize $350,000 of this deferred tax asset, Jensen makes the following entry to adjust this account.

Deferred Tax Asset ($350,000 – $300,000)	50,000	
Income Tax Expense		50,000

Jensen should consider all available evidence, both positive and negative, to determine whether, based on the weight of available evidence, it needs to adjust the deferred tax asset. For example, if Jensen has been experiencing a series of loss years, it reasonably assumes that these losses will continue. Therefore, Jensen will lose the benefit of the future deductible amounts.

Generally, sufficient taxable income arises from temporary taxable differences that will reverse in the future or from a tax-planning strategy that will generate taxable income in the future. **Illustration IFRS19.1** shows how **Ahold** describes its reporting of deferred assets.

ILLUSTRATION IFRS19.1
Deferred Tax Asset Disclosure

Ahold

Note 11. Significant judgment is required in determining whether deferred tax assets are realizable. Ahold determines this on the basis of expected taxable profits arising from recognized deferred tax liabilities and on the basis of budgets, cash flow forecasts, and impairment models. Where utilization is not considered probable, deferred taxes are not recognized.

Carryforward (Non-Recognition) To illustrate non-recognition of a loss carryforward, assume that Groh Inc. has tax benefits of $110,000 associated with a NOL carryback (as discussed in Appendix 19B) and a potential deferred tax asset of $80,000 associated with an operating loss carryforward of $200,000, assuming a future tax rate of 40% ($200,000 × .40). However, if it is probable that Groh will *not* realize the entire NOL carryforward in future years, it does not recognize this deferred tax asset. To illustrate, Groh makes the following journal entry in 2020 to record only the tax refund receivable.

To recognize benefit of loss carryback		
Income Tax Refund Receivable	110,000	
Income Tax Expense (Loss Carryback)		110,000

Illustration IFRS19.2 shows Groh's 2020 income statement presentation.

ILLUSTRATION IFRS19.2

Recognition of Benefit of Loss Carryback Only

Groh Inc.
Income Statement (partial) for 2020

Operating loss before income taxes	$(500,000)
Income tax benefit	
Income tax expense (loss carryback)	110,000
Net loss	$(390,000)

In 2021, assuming that Groh has taxable income of $250,000 (before considering the carryforward), subject to a tax rate of 40 percent, it realizes the deferred tax asset. Groh records the following entries.

To recognize deferred tax asset and loss carryforward		
Deferred Tax Asset	80,000	
Income Tax Expense (Loss Carryforward)		80,000
To record current and deferred income taxes		
Income Tax Expense	100,000	
Deferred Tax Asset		80,000
Income Taxes Payable		20,000

Groh reports the $80,000 Benefit Due to the Loss Carryforward on the 2021 income statement. The company did not recognize it in 2020 because it was probable that it would not be realized. Assuming that Groh derives the income for 2021 from continuing operations, it prepares the income statement as shown in Illustration IFRS19.3.

ILLUSTRATION IFRS19.3

Recognition of Benefit of Loss Carryforward When Realized

Groh Inc.
Income Statement (partial) for 2021

Income before income taxes		$250,000
Income tax expense		
Current	$ 20,000	
Deferred	-0-*	20,000
Net income		$230,000

*Carryforward ($80,000) – Allowance ($80,000)

Another method is to report only one line for total income tax expense of $20,000 on the face of the income statement and disclose the components of income tax expense in the notes to the financial statements.

Statement of Financial Position Classification

Companies classify taxes receivable or payable as current assets or current liabilities. Although current tax assets and liabilities are separately recognized and measured, they are often offset in the statement of financial position. The offset occurs because companies normally have a legally enforceable right to offset a current tax asset (Taxes Receivable) against a current tax liability (Taxes Payable) when they relate to income taxes levied by the same taxation authority. Deferred tax assets and deferred tax liabilities are also separately recognized and measured but may be offset in the statement of financial position. Companies are permitted to offset deferred tax assets and deferred tax liabilities if, and only if (1) the company has a legally enforceable right to offset current tax assets against current tax liabilities, and (2) the deferred tax assets and the deferred tax liabilities relate to income taxes levied by the same tax authority and for the same company.

Similar to GAAP, the net deferred tax asset or net deferred tax liability is reported in the non-current section of the statement of financial position. Deferred tax amounts should not be discounted. The IASB apparently considers discounting to be an unnecessary complication even if the effects are material. To illustrate, assume that K. Scott Company has four deferred tax items at December 31, 2020, as shown in Illustration IFRS19.4.

ILLUSTRATION IFRS19.4
Classification of Temporary Differences

	Resulting Deferred Tax	
Temporary Difference	(Asset)	Liability
1. Rent collected in advance: recognized when a performance obligation is satisfied for accounting purposes and when received for tax purposes.	$(42,000)	
2. Use of straight-line depreciation for accounting purposes and accelerated depreciation for tax purposes.		$214,000
3. Recognition of income on installment sales at the time of sale for accounting purposes and during period of collection for tax purposes.		45,000
4. Warranty liabilities: recognized for accounting purposes at time of sale for tax purposes at time paid.	(12,000)	
Totals	$(54,000)	$259,000

As indicated, K. Scott has a total deferred tax asset of $54,000 and a total deferred tax liability of $259,000. Assuming these two items can be offset, K. Scott reports a deferred tax liability of $205,000 ($259,000 – $54,000) in the non-current liability section of its statement of financial position.

On the Horizon

The IASB and the FASB have worked to address some of the differences in the accounting for income taxes. Some of the issues under discussion are the term "probable" under IFRS for recognition of a deferred tax asset, which might be interpreted to mean "more likely than not." If the term is changed, the reporting for impairments of deferred tax assets will be essentially the same between GAAP and IFRS. In addition, the FASB recently adopted the IFRS classification approach for deferred tax assets and liabilities. Also, GAAP will likely continue to use the enacted tax rate in computing deferred taxes, except in situations where the taxing jurisdiction is not involved. In that case, companies should use IFRS, which is based on enacted rates or substantially enacted tax rates. Finally, the issue of allocation of deferred income taxes to equity for certain transactions under IFRS must be addressed in order to converge with GAAP, which allocates the effects to income. At the time of this printing, deliberations on the income tax project have been suspended indefinitely.

IFRS Self-Test Questions

1. Which of the following is **false**?

   a. Under GAAP, deferred taxes are reported based on the classification of the asset or liability to which it relates.

   b. Under IFRS, all potential liabilities must be recognized.

   c. Under GAAP, the enacted tax rate is used to measure deferred tax assets and liabilities.

   d. Under IFRS, all deferred tax assets and liabilities are classified as non-current.

2. Which of the following statements is **correct** with regard to IFRS and GAAP?

   a. Under GAAP, all potential liabilities related to uncertain tax positions must be recognized.

   b. The tax effects related to certain items are reported in equity under GAAP; under IFRS, the tax effects are charged or credited to income.

   c. IFRS uses an affirmative judgment approach for deferred tax assets, whereas GAAP uses an impairment approach for deferred tax assets.

   d. IFRS classifies deferred taxes based on the classification of the asset or liability to which it relates.

3. Under IFRS:

   a. "probable" is defined as a level of likelihood of at least slightly more than 60%.

   b. a company should reduce a deferred tax asset when it is likely that some or all of it will not be realized by using a valuation allowance.

   c. a company considers only positive evidence when determining whether to recognize a deferred tax asset.

   d. deferred tax assets must be evaluated at the end of each accounting period.

4. Stephens Company has a deductible temporary difference of $2,000,000 at the end of its first year of operations. Its tax rate is 40 percent. Stephens has $1,800,000 of income taxes payable. After a careful review of all available evidence, Stephens determines that it is probable that it will not realize $200,000 of this deferred tax asset. On Stephens Company's statement of financial position at the end of its first year of operations, what is the amount of deferred tax asset?

   a. $2,000,000. **c.** $800,000.
   b. $1,800,000. **d.** $600,000.

5. Lincoln Company has the following four deferred tax items at December 31, 2020. The deferred tax assets and the deferred tax liabilities relate to income taxes levied by the same tax authority.

Temporary Difference	Deferred Tax Asset	Deferred Tax Liability
Rent collected in advance: recognized when a performance obligation is satisfied for accounting purposes and when received for tax purposes.	$652,000	
Use of straight-line depreciation for accounting purposes and accelerated depreciation for tax purposes.		$330,000
Recognition of income on installment sales at the time of sale for accounting purposes and during period of collection for tax purposes.		64,000
Warranty liabilities: recognized for accounting purposes at time of sale for tax purposes at time paid.	37,000	

On Lincoln's December 31, 2020, statement of financial position, it will report:

a. $394,000 non-current deferred tax liability and $689,000 non-current deferred tax asset.

b. $330,000 non-current liability and $625,000 current deferred tax asset.

c. $295,000 non-current deferred tax asset.

d. $295,000 current tax receivable.

IFRS Concepts and Application

IFRS19.1 Where can authoritative IFRS related to the accounting for taxes be found?

IFRS19.2 Briefly describe some of the similarities and differences between GAAP and IFRS with respect to income tax accounting.

IFRS19.3 Describe the current convergence efforts of the FASB and IASB in the area of accounting for taxes.

IFRS19.4 How are deferred tax assets and deferred tax liabilities reported on the statement of financial position under IFRS?

IFRS19.5 Describe the procedure(s) involved in classifying deferred tax amounts on the statement of financial position under IFRS.

IFRS19.6 At December 31, 2020, Hillyard Corporation has a deferred tax asset of $200,000. After a careful review of all available evidence, it is determined that it is probable that $60,000 of this deferred tax asset will not be realized. Prepare the necessary journal entry.

IFRS19.7 Rode Inc. incurred a net operating loss of $500,000 in 2020. Combined income for 2018 and 2019 was $350,000. The tax rate for all years is 20%. Prepare the journal entries to record the benefits of the loss carryforward.

IFRS19.8 Use the information for Rode Inc. given in IFRS19.7. Assume that it is probable that the entire net operating loss carryforward will not be realized in future years. Prepare the journal entry(ies) necessary at the end of 2020.

IFRS19.9 Youngman Corporation has temporary differences at December 31, 2020, that result in the following deferred taxes.

Deferred tax asset	$24,000
Deferred tax liability	69,000

Indicate how these balances would be presented in Youngman's December 31, 2020, statement of financial position.

IFRS19.10 At December 31, 2020, Cascade Company had a net deferred tax liability of $450,000. An explanation of the items that compose this balance is as follows.

Temporary Differences in Deferred Taxes	Resulting Balances
1. Excess of tax depreciation over book depreciation.	$200,000
2. Accrual, for book purposes, of estimated loss contingency from pending lawsuit that is expected to be settled in 2021. The loss will be deducted on the tax return when paid.	$ (50,000)
3. Accrual method used for book purposes and installment method used for tax purposes for an isolated installment sale of an investment.	$300,000

In analyzing the temporary differences, you find that $30,000 of the depreciation temporary difference will reverse in 2021, and $120,000 of the temporary difference due to the installment sale will reverse in 2021. The tax rate for all years is 40%.

Instructions

Indicate the manner in which deferred taxes should be presented on Cascade Company's December 31, 2020, statement of financial position.

IFRS19.11 Callaway Corp. has a deferred tax asset account with a balance of $112,500 at the end of 2020 due to a single cumulative temporary difference of $375,000. At the end of 2021, this same temporary difference has increased to a cumulative amount of $500,000. Taxable income for 2021 is $850,000. The tax rate is 30% for all years.

Instructions

a. Record income tax expense, deferred income taxes, and income taxes payable for 2021, assuming that it is probable that the deferred tax asset will be realized.

b. Assuming that it is probable that $30,000 of the deferred tax asset will not be realized, prepare the journal entry at the end of 2021 to recognize this probability.

Professional Research

IFRS19.12 Kleckner Company started operations in 2016. Although it has grown steadily, the company reported accumulated operating losses of $450,000 in its first four years in business. In the most recent year (2020), Kleckner appears to have turned the corner and reported modest taxable income of $30,000. In addition to a deferred tax asset related to its net operating loss, Kleckner has recorded a deferred tax asset related to product warranties and a deferred tax liability related to accelerated depreciation. Given its past operating results, Kleckner has determined that it is not probable that it will realize any of the deferred tax assets. However, given its improved performance, Kleckner management wonders whether there are any accounting consequences for its deferred tax assets. They would like you to conduct some research on the accounting for recognition of its deferred tax asset.

Instructions

Access the IFRS authoritative literature at the IASB website. (Click on the IFRS tab and then register for free eIFRS access if necessary.) When you have accessed the documents, you can use the search tool in your Internet browser to respond to the following questions. (Provide paragraph citations.)

a. Briefly explain to Kleckner management the importance of future taxable income as it relates to the recognition of deferred tax assets.

b. What are the sources of income that may be relied upon in assessing realization of a deferred tax asset?

c. What are tax-planning strategies? From the information provided, does it appear that Kleckner could employ a tax-planning strategy in evaluating its deferred tax asset?

International Financial Reporting Problem

Marks and Spencer plc (M&S)

IFRS19.13 The financial statements of M&S are presented in Appendix E. The company's complete annual report, including the notes to the financial statements, is available online.

Instructions

Refer to M&S's financial statements and the accompanying notes to answer the following questions.

a. What amounts relative to income taxes does M&S report in its:

   1. 2017 income statement?

   2. 1 April 2017 statement of financial position?

   3. 2017 statement of cash flows?

b. M&S's provision for income taxes in 2016 and 2017 was computed at what effective tax rates? (See the notes to the financial statements.)

c. How much of M&S's 2017 total provision for income taxes was current tax expense, and how much was deferred tax expense?

d. What did M&S report as the significant components (the details) of its 1 April 2017 deferred tax assets and liabilities?

Answers to IFRS Self-Test Questions

1. a **2.** c **3.** d **4.** d **5.** c

CHAPTER **20**

© andersphoto/Shutterstock

Accounting for Pensions and Postretirement Benefits

LEARNING OBJECTIVES

After studying this chapter, you should be able to:

1. Discuss the fundamentals of pension plan accounting.
2. Use a worksheet for employer's pension plan entries.
3. Describe the accounting and amortization of prior service costs.
4. Explain the accounting and amortization for unexpected gains and losses.
5. Describe the requirements for reporting pension plans in financial statements.

PREVIEW OF CHAPTER 20 As the following opening story indicates, the cost of retirement benefits is steep. For example, **British Airways**' pension and healthcare costs for retirees in a recent year totaled $195 million, or approximately $6 per passenger carried. Many other companies are also facing substantial pension and other postretirement expenses and obligations. In this chapter, we discuss the accounting issues related to these benefit plans. The content and organization of the chapter are as follows.

This chapter also includes numerous conceptual and global discussions that are integral to the topics presented here.

ACCOUNTING FOR PENSIONS AND POSTRETIREMENT BENEFITS

Fundamentals of Pension Plan Accounting
- Defined contribution plan
- Defined benefit plan
- Role of actuaries
- Measures of the liability
- Components of pension expense

Using a Pension Worksheet
- 2020 entries and worksheet
- Funded status

Prior Service Cost (PSC)
- Amortization
- 2021 entries and worksheet

Gains and Losses
- Unexpected gains and losses (assets)
- Unexpected gains and losses (liabilities)
- Corridor amortization
- 2022 entries and worksheet
- 2023 entries and worksheet—a comprehensive example

Reporting Pension Plans in Financial Statements
- Assets and liabilities
- Net income
- Comprehensive income
- Note disclosure
- Special issues

Where Have All the Pensions Gone?

Many companies have benefit plans that promise income and other benefits to retired employees in exchange for services during their working years. However, a shift is on from traditional defined benefit plans, in which employers bear the risk of meeting the benefit promises, to plans in which employees bear more of the risk. In some cases, employers are dropping retirement plans altogether. Here are some of the reasons for the shift.

- ***Competition.*** Newer and foreign competitors do not have the same retiree costs that older U.S. companies do. Southwest Airlines does not offer a traditional pension plan, but United has a pension deficit exceeding $100,000 per employee.
- ***Cost.*** Retirees are living longer, and the costs of retirement are higher. Combined with annual retiree healthcare costs, retirement benefits are costing the S&P 500 companies over $25 billion a year and are rising at double-digit rates.
- ***Insurance.*** Pensions are backed by premiums paid to the Pension Benefit Guarantee Corporation (PBGC). When a company fails, the PBGC takes over the plan. But due to a number of significant company failures, the PBGC has run a deficit, with healthy companies subsidizing the weak.
- ***Accounting.*** To bring U.S. standards in line with international rules, accounting rule-makers are considering rules that will require companies to "mark their pensions to market" (value them at market rates). Such a move would increase the reported volatility of the retirement plan and of company financial statements. When Great Britain made this shift, 25 percent of British companies closed their plans to new entrants.

As a result of such factors, it is understandable that experts can think of no major company that has instituted a traditional pension plan in the past decade. What does this mean for you as you evaluate job offers and benefit packages? To start, you should begin building *your own* retirement nest egg, rather than relying on your employer to provide postretirement income and healthcare benefits. Recently, a sample of Americans was asked the following question: When you retire, do you think you will have enough money to live comfortably, or not? The following graph shows a change in responses from nonretired adults from 2005 to 2018.

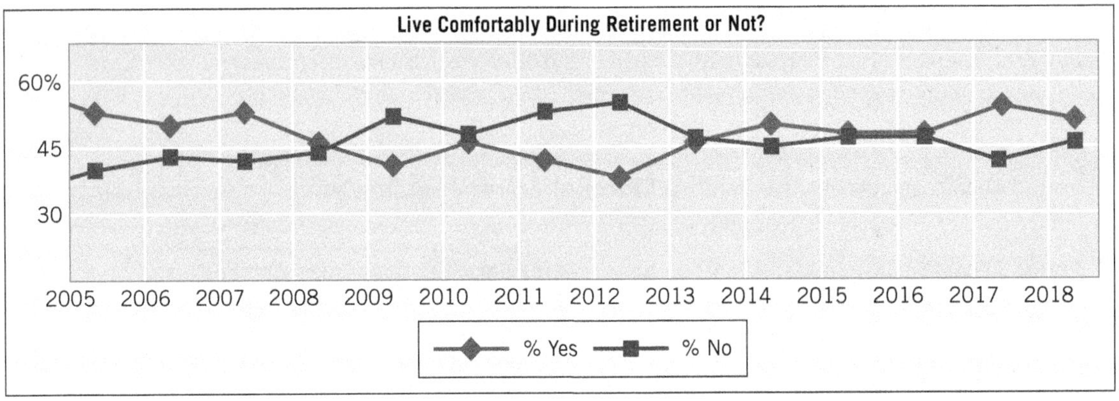

Prior to 2008, a majority of nonretired Americans consistently thought they would be able to live comfortably in retirement. But this dropped to 46 percent early during the U.S. recession in 2008 and stayed below 50 percent until 2014. Most recent data indicate that just over 50 percent of nonretirees thought they would have enough money to live comfortably in retirement. Furthermore, a rising percentage of nonretirees are pessimistic about having enough stashed away when they retire (46 percent in 2018 compared to 42 percent in 2016).

General economic conditions affect how Americans look at retirement. Americans are generally more positive about retirement when the economy is growing. However, the continuing political discussion about the fragility of the country's Social Security and Medicare programs may reduce nonretired Americans' comfort with projections of their monetary resources in their retirement. In addition, many are beginning to realize that retirement at the age of 65 may no longer be possible given the possible extension of social benefits to later ages.

This means that retirement accounts, including individual retirement accounts and defined contribution pensions such as 401(k) plans, will need to become a bigger piece of the pie to fill the gap left by smaller government and employer-sponsored benefits. So get started now with a personal savings strategy to ensure an adequate nest egg at your retirement.

Sources: Nanette Byrnes with David Welch, "The Benefits Trap," *BusinessWeek* (July 19, 2004), pp. 54–72; J. Mauldin, "Angst in America, Part 4: Disappearing Pensions," *Thoughts for the Frontline* (April 16, 2017); and T. Riffkin, "More Americans Think They Will Retire Comfortably," *http://www.gallup.com/poll/168959/americans-think-retire-comfortably.aspx* (May 9, 2018).

Review and Practice

Go to the **Review and Practice** section at the end of the chapter for a targeted summary review and practice problem with solution. Multiple-choice questions with annotated solutions as well as additional exercises and practice problem with solutions are also available online.

Fundamentals of Pension Plan Accounting

LEARNING OBJECTIVE 1

Discuss the fundamentals of pension plan accounting.

A **pension plan** is an arrangement whereby an employer provides benefits (payments) to retired employees for services they provided in their working years. Pension accounting may be divided and separately treated as **accounting for the employer** and **accounting for the pension fund**. The *company* or *employer* is the organization sponsoring the pension plan. It incurs the cost and makes contributions to the pension fund. The *fund* or *plan* is the entity that receives the contributions from the employer, administers the pension assets, and makes the benefit payments to the retired employees (pension recipients). **Illustration 20.1** shows the three entities involved in a pension plan and indicates the flow of cash among them.

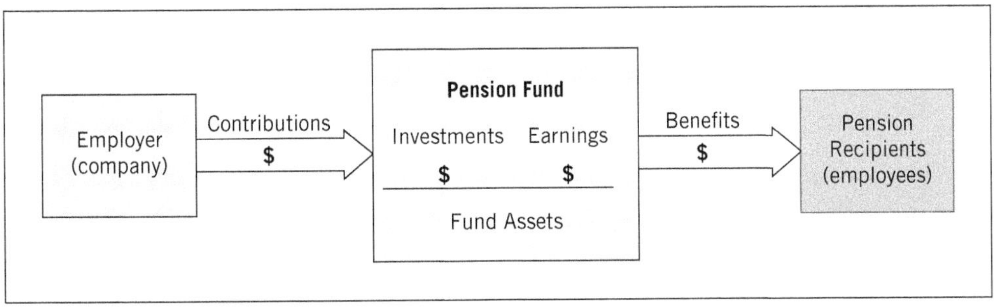

ILLUSTRATION 20.1
Flow of Cash among Pension Plan Participants

A pension plan is **funded** when the employer makes payments to a funding agency.[1] That agency accumulates the assets of the pension fund and makes payments to the recipients as the benefits come due.

[1] When used as a verb, **fund** means to pay to a funding agency (as to fund future pension benefits or to fund pension cost). Used as a noun, it refers to assets accumulated in the hands of a funding agency (trustee) for the purpose of meeting pension benefits when they become due.

Some pension plans are **contributory**. In these, the employees bear part of the cost of the stated benefits or voluntarily make payments to increase their benefits. Other plans are **non-contributory**. In these plans, the employer bears the entire cost. Companies generally design their pension plans so as to take advantage of federal income tax benefits. Plans that offer tax benefits are called **qualified pension plans**. They permit **deductibility of the employer's contributions to the pension fund and tax-free status of earnings from pension fund assets.**

The pension fund should be a separate legal and accounting entity. The pension fund, as a separate entity, maintains a set of books and prepares financial statements. Maintaining records and preparing financial statements for the fund, an activity known as "accounting for employee benefit plans," is not the subject of this chapter.[2] Instead, this chapter explains the pension accounting and reporting problems **of the employer** as the sponsor of a pension plan.

The need to properly administer and account for pension funds becomes apparent when you understand the size of these funds. Listed in Illustration 20.2 are the pension fund assets and pension expenses of six major companies.

ILLUSTRATION 20.2

Pension Funds and Pension Expense

Company ($ in millions)	Size of Pension Fund	2017 Pension Expense (Income)	Pension Expense as % of Pretax Income
General Motors	$74,421	$(1,173)	−9.89%
Hewlett-Packard	10,176	(132)	−4.03
Deere & Company	11,137	106	3.36
Merck	17,560	201	3.08
The Coca-Cola Company	8,371	368	5.46
Molson Coors Brewing	5,946	(68)	−4.91

As Illustration 20.2 indicates, pension expense (income) is a substantial percentage of total pretax income for many companies.[3] The two most common types of pension plans are **defined contribution plans** and **defined benefit plans**, and we look at each of them in the following sections.

Defined Contribution Plan

In a **defined contribution plan**, the employer agrees to contribute to a pension trust a certain sum each period, based on a formula. This formula may consider such factors as age, length of employee service, employer's profits, and compensation level. **The plan defines only the employer's contribution.** It makes no promise regarding the ultimate benefits paid out to the employees. A common form of this plan is a **401(k) plan**.

The size of the pension benefits that the employee finally collects under the plan depends on several factors: the amounts originally contributed to the pension trust, the income accumulated in the trust, and the treatment of forfeitures of funds caused by early

[2]The FASB issued separate guidance covering the accounting and reporting for employee benefit plans. [1] (See the FASB Codification References near the end of the chapter.)

[3]Retirement assets in the 22 major global markets increased 13.1 percent to a record $41.4 trillion in 2017 compared to end-of-year 2016. Pension assets for these 22 markets reached 67 percent of GDP, which represents a 5 percent increase from the 2016 ratio of 62 percent. The largest pension markets are the United States, the United Kingdom, and Japan with 61.4 percent, 7.5 percent, and 7.4 percent, respectively, of total pension assets in the study. The asset growth rate for the United States, United Kingdom, and Japan over 2016 were 12.7 percent, 16.9 percent and 9.7 percent, respectively. See "Global Pension Asset Study—2017," *www.towerswatson.com*.

terminations of other employees. A company usually turns over to an **independent third-party trustee** the amounts originally contributed. The trustee, acting on behalf of the beneficiaries (the participating employees), assumes ownership of the pension assets and is accountable for their investment and distribution. The trust is separate and distinct from the employer.

The accounting for a defined contribution plan is straightforward. The employee gets the benefit of gain (or the risk of loss) from the assets contributed to the pension plan. The employer simply contributes each year based on the formula established in the plan. As a result, the employer's annual cost (pension expense) is simply the amount that it is obligated to contribute to the pension trust. The employer reports a liability on its balance sheet only if it does not make the contribution in full. The employer reports an asset only if it contributes more than the required amount.

In addition to pension expense, the employer must disclose the following for a defined contribution plan: a plan description, including employee groups covered; the basis for determining contributions; and the nature and effect of significant matters affecting comparability from period to period. [2]

Defined Benefit Plan

A **defined benefit plan** outlines the benefits that employees will receive when they retire. These benefits typically are a function of an employee's years of service and of the compensation level in the years approaching retirement.

To meet the defined benefit commitments that will arise at retirement, a company must determine what the contribution should be today (a time value of money computation). Companies may use many different contribution approaches. However, the funding method should provide enough money at retirement to meet the benefits defined by the plan.

The **employees** are the beneficiaries of a defined **contribution** trust, but the **employer** is the beneficiary of a defined **benefit** trust. Under a defined benefit plan, the trust's primary purpose is to safeguard and invest assets so that there will be enough to pay the employer's obligation to the employees. **In form**, the trust is a separate entity. **In substance**, the trust assets and liabilities belong to the employer. That is, **as long as the plan continues, the employer is responsible for the payment of the defined benefits (without regard to what happens in the trust)**. The employer must make up any shortfall in the accumulated assets held by the trust. On the other hand, the employer can recapture any excess accumulated in the trust, either through reduced future funding or through a reversion of funds.

Because a defined benefit plan specifies benefits in terms of uncertain future variables, a company must establish an appropriate funding pattern to ensure the availability of funds at retirement in order to provide the benefits promised. This funding level depends on a number of factors such as turnover, mortality, length of employee service, compensation levels, and interest earnings.

Employers are at risk with defined benefit plans because they must contribute enough to meet the cost of benefits that the plan defines. The expense recognized each period is not necessarily equal to the cash contribution. Similarly, the liability is controversial because its measurement and recognition relate to unknown future variables. Thus, the accounting issues related to this type of plan are complex (see Global View). **Our discussion in the following sections deals primarily with defined benefit plans.**[4]

Global View

Outside the United States, private pension plans are less common because many other nations rely on government-sponsored pension plans. Consequently, accounting for defined benefit pension plans is typically a less important issue elsewhere in the world.

[4]A recent federal law requires employees to participate in an employer-sponsored defined contribution plan unless they explicitly opt out of it. This should help employees build their own nest eggs (as suggested in the opening story) and will contribute to further growth in defined contribution plans. However, note the following three warnings: (1) low-income workers will still not be able to stash enough away, (2) it leaves each participant alone to manage risk, and (3) companies establish a minimum contribution, which too many participants choose to use, instead of a larger contribution.

What Do the Numbers Mean? Which Plan Is Right for You?

Defined contribution plans have become much more popular with employers than defined benefit plans, as indicated in the following chart. One reason is that they are cheaper. Defined contribution plans often cost no more than 3 percent of payroll, whereas defined benefit plans can cost 5 to 6 percent of payroll.

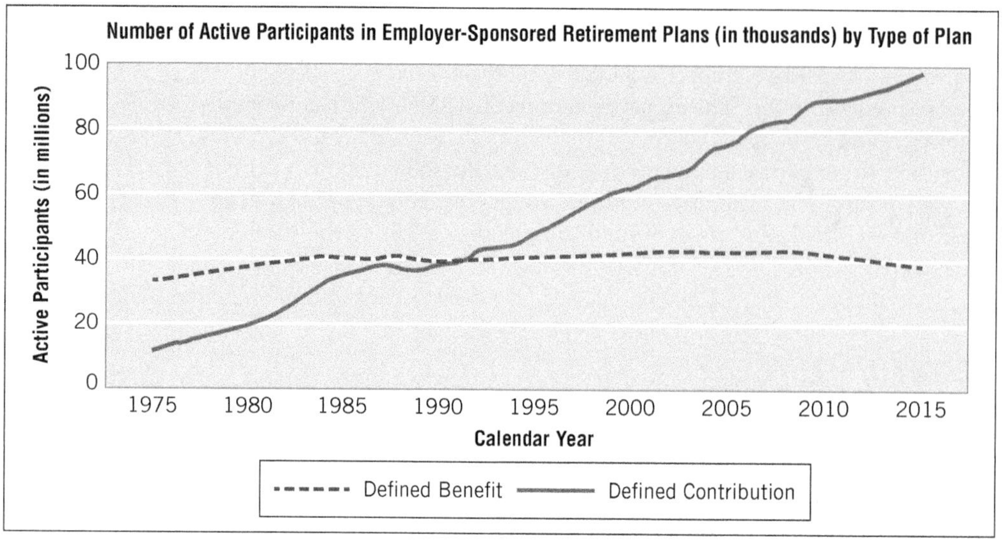

Recent data indicate the total amount of pension assets held by pension plans is $8.1 trillion, which is 67 percent of gross domestic product. In 2015, 35 percent of these assets were in defined contribution plans and 65 percent in defined benefit plans. Pension plan assets have grown approximately 6 percent per year over the period 2004–2015.

Finally, while the chart gives the impression that defined benefit plans are going away, a closer look at the data indicate that, at least for companies in the Russell 3000, more companies reported defined benefit plans over the last 5- to 10-year period. The bottom line is that defined benefit plans have quite a bit of staying power.

Source: U.S. Department of Labor, "Private Pension Plan Bulletin" (February 2018); and J. Ciesielski, "Pension Priorities: Why the Accounting Belongs on FASB's Agenda," *Analyst's Accounting Observer Blog* (February 16, 2017).

The Role of Actuaries in Pension Accounting

The problems associated with pension plans involve complicated mathematical considerations. Therefore, companies engage **actuaries** to ensure that a pension plan is appropriate for the employee group covered.[5] Actuaries are individuals trained through a long and rigorous certification program to assign probabilities to future events and their financial effects. The insurance industry employs actuaries to assess risks and to advise on the setting of premiums and other aspects of insurance policies. Employers rely heavily on actuaries for assistance in developing, implementing, and funding pension funds.

Actuaries make predictions (called *actuarial assumptions*) of mortality rates, employee turnover, interest and earnings rates, early retirement frequency, future salaries, and any other factors necessary to operate a pension plan. They also compute the various pension measures that affect the financial statements, such as the pension obligation, the annual cost of servicing the plan, and the cost of amendments to the plan. In summary, accounting for defined benefit pension plans relies heavily upon information and measurements provided by actuaries.

[5]An actuary's primary purpose is to ensure that the company has established an appropriate funding pattern to meet its pension obligations. This computation involves developing a set of assumptions and continued monitoring of these assumptions to ensure their realism. That the general public has little understanding of what an actuary does is illustrated by the following excerpt from the *Wall Street Journal*: "A polling organization once asked the general public what an actuary was, and received among its more coherent responses the opinion that it was a place where you put dead actors."

Measures of the Liability

In accounting for a company's pension plan, two questions arise. (1) What is the pension obligation that a company should report in the financial statements? (2) What is the pension expense for the period? Attempting to answer the first question has produced much controversy.

Alternative Approaches

Most agree that an employer's **pension obligation** is the deferred compensation obligation it has to its employees for their service under the terms of the pension plan. Measuring that obligation is not so simple, though, because there are alternative ways of measuring it.[6]

One measure of the pension obligation is to base it only on the benefits vested to the employees. **Vested benefits** are those that the employee is entitled to receive even if he or she renders no additional services to the company. Most pension plans require a certain minimum number of years of service to the employer before an employee achieves vested benefits status. Companies compute the **vested benefit obligation** using only vested benefits, at current salary levels.

Another way to measure the obligation uses both vested and nonvested years of service. On this basis, the company computes the deferred compensation amount on all years of employees' service—**both vested and nonvested**—using current salary levels. This measurement of the pension obligation is called the **accumulated benefit obligation**.

A third measure bases the deferred compensation amount on both vested and nonvested service **using future salaries**. This measurement of the pension obligation is called the **projected benefit obligation**. Because future salaries are expected to be higher than current salaries, this approach results in the largest measurement of the pension obligation.

The choice between these measures is critical. The choice affects the amount of a company's pension liability and the annual pension expense reported. **Illustration 20.3** presents the differences in these three measurements.

ILLUSTRATION 20.3

Different Measures of the Pension Obligation

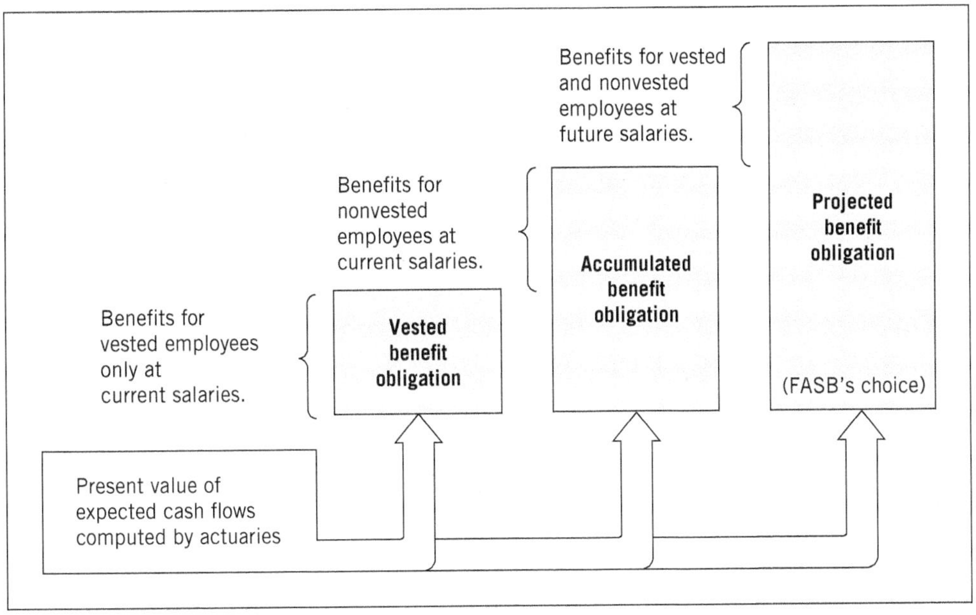

Which of these alternative measures of the pension liability does the profession favor? **The profession adopted the projected benefit obligation—the present value of vested and nonvested benefits accrued to date, based on employees' future**

[6]One measure of the pension obligation is to determine the amount that the **Pension Benefit Guaranty Corporation** would require the employer to pay if it defaulted. (This amount is limited to 30 percent of the employer's net worth.) The accounting profession rejected this approach for financial reporting because it is too hypothetical and ignores the going concern concept.

salary levels.[7] Those in favor of the projected benefit obligation contend that a promise by an employer to pay benefits based on a percentage of the employees' future salaries is far greater than a promise to pay a percentage of their current salary, and such a difference should be reflected in the pension liability and pension expense.

Moreover, companies discount to present value the estimated future benefits to be paid. Minor changes in the interest rate used to discount pension benefits can dramatically affect the measurement of the employer's obligation. For example, a 1 percent decrease in the discount rate can increase pension liabilities 15 percent. Accounting rules require that at each measurement date, a company must determine the appropriate discount rate used to measure the pension liability, based on current interest rates.

Recognition of the Net Funded Status of the Pension Plan

Companies must recognize on their balance sheet the full overfunded or underfunded status of their defined benefit pension plan. [3][8] The **overfunded** or **underfunded status** is measured as the difference between the fair value of the plan assets and the projected benefit obligation.

To illustrate, assume that Coker Company has a projected benefit obligation of $300,000, and the fair value of its plan assets is $210,000. In this case, Coker Company's pension plan is underfunded, and therefore it reports a pension liability of $90,000 ($300,000 – $210,000) on its balance sheet. If instead the fair value of Coker's plan assets were $430,000, it would report a pension asset of $130,000 ($430,000 – $300,000).

What Do the Numbers Mean? Roller Coaster

The chart below shows what has happened to the financial health of pension plans over the last few years. It is a real roller coaster. In 2010, by slowing the growth of pension liabilities and increasing contributions to pension funds, the S&P 500 companies reported a funded status of about 87 percent in 2010, dips in 2012 and 2014, and a climb to about 87 percent again in 2017.

At the turn of the century, when the stock market was strong, pension plans were overfunded. However, the bubble burst, and by 2002 companies in the S&P 1500 saw their pension plans funded at less than reported liabilities. Then, plans bounced back, and by 2007 pension plans were overfunded again. However, due to recent downturns in the wake of the financial crisis, plans are now underfunded again and the future is highly uncertain.

A number of factors cause a fund to change from being overfunded to underfunded. First, low interest rates decimate returns on pension plan assets. Second, using low interest rates to discount the projected benefit payments leads to a higher pension liability. Similarly, as was observed recently, actuaries may revise estimates related to mortality rates or expected salary levels, which could lead to an increase in the projected benefit obligation and more underfunded plans. Finally, more individuals are retiring and living longer, which leads to a depletion of the pension plan assets.

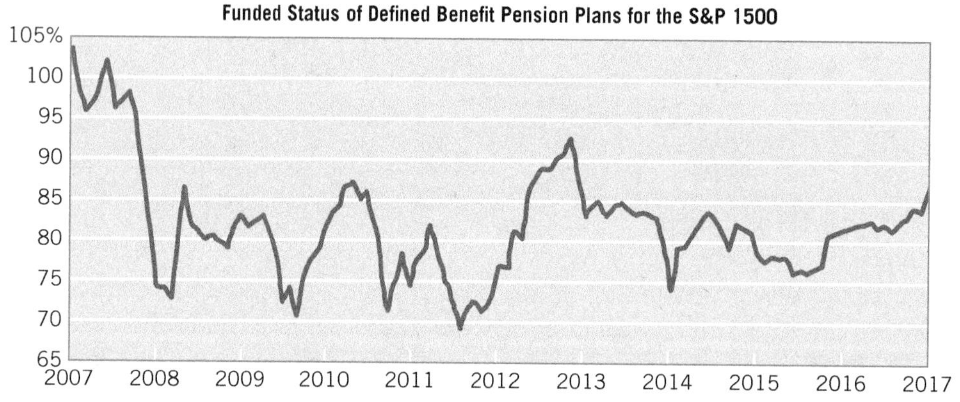

Source: https://www.mercer.com/newsroom/january-1500-pension-funded-status-increased.html (February 6, 2018).

Source: V. Monga, "Longer Lives Cut Premium to Offload Pensions," *Wall Street Journal* (February 3, 2015).

[7]When we use the term "present value of benefits" throughout this chapter, we really mean the *actuarial* present value of benefits. **Actuarial present value** is the amount payable adjusted to reflect the time value of money *and* the probability of payment (by means of decrements for events such as death, disability, withdrawals, or retirement) between the present date and the expected date of payment. For simplicity, though, we use the term "present value" instead of "actuarial present value" in our discussion.

[8]Recognize that GAAP applies to pensions as well as other postretirement benefit plans (OPEBs). Appendix 20A addresses the accounting for OPEBs.

Components of Pension Expense

There is broad agreement that companies should account for pension cost on the **accrual basis.**[9] The profession recognizes that **accounting for pension plans requires measurement of the cost and its identification with the appropriate time periods**. The determination of pension expense, however, is extremely complicated because it is a function of the following components.

1. ***Service cost.*** Service cost is the expense caused by the increase in pension benefits payable (the **projected benefit obligation**) to employees because of their services rendered during the current year. Actuaries compute **service cost** as the present value of the new benefits earned by employees during the year (see **Underlying Concepts**).
2. ***Interest on the liability.*** Because a pension is a deferred compensation arrangement, there is a time value of money factor. As a result, companies record the pension liability on a discounted basis. **Interest expense accrues each year on the projected benefit obligation just as it does on any discounted debt.** The actuary helps to select the interest rate, referred to as the **settlement rate**.
3. ***Actual return on plan assets.*** The return earned by the accumulated pension fund assets in a particular year is relevant in measuring the net cost to the employer of sponsoring an employee pension plan. Therefore, **a company should adjust annual pension expense for interest and dividends that accumulate within the fund, as well as increases and decreases in the fair value of the fund assets.**
4. ***Amortization of prior service cost.*** Pension plan amendments (including initiation of a pension plan) often include provisions to increase benefits (or in rare situations, to decrease benefits) for employee service provided in prior years. A company grants plan amendments with the expectation that it will realize economic benefits in future periods. Thus, **it allocates the cost (prior service cost) of providing these retroactive benefits to pension expense in the future, specifically to the remaining service-years of the affected employees.**
5. ***Gain or loss.*** Volatility in pension expense can result from sudden and large changes in the fair value of plan assets (resulting in differences between the actual return and the expected return on plan assets) and by changes in the projected benefit obligation (which changes when actuaries modify assumptions or when actual experience differs from expected experience). We will discuss this complex computation later in the chapter.

Underlying Concepts

The expense recognition principle and the definition of a liability justify accounting for pension cost on the accrual basis. This requires recording an expense when employees earn the future benefits, and recognizing an existing obligation to pay pensions later based on current services received.

Illustration 20.4 shows the **components of pension expense** and their effect on total pension expense (increase or decrease).

ILLUSTRATION 20.4

Components of Annual Pension Expense

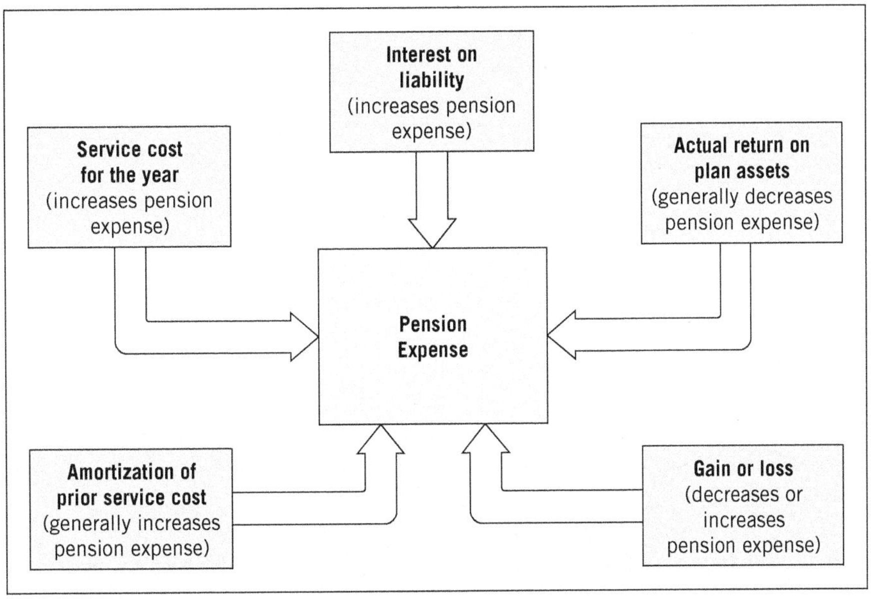

[9]At one time, companies applied the **cash basis** of accounting to pension plans by recognizing the amount paid in a particular accounting period as the pension expense for the period. The problem was that the amount paid or funded in a fiscal period depended on financial management and was too often discretionary. For example, funding could depend on the availability of cash, the level of earnings, or other factors unrelated to the requirements of the plan. Application of the cash basis made it possible to manipulate the amount of pension expense appearing in the income statement simply by varying the cash paid to the pension fund.

Service Cost

The service cost is the **actuarial present value of benefits attributed by the pension benefit formula to employee service during the period**. That is, the actuary predicts the additional benefits that an employer must pay under the plan's benefit formula as a result of the employees' current year's service, and then discounts the cost of those future benefits back to their present value.

The Board concluded that **companies must consider future compensation levels in measuring the present obligation and periodic pension expense if the plan benefit formula incorporates them**. In other words, the present obligation resulting from a promise to pay a benefit of 1 percent of an employee's **final pay** differs from the promise to pay 1 percent of **current pay**. To overlook this fact is to ignore an important aspect of pension expense. Thus, the FASB adopts the **benefits/years-of-service actuarial method, which determines pension expense based on future salary levels**.

Some object to this determination, arguing that a company should have more freedom to select an expense recognition pattern. Others believe that incorporating future salary increases into current pension expense is accounting for events that have not yet happened. They argue that if a company terminates the plan today, it pays only liabilities for accumulated benefits. **Nevertheless, the FASB indicates that the projected benefit obligation provides a more realistic measure of the employer's obligation under the plan on a going concern basis and, therefore, companies should use it as the basis for determining service cost.**

Interest on the Liability

The second component of pension expense is interest on the liability, or interest expense. Because a company defers paying the liability until maturity, the company records it on a discounted basis. The liability then accrues interest over the life of the employee. **The interest component is the interest for the period on the projected benefit obligation outstanding during the period.** The FASB did not address the question of how often to compound the interest cost. To simplify our illustrations and problem materials, we use a simple interest computation, applying the interest rate to the beginning-of-the-year balance of the projected benefit liability.

How do companies determine the interest rate to apply to the pension liability? The Board states that the assumed discount rate should **reflect the rates at which companies can effectively settle pension benefits**. In determining these settlement rates, companies should look to rates of return on high-quality fixed-income investments currently available, whose cash flows match the timing and amount of the expected benefit payments. The objective of selecting the assumed discount rates is to measure a single amount that, if invested in a portfolio of high-quality debt instruments, would provide the necessary future cash flows to pay the pension benefits when due.

Actual Return on Plan Assets

Pension plan assets are usually investments in stocks, bonds, other securities, and real estate that a company holds to earn a reasonable return, generally at minimum risk. Employer contributions and actual returns on pension plan assets increase pension plan assets. Benefits paid to retired employees decrease them. As indicated, the actual return earned on these assets increases the fund balance and correspondingly reduces the employer's net cost of providing employees' pension benefits. That is, the higher the actual return on the pension plan assets, the less the employer has to contribute eventually and, therefore, the less pension expense that it needs to report.

The actual return on the plan assets is the increase in pension funds from interest, dividends, and realized and unrealized changes in the fair value of the plan assets. Companies compute the actual return by adjusting the change in the plan assets for the effects of contributions during the year and benefits paid out during the year. The equation in Illustration 20.5, or a variation thereof, can be used to compute the actual return.

ILLUSTRATION 20.5

Equation for Computing Actual Return

$$\text{Actual Return} = \left(\begin{array}{c}\text{Plan Assets}\\\text{Ending Balance}\end{array} - \begin{array}{c}\text{Plan Assets}\\\text{Beginning Balance}\end{array}\right) - (\text{Contributions} - \text{Benefits Paid})$$

Stated another way, the actual return on plan assets is the difference between the **fair value of the plan assets** at the beginning of the period and at the end of the period, adjusted for contributions and benefit payments. **Illustration 20.6** uses the equation in Illustration 20.5 to compute the actual return, using some assumed amounts.

ILLUSTRATION 20.6

Computation of Actual Return on Plan Assets

Fair value of plan assets at end of period		$5,000,000
Deduct: Fair value of plan assets at beginning of period		4,200,000
Increase in fair value of plan assets		800,000
Deduct: Contributions to plan during period	$500,000	
Less benefits paid during period	300,000	200,000
Actual return on plan assets		$ 600,000

If the actual return on the plan assets is positive (a gain) during the period, a company subtracts it when computing pension expense. If the actual return is negative (a loss) during the period, the company adds it when computing pension expense.[10]

Using a Pension Worksheet

LEARNING OBJECTIVE 2

Use a worksheet for employer's pension plan entries.

We will now illustrate the basic computation of pension expense using the first three components: (1) service cost, (2) interest on the liability, and (3) actual return on plan assets. We discuss the other pension expense components (amortization of prior service cost, and gains and losses) in later sections.

Companies often use a worksheet to record pension-related information. As its name suggests, the worksheet is a working tool. A worksheet is **not** a permanent accounting record. It is neither a journal nor part of the general ledger. The worksheet is merely a device to make it easier to prepare entries and the financial statements.[11] **Illustration 20.7** shows the format of the **pension worksheet.**

ILLUSTRATION 20.7

Basic Format of Pension Worksheet

Pension Worksheet

Home Insert Page Layout Formulas Data Review View

P18 *fx*

	A	B	C	D	E	F
1						
2		General Journal Entries			Memo Record	
3		Annual		Pension	Projected	
4		Pension		Asset/	Benefit	Plan
5	Items	Expense	Cash	Liability	Obligation	Assets
6						
7						
8						
9						

[10]At this point, we use the actual rate of return. Later, for purposes of computing pension expense, we use the expected rate of return.

[11]The use of a pension entry worksheet is recommended and illustrated by Paul B. W. Miller, "The New Pension Accounting (Part 2)," *Journal of Accountancy* (February 1987), pp. 86–94.

The "General Journal Entries" columns of the worksheet (near the center) determine the entries to record in the formal general ledger accounts. The "Memo Record" columns (on the right side) maintain balances in the projected benefit obligation and the plan assets. The difference between the projected benefit obligation and the fair value of the plan assets is the **pension asset/liability**, which is reported in the balance sheet. If the projected benefit obligation is greater than the plan assets, a pension liability occurs. If the projected benefit obligation is less than the plan assets, a pension asset occurs.

On the first line of the worksheet, a company records the beginning balances (if any). It then records subsequent transactions and events related to the pension plan using debits and credits, using both sets of columns as if they were one. For each transaction or event, the debits must equal the credits. **The ending balance in the Pension Asset/Liability column should equal the net balance in the memo record.**

2020 Entries and Worksheet

To illustrate the use of a worksheet and how it helps in accounting for a pension plan, assume that on January 1, 2020, Zarle Company provides the following information related to its pension plan for the year 2020.

- Plan assets, January 1, 2020, are $100,000.
- Projected benefit obligation, January 1, 2020, is $100,000.
- Annual service cost is $9,000.
- Settlement rate is 10 percent.
- Actual return on plan assets is $10,000.
- Funding contributions are $8,000.
- Benefits paid to retirees during the year are $7,000.

Using this data, the worksheet in **Illustration 20.8** presents the beginning balances and all of the pension entries recorded by Zarle in 2020. Zarle records the beginning balances for the projected benefit obligation and the pension plan assets on the first line of the worksheet in the memo record. Because the projected benefit obligation and the plan assets are the same at January 1, 2020, the Pension Asset/Liability account has a zero balance at January 1, 2020.

ILLUSTRATION 20.8

Pension Worksheet—2020

Pension Worksheet—2020

	General Journal Entries			Memo Record	
Items	Annual Pension Expense	Cash	Pension Asset/ Liability	Projected Benefit Obligation	Plan Assets
Balance, Jan. 1, 2020			—	100,000 Cr.	100,000 Dr.
(a) Service cost	9,000 Dr.			9,000 Cr.	
(b) Interest cost	10,000 Dr.			10,000 Cr.	
(c) Actual return	10,000 Cr.				10,000 Dr.
(d) Contributions		8,000 Cr.			8,000 Dr.
(e) Benefits				7,000 Dr.	7,000 Cr.
Journal entry for 2020	9,000 Dr.	8,000 Cr.	1,000 Cr.*		
Balance, Dec. 31, 2020			1,000 Cr.**	112,000 Cr.	111,000 Dr.

*$9,000 – $8,000 = $1,000

**$112,000 – $111,000 = $1,000

Entry (a) in Illustration 20.8 records the service cost component, which increases pension expense by $9,000 and increases the liability (projected benefit obligation) by $9,000. Entry (b) accrues the interest expense component, which increases both the liability and the pension expense by $10,000 (the beginning projected benefit obligation multiplied by the settlement rate of 10 percent). Entry (c) records the actual return on the plan assets, which increases the plan assets and decreases the pension expense. Entry (d) records Zarle's contribution (funding) of assets to the pension fund, thereby decreasing cash by $8,000 and increasing plan assets by $8,000. Entry (e) records the benefit payments made to retirees, which results in equal $7,000 decreases to the plan assets and the projected benefit obligation.

Zarle makes the "formal journal entry" on December 31, which records the pension expense in 2020, as follows.

2020		
Pension Expense	9,000	
Cash		8,000
Pension Asset/Liability		1,000

Funded Status

The credit to Pension Asset/Liability for $1,000 represents the difference between the 2020 pension expense of $9,000 and the amount funded of $8,000. Pension Asset/Liability (credit) is a liability because Zarle underfunds the plan by $1,000. The Pension Asset/Liability account balance of $1,000 also equals the net of the balances in the memo accounts. **Illustration 20.9** shows that the projected benefit obligation exceeds the plan assets by $1,000, which reconciles to the pension liability reported in the balance sheet.

ILLUSTRATION 20.9

Pension Reconciliation Schedule—December 31, 2020

Projected benefit obligation (Credit)	$(112,000)
Plan assets at fair value (Debit)	111,000
Pension asset/liability (Credit)	$ (1,000)

If the net of the memo record balances is a credit, the reconciling amount in the pension asset/liability column will be a credit equal in amount. If the net of the memo record balances is a debit, the pension asset/liability amount will be a debit equal in amount. The worksheet is designed to produce this reconciling feature, which is useful later in the preparation of the financial statements and required note disclosure related to pensions.

In this illustration (for 2020), the debit to Pension Expense exceeds the credit to Cash, resulting in a credit to Pension Asset/Liability—the recognition of a liability. If the credit to Cash exceeded the debit to Pension Expense, Zarle would debit Pension Asset/Liability—the recognition of an asset.

Prior Service Cost (PSC)

LEARNING OBJECTIVE 3

Describe the accounting and amortization of prior service costs.

When either initiating (adopting) or amending a defined benefit plan, a company often provides benefits to employees for years of service before the date of initiation or amendment. As a result of this prior service cost, the projected benefit obligation is increased to recognize this additional liability. In many cases, the increase in the projected benefit obligation is substantial.

Amortization

Should a company report an expense for these prior service costs (PSC) at the time it initiates or amends a plan? The FASB says no. The Board's rationale is that the employer would not provide credit for past years of service unless it expects to receive benefits in the future. As a result, a company should not recognize the retroactive benefits as pension expense in the year of amendment. Instead, **the employer initially records the prior service cost as an adjustment to other comprehensive income. The employer then recognizes the prior service cost as a component of pension expense over the remaining service lives of the employees who are expected to benefit from the change in the plan.**

The cost of the retroactive benefits (including any benefits provided to existing retirees) is the increase in the projected benefit obligation at the date of the amendment. An actuary computes the amount of the prior service cost. Amortization of the prior service cost is also an accounting function performed with the assistance of an actuary.

The Board prefers a years-of-service method that is similar to a units-of-production computation. First, the company computes the total number of service-years to be worked by all of the participating employees. Second, it divides the prior service cost by the total number of service-years, to obtain a cost per service-year (the unit cost). Third, the company multiplies the number of service-years consumed each year by the cost per service-year, to obtain the annual amortization charge.

To illustrate the amortization of the prior service cost under the years-of-service method, assume that Zarle Company's defined benefit pension plan covers 170 employees. In its negotiations with the employees, Zarle Company amends its pension plan on January 1, 2021, and grants $80,000 of prior service costs to its employees. The employees are grouped according to expected years of retirement, as follows.

Group	Number of Employees	Expected Retirement on Dec. 31
A	40	2021
B	20	2022
C	40	2023
D	50	2024
E	20	2025
	170	

Illustration 20.10 shows computation of the service-years per year and the total service-years.

ILLUSTRATION 20.10

Computation of Service-Years

	Service-Years					
Year	A	B	C	D	E	Total
2021	40	20	40	50	20	170
2022		20	40	50	20	130
2023			40	50	20	110
2024				50	20	70
2025					20	20
	40	40	120	200	100	500

Computed on the basis of a prior service cost of $80,000 and a total of 500 service-years for all years, the cost per service-year is $160 ($80,000 ÷ 500). The annual amount of amortization based on a $160 cost per service-year is computed as shown in **Illustration 20.11**.

ILLUSTRATION 20.11

Computation of Annual Prior Service Cost Amortization

Year	Total Service-Years	×	Cost per Service-Year	=	Annual Amortization
2021	170		$160		$27,200
2022	130		160		20,800
2023	110		160		17,600
2024	70		160		11,200
2025	20		160		3,200
	500				$80,000

An alternative method of computing amortization of **prior service cost is permitted. Employers may use straight-line amortization over the average remaining service life of the employees.** In this case, with 500 service-years and 170 employees, the average would be 2.94 years (500 ÷ 170). The annual expense would be $27,211 ($80,000 ÷ 2.94). Using this method, Zarle Company would record expense in 2021, 2022, and 2023 as follows.

Year	Expense
2021	$27,211
2022	27,211
2023	25,578*
	$80,000

*.94 × $27,211

2021 Entries and Worksheet

Continuing the Zarle Company illustration into 2021, we note that the company amends the pension plan on January 1, 2021, to grant employees prior service benefits with a present value of $80,000. Zarle uses the annual amortization amounts, as computed in the previous section using the years-of-service approach ($27,200 for 2021). The following additional facts apply to the pension plan for the year 2021.

- Annual service cost is $9,500.
- Settlement rate is 10 percent.
- Actual return on plan assets is $11,100.
- Annual funding contributions are $20,000.
- Benefits paid to retirees during the year are $8,000.
- Amortization of prior service cost (PSC) using the years-of-service method is $27,200.
- Accumulated other comprehensive income (hereafter referred to as accumulated OCI) on December 31, 2020, is zero.

Illustration 20.12 presents a worksheet of all the pension entries and information recorded by Zarle in 2021. We now add an additional column to the worksheet to record the prior service cost adjustment to other comprehensive income. In addition, as shown in rows 19, 21, and 22, the other comprehensive income amount related to prior service cost is added to accumulated other comprehensive income ("Accumulated OCI") to arrive at a debit balance of $52,800 at December 31, 2021.

ILLUSTRATION 20.12 **Pension Worksheet—2021**

Pension Worksheet—2021

	A	B	C	D	E	F	G
1							
2		General Journal Entries				Memo Record	
3							
4–7	Items	Annual Pension Expense	Cash	Other Comprehensive Income Prior Service Cost	Pension Asset/ Liability	Projected Benefit Obligation	Plan Assets
8	Balance, Dec. 31, 2020				1,000 Cr.	112,000 Cr.	111,000 Dr.
9	(f) Prior service cost			80,000 Dr.		80,000 Cr.	0
10							
11	Balance, Jan. 1, 2021					192,000 Cr.	111,000 Dr.
12	(g) Service cost	9,500 Dr.				9,500 Cr.	
13	(h) Interest cost	19,200 Dr.				19,200 Cr.	
14	(i) Actual return	11,100 Cr.					11,100 Dr.
15	(j) Amortization of PSC	27,200 Dr.		27,200 Cr.			
16	(k) Contributions		20,000 Cr.				20,000 Dr.
17	(l) Benefits					8,000 Dr.	8,000 Cr.
18							
19	Journal entry for 2021	44,800 Dr.	20,000 Cr.	52,800 Dr.	77,600 Cr.		
20							
21	Accumulated OCI, Dec. 31, 2020			0			
22	Balance, Dec. 31, 2021			52,800 Dr.	78,600 Cr.	212,700 Cr.	134,100 Dr.
23							

The first line of the worksheet shows the beginning balances of the Pension Asset/Liability account and the memo accounts. Entry (f) records Zarle's granting of prior service cost, by adding $80,000 to the projected benefit obligation and decreasing other comprehensive income—prior service cost by the same amount. Entries (g), (h), (i), (k), and (l) are similar to the corresponding entries in 2020. To compute the interest cost on the projected benefit obligation for entry (h), we use the beginning projected benefit balance of $192,000, which has been adjusted for the prior service cost amendment on January 1, 2021. Entry (j) records the 2021 amortization of prior service cost by debiting Pension Expense for $27,200 and crediting **Other Comprehensive Income (PSC)** for the same amount.

Zarle makes the following journal entry on December 31 to formally record the 2021 pension expense (the sum of the annual pension expense column), and related pension information.

2021		
Pension Expense	44,800	
Other Comprehensive Income (PSC)	52,800	
Cash		20,000
Pension Asset/Liability		77,600

Because the debits to Pension Expense and to Other Comprehensive Income (PSC) exceed the funding, Zarle credits the Pension Asset/Liability account for the $77,600 difference. That account is a liability. In 2021, as in 2020, the balance of the Pension Asset/Liability account ($78,600) is equal to the net of the balances in the memo accounts, as shown in **Illustration 20.13**.

ILLUSTRATION 20.13

Pension Reconciliation Schedule—December 31, 2021

Projected benefit obligation (Credit)	$(212,700)
Plan assets at fair value (Debit)	134,100
Pension asset/liability (Credit)	$ (78,600)

The reconciliation is the formula that makes the worksheet work. It relates the components of pension accounting, recorded and unrecorded, to one another.

Gains and Losses

LEARNING OBJECTIVE 4

Explain the accounting and amortization for unexpected gains and losses.

Of great concern to companies that have pension plans are the uncontrollable and unexpected swings in pension expense that can result from (1) sudden and large changes in the fair value of plan assets, and (2) changes in actuarial assumptions that affect the amount of the projected benefit obligation. If these gains or losses impact fully the financial statements in the period of realization or incurrence, substantial fluctuations in pension expense result.

Therefore, the FASB decided to reduce the volatility associated with pension expense by using **smoothing techniques** that dampen and in some cases fully eliminate the fluctuations.

Smoothing Unexpected Gains and Losses on Plan Assets

One component of pension expense, actual return on plan assets, reduces pension expense (assuming the actual return is positive). A large change in the actual return can substantially affect pension expense for a year. Assume a company has a 40 percent return in the stock market for the year. Should this substantial, and perhaps one-time, event affect current pension expense?

Actuaries ignore current fluctuations when they develop a funding pattern to pay expected benefits in the future. They develop an **expected rate of return** and multiply it by an asset value weighted over a reasonable period of time to arrive at an **expected return on plan assets**. They then use this return to determine a company's funding pattern.

The FASB adopted the actuary's approach to dampen wide swings that might occur in the actual return. That is, a company includes the **expected return** on the plan assets as a component of pension expense, not the actual return in a given year. To achieve this goal, the company multiplies the expected rate of return by the market-related value of the plan assets. The **market-related asset value** of the plan assets is either the fair value of plan assets or a calculated value that recognizes changes in fair value in a systematic and rational manner. [4][12]

The difference between the expected return and the actual return is referred to as the **unexpected gain or loss**; the FASB uses the term **asset gains and losses**. **Asset gains** occur when actual return exceeds expected return; **asset losses** occur when actual return is less than expected return.

What happens to unexpected gains or losses in the accounting for pensions? Companies record asset gains and asset losses in an account, **Other Comprehensive Income (G/L)**, combining them with gains and losses accumulated in prior years. This treatment is similar to prior service cost. The Board believes this treatment is consistent with the practice of including in

[12]Companies may use different ways of determining the calculated market-related value for different classes of assets. For example, an employer might use fair value for bonds and a five-year moving-average for equities. But companies should consistently apply the manner of determining market-related value from year to year for each asset class. Throughout our Zarle illustrations, we assume that market-related values based on a calculated value and the fair value of plan assets are equal. *For homework purposes, use the fair value of plan assets as the measure for the market-related value.*

other comprehensive income certain changes in value that have not been recognized in net income (for example, unrealized gains and losses on available-for-sale debt securities). [5] In addition, the accounting is simple, transparent, and symmetrical.

To illustrate the computation of an unexpected gain or loss and its related accounting, assume that in 2022, Zarle Company has an actual return on plan assets of $12,000 when the expected return is $13,410 (the expected rate of return of 10% on plan assets times the beginning-of-the-year plan assets). The unexpected asset loss of $1,410 ($12,000 – $13,410) is debited to Other Comprehensive Income (G/L) and credited to Pension Expense. We show treatment of this loss in the worksheet in Illustration 20.18.

What Do the Numbers Mean? Pension Costs Ups and Downs

For some companies, pension plans generate real profits. The plans not only pay for themselves but also increase earnings. This happens when the expected return on pension assets exceed the company's annual costs. At MeadWestvaco, pension income amounted to approximately 27 percent of operating profit. It tallied 11 percent of operating profit at CenturyTel and 9.5 percent at Sun Trust Banks. The issue is important because in these cases management is not driving the operating income—pension income is. And as a result, income can change quickly.

Unfortunately, when the stock market stops booming, pension expense substantially increases for many companies. The reason: Expected return on a smaller asset base no longer offsets pension service costs and interest on the projected benefit obligation. As a result, many companies find it difficult to meet their earnings targets, at a time when meeting such targets is crucial to maintaining the stock price.

Smoothing Unexpected Gains and Losses on the Pension Liability

In estimating the projected benefit obligation (the liability), actuaries make assumptions about such items as mortality rate, retirement rate, turnover rate, disability rate, and salary amounts. Any change in these actuarial assumptions affects the amount of the projected benefit obligation. Seldom does actual experience coincide exactly with actuarial predictions. These unexpected gains or losses from changes in the projected benefit obligation are called **liability gains and losses**.

Companies report liability gains (resulting from unexpected decreases in the liability balance) and liability losses (resulting from unexpected increases) in Other Comprehensive Income (G/L). Companies combine the liability gains and losses in the same Other Comprehensive Income (G/L) account used for asset gains and losses. They accumulate the asset and liability gains and losses from year to year that are not amortized in Accumulated Other Comprehensive Income. This amount is reported on the balance sheet in the stockholders' equity section.

Corridor Amortization

The asset gains and losses and the liability gains and losses can offset each other. As a result, the Accumulated OCI account related to gains and losses may not grow very large. But, it is possible that no offsetting will occur and that the balance in the Accumulated OCI account related to gains and losses will continue to grow.

To limit the growth of the Accumulated OCI account, the FASB invented the **corridor approach** for amortizing the account's accumulated balance when it gets too large. How large is too large? The FASB set a limit of 10 percent of the larger of the beginning balances of the projected benefit obligation or the market-related value of the plan assets. **Above that size, the Accumulated OCI account related to gains and losses is considered too large and must be amortized.**

To illustrate the corridor approach, data for Callaway Co.'s projected benefit obligation and plan assets over a period of six years are shown in Illustration 20.14.

ILLUSTRATION 20.14

Computation of the Corridor

Beginning-of-the-Year Balances	Projected Benefit Obligation	Market-Related Asset Value	Corridor* +/− 10%
2019	$1,000,000	$ 900,000	$100,000
2020	1,200,000	1,100,000	120,000
2021	1,300,000	1,700,000	170,000
2022	1,500,000	2,250,000	225,000
2023	1,700,000	1,750,000	175,000
2024	1,800,000	1,700,000	180,000

*The corridor becomes 10% of the larger (in red type) of the projected benefit obligation or the market-related plan asset value.

How the corridor works becomes apparent when we portray the data graphically, as in **Illustration 20.15**.

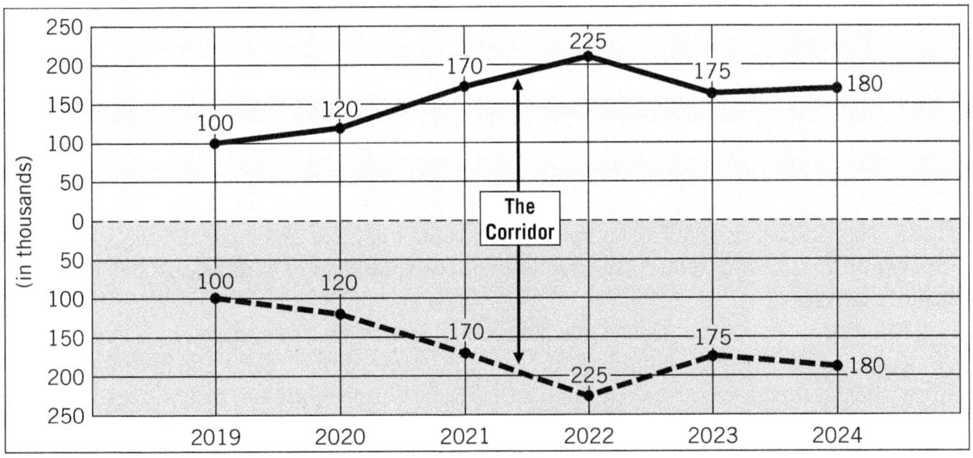

ILLUSTRATION 20.15

Graphic Illustration of the Corridor

If the balance in the Accumulated OCI account related to gains and losses stays within the upper and lower limits of the corridor, no amortization is required. In that case, Callaway carries forward unchanged the accumulated OCI related to gains and losses.

If amortization is required, the minimum amortization is the excess (of the accumulated OCI account above the corridor amount) divided by the average remaining service period of active employees who are expected to receive benefits under the plan. Callaway may use any systematic method of amortization of gains and losses in lieu of the minimum, provided it is greater than the minimum. It must use the method consistently for both gains and losses, and must disclose the amortization method used.

Example of Gains/Losses

In applying the corridor, companies should include amortization of the net gain or loss as a component of pension expense only if, at the **beginning of the year**, the net gain or loss in Accumulated OCI exceeded the corridor. That is, if no net gain or loss exists in Accumulated OCI at the beginning of the period, the company cannot recognize pension expense gains or losses in that period.

To illustrate the amortization of net gains and losses, assume the following information for Soft-White, Inc.

	Beginning of the Year		
	2020	2021	2022
Projected benefit obligation	$2,100,000	$2,600,000	$2,900,000
Market-related asset value	2,600,000	2,800,000	2,700,000

Soft-White recorded in Other Comprehensive Income actuarial losses of $400,000 in 2020 and $300,000 in 2021.

If the average remaining service life of all active employees is 5.5 years, the schedule to amortize the net gain or loss is as shown in Illustration 20.16.

ILLUSTRATION 20.16

Corridor Test and Gain/Loss Amortization Schedule

Year	Projected Benefit Obligation[a]	Plan Assets[a]	Corridor[b]	Accumulated OCI (G/L)[a]	Minimum Amortization of Loss (For Current Year)
2020	$2,100,000	$2,600,000	$260,000	$ -0-	$ -0-
2021	2,600,000	2,800,000	280,000	400,000	21,818[c]
2022	2,900,000	2,700,000	290,000	678,182[d]	70,579[d]

[a]All as of the beginning of the period.
[b]10% of the greater of projected benefit obligation or plan assets' market-related value.
[c]$400,000 − $280,000 = $120,000; $120,000 ÷ 5.5 = $21,818.
[d]$400,000 − $21,818 + $300,000 = $678,182; $678,182 − $290,000 = $388,182; $388,182 ÷ 5.5 = $70,579.

As Illustration 20.16 indicates, the loss recognized in 2021 increased pension expense by $21,818. This amount is small in comparison with the total loss of $400,000. It indicates that the corridor approach dampens the effects (reduces volatility) of these gains and losses on pension expense.

The rationale for the corridor is that gains and losses result from refinements in estimates as well as real changes in economic value. Over time, some of these gains and losses will offset one another. It therefore seems reasonable that Soft-White should not fully recognize gains and losses as a component of pension expense in the period in which they arise.

However, Soft-White should immediately recognize in net income certain gains and losses—if they arise from a single occurrence not directly related to the operation of the pension plan and not in the ordinary course of the employer's business. For example, a gain or loss that is directly related to a plant closing, a disposal of a business component, or a similar event that greatly affects the size of the employee work force should be recognized as a part of the gain or loss associated with that event.

For example, at one time, Bethlehem Steel reported a quarterly loss of $477 million. A great deal of this loss was attributable to future estimated benefits payable to workers who were permanently laid off. In this situation, the loss should be treated as an adjustment to the gain or loss on the plant closing and should not affect pension cost for the current or future periods.

Summary of Calculations for Asset Gain or Loss

The difference between the actual return on plan assets and the expected return on plan assets is the **unexpected asset gain or loss** component. This component defers the difference between the actual return and expected return on plan assets in computing current-year pension expense. Thus, after considering this component, **it is really the expected return on plan assets (not the actual return) that determines current pension expense.**

Companies determine the amortized net gain or loss by amortizing the Accumulated OCI amount related to net gain or loss at the beginning of the year subject to the corridor limitation. In other words, **if the accumulated gain or loss is greater than the corridor, these net gains and losses are subject to amortization**. Soft-White computed this minimum amortization by dividing the net gains or losses subject to amortization by the average remaining service period. When the current-year unexpected gain or loss is combined with the amortized net gain or loss, we determine the current-year gain or loss. Illustration 20.17 summarizes these gain and loss computations.

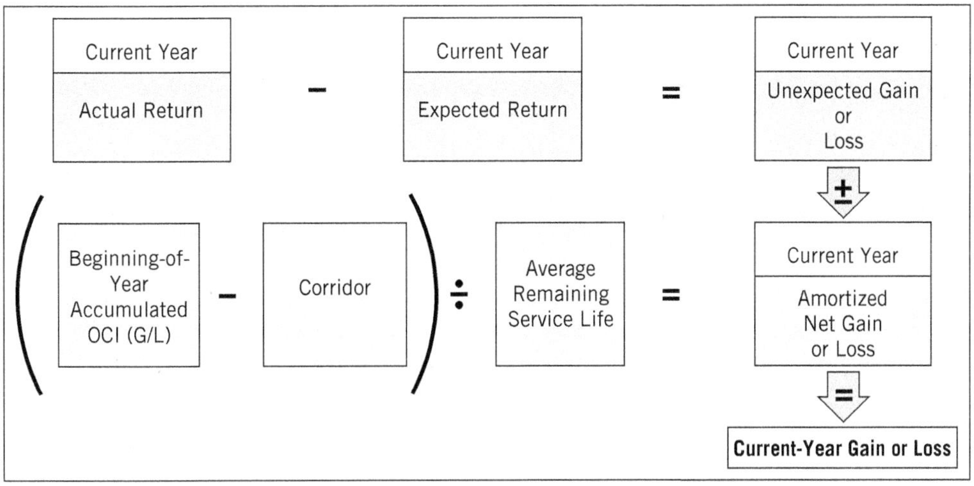

ILLUSTRATION 20.17

Graphic Summary of Gain or Loss Computation

In essence, these gains and losses are subject to *triple* smoothing. That is, companies first smooth the asset gain or loss by using the expected return. Second, they do not amortize the accumulated gain or loss at the beginning of the year unless it is greater than the corridor. Finally, they spread the excess over the remaining service life of existing employees.

Evolving Issue Bye Bye Corridor

Many companies have significant actuarial losses in their pension plans, which are presently deferred through use of the corridor approach. However, companies do have a choice—they may select any method of accounting for these deferred losses as long as it is systematic, rational, and consistently applied, and meets a minimum for recognition in the income statement.

Some companies have shifted away from the corridor approach and recognizing actuarial losses immediately. For example, **AT&T**, **Verizon Communications**, and **Honeywell International** have changed accounting principles from smoothing these losses to recognizing them in the year incurred.

Companies argue this approach provides more transparency for these losses that will directly affect pension expense in the current period (and this accounting is also more similar to IFRS). However, there is a silver lining for these companies—they can charge many of these deferred losses to past years. For example, the table in the adjacent column indicates deferred losses as of 2009 for three major companies.

	Deferred Losses (in billions)	Losses as % of Pension Assets
AT&T	$23.04	49%
Verizon	$12.20	43
Honeywell	$7.57	55

When AT&T changed to immediate recognition in 2010, it restated its previous years. In 2008, for example, AT&T increased its pension cost by $24.9 billion, which led to a net loss of $2.6 billion instead of a profit of $12.9 billion. As a result, in 2010 it recognized a much smaller pension cost of $3 billion. Skeptics suggest that AT&T made this change to charge these losses to prior periods. In other words, does anyone in 2016 care that the profit in 2008 was changed to a loss? In addition, once these losses are charged to prior periods, they no longer affect current and future earnings. **Ford** got on the mark-to-market bandwagon in 2016, taking a $2 billion earnings hit upon adoption.

Although earnings in the future will probably be more volatile due to fluctuations in pension expense, more companies are willing to move in the direction of immediate expensing to eliminate large deferred losses which would be a drag on future income.

Sources: Michael Rapoport, "Rewriting Pension History," *Wall Street Journal* (March 9, 2011); SEI, "Why Are Pension Plan Sponsors Switching to Mark-to-Market Accounting?" (October 2013); and B. Snavely, "Ford Earnings to Take $2 Billion Hit on Accounting Change," *Detroit Free Press* (January 20, 2017).

2022 Entries and Worksheet

Continuing the Zarle Company illustration, the following facts apply to the pension plan for 2022.

- Annual service cost is $13,000.
- Settlement rate is 10 percent; expected earnings rate is 10 percent.

- Actual return on plan assets is $12,000.
- Amortization of prior service cost (PSC) is $20,800.
- Annual funding contributions are $24,000.
- Benefits paid to retirees during the year are $10,500.
- Changes in actuarial assumptions resulted in an end-of-year projected benefit obligation of $265,000.

The worksheet in Illustration 20.18 presents all of Zarle's 2022 pension entries and related information. The first line of the worksheet records the beginning balances that relate to the pension plan. In this case, Zarle's beginning balances are the ending balances from its 2021 pension worksheet in Illustration 20.12.

ILLUSTRATION 20.18 Pension Worksheet—2022

Pension Worksheet—2022

	General Journal Entries					Memo Record	
			Other Comprehensive Income				
Items	Annual Pension Expense	Cash	Prior Service Cost	Gains/Losses	Pension Asset/ Liability	Projected Benefit Obligation	Plan Assets
Balance, Jan. 1, 2022					78,600 Cr.	212,700 Cr.	134,100 Dr.
(m) Service cost	13,000 Dr.					13,000 Cr.	
(n) Interest cost	21,270 Dr.					21,270 Cr.	
(o) Actual return	12,000 Cr.						12,000 Dr.
(p) Unexpected loss	1,410 Cr.			1,410 Dr.			
(q) Amortization of PSC	20,800 Dr.		20,800 Cr.				
(r) Contributions		24,000 Cr.					24,000 Dr.
(s) Benefits						10,500 Dr.	10,500 Cr.
(t) Liability increase				28,530 Dr.		28,530 Cr.	
Journal entry for 2022	41,660 Dr.	24,000 Cr.	20,800 Cr.	29,940 Dr.	26,800 Cr.		
Accumulated OCI, Dec. 31, 2021			52,800 Dr.	0			
Balance, Dec. 31, 2022*			32,000 Dr.	29,940 Dr.	105,400 Cr.	265,000 Cr.	159,600 Dr.
*Accumulated OCI (PSC)	$32,000 Dr.						
Accumulated OCI (G/L)	29,940 Dr.						
Accumulated OCI, Dec. 31, 2022	$61,940 Dr.						

Entries (m), (n), (o), (q), (r), and (s) are similar to the corresponding entries in 2020 or 2021.

Entries (o) and (p) are related. We explained the recording of the actual return in entry (o) in both 2020 and 2021; it is recorded similarly in 2022. In both 2020 and 2021, Zarle assumed that the actual return on plan assets was equal to the expected return on plan assets. In 2022, the expected return of $13,410 (the expected rate of return of 10 percent times the beginning-of-the-year plan assets' balance of $134,100) is higher than the actual return of $12,000. To smooth pension expense, Zarle defers the unexpected loss of $1,410 ($13,410 – $12,000) by debiting the Other Comprehensive Income (G/L) account and crediting Pension Expense. **As a result of this adjustment, the expected return on the plan assets is the amount actually used to compute pension expense.**

Entry (t) records the change in the projected benefit obligation resulting from the change in the actuarial assumptions. As indicated, the actuary has now computed the ending balance to be $265,000. Given the PBO balance at December 31, 2021, and the related transactions during 2022, the PBO balance to date is computed as shown in Illustration 20.19.

December 31, 2021, PBO balance	$212,700
Service cost [entry (m)]	13,000
Interest cost [entry (n)]	21,270
Benefits paid [entry (s)]	(10,500)
December 31, 2022, PBO balance (before liability increases)	$236,470

ILLUSTRATION 20.19

Projected Benefit Obligation Balance (Unadjusted)

The difference between the ending balance of $265,000 and the balance of $236,470 before the liability increase is $28,530 ($265,000 – $236,470). This $28,530 increase in the employer's liability is an unexpected loss. The journal entry on December 31, 2022, to record the pension information is as follows.

Pension Expense	41,660	
Other Comprehensive Income (G/L)	29,940	
Cash		24,000
Other Comprehensive Income (PSC)		20,800
Pension Asset/Liability		26,800

As the 2022 worksheet indicates, the $105,400 balance in the Pension Asset/Liability account at December 31, 2022, is equal to the net of the balances in the memo accounts. Illustration 20.20 shows this computation.

Projected benefit obligation (Credit)	$(265,000)
Plan assets at fair value (Debit)	159,600
Pension asset/liability	$(105,400)

ILLUSTRATION 20.20

Pension Reconciliation Schedule—December 31, 2022

2023 Entries and Worksheet—A Comprehensive Example

Incorporating the corridor computation, we continue the Zarle Company pension plan accounting based on the following facts for 2023.

- Service cost is $16,000.
- Settlement rate is 10 percent; expected rate of return is 10 percent.
- Actual return on plan assets is $22,000.
- Amortization of prior service cost is $17,600.
- Annual funding contributions are $27,000.
- Benefits paid to retirees during the year are $18,000.
- Average service life of all covered employees is 20 years.

Zarle prepares a worksheet to facilitate accumulation and recording of the components of pension expense and maintenance of amounts related to the pension plan. Illustration 20.21 shows that worksheet, which uses the basic data presented above. Beginning-of-the-year 2023 account balances are the December 31, 2022, balances from Zarle's 2022 pension worksheet in Illustration 20.18.

ILLUSTRATION 20.21 Comprehensive Pension Worksheet—2023

Comprehensive Pension Worksheet—2023

Home Insert Page Layout Formulas Data Review View

P18 fx

	A	B	C	D	E	F	G	H
1								
2			**General Journal Entries**				**Memo Record**	
3								
4				Other				
5		Annual		Comprehensive Income		Pension	Projected	
6		Pension		Prior Service		Asset/	Benefit	
7	Items	Expense	Cash	Cost	Gains/Losses	Liability	Obligation	Plan Assets
8	Balance, Dec. 31, 2022					105,400 Cr.	265,000 Cr.	159,600 Dr.
9	(aa) Service cost	16,000 Dr.					16,000 Cr.	
10	(bb) Interest cost	26,500 Dr.					26,500 Cr.	
11	(cc) Actual return	22,000 Cr.						22,000 Dr.
12	(dd) Unexpected gain	6,040 Dr.			6,040 Cr.			
13	(ee) Amortization of PSC	17,600 Dr.		17,600 Cr.				
14	(ff) Contributions		27,000 Cr.					27,000 Dr.
15	(gg) Benefits						18,000 Dr.	18,000 Cr.
16	(hh) Amortization of loss	172 Dr.			172 Cr.			
17								
18	Journal entry for 2023	44,312 Dr.	27,000 Cr.	17,600 Cr.	6,212 Cr.	6,500 Dr.		
19								
20	Accumulated OCI, Dec. 31, 2022			32,000 Dr.	29,940 Dr.			
21	Balance, Dec. 31, 2023*			14,400 Dr.	23,728 Dr.	98,900 Cr.	289,500 Cr.	190,600 Dr.
22								
23	*Accumulated OCI (PSC)	$14,400 Dr.						
24	Accumulated OCI (G/L)	23,728 Dr.						
25	Accumulated OCI, Dec. 31, 2023	$38,128 Dr.						
26								

Worksheet Explanations and Entries

Entries (aa) through (gg) are similar to the corresponding entries previously explained in the prior years' worksheets, with the exception of entry (dd). In 2022, the expected return on plan assets exceeded the actual return, producing an unexpected loss. In 2023, the actual return of \$22,000 exceeds the expected return of \$15,960 (\$159,600 × 10%), resulting in an unexpected gain of \$6,040, entry (dd). By netting the gain of \$6,040 against the actual return of \$22,000, pension expense is affected only by the expected return of \$15,960.

A new entry (hh) in Zarle's worksheet results from application of the corridor test on the accumulated balance of net gain or loss in accumulated other comprehensive income. Zarle Company begins 2023 with a balance in the net loss account of \$29,940. The company applies the corridor test in 2023 to determine whether the balance is excessive and should be amortized. In 2023, the corridor is 10 percent of the larger of the beginning-of-the-year projected benefit obligation of \$265,000 or the plan asset's \$159,600 market-related asset value (assumed to be fair value). The corridor for 2023 is \$26,500 (\$265,000 × 10%). Because the balance in Accumulated OCI is a net loss of \$29,940, the excess (outside the corridor) is \$3,440 (\$29,940 – \$26,500). Zarle amortizes the \$3,440 excess over the average remaining service life of all employees. Given an average remaining service life of 20 years, the amortization in 2023 is \$172 (\$3,440 ÷ 20). In the 2023 pension worksheet, Zarle debits Pension Expense for \$172 and credits that amount to Other Comprehensive Income (G/L). **Illustration 20.22** shows the computation of the \$172 amortization charge.

ILLUSTRATION 20.22

Computation of 2023 Amortization Charge (Corridor Test)

2023 Corridor Test	
Net (gain) or loss at beginning of year in accumulated OCI	$29,940
10% of larger of PBO or market-related asset value of plan assets	(26,500)
Amortizable amount	$ 3,440
Average service life of all employees	20 years
2023 amortization ($3,440 ÷ 20 years)	$172

Zarle formally records pension expense for 2023 as follows.

2023		
Pension Expense	44,312	
Pension Asset/Liability	6,500	
Cash		27,000
Other Comprehensive Income (G/L)		6,212
Other Comprehensive Income (PSC)		17,600

Reporting Pension Plans in Financial Statements

LEARNING OBJECTIVE 5

Describe the requirements for reporting pension plans in financial statements.

As you might suspect, a phenomenon as significant and complex as pensions involves extensive reporting and disclosure requirements. We will cover these requirements in four categories: (1) assets and liabilities, (2) net income, (3) comprehensive income, and (4) the notes to the financial statements.

Assets and Liabilities

Companies must recognize on their balance sheet the overfunded (pension asset) or underfunded (pension liability) status of their defined benefit pension plan. The overfunded or underfunded status is measured as the difference between the fair value of the plan assets and the projected benefit obligation.[13] In Zarle's case, the projected benefit obligation is

[13]Some companies have two or more pension plans. The Board takes the position that **all overfunded plans should be combined** and shown as a pension asset on the balance sheet. Similarly, if the company has two or more underfunded plans, the **underfunded plans are combined and shown as one amount** on the balance sheet.

The FASB rejected the alternative of combining *all* plans and representing the net amount as a single net asset or net liability. The rationale: A company does not have the ability to offset excess assets of one plan against underfunded obligations of another plan. Furthermore, netting all plans is inappropriate because offsetting assets and liabilities is not permitted under GAAP unless a right of offset exists.

greater than the plan assets at December 31, 2023. As a result, Zarle reports a net pension liability. The current portion of a net pension liability represents the amount of benefit payments to be paid in the next 12 months (or operating cycle, if longer), if that amount cannot be funded from existing plan assets. Otherwise, the pension liability is classified as a noncurrent liability.[14]

In the event that the fair value of plan assets exceeds the projected benefit obligation (the plan is overfunded), companies will report a net pension asset. However, no portion of a pension asset is reported as a current asset. That is, the excess of the fair value of the plan assets over the benefit obligation is classified as a noncurrent asset. The rationale for noncurrent classification is that the pension plan assets are restricted. That is, these assets are used to fund the projected benefit obligation, and therefore noncurrent classification is appropriate.

Net Income

Pension expense includes multiple components (service cost, interest cost, return on assets, and amortization of various amounts such as prior service cost and gains and losses) deferred from prior periods. The FASB requires presentation of the components of pension expense as follows.

1. Service cost component is reported as pension expense in income from operations (often as part of compensation expense).
2. Other components of pension expense are generally reported as one net amount in the "Other expenses and losses" section below income from operations. [7]

The rationale for this segregation is that presentation of pension expense as one amount combines amounts that are different in their predictive value, resulting in a presentation that is of limited value to financial statement users. The FASB indicated that service cost is the component that originates from employee service during the current period and has a significantly different effect in terms of information-usefulness compared to other pension expense components.

To illustrate the reporting of pension expense on the income statement, information from Zarle Company's 2023 worksheet (Illustration 20.21) is used. Zarle's worksheet indicates that service cost component of pension expense is $16,000, and other components of pension expense are $28,312 ($44,312 – $16,000). Assuming the following additional information for Zarle Company (sales revenue $2,000,000; cost of goods sold $1,500,000; other operating expenses, excluding pension expense related to service cost $110,000), Illustration 20.23 presents Zarle's income statement for 2023.

ILLUSTRATION 20.23

Income Statement—2023

Zarle Company
Income Statement
For the Year Ended December 31, 2023

Sales revenue	$2,000,000
Cost of goods sold	1,500,000
Gross profit	500,000
Pension expense (service cost)	16,000
Other operating expenses	110,000
Income from operations	374,000
Other expenses and losses	
Pension expense (other components)	28,312
Net income	$ 345,688

[14] At a minimum, companies must disclose the amount of assets allocated to equities, government and corporate bonds, mortgage-backed securities, derivatives, and real estate. Also, information on concentrations of risk must be explained. Finally, fair value disclosures would be required, including classification of amounts into levels of the fair value hierarchy. [6]

If Zarle does not report income from operations, it then has the discretion to report the other components of pension expense wherever it is appropriate. Such presentation should convey the underlying nature of these components and be separated from the service cost component. *For homework purposes, assume that the income statement includes an operating income subtotal.*

Comprehensive Income

In addition to the pension expense reported on the income statement, companies are also required to recognize actuarial gains and losses and prior service costs that originate in the current period in other comprehensive income. Actuarial gains and losses not recognized as part of pension expense are recognized as increases and decreases in other comprehensive income. The same type of accounting is also used for prior service cost. The Board requires that the prior service cost arising in the year of the amendment (which increases the projected benefit obligation) be recognized by an offsetting debit to other comprehensive income. By recognizing both actuarial gains and losses and prior service cost as part of other comprehensive income, the Board believes that the usefulness of financial statements is enhanced.

To illustrate, Zarle Company's 2023 worksheet is used. Zarle's worksheet indicates that both prior service cost of $17,600 and actuarial gains of $6,212 are amortized to pension expense in 2023. The increase in other comprehensive income of $23,812 is computed as shown in **Illustration 20.24**.

ILLUSTRATION 20.24
Computation of Other Comprehensive Income

Prior service cost amortization	$17,600
Gains and losses amortization	6,212
Other comprehensive income	$23,812

Illustration 20.25 shows the computation of comprehensive income for 2023 for Zarle Company.

ILLUSTRATION 20.25
Computation of Comprehensive Income

Net income	$345,688
Other comprehensive income	23,812
Comprehensive income	$369,500

As discussed in Chapter 4, the components of other comprehensive income must be reported in one of two ways: (1) in a second income statement, or (2) in a combined statement of comprehensive income. Regardless of the format used, net income must be added to other comprehensive income to arrive at comprehensive income. *For homework purposes, use the second income statement approach unless stated otherwise.* Earnings per share information related to comprehensive income is not required.

To illustrate the second income statement approach, assume that Zarle Company has reported **a traditional income statement**. The comprehensive income statement is then shown in **Illustration 20.26**.

ILLUSTRATION 20.26
Comprehensive Income Reporting

Zarle Company
Comprehensive Income Statement
For the Year Ended December 31, 2023

Net income		$345,688
Other comprehensive loss		
Actuarial liability loss	$6,212	
Prior service cost	17,600	23,812
Comprehensive income		$369,500

Illustration 20.27 shows the computation of "Accumulated other comprehensive loss" as reported in stockholders' equity at December 31, 2023.

ILLUSTRATION 20.27
Computation of Accumulated Other Comprehensive Income

Accumulated other comprehensive loss, January 1, 2023	$61,940
Other comprehensive income	23,812
Accumulated other comprehensive loss, December 31, 2023	$38,128

Regardless of the display format for the income statement, the accumulated other comprehensive loss is reported in the stockholders' equity section of the balance sheet of Zarle Company as shown in Illustration 20.28. (Illustration 20.28 uses assumed data for the common stock and retained earnings information.)

ILLUSTRATION 20.28
Reporting of Accumulated OCI

Zarle Company
Balance Sheet
As of December 31, 2023
(Stockholders' Equity Section)

Stockholders' equity	
Common stock	$100,000
Retained earnings	60,000
Accumulated other comprehensive loss	38,128
Total stockholders' equity	$121,872

By providing information on the components of comprehensive income as well as total accumulated other comprehensive income, the company communicates all changes in net assets.

In this illustration, it is assumed that the accumulated other comprehensive income at January 1, 2023, is not adjusted for the amortization of any prior service cost or actuarial gains and losses that would change pension expense. As discussed in the earlier examples, these items will be amortized into pension expense in future periods.

Underlying Concepts

Does it make a difference to users of financial statements whether companies recognize pension information in the financial statements or disclose it only in the notes? The FASB was unsure, so in accord with the full disclosure principle, it decided to provide extensive pension plan disclosures.

Within the Notes to the Financial Statements

Pension plans are frequently important to understanding a company's financial position, results of operations, and cash flows. Therefore, a company discloses the following information, either in the body of the financial statements or in the notes (see Underlying Concepts). [8]

1. A schedule showing all the major components of pension expense. ***Rationale:*** Information provided about the components of pension expense helps users better understand how a company determines pension expense. It also is useful in forecasting a company's net income.
2. A reconciliation showing how the projected benefit obligation and the fair value of the plan assets changed from the beginning to the end of the period. ***Rationale:*** Disclosing

the projected benefit obligation, the fair value of the plan assets, and changes in them should help users understand the economics underlying the obligations and resources of these plans. Explaining the changes in the projected benefit obligation and fair value of plan assets in the form of a reconciliation provides a more complete disclosure and makes the financial statements more understandable.

3. A disclosure of the rates used in measuring the benefit amounts (discount rate, expected return on plan assets, rate of compensation). ***Rationale:*** Disclosure of these rates permits users to determine the reasonableness of the assumptions applied in measuring the pension liability and pension expense.
4. A table indicating the allocation of pension plan assets by category (equity securities, debt securities, real estate, and other assets), and showing the percentage of the fair value to total plan assets. In addition, a company must include a narrative description of investment policies and strategies, including the target allocation percentages (if used by the company). ***Rationale:*** Such information helps financial statement users evaluate the pension plan's exposure to market risk and possible cash flow demands on the company. It also will help users better assess the reasonableness of the company's expected rate of return assumption.
5. The **expected benefit payments** to be paid to current plan participants for each of the next five fiscal years and in the aggregate for the five fiscal years thereafter. Also required is disclosure of a company's best **estimate of expected contributions** to be paid to the plan during the next year. ***Rationale:*** These disclosures provide information related to the cash outflows of the company. With this information, financial statement users can better understand the potential cash outflows related to the pension plan. They can better assess the liquidity and solvency of the company, which helps in assessing the company's overall financial flexibility.
6. The nature and amount of changes in plan assets and benefit obligations recognized in net income and in other comprehensive income of each period. ***Rationale:*** This disclosure provides information on pension elements affecting the projected benefit obligation and plan assets and on whether those amounts have been recognized in income or deferred to future periods.
7. The accumulated amount of changes in plan assets and benefit obligations that have been recognized in other comprehensive income. ***Rationale:*** This information indicates the pension-related balances recognized in stockholders' equity, which could affect future income.

In summary, the disclosure requirements are extensive, and purposely so (see **Global View**). One factor that has been a challenge for useful pension reporting has been the lack of consistent terminology. Furthermore, a substantial amount of offsetting is inherent in the measurement of pension expense and the pension liability. These disclosure requirements are designed to address these concerns and take some of the mystery out of pension reporting.[15]

Illustration 20.29 shows the note disclosure of Zarle's pension plan for 2023. Note that this example assumes that the pension liability is noncurrent and that the 2024 adjustment for amortization of the net gain or loss and amortization of prior service cost are the same as 2023.

Global View

The FASB's proposed Accounting Standards Update on presentation of pension expense, if adopted, will align GAAP with IFRS.

[15]As part of its Disclosure Framework project, the FASB has issued Accounting Standards Update (ASU) 2018-14 (August 2018) to improve financial reporting of pensions and other postretirement benefits (discussed in Appendix 20A). This ASU makes defined benefit plan disclosures more useful by adding disclosure requirements (e.g., descriptions of plan benefits and the reasons for significant gains and losses) as requested by users. The ASU also eliminates less-useful disclosures as indicated by users (e.g., the amount of the accumulated benefit obligation).

ILLUSTRATION 20.29

Minimum Note Disclosure of Pension Plan, Zarle Company, 2023

Zarle Company
Notes to the Financial Statements

Note D. The company has a pension plan covering substantially all of its employees. The plan is noncontributory and provides pension benefits that are based on the employee's compensation during the three years immediately preceding retirement. The pension plan's assets consist of cash, stocks, and bonds. The company's funding policy is consistent with the relevant government (ERISA) and tax regulations.

Pension expense for 2023 is comprised of the following components of pension cost.

Components of pension expense

Service cost	$16,000	
Interest on projected benefit obligation	26,500	
Expected return on plan assets	(15,960)	
Amortization of prior service cost	17,600	
Amortization of net loss	172	
Pension expense		$44,312

Amounts recognized in other comprehensive income

Other changes in plan assets and benefit obligations recognized in other comprehensive income		
Net actuarial gain	$ 6,212	
Amortization of prior service cost	17,600	
Total recognized in other comprehensive income		(23,812)
Total recognized in pension expense and other comprehensive income		$20,500

The estimated net actuarial loss and prior service cost for the defined benefit pension plan that will be amortized from accumulated other comprehensive income into pension expense over the next year are estimated to be the same as this year.

The amount recognized as a long-term liability in the balance sheet is as follows:

Amounts recognized in the balance sheet

Noncurrent liability	
Pension liability	$98,900

The amounts recognized in accumulated other comprehensive income related to pensions consist of:

Net actuarial loss	$23,728
Prior service cost	14,400
Total	$38,128

Reconciliations of pension liability and plan assets

Change in benefit obligation	
Benefit obligation at beginning of year	$265,000
Service cost	16,000
Interest cost	26,500
Amendments (Prior service cost)	-0-
Actuarial gain	-0-
Benefits paid	(18,000)
Benefit obligation at end of year	289,500
Change in plan assets	
Fair value of plan assets at beginning of year	159,600
Actual return on plan assets	22,000
Contributions	27,000
Benefits paid	(18,000)
Fair value of plan assets at end of year	190,600
Funded status (liability)	$ 98,900

Funded status of plan

Rates used to estimate plan elements

The weighted-average discount rate used in determining the 2023 projected benefit obligation was 10 percent. The rate of increase in future compensation levels used in computing the 2023 projected benefit obligation was 4.5 percent. The weighted-average expected long-term rate of return on the plan's assets was 10 percent.

Illustrations 20.30 and 20.31 present four-year summaries for the Zarle example related to the key disclosures of pension expense and the funded status of the pension plan (based on the information from the worksheets in Illustrations 20.8, 20.12, 20.18, and 20.21).

ILLUSTRATION 20.30

Summary of Expense Components—2020, 2021, 2022, 2023

Zarle Company

	2020	2021	2022	2023
Components of pension expense				
Service cost	$ 9,000	$ 9,500	$13,000	$16,000
Interest cost	10,000	19,200	21,270	26,500
Expected return on plan assets	(10,000)	(11,100)	(13,410)*	(15,960)*
Amortization of prior service cost	-0-	27,200	20,800	17,600
Amortization of loss	-0-	-0-	-0-	172
Pension expense	$ 9,000	$44,800	$41,660	$44,312

*Note that the expected return must be disclosed, not the actual return. In 2022, the expected return is $13,410, which is the actual gain ($12,000) adjusted by the unrecognized loss ($1,410). In 2023, the expected return is $15,960, which is the actual gain ($22,000) adjusted by the unrecognized gain ($6,040).

ILLUSTRATION 20.31

Pension Reconciliation for Zarle Company—2020, 2021, 2022, 2023

Zarle Company
Pension Reconciliation

	2020	2021	2022	2023
Change in benefit obligation				
Benefit obligation at beginning of year	$100,000	$112,000	$ 212,700	$265,000
Service cost	9,000	9,500	13,000	16,000
Interest cost	10,000	19,200	21,270	26,500
Amendments (Prior service cost)	-0-	80,000	-0-	-0-
Actuarial loss	-0-	-0-	28,530	-0-
Benefits paid	(7,000)	(8,000)	(10,500)	(18,000)
Benefit obligation at end of year	112,000	212,700	265,000	289,500
Change in plan assets				
Fair value of plan assets at beginning of year	100,000	111,000	134,100	159,600
Actual return on plan assets	10,000	11,100	12,000	22,000
Contributions	8,000	20,000	24,000	27,000
Benefits paid	(7,000)	(8,000)	(10,500)	(18,000)
Fair value of plan assets at end of year	111,000	134,100	159,600	190,600
Funded status (Pension asset/liability)	$ (1,000)	$ (78,600)	$(105,400)	$ (98,900)

Special Issues

The Pension Reform Act of 1974

A classic example of the unfortunate consequences of an underfunded pension plan is the 1963 shutdown of the **Studebaker Automobile** operations in South Bend, Indiana, in which 4,500 workers lost 85 percent of their vested benefits. As a result of such situations, the Employee Retirement Income Security Act of 1974—**ERISA**—was passed. The legislation affects virtually every private retirement plan in the United States. It attempts to safeguard employees' pension rights by mandating many pension plan requirements, including minimum funding, participation, and vesting (see **Underlying Concepts**).

These requirements can influence the employers' cash flows significantly. Under this legislation, annual funding is no longer discretionary. An employer now must fund the plan in accordance with an actuarial funding method that over time will be sufficient to pay for all

Underlying Concepts

Many plans are underfunded but still quite viable. For example, at one time **Loews Corp.** had a $159 million shortfall, but also had earnings of $594 million and a good net worth. Thus, the going concern assumption permits us to ignore pension underfundings in some cases because in the long run they are not significant.

pension obligations. If companies do not fund their plans in a reasonable manner, they may be subject to fines and/or loss of tax deductions.[16]

The law requires plan administrators to publish a comprehensive description and summary of their plans, along with detailed annual reports that include many supplementary schedules and statements.

Another important provision of the act is the creation of the **Pension Benefit Guaranty Corporation (PBGC)**. **The PBGC's purpose is to administer terminated plans** and to impose liens on an employer's assets for certain unfunded pension liabilities. If a company terminates its pension plan, the PBGC can effectively impose a lien against the employer's assets for the excess of the present value of guaranteed vested benefits over the pension fund assets. This lien generally has had the status of a tax lien; it takes priority over most other creditorship claims. This section of the act gives the PBGC the power to force an involuntary termination of a pension plan whenever the risks related to nonpayment of the pension obligation seem too great. Because ERISA restricts to 30 percent of net worth the lien that the PBGC can impose, the PBGC must monitor all plans to ensure that net worth is sufficient to meet the pension benefit obligations.

A large number of terminated plans have caused the PBGC to pay out substantial benefits. Currently the PBGC receives its funding from employers, who contribute a certain dollar amount for each employee covered under the plan.[17]

What Do the Numbers Mean? Who Guarantees the Guarantor?

The **Pension Benefit Guaranty Corporation (PBGC)** in a recent annual report indicates that its primary mission is to encourage the continuation and maintenance of voluntary private pension plans. It's an obligation which the PBGC takes seriously. However, the trends are ominous:

- Americans today are spending more years in retirement. They're healthier and more active, which is great news. Unfortunately, pensions haven't kept up.
- Many businesses, for competitive and other reasons, continue to reduce their support for retirement plans. Some have switched from a defined benefit plan to a defined contribution plan which costs less and comes with fewer obligations. Others offer lump-sum cash payments to employees or retirees to settle the employer's obligations.
- Left on their own, many people save less, as well as invest and plan less well. They also pay higher fees and they get lower returns.
- Many people defer retirement but still don't have enough money for retirement—and they're worried. One poll cited by the Senate Health, Education, Labor, and Pensions Committee says that 92 percent of people think there's a retirement crisis. They're right to be concerned.

Add to these concerns that obligations in pension plans today greatly exceed pension assets. Finally, the PBGC has a problem as well—a large deficit in its accounts. The following chart indicates that downward spiral in the net worth of the PBGC over the last 15 years as pension payments have exceeded premiums received.

[16]In 2006, Congress passed the Pension Protection Act. This law has many provisions. One important aspect of the act is that it forced many companies to expedite their contributions to their pension plans. One group estimates that companies in the S&P 500 had to contribute $47 billion to their pension plans when the new rules were fully phased in for 2006. That amount is about 57 percent more than the $30 billion that companies were expecting to contribute to their plans that year. Subsequently, Congress continues to provide pension funding relief. For example, in the "Moving Ahead for Progress in the 21st Century" Act (enacted July 6, 2012), companies can use a higher discount rate based on high-grade bond yields averaged over 25 years, which helps reduce the pension liability and required contributions.

[17]**Pan American Airlines** is a good illustration of how difficult it is to assess when to terminate. When Pan Am filed for bankruptcy in 1991, it had a pension liability of $900 million. From 1983 to 1991, the IRS gave it six waivers so it did not have to make contributions. When Pan Am terminated the plan, there was little net worth left upon which to impose a lien. An additional accounting problem relates to the manner of disclosing the possible termination of a plan. For example, should Pan Am have disclosed a contingent liability for its struggling plan? At present this issue is unresolved, and considerable judgment is needed to analyze a company with these contingent liabilities.

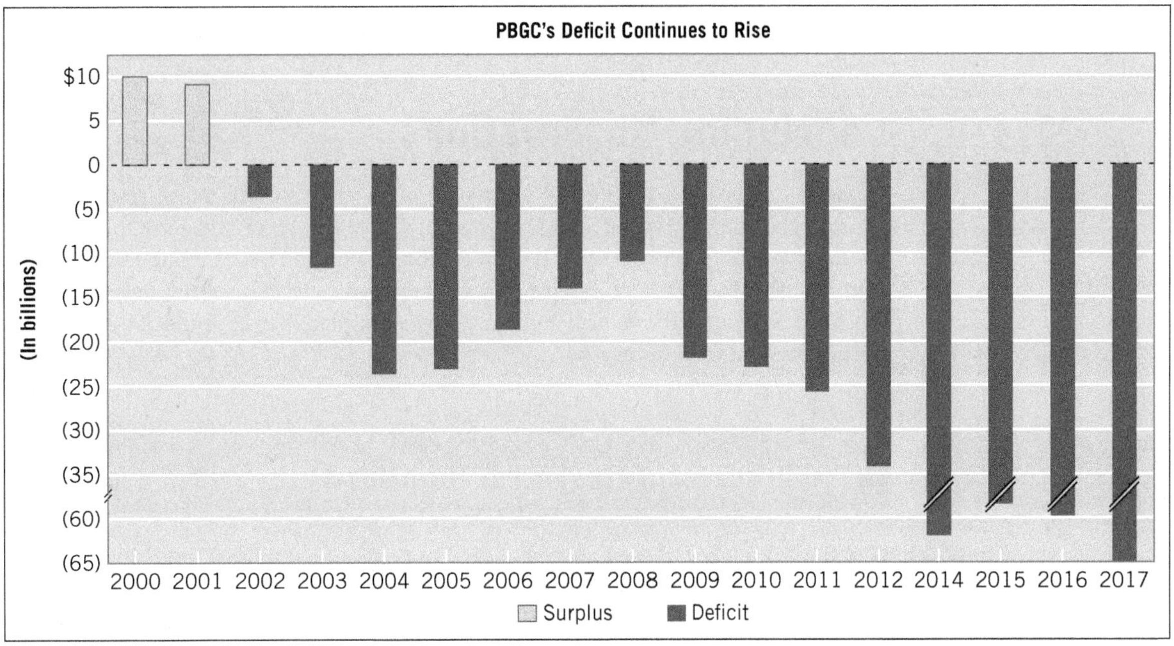

Source: *http://www.pbgc.gov/about/reports/ar2017.html.*

Pension Terminations

A congressman at one time noted, "Employers are simply treating their employee pension plans like company piggy banks, to be raided at will." What this congressman was referring to is the practice of paying off the projected benefit obligation and pocketing any excess. ERISA prevents companies from recapturing excess assets unless they pay participants what is owed to them and then terminate the plan. As a result, companies were buying *annuities* to pay off the pension claimants and then used the excess funds for other corporate purposes.[18]

For example, at one time, pension plan terminations netted $363 million for **Occidental Petroleum Corp.**, $95 million for **Stroh's Brewery Co.**, $58 million for **Kellogg Co.**, and $938 million for **Avaya** (a spinoff of **Lucent Technologies**). Recently, many large companies have terminated their pension plans and captured billions in surplus assets. The U.S. Treasury also benefits: Federal legislation requires companies to pay an excise tax of anywhere from 20 percent to 50 percent on the gains. All of this is quite legal.[19]

The accounting issue that arises from these terminations is whether a company should recognize a gain when pension plan assets revert back to the company (often called **asset reversion** transactions). The issue is complex. In some cases, a company starts a new defined benefit plan after it eliminates the old one. Thus, some contend that there has been no change in substance but merely a change in form. However, the FASB disagrees. It requires recognition

[18]A question exists as to whose money it is. Some argue that the excess funds belong to the employees, not the employer. In addition, given that the funds have been reverting to the employer, critics charge that cost-of-living increases and the possibility of other increased benefits are reduced because companies will be reluctant to use those remaining funds to pay for such increases.

[19]Another way that companies have reduced their pension obligations is through adoption of **cash-balance plans**. These are *hybrid* plans combining features of defined benefit and defined contribution plans. Although these plans permit employees to transfer their pension benefits when they change employers (like a defined contribution plan), they are controversial because the change to a cash-balance plan often reduces benefits to older workers.

The accounting for cash-balance plans is similar to that for defined benefit plans, because employers bear the investment risk in cash-balance plans. However, when an employer adopts a cash-balance plan, the measurement of the future benefit obligation to employees generally is lower, compared to a traditional defined benefit plan. See A. T. Arcady and F. Mellors, "Cash-Balance Conversions," *Journal of Accountancy* (February 2000), pp. 22–28.

in earnings of a gain or loss when the employer settles a pension obligation either by lump-sum cash payments to participants or by purchasing nonparticipating annuity contracts. [9][20]

Concluding Observations

Hardly a day goes by without the financial press analyzing in depth some issue related to pension plans in the United States. This is not surprising, since pension funds exceed over $40 trillion in assets globally. As you have seen, the accounting issues related to pension plans are complex. The FASB has clarified many of these issues which should help users understand the financial implications of a company's pension plans on its financial position, results of operations, and cash flows.

APPENDIX 20A Accounting for Postretirement Benefits

LEARNING OBJECTIVE *6

Identify the differences between pensions and postretirement healthcare benefits.

IBM's adoption of the GAAP requirements on postretirement benefits resulted in a $2.3 billion charge and a historical curiosity—IBM's first-ever quarterly loss. General Electric disclosed that its charge for adoption of the same GAAP rules would be $2.7 billion. AT&T absorbed a $2.1 billion pretax hit for postretirement benefits upon adoption. What is GAAP in this area, and how could its adoption have so grave an impact on companies' earnings?

Accounting Guidance

After a decade of study, the FASB in December 1990 issued GAAP for "Employers' Accounting for Postretirement Benefits Other Than Pensions." [10] It alone was the cause for the large charges to income cited above. These rules cover healthcare and other "welfare benefits" provided to retirees, their spouses, dependents, and beneficiaries.[21] These other welfare benefits include life insurance offered outside a pension plan; medical, dental, and eye care; legal and tax services; tuition assistance; day care; and housing assistance.[22] Because healthcare benefits are the largest of the other postretirement benefits, we use this item to illustrate accounting for postretirement benefits.

For many employers (about 95 percent), these GAAP rules required a change from the predominant practice of accounting for postretirement benefits on a pay-as-you-go (cash) basis to an accrual basis. Similar to pension accounting, the accrual basis necessitates measuring the employer's obligation to provide future benefits and accrual of the cost during the years that the employee provides service.

[20]Some companies have established *pension poison pills* as an anti-takeover measure. These plans require asset reversions from termination of a plan to benefit employees and retirees rather than the acquiring company. For a discussion of pension poison pills, see Eugene E. Comiskey and Charles W. Mulford, "Interpreting Pension Disclosures: A Guide for Lending Officers," *Commercial Lending Review* (Winter 1993–94), Vol. 9, No. 1.

[21]*Accounting Trends and Techniques* indicates that of its 500 surveyed companies, 317 reported benefit plans that provide postretirement healthcare benefits. In response to rising healthcare costs and higher premiums on healthcare insurance, companies are working to get their postretirement benefit costs under control.

[22]"OPEB" is the acronym frequently used to describe postretirement benefits other than pensions. This term came into being before the scope of guidance was narrowed from "other postemployment benefits" to "other postretirement benefits," thereby excluding postemployment benefits related to severance pay or wage continuation to disabled, terminated, or laid-off employees.

One of the reasons companies had not prefunded these benefit plans was that payments to prefund healthcare costs, unlike contributions to a pension trust, are not tax-deductible. Another reason was that postretirement healthcare benefits were once perceived to be a low-cost employee benefit that could be changed or eliminated at will and therefore were not a legal liability. Now, the accounting definition of a liability goes beyond the notion of a legally enforceable claim; the definition now encompasses equitable or constructive obligations as well, making it clear that the postretirement benefit promise is a liability.[23]

Differences Between Pension Benefits and Healthcare Benefits

The FASB used the GAAP rules on pensions as a reference for the accounting prescribed for healthcare and other nonpension postretirement benefits.[24] Why didn't the FASB cover these other types of postretirement benefits in the earlier pension accounting statement? Because the apparent similarities between the two benefits mask some significant differences. **Illustration 20A.1** shows these differences.[25]

ILLUSTRATION 20A.1

Differences Between Pensions and Postretirement Healthcare Benefits

Item	Pensions	Healthcare Benefits
Funding	Generally funded.	Generally **not** funded.
Benefit	Well-defined and level dollar amount.	Generally uncapped and great variability.
Beneficiary	Retiree (maybe some benefit to surviving spouse).	Retiree, spouse, and other dependents.
Benefit payable	Monthly.	As needed and used.
Predictability	Variables are reasonably predictable.	Utilization difficult to predict. Level of cost varies geographically and fluctuates over time.

Two of the differences in Illustration 20A.1 highlight why measuring the future payments for healthcare benefit plans is so much more difficult than for pension plans.

1. Many postretirement plans do not set a limit on healthcare benefits. No matter how serious the illness or how long it lasts, the benefits continue to flow. (Even if the employer uses an insurance company plan, the premiums will escalate according to the increased benefits provided.)
2. The levels of healthcare benefit use and healthcare costs are difficult to predict. Increased longevity, unexpected illnesses (e.g., AIDS, SARS, and avian flu), along with new medical technologies and cures, cause changes in healthcare utilization.

Additionally, although the fiduciary and reporting standards for employee benefit funds under government regulations generally cover healthcare benefits, the stringent minimum vesting, participation, and funding standards that apply to pensions do not apply to healthcare benefits. Nevertheless, as you will learn, many of the basic concepts of pensions, and much of the related accounting terminology and measurement methodology, do apply to other postretirement benefits. Therefore, in the following discussion and illustrations, we point out the similarities and differences in the accounting and reporting for these two types of postretirement benefits.

[23]"Elements of Financial Statements," *Statement of Financial Accounting Concepts No. 6* (Stamford, Conn.: 1985), p. 13, footnote 21.

[24]Other postemployment (but before retirement) benefits include, but are not limited to, salary continuation, disability-related benefits, severance benefits, and continuance of healthcare benefits and life insurance for inactive or former (e.g., terminated, disabled, or deceased) employees or their beneficiaries. These benefits are accounted for similar to accounting for compensated absences (see Chapter 13). [11]

[25]D. Gerald Searfoss and Naomi Erickson, "The Big Unfunded Liability: Postretirement Health-Care Benefits," *Journal of Accountancy* (November 1988), pp. 28–39.

What Do the Numbers Mean? OPEBs—How Big Are They?

For many companies, *other postretirement benefit obligations* (OPEBs) are substantial. Generally, OPEBs are not well funded because companies are not permitted a tax deduction for contributions to the plan assets, as is the case with pensions. That is, the company may not claim a tax deduction until it makes a payment to the participant (pay-as-you-go).

The following are companies with the largest OPEB obligations, indicating their relationship with other financial items.

For Year Ended 12/31/2017	Benefit Obligation (in millions)	% Underfunded	Obligation as a % of Stockholders' Equity
General Motors	$ 6,374	100.00%	17.61%
Ford Motor	6,169	100.00	17.67
AT&T	24,059	75.17	16.94
Verizon Communications	19,460	94.25	43.55
Boeing	6,085	97.65	1,476.94

So, how big are OPEB obligations? REALLY big.

Source: Company reports.

Postretirement Benefits Accounting Provisions

Healthcare and other postretirement benefits for current and future retirees and their dependents are forms of deferred compensation. They are earned through employee service and are subject to accrual during the years an employee is working.

The period of time over which the postretirement benefit cost accrues is called the **attribution period**. It is the period of service during which the employee earns the benefits under the terms of the plan. The attribution period, shown in **Illustration 20A.2** for a hypothetical employee, generally begins when an employee is hired and ends on the date the employee is eligible to receive the benefits and ceases to earn additional benefits by performing service, the vesting date.[26]

ILLUSTRATION 20A.2
Range of Possible Attribution Periods

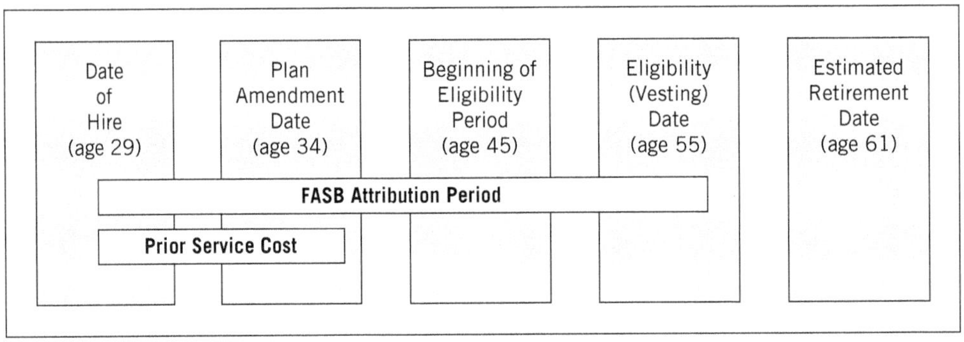

Obligations Under Postretirement Benefits

In defining the obligation for postretirement benefits, the FASB maintained many concepts similar to pension accounting. It also designed some new and modified terms specifically for

[26]This is a benefit-years-of-service approach (the projected unit credit actuarial cost method). The FASB found no compelling reason to switch from the traditional pension accounting approach. It rejected the employee's full service period (i.e., to the estimated retirement date) because it was unable to identify any approach that would appropriately attribute benefits beyond the date when an employee attains full eligibility for those benefits. Employees attain full eligibility by meeting specified age, service, or age and service requirements of the plan.

postretirement benefits. Two of the most important of these specialized terms are (a) expected postretirement benefit obligation and (b) accumulated postretirement benefit obligation.

The **expected postretirement benefit obligation (EPBO)** is the actuarial present value as of a particular date of **all benefits a company expects to pay after retirement to employees and their dependents.** Companies do not record the EPBO in the financial statements, but they do use it in measuring periodic expense.

The **accumulated postretirement benefit obligation (APBO)** is the actuarial present value of **future benefits attributed to employees' services rendered to a particular date**. The APBO is equal to the EPBO for retirees and active employees fully eligible for benefits. Before the date an employee achieves full eligibility, the APBO is only a portion of the EPBO. Or stated another way, the difference between the APBO and the EPBO is the future service costs of active employees who are not yet fully eligible.

Illustration 20A.3 contrasts the EPBO and the APBO. At the date an employee is fully eligible (the end of the attribution period), the APBO and the EPBO for that employee are equal.

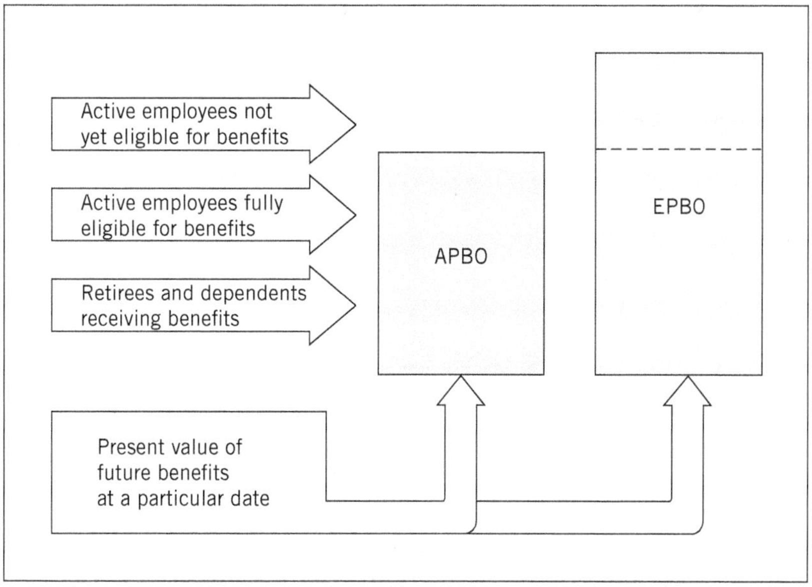

ILLUSTRATION 20A.3

APBO and EPBO Contrasted

Postretirement Expense

Postretirement expense is the employer's annual expense for postretirement benefits. Also called **net periodic postretirement benefit cost**, this expense consists of many of the familiar components used to compute annual pension expense. The components of net periodic postretirement benefit cost are as follows. [12] [27]

1. ***Service cost.*** The portion of the EPBO attributed to employee service during the period.
2. ***Interest cost.*** The increase in the APBO attributable to the passage of time. Companies compute interest cost by applying the beginning-of-the-year discount rate to the beginning-of-the-year APBO, adjusted for benefit payments to be made during the period. The discount rate is based on the rates of return on high-quality, fixed-income investments that are currently available.[28]

[27]See James R. Wilbert and Kenneth E. Dakdduk, "The New FASB 106: How to Account for Postretirement Benefits," *Journal of Accountancy* (August 1991), pp. 36–41.

[28]The FASB concluded that the discount rate for measuring the present value of the postretirement benefit obligation and the service cost component should be the same as that applied to pension measurements. It chose not to label it the *settlement rate*, in order to clarify that the objective of the discount rate is to measure the time value of money.

3. ***Actual return on plan assets.*** The change in the fair value of the plan's assets adjusted for contributions and benefit payments made during the period. Because companies charge or credit the postretirement expense for the gain or loss on plan assets (the difference between the actual and the expected return), this component is actually the expected return.
4. ***Amortization of prior service cost.*** The amortization of the cost of retroactive benefits resulting from plan amendments. The typical amortization period, beginning at the date of the plan amendment, is the remaining service periods through the full eligibility date.
5. ***Gains and losses.*** In general, changes in the APBO resulting from changes in assumptions or from experience different from that assumed. For funded plans, this component also includes the difference between actual return and expected return on plan assets.

Illustrative Accounting Entries

LEARNING OBJECTIVE *7

Contrast accounting for pensions to accounting for other postretirement benefits.

Like pension accounting, the accounting for postretirement plans must recognize in the accounts and in the financial statements effects of several significant items. These items are:

1. Expected postretirement benefit obligation (EPBO).
2. Accumulated postretirement benefit obligation (APBO).
3. Postretirement benefit plan assets.
4. Prior service cost.
5. Net gain or loss.

The EPBO is not recognized in the financial statements or disclosed in the notes. Companies recompute it each year, and the actuary uses it in measuring the annual service cost. Because of the numerous assumptions and actuarial complexity involved in measuring annual service cost, we have omitted these computations of the EPBO.

Similar to pensions, companies must recognize in the financial statements items 2 through 5 listed above. In addition, as in pension accounting, companies must know the exact amount of these items in order to compute postretirement expense. Therefore, companies use the worksheet like that for pension accounting to record both the formal general journal entries and the memo entries.

2020 Entries and Worksheet

To illustrate the use of a worksheet in accounting for a postretirement benefits plan, assume that on January 1, 2020, Quest Company adopts a healthcare benefit plan. The following facts apply to the postretirement benefits plan for the year 2020.

- Plan assets at fair value on January 1, 2020, are zero.
- Actual and expected returns on plan assets are zero.
- Accumulated postretirement benefit obligation (APBO), January 1, 2020, is zero.
- Service cost is $54,000.
- No prior service cost exists.
- Interest cost on the APBO is zero.
- Funding contributions during the year are $38,000.
- Benefit payments to employees from plan are $28,000.

Using that data, the worksheet in Illustration 20A.4 presents the postretirement entries for 2020.

ILLUSTRATION 20A.4
Postretirement Worksheet—2020

Postretirement Worksheet—2020

Items	Annual Postretirement Expense	Cash	Postretirement Asset/Liability	APBO	Plan Assets
	General Journal Entries			Memo Record	
Balance, Jan. 1, 2020					
(a) Service cost	54,000 Dr.			54,000 Cr.	
(b) Contributions		38,000 Cr.			38,000 Dr.
(c) Benefits				28,000 Dr.	28,000 Cr.
Journal entry for 2020	54,000 Dr.	38,000 Cr.	16,000 Cr.*		
Balance, Dec. 31, 2020			16,000 Cr.**	26,000 Cr.	10,000 Dr.

*$54,000 – $38,000 = $16,000
**$26,000 – $10,000 = $16,000

Entry (a) records the service cost component, which increases postretirement expense $54,000 and increases the liability (APBO) $54,000. Entry (b) records Quest's funding of assets to the postretirement fund. The funding decreases cash $38,000 and increases plan assets $38,000. Entry (c) records the benefit payments made to retirees, which results in equal $28,000 decreases to the plan assets and the liability (APBO).

Quest's December 31 adjusting entry formally records the postretirement expense in 2020, as follows.

December 31, 2020

Postretirement Expense	54,000	
Cash		38,000
Postretirement Asset/Liability		16,000

The credit to Postretirement Asset/Liability for $16,000 represents the difference between the APBO and the plan assets. The $16,000 credit balance is a liability because the plan is underfunded. The Postretirement Asset/Liability account balance of $16,000 also equals the net of the balances in the memo accounts.

Illustration 20A.5 shows the funded status reported in the balance sheet. (Notice its similarity to the pension schedule.)

Accumulated postretirement benefit obligation (Credit)	$(26,000)
Plan assets at fair value (Debit)	10,000
Postretirement asset/liability (Credit)	$(16,000)

ILLUSTRATION 20A.5
Postretirement Reconciliation Schedule—December 31, 2020

Recognition of Gains and Losses

Gains and losses represent changes in the APBO or the value of plan assets. These changes result either from actual experience different from that expected or from changes in actuarial assumptions. The amortization of these gains and losses follows the approach used for pensions. That is, the gains and losses are recorded in other comprehensive income.

The Corridor Approach

Consistent with pension accounting, companies amortize the gains and losses in accumulated other comprehensive income as a component of postretirement expense if, at the beginning of the period, they exceed a "corridor" limit. The corridor is measured as the greater of 10 percent of the APBO or 10 percent of the market-related value of plan assets.

The intent of the **corridor approach** is to reduce volatility of postretirement expense by providing a reasonable opportunity for gains and losses to offset over time without affecting net periodic expense.

Amortization Methods

If the company must amortize gains and losses (beyond the corridor) on postretirement benefit plans, the **minimum amortization amount** is the excess gain or loss—in excess of the corridor—divided by the average remaining service life to expected retirement of all active employees. Companies may use any systematic method of amortization provided that: (1) the amount amortized in any period is equal to or greater than the minimum amount, (2) the company applies the method consistently, and (3) the company applies the method similarly for gains and losses.

The company must recompute the amount of gain or loss in accumulated other comprehensive income each year and amortize the gain or loss over the average remaining service life if the net amount exceeds the "corridor."

2021 Entries and Worksheet

Continuing the Quest Company illustration into 2021, the following facts apply to the postretirement benefits plan for the year 2021.

- Actual return on plan assets is $600.
- Expected return on plan assets is $800.
- Discount rate is 8 percent.
- Increase in APBO due to change in actuarial assumptions is $60,000.
- Service cost is $26,000.
- Funding contributions during the year are $18,000.
- Benefit payments to employees during the year are $5,000.
- Average remaining service to expected retirement: 25 years.

The worksheet in **Illustration 20A.6** presents all of Quest's postretirement benefit entries and information for 2021. The beginning balances on the first line of the

ILLUSTRATION 20A.6 Postretirement Benefits Worksheet—2021

Postretirement Benefits Worksheet—2021

Home Insert Page Layout Formulas Data Review View

P18 fx

	A	B	C	D	E	F	G
1							
2		General Journal Entries				Memo Record	
3		Annual		Other			
4		Postretirement		Comprehensive	Postretirement		
5	Items	Expense	Cash	Income (G/L)	Asset/Liability	APBO	Plan Assets
6	Balance, Jan. 1, 2021				16,000 Cr.	26,000 Cr.	10,000 Dr.
7	(d) Service cost	26,000 Dr.				26,000 Cr.	
8	(e) Interest cost	2,080 Dr.				2,080 Cr.	
9	(f) Actual return	600 Cr.					600 Dr.
10	(g) Unexpected loss	200 Cr.		200 Dr.			
11	(h) Contributions		18,000 Cr.				18,000 Dr.
12	(i) Benefits					5,000 Dr.	5,000 Cr.
13	(j) Increase in APBO (Loss)			60,000 Dr.		60,000 Cr.	
14	Journal entry for 2021	27,280 Dr.	18,000 Cr.	60,200 Dr.	69,480 Cr.		
15							
16	Accumulated OCI, Dec. 31, 2020			0			
17	Balance, Dec. 31, 2021			60,200 Dr.	85,480 Cr.	109,080 Cr.	23,600 Dr.
18							

worksheet are the ending balances from Quest's 2020 postretirement benefits worksheet in Illustration 20A.4.

Entries (d), (h), and (i) are similar to the corresponding entries previously explained for 2020. Entry (e) accrues the interest expense component, which increases both the liability and the postretirement expense by $2,080 (the beginning APBO multiplied by the discount rate of 8%). Entries (f) and (g) are related. The expected return of $800 is higher than the actual return of $600. To smooth postretirement expense, Quest defers the unexpected loss of $200 ($800 – $600) by debiting Other Comprehensive Income (G/L) and crediting Postretirement Expense. As a result of this adjustment, the expected return on the plan assets is the amount actually used to compute postretirement expense.

Entry (j) records the change in the APBO resulting from a change in actuarial assumptions. This $60,000 increase in the employer's accumulated liability is an unexpected loss. Quest debits this loss to Other Comprehensive Income (G/L).

On December 31, Quest formally records net periodic expense for 2021 as follows.

December 31, 2021		
Postretirement Expense	27,280	
Other Comprehensive Income (G/L)	60,200	
Cash		18,000
Postretirement Asset/Liability		69,480

The balance of the Postretirement Asset/Liability account at December 31, 2021, is $85,480. This balance is equal to the net of the balances in the memo accounts as shown in the reconciliation schedule in **Illustration 20A.7**.

Accumulated postretirement benefit obligation (Credit)	$(109,080)
Plan assets at fair value (Debit)	23,600
Postretirement asset/liability (Credit)	$ (85,480)

ILLUSTRATION 20A.7

Postretirement Benefits Reconciliation Schedule—December 31, 2021

Amortization of Net Gain or Loss in 2022

Quest has a beginning balance in Accumulated OCI related to losses of $60,200. Therefore, Quest must apply the corridor test for amortization of the balance for 2022. **Illustration 20A.8** shows the computation of the amortization charge for the loss.

2022 Corridor Test	
Accumulated OCI at beginning of year	$60,200
10% of greater of APBO or market-related value of plan assets ($109,080 × .10)	(10,908)
Amortizable amount	$49,292
Average remaining service to expected retirement	25 years
2022 amortization of loss ($49,292 ÷ 25)	$1,972

ILLUSTRATION 20A.8

Computation of Amortization Charge (Corridor Test)—2022

Disclosures in Notes to the Financial Statements

The disclosures required for other postretirement benefit plans are similar to and just as detailed and extensive as those required for pensions. The note disclosure for **Tootsie Roll, Inc.** in **Illustration 20A.9** provides a good example of the extensive disclosure required for other postretirement benefit plans.

ILLUSTRATION 20A.9

Postretirement Benefit Disclosure

Tootsie Roll Industries, Inc.

Notes to Financial Statements

Note 7 Employee Benefit Plans (partial)
Postretirement health care benefit plans:

The Company maintains a post-retirement health benefits plan for a group of "grandfathered" corporate employees. The plan as amended in 2013, generally limited future annual cost increases in health benefits to 3%, restricted this benefit to current employees and retirees with long-term service with the Company, and eliminated all post-retirement benefits for future employees effective April 1, 2014. Post-retirement benefits liabilities (as amended) were $13,497 and $12,128 at December 31, 2017 and 2016, respectively.

Amounts recognized in accumulated other comprehensive loss (pre-tax) at December 31, 2017 are as follows:

Amounts recognized in other comprehensive income

Prior service credit	$(5,519)
Net actuarial loss	(713)
Net amount recognized in accumulated other comprehensive (gain) loss	$(6,232)

The estimated actuarial loss (gain) and prior service credit (gain) to be amortized from accumulated other comprehensive loss (gain) into net periodic benefit cost during 2018 are $(97) and $(1,226), respectively.

The changes in the accumulated postretirement benefit obligation at December 31, 2017 and 2016 consist of the following:

Reconciliation of OPEB liability

	December 31	
	2017	2016
Benefit obligation, beginning of year	$12,128	$11,400
Service cost	323	331
Interest cost	468	462
Actuarial (gain)/loss	897	235
Benefits paid	(319)	(300)
Benefit obligation, end of year	$13,497	$12,128

Net periodic postretirement benefit cost included the following components:

Components of OPEB expense

	2017	2016	2015
Service cost—benefits attributed to service during the period	$ 323	$ 331	$ 441
Interest cost on the accumulated postretirement benefit obligation	468	462	465
Net amortization	(1,462)	(1,642)	(1,451)
Net periodic postretirement benefit cost (income)	$ (671)	$ (849)	$ (545)

Expected benefit payments

The Company estimates future benefit payments will be $603, $525, $556, $598 and $632 in 2018 through 2022, respectively, and a total of $3,647 in 2023 through 2027.

As indicated in Illustration 20A.9, Tootsie Roll shows the impact of the postretirement benefit plan on income, the balance sheet, and the cash flow statement, and it provides information on important assumptions used in the measurement of the postretirement benefit obligation. Also note that given no tax incentives for funding, Tootsie Roll (like many companies) does not have any assets set aside for its other postretirement benefit obligations.

While Tootsie Roll has only an other postretirement benefit plan, many companies sponsor both defined benefit pension and other postretirement plans. Given the similarities in accounting for these plans, companies can combine pension and other postretirement benefit disclosures.[29]

[29]Companies also report assets, liabilities, net income, and comprehensive income elements related to other postretirement plans similar to pensions.

Actuarial Assumptions and Conceptual Issues

Measurement of the EPBO, the APBO, and the net periodic postretirement benefit cost is involved and complex. Due to the uncertainties in forecasting healthcare costs, rates of use, changes in government health programs, and the differences employed in nonmedical assumptions (e.g., discount rate, employee turnover, rate of pre-65 retirement, spouse-age difference), estimates of postretirement benefit costs may have a large margin of error. Is the information relevant, reliable, or verifiable? The FASB concluded that "the obligation to provide postretirement benefits meets the definition of a liability, is representationally faithful, is relevant to financial statement users, and can be measured with sufficient reliability at a justifiable cost." [13] Failure to accrue an obligation and an expense prior to payment of benefits would result in an unfaithful representation of what financial statements should represent.

The FASB took a momentous step by requiring recognition of a postretirement liability. Many opposed the requirement, warning that the GAAP rules would devastate earnings. Others argued that putting these numbers on the balance sheet was inappropriate. Others noted that the requirement would force companies to curtail postretirement benefits to employees.

The authors believe that the FASB deserves special praise. Because the Board addressed this issue, companies now recognize the magnitude of these costs. This recognition has led to efforts to control escalating healthcare costs. As John Ruffle, a former president of the Financial Accounting Foundation noted, "The Board has done American industry a gigantic favor. Over the long term, industry will look back and say thanks."

What Do the Numbers Mean? **Want Some Bad News?**

Many companies have underfunded pension and other postretirement plans. Unfortunately, many governmental entities also have the same problem but on a much larger scale. Here are some examples.

- The actual liabilities of the federal government—including Social Security, Medicare, and federal employees' future retirement benefits—is estimated to be over $100 trillion. When the accrued expenses of the government's entitled programs are counted, we need to collect well over $8 trillion in tax revenues annually. Even if you take all the taxable income of corporations and of individuals earning over approximately $66,000, that still falls short of the $8 trillion.
- A State Budget Crisis Task Force declared underfunded retirement promises as one of the six major threats to states' "fiscal sustainability."
- The annual report from the PEW Charitable Trusts finds that public worker pension funds with heavy state government involvement owed retirees and current workers $4 trillion as of 2016. These funds had about $2.6 trillion in assets, creating a gap of about one-third, or a record $1.4 trillion.

So what does all this have to do with accounting? Similar to the FASB, there is an organization called the Governmental Accounting Standards Board (GASB), which establishes standards of financial accounting and reporting for state and local governmental agencies.

Until recently, the GASB went about its work in relative obscurity. How did the GASB get everyone's attention? It issued new rules [GASB No. 68, *Accounting and Financial Reporting for Pensions—An Amendment of GASB Statement No. 27* (June 2012) and GASB No 74, *Financial Reporting for Postemployment Benefit Plans Other Than Pension Plans* (June 2015)], which requires that governmental units recognize postretirement benefits on their balance sheets on an accrual basis. Some states do not like this requirement and have proposed legislation that will allow them to ignore GASB standards. However, the GASB, with the support of users of government reports, has pushed for the change. They are concerned that without the new requirements, governments will continue to misrepresent the true cost of their retirement-related promises to public employees. In their view, the new accounting rules are in the best interests of municipal bondholders and the public in general. Thus, it appears that the FASB is not the only standard-setter subject to political pressure.

Sources: Chris Cox and Bill Archer, "Why $16 Trillion Only Hints at the True U.S. Debt," *Wall Street Journal* (November 27, 2012); "More Bad News for Public Pensions," *Wall Street Journal* (July 12, 2012); G. Mulvihill, "Report: Many Public Employee Pension Systems Have Massive Unfunded Liabilities," *Naples Daily News* (April 13, 2018); and *http://www.pewtrusts.org/en/research-and-analysis/issue-briefs/2015/07/the-state-pensions-funding-gap-challenges-persist*. For more information on the GASB, go to the GASB website.

Review and Practice

Key Terms Review

accumulated benefit obligation 20-7
*accumulated postretirement benefit obligation (APBO) 20-37
actual return on plan assets 20-10
actuarial present value 20-8(*n*)
actuaries 20-6
asset gains and losses 20-17
*attribution period 20-36
cash-balance plans 20-33(*n*)
components of pension expense 20-9
contributory pension plan 20-4
corridor approach 20-18, 20-40
defined benefit plan 20-5
defined contribution plan 20-4
ERISA 20-31
*expected postretirement benefit obligation (EPBO) 20-37
expected rate of return 20-17
expected return on plan assets 20-17
fair value of plan assets 20-11
funded pension plan 20-3
funded status (overfunded or underfunded) 20-8
interest on the liability (interest expense) 20-10
liability gains and losses 20-18
market-related asset value 20-17
noncontributory pension plan 20-4
Other Comprehensive Income (G/L) 20-17
Other Comprehensive Income (PSC) 20-16
pension asset/liability 20-12
pension plan 20-3
pension worksheet 20-11
prior service cost (PSC) 20-14
projected benefit obligation 20-7
qualified pension plan 20-4
reconciliation 20-28
retroactive benefits 20-14
service cost 20-10
settlement rate 20-10
unexpected gain or loss 20-17
vested benefit obligation 20-7
vested benefits 20-7
years-of-service method 20-14

Learning Objectives Review

1 Discuss the fundamentals of pension plan accounting.

The company or employer is the organization sponsoring the pension plan. It incurs the cost and makes contributions to the pension fund. The fund or plan is the entity that receives the contributions from the employer, administers the pension assets, and makes the benefit payments to the pension recipients (retired employees). The fund should be a separate legal and accounting entity; it maintains a set of books and prepares financial statements.

The two most common types of pension arrangements are as follows. **(1) Defined contribution plans:** The employer agrees to contribute to a pension trust a certain sum each period based on a formula. This formula may consider such factors as age, length of employee service, employer's profits, and compensation level. Only the employer's contribution is defined; no promise is made regarding the ultimate benefits paid out to the employees. **(2) Defined benefit plans:** These plans define the benefits that the employee will receive at the time of retirement. The formula typically provides for the benefits to be a function of the employee's years of service and the compensation level when he or she nears retirement.

Alternative measures for valuing the pension obligation may be used. One measure bases the pension obligation only on the benefits vested to the employees. Vested benefits are those that the employee is entitled to receive even if he or she renders no additional services under the plan. Companies compute the **vested benefit pension obligation** using current salary levels; this obligation includes only vested benefits. Another measure of the obligation, called the **accumulated benefit obligation,** computes the deferred compensation amount based on all years of service performed by employees under the plan—both vested and nonvested—using current salary levels. A third measure, called the **projected benefit obligation,** bases the computation of the deferred compensation amount on both vested and nonvested service using future salaries.

Pension expense is a function of the following components: (1) service cost, (2) interest on the liability, (3) return on plan assets, (4) amortization of prior service cost, and (5) gain or loss.

2 Use a worksheet for employer's pension plan entries.

Companies may use a worksheet unique to pension accounting. This worksheet records both the formal entries and the memo entries to keep track of all the employer's relevant pension plan items and components.

3 Describe the accounting and amortization of prior service costs.

An actuary computes the amount of the prior service cost, and the company then records it as an adjustment to the projected benefit obligation and other comprehensive income. It then amortizes it, generally using a "years-of-service" amortization method, similar to a units-of-production computation. First, the company computes total estimated number of service-years to be worked by all of the participating employees. Second, it divides the accumulated prior service cost by the total number of service-years, to obtain a cost per service-year (the unit cost). Third, the company multiplies the number of service-years consumed each year times the cost per service-year, to obtain the annual amortization charge.

4 **Explain the accounting and amortization for unexpected gains and losses.**

In estimating the projected benefit obligation (the liability), actuaries make assumptions about such items as mortality rate, retirement rate, turnover rate, disability rate, and salary amounts. Any change in these actuarial assumptions affects the amount of the projected benefit obligation. These unexpected gains or losses from changes in the projected benefit obligation are liability gains and losses. Liability gains result from unexpected decreases in the liability balance; liability losses result from unexpected increases. Companies also incur asset gains or losses. Both types of actuarial gains and losses are recorded in other comprehensive income and adjust either the projected benefit obligation or the plan assets.

The FASB set a limit for the size of an accumulated net gain or loss balance. That arbitrarily selected limit (called a **corridor**) is 10 percent of the larger of the beginning balances of the projected benefit obligation or the market-related value of the plan assets. Beyond that limit, an accumulated net gain or loss balance is considered too large and must be amortized. If the balance of the accumulated net gain or loss account stays within the upper and lower limits of the corridor, no amortization is required.

5 **Describe the requirements for reporting pension plans in financial statements.**

Currently, companies must disclose the following pension plan information in their financial statements. (1) The components of pension expense for the period. (2) A schedule showing changes in the benefit obligation and plan assets during the year. (3) The amount of prior service cost and net gains and losses in accumulated OCI, including the estimated prior service cost and gains and losses that will affect net income in the next year. (4) The weighted-average assumed discount rate, the rate of compensation increase used to measure the projected benefit obligation, and the weighted-average expected long-term rate of return on plan assets. (5) A table showing the allocation of pension plan assets by category and the percentage of the fair value to total plan assets. (6) The expected benefit payments for current plan participants for each of the next five fiscal years and for the following five years in aggregate, along with an estimate of expected contributions to the plan during the next year.

*6 **Identify the differences between pensions and postretirement healthcare benefits.**

Pension plans are generally funded, but healthcare benefit plans are not. Pension benefits are generally well-defined and level in amount; healthcare benefits are generally uncapped and variable. Pension benefits are payable monthly; healthcare benefits are paid as needed and used. Pension plan variables are reasonably predictable, whereas healthcare plan variables are difficult to predict.

*7 **Contrast accounting for pensions to accounting for other postretirement benefits.**

Many of the basic concepts, accounting terminology, and measurement methodology that apply to pensions also apply to other postretirement benefit accounting. Because other postretirement benefit plans are unfunded, large obligations can occur. Two significant concepts peculiar to accounting for other postretirement benefits are (1) expected postretirement benefit obligation (EPBO) and (2) accumulated postretirement benefit obligation (APBO).

Enhanced Review and Practice

Go online for multiple-choice questions with solutions, review exercises with solutions, and a full glossary of all key terms.

Practice Problem

Jablonski Corp. sponsors a defined benefit pension plan for its employees. On January 1, 2020, the following balances related to this plan.

Plan assets (market-related value)	$170,000
Projected benefit obligation	340,000
Pension asset/liability	170,000 Cr.
Prior service cost	100,000
OCI—Loss	39,000

As a result of the operation of the plan during 2020, the actuary provided the following additional data at December 31, 2020.

Service cost for 2020	$45,000
Actual return on plan assets in 2020	27,000
Amortization of prior service cost	20,000
Contributions in 2020	85,000
Benefits paid retirees in 2020	51,000
Settlement rate	7%
Expected return on plan assets	8%
Average remaining service life of active employees	10 years

Instructions

a. Compute pension expense for Jablonski Corp. for the year 2020 by preparing a pension worksheet that shows the journal entry for pension expense.

b. Indicate the pension amounts reported in the financial statements.

Solution

a.

Jablonski Corp.
Pension Worksheet—2020

	General Journal Entries					Memo Record	
			Other Comprehensive Income				
Items	Annual Pension Expense	Cash	Prior Service Cost	Gain/Loss	Pension Asset/ Liability	Projected Benefit Obligation	Plan Assets
Balance, Jan. 1, 2020					170,000 Cr.	340,000 Cr.	170,000 Dr.
Service cost	45,000 Dr.					45,000 Cr.	
Interest cost*	23,800 Dr.					23,800 Cr.	
Actual return	27,000 Cr.						27,000 Dr.
Unexpected gain**	13,400 Dr.			13,400 Cr.			
Amortization of PSC	20,000 Dr.		20,000 Cr.				
Amortization of loss***	500 Dr.			500 Cr.			
Contributions		85,000 Cr.					85,000 Dr.
Benefits						51,000 Dr.	51,000 Cr.
Journal entry for 2020	75,700 Dr.	85,000 Cr.	20,000 Cr.	13,900 Cr.	43,200 Dr.		
Accumulated OCI, Dec. 31, 2019			100,000 Dr.	39,000 Dr.			
Balance, Dec. 31, 2020			80,000 Dr.	25,100 Dr.	126,800 Cr.	357,800 Cr.	231,000 Dr.

*$23,800 = $340,000 × .07

**$13,400 = ($170,000 × .08) – $27,000

***

Year	1/1 Projected Benefit Obligation	Value of 1/1 Plan Assets	10% Corridor	Accumulated OCI (G/L), 1/1	Minimum Amortization of Loss for 2020
2020	$340,000	$170,000	$34,000	$39,000	$500****

**** ($39,000 – $34,000) = $5,000 ÷ 10 = $500

2020		
Pension Expense	75,700	
Pension Asset/Liability	43,200	
Other Comprehensive Income (PSC)		20,000
Other Comprehensive Income (G/L)		13,900
Cash		85,000

b. The pension amounts reported in the 2020 financial statements are as follows.

Income Statement

Operating expenses	
Pension expense (service cost)	$45,000
Other income (expenses)	
Pension expense (other components)	$(30,700)

Comprehensive Income Statement

Net income		$ XXXX
Other comprehensive income		
Asset gain	$13,400	
Amortization of loss	500	
Prior service cost amortization	20,000	33,900
Comprehensive income		$ XXXX

Balance Sheet

Liabilities	
Pension liability	$126,800
Stockholders' equity	
Accumulated other comprehensive loss (PSC)	80,000
Accumulated other comprehensive loss (G/L)	25,100

WileyPLUS

Exercises, Problems, Problem Solution Walkthrough Videos, and many more assessment tools and resources are available for practice in WileyPLUS.

Note: All asterisked Questions, Exercises, and Problems relate to material in the appendix to the chapter.

Questions

1. What is a private pension plan? How does a contributory pension plan differ from a noncontributory plan?

2. Differentiate between a defined contribution pension plan and a defined benefit pension plan. Explain how the employer's obligation differs between the two types of plans.

3. Differentiate between "accounting for the employer" and "accounting for the pension fund."

4. The meaning of the term "fund" depends on the context in which it is used. Explain its meaning when used as a noun. Explain its meaning when it is used as a verb.

5. What is the role of an actuary relative to pension plans? What are actuarial assumptions?

6. What factors must be considered by the actuary in measuring the amount of pension benefits under a defined benefit plan?

7. Name three approaches to measuring benefit obligations from a pension plan and explain how they differ.

8. Explain how cash-basis accounting for pension plans differs from accrual-basis accounting for pension plans. Why is cash-basis accounting generally considered unacceptable for pension plan accounting?

9. Identify the five components that comprise pension expense. Briefly explain the nature of each component.

10. What is service cost, and what is the basis of its measurement?

11. In computing the interest component of pension expense, what interest rates may be used?

12. Explain the difference between service cost and prior service cost.

13. What is meant by "prior service cost"? When is prior service cost recognized as pension expense?

14. What are "liability gains and losses," and how are they accounted for?

15. If pension expense recognized in a period exceeds the current amount funded by the employer, what kind of account arises, and how should it be reported in the financial statements? If the reverse occurs—that is, current funding by the employer exceeds the amount recognized as pension expense—what kind of account arises, and how should it be reported?

16. Given the following items and amounts, compute the actual return on plan assets: fair value of plan assets at the beginning of the period $9,500,000, benefits paid during the period $1,400,000, contributions made during the period $1,000,000, and fair value of the plan assets at the end of the period $10,150,000.

17. How does an "asset gain or loss" develop in pension accounting? How does a "liability gain or loss" develop in pension accounting?

18. What is the meaning of "corridor amortization"?

19. At the end of the current period, Agler Inc. had a projected benefit obligation of $400,000 and pension plan assets (at fair value) of $350,000. What are the accounts and amounts that will be reported on the company's balance sheet as pension assets or pension liabilities?

20. At the end of the current year, Pociek Co. has prior service cost of $9,150,000. Where should the prior service cost be reported on the balance sheet?

21. Describe the accounting for actuarial gains and losses.

22. Boey Company reported net income of $25,000 in 2021. It had the following amounts related to its pension plan in 2021: actuarial liability gain $10,000, unexpected asset loss $14,000, accumulated other comprehensive income (G/L) (beginning balance), zero. Determine for 2021 (a) Boey's other comprehensive income, and (b) comprehensive income.

23. Describe the reporting of pension plans for a company with multiple plans, some of which are underfunded and some of which are overfunded.

24. Determine the meaning of the following terms.

a. Contributory plan.

b. Vested benefits.

c. Retroactive benefits.

d. Years-of-service method.

25. A headline in the *Wall Street Journal* stated, "Firms Increasingly Tap Their Pension Funds to Use Excess Assets." What is the accounting issue related to the use of these "excess assets" through plan terminations?

*26. What are postretirement benefits other than pensions?

*27. Why didn't the FASB cover both types of postretirement benefits—pensions and healthcare—in the earlier pension accounting rules?

*28. What are the major differences between postretirement healthcare benefits and pension benefits?

*29. What is the difference between the APBO and the EPBO? What are the components of postretirement expense?

Brief Exercises

BE20.1 **(LO 1)** **AMR Corporation** (parent company of **American Airlines**) reported the following (in millions).

Service cost	$366
Interest on P.B.O.	737
Return on plan assets	593
Amortization of prior service cost	13
Amortization of net loss	154

Compute AMR Corporation's pension expense.

BE20.2 **(LO 1)** For Warren Corporation, year-end plan assets were $2,000,000. At the beginning of the year, plan assets were $1,780,000. During the year, contributions to the pension fund were $120,000, and benefits paid were $200,000. Compute Warren's actual return on plan assets.

BE20.3 **(LO 2)** At January 1, 2020, Hennein Company had plan assets of $280,000 and a projected benefit obligation of the same amount. During 2020, service cost was $27,500, the settlement rate was 10%, actual and expected return on plan assets were $25,000, contributions were $20,000, and benefits paid were $17,500. Prepare a pension worksheet for Hennein Company for 2020.

BE20.4 **(LO 2)** **Campbell Soup Company** reported pension expense of $73 million and contributed $71 million to the pension fund. Prepare Campbell Soup Company's journal entry to record pension expense and funding, assuming Campbell has no OCI amounts.

BE20.5 **(LO 3)** Mancuso Corporation amended its pension plan on January 1, 2020, and granted $160,000 of prior service costs to its employees. The employees are expected to provide 2,000 service years in the future, with 350 service years in 2020. Compute prior service cost amortization for 2020.

BE20.6 **(LO 3)** At December 31, 2020, Besler Corporation had a projected benefit obligation of $560,000, plan assets of $322,000, and prior service cost of $127,000 in accumulated other comprehensive income. Determine the pension asset/liability at December 31, 2020.

BE20.7 **(LO 4)** Shin Corporation had a projected benefit obligation of $3,100,000 and plan assets of $3,300,000 at January 1, 2020. Shin also had a net actuarial loss of $465,000 in accumulated OCI at January 1, 2020. The average remaining service period of Shin's employees is 7.5 years. Compute Shin's minimum amortization of the actuarial loss.

BE20.8 **(LO 5)** Hawkins Corporation has the following balances at December 31, 2020.

Projected benefit obligation	$2,600,000
Plan assets at fair value	2,000,000
Accumulated OCI (PSC)	1,100,000

How should these balances be reported on Hawkins' balance sheet at December 31, 2020?

BE20.9 **(LO 5)** Norton Co. had the following amounts related to its pension plan in 2020.

Actuarial liability loss for 2020	$28,000
Unexpected asset gain for 2020	18,000
Accumulated other comprehensive income (G/L) (beginning balance)	7,000 Cr.

Determine for 2020 (a) Norton's other comprehensive income (loss) and (b) comprehensive income. Net income for 2020 is $26,000; no amortization of gain or loss is necessary in 2020.

*BE20.10 **(LO 6, 7)** Manno Corporation has the following information available concerning its postretirement benefit plan for 2020.

Service cost	$40,000
Interest cost	47,400
Actual and expected return on plan assets	26,900

Compute Manno's 2020 postretirement expense.

*BE20.11 **(LO 6, 7)** For 2020, Sampsell Inc. computed its annual postretirement expense as $240,900. Sampsell's contribution to the plan during 2020 was $180,000. Prepare Sampsell's 2020 entry to record postretirement expense, assuming Sampsell has no OCI amounts.

Exercises

E20.1 **(LO 1, 2)** Excel **(Pension Expense, Journal Entries)** The following information is available for the pension plan of Radcliffe Company for the year 2020.

Actual and expected return on plan assets	$ 15,000
Benefits paid to retirees	40,000
Contributions (funding)	90,000
Interest/discount rate	10%
Prior service cost amortization	8,000
Projected benefit obligation, January 1, 2020	500,000
Service cost	60,000

Instructions

a. Compute pension expense for the year 2020.

b. Prepare the journal entry to record pension expense and the employer's contribution to the pension plan in 2020.

E20.2 **(LO 1, 2, 3)** **(Computation of Pension Expense)** Veldre Company provides the following information about its defined benefit pension plan for the year 2020.

Service cost	$ 90,000
Contribution to the plan	105,000
Prior service cost amortization	10,000
Actual and expected return on plan assets	64,000
Benefits paid	40,000
Plan assets at January 1, 2020	640,000
Projected benefit obligation at January 1, 2020	700,000
Accumulated OCI (PSC) at January 1, 2020	150,000
Interest/discount (settlement) rate	10%

Instructions

Compute the pension expense for the year 2020.

E20.3 **(LO 1, 2, 3)** **(Preparation of Pension Worksheet)** Using the information in E20.2, prepare a pension worksheet inserting January 1, 2020, balances, showing December 31, 2020, balances, and the journal entry recording pension expense.

E20.4 **(LO 1, 2)** **(Basic Pension Worksheet)** The following facts apply to the pension plan of Boudreau Inc. for the year 2020.

Plan assets, January 1, 2020	$490,000
Projected benefit obligation, January 1, 2020	490,000
Settlement rate	8%
Service cost	40,000
Contributions (funding)	25,000
Actual and expected return on plan assets	49,700
Benefits paid to retirees	33,400

Instructions

Using the preceding data, compute pension expense for the year 2020. As part of your solution, prepare a pension worksheet that shows the journal entry for pension expense for 2020 and the year-end balances in the related pension accounts.

E20.5 **(LO 3)** **(Application of Years-of-Service Method)** Andrews Company has five employees participating in its defined benefit pension plan. Expected years of future service for these employees at the beginning of 2020 are as follows.

Employee	Future Years of Service
Jim	3
Paul	4
Nancy	5
Dave	6
Kathy	6

On January 1, 2020, the company amended its pension plan, increasing its projected benefit obligation by $72,000.

Instructions

Compute the amount of prior service cost amortization for the years 2020 through 2025 using the years-of-service method, setting up appropriate schedules.

E20.6 **(LO 1)** **(Computation of Actual Return)** Gingrich Importers provides the following pension plan information.

Fair value of pension plan assets, January 1, 2020	$2,400,000
Fair value of pension plan assets, December 31, 2020	2,725,000
Contributions to the plan in 2020	280,000
Benefits paid retirees in 2020	350,000

Instructions

From the data above, compute the actual return on the plan assets for 2020.

E20.7 **(LO 1, 2, 3)** Excel **(Basic Pension Worksheet)** The following defined pension data of Rydell Corp. apply to the year 2020.

Projected benefit obligation, 1/1/20 (before amendment)	$560,000
Plan assets, 1/1/20	546,200
Pension liability, 1/1/20	13,800
On January 1, 2020, Rydell Corp., through plan amendment, grants prior service benefits having a present value of	120,000
Settlement rate	9%
Service cost	58,000
Contributions (funding)	65,000
Actual (expected) return on plan assets	52,280
Benefits paid to retirees	40,000
Prior service cost amortization for 2020	17,000

Instructions

For 2020, prepare a pension worksheet for Rydell Corp. that shows the journal entry for pension expense and the year-end balances in the related pension accounts.

E20.8 (LO 4) (Application of the Corridor Approach) Kenseth Corp. has the following beginning-of-the-year present values for its projected benefit obligation and market-related values for its pension plan assets.

	Projected Benefit Obligation	Plan Assets Value
2019	$2,000,000	$1,900,000
2020	2,400,000	2,500,000
2021	2,950,000	2,600,000
2022	3,600,000	3,000,000

The average remaining service life per employee in 2019 and 2020 is 10 years and in 2021 and 2022 is 12 years. The net gain or loss that occurred during each year is as follows: 2019, $280,000 loss; 2020, $90,000 loss; 2021, $11,000 loss; and 2022, $25,000 gain. (In working the solution, the gains and losses must be aggregated to arrive at year-end balances.)

Instructions

Using the corridor approach, compute the amount of net gain or loss amortized and charged to pension expense in each of the four years, setting up an appropriate schedule.

E20.9 (LO 5) (Disclosures: Pension Expense and Other Comprehensive Income) Taveras Enterprises provides the following information relative to its defined benefit pension plan.

Balances or Values at December 31, 2020	
Projected benefit obligation	$2,737,000
Accumulated benefit obligation	1,980,000
Fair value of plan assets	2,278,329
Accumulated OCI (PSC)	210,000
Accumulated OCI—Net loss (1/1/20 balance, -0-)	45,680
Pension liability	458,671
Other pension plan data for 2020:	
Service cost	94,000
Prior service cost amortization	42,000
Actual return on plan assets	130,000
Expected return on plan assets	175,680
Interest on January 1, 2020, projected benefit obligation	253,000
Contributions to plan	93,329
Benefits paid	140,000

Instructions

a. Prepare the note disclosing the components of pension expense for the year 2020.

b. Determine the amounts of other comprehensive income and comprehensive income for 2020. Net income for 2020 is $35,000.

c. Compute the amount of accumulated other comprehensive income reported at December 31, 2020.

E20.10 (LO 1, 2, 3, 4) (Pension Worksheet) Webb Corp. sponsors a defined benefit pension plan for its employees. On January 1, 2020, the following balances relate to this plan.

Plan assets	$480,000
Projected benefit obligation	600,000
Pension asset/liability	120,000
Accumulated OCI (PSC)	100,000 Dr.

As a result of the operation of the plan during 2020, the following additional data are provided by the actuary.

Service cost	$90,000
Settlement rate, 9%	
Actual return on plan assets	55,000
Amortization of prior service cost	19,000
Expected return on plan assets	52,000
Unexpected loss from change in projected benefit obligation, due to change in actuarial predictions	76,000
Contributions	99,000
Benefits paid retirees	85,000

Instructions

a. Using the data above, compute pension expense for Webb Corp. for the year 2020 by preparing a pension worksheet.

b. Prepare the journal entry for pension expense for 2020.

E20.11 **(LO 1, 2, 3, 4, 5) (Pension Expense, Journal Entries, Statement Presentation)** Henning Company sponsors a defined benefit pension plan for its employees. The following data relate to the operation of the plan for the year 2020 in which no benefits were paid.

1. The actuarial present value of future benefits earned by employees for services rendered in 2020 amounted to $56,000.
2. The company's funding policy requires a contribution to the pension trustee amounting to $145,000 for 2020.
3. As of January 1, 2020, the company had a projected benefit obligation of $900,000, an accumulated benefit obligation of $800,000, and a debit balance of $400,000 in accumulated OCI (PSC). The fair value of pension plan assets amounted to $600,000 at the beginning of the year. The actual and expected return on plan assets was $54,000. The settlement rate was 9%. No gains or losses occurred in 2020 and no benefits were paid.
4. Amortization of prior service cost was $50,000 in 2020. Amortization of net gain or loss was not required in 2020.

Instructions

a. Determine the amounts of the components of pension expense that should be recognized by the company in 2020.

b. Prepare the journal entry or entries to record pension expense and the employer's contribution to the pension trustee in 2020.

c. Indicate the amounts that would be reported on the income statement and the balance sheet for the year 2020.

E20.12 **(LO 1, 2, 3, 4, 5) (Pension Expense, Journal Entries, Statement Presentation)** Ferreri Company received the following selected information from its pension plan trustee concerning the operation of the company's defined benefit pension plan for the year ended December 31, 2020.

	January 1, 2020	December 31, 2020
Projected benefit obligation	$1,500,000	$1,527,000
Market-related and fair value of plan assets	800,000	1,130,000
Accumulated benefit obligation	1,600,000	1,720,000
Accumulated OCI (G/L)—Net gain	–0–	(200,000)

The service cost component of pension expense for employee services rendered in the current year amounted to $77,000 and the amortization of prior service cost was $120,000. The company's actual funding (contributions) of the plan in 2020 amounted to $250,000. The expected return on plan assets and the actual rate were both 10%; the interest/discount (settlement) rate was 10%. Accumulated other comprehensive income (PSC) had a balance of $1,200,000 on January 1, 2020. Assume no benefits paid in 2020.

Instructions

a. Determine the amounts of the components of pension expense that should be recognized by the company in 2020.

b. Prepare the journal entry to record pension expense and the employer's contribution to the pension plan in 2020.

c. Indicate the pension-related amounts that would be reported on the income statement and the balance sheet for Ferreri Company for the year 2020.

E20.13 **(LO 1, 2, 4) (Computation of Actual Return, Gains and Losses, Corridor Test, and Pension Expense)** Erickson Company sponsors a defined benefit pension plan. The corporation's actuary provides the following information about the plan.

	January 1, 2020	December 31, 2020
Vested benefit obligation	$1,500	$1,900
Accumulated benefit obligation	1,900	2,730
Projected benefit obligation	2,500	3,300
Plan assets (fair value)	1,700	2,620

	January 1, 2020	December 31, 2020
Settlement rate and expected rate of return		10%
Pension asset/liability	$ 800	$?
Service cost for the year 2020		400
Contributions (funding in 2020)		700
Benefits paid in 2020		200

Instructions

a. Compute the actual return on the plan assets in 2020.

b. Compute the amount of the other comprehensive income (G/L) as of December 31, 2020. (Assume the January 1, 2020, balance was zero.)

c. Compute the amount of net gain or loss amortization for 2020 (corridor approach).

d. Compute pension expense for 2020.

E20.14 **(LO 1, 2, 4) (Worksheet for E20.13)** Using the information in E20.13 about Erickson Company's defined benefit pension plan, prepare a 2020 pension worksheet with supplementary schedules of computations. Prepare the journal entries at December 31, 2020, to record pension expense and related pension transactions. Also, indicate the pension amounts reported in the balance sheet.

E20.15 **(LO 1, 2, 5) (Pension Expense, Journal Entries)** Latoya Company provides the following selected information related to its defined benefit pension plan for 2020.

Pension asset/liability (January 1)	$ 25,000 Cr.
Accumulated benefit obligation (December 31)	400,000
Actual and expected return on plan assets	10,000
Contributions (funding) in 2020	150,000
Fair value of plan assets (December 31)	800,000
Settlement rate	10%
Projected benefit obligation (January 1)	700,000
Service cost	80,000

Instructions

a. Compute pension expense and prepare the journal entry to record pension expense and the employer's contribution to the pension plan in 2020. Preparation of a pension worksheet is not required. Benefits paid in 2020 were $35,000.

b. Indicate the pension-related amounts that would be reported in the company's income statement and balance sheet for 2020.

E20.16 **(LO 4) (Amortization of Accumulated OCI (G/L), Corridor Approach, Pension Expense Computation)** The actuary for the pension plan of Gustafson Inc. calculated the following net gains and losses.

Incurred During the Year	(Gain) or Loss
2020	$300,000
2021	480,000
2022	(210,000)
2023	(290,000)

Other information about the company's pension obligation and plan assets is as follows.

As of January 1,	Projected Benefit Obligation	Plan Assets (market-related asset value)
2020	$4,000,000	$2,400,000
2021	4,520,000	2,200,000
2022	5,000,000	2,600,000
2023	4,240,000	3,040,000

Gustafson Inc. has a stable labor force of 400 employees who are expected to receive benefits under the plan. The total service-years for all participating employees is 5,600. The beginning balance of accumulated OCI (G/L) is zero on January 1, 2020. The market-related value and the fair value of plan assets are the same for the 4-year period. Use the average remaining service life per employee as the basis for amortization.

Instructions

(Round to the nearest dollar.)

Prepare a schedule which reflects the minimum amount of accumulated OCI (G/L) amortized as a component of net periodic pension expense for each of the years 2020, 2021, 2022, and 2023. Apply the "corridor" approach in determining the amount to be amortized each year.

E20.17 **(LO 1, 4, 5) (Amortization of Accumulated OCI Balances)** Keeton Company sponsors a defined benefit pension plan for its 600 employees. The company's actuary provided the following information about the plan.

	January 1,	December 31,	
	2020	2020	2021
Projected benefit obligation	$2,800,000	$3,650,000	$4,195,000
Accumulated benefit obligation	1,900,000	2,430,000	2,900,000
Plan assets (fair value and market-related asset value)	1,700,000	2,900,000	3,790,000
Accumulated net (gain) or loss (for purposes of the corridor calculation)	-0-	198,000	(24,000)
Discount rate (current settlement rate)		9%	8%
Actual and expected asset return rate		10%	10%
Contributions		1,030,000	600,000

The average remaining service life per employee is 10.5 years. The service cost component of net periodic pension expense for employee services rendered amounted to $400,000 in 2020 and $475,000 in 2021. The accumulated OCI (PSC) on January 1, 2020, was $1,260,000. No benefits have been paid.

Instructions

(Round to the nearest dollar.)

a. Compute the amount of accumulated OCI (PSC) to be amortized as a component of net periodic pension expense for each of the years 2020 and 2021.

b. Prepare a schedule which reflects the amount of accumulated OCI (G/L) to be amortized as a component of pension expense for 2020 and 2021.

c. Determine the total amount of pension expense to be recognized by Keeton Company in 2020 and 2021.

E20.18 **(LO 1, 2, 3, 4) (Pension Worksheet—Missing Amounts)** The accounting staff of Usher Inc. has prepared the following pension worksheet. Unfortunately, several entries in the worksheet are not decipherable. The company has asked your assistance in completing the worksheet and completing the accounting tasks related to the pension plan for 2020.

Pension Worksheet—Usher Inc.

	General Journal Entries					Memo Record	
Items	Annual Pension Expense	Cash	OCI—Prior Service Cost	OCI—Gain/Loss	Pension Asset/ Liability	Projected Benefit Obligation	Plan Assets
Balance, Jan. 1, 2020					1,100 Cr.	2,800	1,700
Service cost	(1)					500	
Interest cost	(2)					280	
Actual return	(3)						220
Unexpected gain	150			(4)			
Amortization of PSC	(5)		55				
Contributions		800					800
Benefits						200	200
Liability increase				(6)		365	
Journal entry	(7)	(8)	(9)	(10)	(11)		
Accumulated OCI, Dec. 31, 2019			1,100	0			
Balance, Dec. 31, 2020			1,045	215	1,225	3,745	2,520

Instructions

a. Determine the missing amounts in the 2020 pension worksheet, indicating whether the amounts are debits or credits.

b. Prepare the journal entry to record 2020 pension expense for Usher Inc.

c. The accounting staff has heard of a pension accounting procedure called "corridor amortization." Is Usher required to record any amounts for corridor amortization in (1) 2020? In (2) 2021? Explain.

*E20.19 **(LO 6, 7) (Postretirement Benefit Expense Computation)** Kreter Co. provides the following information about its postretirement benefit plan for the year 2020.

Service cost	$ 45,000
Contribution to the plan	10,000
Actual and expected return on plan assets	11,000
Benefits paid	20,000
Plan assets at January 1, 2020	110,000
Accumulated postretirement benefit obligation at January 1, 2020	330,000
Discount rate	8%

Instructions

Compute the postretirement benefit expense for 2020.

*E20.20 **(LO 6, 7) (Postretirement Benefit Worksheet)** Using the information in E20.19, prepare a worksheet inserting January 1, 2020, balances, and showing December 31, 2020, balances. Prepare the journal entry recording postretirement benefit expense.

*E20.21 **(LO 6, 7) (Postretirement Benefit Expense Computation)** Garner Inc. provides the following information related to its postretirement benefits for the year 2020.

Accumulated postretirement benefit obligation at January 1, 2020	$710,000
Actual and expected return on plan assets	34,000
Prior service cost amortization	21,000
Discount rate	10%
Service cost	83,000

Instructions

Compute postretirement benefit expense for 2020.

*E20.22 **(LO 6, 7) (Postretirement Benefit Expense Computation)** Englehart Co. provides the following information about its postretirement benefit plan for the year 2020.

Service cost	$ 90,000
Prior service cost amortization	3,000
Contribution to the plan	56,000
Actual and expected return on plan assets	62,000
Benefits paid	40,000
Plan assets at January 1, 2020	710,000
Accumulated postretirement benefit obligation at January 1, 2020	760,000
Accumulated OCI (PSC) at January 1, 2020	100,000 Dr.
Discount rate	9%

Instructions

Compute the postretirement benefit expense for 2020.

*E20.23 **(LO 6, 7) (Postretirement Benefit Worksheet)** Using the information in E20.22, prepare a worksheet inserting January 1, 2020, balances, showing December 31, 2020, balances, and the journal entry recording postretirement benefit expense.

*E20.24 **(LO 6, 7) (Postretirement Benefit Worksheet—Missing Amounts)** The accounting staff of Holder Inc. has prepared the following postretirement benefit worksheet. Unfortunately, several entries in the worksheet are not decipherable. The company has asked your assistance in completing the worksheet and completing the accounting tasks related to the pension plan for 2020.

Postretirement Benefit Worksheet—Holder Inc.

Home Insert Page Layout Formulas Data Review View

P18 fx

	A	B	C	D	E	F	G
1							
2			General Journal Entries			Memo Record	
3				Other			
4		Annual		Comprehensive	Postretirement		
5	Items	Expense	Cash	Income—PSC	Asset/Liability	APBO	Plan Assets
6	Balance, Jan. 1, 2020				290,000	410,000	120,000
7	Service cost	(1)				56,000	
8	Interest cost	(2)				36,900	
9	Actual/Expected return	(3)					2,000
10	Contributions		66,000				(4)
11	Benefits					5,000	5,000
12	Amortization of PSC	3,000		(5)			
13	Journal entry for 2020	(6)	(7)	(8)	(9)		
14							
15	Accumulated OCI, Dec. 31, 2019			30,000 Dr.			
16	Balance, Dec. 31, 2020			27,000 Dr.	314,900 Cr.	497,900 Cr.	183,000 Dr.
17							

Instructions

a. Determine the missing amounts in the 2020 postretirement worksheet, indicating whether the amounts are debits or credits.

b. Prepare the journal entry to record 2020 postretirement expense for Holder Inc.

c. What discount rate is Holder using in accounting for the interest on its other postretirement benefit plan? Explain.

Problems

P20.1 (LO 1, 2, 3, 4) Excel (2-Year Worksheet) On January 1, 2020, Harrington Company has the following defined benefit pension plan balances.

Projected benefit obligation	$4,500,000
Fair value of plan assets	4,200,000

The interest (settlement) rate applicable to the plan is 10%. On January 1, 2021, the company amends its pension agreement so that prior service costs of $500,000 are created. Other data related to the pension plan are as follows.

	2020	2021
Service cost	$150,000	$180,000
Prior service cost amortization	–0–	90,000
Contributions (funding) to the plan	240,000	285,000
Benefits paid	200,000	280,000
Actual return on plan assets	252,000	260,000
Expected rate of return on assets	6%	8%

Instructions

a. Prepare a pension worksheet for the pension plan for 2020 and 2021.

b. For 2021, prepare the journal entry to record pension-related amounts.

P20.2 (LO 1, 2, 3, 4, 5) Groupwork (3-Year Worksheet, Journal Entries, and Reporting) Jackson Company adopts acceptable accounting for its defined benefit pension plan on January 1, 2019, with the following beginning balances: plan assets $200,000; projected benefit obligation $250,000. Other data relating to 3 years' operation of the plan are as follows.

	2019	2020	2021
Annual service cost	$16,000	$ 19,000	$ 26,000
Settlement rate and expected rate of return	10%	10%	10%
Actual return on plan assets	18,000	22,000	24,000
Annual funding (contributions)	16,000	40,000	48,000
Benefits paid	14,000	16,400	21,000
Prior service cost (plan amended, 1/1/20)		160,000	
Amortization of prior service cost		54,400	41,600
Change in actuarial assumptions establishes a December 31, 2021, projected benefit obligation of:			520,000

Instructions

a. Prepare a pension worksheet presenting all 3 years' pension balances and activities.

b. Prepare the journal entries (from the worksheet) to reflect all pension plan transactions and events at December 31 of each year.

c. Indicate the pension-related amounts reported in the financial statements for 2021.

P20.3 **(LO 1, 2, 3, 4, 5) (Pension Expense, Journal Entries, Amortization of Loss)** Gottschalk Company sponsors a defined benefit plan for its 100 employees. On January 1, 2020, the company's actuary provided the following information.

Accumulated other comprehensive loss (PSC)	$150,000
Pension plan assets (fair value and market-related asset value)	200,000
Accumulated benefit obligation	260,000
Projected benefit obligation	380,000

The average remaining service period for the participating employees is 10 years. All employees are expected to receive benefits under the plan. On December 31, 2020, the actuary calculated that the present value of future benefits earned for employee services rendered in the current year amounted to $52,000; the projected benefit obligation was $490,000; fair value of pension assets was $276,000; the accumulated benefit obligation amounted to $365,000. The expected return on plan assets and the discount rate on the projected benefit obligation were both 10%. The actual return on plan assets is $11,000. The company's current year's contribution to the pension plan amounted to $65,000. No benefits were paid during the year.

Instructions

a. Determine the components of pension expense that the company would recognize in 2020. (With only one year involved, you need not prepare a worksheet.)

b. Prepare the journal entry to record the pension expense and the company's funding of the pension plan in 2020.

c. Compute the amount of the 2020 increase/decrease in gains or losses and the amount to be amortized in 2020 and 2021.

d. Indicate the pension amounts reported in the financial statement as of December 31, 2020.

P20.4 **(LO 1, 2, 3, 4)** Excel **(Pension Expense, Journal Entries for 2 Years)** Gordon Company sponsors a defined benefit pension plan. The following information related to the pension plan is available for 2020 and 2021.

	2020	2021
Plan assets (fair value), December 31	$699,000	$849,000
Projected benefit obligation, January 1	700,000	800,000
Pension asset/liability, January 1	140,000 Cr.	?
Prior service cost, January 1	250,000	240,000
Service cost	60,000	90,000
Actual and expected return on plan assets	24,000	30,000
Amortization of prior service cost	10,000	12,000
Contributions (funding)	115,000	120,000
Accumulated benefit obligation, December 31	500,000	550,000
Interest/settlement rate	9%	9%

Instructions

a. Compute pension expense for 2020 and 2021.

b. Prepare the journal entries to record the pension expense and the company's funding of the pension plan for both years.

P20.5 **(LO 2, 3, 4) (Computation of Pension Expense, Amortization of Net Gain or Loss–Corridor Approach, Journal Entries for 3 Years)** Hiatt Toothpaste Company initiates a defined benefit pension plan for its 50 employees on January 1, 2020. The insurance company which administers the pension plan provided the following selected information for the years 2020, 2021, and 2022.

	For Year Ended December 31,		
	2020	2021	2022
Plan assets (fair value)	$50,000	$ 85,000	$180,000
Accumulated benefit obligation	45,000	165,000	292,000
Projected benefit obligation	60,000	200,000	324,000
Net (gain) loss (for purposes of corridor calculation)	–0–	78,400	81,033
Employer's funding contribution (made at end of year)	50,000	60,000	105,000

There were no balances as of January 1, 2020, when the plan was initiated. The actual and expected return on plan assets was 10% over the 3-year period, but the settlement rate used to discount the company's pension obligation was 13% in 2020, 11% in 2021, and 8% in 2022. The service cost component of net periodic pension expense amounted to the following: 2020, $60,000; 2021, $85,000; and 2022, $119,000. The average remaining service life per employee is 12 years. No benefits were paid in 2020, $30,000 of benefits were paid in 2021, and $18,500 of benefits were paid in 2022 (all benefits paid at end of year).

Instructions

(Round to the nearest dollar.)

a. Calculate the amount of net periodic pension expense that the company would recognize in 2020, 2021, and 2022.

b. Prepare the journal entries to record net periodic pension expense, employer's funding contribution, and related pension amounts for the years 2020, 2021, and 2022.

P20.6 **(LO 3, 4)** Groupwork **(Computation of Prior Service Cost Amortization, Pension Expense, Journal Entries, and Net Gain or Loss)** Aykroyd Inc. has sponsored a noncontributory, defined benefit pension plan for its employees since 1997. Prior to 2020, cumulative net pension expense recognized equaled cumulative contributions to the plan. Other relevant information about the pension plan on January 1, 2020, is as follows.

1. The company has 200 employees. All these employees are expected to receive benefits under the plan. The average remaining service life per employee is 12 years.
2. The projected benefit obligation amounted to $5,000,000 and the fair value of pension plan assets was $3,000,000. The market-related asset value was also $3,000,000. Unrecognized prior service cost was $2,000,000.

On December 31, 2020, the projected benefit obligation and the accumulated benefit obligation were $4,850,000 and $4,025,000, respectively. The fair value of the pension plan assets amounted to $4,100,000 at the end of the year. A 10% settlement rate and a 10% expected asset return rate were used in the actuarial present value computations in the pension plan. The present value of benefits attributed by the pension benefit formula to employee service in 2020 amounted to $200,000. The employer's contribution to the plan assets amounted to $775,000 in 2020. This problem assumes no payment of pension benefits.

Instructions

(Round all amounts to the nearest dollar.)

a. Prepare a schedule, based on the average remaining life per employee, showing the prior service cost that would be amortized as a component of pension expense for 2020, 2021, and 2022.

b. Compute pension expense for the year 2020.

c. Compute the amount of the 2020 increase/decrease in net gains or losses and the amount to be amortized in 2020 and 2021.

d. Prepare the journal entries required to report the accounting for the company's pension plan for 2020.

P20.7 **(LO 2, 3, 4)** **(Pension Worksheet)** Hanson Corp. sponsors a defined benefit pension plan for its employees. On January 1, 2020, the following balances related to this plan.

Plan assets (market-related value)	$520,000
Projected benefit obligation	700,000
Pension asset/liability	180,000 Cr.
Prior service cost	81,000
Net gain or loss (debit)	91,000

As a result of the operation of the plan during 2020, the actuary provided the following additional data for 2020.

Service cost	$108,000
Settlement rate, 9%; expected return rate, 10%	
Actual return on plan assets	48,000
Amortization of prior service cost	25,000
Contributions	133,000
Benefits paid retirees	85,000
Average remaining service life of active employees	10 years

Instructions

Using the preceding data, compute pension expense for Hanson Corp. for the year 2020 by preparing a pension worksheet that shows the journal entry for pension expense. Use the market-related asset value to compute the expected return and for corridor amortization.

P20.8 **(LO 1, 2, 3, 4, 5)** Groupwork **(Comprehensive 2-Year Worksheet)** Lemke Company sponsors a defined benefit pension plan for its employees. The following data relate to the operation of the plan for the years 2020 and 2021.

	2020	2021
Projected benefit obligation, January 1	$600,000	
Plan assets (fair value and market-related value), January 1	410,000	
Pension asset/liability, January 1	190,000 Cr.	
Prior service cost, January 1	160,000	
Service cost	40,000	$ 59,000
Settlement rate	10%	10%
Expected rate of return	10%	10%
Actual return on plan assets	36,000	61,000
Amortization of prior service cost	70,000	50,000
Annual contributions	97,000	81,000
Benefits paid retirees	31,500	54,000
Increase in projected benefit obligation due to changes in actuarial assumptions	87,000	-0-
Accumulated benefit obligation at December 31	721,800	789,000
Average service life of all employees		20 years
Vested benefit obligation at December 31		464,000

Instructions

a. Prepare a pension worksheet presenting both years 2020 and 2021 and accompanying computations and amortization of the loss (2021) using the corridor approach.

b. Prepare the journal entries (from the worksheet) to reflect all pension plan transactions and events at December 31 of each year.

c. For 2021, indicate the pension amounts reported in the financial statements.

P20.9 **(LO 1, 2, 3, 4, 5)** Groupwork **(Comprehensive 2-Year Worksheet)** Hobbs Co. has the following defined benefit pension plan balances on January 1, 2020.

Projected benefit obligation	$4,600,000
Fair value of plan assets	4,600,000

The interest (settlement) rate applicable to the plan is 10%. On January 1, 2021, the company amends its pension agreement so that prior service costs of $600,000 are created. Other data related to the pension plan are:

	2020	2021
Service cost	$150,000	$170,000
Prior service cost amortization	-0-	90,000
Contributions (funding) to the plan	200,000	184,658
Benefits paid	220,000	280,000
Actual return on plan assets	252,000	350,000
Expected rate of return on assets	6%	8%

Instructions

a. Prepare a pension worksheet for the pension plan in 2020.

b. Prepare any journal entries related to the pension plan that would be needed at December 31, 2020.

c. Prepare a pension worksheet for 2021 and any journal entries related to the pension plan as of December 31, 2021.

d. Indicate the pension-related amounts reported in the 2021 financial statements.

P20.10 (LO 1, 2, 3, 4) (Pension Worksheet—Missing Amounts) Kramer Co. has prepared the following pension worksheet. Unfortunately, several entries in the worksheet are not decipherable. The company has asked your assistance in completing the worksheet and completing the accounting tasks related to the pension plan for 2020.

Pension Worksheet—Kramer Co.

	A	B	C	D	E	F	G	H
1								
2		General Journal Entries					Memo Record	
3								
4		Annual Pension		OCI—Prior	OCI—	Pension Asset/	Projected Benefit	
5	Items	Expense	Cash	Service Cost	Gain/Loss	Liability	Obligation	Plan Assets
6	Balance, Jan. 1, 2020					120,000	325,000	205,000 Dr.
7	Service cost	(1)					20,000	
8	Interest cost	(2)					26,000	
9	Actual return	(3)						18,000 Dr.
10	Unexpected loss	2,500			(4)			
11	Amortization of PSC	(5)		35,000				
12	Contributions		41,000					41,000 Dr.
13	Benefits						15,000	15,000 Cr.
14	Increase in PBO				(6)		43,500	
15	Journal entry for 2020	(7)	(8)	(9)	(10)	(11)		
16	Accumulated OCI, Dec. 31, 2019			80,000	0			
17	Balance, Dec. 31, 2020			45,000	46,000	150,500 Cr.	399,500 Cr.	249,000 Dr.
18								

Instructions

a. Determine the missing amounts in the 2020 pension worksheet, indicating whether the amounts are debits or credits.

b. Prepare the journal entry to record 2020 pension expense for Kramer Co.

c. Determine the following for Kramer for 2020: (1) settlement rate used to measure the interest on the liability and (2) expected return on plan assets.

P20.11 (LO 1, 2, 3, 4, 5) (Pension Worksheet) The following data relate to the operation of Kramer Co.'s pension plan in 2021. The pension worksheet for 2020 is provided in P20.10.

Service cost	$59,000
Actual return on plan assets	32,000
Amortization of prior service cost	28,000
Annual contributions	51,000
Benefits paid retirees	27,000
Average service life of all employees	25 years

For 2021, Kramer will use the same assumptions as 2020 for the expected rate of returns on plan assets. The settlement rate for 2021 is 10%.

Instructions

a. Prepare a pension worksheet for 2021 and accompanying computations and amortization of the loss, if any, in 2021 using the corridor approach.

b. Prepare the journal entries (from the worksheet) to reflect all pension plan transactions and events at December 31.

c. Indicate the pension amounts reported in the financial statements.

P20.12 (LO 1, 2, 3, 4, 5) (Pension Worksheet) Larson Corp. sponsors a defined benefit pension plan for its employees. On January 1, 2021, the following balances related to this plan.

Plan assets (market-related value)	$270,000
Projected benefit obligation	340,000
Pension asset/liability	70,000 Cr.
Prior service cost	90,000
OCI—Loss	39,000

As a result of the operation of the plan during 2021, the actuary provided the following additional data for 2021.

Service cost	$45,000
Actual return on plan assets	27,000
Amortization of prior service cost	12,000
Contributions	65,000
Benefits paid retirees	41,000
Settlement rate	7%
Expected return on plan assets	8%
Average remaining service life of active employees	10 years

Instructions

a. Compute pension expense for Larson Corp. for the year 2021 by preparing a pension worksheet that shows the journal entry for pension expense.

b. Indicate the pension amounts reported in the financial statements.

***P20.13 (LO 6, 7) Groupwork (Postretirement Benefit Worksheet)** Hollenbeck Foods Inc. sponsors a postretirement medical and dental benefit plan for its employees. The following balances relate to this plan on January 1, 2020.

Plan assets	$200,000
Expected postretirement benefit obligation	820,000
Accumulated postretirement benefit obligation	200,000
No prior service costs or OCI balances exist.	

As a result of the plan's operation during 2020, the following additional data are provided by the actuary.

Service cost is $70,000
Discount rate is 10%
Contributions to plan are $65,000
Expected return on plan assets is $10,000
Actual return on plan assets is $15,000
Benefits paid to employees are $44,000
Average remaining service to full eligibility: 20 years

Instructions

a. Using the preceding data, compute the net periodic postretirement benefit cost for 2020 by preparing a worksheet that shows the journal entry for postretirement expense and the year-end balances in the related postretirement benefit memo accounts. (Assume that contributions and benefits are paid at the end of the year.)

b. Prepare any journal entries related to the postretirement plan for 2020 and indicate the postretirement amounts reported in the financial statements for 2020.

*P20.14 **(LO 6, 7)** **(Postretirement Benefit Worksheet—2 Years)** Elton Co. has the following postretirement benefit plan balances on January 1, 2020.

Accumulated postretirement benefit obligation	$2,250,000
Fair value of plan assets	2,250,000

The interest (settlement) rate applicable to the plan is 10%. On January 1, 2021, the company amends the plan so that prior service costs of $175,000 are created. Other data related to the plan are:

	2020	2021
Service costs	$ 75,000	$ 85,000
Prior service costs amortization	–0–	12,000
Contributions (funding) to the plan	45,000	35,000
Benefits paid	40,000	45,000
Actual return on plan assets	140,000	120,000
Expected rate of return on assets	8%	6%

Instructions

a. Prepare a worksheet for the postretirement plan in 2020.

b. Prepare any journal entries related to the postretirement plan that would be needed at December 31, 2020.

c. Prepare a worksheet for 2021 and any journal entries related to the postretirement plan as of December 31, 2021.

d. Indicate the postretirement-benefit–related amounts reported in the 2021 financial statements.

Concepts for Analysis

CA20.1 **(LO 1)** **(Pension Terminology and Theory)** Many business organizations have been concerned with providing for the retirement of employees since the late 1800s. Increase in this concern resulted in the establishment of private pension plans in most large companies and in many medium- and small-sized ones.

The substantial growth of these plans, both in numbers of employees covered and in amounts of retirement benefits, has increased the significance of pension costs in relation to the financial position, results of operations, and cash flows of many companies. In examining the costs of pension plans, a CPA encounters certain terms. The components of pension costs that the terms represent must be dealt with appropriately if generally accepted accounting principles are to be reflected in the financial statements of entities with pension plans.

Instructions

a. Define a private pension plan. How does a contributory pension plan differ from a noncontributory plan?

b. Differentiate between "accounting for the employer" and "accounting for the pension fund."

c. Explain the terms "funded" and "pension liability" as they relate to:

1. The pension fund.
2. The employer.

d. 1. Discuss the theoretical justification for accrual recognition of pension costs.

2. Discuss the relative objectivity of the measurement process of accrual versus cash (pay-as-you-go) accounting for annual pension costs.

e. Distinguish among the following as they relate to pension plans.

1. Service cost.
2. Prior service costs.
3. Vested benefits.

CA20.2 **(LO 1)** Writing **(Pension Terminology)** The following items appear on Brueggen Company's financial statements.

1. Under the caption Assets:
   Pension asset/liability.
2. Under the caption Liabilities:
   Pension asset/liability.
3. Under the caption Stockholders' Equity:
   Prior service cost as a component of Accumulated Other Comprehensive Income.
4. On the income statement:
   Pension expense.

Instructions

Explain the significance of each of the items above on corporate financial statements. (*Note:* All items set forth above are not necessarily to be found on the statements of a single company.)

CA20.3 **(LO 1)** **(Basic Terminology)** In examining the costs of pension plans, Helen Kaufman, CPA, encounters certain terms. The components of pension costs that the terms represent must be dealt with appropriately if generally accepted accounting principles are to be reflected in the financial statements of entities with pension plans.

Instructions

a. 1. Discuss the theoretical justification for accrual recognition of pension costs.

2. Discuss the relative objectivity of the measurement process of accrual versus cash (pay-as-you-go) accounting for annual pension costs.

b. Explain the following terms as they apply to accounting for pension plans.

1. Market-related asset value.
2. Projected benefit obligation.
3. Corridor approach.

c. What information should be disclosed about a company's pension plans in its financial statements and its notes?

(AICPA adapted)

CA20.4 **(LO 1)** Writing **(Major Pension Concepts)** Davis Corporation is a medium-sized manufacturer of paperboard containers and boxes. The corporation sponsors a noncontributory, defined benefit pension plan that covers its 250 employees. Sid Cole has recently been hired as president of Davis Corporation. While reviewing last year's financial statements with Carol Dilbeck, controller, Cole expressed confusion about several of the items in the footnote to the financial statements relating to the pension plan. In part, the footnote reads as follows.

> **Note J.** The company has a defined benefit pension plan covering substantially all of its employees. The benefits are based on years of service and the employee's compensation during the last four years of employment. The company's funding policy is to contribute annually the maximum amount allowed under the federal tax code. Contributions are intended to provide for benefits expected to be earned in the future as well as those earned to date.

The net periodic pension expense on Davis Corporation's comparative income statement was $72,000 in 2020 and $57,680 in 2019.

The following are selected figures from the plan's funded status and amounts recognized in the Davis Corporation's Statement of Financial Position at December 31, 2020 ($000 omitted).

Actuarial present value of benefit obligations:	
Accumulated benefit obligation (including vested benefits of $636)	$ (870)
Projected benefit obligation	$(1,200)
Plan assets at fair value	1,050
Projected benefit obligation in excess of plan assets	$ (150)

Given that Davis Corporation's work force has been stable for the last 6 years, Cole could not understand the increase in the net periodic pension expense. Dilbeck explained that the net periodic pension expense consists of several elements, some of which may increase or decrease the net expense.

Instructions

a. The determination of the net periodic pension expense is a function of five elements. List and briefly describe each of the elements.

b. Describe the major difference and the major similarity between the accumulated benefit obligation and the projected benefit obligation.

c. **1.** Explain why pension gains and losses are not recognized on the income statement in the period in which they arise.

2. Briefly describe how pension gains and losses are recognized.

(AICPA adapted)

CA20.5 **(LO 5)** Writing **(Implications of GAAP Rules on Pensions)** Jill Vogel and Pete Dell have to do a class presentation on GAAP rules for reporting pension information. In developing the class presentation, they decided to provide the class with a series of questions related to pensions and then discuss the answers in class. Given that the class has all read the rules related to pension accounting and reporting, they felt this approach would provide a lively discussion. Here are the questions:

1. In an article in *Businessweek* related to pensions, it was reported that the discount rates used by the largest 200 companies for pension reporting ranged from 5% to 11%. How can such a situation exist, and does GAAP alleviate this problem?
2. An article indicated that when GAAP rules were issued related to pensions, it caused an increase in the liability for pensions for approximately 20% of companies. Why might this situation occur?
3. A recent article noted that while "smoothing" is not necessarily an accounting virtue, pension accounting has long been recognized as an exception—an area of accounting in which at least some dampening of market swings is appropriate. This is because pension funds are managed so that their performance is insulated from the extremes of short-term market swings. A pension expense that reflects the volatility of market swings might, for that reason, convey information of little relevance. Are these statements true?
4. Understanding the impact of the changes required in pension reporting requires detailed information about its pension plan(s) and an analysis of the relationship of many factors, particularly the:

   a. Type of plan(s) and any significant amendments.

   b. Plan participants.

   c. Funding status.

   d. Actuarial funding method and assumptions currently used.

   What impact does each of these items have on financial statement presentation?
5. An article noted "You also need to decide whether to amortize gains and losses using the corridor method, or to use some other systematic method. Under the corridor approach, only gains and losses in excess of 10% of the greater of the projected benefit obligation or the plan assets would have to be amortized." What is the corridor method and what is its purpose?

Instructions

What answers do you believe Jill and Pete gave to each of these questions?

CA20.6 **(LO 4)** Writing **(Gains and Losses, Corridor Amortization)** Vickie Plato, accounting clerk in the personnel office of Streisand Corp., has begun to compute pension expense for 2022 but is not sure whether or not she should include the amortization of unrecognized gains/losses. She is currently working with the following beginning-of-the-year present values for the projected benefit obligation and market-related values for the pension plan:

	Projected Benefit Obligation	Plan Assets Value
2019	$2,200,000	$1,900,000
2020	2,400,000	2,500,000
2021	2,900,000	2,600,000
2022	3,900,000	3,000,000

The average remaining service life per employee in 2019 and 2020 is 10 years and in 2021 and 2022 is 12 years. The net gain or loss that occurred during each year is as follows.

2019	$280,000 loss
2020	85,000 loss
2021	12,000 loss
2022	25,000 gain

(In working the solution, you must aggregate the unrecognized gains and losses to arrive at year-end balances.)

Instructions

You are the manager in charge of accounting. Write a memo to Vickie Plato, explaining why in some years she must amortize some of the net gains and losses and in other years she does not need to. In order to explain this situation fully, you must compute the amount of net gain or loss that is amortized and charged to pension expense in each of the 4 years listed above. Include an appropriate amortization schedule, referring to it whenever necessary.

CA20.7 **(LO 4)** Ethics **(Nonvested Employees—An Ethical Dilemma)** Thinken Technology recently merged with College Electronix (CE), a computer graphics company. In performing a comprehensive audit of CE's accounting system, Gerald Ott, internal audit manager for Thinken Technology, discovered that the new subsidiary did not record pension assets and liabilities, subject to GAAP.

The net present value of CE's pension assets was $15.5 million, the vested benefit obligation was $12.9 million, and the projected benefit obligation was $17.4 million. Ott reported this audit finding to Julie Habbe, the newly appointed controller of CE. A few days later, Habbe called Ott for his advice on what to do. Habbe started her conversation by asking, "Can't we eliminate the negative income effect of our pension dilemma simply by terminating the employment of nonvested employees before the end of our fiscal year?"

Instructions

How should Ott respond to Habbe's remark about firing nonvested employees?

Using Your Judgment

Financial Reporting Problem

The Procter & Gamble Company (P&G)

The financial statements of P&G are presented in Appendix B. The company's complete annual report, including the notes to the financial statements, is available online.

Instructions

Refer to P&G's financial statements and the accompanying notes to answer the following questions.

a. What kinds of pension plans does P&G provide its employees?

b. What was P&G's pension expense for 2017, 2016, and 2015 related to its defined benefit plan?

c. What is the impact of P&G's pension plans for 2017 on its financial statements?

d. What information does P&G provide on the target allocation of its pension assets? (Compare the asset allocation for "Pensions and Other Retiree Benefits.") How do the allocations relate to the expected returns on these assets?

Comparative Analysis Case

The Coca-Cola Company and PepsiCo, Inc.

The financial statements of Coca-Cola and PepsiCo are presented in Appendices C and D, respectively. The companies' complete annual reports, including the notes to the financial statements, are available online.

Instructions

Use the companies' financial information to answer the following questions.

a. What kind of pension plans do Coca-Cola and PepsiCo provide their employees?

b. What net periodic pension expense (cost) did Coca-Cola and PepsiCo report in 2017?

c. What is the year-end 2017 funded status of Coca-Cola's and PepsiCo's plans (include international)?

d. What relevant rates were used by Coca-Cola and PepsiCo in computing their pension amounts?

e. Compare the expected benefit payments and contributions for Coca-Cola and PepsiCo.

*Financial Statement Analysis Case

General Electric

A *Wall Street Journal* article discussed a $1.8 billion charge to income made by **General Electric** for postretirement benefit costs. It was attributed to previously unrecognized healthcare and life insurance cost. As financial vice president and controller for Peake, Inc., you found this article interesting because the president recently expressed interest in adopting a postemployment benefit program for Peake's employees, to complement the company's existing defined benefit plan. The president, Martha Beyerlein, wants to know how the expense on the new plan will be determined and what impact the accounting for the plan will have on Peake's financial statements.

Instructions

a. As financial vice president and controller of Peake, Inc., explain the calculation of postemployment benefit expense under GAAP, and indicate how the accounting for the plan will affect Peake's financial statements.

b. Discuss the similarities and differences in the accounting for the other postemployment benefit plan relative to the accounting for the defined benefit plan.

Accounting, Analysis, and Principles

PENCOMP's balance sheet at December 31, 2020, is as follows.

PENCOMP, Inc.
Balance Sheet
As of December 31, 2020

		Liabilities	
Assets		Notes payable	$1,000
Cash	$ 438	Pension liability	344
Inventory	1,800	Total liabilities	1,344
Total current assets	2,238	*Stockholders' equity*	
Plant and equipment	2,000	Common stock	2,000
Accumulated depreciation	(240)	Retained earnings	896
	1,760	Accumulated other comprehensive income	(242)
Total assets	$3,998	Total stockholders' equity	2,654
		Total liabilities and stockholders' equity	$3,998

Additional information concerning PENCOMP's defined benefit pension plan is as follows.

Projected benefit obligation at 12/31/20	$ 820.5
Plan assets (fair value) at 12/31/20	476.5
Unamortized past service cost at 12/31/20	150.0
Amortization of past service cost during 2021	15.0
Service cost for 2021	42.0
Discount rate	10%
Expected rate of return on plan assets in 2021	12%
Actual return on plan assets in 2021	10.4
Contributions to pension fund in 2021	70.0
Benefits paid during 2021	40.0
Expected remaining service life of employees	15.0
Average period to vesting of prior service costs	10.0
Unamortized net loss due to changes in actuarial assumptions and deferred net losses on plan assets at 12/31/20	92.0

Other information about PENCOMP is as follows.

Salary expense, all paid with cash during 2021	$ 700.0
Sales, all for cash	3,000.0
Purchases, all for cash	2,000.0
Inventory at 12/31/21	1,800.0

Property originally cost $2,000 and is depreciated on a straight-line basis over 25 years with no residual value.

Interest on the note payable is 10% annually and is paid in cash on 12/31 of each year.

Dividends declared and paid are $200 in 2021.

Accounting

Prepare an income statement for 2021 and a balance sheet as of December 31, 2021. Also, prepare the pension expense journal entry for the year ended December 31, 2021. Round to the nearest tenth (e.g., round 2.87 to 2.9).

Analysis

Compute return on equity for PENCOMP for 2021 (assume stockholders' equity is equal to year-end average stockholders' equity). Do you think an argument can be made for including some or even all of the change in accumulated other comprehensive income (due to pensions) in the numerator of return on equity? Illustrate that calculation.

Principles

Explain a rationale for why the FASB has (so far) decided to exclude from the current period income statement the effects of pension plan amendments and gains and losses due to changes in actuarial assumptions.

Bridge to the Profession

FASB Codification References

[1] FASB ASC 960. [Predecessor literature: "Accounting and Reporting by Defined Benefit Pension Plans," *Statement of Financial Accounting Standards No. 35* (Stamford, Conn.: FASB, 1979).]

[2] FASB ASC 715-70-50-1. [Predecessor literature: "Employers' Accounting for Pension Plans," *Statement of Financial Accounting Standards No. 87* (Stamford, Conn.: FASB, 1985), paras. 63–66.]

[3] FASB ASC 715-30-25-1. [Predecessor literature: "Employers' Accounting for Defined Benefit Pension and Other Postretirement Plans: An Amendment to SFAS Nos. 87, 88, 106, and 132(R)," *Statement of Financial Accounting Standards No. 158* (Norwalk, Conn.: FASB, 2006).]

[4] FASB ASC 715-30-35-22. [Predecessor literature: "Employers' Accounting for Pension Plans," *Statement of Financial Accounting Standards No. 87* (Stamford, Conn.: FASB, 1985), par. 30.]

[5] FASB ASC 220-10-45-13. [Predecessor literature: "Employers' Accounting for Defined Benefit Pension and Other Postretirement Plans: An Amendment of SFAS Nos. 87, 88, 106, and 132(R)," *Statement of Financial Accounting Standards No. 158* (Norwalk, Conn.: FASB, 2006), par. B41.]

[6] FASB ASC 715-20-50-1. [Predecessor literature: None.]

[7] FASB ASC 715-20-45-3A. [Predecessor literature: None.]

[8] FASB ASC 715-20-50. [Predecessor literature: "Employers' Disclosure about Pensions and Other Postretirement Benefits," *Statement of Financial Accounting Standards No. 132* (Stamford, Conn.: FASB, 1998; revised 2003); and "Employers' Accounting for Defined Benefit Pension and Other Postretirement Plans: An Amendment of SFAS Nos. 87, 88, 106, and 132(R)," *Statement of Financial Accounting Standards No. 158* (Norwalk, Conn.: FASB, 2006).]

[9] FASB ASC 715-30-05-9. [Predecessor literature: "Employers' Accounting for Settlements and Curtailments of Defined Benefit Pension Plans and for Termination Benefits," *Statement of Financial Accounting Standards No. 88* (Stamford, Conn.: FASB, 1985).]

[10] FASB ASC 715-60. [Predecessor literature: "Employers' Accounting for Postretirement Benefits Other Than Pensions," *Statement of Financial Accounting Standards No. 106* (Norwalk, Conn.: FASB, 1990).]

[11] FASB ASC 712-10-05. [Predecessor literature: "Employers' Accounting for Postemployment Benefits," *Statement of Financial Accounting Standards No. 112* (Norwalk, Conn.: FASB, 1992).]

[12] FASB ASC 715-60-35-9. [Predecessor literature: "Employers' Accounting for Postretirement Benefits Other Than Pensions," *Statement of Financial Accounting Standards No. 106* (Norwalk, Conn.: FASB, 1990), paras. 46–66.]

[13] FASB ASC 715-60-25. [Predecessor literature: "Employers' Accounting for Postretirement Benefits Other Than Pensions," *Statement of Financial Accounting Standards No. 106* (Norwalk, Conn.: FASB, 1990), par. 163.]

Codification Exercises

If your school has a subscription to the FASB Codification, log in and prepare responses to the following. Provide Codification references for your responses.

CE20.1 Access the glossary ("Master Glossary") to answer the following.

a. What is an accumulated benefit obligation?

b. What is a defined benefit postretirement plan?

c. What is the definition of "actuarial present value"?

d. What is a prior service cost?

CE20.2 In general, how can an employer choose an appropriate discount rate for its pension plan? What information could an employer use in choosing a discount rate?

CE20.3 If an employer has a defined benefit pension plan, what components would make up its net periodic pension cost?

CE20.4 What information about its pension plan must a publicly traded company disclose in its interim financial statements?

Codification Research Case

Monat Company has grown rapidly since its founding in 2004. To instill loyalty in its employees, Monat is contemplating establishment of a defined benefit plan. Monat knows that lenders and potential investors will pay close attention to the impact of the pension plan on the company's financial statements, particularly any gains or losses that develop in the plan. Monat has asked you to conduct some research on the accounting for gains and losses in a defined benefit plan.

Instructions

If your school has a subscription to the FASB Codification, log in and prepare responses to the following. Provide Codification references for your responses.

a. Briefly describe how pension gains and losses are accounted for.

b. Explain the rationale behind the accounting method described in part (a).

c. What is the related pension asset or liability that will show up on the balance sheet? When will each of these situations occur?

Additional Professional Resources

Go to WileyPLUS for other career-readiness resources, such as career coaching, internship opportunities, and CPAexcel prep.

IFRS Insights

LEARNING OBJECTIVE 8

Compare the accounting for pensions under GAAP and IFRS.

The accounting for various forms of compensation plans under IFRS is found in *IAS 19* ("Employee Benefits") and *IFRS 2* ("Share-Based Payment"). *IAS 19* addresses the accounting for a wide range of compensation elements—wages, bonuses, postretirement benefits, and compensated absences. The underlying concepts for the accounting for postretirement benefits are similar between GAAP and IFRS—both GAAP and IFRS view pensions and other postretirement benefits as forms of deferred compensation. At present, there are significant differences in the specific accounting provisions as applied to these plans.

Relevant Facts

Following are the key similarities and differences between GAAP and IFRS related to pensions.

Similarities

- IFRS and GAAP separate pension plans into defined contribution plans and defined benefit plans. The accounting for defined contribution plans is similar.
- IFRS and GAAP recognize a pension asset or liability as the funded status of the plan (i.e., defined benefit obligation minus the fair value of plan assets). (Note that defined benefit obligation is referred to as the projected benefit obligation in GAAP.)
- IFRS and GAAP compute unrecognized past service cost (PSC) (referred to as prior service cost in GAAP) in the same manner. However, IFRS recognizes past service cost as a component of pension expense in income immediately. GAAP amortizes PSC over the remaining service lives of employees.

Differences

- IFRS and GAAP include interest expense on the liability in pension expense. Regarding asset returns, IFRS reduces pension expense by the amount of interest revenue (based on the discount rate times the beginning value of pension assets). GAAP includes an asset return component based on the expected return on plan assets.
- Under IFRS, companies recognize both liability and asset gains and losses (referred to as remeasurements) in other comprehensive income. These gains and losses are not "recycled" into income in subsequent periods. GAAP recognizes liability and asset gains and losses in "Accumulated other comprehensive income" and amortizes these amounts to income over remaining service lives, using the "corridor approach."
- The accounting for pensions and other postretirement benefit plans is the same under IFRS. GAAP has separate standards for these types of benefits, and significant differences exist in the accounting.

About the Numbers

Accounting for Pensions

Net Defined Benefit Obligation (Asset) As in GAAP, under IFRS the **net defined benefit liability** (asset) is the deficit or surplus related to a defined benefit pension plan. The deficit or surplus is measured as follows.

Defined Benefit Obligation – Fair Value of Plan Assets (if any)

The deficit or surplus is often referred to as the **funded status** of the plan.

If the defined benefit obligation is greater than the plan assets, the pension plan has a deficit. Conversely, if the defined pension obligation is less than the plan assets, the pension plan has a surplus. Illustration IFRS20.1 shows these relationships.

ILLUSTRATION IFRS20.1
Presentation of Funded Status

Deficit		Surplus	
Defined benefit obligation	$1,000,000	Defined benefit obligation	$150,000
Plan assets	900,000	Plan assets	200,000
Net defined benefit obligation	$ 100,000	Net defined benefit asset	$ 50,000

The net defined benefit obligation (asset) is often referred to simply as the pension liability or the pension asset on the statement of financial position.

As indicated, companies should report either a pension asset or pension liability related to a pension plan on the statement of financial position (often referred to as the **net approach**). To illustrate, assume that at year-end Acer Company has a defined pension obligation of $4,000,000 and plan assets of $3,700,000. In this case, Acer reports $300,000 ($4,000,000 – $3,700,000) as a pension liability on its statement of financial position.

Some believe that companies should report separately both the defined benefit obligation and the plan assets on the statement of financial position. This approach (often referred to as the **gross approach**) would report Acer's defined benefit obligation of $4,000,000 and its plan assets of $3,700,000 on the statement of financial position. The IASB disagrees, indicating that offsetting these amounts is consistent with its standard on when assets and liabilities should be netted.[30]

Reporting Changes in the Defined Benefit Obligation (Asset) The IASB requires that all changes in the defined benefit obligation and plan assets in the current period be recognized in comprehensive income. The Board believes that immediate recognition of the effects of these changes in the statement of comprehensive income provides the most understandable and useful information to financial statement users. The IASB requires that companies report changes arising from different elements of pension liabilities and assets in different sections of the statement of comprehensive income, depending on their nature.

In the past, companies often reported only a single pension expense number in the comprehensive income statement. Providing additional segmentation of the **components of pension cost** provides additional transparency about the nature of these costs. The three components are as follows.

- ***Service cost.*** Service cost is either current service cost or past service cost. Current service cost is the increase in the present value of the defined benefit obligation from employee service in the current period. Past service cost is the change in the present value of the defined benefit obligation for employee service for prior periods—generally resulting from a plan amendment (e.g., changes to the plan). This component is reported in the statement of comprehensive income in the operating section of the statement and affects net income.

[30]*IAS 32* states that a financial asset and a financial liability should be offset and the net amount reported in the statement of financial position when a company (a) has a legally enforceable right to set off the recognized amounts and (b) intends either to settle on a net basis, or to realize the asset and settle it simultaneously.

- ***Net interest.*** Net interest is computed by multiplying the discount rate by the funded status of the plan (defined benefit obligation minus plan assets). If the plan has a net defined benefit obligation, the company reports interest expense. Conversely, if it has a net defined benefit asset, it reports interest revenue. This approach is justified on the basis of its simplicity and that any financing costs should be based on the funded status of the plan. This amount is often shown below the operating section of the income statement in the financing section and affects net income.
- ***Remeasurements.*** Remeasurements are gains and losses related to the defined benefit obligation (changes in discount rate or other actuarial assumptions) and gains or losses on the fair value of the plan assets (actual rate of return less interest revenue included in the finance component). This component is reported in other comprehensive income, net of tax. **These remeasurement gains or losses therefore affect comprehensive income but not net income.**

Illustration IFRS20.2 shows the components of changes in the pension liability (asset) and their placement on the statement of comprehensive income.

ILLUSTRATION IFRS20.2

Reporting Changes in the Pension Obligation (Assets)

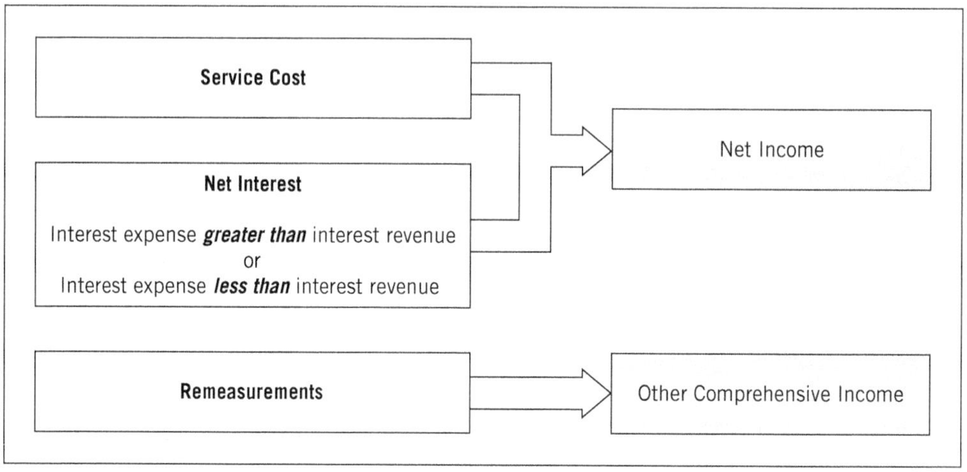

As indicated in Illustration IFRS20.2, service cost and net interest are reported in net income. We discuss determination of each of these components in the following section. Remeasurements, which are reported in other comprehensive income, are discussed in a later section.

Service Cost. To determine current service cost and the related increase in the defined benefit obligation, companies must:

1. Apply an actuarial valuation method.
2. Assign benefits to period of service.
3. Make actuarial assumptions.[31]

In applying an actuarial valuation method, the IASB concluded that **companies must consider future compensation levels in measuring the present obligation and periodic pension expense if the plan benefit formula incorporates them.** In other words, the present obligation resulting from a promise to pay a benefit of 1 percent of an employee's **final pay** differs from the promise to pay 1 percent of **current pay**. To overlook this fact is to ignore an important aspect of pension expense. Thus, the Board adopts the ***projected unit credit method*** **(often referred to as the *benefits/years-of-service method*), which determines pension expense based on future salary levels.**

Some object to this determination, arguing that a company should have more freedom to select an expense recognition pattern. Others believe that incorporating future salary increases into current pension expense is accounting for events that have not yet happened. They argue that if a company terminates the plan today, it pays only liabilities for accumulated benefits. **Nevertheless, the IASB indicates that the defined benefit obligation provides a more realistic measure of the employer's obligation under the plan on a going concern basis and, therefore, companies should use it as the basis for determining service cost.**

[31]As indicated earlier, service cost is comprised of current and past service cost. Determination of past service cost is based on the same actuarial valuation model as that used for current service cost. We discuss recognition of past service cost in a later section.

The assignment of benefits to periods of service is based on the actuarial valuation method. The actuary then allocates the cost of the pension benefits over the expected service life of the company's employees. In determining the proper service cost for a period, the actuary makes actuarial assumptions related to such factors as mortality; rates of employee turnover, disability, and early retirement; discount rate; benefit levels; and future salary levels. While *IAS 19* does not require use of an actuary, given the complexity of these estimates, just about all companies rely on an actuary to determine service cost and related other defined benefit measures.

Net Interest. In computing net interest, companies assume that the discount rate, the net defined benefit obligation, and the pension asset are determined at the beginning of the year.[32] The **discount rate** is based on the yields of high-quality bonds with terms consistent with the company's pension obligation. Net interest is then computed as indicated in the following equation.

Net Interest = **(Defined Benefit Obligation × Discount Rate) − (Plan Assets × Discount Rate)**

That is, net interest is determined by multiplying the net defined pension obligation (asset) by the discount rate.

Because payment of the pension obligation is deferred, companies record the pension liability on a discounted basis. As a result, the liability accrues interest over the service life of the employee (passage of time), which is essentially interest expense (**interest on the liability**). Similarly, companies earn a return on their plan assets. That is, a company assumes that it earns interest based on multiplying the discount rate by the plan assets. While the IASB recognizes that the actual return on plan assets may differ from the assumed interest revenue computed, it believes that the change in plan assets can be divided into an amount that arises from the passage of time and amounts that arise from other changes. As we discuss in the next section, changes not related to the passage of time are reported in other comprehensive income as remeasurements. Thus, the growth in the plan assets should mirror the growth in the defined benefit obligation. In other words, the assumed interest revenue on the plan assets based on the passage of time offsets the interest expense on the defined benefit obligation.

In summary, pension expense is comprised of two components: (1) service cost and (2) net interest. Companies report each of these components in the statement of comprehensive income. In some cases, companies may choose to report these components in one section of the statement of comprehensive income and report total pension expense. Other companies may choose to report the service cost component in operating income and the net interest in a separate section related to financing.[33]

Plan Assets and Actual Return Pension **plan assets** are usually investments in shares, bonds, other securities, and real estate that a company holds to earn a reasonable rate of return. Plan assets are reported at fair value. Companies generally hold these assets in a separate legal entity (a pension fund) that exists only to administer the employee benefit plan. These assets held by the pension fund are therefore not available to the company's own creditors (even in bankruptcy). Employer contributions and the actual return on plan assets increase pension plan assets. **Actual return on plan assets** is the increase in the pension fund assets arising from interest, dividends, and realized and unrealized changes in the fair value of the plan. Benefits paid to retired employees decrease plan assets.

To illustrate, assume that Hasbro Company has pension plan assets of $4,200,000 on January 1, 2020. During 2020, Hasbro contributed $300,000 to the plan and paid out retirement benefits of $250,000. Its actual return on plan assets was $210,000 for the year. Hasbro's plan assets at December 31, 2020, are $4,460,000, computed as shown in **Illustration IFRS20.3**.

ILLUSTRATION IFRS20.3

Determination of Pension Assets

Plan assets, January 1, 2020	$4,200,000
Contributions by Hasbro to plan	300,000
Actual return	210,000
Benefits paid to employees	(250,000)
Plan assets, December 31, 2020	$4,460,000

[32]The IASB indicates that if the beginning of the year amount changes materially (due to contributions to or payments out of the plan), an adjustment to the beginning balances should be made. *For homework purposes, unless information indicates that balances have changed materially, use the beginning of the year balances.*

[33]The IASB does not provide guidance on which of these two approaches is preferred. *For homework purposes, report pension expense as a single total in income from operations in the statement of comprehensive income.*

In some cases, companies compute the actual return by adjusting the change in plan assets for the effect of contributions during the year and benefits paid during the year. The equation in **Illustration IFRS20.4**, or a variation thereof, can be used to compute the actual return.

ILLUSTRATION IFRS20.4

Equation for Computing Actual Return

$$\text{Actual Return} = \left(\text{Plan Assets Ending Balance} - \text{Plan Assets Beginning Balance}\right) - (\text{Contributions} - \text{Benefits Paid})$$

Stated another way, the actual return on plan assets is the difference between the fair value of the plan assets at the beginning of the period and at the end of the period, adjusted for contributions and benefit payments. **Illustration IFRS20.5** uses the equation above to compute actual return, using the information provided in Illustration IFRS20.3.

ILLUSTRATION IFRS20.5

Computation of Actual Return on Plan Assets

Plan assets, December 31, 2020		$4,460,000
Plan assets, January 1, 2020		(4,200,000)
Increase in fair value of plan assets		260,000
Deduct: Contributions to plan	$300,000	
Add: Benefit payments to employees	250,000	(50,000)
Actual return		$ 210,000

In this case, Hasbro has a positive actual return on plan assets. Recently, some pension plans have experienced negative actual returns due to the increased volatility in global securities markets.

Using a Pension Worksheet

We will now illustrate the basic computation of pension expense using the first two components: (1) service cost and (2) net interest. We discuss remeasurements in later sections.

Companies often use a worksheet to record pension-related information. As its name suggests, the worksheet is a working tool. A worksheet is **not** a permanent accounting record: It is neither a journal nor part of the general ledger. The worksheet is merely a device to make it easier to prepare entries and the financial statements.[34] **Illustration IFRS20.6** shows the format of the **pension worksheet**.

ILLUSTRATION IFRS20.6

Basic Format of Pension Worksheet

Pension Worksheet

Home Insert Page Layout Formulas Data Review View

P18 fx

	A	B	C	D	E	F
1						
2		**General Journal Entries**			**Memo Record**	
3		Annual		Pension	Defined	
4		Pension		Asset/	Benefit	
5	Items	Expense	Cash	Liability	Obligation	Plan Assets
6						
7						
8						
9						
10						

The "General Journal Entries" columns of the worksheet (near the middle) determine the entries to record in the formal general ledger accounts. The "Memo Record" columns (on the right side) maintain balances in the defined benefit obligation and the plan assets. The difference between the defined benefit obligation and the fair value of the plan assets is the **pension asset/liability**, which is shown in the statement of financial position. If the defined benefit obligation is greater than the plan assets, a pension liability occurs. If the defined benefit obligation is less than the plan assets, a pension asset occurs.

[34]The use of a pension entry worksheet is recommended and illustrated by Paul B. W. Miller, "The New Pension Accounting (Part 2)," *Journal of Accountancy* (February 1987), pp. 86–94.

On the first line of the worksheet, a company enters the beginning balances (if any). It then records subsequent transactions and events related to the pension plan using debits and credits, using both sets of columns as if they were one. For each transaction or event, the debits must equal the credits. **The ending balance in the Pension Asset/Liability column should equal the net balance in the memo record.**

2020 Entries and Worksheet To illustrate the use of a worksheet and how it helps in accounting for a pension plan, assume that on January 1, 2020, Zarle Company provides the following information related to its pension plan for the year 2020.

- Plan assets, January 1, 2020, are $100,000.
- Defined benefit obligation, January 1, 2020, is $100,000.
- Annual service cost is $9,000.
- Discount rate is 10 percent.
- Funding contributions are $8,000.
- Benefits paid to retirees during the year are $7,000.

Using the data presented above, the worksheet in Illustration IFRS20.7 presents the beginning balances and all of the pension entries recorded by Zarle in 2020. Zarle records the beginning balances for the defined benefit obligation and the pension plan assets on the first line of the worksheet in the memo record. Because the defined benefit obligation and the plan assets are the same at January 1, 2020, the Pension Asset/Liability account has a zero balance at January 1, 2020.

ILLUSTRATION IFRS20.7

Pension Worksheet—2020

Pension Worksheet—2020

Home Insert Page Layout Formulas Data Review View

P18 fx

	A	B	C	D	E	F
1						
2		General Journal Entries			Memo Record	
3		Annual		Pension	Defined	
4		Pension		Asset/	Benefit	
5	Items	Expense	Cash	Liability	Obligation	Plan Assets
6	Balance, Jan. 1, 2020			—	100,000 Cr.	100,000 Dr.
7	(a) Service cost	9,000 Dr.			9,000 Cr.	
8	(b) Interest expense	10,000 Dr.			10,000 Cr.	
9	(c) Interest revenue	10,000 Cr.				10,000 Dr.
10	(d) Contributions		8,000 Cr.			8,000 Dr.
11	(e) Benefits				7,000 Dr.	7,000 Cr.
12						
13	Journal entry for 2020	9,000 Dr.	8,000 Cr.	1,000 Cr.*		
14	Balance, Dec. 31, 2020			1,000 Cr.**	112,000 Cr.	111,000 Dr.
15						
16	*$9,000 – $8,000 = $1,000					
17	**$112,000 – $111,000 = $1,000					

Entry (a) in Illustration IFRS20.7 records the service cost component, which increases pension expense by $9,000 and increases the liability (defined benefit obligation) by $9,000. Entry (b) accrues the interest expense component, which increases both the liability and the pension expense by $10,000 (the beginning defined benefit obligation multiplied by the discount rate of 10 percent). Entry (c) records the interest revenue component, which increases plan assets and decreases pension expense by $10,000. This is computed by multiplying the beginning plan assets by the discount rate of 10 percent. As a result, net interest expense (income) is zero in 2020. Entry (d) records Zarle's contribution (funding) of assets to the pension fund, thereby decreasing cash by $8,000 and increasing plan assets by $8,000. Entry (e) records the benefit payments made to retirees, which results in equal $7,000 decreases to the plan assets and the defined benefit obligation.

Zarle makes the "formal journal entry" on December 31, which records the pension expense in 2020, as follows.

2020		
Pension Expense	9,000	
Cash		8,000
Pension Asset/Liability		1,000

The credit to Pension Asset/Liability for $1,000 represents the difference between the 2020 pension expense of $9,000 and the amount funded of $8,000. Pension Asset/Liability (credit) is a liability because Zarle underfunds the plan by $1,000. The Pension Asset/Liability account balance of $1,000 also equals the net of the balances in the memo accounts. Illustration IFRS20.8 shows that the defined benefit obligation exceeds the plan assets by $1,000, which reconciles to the pension liability reported in the statement of financial position.

ILLUSTRATION IFRS20.8

Pension Reconciliation Schedule—December 31, 2020

Defined benefit obligation (Credit)	$(112,000)
Plan assets at fair value (Debit)	111,000
Pension asset/liability (Credit)	$ (1,000)

If the net of the memo record balances is a credit, the reconciling amount in the Pension Asset/Liability column will be a credit equal in amount. If the net of the memo record balances is a debit, the Pension Asset/Liability amount will be a debit equal in amount. The worksheet is designed to produce this reconciling feature, which is useful later in the preparation of the financial statements and required note disclosure related to pensions.

In this illustration (for 2020), the debit to Pension Expense exceeds the credit to Cash, resulting in a credit to Pension Asset/Liability—the recognition of a liability. If the credit to Cash exceeded the debit to Pension Expense, Zarle would debit Pension Asset/Liability—the recognition of an asset.[35]

Past Service Cost **Past service cost** is the change in the present value of the defined benefit obligation resulting from a plan amendment or a curtailment.[36] For example, a plan amendment arises when a company decides to provide additional benefits to existing employees for past service. Conversely, the company may decide that it is necessary to reduce its benefit package retroactively for existing employees, thereby reducing their pension benefit. A **curtailment** occurs when the company has a significant reduction in the number of employees covered by the plan. Because a curtailment has the same effect as a reduction in benefits due to an amendment to the plan, these situations are accounted for in the same way. Illustration IFRS20.9 summarizes the nature of past service costs.

ILLUSTRATION IFRS20.9

Types of Past Service Costs

Past Service Costs
(Expense in Current Period)

Plan Amendments	Curtailments
• Introduction of a plan. • Withdrawal of a plan. • Changes to a plan.	• Significant reduction in the number of employees covered by the plan.

The accounting for past service cost is straightforward—expense past service cost in the period of the amendment or curtailment. As a result, a substantial increase (decrease) in pension expense and the defined benefit obligation often results when a plan amendment or curtailment occurs. Because current and past service costs relate directly to employment, they are reported in the operating section of the statement of comprehensive income.

Some disagree with the IASB position of expensing these costs in the year a plan is amended or curtailed. They argue that a company would not provide these additional benefits for past years of service unless it expects to receive benefits in the future. According to this reasoning, a company should not recognize the full past service cost in the year of the amendment. Instead, the past service cost should be spread out over the remaining service life of employees who are expected to benefit from the changes in the plan. Others believe that if they are truly past service costs, they should be treated retroactively as an adjustment made to prior periods.

[35]The IASB in *IAS 19* limits the amount of a pension asset that is recognized, based on a recoverability test. This test, which has been further clarified in *IFRIC 14*, limits the amount of the pension asset to the sum of unrecognized actuarial gains and losses (discussed later) and amounts that will be received by the company in the form of refunds or reduction of future contributions. *For purposes of homework, assume that a pension asset, if present, meets the criteria for full recognition.*

[36]The IASB also indicates that gains and losses on non-routine settlements are considered past service costs. A **settlement** is a payment of benefits that is not set out in the terms of the plan.

However, the IASB decided that any changes in the defined benefit obligation or plan assets should be recognized in the current period. To do otherwise is not informative and leads to delayed recognition of costs or reduced benefits which are neither assets nor liabilities.

It is also possible to decrease past service costs by decreasing the defined benefit obligation (referred to as negative past service cost). Negative past service cost arises when an entity changes the benefits attributable to past service cost so that the present value of the defined benefit obligation decreases. In that case, pension expense is decreased. Both positive (increased pension expense) and negative (decreased pension expense) past service cost adjustments are handled in the same manner; that is, adjust pension expense immediately.

2021 Entries and Worksheet Continuing the Zarle Company illustration into 2021, we note that the company amends the pension plan on January 1, 2021, to grant employees past service benefits with a present value of $81,600. The following additional facts apply to the pension plan for the year 2021.

- Annual service cost is $9,500.
- Discount rate is 10 percent.
- Annual funding contributions are $20,000.
- Benefits paid to retirees during the year are $8,000.

Illustration IFRS20.10 presents a worksheet of all the pension entries and information recorded by Zarle in 2021.

ILLUSTRATION IFRS20.10

Pension Worksheet—2021

Pension Worksheet—2021

	A	B	C	D	E	F
1						
2		General Journal Entries			Memo Record	
3		Annual		Pension	Defined	
4		Pension		Asset/	Benefit	
5	Items	Expense	Cash	Liability	Obligation	Plan Assets
6	Balance, Dec. 31, 2020			1,000 Cr.	112,000 Cr.	111,000 Dr.
7	(f) Additional PSC, 1/1/2021	81,600 Dr.			81,600 Cr.	
8	Balance, Jan. 1, 2021				193,600 Cr.	
9	(g) Service cost	9,500 Dr.			9,500 Cr.	
10	(h) Interest expense	19,360 Dr.			19,360 Cr.	
11	(i) Interest revenue	11,100 Cr.				11,100 Dr.
12	(j) Contributions		20,000 Cr.			20,000 Dr.
13	(k) Benefits				8,000 Dr.	8,000 Cr.
14	Journal entry for 2021	99,360 Dr.	20,000 Cr.	79,360 Cr.		
15	Balance, Dec. 31, 2021			80,360 Cr.	214,460 Cr.	134,100 Dr.
16						

The first line of the worksheet shows the beginning balances of the Pension Asset/Liability account and the memo accounts. Entry (f) records Zarle's granting of past service cost, by adding $81,600 to the defined benefit obligation and to Pension Expense. Entry (g) records the current service cost; entry (h) records interest expense for the period. Because the past service cost occurred at the beginning of the year, interest is computed on the January 1, 2021, balance of the defined benefit obligation, adjusted for the past service cost. Interest expense is therefore $19,360 ($193,600 × 10%). Entry (i) records interest revenue for the period of $11,100 ($111,000 × 10%). Entries (j) and (k) are similar to the corresponding entries in 2020.

Zarle makes the following journal entry on December 31 to formally record the 2021 pension expense—the sum of the annual pension expense column.

2021		
Pension Expense	99,360	
Cash		20,000
Pension Asset/Liability		79,360

Because the expense exceeds the funding, Zarle credits the Pension Asset/Liability account for the $79,360 difference. That account is a liability. In 2021, as in 2020, the balance of the Pension

Asset/Liability account ($80,360) is equal to the net of the balances in the memo accounts, as shown in Illustration IFRS20.11.

ILLUSTRATION IFRS20.11

Pension Reconciliation Schedule—December 31, 2021

Defined benefit obligation (Credit)	$(214,460)
Plan assets at fair value (Debit)	134,100
Pension asset/liability (Credit)	$ (80,360)

The **reconciliation** is the formula that makes the worksheet work. It relates the components of pension accounting, recorded and unrecorded, to one another.

Remeasurements Of great concern to companies that have pension plans are the uncontrollable and unexpected swings that can result from (1) sudden and large changes in the fair value of plan assets and (2) changes in actuarial assumptions that affect the amount of the defined benefit obligation. How should these changes (referred to as **remeasurements**) affect the financial statements, most notably pension expense? The IASB believes that the most informative way is to recognize the remeasurement in other comprehensive income. The rationale for this reporting is that the predictive nature of remeasurements is much different than the other two components of pension benefit cost—service cost and net interest.

Remeasurements are generally of two types:

1. Gains and losses on plan assets.
2. Gains and losses on the defined benefit obligation.

Asset Gains and Losses. The gains and losses on plan assets (referred to as **asset gains and losses**) is the difference between the actual return and the interest revenue computed in determining net interest. Asset gains occur when actual returns exceed the interest revenue. Asset losses occur when the actual returns are less than interest revenue. To illustrate, assume that Shopbob Company has plan assets at January 1, 2020, of $100,000. The discount rate for the year is 6 percent, and the actual return on the plan assets for 2020 is $8,000. In 2020, Shopbob should record an asset gain of $2,000, computed as shown in Illustration IFRS20.12.

ILLUSTRATION IFRS20.12

Computation of Asset Gain

Actual return	$8,000
Less: Interest revenue ($100,000 × 6%)	6,000
Asset gain	$2,000

Shopbob therefore debits plan assets for the asset gain of $2,000 and credits Other Comprehensive Income (G/L) for the same amount. If interest revenue exceeds the actual return, Shopbob debits Other Comprehensive Income (G/L) for the asset loss and credits plan assets.

Liability Gains and Losses. In estimating the defined benefit obligation (the liability), actuaries make assumptions about such items as mortality rate, retirement rate, turnover rate, disability rate, and salary amounts. Any change in these actuarial assumptions affects the amount of the defined benefit obligation. Seldom does actual experience coincide exactly with actuarial predictions. These gains or losses from changes in the defined benefit obligation are called **liability gains and losses**.

Companies report liability gains (resulting from unexpected decreases in the liability balance) and liability losses (resulting from unexpected increases in the liability balance) in Other Comprehensive Income (G/L). Companies combine the liability gains and losses in the same Other Comprehensive Income (G/L) account used for asset gains and losses. They accumulate the asset and liability gains and losses from year to year in Accumulated Other Comprehensive Income.[37] This amount is reported on the statement of financial position in the equity section.

[37]The IASB is silent as to whether the account "Accumulated Other Comprehensive Income" should be used instead of another equity account, like Retained Earnings. *For homework purposes, use an Accumulated Other Comprehensive Income account.* The IASB also permits the transfer of the balance in the Accumulated Other Comprehensive Income account to other equity accounts at a later date.

2022 Entries and Worksheet Continuing the Zarle Company illustration, the following facts apply to the pension plan for 2022.

- Annual service cost is $13,000.
- Discount rate is 10 percent.
- Actual return on plan assets is $12,000.
- Annual funding contributions are $24,000.
- Benefits paid to retirees during the year are $10,500.
- Changes in actuarial assumptions establish the end-of-year defined benefit obligation at $265,000.

The worksheet in **Illustration IFRS20.13** presents all of Zarle's 2022 pension entries and related information. The first line of the worksheet records the beginning balances that relate to the pension plan. In this case, Zarle's beginning balances are the ending balances from its 2021 pension worksheet in Illustration IFRS20.10.

ILLUSTRATION IFRS20.13

Pension Worksheet—2022

Pension Worksheet—2022

	A	B	C	D	E	F	G
1							
2		General Journal Entries				Memo Record	
3		Annual			Pension	Defined	
4		Pension		OCI—	Asset/	Benefit	
5	Items	Expense	Cash	Gain/Loss	Liability	Obligation	Plan Assets
6	Balance, Jan. 1, 2022				80,360 Cr.	214,460 Cr.	134,100 Dr.
7	(l) Service cost	13,000 Dr.				13,000 Cr.	
8	(m) Interest expense	21,446 Dr.				21,446 Cr.	
9	(n) Interest revenue	13,410 Cr.					13,410 Dr.
10	(o) Contributions		24,000 Cr.				24,000 Dr.
11	(p) Benefits					10,500 Dr.	10,500 Cr.
12	(q) Asset loss			1,410 Dr.			1,410 Cr.
13	(r) Liability loss			26,594 Dr.		26,594 Cr.	
14	Journal entry for 2022	21,036 Dr.	24,000 Cr.	28,004 Dr.	25,040 Cr.		
15							
16	Accumulated OCI, Dec. 31, 2021			0			
17	Balance, Dec. 31, 2022			28,004 Dr.	105,400 Cr.	265,000 Cr.	159,600 Dr.
18							

Entries (l), (m), (n), (o), and (p) are similar to the corresponding entries in 2020 or 2021. Entries (m) and (n) are related. Entry (m) records the interest expense of $21,446 ($214,460 × 10%). Entry (n) records interest revenue of $13,410 ($134,100 × 10%). Therefore, net interest expense is $8,036 ($21,446 – $13,410). Entries (o) and (p) are recorded similarly in 2022 as those in 2020 and 2021.

Entries (q) and (r) need additional explanation. As indicated, the actual return on plan assets for 2022 was $12,000. However, as indicated in entry (n), pension expense was decreased $13,410 as a result of multiplying the beginning plan assets by the discount rate to arrive at an assumed interest revenue of $13,410. As a result, Zarle has an asset loss of $1,410 ($13,410 – $12,000) because the assumed interest revenue is greater than the actual return. This asset loss is debited to Other Comprehensive Income (G/L) and credited to plan assets. Pension plan assets are then properly stated at their fair value.

Entry (r) records the change in the defined benefit obligation resulting from the changes in the actuarial assumptions related to this obligation. As indicated in the facts above, the actuary has determined that the ending balance in the defined benefit obligation should be $265,000 at December 31, 2022. However, the balance at December 31, 2022, before any adjustment for actuarial gains and losses related to the defined benefit obligation is $238,406, as shown in **Illustration IFRS20.14**.

ILLUSTRATION IFRS20.14

Defined Benefit Obligation Balance (Unadjusted)

December 31, 2021, DBO balance	$214,460
Service cost [entry (l)]	13,000
Interest expense [entry (m)]	21,446
Benefits paid [entry (p)]	(10,500)
December 31, 2022, DBO balance (before liability increases)	$238,406

The difference between the ending balance of $265,000 as determined by the actuary and the present balance of $238,406 is $26,594 (a liability loss on the defined benefit liability). This liability loss is debited to Other Comprehensive Income (G/L) and credited to the defined benefit obligation. After this worksheet adjustment, the defined benefit obligation is stated at its actuarial value of $265,000. The journal entry to record the information related to the pension plan at December 31, 2022, based on the pension worksheet in Illustration IFRS20.13, is as follows.

Pension Expense	21,036	
Other Comprehensive Income (G/L)	28,004	
Cash		24,000
Pension Asset/Liability		25,040

As the 2022 worksheet indicates, the $105,400 balance in the Pension Asset/Liability account at December 31, 2022, is equal to the net of the balances in the memo accounts. Illustration IFRS20.15 shows this computation.

ILLUSTRATION IFRS20.15

Pension Reconciliation Schedule—December 31, 2022

Defined benefit obligation (Credit)	$(265,000)
Plan assets at fair value (Debit)	159,600
Pension asset/liability	$(105,400)

Zarle carries the 2022 ending balances for Pension Asset/Liability and Accumulated Other Comprehensive Income forward as the beginning balances for pension plan accounting in 2023. These balances will be adjusted by changes in the defined benefit obligation and plan assets as shown in the prior examples. For example, assume that Zarle's pension plan had the following activity in 2023:

Service cost	$10,072	Contributions	$32,000
Pension expense	17,450	Benefits	11,000
Asset gain	13,150	Decrease in Pension Asset/Liability	27,700
Discount rate	7%		

The ending balances for the defined benefit obligation and plan assets are $282,622 and $204,922, respectively. These elements are summarized in the partial 2023 pension worksheet shown in Illustration IFRS20.16.

ILLUSTRATION IFRS20.16 Partial Pension Worksheet—2023

Partial Pension Worksheet—2023

	A	B	C	D	E	F	G
1							
2		General Journal Entries				Memo Record	
3–5	Items	Annual Pension Expense	Cash	OCI—Gain/Loss	Pension Asset/ Liability	Defined Benefit Obligation	Plan Assets
6	Balance, Jan. 1, 2023			28,004 Dr.	105,400 Cr.	265,000 Cr.	159,600 Dr.
7							
13							
14	Journal entry for 2023	17,450 Dr.	32,000 Cr.	13,150 Cr.	27,700 Dr.		
15							
16	Accumulated OCI, Jan. 1, 2023			28,004 Dr.			
17	Balance, Dec. 31, 2023			14,854 Dr.	77,700 Cr.	282,622 Cr.	204,922 Dr.
18							

Focusing on the "Journal Entry" row, in 2023 Zarle records pension expense of $17,450 and a decrease in Pension Asset/Liability of $27,700. The reduction in Pension Asset/Liability is due in part to the asset gain of $13,150 recorded in 2023. As a result, Zarle's 2023 ending balances (which become the 2024 beginning balances) are $77,700 for Pension Asset/Liability and Accumulated Other Comprehensive Income $14,854 (beginning Accumulated OCI of $28,004 – gain of $13,150).

On The Horizon

The IASB and the FASB have worked collaboratively on a postretirement benefit project. The recent amendments issued by the IASB moves IFRS closer to GAAP with respect to recognition of the funded status on the statement of financial position. However, as illustrated in the *About the Numbers* section above, significant differences remain in the components of pension expense. While the FASB may consider the recent IASB amendments, which could lead to a converged standard, the FASB does not have a pension project on its technical agenda.

IFRS Self-Test Questions

1. At the end of the current period, Oxford Ltd. has a defined benefit obligation of $195,000 and pension plan assets with a fair value of $110,000. The amount of the vested benefits for the plan is $105,000. What amount related to its pension plan will be reported on the company's statement of financial position?

   a. $5,000. **c.** $85,000.
   b. $90,000. **d.** $20,000.

2. At the end of the current year, Kennedy Co. has a defined benefit obligation of $335,000 and pension plan assets with a fair value of $245,000. The amount of the vested benefits for the plan is $225,000. Kennedy has an actuarial gain of $8,300. What account and amount(s) related to its pension plan will be reported on the company's statement of financial position?

   a. Pension Liability and $74,300.
   b. Pension Liability and $90,000.
   c. Pension Asset and $233,300.
   d. Pension Asset and $110,000.

3. For 2020, Carson Majors Inc. had pension expense of $77 million and contributed $55 million to the pension fund. Which of the following is the journal entry that Carson Majors would make to record pension expense and funding?

a.	Pension Expense	77,000,000	
	Pension Asset/Liability		22,000,000
	Cash		55,000,000
b.	Pension Expense	77,000,000	
	Pension Asset/Liability	22,000,000	
	Cash		99,000,000
c.	Pension Expense	55,000,000	
	Pension Asset/Liability	22,000,000	
	Cash		77,000,000
d.	Pension Expense	22,000,000	
	Pension Asset/Liability	55,000,000	
	Cash		77,000,000

4. At January 1, 2020, Wembley Company had plan assets of $250,000 and a defined benefit obligation of the same amount. During 2020, service cost was $27,500, the discount rate was 10%, actual return on plan assets was $25,000, contributions were $20,000, and benefits paid were $17,500. Based on this information, what would be the defined benefit obligation for Wembley Company at December 31, 2020?

   a. $277,500. **c.** $27,500.
   b. $285,000. **d.** $302,500.

5. Towson Company has experienced tough competition for its talented workforce, leading it to enhance the pension benefits provided to employees. As a result, Towson amended its pension plan on January 1, 2020, and granted past service costs of $250,000. Current service cost for 2020 is $52,000. Interest expense is $18,000, and interest revenue is $5,000. Actual return on assets in 2020 is $3,000. What is Towson's pension expense for 2020?

   a. $65,000. **c.** $317,000.
   b. $302,000. **d.** $315,000.

IFRS Concepts and Application

IFRS20.1 What is net interest? Identify the elements of net interest and explain how they are computed.

IFRS20.2 What is service cost, and what is the basis of its measurement?

IFRS20.3 What is meant by "past service cost"? When is past service cost recognized as pension expense?

IFRS20.4 Bill Haley is learning about pension accounting. He is convinced that in years when companies record liability gains and losses, total comprehensive income will not be affected. Is Bill correct? Explain.

IFRS20.5 At the end of the current year, Joshua Co. has a defined benefit obligation of $335,000 and pension plan assets with a fair value of $345,000. The amount of the vested benefits for the plan is $225,000. Joshua has a liability gain of $8,300 (beginning accumulated OCI is zero). What amount and account(s) related to its pension plan will be reported on the company's statement of financial position?

IFRS20.6 Villa Company has experienced tough competition, leading it to seek concessions from its employees in the company's pension plan. In exchange for promises to avoid layoffs and wage cuts, the employees agreed to receive lower pension benefits in the future. As a result, Villa amended its pension plan on January 1, 2020, and recorded negative past service cost of $125,000. Current service cost for 2020 is $26,000. Interest expense is $9,000, and interest revenue is $2,500. Actual return on assets in 2020 is $1,500. Compute Villa's pension expense in 2020.

IFRS20.7 Tevez Company experienced an actuarial loss of $750 in its defined benefit plan in 2020. For 2020, Tevez's revenues are $125,000, and expenses (excluding pension expense of $14,000, which does not include the actuarial loss) are $85,000. Prepare Tevez's statement of comprehensive income for 2020.

IFRS20.8 The following defined pension data of Doreen Corp. apply to the year 2020.

Defined benefit obligation, 1/1/20 (before amendment)	$560,000
Plan assets, 1/1/20	546,200
Pension asset/liability	13,800 Cr.
On January 1, 2020, Doreen Corp., through plan amendment, grants past service benefits having a present value of	120,000
Discount rate	9%
Service cost	58,000
Contributions (funding)	65,000
Actual return on plan assets	49,158
Benefits paid to retirees	40,000

Instructions

For 2020, prepare a pension worksheet for Doreen Corp. that shows the journal entry for pension expense and the year-end balances in the related pension accounts.

IFRS20.9 Buhl Corp. sponsors a defined benefit pension plan for its employees. On January 1, 2020, the following balances relate to this plan.

Plan assets	$480,000
Defined benefit obligation	600,000
Pension asset/liability	120,000

As a result of the operation of the plan during 2020, the following additional data are provided by the actuary.

Service cost for 2020	$90,000
Discount rate, 6%	
Actual return on plan assets in 2020	55,000
Unexpected loss from change in defined benefit obligation, due to change in actuarial predictions	76,000
Contributions in 2020	99,000
Benefits paid retirees in 2020	85,000

Instructions

a. Using the data above, compute pension expense for Buhl Corp. for the year 2020 by preparing a pension worksheet.

b. Prepare the journal entry for pension expense for 2020.

IFRS20.10 Linda Berstler Company sponsors a defined benefit pension plan. The corporation's actuary provides the following information about the plan.

	January 1, 2020	December 31, 2020
Defined benefit obligation	$2,500	$3,300
Plan assets (fair value)	1,700	2,620
Discount rate		10%
Pension asset/liability	800	?
Service cost for the year 2020		400
Contributions (funding in 2020)		700
Benefits paid in 2020		200

Instructions

a. Compute the actual return on the plan assets in 2020.

b. Compute the amount of other comprehensive income (G/L) as of December 31, 2020. (Assume the January 1, 2020, balance was zero.)

Professional Research

IFRS20.11 Jack Kelly Company has grown rapidly since its founding in 2007. To instill loyalty in its employees, Kelly is contemplating establishment of a defined benefit plan. Kelly knows that lenders and potential investors will pay close attention to the impact of the pension plan on the company's financial statements, particularly any gains or losses that develop in the plan. Kelly has asked you to conduct some research on the accounting for gains and losses in a defined benefit plan.

Instructions

Access the IFRS authoritative literature at the IASB website. (Click on the IFRS tab and then register for free eIFRS access if necessary.) When you have accessed the documents, you can use the search tool in your Internet browser to respond to the following questions. (Provide paragraph citations.)

a. Briefly describe how pension gains and losses are accounted for.

b. Explain the rationale behind the accounting method described in part (a).

c. What is the related pension asset or liability that may show up on the statement of financial position? When will each of these situations occur?

International Financial Reporting Problem

Marks and Spencer plc (M&S)

IFRS20.12 The financial statements of **M&S** are presented in Appendix E. The company's complete annual report, including the notes to the financial statements, is available online.

Instructions

Refer to M&S's financial statements and the accompanying notes to answer the following questions.

a. What kind of pension plan does M&S provide its employees?

b. What was M&S's pension expense for 2017 and 2016?

c. What is the impact of M&S's pension plans for 2017 on its financial statements?

d. What information does M&S provide on the target allocation of its pension assets? How do the allocations relate to the expected returns on these assets?

Answers to IFRS Self-Test Questions

1. c **2.** b **3.** a **4.** b **5.** d

CHAPTER 21

Accounting for Leases

LEARNING OBJECTIVES

After studying this chapter, you should be able to:

1. Describe the environment related to leasing transactions.
2. Explain the accounting for finance leases.
3. Explain the accounting for operating leases.
4. Discuss the accounting and reporting for special features of lease arrangements.

PREVIEW OF CHAPTER 21 The following opening story indicates the increased significance and prevalence of lease arrangements. As a result, the need for uniform accounting and informative reporting of these transactions has intensified. In this chapter, we look at the accounting issues related to leasing. The content and organization of this chapter are as follows.

This chapter also includes numerous conceptual and global discussions that are integral to the topics presented here.

ACCOUNTING FOR LEASES

The Leasing Environment
- Lessees
- Lessee lease advantages
- Lessors
- Lessor lease advantages
- Conceptual nature of a lease
- Finance and operating leases
- Lease classification

Finance Leases
- Lessee accounting and finance lease example
- Lessor accounting
- Sales-type lease example

Operating Leases
- Lessee accounting
- Lessor accounting

Special Lease Accounting Problems
- Residual values
- Other lease adjustments
- Bargain purchase options
- Short-term leases
- Presentation, disclosure, and analysis

Times Are A-Changing

Sir David Tweedie, a former IFRS chairperson, is known for making the following observation about airline accounting. He noted that one day he would like to fly on an airplane that appears on a company's balance sheet. What Sir David was referring to is that many of the airlines such as **United**, **Delta**, and **Southwest** sometimes do not own their aircraft. The airlines lease many of their airplanes due to the favorable accounting treatment they received when they leased rather than purchased. Presented below are the lease percentages for major U.S. airlines in a recent year.

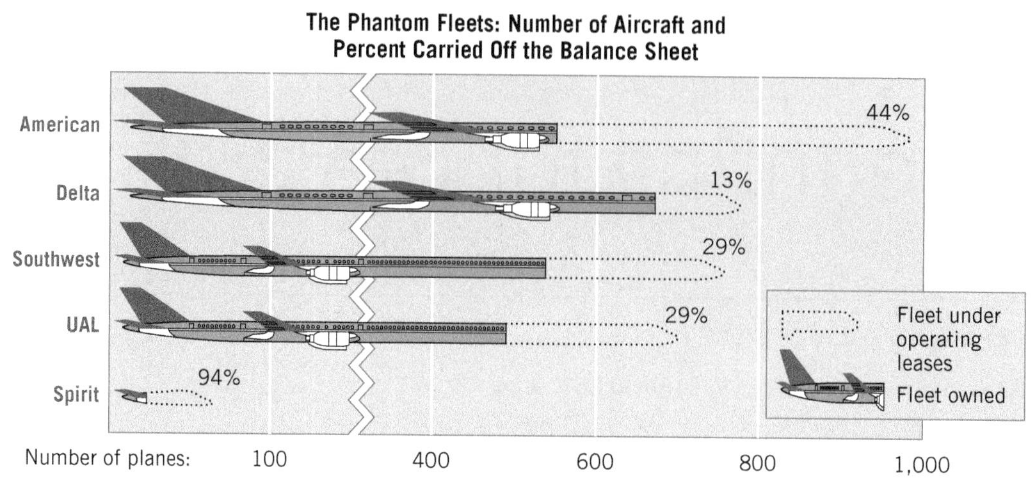

The same held true for many other industries as well. What was this favorable accounting treatment? The previous FASB standard on leasing depended on whether a lease qualified as an operating lease or a finance lease. In an operating lease, companies did not report an asset on their balance sheet for the item they leased, nor did they report a related liability for their lease obligation. Only if the company had a finance lease would companies have to report an asset and a related liability on the balance sheet. However, the FASB has recently issued a standard on leasing that mandates that all companies will have to report both assets and related liabilities for practically all lease arrangements.

The accounting change will have significant impact on many companies' balance sheets. The top 1,000 U.S. public companies alone have nearly $1 trillion in operating lease liabilities. Companies with large off-balance-sheet operating leases will be most affected. For example, here is a list of companies that will have to capitalize a significant number of operating leases.

Balance Sheet Impact
Assets and Liabilities Increases (in millions)

Walgreens Boots Alliance	$32,811	FedEx	$17,874
CVS Health	27,151	United Continental Holdings	16,251
AT&T	25,928	Delta Air Lines	16,236
Amazon	22,848	Walmart	15,366
Verizon Communications	20,734	Bank of America	14,500

So Sir David Tweedie, what we can now say is get ready as your wish is about to come true.

Sources: Adapted from Seth Lubore and Elizabeth MacDonald, "Debt? Who, Me?" *Forbes* (February 18, 2002), p. 56; A. Catanach and E. Ketz, "Still Searching for the 'Rite' Stuff," *Grumpy Old Accountants* (April 30, 2012), *http://blogs.smeal.psu.edu;* "Who Is Most Impacted by the New Lease Accounting Standards? An Analysis of the Fortune 500's Leasing Obligations," *Lease Accelerator* (2016); and Sue Lloyd, "A New Lease on Life," *Investor Perspective* (January 2016).

Review and Practice

Go to the **Review and Practice** section at the end of the chapter for a targeted summary review and practice problem with solution. Multiple-choice questions with annotated solutions as well as additional exercises and practice problem with solutions are also available online.

The Leasing Environment

LEARNING OBJECTIVE 1

Describe the environment related to leasing transactions.

A lease is a contractual agreement between a lessor and a lessee. This arrangement gives the **lessee** the right to use specific property, which is owned by the **lessor**, for a specified period of time. In return for the use of the property, the lessee makes rental payments over the lease term to the lessor.

A Look at the Lessee

Aristotle once said, "Wealth does not lie in ownership but in the use of things!" Clearly, many U.S. companies have decided that Aristotle is right, as they have become heavily involved in leasing assets rather than owning them. For example, according to the Equipment Leasing Association (ELA), the global equipment-leasing market is a $900 billion business, with the United States accounting for about one-third of the global market. The ELA estimates that of the $1.5 trillion in total fixed investment expected from domestic businesses in a recent year, $946 billion (63 percent) was financed through leasing. Remember that these statistics are just for equipment leasing. Add in real estate leasing, which is probably larger, and we are talking about a very large and growing business, one that was at least in part driven by the accounting.

What types of assets are being leased? As the opening story indicated, any type of equipment can be leased, such as railcars, helicopters, bulldozers, barges, CT scanners, computers, and so on. Illustration 21.1 summarizes what several major companies are leasing.

ILLUSTRATION 21.1

What Do Companies Lease?

Company (Ticker)	Description
Gap (GPS)	"We lease most of our store premises and some of our headquarters facilities and distribution centers."
ExxonMobil Corp. (XOM)	"Minimum commitments for operating leases, shown on an undiscounted basis, cover drilling equipment, tankers, service stations, and other properties."
JPMorgan Chase (JPM)	"JPMorgan Chase and its subsidiaries were obligated under a number of noncancelable operating leases for premises and equipment used primarily for banking purposes."
Maytag Corp. (MYG)	"The Company leases real estate, machinery, equipment, and automobiles under operating leases, some of which have renewal options."
McDonald's Corp. (MCD)	"The Company was the lessee at 15,235 restaurant locations through ground leases (the Company leases the land and the Company or franchisee owns the building) and through improved leases (the Company leases land and buildings)."
Starbucks Corp. (SBUX)	"Starbucks leases retail stores, roasting and distribution facilities, and office space under operating leases."
TXU Corp. (TXU)	"TXU Energy Holdings and TXU Electric Delivery have entered into operating leases covering various facilities and properties including generation plant facilities, combustion turbines, transportation equipment, mining equipment, data processing equipment, and office space."
Viacom Inc. (VIA.B)	"The Company has long-term non-cancelable operating lease commitments for office space and equipment, transponders, studio facilities, and vehicles. The Company also enters into leases for satellite transponders."

Source: Company 10-K filings.

The largest group of leased equipment involves information technology equipment, followed by assets in the transportation area (trucks, aircraft, rail), and then construction and agriculture.

Advantages of Leasing—Lessees

From the perspective of the lessee, leasing can provide significant advantages, such as the following:

1. ***100% financing at fixed rates.*** Leases are often signed without requiring any money down from the lessee. This helps the lessee conserve scarce cash—an especially desirable feature for new and developing companies. In addition, lease payments often remain fixed, which protects the lessee against inflation and increases in the cost of money. The following comment explains why companies choose a lease instead of a conventional loan: "Our local bank finally came up to 80 percent of the purchase price but wouldn't go any higher, and they wanted a floating interest rate. We just couldn't afford the down payment, and we needed to lock in a final payment rate we knew we could live with."
2. ***Protection against obsolescence.*** Leasing equipment reduces risk of obsolescence to the lessee and in many cases passes the risk of residual value to the lessor. For example, **Merck** (a pharmaceutical maker) leases computers. Under the lease agreement, Merck may turn in an old computer for a new model at any time, canceling the old lease and writing a new one. The lessor adds the cost of the new lease to the balance due on the old lease, less the old computer's trade-in value. As one treasurer remarked, "Our instinct is to purchase." But if a new computer is likely to come along in a short time, "then leasing is just a heck of a lot more convenient than purchasing." Naturally, the lessor also protects itself by requiring the lessee to pay higher rental payments or provide additional payments if the lessee does not maintain the asset.
3. ***Flexibility.*** Lease agreements may contain less restrictive provisions than other debt agreements. Innovative lessors can tailor a lease agreement to the lessee's special needs. For instance, the duration of the lease—the **lease term**—may be anything from a short period of time to the entire expected economic life of the asset. The rental payments may be level from year to year, or they may increase or decrease in amount. The payment amount may be predetermined or may vary with sales, the prime interest rate, the Consumer Price Index, or some other factor. In most cases, the rent is set to enable the lessor to recover the cost of the asset plus a fair return over the life of the lease.
4. ***Less costly financing.*** Some companies find leasing cheaper than other forms of financing. For example, start-up companies in depressed industries or companies in low tax brackets may lease to claim tax benefits that they might otherwise lose. Depreciation deductions offer no benefit to companies that have little if any taxable income. Through leasing, the leasing companies or financial institutions use these tax benefits. They can then pass some of these tax benefits back to the user of the asset in the form of lower rental payments.

A Look at the Lessor

Who are the lessors that own this property? They generally fall into one of three categories:

1. Banks.
2. Captive leasing companies.
3. Independents.

Banks

Banks are the largest players in the leasing business. They have low-cost funds, which give them the advantage of being able to purchase assets at less cost than their competitors. Banks have been aggressive in the leasing markets. Deciding that there is money to be made in leasing, banks have expanded their product lines in this area. Finally, leasing transactions are now quite standardized, which gives banks an advantage because they do not have to be as innovative in structuring lease arrangements. Thus, banks like **Wells Fargo**, **Chase**, **Citigroup**, and **PNC** have substantial leasing subsidiaries.

Captive Leasing Companies

Captive leasing companies are subsidiaries whose primary business is to perform leasing operations for the parent company. Companies like Caterpillar Financial Services Corp. (for Caterpillar), Ford Motor Credit (for Ford), and IBM Global Financing (for IBM) facilitate the sale of products to consumers. For example, suppose that Sterling Construction Co. wants to acquire a number of earthmovers from Caterpillar. In this case, Caterpillar Financial Services Corp. will offer to structure the transaction as a lease rather than as a purchase. Thus, Caterpillar Financial provides the financing rather than an outside financial institution.

Captive leasing companies have the point-of-sale advantage in finding leasing customers. That is, as soon as Caterpillar receives a possible equipment order, its leasing subsidiary can quickly develop a lease-financing arrangement. Furthermore, the captive lessor has product knowledge that gives it an advantage when financing the parent's product. The current trend is for captives to focus primarily on their companies' products rather than execute general lease financing. For example, Boeing Capital and UPS Capital are two captives that have left the general finance business to focus exclusively on their parent companies' products.

Independents

Independents are the final category of lessors. Their market share has dropped fairly dramatically as banks and captive leasing companies have become more aggressive in the lease-financing area. Independents do not have point-of-sale access, nor do they have a low cost of funds advantage. What they are often good at is developing innovative contracts for lessees. In addition, they are starting to act as captive finance companies for some companies that do not have leasing subsidiaries. For example, International Lease Finance Corp. is one of the world's largest independent lessors. According to recent data from the *Equipment Leasing and Finance Foundation 2015 Annual Report* on new business volume by lessor type, banks hold about 55 percent of the market, followed by captives at 31 percent. Independents had the remaining 14 percent of new business.

Advantages of Leasing—Lessors

Lessors find leasing attractive because:

1. It often provides **profitable interest margins**.
2. It can **stimulate sales** of a lessor's product whether it be from a dealer (lessor) or a manufacturer (lessor).
3. It often provides **tax benefits** to various parties in the lease, which enhances the return to all the parties involved, including the lessor (see Global View). To illustrate, Boeing Aircraft might sell one of its 737 jet planes to a wealthy investor who does not need a plane but could use the tax benefit. The investor (the lessor) then leases the plane to a foreign airline, for which the tax benefit is of no use. Everyone gains. Boeing sells its airplane, the investor receives the tax benefit, and the foreign airline receives a lower rental rate because the lessor is able to use the tax benefit.
4. It can provide a **high residual value to the lessor** upon the return of the property at the end of the lease term. Residual values can sometimes provide large profits. Citigroup at one time estimated that the commercial aircraft it was leasing to the airline industry would have a residual value of 5 percent of their purchase price. It turned out that they were worth 150 percent of their cost—a handsome profit. At the same time, if residual values decline, lessors can suffer losses when less-valuable leased assets are returned at the conclusion of the lease. At one time, automaker Ford took a $2.1 billion write-down on its lease portfolio, when rising gas prices spurred dramatic declines in the resale values of leased trucks and SUVs. Such residual value losses led Chrysler to get out of the leasing business altogether.

> **Global View**
>
> Some companies "double dip" on the international level too. The leasing rules of the lessor's and lessee's countries may differ, permitting both parties to own the asset. Thus, both lessor and lessee receive the tax benefits related to depreciation.

What Do the Numbers Mean? Residual Value Regret

As you have learned, residual value profits are an important driver for the popularity of leasing for lessors, especially for leases of equipment and vehicles. However, the profitability of equipment leasing hinges on the lessors' ability to accurately estimate the residual value of the leased asset at the end of the lease so as to resell the asset at a profit when returned by the lessee. However, **General Motors (GM)** has learned that residual value profits are not guaranteed. Here is what happened.

GM took advantage of a government subsidy for electric vehicles of $7,500 to help drive down the cost of a lease for its electric car, the Chevy Volt. The taxpayer subsidies along with other GM incentives provided for low monthly lease payments, given the estimated residual value, and led to a full two-thirds of all Volt "sales" being attributed to leases. That's about three times the lease rate for the overall industry. The problems for GM started when the Volts came back at the end of the lease. Unfortunately for GM and other electric car enthusiasts, demand for electric cars without the incentives (which expired) were not sustained, and resale values for Volts plummeted.

As a result, rather than reaping residual value profits, GM sustained losses for the Volt lease returns that sold for less than the original expected residual values. It was a double whammy for GM as the already low sales numbers for new Volts were further hurt by the supply of low-priced Volts on the used car lot.

Source: M. Modica, "Chevy Volt Resale Values Plunge as Lease Returns Hit Market," *http://nlpc.org/stories/2014/08/07/chevy-volt-resale-values-plunge-lease-returns-hit-market.*

Conceptual Nature of a Lease

A **lease** is defined as a "contract, or part of a contract, that conveys the right to control the use of identified property, plant or equipment (an identified asset) for a period of time in exchange for consideration." [1] (See the FASB Codification References near the end of the chapter.) A lease therefore conveys the use of an asset from one party (the lessor) to another (the lessee) without transferring ownership. Accounting for lease transactions is controversial, as the following example illustrates.

If **Delta** borrows $47 million on a 10-year note from **Bank of America** to purchase a Boeing 737 jet plane, Delta should report an asset and related liability at that amount on its balance sheet. Similarly if Delta purchases the 737 for $47 million directly from Boeing through an installment purchase over 10 years, it should report an asset and related liability (i.e., it should "capitalize" the installment transaction).

However, what if Delta **leases** the Boeing 737 for 10 years from **International Lease Finance Corp. (ILFC)**—the world's largest lessor of airplanes—through a non-cancelable lease transaction with payments of the same amount as the installment purchase transaction? In that case, opinion differs over how to report this transaction. The various views on **capitalization of leases** are as follows.

1. ***Do not capitalize any leased assets.*** This view considers capitalization inappropriate because Delta does not own the property. Furthermore, a lease is an "**executory**" **contract** requiring continuing performance by both parties. Because companies do not currently capitalize other executory contracts (such as purchase commitments and employment contracts), they should not capitalize leases either.
2. ***Capitalize leases that are similar to installment purchases.*** This view holds that companies should report transactions in accordance with their economic substance. Therefore, if companies capitalize installment purchases, they should also capitalize leases that have similar characteristics. For example, Delta makes the same payments over a 10-year period for either a lease or an installment purchase. Lessees make rental payments, whereas owners make mortgage payments.
3. ***Capitalize all long-term leases.*** This approach requires only the long-term right to use the property in order to capitalize. This property-rights approach capitalizes all long-term leases.
4. ***Capitalize firm leases where the penalty for nonperformance is substantial.*** A final approach advocates capitalizing only "firm" (non-cancelable) contractual rights and obligations. "Firm" means that it is unlikely to avoid performance under the lease without a severe penalty.

In short, the viewpoints range from no capitalization to capitalization of all long-term leases (see Underlying Concepts). The FASB has recently adopted the third approach, which requires companies to capitalize all long-term leases. The only exception to capitalization is that leases covering a term of less than one year do not have to be capitalized. The FASB indicates that the right to use property under the terms of the lease is an asset, and the lessee's commitment to make payments under the lease is a liability.[1] As a result, Delta records the right-of-use of the airplane as an asset on its balance sheet. It also records a liability for its obligation to make payments under the lease.

Underlying Concepts

The issue of how to report leases is the classic case of substance versus form. Although legal title does not technically pass in lease transactions, the benefits from the use of the property do transfer.

Finance and Operating Leases (Lessee)

As you will learn, companies classify lease arrangements as either finance or operating. In either case, **companies capitalize all leased assets and liabilities**. Therefore, the balance sheet for a company that uses either a finance lease or an operating lease will be the same. However, for income statement purposes, the reporting of financial information depends on whether the lease is classified as a finance lease or operating lease.

For a finance lease, the lessee recognizes interest expense on the lease liability over the life of the lease using the effective-interest method and records amortization expense on the right-of-use asset generally on a straight-line basis. A lessee therefore reports both interest expense and amortization of the right-of-use asset on the income statement. As a result, the total expense for the lease transaction is generally higher in the earlier years of the lease arrangement under a finance lease arrangement.

In an operating lease, the lessee also measures interest expense using the effective-interest method. However, the lessee amortizes the right-of-use asset such that the total reported lease expense is the same from period to period. In other words, for operating leases, only a single lease expense (comprised of interest on the liability and amortization of the right-of-use asset) is recognized on the income statement, typically on a straight-line basis. Illustrations of both these approaches are shown in the following sections.

Lease Classification

How do companies determine whether to use the finance method or the operating method? From the lessee's perspective, a lessee should classify a lease based on whether the arrangement is effectively a purchase of the underlying asset. If the lease transfers control (or ownership) of the underlying asset to a lessee, then the lease is classified as a finance lease. In this situation, the lessee takes ownership or consumes the substantial portion of the underlying asset over the lease term. All leases that do not meet any of the finance lease tests are classified as operating leases. In an operating lease, a lessee **obtains the right to use the underlying asset** but not ownership of the asset itself.

For example, a lease may convey use of one floor of an office building for five years. At the end of the lease, the lessee vacates the floor and the lessor can then lease the floor to another tenant. So this lease (an operating lease) conveys right-of-use but not ownership; the lessee controls the leased asset only during the five-year lease. As we will see, the accounting for a lease classified as a finance lease (transfer of control or ownership) or an operating lease (transfer of right-of-use) reflects differences in control conveyed in a lease arrangement.

Illustration 21.2 presents the lease classification tests, which are used to determine whether a company should use the finance lease approach or the operating lease approach.

[1]The FASB believes that the reporting of an asset and liability for a lease arrangement is consistent with its conceptual framework definition of assets and liabilities. That is, assets are probable future economic benefits obtained or controlled by a particular entity as a result of past transactions or events. Liabilities are probable future sacrifices of economic benefits arising from present obligations of a particular entity to transfer assets or provide services to other entities in the future as a result of past transactions or events. See "Elements of Financial Statements," *Statement of Financial Accounting Concepts No. 6* (Stamford, Conn.: FASB, December 1985), pp. ix and x.

ILLUSTRATION 21.2 Lease Classification Tests

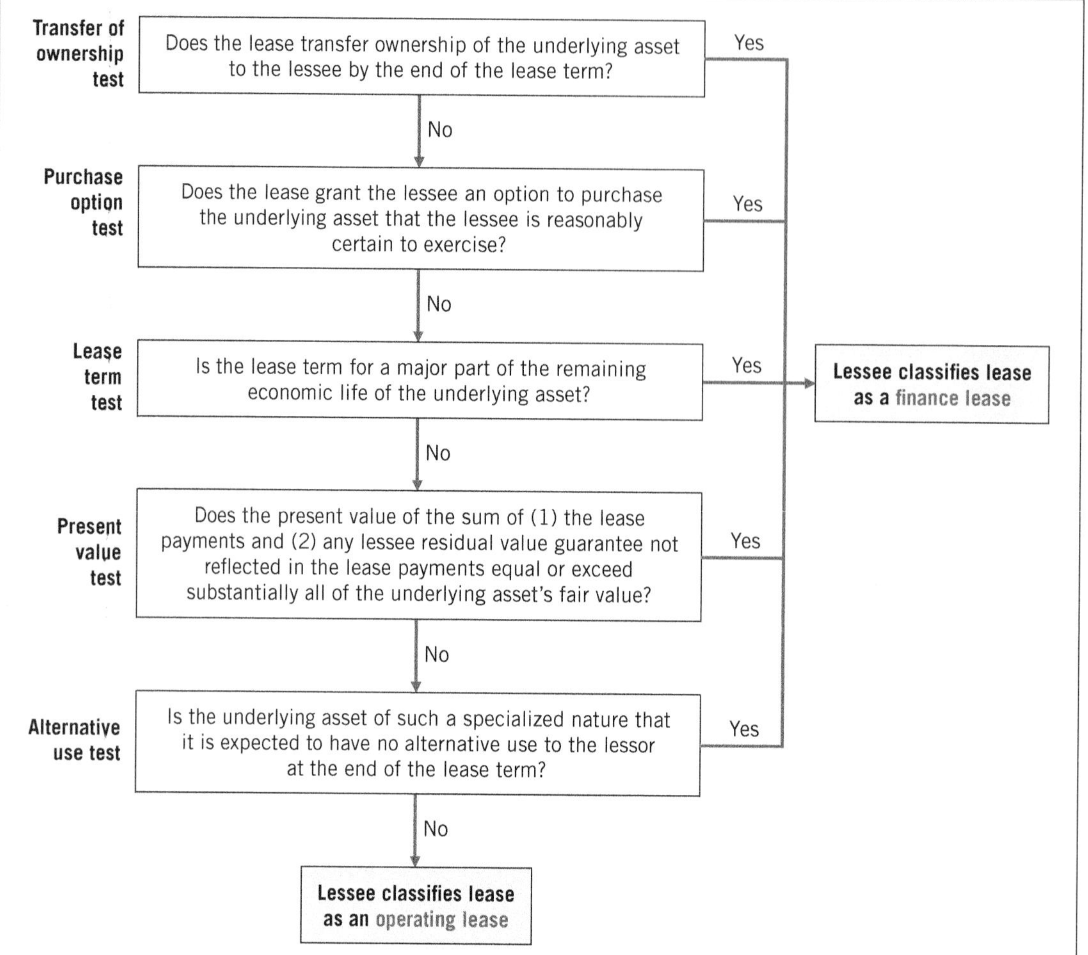

Source: Adapted from *KPMG Leases in Depth* (April 2016), p. 147.

For a lease to be a finance lease, it must be non-cancelable and **meet at least one of the five tests** listed in Illustration 21.2. [2] Otherwise, the lease is an operating lease. Additional explanation of each of the lease classification tests follows.

Transfer of Ownership Test

If the lease transfers ownership of the asset to the lessee, it is a finance lease. This test is not controversial and easily implemented in practice.

Purchase Option Test

A purchase option test is met if it is reasonably certain that the lessee will exercise the option. In other words, the lease purchase option allows the lessee to purchase the property for a price that is significantly lower than the underlying asset's expected fair value at the date the option becomes exercisable (hereafter referred to as a **bargain purchase option**).

For example, assume that Brett's Delivery Service leases a **Honda** Accord for $499 per month for 40 months, with an option to purchase the Accord for $100 at that end of the lease. If the estimated fair value of the Honda Accord is $3,000 at the end of the 40 months, the $100 option is clearly a bargain purchase option. Therefore, Brett's accounts for this lease as a finance lease.

Lease Term Test

When the lease term is a major part of the remaining economic life of the leased asset, companies should use the finance method in accounting for the lease transaction. The question is, what is a major part of the economic life of a leased asset? Although the FASB indicates that companies should use judgment in evaluating the lease term test, it recognizes that additional implementation guidance would be helpful. As a result, the Board establishes an implementation guideline that companies might use. That is, if the lease term is 75 percent or greater of the economic life of the leased asset, the lease meets the **lease term test** and finance lease treatment is appropriate (often referred to as the 75% test).[2] *This guideline should be used for homework purposes.*

Another factor to consider in the lease term test is a bargain renewal option. For example, a lease term is generally considered to be the fixed, non-cancelable term of the lease. However, a **bargain renewal option** allows the lessee to renew the lease for a rental that is lower than the expected fair rental at the time the option becomes exercisable. At the commencement of the lease, the difference between the renewal rental and the expected fair rental must be great enough to make exercise of the option to renew reasonably certain.[3] Thus, companies should include in the lease term any bargain renewal periods.

For example, assume that **Home Depot** leases **Dell** PCs for two years at a rental of $100 per month per computer. In addition, Home Depot can lease these computers for $10 per month per computer for another two years. The lease clearly offers a bargain renewal option, and Home Depot should consider the lease term for these computers to be four years, not two.

Present Value Test

If the present value of the lease payments is reasonably close to the fair value of the asset, a company is effectively purchasing the asset and should therefore use the finance method to account for the lease. Again, the FASB recognizes that determining what is reasonably close often involves significant judgment and therefore provides an implementation guideline (hereafter referred to as the 90% test). This guideline states that if the present value of the lease payments equals or exceeds 90 percent of the fair value of the asset, then a lessee should use the finance method to record the lease. *This guideline should be used for homework purposes.* To apply the present value test, a lessee must determine the amount of lease payments and the appropriate discount rate.

Lease Payments The lease payments generally include the following:

1. ***Fixed payments.*** These are the rental payments that are specified in the lease agreement and fixed over the lease term.
2. ***Variable payments that are based on an index or a rate.*** The lessee should include variable lease payments in the value of the lease liability at the level of the index/rate at the commencement date. When valuing the lease liability, no increases or decreases to future lease payments should be assumed based on increases or decreases in the index or rate. Instead, any difference in the payments due to changes in the index or rate is expensed in the period incurred. **Illustrations 21.3** and **21.4** provide an analysis of variable lease payments.

ILLUSTRATION 21.3
Variable Lease Payments

Including Variable Lease Payments

Facts: On January 1, 2020, Jose Company leases an airplane for 6 years. The annual lease payments are $1,000,000 per year, payable at the beginning of each year (annuity-due basis). In addition, the lease agreement specifies that the lease payment increases by $30,000 every year.

Question: **What are the lease payments in 2021?**

Solution: On January 1, 2021, the lease payment is $1,030,000 ($1,000,000 + $30,000), which is considered a variable payment. Given that the amount of the variable payment is known from year to year (the rate is set at commencement of the lease and in substance fixed), such variable payments are included in calculating the present value of the lease liability.

[2]Companies may lease a used asset in the last 25 percent of its economic life, which raises the question of applying the lease term test for classification of the lease. The FASB's position is that it is inconsistent to require that a lease covering the last few years be recorded as a finance lease by a lessee (or as a sales-type lease by a lessor) when a similar lease of that asset earlier in its economic life would have been classified as an operating lease. This conclusion is debatable because a lessee can direct the use of and obtain substantially all the remaining benefits from a significantly used asset just the same as it can a new or slightly used asset. [3].

[3]Reasonably certain is a high threshold of probability. The FASB intended that parties to a lease account for options only when the lessee has a compelling economic reason to exercise a purchase, renewal, or termination option. [4]

ILLUSTRATION 21.4

Variable Lease Payments

Expensing Variable Lease Payments

Facts: Assume the same information as in Illustration 21.3, except that the lease payments are adjusted each year by a change in the Consumer Price Index (CPI).

Question: **If the CPI is 100 at January 1, 2020, and increases to 104 on January 1, 2021, what is the payment on January 1, 2021?**

Solution: The variable payment on January 1, 2021, is $1,040,000 ($1,000,000 × 1.04). Because the amount of the variable payment from year to year is not known at the lease commencement date, this payment is not included in determining the present value of the lease liability. This additional payment ($40,000) is recognized as an expense in the period it is incurred. Similarly, when lease payments vary with a performance measure (e.g., sales at a store location, asset usage), the variable amounts will be expensed in the period incurred.

3. ***Amounts guaranteed by a lessee under a residual value guarantee.*** Residual value is the expected value of the leased asset at the end of the lease term. A residual value can be guaranteed or unguaranteed. In a guaranteed residual value, the lessee has an obligation to not only return the leased asset at the end of the lease term but also to guarantee that the residual value will be a certain amount. If the lease involves an unguaranteed residual value, the lessee does not have any obligation to the lessor at the end of the lease, except to return the leased asset to the lessor. [5] For classification purposes, the lessee includes the full amount of the residual value guarantee at the end of the lease term in the present value test. The lessee does not consider unguaranteed residual value as part of the present value test.[4]
4. ***Payments related to purchase or termination options that the lessee is reasonably certain to exercise.*** As indicated earlier, if the lease contains a bargain purchase option, the cost of that option should be considered part of the lease payments. Analysis of a termination option is indicated in Illustration 21.5.

ILLUSTRATION 21.5

Termination Option

Analyzing a Termination Option

Facts: Cabrera Company leases a building and land from Worldwide Leasing for 6 years with monthly payments of $10,000. The lease contract allows Cabrera to terminate the lease after 2 years for a total payment of $140,000. At the commencement of the lease, it is reasonably certain that Cabrera will not continue the lease beyond 2 years.

Question: **What are Cabrera's lease payments?**

Solution: In this case, Cabrera should include the cost of the termination option in its calculation of the present value of its lease liability. The total lease payments are therefore $380,000 [($10,000 × 24) + $140,000].

Discount Rate To determine whether the present value of the payments equals or exceeds 90 percent of the fair value of the leased asset, a lessee (like the Delta example presented earlier) should compute the present value of the lease payments using the implicit interest rate. [6] This rate is defined as the discount rate that, at commencement of the lease, causes the aggregate present value of the lease payments and unguaranteed residual value to be equal to the fair value of the leased asset. [7]

[4]As discussed in more detail later, consideration of the guaranteed residual values differs for classification of the lease and measurement of the lease liability.

Delta (a lessee) may find that it is impracticable to determine the implicit rate of the lessor. In the event that it is impracticable to determine the implicit rate, Delta uses its incremental borrowing rate. The **incremental borrowing rate** is the rate of interest the lessee would have to pay on a similar lease or the rate that, at commencement of the lease, the lessee would incur to borrow over a similar term the funds necessary to purchase the asset. The implicit rate of the lessor is generally a more realistic rate to use in determining the amount to report as the asset and related liability for Delta. However, given the difficulty the lessee may have in determining the implicit rate, it is likely that the lessee will use the incremental borrowing rate.[5]

Alternative Use Test

If at the end of the lease term the lessor does not have an alternative use for the asset, the lessee classifies the lease as a finance lease. In this situation, the assumption is that the lessee uses all the benefits from the leased asset and therefore the lessee has essentially purchased the asset.

Lessors sometimes build an asset to meet specifications set by the lessee (referred to as "build-to-suit" arrangements). For example, an equipment manufacturer might build hydraulic lifts to meet unique loading dock configurations of a lessee, like **Amazon.com**. Given the specialty nature of the equipment, only Amazon can use the lifts and it receives substantially all of the benefits of the leased asset, such that the alternative use test is met.

Accounting for Finance Leases

LEARNING OBJECTIVE 2

Explain the accounting for finance leases.

As indicated, the accounting for a lease arrangement by lessees and lessors depends on classification of the lease as a sale of the underlying asset. If the lease is in substance a sale, the lease is classified as a finance lease.

Lessee Accounting for Finance Leases: An Example

To illustrate the accounting for a finance lease, assume that **Caterpillar Financial Services Corp.** (a subsidiary of **Caterpillar**) and **Sterling Construction** sign a lease agreement dated January 1, 2020, that calls for Caterpillar to lease a backhoe to Sterling beginning January 1, 2020. The terms and provisions of the lease agreement and other pertinent data are as follows.

- The term of the lease is five years. The lease agreement is non-cancelable, requiring equal rental payments of $20,711.11 at the beginning of each year (annuity-due basis).
- The backhoe has a fair value at the commencement of the lease of $100,000, an estimated economic life of five years, and a guaranteed residual value of $5,000. (Sterling expects that it is probable that the expected value of the residual value at the end of the lease will be greater than the guaranteed amount of $5,000.)
- The lease contains no renewal options. The backhoe reverts to Caterpillar at the termination of the lease.
- Sterling's incremental borrowing rate is 5 percent per year.

[5]This difficulty arises because, for example, the lessee may not know the residual value used by the lessor, nor the initial direct costs that the lessor incurs.

- Sterling depreciates, on a straight-line basis, similar equipment that it owns.
- Caterpillar sets the annual rental rate to earn a rate of return of 4 percent per year; Sterling is aware of this rate.

Sterling evaluates the lease classification tests as indicated in **Illustration 21.6**.

ILLUSTRATION 21.6
Lease Classification Tests

Test	Assessment
1. Transfer of ownership test	Transfer of ownership does not occur; the asset reverts to Caterpillar at the end of the lease.
2. Purchase option test	There is no purchase option in the lease.
3. Lease term test	The lease term is equal to the economic life of the asset (100 percent). Therefore, **the lease meets the lease term test**.
4. Present value test	The present value of the lease payments is $100,000*, which is 100 percent (greater than or equal to 90 percent) of the fair value of the backhoe. Therefore, **the lease meets the present value test**.
5. Alternative use test	Since the asset is returned to Caterpillar with some residual value, the alternative use test is not met.

*Present value of payments ($20,711.11 × 4.62990 ($PVF\text{-}AD_{5,4\%}$))	$ 95,890.35[6]
Present value of the residual value ($5,000 × .82193 ($PVF_{5,4\%}$))	4,109.65
	$100,000.00

Thus, the lease is classified as a finance lease due to meeting the lease term and present value tests (meeting either one of these tests would suffice). Note that the present value test includes the full amount of the residual value guarantee to determine whether the lease is classified as a financing or operating lease. However, for measurement of the lease liability, Sterling includes **only the expected residual value probable of being owed by the lessee under the residual value guarantee.** [8] Because Sterling believes that it is probable that the expected residual value will be greater than the guaranteed residual value, the guaranteed residual value is not included in the measurement of the lease liability.[7]

Sterling computes the lease liability and the amount capitalized as a right-of-use asset as the present value of the lease payments, as shown in **Illustration 21.7**.

ILLUSTRATION 21.7
Present Value of Lease Payments

Capitalized amount = $20,711.11 × Present value of an annuity due of 1 for 5 periods at 4%
= $20,711.11 × 4.62990 ($PVF\text{-}OA_{5,4\%}$)
= $95,890.35*

*Rounded by $0.02.

Sterling uses Caterpillar's implicit interest rate of 4 percent instead of its incremental borrowing rate of 5 percent because the implicit rate is known to Sterling.[8] Sterling records the lease on its books as follows.

January 1, 2020		
Right-of-Use Asset	95,890.35	
Lease Liability		95,890.35

[6]The computation of the present value is rounded by $0.02. The rounding occurs because the tables from Chapter 6 are used to determine the amounts shown. *For homework and other computations in the text, we use the tables which may to lead to small rounding differences.* In practice, a financial calculator is often used to avoid these rounding differences.

[7]Later in the chapter, we provide an expanded discussion of the relationship between the expected residual value and the guaranteed residual value, and its effect on the measurement of the lease liability.

[8]If Sterling had not known Caterpillar's implicit rate, it would have used its incremental borrowing rate of 5 percent to compute the present value of the lease liability.

Note that Sterling records the obligation at the net amount of $95,890.35 (the present value of the lease payments) rather than at the gross amount of $103,555.55 ($20,711.11 × 5).[9] Sterling then records the **first lease payment** as follows.

	January 1, 2020		
Lease Liability		20,711.11	
Cash			20,711.11

The annual interest expense, applying the effective-interest method, is a function of the outstanding liability as shown in the lease amortization schedule in **Illustration 21.8**.

ILLUSTRATION 21.8

Lease Amortization Schedule

Sterling Construction
Lease Amortization Schedule
Annuity-Due Basis

Date	Annual Lease Payment	Interest (4%) on Liability	Reduction of Lease Liability	Lease Liability
	(a)	(b)	(c)	(d)
1/1/20				$95,890.35
1/1/20	$ 20,711.11	$ -0-	$20,711.11	75,179.24
1/1/21	20,711.11	3,007.17	17,703.94	57,475.30
1/1/22	20,711.11	2,299.01	18,412.10	39,063.20
1/1/23	20,711.11	1,562.53	19,148.58	19,914.62
1/1/24	20,711.11	796.49*	19,914.62	0.00
	$103,555.55	$7,665.20	$95,890.35	

(a) Lease payment as required by lease.
(b) Four percent of the preceding balance of (d) except for 1/1/20; since this is an annuity due, no time has elapsed at the date of the first payment and therefore no interest has accrued.
(c) (a) minus (b).
(d) Preceding balance minus (c).

*Rounded by $0.09.

Each lease payment of $20,711.11 consists of two elements: (1) a reduction of the lease liability and (2) a financing cost (interest expense).[10] The total financing cost (interest expense) over the term of the lease is $7,665.20. This amount is the difference between the present value of the lease payments ($95,890.35) and the actual cash disbursed ($103,555.55). Sterling records **interest expense** for the first year of the lease as follows.

	December 31, 2020		
Interest Expense		3,007.17	
Lease Liability			3,007.17

Amortization of the right-of-use asset over the five-year lease term, applying Sterling's normal depreciation policy (straight-line method), results in the following entry at December 31, 2020.

	December 31, 2020		
Amortization Expense		19,178.07	
Right-of-Use Asset ($95,890.35 ÷ 5 years)			19,178.07

At December 31, 2020, Sterling reports right-of-use assets and related lease liabilities separately from other assets and liabilities on its balance sheet, or discloses these assets and liabilities in the notes to its financial statements.

[9]As discussed, in measuring the liability and right-of-use asset, Sterling does not include the present value of the residual value because the guaranteed amount is not greater than the expected amount. We discuss residual value considerations in more detail in a later section of the chapter.

[10]Because it occurs at the lease commencement date, the first payment does not contain an interest component.

Sterling classifies the portion of the liability due within one year or the operating cycle, whichever is longer, with current liabilities, and the rest with noncurrent liabilities. For example, the current portion of the December 31, 2020, total obligation of $75,179.24 in Sterling's amortization schedule is the amount payable in 2021, or $20,711.11. Note that this current portion is composed of two components: (1) accrued interest on the liability outstanding throughout the year ($3,007.17) and (2) reduction of the initial lease liability ($17,703.94). **Illustration 21.9** shows the presentation of the lease assets and liabilities sections as they relate to lease transactions at December 31, 2020, assuming Sterling chose to present right-of-use assets and lease liabilities separately from other assets and liabilities on the balance sheet.

ILLUSTRATION 21.9
Balance Sheet Presentation

Noncurrent assets	
Right-of-use assets ($95,890.35 – $19,178.07)	$76,712.28
Current liabilities	
Lease liability ($3,007.17 + $17,703.94)	$20,711.11
Noncurrent liabilities	
Lease liability	57,475.30

On its December 31, 2020, income statement, Sterling reports interest expense on the liability and amortization expense related to right-of-use assets, as shown in **Illustration 21.10**.

ILLUSTRATION 21.10
Income Statement Presentation

Expenses	
Interest expense (lease liabilities)	$ 3,007.17
Amortization expense (right-of-use assets)	19,178.07

Sterling records the second lease payment as follows.

January 1, 2021		
Lease Liability ($3,007.17 + $17,703.94)	20,711.11	
Cash		20,711.11

Entries through 2024 follow the pattern above. **Upon expiration of the lease,** Sterling has fully amortized the amount capitalized as a right-of-use asset. It also has fully discharged its lease obligation. At the date the lease expires, both the right-of-use asset account and lease liability account related to Sterling's lease of the backhoe have zero balances. If Sterling does not purchase the backhoe, it returns the equipment to Caterpillar.[11]

If Sterling purchases the equipment from Caterpillar at the termination of the lease at a price of $5,000 and the estimated remaining life of the equipment is two years at that time, it makes the following entry.

January 1, 2025		
Equipment	5,000	
Cash		5,000

Lessor Accounting for Sales-Type Leases

We now turn our attention to the other party involved in the Caterpillar/Sterling lease arrangement—Caterpillar (the lessor). The **lease classification tests for the lessor are**

[11]If Sterling purchases the backhoe during the term of the lease, it accounts for the transaction as a termination of the lease and a purchase of an asset. Thus, it would record any difference between the purchase price and the carrying amount of the lease liability as an adjustment of the carrying amount of the asset. [9]

identical to the tests used by the lessee to determine classification of a lease as a financing or operating lease, as shown in Illustration 21.6. Why use the same criteria for both the lessee and the lessor? The reason is that the tests are used to determine whether the lessee and the lessor have an agreement to transfer control of the asset from one party to the other. If the lessee receives control, then the lessor must have given up control.

The FASB concluded that by meeting any of the lease classification tests in Illustration 21.6, the lessor transfers control of the leased asset and therefore satisfies a performance obligation, which is required for revenue recognition under the FASB's recent standard on revenue. [10] That is, the lessor has, in substance, transferred control of the right-of-use asset and therefore has a **sales-type lease** if the lessee takes ownership or consumes a substantial portion of the underlying asset over the lease term. On the other hand, if the lease does not transfer control (and ownership) of the asset over the lease term, the lessor will generally use the operating approach in accounting for the lease. [11] Although not part of the classification tests, the lessor must also determine whether the collectibility of payments from the lessee is probable. If payments are not probable, the lessor does not record a receivable and does not derecognize the leased asset. Instead, receipt of any lease payments is recorded as a deposit liability. [12][12]

What Do the Numbers Mean? Not So Fast

As an illustration of the importance of the control criteria, consider the case of computer leasing companies, which at one time bought **IBM** equipment, leased the equipment to their customers, and removed the leased assets from their balance sheets. In leasing the assets, the computer lessors stated that they would substitute new IBM equipment if obsolescence occurred (a sales return provision). However, when IBM introduced a new computer line, IBM refused to sell it to the computer leasing companies. As a result, a number of the lessors could not meet their contracts with their customers and had to take back the old equipment. Thus, control had not been fully transferred and the computer leasing companies therefore had to reinstate the assets they had taken off the books. Such a case demonstrates one reason why the lessor classification tests must be aligned with those for revenue recognition.

Accounting Measurement and Presentation

Classification of the lease as either a sales-type or operating lease determines the subsequent accounting by the lessor.[13] For a sales-type lease, the lessor accounts for the lease in a manner similar to the sale of an asset. Under a sales-type lease, the lessor generally records a **Lease Receivable** and eliminates the leased asset. The lease receivable for Sterling is computed as shown in **Illustration 21.11**.[14]

ILLUSTRATION 21.11
Lease Receivable

Lease Receivable	=	**Present Value of Rental Payments**	+	**Present Value of Guaranteed and Unguaranteed Residual Values**

Any selling profit on the transfer of the leased asset is recognized by recording sales revenue and related cost of goods sold at the commencement of the lease. The lessor recognizes

[12]If classified as an operating lease and collectibility is not probable, recognition of lease income is limited to cash received.

[13]We call it a sales-type lease because there is another type of lease for a lessor that uses the finance method, called a "direct financing lease." Direct financing leases are not that common in practice; we discuss this exception in Appendix 21B.

[14]Lease Receivable is often defined as only the present value of the rental payments plus the present value of the guaranteed residual value. In the case in which the lessor has an unguaranteed residual value, the total amount is often referred to as the **net investment** in the lease. Another approach is to report the unguaranteed residual value separately when making the journal entry. *We use the definition in Illustration 21.11 for pedagogical reasons; this definition (including both guaranteed and unguaranteed residual values) should be used in the homework.*

interest revenue on the lease receivable over the life of the lease using the effective-interest method.[15]

Sales-Type Lease Example

To illustrate lessor accounting for a sales-type lease, refer to the preceding Caterpillar/Sterling example. We repeat here the information relevant to Caterpillar in accounting for this lease transaction.

- The term of the lease is five years. The lease agreement is non-cancelable, requiring equal rental payments at the beginning of each year (annuity-due basis).
- The backhoe has a fair value at the commencement of the lease of $100,000, an estimated economic life of five years, and a guaranteed residual value of $5,000. Further, assume the underlying asset (the backhoe) has an $85,000 cost to the dealer, Caterpillar.
- The lease contains no renewal options. The backhoe reverts to Caterpillar at the termination of the lease.
- Collectibility of payments by Caterpillar is probable.
- Caterpillar sets the annual rental payment to earn a rate of return of 4 percent per year (implicit rate) on its investment as shown in **Illustration 21.12**.

ILLUSTRATION 21.12
Lease Payment Calculation

Fair value of leased equipment	$100,000.00
Less: Present value of the residual value ($5,000 × .82193 ($PVF_{5,4\%}$))	4,109.65
Amount to be recovered by lessor through lease payments	$ 95,890.35
Five beginning-of-year lease payments to earn a 4% return ($95,890.35 ÷ 4.62990 ($PVF\text{-}AD_{5,4\%}$))	$ 20,711.11

Caterpillar determines the lease payments based on the implicit rate (rate of return) needed to justify leasing the asset. In establishing this rate of return, Caterpillar considers the credit standing of Sterling, the term of the lease, and whether the residual value is guaranteed or unguaranteed. In the Caterpillar/Sterling example, when a residual value is involved (whether guaranteed or not), Caterpillar does not have to recover as much from the rental payments and therefore the rental payments are less.

The lease meets the criteria for classification as a finance (sales-type) lease because (1) the present value of the lease payments is equal to the fair value of the asset, and (2) the lease term is equal to the economic life of the asset. That is, Sterling will consume substantially the entire underlying asset over the lease term. Caterpillar computes the lease receivable as shown in **Illustration 21.13**.

ILLUSTRATION 21.13
Lease Receivable Calculation

Lease receivable = Present value of the rental payment + Present value of the guaranteed residual value
= $95,890.35 ($20,711.11 × 4.62990 ($PVF\text{-}OA_{5,4\%}$)) + $4,109.65 ($5,000.00 × .82193 ($PVF_{5,4\%}$))
= $100,000.00

Caterpillar then records the lease receivable, cost of goods sold, and sales revenue and removes the leased asset (which prior to the lease was included in Caterpillar's inventory). The journal entry to record this transaction on January 1, 2020, is as follows.

[15]Even if the selling profit is zero (or a net loss), the lessor recognizes sales and cost of goods sold. For a lease classified as operating, the lessor continues to recognize the asset on its books and records lease revenue for payments received from the lease over the lease term.

January 1, 2020

Lease Receivable	100,000	
Cost of Goods Sold	85,000	
Sales Revenue		100,000
Inventory		85,000

As a result, Caterpillar reports a gross profit of $15,000 ($100,000 – $85,000) on its income statement. Caterpillar then prepares a lease amortization schedule, as shown in **Illustration 21.14**, applying the effective-interest method and recognizing interest revenue as a function of the lease receivable balance.

ILLUSTRATION 21.14
Lease Amortization Schedule

Caterpillar Financial
Lease Amortization Schedule
Annuity-Due Basis

Date	Annual Lease Payment	Interest (4%) on Lease Receivable	Reduction of Lease Receivable	Lease Receivable
	(a)	(b)	(c)	(d)
1/1/20				$100,000.00
1/1/20	$ 20,711.11	$ -0-	$ 20,711.11	79,288.89
1/1/21	20,711.11	3,171.56	17,539.55	61,749.34
1/1/22	20,711.11	2,469.97	18,241.14	43,508.20
1/1/23	20,711.11	1,740.33	18,970.78	24,537.42
1/1/24	20,711.11	981.50	19,729.61	4,807.81
1/1/25	5,000.00	192.19*	4,807.81	0.00
	$108,555.55	$8,555.55	$100,000.00	

(a) Lease payment as required by lease.
(b) Four percent of the preceding balance of (d) except for 1/1/20; since this is an annuity due, no time has elapsed at the date of the first payment and therefore no interest has accrued.
(c) (a) minus (b).
(d) Preceding balance minus (c).

*Rounded by $0.12.

On January 1, 2020, Caterpillar records receipt of the first year's lease payment as follows.

January 1, 2020

Cash	20,711.11	
Lease Receivable		20,711.11

On December 31, 2020, Caterpillar recognizes the interest revenue on the lease receivable during the first year through the following entry (see **Underlying Concepts**).

Underlying Concepts

Interest revenue for the lessor may differ from interest expense for the lessee because the lease receivable amount is different than that for the lease liability.

December 31, 2020

Lease Receivable	3,171.56	
Interest Revenue		3,171.56

At December 31, 2020, Caterpillar reports the lease receivable in its balance sheet among current assets and noncurrent assets. It classifies the portion due within one year or the operating cycle, whichever is longer, as a current asset, and the rest with noncurrent assets.

Illustration 21.15 shows Caterpillar's assets section as it relates to the Sterling lease transactions at December 31, 2020.

ILLUSTRATION 21.15
Balance Sheet Presentation

Current assets	
Lease receivable ($3,171.56 + $17,539.55)	$20,711.11
Noncurrent assets (investments)	
Lease receivable	61,749.34

In its income statement for 2020, Caterpillar presents the revenue and expense items shown in **Illustration 21.16**.

ILLUSTRATION 21.16

Income Statement Presentation

Sales	
Sales revenue	$100,000.00
Less: Cost of goods sold	85,000.00
Other revenue	
Interest revenue	3,171.56

The following entries record receipt of the second year's lease payment and recognition of the interest revenue in 2021.

January 1, 2021		
Cash	20,711.11	
Lease Receivable		20,711.11

December 31, 2021		
Lease Receivable	2,469.97	
Interest Revenue		2,469.97

Journal entries through 2024 follow the same pattern, except for the year 2024. In 2024, the final lease payment is made on January 1, 2024, but the asset is not returned to Caterpillar until January 1, 2025.

Caterpillar makes the following entry on December 31, 2024.

December 31, 2024		
Lease Receivable	192.19	
Lease Revenue		192.19

As a result, interest revenue of $192.19 is recognized for the year 2024 as the residual value accretes up to $5,000 at the end of the lease. At January 1, 2025, when the leased asset is returned to Caterpillar, the Lease Receivable account is reduced to zero and the asset returned is recorded in inventory, as follows.

January 1, 2025		
Inventory	5,000	
Lease Receivable		5,000

Accounting for Operating Leases

LEARNING OBJECTIVE 3

Explain the accounting for operating leases.

Lessee Accounting for Operating Leases

If a lease does not meet any of the lease classification tests for a finance lease, a lessee should classify it as an operating lease. For leases classified as operating, the lessee records a right-of-use asset and lease liability at commencement of the lease, similar to the finance lease approach. However, unlike a finance lease, the lessee records the same amount for lease expense each period over the lease term (often referred to as the straight-line method for expense measurement).

Companies continue to use the effective-interest method for amortizing the lease liability. However, instead of reporting interest expense, a lessee reports interest on the lease liability as part of Lease Expense. In addition, the lessee no longer reports amortization expense related to the right-of-use asset. Instead, it "plugs" in an amount that increases the Lease Expense account so that it is the same amount from period to period. This plugged amount then reduces the right-of-use asset, such that both the right-of-use asset and the lease liability are amortized to zero at the end of the lease.[16]

To illustrate operating lease accounting for a lessee, assume that Josway Disposal Inc. (lessor) and Traylor Stores Inc. (lessee) sign a lease agreement dated January 1, 2020. The lease agreement specifies that Josway will grant right-of-use of one of its standard cardboard compactors (is not of a specialized nature) at one of Traylor's locations. Information relevant to the lease is as follows.

- The lease agreement is non-cancelable with a term of three years.
- The compactor has a cost and fair value at commencement of the lease of $60,000, an estimated economic life of five years, and a residual value at **the end of the lease** of $12,000 (unguaranteed).
- The lease contains no renewal options. The compactor reverts to Josway at the termination of the lease.
- The implicit rate of Josway (the lessor) is 6 percent and is known by Traylor.

Josway determines the rental payments such that it earns rate of return of 6 percent per year on its investment, as shown in **Illustration 21.17**.

ILLUSTRATION 21.17

Computation of Lease Payments

Fair value of leased equipment	$60,000.00
Less: Present value of the residual value ($12,000 × .83962 ($PVF_{3,6\%}$))	10,075.44
Amount to be recovered by lessor through lease payments	$49,924.56
Three beginning-of-year lease payments to earn a 6% return ($49,924.56 ÷ 2.83339 ($PVF\text{-}AD_{3,6\%}$))	$17,620.08

Traylor classifies the lease as an operating lease because none of the finance lease tests are met, as shown in **Illustration 21.18**.

ILLUSTRATION 21.18

Lease Classification Tests

Test	Assessment
1. Transfer of ownership test	Transfer of ownership does not occur; the asset reverts to Josway at the end of the lease.
2. Purchase option test	There is no purchase option in the lease.
3. Lease term test	The lease term is 60 percent (3 ÷ 5) of the economic life of the asset, which is less than a major part of the life of the asset (75 percent).
4. Present value test	The present value of the lease payments is $49,924.56*, which is 83.2% ($49,924.56 ÷ $60,000) of the fair value of the compactor. Therefore, the lease does not meet the present value test.
5. Alternative use test	As indicated, the equipment is not of a specialized nature and is expected to have use to Josway when returned at the end of the lease.

*$17,620.08 × 2.83339 ($PVF\text{-}AD_{3,6\%}$)

Traylor makes the following entry to record this operating lease.

January 1, 2020

Right-of-Use Asset	49,924.56	
Lease Liability		49,924.56

[16]The FASB indicates that reporting a single operating cost in the income statement more appropriately reflects the economics of an operating lease than the separate recognition of interest and amortization used in a finance lease. The rationale for this approach is that an operating lease grants different rights to the lessee. The different rights are that in an operating lease, the lessee is not exposed to nor benefits from any value changes in the right-of-use asset over the term of the lease. [13]

In addition, Traylor records the first payment, as follows.

January 1, 2020		
Lease Liability	17,620.08	
Cash		17,620.08

Traylor then prepares a lease amortization schedule, as shown in Illustration 21.19, applying the effective-interest method and measuring interest on the liability as a function of the lease liability balance, with related amortization of the lease liability.

ILLUSTRATION 21.19

Lease Amortization Schedule

Traylor Stores Inc.
Lease Amortization Schedule
Annuity-Due Basis

Date	Annual Lease Payment	Interest (6%) on Liability	Reduction of Lease Liability	Lease Liability
	(a)	(b)	(c)	(d)
1/1/20				$49,924.56
1/1/20	$17,620.08	$ -0-	$17,620.08	32,304.48
1/1/21	17,620.08	1,938.27	15,681.81	16,622.67
1/1/22	17,620.08	997.41*	16,622.67	0.00
	$52,860.24	$2,935.68	$49,924.56	

(a) Lease payment as required by lease.
(b) Six percent of the preceding balance of (d) except for 1/1/20; since this is an annuity due, no time has elapsed at the date of the first payment and therefore no interest has accrued.
(c) (a) minus (b).
(d) Preceding balance minus (c).

*Rounded by $0.05.

To record equal amounts of lease expense each period under the straight-line approach, the lessee computes interest on the lease liability (as shown in Illustration 21.19) and then amortizes the right-of-use asset in a manner that results in equal amounts of lease expense in each period. Traylor computes the straight-line lease expense each year as presented in the lease expense schedule in Illustration 21.20.

ILLUSTRATION 21.20

Lease Expense Schedule

Traylor Stores Inc.
Lease Expense Schedule

Date	(A) Lease Expense (Straight-Line)	(B) Interest (6%) on Liability	(C) Amortization of ROU Asset (A – B)	(D) Carrying Value of ROU Asset (D – C)
1/1/20				$49,924.56
12/31/20	$17,620.08	$1,938.27	$15,681.81	34,242.75
12/31/21	17,620.08	997.41	16,622.67	17,620.08
12/31/22	17,620.08		17,620.08	0.00
	$52,860.24	$2,935.68	$49,924.56	

As shown in Illustration 21.20, Traylor does the following to record straight-line expense related to its operating lease.

1. Traylor makes lease payments totaling $52,860.24 to Josway. Traylor divides the $52,860.24 by the lease term of three years to compute its straight-line annual lease expense of $17,620.08 (Column A).
2. Traylor records part of its annual lease expense based on interest related to amortizing its lease liability according to the lease amortization schedule provided in Illustration 21.19 [Column (b)].

3. Traylor deducts that amount of interest on the liability from the straight-line lease expense to arrive at the amount of amortization of the right-of-use asset (Column C).
4. Traylor determines the carrying value of the right-of-use asset by deducting the amortization of the right-of-use asset each reporting period (Column D).

Traylor prepares journal entries during the lease term to record lease expense, which is comprised of interest on the lease liability and the amortization of the right-of-use asset. Traylor makes the following entry to record lease expense in 2020 on December 31, 2020.

December 31, 2020		
Lease Expense	17,620.08	
Right-of-Use Asset ($17,620.08 – $1,938.27)		15,681.81
Lease Liability		1,938.27

As indicated in Illustration 21.20, Traylor accrues interest ($1,938.27) and amortizes the right-of-use asset ($15,681.81). As a result, Traylor records a single lease expense amount of $17,620.08 for the year 2020. The second lease payment on January 1, 2021, is as follows.

January 1, 2021		
Lease Liability ($1,938.27 + $15,681.81)	17,620.08	
Cash		17,620.08

Journal entries in subsequent periods follow the same pattern, using the amounts presented in Illustration 21.20. The entry to record lease expense in the second year of the lease is as follows.

December 31, 2021		
Lease Expense	17,620.08	
Right-of-Use Asset ($17,620.08 – $997.41)		16,622.67
Lease Liability		997.41

Traylor records a single lease expense amount of $17,620.08, comprised of interest on the lease liability ($997.41 in 2021) and amortization of the right-of-use asset ($16,622.67 in 2021). The third and final lease payment is made on January 1, 2022, as follows.

January 1, 2022		
Lease Liability ($997.41 + $16,622.67)	17,620.08	
Cash		17,620.08

Traylor makes the following entry to record lease expense for 2022, the third year of the lease.

December 31, 2022		
Lease Expense	17,620.08	
Right-of-Use Asset		17,620.08

Following this entry, the right-of-use asset has been fully amortized. As summarized in the lease expense schedule in Illustration 21.20, the total lease expense for the three years is comprised of the amortization of the right-of-use asset of $49,924.56 plus interest related to the lease liability of $2,935.68, for a total lease expense of $52,860.24. Traylor presents the interest and right-of-use asset amortization related to the lease as a **single lease (operating) expense** in the income statement each year.

Lessor Accounting for Operating Leases

To illustrate lessor accounting for an operating lease, refer to the previously discussed lease agreement between Josway Disposal Inc. and Traylor Stores Inc. for the use of one of Josway's standard cardboard compactors. Information relevant to the lease is as follows.

- The term of the lease is three years. The lease agreement is non-cancelable, requiring three annual rental payments of $17,620.08, with the first payment on January 1, 2020 (annuity-due basis).

- The compactor has a cost and fair value at commencement of the lease of $60,000, an estimated economic life of five years, and a residual value at the end of the lease of $12,000 (unguaranteed). Josway depreciates assets, such as this compactor, using double-declining-balance.
- The lease contains no renewal options. The compactor reverts to Josway at the termination of the lease.
- The implicit rate of the lessor is known by Traylor. Traylor's incremental borrowing rate is 6 percent. Josway sets the annual rental rate to earn a rate of return of 6 percent per year (implicit rate) on its investment, as shown in Illustration 21.17.

Applying the same classification tests used by Traylor (see Illustration 21.18), Josway classifies the lease as an operating lease because none of the finance lease tests are met. Under the operating method, Josway (the lessor) continues to recognize the asset on its balance sheet and recognizes lease revenue (generally on a straight-line basis) in each period.

To illustrate the operating method for the Josway/Traylor lease, Josway records the lease payment on a straight-line basis on January 1, 2020, 2021, and 2022, as follows.

January 1, 2020, 2021, and 2022		
Cash	17,620.08	
Unearned Lease Revenue		17,620.08

On December 31, 2020, 2021, and 2022, Josway records the recognition of the revenue each period as follows.

Unearned Lease Revenue	17,620.08	
Lease Revenue		17,620.08

Underlying Concepts

Since the lessor owns the underlying asset, it depreciates the compactor over its entire useful life.

Josway also records depreciation expense on the leased equipment (assuming double-declining-balance, given a cost basis of $60,000, and a five-year economic life), as follows (see **Underlying Concepts**).

Depreciation Expense ($60,000 × .40)	24,000.00	
Accumulated Depreciation—Equipment		24,000.00

In addition to depreciation expense, Josway records other costs related to the lease arrangement, such as insurance, maintenance, and taxes in the period incurred. Josway classifies the leased equipment and accompanying accumulated depreciation as Leased Assets.

Special Lease Accounting Problems

LEARNING OBJECTIVE 4

Discuss the accounting and reporting for special features of lease arrangements.

The features of lease arrangements that cause unique accounting problems are:

1. Residual values.
2. Other lease adjustments.
3. Bargain purchase options.
4. Short-term leases.
5. Presentation, disclosure, and analysis.

Residual Values

Lessee Perspective—Guaranteed Residual Value

In the Caterpillar/Sterling lease discussed earlier, the residual value was guaranteed by the lessee. This guaranteed residual value did not affect the computation of the lease liability, however, because it was probable that the expected residual value was greater than the guaranteed residual value. In other words, Sterling did not report a liability related to this guarantee because Sterling expects that it will not have to make a cash payment at the end of the lease. Sterling will simply return the backhoe to Caterpillar at the end of the lease.

The guidelines for accounting for a guaranteed residual value are as follows. [14]

1. If it is probable that the expected residual value is equal to or greater than the guaranteed residual value, the lessee should not include the guaranteed residual value in the computation of the lease liability.
2. If it is probable that the expected residual value is less than the guaranteed residual value, the difference between the expected and guaranteed residual values should be included in computation of the lease liability.

To illustrate a situation where the expected residual value is below the guaranteed residual value, assume in the earlier Caterpillar/Sterling example that it is probable that the residual value will be $3,000 instead of the guaranteed amount of $5,000. If Sterling estimates the residual value of the backhoe at the end of the lease to be $3,000, Sterling includes $2,000 ($5,000 – $3,000) as an additional lease payment in determining the lease liability and right-of-use asset. Illustration 21.21 shows the computation of the lease liability/right-of-use asset for Sterling in this situation.

ILLUSTRATION 21.21

Computation of Lessee's Capitalized Amount—Guaranteed Residual Value

Sterling's Capitalized Amount (4% Rate)
Annuity-Due Basis, Including Guaranteed Residual Value

Present value of five annual rental payments ($20,711.11 × 4.62990 ($PVF\text{-}AD_{5,4\%}$))	$95,890.35*
Present value of probable residual value payment of $2,000 due five years after date of commencement ($2,000 × .82193 ($PVF_{5,4\%}$))	1,643.86
Lessee's lease liability/right-of use asset	$97,534.21

*Rounded by $0.02.

Sterling makes the following entries to record the lease and the first payment.

January 1, 2020		
Right-of-Use Asset	97,534.21	
Lease Liability		97,534.21
(To record the right-of-use asset and related liability at commencement of the lease)		
Lease Liability	20,711.11	
Cash		20,711.11
(To record first lease payment)		

Sterling prepares a lease amortization schedule to show interest expense and related amortization of the lease liability over the five-year period. The schedule, shown in Illustration 21.22, is based on an expected residual value payment of $2,000 ($5,000 – $3,000) at the end of five years.

ILLUSTRATION 21.22

Lease Amortization Schedule for Lessee—Guaranteed Residual Value

Sterling Construction
Lease Amortization Schedule—Guaranteed Residual Value
Annuity-Due Basis

Date	Annual Lease Payment	Interest (4%) on Liability	Reduction of Lease Liability	Lease Liability
	(a)	(b)	(c)	(d)
1/1/20				$97,534.21
1/1/20	$ 20,711.11	$ -0-	$20,711.11	76,823.10
1/1/21	20,711.11	3,072.92	17,638.19	59,184.91
1/1/22	20,711.11	2,367.40	18,343.71	40,841.20
1/1/23	20,711.11	1,633.65	19,077.46	21,763.74
1/1/24	20,711.11	870.55	19,840.56	1,923.18
1/1/25	2,000.00	76.82*	1,923.18	0.00
	$105,555.55	$8,021.34	$97,534.21	

(a) Lease payment as required by lease.
(b) Four percent of the preceding balance of (d) except for 1/1/20; since this is an annuity due, no time has elapsed at the date of the first payment and therefore no interest has accrued.
(c) (a) minus (b).
(d) Preceding balance minus (c).

*Rounded by $0.11.

Illustration 21.23 shows, in comparative form, Sterling's entries for the first two years of the lease when:

1. Sterling expects to pay $2,000 at the end of the lease related to the guaranteed residual value (see Illustration 21.22).
2. Sterling does not expect to owe an additional payment for the guaranteed residual value (see Illustration 21.8).

ILLUSTRATION 21.23 **Journal Entries—Guaranteed Residual Value**

Guaranteed Residual Value ($2,000 expected payment)			Guaranteed Residual Value (no expected payment)		
Capitalization of lease (January 1, 2020):					
Right-of-Use Asset	97,534.21		Right-of-Use Asset	95,890.35	
Lease Liability		97,534.21	Lease Liability		95,890.35
First payment (January 1, 2020):					
Lease Liability	20,711.11		Lease Liability	20,711.11	
Cash		20,711.11	Cash		20,711.11
Adjusting entry for accrued interest (December 31, 2020):					
Interest Expense	3,072.92		Interest Expense	3,007.17	
Lease Liability		3,072.92	Lease Liability		3,007.17
Entry to record amortization of the ROU asset (December 31, 2020):					
Amortization Expense	19,506.84		Amortization Expense	19,178.07	
Right-of-Use Asset		19,506.84	Right-of-Use Asset		19,178.07
($97,534.21 ÷ 5 years)			($95,890.35 ÷ 5 years)		
Second payment (January 1, 2021):					
Lease Liability	20,711.11		Lease Liability	20,711.11	
($3,072.92 + $17,638.19)			($3,007.17 + $17,703.94)		
Cash		20,711.11	Cash		20,711.11

Following similar entries in subsequent years of the lease and using the amounts in Illustration 21.22, at the end of the lease term (January 1, 2025), Sterling returns the asset to Caterpillar and makes the entries shown in Illustration 21.24 under the two situations.

ILLUSTRATION 21.24 **Final Payments—Guaranteed and Unguaranteed Residual Value**

Guaranteed Residual Value ($2,000 expected payment)			Guaranteed Residual Value (no expected payment)
Final payment (January 1, 2025):			
Lease Liability	2,000.00		No entry
Cash		2,000.00	

Following the entries summarized in Illustrations 21.23 and 21.24, the Right-of-Use Asset and the Lease Liability accounts have been fully amortized and have zero balances. If at the end of the lease (January 1, 2025) Sterling has no additional obligations under the residual value guarantee, no further entries are needed.

However, if the fair value of the underlying asset is less than the expected residual value, such that Sterling will have to further compensate Caterpillar under the residual value guarantee, Sterling will record a loss. For example, assume that due to poor maintenance of the backhoe, Sterling and Caterpillar agree that the fair value of the asset is sufficiently below the expected fair value such that Sterling must pay an additional $1,000 upon returning the backhoe to Caterpillar on January 1, 2025. In this case, Sterling reports a loss of $1,000, as reflected in the following journal entry.

January 1, 2025		
Lease Liability	2,000	
Loss on Lease (Residual Value Guarantee)	1,000	
Cash		3,000

Lessee Perspective—Unguaranteed Residual Value

A lessee does not include an unguaranteed residual value in the computation of the lease liability, whether it is a finance lease or an operating lease. At the end of the lease, the lessee simply returns the leased asset to the lessor without any other payment. The Josway/Trayor operating lease example illustrates the lessee accounting for an unguaranteed residual value.

Lessor Perspective—Guaranteed Residual Value

In the Sterling/Caterpillar example, Sterling guaranteed a residual value of $5,000. In computing the amount to be recovered from the rental payments, the present value of the residual value was subtracted from the fair value of the backhoe to arrive at the amount to be recovered by the lessor. Illustration 21.25 shows this computation.

ILLUSTRATION 21.25
Lease Payment Calculation

Amount to be recovered by lessor through lease payments	$95,890.35
Five beginning-of-year lease payments to earn a 4% return ($95,890.35 ÷ 4.62990 ($PVF\text{-}AD_{5,4\%}$))	$20,711.11

The computation in Illustration 21.25 is the same whether the residual value is guaranteed or unguaranteed.

The Caterpillar/Sterling lease agreement accounted for the lease as a sales-type lease. Caterpillar therefore recorded sales revenue and related cost of goods sold at lease commencement. Caterpillar accounts for the guaranteed residual value as part of sales revenue because the lessor receives this amount at the end of the lease either in cash or in the residual value returned.

Lessor Perspective—Unguaranteed Residual Value

What happens if the residual value for Caterpillar is unguaranteed? In this case, there is less certainty that the unguaranteed residual portion of the asset has been "sold." Therefore, the lessor recognizes sales revenue and cost of goods sold only for the portion of the asset for which recovery is assured. To account for this uncertainty, both sales revenue and cost of goods sold are reduced by the present value of the unguaranteed residual value. Given that the amount subtracted from sales revenue and cost of goods sold are the same, the gross profit computed will still be the same amount as when a guaranteed residual value exists.

To compare a sales-type lease with a guaranteed residual value to one with an unguaranteed residual value, assume the same facts as in the Caterpillar/Sterling lease situation. That is:

1. The sales price is $100,000.
2. The expected residual value is $5,000 (the present value of which is $4,109.65).
3. The leased equipment has an $85,000 cost to the dealer, Caterpillar.

Illustration 21.26 shows the computation of the amounts relevant to a sales-type lease, under both a guaranteed and unguaranteed residual value situation.

ILLUSTRATION 21.26

Computation of Lease Amounts by Caterpillar Financial—Sales-Type Lease

	Guaranteed Residual Value	Unguaranteed Residual Value
Lease receivable	$100,000 [$20,711.11 × 4.62990 ($PVF\text{-}AD_{5,4\%}$) + $5,000 × .82193 ($PVF_{5,4\%}$)]	Same
Sales price of the asset	$100,000	$95,890.35 ($100,000 – $4,109.65)
Cost of goods sold	$85,000	$80,890.35 ($85,000.00 – $4,109.65)
Gross profit	$15,000 ($100,000 – $85,000)	$15,000 ($95,890.35 – $80,890.35)

Caterpillar records the same gross profit ($15,000) at the point of sale whether the residual value is guaranteed or unguaranteed. However, the amounts recorded for sales revenue and the cost of goods sold are different between the guaranteed and unguaranteed situations. The reason for the difference is the uncertainty surrounding the realization of the unguaranteed residual value. Unlike the guaranteed residual value situation, where the lessor knows that it will receive the full amount of the guarantee at the end of the lease, in an unguaranteed residual value situation the lessor is not sure what it will receive at the end of the lease regarding the residual value. That is, due to the uncertainty surrounding the realization of the unguaranteed residual value, sales revenue and related cost of goods sold are reduced by the present value of the residual value. This results in **the sales revenue and cost of goods sold amounts being reported at different amounts under an unguaranteed residual value situation.**

Caterpillar makes the entries with respect to the lease arrangement under guaranteed and unguaranteed residual value situations as shown in Illustration 21.27.

ILLUSTRATION 21.27 Entries for Guaranteed and Unguaranteed Residual Values—Sales-Type Lease

	Guaranteed Residual Value			Unguaranteed Residual Value		
	To record sales-type lease at commencement (January 1, 2020):					
Sales and cost of goods sold differ; gross profit the same	Cost of Goods Sold	85,000.00		Cost of Goods Sold	80,890.35	
	Lease Receivable	100,000.00		Lease Receivable	100,000.00	
	Sales Revenue		100,000.00	Sales Revenue		95,890.35
	Inventory		85,000.00	Inventory		85,000.00
	To record receipt of the first lease payment (January 1, 2020):					
Lease receipt the same	Cash	20,711.11		Cash	20,711.11	
	Lease Receivable		20,711.11	Lease Receivable		20,711.11
	To recognize interest revenue during the first year (December 31, 2020):					
Accrual of interest the same	Lease Receivable	3,171.56		Lease Receivable	3,171.56	
	Interest Revenue		3,171.56	Interest Revenue		3,171.56
	To record receipt of the second lease payment (January 1, 2021):					
Lease receipt the same	Cash	20,711.11		Cash	20,711.11	
	Lease Receivable ($3,171.56 + $17,539.56)		20,711.11	Lease Receivable ($3,171.56 + $17,539.56)		20,711.11
	To recognize interest revenue during the second year (December 31, 2021):					
Accrual of interest the same	Lease Receivable	2,469.97		Lease Receivable	2,469.97	
	Interest Revenue		2,469.97	Interest Revenue		2,469.97
	To record receipt of residual value at $3,000 end of lease term (January 1, 2025):					
Guaranteed does not result in loss; unguaranteed does	Inventory	3,000.00		Inventory	3,000.00	
	Cash	2,000.00		Loss on Lease	2,000.00	
	Lease Receivable		5,000.00	Lease Receivable		5,000.00

Illustration 21.28 provides a summary of the accounting treatment for guaranteed and unguaranteed residual values by lessees and lessors related to the present value classification test and the measurement of the lease liability and receivable.

ILLUSTRATION 21.28 Summary of Treatment of Residual Values

	Unguaranteed Residual Value	Guaranteed Residual Value
LESSEE		
Classification Test	Ignore	Include full amount of residual value in present value test
Measurement of Liability	Ignore	• If expected value of residual value >/= to guaranteed residual value, ignore • If expected value of residual value </= to guaranteed residual value, include the present value of the difference between the expected and guaranteed residual value in computation of lease liability
LESSOR		
Classification Test	Ignore	Include
Measurement of Receivable	Include	Include

Note: When residual value is not guaranteed in a sales-type lease, lessor reduces Sales Revenue and Cost of Goods Sold by the present value of the unguaranteed residual value.

Other Lease Adjustments

Additional lease adjustments that affect the measurement of lease assets and liabilities relate to the following:

1. Executory costs.
2. Lease prepayments and incentives.
3. Initial direct costs.

Executory Costs

Executory costs are normal expenses associated with owning a leased asset, such as property insurance and property taxes. The accounting for executory costs depends on how the lease is structured, that is, whether the lease is a gross lease or a net lease. In a gross lease, the payments to the lessor are fixed as part of the rental payments in the contract. In a net lease, the lessee makes variable payments to a third party or to the lessor directly for the executory costs. Illustration 21.29 provides examples of these two situations.

ILLUSTRATION 21.29

Executory Cost Example

Gross versus Net Leases

Facts: Ortiz Company enters into a lease arrangement to lease a retail space in a shopping mall from Bryant Inc. The lease term is 2 years with monthly payments of $15,000 per month. Ortiz does not have any obligation to pay any of the property taxes or property insurance on the retail space. Ortiz estimates that Bryant is paying approximately $1,500 per month related to these executory costs.

***Question:* How should Ortiz account for the executory costs in this situation?**

Solution: Ortiz and Bryant have a gross lease arrangement in that the property taxes and property insurance are included in the rental payments made by Ortiz. In this arrangement, the payment for the executory costs are fixed (per the rental agreement) and should be included in the computation of the lease liability.

Now assume that Ortiz agrees to a lease arrangement in which it must reimburse the lessor for the property taxes and property insurance, or pay a relevant third party directly. In this case, Ortiz and Bryant have a net lease arrangement because the lessee makes variable payments to a third party or to the lessor for the executory costs. In this case, Ortiz is responsible for paying directly the executory costs and therefore it is a variable payment which is expensed in the period incurred (not included in the lease liability and right-of-use assets).

Note that including executory costs in the measurement of the lease liability and related right-of-use asset may lead to inflated values on the balance sheet in comparison to lessees who do not capitalize these costs. Thus, the way parties structure the payment of executory costs (i.e., variable or fixed) can have potentially material implications with regard to the values that appear on the balance sheet.

In summary, executory costs included in the fixed payments required by the lessor should be included in lease payments for purposes of measuring the lease liability. Payments by the lessee made directly to the taxing authority or insurance provider are considered variable payments and are expensed as incurred. [15]

Lease Prepayments and Incentives

For all leases at the commencement date, the lease liability is the starting point to determine the amount to record for the right-of-use asset. Companies adjust the right-of-use asset for any lease prepayments, lease incentives, and initial direct costs made prior to or at the commencement date. These adjustments determine the amount to report as the right-of-use asset at the lease commencement date as follows.

1. Lease prepayments made by the lessee **increase** the right-of-use asset.
2. Lease incentive payments made by the lessor to the lessee **reduce** the right-of-use asset.
3. Initial direct costs incurred by the lessee (discussed in the next section) **increase** the right-of-use asset.

Illustration 21.30 identifies the adjustments made to the lease liability balance to determine the proper amount to report for the right-of-use asset.

ILLUSTRATION 21.30

Right-of-Use Asset Adjustments

Initial Measurement of Lease Liability	+	Prepaid Lease Payments	−	Lease Incentives Received	+	Initial Direct Costs	=	Right-of-Use Asset

Initial Direct Costs

Initial direct costs are incremental costs of a lease that would not have been incurred had the lease not been executed. [16] Costs directly or indirectly attributable to negotiating and arranging the lease (e.g., external legal costs to draft or negotiate a lease or an allocation of internal legal costs) are not considered initial direct costs. Illustration 21.31 provides examples of costs included and excluded from initial direct costs from the lessee and lessor side.[17]

ILLUSTRATION 21.31

Initial Direct Costs

Included	Excluded
• Commissions (including payments to employees acting as selling agents) • Legal fees resulting from the execution of the lease • Lease document preparation costs incurred after the execution of the lease • Consideration paid for a guarantee of residual value by an unrelated third party	• Employee salaries • Internal engineering costs • Legal fees for services rendered before the execution of the lease • Negotiating lease term and conditions • Advertising • Depreciation • Costs related to an idle asset

Initial direct costs incurred by the lessee are included in the cost of the right-of-use asset but are not recorded as part of the lease liability.

Illustration 21.32 provides an example of the computation of the right-of-use asset with initial direct costs.

[17]Adapted from PricewaterhouseCoopers, *Leases—2016* (*www.pwc.com*), p. 4-4.

ILLUSTRATION 21.32

Computation of Right-of-Use Asset

Right-of-Use Cost Analysis

Facts: Mangan Company leases from DeMallie Co. solar equipment for 8 years starting on January 1, 2020. The lease is a finance/sales-type lease. The terms of the lease are as follows.

1. DeMallie will pay Mangan $30,000 as a cash incentive for entering the lease by January 1, 2020.
2. DeMallie pays initial direct costs of $5,000 for legal fees related to the execution of the lease.
3. Mangan incurred $1,500 of initial direct costs (commission paid to lease negotiator) which are payable by January 1, 2020.
4. Mangan must pay not only the first rental payment of $10,000 on January 1, 2021, but has to prepay the last month's rental payment on December 31, 2020.
5. The initial measurement of the liability is $400,000.

***Question:* What is the amount to be reported for Mangan's right-of-use asset at the commencement date?**

Solution: The measurement of the right-of-use asset for Mangan is as follows.

Initial measurement of the lease liability	$400,000
Cash incentive received from DeMallie (lessor)	(30,000)
Initial direct costs (commission paid to lease negotiator)	1,500
Prepayments made by Mangan to DeMallie before the lease commencement	10,000
Measurement of right-of-use asset at January 1, 2020	$381,500

Mangan therefore reports the right-of-use asset at $381,500.

DeMaille (the lessor) expenses its initial direct costs in the period incurred, given DeMaille reported a gross profit related to its sale-type lease.

For lessors, initial direct costs often are more significant because they are usually the party that solicits lessees as part of their sales activities. As a result, lessors often engage attorneys to prepare the legal documents, as well as pay commissions incurred in connection with the execution of a lease.

Lessor accounting for initial direct costs depends on the type of lease. [17]

- For **operating leases**, a lessor defers the initial direct costs and amortizes them as expenses over the term of the lease.
- For **sales-type leases**, the lessor expenses initial direct costs at lease commencement (in **the period** in which it recognizes the profit on the sale). An exception is when there is no selling profit or loss on the transaction. If there is no selling profit or loss, the initial direct costs are deferred and recognized over the lease term.

Lessors commonly also incur **internal costs** related to leasing activities. Examples are activities the lessor performs for advertising, servicing existing leases, and establishing and monitoring credit policies, as well as the costs for supervision and administration or for expenses such as rent and depreciation. **Internal direct costs should not be included in initial direct costs.** Such costs would have been incurred regardless of whether a lease was executed. As a result, internal direct costs are generally expensed as incurred.

Bargain Purchase Options

As stated earlier, a **bargain purchase option** allows the lessee to purchase the leased property for a future price that is substantially lower than the asset's expected future fair value. This price is so favorable at the lease's commencement that the future exercise of the option appears to be reasonably certain. If a bargain purchase option exists, **the lessee must increase the present value of the lease payments by the present value of the option price.**

For example, assume that Sterling Construction (see Illustration 21.22) had an option to buy the leased equipment for $2,000 at the end of the five-year lease term. At that point, Sterling and Caterpillar expect the fair value to be $18,000. The significant difference between the option price and the fair value creates a bargain purchase option as the exercise of that option is reasonably certain.

A bargain purchase option affects the accounting for leases in the same way as a guaranteed residual value with a probable amount to be owed. In other words, with a guaranteed residual value, the lessee is expected to make an additional payment related to the residual value at the end of the lease. Similarly, the cost of a bargain purchase option is expected to be paid by the lessee. Therefore, the computations, amortization schedule, and entries prepared for this $2,000 bargain purchase option are identical to those shown for the $2,000 probable amount to be owed under the guaranteed residual value (see Illustrations 21.22, 21.23, and 21.24).

The only difference between the accounting treatment for a bargain purchase option and a guaranteed residual value of identical amounts and circumstances is in the **computation of the annual amortization**. In the case of a guaranteed residual value, Sterling amortizes the right-of-use asset over the lease term. In the case of a bargain purchase option, it uses the **economic life** of the underlying asset, given that the lessee takes ownership of the asset.

Short-Term Leases

A short-term lease is a **lease** that, at the **commencement date**, has a **lease term** of 12 months or less. Rather than recording a right-of-use asset and lease liability, lessees may elect to expense the lease payments as incurred. [18]

Leases may include options to either extend the term of the lease (a renewal option) or to terminate the lease prior to the contractually defined lease expiration date (a termination option). In these situations, renewal or termination options that are reasonably certain of exercise by the lessee are included in the lease term. Therefore, a one-year lease with a renewal option that the lessee is reasonably certain to exercise is not a short-term lease. Illustration 21.33 provides an example of two short-term lease situations.[18]

ILLUSTRATION 21.33
Short-Term Lease Examples

Short-Term Leases

Facts:

a. Thomas Company (lessee) enters into an arrangement to lease a crane for a 6-month period, with the option to extend the term for up to 9 additional months (in 3-month increments). After considering the nature of the project, Thomas determines that it expects to use the crane for only 9 months and is therefore reasonably certain that it will exercise only one of the 3-month renewal options.

b. Thomas Company enters into the same arrangement as in part (a) but the project for which the crane is being used is now expected to take 15 months to complete. After considering the nature of the project, Thomas determines that it expects to use the crane for 15 months and is therefore reasonably certain that it will exercise all three renewal options.

***Question:* How would Thomas report these two situations?**

Solutions:

a. Since the lease term is not more than 12 months, Thomas is able to elect the short-term lease exception because the lease term is not more than 12 months as it does not expect to exercise the renewal option.

b. The expected lease term is greater than 12 months because Thomas expects to exercise all three renewal options. Thus, Thomas is not able to apply the short-term lease exception and must record a right-of-use asset and related lease liability.

Presentation, Disclosure, and Analysis

Presentation

Presented in Illustration 21.34 is a summary of how the **lessee** reports the information related to finance and operating leases in the financial statements.

[18]Adapted from PricewaterhouseCoopers, *Leases –2016* (*www.pwc.com*), Chapter 4.

ILLUSTRATION 21.34

Presentation in Financial Statements—Lessee

	Balance Sheet	Income Statement
Finance Lease	Right-of-use asset Lease liability	Amortization expense Interest expense
Operating Lease	Right-of-use asset Lease liability	Lease expense

Presented in Illustration 21.35 is a summary of **lessor** presentation of lease information in the financial statements.

ILLUSTRATION 21.35

Presentation in Financial Statements—Lessor

	Balance Sheet	Income Statement
Sales-Type Lease	Lease receivable presented separate from other assets Derecognize the leased asset	Interest revenue Selling profit or loss
Operating Lease	Continue to recognize assets subject to operating leases as property, plant, and equipment	Revenue generally recognized on a straight-line basis Depreciation expense on the leased asset

Disclosure

Lessees and lessors must also provide additional qualitative and quantitative disclosures to help financial statement users assess the amount, timing, and uncertainty of future cash flows. These disclosures are intended to supplement the amounts provided in the financial statements. Qualitative disclosures to be provided by both lessees and lessors are summarized in Illustration 21.36. [19]

ILLUSTRATION 21.36

Qualitative Lease Disclosures

- Nature of its leases, including general description of those leases.
- How variable lease payments are determined.
- Existence and terms and conditions for options to extend or terminate the lease and for residual value guarantees.
- Information about significant assumptions and judgments (e.g., discount rates).

Illustration 21.37 presents the type of quantitative information that should be disclosed for **the lessee**.

ILLUSTRATION 21.37

Lessee Quantitative Disclosures

- Total lease cost.
- Finance lease cost, segregated between the amortization of the right-of-use assets and interest on the lease liabilities.
- Operating and short-term lease cost.
- Weighted-average remaining lease term and weighted-average discount rate (segregated between finance and operating leases).
- Maturity analysis of finance and operating lease liabilities, on an annual basis for a minimum of each of the next five years, the sum of the undiscounted cash flows for all years thereafter.

Illustration 21.38 presents a sample disclosure typical of a lessee having both finance leases and operating leases.

ILLUSTRATION 21.38 Lessee Sample Disclosure

Note 12: Leases

Description of leased assets

The Company has long-term leases for stores and equipment. Aggregate minimum annual rentals at December 31, 2021 and 2020, under non-cancelable leases are as follows (dollar amounts in thousands):

Lease costs, segregation of finance, operating, and short-term lease costs

	Year Ending December 31	
	2021	2020
Lease Cost		
Finance lease cost		
Amortization of right-of-use assets	$ 600	$ 525
Interest on lease liabilities	150	110
Operating lease cost	1,000	900
Short-term lease cost	50	40
Variable lease cost	75	60
Total lease cost	$1,875	$1,635
Other Information		
(Gains) and losses on sale and leaseback transactions, net	$ (8)	$ 5
Cash paid for amounts included in the measurement of lease liabilities for finance leases		
Operating cash flows	1,400	1,300
Financing cash flows	200	170
Cash paid for amounts included in the measurement of lease liabilities for operating leases		
Operating cash flows	800	635
Right-of-use assets obtained in exchange for new finance lease liabilities	475	515
Right-of-use assets obtained in exchange for new operating lease liabilities	150	175
Weighted-average remaining lease term—finance leases	9.7 years	2.9 years
Weighted-average remaining lease term—operating leases	5.2 years	5.4 years
Weighted-average discount rate—finance leases	5.8%	6.0%
Weighted-average discount rate—operating	6.1%	6.3%

Weighted-average lease term

Weighted-average discount rate

Maturity Analysis

Maturity analysis

The Company has long-term leases for stores and equipment. Aggregate minimum annual rentals at December 31 under non-cancelable leases are as follows (dollar amounts in thousands):

	Operating	Finance
2022	$ 1,759	$ 504
2023	1,615	476
2024	1,482	444
2025	1,354	408
2026	1,236	370
Thereafter	10,464	3,252
Total payments	$17,910	$5,454

Illustration 21.39 shows the type of quantitative information that should be disclosed for **the lessor**.

ILLUSTRATION 21.39

Lessor Quantitative Disclosures

- Lease-related income, including profit and loss recognized at lease commencement for sales-type and direct financing leases, and interest income.
- Income from variable lease payments not included in the lease receivable.
- The components of the net investment in sales-type and direct financing leases, including the carrying amount of the lease receivable, the unguaranteed residual asset, and any deferred profit on direct financing leases.
- A maturity analysis for operating lease payments and a separate maturity analysis for the lease receivable (sales-type and direct financing leases).
- Management approaches for risk associated with residual value of leased assets (e.g., buyback agreements or third-party insurance).

Illustration 21.40 provides a sample **lessor** disclosure.

ILLUSTRATION 21.40 Disclosure of Leases by Lessor

Note 11: Sales-Type Lease Receivables and Operating Leases

Financing receivables represent sales-type leases resulting from the marketing of our products. These receivables typically have terms from two to five years and are usually collateralized by a security interest in the underlying assets. Financing receivables also include billed receivables from operating leases. The components of net financing receivables, which are included in financing receivables and long-term financing receivables and other assets, were as follows for the following fiscal years ended December 31: — Description of leased assets

	2021	2020	
Lease Income			
Interest income	$ 612	$ 685	Lease income
Gross profit on sales-type leases	2,645	2,813	
Total lease-related income	$3,257	$3,498	
Lease Receivables			
Minimum lease payments receivable	$6,982	$7,505	Net investment
Allowance for doubtful accounts	(111)	(131)	
Unguaranteed residual value	235	252	
Unearned income	(547)	(604)	
Financing receivables, net	6,559	7,022	
Less current portion	(2,946)	(3,144)	
Amounts due after one year, net	$3,613	$3,878	

As of December 31, 2021, scheduled maturities of lease payments receivable were as follows for the following fiscal years ended December 31:

	2022	2023	2024	2025	2026	Thereafter	Total	
Scheduled maturities of lease payments receivable	$3,220	$1,959	$1,112	$483	$174	$34	$6,982	Maturity analysis

Equipment leased to customers under operating leases was $4.0 billion at December 31, 2021, and $3.8 billion at December 31, 2020, and is included in machinery and equipment. Accumulated depreciation on equipment under lease was $1.4 billion at December 31, 2021, and $1.5 billion at December 31, 2020. As of December 31, 2021, future rentals on non-cancelable operating leases related to leased equipment were as follows for the following fiscal years ended December 31:

	2022	2023	2024	2025	2026	Thereafter	Total	
Minimum future rentals on non-cancelable operating leases	$1,487	$958	$467	$156	$50	$6	$3,124	Maturity analysis

Analysis

Many companies that lease are likely to see their balance sheets grow substantially over the next few years as a result of implementing the new standard on leasing. Estimates as to its dollar impact on the assets and liabilities of companies vary, but it will be in the trillions of dollars. For example, here are the possible effects on the assets and liabilities for the following five companies (in millions) as a result of capitalizing lease assets and related liabilities: (1) Walgreens, $33,721; (2) AT&T, $31,047; (3) CVS Health, $27,282; (4) Wal-Mart Stores, $17,910; and FedEx Corporation, $16,385.

Some contend that "grossing up" the assets and liabilities on companies' balance sheets will not have any significant impact on analysis, based on information in the financial statements. Their rationale is that stockholders' equity does not change substantially, nor will net income. In addition, it is argued that users can determine the obligations that lessees are incurring by examining the notes to the financial statements.

These assertions are debatable. With the increase in the assets and liabilities as a result of the new standard, a number of financial metrics used to measure the profitability and solvency of companies will change, which could create challenges when performing financial analysis. On the profitability side, return on assets will decrease because a company's assets will increase, but net income will often be the same. Furthermore, analysts commonly focus on income subtotals, such as earnings before interest, taxes, and depreciation and amortization (EBIDTA), which likely will require some adjustments as companies amortize right-of-use assets. On the solvency side, the debt to equity ratio will increase, and the interest coverage ratio will decrease. In addition, recent studies indicate that using only note disclosures to determine lease obligations have understated their numerical impact.[19]

One thing is certain—the grossing up of the assets and liabilities related to lease arrangements will have significant consequences on the organizational, operational, and contractual side. Examples are:

1. States often levy taxes based on property amounts, which will now be higher.
2. Performance metrics to evaluate management may have to change for companies, particularly when growth rates in assets are used or returns on assets are used to measure performance.
3. Companies may have contracts with the government for which reimbursement is based on rent expense, which may change the compensation agreement.
4. Debt covenants might require revisions.

Given the pervasiveness and magnitude of the changes, it is not surprising that the FASB is permitting an extended implementation window to allow companies and users of financial statements to adapt to the new standard.

Evolving Issue **Bring It On!**

As discussed in the opening story, the lease accounting rules will bring a significant amount of lease-related assets and liabilities onto lessee balance sheets. Recent estimates for the largest 100 U.S. companies put the number at over $539 billion. Most agree this is a good result—applying the "right-of-use" model will result in reporting more relevant and representationally faithful information about leasing arrangements, which is a big win for investors and creditors. As the chairperson of the IASB remarked, ". . . a financing, in the form of a loan to purchase an asset . . . then is recorded. Call it a lease and miraculously it does not show up in your books. In my book, if it looks like a duck, swims like a duck, and quacks like a duck, then it probably is a duck. So is the case with debt—leasing or otherwise."

At the same time, an analysis of the new rules and how they might impact the advantages of leasing presented in the following table suggests that many of the advantages of leases will remain after implementation of the new rules.

Reason for Leasing	Details	Status After Proposed New Rules Implemented
Funding source	Additional capital source, 100% financing, fixed rate, level payments, longer terms.	Still a major benefit versus a purchase—fixed rate, level payments—especially for smaller companies with limited sources of capital.
Low-cost capital	Low payments/rate due to tax benefits, residual and lessor's comparatively low cost of funds.	Still a benefit versus a loan.
Tax benefits	Lessee cannot use tax benefits and lease versus buy shows lease option offers lowest after tax cost.	Still a benefit.
Manage need for assets/ residual risk transfer	Lessee has flexibility to return asset.	Still a benefit.
Convenience	Quick and convenient financing process often available at point-of-sale.	Still a benefit.
Regulatory	Can help in meeting capital requirements.	Still a partial benefit if the capitalized amount is less than the cost of the asset as it is in many leases due to residuals assumed and tax benefits.
Accounting	Asset and liability off-balance-sheet.	Still a partial benefit if the capitalized amount is less than the cost of the asset as it is in many leases due to residuals assumed and tax benefits.

Sources: Equipment Leasing & Finance Foundation, *2016 State of the Equipment Finance Industry Report*; M. Murphy, "The Big Number: $539 Billion," *Wall Street Journal* (January 16, 2016); Hans Hoogervorst, "Harmonisation and Global Economic Consequences," Public lecture at the London School of Economics (November 6, 2012); and R. Petta, "Telecom Industry Update: Benefits of Financing Remain with Lease Accounting Changes," *Knowledge, Leasing/Finance* (*http://www.telecomreseller.com/2016/05/09/telecom-industry-update-benefits-of-financing-remain-with-lease-accounting-changes/*).

[19]Pepa Kraft, "Rating Agency Adjustment to GAAP Financial Statements and Their Effect on Ratings and Credit Spreads," *The Accounting Review* (March 2015), Vol. 90, No. 2, pp 641–674. In addition, a study by J.P. Morgan showed significant variation in the range of analysts' estimates of the underlying lease obligations under the new rules. See P. Elwin and S. C. Fernandes, "Leases on B/S from 2017? Retailers and Transport Will Be Hit Hard in Leverage Terms," *Global Equity Research*, J.P. Morgan Securities (May 17, 2013).

APPENDIX 21A Sale-Leasebacks

LEARNING OBJECTIVE *5

Describe the lessee's accounting for sale-leaseback transactions.

In a **sale-leaseback** arrangement, a company (the seller-lessee) transfers an asset to another company (the buyer-lessor) and then leases that asset back from the buyer-lessor. For example, **Darden Restaurants** sold off its Red Lobster division to **Golden Gate Capital** (a private equity firm) for $2.1 billion recently and then leased these restaurants back from Golden Gate Capital. This transaction is shown in **Illustration 21A.1**.

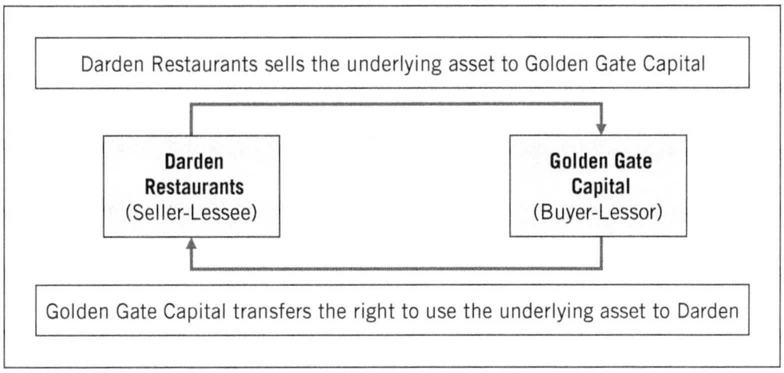

ILLUSTRATION 21A.1
Sale-Leaseback

Why do companies like Darden Restaurants engage in sale-leaseback transactions? Some major reasons are:

1. Darden can use the cash that otherwise would be tied up in property to expand its operations. At the same time, it continues to use the property through the lease term.
2. Darden can structure the lease arrangement so issues such as repurchase provisions, refinancing issues, and conventional financing costs are minimized.
3. Darden may receive a tax advantage because entire rental payments are tax-deductible, whereas under a conventional financing, only interest and depreciation can be deducted. If the lease has a significant land component (land is not depreciable) or if the fair value of the property is much greater than the carrying value of the property (depreciation limited to cost of property), then the sale lease-back arrangement generally reduces tax payments.

The advantages to Golden Gate Capital (buyer-lessor) are that it generally can earn a higher rate of return under a sale-leaseback than under traditional financing. In addition, during the lease term, Golden Gate is protected from a downturn in the real estate market and may have an inflation hedge, provided the property appreciates in value.

Sale-leasebacks are common and the dollar amounts related to these transactions are significant (approximately $15 billion per year). Financial institutions (e.g., **Bank of America** and **First Chicago**) have used this technique for their administrative offices, public utilities (e.g., **Ohio Edison** and **Pinnacle West Corporation**) for their generating plants, and airlines (such as **Alaska Air Group**) for their aircraft.

Accounting Issues in Sale-Leaseback Transactions

When Darden transferred the Red Lobster restaurants to Golden Gate Capital and then leased them back, the accounting issue is whether the transaction is a sale or a financing. To determine whether it is a sale, revenue recognition guidelines are used. That is, if control has passed from seller to buyer, then a sale has occurred. Conversely, if control has not passed from seller to buyer, the transaction is recorded as a financing (often referred to as a failed sale). [20] Illustration 21A.2 highlights these two approaches.

ILLUSTRATION 21A.2

Sale-Leaseback Accounting

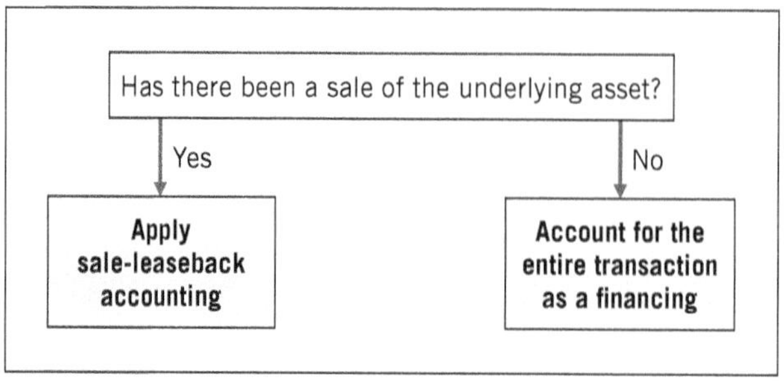

Sale Transaction

As indicated, if Darden (seller-lessee) **gives up control** of the Red Lobster restaurants, the transaction is a sale. In a sale, **gain or loss recognition** is appropriate. Darden then records the transaction as follows.

1. Increases cash and reduces the carrying value of the asset to zero (referred to as derecognizing the asset).
2. Recognizes a gain or loss as appropriate.
3. Accounts for the leaseback in accordance with lease accounting guidance used in this chapter.

For example, assume that Scott Paper sells one of its buildings having a carrying value of $580,000 (building $800,000 less accumulated depreciation $220,000) to General Electric for $623,110. It then leases the building back from General Electric for $50,000 a year, for eight of the building's 15 years of remaining economic life. Assume that the present value of these lease payments is equal to $310,000, such that the lease is classified as an operating lease. Scott Paper makes the following entries to record the sale-leaseback.

Cash	623,110	
Accumulated Depreciation—Buildings	220,000	
Buildings		800,000
Gain on Disposal of Plant Assets		43,110
($623,110 – $580,000)		

In addition, Scott makes an entry to record the operating lease from General Electric as follows.

Right-of-Use Asset	310,000	
Lease Liability		310,000

Underlying Concepts

A sale-leaseback under a financing transaction is similar in substance to the parking of inventories (discussed in Chapter 8). The ultimate economic benefits remain under the control of the "seller-lessee," so revenue (gain) should not be recognized.

Financing Transaction (Failed Sale)

Scott Paper does not record a sale in the above transaction if the lease from General Electric is classified as a finance lease. The reason: if any of the lease classification tests are met, Scott, not General Electric, controls (owns) the asset. If Scott **continues to control the building, it should not record a sale nor recognize a gain or loss** on the transaction (see Underlying Concepts). In essence, Scott Paper is borrowing money from General Electric (often referred to as a financing or a failed sale). In a financing (failed sale), Scott:

- Does not reduce the carrying value of the building.
- Continues to depreciate the building as if it was the legal owner.
- Recognizes the sale proceeds from General Electric as a financial liability.

The entry to record the financing is as follows.

Cash	623,110	
Notes Payable		623,110

Sale-Leaseback Example

To illustrate the accounting treatment accorded a sale-leaseback transaction over the lease term, assume that **American Airlines** on January 1, 2020, sells a used, standard-design Boeing 757 having a carrying amount on its books of $30,000,000 to **CitiCapital** for $33,000,000. American immediately leases the aircraft back under the following conditions.

- The term of the lease is seven years. The lease agreement is non-cancelable, requiring equal rental payments of $4,881,448 at the end of each year (ordinary annuity basis), beginning December 31, 2020.
- The lease contains no renewal or purchase options. The plane reverts to CitiCapital at the termination of the lease.
- The aircraft has a fair value of $33,000,000 on January 1, 2020, and an estimated remaining economic life of 10 years. The residual value (unguaranteed) at the end of the lease is $13,000,000.
- The annual payments assure the lessor an 8 percent return (which is the same as American's incremental borrowing rate).

Applying the classification tests, the lease-back of the airplane is classified as an operating lease because none of the sales-type lease criteria are met, as indicated in **Illustration 21A.3**.

ILLUSTRATION 21A.3
Lease Classification Tests

Test	Assessment
1. Transfer of ownership test	Transfer of ownership does not occur; the asset reverts to CitiCapital at the end of the lease.
2. Purchase option test	There is no purchase option in the lease.
3. Lease term test	The lease term is 70 percent (7 ÷ 10) of the remaining economic life of the asset, which is less than the major part of the life of the asset (75 percent).
4. Present value test	The present value of the lease payments is $25,414,625*, which is 77 percent ($25,414,625 ÷ $33,000,000) of the fair value of the aircraft, or less than 90 percent. Therefore, the lease does not meet the present value test.
5. Alternative use test	As indicated, the equipment is not of a specialized nature and is expected to have use to CitiCapital when returned at the end of the lease.

*$4,881,448 × 5.20637 ($PVF\text{-}OA_{7,8\%}$)

Thus, this arrangement is accounted for as a sale, rather than a failed sale, because the leaseback does not transfer control of the asset back to American; that is, only the right-of-use for seven years is granted through the lease. **Illustration 21A.4** presents the typical journal entries to record the sale-leaseback transactions for American and CitiCapital for the first two years of the lease.

ILLUSTRATION 21A.4 Comparative Entries for Sale-Leaseback for Lessee and Lessor

American Airlines (Lessee)			CitiCapital (Lessor)		
Sale of aircraft by American to CitiCapital (January 1, 2020):					
Cash	33,000,000		Aircraft	33,000,000	
Gain on Disposal of Plant Assets		3,000,000	Cash		33,000,000
Aircraft		30,000,000			
Right-of-Use Asset	25,414,625				
Lease Liability		25,414,625			
First lease payment (December 31, 2020):					
Lease Expense ($2,033,170 + $2,848,278)	4,881,448		Cash	4,881,448	
Lease Liability (Schedule A)	2,848,278		Lease Revenue		4,881,448
Right-of-Use Asset (Schedule B)		2,848,278			
Cash		4,881,448			
Depreciation expense on the aircraft (December 31, 2020):					
No entry			Depreciation expense ($33,000,000 ÷ 10)	3,300,000	
			Accumulated Depreciation – Leased Equipment		3,300,000
Second lease payment (December 31, 2021):					
Lease Expense ($1,805,308 + $3,076,140)	4,881,448		Cash	4,881,448	
Lease Liability	3,076,140		Lease Revenue		4,881,448
Right-of-Use Asset		3,076,140			
Cash		4,881,448			
Depreciation expense on the aircraft (December 31, 2021):					
No entry			Depreciation expense ($33,000,000 ÷ 10)	3,300,000	
			Accumulated Depreciation—Leased Equipment		3,300,000

Schedule A: Partial Lease Amortization Schedule

Date	Annual Lease Payment	Interest (8%) on Liability	Reduction of Lease Liability	Lease Liability
Jan. 2020				$25,414,625
Dec. 2020	$4,881,448	$2,033,170	$2,848,278	22,566,347
Dec. 2021	4,881,448	1,805,308	3,076,140	19,490,207

Schedule B: Partial Lease Expense Schedule

Date	(A) Lease Expense (Straight-Line)	(B) Interest (8%) on Liability	(C) Amortization of ROU Asset (A − B)	(D) Carrying Value of ROU Asset (D − C)
Jan. 2020				$25,414,625
Dec. 2020	$4,881,448	$ 2,033,170	$2,848,278	22,566,347
Dec. 2021	4,881,448	1,805,308	3,076,140	19,490,207

As indicated, under the operating method, American amortizes the lease liability and right-of-use asset, resulting in straight-line expense recognition. CitiCapital (the buyer-lessor) continues to recognize the asset on its balance sheet and recognizes equal amounts of rental revenue (straight-line basis) in each period. It **depreciates the leased asset generally on a straight-line basis**.

APPENDIX 21B Direct Financing Lease (Lessor)

LEARNING OBJECTIVE *6

Describe the lessor's accounting for a direct financing lease.

Lessors account for a lease as a sales-type lease if the lease transfers control of the underlying asset to the lessee, based on meeting one of the lease classification tests presented in Illustration 21.2. Leases that do not meet any of the classification tests are generally recorded as operating leases. However, lessors use a third lease classification—a **direct financing lease**—in one special situation. This situation occurs when the lessor **relinquishes control of the asset** to the lessee but there is also involvement of a third party. [21] This situation is common when a third-party residual value guarantee is involved. **Illustration 21B.1** illustrates the decision process for direct financing lease classification.

ILLUSTRATION 21B.1 Direct Financing Lease Classification

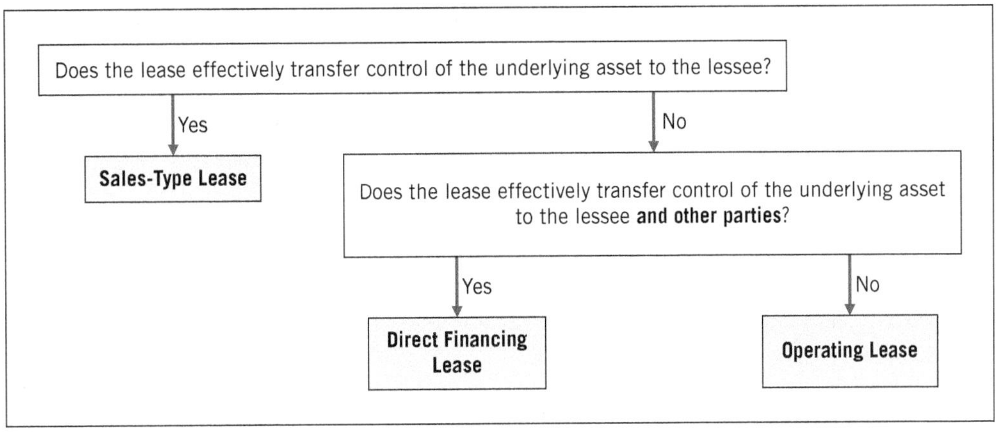

For example, in the Josway/Traylor compactor lease, both parties classified the lease as an operating lease because none of the transfer of control criteria were met. A condition of that agreement was that the residual value was not guaranteed by the lessee. It turns out that if the residual value was guaranteed by Traylor, the 90% test would be met and Josway and Traylor would account for this lease as a finance (sales-type) lease. However if Josway (the lessor) obtains the **residual value guarantee from a third party, Josway (the lessor) classifies the lease as a direct financing lease, not a sales-type lease.**[20]

Direct Financing Lease Accounting

The basic difference between a direct financing lease and a sales-type lease relates to the profit on the sale. In a sales-type lease, the profit is recognized immediately. **In a direct financing lease, the profit is deferred and recognized over the life of the lease.**[21]

[20]For classification as a direct financing lease, it must be probable that the lessor will collect the lease payments and any amounts related to the residual value guarantee(s).

[21]Losses at commencement of a direct financing lease are recognized immediately. [22]

This accounting—with no selling profit recognized at the commencement of a direct financing lease—aligns with revenue recognition criteria because the lease does not transfer complete control of the underlying asset to the lessee. However, the lessor transfers substantially all the risks and rewards of ownership through the right-of-use of the underlying asset to one or more third parties. That is, in a direct financing lease, **the presence of a third-party guarantee effectively converts the lessor's risk arising from the underlying asset into a credit risk**. Given that the lessor now has credit risk, the FASB concluded that the lessor should not be permitted to recognize gross profit on the lease at the commencement of the lease. Instead, the lessor should defer the profit and recognize this profit over the life of the lease arrangement.[22] [23]

Direct Financing Lease Example

Assume that Ormand Company (the lessor) enters into a lease agreement with Amazon.com for the use of one of Ormand's standard motorized warehouse package pickers. Information relevant to the lease is as follows.

- The lease commencement date is January 1, 2020, with a term of three years. The lease agreement is non-cancelable, requiring equal rental payments at the end of each year (ordinary annuity).
- The picker has a fair value at commencement of the lease of $30,000 and a carrying value of $28,000, with an estimated residual value of $6,000 at the end of the lease. The picker has an estimated economic life of five years. Amazon provides a **guarantee that the residual value of the picker will be at least $6,000 at the end of the lease.**
- The lease contains no renewal options, and the picker reverts to Ormand at the termination of the lease.
- Ormand sets the annual rental rate to earn a rate of return of 6 percent per year (implicit rate) on its investment, as shown in Illustration 21B.2.

ILLUSTRATION 21B.2

Computation of Lease Payments

Fair value of leased equipment	$30,000.00
Less: Present value of the residual value ($6,000 × .83962 ($PVF_{3,6\%}$))	5,037.72
Amount to be recovered by lessor through lease payments	$24,962.28
Three end-of-year lease payments to earn a 6% return ($24,962.28 ÷ 2.67301 ($PVF\text{-}OA_{3,6\%}$))	$ 9,338.64

Evaluation of the classification tests, based on these facts, indicates that this lease is classified as a sales-type lease for Ormand because the present value test is met, as indicated in Illustration 21B.3.

Note that the residual value guarantee is provided by the lessee and therefore is included in the lease payments used in the present value test for classification purposes. Ormand accounts for the lease as a sale-type lease, recording a lease receivable and reducing the carrying value of the underlying asset (Inventory) to zero.

For a sales-type lease, Ormond makes the following journal entry at the beginning of the lease.

Lease Receivable	30,000	
Cost of Goods Sold	28,000	
Sales Revenue		30,000
Inventory		28,000

[22]In addition, lessor initial direct costs are deferred and amortized over the life of the lease.

ILLUSTRATION 21B.3
Lease Classification Tests

Test	Assessment
1. Transfer of ownership test	Transfer of ownership does not occur; the asset reverts to Ormand at the end of the lease.
2. Purchase option test	There is no purchase option in the lease.
3. Lease term test	The lease term is 60 percent (3 ÷ 5) of the economic life of the asset, which is less than the major part of the life of the asset (75 percent).
4. Present value test	The present value of the lease payments is $30,000.00*, which is 100 percent ($30,000 ÷ $30,000, which is greater than or equal to 90 percent) of the fair value of the picker. Therefore, **the lease meets the present value test.**
5. Alternative use test	As indicated, the equipment is not of a specialized nature and is expected to have use to Ormand when returned at the end of the lease.

*Present value of rental payments plus residual value guarantee discounted at 6%:

Present value of five annual rental payments ($9,338.64 × 2.67301 ($PVF\text{-}OA_{3,6\%}$))	$24,962.28
Present value of guaranteed residual value of $6,000 at end of the lease ($6,000 × .83962 ($PVF_{3,6\%}$))	5,037.72
	$30,000.00

On January 1, 2020, Ormand therefore reports gross profit on the sale of the package picker of $2,000 ($30,000 – $28,000). In subsequent periods, Ormand reduces the lease receivable by the payments received and recognizes interest revenue using the 6 percent implicit rate.

On the other hand, if the residual value is **guaranteed by an unrelated third party, the lessor classifies the lease as a direct financing lease.** Ormand uses the direct financing method because, as discussed earlier, the lessor still maintains some control of the asset. That is, as a result of a third-party guarantee, the lessor does not effectively transfer all risks and rewards (control) of the underlying asset (until all residual value guarantees are satisfied). In this situation, and consistent with other revenue recognition concepts, sales revenue and related cost of goods sold are not recognized. Instead Ormand recognizes a deferred gross profit of $2,000, which is the difference between the fair value of the property ($30,000) and the carrying amount of the asset ($28,000). This deferred gross profit reduces the lease receivable in the lease, as shown in **Illustration 21B.4** for the Ormand/Amazon lease.

ILLUSTRATION 21B.4
Net Investment, Direct Financing Lease

Lease Receivable	–	**Deferred Gross Profit**	=	**Net Lease Receivable**
$30,000	–	$2,000	=	$28,000

On January 1, 2020, Ormand makes the following entry to record the direct financing lease.

January 1, 2020		
Lease Receivable	30,000	
Deferred Gross Profit		2,000
Inventory		28,000

Subsequent accounting for the direct financing lease is based on a discount rate that will amortize the net lease receivable to zero over the life of the lease. That is, in a direct financing lease, the rate used to amortize the lower net lease receivable (lease receivable less deferred gross profit) will be higher. This results because the rate includes interest revenue on the lease receivable and revenue from amortizing deferred gross profit. In other words, consider the following.

1. In a normal sale, Ormand would receive lease payments over the life of the lease which, on a present value basis, equals the lease receivable of $30,000 (a 6% rate of return). Interest on the lease receivable over the life of the lease is therefore $4,015.92. This computation is shown in **Illustration 21B.5**.

ILLUSTRATION 21B.5

Sale-Type Lease Amortization

Ormand Company
Sales-Type Lease Amortization Schedule
Ordinary Annuity Basis

Date	Annual Lease Payment	Interest (6%) on Receivable	Reduction of Lease Receivable	Lease Receivable
	(a)	(b)	(c)	(d)
1/1/20				$30,000.00
12/31/20	$ 9,338.64	$1,800.00	$ 7,538.64	22,461.36
12/31/21	9,338.64	1,347.68	7,990.96	14,470.40
12/31/22	9,338.64	868.24*	8,470.40	6,000.00
12/31/23	6,000.00	-0-	6,000.00	0.00
	$34,015.92	$4,015.92	$30,000.00	

(a) Lease payment as required by lease.
(b) 6 percent of the preceding balance of (d).
(c) (a) minus (b).

*Rounded by $0.02.

2. In a direct financing arrangement, Ormand receives the same lease payments, which on a present value basis equals $28,000 (a 9.5% rate of return).[23] This computation is shown in Illustration 21B.6.

ILLUSTRATION 21B.6

Direct Financing Lease Amortization

Ormand Company
Direct Financing Lease Amortization Schedule
Ordinary Annuity Basis

Date	Annual Lease Payment	Interest (9.5%) on Receivable	Reduction of Net Lease Receivable	Net Lease Receivable
	(a)	(b)	(c)	(d)
1/1/20				$28,000.00
12/31/20	$ 9,338.64	$2,660.00	$ 6,678.64	21,321.36
12/31/21	9,338.64	2,025.53	7,313.11	14,008.25
12/31/22	9,338.64	1,330.39*	8,008.25	6,000.00
12/31/23	6,000.00		6,000.00	0.00
	$34,015.92	$6,015.92	$28,000.00	

(a) Lease payment as required by lease.
(b) 9.5 percent of the preceding balance of (d).
(c) (a) minus (b).
(d) Preceding balance minus (c).

*Rounded by $0.39

As shown in Illustration 21B.6, Ormand then records Lease Revenue based on a discount rate of 9.5 percent applied to the net lease receivable balance. In this case, the revenue on the lease receivable is $6,015.92, which is $2,000 ($6,015.92 – $4,015.92) higher than under Illustration 21B.5. The difference results because the total lease revenue each year of the lease is comprised of interest revenue on the lease receivable plus the recognition of a portion of

[23]The 9.5% rate is determined through trial and error or with a financial calculator to arrive at a discount rate for present values of the residual value (single sum) and payments (annuity), such that the net lease receivable, including the deferred gross profit, is amortized to zero (given the lease payments, as computed on the lease receivable of $30,000 and a 6% rate).

deferred gross profit. Ormand makes the following entry in 2020, based on the amounts presented in Illustration 21B.6.[24]

December 31, 2020		
Cash	9,338.64	
Deferred Gross Profit ($2,660 – $1,800)	860.00	
Lease Revenue		2,660.00
Lease Receivable		7,538.64

Ormand reports the following information related to the direct financing lease at December 31, 2020, either in the balance sheet or notes to the financial statements, as shown in Illustration 21B.7.

ILLUSTRATION 21B.7

Direct Financing Lease Balances

Leases	
Lease receivable ($30,000.00 – $7,538.64)	$22,461.36
Less: Deferred gross profit ($2,000 – $860)	1,140.00
Net lease receivable	$21,321.36

Ormand makes the following entries for payments in 2021 and 2022.

December 31, 2021		
Cash	9,338.64	
Deferred Gross Profit ($2,025.53 – $1,347.68)	677.85	
Lease Revenue		2,025.53
Lease Receivable		7,990.96

December 31, 2022		
Cash	9,338.64	
Deferred Gross Profit ($1,330.39 – $868.24)	462.15	
Lease Revenue		1,330.39
Lease Receivable		8,470.40

After the entry on December 31, 2022, to recognize interest revenue, Lease Receivable has a balance of $6,000, which equals the guaranteed residual value (the deferred gross profit has been fully amortized).

Assuming the underlying asset has a fair value of $6,000 at the end of the lease, Ormand makes the following entry.[25]

December 31, 2022		
Inventory	6,000.00	
Lease Receivable		6,000.00

[24]The reduction in deferred gross profit each year equals the difference in yearly amounts of interest revenue at 6% and 9.5%, as shown in column (b) of Illustrations 21B.5 and Illustration 21B.6, as indicated in the following table.

Date	Interest (6%) on Receivable (a)	Lease Revenue (9.5%) (b)	Reduction in Deferred Gross Profit (b) – (a)	Deferred Gross Profit Balance
1/1/20				$2,000.00
12/31/20	$1,800.00	$2,660.00	$860.00	1,140.00
12/31/21	1,347.68	2,025.53	677.85	462.15
12/31/22	868.24	1,330.39	462.15	0

A Lease Revenue account is used because both deferred gross profit and interest are recognized.

[25]If the fair value of the leased asset is less than $6,000—e.g., $5,000 upon return—Ormand receives $1,000 from the third-party guarantor to compensate for the decline in the value of the asset below the guaranteed residual value. If the asset returned has a fair value in excess of $6,000, Ormand records the asset at the carrying amount of the residual value, and the gain is unrealized until the asset is sold.

APPENDIX **21C**

Comprehensive Examples

LEARNING OBJECTIVE *7

Apply lessee and lessor accounting to finance and operating leases.

This appendix presents a comprehensive illustration of lessee and lessor accounting for a lease arrangement when classified as a finance/sales-type or operating lease.

Lease Terms: Scenario 1

Parker Shipping Co. (lessee) leases a standard hydraulic lift from Stoughton Trailers Inc. (the lessor) that will be installed at one of Parker's loading docks. The lease, signed on January 1, 2020, specifies that Stoughton grants right-of-use of the lift to Parker under the following terms:

- The lease agreement is non-cancelable with a term of four years, requiring equal rental payments of $11,182.24 at the beginning of each year of the lease (annuity-due basis).
- The lift has a fair value at commencement of the lease of $40,000, an **estimated economic life of four years, and no residual value**. The cost of the lift on Stoughton's books is $30,000.
- The lease contains no renewal options. The lift reverts to Stoughton at the termination of the lease.
- The implicit rate of the lessor is 8 percent and is known by Parker. Stoughton sets the annual rental as shown in Illustration 21C.1.

ILLUSTRATION 21C.1
Lease Payment Calculation

Fair value of leased equipment	$40,000.00
Less—present value of the residual value	0.00
Amount to be recovered by lessor through lease payments	$40,000.00
Four beginning-of-year lease payments to earn an 8% return ($40,000 ÷ 3.57710 ($PVF\text{-}AD_{4,8\%}$))	$11,182.24

Lease Classification

The lease is classified as a finance/sales-type lease by Parker/Stoughton, as indicated by the analysis in Illustration 21C.2.

ILLUSTRATION 21C.2
Lease Classification Tests

Test	Assessment
1. Transfer of ownership test	Transfer of ownership does not occur; the asset reverts to Stoughton at the end of the lease.
2. Purchase option test	There is no bargain purchase option in the lease.
3. Lease term test	The lease term is equal to the economic life of the asset (100 percent). Therefore, **the lease meets the lease term test.**
4. Present value test	The present value of the lease payments is $40,000*, which is 100 percent (greater than or equal to 90 percent) of the fair value of the hydraulic lift. Therefore, **the lease meets the present value test.**
5. Alternative use test	As indicated, the hydraulic lift will be completely used up at the end of the lease; it will not have use to Stoughton at the end of the lease.

*$11,182.24 × 3.57710 ($PVF\text{-}AD_{4,8\%}$) = $40,000.00

Thus, the lease is classified as a finance/sales-type lease due to meeting the lease term, present value, and alternative use tests (any one is sufficient).

Accounting for Finance Lease

The accounting for the lease liability (Parker) and lease receivable (Stoughton) is based on the amounts reported in the amortization schedule presented in **Illustration 21C.3**.[26]

ILLUSTRATION 21C.3
Lease Liability Amortization Schedule

Parker Shipping/Stoughton Trailers
Lease Amortization Schedule
Annuity-Due Basis

Date	Annual Lease Payment	Interest (8%) on Liability/ Receivable	Reduction of Lease Liability/ Receivable	Lease Liability/ Receivable
	(a)	(b)	(c)	(d)
1/1/20				$40,000.00
1/1/20	$11,182.24	$ -	$11,182.24	28,817.76
1/1/21	11,182.24	2,305.42	8,876.82	19,940.94
1/1/22	11,182.24	1,595.28	9,586.96	10,353.98
1/1/23	11,182.24	828.26*	10,353.98	0.00
	$44,728.96	$4,728.96	$40,000.00	

(a) Lease payment as required by lease.
(b) 8 percent of the preceding balance of (d) except for 1/1/20; since this is an annuity due, no time has elapsed at the date of the first payment and therefore no interest has accrued.
(c) (a) minus (b).
(d) Preceding balance minus (c).

*Rounded by $0.06.

Entries for Parker (lessee) and Stoughton (lessor) over the life of the lease are presented in **Illustration 21C.4**, based on the amounts reported in the amortization schedule in Illustration 21C.3.

ILLUSTRATION 21C.4 Lessee/Lessor Entries for Finance/Sales-Type Lease

Parker Shipping (Lessee)			Stoughton Trailers (Lessor)		
Lease commencement/first payment (January 1, 2020):					
Right-of-Use Asset	40,000.00		Lease Receivable	40,000.00	
Lease Liability		40,000.00	Cost of Goods Sold	30,000.00	
			Inventory		30,000.00
			Sales Revenue		40,000.00
Lease Liability	11,182.24		Cash	11,182.24	
Cash		11,182.24	Lease Receivable		11,182.24
Interest accrual and amortization expense (December 31, 2020):					
Interest Expense	2,305.42		Lease Receivable	2,305.42	
Lease Liability		2,305.42	Interest Revenue		2,305.42
Amortization Expense	10,000.00				
Right-of-Use Asset ($40,000 ÷ 4 years)		10,000.00	No entry		

Parker: Balance Sheet		Parker: Income Statement		Stoughton: Balance Sheet		Stoughton: Income Statement	
Noncurrent assets		Interest expense	$ 2,305.42	Current assets		Sales revenue	$40,000.00
Right-of-use assets	$30,000.00	Amortization expense	10,000.00	Lease receivable	$11,182.24	Cost of goods sold	30,000.00
Current liabilities				Noncurrent assets		Interest revenue	2,305.42
Lease liability	11,182.24			Lease receivable	19,940.94		
Noncurrent liabilities							
Lease liability	19,940.94						

(continued)

[26]The same amortization schedule can be used for the lessee and lessor because there is no residual value and Parker knows the implicit rate used by the lessor is setting the payments.

ILLUSTRATION 21C.4 *(continued)*

Parker Shipping (Lessee)			Stoughton Trailers (Lessor)		
Second lease payment (January 1, 2021):					
Lease Liability ($8,876.82 + $2,305.42)	11,182.24		Cash	11,182.24	
Cash		11,182.24	Lease Receivable		11,182.24
Interest accrual and amortization expense (December 31, 2021):					
Interest Expense	1,595.28		Lease Receivable	1,595.28	
Lease Liability		1,595.28	Interest Revenue		1,595.28
Amortization Expense	10,000.00			No entry	
Right-of-Use Asset ($40,000 ÷ 4 years)		10,000.00			

Balance Sheet		Income Statement		Balance Sheet		Income Statement	
Noncurrent assets		Interest expense	$ 1,595.28	Current assets		Interest revenue	$1,595.28
Right-of-use assets	$20,000.00	Amortization expense	10,000.00	Lease receivable	$11,182.24		
Current liabilities				Noncurrent assets			
Lease liability	11,182.24			Lease receivable	10,353.98		
Noncurrent liabilities							
Lease liability	10,353.98						

Parker Shipping (Lessee)			Stoughton Trailers (Lessor)		
Third lease payment (January 1, 2022):					
Lease Liability ($9,586.96 + $ 1,595.28)	11,182.24		Cash	11,182.24	
Cash		11,182.24	Lease Receivable		11,182.24
Interest accrual and amortization expense (December 31, 2022):					
Interest Expense	828.26		Lease Receivable	828.26	
Lease Liability		828.26	Interest Revenue		828.26
Amortization Expense	10,000.00				
Right-of-Use Asset ($40,000 ÷ 4 years)		10,000.00		No entry	

Balance Sheet		Income Statement		Balance Sheet		Income Statement	
Noncurrent assets		Interest expense	$ 828.26	Current assets		Interest revenue	$828.26
Right-of-use assets	$10,000.00	Amortization expense	10,000.00	Lease receivable	$11,182.24		
Current liabilities							
Lease liability	$11,182.24						

Parker Shipping (Lessee)			Stoughton Trailers (Lessor)		
Fourth lease payment (January 1, 2023):					
Lease Liability ($10,353.98 + $ 828.26)	11,182.24		Cash	11,182.24	
Cash		11,182.24	Lease Receivable		11,182.24

Lease Terms: Scenario 2

Now consider the following revised terms of the lease between Parker Shipping Co. and Stoughton Trailers Inc. for the right-of-use of a hydraulic lift. The lease, signed on January 1, 2020, specifies that Stoughton grants right-of-use of the lift to Parker under the following terms.

- The lease agreement is non-cancelable with a term of four years, requiring equal rental payments of $9,538.39 with the first payment on January 1, 2020 (annuity-due basis).
- The lift has a fair value at commencement of the lease of $40,000, an estimated **economic life of six years**. The lift has **a residual value** at the end of the lease of **$8,000 (unguaranteed)**. The cost of the lift on Stoughton's books is $30,000.

- The lease contains no renewal options. The lift reverts to Stoughton at the termination of the lease.
- The implicit rate of Stoughton (the lessor) is 8 percent and is known by Parker.

Stoughton determines the rental payments such that it earns a rate of return of 8 percent per year (implicit rate) on its investment, as shown in **Illustration 21C.5**.

ILLUSTRATION 21C.5
Computation of Lease Payments

Fair value of leased equipment	$40,000.00
Less: Present value of the residual value ($8,000 × .73503($PV_{4,8\%}$))	5,880.24
Amount to be recovered by lessor through lease payments	$34,119.76
Four beginning-of-year lease payments to earn an 8% return ($34,119.76 ÷ 3.57710 ($PVF\text{-}AD_{4,8\%}$))	$ 9,538.39

Lease Classification

The lease is classified as an operating lease by Parker and Stoughton, as indicated by the analysis in **Illustration 21C.6**.

ILLUSTRATION 21C.6
Lease Classification Tests

Test	Assessment
1. Transfer of ownership test	Transfer of ownership does not occur; the asset reverts to Stoughton at the end of the lease.
2. Purchase option test	There is no bargain purchase option in the lease.
3. Lease term test	The lease term is 66.67 percent (4 ÷ 6) of the economic life of the asset, which is less than the major part of the life of the asset (75 percent).
4. Present value test	The present value of the lease payments is $34,119.76*, which is 85.3 percent ($34,119.76 ÷ $40,000) of the fair value of the lift. Therefore, it does not meet the present value test.
5. Alternative use test	As indicated, the equipment is not of a specialized nature and is expected to have use to Stoughton when returned at the end of the lease.

*$9,538.39 × 3.57710 ($PVF\text{-}AD_{4,8\%}$)

Thus, the lease is classified as an operating lease by both the lessee and lessor, as none of the classification tests are met.

Lessee Accounting—Operating Lease

Parker makes the following entry to record this operating lease and the first payment.

January 1, 2020		
Right-of-Use Asset	34,119.76	
Lease Liability		34,119.76
(To record right-of-use asset and related liability)		
Lease Liability	9,538.39	
Cash		9,538.39
(To record first payment)		

Illustration 21C.7 shows the interest expense and amortization of the lease liability, applying the effective-interest method.

ILLUSTRATION 21C.7

Lease Amortization Schedule

Parker Shipping Co.
Lease Amortization Schedule
Annuity-Due Basis

Date	Annual Lease Payment	Interest (8%) on Liability	Reduction of Lease Liability	Lease Liability
	(a)	(b)	(c)	(d)
1/1/20				$34,119.76
1/1/20	$ 9,538.39	$ -0-	9,538.39	24,581.37
1/1/21	9,538.39	1,966.51	7,571.88	17,009.49
1/1/22	9,538.39	1,360.76	8,177.63	8,831.86
1/1/23	9,538.39	706.53*	8,831.86	0.00
	$38,153.56	$4,033.80	$34,119.76	

(a) Lease payment as required by lease.
(b) 8 percent of the preceding balance of (d) except for 1/1/20; since this is an annuity due, no time has elapsed at the date of the first payment and therefore no interest has accrued.
(c) (a) minus (b).
(d) Preceding balance minus (c).
*Rounded by $0.02.

Parker computes straight-line expense and amortization on its right-of-use asset for each year of the lease, as presented in Illustration 21C.8.

ILLUSTRATION 21C.8

Lease Expense Schedule

Parker Shipping Co.
Lease Expense Schedule

Date	(A) Lease Expense (Straight-Line)	(B) Interest (8%) on Liability	(C) Amortization of ROU Asset (A – B)	(D) Carrying Value of ROU Asset (D – C)
12/31/19				$34,119.76
12/31/20	$ 9,538.39	$1,966.51	$ 7,571.88	26,547.88
12/31/21	9,538.39	1,360.76	8,177.63	18,370.25
12/31/22	9,538.39	706.53	8,831.86	9,538.39
12/31/23	9,538.39		9,538.39	0.00
	$38,153.56	$4,033.80	$34,119.76	

As indicated, the annual lease expense equals interest related to amortizing its lease liability plus amortization of the right-of-use asset. Parker decreases the right-of-use asset's book value each year by an amount (a plug) such that total annual lease expense is $9,538.39. The journal entries by Parker over the life of the lease are presented in Illustration 21C.9.

After the entry for the final payment on December 31, 2023, the lease liability and right-of-use asset are fully amortized. The lease expense for the four years ($38,153.56) is comprised of amortization of the right of-use asset of $34,119.76 plus interest associated with the amortization of the lease liability of $4,033.80. Parker combines interest on the liability and amortization of the right-of-use asset to report lease expense on the income statement over the life of the lease.

ILLUSTRATION 21C.9

Lessee Operating Lease Entries

Parker Shipping (Lessee)

Recognize lease expense, record amortization (December 31, 2020):

Lease Expense	9,538.39	
Right-of-Use Asset		7,571.88
Lease Liability		1,966.51

Balance Sheet		Income Statement	
Noncurrent assets		Lease expense	$9,538.39
Right-of-use assets	$26,547.88		
Current liabilities			
Lease liability	$9,538.39		
Noncurrent liabilities			
Lease liability	17,009.49		

Record second lease payment (January 1, 2021):

Lease Liability	9,538.39	
Cash		9,538.39

Recognize lease expense, record amortization (December 31, 2021):

Lease Expense	9,538.39	
Right-of-Use Asset		8,177.63
Lease Liability		1,360.76

Balance Sheet		Income Statement	
Noncurrent assets		Lease expense	$9,538.39
Right-of-use assets	$18,370.25		
Current liabilities			
Lease liability	$9,538.39		
Noncurrent liabilities			
Lease liability	8,831.86		

Record third lease payment (January 1, 2022):

Lease Liability	9,538.39	
Cash		9,538.39

Recognize lease expense, record amortization (December 31, 2022):

Lease Expense	9,538.39	
Right-of-Use Asset		8,831.86
Lease Liability		706.53

Balance Sheet		Income Statement	
Noncurrent assets		Lease expense	$9,538.39
Right-of-use assets	$9,538.39		
Current liabilities			
Lease liability	$9,538.39		

Record lease payment (January 1, 2023):

Lease Liability	9,538.39	
Cash		9,538.39

Recognize lease expense, record amortization (December 31, 2023):

Lease Expense	9,538.39	
Right-of-Use Asset		9,538.39

Lessor Accounting—Operating Lease

As shown in the evaluation of the classification tests in Illustration 21C.6, Stoughton classifies the lease as an operating lease because none of the sales-type lease criteria are met. Stoughton's entries throughout the lease are presented in Illustration 21C.10.

ILLUSTRATION 21C.10

Lessor Entries for Operating Lease

Stoughton Trailers (Lessor)		
Lease payments (January 1, 2020, 2021, 2022, 2023):		
Cash	9,538.39	
Unearned Revenue		9,538.39
Recognize lease revenue, record depreciation (December 31, 2020, 2021, 2022, 2023):		
Unearned Revenue (leases)	9,538.39	
Lease Revenue		9,538.39
Depreciation Expense ($30,000 ÷ 6)	5,000	
Accumulated Depreciation—Equipment		5,000

Under the operating method, Stoughton (the lessor) continues to recognize the asset on its balance sheet and recognizes equal amounts of rental revenue (straight-line basis) in each period. It depreciates the leased asset generally on a straight-line basis over the asset's remaining economic life. In addition to the depreciation charge, Stoughton reports lease revenue separately from other revenues in its income statement or notes to its financial statements. A lessor should classify the leased equipment and accompanying accumulated depreciation separately from plant assets it owns as Equipment Leased to Others or Investment in Leased Property.

Review and Practice

Key Terms Review

Learning Objectives Review

1 Describe the environment related to leasing transactions.

A lease is a contract that conveys the right to control the use of identified property, plant, or equipment (an identified asset) for a period of time in exchange for consideration. The advantages of lease transactions for lessees are (1) 100 percent financing, (2) protection against obsolescence, (3) flexibility, and (4) less costly financing. Lessors leasing benefits relate to (1) profitable interest margins, (2) stimulation of product sales, (3) tax benefits and efficient tax sharing, and (4) residual value profits. Lessees classify a lease as a finance lease if it meets one or more of the following tests: (1) the lease transfers ownership of the property to the lessee, (2) the lease contains an option to purchase the underlying asset that the lessee is reasonably certain to exercise, (3) the lease term is a major part (75%) of the remaining economic life of the underlying asset, (4) the present value of the lease payments equals or exceeds substantially all (90%) of the underlying asset's fair value, and (5) the lessor does not have an alternative use for the asset at the end of the lease. Lessors evaluate the same tests as lessees to determine the classification of a lease as sales-type or operating.

2 Explain the accounting for finance leases.

For a finance/sales-type lease, the lessee records a right-of-use asset and related liability at the commencement of the lease. The lessee recognizes interest expense on the lease liability over the life of the lease using the effective-interest method and records amortization expense on the right-of-use asset. The lessor determines the lease payments, based on the rate of return—the implicit rate—needed to justify leasing the asset, taking into account the credit standing of the lessee, the length of the lease, and the status of the residual value (guaranteed versus unguaranteed). For a sales-type lease, the lessor accounts for the lease in a manner similar to the sale of an asset. At lease commencement, the lessor takes the asset off the books and records a receivable equal to the present value of the lease payments. Any dealer or manufacturer selling profit on the transfer of the leased asset is recognized in income at commencement of the lease. The lessor recognizes interest revenue on the lease receivable over the life of the lease using the effective-interest method.

3 Explain the accounting for operating leases.

In an operating lease, a lessee obtains control of only **the use of the underlying asset but not ownership of the underlying asset itself**. Lessees and lessors classify and account for all leases that fail to meet all of the five classification tests as operating leases. Lessees account for operating leases using the straight-line, single-lease cost approach. Lease expense is recorded using the straight-line approach for operating leases. To achieve a single operating cost that is constant from period to period, companies continue to use the effective-interest method for amortizing the lease liability. However, instead of reporting interest expense, a lessee reports interest on the lease liability as part of Lease Expense. In addition, the lessee no longer reports amortization expense related to the right-of-use asset. Instead, it "plugs" in an amount that increases the Lease Expense account so that it is the same amount from period to period. This plugged amount then reduces the right-of-use asset, such that both the right-of-use asset and the lease liability are amortized to zero at the end of the lease. Under the operating method, lessors continue to recognize the asset on the balance sheet and record equal amounts of lease revenue (straight-line basis) in each period. It depreciates the leased asset generally on a straight-line basis.

4 Discuss the accounting and reporting for special features of lease arrangements.

The features of lease arrangements that cause unique accounting problems are (1) residual values, (2) other lease adjustments (including initial direct costs), (3) bargain purchase options, (4) short-term leases (lessee), and (5) presentation, disclosure, and analysis.

The Effect of Residual Values, Guaranteed and Unguaranteed. In setting the lease payments, lessors work under the assumption that the residual value at the end of the lease term will be realized whether guaranteed or unguaranteed. This ensures that the lessor will recover the same net investment whether the residual value is guaranteed or unguaranteed. Whether the estimated residual value is guaranteed or unguaranteed is of both economic and accounting consequence to the lessee. The accounting consequence is that the lease payments, the basis for classification, include the guaranteed residual value but exclude the unguaranteed residual value. For measuring the lessee's lease liability and right-of-use asset, however, only the amount of the guaranteed residual value that is probable to be paid under the guarantee is included in the lease payments to be capitalized. In effect, the guaranteed residual value is an additional lease payment that the lessee will pay in property or cash, or both, at the end of the lease term. An unguaranteed residual value from the lessee's viewpoint is the same as no residual value in terms of its effect upon the lessee's method of computing the lease payments and the capitalization of the leased asset and the lease liability. See Illustration 21.28 for a summary.

Other Lease Adjustments. The lease liability is the starting point to determine the amount to record for the right-of-use asset. Companies adjust the measurement of the right-of-use asset as follows: (1) lease prepayments made by the lessee increase the right-of-use asset, (2) lease incentive payments made by the lessor to the lessee reduce the right-of-use asset, and (3) initial direct costs incurred by the lessee increase the right-of-use asset. Incremental costs of a lease that would not have been incurred had the lease not been executed are included in the cost of the right-of-use asset but should not be recorded as part of the lease liability. For operating leases, lessors defer initial direct costs and amortize them as expenses over the term of the lease. For sales-type leases, lessors generally expense initial direct costs at lease commencement. Lessor internal costs are not included in initial direct costs and are expensed as incurred.

Bargain Purchase Option. A bargain purchase option increases the present value of the lease payments by the present value of the option price for the lessee. In computing annual amortization of the right-of-use asset with this type of option, the lessee uses the economic life of the underlying asset.

Short-Term Leases. A short-term lease is a lease that, at the commencement date, has a lease term of 12 months or less. Rather than recording a right-of-use asset and lease liability, lessees may elect to forego recognition of a right-of-use asset and lease liability. If this election is taken, the lease payments are recognized in net income on a straight-line basis over the lease term. Variable lease payments for short-term leases should be recorded in the period in which the obligation for the payment is incurred.

Presentation, Disclosure, and Analysis. Presentation and disclosure by lessors and lessees of amounts related to leases vary depending on whether leases are classified as finance/sales-type or operating. See Illustrations 21.34 and 21.35 (presentation in the balance sheet and income statement) and Illustrations 21.36, 21.37, 21.38, and 21.39 (disclosures in the notes to the financial statements) for summaries of presentation and disclosure requirements. Expanded recognition of lease assets and liabilities under the new lease accounting rules have the potential to result in significant impacts on analysis, based on information in the financial statements. A number of financial metrics used to measure the profitability and solvency of companies (return on assets and debt to equity ratios) will change, which could create challenges when performing financial analysis.

***5 Describe the lessee's accounting for sale-leaseback transactions.**

In a sale-leaseback arrangement, a company (the seller-lessee) transfers an asset to another company (the buyer-lessor) and then leases that asset back from the buyer-lessor. If the leaseback is classified as a finance/sales-type lease, the sale is not recognized (referred to as a failed sale) because the seller-lessee continues to control the asset—the transaction is accounted for as a financing arrangement. If the leaseback is classified as an operating lease, sale-leaseback accounting is appropriate. Under sale-leaseback accounting, gross profit on the sale is recognized and the leaseback is accounted for as an operating lease with recognition of a right-of-use asset, lease liability, and subsequent amortization, resulting in straight-line expense recognition. The buyer-lessor continues to recognize the asset on its balance sheet and recognizes equal amounts of lease revenue (straight-line basis) in each period. It depreciates the leased asset generally on a straight-line basis.

***6 Describe the lessor's accounting for a direct financing lease.**

In a direct financing lease, the lessee does not **obtain ownership control** of the asset, but the lessor **relinquishes control**. That is, the lessee controls use of the asset during the lease but will return the asset to the lessor at the end of the lease. However, the lessor will recover the value of the asset through lease payments **plus the third-party residual value guarantee**. In this situation, rather than following operating lease accounting: (1) the lessor derecognizes the underlying asset and recognizes a net investment in the lease (which consists of the lease receivable, unguaranteed residual asset, and deferred gross profit), and (2) the lessor gross profit is deferred and amortized into income over the lease term.

***7 Apply lessee and lessor accounting to finance and operating leases.**

Companies must understand and correctly apply the procedures for classifying and accounting for lease arrangements.

Enhanced Review and Practice

Go online for multiple-choice questions with solutions, review exercises with solutions, and a full glossary of all key terms.

Practice Problem

Morgan Bakeries is involved in four different lease situations. Each of these leases is noncancelable, and in no case does Morgan receive title to the properties leased during or at the end of the lease term. All leases start on January 1, 2020, with the first rental due at the beginning of the year. For each lease, assume that the lessors have alternative use for the assets at the end of the lease unless ownership transfers to the lessee. Additional information is shown in the following table.

	(a) Harmon, Inc.	(b) Arden's Oven Co.	(c) Mendota Truck Co.	(d) Appleland Computer
Type of property	Cabinets	Oven	Truck	Computer
Yearly rental	$6,000	$12,000	$5,189.31	$2,640.35
Lease term (years)	20	10	3	3
Estimated economic life	30	25	4	5
Purchase option	None	$75,000 at end of 10 years $4,000 at end of 15 years	None	$3,000 at end of 3 years, which approximates fair value
Renewal option	None	5-year renewal at $12,000 per year after 10 years, reasonably certain to be exercised if the purchase option is not	None	1 year at $1,500; no penalty for nonrenewal; standard renewal clause
Fair value at commencement of lease	$75,000	$120,000	$20,000	$10,000
Cost of asset to lessor	$60,000	$100,000	$15,000	$10,000

	(a) Harmon, Inc.	(b) Arden's Oven Co.	(c) Mendota Truck Co.	(d) Appleland Computer
Residual value				
Guaranteed	-0-	-0-	$7,000 (the amount expected to be paid)	-0-
Unguaranteed	$35,000	-0-	-0-	$3,000
Incremental borrowing rate of lessee	8%	8%	8%	8%
Present value of rental payments				
Using incremental borrowing rate of lessee	$63,621.60	$112,191.84	$20,000	$7,618.51
Using implicit rate of lessor	Not known	Not known	Not known	Known by lessee (6%), $7,481.14
Estimated fair value at end of lease term	$35,000	$80,000 at end of 10 years $60,000 at end of 15 years	Not available	$3,000

Instructions

For each lease arrangement, determine the correct classification of the lease and prepare the journal entry at its commencement.

Solution

a. Analysis of the Harmon, Inc. lease:

1. **Transfer of title?** No.
2. **Bargain purchase option?** No.
3. **Economic life test (75% test):** The lease term is 20 years and the estimated economic life is 30 years. Thus, it **does not** meet the 75% test.
4. **Present value test (90% test):** No; the present value of the rental payments of $63,621,60 is less than 90 percent of the fair value of the underlying asset as shown below.

Fair value	$75,000	Rental payments	$ 6,000
Rate	× .90	PV of annuity due for 20 years at 8%	× 10.60360
90% of fair value	$67,500	PV of rental payments	$63,621.60

Both Morgan and Harmon should account for this lease as an operating lease. They make the following January 1, 2020, entries.

Morgan Bakeries (Lessee)			Harmon, Inc. (Lessor)		
Right-of-Use Asset	63,621.60		Cash	6,000	
Lease Liability		63,621.60	Rent Revenue		6,000
Lease Liability	6,000.00				
Cash		6,000.00			

b. Analysis of the Arden's Oven Co. lease:

1. **Transfer of title?** No.
2. **Bargain purchase option?** The $75,000 option at the end of 10 years does not appear to be sufficiently lower than the expected fair value of $80,000 to make it reasonably assured that it will be exercised. However, given that the renewal option is reasonably certain to be exercised, the parties also consider the $4,000 purchase option at the end of 15 years. Since the fair value

is expected to be $60,000 at the end of 15 years, the $4,000 option appears to be a bargain and test 2 (bargain purchase option) is therefore met. Note that both the guaranteed and the unguaranteed residual values are assigned zero values because the lessor does not expect to repossess the leased asset.

3. **Economic life test (75% test):** Given that the renewal option exists, the lease term is the initial lease period of 10 years plus the 5-year renewal option. Even though the lease term is now considered to be 15 years, the lease term test is still not met because 75 percent of the economic life of 25 years is 18.75 years.
4. **Present value test (90% test):**

Fair value	$120,000	Rental payments	$ 12,000
Rate	× .90	PV of annuity due for	
90% of fair value	$108,000	15 years at 8%	× 9.24424
		PV of rental payments	$110,930.88

PV of bargain purchase option: = $4,000 × ($PVF_{15,8\%}$) = $4,000 × .31524 = $1,260.96

PV of rental payments	$110,930.88
PV of bargain purchase option	1,260.96
PV of lease payments	$112,191.84

The present value of the lease payments is greater than 90 percent of the fair value. Therefore, the lease does meet the 90% test.

Morgan should account for this as a finance lease, and Arden as a sales-type lease, because the lease meets both tests 2 and 4. The following entries are made on January 1, 2020.

Morgan Bakeries (Lessee)			Arden's Oven Co. (Lessor)		
Right-of Use Asset (oven)	112,191.84		Lease Receivable	120,000	
Lease Liability		112,191.84	Cost of Goods Sold	100,000	
Lease Liability	12,000.00		Inventory		100,000
Cash		12,000.00	Sales Revenue		120,000
			Cash	12,000	
			Lease Receivable		12,000

Morgan would amortize the right-of-use asset over its economic life of 25 years, given the bargain purchase option. The Lease Receivable amount of $120,000 recorded by Arden is different than the Lease Liability amount of $112,191.84 recorded by Morgan. The reason for this difference is that the implicit rate used by Arden is lower than the incremental borrowing rate of 8% used by Morgan.

c. Analysis of the Mendota Truck Co. lease:

1. **Transfer of title?** No.
2. **Bargain purchase option?** No.
3. **Economic life test (75% test):** The lease term is 3 years and the estimated economic life is 4 years. Thus, it **does** meet the 75% test (3 ÷ 4 = 75%).
4. **Present value test (90% test):**

Fair value	$20,000	Rental payments	$5,189.31
Rate	× .90	PV of annuity due for	
90% of fair value	$18,000	3 years at 8%	× 2.78326
		PV of rental payments	$14,443.19*

*Adjusted for $0.01 due to rounding.

PV of guaranteed residual value = $7,000 × ($PVF_{3,\,8\%}$) = $7,000 × .79383 = $5,556.81

PV of rental payments	$14,443.19
PV of guaranteed residual value	5,556.81
PV of lease payments	$20,000.00

The present value of the lease payments is greater than 90 percent of the fair value. Therefore, the lease meets the 90% test.

The following entries are made on January 1, 2020.

Morgan Bakeries (Lessee)			Mendota Truck Co. (Lessor)		
Right-of-Use Asset (truck)	20.000.00		Lease Receivable	20,000	
Lease Liability		20.000.00	Cost of Goods Sold	15,000	
Lease Liability	5,189.31		Trucks		15,000
Cash		5,189.31	Sales Revenue		20,000
			Cash	5,189.31	
			Lease Receivable		5,189.31

This is a sales-type lease for Mendota. Morgan amortizes the right-of-use asset over 3 years.

d. Analysis of the Appleland Computer lease:

1. **Transfer of title?** No.
2. **Bargain purchase option?** No. The option to purchase at the end of 3 years at approximate fair value is clearly not a bargain.
3. **Economic life test (75% test):** The lease term is 3 years, and no bargain renewal period exists as it is simply a standard renewal clause which is not reasonably certain to be exercised. Therefore, the 75% test is not met (3 ÷ 5 = 60%).
4. **Recovery of investment test (90% test):**

Fair value	$10,000	Rental payments	$2,640.35
Rate	× .90	PV of annuity-due factor for 3 years at 6%	× 2.83339
90% of fair value	$ 9,000	PV of lease payments using implicit borrowing rate	$7,481.14

The present value of the lease payments using the implicit borrowing rate is $7,481.14. Because the present value of the lease payments is lower than 90 percent of the fair value, the lease does **not** meet the present value test.

The entries made for an operating lease on January 1, 2020, are as follows.

Morgan Bakeries (Lessee)			Appleland Computer (Lessor)		
Right-of-Use Asset (truck)	7,481.14		Cash	2,640.35	
Lease Liability		7,481.14	Lease Revenue		2,640.35
Lease Liability	2,640.35				
Cash		2,640.35			

WileyPLUS

Exercises, Problems, Problem Solution Walkthrough Videos, and many more assessment tools and resources are available for practice in WileyPLUS.

Note: All asterisked Questions, Exercises, and Problems relate to material in the appendices to the chapter.

Questions

1. What are the major lessor groups in the United States? What advantage does a captive leasing subsidiary have in a leasing arrangement?

2. Bradley Co. is expanding its operations and is in the process of selecting the method of financing this program. After some investigation, the company determines that it may (1) issue bonds and with the proceeds purchase the needed assets, or (2) lease the assets on a long-term basis. Without knowing the comparative costs involved, answer these questions:

a. What are the possible advantages of leasing the assets instead of owning them?

b. What are the possible disadvantages of leasing the assets instead of owning them?

c. How will the balance sheet be different if Bradley Co. leases the assets rather than purchasing them?

3. What are the major advantages to a lessor for becoming involved in a leasing arrangement?

4. From a lessee perspective, distinguish between a finance lease and an operating lease.

5. Identify the lease classification tests and how they are applied.

6. Morgan Handley and Tricia Holbrook are discussing the new leasing standard. Morgan believes the standard requires that the lessee use the implicit rate of the lessor in computing the present value of its lease liability. Tricia is not sure if Morgan is correct. Explain the discount rate that the lessee should use to compute its lease liability.

7. Explain which of following would result in the lessee classifying the lease as a finance lease.

a. The lease is for a major part of the economic life of the asset.

b. The lease term is for 12 months or less.

c. The lease transfers ownership of the asset at the end of the lease.

8. Paul Singer indicated that "all leases must now be capitalized on the balance sheet." Is this statement correct? Explain.

9. Describe the following terms: (a) residual value, (b) guaranteed residual value, and (c) initial direct costs.

10. Explain the following concepts: (a) bargain purchase option and (b) bargain renewal option.

11. What payments are included in the lease liability?

12. Wonda Stone read somewhere that a residual value guarantee is used for computing the present value of lease payments for lease classification purposes but is treated differently when measuring its lease liability. Is Wonda correct in her interpretation? Explain.

13. Identify the amounts included in the measurement of the right-of-use asset.

14. Harcourt Company enters into a lease agreement with Brunsell Inc. to lease office space for a term of 72 months. Lease payments during the first year are $5,000 per month. Each year thereafter, the lease payments increase by an amount equivalent to the percentage increase in the Consumer Price Index (CPI). For example, if the CPI increases 2% in the second year, the monthly payment increases to $5,100. In the second year, the CPI increases by 3%. What are the lease payment amounts used to record this lease in the second year?

15. Describe the accounting procedures involved in applying the operating lease method by a lessee.

16. Describe the accounting procedures involved in applying the finance lease method by a lessee.

17. Explain the difference in lessee income statement and balance sheet presentation for a finance versus an operating lease.

18. Dr. Alice Foyle (lessee) has a non-cancelable, 20-year lease with Brownback Realty Inc. (lessor) for the use of a medical building. Taxes, insurance, and maintenance are paid by the lessee in addition to the fixed annual payments, of which the present value is equal to the fair value of the leased property. At the end of the lease period, title becomes the lessee's at a nominal price. Considering the terms of this lease, comment on the nature of the lease transaction and the accounting treatment that should be accorded it by the lessee.

19. Identify the lease classifications for lessors and the criteria that must be met for each classification. What is the relevance of revenue recognition criteria for lessor accounting for leases?

20. What is the difference between a lease receivable and a net investment in the lease?

21. Explain the accounting involved in applying the operating lease method by a lessor.

22. Explain the difference in lessor income statement presentation for a sales-type versus operating lease.

23. Walker Company is a manufacturer and lessor of computer equipment. What should be the nature of its lease arrangements with lessees if the company wishes to account for its lease transactions as sales-type leases?

24. Metheny Corporation's lease arrangements qualify as sales-type leases at the time of entering into the transactions. How should the corporation recognize sales revenue and cost of goods sold in these situations?

25. Packer Company (the lessor) concludes that its lease meets one of the tests to be classified as a sales-type lease. However, collection of lease payments is not probable. In this case, how should Packer account for any lease payments received?

26. The residual value is the estimated fair value of the leased property at the end of the lease term.

a. Of what significance is (1) an unguaranteed and (2) a guaranteed residual value in the lessee's accounting for a finance lease transaction?

b. Distinguish between lease payments used to determine lease classification compared to lease payments for measuring the lease liability.

27. Of what significance is (a) an unguaranteed and (b) a guaranteed residual value in the lessor's accounting for a sales-type lease transaction?

28. Describe the effect on the lessee of a "bargain purchase option" on accounting for a finance lease transaction.

29. What are "initial direct costs" and how are they accounted for by lessees and lessors?

30. What is a short-term lease? Describe lessee accounting for a short-term lease.

31. What disclosures should be made by lessees and lessors related to future lease payments?

*32. What is the nature of a "sale-leaseback" transaction?

*33. Sanchez Company (seller-lessee) enters into a sale-leaseback to sell its corporate headquarters for $18 million to Harper Bank. The carrying value of the headquarters at the date of sale is $14 million. Sanchez then leases back the headquarters in exchange for $180,000 per year in rental payments. The leaseback is considered an operating lease. How should Sanchez account for this sale?

*34. Explain the distinction between a direct financing lease and a sales-type lease for a lessor.

*35. Explain the differences in revenue recognition for the lessor in a sales-type lease, a direct financing lease, and an operating lease.

*36. Describe the accounting procedures involved in applying the direct financing method by a lessor.

Brief Exercises

BE21.1 **(LO 2)** Callaway Golf Co. leases telecommunications equipment from Photon Company. Assume the following data for equipment leased from Photon Company. The lease term is 5 years and requires equal rental payments of $31,000 at the beginning of each year. The equipment has a fair value at the commencement of the lease of $150,000, an estimated useful life of 8 years, and a guaranteed residual value at the end of the lease of $15,500. Photon set the annual rental to earn a rate of return of 6%, and this fact is known to Callaway. The lease does not transfer title or contain a bargain purchase option, and is not a specialized asset. How should Callaway classify this lease?

BE21.2 **(LO 2)** Jelly Co. processes jam and sells it to the public. Jelly leases equipment used in its production processes from Squishy, Inc. This year, Jelly leases a new piece of equipment from Squishy. The lease term is 5 years and requires equal rental payments of $15,000 at the beginning of each year. In addition, there is a renewal option to allow Jelly to keep the equipment one extra year for a payment at the end of the fifth year of $10,000 (which Jelly is reasonably certain it will exercise). The equipment has a fair value at the commencement of the lease of $76,024 and an estimated useful life of 7 years. Squishy set the annual rental to earn a rate of return of 5%, and this fact is known to Jelly. The lease does not transfer title, does not contain a bargain purchase option, and the equipment is not of a specialized nature. How should Jelly classify this lease?

BE21.3 **(LO 2)** Samson Company leases a building and land. The lease term is 6 years and the annual fixed payments are $800,000. The lease arrangement gives Samson the right to purchase the building and land for $11,000,000 at the end of the lease. Based on an economic analysis of the lease at the commencement date, Samson is reasonably certain that the fair value of the leased assets at the end of lease term will be much higher than $11,000,000. What are the total lease payments in this lease arrangement?

BE21.4 **(LO 2, 4)** Fieger Company leases equipment for 8 years with an annual rental of $2,000 per year or $16,000 in total. General Leasing (the lessor) agrees to provide Fieger with $300 for the first 2 years of the lease to defray needed repairs to the equipment. Determine the lease payments that Fieger will pay for the first 3 years of the lease agreement.

BE21.5 **(LO 1)** Sanders Fashion Company enters into a lease arrangement with Highpoint Leasing for 5 years. Sanders agrees to pay 4% of its net sales as a variable lease payment. Sanders does not pay any fixed payments. Sanders is a highly successful company that has achieved over $1,000,000 in net sales over the last 7 years. Both Sanders and Highpoint forecast that net sales will be a much greater amount than $1,000,000 in subsequent years. As a result, it is highly certain that Sanders will make payments of at least $40,000 ($1,000,000 × .04) each year. What is the lease payment amount Sanders should use to record its right-of-use asset?

BE21.6 **(LO 2)** Waterworld Company leased equipment from Costner Company, beginning on December 31, 2019. The lease term is 4 years and requires equal rental payments of $41,933 at the beginning of each year of the lease, starting on the commencement date (December 31, 2019). The equipment has a fair value at the commencement date of the lease of $150,001, an estimated useful life of 4 years, and no estimated residual value. The appropriate interest rate is 8%. Prepare Waterworld's 2019 and 2020 journal entries, assuming Waterworld depreciates similar equipment it owns on a straight-line basis.

BE21.7 **(LO 2)** Rick Kleckner Corporation recorded a right-of-use asset for $300,000 as a result of a finance lease on December 31, 2019. Kleckner's incremental borrowing rate is 8%, and the implicit rate of the lessor was not known at the commencement of the lease. Kleckner made the first lease payment of $48,337 on December 31, 2019. The lease requires eight annual payments. The equipment has a useful life of 8 years with no residual value. Prepare Kleckner's December 31, 2020, entries.

BE21.8 **(LO 2, 4)** Cardinal Company is negotiating to lease a piece of equipment to MTBA, Inc. MTBA requests that the lease be for 9 years. The equipment has a useful life of 10 years. Cardinal wants a guarantee that the residual value of the equipment at the end of the lease is at least $5,000. MTBA agrees to guarantee a residual value of this amount though it expects the residual value of the equipment to be only $2,500 at the end of the lease term. If the fair value of the equipment at lease commencement is $70,000, what would be the amount of the annual rental payments Cardinal demands of MTBA, assuming each payment will be made at the beginning of each year and Cardinal wishes to earn a rate of return on the lease of 8%?

BE21.9 **(LO 1, 4)** Mequon Inc. wishes to lease machinery to Thiensville Company. Thiensville wants the machinery for 4 years, although it has a useful life of 10 years. The machinery has a fair value at the commencement of the lease of $47,000, and Mequon expects the machinery to have a residual value at the end of the lease term of $30,000. However, Thiensville does not guarantee any part of the residual value. Thiensville does expect that the residual value will be $45,000 instead of $30,000. What would be the amount of the annual rental payments Mequon demands of Thiensville, assuming each payment will be made at the end of each year and Mequon wishes to earn a rate of return on the lease of 6%?

BE21.10 (LO 2) Assume that **IBM** leased equipment that was carried at a cost of $120,000 to Swander Company. The term of the lease is 6 years beginning December 31, 2019, with equal rental payments of $30,044 beginning December 31, 2019. The fair value of the equipment at commencement of the lease is $150,001. The equipment has a useful life of 6 years with no salvage value. The lease has an implicit interest rate of 8%, no bargain purchase option, and no transfer of title. Collectibility of lease payments for IBM is probable. Prepare Swander's December 31, 2019, journal entries at commencement of the lease.

BE21.11 (LO 2) Use the information for **IBM** from BE21.10. Assume the sales-type lease was recorded at a present value of $150,000. Prepare IBM's December 31, 2020, entry to record the lease transaction with Swander Company.

BE21.12 (LO 2) Geiberger Corporation manufactures drones. On December 31, 2019, it leased to Althaus Company a drone that had cost $120,000 to manufacture. The lease agreement covers the 5-year useful life of the drone and requires five equal annual rentals of $40,800 payable each December 31, beginning December 31, 2019. An interest rate of 8% is implicit in the lease agreement. Collectibility of the rentals is probable. Prepare Geiberger's December 31, 2019, journal entries.

BE21.13 (LO 2) Use the information for Geiberger Corporation from BE21.12, except assume the collectibility of the rentals is not probable. Prepare any journal entries for Geiberger on December 31, 2019.

BE21.14 (LO 2) Kubby Company specializes in leasing large storage units to other businesses. Kubby entered a contract to lease a storage unit to Riskey, Inc. for 4 years when that particular storage unit had a remaining useful life of 5 years. The fair value of the unit was $10,000 at the commencement of the lease on January 1, 2020. The present value of the five equal rental payments of $2,507 at the start of each year, plus the present value of a guaranteed residual value of $1,000, equals the fair value of $10,000, Kubby's implicit rate of return on the lease of 6%. The following is a correct, complete amortization schedule created by Kubby.

Date	Lease Payment	Interest (6%) on Outstanding Lease Receivable	Reduction of Lease Receivable	Balance of Lease Receivable
1/1/20				$10,000
1/1/20	$ 2,507		$ 2,507	7,493
1/1/21	2,507	$ 450	2,057	5,436
1/1/22	2,507	326	2,181	3,255
1/1/23	2,507	195	2,312	943
12/31/23	1,000	57	943	0
	$11,028	$1,028	$10,000	

Given the above schedule, make the appropriate entries at December 31, 2023, to record the accrual of interest and the return of the storage unit to Kubby (assuming the unit is returned on December 31, 2023, at the expected and guaranteed residual value of $1,000).

BE21.15 (LO 3) LeBron James (LBJ) Corporation agrees on January 1, 2020, to lease equipment from Cavaliers, Inc. for 3 years. The lease calls for annual lease payments of $23,000 at the beginning of each year. The lease does not transfer ownership, nor does it contain a bargain purchase option, and is not a specialized asset. In addition, the useful life of the equipment is 10 years, and the present value of the lease payments is less than 90% of the fair value of the equipment. Prepare LBJ's journal entries on January 1, 2020 (commencement of the operating lease), and on December 31, 2020. Assume the implicit rate used by the lessor is unknown, and LBJ's incremental borrowing rate is 6%.

BE21.16 (LO 3) Kingston Corporation leases equipment from Falls Company on January 1, 2020. The lease agreement does not transfer ownership, contain a bargain purchase option, and is not a specialized asset. It covers 3 years of the equipment's 8-year useful life, and the present value of the lease payments is less than 90% of the fair value of the asset leased. Prepare Kingston's journal entries on January 1, 2020, and December 31, 2020. Assume the annual lease payment is $35,000 at the beginning of each year, and Kingston's incremental borrowing rate is 6%, which is the same as the lessor's implicit rate.

BE21.17 (LO 3) Use the information for Kingston Corporation from BE21.16. Prepare all the necessary journal entries for Falls Company (the lessor) for 2020, assuming the equipment is carried at a cost of $200,000.

BE21.18 (LO 3) Rodgers Corporation agrees on January 1, 2020, to lease equipment from Packers, Inc. for 3 years. The lease calls for annual lease payments of $12,000 at the beginning of each year. The lease does not transfer ownership, contain a bargain purchase option, and is not a specialized asset. In addition, the economic life of the equipment is 10 years, and the present value of the lease payments is less than 90% of the fair value of the equipment. Prepare Rodgers' journal entries on January 1, 2020 (commencement of the operating lease), and on December 31, 2020. Assume the implicit rate used by the lessor is 8%, and this is known to Rodgers.

BE21.19 (LO 3) Use the information for Rodgers Corporation and Packers, Inc. from BE21.18. Assume that for Packers, Inc., the lessor, the collectibility of the lease payments is probable, and the fair value and cost of the equipment is $60,000. Prepare Packers' 2020 journal entries, assuming the company uses straight-line depreciation and no salvage value.

BE21.20 (LO 4) On December 31, 2019, Escapee Company leased machinery from Terminator Corporation for an agreed-upon lease term of 3 years. Escapee agreed to make annual lease payments of $17,000, beginning on December 31, 2019. The expected residual value of the machinery at the end of the lease term is $9,000, though Escapee does not guarantee any residual value to Terminator. What amount will Escapee record as its lease liability on December 31, 2019, if its incremental borrowing rate is 6% and the implicit rate of the lease is unknown?

BE21.21 (LO 4) Use the information for Escapee Company from BE21.20. Assume the same facts, except Escapee guarantees a residual value of $9,000 at the end of the lease term, which equals the expected residual value of the machinery. (a) Does this change your answer from BE21.20? (b) What if the expected residual value at the end of the lease term is $5,000 and Escapee guarantees a residual of $9,000?

BE21.22 (LO 4) Indiana Jones Corporation enters into a 6-year lease of equipment on December 31, 2019, which requires six annual payments of $40,000 each, beginning December 31, 2019. In addition, Indiana Jones guarantees the lessor a residual value of $20,000 at the end of the lease. However, Indiana Jones believes it is probable that the expected residual value at the end of the lease term will be $10,000. The equipment has a useful life of 6 years. Prepare Indiana Jones' December 31, 2019, journal entries, assuming the implicit rate of the lease is 6% and this is known to Indiana Jones.

BE21.23 (LO 4) Use the information for Indiana Jones Corporation from BE21.22. Assume that for Lost Ark Company, the lessor, collectibility of lease payments is probable and the carrying amount of the equipment is $180,000. Prepare Lost Ark's 2019 and 2020 journal entries.

BE21.24 (LO 4) Forrest, Inc. has entered an agreement to lease an old warehouse with a useful life of 5 years and a fair value of $20,000 from United Corporation. The agreement stipulates the following.

- Rental payments of $4,638 are to be made at the start of each year of the 5-year lease. No residual value is expected at the end of the lease.
- Forrest must reimburse United each year for any real estate taxes incurred for the year. Last year, the cost of real estate taxes was $700, though these costs vary from year to year.
- Forrest must make a payment of $500 with the rental payment each period to cover the insurance United has on the warehouse.
- Forrest paid legal fees of $1,000 in executing the lease.

Assuming Forrest's incremental borrowing rate is 8% and the rate implicit in the lease is unknown, prepare the journal entry to record the initial lease liability and right-of-use asset for Forrest.

BE21.25 (LO 4) Bucky Corporation entered into an operating lease agreement to lease equipment from Badger, Inc. on January 1, 2020. The lease calls for annual lease payments of $30,000, beginning on January 1, for each of the 3 years of the lease. In addition, Badger will pay Bucky $5,000 as a cash incentive for entering the lease by January 1, 2020. In relation to the lease agreement, Bucky incurred the following costs.

Salaries of employees involved in the investigation of the lease	$2,000
Lease document preparation costs incurred after execution of the lease	500

Bucky's incremental borrowing rate is 8%. If the value of the lease liability is $83,498, what amount will Bucky record as the value of the right-of-use asset on January 1, 2020, at commencement of the operating lease?

BE21.26 (LO 4) Homestead Corporation entered into an operating lease to lease equipment from Highlander, Inc. on January 1, 2020. The lease calls for annual lease payments of $10,000, beginning on December 31, for each of the 5 years of the lease. In addition, Highlander, Inc. will pay Homestead Corporation $2,000 as a cash incentive for entering the lease by December 31. In relation to the lease agreement, Homestead incurred the following costs.

Commissions for selling agents	$ 900
Internal engineering costs	500
Legal fees resulting from the execution of the lease	3,000

Homestead's incremental borrowing rate is 6%. If the value of the lease liability is $44,651, what amount will Homestead record as the value of the right-of-use asset on January 1, 2020, at commencement of the operating lease?

BE21.27 **(LO 4)** Debbink Co. leased machinery from Young, Inc. on January 1, 2020. The lease term was for 8 years, with equal annual rental payments of $5,300 at the beginning of each year. In addition, the lease provides an option to purchase the machinery at the end of the lease term for $2,000, which Debbink is reasonably certain it will exercise as it believes the fair value of the machinery will be at least $6,000. The machinery has a useful life of 10 years and a fair value of $36,000. The implicit rate of the lease is not known to Debbink. Debbink's incremental borrowing rate is 8%. Prepare Debbink's 2020 journal entries.

BE21.28 **(LO 4)** Brent Corporation owns equipment that cost $80,000 and has a useful life of 8 years with no salvage value. On January 1, 2020, Brent leases the equipment to Havaci Inc. for one year for one rental payment of $15,000 on January 1. Assuming Havaci (lessee) elects to use the short-term lease exception, prepare Havaci's 2020 journal entries.

*BE21.29 **(LO 5)** On January 1, 2020, Irwin Animation sold a truck to Peete Finance for $35,000 and immediately leased it back. The truck was carried on Irwin's books at $28,000. The term of the lease is 3 years, there is no bargain purchase option, and title does not transfer to Irwin at lease-end. The lease requires three equal rental payments of $8,696 at the end of each year (first payment on January 1, 2021). The appropriate rate of interest is 6%, the truck has a useful life of 5 years, and the residual value at the end of the lease term is expected to be $14,000, none of which is guaranteed. Prepare Irwin's 2020 journal entries.

*BE21.30 **(LO 5)** Assume the same facts as BE21.29, except the lease term is now 5 years and the five annual rental payments are $8,309, with no expected residual value at the end of the lease term. Prepare Irwin's 2020 journal entries assuming these new facts.

*BE21.31 **(LO 6)** Bulls, Inc. leases a piece of equipment to Bucks Company on January 1, 2020. The contract stipulates a lease term of 5 years, with equal annual rental payments of $4,523 at the end of each year. Ownership does not transfer at the end of the lease term, there is no bargain purchase option, and the asset is not of a specialized nature. The asset has a fair value of $30,000, a book value of $27,000, and a useful life of 8 years. At the end of the lease term, Bulls expects the residual value of the asset to be $12,000, and this amount is guaranteed by a third party. Assuming Bulls wants to earn a 4% return on the lease and collectibility of the lease payments is probable, record its journal entry at the commencement of the lease on January 1, 2020.

*BE21.32 **(LO 6)** Use the information for Bulls, Inc. from BE21.31. Assume that the lease receivable is $30,000, deferred gross profit is $3,000, and the rate of return to amortize the net lease receivable to zero is 7.11%. Prepare Bulls' journal entry at the end of the first year of the lease to record the receipt of the first lease payment.

Exercises

E21.1 **(LO 1, 4)** **(Lessee Entries; Finance Lease with No Residual Value)** DU Journeys enters into an agreement with Traveler Inc. to lease a car on December 31, 2019. The following information relates to this agreement.

1. The term of the non-cancelable lease is 3 years with no renewal or bargain purchase option. The remaining economic life of the car is 3 years, and it is expected to have no residual value at the end of the lease term.
2. The fair value of the car was $15,000 at commencement of the lease.
3. Annual payments are required to be made on December 31 at the end of each year of the lease, beginning December 31, 2020. The first payment is to be of an amount of $5,552.82, with each payment increasing by a constant rate of 5% from the previous payment (i.e., the second payment will be $5,830.46 and the third and final payment will be $6,121.98).
4. DU Journeys' incremental borrowing rate is 8%. The rate implicit in the lease is unknown.
5. DU Journeys uses straight-line depreciation for all similar cars.

Instructions

a. Prepare DU Journeys' journal entries for 2019, 2020, and 2021.

b. Assume, instead of a constant rate of increase, the annual lease payments will increase according to the Consumer Price Index (CPI). At its current level, the CPI stipulates that the first rental payment should be $5,820. What would be the impact on the journal entries made by DU Journeys at commencement of the lease, as well as for subsequent years?

E21.2 **(LO 2, 4)** **(Lessee Entries; Finance Lease with Unguaranteed Residual Value)** On December 31, 2019, Burke Corporation signed a 5-year, non-cancelable lease for a machine. The terms of the lease called for Burke to make annual payments of $8,668 at the beginning of each year, starting December 31, 2019. The machine has an estimated useful life of 6 years and a $5,000 unguaranteed residual value. The machine reverts back to the lessor at the end of the lease term. Burke uses the straight-line method of depreciation for all of its plant assets. Burke's incremental borrowing rate is 5%, and the lessor's implicit rate is unknown.

Instructions

a. What type of lease is this? Explain.

b. Compute the present value of the lease payments.

c. Prepare all necessary journal entries for Burke for this lease through December 31, 2020.

E21.3 **(LO 2, 4)** **(Lessee Computations and Entries; Finance Lease with Guaranteed Residual Value)** Delaney Company leases an automobile with a fair value of $10,000 from Simon Motors, Inc., on the following terms.

1. Non-cancelable term of 50 months.
2. Rental of $200 per month (at the beginning of each month). (The present value at 0.5% per month is $8,873.)
3. Delaney guarantees a residual value of $1,180 (the present value at 0.5% per month is $920). Delaney expects the probable residual value to be $1,180 at the end of the lease term.
4. Estimated economic life of the automobile is 60 months.
5. Delaney's incremental borrowing rate is 6% a year (0.5% a month). Simon's implicit rate is unknown.

Instructions

a. What is the nature of this lease to Delaney?

b. What is the present value of the lease payments to determine the lease liability?

c. Based on the original fact pattern, record the lease on Delaney's books at the date of commencement.

d. Record the first month's lease payment (at commencement of the lease).

e. Record the second month's lease payment.

f. Record the first month's amortization on Delaney's books (assume straight-line).

g. Suppose that instead of $1,180, Delaney expects the residual value to be only $500 (the guaranteed amount is still $1,180). How does the calculation of the present value of the lease payments change from part b?

E21.4 **(LO 2, 4)** Excel **(Lessee Entries; Finance Lease and Unguaranteed Residual Value)** Assume that on December 31, 2019, **Kimberly-Clark Corp.** signs a 10-year, non-cancelable lease agreement to lease a storage building from Sheffield Storage Company. The following information pertains to this lease agreement.

1. The agreement requires equal rental payments of $71,830 beginning on December 31, 2019.
2. The fair value of the building on December 31, 2019, is $525,176.
3. The building has an estimated economic life of 12 years, a guaranteed residual value of $10,000, and an expected residual value of $7,000. Kimberly-Clark depreciates similar buildings on the straight-line method.
4. The lease is nonrenewable. At the termination of the lease, the building reverts to the lessor.
5. Kimberly-Clark's incremental borrowing rate is 8% per year. The lessor's implicit rate is not known by Kimberly-Clark.

Instructions

a. Prepare the journal entries on the lessee's books to reflect the signing of the lease agreement and to record the payments and expenses related to this lease for the years 2019, 2020, and 2021. Kimberly-Clark's fiscal year-end is December 31.

b. Suppose the same facts as above, except that Kimberly-Clark incurred legal fees resulting from the execution of the lease of $5,000, and received a lease incentive from Sheffield to enter the lease of $1,000. How would the initial measurement of the lease liability and right-of-use asset be affected under this situation?

c. Suppose that in addition to the $71,830 annual rental payments, Kimberly-Clark is also required to pay $5,000 for insurance costs each year on the building directly to the lessor, Sheffield Storage. How would this executory cost affect the initial measurement of the lease liability and right-of-use asset?

d. Return to the original facts in the problem. Now suppose that, at the end of the lease term, Kimberly-Clark took good care of the asset and Sheffield agrees that the fair value of the asset is actually $10,000. Record the entry for Kimberly-Clark at the end of the lease to return control of the storage building to Sheffield (assuming the accrual of interest on the lease liability has already been made).

E21.5 **(LO 2, 4)** **(Computation of Rental; Journal Entries for Lessor)** Morgan Leasing Company signs an agreement on January 1, 2020, to lease equipment to Cole Company. The following information relates to this agreement.

1. The term of the non-cancelable lease is 6 years with no renewal option. The equipment has an estimated economic life of 6 years.
2. The cost of the asset to the lessor is $245,000. The fair value of the asset at January 1, 2020, is $245,000.
3. The asset will revert to the lessor at the end of the lease term, at which time the asset is expected to have a residual value of $24,335, none of which is guaranteed.
4. The agreement requires equal annual rental payments, beginning on January 1, 2020.
5. Collectibility of the lease payments by Morgan is probable.

Instructions

(Round all numbers to the nearest cent.)

a. Assuming the lessor desires an 8% rate of return on its investment, calculate the amount of the annual rental payment required. (Round to the nearest dollar.)

b. Prepare an amortization schedule that is suitable for the lessor for the lease term.

c. Prepare all of the journal entries for the lessor for 2020 and 2021 to record the lease agreement, the receipt of lease payments, and the recognition of revenue. Assume the lessor's annual accounting period ends on December 31, and it does not use reversing entries.

E21.6 **(LO 2, 4)** **(Lessor Entries; Sales-Type Lease with Option to Purchase)** Castle Leasing Company signs a lease agreement on January 1, 2020, to lease electronic equipment to Jan Way Company. The term of the non-cancelable lease is 2 years, and payments are required at the end of each year. The following information relates to this agreement.

1. Jan Way has the option to purchase the equipment for $16,000 upon termination of the lease. It is not reasonably certain that Jan Way will exercise this option.
2. The equipment has a cost of $120,000 and fair value of $160,000 to Castle Leasing. The useful economic life is 2 years, with a residual value of $16,000.
3. Castle Leasing desires to earn a return of 5% on its investment.
4. Collectibility of the payments by Castle Leasing is probable.

Instructions

a. Prepare the journal entries on the books of Castle Leasing to reflect the payments received under the lease and to recognize income for the years 2020 and 2021.

b. Assuming that Jan Way exercises its option to purchase the equipment on December 31, 2021, prepare the journal entry to record the sale on Castle Leasing's books.

E21.7 **(LO 2, 4)** **(Type of Lease; Amortization Schedule)** Macinski Leasing Company leases a new machine to Sharrer Corporation. The machine has a cost of $70,000 and fair value of $95,000. Under the 3-year, non-cancelable contract, Sharrer will receive title to the machine at the end of the lease. The machine has a 3-year useful life and no residual value. The lease was signed on January 1, 2020. Macinski expects to earn an 8% return on its investment, and this implicit rate is known by Sharrer. The annual rentals are payable on each December 31, beginning December 31, 2020.

Instructions

a. Discuss the nature of the lease arrangement and the accounting method that each party to the lease should apply.

b. Prepare an amortization schedule that would be suitable for both the lessor and the lessee and that covers all the years involved.

c. Prepare the journal entry at commencement of the lease for Macinski.

d. Prepare the journal entry at commencement of the lease for Sharrer.

e. Prepare the journal entry at commencement of the lease for Sharrer, assuming (1) Sharrer does not know Macinski's implicit rate (Sharrer's incremental borrowing rate is 9%), and (2) Sharrer incurs initial directs costs of $10,000.

E21.8 **(LO 2, 4)** Excel **(Lessor Entries; Sales-Type Lease)** Crosley Company, a machinery dealer, leased a machine to Dexter Corporation on January 1, 2020. The lease is for an 8-year period and requires equal annual payments of $35,004 at the beginning of each year. The first payment is received on January 1, 2020. Crosley had purchased the machine during 2019 for $160,000. Collectibility of lease payments by Crosley is probable. Crosley set the annual rental to ensure a 6% rate of return. The machine has an economic life of 10 years with no residual value and reverts to Crosley at the termination of the lease.

Instructions

a. Compute the amount of the lease receivable.

b. Prepare all necessary journal entries for Crosley for 2020.

c. Suppose the collectibility of the lease payments was not probable for Crosley. Prepare all necessary journal entries for the company in 2020.

d. Suppose at the end of the lease term, Crosley receives the asset and determines that it actually has a fair value of $1,000 instead of the anticipated residual value of $0. Record the entry to recognize the receipt of the asset for Crosley at the end of the lease term.

E21.9 **(LO 2, 4)** **(Lessee Entries; Initial Direct Costs)** Use the information for Crosley Company in E21.8. Assume that Dexter Corporation does not know the rate implicit in the lease used by Crosley, and Dexter's incremental borrowing rate is 8%. In addition, assume that Dexter incurs initial direct costs of $15,000.

Instructions

a. Compute the amount of the lease liability and right-of-use asset for Dexter.

b. Prepare all necessary journal entries for Dexter for 2020.

E21.10 **(LO 2, 4)** **(Lessee Entries with Bargain Purchase Option)** The following facts pertain to a non-cancelable lease agreement between Mooney Leasing Company and Rode Company, a lessee.

Commencement date	May 1, 2020
Annual lease payment due at the beginning of each year, beginning with May 1, 2020	$20,471.94
Bargain purchase option price at end of lease term	$ 4,000.00
Lease term	5 years
Economic life of leased equipment	10 years
Lessor's cost	$65,000.00
Fair value of asset at May 1, 2020	$91,000.00
Lessor's implicit rate	8%
Lessee's incremental borrowing rate	8%
The collectibility of the lease payments by Mooney is probable.	

Instructions

(Round all numbers to the nearest cent.)

a. Discuss the nature of this lease to Rode.

b. Discuss the nature of this lease to Mooney.

c. Prepare a lease amortization schedule for Rode for the 5-year lease term.

d. Prepare the journal entries on the lessee's books to reflect the signing of the lease agreement and to record the payments and expenses related to this lease for the years 2020 and 2021. Rode's annual accounting period ends on December 31. Reversing entries are used by Rode.

E21.11 **(LO 2, 4)** **(Lessor Entries with Bargain Purchase Option)** A lease agreement between Mooney Leasing Company and Rode Company is described in E21.10.

Instructions

Refer to the data in E21.10 and do the following for the lessor. (Round all numbers to the nearest cent.)

a. Compute the amount of the lease receivable at commencement of the lease.

b. Prepare a lease amortization schedule for Mooney for the 5-year lease term.

c. Prepare the journal entries to reflect the signing of the lease agreement and to record the receipts and income related to this lease for the years 2020 and 2021. The lessor's accounting period ends on December 31. Reversing entries are not used by Mooney.

d. Suppose the collectibility of the lease payments was not probable for Mooney. Prepare all necessary journal entries for the company in 2020.

E21.12 **(LO 2, 4) (Lessee-Lessor Entries; Sales-Type Lease with Bargain Purchase Option)** On January 1, 2020, Bensen Company leased equipment to Flynn Corporation. The following information pertains to this lease.

1. The term of the non-cancelable lease is 6 years. At the end of the lease term, Flynn has the option to purchase the equipment for $1,000, while the expected residual value at the end of the lease is $5,000.
2. Equal rental payments are due on January 1 of each year, beginning in 2020.
3. The fair value of the equipment on January 1, 2020, is $150,000, and its cost is $120,000.
4. The equipment has an economic life of 8 years. Flynn depreciates all of its equipment on a straight-line basis.
5. Bensen set the annual rental to ensure a 5% rate of return. Flynn's incremental borrowing rate is 6%, and the implicit rate of the lessor is unknown.
6. Collectibility of lease payments by the lessor is probable.

Instructions

(Both the lessor and the lessee's accounting periods end on December 31.)

a. Discuss the nature of this lease to Bensen and Flynn.

b. Calculate the amount of the annual rental payment.

c. Prepare all the necessary journal entries for Bensen for 2020.

d. Suppose the collectibility of the lease payments was not probable for Bensen. Prepare all necessary journal entries for the company in 2020.

e. Prepare all the necessary journal entries for Flynn for 2020.

f. Discuss the effect on the journal entry for Flynn at lease commencement, assuming initial direct costs of $2,000 are incurred by Flynn to negotiate the lease.

E21.13 **(LO 2, 4) (Lessee-Lessor Entries; Sales-Type Lease; Guaranteed Residual Value)** Phelps Company leases a building to Walsh, Inc. on January 1, 2020. The following facts pertain to the lease agreement.

1. The lease term is 5 years, with equal annual rental payments of $4,703 at the beginning of each year.
2. Ownership does not transfer at the end of the lease term, there is no bargain purchase option, and the asset is not of a specialized nature.
3. The building has a fair value of $23,000, a book value to Phelps of $16,000, and a useful life of 6 years.
4. At the end of the lease term, Phelps and Walsh expect there to be an unguaranteed residual value of $4,000.
5. Phelps wants to earn a return of 8% on the lease, and collectibility of the payments is probable. This rate is known by Walsh.

Instructions

a. How would Phelps (lessor) and Walsh (lessee) classify this lease? How would Phelps initially measure the lease receivable, and how would Walsh initially measure the lease liability and right-of-use asset?

b. Using the original facts of the lease, show the journal entries to be made by both Phelps and Walsh in 2020.

c. Suppose the entire expected residual value of $4,000 is guaranteed by Walsh. How will this change your answer to part a?

d. Assume the same facts as part c, except the expected residual value is $3,000. Does your answer change?

E21.14 **(LO 2, 4) (Lessee Entries; Initial Direct Costs)** Use the information for the Phelps/Walsh lease in E21.13, except that Walsh was unaware of the implicit rate used in the lease by Phelps and has an incremental borrowing rate of 9%.

Instructions

How would your answer to E21.13(a) change?

E21.15 (LO 2, 4) (Amortization Schedule and Journal Entries for Lessee) Laura Leasing Company signs an agreement on January 1, 2020, to lease equipment to Plote Company. The following information relates to this agreement.

1. The term of the non-cancelable lease is 3 years with no renewal option. The equipment has an estimated economic life of 5 years.
2. The fair value of the asset at January 1, 2020, is $80,000.
3. The asset will revert to the lessor at the end of the lease term, at which time the asset is expected to have a residual value of $7,000, none of which is guaranteed.
4. The agreement requires equal annual rental payments of $25,562.96 to the lessor, beginning on January 1, 2020.
5. The lessee's incremental borrowing rate is 5%. The lessor's implicit rate is 4% and is unknown to the lessee.
6. Plote uses the straight-line depreciation method for all equipment.

Instructions

(Round all numbers to the nearest cent.)

a. Prepare an amortization schedule that would be suitable for the lessee for the lease term.

b. Prepare all of the journal entries for the lessee for 2020 and 2021 to record the lease agreement, the lease payments, and all expenses related to this lease. Assume the lessee's annual accounting period ends on December 31.

E21.16 (LO 3, 4) (Amortization Schedule and Journal Entries for Lessee) Use the information pertaining to Laura Leasing Company and Plote Company from E21.15. Assume that the expected residual value at the end of the lease is $10,000, such that the payments are $24,638.87.

Instructions

Prepare all of the journal entries for the lessee for 2020 to record the lease agreement, the lease payments, and all expenses related to this lease. Assume the lessee's annual accounting period ends on December 31.

E21.17 (LO 3, 4) (Accounting for an Operating Lease) On January 1, 2020, Nelson Co. leased a building to Wise Inc. The relevant information related to the lease is as follows.

1. The lease arrangement is for 10 years. The building is expected to have a residual value at the end of the lease of $3,500,000 (unguaranteed).
2. The leased building has a cost of $4,000,000 and was purchased for cash on January 1, 2020.
3. The building is depreciated on a straight-line basis. Its estimated economic life is 50 years with no salvage value.
4. Lease payments are $275,000 per year and are made at the beginning of the year.
5. Wise has an incremental borrowing rate of 8%, and the rate implicit in the lease is unknown to Wise.
6. Both the lessor and the lessee are on a calendar-year basis.

Instructions

a. Prepare the journal entries that Nelson should make in 2020.

b. Prepare the journal entries that Wise should make in 2020.

c. If Wise paid $30,000 to a real estate broker on January 1, 2020, as a fee for finding the lessor, what is the initial measurement of the right-of-use asset? Explain.

E21.18 (LO 3, 4) (Accounting for an Operating Lease) On January 1, 2020, a machine was purchased for $900,000 by Young Co. The machine is expected to have an 8-year life with no salvage value. It is to be depreciated on a straight-line basis. The machine was leased to St. Leger Inc. for 3 years on January 1, 2020, with annual rent payments of $150,955 due at the beginning of each year, starting January 1, 2020. The machine is expected to have a residual value at the end of the lease term of $562,500, though this amount is unguaranteed.

Instructions

a. How much should Young report as income before income tax on this lease for 2020?

b. Record the journal entries St. Leger would record for 2020 on this lease, assuming its incremental borrowing rate is 6% and the rate implicit in the lease is unknown.

c. Suppose the lease was only for one year (only one payment of the same amount at commencement of the lease), with a renewal option at market rates at the end of the lease, and St. Leger elects to use the short-term lease exception. Record the journal entries St. Leger would record for 2020 on this lease.

E21.19 **(LO 3, 4) (Accounting for an Operating Lease)** Kaluzniak Corporation leased equipment to Moeller, Inc. on January 1, 2020. The lease agreement called for annual rental payments of $1,137 at the beginning of each year of the 3-year lease. The equipment has an economic useful life of 7 years, a fair value of $7,000, a book value of $5,000, and Kaluzniak expects a residual value of $4,500 at the end of the lease term. Kaluzniak set the lease payments with the intent of earning a 6% return, though Moeller is unaware of the rate implicit in the lease and has an incremental borrowing rate of 8%. There is no bargain purchase option, ownership of the lease does not transfer at the end of the lease term, and the asset is not of a specialized nature.

Instructions

a. Describe the nature of the lease to both Kaluzniak and Moeller.

b. Prepare all necessary journal entries for Moeller in 2020. Moeller uses straight-line depreciation.

c. How would the measurement of the lease liability and right-of-use asset be affected if, as a result of the lease contract, Moeller was also required to pay $500 in commissions, prepay $750 in addition to the first rental payment, and pay $200 of insurance each year?

d. Suppose, instead of a 3-year lease term, Moeller and Kaluzniak agree to a one-year lease with a payment of $1,137 at the start of the lease. Prepare all necessary journal entries for Moeller in 2020.

E21.20 **(LO 3, 4) (Accounting for an Operating Lease)** Use the information for Kaluzniak Corporation and Moeller, Inc. from E21.19.

Instructions

a. Explain (and show calculations) how Kaluzniak arrived at the amount of the rental payments used in the lease agreement.

b. Prepare the entries for Kaluzniak for 2020.

c. How would Kaluzniak's accounting in part a change if it incurred legal fees of $700 to execute the lease documents and $500 in advertising expenses for the year in connection with the lease?

E21.21 **(LO 3, 4) (Accounting for an Operating Lease)** Rauch Incorporated leases a piece of equipment to Donahue Corporation on January 1, 2020. The lease agreement called for annual rental payments of $4,892 at the beginning of each year of the 4-year lease. The equipment has an economic useful life of 6 years, a fair value of $25,000, a book value of $20,000, and both parties expect a residual value of $8,250 at the end of the lease term, though this amount is not guaranteed. Rauch set the lease payments with the intent of earning a 5% return, and Donahue is aware of this rate. There is no bargain purchase option, ownership of the lease does not transfer at the end of the lease term, and the asset is not of a specialized nature.

Instructions

a. Describe the nature of the lease to both Rauch and Donahue.

b. Prepare the lease amortization schedule(s) for Donahue for all 4 years of the lease.

c. Prepare the journal entries for Donahue for 2020 and 2021.

d. Suppose Donahue incurs initial direct costs of $750 related to the lease. Prepare the journal entries for 2020.

e. Explain how a fully guaranteed residual value by Donahue would change the accounting for the company. The expected residual value is $9,000.

f. Explain how a bargain renewal option for one extra year at the end of the lease term would change the accounting of the lease for Donahue.

E21.22 **(LO 3, 4) (Accounting for an Operating Lease)** Use the information for Rauch Incorporated and Donahue Corporation from E21.21.

Instructions

a. Explain (and show calculations) how Rauch arrived at the amount of the rental payments used in the lease agreement.

b. Prepare the entries for Rauch for 2020.

c. Suppose that instead of $8,250, Rauch expects the residual value at the end of the lease to be $5,000, but Donahue agrees to guarantee a residual value of $8,250. All other facts being equal, how would Rauch change the amount of the annual rental payments, if at all?

d. Explain how a fully guaranteed residual value by Donahue would change the accounting for Rauch, the lessor.

e. Explain how a bargain renewal option for one extra year at the end of the lease term would change the accounting of the lease for Rauch, the lessor.

*E21.23 **(LO 5)** **(Sale-Leaseback)** Assume that on January 1, 2020, **Elmer's Restaurants** sells a computer system to Liquidity Finance Co. for $680,000 and immediately leases back the computer system. The relevant information is as follows.

1. The computer was carried on Elmer's books at a value of $600,000.
2. The term of the non-cancelable lease is 3 years; title will not transfer to Elmer's, and the expected residual value at the end of the lease is $450,000, all of which is unguaranteed.
3. The lease agreement requires equal rental payments of $115,970 at the beginning of each year.
4. The incremental borrowing rate for Elmer's is 8%. Elmer's is aware that Liquidity Finance set the annual rental to ensure a rate of return of 8%.
5. The computer has a fair value of $680,000 on January 1, 2020, and an estimated economic life of 10 years.

Instructions

Prepare the journal entries for both the lessee and the lessor for 2020 to reflect the sale and leaseback agreement.

*E21.24 **(LO 5)** **(Lessee-Lessor, Sale-Leaseback)** Respond to the requirements in each situation.

Instructions

a. On January 1, 2020, Zarle Inc. sold computer equipment to Daniell Co. The sales price of the equipment was $520,000 and its carrying amount is $400,000. Record any journal entries necessary for Zarle from the sale of the computer equipment in 2020.

b. Use the information from part a. Assume that, on the same day the sale occurred, Zarle enters into an agreement to lease the equipment from Daniell for 10 years with annual lease payments of $67,342.42 at the end of each year, beginning on December 31, 2020. If Zarle has an incremental borrowing rate of 5% and the equipment has an economic useful life of 10 years, record any journal entries necessary for Zarle from the sale and leaseback of computer equipment in 2020.

c. Use the information from part b. Now, instead of 10 years, the lease term is only 3 years with annual lease payments of $67,342.42 at the beginning of each year. Record any journal entries necessary for Zarle from the sale and leaseback of computer equipment in 2020.

*E21.25 **(LO 6)** **(Direct Financing Lease)** Giannis Corporation leases a building to Jabari, Inc. on January 1, 2020. The following facts pertain to the lease agreement.

1. The lease term is 10 years with equal annual rental payments of $3,449 at the end of each year.
2. Ownership does not transfer at the end of the lease term, there is no bargain purchase option, and the asset is not of a specialized nature.
3. The building has a fair value of $34,000, a book value to Giannis of $22,000, and a useful life of 15 years.
4. At the end of the lease term, Giannis and Jabari expect the residual value of the building to be $12,000, and this amount is guaranteed by Money, Inc., a third party.
5. Giannis wants to earn a 5% return on the lease, and collectibility of the payments is probable.

Instructions

a. Describe the nature of this lease to both Giannis and Jabari.

b. Assume the present value of lease payments and third-party guarantee is $34,000 and the rate of return to amortize the net lease receivable to zero is 13.24%. Prepare the amortization schedules Giannis would use to amortize the net lease receivable to zero.

c. Prepare the journal entries to record the entries for Giannis for 2020 and 2021.

d. Prepare the journal entries for Jabari (the lessee) for 2020 and 2021, assuming the rate implicit in the lease is known to Jabari.

e. Suppose the leased asset had a shorter economic life of 8 years, the lease agreement was only for 5 years, and the residual value of $12,000 guaranteed by Money, Inc. remained the same. Would the rate of return required to amortize the net lease receivable to zero increase, decrease, or stay the same? Explain.

f. Suppose, instead of Money, Inc., Jabari guarantees the residual value itself. How would this affect the classification of this lease agreement for both Giannis and Jabari? Describe the impact that any change in classification would have on revenue recognition for Giannis.

Problems

P21.1 (LO 2, 4) **(Lessee Entries, Finance Lease)** The following facts pertain to a non-cancelable lease agreement between Faldo Leasing Company and Vance Company, a lessee.

Commencement date	January 1, 2020
Annual lease payment due at the beginning of each year, beginning with January 1, 2020	$113,864
Residual value of equipment at end of lease term, guaranteed by the lessee	$50,000
Expected residual value of equipment at end of lease term	$45,000
Lease term	6 years
Economic life of leased equipment	6 years
Fair value of asset at January 1, 2020	$600,000
Lessor's implicit rate	8%
Lessee's incremental borrowing rate	8%

The asset will revert to the lessor at the end of the lease term. The lessee uses the straight-line amortization for all leased equipment.

Instructions

a. Prepare an amortization schedule that would be suitable for the lessee for the lease term.

b. Prepare all of the journal entries for the lessee for 2020 and 2021 to record the lease agreement, the lease payments, and all expenses related to this lease. Assume the lessee's annual accounting period ends on December 31.

c. Suppose Vance received a lease incentive of $5,000 from Faldo Leasing to enter the lease. How would the initial measurement of the lease liability and right-of-use asset be affected? What if Vance prepaid rent of $5,000 to Faldo?

P21.2 (LO 2, 4) **(Lessee Entries and Balance Sheet Presentation, Finance Lease)** On January 1, 2020, Cage Company contracts to lease equipment for 5 years, agreeing to make a payment of $120,987 at the beginning of each year, starting January 1, 2020. The leased equipment is to be capitalized at $550,000. The asset is to be amortized on a double-declining-balance basis, and the obligation is to be reduced on an effective-interest basis. Cage's incremental borrowing rate is 6%, and the implicit rate in the lease is 5%, which is known by Cage. Title to the equipment transfers to Cage at the end of the lease. The asset has an estimated useful life of 5 years and no residual value.

Instructions

a. Explain the probable relationship of the $550,000 amount to the lease arrangement.

b. Prepare the journal entry or entries that Cage should record on January 1, 2020.

c. Prepare the journal entries to record amortization of the leased asset and interest expense for the year 2020.

d. Prepare the journal entry to record the lease payment of January 1, 2021, assuming reversing entries are not made.

e. What amounts will appear on the lessee's December 31, 2020, balance sheet relative to the lease contract?

f. How would the value of the lease liability in part b change if Cage also agreed to pay the fixed annual insurance on the equipment of $2,000 at the same time as the rental payments?

P21.3 (LO 2, 4) Groupwork **(Lessee Entries and Balance Sheet Presentation, Finance Lease)** Ludwick Steel Company, as lessee, signed a lease agreement for equipment for 5 years, beginning December 31, 2020. Annual rental payments of $40,000 are to be made at the beginning of each lease year (December 31). The interest rate used by the lessor in setting the payment schedule is 6%; Ludwick's incremental borrowing rate is 8%. Ludwick is unaware of the rate being used by the lessor. At the end of the lease, Ludwick has the option to buy the equipment for $5,000, considerably below its estimated fair value at that time. The equipment has an estimated useful life of 7 years, with no salvage value. Ludwick uses the straight-line method of depreciation on similar owned equipment.

Instructions

a. Prepare the journal entry or entries, with explanations, that Ludwick should record on December 31, 2020.

b. Prepare the journal entry or entries, with explanations, that Ludwick should record on December 31, 2021. (Prepare the lease amortization schedule for all five payments.)

c. Prepare the journal entry or entries, with explanations, that Ludwick should record on December 31, 2022.

d. What amounts would appear on Ludwick's December 31, 2022, balance sheet relative to the lease arrangement?

P21.4 **(LO 2)** **(Lessee Entries, Finance Lease with Monthly Payments)** Shapiro Inc. was incorporated in 2019 to operate as a computer software service firm, with an accounting fiscal year ending August 31. Shapiro's primary product is a sophisticated online inventory-control system; its customers pay a fixed fee plus a usage charge for using the system.

Shapiro has leased a large, Alpha-3 computer system from the manufacturer. The lease calls for a monthly rental of $40,000 for the 144 months (12 years) of the lease term. The estimated useful life of the computer is 15 years.

All rentals are payable on the first day of the month beginning with August 1, 2020, the date the computer was installed and the lease agreement was signed. The lease is non-cancelable for its 12-year term, and it is secured only by the manufacturer's chattel lien on the Alpha-3 system.

This lease is to be accounted for as a finance lease by Shapiro, and it will be amortized by the straight-line method. Borrowed funds for this type of transaction would cost Shapiro 6% per year (0.5% per month). Following is a schedule of the present value of an annuity due for selected periods discounted at 0.5% per period when payments are made at the beginning of each period.

Periods (months)	Present Value of an Annuity Due Discounted at 0.5% per Period
1	1.000
2	1.995
3	2.985
143	102.497
144	102.987

Instructions

Prepare all entries Shapiro should make in its accounting records during August 2020 relating to this lease. Give full explanations and show supporting computations for each entry. Remember, August 31, 2020, is the end of Shapiro's fiscal accounting period, and it will be preparing financial statements on that date. Do not prepare closing entries.

P21.5 **(LO 2, 4)** **(Basic Lessee Accounting with Difficult PV Calculation)** In 2019, Grishell Trucking Company negotiated and closed a long-term lease contract for newly constructed truck terminals and freight storage facilities. The buildings were erected to the company's specifications on land owned by the company. On January 1, 2020, Grishell Trucking took possession of the lease properties.

Although the terminals have a composite useful life of 40 years, the non-cancelable lease runs for 20 years from January 1, 2020, with a bargain purchase option available upon expiration of the lease.

The 20-year lease is effective for the period January 1, 2020, through December 31, 2039. Rental payments of $800,000 are payable to the lessor on January 1 of each of the first 10 years of the lease term. Advance rental payments of $320,000 are due on January 1 for each of the last 10 years of the lease. The company has an option to purchase all of these leased facilities for $1 on December 31, 2039. The lease was negotiated to assure the lessor a 6% rate of return.

Instructions

a. Prepare a schedule to compute for Grishell Trucking the present value of the terminal facilities and related obligation at January 1, 2020.

b. Assuming that the present value of terminal facilities and related obligation at January 1, 2020, was $7,635,410, prepare journal entries for Grishell Trucking to record the:

1. Cash payment to the lessor on January 1, 2022.
2. Amortization of the cost of the leased properties for 2022, using the straight-line method and assuming a zero salvage value.
3. Accrual of interest expense at December 31, 2022.

Selected present value factors are as follows.

Periods	For an Ordinary Annuity of $1 at 6%	For $1 at 6%
1	.943396	.943396
2	1.833393	.889996
8	6.209794	.627412
9	6.801692	.591898
10	7.360087	.558395
19	11.158117	.330513
20	11.469921	.311805

P21.6 **(LO 2, 4)** **(Lessee-Lessor Entries, Finance Lease with a Guaranteed Residual Value)** Glaus Leasing Company agrees to lease equipment to Jensen Corporation on January 1, 2020. The following information relates to the lease agreement.

1. The term of the lease is 7 years with no renewal option, and the machinery has an estimated economic life of 9 years.
2. The cost of the machinery is $525,000, and the fair value of the asset on January 1, 2020, is $700,000.
3. At the end of the lease term, the asset reverts to the lessor and has a guaranteed residual value of $50,000. Jensen estimates that the expected residual value at the end of the lease term will be $50,000. Jensen amortizes all of its leased equipment on a straight-line basis.
4. The lease agreement requires equal annual rental payments, beginning on January 1, 2020.
5. The collectibility of the lease payments is probable.
6. Glaus desires a 5% rate of return on its investments. Jensen's incremental borrowing rate is 6%, and the lessor's implicit rate is unknown.

Instructions

(Assume the accounting period ends on December 31.)

a. Discuss the nature of this lease for both the lessee and the lessor.

b. Calculate the amount of the annual rental payment required.

c. Compute the value of the lease liability to the lessee.

d. Prepare the journal entries Jensen would make in 2020 and 2021 related to the lease arrangement.

e. Prepare the journal entries Glaus would make in 2020 and 2021 related to the lease arrangement.

f. Suppose Jensen expects the residual value at the end of the lease term to be $40,000 but still guarantees a residual of $50,000. Compute the value of the lease liability at lease commencement.

P21.7 **(LO 2, 4)** **(Lessor Computations and Entries, Sales-Type Lease with Guaranteed Residual Value)** Amirante Inc. manufactures an X-ray machine with an estimated life of 12 years and leases it to Chambers Medical Center for a period of 10 years. The normal selling price of the machine is $495,678, and its guaranteed residual value at the end of the non-cancelable lease term is estimated to be $15,000. The hospital will pay rents of $60,000 at the beginning of each year. Amirante incurred costs of $300,000 in manufacturing the machine and $14,000 in legal fees directly related to the signing of the lease. Amirante has determined that the collectibility of the lease payments is probable and that the implicit interest rate is 5%.

Instructions

a. Discuss the nature of this lease in relation to the lessor and compute the amount of each of the following items.

   1. Lease receivable at commencement of the lease.
   2. Sales price.
   3. Cost of sales.

b. Prepare a 10-year lease amortization schedule for Amirante, the lessor.

c. Prepare all of the lessor's journal entries for the first year.

P21.8 **(LO 2, 4)** **(Lessee Computations and Entries, Finance Lease with Guaranteed Residual Value)** Assume the same data as in P21.7 and that Chambers Medical Center has an incremental borrowing rate of 5% and an expected residual value at the end of the lease of $10,000.

Instructions

a. Discuss the nature of this lease in relation to the lessee, and compute the amount of the initial lease liability.

b. Prepare a 10-year lease amortization schedule.

c. Prepare all of the lessee's journal entries for the first year.

d. Suppose Chambers Medical Center incurred $7,000 of document preparation costs after the execution of the lease. How would the initial measurement of the lease liability and right-of-use asset be affected?

P21.9 **(LO 2, 4)** Groupwork **(Lessor Computations and Entries, Sales-Type Lease with Unguaranteed Residual Value)** George Company manufactures a check-in kiosk with an estimated economic life of 12 years and leases it to National Airlines for a period of 10 years. The normal selling price of the equipment is $299,140, and its unguaranteed residual value at the end of the lease term is estimated to be $20,000. National will pay annual payments of $40,000 at the beginning of each year. George incurred costs of $180,000 in manufacturing the equipment and $4,000 in sales commissions in closing the lease. George has determined that the collectibility of the lease payments is probable and that the implicit interest rate is 8%.

Instructions

a. Discuss the nature of this lease in relation to the lessor and compute the amount of each of the following items.

1. Lease receivable.
2. Sales price.
3. Cost of goods sold.

b. Prepare a 10-year lease amortization schedule for George, the lessor.

c. Prepare all of the lessor's journal entries for the first year.

P21.10 **(LO 2, 4)** **(Lessee Computations and Entries, Finance Lease with Unguaranteed Residual Value)** Assume the same data as in P21.9, with National Airlines having an incremental borrowing rate of 8%.

Instructions

a. Discuss the nature of this lease in relation to the lessee, and compute the amount of the initial lease liability.

b. Prepare a 10-year lease amortization schedule.

c. Prepare all of the lessee's journal entries for the first year. Assume straight-line depreciation.

P21.11 **(LO 2, 4)** Groupwork **(Lessee-Lessor Accounting for Residual Values)** Goring Dairy leases its milking equipment from King Finance Company under the following lease terms.

1. The lease term is 10 years, non-cancelable, and requires equal rental payments of $30,300 due at the beginning of each year starting January 1, 2020.
2. The equipment has a fair value at the commencement of the lease (January 1, 2020) of $242,741 and a cost of $180,000 on King Finance's books. It also has an estimated economic life of 15 years and an expected residual value of $45,000, though Goring Dairy has guaranteed a residual value of $50,000 to King Finance.
3. The lease contains no renewal options, and the equipment reverts to King Finance upon termination of the lease. The equipment is not of a specialized use.
4. Goring Dairy's incremental borrowing rate is 8% per year. The implicit rate is also 8%.
5. Goring Dairy depreciates similar equipment that it owns on a straight-line basis.
6. Collectibility of the payments is probable.

Instructions

a. Evaluate the criteria for classification of the lease, and describe the nature of the lease. In general, discuss how the lessee and lessor should account for the lease transaction.

b. Prepare the journal entries for the lessee and lessor at January 1, 2020, and December 31, 2020 (the lessee's and lessor's year-end). Assume no reversing entries.

c. What would have been the amount of the initial lease liability recorded by the lessee upon the commencement of the lease if:

1. The residual value of $50,000 had been guaranteed by a third party, not the lessee?
2. The residual value of $50,000 had not been guaranteed at all?

d. On the lessor's books, what would be the amount recorded as the lease receivable at the commencement of the lease, assuming:

1. The residual value of $50,000 had been guaranteed by a third party?

2. The residual value of $50,000 had not been guaranteed at all?

P21.12 **(LO 2, 4) (Lessee-Lessor Entries, Balance Sheet Presentation, Finance and Sales-Type Lease)** Winston Industries and Ewing Inc. enter into an agreement that requires Ewing Inc. to build three diesel-electric engines to Winston's specifications. Upon completion of the engines, Winston has agreed to lease them for a period of 10 years and to assume all costs and risks of ownership. The lease is non-cancelable, becomes effective on January 1, 2020, and requires annual rental payments of $384,532 each January 1, starting January 1, 2020.

Winston's incremental borrowing rate is 8%. The implicit interest rate used by Ewing and known to Winston is 6%. The total cost of building the three engines is $2,600,000. The economic life of the engines is estimated to be 10 years, with residual value set at zero. Winston depreciates similar equipment on a straight-line basis. At the end of the lease, Winston assumes title to the engines. Collectibility of the lease payments is probable.

Instructions

a. Discuss the nature of this lease transaction from the viewpoints of both lessee and lessor.

b. Prepare the journal entry or entries to record the transaction on January 1, 2020, on the books of Winston (the lessee).

c. Prepare the journal entry or entries to record the transaction on January 1, 2020, on the books of Ewing (the lessor).

d. Prepare the journal entries for both the lessee and lessor to record the first rental payment on January 1, 2020.

e. Prepare the journal entries for both the lessee and lessor to record any entries needed in connection with the lease at December 31, 2020. (Prepare a lease amortization schedule for 2 years.)

f. Show the items and amounts that would be reported on the balance sheet (not notes) at December 31, 2020, for both the lessee and the lessor.

g. Assume that Winston incurs legal fees related to the execution of the lease of $30,000. In addition, assume Winston receives a lease incentive from Ewing of $50,000 to enter the lease. How will this affect your answer to part b?

P21.13 **(LO 2, 4)** Excel **(Balance Sheet and Income Statement Disclosure—Lessee)** The following facts pertain to a non-cancelable lease agreement between Alschuler Leasing Company and McKee Electronics, a lessee, for a computer system.

Commencement date	October 1, 2020
Lease term	6 years
Economic life of leased equipment	6 years
Fair value of asset at October 1, 2020	$313,043
Book value of asset at October 1, 2020	$280,000
Residual value at end of lease term	-0-
Lessor's implicit rate	8%
Lessee's incremental borrowing rate	8%
Annual lease payment due at the beginning of each year, beginning with October 1, 2020	$62,700

The collectibility of the lease payments is probable by the lessor. The asset will revert to the lessor at the end of the lease term. The straight-line depreciation method is used for all equipment.

The following amortization schedule has been prepared correctly for use by both the lessor and the lessee in accounting for this lease. The lease is to be accounted for properly as a finance lease by the lessee and as a sales-type lease by the lessor.

Date	Lease Payment/ Receipt	Interest (8%) on Unpaid Liability/ Receivable	Reduction of Lease Liability/Receivable	Balance of Lease Liability/Receivable
10/01/20				$313,043
10/01/20	$ 62,700		$ 62,700	250,343
10/01/21	62,700	$20,027	42,673	207,670
10/01/22	62,700	16,614	46,086	161,584
10/01/23	62,700	12,927	49,773	111,811
10/01/24	62,700	8,945	53,755	58,056
10/01/25	62,700	4,644	58,056	-0-
	$376,200	$63,157	$313,043	

Instructions

a. Assuming the lessee's accounting period ends on September 30, answer the following questions with respect to this lease agreement.

1. What items and amounts will appear on the lessee's income statement for the year ending September 30, 2021?
2. What items and amounts will appear on the lessee's balance sheet at September 30, 2021?
3. What items and amounts will appear on the lessee's income statement for the year ending September 30, 2022?
4. What items and amounts will appear on the lessee's balance sheet at September 30, 2022?

b. Assuming the lessee's accounting period ends on December 31, answer the following questions with respect to this lease agreement.

1. What items and amounts will appear on the lessee's income statement for the year ending December 31, 2020?
2. What items and amounts will appear on the lessee's balance sheet at December 31, 2020?
3. What items and amounts will appear on the lessee's income statement for the year ending December 31, 2021?
4. What items and amounts will appear on the lessee's balance sheet at December 31, 2021?

P21.14 **(LO 2, 4)** Excel **(Balance Sheet and Income Statement Disclosure—Lessor)** Assume the same information as in P21.13.

Instructions

a. Assuming the lessor's accounting period ends on September 30, answer the following questions with respect to this lease agreement.

1. What items and amounts will appear on the lessor's income statement for the year ending September 30, 2021?
2. What items and amounts will appear on the lessor's balance sheet at September 30, 2021?
3. What items and amounts will appear on the lessor's income statement for the year ending September 30, 2022?
4. What items and amounts will appear on the lessor's balance sheet at September 30, 2022?

b. Assuming the lessor's accounting period ends on December 31, answer the following questions with respect to this lease agreement.

1. What items and amounts will appear on the lessor's income statement for the year ending December 31, 2020?
2. What items and amounts will appear on the lessor's balance sheet at December 31, 2020?
3. What items and amounts will appear on the lessor's income statement for the year ending December 31, 2021?
4. What items and amounts will appear on the lessor's balance sheet at December 31, 2021?

P21.15 **(LO 2, 3)** **(Finance and Operating Lease)** Anthony Incorporated leases a piece of machinery to Irving Company on January 1, 2020, under the following terms.

1. The lease is to be for 4 years with rental payments of $12,471 to be made at the beginning of each year.
2. The machinery' has a fair value of $67,000, a book value of $50,000, and an economic life of 10 years.
3. At the end of the lease term, both parties expect the machinery to have a residual value of $25,000. To protect against a large loss, Anthony requests Irving to guarantee $17,500 of the residual value, which Irving agrees to do.
4. The lease does not transfer ownership at the end of the lease term, does not have any bargain purchase options, and the asset is not of a specialized nature.
5. The implicit rate is 5%, which is known by Irving.
6. Collectibility of the payments is probable.

Instructions

a. Evaluate the criteria for classification of the lease, and describe the nature of the lease.

b. Prepare the journal entries for Irving for the year 2020.

c. Prepare the journal entries for Anthony for the year 2020.

d. Suppose Irving did not guarantee any amount of the expected residual value. How would your answers to parts a–c change?

P21.16 (LO 3) (Operating Lease) Lewis Corporation entered into a lease agreement on January 1, 2020, to provide Dawkins Company with a piece of machinery. The terms of the lease agreement were as follows.

1. The lease is to be for 3 years with rental payments of $10,521 to be made at the beginning of each year.
2. The machinery has a fair value of $55,000, a book value of $40,000, and an economic life of 8 years.
3. At the end of the lease term, both parties expect the machinery to have a residual value of $30,000, none of which is guaranteed.
4. The lease does not transfer ownership at the end of the lease term, does not have a bargain purchase option, and the asset is not of a specialized nature.
5. The implicit rate is 6%, which is known by Dawkins.
6. Collectibility of the payments is probable.

Instructions

a. Evaluate the criteria for classification of the lease, and describe the nature of the lease.

b. Prepare the amortization schedules Dawkins will use over the lease term.

c. Prepare the 2020 journal entries for Dawkins.

d. Prepare the 2020 journal entries for Lewis.

e. Suppose the lease were only for one year instead of 3 years, with just one lease payment at the beginning of the lease term. Prepare any journal entries Dawkins would need, assuming it elects to use the short-term lease option.

P21.17 (LO 3) Groupwork (Lessee-Lessor Entries, Operating Lease with an Unguaranteed Residual Value) Cleveland Inc. leased a new crane to Abriendo Construction under a 5-year, non-cancelable contract starting January 1, 2020. Terms of the lease require payments of $48,555 each January 1, starting January 1, 2020. The crane has an estimated life of 7 years, a fair value of $240,000, and a cost to Cleveland of $240,000. The estimated fair value of the crane is expected to be $45,000 (unguaranteed) at the end of the lease term. No bargain purchase or renewal options are included in the contract, and it is not a specialized asset. Both Cleveland and Abriendo adjust and close books annually at December 31. Collectibility of the lease payments is probable. Abriendo's incremental borrowing rate is 8%, and Cleveland's implicit interest rate of 8% is known to Abriendo.

Instructions

a. Identify the type of lease involved and give reasons for your classification. Discuss the accounting treatment that should be applied by both the lessee and the lessor.

b. Prepare all the entries related to the lease contract and leased asset for the year 2020 for the lessee and lessor, assuming Abriendo uses straight-line amortization for all similar leased assets, and Cleveland depreciates the asset on a straight-line basis with a salvage value of $15,000.

c. Discuss what should be presented in the balance sheet, the income statement, and the related notes of both the lessee and the lessor at December 31, 2020.

Concepts for Analysis

CA21.1 (LO 2, 4) Writing (Lessee Accounting and Reporting) On January 1, 2020, Evans Company entered into a non-cancelable lease for a machine to be used in its manufacturing operations. The lease transfers control of the machine to Evans by the end of the lease term. The term of the lease is 8 years, which equals the useful life of the asset. The lease payment made by Evans on January 1, 2020, was one of eight equal annual payments. At the commencement of the lease, the criteria established for classification as a finance lease by the lessee were met.

Instructions

a. What is the theoretical basis for the accounting standard that requires certain long-term leases to be capitalized by the lessee? Do not discuss the specific criteria for classifying a specific lease as a finance lease.

b. How should Evans account for this lease at its commencement?

c. What expenses directly related to lease liability and right-of-use asset will Evans incur during the first year of the lease, and how will these expenses be determined?

d. How should Evans report the lease transaction on its December 31, 2020, balance sheet?

CA21.2 **(LO 2, 4) (Lessor and Lessee Accounting and Disclosure)** Sylvan Inc. entered into a non-cancelable lease arrangement with Breton Leasing Corporation for a certain machine. Breton's primary business is leasing. Sylvan will lease the machine for a period of 3 years, which is 50% of the machine's economic life. Breton will take possession of the machine at the end of the initial 3-year lease and lease it to another, smaller company that does not need the most current version of the machine. Sylvan does not guarantee any residual value for the machine and will not purchase the machine at the end of the lease term. Sylvan's incremental borrowing rate is 10%, and the implicit rate in the lease is 9%. Sylvan has no way of knowing the implicit rate used by Breton. Using either rate, the present value of the lease payments is between 90% and 100% of the fair value of the machine at the date of the lease agreement. Breton is reasonably certain that Sylvan will pay all lease payments.

Instructions

a. With respect to Sylvan (the lessee), answer the following.

1. What type of lease has been entered into? Explain the reason for your answer.
2. How should Sylvan compute the appropriate amount to be recorded for the lease or asset acquired?
3. What accounts will be created or affected by this transaction, and how will the lease or asset and other costs related to the transaction be recorded in earnings?
4. What disclosures must Sylvan make regarding this leased asset?

b. With respect to Breton (the lessor), answer the following.

1. What type of leasing arrangement has been entered into? Explain the reason for your answer.
2. How should this lease be recorded by Breton, and how are the appropriate amounts determined?
3. How should Breton determine the appropriate amount of revenue to be recognized from each lease payment?
4. What disclosures must Breton make regarding this lease?

CA21.3 **(LO 2) (Lessee Capitalization Tests)** On January 1, Santiago Company, a lessee, entered into three non-cancelable leases for new equipment, Lease L, Lease M, and Lease N. None of the three leases transfers ownership of the equipment to Santiago at the end of the lease term. For each of the three leases, the present value at the beginning of the lease term of the lease payments is 75% of the fair value of the equipment. The following information is specific to each lease.

1. Lease L does not contain a bargain purchase option. The lease term is equal to 80% of the estimated economic life of the equipment.
2. Lease M contains a bargain purchase option. The lease term is equal to 50% of the estimated economic life of the equipment.
3. Lease N does not contain a bargain purchase option. The lease term is equal to 50% of the estimated economic life of the equipment.

Instructions

a. How should Santiago classify each of the three leases above, and why? Discuss the rationale for your answer.

b. What amount, if any, should Santiago record as a liability at commencement of the lease for each of the three leases above?

c. Assuming that the lease payments are made on a straight-line basis, how should Santiago record each lease payment for each of the three leases above?

CA21.4 **(LO 2, 3) (Comparison of Different Types of Accounting by Lessee and Lessor)**

Part 1: Finance leases and operating leases are the two classifications of leases described in FASB pronouncements from the standpoint of the **lessee**.

Instructions

a. Describe how a finance lease would be accounted for by the lessee both at the commencement of the lease and during the first year of the lease, assuming the lease transfers ownership of the property to the lessee by the end of the lease.

b. Describe how an operating lease would be accounted for by the lessee both at the commencement of the lease and during the first year of the lease, assuming equal monthly payments are made by the lessee at the beginning of each month of the lease.

Do **not** discuss the criteria for distinguishing between finance leases and operating leases.

Part 2: Sales-type leases and operating leases are two of the classifications of leases described in FASB pronouncements from the standpoint of the **lessor**.

Instructions

Compare and contrast a sales-type lease with an operating lease as follows.

a. Lease receivable.

b. Recognition of interest revenue.

c. Gross profit.

Do **not** discuss the criteria for distinguishing between the leases described above and operating leases.

CA21.5 **(LO 4)** Ethics **(Lease Capitalization, Bargain Purchase Option)** Baden Corporation entered into a lease agreement for 100 photocopy machines for its corporate headquarters. The lease agreement qualifies as an operating lease except there is a bargain purchase option. After the 5-year lease term, the corporation can purchase each copier for $1,000, when the anticipated fair value is $2,500.

Jerry Suffolk, the financial vice president, thinks the financial statements must recognize the lease agreement as a finance lease because of the bargain purchase option. The controller, Diane Buchanan, disagrees: "Although I don't know much about the copiers themselves, there is a way to avoid recording the lease liability." She argues that the corporation might claim that copier technology advances rapidly and that by the end of the lease term, the machines will most likely not be worth the $1,000 bargain price.

Instructions

a. What ethical issue is at stake?

b. Should the controller's argument be accepted if she does not really know much about copier technology? Would it make a difference if the controller were knowledgeable about the rate of change in copier technology?

c. What should Suffolk do?

CA21.6 **(LO 2, 4)** Writing **(Short-Term Lease vs. Finance Lease)** You are auditing the December 31, 2020, financial statements of Hockney, Inc., manufacturer of novelties and party favors. During your inspection of the company garage, you discovered that a used automobile not listed in the equipment subsidiary ledger is parked there. You ask Stacy Reeder, plant manager, about the vehicle, and she tells you that the company did not list the automobile because the company was only leasing it and elected to use the short-term lease accounting option for the lease. The lease agreement was entered into on January 1, 2020, with Crown New and Used Cars.

You decide to review the lease agreement to ensure that the lease should be afforded short-term lease treatment, and you discover the following lease terms.

1. Non-cancelable term of 2 years.
2. Rental of $3,240 per year (at the end of each year). (The present value at 8% per year is $5,778.)
3. Expected residual value after 2 years is $500. (The present value at 8% per year is $429.) Hockney guarantees the residual value of $500.
4. Estimated economic life of the automobile is 2.5 years.
5. Hockney's incremental borrowing rate is 8% per year.

Instructions

You are a senior auditor writing a memo to your supervisor, the audit partner in charge of this audit, to discuss the above situation. Be sure to include (a) why you inspected the lease agreement, (b) what you determined about the lease, and (c) how you advised your client to account for this lease. Explain every journal entry that you believe is necessary to record this lease properly on the client's books. (It is also necessary to include the fact that you communicated this information to your client.)

*CA21.7 **(LO 5)** **(Sale-Leaseback)** On January 1, 2020, Perriman Company transferred equipment for cash and leased it back. As seller-lessee, Perriman retained the right to substantially all of the remaining use of the equipment. The term of the lease is 8 years.

Instructions

a. What is the major issue related to sale-leaseback accounting?

b. 1. How should Perriman account for the sale portion of the sale-leaseback transaction at January 1, 2020?

2. How should Perriman account for the leaseback portion of the sale-leaseback transaction at January 1, 2020?

Using Your Judgment

Note that P&G, Delta Air Lines, Southwest Airlines, and Wal-Mart have not yet adopted the new lease accounting rules. As a result, in the financial statements referred to below, finance leases are referred to as "capital," and assets and liabilities related to operating leases are not recognized on the balance sheet.

Financial Reporting Problem

The Procter & Gamble Company (P&G)

The financial statements of **P&G** are presented in Appendix B. The company's complete annual report, including the notes to the financial statements, is available online.

Instructions

Refer to P&G's financial statements, accompanying notes, and management's discussion and analysis to answer the following questions.

a. What types of leases are used by P&G?

b. What amount of capital leases was reported by P&G in total and for less than one year?

c. What minimum annual rental commitments under all non-cancelable leases at June 30, 2017, did P&G disclose?

Comparative Analysis Case

Delta Air Lines and Southwest Airlines

The financial statements and notes to the financial statements for **Delta Air Lines** and **Southwest Airlines** can be found online.

Instructions

Use information found in the companies' financial reports to answer the following questions.

a. What types of leases are used by Southwest and Delta and on what assets are these leases primarily used?

b. How long-term are some of Southwest's leases? What are some of the characteristics or provisions of Southwest's (as lessee) leases?

c. What did Southwest report in 2017 as its future minimum annual rental commitments under non-cancelable leases?

d. At year-end 2017, what was the present value of the minimum rental payments under Southwest's capital leases? How much imputed interest was deducted from the future minimum annual rental commitments to arrive at the present value?

e. What were the amounts and details reported by Southwest for rental expense in 2017, 2016, and 2015?

f. How does Delta's use of leases compare with Southwest's?

Financial Statement Analysis Case

Wal-Mart Stores, Inc.

The following are the financial statement disclosures from the January 31, 2018, annual report of **Wal-Mart Stores, Inc.**

Wal-Mart Stores, Inc.
(dollar amounts in millions)

Description and amount of lease obligations

	Jan. 31, 2018	Jan. 31, 2017
Current Liabilities		
Capital lease and financing obligations due within one year	$ 667	$ 565
Noncurrent Liabilities		
Long-term capital lease and financing obligations	$6,780	$6,003

General description and amount of lease rental expense

Note 11: Commitments

The Company has long-term leases for stores and equipment. Rentals (including amounts applicable to taxes, insurance, maintenance, other operating expenses and contingent rentals) under operating leases and other short-term rental arrangements were $2.9 billion, $2.6 billion and $2.5 billion in fiscal 2018, 2017 and 2016, respectively.

Aggregate minimum annual rentals at January 31, 2018, under non-cancelable leases are as follows (dollar amounts in millions):

Description and amounts of leased assets

Nature, timing, and amounts of cash outflows

Fiscal Year	Operating Leases	Capital Lease and Financial Obligations
2019	1,933	1,039
2020	1,718	987
2021	1,532	942
2022	1,381	843
2023	1,158	696
Thereafter	7,644	5,423
Total minimum rentals	15,366	9,930
Less estimated executory costs		27
Net minimum lease payments		9,903
Noncash gain on future termination of financing obligations		1,111
Less imputed interest		−3,567
Present value of minimum lease payments		$7,447

Certain of the Company's leases provide for the payment of contingent rentals based on a percentage of sales. Such contingent rentals were not material for fiscal 2018, 2017 and 2016. Substantially all of the Company's store leases have renewal options, some of which may trigger an escalation in rentals.

Instructions

Answer the following questions related to these disclosures.

a. What is the total obligation under capital leases and financial obligations at January 31, 2018, for Wal-Mart?

b. What is the total rental expense reported for leasing activity for the year ended January 31, 2018, for Wal-Mart?

c. What is the present value of minimum lease payments related to capital leases and financial obligations at January 31, 2018?

Accounting, Analysis, and Principles

Salaur Company, a risky start-up, is evaluating a lease arrangement being offered by TSP Company for use of a standard computer system. The lease is non-cancelable, and in no case does Salaur receive title to the computers during or at the end of the lease term. TSP will lease the returned computers to other customers. The lease starts on January 1, 2020, with the first rental payment due on January 1, 2020. Additional information related to the lease and the underlying leased asset is as follows.

Yearly rental	$3,057.25
Lease term	3 years
Estimated economic life	5 years
Purchase option	$3,000 at end of 3 years, which approximates fair value
Renewal option	1 year at $1,500; no penalty for nonrenewal; standard renewal clause
Fair value at commencement	$10,000
Cost of asset to lessor	$8,000
Residual value:	
Guaranteed	-0-
Unguaranteed	$3,000
Lessor's implicit rate (known by the lessee)	12%
Estimated fair value at end of lease	$3,000

Accounting

a. Analyze the lease classification tests for this lease for Salaur. Prepare the journal entries for Salaur for 2020.

b. Repeat the requirements in part a, assuming Salaur has the option to purchase the system at the end of the lease for $100.

Analysis

Briefly discuss the impact of the accounting for this lease as a finance or operating lease for two common ratios: return on assets and debt to total assets.

Principles

What fundamental quality of useful information is being addressed when a company like Salaur capitalizes all leases with terms of one year or longer?

Bridge to the Profession

FASB Codification References

[1] FASB ASC 842 (Glossary). [Predecessor literature: None.]
[2] FASB ASC 842-10-25-2. [Predecessor literature: None.]
[3] FASB ASU 2016-2 [BC 71(c).] [Predecessor literature: None.]
[4] FASB ASU 2016-2 (BC 194, 197, 218). [Predecessor literature: None.]
[5] FASB ASC 842 (Glossary). [Predecessor literature: None.]
[6] FASB ASC 842-20-30-3. [Predecessor literature: None.]
[7] FASB ASC 842 (Glossary). [Predecessor literature: None.]
[8] FASB ASC 842-10-30-5(f). [Predecessor literature: None.]
[9] FASB ASC 842-20-40-2. [Predecessor literature: None.]
[10] FASB ASU 2016-2 (BC 93). [Predecessor literature: None.]
[11] FASB ASC 842-10-25-3(a). [Predecessor literature: None.]
[12] FASB ASC 842-30-25-3(b). [Predecessor literature: None.]
[13] FASB ASU 2016-2 (BC 61). [Predecessor literature: None.]
[14] FASB ASC 842-10-55-34 to 36. [Predecessor literature: None.]
[15] FASB ASC 842-10-15-30. [Predecessor literature: None.]
[16] FASB ASC 842 (Glossary). [Predecessor literature: None.]
[17] FASB ASC 842-30-25-1(c), 8, 10. [Predecessor literature: None.]
[18] FASB ASC 842-20-25-2. [Predecessor literature: None.]
[19] FASB ASC 842-20-50 and 842-30-50. [Predecessor literature: None.]
[20] FASB ASC 842-40-25, 842-40-30, and 842-40-50. [Predecessor literature: None.]
[21] FASB ASC 842-10-25-3; ASU 2016 2 (BC95 96). [Predecessor literature: None.]
[22] FASB ASC 842-30-25-9. [Predecessor literature: None.]
[23] FASB ASC 842-30-25-8. [Predecessor literature: None.]

Codification Exercises

If your school has a subscription to the FASB Codification, log in and prepare responses to the following. Provide Codification references for your responses.

CE21.1 Access the glossary ("Master Glossary") to answer the following.

a. What is the "commencement date"?

b. What is the definition of "incremental borrowing rate"?

c. What is an unguaranteed residual asset?

d. What are variable lease payments?

CE21.2 What comprises lease payments? What is excluded?

CE21.3 What information should a lessee disclose about its finance leases in its financial statements and footnotes?

CE21.4 How should a lessor measure its net investment in either a sales-type lease or a direct financing lease?

Codification Research Case

Daniel Hardware Co. is considering alternative financing arrangements for equipment used in its warehouses. Besides purchasing the equipment outright, Daniel is also considering a lease. Accounting for the outright purchase is fairly straightforward, but because Daniel has not used equipment leases in the past, the accounting staff is less informed about the specific accounting rules for leases. The staff is aware of some general lease rules related to "right-of-use," but they are unsure how the accounting rules apply to their situation. Daniel has asked you to conduct some research on these items related to lease capitalization criteria.

Instructions

If your school has a subscription to the FASB Codification, log in and prepare responses to the following. Provide Codification references for your responses.

a. What is included is the measurement of (1) the lease liability and (2) the right-of-use asset?

b. Besides the non-cancelable term of the lease, what other considerations determine the "lease term"?

c. When should a lessee account for a lease modification? What procedures are followed?

Additional Professional Resources

Go to WileyPLUS for other career-readiness resources, such as career coaching, internship opportunities, and CPAexcel prep.

IFRS Insights

LEARNING OBJECTIVE 8

Compare the accounting for leases under GAAP and IFRS.

Leasing is a global business. Lessors and lessees enter into arrangements with one another without regard to national boundaries. Although GAAP and IFRS for leasing are not identical, both the FASB and the IASB decided that prior lease accounting did not provide the most useful, transparent, and complete information about leasing transactions. In response, the FASB and IASB worked together on a lease accounting project. The IASB issued *IFRS 16, Leases* in January 2016. Many of the requirements in the new FASB standard are the same as those in *IFRS 16*. The main differences between GAAP and IFRS under the new rules are in relation to the lessee accounting model. Specifically, IFRS does not make a distinction between finance leases and operating leases in the financial statements. As a result, lessees account for all leases using the finance lease method.

Relevant Facts

Following are the key similarities and differences between GAAP and IFRS related to the accounting for leases.

Similarities

- Both GAAP and IFRS share the same objective of recording leases by lessees and lessors according to their economic substance—that is, according to the definitions of assets and liabilities.
- Much of the terminology for lease accounting in IFRS and GAAP is the same.
- Both GAAP and IFRS require lessees to recognize a right-of-use asset and related lease liability for leases with terms longer than one year.
- Under both IFRS and GAAP, lessors use the same general criteria (consistent with the recent standard on revenue) to determine if there is transfer of control of the underlying asset and if lessors classify leases as sales-type or operating.
- GAAP and IFRS have similar qualitative and quantitative disclosure requirements for lessees.

Differences

- There is no classification test for lessees under *IFRS 16*. Thus, lessees account for all leases using the finance lease method—that is, leases classified as operating leases under GAAP will be accounted for differently compared to IFRS (see example in About the Numbers section below).
- IFRS allows alternative measurement bases for the right-of-use asset (e.g., the revaluation model, in accordance with *IAS 16, Property, Plant and Equipment*).
- In addition to the short-term lease exception, IFRS has an additional lessee recognition and measurement exemption for leases of assets of low value (e.g., personal computers, small office furniture).

- IFRS does not include any explicit guidance on collectibility of the lease payments by lessors and amounts necessary to satisfy a residual value guarantee.
- IFRS does not distinguish between sales-type and direct financing leases for lessors. Therefore, *IFRS 16* permits recognition of selling profit on direct financing leases at lease commencement.
- IFRS applies to leases of any asset, whether tangible plant, property, or intangible assets. GAAP applies only to tangible plant property.
- IFRS uses the same model for leases for both lessees and lessors, whereas GAAP uses a different model for lessees and lessors.

About the Numbers

A **lease** is defined as "a contract, or part of a contract, that conveys the right to control the use of an identified property, plant or equipment (an identified asset) for a period of time in exchange for consideration." A lease therefore conveys use of an asset from one party (the lessor) to another (the lessee) without transferring ownership. Accounting for lease transactions is controversial as the following example illustrates.

If **Air France** borrows $47 million on a 10-year note from **Bank of America** to purchase a Boeing 737 jet plane, Air France should report an asset and related liability at that amount on its statement of financial position. Similarly, if Air France purchases the 737 for $47 million directly from Boeing through an installment purchase over 10 years, it should report an asset and related liability (i.e., it should "capitalize" the installment transaction).

However, what if Air France **leases** the Boeing 737 for 10 years from **International Lease Finance Corp. (ILFC)**—the world's largest lessor of airplanes—through a non-cancelable lease transaction with payments of the same amount as the installment purchase transaction? In that case, opinion differs over how to report this transaction. Views on the appropriate accounting range from no capitalization to capitalization of all long-term leases.

The IASB now requires companies to capitalize all leases. The only exceptions to this guideline are that leases covering a term of less than one year or leases under $5,000 do not have to be capitalized. The IASB indicates that the right to use property under the terms of the lease is an asset, and the lessee's obligation to make payments under the lease is a liability. As a result, Air France records the right-of-use of the airplane as an asset on its statement of financial position. It also records a liability for its obligation to make payments under the lease.

Lessee Accounting

Lessees use the finance lease method to account for all non-cancelable leases, by recording a right-of-use asset and related lease liability. The lessee recognizes interest expense on the lease liability over the life of the lease using the effective-interest method and records depreciation expense on the right-of-use asset. This accounting is applied whether the lease arrangement is effectively a purchase of the underlying asset (Air France's lease with ILFC above) or the lessee **obtains control of only the use of the underlying asset**, but not the underlying asset itself. For example, a lease may convey use of one floor of an office building for five years. At the end of the lease, the lessee vacates the floor and the lessor can then lease the floor to another tenant. In this situation, the lease conveys right-of-use but not ownership. However, lessee accounting for leases that transfer ownership or transfer control is the same.

Lessee Accounting at Commencement

At commencement of the lease, lessees record a right-of-use asset and lease liability. The measurement of the right-of-use asset depends on the lease liability. The lease liability is computed as the present value of the lease payments. An asset for the right-of-use of the underlying asset (i.e., the right-of-use asset) is equal to the lease liability, adjusted for prepaid rent (less lease incentives received from the lessor), and any initial direct costs.[27]

Subsequent Lessee Accounting

Throughout the term of the lease, a lessee, like Air France, uses the **effective-interest method** to allocate each lease payment between principal and interest on the lease liability. This method produces a periodic interest expense equal to a constant percentage of the carrying value of the lease obligation. When applying the effective-interest method to finance leases, Air France must use the same discount rate (the implicit rate) that determines the present value of the lease payments.

[27]Determination of elements of the lease liability (lease payment, discounts. rate) and the right-of-use asset is the same under IFRS and GAAP.

Depreciation of the right-of-use asset is accounted for similar to other non-financial assets. That is, the lessee should depreciate the right-of-use asset using an approach that reflects the consumption of the economic benefits of the leased asset. Generally, companies use the straight-line method for recording the consumption of a right-of-use asset. One troublesome aspect of accounting for the depreciation of the right-of-use asset relates to the depreciable life. If the lease agreement transfers ownership of the asset to Air France or if the lease contains a bargain purchase option at the end of the lease, Air France depreciates the aircraft consistent with its normal depreciation policy for other aircraft, **using the economic life of the asset**. On the other hand, if the lease does not transfer ownership and does not contain a bargain purchase option at the end of the lease, then Air France depreciates it over the **term of the lease**. In this case, the aircraft reverts to ILFC after a certain period of time.

Recognizing the interest on the lease liability coupled with the depreciation of the right-of-use asset will **generally result in higher total expense in the earlier years and lower total expense in the later years of the lease**.

Lease Accounting Example

To illustrate lessee accounting for a lease that conveys right-of-use but not ownership, assume that Hathaway Disposal Inc. (lessor) and **Marks and Spencer plc (M&S)** (the lessee) sign a lease agreement dated January 1, 2020. The lease agreement specifies that Hathaway will grant right-of-use of one of its standard cardboard compactors for use at one of M&S's stores. Information relevant to the lease is as follows.

- The term of the lease is three years. The lease agreement is non-cancelable, requiring equal rental payments of $17,620.08 at the beginning of each year of the lease (annuity-due basis).
- The compactor has a cost and fair value at commencement of the lease of $60,000, an estimated economic life of seven years, and a residual value of $12,000 (unguaranteed).
- The lease contains no renewal options, and the compactor reverts to Hathaway at the termination of the lease.
- The implicit rate of the lessor is not known by M&S. M&S's incremental borrowing rate is 6 percent.

Under this lease arrangement, M&S has right of use of the compactor for three years and will return the asset to Hathaway at the end of the lease; Hathaway retains ownership of the compactor. The present value of the lease payments for M&S in this situation is $49,924.56 ($17,620.08 × 2.83339). M&S makes the following entries to record the lease and the first payment.

January 1, 2020		
Right-of-Use Asset	49,924.56	
Lease Liability		49,924.56
(To record the right-of-use asset and related liability at commencement of the lease)		
Lease Liability	17,620.08	
Cash		17,620.08
(To record first lease payment)		

M&S prepares a lease amortization schedule to show interest expense and related amortization of the lease liability over the three-year period, as shown in **Illustration IFRS21.1**.

ILLUSTRATION IFRS21.1

Lease Amortization Schedule for Lessee

Marks and Spencer plc
Lease Amortization Schedule
Annuity-Due Basis

Date	Lease Payment (a)	Interest (6%) on Liability (b)	Reduction of Lease Liability (c)	Lease Liability (d)
1/1/20				$49,924.56
1/1/20	$17,620.08	$ -0-	$17,620.08	32,304.48
1/1/21	17,620.08	1,938.27	15,681.81	16,622.67
1/1/22	17,620.08	997.41*	16,622.67	0.00
	$52,860.24	$2,935.68	$49,924.56	

(a) Lease payment as required by lease.
(b) 6 percent of the preceding balance of (d) except for 1/1/20; since this is an annuity due, no time has elapsed at the date of the first payment and therefore no interest has accrued.
(c) (a) minus (b).
(d) Preceding balance minus (c).

*Rounded by $0.05.

The journal entries to be prepared by M&S throughout the lease to record lease expense and amortization of the lease liability and depreciation of the right-of-use asset are as follows, using the amounts presented in Illustration IFRS21.2.

ILLUSTRATION IFRS21.2
Journal Entries by Lessee

Marks and Spencer plc (Lessee)		
Recognize lease expense, record amortization (December 31, 2020):		
Interest Expense	1,938.27	
Lease Liability		1,938.27
Depreciation Expense	16,641.52	
Accumulated Depreciation (Right-of-Use Asset) ($49,924.56 ÷ 3)		16,641.52
Record second lease payment (January 1, 2021):		
Lease Liability ($1,938.27 + $15,681.81)	17,620.08	
Cash		17,620.08
Recognize lease expense, record amortization (December 31, 2021):		
Interest Expense	997.41	
Lease Liability		997.41
Depreciation Expense	16,641.52	
Accumulated Depreciation (Right-of-Use Asset) ($49,924.56 ÷ 3)		16,641.52
Record third lease payment (January 1, 2022):		
Lease Liability ($997.41 + $16,622.67)	17,620.08	
Cash		17,620.08
Record amortization (December 31, 2022):		
Depreciation Expense	16,641.52	
Accumulated Depreciation (Right-of-Use Asset) ($49,924.56 ÷ 3)		16,641.52

Following these entries, as indicated in Illustration IFRS21.1, the lease liability and the right-of-use asset have zero balances.[28] M&S returns the asset to Hathaway.

On the Horizon

Lease accounting is one of the areas identified in the IASB/FASB Memorandum of Understanding. The Boards have developed rules based on "right-of-use" (ROU) which require that all leases with terms longer than one year be recorded on the statement of financial position/balance sheet. The IASB has decided on a single approach for lessee accounting. Under the IASB approach, a lessee accounts for all leases as finance leases, recognizing depreciation of the ROU asset separately from interest on the lease liability. The FASB reached a different conclusion on the expense recognition for operating-type leases. Under the FASB model, the income effects will reflect a straight-line expense pattern, reported as a single total lease expense. The Boards are generally converged with respect to lessor accounting.

IFRS Self-Test Questions

1. Which of the following is **false** with respect to lease accounting under IFRS?

   a. IFRS require lessees to recognize a right-of-use asset and related lease liability for leases with terms longer than one year.

   b. IFRS does not include any explicit guidance on collectibility of the lease payments by lessors and amounts necessary to satisfy a residual value guarantee.

   c. IFRS does not permit recognition of selling profit on direct financing leases at lease commencement.

   d. IFRS uses essentially the same lessor accounting model as GAAP for leases classified as sales-type or operating.

2. Under IFRS:

   a. lessees and lessors recognize right-of-use assets.

   b. lessees always use the operating method.

[28]Under GAAP, this lease is classified as an operating lease and lease expense is be recognized on a straight-line basis. Lessor accounting for an operating lease under IFRS and GAAP is essentially the same; that is, the lessor records Lease Revenue in each year of the lease on a straight-line basis.

c. lessees always recognize a right-of-use asset and lease liability for leases with terms less than one year.

d. lessors do not distinguish between sales-type and direct financing leases.

3. All of the following are similarities with respect to the accounting for leases, under IFRS and GAAP, **except**:

a. lessees recognize a right-of-use asset and related lease liability for leases with terms longer than one year.

b. lessees use the same general lease classification criteria to determine if lessees classify leases as finance or operating.

c. lessors under IFRS and GAAP use the same model to account for sales-type leases.

d. GAAP and IFRS have similar qualitative and quantitative disclosure requirements for lessees and lessors.

4. Under IFRS:

a. lessees may use alternative measurement bases (e.g., revaluation accounting) for the right-of-use asset.

b. different measurement bases may be used for the right-of-use asset but only for leases with terms less than one year.

c. the same guidance on collectibility of the lease payments is used by lessors as in GAAP.

d. lessors are required to defer gross profit on direct financing leases.

5. All of the following are differences with respect to the accounting for leases, under IFRS and GAAP, **except**:

a. IFRS has an additional lessee recognition and measurement exemption for leases of assets of low value (GAAP does not).

b. IFRS allows alternative measurement bases for the right-of-use asset (e.g., the revaluation model).

c. under IFRS, lessees use the same tests to determine if a lease should be classified as finance or operating.

d. IFRS permits recognition of selling profit on direct financing leases at lease commencement.

IFRS Concepts and Application

IFRS21.1 Where can authoritative IFRS related to the accounting for leases be found?

IFRS21.2 Briefly describe some of the similarities and differences between GAAP and IFRS with respect to the accounting for leases.

IFRS21.3 Outline the accounting procedures (the finance lease method) for a lease by a lessee.

IFRS21.4 Kleckner Corporation recorded a lease at $300,000 on December 31, 2019. Kleckner's incremental borrowing rate is 8%, and the implicit rate of the lessor is not known. Kleckner made the first lease payment of $48,337 on December 31, 2019. The lease requires eight annual payments. The equipment has a useful life of 8 years with no residual value. Prepare Kleckner's December 31, 2020, adjusting entries.

IFRS21.5 Use the information for Kleckner Corporation from IFRS21.4. Assume that at December 31, 2020, Kleckner made an adjusting entry to accrue interest expense of $20,133 on the lease. Prepare Kleckner's January 1, 2021, journal entry to record the second lease payment of $48,337.

IFRS21.6 Delaney Company leases an automobile with a fair value of $10,000 from Simon Motors, Inc., on the following terms.

1. Non-cancelable term of 50 months.
2. Rental of $200 per month at the beginning of each month. (The present value at 0.5% per month is $8,873.)
3. Estimated economic life of the automobile is 60 months.
4. Delaney's incremental borrowing rate is 6% a year (0.5% a month). Simon's implicit rate is unknown.

Instructions

a. What is the present value of the lease payments to determine the lease liability?

b. Record the lease on Delaney's books at the commencement date.

c. Record the first month's lease payment (at commencement of the lease).

d. Record the second month's lease payment.

e. Record the first month's depreciation on Delaney's books (assume straight-line).

IFRS21.7 On January 1, 2020, a machine was purchased for $900,000 by Young Co. The machine is expected to have an 8-year life with no residual value. It is to be depreciated on a straight-line basis. The machine was leased to St. Ledger Inc. for 3 years on January 1, 2020, with annual rent payments of $150,955 due each December 31, though St. Ledger was required to prepay the last year's rent on the commencement date. The machine is expected to have a residual value at the end of the lease term of $562,500, though this amount is unguaranteed.

Instructions

a. Record the journal entries St. Ledger would record for 2020 on this lease, assuming its incremental borrowing rate is 6% and the implicit rate is unknown.

b. Suppose the lease was only for one year (only one payment of the same amount at the commencement of the lease), with a renewal option at market rates at the end of the lease, and St. Ledger elects to use the short-term lease exception. Record the journal entries St. Ledger would record for 2020 on this lease.

c. How much should Young report as income before income tax on this operating lease for 2020?

Professional Research

IFRS21.8 Daniel Hardware Co. is considering alternative financing arrangements for equipment used in its warehouses. Besides purchasing the equipment outright, Daniel is also considering a lease. Accounting for the outright purchase is fairly straightforward, but because Daniel has not used equipment leases in the past, the accounting staff is less informed about the specific accounting rules for leases. The staff is aware of some general lease rules related to "right-of-use," but they are unsure how the accounting rules apply to their situation. Daniel has asked you to conduct some research on these items related to lease capitalization criteria.

Instructions

Access the IFRS authoritative literature at the IASB website. (Click on the IFRS tab and then register for free eIFRS access if necessary.) When you have accessed the documents, you can use the search tool in your Internet browser to respond to the following questions. (Provide paragraph citations.)

a. What is included is the measurement of (1) the lease liability and (2) the right-of-use asset?

b. Besides the non-cancelable term of the lease, what are other considerations in determining the "lease term?"

c. When should a lessee account for a lease modification? What procedures are followed?

International Financial Reporting Problem

Marks and Spencer plc (M&S)

IFRS21.9 The financial statements of M&S are presented in Appendix E. The company's complete annual report, including the notes to the financial statements, is available online.

Instructions

Refer to M&S's financial statements and the accompanying notes to answer the following questions.

a. What types of leases are used by M&S?

b. What amount of finance leases was reported by M&S in total and for less than one year?

c. What minimum annual rental commitments under all non-cancelable leases at 1 April 2017 did M&S disclose?

Answers to IFRS Self-Test Questions

1. c **2.** d **3.** b **4.** a **5.** c

CHAPTER 22

Accounting Changes and Error Analysis

LEARNING OBJECTIVES

After studying this chapter, you should be able to:

1. Discuss the types of accounting changes and the accounting for changes in accounting principles.
2. Describe the accounting for changes in estimates and changes in the reporting entity.
3. Describe the accounting for correction of errors.
4. Analyze the effects of errors.

PREVIEW OF CHAPTER 22 As the following opening story indicates, changes in accounting principles and errors in financial information have persisted in recent years and can leave investors in the dark. When these changes occur, companies must follow specific accounting and reporting requirements. In addition, to ensure comparability among companies, the FASB has standardized reporting of accounting changes, accounting estimates, error corrections, and related earnings per share information. In this chapter, we discuss these reporting standards, which help investors better understand a company's financial condition. The content and organization of the chapter are as follows.

This chapter also includes numerous conceptual and global discussions that are integral to the topics presented here.

ACCOUNTING CHANGES AND ERROR ANALYSIS

Accounting Changes
- Background
- Changes in accounting principle
- Impracticability

Other Changes
- Changes in accounting estimates
- Changes in reporting entity

Accounting Errors
- Example
- Summary

Error Analysis
- Balance sheet errors
- Income statement errors
- Balance sheet and income statement errors
- Comprehensive example
- Preparation of statements with error corrections

In the Dark

The FASB's conceptual framework describes comparability (including consistency) as one of the qualitative characteristics that contributes to the usefulness of accounting information. Unfortunately, companies are finding it difficult to maintain comparability and consistency due to the numerous changes in accounting principles mandated by the FASB. In addition, a number of companies have faced restatements due to errors in their financial statements. For example, the table below shows types and percentages of adjustments required for 300 material errors in a recent year.

Tax expense/benefit/deferral/other (*FAS 109*)	19.9%	Acquisitions, mergers, disposals, and reorganization accounting	4.8%
Revenue recognition	13.4	Consolidation and off-balance-sheet	4.8
Liabilities, payables, reserves, and accrual estimate failures	7.1	PPE, intangible or fixed asset (value/diminution)	4.3
Expense (payroll, SGA, other) recording	6.3	Depreciation, depletion, or amortization errors	4.3
Inventory, vendor, and/or cost of sales	5.8	Accounts/loans receivable, investments, and cash	4.0
Foreign, related-party, affiliated, or subsidiary	5.6	Other (e.g., leases, capitalization of expenditures, pensions, investments, derivatives, gain/loss recognition, debt/equity classifications, and cash flow statement classifications)	8.8
Deferred, stock-based, and/or executive compensation	5.6		
Debt, quasi-debt, warrants, and equity (BCF) security	5.3		

Although the percentage of companies reporting material changes or errors is small, readers of financial statements still must be careful. The reason: The amounts in the financial statements may have changed due to changing accounting principles and/or restatements. The following chart indicates the recent trends in restatements.

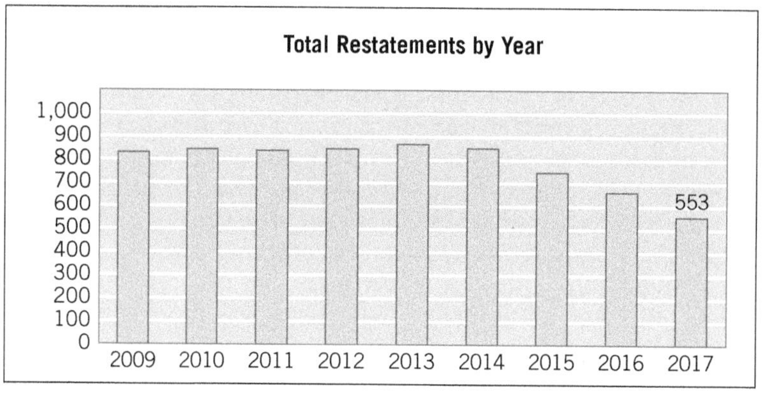

There is much good news in the chart. Restatements took another downward dip in 2017, indicating another year of incremental improvement in the quality of financial reporting. The total number of restatements declined in 2017 for the fifth consecutive year, from 873 in 2013 to 553 in 2017. However, investors can be in the dark when a company has an error that requires restatement. It may take some time for companies to sort out the source of an error, prepare corrected statements, and get auditor sign-off.

This period—referred to as a "dark period"—is the length of time between a company's discovery that it will need to restate financial data and the subsequent disclosure of the restatement's effect on earnings. One study indicated that companies with financial experts on the audit committee have shorter dark periods but only when such financial expertise relates specifically to accounting. The study suggests that both the auditor and the audit committee expertise are associated with the timely disclosure of restatement details.

These dark periods have caught the attention of policy-setters and were a topic of discussion of the Committee for Improvements in Financial Reporting (CIFR). As one member of CIFR noted, "The dark period is bad for users." As a result, the committee has proposed that for some errors, companies might not need to go through the pain of restatement, but enhanced disclosures about errors are needed.

Sources: J. Schmidt and M. Wilkins, "Bringing Darkness to Light: The Influence of Auditor Quality and Audit Committee Expertise on the Timeliness of Financial Statement Restatement Disclosures," *Auditing: A Journal of Practice and Theory* (February 2013); B. Badertscher and J. Burks, "Accounting Restatements and the Timeliness of Disclosures," *Accounting Horizons* (December 2011), pp. 609–629; and "2017 Financial Restatements: A Seventeen Year Comparison," *Audit Analytics* (June 2018).

Review and Practice

Go to the **Review and Practice** section at the end of the chapter for a targeted summary review and practice problem with solution. Multiple-choice questions with annotated solutions as well as additional exercises and practice problem with solutions are also available online.

Accounting Changes

LEARNING OBJECTIVE 1

Discuss the types of accounting changes and the accounting for changes in accounting principles.

Background

Accounting alternatives diminish the comparability of financial information between periods and between companies; they also obscure useful historical trend data. For example, if **Ford** revises its estimates for equipment useful lives, depreciation expense for the current year will not be comparable to depreciation expense reported by Ford in prior years. Similarly, if **OfficeMax** changes to FIFO inventory pricing while **Staples** uses LIFO, it will be difficult to compare these companies' reported results. A reporting framework helps preserve comparability when there is an accounting change (see **Underlying Concepts**).

The FASB has established a reporting framework, which involves three types of accounting changes. [1] (See the FASB Codification References near the end of the chapter.) The three types of accounting changes are:

1. *Change in accounting principle.* A change from one generally accepted accounting principle to another one. For example, a company may change its inventory valuation method from LIFO to average-cost.
2. *Change in accounting estimate.* A change that occurs as the result of new information or additional experience. For example, a company may change its estimate of the useful lives of depreciable assets.
3. *Change in reporting entity.* A change from reporting as one type of entity to another type of entity. As an example, a company might change the subsidiaries for which it prepares consolidated financial statements.

> **Underlying Concepts**
>
> While changes in accounting may enhance the qualitative characteristic of *usefulness*, these changes may adversely affect the enhancing characteristics of *comparability* and *consistency.*

A fourth category necessitates changes in accounting, though it is not classified as an accounting change.

4. *Errors in financial statements.* Errors result from mathematical mistakes, mistakes in applying accounting principles, or oversight or misuse of facts that existed when preparing the financial statements. For example, a company may incorrectly apply the retail inventory method for determining its final inventory value.

The FASB classifies changes in these categories because each category involves different methods of recognizing changes in the financial statements. In this chapter, we discuss these classifications. We also explain how to report each item in the accounts and how to disclose the information in comparative statements.

Changes in Accounting Principle

By definition, a change in accounting principle **involves a change from one generally accepted accounting principle to another**. For example, a company might change the basis of inventory pricing from average-cost to LIFO. Or, it might change its method of revenue recognition for long-term construction contracts from the completed-contract to the percentage-of-completion method.

Companies must carefully examine each circumstance to ensure that a change in principle has actually occurred. **Adoption of a new principle** in recognition of events that have occurred for the first time or that were previously immaterial is not an accounting change. For example, a change in accounting principle has not occurred when a company adopts an inventory method (e.g., FIFO) for **newly** acquired items of inventory, even if FIFO differs from that used for **previously recorded** inventory. Another example is certain marketing expenditures that were previously immaterial and expensed in the period incurred. It would not be considered a change in accounting principle if they become material and so may be acceptably deferred and amortized.

Finally, what if a company previously followed an accounting principle that was not acceptable? Or what if the company applied a principle incorrectly? In such cases, the profession considers a change to a generally accepted accounting principle **a correction of an error**. For example, a switch from the cash (income tax) basis of accounting to the accrual basis is a correction of an error. Or, if a company deducted salvage value when computing double-declining depreciation on plant assets and later recomputed depreciation without deducting estimated salvage value, it has corrected an error.

There are three possible approaches for reporting changes in accounting principles:

1. ***Report changes currently.*** In this approach, companies report the cumulative effect of the change in the current year's income statement as an irregular item. The cumulative effect is the difference in prior years' income between the newly adopted and prior accounting method. Under this approach, the effect of the change on prior years' income appears only in the current-year income statement. The company does not change **prior year financial statements**.

   Advocates of this position argue that changing prior years' financial statements results in a loss of confidence in financial reports. How do investors react when told that the earnings computed three years ago are now entirely different? Changing prior periods, if permitted, also might upset contractual arrangements based on the old figures. For example, profit-sharing arrangements computed on the old basis might have to be recomputed and completely new distributions made, creating numerous legal problems. Many practical difficulties also exist. The cost of changing prior period financial statements may be excessive, or determining the amount of the prior period effect may be impossible on the basis of available data.
2. ***Report changes retrospectively.*** Retrospective application refers to the application of a different accounting principle to recast previously issued financial statements—**as if the new principle had always been used**. In other words, the company "goes back" and adjusts **prior years' statements** on a basis consistent with the newly adopted principle. The company shows any cumulative effect of the change as an adjustment to beginning retained earnings of the earliest year presented.

   Advocates of this position argue that retrospective application ensures comparability. Think for a moment what happens if this approach is not used. The year *previous* to the change will be on the old method, the year *of the change* will report the entire cumulative adjustment, and the *following* year will present financial statements on the new basis without the cumulative effect of the change. Such lack of consistency fails to provide meaningful earnings-trend data and other financial relationships necessary to evaluate the business.

3. ***Report changes prospectively (in the future).*** In this approach, previously reported results remain. As a result, companies do not adjust opening balances to reflect the change in principle. Advocates of this position argue that once management presents financial statements based on acceptable accounting principles, they are final. Management cannot change prior periods by adopting a new principle. According to this line of reasoning, the current-period cumulative adjustment is not appropriate because that approach includes amounts that have little or no relationship to the current year's income or economic events (see Global View).

Global View

IFRS (*IAS 8*) generally requires retrospective application to prior years for accounting changes. However, *IAS 8* permits the prospective method if a company cannot reasonably determine the amounts to which to restate prior periods.

Given these three possible approaches, which does the accounting profession prefer? The FASB **requires that companies use the retrospective approach**. Why? Because it provides financial statement users with more useful information than the cumulative-effect or prospective approaches. [2] The rationale is that changing the prior statements to be on the same basis as the newly adopted principle results in greater consistency across accounting periods. Users can then better compare results from one period to the next.[1]

What Do the Numbers Mean? Quite a Change

The cumulative-effect approach results in a loss of comparability. Also, reporting the cumulative adjustment in the period of the change can significantly affect net income, resulting in a misleading income figure. For example, at one time Chrysler Corporation changed its inventory accounting from LIFO to FIFO. If Chrysler had used the cumulative-effect approach, it would have reported a $53,500,000 adjustment to net income. That adjustment would have resulted in net income of $45,900,000, instead of a net loss of $7,600,000.

A second case: In the early 1980s, the railroad industry switched from the retirement-replacement method of depreciating railroad equipment to more generally used methods such as straight-line depreciation. Using cumulative treatment, railroad companies would have made substantial adjustments to income in the period of change. Many in the industry argued that including such large cumulative-effect adjustments in the current year would distort the information and make it less useful.

Such situations lend support to retrospective application so that comparability is maintained.

Retrospective Accounting Change Approach

A presumption exists that once a company adopts an accounting principle, it should not change. That presumption is understandable, given the idea that consistent use of an accounting principle enhances the usefulness of financial statements. However, the environment continually changes, and companies change in response. Recent standards on such subjects as stock options, exchanges of nonmonetary assets, and revenue recognition indicate that changes in accounting principle will continue to occur.

When a company changes an accounting principle, it should report the change using retrospective application (see Underlying Concepts). In general terms, here is what it must do:

Underlying Concepts

Retrospective application contributes to comparability.

1. ***It adjusts its financial statements for each prior period presented.*** Thus, financial statement information about prior periods is on the same basis as the new accounting principle.
2. ***It adjusts the carrying amounts of assets and liabilities as of the beginning of the first year presented.*** By doing so, these accounts reflect the cumulative effect on periods prior to those presented of the change to the new accounting principle. The company also makes an offsetting adjustment to the opening balance of retained earnings or other appropriate component of stockholders' equity or net assets as of the beginning of the first year presented.

[1]Adoption of the retrospective approach contributes to international accounting convergence. As discussed throughout the text, the FASB and the IASB have collaborated to converge around high-quality solutions to resolve differences between GAAP and IFRS. By adopting the retrospective approach, which is the method used in IFRS, the FASB agreed that this approach is superior to the current approach.

For example, assume that Target decides to change its inventory valuation method in 2020 from the retail inventory method (FIFO) to the retail inventory method (average-cost). It provides comparative information for 2018 and 2019 based on the new method. Target also would adjust its assets, liabilities, and retained earnings for periods prior to 2018 and report these amounts in the 2018 financial statements, when it prepares comparative financial statements.

Retrospective Accounting Change: Long-Term Contracts To illustrate the retrospective approach, assume that Denson Company has accounted for its income from long-term construction contracts at a point in time using the completed-contract method. In 2020 as a result of adopting the new revenue standard, the company changed to recognizing revenue over time (percentage-of-completion method). Management believes this approach provides a more appropriate measure of the income earned. For tax purposes, the company uses the completed-contract method and plans to continue doing so in the future. (We assume a 20% enacted tax rate.)

Illustration 22.1 shows portions of three income statements for 2018–2020—for both the completed-contract and percentage-of-completion methods (2018 was Denson's first year of operations in the construction business).

ILLUSTRATION 22.1

Comparative Income Statements for Completed-Contract versus Percentage-of-Completion Methods

Completed-Contract Method
Denson Company
Income Statement (partial)
For the Year Ended December 31

	2018	2019	2020
Income before income tax	$400,000	$160,000	$190,000
Income tax (20%)	80,000	32,000	38,000
Net income	$320,000	$128,000	$152,000

Percentage-of-Completion Method
Denson Company
Income Statement (partial)
For the Year Ended December 31

	2018	2019	2020
Income before income tax	$600,000	$180,000	$200,000
Income tax (20%)	120,000	36,000	40,000
Net income	$480,000	$144,000	$160,000

To record a change from the completed-contract to the percentage-of-completion method, we analyze the various effects, as Illustration 22.2 shows.

ILLUSTRATION 22.2

Data for Retrospective Change Example

	Pretax Income from		Difference in Income		
Year	Percentage-of-Completion	Completed-Contract	Difference	Tax Effect 20%	Income Effect (net of tax)
Prior to 2019	$600,000	$400,000	$200,000	$40,000	$160,000
In 2019	180,000	160,000	20,000	4,000	16,000
Total at beginning of 2020	$780,000	$560,000	$220,000	$44,000	$176,000
Total in 2020	$200,000	$190,000	$ 10,000	$ 2,000	$ 8,000

The entry to record the change at the beginning of 2020 would be:

Construction in Process	220,000	
Deferred Tax Liability		44,000
Retained Earnings		176,000

The Construction in Process account increases by $220,000 (as indicated in the first column under "Difference in Income" in Illustration 22.2). The credit to Retained Earnings of $176,000 reflects the cumulative income effects prior to 2020 (third column under "Difference in Income" in Illustration 22.2). The company credits Retained Earnings because prior years' income is closed to this account each year. The credit to Deferred Tax Liability represents the adjustment to prior years' tax expense. The company now recognizes that amount, $44,000, as a tax liability for future taxable amounts. That is, in future periods, taxable income will be higher than book income as a result of current temporary differences. Therefore, Denson must report a deferred tax liability in the current year.

What Do the Numbers Mean? Change Management

Halliburton offers a case study in the importance of good reporting of an accounting change. Note that Halliburton uses percentage-of-completion accounting for its long-term construction-services contracts. The SEC questioned the company about its change in accounting for disputed claims.

Prior to the year of the change, Halliburton took a very conservative approach to its accounting for disputed claims. That is, the company waited until all disputes were resolved before recognizing associated revenues. In contrast, in the year of the change, the company recognized revenue for disputed claims before their resolution, using estimates of amounts expected to be recovered. Such revenue and its related profit are more tentative and subject to possible later adjustment. The accounting method adopted is more aggressive than the company's former policy but is within the boundaries of GAAP.

It appears that the problem with Halliburton's accounting stems more from how the company handled its accounting change than from the new method itself. That is, Halliburton did not provide in its annual report in the year of the change an explicit reference to its change in accounting method. In fact, rather than stating its new policy, the company simply deleted the sentence that described how it accounted for disputed claims. Then later, in its next year's annual report, the company stated its new accounting policy. Similar transparency concerns were also raised when companies, like **Hawthorn Bancshares**, did not provide sufficient explanation about their changes to fair value accounting for their mortgage servicing rights. More recently, the SEC admonished companies to provide sufficient disclosure of judgments related to adoption of the revenue recognition standard.

When companies make such changes in accounting, investors need to be informed about the change and about its effects on the financial results. With such information, investors and analysts can compare current results with those of prior periods and can make a more informed assessment about the company's future prospects.

Sources: Adapted from "Accounting Ace Charles Mulford Answers Accounting Questions," *Wall Street Journal Online* (June 7, 2002); J. Arnold, B. Blisard, and J. Duggan, "Dealing with the Implications of Accounting Change," *FEI Magazine* (November 2012); and Tatyana Shumsky, "SEC Spotlights Areas of Subjective Judgment in Letters to Early Adopters of Revenue Rules," *Wall Street Journal* (November 5, 2018).

Reporting a Change in Principle The disclosure of accounting changes is particularly important. Financial statement readers want consistent information from one period to the next. Such consistency ensures the usefulness of financial statements. The major disclosure requirements are as follows.

1. The nature of and reason for the change in accounting principle. This must include an explanation of why the newly adopted accounting principle is preferable.
2. The method of applying the change, and:
    a. A description of the prior period information that has been retrospectively adjusted, if any.
    b. The effect of the change on income from continuing operations, net income (or other appropriate captions of changes in net assets or performance indicators), any other affected line item, and any affected per share amounts for the current period and for any prior periods retrospectively adjusted.
    c. The cumulative effect of the change on retained earnings or other components of equity or net assets in the statement of financial position as of the beginning of the earliest period presented.[2]

[2]Presentation of the effect on financial statement subtotals and totals other than income from continuing operations and net income (or other appropriate captions of changes in the applicable net assets or performance indicator) is not required. [3]

To illustrate, Denson will prepare comparative financial statements for 2019 and 2020 using the percentage-of-completion method (the new construction accounting method). Illustration 22.3 indicates how Denson presents this information.

ILLUSTRATION 22.3

Comparative Information Related to Accounting Change (Percentage-of-Completion)

Denson Company
Income Statement (partial)
For the Year Ended

	2020	2019 As Adjusted (Note A)
Income before income tax	$200,000	$180,000
Income tax (20%)	40,000	36,000
Net income	$160,000	$144,000

Note A: Change in Method of Accounting for Long-Term Contracts. The company has accounted for revenue and costs for long-term construction contracts by the percentage-of-completion method in 2020, whereas in all prior years, revenue and costs were determined by the completed-contract method. The new method of accounting for long-term contracts was adopted to recognize . . . [state justification for change in accounting principle] . . . and financial statements of prior years have been restated to apply the new method retrospectively. For income tax purposes, the completed-contract method has been continued. The effect of the accounting change on income of 2020 was an increase of $8,000 net of related taxes and on income of 2019 as previously reported was an increase of $16,000 net of related taxes. The balances of retained earnings for 2019 and 2020 have been adjusted for the effect of applying retrospectively the new method of accounting. As a result of the accounting change, retained earnings as of January 1, 2019, increased by $160,000 compared to that reported using the completed-contract method.

As Illustration 22.3 shows, Denson Company reports net income under the newly adopted percentage-of-completion method for both 2019 and 2020. The company retrospectively adjusted the 2019 income statement to report the information on a percentage-of-completion basis. Also, the note to the financial statements indicates the nature of the change, why the company made the change, and the years affected.

In addition, companies are required to provide data on important differences between the amounts reported under percentage-of-completion versus completed-contract. When identifying the significant differences, some companies show the *entire* financial statements and line-by-line differences between percentage-of-completion and completed-contract. However, most companies will show only line-by-line differences. For example, Denson would show the differences in construction in process, retained earnings, gross profit, and net income for 2019 and 2020 under the completed-contract and percentage-of-completion methods.

Retained Earnings Adjustment As indicated earlier, one of the disclosure requirements is to show the cumulative effect of the change on retained earnings as of the beginning of the earliest period presented. For Denson Company, that date is January 1, 2019. Denson disclosed that information by means of a narrative description (see Note A in Illustration 22.3). Denson also would disclose this information in its retained earnings statement. Assuming a retained earnings balance of $1,360,000 at the beginning of 2018, Illustration 22.4 shows Denson's retained earnings statement under the completed- contract method—that is, before giving effect to the change in accounting principle. (The income information comes from Illustration 22.1.)

ILLUSTRATION 22.4

Retained Earnings Statement Before Retrospective Change

Denson Company
Retained Earnings Statement
For the Year Ended

	2020	2019	2018
Retained earnings, January 1	$1,808,000	$1,680,000	$1,360,000
Net income	152,000	128,000	320,000
Retained earnings, December 31	$1,960,000	$1,808,000	$1,680,000

If Denson presents comparative statements for 2019 and 2020 under percentage-of-completion, then it must change the beginning balance of retained earnings at January 1,

2019. The difference between the retained earnings balances under completed-contract and percentage-of-completion is computed as follows.

Retained earnings, January 1, 2019 (percentage-of-completion)	$1,840,000
Retained earnings, January 1, 2019 (completed-contract)	(1,680,000)
Cumulative-effect difference	$ 160,000

The $160,000 difference is the cumulative effect. Illustration 22.5 shows a comparative retained earnings statement for 2019 and 2020, giving effect to the change in accounting principle to percentage-of-completion.

ILLUSTRATION 22.5

Retained Earnings Statement After Retrospective Application

Denson Company
Retained Earnings Statement
For the Year Ended

	2020	2019
Retained earnings, January 1, as reported	—	$1,680,000
Add: Adjustment for the cumulative effect on prior years of applying retrospectively the new method of accounting for construction contracts		160,000
Retained earnings, January 1, as adjusted	$1,984,000	1,840,000
Net income	160,000	144,000
Retained earnings, December 31	$2,144,000	$1,984,000

Denson adjusted the beginning balance of retained earnings on January 1, 2019, for the excess of percentage-of-completion net income over completed-contract net income in 2018. This comparative presentation indicates the type of adjustment that a company needs to make. It follows that this adjustment could be much larger if a number of prior periods were involved.

Retrospective Accounting Change: Inventory Methods As a second illustration of the retrospective approach, assume that Lancer Company has accounted for its inventory using the LIFO method. In 2020, the company changes to the FIFO method because management believes this approach provides a more appropriate reporting of its inventory costs. Illustration 22.6 provides additional information related to Lancer Company.

ILLUSTRATION 22.6

Lancer Company Information

1. Lancer Company started its operations on January 1, 2018. At that time, stockholders invested $100,000 in the business in exchange for common stock.
2. All sales, purchases, and operating expenses for the period 2018–2020 are cash transactions. Lancer's cash flows over this period are as follows.

	2018	2019	2020
Sales	$300,000	$300,000	$300,000
Purchases	90,000	110,000	125,000
Operating expenses	100,000	100,000	100,000
Cash flow from operations	$110,000	$ 90,000	$ 75,000

3. Lancer has used the LIFO method for financial reporting since its inception.
4. Inventory determined under LIFO and FIFO for the period 2018–2020 is as follows.

	LIFO Method	FIFO Method	Difference
January 1, 2018	$ 0	$ 0	$ 0
December 31, 2018	10,000	12,000	2,000
December 31, 2019	20,000	25,000	5,000
December 31, 2020	32,000	39,000	7,000

(continued)

ILLUSTRATION 22.6
(continued)

5. Cost of goods sold under LIFO and FIFO for the period 2018–2020 are as follows.

	Cost of Goods Sold		
	LIFO	FIFO	Difference
2018	$ 80,000	$ 78,000	$2,000
2019	100,000	97,000	3,000
2020	113,000	111,000	2,000

6. Earnings per share information is not required on the income statement.
7. All tax effects for this illustration should be ignored.

Given the information about Lancer Company, Illustration 22.7 shows its income statement, retained earnings statement, balance sheet, and statement of cash flows for 2018–2020 under LIFO.

ILLUSTRATION 22.7
Lancer Financial Statements (LIFO)

Lancer Company
Income Statement
For the Year Ended December 31

	2018	2019	2020
Sales	$300,000	$300,000	$300,000
Cost of goods sold (LIFO)	80,000	100,000	113,000
Operating expenses	100,000	100,000	100,000
Net income	$120,000	$100,000	$ 87,000

Lancer Company
Retained Earnings Statement
For the Year Ended December 31

	2018	2019	2020
Retained earnings (beginning)	$ 0	$120,000	$220,000
Add: Net income	120,000	100,000	87,000
Retained earnings (ending)	$120,000	$220,000	$307,000

Lancer Company
Balance Sheet
At December 31

	2018	2019	2020
Cash	$210,000	$300,000	$375,000
Inventory (LIFO)	10,000	20,000	32,000
Total assets	$220,000	$320,000	$407,000
Common stock	$100,000	$100,000	$100,000
Retained earnings	120,000	220,000	307,000
Total liabilities and stockholders' equity	$220,000	$320,000	$407,000

Lancer Company
Statement of Cash Flows
For the Year Ended December 31

	2018	2019	2020
Cash flows from operating activities			
Sales	$300,000	$300,000	$300,000
Purchases	90,000	110,000	125,000
Operating expenses	100,000	100,000	100,000
Net cash provided by operating activities	110,000	90,000	75,000
Cash flows from financing activities			
Issuance of common stock	100,000	—	—
Net increase in cash	210,000	90,000	75,000
Cash at beginning of year	0	210,000	300,000
Cash at end of year	$210,000	$300,000	$375,000

As Illustration 22.7 indicates, under LIFO Lancer Company reports $120,000 net income in 2018, $100,000 net income in 2019, and $87,000 net income in 2020. The amount of inventory reported on Lancer's balance sheet reflects LIFO costing.

Illustration 22.8 shows Lancer's income statement, retained earnings statement, balance sheet, and statement of cash flows for 2018–2020 under **FIFO**. You can see that **the cash flow statement under FIFO is the same as under LIFO**. Although the net incomes are different in each period, there is no cash flow effect from these differences in net income. (If we considered income taxes, a cash flow effect would result.)

ILLUSTRATION 22.8
Lancer Financial Statements (FIFO)

Lancer Company
Income Statement
For the Year Ended December 31

	2018	2019	2020
Sales	$300,000	$300,000	$300,000
Cost of goods sold (FIFO)	78,000	97,000	111,000
Operating expenses	100,000	100,000	100,000
Net income	$122,000	$103,000	$ 89,000

Lancer Company
Retained Earnings Statement
For the Year Ended December 31

	2018	2019	2020
Retained earnings (beginning)	$ 0	$122,000	$225,000
Add: Net income	122,000	103,000	89,000
Retained earnings (ending)	$122,000	$225,000	$314,000

Lancer Company
Balance Sheet
At December 31

	2018	2019	2020
Cash	$210,000	$300,000	$375,000
Inventory (FIFO)	12,000	25,000	39,000
Total assets	$222,000	$325,000	$414,000
Common stock	$100,000	$100,000	$100,000
Retained earnings	122,000	225,000	314,000
Total liabilities and stockholders' equity	$222,000	$325,000	$414,000

Lancer Company
Statement of Cash Flows
For the Year Ended December 31

	2018	2019	2020
Cash flows from operating activities			
Sales	$300,000	$300,000	$300,000
Purchases	90,000	110,000	125,000
Operating expenses	100,000	100,000	100,000
Net cash provided by operating activities	110,000	90,000	75,000
Cash flows from financing activities			
Issuance of common stock	100,000	—	—
Net increase in cash	210,000	90,000	75,000
Cast at beginning of year	0	210,000	300,000
Cash at end of year	$210,000	$300,000	$375,000

Compare the financial statements reported in Illustration 22.7 and Illustration 22.8. You can see that under retrospective application, the change to FIFO inventory valuation affects reported inventories, cost of goods sold, net income, and retained earnings. In the following sections, we discuss the accounting and reporting of Lancer's accounting change from LIFO to FIFO.

Given the information provided in Illustrations 22.6, 22.7, and 22.8, we now are ready to account for and report on the accounting change.

Our first step is to adjust the financial records for the change from LIFO to FIFO. To do so, we perform the analysis in **Illustration 22.9**.

ILLUSTRATION 22.9

Data for Recording Change in Accounting Principle

Year	Net Income LIFO	Net Income FIFO	Difference in Income
2018	$120,000	$122,000	$2,000
2019	100,000	103,000	3,000
Total at beginning of 2020	$220,000	$225,000	$5,000
Total in 2020	$ 87,000	$ 89,000	$2,000

The entry to record the change to the FIFO method at the beginning of 2020 is as follows.

Inventory	5,000	
Retained Earnings		5,000

The change increases the Inventory account by $5,000. This amount represents the difference between the ending inventory at December 31, 2019, under LIFO ($20,000) and the ending inventory under FIFO ($25,000). The credit to Retained Earnings indicates the amount needed to change the prior year's income, assuming that Lancer had used FIFO in previous periods.

Reporting a Change in Principle Lancer Company will prepare comparative financial statements for 2019 and 2020 using FIFO (the new inventory method). **Illustration 22.10** indicates how Lancer might present this information.

ILLUSTRATION 22.10

Comparative Information Related to Accounting Change (FIFO)

Lancer Company
Income Statement
For the Year Ended December 31

	2020	2019 As adjusted (Note A)
Sales	$300,000	$300,000
Cost of goods sold	111,000	97,000
Operating expenses	100,000	100,000
Net income	$ 89,000	$103,000

Note A

Nature and reason for change; description of prior period information adjusted

Change in Method of Accounting for Inventory Valuation On January 1, 2020, Lancer Company elected to change its method of valuing its inventory to the FIFO method; in all prior years, inventory was valued using the LIFO method. The Company adopted the new method of accounting for inventory to better report cost of goods sold in the year incurred. Comparative financial statements of prior years have been adjusted to apply the new method retrospectively. The following financial statement line items for years 2020 and 2019 were affected by the change in accounting principle.

Effect of change on key performance indicators

	2020 LIFO	2020 FIFO	2020 Difference	2019 LIFO	2019 FIFO	2019 Difference
Balance Sheet						
Inventory	$ 32,000	$ 39,000	$7,000	$ 20,000	$ 25,000	$5,000
Retained earnings	307,000	314,000	7,000	220,000	225,000	5,000
Income Statement						
Cost of goods sold	$113,000	$111,000	$2,000	$100,000	$ 97,000	$3,000
Net income	87,000	89,000	2,000	100,000	103,000	3,000
Statement of Cash Flows						
(no effect)						

Cumulative effect on retained earnings

As a result of the accounting change, retained earnings as of January 1, 2019, increased from $120,000, as originally reported using the LIFO method, to $122,000 using the FIFO method.

As Illustration 22.10 shows, Lancer Company reports net income under the newly adopted FIFO method for both 2019 and 2020. The company retrospectively adjusted the 2019 income statement to report the information on a FIFO basis. In addition, the note to the financial statements indicates the nature of the change, why the company made the change, and the years affected. The note also provides data on important differences between the amounts reported under LIFO versus FIFO. (When identifying the significant differences, some companies show the *entire* financial statements and line-by-line differences between LIFO and FIFO.)

Retained Earnings Adjustment As indicated earlier, one of the disclosure requirements is to show the cumulative effect of the change on retained earnings as of the beginning of the earliest period presented. For Lancer Company, that date is January 1, 2019. Lancer disclosed that information by means of a narrative description (see Note A in Illustration 22.10). Lancer also would disclose this information in its retained earnings statement. **Illustration 22.11** shows Lancer's retained earnings statement under LIFO—that is, before giving effect to the change in accounting principle. (This information comes from Illustration 22.7.)

ILLUSTRATION 22.11
Retained Earnings Statements (LIFO)

	2020	2019	2018
Retained earnings, January 1	$220,000	$120,000	$ 0
Net income	87,000	100,000	120,000
Retained earnings, December 31	$307,000	$220,000	$120,000

If Lancer presents comparative statements for 2019 and 2020 under FIFO, then it must change the beginning balance of retained earnings at January 1, 2019. The difference between the retained earnings balances under LIFO and FIFO is computed as follows.

Retained earnings, January 1, 2019 (FIFO)	$122,000
Retained earnings, January 1, 2019 (LIFO)	(120,000)
Cumulative effect difference	$ 2,000

The $2,000 difference is the cumulative effect. **Illustration 22.12** shows a comparative retained earnings statement for 2019 and 2020, giving effect to the change in accounting principle to FIFO.

ILLUSTRATION 22.12
Retained Earnings Statements After Retrospective Application

	2020	2019
Retained earnings, January 1, as reported		$120,000
Add: Adjustment for the cumulative effect on prior years of applying retrospectively the new method of accounting for inventory		2,000
Retained earnings, January 1, as adjusted	$225,000	122,000
Net income	89,000	103,000
Retained earnings, December 31	$314,000	$225,000

Lancer adjusted the beginning balance of retained earnings on January 1, 2019, for the excess of FIFO net income over LIFO net income in 2018. This comparative presentation indicates the type of adjustment that a company needs to make. It follows that the amount of this adjustment could be much larger if a number of prior periods were involved.

Direct and Indirect Effects of Changes

Are there other effects that a company should report when it makes a change in accounting principle? For example, what happens when a company like Lancer has a bonus plan based on net income and the prior year's net income changes when FIFO is retrospectively applied? Should Lancer also change the reported amount of bonus expense? Or what happens if we had not ignored income taxes in the Lancer example? Should Lancer adjust net income, given that taxes will be different under LIFO and FIFO in prior periods? The answers depend on whether the effects are direct or indirect.

Direct Effects The FASB takes the position that companies should retrospectively apply the **direct effects of a change in accounting principle**. An example of a **direct effect** is an adjustment to an inventory balance as a result of a change in the inventory valuation method. For example, Lancer Company should change the inventory amounts in prior periods to indicate the change to the FIFO method of inventory valuation. Another inventory-related example would be an impairment adjustment resulting from applying the lower-of-cost-or-net realizable value or the lower-of-cost-or-market test to the adjusted inventory balance. Related changes, such as deferred income tax effects of the impairment adjustment, are also considered direct effects. This entry was illustrated in the Denson example, in which the change to percentage-of-completion accounting resulted in recording a deferred tax liability.

Indirect Effects In addition to direct effects, companies can have **indirect effects related to a change in accounting principle**. An **indirect effect** is any change to current or future cash flows of a company that results from making a change in accounting principle that is applied retrospectively (see Global View). An example of an indirect effect is a change in profit-sharing or royalty payment that is based on a reported amount such as revenue or net income. **Indirect effects do not change prior period amounts.**

> **Global View**
>
> IFRS does not explicitly address the accounting and disclosure of indirect effects.

For example, let's assume that Lancer has an employee profit-sharing plan based on net income. As Illustration 22.9 showed, Lancer would report higher income in 2018 and 2019 if it used the FIFO method. In addition, let's assume that the profit-sharing plan requires that Lancer pay the incremental amount due based on the FIFO income amounts. In this situation, Lancer reports this additional expense **in the current period**; it would not change prior periods for this expense. If the company prepares comparative financial statements, it follows that it does not recast the prior periods for this additional expense.[3]

If the terms of the profit-sharing plan indicate that *no payment is necessary* in the current period due to this change, then the company need not recognize additional profit-sharing expense in the current period. Neither does it change amounts reported for prior periods.

When a company recognizes the indirect effects of a change in accounting principle, it includes in the financial statements a description of the indirect effects. In doing so, it discloses the amounts recognized in the current period and related per share information.

Impracticability

It is not always possible for companies to determine how they would have reported prior periods' financial information under retrospective application of an accounting principle change. Retrospective application is considered **impracticable** if a company cannot determine the prior period effects using every reasonable effort to do so.

[3]The rationale for this approach is that companies should recognize, in the period the adoption occurs (not the prior period), the effect on the cash flows that is caused by the adoption of the new accounting principle. That is, the accounting change is a necessary "past event" in the definition of an asset or liability that gives rise to the accounting recognition of the indirect effect in the current period. [4]

Companies should not use retrospective application if one of the following conditions exists:

1. The company cannot determine the effects of the retrospective application.
2. Retrospective application requires assumptions about management's intent in a prior period.
3. Retrospective application requires significant estimates for a prior period, and the company cannot objectively verify the necessary information to develop these estimates.

If any of the above conditions exists, it is deemed impracticable to apply the retrospective approach. In this case, the company **prospectively applies** the new accounting principle as of the earliest date it is practicable to do so. [5]

For example, assume that Williams Company changed its inventory method from FIFO to LIFO, effective January 1, 2021. Williams prepares statements on a calendar-year basis and has used the FIFO method since its inception. Williams judges it impracticable to retrospectively apply the new method. This is generally the case for this change in principle because determining prior period effects would require subjective assumptions about the LIFO layers established in prior periods. These assumptions would ordinarily result in the computation of a number of different earnings figures.

As a result, the only adjustment necessary may be to restate the beginning inventory to a cost basis from a lower-of-cost-or-market approach (which establishes the beginning LIFO layer). Williams must disclose only the effect of the change on the results of operations in the period of change. Also, the company should explain the reasons for omitting the computations of the cumulative effect for prior years. Finally, it should disclose the justification for the change to LIFO. [6][4] **Illustration 22.13**, from the annual report of **The Quaker Oats Company**, shows the type of disclosure needed.

ILLUSTRATION 22.13

Disclosure of Change to LIFO

The Quaker Oats Company

Note 1 (In Part): Summary of Significant Accounting Policies

Inventories. Inventories are valued at the lower of cost or market, using various cost methods, and include the cost of raw materials, labor and overhead. The percentage of year-end inventories valued using each of the methods is as follows:

June 30	Current Year	Prior Year
Average quarterly cost	21%	54%
Last-in, first-out (LIFO)	65%	29%
First-in, first-out (FIFO)	14%	17%

Effective July 1, the Company adopted the LIFO cost flow assumption for valuing the majority of remaining U.S. Grocery Products inventories. The Company believes that the use of the LIFO method better matches current costs with current revenues. The cumulative effect of this change on retained earnings at the beginning of the year is not determinable, nor are the pro-forma effects of retroactive application of LIFO to prior years. The effect of this change on current-year fiscal results was to decrease net income by $16.0 million, or $.20 per share.

If the LIFO method of valuing certain inventories were not used, total inventories would have been $60.1 million higher in the current year, and $24.0 million higher in the prior year.

Other Accounting Changes

LEARNING OBJECTIVE 2

Describe the accounting for changes in estimates and changes in the reporting entity.

[4] In practice, many companies defer the formal adoption of LIFO until year-end. Management thus has an opportunity to assess the impact that a change to LIFO will have on the financial statements and to evaluate the desirability of a change for tax purposes. As indicated in Chapter 8, many companies use LIFO because of the advantages of this inventory valuation method in a period of inflation.

Changes in Accounting Estimates

To prepare financial statements, companies must estimate the effects of future conditions and events. For example, the following items require estimates.

1. Uncollectible receivables.
2. Inventory obsolescence.
3. Useful lives and salvage values of assets.
4. Periods benefited by deferred costs.
5. Liabilities for warranty costs and income taxes.
6. Recoverable mineral reserves.
7. Change in depreciation methods.

A company cannot perceive future conditions and events and their effects with certainty. Therefore, estimation requires the exercise of judgment. Accounting estimates will change as new events occur, as a company acquires more experience, or as it obtains additional information.

Prospective Reporting

Companies report prospectively changes in accounting estimates. That is, companies should not adjust previously reported results for changes in estimates. Instead, they account for the effects of all changes in estimates in (1) the period of change if the change affects that period only, or (2) the period of change and future periods if the change affects both. The FASB views changes in estimates as **normal recurring corrections and adjustments**, the natural result of the accounting process. It prohibits retrospective treatment.

The circumstances related to a change in estimate differ from those for a change in accounting principle. If companies reported changes in estimates retrospectively, continual adjustments of prior years' income would occur. It seems proper to accept the view that, because new conditions or circumstances exist, the revision fits the new situation (not the old one). Companies should therefore handle such a revision in the current and future periods.

To illustrate, Underwriters Labs Inc. purchased for $300,000 a building that it originally estimated to have a useful life of 15 years and no salvage value. It recorded depreciation for 5 years on a straight-line basis. On January 1, 2020, Underwriters Labs revises the estimate of the useful life. It now considers the asset to have a total life of 25 years. (Assume that the useful life for financial reporting and tax purposes and depreciation method are the same.) Illustration 22.14 shows the accounts at the beginning of the sixth year.

ILLUSTRATION 22.14
Book Value after Five Years' Depreciation

Buildings	$300,000
Less: Accumulated depreciation—buildings (5 × $20,000)	100,000
Book value of building	$200,000

Underwriters Labs records depreciation for the year 2020 as follows.

Depreciation Expense	10,000	
Accumulated Depreciation—Buildings		10,000

The company computes the $10,000 depreciation charge as shown in Illustration 22.15.

ILLUSTRATION 22.15
Depreciation after Change in Estimate

$$\frac{\textbf{Book Value of Asset}}{\textbf{Remaining Service Life}} = \textbf{Depreciation Charge}$$

$$\frac{\$200{,}000}{(25 \text{ years} - 5 \text{ years})} = \$10{,}000$$

Companies sometime find it difficult to differentiate between a change in estimate and a change in accounting principle. Is it a change in principle or a change in estimate when a company changes from deferring and amortizing marketing costs to expensing them as incurred because future benefits of these costs have become doubtful? If it is impossible to determine whether a change in principle or a change in estimate has occurred, the rule is this: **Consider the change as a change in estimate.** This is often referred to as a **change in estimate effected by a change in accounting principle**.

Another example of a change in estimate effected by a change in principle is a change in depreciation (as well as amortization or depletion) methods. Because companies change depreciation methods based on changes in estimates about future benefits from long-lived assets, it is not possible to separate the effect of the accounting principle change from that of the estimates. **As a result, companies account for a change in depreciation methods as a change in estimate effected by a change in accounting principle.** [7]

A similar problem occurs in differentiating between a change in estimate and a correction of an error, although here the answer is more clear-cut. How does a company determine whether it overlooked the information in earlier periods (an error), or whether it obtained new information (a change in estimate)? Proper classification is important because the accounting treatment differs for corrections of errors versus changes in estimates. The general rule is this: **Companies should consider careful estimates that later prove to be incorrect as changes in estimate.** Only when a company obviously computed the estimate incorrectly because of lack of expertise or in bad faith should it consider the adjustment an error. There is no clear demarcation line here. Companies must use good judgment in light of all the circumstances.[5]

Disclosures

Illustration 22.16 shows disclosure of a change in estimated useful lives, which appeared in the annual report of **Ampco–Pittsburgh Corporation**.

ILLUSTRATION 22.16
Disclosure of Change in Estimated Useful Lives

Ampco–Pittsburgh Corporation

Note 11: Change in Accounting Estimate. The Corporation revised its estimate of the useful lives of certain machinery and equipment. Previously, all machinery and equipment, whether new when placed in use or not, were in one class and depreciated over 15 years. The change principally applies to assets purchased new when placed in use. Those lives are now extended to 20 years. These changes were made to better reflect the estimated periods during which such assets will remain in service. The change had the effect of reducing depreciation expense and increasing net income by approximately $991,000 ($.10 per share).

For the most part, companies need not disclose changes in accounting estimates made as part of normal operations, such as bad debt allowances or inventory obsolescence, unless such changes are material. However, for a change in estimate that affects several periods (such as a change in the service lives of depreciable assets), companies should disclose the effect on income from continuing operations and related per share amounts of the current period. When a company has a change in estimate effected by a change in accounting principle, it must indicate why the new method is preferable. In addition, companies are subject to all other disclosure guidelines established for changes in accounting principle.

[5]In evaluating reasonableness, the auditor should use one or a combination of the following approaches.

a. Review and test the process used by management to develop the estimate.
b. Develop an independent expectation of the estimate to corroborate the reasonableness of management's estimate.
c. Review subsequent events or transactions occurring prior to completion of fieldwork.

See AU-C Section 540, "Auditing Accounting Estimates, Including Fair Value Accounting Estimates, and Related Disclosures," *Statement on Auditing Standards No. 122*. Effective for audits of financial statements for periods ending on or after December 15, 2012. [Predecessor literature: "Auditing Accounting Estimates," *Statement on Auditing Standards No. 57* (New York: AICPA, 1988).]

What Do the Numbers Mean? Why Now?

For many years, **Intel** has been the leader in innovation related to semiconductors. Recently, Intel said longer product cycles mean it will now depreciate its machinery and equipment more slowly, giving them a useful life of five years instead of four years. So, is this a big deal?

Looking at the issue from an accounting perspective, changing the useful life of its machinery and equipment means that Intel will record $1.5 billion less in depreciation expense in the current period, which is approximately 10 percent of its pretax income from the previous year. The number is substantial as it is the largest depreciation-related change with a positive effect on income in many years. Therefore, it is not surprising that some express concern about the comparability of the financial information between the year of change and preceding years.

This is especially important when considering the effect of the depreciation charge on net income. That is, this change in accounting may signal trouble for the company and the semiconductor industry. In the last few years, many other semiconductor companies have lengthened the useful lives of their machinery and equipment—and financial statement readers must ask why. The answer is that it may signal that innovation is slowing in the industry, which some suggest is worrisome and not a sign of strength.

Sources: M. Murphy, "Moore's Law Meets GAAP Accounting at Intel," *Wall Street Journal* (April 5, 2015); and O. Usvyatsky and J. Pakaluk, "What Depreciation at Intel Says About Moore's Law," *Audit Analytics* (April 5, 2016).

Changes in Reporting Entity

Occasionally, companies make changes that result in different reporting entities. In such cases, companies report the change by **changing the financial statements of all prior periods presented**. The revised statements show the financial information for the **new reporting entity** for all periods.

Examples of a change in reporting entity are:

1. Presenting consolidated statements in place of statements of individual companies.
2. Changing specific subsidiaries that constitute the group of companies for which the entity presents consolidated financial statements.
3. Changing the companies included in combined financial statements.
4. Changing the cost, equity, or consolidation method of accounting for subsidiaries and investments.[6] In this case, a change in the reporting entity does not result from creation, cessation, purchase, or disposition of a subsidiary or other business unit.

In the year in which a company changes a reporting entity, it should disclose in the financial statements the nature of the change and the reason for it. It also should report, for all periods presented, the effect of the change on income from continuing operations, net income, and earnings per share. These disclosures need not be repeated in subsequent periods' financial statements.

Illustration 22.17 shows a note disclosing a change in reporting entity, from the annual report of **Hewlett-Packard Company**.

ILLUSTRATION 22.17
Disclosure of Change in Reporting Entity

Hewlett-Packard Company

Note: Accounting and Reporting Changes (In Part)

Consolidation of Hewlett-Packard Finance Company. The company implemented a new accounting pronouncement on consolidations. With the adoption of this new pronouncement, the company consolidated the accounts of Hewlett-Packard Finance Company (HPFC), a wholly owned subsidiary previously accounted for under the equity method, with those of the company. The change resulted in an increase in consolidated assets and liabilities but did not have a material effect on the company's financial position. Since HPFC was previously accounted for under the equity method, the change did not affect net earnings. Prior years' consolidated financial information has been restated to reflect this change for comparative purposes.

[6] An exception to retrospective application occurs when changing from the equity method. We provide an expanded illustration of the accounting for a change from or to the equity method in Appendix 22A.

Accounting Errors

LEARNING OBJECTIVE 3

Describe the accounting for correction of errors.

No business, large or small, is immune from errors. As the opening story discusses, the number of accounting errors that lead to restatement has stabilized in recent years. However, without accounting and disclosure guidelines for the reporting of errors, investors can be left in the dark about the effects of errors.

Certain errors, such as misclassifications of balances within a financial statement, are not as significant to investors as other errors. For example, significant errors would be those resulting in overstating assets or income. However, investors should know the potential impact of all errors. Even "harmless" misclassifications can affect important ratios. Also, some errors could signal important weaknesses in internal controls that could lead to more significant errors.

In general, accounting errors include the following types:

1. A change from an accounting principle that is **not** generally accepted to an accounting principle that is acceptable. The rationale is that the company incorrectly presented prior periods because of the application of an improper accounting principle. For example, a company may change from the cash (income tax) basis of accounting to the accrual basis.
2. Mathematical mistakes, such as incorrectly totaling the inventory count sheets when computing the inventory value.
3. Changes in estimates that occur because a company did not prepare the estimates in good faith. For example, a company may have adopted a clearly unrealistic depreciation rate.
4. An oversight, such as the failure to accrue or defer certain expenses and revenues at the end of the period.
5. A misuse of facts, such as the failure to use salvage value in computing the depreciation base for the straight-line approach.
6. The incorrect classification of a cost as an expense instead of an asset, and vice versa.

Accounting errors occur for a variety of reasons. **Illustration 22.18** indicates 11 major categories of accounting errors that drive restatements.

ILLUSTRATION 22.18 Accounting-Error Types

Accounting Category	Type of Restatement
Expense recognition	Recording expenses in the incorrect period or for an incorrect amount.
Revenue recognition	Improper revenue accounting. This category includes instances in which revenue was improperly recognized, questionable revenues were recognized, or any other number of related errors that led to misreported revenue.
Misclassification	Misclassifying significant accounting items on the balance sheet, income statement, or statement of cash flows. These include restatements due to misclassification of short- or long-term accounts or those that impact cash flows from operations.
Equity—other	Improper accounting for EPS, restricted stock, warrants, and other equity instruments.
Allowances/contingencies	Errors involving bad debts related to accounts receivable, inventory reserves, income tax allowances, and loss contingencies.
Long-lived assets	Asset impairments of property, plant, and equipment; goodwill; or other related items.
Taxes	Errors involving correction of tax provision, improper treatment of tax liabilities, and other tax-related items.
Equity—other comprehensive income	Improper accounting for comprehensive income equity transactions including foreign currency items, unrealized gains and losses on certain investments in debt securities and derivatives.
Inventory	Inventory costing valuations, quantity issues, and cost of sales adjustments.
Equity—stock options	Improper accounting for employee stock options.
Other	Any restatement not covered by the listed categories including those related to improper accounting for acquisitions or mergers.

Sources: T. Baldwin and D. Yoo, "Restatements—Traversing Shaky Ground," *Trend Alert*, Glass Lewis & Co. (June 2, 2005), p. 8; and "2017 Financial Restatements Review," *Audit Analytics* (June 2018).

As soon as a company discovers an error, it must correct the error. Companies record **corrections of errors** from prior periods as an adjustment to the beginning balance of retained earnings in the current period. Such corrections are called **prior period adjustments**.[7] [8]

If it presents comparative statements, a company should restate the prior statements affected, to correct for the error.[8] The company need not repeat the disclosures in the financial statements of subsequent periods.

What Do the Numbers Mean? Can I Get My Money Back?

When companies report restatements, investors usually lose money. What should investors do if a company misleads them by misstating its financial results? Join other investors in a class-action suit against the company and in some cases, the auditor.

Class-action activity has picked up in recent years, and settlements can be large. To find out about class actions, investors can go online to see if they are eligible to join any class actions. Below are some recent examples.

Company	Settlement Amount
Takata	$200 million
Facebook	$ 10 million
Goldman Sachs	$ 41 million

The amounts reported are *before* attorney's fees, which can range from 15 to 30 percent of the total. Also, investors may owe taxes if the settlement results in a capital gain on the investment. Thus, investors can get back some of the money they lost due to restatements, but they should be prepared to pay an attorney and the government first.

Sources: Adapted from C. Coolidge, "Lost and Found," *Forbes* (October 1, 2001), pp. 124–125; data from *www.lawyersandsettlements.com* as of spring 2018.

Example of Error Correction

To illustrate, in 2021 the bookkeeper for Selectro Company discovered an error. In 2020, the company failed to record $20,000 of depreciation expense on a newly constructed building. This building is the only depreciable asset Selectro owns. The company correctly included the depreciation expense in its tax return and correctly reported its income taxes payable. **Illustration 22.19** presents Selectro's income statement for 2020 (starting with income before depreciation expense) with and without the error.

ILLUSTRATION 22.19
Error Correction Comparison

Selectro Company
Income Statement
For the Year Ended December 31, 2020

		Without Error		With Error
Income before depreciation expense		$100,000		$100,000
Depreciation expense		20,000		-0-
Income before income tax		80,000		100,000
Current income tax expense	$16,000		$16,000	
Deferred income tax expense	-0-	16,000	4,000	20,000
Net income		$ 64,000		$ 80,000

Illustration 22.20 shows the entries that Selectro should have made and did make for recording depreciation expense and income taxes.

[7] See Mark L. Defond and James Jiambalvo, "Incidence and Circumstances of Accounting Errors," *The Accounting Review* (July 1991) for examples of different types of errors and why these errors might have occurred.

[8] The term **restatement** is used for the process of revising previously issued financial statements to reflect the correction of an error. This distinguishes an error correction from a change in accounting principle. [9] Some restatements—so-called "Little r" restatements—are distinguished from the restatements discussed here ("Big R" restatements), which require special reporting. Little r restatements arise when a company's *immaterial* errors accumulate to a material error in a given year. In a Little r restatement, the company must disclose the correction in the footnotes of the current-period financial statements (i.e., the financial statements that reflect the correction) but would not have to amend prior accounting reports. See C. Tan and S. Young, "An Analysis of 'Little r' Restatements," *Accounting Horizons* (September 2015).

ILLUSTRATION 22.20
Error Entries

Entries Company Should Have Made (Without Error)			Entries Company Did Make (With Error)		
Depreciation Expense	20,000		No entry made for depreciation		
Accumulated Depreciation—Buildings		20,000			
Income Tax Expense	16,000		Income Tax Expense	20,000	
Income Taxes Payable		16,000	Deferred Tax Liability		4,000
			Income Taxes Payable		16,000

As Illustration 22.20 indicates, the $20,000 omission error in 2020 results in the following effects.

Income Statement Effects
Depreciation expense (2020) is understated $20,000.
Income tax expense (2020) is overstated $4,000 ($20,000 × .20).
Net income (2020) is overstated $16,000 ($80,000 − $64,000).

Balance Sheet Effects
Accumulated depreciation—buildings is understated $20,000.
Deferred tax liability is overstated $4,000 ($20,000 × .20).

To make the proper correcting entry in 2021, Selectro should recognize that net income in 2020 is overstated by $16,000, the Deferred Tax Liability is overstated by $4,000, and Accumulated Depreciation—Buildings is understated by $20,000. The entry to correct this error in 2021 is as follows.

Retained Earnings	16,000	
Deferred Tax Liability	4,000	
Accumulated Depreciation—Buildings		20,000

The debit to Retained Earnings results because net income for 2020 is overstated. The debit to Deferred Tax Liability is made to remove this account, which was caused by the error. The credit to Accumulated Depreciation—Buildings reduces the book value of the building to its proper amount. Selectro will make the same journal entry to record the correction of the error in 2021 whether it prepares single-period (noncomparative) or comparative financial statements.

Single-Period Statements

To demonstrate how to show this information in a single-period statement, assume that Selectro Company has a beginning retained earnings balance at January 1, 2021, of $350,000. The company reports net income of $400,000 in 2021. Illustration 22.21 shows Selectro's retained earnings statement for 2021.

ILLUSTRATION 22.21
Reporting an Error—Single-Period Financial Statement

Selectro Company
Retained Earnings Statement
For the Year Ended December 31, 2021

Retained earnings, January 1, as reported		$350,000
Correction of an error (depreciation)	$20,000	
Less: Applicable income tax reduction	4,000	(16,000)
Retained earnings, January 1, as adjusted		334,000
Add: Net income		400,000
Retained earnings, December 31		$734,000

The balance sheet in 2021 would not have any deferred tax liability related to the building, and Accumulated Depreciation—Buildings is now restated at a higher amount. The income statement would not be affected.

Comparative Statements

If preparing comparative financial statements, a company should make adjustments to correct the amounts for all affected accounts reported in the statements for **all periods** reported. The company should restate the data to the correct basis for each year presented. It should **show any catch-up adjustment as a prior period adjustment to retained earnings for the earliest period it reported**. These requirements are essentially the same as those for reporting a change in accounting principle.

For example, in the case of Selectro, the error of omitting the depreciation of $20,000 in 2020, discovered in 2021, results in the restatement of the 2020 financial statements. Illustration 22.22 shows the accounts that Selectro restates in the 2020 financial statements.

ILLUSTRATION 22.22

Reporting an Error—Comparative Financial Statements

In the balance sheet:	
Accumulated depreciation—buildings	$20,000 increase
Deferred tax liability	$ 4,000 decrease
Retained earnings, ending balance	$16,000 decrease
In the income statement:	
Depreciation expense—buildings	$20,000 increase
Income tax expense	$ 4,000 decrease
Net income	$16,000 decrease
In the retained earnings statement:	
Retained earnings, ending balance (due to lower net income for the period)	$16,000 decrease

Selectro prepares the 2021 financial statements in comparative form with those of 2020 **as if the error had not occurred**. In addition, Selectro must disclose that it has restated its previously issued financial statements, and it describes the nature of the error. Selectro also must disclose the following.

1. The effect of the correction on each financial statement line item and any per share amounts affected for each prior period presented.
2. The cumulative effect of the change on retained earnings or other appropriate components of equity or net assets in the statement of financial position, as of the beginning of the earliest period presented. [10]

Summary of Accounting Changes and Correction of Errors

Underlying Concepts

Neutrality is an important element of faithful representation.

Having guidelines for reporting accounting changes and corrections has helped resolve several significant and long-standing accounting problems. Yet, because of diversity in situations and characteristics of the items encountered in practice, use of professional judgment is of paramount importance. In applying these guidelines, the primary objective is to serve the users of the financial statements. Achieving this objective requires accuracy, full disclosure, and an absence of misleading inferences (see Underlying Concepts).

Illustration 22.23 summarizes the main distinctions and treatments presented in the discussion in this chapter.

Changes in accounting principle are appropriate **only** when a company demonstrates that the newly adopted generally accepted accounting principle is **preferable** to the existing one. Companies and accountants determine preferability on the basis of whether the new principle constitutes an **improvement in financial reporting**, not on the basis of the income tax effect alone.[9]

[9]A change in accounting principle, a change in the reporting entity (special type of change in accounting principle), and a correction of an error require an explanatory paragraph in the auditor's report discussing lack of consistency from one period to the next. A change in accounting estimate does not affect the auditor's opinion relative to consistency. However, if the change in estimate has a material effect on the financial statements, disclosure may still be required. Error correction not involving a change in accounting principle does not require disclosure relative to consistency.

ILLUSTRATION 22.23

Summary of Guidelines for Accounting Changes and Errors

Changes in Accounting Principle

Employ the retrospective approach by:

a. Changing the financial statements of all prior periods presented.

b. Disclosing in the year of the change the effect on net income and earnings per share for all prior periods presented.

c. Reporting an adjustment to the beginning retained earnings balance in the retained earnings statement in the earliest year presented.

If impracticable to determine the prior period effect (e.g., change to LIFO):

a. Do not change prior years' income.

b. Use opening inventory in the year the method is adopted as the base-year inventory for all subsequent LIFO computations.

c. Disclose the effect of the change on the current year, and the reasons for omitting the computation of the cumulative effect and pro forma amounts for prior years.

Changes in Accounting Estimate

Employ the current and prospective approach by:

a. Reporting current and future financial statements on the new basis.

b. Presenting prior period financial statements as previously reported.

c. Making no adjustments to current-period opening balances for the effects in prior periods.

Changes in Reporting Entity

Employ the retrospective approach by:

a. Restating the financial statements of all prior periods presented.

b. Disclosing in the year of change the effect on net income and earnings per share data for all prior periods presented.

Changes Due to Error

Employ the restatement approach by:

a. Correcting all prior period statements presented.

b. Restating the beginning balance of retained earnings for the first period presented when the error effects occur in a period prior to the first period presented.

But it is not always easy to determine an improvement in financial reporting. **How does one measure preferability or improvement?** Such measurement varies from company to company. Quaker Oats Company, for example, argued that a change in accounting principle to LIFO inventory valuation "better matches current costs with current revenues" (see Illustration 22.13). Conversely, another company might change from LIFO to FIFO because it wishes to report a more realistic ending inventory. How do you determine which is the better of these two arguments? Determining the preferable method requires some "standard" or "objective." Because no universal standard or objective is generally accepted, the problem of determining preferability continues to be difficult.

Initially, the SEC took the position that the auditor should indicate whether a change in accounting principle was preferable. The SEC has since modified this approach, noting that greater reliance may be placed on management's judgment in assessing preferability. Even though the preferability criterion is difficult to apply, the general guidelines have acted as a deterrent to capricious changes in accounting principles.[10] **If a FASB rule creates a new principle, expresses preference for, or rejects a specific accounting principle, a change is considered clearly acceptable.**

[10]If management has not provided reasonable justification for the change in accounting principle, the auditor should express a qualified opinion. Or, if the effect of the change is sufficiently material, the auditor should express an adverse opinion on the financial statements. See AU-C Section 508, "Reports on Audited Financial Statements," *Statement on Auditing Standards No. 122.* Effective for audits of financial statements for periods ending on or after December 15, 2012. [Predecessor literature: "Reports on Audited Financial Statements," *Statement on Auditing Standards No. 58* (New York: AICPA, 1988).]

What Do the Numbers Mean? What's Your Motivation?

Difficult as it is to determine which accounting standards have the strongest conceptual support, other complications make the process even more complex. These complications stem from the fact that managers have self-interest in how the financial statements make the company look. They naturally wish to show their financial performance in the best light.

Research provides insights into why companies may prefer certain accounting methods. Some of these reasons are as follows.

1. ***Political costs.*** As companies become larger and more politically visible, politicians and regulators devote more attention to them. The larger the firm, the more likely it is to become subject to regulation such as antitrust, and the more likely it is to be required to pay higher taxes. Therefore, companies that are politically visible may seek to report low income numbers, to avoid the scrutiny of regulators. In addition, other constituents, such as labor unions, may be less willing to ask for wage increases if reported income is low. Researchers have found that the larger the company, the more likely it is to adopt income-decreasing approaches in selecting accounting methods.
2. ***Capital structure.*** A number of studies have indicated that the capital structure of the company can affect the selection of accounting methods. For example, a company with a high debt to equity ratio is more likely to be constrained by debt covenants. The debt covenant may indicate that the company cannot pay dividends if retained earnings fall below a certain level. As a result, such a company is more likely to select accounting methods that will increase net income.
3. ***Bonus payments.*** Studies have found that if compensation plans tie managers' bonus payments to income, management will select accounting methods that maximize their bonus payments.
4. ***Smooth earnings.*** Substantial earnings increases attract the attention of politicians, regulators, and competitors. In addition, large increases in income are difficult to achieve in following years. Further, executive compensation plans would use these higher numbers as a baseline and make it difficult for managers to earn bonuses in subsequent years. Conversely, investors and competitors might view large decreases in earnings as a signal that the company is in financial trouble. Also, substantial decreases in income raise concerns on the part of stockholders, lenders, and other interested parties about the competency of management. For all these reasons, companies have an incentive to "manage" or "smooth" earnings. In general, management tends to believe that a steady 10 percent growth a year is much better than a 30 percent growth one year and a 10 percent decline the next. In other words, managers usually prefer a gradually increasing income report and sometimes change accounting methods to ensure such a result.

Management pays careful attention to the accounting it follows and often changes accounting methods, not for conceptual reasons, but for economic reasons. As indicated throughout this text, such arguments have come to be known as **economic consequences** arguments. These arguments focus on the supposed impact of the accounting method on the behavior of investors, creditors, competitors, governments, or managers of the reporting companies themselves.

To counter these pressures, standard-setters such as the FASB have declared, as part of their conceptual framework, that they will assess the merits of proposed standards from a position of **neutrality**. That is, they evaluate the soundness of standards on the basis of conceptual soundness, not on the grounds of possible impact on behavior. It is not the FASB's place to choose standards according to the kinds of behavior it wishes to promote and the kinds it wishes to discourage.

Sources: Ross L. Watts and Jerold L. Zimmerman, "Positive Accounting Theory: A Ten-Year Perspective," *The Accounting Review* (January 1990); and O. Douglas Moses, "Income Smoothing and Incentives: Empirical Tests Using Accounting Changes," *The Accounting Review* (April 1987).

Error Analysis

LEARNING OBJECTIVE 4

Analyze the effects of errors.

In this section, we show some additional types of accounting errors. Companies generally do not correct for errors that do not have a significant effect on the presentation of the financial statements. For example, should a company with a total annual payroll of $1,750,000 and net income of $940,000 correct its financial statements if it finds it failed to record accrued wages of $5,000? No—it would not consider this error significant or material.

Obviously, defining materiality is difficult, and managers and auditors must use experience and judgment to determine whether adjustment is necessary for a given error. We assume **all errors discussed in this section to be material and to require adjustment**. (Also, we ignore all tax effects in this section.)

Companies must answer three questions in error analysis:

1. What type of error is involved?
2. What entries are needed to correct for the error?
3. After discovery of the error, how are financial statements to be restated?

As indicated earlier, companies treat errors **as prior period adjustments and report them in the current year as adjustments to the beginning balance of Retained Earnings**. If a company presents comparative statements, it restates the prior affected statements to correct for the error.

Balance Sheet Errors

Balance sheet errors affect only the presentation of an asset, liability, or stockholders' equity account. Examples are the classification of a short-term receivable as part of the investment section, the classification of a note payable as an account payable, and the classification of plant assets as inventory.

When the error is discovered, the company reclassifies the item to its proper position. If the company prepares comparative statements that include the error year, it should correctly restate the balance sheet for the error year.

Income Statement Errors

Income statement errors involve the improper classification of revenues or expenses. Examples include recording interest revenue as part of sales, purchases as bad debt expense, and depreciation expense as interest expense. An income statement classification error has no effect on the balance sheet and **no effect on net income**.

A company must make a reclassification entry when it discovers the error, if it makes the discovery in the same year in which the error occurs. If the error occurred in prior periods, the company does not need to make a reclassification entry at the date of discovery because the accounts for the current year are correctly stated. (Remember that the company has closed the income statement accounts from the prior period to retained earnings.) If the company prepares comparative statements that include the error year, it restates the income statement for the error year.

Balance Sheet and Income Statement Errors

The third type of error involves both the balance sheet and income statement. For example, assume that the bookkeeper overlooked accrued wages payable at the end of the accounting period. The effect of this error is to understate expenses, understate liabilities, and overstate net income for that period of time. This type of error affects both the balance sheet and the income statement. We classify this type of error in one of two ways—counterbalancing or noncounterbalancing.

Counterbalancing errors are those that will be offset or corrected over two periods. For example, the failure to record accrued wages is a counterbalancing error because over a two-year period the error will no longer be present. In other words, the failure to record accrued wages in the previous period means (1) net income for the first period is overstated, (2) accrued wages payable (a liability) is understated, and (3) wages expense is understated. In the next period, net income is understated, accrued wages payable (a liability) is correctly stated, and wages expense is overstated. For the two **years combined**: (1) net income is correct, (2) wages expense is correct, and (3) accrued wages payable at the end of the second year is correct. Most errors in accounting that affect both the balance sheet and income statement are counterbalancing errors.

Noncounterbalancing errors are those that are not offset in the next accounting period. An example would be the failure to capitalize equipment that has a useful life of five years. If we expense this asset immediately, expenses will be overstated in the first period but understated in the next four periods. At the end of the second period, the effect of the error is not fully offset. Net income is correct in the aggregate only at the end of five years because the asset is fully depreciated at this point. Thus, **noncounterbalancing errors are those that take longer than two periods to correct themselves**.

Only in rare instances is an error never reversed. An example would be if a company initially expenses land. Because land is not depreciable, theoretically the error is never offset, unless the land is sold.

Counterbalancing Errors

We illustrate the usual types of counterbalancing errors in the following sections. In studying these illustrations, keep in mind a couple of points.

First, determine whether the company has closed the books for the period in which the error is found:

1. If the company has closed the books in the current year:
   a. If the error is already counterbalanced, no entry is necessary.
   b. If the error is not yet counterbalanced, make an entry to adjust the present balance of retained earnings.
2. If the company has not closed the books in the current year:
   a. If the error is already counterbalanced, make an entry to correct the error in the current period and to adjust the beginning balance of Retained Earnings.
   b. If the error is not yet counterbalanced, make an entry to adjust the beginning balance of Retained Earnings.

Second, if the company presents comparative statements, it must restate the amounts for comparative purposes. **Restatement is necessary even if a correcting journal entry is not required.**

To illustrate, assume that Sanford Cement Co. failed to accrue revenue in 2018 when it fulfilled its performance obligation, but recorded the revenue in 2019 when it received payment. The company discovered the error in 2021. It does not need to make an entry to correct for this error because the effects have been counterbalanced by the time Sanford discovered the error in 2021. However, if Sanford presents comparative financial statements for 2018 through 2021, it must **restate the accounts and related amounts for the years 2018 and 2019 for financial reporting purposes**.

The sections that follow demonstrate the accounting for the usual types of counterbalancing errors.

Failure to Record Accrued Wages On December 31, 2020, Hurley Enterprises did not accrue wages in the amount of $1,500. The entry in 2021 to correct this error, assuming Hurley has not closed the books for 2021, is:

Retained Earnings	1,500	
Salaries and Wages Expense		1,500

The rationale for this entry is as follows. (1) When Hurley pays the 2020 accrued wages in 2021, it makes an additional debit of $1,500 to 2021 Salaries and Wages Expense. (2) Salaries and Wages Expense—2021 is overstated by $1,500. (3) Because the company did not record 2020 accrued wages as Salaries and Wages Expense in 2020, the net income for 2020 was overstated by $1,500. (4) Because 2020 net income is overstated by $1,500, the Retained Earnings account is overstated by $1,500 (because net income is closed to Retained Earnings).

If Hurley has closed the books for 2021, it makes no entry because the error is counterbalanced.

Failure to Record Prepaid Expenses In January 2020, Hurley Enterprises purchased a two-year insurance policy costing $1,000. It debited Insurance Expense, and credited Cash. The company made no adjusting entries at the end of 2020.

The entry on December 31, 2021, to correct this error, assuming Hurley has not closed the books for 2021, is:

Insurance Expense	500	
Retained Earnings		500

If Hurley has closed the books for 2021, it makes no entry because the error is counterbalanced.

Understatement of Unearned Revenue On December 31, 2020, Hurley Enterprises received $50,000 as a prepayment for renting certain office space for the following year. At the time of receipt of the rent payment, the company recorded a debit to Cash and a credit to Rent Revenue. It made no adjusting entry as of December 31, 2020. The entry on December 31, 2021, to correct for this error, assuming that Hurley has not closed the books for 2021, is:

Retained Earnings	50,000	
Rent Revenue		50,000

If Hurley has closed the books for 2021, it makes no entry because the error is counterbalanced.

Overstatement of Accrued Revenue On December 31, 2020, Hurley Enterprises accrued as interest revenue $8,000 that applied to 2021. On that date, the company recorded a debit to Interest Receivable and a credit to Interest Revenue. The entry on December 31, 2021, to correct for this error, assuming that Hurley has not closed the books for 2021, is:

Retained Earnings	8,000	
Interest Revenue		8,000

If Hurley has closed the books for 2021, it makes no entry because the error is counterbalanced.

Overstatement of Purchases Hurley's accountant recorded a purchase of merchandise for $9,000 in 2020 that applied to 2021. The physical inventory for 2020 was correctly stated. The company uses the periodic inventory method. The entry on December 31, 2021, to correct for this error, assuming that Harley has not closed the books for 2021, is:

Purchases	9,000	
Retained Earnings		9,000

If Hurley has closed the books for 2021, it makes no entry because the error is counterbalanced.

Noncounterbalancing Errors

The entries for noncounterbalancing errors are more complex. Companies must make correcting entries, even if they have closed the books.

Failure to Record Depreciation Assume that on January 1, 2020, Hurley Enterprises purchased a machine for $10,000 that had an estimated useful life of five years. The accountant incorrectly expensed this machine in 2020, but discovered the error in 2021. If we assume that Hurley uses straight-line depreciation on this asset, the entry on December 31, 2021, to correct for this error, given that Hurley has or has not closed the books, is as follows.

Hurley has not closed the books for 2021:

Equipment	10,000	
Depreciation Expense	2,000	
Retained Earnings		8,000*
Accumulated Depreciation—Equipment (.20 × $10,000 × 2)		4,000

*Overstatement of expense in 2020	$10,000
Proper depreciation for 2020 (.20 × $10,000)	(2,000)
Retained earnings understated as of Dec. 31, 2020	$ 8,000

Hurley has closed the books for 2021:

Equipment	10,000	
Retained Earnings		6,000*
Accumulated Depreciation—Equipment		4,000

*Retained earnings understated as of Dec. 31, 2020	$ 8,000
Proper depreciation for 2021 (.20 × $10,000)	(2,000)
Retained earnings understated as of Dec. 31, 2021	$ 6,000

Failure to Adjust for Bad Debts Companies sometimes use a specific charge-off method in accounting for bad debt expense when a percentage of sales is more appropriate. They then make adjustments to change from the specific write-off method to some type of allowance method. For example, assume that Hurley Enterprises has recognized bad debt expense when it has the following uncollectible debts.

	2020	2021
From 2020 sales	$550	$690
From 2021 sales		700

Hurley estimates that it will charge off an additional $1,400 in 2022, of which $300 is applicable to 2020 sales and $1,100 to 2021 sales. The entry on December 31, 2021, assuming that Hurley has or has not closed the books for 2021, is as follows.

Hurley has not closed the books in 2021:

Bad Debt Expense	410	
Retained Earnings	990	
Allowance for Doubtful Accounts		1,400

Allowance for doubtful accounts: Additional $300 for 2020 sales and $1,100 for 2021 sales.

Bad debts and retained earnings balance:

	2020	2021
Bad debts charged for	$1,240*	$ 700
Additional bad debts anticipated in 2022	300	1,100
Proper bad debt expense	1,540	1,800
Charges currently made to each period	(550)	(1,390)
Bad debt adjustment	$ 990	$ 410

*$550 + $690 = $1,240

Hurley has closed the books for 2021:

Retained Earnings	1,400	
Allowance for Doubtful Accounts		1,400

Comprehensive Example: Numerous Errors

In some circumstances, a combination of errors occurs. The company therefore prepares a worksheet to facilitate the analysis. The following problem demonstrates use of the worksheet. The mechanics of its preparation should be obvious from the solution format. The income statements of Hudson Company for the years ended December 31, 2019, 2020, and 2021, indicate the following net incomes.

2019	$17,400
2020	20,200
2021	11,300

An examination of the accounting records for these years indicates that Hudson Company made several errors in arriving at the net income amounts reported:

1. The company consistently omitted from the records wages earned by workers but not paid at December 31. The amounts omitted were:

December 31, 2019	$1,000
December 31, 2020	1,400
December 31, 2021	1,600

When paid in the year following that in which they were earned, Hudson recorded these amounts as expenses.

2. The company overstated merchandise inventory on December 31, 2019, by $1,900 as the result of errors made in the footings and extensions on the inventory sheets.
3. On December 31, 2020, Hudson expensed prepaid insurance of $1,200, applicable to 2021.
4. The company did not record on December 31, 2020, interest receivable in the amount of $240.
5. On January 2, 2020, Hudson sold for $1,800 a piece of equipment costing $3,900. At the date of sale, the equipment had accumulated depreciation of $2,400. The company recorded the cash received as Miscellaneous Income in 2020. In addition, the company continued to record depreciation for this equipment in both 2020 and 2021 at the rate of 10 percent of cost.

The first step in preparing the worksheet is to prepare a schedule showing the reported net income amounts for the years ended December 31, 2019, 2020, and 2021. Each correction of the amount originally reported is clearly labeled. The next step is to indicate the balance sheet accounts affected as of December 31, 2021. **Illustration 22.24** shows the completed worksheet for Hudson Company.

ILLUSTRATION 22.24 **Worksheet to Correct Income and Balance Sheet Errors**

Hudson Company

Home Insert Page Layout Formulas Data Review View

P18 *fx*

	A	B	C	D	E	F	G	H
1			**Hudson Company**					
2			**Worksheet to Correct Income and**					
3			**Balance Sheet Errors**					
4			Worksheet Analysis of Changes in Net Income				Balance Sheet Correction at December 31, 2021	
5		2019	2020	2021	Totals	Debit	Credit	Account
6	Net income as reported	$17,400	$20,200	$11,300	$48,900			
7	Wages unpaid, 12/31/19	(1,000)	1,000		–0–			
8	Wages unpaid, 12/31/20		(1,400)	1,400	–0–			
9	Wages unpaid, 12/31/21			(1,600)	(1,600)		$1,600	Salaries and Wages Payable
10	Inventory overstatement, 12/31/19	(1,900)	1,900		–0–			
11	Prepaid insurance, 12/31/20		1,200	(1,200)	–0–			
12	Interest receivable, 12/31/20		240	(240)	–0–			
13	Correction for entry made upon sale of equipment, 1/2/20[a]		(1,500)		(1,500)	$2,400		Accumulated Depreciation—Equipment
							3,900	Equipment
14	Overcharge of depreciation, 2020		390		390	390		Accumulated Depreciation—Equipment
15	Overcharge of depreciation, 2021			390	390	390		Accumulated Depreciation—Equipment
16	Corrected net income	$14,500	$22,030	$10,050	$46,580			
17	[a]Cost	$ 3,900						
18	Less: Accumulated depreciation	2,400						
19	Book value	1,500						
20	Less: Proceeds from sale	1,800						
21	Gain on sale	300						
22	Income reported	(1,800)						
23	Adjustment	$(1,500)						

The correcting entries on December 31, 2021, assuming the books have not or have been closed, are as follows.

Hudson Company has not closed the books for 2021:

Retained Earnings	1,400	
Salaries and Wages Expense		1,400
(To correct improper charge to Salaries and Wages Expense for 2021)		
Salaries and Wages Expense	1,600	
Salaries and Wages Payable		1,600
(To record proper wages expense for 2021)		
Insurance Expense	1,200	
Retained Earnings		1,200
(To record proper insurance expense for 2021)		
Interest Revenue	240	
Retained Earnings		240
(To correct improper credit to Interest Revenue in 2021)		
Retained Earnings	1,500	
Accumulated Depreciation—Equipment	2,400	
Equipment		3,900
(To record write-off of equipment in 2020 and adjustment of Retained Earnings)		
Accumulated Depreciation—Equipment	780	
Depreciation Expense		390
Retained Earnings		390
(To correct improper charge for depreciation expense in 2020 and 2021)		

Hudson Company has closed the books for 2021:

Retained Earnings	1,600	
Salaries and Wages Payable		1,600
(To record proper wage expense for 2021)		
Retained Earnings	1,500	
Accumulated Depreciation—Equipment	2,400	
Equipment		3,900
(To record write-off of equipment in 2020 and adjustment of Retained Earnings)		
Accumulated Depreciation—Equipment	780	
Retained Earnings		780
(To correct improper charge for depreciation expense in 2020 and 2021)		

What Do the Numbers Mean? Guard the Financial Statements!

Restatements sometimes occur because of financial fraud. Financial frauds involve the intentional misstatement or omission of material information in the organization's financial reports. Common methods of financial fraud manipulation include recording fictitious revenues, concealing liabilities or expenses, and artificially inflating reported assets.

Of the three primary categories of occupational fraud, asset misappropriations are by far the most common, occurring in 89 percent of the cases. However, they are also the least costly, causing a median loss of $114,000. Corruption schemes are the next most common form of occupational fraud; 38 percent of the cases involved some form of corrupt act. These schemes resulted in a median loss to the victim organizations of $250,000. The least common and most costly form of occupational fraud is financial statement fraud, which occurred in 10 percent of the cases and caused a median loss of $800,000. The following chart indicates the types of occupational fraud committed and the median loss for each category.

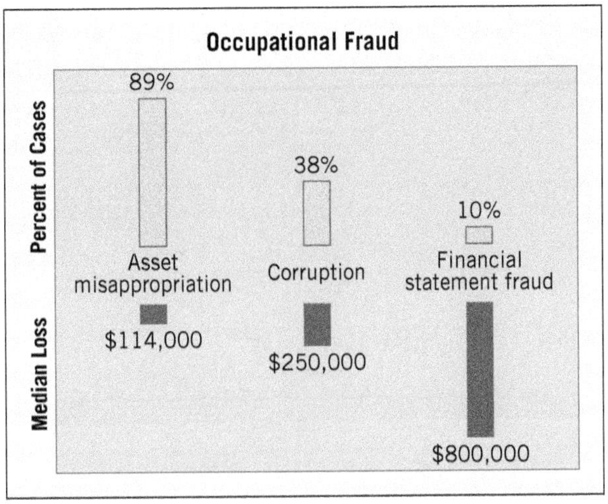

Here are the most common types of financial statement fraud:

1. Revenue recognition.
2. Irregularities associated with foreign subsidiaries and affiliates of U.S. companies.
3. Misclassifications of accounts, such as cash, investments, receivables, and allowances for doubtful accounts.
4. Inappropriate determination of inventory costs, cost of sales, and the inventory balances at year-end.
5. Expense recording issues.
6. Identification of liabilities on the balance sheet.

Sources: *Report to the Nations on Occupational Fraud and Abuse, 2018 Global Fraud Study*, Association of Certified Fraud Examiners (2018), p. 10; C. McDonald, "Fraud Reports Climb Still Higher," *CFO.com* (September 26, 2012); and F. Alali and I. Wang, "Characteristics of Financial Statements and Frauds," *CPA Journal* (November 11, 2017).

Preparation of Financial Statements with Error Corrections

Up to now, our discussion of error analysis has focused on identifying the type of error involved and accounting for its correction in the records. We have noted that companies must present the correction of the error on comparative financial statements.

The following example illustrates how a company would restate a typical year's financial statements, given many different errors.

Dick & Wally's Outlet is a small retail outlet in the town of Holiday. Lacking expertise in accounting, the company does not keep adequate records, and numerous errors occurred in recording accounting information.

1. The bookkeeper inadvertently failed to record a cash receipt of $1,000 on the sale of merchandise in 2021.
2. Accrued wages expense at the end of 2020 was $2,500; at the end of 2021, $3,200. The company does not accrue for wages; all wages are charged to Administrative Expenses.
3. The company had not set up an allowance for estimated uncollectible receivables. Dick and Wally decided to set up such an allowance for the estimated probable losses, as of December 31, 2021, for 2020 accounts of $700, and for 2021 accounts of $1,500. They also decided to correct the charge against each year so that it shows the losses (actual and estimated) relating to that year's sales. The company has written off accounts to bad debt expense (selling expense) as follows.

	In 2020	In 2021
2020 accounts	$400	$2,000
2021 accounts		1,600

4. Prepaid insurance not recorded at the end of 2020 was $600, and at the end of 2021, $400. All insurance is charged to Administrative Expenses.
5. An account payable of $6,000 should have been a note payable.
6. During 2020, the company sold for $7,000 an asset that cost $10,000 and had a book value of $4,000. At the time of sale, Cash was debited and Miscellaneous Income was credited for $7,000.
7. As a result of the last transaction, the company overstated depreciation expense (an administrative expense) in 2020 by $800 and in 2021 by $1,200.

Illustration 22.25 presents a worksheet that begins with the unadjusted trial balance of Dick & Wally's Outlet. You can determine the correcting entries and their effect on the financial statements by examining the worksheet.

ILLUSTRATION 22.25 **Worksheet to Analyze Effect of Errors in Financial Statements**

Dick & Wally's Outlet

Home Insert Page Layout Formulas Data Review View

P18 *fx*

Dick & Wally's Outlet
Worksheet Analysis to Adjust Financial Statements for the Year 2021

	A	B	C	D	E	F	G	H	I	J
5		Trial Balance					Income Statement		Balance Sheet	
6		Unadjusted		Adjustments			Adjusted		Adjusted	
7		Dr.	Cr.		Dr.	Cr.	Dr.	Cr.	Dr.	Cr.
8	Cash	3,100		(1)	1,000				4,100	
9	Accounts Receivable	17,600							17,600	
10	Notes Receivable	8,500							8,500	
11	Inventory	34,000							34,000	
12	Property, Plant, and Equipment	112,000				(6) 10,000[a]			102,000	
13	Accumulated Depreciation—Equipment		83,500	(6) (7)	6,000[a] 2,000					75,500
14										
15	Investments	24,300							24,300	
16	Accounts Payable		14,500	(5)	6,000					8,500
17	Notes Payable		10,000			(5) 6,000				16,000
18	Capital Stock		43,500							43,500
19	Retained Earnings		20,000	(3)	2,700[b]					
20				(6)	4,000[a]	(4) 600				
21				(2)	2,500	(7) 800				12,200
22	Sales Revenue		94,000			(1) 1,000		95,000		
23	Cost of Goods Sold	21,000					21,000			
24	Selling Expenses	22,000				(3) 500[b]	21,500			
25	Administrative Expenses	23,000		(2)	700	(4) 400	22,700			
26				(4)	600	(7) 1,200				
27	Totals	265,500	265,500							
28										
29	Salaries and Wages Payable					(2) 3,200				3,200
30	Allowance for Doubtful Accounts					(3) 2,200[b]				2,200
32	Prepaid Insurance			(4)	400				400	
33	Net Income						29,800			29,800
34	Totals				25,900	25,900	95,000	95,000	190,900	190,900
35										

Computations:

[a]Machinery

Proceeds from sale	$ 7,000
Book value of machinery	(4,000)
Gain on sale	3,000
Less: Income credited	7,000
Retained earnings adjustment	$(4,000)

[b]Bad Debts

	2020	2021
Bad debts charged for	$2,400	$1,600
Additional bad debts anticipated	700	1,500
	3,100	3,100
Charges currently made to each year	(400)	(3,600)
Bad debt adjustment	$2,700	$ (500)

APPENDIX 22A Changing from or to the Equity Method

LEARNING OBJECTIVE *5

Make the computations and prepare the entries necessary to record a change from or to the equity method of accounting.

As noted in the chapter, companies generally should report an accounting change that results in financial statements for a different entity by **changing the financial statements of all prior periods presented**.

An example of a change in reporting entity is when a company's level of ownership or influence changes, such as when it changes from or to the equity method. When changing **to** the equity method, companies use retrospective application. Companies treat a change **from** the equity method prospectively. We present examples of these changes in entity in the following two sections.

Change from the Equity Method

If the investor level of influence or ownership falls below that necessary for continued use of the equity method, a company must change from the equity method to the fair value method. The earnings or losses that the investor previously recognized under the equity method should **remain as part of the carrying amount** of the investment, with no retrospective application to the new method.

When a company changes **from the equity method to the fair value method, the cost basis for accounting purposes is the carrying amount of the investment at the date of the change**. The investor applies the new method in its entirety once the equity method is no longer appropriate. At the next reporting date, the investor should record the unrealized holding gain or loss to recognize the difference between the carrying amount and fair value.[11]

Dividends in Excess of Earnings

In subsequent periods, dividends received by the investor company may exceed its share of the investee's earnings for such periods (all periods following the change in method). To the extent that they do so, the investor company should account for such dividends as a **reduction of the investment carrying amount**, rather than as revenue. The reason: Dividends in excess of earnings are viewed as a liquidating dividend, with this excess then accounted for as a reduction of the equity investment.

To illustrate, assume that on January 1, 2019, Investor Company purchased 250,000 shares of Investee Company's 1,000,000 shares of outstanding stock for $8,500,000. Investor correctly accounted for this investment using the equity method. After accounting for dividends received and investee net income, in 2019 Investor reported its investment in Investee Company at $8,780,000 at December 31, 2019. On January 2, 2020, Investee Company sold 1,500,000 additional shares of its own common stock to the public, thereby reducing Investor Company's ownership from 25 percent to 10 percent. Illustration 22A.1 shows the net income (or loss) and dividends of Investee Company for the years 2020 through 2022.

[11] A retrospective application for this type of change is impracticable in many cases. Determining fair values on a portfolio basis for securities in previous periods may be quite difficult. As a result, prospective application is used.

ILLUSTRATION 22A.1

Income Earned and Dividends Received

Year		Investor's Share of Investee Income (Loss)	Investee Dividends Received by Investor
2020		$600,000	$ 400,000
2021		350,000	400,000
2022		-0-	210,000
	Totals	$950,000	$1,010,000

Assuming a change from the equity method to the fair value method as of January 2, 2020, Investor Company's reported investment in Investee Company and its reported income would be as shown in **Illustration 22A.2**.

ILLUSTRATION 22A.2

Impact on Investment Carrying Amount

Year	Dividend Revenue Recognized	Cumulative Excess of Share of Earnings over Dividends Received	Investment at December 31
2020	$400,000	$200,000[a]	$8,780,000
2021	400,000	150,000[b]	8,780,000
2022	150,000	(60,000)[c]	$8,780,000 – $60,000 = $8,720,000

[a]$600,000 – $400,000 = $200,000
[b]($350,000 – $400,000) + $200,000 = $150,000
[c]$150,000 – $210,000 = $(60,000)

Investor Company would record the dividends and earnings data for the three years subsequent to the change in methods as shown by the following entries.

2020 and 2021

Cash	400,000	
Dividend Revenue		400,000
(To record dividend received from Investee Company)		

2022

Cash	210,000	
Equity Investments		60,000
Dividend Revenue		150,000
(To record dividend revenue from Investee Company in 2022 and to recognize cumulative excess of dividends received over share of Investee earnings in periods subsequent to change from the equity method)		

Change to the Equity Method

When converting to the equity method, companies use the prospective approach. Recall that under this approach, companies do not adjust opening balances to reflect the change in principle on prior reported results. Instead, they account for the effects of the change in (1) the period of change if the change affects that period only, or (2) the period of change and future periods if the change affects both. In applying the prospective approach to the change to the equity method, the investor company should add the cost of acquiring the additional interest in the investee company to the cost basis of their previously held interest (the present stock holding). [11][12]

For example, assume that Exact Technology on January 1, 2020, purchases a 10 percent stock interest in Cellular4D that costs $850,000. Exact Technology uses the fair value method to account for its interest in Cellular4D by adjusting its cost basis to fair value at the end of a reporting period. The entry to record the purchase of Cellular4D on January 1, 2020, is as follows.

January 1, 2020		
Equity Investment	850,000	
Cash		850,000
(To record the purchase of a 10% interest in Cellular4D)		

At December 31, 2020, the fair value of Exact Technology's investment is $1,000,000. The entry to record the excess of the fair value over its cost for Exact Technology's investment is as follows.

December 31, 2020		
Fair Value Adjustment	150,000	
Unrealized Holding Gain or Loss—Income ($1,000,000 – $850,000)		150,000
(To record increase in value of securities)		

On January 1, 2021, Exact Technology now purchases an additional 20 percent stock interest in Cellular4D for $4,000,000. Because of this additional investment, Exact Technology now exerts significant influence over the operations of Cellular4D. Exact Technology must use the equity method to account for this investment. Exact Technology adds the cost of acquiring the additional interest in Cellular4D of $4,000,000 to its original cost basis of $850,000 to determine a new cost basis in Cellular4D of $4,850,000 ($4,000,000 + $850,000).

Exact Technology makes the following entry to record this additional investment in Cellular4D.

January 1, 2021		
Equity Investment (Cellular4D)	4,000,000	
Cash		4,000,000
(To record the purchase of the additional interest in Cellular4D)		

Exact Technology then reclassifies its existing balance in the investment account as follows.

January 1, 2021		
Equity Investment (Cellular4D)	850,000	
Equity Investment		850,000
(To reclassify initial 10% interest to equity method)		

In addition, Exact Technology must adjust the fair value accounts when it changes to the equity method. The entry to record this transaction is as follows.

January 1, 2021		
Retained Earnings	150,000	
Fair Value Adjustment ($1,000,000 – $850,000)		150,000
(To eliminate fair value accounts for change to equity method)		

Exact Technology now reports an equity investment at $4,850,000. Subsequently, Exact Technology will adjust the cost basis of $4,850,000 for changes in the net income and dividends of Cellular4D under the equity method as discussed in Chapter 17.

[12]At one time, when an investment qualified for use of the equity method because of an increase in the level of ownership interest or degree of influence, the investor had to retroactively restate the investment, results of operations, and retained earnings, which often was a very complex task. The FASB decided that the retroactive method was too costly and time-consuming to implement, and of little benefit to users. See *FASB Accounting Standards Update No. 2016-07*, "Simplifying the Transition to the Equity Method of Accounting" (March 2016).

Review and Practice

Key Terms Review

Learning Objectives Review

1 Discuss the types of accounting changes and the accounting for changes in accounting principles.

The three different types of accounting changes are as follows. (1) *Change in accounting principle*: a change from one generally accepted accounting principle to another generally accepted accounting principle. (2) *Change in accounting estimate:* a change that occurs as the result of new information or as additional experience is acquired. (3) *Change in reporting entity:* a change from reporting as one type of entity to another type of entity.

A **change in accounting principle** involves a change from one generally accepted accounting principle to another. A change in accounting principle is not considered to result from the adoption of a new principle in recognition of events that have occurred for the first time or that were previously immaterial. If the accounting principle previously followed was not acceptable or if the principle was applied incorrectly, a change to a generally accepted accounting principle is considered a correction of an error.

The general requirement for changes in accounting principle is **retrospective application**. Under retrospective application, companies change prior years' financial statements on a basis consistent with the newly adopted principle. They treat any part of the effect attributable to years prior to those presented as an adjustment of the earliest retained earnings presented. However, retrospective application is impracticable if the prior period effect cannot be determined using every reasonable effort to do so. For example, in changing to LIFO, the base-year inventory for all subsequent LIFO calculations is generally the opening inventory in the year the company adopts the method. There is no restatement of prior years' income because it is often too impractical to do so.

2 Describe the accounting for changes in estimates and changes in the reporting entity.

Companies report changes in estimates prospectively. That is, companies should make no changes in previously reported results. They do not adjust opening balances nor change financial statements of prior periods.

An accounting change that results in financial statements that are actually the statements of a different entity should be reported by restating the financial statements of all prior periods presented, to show the financial information for the new reporting entity for all periods.

3 Describe the accounting for correction of errors.

Companies must correct errors as soon as they discover them, by proper entries in the accounts, and report them in the financial statements. The profession requires that a company treat corrections of errors as prior period adjustments, record them in the year in which it discovered the errors, and report them in the financial statements in the proper periods. If presenting comparative statements, a company should restate the prior statements affected to correct for the errors. The company need not repeat the disclosures in the financial statements of subsequent periods.

4 Analyze the effects of errors.

Three types of errors can occur. (1) *Balance sheet errors*, which affect only the presentation of an asset, liability, or stockholders' equity account. (2) *Income statement errors*, which affect only the presentation of revenue, expense, gain, or loss accounts in the income statement. (3) *Balance sheet and income statement errors*, which involve both the balance sheet and income statement. Errors are classified into two types. (1) *Counterbalancing errors* are offset or corrected over two periods. (2) *Noncounterbalancing errors* are not offset in the next accounting period and take longer than two periods to correct themselves.

*5 Make the computations and prepare the entries necessary to record a change from or to the equity method of accounting.

When changing *from* the equity method to the fair value method, the cost basis for accounting purposes is the carrying amount used for the investment at the date of change. The investor company applies the new method in its entirety once the equity method is no longer appropriate. When changing *to* the equity method, companies use the prospective approach by adding the cost of acquiring the additional interest in the investee company to the cost basis of their previously held interest.

As an aid to understanding accounting changes, we provide the following glossary.

Key Terms Related to Accounting Changes

1. **Accounting Change.** A change in (1) an accounting principle, (2) an accounting estimate, or (3) the reporting entity. The correction of an error in previously issued financial statements is not an accounting change.
2. **Change in Accounting Principle.** A change from one generally accepted accounting principle to another generally accepted accounting principle when two or more generally accepted accounting principles apply or when the accounting principle formerly used is no longer generally accepted.
3. **Change in Accounting Estimate.** A change that has the effect of adjusting the carrying amount of an existing asset or liability or altering the subsequent accounting for existing or future assets or liabilities. Changes in accounting estimates result from new information.
4. **Change in Accounting Estimate Effected by a Change in Accounting Principle.** A change in accounting estimate that is inseparable from the effect of a related change in accounting principle.
5. **Change in Reporting Entity.** A change that results in financial statements that, in effect, are those of a different reporting entity.
6. **Direct Effects of a Change in Accounting Principle.** Those recognized changes in assets or liabilities necessary to effect a change in accounting principle.
7. **Error in Previously Issued Financial Statements.** An error in recognition, measurement, presentation, or disclosure in financial statements resulting from mathematical mistakes, mistakes in the application of GAAP, or oversight or misuse of facts that existed at the time the financial statements were prepared. A change from an accounting principle that is not generally accepted to one that is generally accepted is a correction of an error.
8. **Indirect Effects of a Change in Accounting Principle.** Any changes to current or future cash flows of an entity that result from making a change in accounting principle that is applied retrospectively.
9. **Restatement.** The process of revising previously issued financial statements to reflect the correction of an error in those financial statements.
10. **Retrospective Application.** The application of a different accounting principle to one or more previously issued financial statements, or to the statement of financial position at the beginning of the current period, as if that principle had always been used, or a change to financial statements of prior accounting periods to present the financial statements of a new reporting entity as if it had existed in those prior years. [12]

Enhanced Review and Practice

Go online for multiple-choice questions with solutions, review exercises with solutions, and a full glossary of all key terms.

Practice Problem

Wangerin Company is in the process of adjusting and correcting its books at the end of 2020. In reviewing its records, the following information is compiled.

1. At December 31, 2020, Wangerin decided to change the depreciation method on its office equipment from double-declining-balance to straight-line. The equipment had an original cost of $200,000 when purchased on January 1, 2018. It has a 10-year useful life and no salvage value. Depreciation expense recorded prior to 2020 under the double-declining-balance method was $72,000. Wangerin has already recorded 2020 depreciation expense of $25,600 using the double-declining-balance method.
2. Before 2020, Wangerin accounted for its income from long-term construction contracts on the completed-contract basis. Early in 2020, Wangerin changed to the percentage-of-completion basis for accounting purposes. It continues to use the completed-contract method for tax purposes. Income for 2020 has been recorded using the percentage-of-completion method. The following information is available.

	Pretax Income from	
	Percentage-of-Completion	Completed-Contract
Prior to 2020	$450,000	$315,000
2020	180,000	60,000

3. Insurance for a 12-month period purchased on November 1 of this year was charged to insurance expense in the amount of $3,300 because "the amount of the check is about the same every year."
4. Reported sales revenue for the year is $1,908,000. This includes all sales taxes collected for the year. The sales tax rate is 6%. Because the sales tax is forwarded to the state's Department of Revenue, the Sales Tax Expense account is debited. The bookkeeper thought that "the sales tax is a selling expense." At the end of the current year, the balance in the Sales Tax Expense account is $103,400.

Instructions

Prepare the journal entries necessary at December 31, 2020, to record the above corrections and changes. The books are still open for 2020. The income tax rate is 20%. Wangerin has not yet recorded its 2020 income tax expense and payable amounts so current-year tax effects may be ignored. Prior-year tax effects must be considered in item 2.

Solution

1.	Accumulated Depreciation—Equipment	9,600	
	Depreciation Expense		9,600*
	*Equipment cost	$200,000	
	Depreciation before 2020	(72,000)	
	Book value	$128,000	
	Depreciation recorded	$ 25,600	
	Depreciation to be taken ($128,000 ÷ 8)	(16,000)	
	Difference	$ 9,600	
2.	Construction In Process	135,000	
	Deferred Tax Liability		27,000*
	Retained Earnings		108,000
	*($450,000 – $315,000) × .20		
3.	Prepaid Insurance ($3,300 × 10/12)	2,750	
	Insurance Expense		2,750
4.	Sales Revenue [$1,908,000 ÷ (1.00 + .06) × .06]	108,000	
	Sales Taxes Payable		108,000
	Sales Taxes Payable	103,400	
	Sales Tax Expense		103,400

WileyPLUS

Exercises, Problems, Problem Solution Walkthrough Videos, and many more assessment tools and resources are available for practice in WileyPLUS.

Note: All asterisked Questions, Exercises, and Problems relate to material in the appendix to the chapter.

Questions

1. In recent years, the *Wall Street Journal* has indicated that many companies have changed their accounting principles. What are the major reasons why companies change accounting methods?

2. State how each of the following items is reflected in the financial statements.

   a. Change from FIFO to LIFO method for inventory valuation purposes.
   b. Charge for failure to record depreciation in a previous period.
   c. Litigation won in current year, related to prior period.
   d. Change in the realizability of certain receivables.
   e. Write-off of receivables.
   f. Change from the percentage-of-completion to the completed-contract method for reporting net income.

3. Discuss briefly the three approaches that have been suggested for reporting changes in accounting principles.

4. Identify and describe the approach the FASB requires for reporting changes in accounting principles.

5. What is the indirect effect of a change in accounting principle? Briefly describe the reporting of the indirect effects of a change in accounting principle.

6. Define a change in estimate and provide an illustration. When is a change in accounting estimate effected by a change in accounting principle?

7. Lenexa State Bank has followed the practice of capitalizing certain marketing costs and amortizing these costs over their expected life. In the current year, the bank determined that the future benefits from these costs were doubtful. Consequently, the bank adopted the policy of expensing these costs as incurred. How should the bank report this accounting change in the comparative financial statements?

8. Indicate how the following items are recorded in the accounting records in the current year of Coronet Co.

a. Impairment of goodwill.

b. A change in depreciating plant assets from accelerated to the straight-line method.

c. Large write-off of inventories because of obsolescence.

d. Change from the cash basis to accrual basis of accounting.

e. Change from LIFO to FIFO method for inventory valuation purposes.

f. Change in the estimate of service lives for plant assets.

9. Whittier Construction Co. had followed the practice of expensing all materials assigned to a construction job without recognizing any salvage inventory. On December 31, 2020, it was determined that salvage inventory should be valued at $52,000. Of this amount, $29,000 arose during the current year. How does this information affect the financial statements to be prepared at the end of 2020?

10. Parsons Inc. has proposed a change from one inventory accounting method to another for financial reporting purposes. The auditor indicates that a change would be permitted only if it is to a preferable method. What difficulties develop in assessing preferability?

11. Discuss how a change to the LIFO method of inventory valuation is handled when it is impracticable to determine previous LIFO inventory amounts.

12. How should consolidated financial statements be reported this year when statements of individual companies were presented last year?

13. Simms Corp. controlled four domestic subsidiaries and one foreign subsidiary. Prior to the current year, Simms Corp. had excluded the foreign subsidiary from consolidation. During the current year, the foreign subsidiary was included in the financial statements. How should this change in accounting entity be reflected in the financial statements?

14. Distinguish between counterbalancing and noncounterbalancing errors. Give an example of each.

15. Discuss and illustrate how a correction of an error in previously issued financial statements should be handled.

16. Prior to 2020, Heberling Inc. excluded manufacturing overhead costs from work in process and finished goods inventory. These costs have been expensed as incurred. In 2020, the company decided to change its accounting methods for manufacturing inventories to full costing by including these costs as product costs. Assuming that these costs are material, how should this change be reflected in the financial statements for 2019 and 2020?

17. Elliott Corp. failed to record accrued salaries for 2019, $2,000; 2020, $2,100; and 2021, $3,900. What is the amount of the overstatement or understatement of Retained Earnings at December 31, 2022?

18. In January 2020, installation costs of $6,000 on new machinery were charged to Maintenance and Repairs Expense. Other costs of this machinery of $30,000 were correctly recorded and have been depreciated using the straight-line method with an estimated life of 10 years and no salvage value. At December 31, 2021, it is decided that the machinery has a remaining useful life of 20 years, starting with January 1, 2021. What entry(ies) should be made in 2021 to correctly record transactions related to machinery, assuming the machinery has no salvage value? The books have not been closed for 2021 and depreciation expense has not yet been recorded for 2021.

19. On January 2, 2020, $100,000 of 11%, 10-year bonds were issued for $97,000. The $3,000 discount was charged to Interest Expense. The bookkeeper, Mark Landis, records interest only on the interest payment dates of January 1 and July 1. What is the effect on reported net income for 2020 of this error, assuming straight-line amortization of the discount? What entry is necessary to correct for this error, assuming that the books are not closed for 2020?

20. An entry to record Purchases and related Accounts Payable of $13,000 for merchandise purchased on December 23, 2021, was recorded in January 2022. This merchandise was not included in inventory at December 31, 2021. What effect does this error have on reported net income for 2021? What entry should be made to correct for this error, assuming that the books are not closed for 2021?

21. Equipment was purchased on January 2, 2020, for $24,000, but no portion of the cost has been charged to depreciation. The corporation wishes to use the straight-line method for these assets, which have been estimated to have a life of 10 years and no salvage value. What effect does this error have on net income in 2020? What entry is necessary to correct for this error, assuming that the books are not closed for 2020?

Brief Exercises

BE22.1 **(LO 1)** At the beginning of 2020, Wertz Construction Company changed from the completed-contract method to recognizing revenue over time (percentage-of-completion) for financial reporting purposes. The company will continue to use the completed-contract method for tax purposes. For years prior to 2020, pretax income under the two methods was as follows: percentage-of-completion $120,000, and completed-contract $80,000. The tax rate is 20%. Prepare Wertz's 2020 journal entry to record the change in accounting principle.

BE22.2 **(LO 1)** Refer to the accounting change by Wertz Construction Company in BE22.1. Wertz has a profit-sharing plan, which pays all employees a bonus at year-end based on 1% of pretax income. Compute the indirect effect of Wertz's change in accounting principle that will be reported in the 2020 income statement, assuming that the profit-sharing contract explicitly requires adjustment for changes in income numbers.

BE22.3 **(LO 1)** Shannon, Inc., changed from the LIFO cost flow assumption to the FIFO cost flow assumption in 2020. The increase in the prior year's income before taxes is $1,200,000. The tax rate is 20%. Prepare Shannon's 2020 journal entry to record the change in accounting principle.

BE22.4 **(LO 1)** Tedesco Company changed depreciation methods in 2020 from double-declining-balance to straight-line. Depreciation prior to 2020 under double-declining-balance was $90,000, whereas straight-line depreciation prior to 2020 would have been $50,000. Tedesco's depreciable assets had a cost of $250,000 with a $40,000 salvage value, and an 8-year remaining useful life at the beginning of 2020. Prepare the 2020 journal entries, if any, related to Tedesco's depreciable assets.

BE22.5 **(LO 2)** Sesame Company purchased a computer system for $74,000 on January 1, 2019. It was depreciated based on a 7-year life and an $18,000 salvage value. On January 1, 2021, Sesame revised these estimates to a total useful life of 4 years and a salvage value of $10,000. Prepare Sesame's entry to record 2021 depreciation expense. Sesame uses straight-line depreciation.

BE22.6 **(LO 3)** In 2020, Bailey Corporation discovered that equipment purchased on January 1, 2018, for $50,000 was expensed at that time. The equipment should have been depreciated over 5 years, with no salvage value. The effective tax rate is 30%. Prepare Bailey's 2020 journal entry to correct the error. Bailey uses straight-line depreciation.

BE22.7 **(LO 3)** At January 1, 2020, Beidler Company reported retained earnings of $2,000,000. In 2020, Beidler discovered that 2019 depreciation expense was understated by $400,000. In 2020, net income was $900,000 and dividends declared were $250,000. The tax rate is 20%. Prepare a 2020 retained earnings statement for Beidler Company.

BE22.8 **(LO 3)** Indicate the effect—Understate, Overstate, No Effect—that each of the following errors has on 2020 net income and 2021 net income.

	2020	2021
a. Equipment (with a useful life of 5 years) was purchased and expensed in 2018.	____	____
b. Wages payable were not recorded at 12/31/20.	____	____
c. Equipment purchased in 2020 was expensed.	____	____
d. 2020 ending inventory was overstated.	____	____
e. Patent amortization was not recorded in 2021.	____	____

BE22.9 **(LO 1, 2)** Roundtree Manufacturing Co. is preparing its year-end financial statements and is considering the accounting for the following items.

1. The vice president of sales had indicated that one product line has lost its customer appeal and will be phased out over the next 3 years. Therefore, a decision has been made to lower the estimated lives on related production equipment from the remaining 5 years to 3 years.
2. The Hightone Building was converted from a sales office to offices for the Accounting Department at the beginning of this year. Therefore, the expense related to this building will now appear as an administrative expense rather than a selling expense on the current year's income statement.
3. Estimating the lives of new products in the Leisure Products Division has become very difficult because of the highly competitive conditions in this market. Therefore, the practice of deferring and amortizing preproduction costs has been abandoned in favor of expensing such costs as they are incurred.

Identify and explain whether each of the above items is a change in principle, a change in estimate, or an error.

BE22.10 **(LO 1, 3)** Palmer Co. is evaluating the appropriate accounting for the following items.

1. Management has decided to switch from the FIFO inventory valuation method to the LIFO inventory valuation method for all inventories.
2. When the year-end physical inventory adjustment was made for the current year, the controller discovered that the prior year's physical inventory sheets for an entire warehouse were mislaid and excluded from last year's count.
3. Palmer's Custom Division manufactures large-scale, custom-designed machinery on a contract basis. Management decided to switch from the completed-contract method to the percentage-of-completion method of accounting for long-term contracts.

Identify and explain whether each of the above items is a change in accounting principle, a change in estimate, or an error.

*BE22.11 **(LO 5)** Simmons Corporation owns stock of Armstrong, Inc. Prior to 2020, the investment was accounted for using the equity method. In early 2020, Simmons sold part of its investment in Armstrong, and began using the fair value method. In 2020, Armstrong earned net income of $80,000 and paid dividends of $95,000. Prepare Simmons's entries related to Armstrong's net income and dividends, assuming Simmons now owns 10% of Armstrong's stock.

*BE22.12 **(LO 5)** Oliver Corporation has owned stock of Conrad Corporation since 2017. At December 31, 2020, its balances related to this investment were:

Equity Investments	$185,000
Fair Value Adjustment	34,000 Dr.

On January 1, 2021, Oliver purchased additional stock of Conrad Company for $475,000 and now has significant influence over Conrad. Prepare Oliver's journal entries to record the purchase of the investment and the change to the equity method.

Exercises

E22.1 **(LO 1)** **(Change in Principle—Long-Term Contracts)** Pam Erickson Construction Company changed from the completed-contract to the percentage-of-completion method of accounting for long-term construction contracts during 2021. For tax purposes, the company employs the completed-contract method and will continue this approach in the future. (*Hint:* Adjust all tax consequences through the Deferred Tax Liability account.) The appropriate information related to this change is as follows.

	Pretax Income from		
	Percentage-of-Completion	Completed-Contract	Difference
2020	$780,000	$590,000	$190,000
2021	700,000	480,000	220,000

Instructions

a. Assuming that the tax rate is 20%, what is the amount of net income that would be reported in 2021?

b. What entry(ies) are necessary to adjust the accounting records for the change in accounting principle?

E22.2 **(LO 1)** **(Change in Principle—Inventory Methods)** Holder-Webb Company began operations on January 1, 2018, and uses the average-cost method of pricing inventory. Management is contemplating a change in inventory methods for 2021. The following information is available for the years 2018–2020.

	Net Income Computed Using		
	Average-Cost Method	FIFO Method	LIFO Method
2018	$15,000	$19,000	$12,000
2019	18,000	23,000	14,000
2020	20,000	25,000	17,000

Instructions

(Ignore all tax effects.)

a. Prepare the journal entry necessary to record a change from the average-cost method to the FIFO method in 2021.

b. Determine net income to be reported for 2018, 2019, and 2020, after giving effect to the change in accounting principle.

c. Assume Holder-Webb Company used the LIFO method instead of the average-cost method during the years 2018–2020. In 2021, Holder-Webb changed to the FIFO method. Prepare the journal entry necessary to record the change in principle.

E22.3 **(LO 1)** **(Accounting Change)** Taveras Co. decides at the beginning of 2020 to adopt the FIFO method of inventory valuation. Taveras had used the LIFO method for financial reporting since its inception on January 1, 2018, and had maintained records adequate to apply the FIFO method retrospectively. Taveras concluded that FIFO is the preferable inventory method because it reflects the current cost of inventory on the balance sheet. The following table presents the effects of the change in accounting principles on inventory and cost of goods sold.

	Inventory Determined by		Cost of Goods Sold Determined by	
Date	LIFO Method	FIFO Method	LIFO Method	FIFO Method
January 1, 2018	$ 0	$ 0	$ 0	$ 0
December 31, 2018	100	80	800	820
December 31, 2019	200	240	1,000	940
December 31, 2020	320	390	1,130	1,100

Other information:

1. For each year presented, sales are $3,000 and operating expenses are $1,000.
2. Taveras provides two years of financial statements. Earnings per share information is not required.

Instructions

a. Prepare income statements under LIFO and FIFO for 2018, 2019, and 2020.

b. Prepare income statements reflecting the retrospective application of the accounting change from the LIFO method to the FIFO method for 2020 and 2019.

c. Prepare the note to the financial statements describing the change in method of inventory valuation. In the note, indicate the income statement line items for 2020 and 2019 that were affected by the change in accounting principle.

d. Prepare comparative retained earnings statements for 2019 and 2020 under FIFO. Retained earnings reported under LIFO are as follows:

	Retained Earnings Balance
December 31, 2018	$1,200
December 31, 2019	2,200
December 31, 2020	3,070

E22.4 **(LO 1)** **(Accounting Change)** Gordon Company started operations on January 1, 2015, and has used the FIFO method of inventory valuation since its inception. In 2021, it decides to switch to the average-cost method. You are provided with the following information.

	Net Income		Retained Earnings (Ending Balance)
	Under FIFO	Under Average-Cost	Under FIFO
2015	$100,000	$ 90,000	$100,000
2016	70,000	65,000	160,000
2017	90,000	80,000	235,000
2018	120,000	130,000	340,000
2019	300,000	290,000	590,000
2020	305,000	310,000	780,000

Instructions

a. What is the beginning retained earnings balance at January 1, 2017, if Gordon prepares comparative financial statements starting in 2017?

b. What is the beginning retained earnings balance at January 1, 2020, if Gordon prepares comparative financial statements starting in 2020?

c. What is the beginning retained earnings balance at January 1, 2021, if Gordon prepares single-period financial statements for 2021?

d. What is the net income reported by Gordon in the 2020 income statement if it prepares comparative financial statements starting with 2018?

E22.5 **(LO 1)** **(Accounting Change)** Presented below are income statements prepared on a LIFO and FIFO basis for Kenseth Company, which started operations on January 1, 2019. The company presently uses the LIFO method of pricing its inventory and has decided to switch to the FIFO method in 2020. The FIFO income statement is computed in accordance with the requirements of GAAP. Kenseth's profit-sharing agreement with its employees indicates that the company will pay employees 10% of income before profit-sharing. Income taxes are ignored.

	LIFO Basis		FIFO Basis	
	2020	2019	2020	2019
Sales	$3,000	$3,000	$3,000	$3,000
Cost of goods sold	1,130	1,000	1,100	940
Operating expenses	1,000	1,000	1,000	1,000
Income before profit-sharing	870	1,000	900	1,060
Profit-sharing expense	87	100	96	100
Net income	$ 783	$ 900	$ 804	$ 960

Instructions

Answer the following questions.

a. If comparative income statements are prepared, what net income should Kenseth report in 2019 and 2020?

b. Explain why, under the FIFO basis, Kenseth reports $100 in 2019 and $96 in 2020 for its profit-sharing expense.

c. Assume that Kenseth has a beginning balance of retained earnings at January 1, 2020, of $900 using the LIFO method. The company declared and paid dividends of $500 in 2020. Prepare the -retained earnings statement for 2020, assuming that Kenseth has switched to the FIFO method.

E22.6 **(LO 1)** **(Change in Principle—Long-Term Contracts)** Cullen Construction Company, which began operations in 2020, changed from the completed-contract to the percentage-of-completion method of accounting for long-term construction contracts during 2021. For tax purposes, the company employs the completed-contract method and will continue this approach in the future. The appropriate information related to this change is as follows.

	Pretax Income from		
	Percentage-of-Completion	Completed-Contract	Difference
2020	$880,000	$590,000	$290,000
2021	900,000	480,000	420,000

Instructions

a. Assuming that the tax rate is 20%, what is the amount of net income that would be reported in 2021?

b. What entry(ies) are necessary to adjust the accounting records for the change in accounting principle?

E22.7 **(LO 1)** **(Various Changes in Principle—Inventory Methods)** Below is the net income of Anita Ferreri Instrument Co., a private corporation, computed under the three inventory methods using a periodic system.

	FIFO	Average-Cost	LIFO
2018	$26,000	$24,000	$20,000
2019	30,000	25,000	21,000
2020	28,000	27,000	24,000
2021	34,000	30,000	26,000

Instructions

(Ignore tax considerations.)

a. Assume that in 2021 Ferreri decided to change from the FIFO method to the average-cost method of pricing inventories. Prepare the journal entry necessary for the change that took place during 2021, and show net income reported for 2018, 2019, 2020, and 2021.

b. Assume that in 2021 Ferreri, which had been using the LIFO method since incorporation in 2018, changed to the FIFO method of pricing inventories. Prepare the journal entry necessary to record the change in 2021 and show net income reported for 2018, 2019, 2020, and 2021.

E22.8 **(LO 2)** **(Accounting Changes—Depreciation)** Kathleen Cole Inc. acquired the following assets in January of 2018.

Equipment, estimated service life, 5 years; salvage value, $15,000	$525,000
Building, estimated service life, 30 years; no salvage value	$693,000

The equipment has been depreciated using the sum-of-the-years'-digits method for the first 3 years for financial reporting purposes. In 2021, the company decided to change the method of computing depreciation to the straight-line method for the equipment, but no change was made in the estimated service life or salvage value. It was also decided to change the total estimated service life of the building from 30 years to 40 years, with no change in the estimated salvage value. The building is depreciated on the straight-line method.

Instructions

a. Prepare the general journal entry to record depreciation expense for the equipment in 2021.

b. Prepare the journal entry to record depreciation expense for the building in 2021. (Round all computations to two decimal places.)

E22.9 (LO 2, 3) (Change in Estimate and Error; Financial Statements) Presented below are the comparative income and retained earnings statements for Denise Habbe Inc. for the years 2020 and 2021.

	2021	2020
Sales	$340,000	$270,000
Cost of sales	200,000	142,000
Gross profit	140,000	128,000
Expenses	88,000	50,000
Net income	$ 52,000	$ 78,000
Retained earnings (Jan. 1)	$125,000	$ 72,000
Net income	52,000	78,000
Dividends	(30,000)	(25,000)
Retained earnings (Dec. 31)	$147,000	$125,000

The following additional information is provided:

1. In 2021, Denise Habbe Inc. decided to switch its depreciation method from sum-of-the-years' digits to the straight-line method. The assets were purchased at the beginning of 2020 for $100,000 with an estimated useful life of 4 years and no salvage value. (The 2021 income statement contains depreciation expense of $30,000 on the assets purchased at the beginning of 2020.)
2. In 2021, the company discovered that the ending inventory for 2020 was overstated by $24,000; ending inventory for 2021 is correctly stated.

Instructions

Prepare the revised retained earnings statement for 2020 and 2021, assuming comparative statements. (Ignore income taxes.)

E22.10 (LO 1, 2, 3) (Accounting for Accounting Changes and Errors) Listed below are various types of accounting changes and errors.

______ 1. Change in a plant asset's salvage value.
______ 2. Change due to overstatement of inventory.
______ 3. Change from sum-of-the-years'-digits to straight-line method of depreciation.
______ 4. Change from presenting unconsolidated to consolidated financial statements.
______ 5. Change from LIFO to FIFO inventory method.
______ 6. Change in the rate used to compute warranty costs.
______ 7. Change from an unacceptable accounting principle to an acceptable accounting principle.
______ 8. Change in a patent's amortization period.
______ 9. Change from completed-contract to percentage-of-completion method on construction contracts.
______ 10. Change from FIFO to average-cost inventory method.

Instructions

For each change or error, indicate how it would be accounted for using the following code letters:

a. Accounted for prospectively.
b. Accounted for retrospectively.
c. Neither of the above.

E22.11 (LO 2, 3) Excel (Error and Change in Estimate—Depreciation) Joy Cunningham Co. purchased a machine on January 1, 2018, for $550,000. At that time, it was estimated that the machine would have a 10-year life and no salvage value. On December 31, 2021, the firm's accountant found that the entry for depreciation expense had been omitted in 2019. In addition, management has informed the accountant that the company plans to switch to straight-line depreciation, starting with the year 2021. At present, the company uses the sum-of-the-years'-digits method for depreciating equipment.

Instructions

Prepare the general journal entries that should be made at December 31, 2021, to record these events. (Ignore tax effects.)

E22.12 (LO 2) (Depreciation Changes) On January 1, 2017, Jackson Company purchased a building and equipment that have the following useful lives, salvage values, and costs.

Building, 40-year estimated useful life, $50,000 salvage value, $800,000 cost
Equipment, 12-year estimated useful life, $10,000 salvage value, $100,000 cost

The building has been depreciated under the double-declining-balance method through 2020. In 2021, the company decided to switch to the straight-line method of depreciation. Jackson also decided to change the total useful life of the equipment to 9 years, with a salvage value of $5,000 at the end of that time. The equipment is depreciated using the straight-line method.

Instructions

a. Prepare the journal entry(ies) necessary to record the depreciation expense on the building in 2021.

b. Compute depreciation expense on the equipment for 2021.

E22.13 **(LO 2)** Excel **(Change in Estimate—Depreciation)** Peter M. Dell Co. purchased equipment for $510,000 which was estimated to have a useful life of 10 years with a salvage value of $10,000 at the end of that time. Depreciation has been entered for 7 years on a straight-line basis. In 2021, it is determined that the total estimated life should be 15 years with a salvage value of $5,000 at the end of that time.

Instructions

a. Prepare the entry (if any) to correct the prior years' depreciation.

b. Prepare the entry to record depreciation for 2021.

E22.14 **(LO 2)** **(Change in Estimate—Depreciation)** Gerald Englehart Industries changed from the double-declining-balance to the straight-line method in 2021 on all its equipment. There was no change in the assets' salvage values or useful lives. Plant assets, acquired on January 2, 2018, had an original cost of $1,600,000, with a $100,000 salvage value and an 8-year estimated useful life. Income before depreciation expense was $270,000 in 2020 and $300,000 in 2021.

Instructions

a. Prepare the journal entry(ies) to record depreciation expense in 2021.

b. Starting with income before depreciation expense, prepare the remaining portion of the income statement for 2020 and 2021.

E22.15 **(LO 3)** **(Error Correction Entries)** The first audit of the books of Bruce Gingrich Company was made for the year ended December 31, 2021. In examining the books, the auditor found that certain items had been overlooked or incorrectly handled in the last 3 years. These items are:

1. At the beginning of 2019, the company purchased a machine for $510,000 (salvage value of $51,000) that had a useful life of 6 years. The bookkeeper used straight-line depreciation but failed to deduct the salvage value in computing the depreciation base for the 3 years.
2. At the end of 2020, the company failed to accrue sales salaries of $45,000.
3. A tax lawsuit that involved the year 2019 was settled late in 2021. It was determined that the company owed an additional $85,000 in taxes related to 2019. The company did not record a liability in 2019 or 2020 because the possibility of loss was considered remote, and charged the $85,000 to a loss account in 2021.
4. Gingrich Company purchased a copyright from another company early in 2019 for $45,000. Gingrich had not amortized the copyright because its value had not diminished. The copyright has a useful life at purchase of 20 years.
5. In 2021, the company wrote off $87,000 of inventory considered to be obsolete; this loss was charged directly to Retained Earnings.

Instructions

Prepare the journal entries necessary in 2021 to correct the books, assuming that the books have not been closed. Disregard effects of corrections on income tax.

E22.16 **(LO 3)** **(Error Analysis and Correcting Entry)** You have been engaged to review the financial statements of Gottschalk Corporation. In the course of your examination, you conclude that the bookkeeper hired during the current year is not doing a good job. You notice a number of irregularities as follows.

1. Year-end wages payable of $3,400 were not recorded because the bookkeeper thought that "they were immaterial."
2. Accrued vacation pay for the year of $31,100 was not recorded because the bookkeeper "never heard that you had to do it."
3. Insurance for a 12-month period purchased on November 1 of this year was charged to insurance expense in the amount of $2,640 because "the amount of the check is about the same every year."

4. Reported sales revenue for the year is $2,120,000. This includes all sales taxes collected for the year. The sales tax rate is 6%. Because the sales tax is forwarded to the state's Department of Revenue, the Sales Tax Expense account is debited. The bookkeeper thought that "the sales tax is a selling expense." At the end of the current year, the balance in the Sales Tax Expense account is $103,400.

Instructions

Prepare the necessary correcting entries, assuming that Gottschalk uses a calendar-year basis.

E22.17 **(LO 3)** **(Error Analysis and Correcting Entry)** The reported net incomes for the first 2 years of Sandra Gustafson Products, Inc., were as follows: 2020, $147,000; 2021, $185,000. Early in 2022, the following errors were discovered.

1. Depreciation of equipment for 2020 was overstated $17,000.
2. Depreciation of equipment for 2021 was understated $38,500.
3. December 31, 2020, inventory was understated $50,000.
4. December 31, 2021, inventory was overstated $16,200.

Instructions

Prepare the correcting entry necessary when these errors are discovered. Assume that the books are closed. (Ignore income tax considerations.)

E22.18 **(LO 3, 4)** **(Error Analysis)** Peter Henning Tool Company's December 31 year-end financial statements contained the following errors.

	December 31, 2020	December 31, 2021
Ending inventory	$9,600 understated	$8,100 overstated
Depreciation expense	$2,300 understated	—

An insurance premium of $66,000 was prepaid in 2020 covering the years 2020, 2021, and 2022. The entire amount was charged to expense in 2020. In addition, on December 31, 2021, fully depreciated machinery was sold for $15,000 cash, but the entry was not recorded until 2022. There were no other errors during 2020 or 2021, and no corrections have been made for any of the errors. (Ignore income tax considerations.)

Instructions

a. Compute the total effect of the errors on 2021 net income.

b. Compute the total effect of the errors on the amount of Henning's working capital at December 31, 2021.

c. Compute the total effect of the errors on the balance of Henning's retained earnings at December 31, 2021.

E22.19 **(LO 3, 4)** **(Error Analysis; Correcting Entries)** A partial trial balance of Julie Hartsack Corporation is as follows on December 31, 2021.

	Dr.	Cr.
Supplies	$ 2,700	
Salaries and wages payable		$ 1,500
Interest receivable	5,100	
Prepaid insurance	90,000	
Unearned rent		–0–
Interest payable		15,000

Additional adjusting data:

1. A physical count of supplies on hand on December 31, 2021, totaled $1,100.
2. Through oversight, the Salaries and Wages Payable account was not changed during 2021. Accrued salaries and wages on December 31, 2021, amounted to $4,400.
3. The Interest Receivable account was also left unchanged during 2021. Accrued interest on investments amounts to $4,350 on December 31, 2021.
4. The unexpired portions of the insurance policies totaled $65,000 as of December 31, 2021.
5. $28,000 was received on January 1, 2021, for the rent of a building for both 2021 and 2022. The entire amount was credited to rent revenue.

6. Depreciation on equipment for the year was erroneously recorded as $5,000 rather than the correct figure of $50,000.
7. A further review of depreciation calculations of prior years revealed that equipment depreciation of $7,200 was not recorded. It was decided that this oversight should be corrected by a prior period adjustment.

Instructions

a. Assuming that the books have not been closed, what are the adjusting entries necessary at December 31, 2021? (Ignore income tax considerations.)

b. Assuming that the books have been closed, what are the adjusting entries necessary at December 31, 2021? (Ignore income tax considerations.)

c. Repeat the requirements for items 6 and 7, taking into account income tax effects (40% tax rate) and assuming that the books have been closed.

E22.20 **(LO 3, 4)** **(Error Analysis)** The before-tax income for Lonnie Holdiman Co. for 2020 was $101,000 and $77,400 for 2021. However, the accountant noted that the following errors had been made:

1. Sales for 2020 included amounts of $38,200 which had been received in cash during 2020, but for which the related products were delivered in 2021. Title did not pass to the purchaser until 2021.
2. The inventory on December 31, 2020, was understated by $8,640.
3. The bookkeeper in recording interest expense for both 2020 and 2021 on bonds payable made the following entry on an annual basis.

Interest Expense	15,000	
Cash		15,000

The bonds have a face value of $250,000 and pay a stated interest rate of 6%. They were issued at a discount of $15,000 on January 1, 2020, to yield an effective-interest rate of 7%. (Assume that the effective-yield method should be used.)

4. Ordinary repairs to equipment had been erroneously charged to the Equipment account during 2020 and 2021. Repairs in the amount of $8,500 in 2020 and $9,400 in 2021 were so charged. The company applies a rate of 10% to the balance in the Equipment account at the end of the year in its determination of depreciation charges.

Instructions

Prepare a schedule showing the determination of corrected income before taxes for 2020 and 2021.

E22.21 **(LO 3, 4)** **(Error Analysis)** When the records of Debra Hanson Corporation were reviewed at the close of 2021, the following errors were discovered. For each item, indicate by a check mark in the appropriate column whether the error resulted in an overstatement, an understatement, or had no effect on net income for the years 2020 and 2021.

	2020			2021		
Item	Over-statement	Under-statement	No Effect	Over-statement	Under-statement	No Effect
1. Failure to record amortization of patent in 2021.						
2. Failure to record the correct amount of ending 2020 inventory. The amount was understated because of an error in calculation.						
3. Failure to record merchandise purchased in 2020. Merchandise was also omitted from ending inventory in 2020 but was not yet sold.						

(continued)

(continued)

Item	2020			2021		
	Over-statement	Under-statement	No Effect	Over-statement	Under-statement	No Effect
4. Failure to record accrued interest on notes payable in 2020; that amount was recorded when paid in 2021.						
5. Failure to reflect supplies on hand on balance sheet at end of 2020.						

*E22.22 **(LO 5) (Change from Fair Value to Equity)** On January 1, 2020, Beyonce Co. purchased 25,000 shares (a 10% interest) in Elton John Corp. for $1,400,000. At the time, the book value and the fair value of John's net assets were $13,000,000.

On July 1, 2021, Beyonce paid $3,040,000 for 50,000 additional shares of John common stock, which represented a 20% investment in John. As a result of this transaction, Beyonce owns 30% of John and can exercise significant influence over John's operating and financial policies.

John reported the following net income and declared and paid the following dividends.

	Net Income	Dividend per Share
Year ended 12/31/20	$700,000	None
Six months ended 6/30/21	500,000	None
Six months ended 12/31/21	815,000	$1.55

Instructions

Determine the ending balance that Beyonce Co. should report as its investment in John Corp. at the end of 2021.

*E22.23 **(LO 5) (Change from Equity to Fair Value)** Aykroyd Corp. was a 30% owner of Martin Company, holding 210,000 shares of Martin's common stock on December 31, 2019. The investment account had the following entries.

Investment in Martin

1/1/18 Cost	$3,180,000	12/6/18 Dividend received	$150,000
12/31/18 Share of income	390,000	12/5/19 Dividend received	240,000
12/31/19 Share of income	510,000		

On January 2, 2020, Aykroyd sold 126,000 shares of Martin for $3,440,000, thereby losing its significant influence. During the year 2020, Martin experienced the following results of operations and paid the following dividends to Aykroyd.

	Martin Income (Loss)	Dividends Paid to Aykroyd
2020	$300,000	$50,400

At December 31, 2020, the fair value of Martin shares held by Aykroyd is $1,570,000. This is the first reporting date since the January 2 sale.

Instructions

a. What effect does the January 2, 2020, transaction have upon Aykroyd's accounting treatment for its investment in Martin?

b. Compute the carrying amount of the investment in Martin as of December 31, 2020 (prior to any fair value adjustment).

c. Prepare the adjusting entry on December 31, 2020, applying the fair value method to Aykroyd's long-term investment in Martin Company securities.

Problems

P22.1 (LO 1) (Change in Principle—Inventory—Periodic) The management of Utrillo Instrument Company had concluded, with the concurrence of its independent auditors, that results of operations would be more fairly presented if Utrillo changed its method of pricing inventory from last-in, first-out (LIFO) to average-cost in 2020. Given below is the 5-year summary of income under LIFO and a schedule of what the inventories would be if stated on the average-cost method.

Utrillo Instrument Company
Statement of Income and Retained Earnings
For the Years Ended May 31

	2016	2017	2018	2019	2020
Sales—net	$13,964	$15,506	$16,673	$18,221	$18,898
Cost of goods sold					
Beginning inventory	1,000	1,100	1,000	1,115	1,237
Purchases	13,000	13,900	15,000	15,900	17,100
Ending inventory	(1,100)	(1,000)	(1,115)	(1,237)	(1,369)
Total	12,900	14,000	14,885	15,778	16,968
Gross profit	1,064	1,506	1,788	2,443	1,930
Administrative expenses	700	763	832	907	989
Income before taxes	364	743	956	1,536	941
Income taxes (50%)	182	372	478	768	471
Net income	182	371	478	768	470
Retained earnings—beginning	1,206	1,388	1,759	2,237	3,005
Retained earnings—ending	$ 1,388	$ 1,759	$ 2,237	$ 3,005	$ 3,475
Earnings per share	$1.82	$3.71	$4.78	$7.68	$4.70

Schedule of Inventory Balances Using Average-Cost Method
For the Years Ended May 31

2015	2016	2017	2018	2019	2020
$1,010	$1,124	$1,101	$1,270	$1,500	$1,720

Instructions

Prepare comparative statements for the 5 years, assuming that Utrillo changed its method of inventory pricing to average-cost. Indicate the effects on net income and earnings per share for the years involved. Utrillo Instruments started business in 2015. (All amounts except EPS are rounded up to the nearest dollar.)

P22.2 (LO 1, 2, 3) Excel Groupwork (Change in Estimate and Error Correction) Holtzman Company is in the process of preparing its financial statements for 2020. Assume that no entries for depreciation have been recorded in 2020. The following information related to depreciation of fixed assets is provided to you.

1. Holtzman purchased equipment on January 2, 2017, for $85,000. At that time, the equipment had an estimated useful life of 10 years with a $5,000 salvage value. The equipment is depreciated on a straight-line basis. On January 2, 2020, as a result of additional information, the company determined that the equipment has a remaining useful life of 4 years with a $3,000 salvage value.
2. During 2020, Holtzman changed from the double-declining-balance method for its building to the straight-line method. The building originally cost $300,000. It had a useful life of 10 years and a salvage value of $30,000. The following computations present depreciation on both bases for 2018 and 2019.

	2019	2018
Straight-line	$27,000	$27,000
Declining-balance	48,000	60,000

3. Holtzman purchased a machine on July 1, 2018, at a cost of $120,000. The machine has a salvage value of $16,000 and a useful life of 8 years. Holtzman's bookkeeper recorded straight-line depreciation in 2018 and 2019 but failed to consider the salvage value.

Instructions

a. Prepare the journal entries to record depreciation expense for 2020 and correct any errors made to date related to the information provided. (Ignore taxes.)

b. Show comparative net income for 2019 and 2020. Income before depreciation expense was $300,000 in 2020, and was $310,000 in 2019. (Ignore taxes.)

P22.3 **(LO 1, 2, 3) (Comprehensive Accounting Change and Error Analysis Problem)** Botticelli Inc. was organized in late 2018 to manufacture and sell hosiery. At the end of its fourth year of operation, the company has been fairly successful, as indicated by the following reported net incomes.

2018	$140,000[a]	2020	$205,000
2019	160,000[b]	2021	276,000

[a]Includes a $10,000 increase because of change in bad debt experience rate.
[b]Includes a gain of $30,000.

The company has decided to expand operations and has applied for a sizable bank loan. The bank officer has indicated that the records should be audited and presented in comparative statements to facilitate analysis by the bank. Botticelli Inc. therefore hired the auditing firm of Check & Doublecheck Co. and has provided the following additional information.

1. In early 2019, Botticelli Inc. changed its estimate from 2% of receivables to 1% on the amount of bad debt expense to be charged to operations. Bad debt expense for 2018, if a 1% rate had been used, would have been $10,000. The company therefore restated its net income for 2018.
2. In 2021, the auditor discovered that the company had changed its method of inventory pricing from LIFO to FIFO. The effect on the income statements for the previous years is as follows.

	2018	2019	2020	2021
Net income unadjusted—LIFO basis	$140,000	$160,000	$205,000	$276,000
Net income unadjusted—FIFO basis	155,000	165,000	215,000	260,000
	$ 15,000	$ 5,000	$ 10,000	$ (16,000)

3. In 2021, the auditor discovered that:
   a. The company incorrectly overstated the ending inventory (under both LIFO and FIFO) by $14,000 in 2020.
   b. A dispute developed in 2019 with the Internal Revenue Service over the deductibility of entertainment expenses. In 2018, the company was not permitted these deductions, but a tax settlement was reached in 2021 that allowed these expenses. As a result of the court's finding, tax expenses in 2021 were reduced by $60,000.

Instructions

a. Indicate how each of these changes or corrections should be handled in the accounting records. (Ignore income tax considerations.)

b. Present net income as reported in comparative income statements for the years 2018 to 2021.

P22.4 **(LO 1, 2, 3) (Error Corrections and Accounting Changes)** Penn Company is in the process of adjusting and correcting its books at the end of 2020. In reviewing its records, the following information is compiled.

1. Penn has failed to accrue sales commissions payable at the end of each of the last 2 years, as follows.

December 31, 2019	$3,500
December 31, 2020	$2,500

2. In reviewing the December 31, 2020, inventory, Penn discovered errors in its inventory-taking procedures that have caused inventories for the last 3 years to be incorrect, as follows.

December 31, 2018	Understated	$16,000
December 31, 2019	Understated	$19,000
December 31, 2020	Overstated	$ 6,700

Penn has already made an entry that established the incorrect December 31, 2020, inventory amount.

3. At December 31, 2020, Penn decided to change the depreciation method on its office equipment from double-declining-balance to straight-line. The equipment had an original cost of $100,000 when purchased on January 1, 2018. It has a 10-year useful life and no salvage value. Depreciation expense recorded prior to 2020 under the double-declining-balance method was $36,000. Penn has already recorded 2020 depreciation expense of $12,800 using the double-declining-balance method.

4. Before 2020, Penn accounted for its income from long-term construction contracts on the completed-contract basis. Early in 2020, Penn changed to the percentage-of-completion basis for accounting purposes. It continues to use the completed-contract method for tax purposes. Income for 2020 has been recorded using the percentage-of-completion method. The following information is available.

	Pretax Income	
	Percentage-of-Completion	Completed-Contract
Prior to 2020	$150,000	$105,000
2020	60,000	20,000

Instructions

Prepare the journal entries necessary at December 31, 2020, to record the above corrections and changes. The books are still open for 2020. The income tax rate is 20%. Penn has not yet recorded its 2020 income tax expense and payable amounts so current-year tax effects may be ignored. Prior-year tax effects must be considered in item 4.

P22.5 **(LO 1, 2)** Groupwork Ethics **(Accounting Changes)** Aston Corporation performs year-end planning in November of each year before its calendar year ends in December. The preliminary estimated net income is $4,800,000. The CFO, Rita Warren, meets with the company president, J. B. Aston, to review the projected numbers. She presents the following projected information.

Aston Corporation
Projected Income Statement
For the Year Ended December 31, 2020

Sales		$28,995,000
Interest revenue		5,000
Cost of goods sold	$14,000,000	
Depreciation	2,600,000	
Operating expenses	6,400,000	23,000,000
Income before income tax		6,000,000
Income tax		1,200,000
Net income		$ 4,800,000

Aston Corporation
Selected Balance Sheet Information
At December 31, 2020

Estimated cash balance	$ 5,000,000
Available-for-sale debt investments (at cost)	10,000,000
Fair value adjustment (1/1/20)	—0—

Estimated fair value at December 31, 2020:

Security	Cost	Estimated Fair Value
A	$ 2,000,000	$ 2,200,000
B	4,000,000	3,900,000
C	3,000,000	3,100,000
D	1,000,000	1,800,000
Total	$10,000,000	$11,000,000

Other information at December 31, 2020:

Equipment	$3,000,000
Accumulated depreciation (5-year SL)	1,200,000
New robotic equipment (purchased 1/1/20)	5,000,000
Accumulated depreciation (5-year DDB)	2,000,000

The corporation has never used robotic equipment before, and Warren assumed an accelerated method because of the rapidly changing technology in robotic equipment. The company normally uses straight-line depreciation for production equipment.

Aston explains to Warren that it is important for the corporation to show a $7,000,000 income before taxes because Aston receives a $1,000,000 bonus if the income before taxes and bonus reaches $7,000,000. Aston also does not want the company to pay more than $1,200,000 in income taxes to the government.

Instructions

a. What can Warren do within GAAP to accommodate the president's wishes to achieve $7,000,000 in income before taxes and bonus? Present the revised income statement based on your decision.

b. Are the actions ethical? Who are the stakeholders in this decision, and what effect do Warren's actions have on their interests?

P22.6 **(LO 1, 3, 4)** Excel **(Accounting Change and Error Analysis)** On December 31, 2020, before the books were closed, the management and accountants of Madrasa Inc. made the following determinations about three pieces of equipment.

1. Equipment A was purchased January 2, 2017. It originally cost $540,000 and, for depreciation purposes, the straight-line method was originally chosen. The asset was originally expected to be useful for 10 years and have a zero salvage value. In 2020, the decision was made to change the depreciation method from straight-line to sum-of-the-years'-digits, and the estimates relating to useful life and salvage value remained unchanged.
2. Equipment B was purchased January 3, 2016. It originally cost $180,000 and, for depreciation purposes, the straight-line method was chosen. The asset was originally expected to be useful for 15 years and have a zero residual value. In 2020, the decision was made to shorten the total life of this asset to 9 years and to estimate the residual value at $3,000.
3. Equipment C was purchased January 5, 2016. The asset's original cost was $160,000, and this amount was entirely expensed in 2016. This particular asset has a 10-year useful life and no residual value. The straight-line method was chosen for depreciation purposes.

Additional data:

1. Income in 2020 before depreciation expense amounted to $400,000.
2. Depreciation expense on assets other than A, B, and C totaled $55,000 in 2020.
3. Income in 2019 was reported at $370,000.
4. Ignore all income tax effects.
5. 100,000 shares of common stock were outstanding in 2019 and 2020.

Instructions

a. Prepare all necessary entries in 2020 to record these determinations.

b. Prepare comparative retained earnings statements for Madrasa Inc. for 2019 and 2020. The company had retained earnings of $200,000 at December 31, 2018.

P22.7 **(LO 3, 4)** Groupwork **(Error Corrections)** You have been assigned to examine the financial statements of Zarle Company for the year ended December 31, 2020. You discover the following situations.

1. Depreciation of $3,200 for 2020 on delivery vehicles was not recorded.
2. The physical inventory count on December 31, 2019, improperly excluded merchandise costing $19,000 that had been temporarily stored in a public warehouse. Zarle uses a periodic inventory system.
3. A collection of $5,600 on account from a customer received on December 31, 2020, was not recorded until January 2, 2021.
4. In 2020, the company sold for $3,700 fully depreciated equipment that originally cost $25,000. The company credited the proceeds from the sale to the Equipment account.
5. During November 2020, a competitor company filed a patent-infringement suit against Zarle claiming damages of $220,000. The company's legal counsel has indicated that an unfavorable verdict is probable and a reasonable estimate of the court's award to the competitor is $125,000. The company has not reflected or disclosed this situation in the financial statements.
6. Zarle has a portfolio of trading investments. No entry has been made to adjust to market. Information on cost and fair value is as follows.

	Cost	Fair Value
December 31, 2019	$95,000	$95,000
December 31, 2020	$84,000	$82,000

7. At December 31, 2020, an analysis of payroll information shows accrued salaries of $12,200. The Salaries and Wages Payable account had a balance of $16,000 at December 31, 2020, which was unchanged from its balance at December 31, 2019.
8. A large piece of equipment was purchased on January 3, 2020, for $40,000 and was charged to Maintenance and Repairs Expense. The equipment is estimated to have a service life of 8 years and no residual value. Zarle normally uses the straight-line depreciation method for this type of equipment.
9. A $12,000 insurance premium paid on July 1, 2019, for a policy that expires on June 30, 2022, was charged to insurance expense.
10. A trademark was acquired at the beginning of 2019 for $50,000. No amortization has been recorded since its acquisition. The maximum allowable amortization period is 10 years.

Instructions

Assume the trial balance has been prepared but the books have not been closed for 2020. Assuming all amounts are material, prepare journal entries showing the adjustments that are required. (Ignore income tax considerations.)

P22.8 **(LO 3, 4)** **Groupwork** **(Comprehensive Error Analysis)** On March 5, 2021, you were hired by Hemingway Inc., a closely held company, as a staff member of its newly created internal auditing department. While reviewing the company's records for 2019 and 2020, you discover that no adjustments have yet been made for the following items.

Items

1. Interest income of $14,100 was not accrued at the end of 2019. It was recorded when received in February 2020.
2. A computer costing $4,000 was expensed when purchased on July 1, 2019. It is expected to have a 4-year life with no salvage value. The company typically uses straight-line depreciation for all fixed assets.
3. Research and development costs of $33,000 were incurred early in 2019. They were capitalized and were to be amortized over a 3-year period. Amortization of $11,000 was recorded for 2019 and $11,000 for 2020.
4. On January 2, 2019, Hemingway leased a building for 5 years at a monthly rental of $8,000. On that date, the company paid the following amounts, which were expensed when paid.

Security deposit	$20,000
First month's rent	8,000
Last month's rent	8,000
	$36,000

5. The company received $36,000 from a customer at the beginning of 2019 for services that it is to perform evenly over a 3-year period beginning in 2019. None of the amount received was reported as unearned revenue at the end of 2019.
6. Merchandise inventory costing $18,200 was in the warehouse at December 31, 2019, but was incorrectly omitted from the physical count at that date. The company uses the periodic inventory method.

Instructions

Indicate the effect of any errors on the net income figure reported on the income statement for the year ending December 31, 2019, and the retained earnings figure reported on the balance sheet at December 31, 2020. Assume all amounts are material, and ignore income tax effects. Using the following format, enter the appropriate dollar amounts in the appropriate columns. Consider each item independent of the other items. It is not necessary to total the columns on the grid.

	Net Income for 2019		Retained Earnings at 12/31/20	
Item	Understated	Overstated	Understated	Overstated

(CIA adapted)

P22.9 (LO 3, 4) (Error Analysis) Lowell Corporation has used the accrual basis of accounting for several years. A review of the records, however, indicates that some expenses and revenues have been handled on a cash basis because of errors made by an inexperienced bookkeeper. Income statements prepared by the bookkeeper reported $29,000 net income for 2019 and $37,000 net income for 2020. Further examination of the records reveals that the following items were handled improperly.

1. Rent was received from a tenant in December 2019. The amount, $1,000, was recorded as revenue at that time even though the rental pertained to 2020.
2. Salaries and wages payable on December 31 have been consistently omitted from the records of that date and have been entered as expenses when paid in the following year. The amounts of the accruals recorded in this manner were:

December 31, 2018	$1,100
December 31, 2019	1,200
December 31, 2020	940

3. Invoices for supplies purchased have been charged to expense accounts when received. Inventories of supplies on hand at the end of each year have been ignored, and no entry has been made for them.

December 31, 2018	$1,300
December 31, 2019	940
December 31, 2020	1,420

Instructions

Prepare a schedule that will show the corrected net income for the years 2019 and 2020. All items listed should be labeled clearly. (Ignore income tax considerations.)

P22.10 (LO 3, 4) (Error Analysis and Correcting Entries) You have been asked by a client to review the records of Roberts Company, a small manufacturer of precision tools and machines. Your client is interested in buying the business, and arrangements have been made for you to review the accounting records. Your examination reveals the following information.

1. Roberts Company commenced business on April 1, 2018, and has been reporting on a fiscal year ending March 31. The company has never been audited, but the annual statements prepared by the bookkeeper reflect the following income before closing and before deducting income taxes.

Year Ended March 31	Income Before Taxes
2019	$ 71,600
2020	111,400
2021	103,580

2. A relatively small number of machines have been shipped on consignment. These transactions have been recorded as ordinary sales and billed as such. On March 31 of each year, machines billed and in the hands of consignees amounted to:

2019	$6,500
2020	none
2021	5,590

Sales price was determined by adding 25% to cost. Assume that the consigned machines are sold the following year.

3. On March 30, 2020, two machines were shipped to a customer on a C.O.D. basis. The sale was not entered until April 5, 2020, when cash was received for $6,100. The machines were not included in the inventory at March 31, 2020. (Title passed on March 30, 2020.)
4. All machines are sold subject to a 5-year warranty. It is estimated that the expense ultimately to be incurred in connection with the warranty will amount to ½ of 1% of sales. The company has charged an expense account for warranty costs incurred.

Sales per books and warranty costs were as follows.

Year Ended March 31	Sales	Warranty Expense for Sales Made in 2019	2020	2021	Total
2019	$ 940,000	$760			$ 760
2020	1,010,000	360	$1,310		1,670
2021	1,795,000	320	1,620	$1,910	3,850

5. Bad debts have been recorded on a direct write-off basis. Experience of similar enterprises indicates that losses will approximate 1% of receivables. Bad debts written off were:

	Bad Debts Incurred on Sales Made in				
	2019	2020	2021	Total	Bad Debt Expense Based on 1% of Receivables
2019	$750			$ 750	$2,334
2020	800	$ 520		1,320	2,557
2021	350	1,800	$1,700	3,850	4,458

6. The bank deducts 6% on all contracts financed. Of this amount, ½% is placed in a reserve to the credit of Roberts Company that is refunded to Roberts as finance contracts are paid in full. (Thus, Roberts should have a receivable for these payments and should record revenue when the net balance is remitted each year.) The reserve established by the bank has not been reflected in the books of Roberts. The excess of credits over debits (net increase) to the reserve account with Roberts on the books of the bank for each fiscal year were as follows.

2019	$ 3,000
2020	3,900
2021	5,100
	$12,000

7. Commissions on sales have been entered when paid. Commissions payable on March 31 of each year were as follows.

2019	$1,400
2020	900
2021	1,120

8. A review of the corporate minutes reveals the manager is entitled to a bonus of 1% of the income before deducting income taxes and the bonus. The bonuses have never been recorded or paid.

Instructions

a. Present a schedule showing the revised income before income taxes for each of the years ended March 31, 2019, 2020, and 2021. (Make computations to the nearest whole dollar.)

b. Prepare the journal entry or entries you would give the bookkeeper to correct the books. Assume the books have not yet been closed for the fiscal year ended March 31, 2021. Disregard correction of income taxes.

(AICPA adapted)

*P22.11 **(LO 5)** **(Fair Value to Equity Method with Goodwill)** On January 1, 2020, Millay Inc. paid $700,000 for 10,000 shares of Genso Company's voting common stock, which was a 10% interest in Genso. Millay does not have the ability to exercise significant influence over the operating and financial policies of Genso. Millay received dividends of $1.50 per share from Genso on October 1, 2020. Genso reported net income of $550,000 for the year ended December 31, 2020. The cost and fair value of Genso common stock was the same at December 31, 2020.

On July 1, 2021, Millay paid $2,325,000 for 30,000 additional shares of Genso Company's voting common stock, which represents an additional 30% investment in Genso. As a result of this transaction, Millay has the ability to exercise significant influence over the operating and financial policies of Genso. Millay received dividends of $2.00 per share from Genso on April 1, 2021, and $2.50 per share on October 1, 2021. Genso reported net income of $650,000 for the year ended December 31, 2021, and $350,000 for the 6 months ended December 31, 2021.

Instructions

(For both purchases, assume any excess of cost over book value is due to goodwill.)

a. Prepare a schedule showing the income or loss before income taxes for the year ended December 31, 2020, that Millay should report from its investment in Genso in its income statement issued in March 2021.

b. During March 2022, Millay issues comparative financial statements for 2020 and 2021. Prepare schedules showing the income or loss before income taxes for the years ended December 31, 2020 and 2021, that Millay should report from its investment in Genso.

(AICPA adapted)

*P22.12 **(LO 5)** **(Change from Fair Value to Equity Method)** On January 3, 2019, Martin Company purchased for $500,000 cash a 10% interest in Renner Corp. The fair value of Martin's investment in Renner securities is as follows: December 31, 2019, $560,000, and December 31, 2020, $515,000. On January 2, 2021, Martin purchased an additional 30% of Renner's stock for $1,545,000 cash.

During 2019, 2020, and 2021, the following occurred.

	Renner Net Income	Dividends Paid by Renner to Martin
2019	$350,000	$15,000
2020	450,000	20,000
2021	550,000	70,000

Instructions

On the books of Martin Company, prepare all journal entries in 2019, 2020, and 2021 that relate to its investment in Renner Corp., reflecting the data above and a change from the fair value method to the equity method.

Concepts for Analysis

CA22.1 **(LO 1, 2, 3)** **Groupwork** **(Analysis of Various Accounting Changes and Errors)** Mathys Inc. has recently hired a new independent auditor, Karen Ogleby, who says she wants "to get everything straightened out." Consequently, she has proposed the following accounting changes in connection with Mathys Inc.'s 2020 financial statements.

1. At December 31, 2019, the client had a receivable of $820,000 from Hendricks Inc. on its balance sheet. Hendricks Inc. has gone bankrupt, and no recovery is expected. The client proposes to write off the receivable as a prior period item.
2. The client proposes the following changes in depreciation policies.
   a. For office furniture and fixtures, it proposes to change from a 10-year useful life to an 8-year life. If this change had been made in prior years, retained earnings at December 31, 2019, would have been $250,000 less. The effect of the change on 2020 income alone is a reduction of $60,000.
   b. For its new equipment in the leasing division, the client proposes to adopt the sum-of-the-years'-digits depreciation method. The client had never used SYD before. The first year the client operated a leasing division was 2020. If straight-line depreciation were used, 2020 income would be $110,000 greater.
3. In preparing its 2019 statements, one of the client's bookkeepers overstated ending inventory by $235,000 because of a mathematical error. The client proposes to treat this item as a prior period adjustment.
4. In the past, the client has spread preproduction costs in its furniture division over 5 years. Because its latest furniture is of the "fad" type, it appears that the largest volume of sales will occur during the first 2 years after introduction. Consequently, the client proposes to amortize preproduction costs on a per-unit basis, which will result in expensing most of such costs during the first 2 years after the furniture's introduction. If the new accounting method had been used prior to 2020, retained earnings at December 31, 2019, would have been $375,000 less.
5. For the nursery division, the client proposes to switch from FIFO to LIFO inventories because it believes that LIFO will provide a better matching of current costs with revenues. The effect of making this change on 2020 earnings will be an increase of $320,000. The client says that the effect of the change on December 31, 2019, retained earnings cannot be determined.
6. To achieve an appropriate recognition of revenues and expenses in its building construction division, the client proposes to switch from the completed-contract method of accounting to the percentage-of-completion method. Had the percentage-of-completion method been employed in all prior years, retained earnings at December 31, 2019, would have been $1,075,000 greater.

Instructions

a. For each of the changes described above, decide whether:
   1. The change involves an accounting principle, accounting estimate, or correction of an error.
   2. Restatement of opening retained earnings is required.

b. What would be the proper adjustment to the December 31, 2019, retained earnings?

CA22.2 **(LO 1, 2, 3) (Analysis of Various Accounting Changes and Errors)** Various types of accounting changes can affect the financial statements of a business enterprise differently. Assume that the following list describes changes that have a material effect on the financial statements for the current year of your business enterprise.

1. A change from the completed-contract method to the percentage-of-completion method of accounting for long-term construction-type contracts.
2. A change in the estimated useful life of previously recorded fixed assets as a result of newly acquired information.
3. A change from deferring and amortizing preproduction costs to recording such costs as an expense when incurred because future benefits of the costs have become doubtful. The new accounting method was adopted in recognition of the change in estimated future benefits.
4. A change from including the employer share of FICA taxes with payroll tax expenses to including it with "Retirement benefits" on the income statement.
5. Correction of a mathematical error in inventory pricing made in a prior period.
6. A change from presentation of statements of individual companies to presentation of consolidated statements.
7. A change in the method of accounting for leases for tax purposes to conform with the financial accounting method. As a result, both deferred and current taxes payable changed substantially.
8. A change from the FIFO method of inventory pricing to the LIFO method of inventory pricing.

Instructions

Identify the type of change that is described in each item above and indicate whether the prior year's financial statements should be recast when presented in comparative form with the current year's financial statements.

CA22.3 **(LO 1, 2, 3) (Analysis of Three Accounting Changes and Errors)** The following are three independent, unrelated sets of facts relating to accounting changes.

Situation 1: Sanford Company is in the process of having its first audit. The company has used the cash basis of accounting for revenue recognition. Sanford president, B. J. Jimenez, is willing to change to the accrual method of revenue recognition.

Situation 2: Hopkins Co. decides in January 2021 to change from FIFO to weighted-average pricing for its inventories.

Situation 3: Marshall Co. determined that the depreciable lives of its fixed assets are too long at present to fairly match the cost of the fixed assets with the revenue produced. The company decided at the beginning of the current year to reduce the depreciable lives of all of its existing fixed assets by 5 years.

Instructions

For each of the situations described, provide the information indicated below.

a. Type of accounting change.
b. Manner of reporting the change under current generally accepted accounting principles, including a discussion where applicable of how amounts are computed.
c. Effect of the change on the balance sheet and income statement.

CA22.4 **(LO 1, 2, 3) Writing (Analysis of Various Accounting Changes and Errors)** Katherine Irving, controller of Lotan Corp., is aware of a pronouncement on accounting changes. After reading the pronouncement, she is confused about what action should be taken on the following items related to Lotan Corp. for the year 2020.

1. In 2020, Lotan decided to change its policy on accounting for certain marketing costs. Previously, the company had chosen to defer and amortize all marketing costs over at least 5 years because Lotan believed that a return on these expenditures did not occur immediately. Recently, however, the time differential has considerably shortened, and Lotan is now expensing the marketing costs as incurred.
2. In 2020, the company examined its entire policy relating to the depreciation of plant equipment. Plant equipment had normally been depreciated over a 15-year period, but recent experience has indicated that the company was incorrect in its estimates and that the assets should be depreciated over a 20-year period.
3. One division of Lotan Corp., Hawthorne Co., has consistently shown an increasing net income from period to period. On closer examination of its operating statement, it is noted that bad debt

expense and inventory obsolescence charges are much lower than in other divisions. In discussing this with the controller of this division, it has been learned that the controller has increased his net income each period by knowingly making low estimates related to the write-off of receivables and inventory.

4. In 2020, the company purchased new machinery that should increase production dramatically. The company has decided to depreciate this machinery on an accelerated basis, even though other machinery is depreciated on a straight-line basis.
5. All equipment sold by Lotan is subject to a 3-year warranty. It has been estimated that the expense ultimately to be incurred on these machines is 1% of sales. In 2020, because of a production breakthrough, it is now estimated that ½ of 1% of sales is sufficient. In 2018 and 2019, warranty expense was computed as $64,000 and $70,000, respectively. The company now believes that these warranty costs should be reduced by 50%.
6. In 2020, the company decided to change its method of inventory pricing from average-cost to the FIFO method. The effect of this change on prior years is to increase 2018 income by $65,000 and increase 2019 income by $20,000.

Instructions

Katherine Irving has come to you, as her CPA, for advice about the situations above. Prepare a report, indicating the appropriate accounting treatment that should be given for each of these situations.

CA22.5 **(LO 1, 2)** Writing **(Change in Principle, Estimate)** As a certified public accountant, you have been contacted by Joe Davison, CEO of Sports-Pro Athletics, Inc., a manufacturer of a variety of athletic equipment. He has asked you how to account for the following changes.

1. Sports-Pro appropriately changed its depreciation method for its machinery from the double-declining-balance method to the units-of-production method effective January 1, 2020.
2. Effective January 1, 2020, Sports-Pro appropriately changed the salvage values used in computing depreciation for its office equipment.
3. On December 31, 2020, Sports-Pro appropriately changed the specific subsidiaries constituting the group of companies for which consolidated financial statements are presented.

Instructions

Write a 1–1.5 page letter to Joe Davison explaining how each of the above changes should be presented in the December 31, 2020, financial statements.

CA22.6 **(LO 2)** Ethics **(Change in Estimate)** Mike Crane is an audit senior of a large public accounting firm who has just been assigned to the Frost Corporation's annual audit engagement. Frost has been a client of Crane's firm for many years. Frost is a fast-growing business in the commercial construction industry. In reviewing the fixed asset ledger, Crane discovered a series of unusual accounting changes, in which the useful lives of assets, depreciated using the straight-line method, were substantially lowered near the midpoint of the original estimate. For example, the useful life of one dump truck was changed from 10 to 6 years during its fifth year of service. Upon further investigation, Mike was told by Kevin James, Frost's accounting manager, "I don't really see your problem. After all, it's perfectly legal to change an accounting estimate. Besides, our CEO likes to see big earnings!"

Instructions

Answer the following questions.

a. What are the ethical issues concerning Frost's practice of changing the useful lives of fixed assets?
b. Who could be harmed by Frost's unusual accounting changes?
c. What should Crane do in this situation?

Using Your Judgment

Financial Reporting Problem

The Procter & Gamble Company (P&G)

The financial statements of P&G are presented in Appendix B. The company's complete annual report, including the notes to the financial statements, is available online.

Instructions

Refer to P&G's financial statements and the accompanying notes to answer the following questions.

a. Were there changes in accounting principles reported by P&G during the three years covered by its income statements (2015–2017)? If so, describe the nature of the change and the year of change.

b. What types of estimates did P&G discuss in 2017?

Comparative Analysis Case

The Coca-Cola Company and PepsiCo, Inc.

The financial statements of **Coca-Cola** and **PepsiCo** are presented in Appendices C and D, respectively. The companies' complete annual reports, including the notes to the financial statements, are available online.

Instructions

Use the companies' financial information to answer the following questions.

a. Identify the changes in accounting principles reported by Coca-Cola during the 3 years covered by its income statements (2015–2017). Describe the nature of the change and the year of change.

b. Identify the changes in accounting principles reported by PepsiCo during the 3 years covered by its income statements (2015–2017). Describe the nature of the change and the year of change.

c. What types of estimates did PepsiCo discuss in 2017?

Accounting, Analysis, and Principles

In preparation for significant expansion of its international operations, ABC Co. has adopted a plan to gradually shift to the same accounting methods as used by its international competitors. Part of this plan includes a switch from LIFO inventory accounting to FIFO (recall that IFRS does not allow LIFO). ABC decides to make the switch to FIFO at January 1, 2020. The following data pertains to ABC's 2020 financial statements (in millions of dollars).

Sales	$550
Inventory purchases	350
12/31/20 inventory (using FIFO)	580
Compensation expense	17

All sales and purchases were with cash. All of 2020's compensation expense was paid with cash. (Ignore taxes.) ABC's property, plant, and equipment cost $400 million and has an estimated useful life of 10 years with no salvage value.

ABC Co. reported the following for fiscal 2019 (in millions of dollars):

ABC Co.
Balance Sheet
At December 31, 2019

	2019	**2018**		**2019**	**2018**
Cash	$ 365	$ 200	Common stock	$ 500	$ 500
Inventory	500	480	Retained earnings	685	540
Property, plant, and equipment	400	400			
Accumulated depreciation	(80)	(40)			
Total assets	$1,185	$1,040	Total equity	$1,185	$1,040

ABC Co.
Income Statement
For the Year Ended December 31, 2019

	2019
Sales	$ 500
Cost of goods sold	(300)
Depreciation expense	(40)
Compensation expense	(15)
Net income	$ 145

Summary of Significant Accounting Policies

Inventory: The company accounts for inventory by the LIFO method. The current cost of the company's inventory, which approximates FIFO, was $60 and $50 higher at the end of fiscal 2019 and 2018, respectively, than those reported in the balance sheet.

Accounting

Prepare ABC's December 31, 2020, balance sheet and an income statement for the year ended December 31, 2020. In columns beside 2020's numbers, include 2019's numbers *as they would appear in the 2020 financial statements* for comparative purposes.

Analysis

Compute ABC's inventory turnover for 2019 and 2020 under both LIFO and FIFO. Assume averages are equal to year-end balances where necessary. What causes the differences in this ratio between LIFO and FIFO?

Principles

Briefly explain, in terms of the principles discussed in Chapter 2, why GAAP requires that companies that change accounting methods recast prior year's financial statement data.

Bridge to the Profession

FASB Codification References

[1] FASB ASC 250-10-05-1. [Predecessor literature: "Accounting Changes and Error Corrections," *Statement of Financial Accounting Standards No. 154* (Stamford, Conn.: FASB, 2005).]

[2] FASB ASC 250-10-05-2. [Predecessor literature: "Accounting Changes and Error Corrections," *Statement of Financial Accounting Standards No. 154* (Stamford, Conn.: FASB, 2005).]

[3] FASB ASC 250-10-50-1. [Predecessor literature: "Accounting Changes and Error Corrections," *Statement of Financial Accounting Standards No. 154* (Stamford, Conn.: FASB, 2005), par. 17.]

[4] FASB ASC 250-10-50-1. [Predecessor literature: "Accounting Changes and Error Corrections," *Statement of Financial Accounting Standards No. 154* (Stamford, Conn.: FASB, 2005), par. B19.]

[5] FASB ASC 250-10-45-6. [Predecessor literature: "Accounting Changes and Error Corrections," *Statement of Financial Accounting Standards No. 154* (Stamford, Conn.: FASB, 2005), paras. 8–11.]

[6] FASB ASC 250-10-50-1. [Predecessor literature: "Accounting Changes and Error Corrections," *Statement of Financial Accounting Standards No. 154* (Stamford, Conn.: FASB, 2005), par. 17.]

[7] FASB ASC 250-10-45-18. [Predecessor literature: "Accounting Changes and Error Corrections," *Statement of Financial Accounting Standards No. 154* (Stamford, Conn.: FASB, 2005), par. 20.]

[8] FASB ASC 250-10-45-24. [Predecessor literature: "Prior Period Adjustments," *Statement of Financial Accounting Standards No. 16* (Stamford, Conn.: FASB, 1977), p. 5.]

[9] FASB ASC 250-10-50-4. [Predecessor literature: "Accounting Changes and Error Corrections," *Statement of Financial Accounting Standards No. 154* (Stamford, Conn.: FASB, 2005), par. 2.]

[10] FASB ASC 250-10-50-7. [Predecessor literature: "Accounting Changes and Error Corrections," *Statement of Financial Accounting Standards No. 154* (Stamford, Conn.: FASB, 2005), par. 26.]

[11] FASB ASC 323-10-35-3 and ASC 323-10-65-2. [Predecessor literature: "The Equity Method of Accounting for Investments in Common Stock," *Opinions of the Accounting Principles Board No. 18* (New York: AICPA, 1971), par. 17.]

[12] FASB ASC 250-10-50-1. [Predecessor literature: "Accounting Changes and Error Corrections," *Statement of Financial Accounting Standards No. 154* (Stamford, Conn.: FASB, 2005), par. 2.]

Codification Exercises

If your school has a subscription to the FASB Codification, log in and prepare responses to the following. Provide Codification references for your responses.

CE22.1 Access the glossary ("Master Glossary") to answer the following.

a. What is a change in accounting estimate?

b. What is a change in accounting principle?

c. What is a restatement?

d. What is the definition of "retrospective application"?

CE22.2 When a company has to restate its financial statements to correct an error, what information must the company disclose?

CE22.3 What reporting requirements does retrospective application require?

CE22.4 If a company registered with the SEC justifies a change in accounting method as preferable under the circumstances, and the circumstances change, can that company switch back to its prior method of accounting before the change? Why or why not?

Codification Research Case

As part of the year-end accounting process and review of operating policies, Cosper Co. is considering a change in the accounting for its equipment from the straight-line method to an accelerated method. Your supervisor wonders how the company will report this change in principle. He read in a newspaper article that the FASB has issued a standard in this area and has changed GAAP for a "change in estimate that is effected by a change in accounting principle." (Thus, the accounting may be different from what he learned in intermediate accounting.) Your supervisor wants you to research the authoritative guidance on a change in accounting principle related to depreciation methods.

Instructions

If your school has a subscription to the FASB Codification, log in and prepare responses to the following. Provide Codification references for your responses.

a. What are the accounting and reporting guidelines for a change in accounting principle related to depreciation methods?

b. What are the conditions that justify a change in depreciation method, as contemplated by Cosper Co.?

c. What guidance does the SEC provide concerning the impact that recently issued accounting standards will have on the financial statements in a future period?

Additional Professional Resources

Go to WileyPLUS for other career-readiness resources, such as career coaching, internship opportunities, and CPAexcel prep.

IFRS Insights

LEARNING OBJECTIVE 6

Compare the procedures for accounting changes and error analysis under GAAP and IFRS.

The IFRS addressing accounting and reporting for changes in accounting principles, changes in estimates, and errors is *IAS 8* ("Accounting Policies, Changes in Accounting Estimates and Errors"). Various presentation issues related to restatements are addressed in *IAS 1* ("Presentation of Financial Statements"). As indicated in the chapter, the FASB has issued guidance on changes in accounting principles, changes in estimates, and corrections of errors, which essentially converges GAAP to *IAS 8*.

Relevant Facts

Following are the key similarities and differences between GAAP and IFRS related to the procedures for accounting changes.

Similarities

- The accounting for changes in estimates is similar between GAAP and IFRS.
- Under GAAP and IFRS, if determining the effect of a change in accounting policy is considered impracticable, then a company should report the effect of the change in the period in which it believes it practicable to do so, which may be the current period.

Differences

- One area in which GAAP and IFRS differ is the reporting of error corrections in previously issued financial statements. While both sets of standards require restatement, GAAP is an absolute standard—that is, there is no exception to this rule.
- Under IFRS, the impracticality exception applies both to changes in accounting principles and to the correction of errors. Under GAAP, this exception applies only to changes in accounting principle.
- IFRS (*IAS 8*) does not specifically address the accounting and reporting for indirect effects of changes in accounting principles. As indicated in the chapter, GAAP has detailed guidance on the accounting and reporting of indirect effects.

About the Numbers

Direct and Indirect Effects of Changes

Are there other effects that a company should report when it makes a change in accounting policy? For example, what happens when a company like Lancer (as discussed in the chapter) has a bonus plan based on net income and the prior year's net income changes when FIFO is retrospectively applied? Should Lancer also change the reported amount of bonus expense? Or, what happens if we had not ignored income taxes in the Lancer example? Should Lancer adjust net income, given that taxes will be different under average-cost and FIFO in prior periods? The answers depend on whether the effects are direct or indirect.

Direct Effects Similar to GAAP, IFRS indicates that companies should retrospectively apply the **direct effects of a change in accounting policy**. An example of a **direct effect** is an adjustment to an inventory balance as a result of a change in the inventory valuation method. For example, referring to Lancer Company, Lancer should change the inventory amounts in prior periods to indicate the change to the FIFO method of inventory valuation. Another inventory-related example would be an impairment adjustment resulting from applying the lower-of-cost-or-net realizable value test to the adjusted inventory balance. Related changes, such as deferred income tax effects of the impairment adjustment, are also considered direct effects. This entry was illustrated in the Denson example in the chapter, in which the change to percentage-of-completion accounting resulted in recording a deferred tax liability.

Indirect Effects In addition to direct effects, companies can have **indirect effects related to a change in accounting policy**. An **indirect effect** is any change to current or future cash flows of a company that results from making a change in accounting policy that is applied retrospectively. An example of an indirect effect is a change in profit-sharing or royalty payment that is based on a reported amount such as revenue or net income. The IASB is silent on what to do in this situation. GAAP (likely because its standard in this area was issued after *IAS 8*) requires that indirect effects do not change prior period amounts.

For example, let's assume that Lancer Company has an employee profit-sharing plan based on net income and it changed from the weighted-average inventory method to FIFO in 2020. Lancer reports higher income in 2019 and 2020 if it used the FIFO method. In addition, let's assume that the profit-sharing plan requires that Lancer pay the incremental amount due based on the FIFO income amounts. In this situation, Lancer reports this additional expense **in the current period**; it would not change prior periods for this expense. If the company prepares comparative financial statements, it follows that it does not recast the prior periods for this additional expense. If the terms of the profit-sharing plan indicate that *no payment is necessary* in the current period due to this change, then the company need not recognize additional profit-sharing expense in the current period. Neither does it change amounts reported for prior periods.

When a company recognizes the indirect effects of a change in accounting policy, it includes in the financial statements a description of the indirect effects. In doing so, it discloses the amounts recognized in the current period and related per share information.

Impracticability

It is not always possible for companies to determine how they would have reported prior periods' financial information under retrospective application of an accounting policy change. Retrospective application is considered **impracticable** if a company cannot determine the prior period effects using every reasonable effort to do so.

Companies should not use retrospective application if one of the following conditions exists:

1. The company cannot determine the effects of the retrospective application.
2. Retrospective application requires assumptions about management's intent in a prior period.
3. Retrospective application requires significant estimates for a prior period, and the company cannot objectively verify the necessary information to develop these estimates.

If any of the above conditions exists, it is deemed impracticable to apply the retrospective approach. In this case, the company prospectively applies the new accounting policy as of the earliest date it is practicable to do so.

For example, assume that Williams Company changed its accounting policy for depreciable assets so as to more fully apply component depreciation under revaluation accounting. Unfortunately, the company does not have detailed accounting records to establish a basis for the components of these assets. As a result, Williams determines it is not practicable to account for the change to full component depreciation using the retrospective application approach. It therefore applies the policy prospectively, starting at the beginning of the current year.

Williams must disclose only the effect of the change on the results of operations in the period of change. Also, the company should explain the reasons for omitting the computations of the cumulative effect for prior years. Finally, it should disclose the justification for the change to component depreciation.

On the Horizon

For the most part, IFRS and GAAP are similar in the area of accounting changes and reporting the effects of errors. Thus, there is no active project in this area. A related development involves the presentation of comparative data. Under IFRS, when a company prepares financial statements on a new basis, two years of comparative data are reported. GAAP requires comparative information for a three-year period. Use of the shorter comparative data period could be an issue when U.S. companies adopt IFRS.

IFRS Self-Test Questions

1. Which of the following is **false**?
   a. GAAP and IFRS have the same absolute standard regarding the reporting of error corrections in previously issued financial statements.
   b. The accounting for changes in estimates is similar between GAAP and IFRS.
   c. Under IFRS, the impracticability exception applies both to changes in accounting principles and to the correction of errors.
   d. GAAP has detailed guidance on the accounting and reporting of indirect effects; IFRS does not.

2. Which of the following is **not** classified as an accounting change by IFRS?
   a. Change in accounting policy.
   b. Change in accounting estimate.
   c. Errors in financial statements.
   d. None of the above.

3. IFRS requires companies to use which method for reporting changes in accounting policies?
   a. Cumulative effect approach.
   b. Retrospective approach.
   c. Prospective approach.
   d. Averaging approach.

4. Under IFRS, the retrospective approach should not be used if:
   a. retrospective application requires assumptions about management's intent in a prior period.
   b. the company does not have trained staff to perform the analysis.
   c. the effects of the change have counterbalanced.
   d. the effects of the change have not counterbalanced.

5. Which of the following is **true** regarding whether IFRS specifically addresses the accounting and reporting for effects of changes in accounting policies?

	Direct Effects	Indirect Effects
a.	Yes	Yes
b.	No	No
c.	No	Yes
d.	Yes	No

IFRS Concepts and Application

IFRS22.1 Where can authoritative IFRS related to accounting changes be found?

IFRS22.2 Briefly describe some of the similarities and differences between GAAP and IFRS with respect to reporting accounting changes.

IFRS22.3 How might differences in presentation of comparative data under GAAP and IFRS affect adoption of IFRS by U.S. companies?

IFRS22.4 What is the indirect effect of a change in accounting policy? Briefly describe the approach to reporting the indirect effects of a change in accounting policy under IFRS.

IFRS22.5 Discuss how a change in accounting policy is handled when it is impracticable to determine previous amounts.

IFRS22.6 Joblonsky Inc. has recently hired a new independent auditor, Karen Ogleby, who says she wants "to get everything straightened out." Consequently, she has proposed the following accounting changes in connection with Joblonsky Inc.'s 2020 financial statements.

1. At December 31, 2019, the client had a receivable of $820,000 from Hendricks Inc. on its statement of financial position. Hendricks Inc. has gone bankrupt, and no recovery is expected. The client proposes to write off the receivable as a prior period item.
2. The client proposes the following changes in depreciation policies.
   a. For office furniture and fixtures, it proposes to change from a 10-year useful life to an 8-year life. If this change had been made in prior years, retained earnings at December 31, 2019, would have been $250,000 less. The effect of the change on 2020 income alone is a reduction of $60,000.
   b. For its new equipment in the leasing division, the client proposes to adopt the sum-of-the-years'-digits depreciation method. The client had never used SYD before. The first year the client operated a leasing division was 2020. If straight-line depreciation were used, 2020 income would be $110,000 greater.
3. In preparing its 2019 statements, one of the client's bookkeepers overstated ending inventory by $235,000 because of a mathematical error. The client proposes to treat this item as a prior period adjustment.

4. In the past, the client has spread preproduction costs in its furniture division over 5 years. Because its latest furniture is of the "fad" type, it appears that the largest volume of sales will occur during the first 2 years after introduction. Consequently, the client proposes to amortize preproduction costs on a per-unit basis, which will result in expensing most of such costs during the first 2 years after the furniture's introduction. If the new accounting method had been used prior to 2020, retained earnings at December 31, 2019, would have been $375,000 less.
5. For the nursery division, the client proposes to switch from FIFO to average-cost inventories because it believes that average-cost will provide a better income measure. The effect of making this change on 2020 earnings will be an increase of $320,000. The client says that the effect of the change on December 31, 2019, retained earnings cannot be determined.
6. To achieve an appropriate recognition of revenues and expenses in its building construction division, the client proposes to switch from the cost-recovery method of accounting to the percentage-of-completion method. Had the percentage-of-completion method been employed in all prior years, retained earnings at December 31, 2019, would have been $1,075,000 greater.

Instructions

a. For each of the changes described above, decide whether:
   1. The change involves an accounting policy, accounting estimate, or correction of an error.
   2. Restatement of opening retained earnings is required.

b. What would be the proper adjustment to the December 31, 2019, retained earnings?

Professional Research

IFRS22.7 As part of the year-end accounting process and review of operating policies, Tokar Co. is considering a change in the accounting for its equipment from the straight-line method to an accelerated method. Your supervisor wonders how the company will report this change in accounting. It has been a few years since he took intermediate accounting, and he cannot remember whether this change would be treated in a retrospective or prospective manner. Your supervisor wants you to research the authoritative guidance on a change in accounting policy related to depreciation methods.

Instructions

Access the IFRS authoritative literature at the IASB website. (Click on the IFRS tab and then register for free eIFRS access if necessary.) When you have accessed the documents, you can use the search tool in your Internet browser to respond to the following questions. (Provide paragraph citations.)

a. What are the accounting and reporting guidelines for a change in accounting policy related to depreciation methods?

b. What are the conditions that justify a change in depreciation method, as contemplated by Tokar Co.?

International Financial Reporting Problem

Marks and Spencer plc (M&S)

IFRS22.8 The financial statements of **M&S** are presented in Appendix E. The company's complete annual report, including the notes to the financial statements, is available online.

Instructions

Refer to M&S's financial statements and the accompanying notes to answer the following questions.

a. Were there changes in accounting policies reported by M&S during the two years covered by its income statements (2016–2017)? If so, describe the nature of the change and the year of change.

b. What types of estimates did M&S discuss in 2017?

Answers to IFRS Self-Test Questions

1. a **2.** c **3.** b **4.** a **5.** d

CHAPTER **23**

© andersphoto/Shutterstock

Statement of Cash Flows

LEARNING OBJECTIVES

After studying this chapter, you should be able to:

1. Describe the usefulness and format of the statement of cash flows.
2. Prepare a statement of cash flows.
3. Contrast the direct and indirect methods of calculating net cash flow from operating activities.
4. Discuss special problems in preparing a statement of cash flows.
5. Explain the use of a worksheet in preparing a statement of cash flows.

PREVIEW OF CHAPTER 23 As the following opening story indicates, examination of **W. T. Grant**'s cash flows from operations would have shown the financial inflexibility that eventually caused the company's bankruptcy. This chapter explains the main components of a statement of cash flows and the types of information it provides. The content and organization of the chapter are as follows.

This chapter also includes numerous conceptual and global discussions that are integral to the topics presented here.

STATEMENT OF CASH FLOWS

Statement of Cash Flows
- Usefulness of statement
- Classification of cash flows
- Format of statement

Preparing the Statement of Cash Flows
- Illustrations—Tax Consultants Inc.
- Sources of information
- Net cash flow from operating activities—direct method

Special Problems in Statement Preparation
- Adjustments to net income
- Accounts receivable (net)
- Other working capital changes
- Net losses
- Significant noncash transactions

Use of a Worksheet
- Preparation of worksheet
- Analysis of transactions
- Preparation of final statement

Show Me the Money!

Investors usually look to net income as a key indicator of a company's financial health and future prospects. The following graph shows the net income of one company over a seven-year period.

The company showed a pattern of consistent profitability and even some periods of income growth. Between years 1 and 4, net income for this company grew by 32 percent,

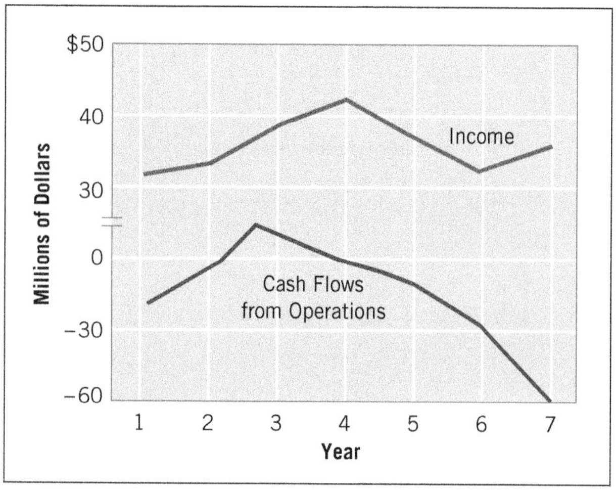

from $31 million to $41 million. Would you expect its profitability to continue? The company had consistently paid dividends and interest. Would you expect it to continue to do so? Investors answered these questions by buying the company's stock. Eighteen months later, this company—**W. T. Grant**—filed for bankruptcy, in what was then the largest bankruptcy filing in the United States.

How could this happen? As indicated by the second line in the graph, the company had experienced several years of negative cash flow from its operations, even though it reported profits. How can a company have negative cash flows while reporting profits? The answer lays partly in the fact that W. T. Grant was having trouble collecting the receivables from its credit sales, causing cash flow to be less than net income. Investors who analyzed the cash flows would have been likely to find an early warning signal of W. T. Grant's operating problems.

Investors can also look to cash flow information to sniff out companies that can be good buys. As one analyst stated when it comes to valuing stocks: "Show me the money!" Here's the thinking behind that statement. Start with the "cash flows from operations" reported in the statement of cash flows, which (as you will learn in this chapter) consists of net income with noncash charges (like depreciation and deferred taxes) added back and cash-draining events (like an inventory pile-up) taken out. Now subtract capital expenditures and dividends. What you're left with is free cash flow (as discussed in Chapter 5).

Many analysts like companies trading at low multiples of their free cash flow—low, that is, in relation to rivals today or the same company in past years. Why? They know that reported earnings can be misleading. Case in point: Computer-game firm **Activision Blizzard** reported net income of $113 million in a recent year. But it did better than that. It took in an additional $300 million, mostly for subscriptions to online multiplayer games. It gets the cash now but records the revenue only over time, as the subscriptions run out. A couple of investment houses put this stock on their buy list on the strength of its cash flows.

In contrast, **Moody's Investors Service** downgraded **Tesla**'s debt, citing persistently negative cash flow and continued production issues with the Model 3 mass-market sedan. Moody's is keeping a negative outlook on the credit due to "the likelihood that Tesla will have to undertake a large, near-term capital raise in order to refund maturing obligations and avoid a liquidity shortfall." And **Boeing** experienced a 3 percent decline in its stock price in a recent quarter when it reported decent operating profits but declining free cash flow (mostly due to share buybacks and increased capital expenditures). Analysts said the cash outflow spurred investors to sell.

So watch cash flow—to get an indicator of companies headed for trouble, as well as companies that may be undervalued.

Sources: Adapted from James A. Largay III and Clyde P. Stickney, "Cash Flows, Ratio Analysis, and the W. T. Grant Company Bankruptcy," *Financial Analysts Journal* (July–August 1980), p. 51; D. Fisher, "Cash Doesn't Lie," *Forbes* (April 12, 2010), pp. 52–55; J. Benkoe, "Show Me the Money," *The New York Times* (April 22, 2015); and C. Grant, "The Clock Is Ticking Faster at Tesla," *Wall Street Journal* (March 28, 2018).

Review and Practice

Go to the **Review and Practice** section at the end of the chapter for a targeted summary review and practice problem with solution. Multiple-choice questions with annotated solutions as well as additional exercises and practice problem with solutions are also available online.

Statement of Cash Flows

LEARNING OBJECTIVE 1

Describe the usefulness and format of the statement of cash flows.

The primary purpose of the **statement of cash flows** is to provide information about a company's cash receipts and cash payments during a period. A secondary objective is to provide cash-basis information about the company's operating, investing, and financing activities. The statement of cash flows therefore reports cash receipts, cash payments, and net change in cash resulting from a company's operating, investing, and financing activities during a period. Its format reconciles the beginning and ending cash balances for the period.

Usefulness of the Statement of Cash Flows

The statement of cash flows provides information to help investors, creditors, and others assess the following [1]. (See the FASB Codification References near the end of the chapter.)

1. ***The entity's ability to generate future cash flows.*** A primary objective of financial reporting is to provide information with which to predict the amounts, timing, and uncertainty of future cash flows. By examining relationships between items such as sales and net cash flow from operating activities, or net cash flow from operating activities and increases or decreases in cash, it is possible to better predict the future cash flows than is possible using accrual-basis data alone.
2. ***The entity's ability to pay dividends and meet obligations.*** Simply put, cash is essential. Without adequate cash, a company cannot pay employees, settle debts, pay out dividends, or acquire equipment. A statement of cash flows indicates where the company's cash comes from and how the company uses its cash. Employees, creditors, stockholders, and customers should be particularly interested in this statement, because it alone shows the flows of cash in a business (see **Underlying Concepts**).
3. ***The reasons for the difference between net income and net cash flow from operating activities.*** The net income number is important: It provides information on the performance of a company from one period to another. But some people are critical of accrual-basis net income because companies must make estimates to arrive at it. Such is not the case with cash. Thus, as the opening story showed, financial statement readers can benefit from knowing why a company's net income and net cash flow from operating activities differ, and can assess for themselves the reliability of the income number.
4. ***The cash and noncash investing and financing transactions during the period.*** Besides operating activities, companies undertake investing and financing transactions. *Investing* activities include the purchase and sale of assets other than a company's products or services. *Financing* activities include borrowings and repayments of borrowings, investments by owners, and distributions to owners. By examining a company's investing and financing activities, a financial statement reader can better understand why assets and liabilities increased or decreased during the period. For example, by reading the statement of cash flows, the reader might find answers to the following questions:
   - Why did cash decrease for **Home Depot** when it reported net income for the period?
   - How much did **Southwest Airlines** spend on property, plant, and equipment last year?
   - Did dividends paid by **Campbell's Soup** increase?
   - How much money did **Coca-Cola** borrow last year?
   - How much cash did **Hewlett-Packard** use to repurchase its common stock?

Underlying Concepts

Reporting information in the statement of cash flows contributes to meeting the objective of financial reporting.

Classification of Cash Flows

The statement of cash flows classifies cash receipts and cash payments by operating, investing, and financing activities.[1] Transactions and other events characteristic of each kind of activity are as follows.

1. **Operating activities** involve the cash effects of transactions that enter into the determination of net income, such as cash receipts from sales of goods and services, and cash payments to suppliers and employees for acquisitions of inventory and expenses.
2. **Investing activities** generally involve long-term assets and include (a) making and collecting loans, and (b) acquiring and disposing of investments and productive long-lived assets.
3. **Financing activities** involve liability and stockholders' equity items and include (a) obtaining cash from creditors and repaying the amounts borrowed, and (b) obtaining capital from owners and providing them with a return on, and a return of, their investment.

Illustration 23.1 classifies the typical cash receipts and payments of a company according to operating, investing, and financing activities. The operating activities category is the most important. It shows the cash provided by company operations. This source of cash is generally considered to be the best measure of a company's ability to generate enough cash to continue as a going concern.

ILLUSTRATION 23.1

Classification of Typical Cash Inflows and Outflows

Operating Cash inflows From sales of goods or services. From returns on loans (interest) and on equity securities (dividends). Cash outflows To suppliers for inventory. To employees for services. To government for taxes. To lenders for interest. To others for expenses.	**Income Statement Items**
Investing Cash inflows From sale of property, plant, and equipment. From sale of debt or equity securities of other entities. From collection of principal on loans to other entities. Cash outflows To purchase property, plant, and equipment. To purchase debt or equity securities of other entities. To make loans to other entities.	**Generally Long-Term Asset Items**
Financing Cash inflows From sale of equity securities. From issuance of debt (bonds and notes). Cash outflows To stockholders as dividends. To redeem long-term debt or reacquire capital stock.	**Generally Long-Term Liability and Equity Items**

Global View

According to IFRS, companies can define "cash and cash equivalents" as "net monetary assets"—that is, as "cash and demand deposits and highly liquid investments less short-term borrowings."

[1]The basis recommended by the FASB for the statement of cash flows is actually "cash and cash equivalents." **Cash equivalents** are short-term, highly liquid investments that are both (a) readily convertible to known amounts of cash, and (b) so near their maturity that they present insignificant risk of changes in interest rates. Generally, only investments with original maturities of three months or less qualify under this definition. Examples of cash equivalents are Treasury bills, commercial paper, and money market funds purchased with cash that is in excess of immediate needs.

Although we use the term "cash" throughout our discussion and illustrations, we mean cash and cash equivalents when reporting the cash flows and the net increase or decrease in cash (see Global View).

Note the following general guidelines about the classification of cash flows.

1. Operating activities involve income statement items.
2. Investing activities involve cash flows resulting from changes in investments and long-term asset items.
3. Financing activities involve cash flows resulting from changes in long-term liability and stockholders' equity items.

Companies classify some cash flows relating to investing or financing activities as operating activities.[2] For example, companies classify receipts of investment income (interest and dividends) and payments of interest to lenders as operating activities. Why are these considered operating activities? Companies report these items in the income statement, where the results of operations are shown.

Conversely, companies classify some cash flows relating to operating activities as investing or financing activities. For example, a company classifies the cash received from the sale of property, plant, and equipment as an investing activity, while it excludes the effects of any related gain or loss in net cash flow from operating activities. Likewise, a gain or loss on the payment (extinguishment) of debt is generally part of the cash outflow related to the repayment of the amount borrowed. It therefore is a financing activity.

What Do the Numbers Mean? How's My Cash Flow?

To evaluate overall cash flow, it is useful to understand where in the product life cycle a company is. Generally, companies move through several stages of development, which have implications for cash flow. As the following graph shows, the pattern of cash flows from operating, financing, and investing activities will vary depending on the stage of the product life cycle.

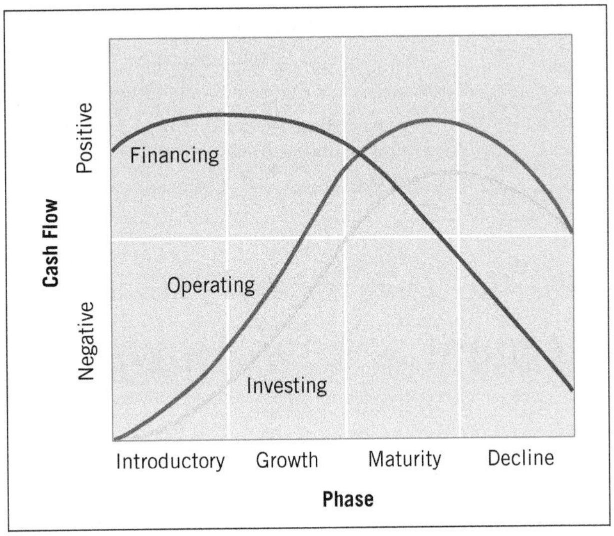

In the introductory phase, the product is likely not generating much revenue (operating cash flow is negative). Because the company is making heavy investments to get a product off the ground, cash flow from investment is negative, and financing cash flows are positive.

As the product moves to the growth and maturity phases, these cash flow relationships reverse. The product generates more cash flow from operations, which can be used to cover investments needed to support the product, and less cash is needed from financing. So is a negative operating cash flow bad? Not always. It depends on the product life cycle.

Source: Adapted from Paul D. Kimmel, Jerry J. Weygandt, and Donald E. Kieso, *Financial Accounting: Tools for Business Decision Making*, 8th ed. (New York: John Wiley & Sons, 2016), p. 607.

[2]Banks and brokers must classify cash flows from purchases and sales of loans and securities specifically for resale and carried at fair value **as operating activities**. This requirement recognizes that for these firms these assets are similar to inventory in other businesses. [2]

Format of the Statement of Cash Flows

The three activities we discussed above constitute the general format of the statement of cash flows. The operating activities section always appears first. It is followed by the investing activities section and then the financing activities section.

A company reports the individual inflows and outflows from investing and financing activities separately. That is, a company reports them gross, not netted against one another. Thus, a cash outflow from the purchase of property is reported separately from the cash inflow from the sale of property. Similarly, a cash inflow from the issuance of debt is reported separately from the cash outflow from its retirement.

The net increase or decrease in cash reported during the period should reconcile the beginning and ending cash balances as reported in the comparative balance sheets. The general format of the statement of cash flows presents the results of the three activities discussed previously–operating, investing, and financing. Illustration 23.2 shows a widely used form of the statement of cash flows (see Global View).

Global View

Both IFRS and GAAP specify that companies must classify cash flows as operating, investing, or financing.

ILLUSTRATION 23.2

Format of the Statement of Cash Flows

Company Name
Statement of Cash Flows
Period Covered

Cash flows from operating activities		
Net income		XXX
Adjustments to reconcile net income to net cash provided (used) by operating activities:		
(List of individual items)	XX	XX
Net cash provided (used) by operating activities		XXX
Cash flows from investing activities		
(List of individual inflows and outflows)	XX	
Net cash provided (used) by investing activities		XXX
Cash flows from financing activities		
(List of individual inflows and outflows)	XX	
Net cash provided (used) by financing activities		XXX
Net increase (decrease) in cash		XXX
Cash at beginning of period		XXX
Cash at end of period		XXX

Preparing the Statement of Cash Flows

LEARNING OBJECTIVE 2

Prepare a statement of cash flows.

Companies prepare the statement of cash flows differently from the three other basic financial statements. For one thing, it is not prepared from an adjusted trial balance. The statement of cash flows requires detailed information concerning the changes in account balances that occurred between two points in time. An adjusted trial balance will not provide the necessary data. Second, the statement of cash flows deals with cash receipts and payments. As a result, the company must adjust the effects of the use of accrual accounting to determine cash flows. The information to prepare this statement usually comes from three sources:

1. **Comparative balance sheets** provide the amount of the changes in assets, liabilities, and equities from the beginning to the end of the period.
2. **Current income statement data** help determine the amount of cash provided by or used by operations during the period.

3. **Selected transaction data** from the general ledger provide additional detailed information needed to determine how the company provided or used cash during the period.

Preparing the statement of cash flows from the data sources above involves three major steps:

Step 1. *Determine the change in cash.* This procedure is straightforward. A company can easily compute the difference between the beginning and the ending cash balance from examining its comparative balance sheets.

Step 2. *Determine the net cash flow from operating activities.* This procedure is complex. It involves analyzing not only the current year's income statement but also comparative balance sheets as well as selected transaction data.

Step 3. *Determine net cash flows from investing and financing activities.* A company must analyze all other changes in the balance sheet accounts to determine their effects on cash.

On the following pages, we work through these three steps in the process of preparing the statement of cash flows for Tax Consultants Inc. over several years.

Illustrations—Tax Consultants Inc.

We show the steps in preparing the statement of cash flows using data for Tax Consultants Inc. To begin, we use the **first year of operations** for Tax Consultants Inc. The company started on January 1, 2019, when it issued 60,000 shares of $1 par value common stock for $60,000 cash. The company rented its office space, furniture, and equipment, and performed tax consulting services throughout the first year. The comparative balance sheets at the beginning and end of the year 2019 appear in **Illustration 23.3**.

ILLUSTRATION 23.3

Comparative Balance Sheets, Tax Consultants Inc., Year 1

Tax Consultants Inc.
Comparative Balance Sheets

Assets	Dec. 31, 2019	Jan. 1, 2019	Change Increase/Decrease
Cash	$49,000	$-0-	$49,000 Increase
Accounts receivable	36,000	-0-	36,000 Increase
Total	$85,000	$-0-	
Liabilities and Stockholders' Equity			
Accounts payable	$ 5,000	$-0-	$ 5,000 Increase
Common stock ($1 par)	60,000	-0-	60,000 Increase
Retained earnings	20,000	-0-	20,000 Increase
Total	$85,000	$-0-	

Illustration 23.4 shows the income statement and additional information for Tax Consultants.

ILLUSTRATION 23.4

Income Statement, Tax Consultants Inc., Year 1

Tax Consultants Inc.
Income Statement
For the Year Ended December 31, 2019

Revenues	$125,000
Operating expenses	85,000
Income before income taxes	40,000
Income tax expense	6,000
Net income	$ 34,000

Additional Information
Examination of selected data indicates that a dividend of $14,000 was declared and paid during the year.

Step 1: Determine the Change in Cash

To prepare a statement of cash flows, the first step is to **determine the change in cash.** This is a simple computation. Tax Consultants had no cash on hand at the beginning of the year 2019. It had $49,000 on hand at the end of 2019. Thus, cash changed (increased) in 2019 by $49,000.

Step 2: Determine Net Cash Flow from Operating Activities

To determine net cash flow from operating activities,[3] companies adjust net income in numerous ways. A useful starting point is to understand why net income must be converted to net cash provided by operating activities.

Under generally accepted accounting principles, most companies use the accrual basis of accounting. As you have learned, this basis requires that companies record revenue when a performance obligation is met and record expenses when incurred. For example, revenues may include credit sales for which the company has not yet collected cash, or expenses incurred may include some items that the company has not yet paid in cash. Thus, under the accrual basis of accounting, net income is not the same as net cash flow from operating activities.

To arrive at net cash flow from operating activities, a company must determine revenues and expenses on a **cash basis. It does this by eliminating the effects of income statement transactions that do not result in an increase or decrease in cash.** Illustration 23.5 shows the relationship between net income and net cash flow from operating activities.

ILLUSTRATION 23.5

Net Income versus Net Cash Flow from Operating Activities

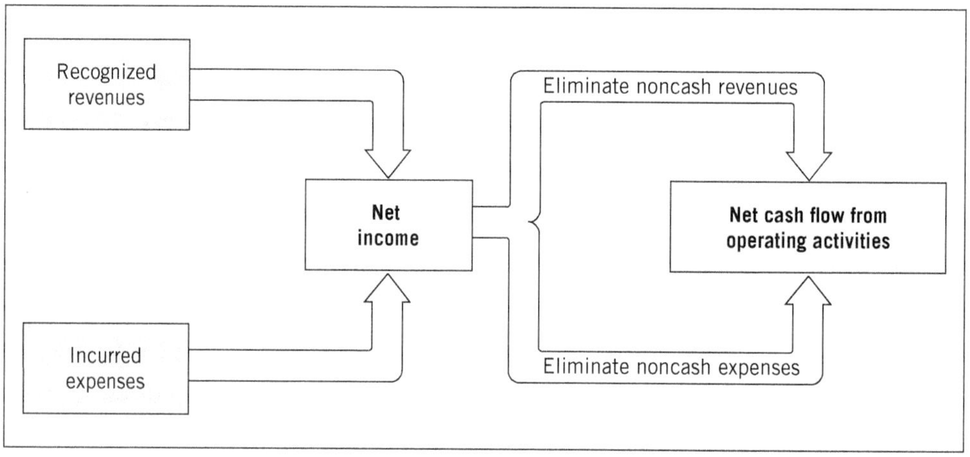

In this chapter, we use the term net income to refer to accrual-based net income. A company may convert net income to net cash flow from operating activities through either a direct method or an indirect method. Due to its widespread use in practice, in the following sections we illustrate use of the indirect method. Later in the chapter, we describe the direct method and discuss the advantages and disadvantages of the two methods.[4]

The indirect method (or **reconciliation method**) starts with net income and converts it to net cash flow from operating activities. In other words, **the indirect method adjusts net income for items that affected reported net income but did not affect cash.** To compute net cash flow from operating activities, a company adds back noncash charges in the income statement to net income and deducts noncash credits. We explain the two adjustments to net income for Tax Consultants, namely, the increases in accounts receivable and accounts payable, as follows.

[3] "Net cash flow from operating activities" is a generic phrase, replaced in the statement of cash flows with either "Net cash **provided by** operating activities" if operations increase cash, or "Net cash **used by** operating activities" if operations decrease cash.

[4] *Accounting Trends and Techniques* indicates that out of its 500 surveyed companies, 495 (99 percent) used the indirect method, and only 5 used the direct method. *In doing homework assignments, you should follow instructions for use of either the direct or indirect method.*

Increase in Accounts Receivable—Indirect Method Tax Consultants' accounts receivable increased by $36,000 (from $0 to $36,000) during the year. For Tax Consultants, this means that cash receipts were $36,000 lower than revenues. The Accounts Receivable account in Illustration 23.6 shows that Tax Consultants had $125,000 in revenues (as reported on the income statement), but it collected only $89,000 in cash.

ILLUSTRATION 23.6
Analysis of Accounts Receivable

Accounts Receivable				
1/1/19	Balance	-0-	Receipts from customer	89,000
	Revenues	125,000		
12/31/19	Balance	36,000		

As shown in Illustration 23.7, to adjust net income to net cash provided by operating activities, Tax Consultants must deduct the increase of $36,000 in accounts receivable from net income. When the Accounts Receivable balance *decreases*, cash receipts are higher than revenue recognized under the accrual basis. Therefore, the company adds to net income the amount of the decrease in accounts receivable to arrive at net cash provided by operating activities.

Increase in Accounts Payable—Indirect Method When accounts payable increase during the year, expenses on an accrual basis exceed those on a cash basis. Why? Because Tax Consultants incurred expenses, but some of the expenses are not yet paid. To convert net income to net cash flow from operating activities, Tax Consultants must add back the increase of $5,000 in accounts payable to net income.

As a result of the accounts receivable and accounts payable adjustments, Tax Consultants determines net cash provided by operating activities is $3,000 for the year 2019. Illustration 23.7 shows this computation.

ILLUSTRATION 23.7
Computation of Net Cash Flow from Operating Activities, Year 1—Indirect Method

Net income		$ 34,000
Adjustments to reconcile net income to net cash provided by operating activities:		
Increase in accounts receivable	$(36,000)	
Increase in accounts payable	5,000	(31,000)
Net cash provided by operating activities		$ 3,000

What Do the Numbers Mean? Earnings and Cash Flow Management?

Investors must be vigilant in their monitoring of management incentives to manipulate both earnings and cash flows. That is, financial success is dependent not only on a company's ability to generate revenues and earnings, but also cash flow. A company that shows profits but is unable to generate cash will also experience waning investor enthusiasm.

Thus, management has an incentive to make operating cash flow look good because Wall Street has paid a premium for companies that generate a lot of cash from operations, rather than through borrowings. However, similar to earnings, companies have ways to pump up cash flow from operations.

One way that companies can boost their operating cash flow is by "securitizing" receivables. That is, companies can speed up cash collections by selling their receivables. For example, Federated Department Stores reported a $2.2 billion increase in cash flow from operations. This seems impressive until you read the fine print, which indicates that a big part of the increase was due to the sale of receivables. As discussed in this section, decreases in accounts receivable increase cash flow from operations. So while it appeared that Federated's core operations had improved, the company really did little more than accelerate collections of its receivables. In fact, the cash flow from the securitizations represented more than half of Federated's operating cash flow.

Some securitizations, such as those executed by Kraft-Heinz and AT&T, include cash flows from so-called "beneficial interests," which may or may not result in an increase in operating cash flows. In response to possible overstatement of operating cash flows from such securitizations, the FASB recently tightened rules to classify as operating cash flows only those directly related to the sale. Other cash flows related to beneficial interests must be disclosed as a noncash investing activity. The new rules resulted in a significant drop in cash flow from operations for Kraft-Heinz and AT&T. Thus, in evaluating the quality of accounting, investors must keep an eye on the quality of earnings *and* cash flows.

Source: Adapted from Ann Tergesen, "Cash Flow Hocus Pocus," *BusinessWeek* (July 16, 2002), pp. 130–131. See also C. Mulford and A. Lopez de Mesa, *Cash Flow Trends and Their Fundamental Drivers: Comprehensive Industry Review*, Georgia Tech Financial Analysis Lab (October 2, 2012); and M. Rappaport, "Why Kraft-Heinz's Cash Flow Is Getting Sliced," *Wall Street Journal* (April 2, 2018).

Step 3: Determine Net Cash Flows from Investing and Financing Activities

After Tax Consultants has computed the net cash provided by operating activities, the next step is to determine whether any other changes in balance sheet accounts caused an increase or decrease in cash.

For example, an examination of the remaining balance sheet accounts for Tax Consultants shows increases in both common stock and retained earnings. The common stock increase of $60,000 resulted from the issuance of common stock for cash. The issuance of common stock is reported in the statement of cash flows as a receipt of cash from a financing activity.

Two items caused the retained earnings increase of $20,000:

1. Net income of $34,000 increased retained earnings.
2. Declaration of $14,000 of dividends decreased retained earnings.

Tax Consultants has converted net income into net cash flow from operating activities, as explained earlier. The additional data indicate that it paid the dividend. Thus, the company reports the dividend payment as a cash outflow, classified as a financing activity.

Statement of Cash Flows—2019

We are now ready to prepare the statement of cash flows. The statement starts with the operating activities section. Tax Consultants uses the indirect method to report net cash flow from operating activities.

Illustration 23.8 shows the statement of cash flows for Tax Consultants Inc., for year 1 (2019).

ILLUSTRATION 23.8

Statement of Cash Flows, Tax Consultants Inc., Year 1

Tax Consultants Inc.
Statement of Cash Flows
For the Year Ended December 31, 2019

Cash flows from operating activities		
Net income		$ 34,000
Adjustments to reconcile net income to net cash provided by operating activities:		
Increase in accounts receivable	$(36,000)	
Increase in accounts payable	5,000	(31,000)
Net cash provided by operating activities		3,000
Cash flows from financing activities		
Issuance of common stock	60,000	
Payment of cash dividends	(14,000)	
Net cash provided by financing activities		46,000
Net increase in cash		49,000
Cash, January 1, 2019		-0-
Cash, December 31, 2019		$ 49,000

As indicated, the $60,000 increase in common stock results in a financing activity cash inflow. The payment of $14,000 in cash dividends is a financing activity outflow of cash. The $49,000 increase in cash reported in the statement of cash flows agrees with the increase of $49,000 shown in the comparative balance sheets as the change in the Cash account.

Illustration—2020

Tax Consultants Inc. continued to grow and prosper in its second year of operations. The company purchased land, building, and equipment, and revenues and net income increased substantially over the first year. Illustrations 23.9 and 23.10 present information related to the second year of operations for Tax Consultants Inc.

ILLUSTRATION 23.9

Comparative Balance Sheets, Tax Consultants Inc., Year 2

Tax Consultants Inc.
Comparative Balance Sheets
As of December 31

Assets	2020	2019	Change Increase/Decrease
Cash	$ 37,000	$49,000	$ 12,000 Decrease
Accounts receivable	26,000	36,000	10,000 Decrease
Prepaid expenses	6,000	-0-	6,000 Increase
Land	70,000	-0-	70,000 Increase
Buildings	200,000	-0-	200,000 Increase
Accumulated depreciation—buildings	(11,000)	-0-	11,000 Increase
Equipment	68,000	-0-	68,000 Increase
Accumulated depreciation—equipment	(10,000)	-0-	10,000 Increase
Total	$386,000	$85,000	
Liabilities and Stockholders' Equity			
Accounts payable	$ 40,000	$ 5,000	$ 35,000 Increase
Bonds payable	150,000	-0-	150,000 Increase
Common stock ($1 par)	60,000	60,000	-0-
Retained earnings	136,000	20,000	116,000 Increase
Total	$386,000	$85,000	

ILLUSTRATION 23.10

Income Statement, Tax Consultants Inc., Year 2

Tax Consultants Inc.
Income Statement
For the Year Ended December 31, 2020

Revenues		$492,000
Operating expenses (excluding depreciation)	$269,000	
Depreciation expense	21,000	290,000
Income from operations		202,000
Income tax expense		68,000
Net income		$134,000

Additional Information

(a) The company declared and paid an $18,000 cash dividend.
(b) The company obtained $150,000 cash through the issuance of long-term bonds.
(c) Land, building, and equipment were acquired for cash.

Step 1: Determine the Change in Cash To prepare a statement of cash flows from the available information, the first step is to determine the change in cash. As indicated from the information presented, cash decreased $12,000 ($49,000 – $37,000).

Step 2: Determine Net Cash Flow from Operating Activities—Indirect Method Using the indirect method, we adjust net income of $134,000 on an accrual basis to arrive at net cash flow from operating activities. Explanations for the adjustments to net income follow.

- ***Decrease in Accounts Receivable.*** Accounts receivable decreased during the period because cash receipts (cash-basis revenues) are higher than revenues reported on an accrual basis. To convert net income to net cash flow from operating activities, the decrease of $10,000 in accounts receivable must be added to net income.

- ***Increase in Prepaid Expenses.*** When prepaid expenses (assets) increase during a period, expenses on an accrual-basis income statement are lower than they are on a cash-basis income statement. The reason: Tax Consultants has made cash payments in the current period, but expenses (as charges to the income statement) have been deferred to future periods. To convert net income to net cash flow from operating activities, the company must deduct from net income the increase of $6,000 in prepaid expenses. An increase in prepaid expenses results in a decrease in cash during the period.
- ***Increase in Accounts Payable.*** Like the increase in 2019, Tax Consultants must add the 2020 increase of $35,000 in accounts payable to net income, to convert to net cash flow from operating activities. The company incurred a greater amount of expense than the amount of cash it disbursed.
- ***Depreciation Expense (Increase in Accumulated Depreciation).*** The purchase of depreciable assets is a use of cash, shown in the investing section in the year of acquisition. Tax Consultants' depreciation expense of $21,000 (also represented by the increase in accumulated depreciation) is a noncash charge; the company adds it back to net income, to arrive at net cash flow from operating activities. The $21,000 is the sum of the $11,000 depreciation on the building plus the $10,000 depreciation on the equipment.

Certain other periodic charges to expense do not require the use of cash. Examples are the amortization of intangible assets and depletion expense. Such charges are treated in the same manner as depreciation. Companies frequently list depreciation and similar noncash charges as the first adjustments to net income in the statement of cash flows.

As a result of the foregoing items, net cash provided by operating activities is $194,000 as shown in Illustration 23.11.

ILLUSTRATION 23.11

Computation of Net Cash Flow from Operating Activities, Year 2—Indirect Method

Net income		$134,000
Adjustments to reconcile net income to net cash provided by operating activities:		
Depreciation expense	$21,000	
Decrease in accounts receivable	10,000	
Increase in prepaid expenses	(6,000)	
Increase in accounts payable	35,000	60,000
Net cash provided by operating activities		$194,000

Step 3: Determine Net Cash Flows from Investing and Financing Activities

After you have determined the items affecting net cash provided by operating activities, the next step involves analyzing the remaining changes in balance sheet accounts. Tax Consultants Inc. analyzed the following accounts.

- ***Increase in Land.*** As indicated from the change in the Land account, the company purchased land of $70,000 during the period. This transaction is an investing activity, reported as a use of cash.
- ***Increase in Buildings and Related Accumulated Depreciation.*** As indicated in the additional data and from the change in the Buildings account, Tax Consultants acquired an office building using $200,000 cash. This transaction is a cash outflow, reported in the investing section. The $11,000 increase in accumulated depreciation results from recording depreciation expense on the building. As indicated earlier, the reported depreciation expense has no effect on the amount of cash.

- ***Increase in Equipment and Related Accumulated Depreciation.*** An increase in equipment of $68,000 resulted because the company used cash to purchase equipment. This transaction is an outflow of cash from an investing activity. The depreciation expense entry for the period explains the increase in Accumulated Depreciation—Equipment.
- ***Increase in Bonds Payable.*** The Bonds Payable account increased $150,000. Cash received from the issuance of these bonds represents an inflow of cash from a financing activity.
- ***Increase in Retained Earnings.*** Retained earnings increased $116,000 during the year. Two factors explain this increase. (1) Net income of $134,000 increased retained earnings, and (2) dividends of $18,000 decreased retained earnings. As indicated earlier, the company adjusts net income to net cash provided by operating activities in the operating activities section. Payment of the dividends is a financing activity that involves a cash outflow.

Statement of Cash Flows—2020 Combining the foregoing items, we get the statement of cash flows for 2020 for Tax Consultants Inc., shown in **Illustration 23.12**, using the indirect method to compute net cash flow from operating activities.

ILLUSTRATION 23.12

Statement of Cash Flows, Tax Consultants Inc., Year 2

Tax Consultants Inc.
Statement of Cash Flows
For the Year Ended December 31, 2020

Cash flows from operating activities		
Net income		$ 134,000
Adjustments to reconcile net income to net cash provided by operating activities:		
Depreciation expense	$ 21,000	
Decrease in accounts receivable	10,000	
Increase in prepaid expenses	(6,000)	
Increase in accounts payable	35,000	60,000
Net cash provided by operating activities		194,000
Cash flows from investing activities		
Purchase of land	(70,000)	
Purchase of building	(200,000)	
Purchase of equipment	(68,000)	
Net cash used by investing activities		(338,000)
Cash flows from financing activities		
Issuance of bonds	150,000	
Payment of cash dividends	(18,000)	
Net cash provided by financing activities		132,000
Net decrease in cash		(12,000)
Cash, January 1, 2020		49,000
Cash, December 31, 2020		$ 37,000

Illustration—2021

Our third example, covering the 2021 operations of Tax Consultants Inc., is more complex. It again uses the indirect method to compute and present net cash flow from operating activities.

Tax Consultants Inc. experienced continued success in 2021 and expanded its operations to include the sale of computer software used in tax-return preparation and tax planning. Thus, inventory is a new asset appearing in the company's December 31, 2021, balance sheet. **Illustrations 23.13** and **23.14** show the comparative balance sheets, income statements, and selected data for 2021.

ILLUSTRATION 23.13

Comparative Balance Sheets, Tax Consultants Inc., Year 3

Tax Consultants Inc.
Comparative Balance Sheets
As of December 31

Assets	2021	2020	Change Increase/Decrease
Cash	$ 54,000	$ 37,000	$ 17,000 Increase
Accounts receivable	68,000	26,000	42,000 Increase
Inventory	54,000	–0–	54,000 Increase
Prepaid expenses	4,000	6,000	2,000 Decrease
Land	45,000	70,000	25,000 Decrease
Buildings	200,000	200,000	–0–
Accumulated depreciation—buildings	(21,000)	(11,000)	10,000 Increase
Equipment	193,000	68,000	125,000 Increase
Accumulated depreciation—equipment	(28,000)	(10,000)	18,000 Increase
Totals	$569,000	$386,000	
Liabilities and Stockholders' Equity			
Accounts payable	$ 33,000	$ 40,000	$ 7,000 Decrease
Bonds payable	110,000	150,000	40,000 Decrease
Common stock ($1 par)	220,000	60,000	160,000 Increase
Retained earnings	206,000	136,000	70,000 Increase
Totals	$569,000	$386,000	

ILLUSTRATION 23.14

Income Statement, Tax Consultants Inc., Year 3

Tax Consultants Inc.
Income Statement
For the Year Ended December 31, 2021

Revenues		$890,000
Cost of goods sold	$465,000	
Operating expenses	221,000	
Interest expense	12,000	
Loss on sale of equipment	2,000	700,000
Income from operations		190,000
Income tax expense		65,000
Net income		$125,000

Additional Information

(a) Operating expenses include depreciation expense of $33,000 and expiration of prepaid expenses of $2,000.
(b) Land was sold at its book value for cash.
(c) Cash dividends of $55,000 were declared and paid.
(d) Interest expense of $12,000 was paid in cash.
(e) Equipment with a cost of $166,000 was purchased for cash. Equipment with a cost of $41,000 and a book value of $36,000 was sold for $34,000 cash.
(f) Bonds were redeemed at their book value for cash.
(g) Common stock ($1 par) was issued for cash.

Step 1: Determine the Change in Cash The first step in the preparation of the statement of cash flows is to determine the change in cash. As the comparative balance sheets show, cash increased $17,000 in 2021.

Step 2: Determine Net Cash Flow from Operating Activities—Indirect Method We explain the adjustments to net income of $125,000 as follows.

- ***Increase in Accounts Receivable.*** The increase in accounts receivable of $42,000 represents recorded accrual-basis revenues in excess of cash collections in 2021. The company deducts this increase from net income to convert from the accrual basis to the cash basis.
- ***Increase in Inventory.*** The $54,000 increase in inventory represents an operating use of cash, not an expense. Tax Consultants therefore deducts this amount from net income

to arrive at net cash flow from operations. In other words, when inventory purchased exceeds inventory sold during a period, cost of goods sold on an accrual basis is lower than on a cash basis.

- ***Decrease in Prepaid Expenses.*** The $2,000 decrease in prepaid expenses represents a charge to the income statement for which Tax Consultants made no cash payment in the current period. The company adds back the decrease to net income, to arrive at net cash flow from operating activities.
- ***Decrease in Accounts Payable.*** When accounts payable decrease during the year, cost of goods sold and expenses on a cash basis are higher than they are on an accrual basis. To convert net income to net cash flow from operating activities, the company must deduct the $7,000 decrease in accounts payable from net income.
- ***Depreciation Expense (Increase in Accumulated Depreciation).*** Accumulated Depreciation—Buildings increased $10,000 ($21,000 – $11,000). The Buildings account did not change during the period, which means that Tax Consultants recorded depreciation expense of $10,000 in 2021.

  Accumulated Depreciation—Equipment increased by $18,000 ($28,000 – $10,000) during the year. But Accumulated Depreciation—Equipment decreased by $5,000 as a result of the sale during the year. Thus, depreciation for the year was $23,000. The company reconciled Accumulated Depreciation—Equipment as follows.

Beginning balance	$10,000
Add: Depreciation for 2021	23,000
	33,000
Deduct: Sale of equipment	5,000
Ending balance	$28,000

  The company must add back to net income the total depreciation of $33,000 ($10,000 + $23,000) charged to the income statement, to determine net cash flow from operating activities.
- ***Loss on Sale of Equipment.*** Tax Consultants Inc. sold for $34,000 equipment that cost $41,000 and had a book value of $36,000. As a result, the company reported a loss of $2,000 on its sale. To arrive at net cash flow from operating activities, it must add back to net income the loss on the sale of the equipment. The reason is that the loss is a noncash charge to the income statement. The loss did not reduce cash, but it did reduce net income.[5]

From the foregoing items, the company prepares the operating activities section of the statement of cash flows, as shown in **Illustration 23.15**.

ILLUSTRATION 23.15

Operating Activities Section of Cash Flow Statement

Cash flows from operating activities		
Net income		$125,000
Adjustments to reconcile net income to net cash provided by operating activities:		
Depreciation expense	$ 33,000	
Loss on sale of equipment	2,000	
Increase in accounts receivable	(42,000)	
Increase in inventory	(54,000)	
Decrease in prepaid expenses	2,000	
Decrease in accounts payable	(7,000)	(66,000)
Net cash provided by operating activities		59,000

[5]A similar adjustment is required for unrealized gains or losses recorded on trading debt investments, equity investments, or other financial assets and liabilities accounted for under the fair value option. Marking these assets and liabilities to fair value results in an increase or decrease in income, but there is no effect on cash flows.

Step 3: Determine Net Cash Flows from Investing and Financing Activities By analyzing the remaining changes in the balance sheet accounts, Tax Consultants identifies cash flows from investing and financing activities.

- ***Land.*** Land decreased $25,000 during the period. As indicated from the information presented, the company sold land for cash at its book value. This transaction is an investing activity, reported as a $25,000 source of cash.
- ***Equipment.*** An analysis of the Equipment account indicates the following.

Beginning balance	$ 68,000
Purchase of equipment	166,000
	234,000
Deduct: Sale of equipment	41,000
Ending balance	$193,000

The company used cash to purchase equipment with a fair value of $166,000—an investing transaction reported as a cash outflow. The sale of the equipment for $34,000 is also an investing activity, but one that generates a cash inflow.

- ***Bonds Payable.*** Bonds payable decreased $40,000 during the year. As indicated from the additional information, the company redeemed the bonds at their book value. This financing transaction used $40,000 of cash.
- ***Common Stock.*** The Common Stock account increased $160,000 during the year. As indicated from the additional information, Tax Consultants issued common stock of $160,000 at par. This financing transaction provided cash of $160,000.
- ***Retained Earnings.*** Retained earnings changed $70,000 ($206,000 – $136,000) during the year. The $70,000 change in retained earnings results from net income of $125,000 from operations and the financing activity of paying cash dividends of $55,000.

Statement of Cash Flows—2021 Tax Consultants Inc. combines the foregoing items to prepare the statement of cash flows shown in **Illustration 23.16**.

ILLUSTRATION 23.16

Statement of Cash Flows, Tax Consultants Inc., Year 3

Tax Consultants Inc.
Statement of Cash Flows
For the Year Ended December 31, 2021

Cash flows from operating activities		
Net income		$ 125,000
Adjustments to reconcile net income to net cash provided by operating activities:		
Depreciation expense	$ 33,000	
Loss on sale of equipment	2,000	
Increase in accounts receivable	(42,000)	
Increase in inventory	(54,000)	
Decrease in prepaid expenses	2,000	
Decrease in accounts payable	(7,000)	(66,000)
Net cash provided by operating activities		59,000
Cash flows from investing activities		
Sale of land	25,000	
Sale of equipment	34,000	
Purchase of equipment	(166,000)	
Net cash used by investing activities		(107,000)
Cash flows from financing activities		
Redemption of bonds	(40,000)	
Sale of common stock	160,000	
Payment of dividends	(55,000)	
Net cash provided by financing activities		65,000
Net increase in cash		17,000
Cash, January 1, 2021		37,000
Cash, December 31, 2021		$ 54,000

Sources of Information for the Statement of Cash Flows

Important points to remember in the preparation of the statement of cash flows are these:

1. Comparative balance sheets provide the basic information from which to prepare the report. Additional information obtained from analyses of specific accounts is also included.
2. An analysis of the Retained Earnings account is necessary. The net increase or decrease in Retained Earnings without any explanation is a meaningless amount in the statement. Without explanation, it might represent the effect of net income, dividends declared, or prior period adjustments.
3. The statement includes all changes that have passed through cash or have resulted in an increase or decrease in cash.
4. Write-downs, amortization charges, and similar "book" entries, such as depreciation of plant assets, represent neither inflows nor outflows of cash because they have no effect on cash. To the extent that they have entered into the determination of net income, however, the company must add them back to or subtract them from net income, to arrive at net cash provided (used) by operating activities.

Indirect Method—Additional Adjustments

For consistency and comparability and because it is the most widely used method in practice, we used the indirect method in the Tax Consultants' illustrations. We determined net cash flow from operating activities by adding back to or deducting from net income those items that had no effect on cash. Illustration 23.17 presents a more complete set of common adjustments that companies make to net income to arrive at net cash flow from operating activities.

ILLUSTRATION 23.17

Adjustments Needed to Determine Net Cash Flow from Operating Activities—Indirect Method

Net Income

Additions	Deductions
Depreciation expense	Amortization of premium on bonds payable
Amortization of intangibles and deferred charges	Decrease in deferred income tax liability
Amortization of discount on bonds payable	Income on investment in common stock using equity method
Increase in deferred income tax liability	Gain on sale of plant assets
Loss on investment in common stock using equity method	Increase in receivables
Loss on sale of plant assets	Increase in inventory
Loss on impairment of assets	Increase in prepaid expenses
Decrease in receivables	Decrease in accounts payable
Decrease in inventory	Decrease in accrued liabilities
Decrease in prepaid expenses	
Increase in accounts payable	
Increase in accrued liabilities	

=

Net Cash Flow from Operating Activities

The additions and deductions in Illustration 23.17 reconcile net income to net cash flow from operating activities, illustrating why the indirect method is also called the reconciliation method.

Net Cash Flow from Operating Activities—Direct Method

LEARNING OBJECTIVE 3

Contrast the direct and indirect methods of calculating net cash flow from operating activities.

Two different methods are available to adjust income from operations on an accrual basis to net cash flow from operating activities. We showed the indirect method in the Tax Consultants' illustrations in the prior sections.

The **direct method** reports cash receipts and cash disbursements from operating activities. The difference between these two amounts is the net cash flow from operating activities. In other words, the direct method deducts operating cash disbursements from operating cash receipts. The direct method results in the presentation of a condensed cash receipts and cash disbursements statement.

As indicated from the accrual-based income statement (see Illustration 23.4), Tax Consultants reported revenues of $125,000. However, because the company's accounts receivable increased during 2019 by $36,000, the company collected only $89,000 ($125,000 – $36,000) in cash from these revenues. Similarly, Tax Consultants reported operating expenses of $85,000. However, accounts payable increased during the period by $5,000. Assuming that these payables relate to operating expenses, cash operating expenses were $80,000 ($85,000 – $5,000). Because no taxes payable exist at the end of the year, the company must have paid $6,000 income tax expense for 2019 in cash during the year. Tax Consultants computes net cash flow from operating activities as shown in **Illustration 23.18**.

ILLUSTRATION 23.18

Computation of Net Cash Flow from Operating Activities, Year 1—Direct Method

Cash collected from revenues	$89,000
Cash payments for expenses	80,000
Income before income taxes	9,000
Cash payments for income taxes	6,000
Net cash provided by operating activities	$ 3,000

"Net cash provided by operating activities" is the equivalent of cash basis net income. ("Net cash used by operating activities" is equivalent to cash basis net loss.)

The FASB encourages use of the direct method and permits use of the indirect method. Yet, if the direct method is used, the Board requires that companies provide in a separate schedule a reconciliation of net income to net cash flow from operating activities. Therefore, under either method, companies must prepare and report information from the indirect (reconciliation) method.

Direct Method—Expanded Example

Under the direct method, the statement of cash flows reports net cash flow from operating activities as major classes of *operating cash receipts* (e.g., cash collected from customers and cash received from interest and dividends) and *cash disbursements* (e.g., cash paid to suppliers for goods, to employees for services, to creditors for interest, and to government authorities for taxes).

We illustrate the direct method here in more detail to help you understand the difference between accrual-based income and net cash flow from operating activities. This example also illustrates the data needed to apply the direct method. Emig Company, which began business on January 1, 2020, has the selected balance sheet information shown in **Illustration 23.19**.

ILLUSTRATION 23.19

Balance Sheet Accounts, Emig Co.

	December 31, 2020	January 1, 2020
Cash	$159,000	-0-
Accounts receivable	15,000	-0-
Inventory	160,000	-0-
Prepaid expenses	8,000	-0-
Property, plant, and equipment (net)	90,000	-0-
Accounts payable	60,000	-0-
Accrued expenses payable	20,000	-0-

Emig Company's December 31, 2020, income statement and additional information are presented in **Illustration 23.20**.

ILLUSTRATION 23.20

Income Statement, Emig Co.

Sales revenue		$780,000
Cost of goods sold		450,000
Gross profit		330,000
Operating expenses	$160,000	
Depreciation	10,000	170,000
Income before income taxes		160,000
Income tax expense		48,000
Net income		$112,000

Additional Information

(a) Dividends of $70,000 were declared and paid in cash.
(b) The accounts payable increase resulted from the purchase of merchandise inventory.
(c) Prepaid expenses and accrued expenses payable relate to operating expenses.

Under the **direct method**, companies compute net cash provided by operating activities by **adjusting each item in the income statement** from the accrual basis to the cash basis. To simplify and condense the operating activities section, only major classes of operating cash receipts and cash payments are reported. As **Illustration 23.21** shows, the difference between these major classes of cash receipts and cash payments is the net cash provided by operating activities.

ILLUSTRATION 23.21 **Major Classes of Cash Receipts and Payments**

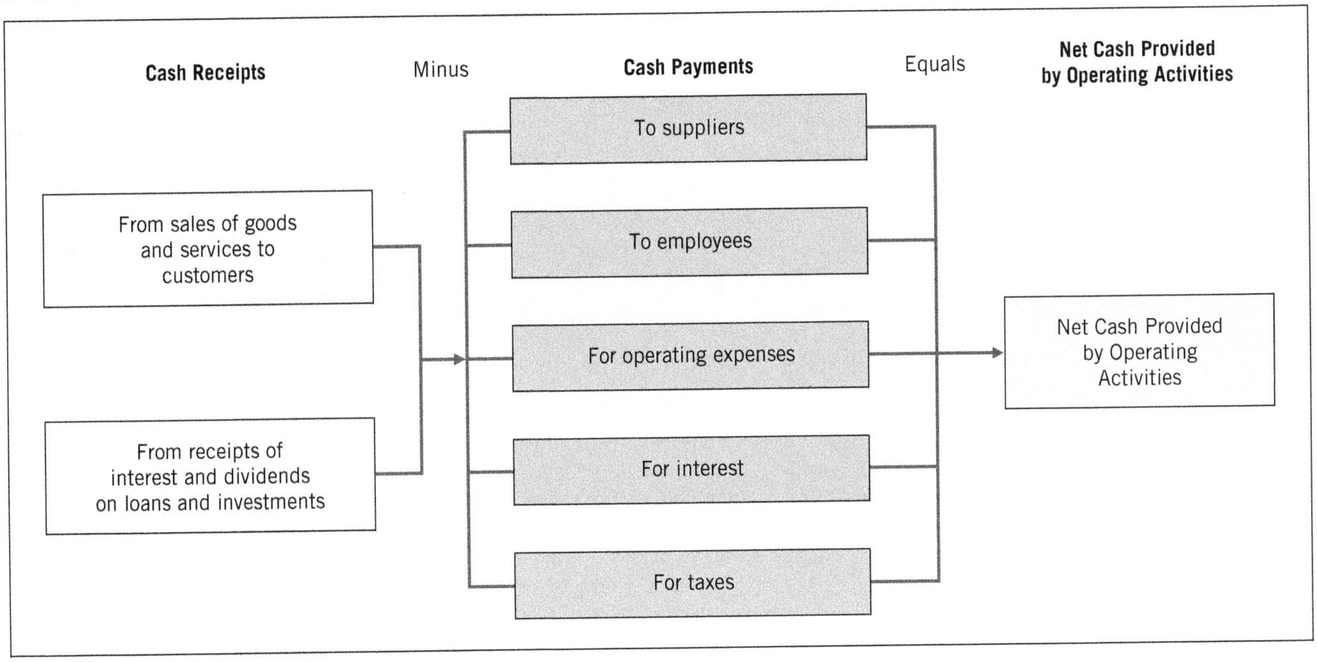

An efficient way to apply the direct method is to analyze the revenues and expenses reported in the income statement in the order in which they are listed. The company then determines cash receipts and cash payments related to these revenues and expenses. In the following sections, we present the direct method adjustments for Emig Company in 2020, to determine net cash provided by operating activities.

Cash Receipts from Customers The income statement for Emig Company reported revenues from customers of $780,000. To determine cash receipts from customers, the company considers the change in accounts receivable during the year.

When accounts receivable increase during the year, revenues on an accrual basis are higher than cash receipts from customers. In other words, operations led to increased revenues, but not all of these revenues resulted in cash receipts. To determine the amount of increase in cash receipts, deduct the amount of the increase in accounts receivable from the total sales revenue. Conversely, a decrease in accounts receivable is added to sales revenue because cash receipts from customers then exceed sales revenue.

For Emig Company, accounts receivable increased $15,000. Thus, cash receipts from customers were $765,000, computed as follows.

Sales revenue	$780,000
Deduct: Increase in accounts receivable	15,000
Cash receipts from customers	$765,000

Emig could also determine cash receipts from customers by analyzing the Accounts Receivable account as shown below.

Accounts Receivable

1/1/20	Balance	–0–	Receipts from customers	765,000
	Sales revenue	780,000		
12/31/20	Balance	15,000		

Illustration 23.22 shows the relationships between cash receipts from customers, sales revenue, and changes in accounts receivable.

ILLUSTRATION 23.22

Formula to Compute Cash Receipts from Customers

Cash Receipts from Customers	=	**Sales Revenue**	**+ Decrease in Accounts Receivable** or **– Increase in Accounts Receivable**

Cash Payments to Suppliers Emig Company reported cost of goods sold on its income statement of $450,000. To determine cash payments to suppliers, the company first finds purchases for the year, by adjusting cost of goods sold for the change in inventory. When inventory increases during the year, purchases this year exceed cost of goods sold. As a result, the company adds the increase in inventory to cost of goods sold, to arrive at purchases.

In 2020, Emig Company's inventory increased $160,000. The company computes purchases as follows.

Cost of goods sold	$450,000
Add: Increase in inventory	160,000
Purchases	$610,000

After computing purchases, Emig determines cash payments to suppliers by adjusting purchases for the change in accounts payable. When accounts payable increase during the year, purchases on an accrual basis are higher than they are on a cash basis. As a result, the company deducts from purchases the increase in accounts payable to arrive at cash payments to suppliers. Conversely, if cash payments to suppliers exceed purchases, Emig adds to purchases the decrease in accounts payable. Cash payments to suppliers were $550,000, computed as follows.

Purchases	$610,000
Deduct: Increase in accounts payable	60,000
Cash payments to suppliers	$550,000

Emig also can determine cash payments to suppliers by analyzing Accounts Payable, as shown below.

Accounts Payable

Payments to suppliers	550,000	1/1/20	Balance	–0–
			Purchases	610,000
		12/31/20	Balance	60,000

Illustration 23.23 shows the relationships between cash payments to suppliers, cost of goods sold, changes in inventory, and changes in accounts payable.

Cash Payments to Suppliers	=	Cost of Goods Sold	{ + Increase in Inventory or − Decrease in Inventory }	{ + Decrease in Accounts Payable or − Increase in Accounts Payable }

ILLUSTRATION 23.23

Formula to Compute Cash Payments to Suppliers

Cash Payments for Operating Expenses Emig reported operating expenses of $160,000 on its income statement. To determine the cash paid for operating expenses, it must adjust this amount for any changes in prepaid expenses and accrued expenses payable.

For example, when prepaid expenses increased $8,000 during the year, cash paid for operating expenses was $8,000 higher than operating expenses reported on the income statement. To convert operating expenses to cash payments for operating expenses, the company adds to operating expenses the increase of $8,000. Conversely, if prepaid expenses decrease during the year, it deducts from operating expenses the amount of the decrease.

Emig also must adjust operating expenses for changes in accrued expenses payable. When accrued expenses payable increase during the year, operating expenses on an accrual basis are higher than they are on a cash basis. As a result, the company deducts from operating expenses an increase in accrued expenses payable, to arrive at cash payments for operating expenses. Conversely, it adds to operating expenses a decrease in accrued expenses payable, because cash payments exceed operating expenses.

Emig's cash payments for operating expenses were $148,000, computed as follows.

Operating expenses	$160,000
Add: Increase in prepaid expenses	8,000
Deduct: Increase in accrued expenses payable	20,000
Cash payments for operating expenses	$148,000

The relationships among cash payments for operating expenses, changes in prepaid expenses, and changes in accrued expenses payable are shown in Illustration 23.24.

Cash Payments for Operating Expenses	=	Operating Expenses	{ + Increase in Prepaid Expense or − Decrease in Prepaid Expense }	{ + Decrease in Accrued Expenses Payable or − Increase in Accrued Expenses Payable }

ILLUSTRATION 23.24

Formula to Compute Cash Payments for Operating Expenses

Note that the company did not consider depreciation expense because it is a noncash charge.

Cash Payments for Income Taxes The income statement for Emig shows income tax expense of $48,000. This amount equals the cash paid. How do we know that? Because the comparative balance sheet indicated no income taxes payable (or deferred tax assets or liabilities) at either the beginning or end of the year.

Summary of Net Cash Flow from Operating Activities—Direct Method

The schedule presented in Illustration 23.25 summarizes the computations shown above.

ILLUSTRATION 23.25

Accrual Basis to Cash Basis

Accrual Basis			Adjustment	Add (Subtract)	Cash Basis
Sales revenue	$780,000	−	Increase in accounts receivable	$ (15,000)	$765,000
Cost of goods sold	450,000	+	Increase in inventory	160,000	
		−	Increase in accounts payable	(60,000)	550,000
Operating expenses	160,000	+	Increase in prepaid expenses	8,000	
		−	Increase in accrued expenses payable	(20,000)	148,000
Depreciation expense	10,000	−	Depreciation expense	(10,000)	-0-
Income tax expense	48,000				48,000
Total expense	668,000				746,000
Net income	$112,000		Net cash provided by operating activities		$ 19,000

Illustration 23.26 shows the presentation of the direct method for reporting net cash flow from operating activities for the Emig Company illustration.

ILLUSTRATION 23.26

Operating Activities Section—Direct Method, 2020

Emig Company
Statement of Cash Flows (partial)

Cash flows from operating activities		
Cash received from customers		$765,000
Cash payments:		
To suppliers	$550,000	
For operating expenses	148,000	
For income taxes	48,000	746,000
Net cash provided by operating activities		$ 19,000

If Emig Company uses the direct method to present the net cash flow from operating activities, it must provide in a separate schedule the reconciliation of net income to net cash provided by operating activities. The reconciliation assumes the identical form and content of the indirect method of presentation, as shown in Illustration 23.27.

ILLUSTRATION 23.27

Reconciliation of Net Income to Net Cash Provided by Operating Activities

Emig Company
Reconciliation

Net income		$112,000
Adjustments to reconcile net income to net cash provided by operating activities:		
Depreciation expense	$ 10,000	
Increase in accounts receivable	(15,000)	
Increase in inventory	(160,000)	
Increase in prepaid expenses	(8,000)	
Increase in accounts payable	60,000	
Increase in accrued expense payable	20,000	(93,000)
Net cash provided by operating activities		$ 19,000

When the direct method is used, the company may present this reconciliation at the bottom of the statement of cash flows or in a separate schedule.

Evolving Issue Direct versus Indirect

The most contentious decision that the FASB faced related to cash flow reporting was choosing between the direct method and the indirect method of determining net cash flow from operating activities. Companies lobbied *against* the direct method, urging adoption of the indirect method. However, commercial lending officers expressed to the FASB a strong preference in favor of the direct method. What are the arguments in favor of each of the methods?

In Favor of the Direct Method

The principal advantage of the direct method is that **it shows operating cash receipts and payments.** Thus, it is more consistent with the objective of a statement of cash flows—to provide information about cash receipts and cash payments—than the indirect method, which does not report operating cash receipts and payments.

Supporters of the direct method contend that knowledge of the specific sources of operating cash receipts and the purposes for which operating cash payments were made in past periods is useful in estimating future operating cash flows. Furthermore, information about amounts of major classes of operating cash receipts and payments is more useful than information only about their arithmetic sum (the net cash flow from operating activities). Such information is more revealing of a company's ability (1) to generate sufficient cash from operating activities to pay its debts, (2) to reinvest in its operations, and (3) to make distributions to its owners. [3]

Indeed, a comprehensive review of academic research related to direct method cash flow presentation indicates that financial statement users prefer the direct method and that the direct method generally provides decision-useful information. That is, the direct method information is reflected in stock prices indicating that users appear to utilize this information when available.

Many companies indicate that they do not currently collect information in a manner that allows them to determine amounts such as cash received from customers or cash paid to suppliers directly from their accounting systems. But supporters of the direct method contend that the incremental cost of determining operating cash receipts and payments is not significant.

In Favor of the Indirect Method

The principal advantage of the indirect method is that **it focuses on the differences between net income and net cash flow from operating activities**. That is, it provides a useful link between the statement of cash flows and the income statement and balance sheet.

Many companies contend that it is less costly to adjust net income to net cash flow from operating activities (indirect) than it is to report gross operating cash receipts and payments (direct). Supporters of the indirect method also state that the direct method, which effectively reports income statement information on a cash rather than an accrual basis, may erroneously suggest that net cash flow from operating activities is as good as, or better than, net income as a measure of performance.

In their joint financial statement presentation project, the FASB and the IASB proposed to allow only the direct method. However, there has been significant pushback on this proposal, which suggests that the choice of either the direct or indirect method will continue to be available.

Source: J. Hales and S. Orpurt, "A Review of Academic Research on the Reporting of Cash Flows from Operations," *Accounting Horizons* (September 2013), pp. 539–578. See also the FASB website: click on Projects and then Search on Inactive Joint FASB/IASB Projects. See also T. Whitehouse, "FASB Proposal May Foreshadow Changes to Cash Flow Rules," *www.complianceweek.com* (April 24, 2015).

Special Reporting Rules Applying to Direct and Indirect Methods

Companies that use the direct method are required, at a minimum, to report separately the following classes of operating cash receipts and payments (see Global View):

Receipts

1. Cash collected from customers (including lessees, licensees, etc.).
2. Interest and dividends received.
3. Other operating cash receipts, if any.

Payments

1. Cash paid to employees and suppliers of goods or services (including suppliers of insurance, advertising, etc.).
2. Interest paid.
3. Income taxes paid.
4. Other operating cash payments, if any.

The FASB encourages companies to provide further breakdowns of operating cash receipts and payments that they consider meaningful.

Companies using the indirect method must disclose separately changes in inventory, receivables, and payables in order to reconcile net income to net cash flow from operating activities. In addition, they must disclose, elsewhere in the financial statements or in accompanying notes, interest paid (net of amount capitalized) and income taxes paid.[6] The FASB requires these separate and additional disclosures so that users may approximate the direct method. Also, an acceptable alternative presentation of the indirect method is to report net cash flow from operating activities as a single line item in the statement of cash flows and to present the reconciliation details elsewhere in the financial statements.

Global View

Consolidated statements of cash flows may be of limited use to analysts evaluating multinational companies. Without disaggregation, users of such statements are not able to determine "where in the world" the funds are sourced and used.

[6]*Accounting Trends and Techniques* indicates that of the 500 companies surveyed, 207 disclosed interest paid in notes to the financial statements, 257 disclosed interest paid at the bottom of the statement of cash flows, 7 disclosed interest paid within the statement of cash flows, and 29 reported no separate amount. Income taxes paid during the year were disclosed in a manner similar to interest payments.

Finally, the FASB **encourages** the use of the direct method over the indirect method. If a company uses the direct method of reporting net cash flow from operating activities, the FASB **requires** that the company provide in a separate schedule a reconciliation of net income to net cash flow from operating activities. If a company uses the indirect method, it can either report the reconciliation within the statement of cash flows or can provide it in a separate schedule, with the statement of cash flows reporting only the **net** cash flow from operating activities. [4]

Special Problems in Statement Preparation

LEARNING OBJECTIVE 4

Discuss special problems in preparing a statement of cash flows.

We discussed some of the special problems related to preparing the statement of cash flows in connection with the preceding illustrations. Other problems that arise with some frequency in the preparation of this statement include the following.

1. Adjustments to net income.
2. Accounts receivable (net).
3. Other working capital changes.
4. Net losses.
5. Significant noncash transactions.

Adjustments to Net Income

Depreciation and Amortization

Depreciation expense is the most common adjustment to net income that companies make to arrive at net cash flow from operating activities. But there are numerous other noncash expense or revenue items. Examples of expense items that companies must add back to net income are the **amortization of limited-life intangible assets** such as patents, and the **amortization of deferred costs** such as bond issue costs. These charges to expense involve expenditures made in prior periods that a company amortizes currently. These charges reduce net income without affecting cash in the current period.

Also, **amortization of bond discount or premium** on long-term bonds payable affects the amount of interest expense. However, neither affects cash. As a result, a company should add back discount amortization and subtract premium amortization from net income to arrive at net cash flow from operating activities.

Postretirement Benefit Costs

If a company has postretirement costs such as an employee pension plan, chances are that the pension expense recorded during a period will either be higher or lower than the cash funded. It will be higher when there is an increase in the unfunded liability and will be lower when there is a decrease. When the expense is higher or lower than the cash paid, **the company must adjust net income by the difference between cash paid and the expense reported** in computing net cash flow from operating activities.

Changes in Deferred Income Taxes

Changes in deferred income taxes affect net income but have no effect on cash. For example, **Delta Air Lines** reported an increase in its liability for deferred taxes of approximately $1.2 billion. This change in the liability increased tax expense and decreased net income, but did not affect cash. Therefore, Delta added back $1.2 billion to net income on its statement of cash flows.

Equity Method of Accounting

Another common adjustment to net income is **a change related to an investment in common stock** when recording income or loss under the equity method. Recall that under the equity method, the investor (1) debits the investment account and credits revenue for its share of the investee's net income, and (2) credits dividends received to the investment account. Therefore, the net increase in the investment account does not affect cash flow. A company must deduct the net increase from net income to arrive at net cash flow from operating activities.

Assume that Victor Co. owns 40 percent of Milo Inc. During the year, Milo reports net income of $100,000 and pays a cash dividend of $30,000. Victor reports this in its statement of cash flows as a deduction from net income in the following manner—Equity in earnings of Milo, net of dividends, $28,000 [($100,000 − $30,000) × .40].

Losses and Gains

Realized Losses and Gains In the illustration for Tax Consultants, the company experienced a loss of $2,000 from the sale of equipment. The company added this loss to net income to compute net cash flow from operating activities because **the loss is a noncash charge in the income statement.**

If Tax Consultants experiences a **gain** from a sale of equipment, it too requires an adjustment to net income. Because a company reports the gain in the statement of cash flows as part of the cash proceeds from the sale of equipment under investing activities, **it deducts the gain from net income to avoid double-counting**—once as part of net income and again as part of the cash proceeds from the sale.

To illustrate, assume that Lynch Co. had land with a carrying value of $100,000 that it sold for $110,000, resulting in a gain of $10,000. In the statement of cash flows (indirect method), the company would deduct the $10,000 gain from net income in the operating activities section. It would report the $110,000 cash inflow from the sale as an investing activity, as follows.

Cash flows from investing activities	
Sale of land	$110,000

Unrealized Losses and Gains Unrealized losses and gains often result for investments in debt and equity securities. For example, assume that **Target** purchases the following three investments on January 10, 2020:

1. Debt investment for $1 million that is classified as trading. During 2020, the debt investment has an unrealized holding gain of $110,000 (recorded in net income).
2. Debt investment for $600,000 that is classified as available-for-sale. During 2020, the available-for-sale debt investment has an unrealized holding loss of $50,000 (recorded in other comprehensive income).
3. Equity investment for $200,000 in the stock of Groesch Company (the number of shares purchased represents less than 20 percent of Groesch common stock). During 2020, the Groesch investment has an unrealized holding gain of $15,000 (recorded in net income).

For Target, the unrealized holding gain of $110,000 on the debt investment increases net income but does not increase net cash flow from operating activities. As a result, the unrealized holding gain of $110,000 is deducted from net income to compute net cash flow from operating activities.

On the other hand, the unrealized holding loss of $50,000 that Target incurs on the available-for-sale debt investment does not affect net income or cash flows—this loss is reported in the other comprehensive income section. As a result, no adjustment to net income is necessary in computing net cash flow from operating activities.

Finally, the unrealized holding gain of $15,000 on the equity investment increases net income but does not increase net cash flow from operating activities. As a result, the unrealized holding gain of $15,000 is deducted from net income to compute net cash flow from operating activities.

Thus, the general rule is that unrealized holding gains or losses that affect net income must be adjusted to determine net cash flow from operating activities. Conversely, unrealized holding gains or losses that do not affect net income are not adjusted to determine net cash flow from operating activities.

Stock Options

Recall for share-based compensation plans that companies are required to use the fair value method to determine total compensation cost. The compensation cost is then recognized as an expense in the periods in which the employee provides services. When Compensation Expense is debited, Paid-in Capital—Stock Options is often credited. Cash is not affected by recording the expense. **Therefore, the company must increase net income by the amount of compensation expense from stock options in computing net cash flow from operating activities.**

To illustrate how this information should be reported on a statement of cash flows, assume that First Wave Inc. grants 5,000 options to its CEO, Ann Johnson. Each option entitles Johnson to purchase one share of First Wave's $1 par value common stock at $50 per share at any time in the next two years (the service period). The fair value of the options is $200,000. First Wave records compensation expense in the first year as follows.

Compensation Expense ($200,000 ÷ 2)	100,000	
Paid-in Capital—Stock Options		100,000

In addition, if we assume that First Wave has a 20 percent tax rate, it would recognize a deferred tax asset of $20,000 ($100,000 × .20) in the first year as follows.

Deferred Tax Asset	20,000	
Income Tax Expense		20,000

Therefore, on the statement of cash flows for the first year, First Wave reports the following (assuming a net income of $600,000).

Net income	$600,000
Adjustments to reconcile net income to net cash provided by operating activities:	
Share-based compensation expense	100,000
Increase in deferred tax asset	(20,000)

As shown in First Wave's statement of cash flows, it adds the share-based compensation expense to net income because it is a noncash expense. The increase in the deferred tax asset and the related reduction in income tax expense increase net income. Although the negative income tax expense increases net income, it does not increase cash. Therefore, it should be deducted.

Subsequently, if Ann Johnson exercises her options, First Wave reports "Cash provided by exercise of stock options" in the financing section of the statement of cash flows.[7]

[7]Companies receive a tax deduction related to share-based compensation plans at the time employees exercise their options. The amount of the deduction is equal to the difference between the market price of the stock and the exercise price at the date the employee purchases the stock, which in most cases is much larger than the total compensation expense recorded. When the tax deduction exceeds the total compensation recorded, this provides an additional cash inflow to the company. For example, in a recent year **Cisco Systems** reported an additional cash inflow related to its stock-option plans equal to $537 million. Under current GAAP, this tax-related cash inflow is reported in the operating section of the statement of cash flows. [5]

Unusual and Infrequent Items

Companies should report **either as investing activities or as financing activities** cash flows from unusual and infrequent transactions and other events whose effects are included in net income but which are not related to operations.

For example, assume that Tax Consultants had land with a carrying value of $200,000, which was condemned by the state of Maine for a highway project. The condemnation proceeds received were $205,000, resulting in a gain of $5,000 less $2,000 of taxes. In the statement of cash flows (indirect method), the company would deduct the $5,000 gain from net income in the operating activities section. It would report the $205,000 cash inflow from the condemnation as an investing activity, as follows.

Cash flows from investing activities	
Condemnation of land	$205,000

Note that Tax Consultants handles the gain at its **gross** amount ($5,000), not net of tax. The company reports the cash received in the condemnation as an investing activity at $205,000, also exclusive of the tax effect.

The FASB requires companies to classify **all income taxes paid as operating cash outflows**. Some suggested that income taxes paid be allocated to investing and financing transactions. But the Board decided that allocation of income taxes paid to operating, investing, and financing activities would be so complex and arbitrary that the benefits, if any, would not justify the costs involved (see **Underlying Concepts**). Under both the direct method and the indirect method, companies must disclose the total amount of income taxes paid.[8]

Underlying Concepts

By rejecting the requirement to allocate taxes to the various activities, the FASB invoked the cost constraint. The information would be beneficial, but the cost of providing such information would exceed the benefits of providing it.

Accounts Receivable (Net)

Up to this point, we assumed no allowance for doubtful accounts—a contra account—to offset accounts receivable. However, if a company needs an allowance for doubtful accounts, how does that allowance affect the company's determination of net cash flow from operating activities? For example, assume that Redmark Co. reports net income of $40,000. It has the accounts receivable balances as shown in **Illustration 23.28**.

ILLUSTRATION 23.28

Accounts Receivable Balances, Redmark Co.

	2020	2019	Change Increase/Decrease
Accounts receivable	$105,000	$90,000	$15,000 Increase
Allowance for doubtful accounts	(10,000)	(4,000)	6,000 Increase
Accounts receivable (net)	$ 95,000	$86,000	9,000 Increase

Indirect Method

Because an increase in Allowance for Doubtful Accounts results from a charge to bad debt expense, a company should add back an increase in Allowance for Doubtful Accounts to net income to arrive at net cash flow from operating activities. **Illustration 23.29** shows one method for presenting this information in a statement of cash flows.

[8]For an insightful article on some weaknesses and limitations in the statement of cash flows, see Hugo Nurnberg, "Inconsistencies and Ambiguities in Cash Flow Statements Under *FASB Statement No. 95*," *Accounting Horizons* (June 1993), pp. 60–73. Nurnberg identifies the inconsistencies caused by the three-way classification of all cash receipts and cash payments, gross versus net of tax, the ambiguous disclosure requirements for noncash investing and financing transactions, and the ambiguous presentation of third-party financing transactions. See also Paul B. W. Miller and Bruce P. Budge, "Nonarticulation in Cash Flow Statements and Implications for Education, Research, and Practice," *Accounting Horizons* (December 1996), pp. 1–15; and Charles Mulford and Michael Ely, "Calculating Sustainable Cash Flow: A Study of the S&P 100," *Georgia Tech Financial Analysis Lab* (October 2004).

ILLUSTRATION 23.29

Presentation of Allowance for Doubtful Accounts—Indirect Method

Redmark Co.
Statement of Cash Flows (partial)
For the Year 2020

Cash flows from operating activities		
Net income		$40,000
Adjustments to reconcile net income to net cash provided by operating activities:		
Increase in accounts receivable	$(15,000)	
Increase in allowance for doubtful accounts	6,000	(9,000)
		$31,000

As we indicated, the increase in the Allowance for Doubtful Accounts balance results from a charge to bad debt expense for the year. Because bad debt expense is a noncash charge, a company must add it back to net income in arriving at net cash flow from operating activities.

Instead of separately analyzing the allowance account, a shortcut approach is to net the allowance balance against the receivable balance and compare the change in accounts receivable on a net basis. Illustration 23.30 shows this presentation.

ILLUSTRATION 23.30

Net Approach to Allowance for Doubtful Accounts—Indirect Method

Redmark Co.
Statement of Cash Flows (partial)
For the Year 2020

Cash flows from operating activities	
Net income	$40,000
Adjustments to reconcile net income to net cash provided by operating activities:	
Increase in accounts receivable (net)	(9,000)
	$31,000

This shortcut procedure works also if the change in the allowance account results from a write-off of accounts receivable. This reduces both Accounts Receivable and Allowance for Doubtful Accounts. No effect on cash flows occurs. *Because of its simplicity, use the net approach for your homework assignments.*

Direct Method

If using the direct method, a company **should not net** Allowance for Doubtful Accounts against Accounts Receivable. To illustrate, assume that Redmark Co.'s net income of $40,000 consisted of the items shown in Illustration 23.31.

ILLUSTRATION 23.31

Income Statement, Redmark Co.

Redmark Co.
Income Statement
For the Year 2020

Sales revenue		$100,000
Expenses		
Salaries	$46,000	
Utilities	8,000	
Bad debts	6,000	60,000
Net income		$ 40,000

If Redmark deducts the $9,000 increase in accounts receivable (net) from sales for the year, it would report cash sales at $91,000 ($100,000 – $9,000) and cash payments for operating expenses at $60,000. Both items would be misstated: Cash sales should be reported at $85,000 ($100,000 – $15,000), and total cash payments for operating expenses should be reported at $54,000 ($60,000 – $6,000). Illustration 23.32 shows the proper presentation.

ILLUSTRATION 23.32
Bad Debts—Direct Method

Redmark Co.
Statement of Cash Flows (partial)
For the Year 2020

Cash flows from operating activities		
Cash received from customers		$85,000
Salaries paid	$46,000	
Utilities paid	8,000	54,000
Net cash provided by operating activities		$31,000

An added complication develops when a company writes off accounts receivable. Simply adjusting sales for the change in accounts receivable will not provide the proper amount of cash sales. The reason is that the write-off of the accounts receivable is not a cash collection. Thus, an additional adjustment is necessary.

What Do the Numbers Mean? Not What It Seems

The controversy over direct and indirect methods highlights the importance that the market attributes to operating cash flow. By showing an improving cash flow, a company can give a favorable impression of its ongoing operations. For example, **WorldCom** concealed declines in its operations by capitalizing certain operating expenses—to the tune of $3.8 billion! This practice not only "juiced up" income but also made it possible to report the cash payments in the investing section of the cash flow statement rather than as a deduction from operating cash flow.

The SEC recently addressed a similar cash flow classification issue with automakers like **Ford**, **GM**, and **Chrysler**. For years, automakers classified lease receivables and other dealer-financing arrangements as investment cash flows. Thus, they reported an increase in lease or loan receivables from cars sold as a use of cash in the investing section of the statement of cash flows. The SEC objected and now requires automakers to report these receivables as operating cash flows, since the leases and loans are used to facilitate car sales. At GM, these reclassifications reduced its operating cash flows from $7.6 billion to $3 billion in the year before the change.

In the banking industry, how banks classify their investments, deposits, and cash flow from acquisitions results in huge swings in operating cash flows, both downward (**Bank of America**) and upward (**KeyCorp**). According to one analyst, "As it stands now, banks can't be reliably compared to each other by their recorded cash flow from operations . . . operating cash flow for a bank is basically meaningless." Another questionable cash flow classification for banks is the characterization of increases and decreases in deposits as a financing cash flow. Many analysts believe customer-driven deposits should be accounted for under operating cash flow (rather than as a financing cash flow) since "the very health of a bank's operations depends on its deposit base and its ability to attract a growing stream of deposits." So while the overall cash flow—from operations, investing, and financing—remained the same, operating cash flow at these companies looked better than it really was.

In response to cash flow classification debates, the FASB, working with the Emerging Issues Task Force, issued guidance to address diversity in practice related to cash flow reporting. [6] The eight topics addressed ranged from the reporting of beneficial interests of securitization transactions (discussed in the earlier What Do the Numbers Mean? box entitled "Earnings and Cash Flow Management?") to cash flows from debt prepayments. These issues are generally beyond the topics addressed in this course.

Sources: Peter Elstrom, "How to Hide $3.8 Billion in Expenses," *BusinessWeek Online* (July 8, 2002); Judith Burns, "SEC Tells US Automakers to Retool Cash-Flow Accounting," *Wall Street Journal Online* (February 28, 2005); Sarah Johnson, "Cash Flow: A Better Way to Know Your Bank?" *CFO.com* (July 9, 2009); D. Katz, "FASB Revisits the Cash Flow Statement," *CFO.com* (September 30, 2014); and J. Ciesielski, "Statement of Cash Flows Fixes," *The Analyst's Accounting Observer* (November 21, 2016).

Other Working Capital Changes

Up to this point, we showed how companies handled all of the changes in working capital items (current asset and current liability items) as adjustments to net income in determining net cash flow from operating activities. You must be careful, however, because **some changes**

in working capital, although they affect cash, do not affect net income. Generally, these are investing or financing activities of a current nature.

One activity is the purchase of **short-term available-for-sale debt securities.** For example, the purchase of short-term available-for-sale debt securities for $50,000 cash has no effect on net income but it does cause a $50,000 decrease in cash. A company reports this transaction as a cash flow from investing activities as follows. [7]

Cash flows from investing activities	
Purchase of short-term available-for-sale debt securities	$(50,000)

What about **trading securities?** Because companies hold these investments principally for the purpose of selling them in the near term, companies should classify the cash flows from purchases and sales of trading securities as cash flows from **operating activities.** [8][9]

Another example is the issuance of a **short-term nontrade note payable** for cash. This change in a working capital item has no effect on income from operations but it increases cash by the amount of the note payable. For example, a company reports the issuance of a $10,000 short-term note payable for cash in the statement of cash flows as follows.

Cash flows from financing activities	
Issuance of short-term note	$10,000

Another change in a working capital item that has no effect on income from operations or on cash is a **cash dividend payable.** Although a company will report the cash dividends when paid as a financing activity, it does not report the declared but unpaid dividend on the statement of cash flows.

Net Losses

If a company reports a net loss instead of a net income, it must adjust the net loss for those items that do not result in a cash inflow or outflow. The net loss, after adjusting for the charges or credits not affecting cash, may result in a negative or a positive cash flow from operating activities.

For example, if the net loss is $50,000 and the total amount of charges to add back is $60,000, then net cash provided by operating activities is $10,000. **Illustration 23.33** shows this computation.

ILLUSTRATION 23.33

Computation of Net Cash Flow from Operating Activities—Cash Inflow

Net loss		$(50,000)
Adjustments to reconcile net income to net cash provided by operating activities:		
Depreciation of plant assets	$55,000	
Amortization of patents	5,000	60,000
Net cash provided by operating activities		$ 10,000

If the company experiences a net loss of $80,000 and the total amount of the charges to add back is $25,000, the presentation appears as shown in **Illustration 23.34**.

[9]If the basis of the statement of cash flows is **cash and cash equivalents** and the short-term investment is considered a cash equivalent, then a company reports nothing in the statement because the transaction does not affect the balance of cash and cash equivalents. The Board notes that cash purchases of short-term investments generally are part of the company's cash management activities rather than part of its operating, investing, or financing activities.

Net loss	$(80,000)
Adjustments to reconcile net income to net cash used by operating activities:	
Depreciation of plant assets	25,000
Net cash used by operating activities	$(55,000)

ILLUSTRATION 23.34

Computation of Net Cash Flow from Operating Activities—Cash Outflow

Although not illustrated in this chapter, a negative cash flow may result even if the company reports a net income.

Significant Noncash Transactions

Because the statement of cash flows reports only the effects of operating, investing, and financing activities in terms of cash flows, it omits some **significant noncash transactions** and other events that are investing or financing activities. Among the more common of these noncash transactions that a company should report or disclose in some manner are the following.

1. Acquisition of assets by assuming liabilities (including capital lease obligations) or by issuing equity securities.
2. Exchanges of nonmonetary assets.
3. Refinancing of long-term debt.
4. Conversion of debt or preferred stock to common stock.
5. Issuance of equity securities to retire debt.

A company does not incorporate these noncash items in the statement of cash flows. If material in amount, these disclosures may be either narrative or summarized in a separate schedule at the bottom of the statement, or they may appear in a separate note or supplementary schedule to the financial statements.[10] **Illustration 23.35** shows the presentation of these significant noncash transactions or other events in a separate schedule at the bottom of the statement of cash flows.

Net increase in cash	$3,717,000
Cash at beginning of year	5,208,000
Cash at end of year	$8,925,000
Noncash investing and financing activities	
Purchase of land and building through issuance of 250,000 shares of common stock	$1,750,000
Exchange of Steadfast, NY, land for Bedford, PA, land	$2,000,000
Conversion of 7% bonds to 50,000 shares of common stock	$500,000

ILLUSTRATION 23.35

Schedule Presentation of Noncash Investing and Financing Activities

Or, companies may present these noncash transactions in a separate note, as shown in **Illustration 23.36**.

[10]Some noncash investing and financing activities are part cash and part noncash. Companies should report only the cash portion on the statement of cash flows. The noncash component should be reported at the bottom of the statement or in a separate note. A study of significant noncash investing and financing activities found that the effects of these transactions—debt issued for capital assets and capital lease financing of capital assets—can have a significant effect on analysts' assessments of capital expenditures and free cash flow. Given the importance of noncash capital expenditures to calculations of free cash flow, the authors encourage the FASB to revise its stance regarding the exclusion of all noncash activities from the statement of cash flows. See C. Mulford and H. Nicholson, "Measuring the Effects of Non-Cash Investing and Financing Activities," *Journal of Applied Research in Accounting and Finance* (Vol. 9, No. 1, 2014), pp. 27–43.

ILLUSTRATION 23.36

Note Presentation of Noncash Investing and Financing Activities

Note G: Significant noncash transactions. During the year, the company engaged in the following significant noncash investing and financing transactions:

Issued 250,000 shares of common stock to purchase land and building	$1,750,000
Exchanged land in Steadfast, NY, for land in Bedford, PA	$2,000,000
Converted 7% bonds to 50,000 shares of common stock	$500,000

Companies do not generally report certain other significant noncash transactions or other events in conjunction with the statement of cash flows. Examples of these types of transactions are **stock dividends, stock splits, and restrictions on retained earnings**. Companies generally report these items, neither financing nor investing activities, in conjunction with the statement of stockholders' equity or schedules and notes pertaining to changes in capital accounts.

What Do the Numbers Mean? Better Than ROA?

As you have learned in your study of accounting, both accounting income (measured under accrual-accounting principles) and cash flow from operations can provide useful information. However, both measures are sometimes criticized. Accounting income is sometimes faulted for the multitude of judgments required to determine revenues and expenses. In addition, many companies can boost an earnings-based metric, return on equity, by piling on debt which also makes the company riskier, not better. On the other hand, cash flow performance metrics are criticized because they do not follow the revenue and expense recognition principles.

So what's a better way to measure how profitable companies really are? Or, adopting master investor Warren Buffett's view of investing: How do you find companies that consistently generate big returns on invested capital? Recently, a new measure of profitability, "COROA"—for cash operating return on assets—has been proposed to provide a better performance metric. The idea is to measure management's ability to generate pure cash returns, not cash expected in the future, on every dollar invested in property, plant, and equipment; R&D centers; inventories; and all other assets.

Specifically, COROA is computed by starting with the cash flow from operations amount and then adding back cash taxes and cash interest to calculate pure operating cash flows. That's the dollar amount that the company actually puts in its coffers during the year—and which could be used to pay dividends, make "investments" by purchasing companies or divisions, and fund capital expenditures, especially those that propel growth. That's the numerator. Adjustments for taxes and interest are fundamental to this COROA measure. This is because falling taxes can create the illusion of ongoing progress. Interest is added back because it primarily reflects the level of leverage but has nothing to do with how well management is managing their assets.

The denominator consists of every dollar spent on the assets that produce those operating cash flows. To calculate that figure, take "total assets" from the balance sheet and add "accumulated depreciation" to account for operating assets that are still being used to make cars, semiconductors, or other products that, for accounting purposes, are fully expensed.

Thus, COROA—adjusted cash flow from operations as a percentage of total assets—is the ratio to keep an eye on. It's the best measure of pure profitability. If the number has been high for a while and is either staying high or improving, evidence is strong that the company is generating strong returns from its new investments. That's the quality that Buffett looks for. And according to accounting guru Jack Ciesielski, it's all about cash. "What's more important in the world than cash?" he asks. "Why, it's *more* cash, of course."

Source: S. Tully, "A Top Accounting Guru's Compelling New Measure for Profitability," *Fortune* (March 10, 2014).

Use of a Worksheet

LEARNING OBJECTIVE 5

Explain the use of a worksheet in preparing a statement of cash flows.

When numerous adjustments are necessary or other complicating factors are present, companies often use **a worksheet to assemble and classify the data that will appear on the statement of cash flows**. The worksheet is merely a device that aids in the preparation of the statement. Its use is optional. Illustration 23.37 shows the skeleton format of the worksheet for preparation of the statement of cash flows using the indirect method.

ILLUSTRATION 23.37

Format of Worksheet for Preparation of Statement of Cash Flows

XYZ Company

Home Insert Page Layout Formulas Data Review View

P18 *fx*

	A	B	C	D	E
1					
2	**XYZ Company**				
3	**Statement of Cash Flows for the Year Ended...**				
4	Balance Sheet Accounts	End of Prior Year Balances	Reconciling Items Debits	Reconciling Items Credits	End of Current Year Balances
5	Debit balance accounts	XX	XX	XX	XX
6		XX	XX	XX	XX
7	Totals	XXX			XXX
8	Credit balance accounts	XX	XX	XX	XX
9		XX	XX	XX	XX
10	Totals	XXX			XXX
11	Statement of Cash Flows Effects				
12	Operating activities				
13	Net income		XX		
14	Adjustments		XX	XX	
15	Investing activities				
16	Receipts and payments		XX	XX	
17	Financing activities				
18	Receipts and payments		XX	XX	
19	Totals		XXX	XXX	
20	Increase (decrease) in cash		(XX)	XX	
21	Totals		XXX	XXX	
22					

The following guidelines are important in using a worksheet.

1. In the balance sheet accounts section, **list accounts with debit balances separately from those with credit balances**. This means, for example, that Accumulated Depreciation is listed under credit balances and not as a contra account under debit balances. Enter the beginning and ending balances of each account in the appropriate columns. Then, enter the transactions that caused the change in the account balance during the year as reconciling items in the two middle columns.

   After all reconciling items have been entered, each line pertaining to a balance sheet account should foot across. That is, the beginning balance plus or minus the reconciling item(s) must equal the ending balance. When this agreement exists for all balance sheet accounts, all changes in account balances have been reconciled.

2. The bottom portion of the worksheet consists of the operating, investing, and financing activities sections. Accordingly, it provides the information necessary to prepare the formal statement of cash flows. **Enter inflows of cash as debits in the reconciling columns, and outflows of cash as credits in the reconciling columns.** Thus, in this section, a company would enter the sale of equipment for cash at book value as a debit under inflows of cash from investing activities. Similarly, it would enter the purchase of land for cash as a credit under outflows of cash from investing activities.

3. **Do not enter in any journal or post to any account the reconciling items shown in the worksheet.** These items do not represent either adjustments or corrections of the balance sheet accounts. They are used only to facilitate the preparation of the statement of cash flows.

Preparation of the Worksheet

The preparation of a worksheet involves the following steps.

Step 1. Enter the balance sheet accounts and their beginning and ending balances in the balance sheet accounts section.

Step 2. Enter the data that explain the changes in the balance sheet accounts (other than cash) and their effects on the statement of cash flows in the reconciling columns of the worksheet.

Step 3. Enter the increase or decrease in cash on the cash line and at the bottom of the worksheet. This entry should enable the totals of the reconciling columns to be in agreement.

To illustrate the preparation and use of a worksheet and to illustrate the reporting of some of the special problems discussed in the prior section, we present a comprehensive example for Satellite Corporation. Again, the indirect method serves as the basis for the computation of net cash provided by operating activities. Illustrations 23.38 and 23.39 present the balance sheet, combined statement of income and retained earnings, and additional information for Satellite Corporation.

ILLUSTRATION 23.38

Comparative Balance Sheet, Satellite Corporation

Satellite Corporation

Comparative Balance Sheet–December 31, 2020 and 2019

Assets	2020	2019	Increase or (Decrease)
Cash	$ 59,000	$ 66,000	$ (7,000)
Accounts receivable (net)	104,000	51,000	53,000
Inventory	493,000	341,000	152,000
Prepaid expenses	16,500	17,000	(500)
Investment in Porter Co. (equity method)	18,500	15,000	3,500
Land	131,500	82,000	49,500
Equipment	187,000	142,000	45,000
Accumulated depreciation—equipment	(29,000)	(31,000)	(2,000)
Buildings	262,000	262,000	–
Accumulated depreciation—buildings	(74,100)	(71,000)	3,100
Trademarks	7,600	10,000	(2,400)
Total assets	$1,176,000	$884,000	
Liabilities			
Accounts payable	$ 132,000	$131,000	$ 1,000
Accrued liabilities	43,000	39,000	4,000
Income taxes payable	3,000	16,000	(13,000)
Notes payable (long-term)	60,000	–	60,000
Bonds payable	100,000	100,000	–
Premium on bonds payable	7,000	8,000	(1,000)
Deferred tax liability (long-term)	9,000	6,000	3,000
Total liabilities	354,000	300,000	
Stockholders' Equity			
Common stock ($1 par)	60,000	50,000	10,000
Paid-in capital in excess of par—common stock	187,000	38,000	149,000
Retained earnings	592,000	496,000	96,000
Treasury stock	(17,000)	–	17,000
Total stockholders' equity	822,000	584,000	
Total liabilities and stockholders' equity	$1,176,000	$884,000	

ILLUSTRATION 23.39

Income and Retained Earnings Statements, Satellite Corporation

Satellite Corporation
Combined Statement of Income and Retained Earnings
For the Year Ended December 31, 2020

Net sales		$526,500
Other revenue		3,500
Total revenues		530,000
Expense		
Cost of goods sold	$310,000	
Selling and administrative expenses	47,000	
Other expenses and losses	12,000	
Total expenses		369,000
Other gains and losses		
Gain on condemnation of land		8,000
Income before income taxes		169,000
Income taxes		
Current	49,000	
Deferred	3,000	52,000
Net income		117,000
Retained earnings, January 1		496,000
Less:		
Cash dividends	6,000	
Stock dividend	15,000	21,000
Retained earnings, December 31		$592,000
Per share:		
Net income		$2.13

Additional Information

(a) Other revenue of $3,500 represents Satellite's equity share in the net income of Porter Co., an equity investee. Satellite owns 22% of Porter Co.

(b) An analysis of the equipment account and related accumulated depreciation indicates the following:

	Equipment Dr./(Cr.)	Accum. Dep. Dr./(Cr.)	Gain or (Loss)
Balance at end of 2019	$142,000	$(31,000)	
Purchases of equipment	53,000		
Sale of equipment	(8,000)	2,500	$(1,500)
Depreciation for the period		(11,500)	
Major repair charged to accumulated depreciation		11,000	
Balance at end of 2020	$187,000	$(29,000)	

(c) Land in the amount of $60,000 was purchased through the issuance of a long-term note; in addition, certain parcels of land costing $10,500 were condemned. The state government paid Satellite $18,500, resulting in an $8,000 gain.

(d) The change in the Accumulated Depreciation—Buildings, Trademarks, and Premium on Bonds Payable accounts resulted from depreciation and amortization entries.

(e) An analysis of the paid-in capital accounts in stockholders' equity discloses the following.

	Common Stock	Paid-In Capital in Excess of Par—Common Stock
Balance at end of 2019	$50,000	$ 38,000
Issuance of 2% stock dividend	1,000	14,000
Sale of stock for cash	9,000	135,000
Balance at end of 2020	$60,000	$187,000

(f) Interest paid (net of amount capitalized) is $9,000; income taxes paid is $47,000.

The discussion that follows provides additional explanations related to the preparation of the worksheet shown in **Illustration 23.40**.

ILLUSTRATION 23.40

Completed Worksheet for Preparation of Statement of Cash Flows, Satellite Corporation

Satellite Corporation

Home Insert Page Layout Formulas Data Review View

P18 fx

Satellite Corporation
Worksheet for Preparation of Statement of Cash Flows
for the Year Ended December 31, 2020

	A	B	C	D	E	F	G
5		Balance 12/31/19		Reconciling Items–2020 Dr.		Cr.	Balance 12/31/20
6	Debits						
7	Cash	$ 66,000			(18)	$ 7,000	$ 59,000
8	Accounts receivable (net)	51,000	(4)	$ 53,000			104,000
9	Inventory	341,000	(5)	152,000			493,000
10	Prepaid expenses	17,000			(6)	500	16,500
11	Investment in Porter Co. (equity method)	15,000	(7)	3,500			18,500
12	Land	82,000	(8)	60,000	(9)	10,500	131,500
13	Equipment	142,000	(10)	53,000	(11)	8,000	187,000
14	Buildings	262,000					262,000
15	Trademarks	10,000			(14)	2,400	7,600
16	Treasury stock		(17)	17,000			17,000
17	Total debits	$986,000					$1,296,100
18	Credits						
19	Accum. depr.–equipment	$ 31,000	(11)	2,500	(12)	11,500	
20			(13)	11,000			$ 29,000
21	Accum. depr.–buildings	71,000			(14)	3,100	74,100
22	Accounts payable	131,000			(15)	1,000	132,000
23	Accrued liabilities	39,000			(15)	4,000	43,000
24	Income taxes payable	16,000	(15)	13,000			3,000
25	Notes payable	-0-			(8)	60,000	60,000
26	Bonds payable	100,000					100,000
27	Premium on bonds payable	8,000	(15)	1,000			7,000
28	Deferred tax liability	6,000			(15)	3,000	9,000
29	Common stock	50,000			(2)	1,000	
30					(16)	9,000	60,000
31	Paid-in capital in excess of	38,000			(2)	14,000	
32	par—common stock				(16)	135,000	187,000
33	Retained earnings	496,000	(2)	15,000	(1)	117,000	
34			(3)	6,000			592,000
35	Total credits	$986,000					$1,296,100
36	Statement of Cash Flows Effects						
37	Operating activities						
38	Net income		(1)	117,000			
39	Increase in accounts receivable (net)				(4)	53,000	
40	Increase in inventory				(5)	152,000	
41	Decrease in prepaid expenses		(6)	500			
42	Equity in earnings of Porter Co.				(7)	3,500	
43	Gain on condemnation of land				(9)	8,000	
44	Loss on sale of equipment		(11)	1,500			
45	Depr. expense–equipment		(12)	11,500			
46	Depr. expense–buildings		(14)	3,100			
47	Amortization of trademarks		(14)	2,400			
48	Increase in accounts payable		(15)	1,000			
49	Increase in accrued liabilities		(15)	4,000			
50	Increase in deferred tax liability		(15)	3,000			
51	Decrease in income taxes payable				(15)	13,000	
52	Amortization of bond premium				(15)	1,000	
53	Investing activities						
54	Proceeds from condemnation of land		(9)	18,500			
55	Purchase of equipment				(10)	53,000	
56	Sale of equipment		(11)	4,000			
57	Major repairs of equipment				(13)	11,000	
58	Financing activities						
59	Payment of cash dividend				(3)	6,000	
60	Issuance of common stock		(16)	144,000			
61	Purchase of treasury stock				(17)	17,000	
62	Totals			697,500		704,500	
63	Decrease in cash		(18)	7,000			
64	Totals			$704,500		$704,500	
65							

Analysis of Transactions

The following discussion explains the individual adjustments that appear on the worksheet in Illustration 23.40. Because cash is the basis for the analysis, Satellite reconciles the Cash account last. Because income is the first item that appears on the statement of cash flows, it is handled first.

Change in Retained Earnings

Net income for the period is $117,000. The entry for it on the worksheet is as follows.

	(1)	
Operating—Net Income	117,000	
Retained Earnings		117,000

Satellite reports net income on the bottom section of the worksheet. This **is the starting point for preparation of the statement of cash flows (under the indirect method)**.

A stock dividend and a cash dividend also affected retained earnings. The retained earnings statement reports a stock dividend of $15,000. The worksheet entry for this transaction is as follows.

	(2)	
Retained Earnings	15,000	
Common Stock		1,000
Paid-in Capital in Excess of Par—Common Stock		14,000

Retained Earnings

(2)	15,000	Bal.	496,000
(3)	6,000	(1)	117,000
		Bal.	592,000

The issuance of stock dividends is not a cash operating, investing, or financing item. Therefore, **although the company enters this transaction on the worksheet for reconciling purposes, it does not report it in the statement of cash flows.**

The $6,000 cash dividend paid represents a financing activity cash outflow. Satellite makes the following worksheet entry:

	(3)	
Retained Earnings	6,000	
Financing—Cash Dividends		6,000

The company reconciles the beginning and ending balances of retained earnings by entry of the three items above.

Accounts Receivable (Net)

The increase in accounts receivable (net) of $53,000 represents adjustments that did not result in cash inflows during 2020. As a result, the company would deduct from net income the increase of $53,000. Satellite makes the following worksheet entry.

	(4)	
Accounts Receivable (net)	53,000	
Operating—Increase in Accounts Receivable (net)		53,000

Inventory

The increase in inventory of $152,000 represents an operating use of cash. The incremental investment in inventory during the year reduces cash without increasing the cost of goods sold. Satellite makes the following worksheet entry.

	(5)	
Inventory	152,000	
Operating—Increase in Inventory		152,000

Prepaid Expense

The decrease in prepaid expenses of $500 represents a charge in the income statement for which there was no cash outflow in the current period. Satellite should add that amount back to net income through the following entry.

(6)		
Operating—Decrease in Prepaid Expenses	500	
Prepaid Expenses		500

Investment in Stock

Satellite's investment in the stock of Porter Co. increased $3,500. This amount reflects Satellite's share of net income earned by Porter (its equity investee) during the current year. Although Satellite's revenue and therefore its net income increased $3,500 by recording Satellite's share of Porter Co.'s net income, no cash (dividend) was provided. Satellite makes the following worksheet entry.

(7)		
Equity Investments (Porter Co.)	3,500	
Operating—Equity in Earnings of Porter Co.		3,500

Land

Satellite purchased land in the amount of $60,000 through the issuance of a long-term note payable. This transaction did not affect cash. It is a significant noncash investing/financing transaction that the company would disclose either in a separate schedule below the statement of cash flows or in the accompanying notes. Satellite makes the following entry to reconcile the worksheet.

(8)		
Land	60,000	
Notes Payable		60,000

Land

Bal.	82,000	**(9)**	10,500
(8)	60,000		
Bal.	**131,500**		

In addition to the noncash transaction involving the issuance of a note to purchase land, the Land account was decreased by the condemnation proceedings. The following worksheet entry records the receipt of $18,500 for land having a book value of $10,500.

(9)		
Investing—Proceeds from Condemnation of Land	18,500	
Land		10,500
Operating—Gain on Condemnation of Land		8,000

In reconciling net income to net cash flow from operating activities, Satellite deducts from net income the gain of $8,000. The reason is that the transaction that gave rise to the gain is an item whose cash effect is already classified as an investing cash inflow. The Land account is now reconciled.

Equipment and Accumulated Depreciation

An analysis of Equipment and Accumulated Depreciation—Equipment shows that a number of transactions have affected these accounts. The company purchased equipment in the amount of $53,000 during the year. Satellite records this transaction on the worksheet as follows.

(10)		
Equipment	53,000	
Investing—Purchase of Equipment		53,000

In addition, Satellite sold at a loss of $1,500 equipment with a book value of $5,500. It records this transaction as follows.

(11)		
Investing—Sale of Equipment	4,000	
Operating—Loss on Sale of Equipment	1,500	
Accumulated Depreciation—Equipment	2,500	
Equipment		8,000

Equipment

Bal.	142,000	**(11)**	8,000
(10)	53,000		
Bal.	187,000		

The proceeds from the sale of the equipment provided cash of $4,000. In addition, the loss on the sale of the equipment has reduced net income but did not affect cash. Therefore, the company adds back to net income the amount of the loss, in order to accurately report cash provided by operating activities.

Satellite reported depreciation on the equipment at $11,500 and recorded it on the worksheet as follows.

(12)		
Operating—Depreciation Expense—Equipment	11,500	
Accumulated Depreciation—Equipment		11,500

The company adds depreciation expense back to net income because that expense reduced income but did not affect cash.

Finally, the company made a major repair to the equipment. It charged this expenditure, in the amount of $11,000, to Accumulated Depreciation—Equipment. This expenditure required cash, and so Satellite makes the following worksheet entry.

Accumulated Depreciation—Equipment

(11)	2,500	Bal.	31,000
(13)	11,000	**(12)**	11,500
		Bal.	29,000

(13)		
Accumulated Depreciation—Equipment	11,000	
Investing—Major Repairs of Equipment		11,000

After adjusting for the foregoing items, Satellite has reconciled the balances in the Equipment and related Accumulated Depreciation—Equipment accounts.

Building Depreciation and Amortization of Trademarks

Depreciation expense on the buildings of $3,100 and amortization of trademarks of $2,400 are both expenses in the income statement that reduced net income but did not require cash outflows in the current period. Satellite makes the following worksheet entry.

(14)		
Operating—Depreciation Expense—Buildings	3,100	
Operating—Amortization of Trademarks	2,400	
Accumulated Depreciation—Buildings		3,100
Trademarks		2,400

Other Noncash Charges or Credits

Analysis of the remaining accounts indicates that changes in the Accounts Payable, Accrued Liabilities, Income Taxes Payable, Premium on Bonds Payable, and Deferred Tax Liability balances resulted from charges or credits to net income that did not affect cash. The company should individually analyze each of these items and enter them in the worksheet. The following compound entry summarizes these noncash, income-related items.

(15)

Income Taxes Payable	13,000	
Premium on Bonds Payable	1,000	
Operating—Increase in Accounts Payable	1,000	
Operating—Increase in Accrued Liabilities	4,000	
Operating—Increase in Deferred Tax Liability	3,000	
Operating—Decrease in Income Taxes Payable		13,000
Operating—Amortization of Bond Premium		1,000
Accounts Payable		1,000
Accrued Liabilities		4,000
Deferred Tax Liability		3,000

Common Stock and Related Accounts

Comparison of the Common Stock balances and the Paid-in Capital in Excess of Par—Common Stock balances shows that transactions during the year affected these accounts. First, Satellite issues a stock dividend of 2 percent to stockholders. As the discussion of worksheet entry (2) indicated, no cash was provided or used by the stock dividend transaction. In addition to the shares issued via the stock dividend, Satellite sold shares of common stock at $16 per share. The company records this transaction as follows.

Common Stock

	Bal.	50,000
	(2)	1,000
	(16)	9,000
	Bal.	60,000

(16)

Financing—Sale of Common Stock	144,000	
Common Stock		9,000
Paid-in Capital in Excess of Par—Common Stock		135,000

Paid-in Capital in Excess of Par—Common Stock

	Bal.	38,000
	(2)	14,000
	(16)	135,000
	Bal.	187,000

Also, the company purchased shares of its common stock in the amount of $17,000. It records this transaction on the worksheet as follows.

(17)

Treasury Stock	17,000	
Financing—Purchase of Treasury Stock		17,000

Final Reconciling Entry

The final entry to reconcile the change in cash and to balance the worksheet is shown below. The $7,000 amount is the difference between the beginning and ending cash balance.

(18)

Decrease in Cash	7,000	
Cash		7,000

Once the company has determined that the differences between the beginning and ending balances per the worksheet columns have been accounted for, it can total the reconciling transactions columns, and they should balance. Satellite can prepare the statement of cash flows entirely from the items and amounts that appear at the bottom of the worksheet under "Statement of Cash Flows Effects."

Preparation of Final Statement

Illustration 23.41 presents a formal statement of cash flows prepared from the data compiled in the lower portion of the worksheet shown in Illustration 23.40.

ILLUSTRATION 23.41

Statement of Cash Flows, Satellite Corporation

Satellite Corporation
Statement of Cash Flows
For the Year Ended December 31, 2020

Cash flows from operating activities		
Net income		$117,000
Adjustments to reconcile net income to net cash used by operating activities:		
Depreciation expense	$ 14,600	
Amortization of trademarks	2,400	
Amortization of bond premium	(1,000)	
Equity in earnings of Porter Co.	(3,500)	
Gain on condemnation of land	(8,000)	
Loss on sale of equipment	1,500	
Increase in deferred tax liability	3,000	
Increase in accounts receivable (net)	(53,000)	
Increase in inventory	(152,000)	
Decrease in prepaid expenses	500	
Increase in accounts payable	1,000	
Increase in accrued liabilities	4,000	
Decrease in income taxes payable	(13,000)	(203,500)
Net cash used by operating activities		(86,500)
Cash flows from investing activities		
Proceeds from condemnation of land	18,500	
Purchase of equipment	(53,000)	
Sale of equipment	4,000	
Major repairs of equipment	(11,000)	
Net cash used by investing activities		(41,500)
Cash flows from financing activities		
Payment of cash dividend	(6,000)	
Issuance of common stock	144,000	
Purchase of treasury stock	(17,000)	
Net cash provided by financing activities		121,000
Net decrease in cash		(7,000)
Cash, January 1, 2020		66,000
Cash, December 31, 2020		$ 59,000

Supplemental Disclosures of Cash Flow Information:

Cash paid during the year for:	
Interest (net of amount capitalized)	$ 9,000
Income taxes	$ 47,000

Supplemental Schedule of Noncash Investing and Financing Activities:

Purchase of land for $60,000 in exchange for a $60,000 long-term note.

Review and Practice

Key Terms Review

cash equivalents 23-4(*n*)
direct method 23-18
financing activities 23-4
indirect method 23-8
investing activities 23-4
operating activities 23-4
significant noncash transactions 23-31
statement of cash flows 23-3

Learning Objectives Review

1 Describe the usefulness and format of the statement of cash flows.

The primary purpose of the statement of cash flows is to provide information about cash receipts and cash payments of an entity during a period. A secondary objective is to report the entity's operating, investing, and financing activities during the period.

Companies classify cash flows as follows. (1) **Operating activities**—transactions that result in the revenues, expenses, gains, and losses that determine net income. (2) **Investing activities**—lending money and collecting on those loans, and acquiring and disposing of investments, plant assets, and intangible assets. (3) **Financing activities**—obtaining cash from creditors and repaying loans, issuing and reacquiring capital stock, and paying cash dividends.

2 Prepare a statement of cash flows.

(1) *Determine the change in cash*. This is the difference between the beginning and the ending cash balance shown on the comparative balance sheets. (2) *Determine the net cash flow from operating activities*. This procedure is complex; it involves analyzing not only the current year's income statement but also the comparative balance sheets and the selected transaction data. (3) *Determine cash flows from investing and financing activities*. Analyze all other changes in the balance sheet accounts to determine the effects on cash.

Companies must adjust net income on an accrual basis to determine net cash flow from operating activities because some expenses and losses do not cause cash outflows, and some revenues and gains do not provide cash inflows. Once a company has computed the net cash flow from operating activities, the next step is to determine whether any other changes in balance sheet accounts caused an increase or decrease in cash. Net cash flows from investing and financing activities can be determined primarily by examining the changes in noncurrent balance sheet accounts.

The information to prepare the statement usually comes from three sources. (1) *Comparative balance sheets*: Information in these statements indicates the amount of the changes in assets, liabilities, and equities during the period. (2) *Current income statement*: Information in this statement is used in determining the cash provided by operations during the period. (3) *Selected transaction data*: These data from the general ledger provide additional detailed information needed to determine how cash was provided or used during the period.

3 Contrast the direct and indirect methods of calculating net cash flow from operating activities.

Under the direct approach, companies calculate the major classes of operating cash receipts and cash disbursements. Companies summarize the computations in a schedule of changes from the accrual- to the cash-basis income statement. Presentation of the direct approach of reporting net cash flow from operating activities takes the form of a condensed cash-basis income statement. The indirect method adds back to net income the noncash expenses and losses and subtracts the noncash revenues and gains.

4 Discuss special problems in preparing a statement of cash flows.

These special problems are (1) adjustments to income (depreciation and amortization, postretirement benefit costs, change in deferred income taxes, equity method of accounting, losses and gains, stock options, unusual and infrequent items); (2) accounts receivable (net); (3) other working capital changes; (4) net losses; and (5) significant noncash transactions.

5 Explain the use of a worksheet in preparing a statement of cash flows.

When numerous adjustments are necessary or other complicating factors are present, companies often use a worksheet to assemble and classify the data that will appear on the statement of cash flows. The worksheet is merely a device that aids in the preparation of the statement. Its use is optional.

Enhanced Review and Practice

Go online for multiple-choice questions with solutions, review exercises with solutions, and a full glossary of all key terms.

Practice Problem

Data presented below are from the records of Antonio Brasileiro Company.

	December 31, 2020	December 31, 2019
Cash	$ 15,000	$ 8,000
Current assets other than cash	85,000	60,000
Long-term investments	10,000	53,000
Plant assets	335,000	215,000
	$445,000	$336,000

	December 31, 2020	December 31, 2019
Accumulated depreciation	$ 20,000	$ 40,000
Current liabilities	40,000	22,000
Bonds payable	75,000	-0-
Common stock	254,000	254,000
Retained earnings	56,000	20,000
	$445,000	$336,000

Additional information:

1. In 2020, the company sold for $34,000 available-for-sale debt investments carried at a cost of $43,000 on December 31, 2020. No unrealized gains or losses were recorded on this investment in 2020.
2. In 2020, the company sold for $8,000 plant assets that cost $50,000 and were 80% depreciated. The loss was incorrectly charged directly to Retained Earnings.
3. Net income as reported on the income statement for the year was $48,000.
4. The company paid dividends totaling $10,000.
5. Depreciation charged for the year was $20,000.

Instructions

Prepare a statement of cash flows for the year 2020 using the indirect method.

Solution

Antonio Brasileiro Company
Statement of Cash Flows
For the Year Ended December 31, 2020
Indirect Method

Cash flows from operating activities		
Net income ($48,000 – $2,000 loss on plant assets)		$ 46,000
Adjustments to reconcile net income to net cash provided by operating activities:		
Depreciation expense	$ 20,000	
Loss on sale of investments	9,000	
Loss on sale of plant assets	2,000	
Increase in current assets other than cash	(25,000)	
Increase in current liabilities	18,000	24,000
Net cash provided by operating activities		70,000
Cash flows from investing activities		
Sale of plant assets	8,000	
Sale of investments	34,000	
Purchase of plant assets*	(170,000)	
Net cash used by investing activities		(128,000)
Cash flows from financing activities		
Issuance of bonds payable	75,000	
Payment of dividends	(10,000)	
Net cash provided by financing activities		65,000
Net increase in cash		7,000
Cash balance, January 1, 2020		8,000
Cash balance, December 31, 2020		$ 15,000

*Supporting computation (purchase of plant assets):

Plant assets, December 31, 2020	$335,000
Less: Plant assets, December 31, 2019	215,000
Net change	120,000
Plant assets sold	50,000
Plant assets purchased	$170,000

WileyPLUS

Exercises, Problems, Problem Solution Walkthrough Videos, and many more assessment tools and resources are available for practice in WileyPLUS.

Questions

1. What is the purpose of the statement of cash flows? What information does it provide?

2. Of what use is the statement of cash flows?

3. Differentiate between investing activities, financing activities, and operating activities.

4. What are the major sources of cash (inflows) in a statement of cash flows? What are the major uses (outflows) of cash?

5. Identify and explain the major steps involved in preparing the statement of cash flows.

6. Identify the following items as (1) operating, (2) investing, or (3) financing activities: purchase of land, payment of dividends, cash sales, and purchase of treasury stock.

7. Unlike the other major financial statements, the statement of cash flows is not prepared from the adjusted trial balance. From what sources does the information to prepare this statement come, and what information does each source provide?

8. Why is it necessary to convert accrual-based net income to a cash basis when preparing a statement of cash flows?

9. Differentiate between the direct method and the indirect method by discussing each method.

10. Broussard Company reported net income of $3.5 million in 2020. Depreciation for the year was $520,000, accounts receivable increased $500,000, and accounts payable increased $300,000. Compute net cash flow from operating activities using the indirect method.

11. Collinsworth Co. reported sales on an accrual basis of $100,000. If accounts receivable increased $30,000 and the allowance for doubtful accounts increased $9,000 after a write-off of $2,000, compute cash sales.

12. Your roommate is puzzled. During the last year, the company in which she is a stockholder reported a net loss of $675,000, yet its cash increased $321,000 during the same period of time. Explain to your roommate how this situation could occur.

13. The board of directors of Tirico Corp. declared cash dividends of $260,000 during the current year. If dividends payable was $85,000 at the beginning of the year and $90,000 at the end of the year, how much cash was paid in dividends during the year?

14. Explain how the amount of cash payments to suppliers is computed under the direct method.

15. The net income for Fallon Company for 2020 was $320,000. During 2020, depreciation on plant assets was $124,000, amortization of patent was $40,000, and the company incurred a loss on sale of plant assets of $21,000. Compute net cash flow from operating activities.

16. Each of the following items must be considered in preparing a statement of cash flows for Blackwell Inc. for the year ended December 31, 2020. State where each item is to be shown in the statement, if at all.

- **a.** Plant assets that had cost $18,000 6½ years before and were being depreciated on a straight-line basis over 10 years with no estimated scrap value were sold for $4,000.
- **b.** During the year, 10,000 shares of common stock with a stated value of $20 a share were issued for $41 a share.
- **c.** Uncollectible accounts receivable in the amount of $22,000 were written off against Allowance for Doubtful Accounts.
- **d.** The company sustained a net loss for the year of $50,000. Depreciation amounted to $22,000, and a gain of $9,000 was realized on the sale of available-for-sale debt securities for $38,000 cash.

17. Classify the following items as (1) operating, (2) investing, (3) financing, or (4) significant noncash investing and financing activities, using the direct method.

- **a.** Cash payments to employees.
- **b.** Redemption of bonds payable.
- **c.** Sale of building at book value.
- **d.** Cash payments to suppliers.
- **e.** Exchange of equipment for furniture.
- **f.** Issuance of preferred stock.
- **g.** Cash received from customers.
- **h.** Purchase of treasury stock.
- **i.** Issuance of bonds for land.
- **j.** Payment of dividends.
- **k.** Purchase of equipment.
- **l.** Cash payments for operating expenses.

18. Stan Conner and Mark Stein were discussing the presentation format of the statement of cash flows of Bombeck Co. At the bottom of Bombeck's statement of cash flows was a separate section entitled "Noncash investing and financing activities." Give three examples of significant noncash transactions that would be reported in this section.

19. During 2020, Simms Company redeemed $2,000,000 of bonds payable for $1,880,000 cash. Indicate how this transaction would be reported on a statement of cash flows, if at all.

20. What are some of the arguments in favor of using the indirect (reconciliation) method as opposed to the direct method for reporting a statement of cash flows?

21. Why is it desirable to use a worksheet when preparing a statement of cash flows? Is a worksheet required to prepare a statement of cash flows?

Brief Exercises

BE23.1 **(LO 1)** Novak Corporation is preparing its 2020 statement of cash flows, using the indirect method. Presented below is a list of items that may affect the statement. Using the code below, indicate how each item will affect Novak's 2020 statement of cash flows.

Code Letter	Effect
A	Added to net income in the operating section
D	Deducted from net income in the operating section
R-I	Cash receipt in investing section
P-I	Cash payment in investing section
R-F	Cash receipt in financing section
P-F	Cash payment in financing section
N	Noncash investing and financing activity

Items

_____ **a.** Purchase of land and building.

_____ **b.** Decrease in accounts receivable.

_____ **c.** Issuance of stock.

_____ **d.** Depreciation expense.

_____ **e.** Sale of land at book value.

_____ **f.** Sale of land at a gain.

_____ **g.** Payment of dividends.

_____ **h.** Increase in accounts receivable.

_____ **i.** Purchase of available-for-sale debt investment.

_____ **j.** Increase in accounts payable.

_____ **k.** Decrease in accounts payable.

_____ **l.** Loan from bank by signing note.

_____ **m.** Purchase of equipment using a note.

_____ **n.** Increase in inventory.

_____ **o.** Issuance of bonds.

_____ **p.** Redemption of bonds payable.

_____ **q.** Sale of equipment at a loss.

_____ **r.** Purchase of treasury stock.

BE23.2 **(LO 2)** Wainwright Corporation had the following activities in 2020.

1. Sale of land $180,000.
2. Purchase of inventory $845,000.
3. Purchase of treasury stock $72,000.
4. Purchase of equipment $415,000.
5. Issuance of common stock $320,000.
6. Purchase of available-for-sale debt securities $59,000.

Compute the amount Wainwright should report as net cash provided (used) by investing activities in its 2020 statement of cash flows.

BE23.3 **(LO 2)** Stansfield Corporation had the following activities in 2020.

1. Payment of accounts payable $770,000.
2. Issuance of common stock $250,000.
3. Payment of dividends $350,000.
4. Collection of note receivable $100,000.
5. Issuance of bonds payable $510,000.
6. Purchase of treasury stock $46,000.

Compute the amount Stansfield should report as net cash provided (used) by financing activities in its 2020 statement of cash flows.

BE23.4 **(LO 2, 3)** Bloom Corporation had the following 2020 income statement.

Sales revenue	$200,000
Cost of goods sold	120,000
Gross profit	80,000
Operating expenses (includes depreciation of $21,000)	50,000
Net income	$ 30,000

The following accounts increased during 2020: Accounts Receivable $12,000, Inventory $11,000, and Accounts Payable $13,000. Prepare the cash flows from operating activities section of Bloom's 2020 statement of cash flows using the direct method.

BE23.5 **(LO 2, 3)** Use the information from BE23.4 for Bloom Corporation. Prepare the cash flows from operating activities section of Bloom's 2020 statement of cash flows using the indirect method.

BE23.6 **(LO 3)** At January 1, 2020, Eikenberry Inc. had accounts receivable of $72,000. At December 31, 2020, accounts receivable is $54,000. Sales revenue for 2020 total $420,000. Compute Eikenberry's 2020 cash receipts from customers.

BE23.7 (LO 3) Moxley Corporation had January 1 and December 31 balances as follows.

	1/1/20	12/31/20
Inventory	$95,000	$113,000
Accounts payable	61,000	69,000

For 2020, cost of goods sold was $500,000. Compute Moxley's 2020 cash payments to suppliers.

BE23.8 (LO 2) In 2020, Elbert Corporation had net cash provided by operating activities of $531,000, net cash used by investing activities of $963,000, and net cash provided by financing activities of $585,000. At January 1, 2020, the cash balance was $333,000. Compute December 31, 2020, cash.

BE23.9 (LO 2, 3) Colbert Corporation had the following 2020 income statement.

Revenues	$100,000
Expenses	60,000
Net income	$ 40,000

In 2020, Colbert had the following activity in selected accounts.

Accounts Receivable

1/1/20	20,000	1,000	Write-offs
Revenues	100,000	90,000	Collections
12/31/20	29,000		

Allowance for Doubtful Accounts

Write-offs	1,000	1,200	1/1/20
		1,840	Bad debt expense
		2,040	12/31/20

Prepare Colbert's cash flows from operating activities section of the statement of cash flows using (a) the direct method and (b) the indirect method.

BE23.10 (LO 3) Hendrickson Corporation reported net income of $50,000 in 2020. Depreciation expense was $17,000. The following working capital accounts changed.

Accounts receivable	$11,000 increase
Available-for-sale debt securities	16,000 increase
Inventory	7,400 increase
Nontrade note payable	15,000 decrease
Accounts payable	12,300 increase

Compute net cash provided by operating activities.

BE23.11 (LO 3) In 2020, Wild Corporation reported a net loss of $70,000. Wild's only net income adjustments were depreciation expense $81,000, and increase in accounts receivable $8,100. Compute Wild's net cash provided (used) by operating activities.

BE23.12 (LO 4) In 2020, Leppard Inc. issued 1,000 shares of $10 par value common stock for land worth $40,000.

a. Prepare Leppard's journal entry to record the transaction.

b. Indicate the effect the transaction has on cash.

c. Indicate how the transaction is reported on the statement of cash flows.

BE23.13 (LO 5) Indicate in general journal form how the items below would be entered in a worksheet for the preparation of the statement of cash flows.

a. Net income is $317,000.

b. Cash dividends declared and paid totaled $120,000.

c. Equipment was purchased for $114,000.

d. Equipment that originally cost $40,000 and had accumulated depreciation of $32,000 was sold for $10,000.

Exercises

E23.1 (LO 1) (Classification of Transactions) Red Hot Chili Peppers Co. had the following activity in its most recent year of operations.

a. Purchase of equipment.

b. Redemption of bonds payable.

c. Sale of building.

d. Depreciation.

e. Exchange of equipment for furniture.

f. Issuance of common stock.

g. Amortization of intangible assets.
h. Purchase of treasury stock.
i. Issuance of bonds for land.
j. Payment of dividends.
k. Increase in interest receivable on notes receivable.
l. Pension expense exceeds amount funded.

Instructions

Classify the items as (1) operating—add to net income; (2) operating—deduct from net income; (3) investing; (4) financing; or (5) significant noncash investing and financing activities. Use the indirect method.

E23.2 **(LO 1, 2)** **(Statement Presentation of Transactions—Indirect Method)** Each of the following items must be considered in preparing a statement of cash flows (indirect method) for Turbulent Indigo Inc. for the year ended December 31, 2020.

a. Plant assets that had cost $20,000 6 years before and were being depreciated on a straight-line basis over 10 years with no estimated scrap value were sold for $5,300.

b. During the year, 10,000 shares of common stock with a stated value of $10 a share were issued for $43 a share.

c. Uncollectible accounts receivable in the amount of $27,000 were written off against Allowance for Doubtful Accounts.

d. The company sustained a net loss for the year of $50,000. Depreciation amounted to $22,000, and a gain of $9,000 was realized on the sale of land for $39,000 cash.

e. A 3-month U.S. Treasury bill was purchased for $100,000. The company uses a cash and cash equivalent basis for its cash flow statement.

f. Patent amortization for the year was $20,000.

g. The company exchanged common stock for a 70% interest in Tabasco Co. for $900,000.

h. During the year, treasury stock costing $47,000 was purchased.

Instructions

State where each item is to be shown in the statement of cash flows, if at all.

E23.3 **(LO 2, 3)** Excel **(Preparation of Operating Activities Section—Indirect Method, Periodic Inventory)** The income statement of Vince Gill Company is shown below.

Vince Gill Company
Income Statement
For the Year Ended December 31, 2020

Sales revenue		$6,900,000
Cost of goods sold		
Beginning inventory	$1,900,000	
Purchases	4,400,000	
Goods available for sale	6,300,000	
Ending inventory	1,600,000	
Cost of goods sold		4,700,000
Gross profit		2,200,000
Operating expenses		
Selling expenses	450,000	
Administrative expenses	700,000	1,150,000
Net income		$1,050,000

Additional information:

1. Accounts receivable decreased $360,000 during the year.
2. Prepaid expenses increased $170,000 during the year.
3. Accounts payable to suppliers of merchandise decreased $275,000 during the year.
4. Accrued expenses payable decreased $100,000 during the year.
5. Administrative expenses include depreciation expense of $60,000.

Instructions

Prepare the operating activities section of the statement of cash flows for the year ended December 31, 2020, for Vince Gill Company, using the indirect method.

E23.4 **(LO 2, 3)** Excel **(Preparation of Operating Activities Section—Direct Method)** Data for the Vince Gill Company are presented in E23.3.

Instructions

Prepare the operating activities section of the statement of cash flows using the direct method.

E23.5 **(LO 2, 3)** **(Preparation of Operating Activities Section—Direct Method)** Krauss Company's income statement for the year ended December 31, 2020, contained the following condensed information.

Service revenue		$840,000
Operating expenses (excluding depreciation)	$624,000	
Depreciation expense	60,000	
Loss on sale of equipment	26,000	710,000
Income before income taxes		130,000
Income tax expense		40,000
Net income		$ 90,000

Krauss's balance sheet contained the following comparative data at December 31.

	2020	2019
Accounts receivable	$37,000	$54,000
Accounts payable	41,000	31,000
Income taxes payable	4,000	8,500

(Accounts payable pertains to operating expenses.)

Instructions

Prepare the operating activities section of the statement of cash flows using the direct method.

E23.6 **(LO 2, 3)** **(Preparation of Operating Activities Section—Indirect Method)** Data for Krauss Company are presented in E23.5.

Instructions

Prepare the operating activities section of the statement of cash flows using the indirect method.

E23.7 **(LO 2, 3)** **(Computation of Operating Activities—Direct Method)** Presented below are two independent situations.

Situation A: Annie Lennox Co. reports revenues of $200,000 and operating expenses of $110,000 in its first year of operations, 2020. Accounts receivable and accounts payable at year-end were $71,000 and $29,000, respectively. Assume that the accounts payable related to operating expenses. (Ignore income taxes.)

Instructions

Using the direct method, compute net cash provided by operating activities.

Situation B: The income statement for Blues Traveler Company shows cost of goods sold $310,000 and operating expenses (exclusive of depreciation) $230,000. The comparative balance sheet for the year shows that inventory increased $26,000, prepaid expenses decreased $8,000, accounts payable (related to merchandise) decreased $17,000, and accrued expenses payable increased $11,000.

Instructions

Compute (a) cash payments to suppliers and (b) cash payments for operating expenses.

E23.8 **(LO 2, 3)** **(Schedule of Net Cash Flow from Operating Activities—Indirect Method)** Ballard Co. reported $145,000 of net income for 2020. The accountant, in preparing the statement of cash flows, noted the following items occurring during 2020 that might affect cash flows from operating activities.

1. Ballard purchased 100 shares of treasury stock at a cost of $20 per share. These shares were then resold at $25 per share.
2. Ballard sold 100 shares of IBM common at $200 per share. The acquisition cost of these shares was $145 per share. There were no unrealized gains or losses recorded on this investment in 2020.
3. Ballard revised its estimate for bad debts. Before 2020, Ballard's bad debt expense was 1% of its receivables. In 2020, this percentage was increased to 2%. Net accounts receivable decreased by $12,000 during 2020.

4. Ballard issued 500 shares of its $10 par common stock for a patent. The market price of the shares on the date of the transaction was $23 per share.
5. Depreciation expense is $39,000.
6. Ballard Co. holds 40% of the Nirvana Company's common stock as a long-term investment. Nirvana Company reported $27,000 of net income for 2020.
7. Nirvana Company paid a total of $2,000 of cash dividends to all investees in 2020.
8. Ballard declared a 10% stock dividend. One thousand shares of $10 par common stock were distributed. The market price at date of issuance was $20 per share.

Instructions

Prepare a schedule that shows the net cash flow from operating activities using the indirect method. Assume no items other than those listed above affected the computation of 2020 net cash flow from operating activities.

E23.9 **(LO 2, 3)** **(SCF—Direct Method)** Los Lobos Corp. uses the direct method to prepare its statement of cash flows. Los Lobos's trial balances at December 31, 2020 and 2019, are as follows.

	December 31	
	2020	2019
Debits		
Cash	$ 35,000	$ 32,000
Accounts receivable	33,000	30,000
Inventory	31,000	47,000
Property, plant, and equipment	100,000	95,000
Unamortized bond discount	4,500	5,000
Cost of goods sold	250,000	380,000
Selling expenses	141,500	172,000
General and administrative expenses	137,000	151,300
Interest expense	4,300	2,600
Income tax expense	20,400	61,200
	$756,700	$976,100
Credits		
Allowance for doubtful accounts	$ 1,300	$ 1,100
Accumulated depreciation—plant assets	16,500	15,000
Accounts payable	25,000	15,500
Income taxes payable	21,000	29,100
Deferred tax liability	5,300	4,600
8% callable bonds payable	45,000	20,000
Common stock	50,000	40,000
Paid-in capital in excess of par	9,100	7,500
Retained earnings	44,700	64,600
Sales revenue	538,800	778,700
	$756,700	$976,100

Additional information:

1. Los Lobos purchased $5,000 in equipment during 2020.
2. Los Lobos allocated one-third of its depreciation expense to selling expenses and the remainder to general and administrative expenses.
3. Bad debt expense for 2020 was $5,000, and write-offs of uncollectible accounts totaled $4,800.

Instructions

Determine what amounts Los Lobos should report in its statement of cash flows for the year ended December 31, 2020, for the following items.

a. Cash collected from customers.
b. Cash paid to suppliers.
c. Cash paid for interest.
d. Cash paid for income taxes.
e. Cash paid for selling expenses.

E23.10 **(LO 1, 4)** **(Classification of Transactions)** Following are selected balance sheet accounts of Allman Bros. Corp. at December 31, 2020 and 2019, and the increases or decreases in each account from 2019 to 2020. Also presented is selected income statement information for the year ended December 31, 2020, and additional information.

	2020	2019	Increase (Decrease)
Selected balance sheet accounts:			
Assets			
Accounts receivable	$ 34,000	$ 24,000	$ 10,000
Property, plant, and equipment	277,000	247,000	30,000
Accumulated depreciation—plant assets	(178,000)	(167,000)	(11,000)
Liabilities and stockholders' equity			
Bonds payable	$ 49,000	$ 46,000	$ 3,000
Dividends payable	8,000	5,000	3,000
Common stock, $1 par	22,000	19,000	3,000
Additional paid-in capital	9,000	3,000	6,000
Retained earnings	104,000	91,000	13,000

Selected income statement information for the year ended December 31, 2020:

Sales revenue	$ 155,000
Depreciation	33,000
Gain on sale of equipment	14,500
Net income	31,000

Additional information:

1. During 2020, equipment costing $45,000 was sold for cash.
2. Accounts receivable relate to sales of merchandise.
3. During 2020, $20,000 of bonds payable were issued in exchange for property, plant, and equipment. There was no amortization of bond discount or premium.

Instructions

Determine the category (operating, investing, or financing) and the amount that should be reported in the statement of cash flows for the following items.

a. Payments for purchase of property, plant, and equipment.

b. Proceeds from the sale of equipment.

c. Cash dividends paid.

d. Redemption of bonds payable.

E23.11 **(LO 2)** **(SCF—Indirect Method)** Condensed financial data of Pat Metheny Company for 2020 and 2019 are presented below.

Pat Metheny Company
Comparative Balance Sheet
As of December 31, 2020 and 2019

	2020	2019
Cash	$1,800	$1,150
Receivables	1,750	1,300
Inventory	1,600	1,900
Plant assets	1,900	1,700
Accumulated depreciation	(1,200)	(1,170)
Long-term investments (held-to-maturity)	1,300	1,420
	$7,150	$6,300
Accounts payable	$1,200	$ 900
Accrued liabilities	200	250
Bonds payable	1,400	1,550
Common stock	1,900	1,700
Retained earnings	2,450	1,900
	$7,150	$6,300

Pat Metheny Company
Income Statement
For the Year Ended December 31, 2020

Sales revenue	$6,900
Cost of goods sold	4,700
Gross margin	2,200
Selling and administrative expense	930
Income from operations	1,270
Other revenues and gains	
Gain on sale of investments	80
Income before tax	1,350
Income tax expense	540
Net income	810
Cash dividends	260
Income retained in business	$ 550

Additional information:

During the year, $70 of common stock was issued in exchange for plant assets. No plant assets were sold in 2020.

Instructions

Prepare a statement of cash flows using the indirect method.

E23.12 **(LO 2)** **(SCF—Direct Method)** Data for Pat Metheny Company are presented in E23.11.

Instructions

Prepare a statement of cash flows using the direct method. (Do not prepare a reconciliation schedule.)

E23.13 **(LO 2, 3)** **(SCF—Direct Method)** Brecker Inc., a greeting card company, had the following statements prepared as of December 31, 2020.

Brecker Inc.
Comparative Balance Sheet
As of December 31, 2020 and 2019

	12/31/20	12/31/19
Cash	$ 6,000	$ 7,000
Accounts receivable	62,000	51,000
Short-term debt investments (available-for-sale)	35,000	18,000
Inventory	40,000	60,000
Prepaid rent	5,000	4,000
Equipment	154,000	130,000
Accumulated depreciation—equipment	(35,000)	(25,000)
Copyrights	46,000	50,000
Total assets	$313,000	$295,000
Accounts payable	$ 46,000	$ 40,000
Income taxes payable	4,000	6,000
Salaries and wages payable	8,000	4,000
Short-term loans payable	8,000	10,000
Long-term loans payable	60,000	69,000
Common stock, $10 par	100,000	100,000
Contributed capital, common stock	30,000	30,000
Retained earnings	57,000	36,000
Total liabilities and stockholders' equity	$313,000	$295,000

Brecker Inc.
Income Statement
For the Year Ending December 31, 2020

Sales revenue		$338,150
Cost of goods sold		175,000
Gross profit		163,150
Operating expenses		120,000
Operating income		43,150
Interest expense	$11,400	
Gain on sale of equipment	2,000	9,400
Income before tax		33,750
Income tax expense		6,750
Net income		$ 27,000

Additional information:

1. Dividends in the amount of $6,000 were declared and paid during 2020.
2. Depreciation expense and amortization expense are included in operating expenses.
3. No unrealized gains or losses have occurred on the investments during the year.
4. Equipment that had a cost of $20,000 and was 70% depreciated was sold during 2020.

Instructions

Prepare a statement of cash flows using the direct method. (Do not prepare a reconciliation schedule.)

E23.14 **(LO 2)** **(SCF—Indirect Method)** Data for Brecker Inc. are presented in E23.13.

Instructions

Prepare a statement of cash flows using the indirect method.

E23.15 **(LO 2)** **(SCF—Indirect Method)** The following data are taken from the records of Alee Company.

	December 31, 2020	December 31, 2019
Cash	$ 15,000	$ 8,000
Current assets other than cash	85,000	60,000
Long-term debt investments	10,000	53,000
Plant assets	335,000	215,000
	$445,000	$336,000
Accumulated depreciation	$ 20,000	$ 40,000
Current liabilities	40,000	22,000
Bonds payable	75,000	-0-
Common stock	254,000	254,000
Retained earnings	56,000	20,000
	$445,000	$336,000

Additional information:

1. Held-to-maturity debt securities carried at a cost of $43,000 on December 31, 2019, were sold in 2020 for $34,000. The loss (not unusual) was incorrectly charged directly to Retained Earnings.
2. Plant assets that cost $50,000 and were 80% depreciated were sold during 2020 for $8,000. The loss was incorrectly charged directly to Retained Earnings.
3. Net income as reported on the income statement for the year was $57,000.
4. Dividends paid amounted to $10,000.
5. Depreciation charged for the year was $20,000.

Instructions

Prepare a statement of cash flows for the year 2020 using the indirect method.

E23.16 **(LO 1, 2)** **(Cash Provided by Operating, Investing, and Financing Activities)** The balance sheet data of Brown Company at the end of 2020 and 2019 follow.

	2020	2019
Cash	$ 30,000	$ 35,000
Accounts receivable (net)	55,000	45,000
Inventory	65,000	45,000
Prepaid expenses	15,000	25,000
Equipment	90,000	75,000
Accumulated depreciation—equipment	(18,000)	(8,000)
Land	70,000	40,000
	$307,000	$257,000
Accounts payable	$ 65,000	$ 52,000
Accrued expenses	15,000	18,000
Notes payable—bank, long-term	–0–	23,000
Bonds payable	30,000	–0–
Common stock, $10 par	189,000	159,000
Retained earnings	8,000	5,000
	$307,000	$257,000

Land was acquired for $30,000 in exchange for common stock, par $30,000, during the year; all equipment purchased was for cash. Equipment costing $10,000 was sold for $3,000; book value of the equipment was $6,000. Cash dividends of $10,000 were declared and paid during the year.

Instructions

Compute net cash provided (used) by:

a. Operating activities.

b. Investing activities.

c. Financing activities.

E23.17 **(LO 2)** **(SCF—Indirect Method and Balance Sheet)** Jobim Inc. had the following condensed balance sheet at the end of operations for 2019.

Jobim Inc.
Balance Sheet
December 31, 2019

Cash	$ 8,500	Current liabilities	$ 15,000
Current assets other than cash	29,000	Long-term notes payable	25,500
Equity investments	20,000	Bonds payable	25,000
Plant assets (net)	67,500	Common stock	75,000
Land	40,000	Retained earnings	24,500
	$165,000		$165,000

During 2020, the following occurred.

1. A tract of land was purchased for $9,000.
2. Bonds payable in the amount of $15,000 were redeemed at par.
3. An additional $10,000 in common stock was issued at par.
4. Dividends totaling $9,375 were paid to stockholders.
5. Net income was $35,250 after allowing depreciation of $13,500.
6. Land was purchased through the issuance of $22,500 in bonds.
7. Jobim Inc. sold part of its investment portfolio for $12,875. This transaction resulted in a gain of $2,000 for the company. No unrealized gains or losses were recorded on these investments in 2020.
8. Both current assets (other than cash) and current liabilities remained at the same amount.

Instructions

a. Prepare a statement of cash flows for 2020 using the indirect method.

b. Prepare the condensed balance sheet for Jobim Inc. as it would appear at December 31, 2020.

E23.18 **(LO 2, 4)** **(Partial SCF—Indirect Method)** The accounts below appear in the ledger of Anita Baker Company.

	Retained Earnings	Dr.	Cr.	Bal.
Jan. 1, 2020	Credit Balance			$ 42,000
Aug. 15	Dividends (cash)	$15,000		27,000
Dec. 31	Net Income for 2020		$40,000	67,000

	Equipment	Dr.	Cr.	Bal.
Jan. 1, 2020	Debit Balance			$140,000
Aug. 3	Purchase of Equipment	$62,000		202,000
Sept. 10	Cost of Equipment Constructed	48,000		250,000
Nov. 15	Equipment Sold		$56,000	194,000

	Accumulated Depreciation—Equipment	Dr.	Cr.	Bal.
Jan. 1, 2020	Credit Balance			$ 84,000
Apr. 8	Major Repairs	$21,000		63,000
Nov. 15	Accum. Depreciation on Equipment Sold	25,200		37,800
Dec. 31	Depreciation for 2020		$16,800	54,600

Instructions

From the postings in the accounts above, indicate how the information is reported on a statement of cash flows by preparing a partial statement of cash flows using the indirect method. The loss on sale of equipment (November 15) was $5,800.

E23.19 **(LO 5)** **(Worksheet Analysis of Selected Accounts)** Data for Anita Baker Company are presented in E23.18.

Instructions

Prepare entries in journal form for all adjustments that should be made on a worksheet for a statement of cash flows.

E23.20 **(LO 5)** **(Worksheet Analysis of Selected Transactions)** The transactions below took place during the year 2020.

1. Convertible bonds payable with a par value of $300,000 were exchanged for unissued common stock with a par value of $300,000. The market price of both types of securities was par.
2. The net income for the year was $410,000.
3. Depreciation expense for the building was $90,000.
4. Some old office equipment was traded in on the purchase of some dissimilar office equipment, and the following entry was made.

Equipment	50,000	
Accum. Depreciation—Equipment	30,000	
Equipment		40,000
Cash		34,000
Gain on Disposal of Plant Assets		6,000

The Gain on Disposal of Plant Assets was included in income before income taxes.

5. Dividends in the amount of $123,000 were declared. They are payable in January of next year.

Instructions

Show by journal entries the adjustments that would be made on a worksheet for a statement of cash flows.

E23.21 **(LO 5)** **(Worksheet Preparation)** Below is the comparative balance sheet for Stevie Wonder Corporation.

	Dec. 31, 2020	Dec. 31, 2019
Cash	$ 16,500	$ 21,000
Short-term investments	25,000	19,000
Accounts receivable	43,000	45,000
Allowance for doubtful accounts	(1,800)	(2,000)
Prepaid expenses	4,200	2,500
Inventory	81,500	65,000

	Dec. 31, 2020	Dec. 31, 2019
Land	$ 50,000	$ 50,000
Buildings	125,000	73,500
Accumulated depreciation—buildings	(30,000)	(23,000)
Equipment	53,000	46,000
Accumulated depreciation—equipment	(19,000)	(15,500)
Delivery equipment	39,000	39,000
Accumulated depreciation—delivery equipment	(22,000)	(20,500)
Patents	15,000	-0-
	$379,400	$300,000

	Dec. 31, 2020	Dec. 31, 2019
Accounts payable	$ 26,000	$ 16,000
Short-term notes payable (trade)	4,000	6,000
Accrued payables	3,000	4,600
Mortgage payable	73,000	53,400
Bonds payable	50,000	62,500
Common stock	140,000	102,000
Paid-in capital in excess of par	10,000	4,000
Retained earnings	73,400	51,500
	$379,400	$300,000

Dividends in the amount of $15,000 were declared and paid in 2020.

Instructions

From this information, prepare a worksheet for a statement of cash flows. Make reasonable assumptions as appropriate. The short-term investments are considered available-for-sale debt securities and no unrealized gains or losses have occurred on these securities.

Problems

P23.1 **(LO 2, 4)** **(SCF—Indirect Method)** The following are Sullivan Corp.'s comparative balance sheet accounts at December 31, 2020 and 2019, with a column showing the increase (decrease) from 2019 to 2020.

Comparative Balance Sheets

	2020	2019	Increase (Decrease)
Cash	$ 815,000	$ 700,000	$115,000
Accounts receivable	1,128,000	1,168,000	(40,000)
Inventory	1,850,000	1,715,000	135,000
Property, plant, and equipment	3,307,000	2,967,000	340,000
Accumulated depreciation	(1,165,000)	(1,040,000)	(125,000)
Investment in Myers Co.	310,000	275,000	35,000
Loan receivable	250,000	—	250,000
Total assets	$6,495,000	$5,785,000	$710,000
Accounts payable	$1,015,000	$ 955,000	$ 60,000
Income taxes payable	30,000	50,000	(20,000)
Dividends payable	80,000	100,000	(20,000)
Lease liability	400,000	—	400,000
Common stock, $1 par	500,000	500,000	—
Paid-in capital in excess of par—common stock	1,500,000	1,500,000	—
Retained earnings	2,970,000	2,680,000	290,000
Total liabilities and stockholders' equity	$6,495,000	$5,785,000	$710,000

Additional information:

1. On December 31, 2019, Sullivan acquired 25% of Myers Co.'s common stock for $275,000. On that date, the carrying value of Myers's assets and liabilities, which approximated their fair values, was

$1,100,000. Myers reported income of $140,000 for the year ended December 31, 2020. No dividend was paid on Myers's common stock during the year.

2. During 2020, Sullivan loaned $300,000 to TLC Co., an unrelated company. TLC made the first semi-annual principal repayment of $50,000, plus interest at 10%, on December 31, 2020.
3. On January 2, 2020, Sullivan sold equipment costing $60,000, with a carrying amount of $38,000, for $40,000 cash.
4. On December 31, 2020, Sullivan entered into a capital lease for an office building. The present value of the annual rental payments is $400,000, which equals the fair value of the building. Sullivan made the first rental payment of $60,000 when due on January 2, 2021.
5. Net income for 2020 was $370,000.
6. Sullivan declared and paid the following cash dividends for 2020 and 2019.

	2020	2019
Declared	December 15, 2020	December 15, 2019
Paid	February 28, 2021	February 28, 2020
Amount	$80,000	$100,000

Instructions

Prepare a statement of cash flows for Sullivan Corp. for the year ended December 31, 2020, using the indirect method.

(AICPA adapted)

P23.2 **(LO 2, 4)** Excel Groupwork **(SCF—Indirect Method)** The comparative balance sheets for Hinckley Corporation show the following information.

	December 31	
	2020	2019
Cash	$ 33,500	$13,000
Accounts receivable	12,250	10,000
Inventory	12,000	9,000
Available-for-sale debt investments	–0–	3,000
Buildings	–0–	29,750
Equipment	45,000	20,000
Patents	5,000	6,250
	$107,750	$91,000
Allowance for doubtful accounts	$ 3,000	$ 4,500
Accumulated depreciation—equipment	2,000	4,500
Accumulated depreciation—building	–0–	6,000
Accounts payable	5,000	3,000
Dividends payable	–0–	5,000
Notes payable, short-term (nontrade)	3,000	4,000
Long-term notes payable	31,000	25,000
Common stock	43,000	33,000
Retained earnings	20,750	6,000
	$107,750	$91,000

Additional data related to 2020 are as follows.

1. Equipment that had cost $11,000 and was 40% depreciated at time of disposal was sold for $2,500.
2. $10,000 of the long-term note payable was paid by issuing common stock.
3. Cash dividends paid were $5,000.
4. On January 1, 2020, the building was completely destroyed by a flood. Insurance proceeds on the building were $30,000 (net of $2,000 taxes).
5. Debt investments (available-for-sale) were sold at $1,700 above their cost. The company has made similar sales and investments in the past.
6. Cash was paid for the acquisition of equipment.
7. A long-term note for $16,000 was issued for the acquisition of equipment.
8. Interest of $2,000 and income taxes of $6,500 were paid in cash.

Instructions

Prepare a statement of cash flows using the indirect method.

P23.3 (LO 2) Excel (SCF—Direct Method) Mortonson Company has not yet prepared a statement of cash flows for the 2020 fiscal year. Comparative balance sheets as of December 31, 2019 and 2020, and a statement of income and retained earnings for the year ended December 31, 2020, are presented as follows.

Mortonson Company
Statement of Income and Retained Earnings
For the Year Ended December 31, 2020
($000 omitted)

Sales revenue		$3,800
Expenses		
Cost of goods sold	$1,200	
Salaries and benefits	725	
Heat, light, and power	75	
Depreciation	80	
Property taxes	19	
Patent amortization	25	
Miscellaneous expenses	10	
Interest	30	2,164
Income before income taxes		1,636
Income taxes		818
Net income		818
Retained earnings—Jan. 1, 2020		310
		1,128
Stock dividend declared and issued		600
Retained earnings—Dec. 31, 2020		$ 528

Mortonson Company
Comparative Balance Sheets
As of December 31
($000 omitted)

Assets	2020	2019
Current assets		
Cash	$ 333	$ 100
U.S. Treasury notes (available-for-sale)	10	50
Accounts receivable	780	500
Inventory	720	560
Total current assets	1,843	1,210
Long-term assets		
Land	150	70
Buildings and equipment	910	600
Accumulated depreciation—buildings and equipment	(200)	(120)
Patents (less amortization)	105	130
Total long-term assets	965	680
Total assets	$2,808	$1,890
Liabilities and Stockholders' Equity		
Current liabilities		
Accounts payable	$ 420	$ 330
Income taxes payable	40	30
Notes payable	320	320
Total current liabilities	780	680
Long-term notes payable—due 2022	200	200
Total liabilities	980	880
Stockholders' equity		
Common stock	1,300	700
Retained earnings	528	310
Total stockholders' equity	1,828	1,010
Total liabilities and stockholders' equity	$2,808	$1,890

Instructions

Prepare a statement of cash flows using the direct method. Changes in accounts receivable and accounts payable relate to sales and cost of goods sold. Do not prepare a reconciliation schedule.

(CMA adapted)

P23.4 **(LO 2, 4)** **(SCF—Direct Method)** Michaels Company had available at the end of 2020 the following information.

Michaels Company
Comparative Balance Sheets
As of December 31, 2020 and 2019

	2020	2019
Cash	$ 10,000	$ 4,000
Accounts receivable	20,500	12,950
Short-term investments	22,000	30,000
Inventory	42,000	35,000
Prepaid rent	3,000	12,000
Prepaid insurance	2,100	900
Supplies	1,000	750
Land	125,000	175,000
Buildings	350,000	350,000
Accumulated depreciation—buildings	(105,000)	(87,500)
Equipment	525,000	400,000
Accumulated depreciation—equipment	(130,000)	(112,000)
Patents	45,000	50,000
Total assets	$910,600	$871,100
Accounts payable	$ 22,000	$ 32,000
Income taxes payable	5,000	4,000
Salaries and wages payable	5,000	3,000
Short-term notes payable	10,000	10,000
Long-term notes payable	60,000	70,000
Bonds payable	400,000	400,000
Premium on bonds payable	20,303	25,853
Common stock	240,000	220,000
Paid-in capital in excess of par—common stock	25,000	17,500
Retained earnings	123,297	88,747
Total liabilities and stockholders' equity	$910,600	$871,100

Michaels Company
Income Statement and Dividend Information
For the Year Ended December 31, 2020

Sales revenue		$1,160,000
Cost of goods sold		748,000
Gross margin		412,000
Operating expenses		
Selling expenses	$ 79,200	
Administrative expenses	156,700	
Depreciation/Amortization expense	40,500	
Total operating expenses		276,400
Income from operations		135,600
Other revenues/expenses		
Gain on sale of land	8,000	
Gain on sale of short-term investment	4,000	
Dividend revenue	2,400	
Interest expense	(51,750)	(37,350)
Income before taxes		98,250
Income tax expense		39,400
Net income		58,850
Dividends to common stockholders		(24,300)
To retained earnings		$ 34,550

Instructions

Prepare a statement of cash flows for Michaels Company using the direct method accompanied by a reconciliation schedule. Assume the short-term investments are debt securities, classified as available-for-sale.

P23.5 **(LO 2, 4) (SCF—Indirect Method)** You have completed the field work in connection with your audit of Alexander Corporation for the year ended December 31, 2020. The balance sheet accounts at the beginning and end of the year are shown below.

	Dec. 31, 2020	Dec. 31, 2019	Increase or (Decrease)
Cash	$ 277,900	$ 298,000	($20,100)
Accounts receivable	469,424	353,000	116,424
Inventory	741,700	610,000	131,700
Prepaid expenses	12,000	8,000	4,000
Investment in subsidiary	110,500	–0–	110,500
Cash surrender value of life insurance	2,304	1,800	504
Machinery	207,000	190,000	17,000
Buildings	535,200	407,900	127,300
Land	52,500	52,500	–0–
Patents	69,000	64,000	5,000
Copyrights	40,000	50,000	(10,000)
Bond discount and issue costs	4,502	–0–	4,502
	$2,522,030	$2,035,200	$486,830
Income taxes payable	$ 90,250	$ 79,600	$ 10,650
Accounts payable	299,280	280,000	19,280
Dividends payable	70,000	–0–	70,000
Bonds payable—8%	125,000	–0–	125,000
Bonds payable—12%	–0–	100,000	(100,000)
Allowance for doubtful accounts	35,300	40,000	(4,700)
Accumulated depreciation—buildings	424,000	400,000	24,000
Accumulated depreciation—machinery	173,000	130,000	43,000
Premium on bonds payable	–0–	2,400	(2,400)
Common stock—no par	1,176,200	1,453,200	(277,000)
Paid-in capital in excess of par—common stock	109,000	–0–	109,000
Retained earnings—unappropriated	20,000	(450,000)	470,000
	$2,522,030	$2,035,200	$486,830

Statement of Retained Earnings
For the Year Ended December 31, 2020

January	1, 2020	Balance (deficit)	$(450,000)
March	31, 2020	Net income for first quarter of 2020	25,000
April	1, 2020	Transfer from paid-in capital	425,000
		Balance	–0–
December	31, 2020	Net income for last three quarters of 2020	90,000
		Dividend declared—payable January 21, 2021	(70,000)
		Balance	$ 20,000

Your working papers from the audit contain the following information:

1. On April 1, 2020, the existing deficit was written off against paid-in capital created by reducing the stated value of the no-par stock.
2. On November 1, 2020, 29,600 shares of no-par stock were sold for $257,000. The board of directors voted to regard $5 per share as stated capital.
3. A patent was purchased for $15,000.
4. During the year, machinery that had a cost basis of $16,400 and on which there was accumulated depreciation of $5,200 was sold for $9,000. No other plant assets were sold during the year.
5. The 12%, 20-year bonds were dated and issued on January 2, 2008. Interest was payable on June 30 and December 31. They were sold originally at 106. These bonds were redeemed at 100.9 plus accrued interest on March 31, 2020.

6. The 8%, 40-year bonds were dated January 1, 2020, and were sold on March 31 at 97 plus accrued interest. Interest is payable semiannually on June 30 and December 31. Expense of issuance was $839.
7. Alexander Corporation acquired 70% control in Crimson Company on January 2, 2020, for $100,000. The income statement of Crimson Company for 2020 shows a net income of $15,000.
8. Major repairs to buildings of $7,200 were charged to Accumulated Depreciation—Buildings.
9. Interest paid in 2020 was $10,500 and income taxes paid were $34,000.

Instructions

From the information given, prepare a statement of cash flows using the indirect method. A worksheet is not necessary, but the principal computations should be supported by schedules or general ledger accounts. The company uses straight-line amortization for bond interest.

P23.6 **(LO 2, 3, 4) (SCF—Indirect Method, and Net Cash Flow from Operating Activities, Direct Method)** Comparative balance sheet accounts of Marcus Inc. are presented below.

Marcus Inc.
Comparative Balance Sheet Accounts
As of December 31, 2020 and 2019

	December 31	
Debit Accounts	2020	2019
Cash	$ 42,000	$ 33,750
Accounts Receivable	70,500	60,000
Inventory	30,000	24,000
Equity investments	22,250	38,500
Machinery	30,000	18,750
Buildings	67,500	56,250
Land	7,500	7,500
	$269,750	$238,750
Credit Accounts		
Allowance for Doubtful Accounts	$ 2,250	$ 1,500
Accumulated Depreciation—Machinery	5,625	2,250
Accumulated Depreciation—Buildings	13,500	9,000
Accounts Payable	35,000	24,750
Accrued Payables	3,375	2,625
Long-Term Notes Payable	21,000	31,000
Common Stock, no-par	150,000	125,000
Retained Earnings	39,000	42,625
	$269,750	$238,750

Additional data (ignoring taxes):

1. Net income for the year was $42,500.
2. Cash dividends declared and paid during the year were $21,125.
3. A 20% stock dividend was declared during the year. $25,000 of retained earnings was capitalized.
4. Equity investments (level of ownership is less than 20%) that cost $25,000 were sold during the year for $28,750. No unrealized gains and losses were recorded on these investments in 2020.
5. Machinery that cost $3,750, on which $750 of depreciation had accumulated, was sold for $2,200.

Marcus's 2020 income statement follows (ignoring taxes).

Sales revenue		$540,000
Less: Cost of goods sold		380,000
Gross margin		160,000
Less: Operating expenses (includes $8,625 depreciation and $5,400 bad debts)		120,450
Income from operations		39,550
Other: Gain on sale of investments	$3,750	
Loss on sale of machinery	(800)	2,950
Net income		$ 42,500

Instructions

a. Compute net cash flow from operating activities using the direct method.

b. Prepare a statement of cash flows using the indirect method.

P23.7 **(LO 2, 3, 4)** Groupwork **(SCF—Direct and Indirect Methods from Comparative Financial Statements)** Chapman Company, a major retailer of bicycles and accessories, operates several stores and is a publicly traded company. The comparative balance sheet and income statement for Chapman as of May 31, 2020, are as follows. The company is preparing its statement of cash flows.

Chapman Company
Comparative Balance Sheet
As of May 31

	2020	2019
Current assets		
Cash	$ 28,250	$ 20,000
Accounts receivable	75,000	58,000
Inventory	220,000	250,000
Prepaid expenses	9,000	7,000
Total current assets	332,250	335,000
Plant assets		
Plant assets	600,000	502,000
Less: Accumulated depreciation—plant assets	150,000	125,000
Net plant assets	450,000	377,000
Total assets	$782,250	$712,000
Current liabilities		
Accounts payable	$123,000	$115,000
Salaries and wages payable	47,250	72,000
Interest payable	27,000	25,000
Total current liabilities	197,250	212,000
Long-term debt		
Bonds payable	70,000	100,000
Total liabilities	267,250	312,000
Stockholders' equity		
Common stock, $10 par	370,000	280,000
Retained earnings	145,000	120,000
Total stockholders' equity	515,000	400,000
Total liabilities and stockholders' equity	$782,250	$712,000

Chapman Company
Income Statement
For the Year Ended May 31, 2020

Sales revenue	$1,255,250
Cost of goods sold	722,000
Gross profit	533,250
Expenses	
Salaries and wages expense	252,100
Interest expense	75,000
Depreciation expense	25,000
Other expenses	8,150
Total expenses	360,250
Operating income	173,000
Income tax expense	43,000
Net income	$ 130,000

The following is additional information concerning Chapman's transactions during the year ended May 31, 2020.

1. All sales during the year were made on account.
2. All merchandise was purchased on account, comprising the total accounts payable account.
3. Plant assets costing $98,000 were purchased by paying $28,000 in cash and issuing 7,000 shares of stock.
4. The "other expenses" are related to prepaid items.
5. All income taxes incurred during the year were paid during the year.
6. In order to supplement its cash, Chapman issued 2,000 shares of common stock at par value.
7. Cash dividends of $105,000 were declared and paid at the end of the fiscal year.

Instructions

a. Compare and contrast the direct method and the indirect method for reporting cash flows from operating activities.

b. Prepare a statement of cash flows for Chapman Company for the year ended May 31, 2020, using the direct method. Be sure to support the statement with appropriate calculations. (A reconciliation of net income to net cash provided is not required.)

c. Using the indirect method, calculate only the net cash flow from operating activities for Chapman Company for the year ended May 31, 2020.

P23.8 **(LO 2, 4)** **(SCF—Direct and Indirect Methods)** Comparative balance sheet accounts of Sharpe Company are presented below.

Sharpe Company
Comparative Balance Sheet Accounts
As of December 31

Debit Balances	2020	2019
Cash	$ 70,000	$ 51,000
Accounts Receivable	155,000	130,000
Inventory	75,000	61,000
Debt investments (available-for-sale)	55,000	85,000
Equipment	70,000	48,000
Buildings	145,000	145,000
Land	40,000	25,000
Totals	$610,000	$545,000
Credit Balances		
Allowance for Doubtful Accounts	$ 10,000	$ 8,000
Accumulated Depreciation—Equipment	21,000	14,000
Accumulated Depreciation—Buildings	37,000	28,000
Accounts Payable	66,000	60,000
Income Taxes Payable	12,000	10,000
Long-Term Notes Payable	62,000	70,000
Common Stock	310,000	260,000
Retained Earnings	92,000	95,000
Totals	$610,000	$545,000

Additional data:

1. Equipment that cost $10,000 and was 60% depreciated was sold in 2020.
2. Cash dividends were declared and paid during the year.
3. Common stock was issued in exchange for land.
4. Debt investments that cost $35,000 were sold during the year.
5. There were no write-offs of uncollectible accounts during the year.

Sharpe's 2020 income statement is as follows.

Sales revenue		$950,000
Less: Cost of goods sold		600,000
Gross profit		350,000
Less: Operating expenses (includes depreciation expense and bad debt expense)		250,000
Income from operations		100,000
Other revenues and expenses		
Gain on sale of investments	$15,000	
Loss on sale of equipment	(3,000)	12,000
Income before taxes		112,000
Income taxes		45,000
Net income		$ 67,000

Instructions

a. Compute net cash provided by operating activities under the direct method.

b. Prepare a statement of cash flows using the indirect method.

P23.9 **(LO 2, 4)** **(Indirect SCF)** Dingel Corporation has contracted with you to prepare a statement of cash flows. The controller has provided the following information.

	December 31	
	2020	2019
Cash	$ 38,500	$13,000
Accounts receivable	12,250	10,000
Inventory	12,000	10,000
Equity investments	-0-	3,000
Buildings	-0-	29,750
Equipment	40,000	20,000
Copyrights	5,000	5,250
Totals	$107,750	$91,000
Allowance for doubtful accounts	$ 3,000	$ 4,500
Accumulated depreciation—equipment	2,000	4,500
Accumulated depreciation—buildings	-0-	6,000
Accounts payable	5,000	4,000
Dividends payable	-0-	5,000
Notes payable, short-term (nontrade)	3,000	4,000
Long-term notes payable	36,000	25,000
Common stock	38,000	33,000
Retained earnings	20,750	5,000
	$107,750	$91,000

Additional data related to 2020 are as follows.

1. Equipment that had cost $11,000 and was 30% depreciated at time of disposal was sold for $2,500.
2. $5,000 of the long-term note payable was paid by issuing common stock.
3. Cash dividends paid were $5,000.
4. On January 1, 2020, the building was completely destroyed by a flood. Insurance proceeds on the building were $33,000 (net of $4,000 taxes).
5. Equity investments (ownership is less than 20% of total shares) were sold at $1,500 above their cost. No unrealized gains or losses were recorded in 2020.
6. Cash and a long-term note for $16,000 were given for the acquisition of equipment.
7. Interest of $2,000 and income taxes of $5,000 were paid in cash.

Instructions

a. Use the indirect method to analyze the above information and prepare a statement of cash flows for Dingel.

b. What would you expect to observe in the operating, investing, and financing sections of a statement of cash flows of:

1. A severely financially troubled firm?
2. A recently formed firm that is experiencing rapid growth?

Concepts for Analysis

CA23.1 **(LO 2, 4)** **Writing** **(Analysis of Improper SCF)** The following statement was prepared by Maloney Corporation's accountant.

Maloney Corporation
Statement of Sources and Application of Cash
For the Year Ended September 30, 2020

Sources of cash	
Net income	$111,000
Depreciation and depletion	70,000
Increase in long-term debt	179,000
Changes in current receivables and inventories, less current liabilities (excluding current maturities of long-term debt)	14,000
	$374,000
Application of cash	
Cash dividends	$ 60,000
Expenditure for property, plant, and equipment	214,000
Investments and other uses	20,000
Change in cash	80,000
	$374,000

The following additional information relating to Maloney Corporation is available for the year ended September 30, 2020.

1. Salaries and wages expense attributable to stock option plans was $25,000 for the year.
2. Expenditures for property, plant, and equipment — $250,000
   Proceeds from retirements of property, plant, and equipment — 36,000
   Net expenditures — $214,000
3. A stock dividend of 10,000 shares of Maloney Corporation common stock was distributed to common stockholders on April 1, 2020, when the per share market price was $7 and par value was $1.
4. On July 1, 2020, when its market price was $6 per share, 16,000 shares of Maloney Corporation common stock were issued in exchange for 4,000 shares of preferred stock.
5. Depreciation expense — $ 65,000
   Depletion expense — 5,000
   — $ 70,000
6. Increase in long-term debt — $620,000
   Less: Redemption of debt — 441,000
   Net increase — $179,000

Instructions

a. In general, what are the objectives of a statement of the type shown above for Maloney Corporation? Explain.

b. Identify the weaknesses in the form and format of Maloney Corporation's statement of cash flows without reference to the additional information. (Assume adoption of the indirect method.)

c. For each of the six items of additional information for the statement of cash flows, indicate the preferable treatment and explain why the suggested treatment is preferable.

(AICPA adapted)

CA23.2 **(LO 2, 4)** **Groupwork** **(SCF Theory and Analysis of Improper SCF)** Teresa Ramirez and Lenny Traylor are examining the following statement of cash flows for Pacific Clothing Store's first year of operations.

Pacific Clothing Store Statement of Cash Flows For the Year Ended January 31, 2020	
Sources of cash	
From sales of merchandise	$ 382,000
From sale of common stock	380,000
From sale of investment	120,000
From depreciation	80,000
From issuance of note for truck	30,000
From interest on investments	8,000
Total sources of cash	1,000,000
Uses of cash	
For purchase of fixtures and equipment	330,000
For merchandise purchased for resale	253,000
For operating expenses (including depreciation)	170,000
For purchase of investment	95,000
For purchase of truck by issuance of note	30,000
For purchase of treasury stock	10,000
For interest on note	3,000
Total uses of cash	891,000
Net increase in cash	$ 109,000

Teresa claims that Pacific's statement of cash flows is an excellent portrayal of a superb first year, with cash increasing $109,000. Lenny replies that it was not a superb first year—that the year was an operating failure, the statement was incorrectly presented, and $109,000 is not the actual increase in cash.

Instructions

a. With whom do you agree, Teresa or Lenny? Explain your position.

b. Using the data provided, prepare a statement of cash flows in proper indirect method form. The only noncash items in income are depreciation and the gain from the sale of the investment (purchase and sale are related).

CA23.3 **(LO 2, 4)** **(SCF Theory and Analysis of Transactions)** Ashley Company is a young and growing producer of electronic measuring instruments and technical equipment. You have been retained by Ashley to advise it in the preparation of a statement of cash flows using the indirect method. For the fiscal year ended October 31, 2020, you have obtained the following information concerning certain events and transactions of Ashley.

1. The amount of reported earnings for the fiscal year was $700,000, which included a deduction for a loss of $110,000 (see item 5 below).
2. Depreciation expense of $315,000 was included in the income statement.
3. Uncollectible accounts receivable of $40,000 were written off against the allowance for doubtful accounts. Also, $51,000 of bad debt expense was included in determining income for the fiscal year, and the same amount was added to the allowance for doubtful accounts.
4. A gain of $6,000 was realized on the sale of a machine. It originally cost $75,000, of which $30,000 was undepreciated on the date of sale.
5. On April 1, 2020, lightning caused an uninsured building loss of $110,000 ($180,000 loss, less reduction in income taxes of $70,000). This loss was included in determining income as indicated in item 1 above.
6. On July 3, 2020, building and land were purchased for $700,000. Ashley gave in payment $75,000 cash, $200,000 market price of its unissued common stock, and signed a $425,000 mortgage note payable.
7. On August 3, 2020, $800,000 face value of Ashley's 10% convertible debentures was converted into $150,000 par value of its common stock. The bonds were originally issued at face value.

Instructions

Explain whether each of the seven numbered items above is a cash inflow or outflow, and explain how it should be disclosed in Ashley's statement of cash flows for the fiscal year ended October 31, 2020. If any item is neither an inflow nor an outflow of cash, explain why it is not, and indicate the disclosure, if any, that should be made of the item in Ashley's statement of cash flows for the fiscal year ended October 31, 2020.

CA23.4 **(LO 2, 4)** **Groupwork** **(Analysis of Transactions' Effect on SCF)** Each of the following items must be considered in preparing a statement of cash flows for Cruz Fashions Inc. for the year ended December 31, 2020.

1. Fixed assets that had cost $20,000 6½ years before and were being depreciated on a 10-year basis, with no estimated scrap value, were sold for $4,750.
2. During the year, goodwill of $15,000 was considered impaired and was completely written off to expense.
3. During the year, 500 shares of common stock with a stated value of $25 a share were issued for $32 a share.
4. The company sustained a net loss for the year of $2,100. Depreciation amounted to $2,000 and patent amortization was $400.
5. Uncollectible accounts receivable in the amount of $2,000 were written off against Allowance for Doubtful Accounts.
6. Debt investments (available-for-sale) that cost $12,000 when purchased 4 years earlier were sold for $10,600.
7. Bonds payable with a par value of $24,000 on which there was an unamortized bond premium of $2,000 were redeemed at 101.

Instructions

For each item, state where it is to be shown in the statement and then how you would present the necessary information, including the amount. Consider each item to be independent of the others. Assume that correct entries were made for all transactions as they took place.

CA23.5 **(LO 1, 2)** **(Purpose and Elements of SCF)** GAAP requires the statement of cash flows be presented when financial statements are prepared.

Instructions

a. Explain the purposes of the statement of cash flows.
b. List and describe the three categories of activities that must be reported in the statement of cash flows.
c. Identify and describe the two methods that are allowed for reporting cash flows from operations.
d. Describe the financial statement presentation of noncash investing and financing transactions. Include in your description an example of a noncash investing and financing transaction.

CA23.6 **(LO 1, 2, 3)** **Ethics** **(Cash Flow Reporting)** Brockman Guitar Company is in the business of manufacturing top-quality, steel-string folk guitars. In recent years, the company has experienced working capital problems resulting from the procurement of factory equipment, the unanticipated buildup of receivables and inventories, and the payoff of a balloon mortgage on a new manufacturing facility. The founder and president of the company, Barbara Brockman, has attempted to raise cash from various financial institutions, but to no avail because of the company's poor performance in recent years. In particular, the company's lead bank, First Financial, is especially concerned about Brockman's inability to maintain a positive cash position. The commercial loan officer from First Financial told Barbara, "I can't even consider your request for capital financing unless I see that your company is able to generate positive cash flows from operations."

Thinking about the banker's comment, Barbara came up with what she believes is a good plan: With a more attractive statement of cash flows, the bank might be willing to provide long-term financing. To "window dress" cash flows, the company can sell its accounts receivables to factors and liquidate its raw materials inventories. These rather costly transactions would generate lots of cash. As the chief accountant for Brockman Guitar, it is your job to tell Barbara what you think of her plan.

Instructions

Answer the following questions.

a. What are the ethical issues related to Barbara Brockman's idea?
b. What would you tell Barbara Brockman?

Using Your Judgment

Financial Reporting Problem

The Procter & Gamble Company (P&G)

The financial statements of **P&G** are presented in Appendix B. The company's complete annual report, including the notes to the financial statements, is available online.

Instructions

Refer to P&G's financial statements and the accompanying notes to answer the following questions.

a. Which method of computing net cash provided by operating activities does P&G use? What were the amounts of net cash provided by operating activities for the years 2015, 2016, and 2017? Which two items were most responsible for the decrease in net cash provided by operating activities in 2017?

b. What was the most significant item in the cash flows used for investing activities section in 2017? What was the most significant item in the cash flows used for financing activities section in 2017?

c. Where is "deferred income taxes" reported in P&G's statement of cash flows? Why does it appear in that section of the statement of cash flows?

d. Where is depreciation reported in P&G's statement of cash flows? Why is depreciation added to net income in the statement of cash flows?

Comparative Analysis Case

The Coca-Cola Company and PepsiCo, Inc.

The financial statements of **Coca-Cola** and **PepsiCo** are presented in Appendices C and D, respectively. The companies' complete annual reports, including the notes to the financial statements, are available online.

Instructions

Use the companies' financial information to answer the following questions.

a. What method of computing net cash provided by operating activities does Coca-Cola use? What method does PepsiCo use? What were the amounts of cash provided by operating activities reported by Coca-Cola and PepsiCo in 2017?

b. What was the most significant item reported by Coca-Cola and PepsiCo in 2017 in their investing activities sections? What is the most significant item reported by Coca-Cola and PepsiCo in 2017 in their financing activities sections?

c. What were these two companies' trends in net cash provided by operating activities over the period 2015 to 2017?

d. Where is "depreciation and amortization" reported by Coca-Cola and PepsiCo in their statements of cash flows? What is the amount and why does it appear in that section of the statement of cash flows?

e. Based on the information contained in Coca-Cola's and PepsiCo's financial statements, compute the following 2017 ratios for each company. These ratios require the use of statement of cash flows data. (These ratios were covered in Chapter 5.)

1. Current cash debt coverage.
2. Cash debt coverage.

f. What conclusions concerning the management of cash can be drawn from the ratios computed in (e)?

Financial Statement Analysis Case

Vermont Teddy Bear Co.

Founded in the early 1980s, the **Vermont Teddy Bear Co.** designs and manufactures American-made teddy bears and markets them primarily as gifts called Bear-Grams or Teddy Bear-Grams. Bear-Grams are personalized teddy bears delivered directly to the recipient for special occasions such as birthdays and anniversaries. The Shelburne, Vermont, company's primary markets are New York, Boston, and Chicago. Sales have jumped dramatically in recent years. Such dramatic growth has significant implications for cash flows. Provided below are the cash flow statements for two recent years for the company.

	Current Year	Prior Year
Cash flows from operating activities:		
Net income	$ 17,523	$ 838,955
Adjustments to reconcile net income to net cash provided by operating activities		
Deferred income taxes	(69,524)	(146,590)
Depreciation and amortization	316,416	181,348
Changes in assets and liabilities:		
Accounts receivable, trade	(38,267)	(25,947)
Inventories	(1,599,014)	(1,289,293)
Prepaid and other current assets	(444,794)	(113,205)
Deposits and other assets	(24,240)	(83,044)
Accounts payable	2,017,059	(284,567)
Accrued expenses	61,321	170,755
Accrued interest payable, debentures	—	(58,219)
Other	—	(8,960)
Income taxes payable	—	117,810
Net cash provided by (used for) operating activities	236,480	(700,957)
Net cash used for investing activities	(2,102,892)	(4,422,953)
Net cash (used for) provided by financing activities	(315,353)	9,685,435
Net change in cash and cash equivalents	$(2,181,765)	$ 4,561,525
Other information:		
Current liabilities	$ 4,055,465	$ 1,995,600
Total liabilities	4,620,085	2,184,386
Net sales	20,560,566	17,025,856

Instructions

a. Note that net income in the current year was only $17,523 compared to prior-year income of $838,955, but net cash flow from operating activities was $236,480 in the current year and a negative $700,957 in the prior year. Explain the causes of this apparent paradox.

b. Evaluate Vermont Teddy Bear's liquidity, solvency, and profitability for the current year using cash flow-based ratios.

Accounting, Analysis, and Principles

The income statement for the year ended December 31, 2020, for Laskowski Manufacturing Company contains the following condensed information.

Laskowski Co.
Income Statement

Revenues		$6,583,000
Operating expenses (excluding depreciation)	$4,920,000	
Depreciation expense	880,000	5,800,000
Income before income tax		783,000
Income tax expense		353,000
Net income		$ 430,000

Included in operating expenses is a $24,000 loss resulting from the sale of machinery for $270,000 cash. The company purchased machinery at a cost of $750,000.

Laskowski reports the following balances on its comparative balance sheets at December 31.

Laskowski Co.
Comparative Balance Sheets (partial)

	2020	2019
Cash	$672,000	$130,000
Accounts receivable	775,000	610,000
Inventory	834,000	867,000
Accounts payable	521,000	501,000

Income tax expense of $353,000 represents the amount paid in 2020. Dividends declared and paid in 2020 totaled $200,000.

Accounting

Prepare the statement of cash flows using the indirect method.

Analysis

Laskowski has an aggressive growth plan, which will require significant investments in plant and equipment over the next several years. Preliminary plans call for an investment of over $500,000 in the next year. Compute Laskowski's free cash flow (from Chapter 5) and use it to evaluate the investment plans with the use of only internally generated funds.

Principles

How does the statement of cash flows contribute to achieving the objective of financial reporting?

Bridge to the Profession

FASB Codification References

[1] FASB ASC 230-10-10-2. [Predecessor literature: "The Statement of Cash Flows," *Statement of Financial Accounting Standards No. 95* (Stamford, Conn.: FASB, 1987), paras. 4 and 5.]

[2] FASB ASC 230-10-45-18 through 21. [Predecessor literature: "Statement of Cash Flows—Exemption of Certain Enterprises and Classification of Cash Flows from Certain Securities Acquired for Resale (amended)," *Statement of Financial Accounting Standards No. 102* (February 1989).]

[3] FASB ASC 230-10-45-25. [Predecessor literature: "Statement of Cash Flows," *Statement of Financial Accounting Standards No. 95* (Stamford, Conn.: FASB, 1987), paras. 107 and 111.]

[4] FASB ASC 230-10-45-31. [Predecessor literature: "The Statement of Cash Flows," *Statement of Financial Accounting Standards No. 95* (Stamford, Conn.: FASB, 1987), paras. 27 and 30.]

[5] FASB ASC 230-10-45-14. [Predecessor literature: "Share-Based Payment," *Statement of Financial Accounting Standard No. 123(R)* (Norwalk, Conn.: FASB, 2004), par. 68.]

[6] FASB ASC 230-10 with a link to transition paragraph 230-10-65-2. [Predecessor literature: None.]

[7] FASB ASC 320-10-45-11. [Predecessor literature: "Accounting for Certain Investments in Debt and Equity Securities," *Statement of Financial Accounting Standards No. 115* (Norwalk, Conn.: 1993), par. 118.]

[8] FASB ASC 320-10-45-11. [Predecessor literature: "Accounting for Certain Investments in Debt and Equity Securities," *Statement of Financial Accounting Standards No. 115* (Norwalk, Conn.: 1993), par. 118.]

Codification Exercises

If your school has a subscription to the FASB Codification, log in and prepare responses to the following. Provide Codification references for your responses.

CE23.1 Access the glossary ("Master Glossary") to answer the following.

a. What are cash equivalents?

b. What are financing activities?

c. What are investing activities?

d. What are operating activities?

CE23.2 Name five cash inflows that would qualify as a "financing activity."

CE23.3 How should cash flows from purchases, sales, and maturities of available-for-sale debt securities be classified and reported in the statement of cash flows?

CE23.4 Do companies need to disclose information about investing and financing activities that do not affect cash receipts or cash payments? If so, how should such information be disclosed?

Codification Research Case

As part of the year-end accounting process for your company, you are preparing the statement of cash flows according to GAAP. One of your team, a finance major, believes the statement should be prepared to report the change in working capital, because analysts many times use working capital in ratio analysis. Your supervisor would like research conducted to verify the basis for preparing the statement of cash flows.

Instructions

If your school has a subscription to the FASB Codification, log in and prepare responses to the following. Provide Codification references for your responses.

a. What is the primary objective for the statement of cash flows? Is working capital the basis for meeting this objective?

b. What information is provided in a statement of cash flows?

c. List some of the typical cash inflows and outflows from operations.

Additional Professional Resources

Go to WileyPLUS for other career-readiness resources, such as career coaching, internship opportunities, and CPAexcel prep.

IFRS Insights

LEARNING OBJECTIVE 6

Compare the statement of cash flows under GAAP and IFRS.

As in GAAP, the statement of cash flows is a required statement for IFRS. In addition, the content and presentation of a U.S. statement of cash flows is similar to one used for IFRS. However, the disclosure requirements related to the statement of cash flows are more extensive under GAAP. *IAS* 7 ("Cash Flow Statements") provides the overall IFRS requirements for cash flow information.

Relevant Facts

Following are the key similarities and differences between GAAP and IFRS related to the statement of cash flows.

Similarities

- Both GAAP and IFRS require that companies prepare a statement of cash flows.
- Both IFRS and GAAP require that the statement of cash flows should have three major sections—operating, investing, and financing—along with changes in cash and cash equivalents.
- Similar to GAAP, the cash flow statement can be prepared using either the indirect or direct method under IFRS. For both IFRS and GAAP, most companies use the indirect method for reporting net cash flow from operating activities.
- The definition of cash equivalents used in IFRS is similar to that used in GAAP.

Differences

- A major difference in the definition of cash and cash equivalents is that in certain situations, bank overdrafts are considered part of cash and cash equivalents under IFRS (which is not the case in GAAP). Under GAAP, bank overdrafts are classified as financing activities.
- IFRS requires that non-cash investing and financing activities be excluded from the statement of cash flows. Instead, these non-cash activities should be reported elsewhere. This requirement is interpreted to mean that non-cash investing and financing activities should be disclosed in the notes to the financial statements instead of in the financial statements. Under GAAP, companies may present this information in the cash flow statement.
- One area where there can be substantive differences between IFRS and GAAP relates to the classification of interest, dividends, and taxes. IFRS provides more alternatives for disclosing these items, while GAAP requires that except for dividends paid (which are classified as a financing activity), these items are all reported as operating activities.

About the Numbers

Significant Non-Cash Transactions

Because the statement of cash flows reports only the effects of operating, investing, and financing activities in terms of cash flows, it omits some **significant non-cash transactions** and other events that are investing or financing activities. Among the more common of these non-cash transactions that a company should report or disclose in some manner are the following.

1. Acquisition of assets by assuming liabilities (including finance lease obligations) or by issuing equity securities.
2. Exchanges of non-monetary assets.
3. Refinancing of long-term debt.
4. Conversion of debt or preference shares to ordinary shares.
5. Issuance of equity securities to retire debt.

Investing and financing transactions that do not require the use of cash are excluded from the statement of cash flows. If material in amount, these disclosures may be either narrative or summarized in a separate schedule. This schedule may appear in a separate note or supplementary schedule to the financial statements.

Illustration IFRS23.1 shows the presentation of these significant non-cash transactions or other events in a separate schedule in the notes to the financial statements.

ILLUSTRATION IFRS23.1

Note Presentation of Non-Cash Investing and Financing Activities

Note G: Significant non-cash transactions. During the year, the company engaged in the following significant non-cash investing and financing transactions:

Issued 250,000 ordinary shares to purchase land and building	$1,750,000
Exchanged land in Steadfast, New York, for land in Bedford, Pennsylvania	$2,000,000
Converted 7% bonds to 50,000 ordinary shares	$ 500,000

Companies do not generally report certain other significant non-cash transactions or other events in conjunction with the statement of cash flows. Examples of these types of transactions are **share dividends, share splits, and restrictions on retained earnings**. Companies generally report these items, neither financing nor investing activities, in conjunction with the statement of changes in equity or schedules and notes pertaining to changes in equity accounts.

Special Disclosures

IAS 7 indicates that cash flows related to interest received and paid, and dividends received and paid, should be separately disclosed in the statement of cash flows. IFRS allows flexibility in how these items are classified in the statement of cash flows. However, each item should be classified in a consistent manner from period to period as operating, investing, or financing cash flows. *For homework purposes, classify interest received and paid and dividends received as part of cash flows from operating activities and dividends paid as cash flows from financing activities.* The justification for reporting the first three items in cash flows from operating activities is that each item affects net income. Dividends paid, however, do not affect net income and are often considered a cost of financing.

Companies should also disclose income taxes paid separately in the cash flows from operating activities unless they can be separately identified as part of investing or financing activities. While tax expense may be readily identifiable with investing or financing activities, the related tax cash flows are often impracticable to identify and may arise in a different period from the cash flows of the underlying transaction. Therefore, taxes paid are usually classified as cash flows from operating activities. IFRS requires that the cash paid for taxes, as well as cash flows from interest and dividends received and paid, be disclosed. The category (operating, investing, or financing) that each item was included in must be disclosed as well.

An example of such a disclosure from the notes to **Daimler**'s financial statements is provided in **Illustration IFRS23.2**.

ILLUSTRATION IFRS23.2

Note Disclosure of Interest, Taxes, and Dividends

Daimler

Cash flows included in cash used for/provided by operating activities:

(In millions of euros)	2017	2016
Interest paid	(304)	(299)
Interest received	187	211
Dividends received from equity-method investments	843	103
Dividends received from other shareholdings	52	85

Other companies choose to report these items directly in the statement of cash flows. In many cases, companies start with income before income taxes and then show income taxes paid as a separate item. In addition, they often add back interest expense on an accrual basis and then subtract interest paid. Reporting these items in the operating activities section is shown for Mermel Company in **Illustration IFRS23.3**.

ILLUSTRATION IFRS23.3

Reporting of Interest, Taxes, and Dividends in the Operating Section

Mermel Company
Statement of Cash Flows ($000,000)
(Operating Activities Section Only)

Income before income tax		$ 4,000
Adjustments to reconcile income before income tax to net cash provided by operating activities:		
Depreciation expense	$1,000	
Interest expense	500	
Investment revenue (dividends)	(650)	
Decrease in inventories	1,050	
Increase in trade receivables	(310)	1,590
Cash generated from operations		5,590
Interest paid	(300)	
Income taxes paid	(760)	(1,060)
Net cash provided by operating activities		$ 4,530

Companies often provide a separate section to identify interest and income taxes paid.

On the Horizon

The IASB and the FASB have worked on a project on the presentation and organization of information in the financial statements. With respect to the cash flow statement specifically, the notion of *cash equivalents* will probably not be retained. The definition of cash in the existing literature would be retained, and the statement of cash flows would present information on changes in cash only. In addition, the IASB and FASB favor presentation of operating cash flows using the direct method only. This approach is generally opposed by the preparer community. The project is currently on hold.

IFRS Self-Test Questions

1. Which of the following is **true** regarding the statement of cash flows under IFRS?

 a. The statement of cash flows has two major sections—operating and non-operating.

 b. The statement of cash flows has two major sections—financing and investing.

 c. The statement of cash flows has three major sections—operating, investing, and financing.

 d. The statement of cash flows has three major sections—operating, non-operating, and financing.

2. In the case of a bank overdraft:

 a. GAAP typically includes the amount in cash and cash equivalents.

 b. IFRS typically includes the amount in cash equivalents but not in cash.

 c. GAAP typically treats the overdraft as a liability, and reports the amount in the financing section of the statement of cash flows.

 d. IFRS typically treats the overdraft as a liability, and reports the amount in the investing section of the statement of cash flows.

3. Under IFRS, significant non-cash transactions:

 a. are classified as operating, if they are related to income items.

 b. are excluded from the statement of cash flows and disclosed in a narrative form or summarized in a separate schedule.

 c. are classified as an investing or financing activity.

 d. are classified as an operating activity, unless they can be specifically identified with financing or investing activities.

4. For purposes of the statement of cash flows, under IFRS interest paid is treated as:

 a. an operating activity in all cases.

 b. an investing or operating activity, depending on use of the borrowed funds.

 c. either a financing or investing activity.

 d. either an operating or financing activity, but treated consistently from period to period.

5. For purposes of the statement of cash flows, under IFRS income taxes paid are treated as:

 a. cash flows from operating activities unless they can be separately identified as part of investing or financing activities.

 b. an operating activity in all cases.

 c. an investing or operating activity, depending on whether a refund is received.

 d. either operating, financing, or investing activity, but treated consistently to other companies in the same industry.

IFRS Concepts and Application

IFRS23.1 Where can authoritative IFRS related to the statement of cash flows be found?

IFRS23.2 Briefly describe some of the similarities and differences between GAAP and IFRS with respect to cash flow reporting.

IFRS23.3 What are some of the key obstacles for the FASB and IASB within their accounting guidance in the area of cash flow reporting? Explain.

IFRS23.4 Stan Conner and Mark Stein were discussing the statement of cash flows of Bombeck Co. In the notes to the statement of cash flows was a schedule entitled "Non-cash investing and financing activities." Give three examples of significant non-cash transactions that would be reported in this schedule.

IFRS23.5 Springsteen Co. had the following activity in its most recent year of operations.

- **a.** Pension expense exceeds amount funded.
- **b.** Redemption of bonds payable.
- **c.** Sale of building at book value.
- **d.** Depreciation.
- **e.** Exchange of equipment for furniture.
- **f.** Issuance of ordinary shares.
- **g.** Amortization of intangible assets.
- **h.** Purchase of treasury shares.
- **i.** Issuance of bonds for land.
- **j.** Payment of dividends.
- **k.** Increase in interest receivable on notes receivable.
- **l.** Purchase of equipment.

Instructions

Classify the items as (1) operating—add to net income, (2) operating—deduct from net income, (3) investing, (4) financing, or (5) significant non-cash investing and financing activities. Use the indirect method.

IFRS23.6 Following are selected statement of financial position accounts of Sander Bros. Corp. at December 31, 2020 and 2019, and the increases or decreases in each account from 2019 to 2020. Also presented is selected income statement information for the year ended December 31, 2020, and additional information.

Selected statement of financial position accounts	2020	2019	Increase (Decrease)
Assets			
Property, plant, and equipment	$277,000	$247,000	$30,000
Accumulated depreciation	(178,000)	(167,000)	(11,000)
Accounts receivable	34,000	24,000	10,000
Equity and liabilities			
Share capital—ordinary, $1 par	$ 22,000	$ 19,000	$ 3,000
Share premium—ordinary	9,000	3,000	6,000
Retained earnings	104,000	91,000	13,000
Bonds payable	49,000	46,000	3,000
Dividends payable	8,000	5,000	3,000

Selected income statement information for the year ended December 31, 2020

Sales revenue	$155,000
Depreciation	38,000
Gain on sale of equipment	14,500
Net income	31,000

Additional information:

1. During 2020, equipment costing $45,000 was sold for cash.
2. Accounts receivable relate to sales of merchandise.
3. During 2020, $25,000 of bonds payable were issued in exchange for property, plant, and equipment.

There was no amortization of bond discount or premium.

Instructions

Determine the category (operating, investing, or financing) and the amount that should be reported in the statement of cash flows for the following items.

- **a.** Payments for purchase of property, plant, and equipment.
- **b.** Proceeds from the sale of equipment.

c. Cash dividends paid.

d. Redemption of bonds payable.

IFRS23.7 Dingel Corporation has contracted with you to prepare a statement of cash flows. The controller has provided the following information.

	December 31	
	2020	2019
Buildings	$ -0-	$29,750
Equipment	45,000	20,000
Patents	5,000	6,250
Investments	-0-	3,000
Inventory	12,000	9,000
Accounts receivable	12,250	10,000
Cash	33,500	13,000
	$107,750	$91,000
Share capital—ordinary	$ 43,000	$33,000
Retained earnings	20,750	6,000
Allowance for doubtful accounts	3,000	4,500
Accumulated depreciation on equipment	2,000	4,500
Accumulated depreciation on buildings	-0-	6,000
Accounts payable	5,000	3,000
Dividends payable	-0-	5,000
Long-term notes payable	31,000	25,000
Notes payable, short-term (non-trade)	3,000	4,000
	$107,750	$91,000

Additional data related to 2020 are as follows.

1. Equipment that had cost $11,000 and was 40% depreciated at time of disposal was sold for $2,500.
2. $10,000 of the long-term notes payable was paid by issuing ordinary shares.
3. Cash dividends paid were $5,000.
4. On January 1, 2020, the building was completely destroyed by a flood. Insurance proceeds on the building were $32,000.
5. Equity investments (non-trading) were sold at $1,700 above their cost.
6. Cash was paid for the acquisition of equipment.
7. A long-term note for $16,000 was issued for the acquisition of equipment.
8. Interest of $2,000 and income taxes of $6,500 were paid in cash.

Instructions

Prepare a statement of cash flows using the indirect method.

Professional Research

IFRS23.8 As part of the year-end accounting process for your company, you are preparing the statement of cash flows according to IFRS. One of your team, a finance major, believes the statement should be prepared to report the change in working capital because analysts many times use working capital in ratio analysis. Your supervisor would like research conducted to verify the basis for preparing the statement of cash flows.

Instructions

Access the IFRS authoritative literature at the IASB website. (Click on the IFRS tab and then register for free eIFRS access if necessary.) When you have accessed the documents, you can use the search tool in your Internet browser to respond to the following questions. (Provide paragraph citations.)

a. What is the primary objective for the statement of cash flows? Is working capital the basis for meeting this objective?

b. What information is provided in a statement of cash flows?

c. List some of the typical cash inflows and outflows from operations.

International Financial Reporting Problem

Marks and Spencer plc (M&S)

IFRS23.9 The financial statements of **M&S** are presented in Appendix E. The company's complete annual report, including the notes to the financial statements, is available online.

Instructions

Refer to M&S's financial statements and the accompanying notes to answer the following questions.

a. Which method of computing net cash provided by operating activities does M&S use? What were the amounts of net cash provided by operating activities for the years 2016 and 2017? Which two items were most responsible for the increase in net cash provided by operating activities in 2017?

b. What was the most significant item in the cash flows used for investing activities section in 2017? What was the most significant item in the cash flows used for financing activities section in 2017?

c. Where is "deferred income taxes" reported in M&S's statement of cash flows? Why does it appear in that section of the statement of cash flows?

d. Where is depreciation reported in M&S's statement of cash flows? Why is depreciation added to net income in the statement of cash flows?

Answers to IFRS Self-Test Questions

1. c **2.** c **3.** b **4.** d **5.** a

CHAPTER **24**

© andersphoto/Shutterstock

Full Disclosure in Financial Reporting

LEARNING OBJECTIVES

After studying this chapter, you should be able to:

1. Review the full disclosure principle and describe how it is implemented.
2. Discuss the disclosure requirements for related-party transactions, post-balance-sheet events, major business segments, and interim reporting.
3. Identify the major disclosures in the auditor's report and understand management's responsibilities for the financial statements.
4. Identify reporting issues related to fraudulent financial reporting and financial forecasts.

PREVIEW OF CHAPTER 24 As the following opening story indicates, our markets will not function properly without transparent, complete, and truthful reporting of financial performance. Investors and other interested parties need to read and understand all aspects of financial reporting—the financial statements, the notes, the president's letter, and management's discussion and analysis. In this chapter, we cover the full disclosure principle in more detail and examine disclosures that must accompany financial statements so that they are not misleading. The content and organization of this chapter are as follows.

This chapter also includes numerous conceptual and global discussions that are integral to the topics presented here.

FULL DISCLOSURE IN FINANCIAL REPORTING

Full Disclosure Principle
- Increase in reporting requirements
- Differential disclosure
- Notes to the financial statements

Disclosure Issues
- Related parties
- Post-balance-sheet events
- Diversified companies
- Interim reports

Auditor's and Management's Reports
- Auditor's report
- Management's reports

Current Reporting Issues
- Fraudulent financial reporting
- Internet financial reporting
- Reporting on forecasts and projections
- Criteria for accounting and reporting choices

High-Quality Financial Reporting—Always in Fashion

Here are excerpts from leading experts regarding the importance of high-quality financial reporting:

Warren E. Buffett, Chairman and Chief Executive Officer, Berkshire Hathaway Inc.:

Financial reporting for Berkshire Hathaway, and for me personally, is the beginning of every decision that we make around here in terms of capital. I'm punching out 10-Ks and 10-Qs every single day. We look at the numbers and try to evaluate the quality of the financial reporting, and then we try to figure out what that means for the bonds and stocks that we're looking at, and thinking of either buying or selling.

Judy Lewent, former Executive Vice President and Chief Financial Officer, Merck & Co., Inc.:

. . . standards, when properly implemented, drive excellence. I can make a parallel to the pharmaceutical industry. If you look around the world at where innovations come from, economists have studied and seen that where regulatory standards are the highest is where innovation is also the highest.

Floyd Norris, Chief Financial Correspondent, The New York Times:

We are in a situation now in our society where the temptations to provide "bad" financial reporting are probably greater than they used to be. The need to get the stock price up, or to keep it up, is intense. So, the temptation to play games, the temptation to manage earnings—some of which can be legitimate and some of which cannot be—is probably greater than it used to be.

Abby Joseph Cohen, President, Global Markets Institute, Goldman, Sachs & Co.:

High-quality financial reporting is perhaps the most important thing we can expect from companies. For investors to make good decisions—whether those investors are buying stocks or bonds or making private investments—they need to know the truth. And we think that when information is as clear as possible and is reported as frequently as makes sense, investors can do their jobs as best they can.

We can also get insight into the importance of high-quality reporting based on the market assessment of companies perceived to have poor-quality reporting. At one time, Coach, Inc. stopped reporting as separate items sales from regular stores (full price) and factory outlets. As a result, readers of its financial statements had a hard time determining the source of Coach's sales growth. Analysts were especially concerned that the less-transparent reporting might obscure slowing sales at its regular stores, as consumers cut down on luxury goods in a sluggish economy. Did Coach's stock price suffer as a result of this lower-quality reporting? You bet, as shown in the adjacent price graph.

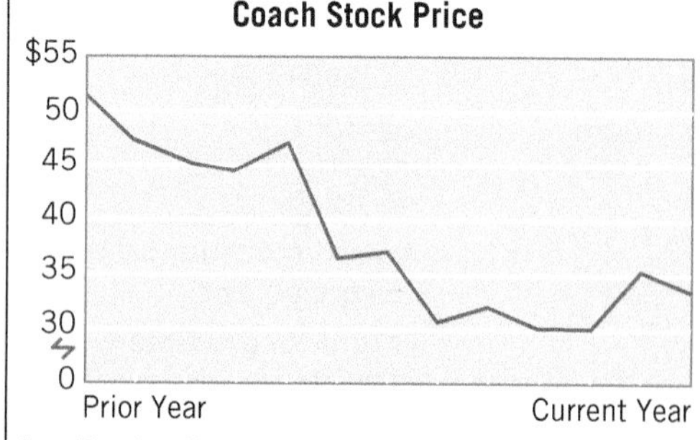

Data: Bloomberg Financial Markets.

In the year following the change in reporting, Coach's stock price was down 34 percent. As one analyst noted, "It's never a good sign when you reduce transparency . . . It's a sign of weakness."

Another example is the recent case of Sunrun. Company insiders at this solar-energy company admitted to manipulating a key sales metric around the time of the company's initial public offering (IPO). The former managers say they were told by their superiors to hold off on internally reporting hundreds of customers who canceled their contracts during a roughly five-month period in the middle of that year. Sunrun and other solar companies typically give homeowners at least several days to back out of a contract before their home-energy systems are installed. Hiding the canceled contracts made the company's sales figures appear stronger. As one manager noted, "The big internal push was to cram as many sales as we could through the pipeline." When discovered—shortly after the IPO—the market response was predictable. As shown in the following graph, similar to the Coach example, Sunrun's share price has declined substantially since its IPO.

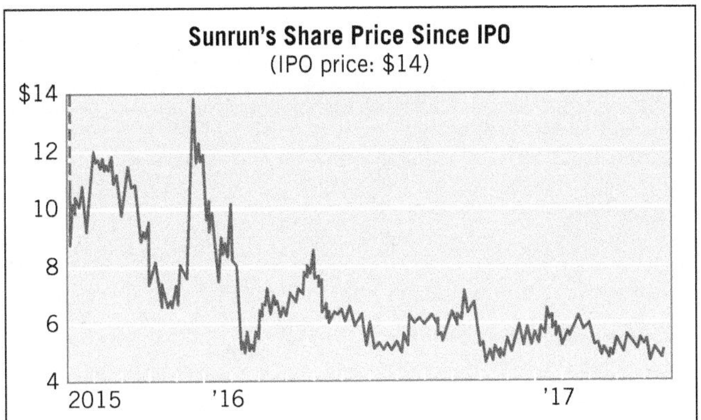

Sources: FactSet, *Wall Street Journal.*

In short, these examples illustrate why high-quality reporting is always in fashion—for companies, investors, and the capital markets. And, as the Coach and Sunrun examples illustrate, full disclosure is at the heart of high-quality reporting.

Source: Excerpts taken from video entitled "Financially Correct with Ben Stein," Financial Accounting Standards Board (Norwalk, Conn.: FASB, 2002). By permission. See also J. Porter, "As Belts Tighten, Coach Feels the Pinch," *BusinessWeek* (May 29, 2008), p. 66; and K. Grind, "Solar Company Sunrun Was Manipulating Sales Data, Say Former Managers," *Wall Street Journal* (May 22, 2017).

Review and Practice

Go to the **Review and Practice** section at the end of the chapter for a targeted summary review and practice problem with solution. Multiple-choice questions with annotated solutions as well as additional exercises and practice problem with solutions are also available online.

Full Disclosure Principle

LEARNING OBJECTIVE 1

Review the full disclosure principle and describe how it is implemented.

According to the FASB Conceptual Framework, some useful information is best provided in the financial statements, and some is best provided by other means. For example, earnings and cash flows are readily available in financial statements—but investors might do better to look at comparisons to other companies in the same industry, found in news articles or brokerage house reports.

FASB rules directly affect financial statements, notes to the financial statements, and supplementary information. Other types of information found in the annual report, such as management's discussion and analysis, are not subject to FASB rules. **Illustration 24.1** indicates the various types of financial information.

As Chapter 2 indicated, the profession has adopted a **full disclosure principle**. The full disclosure principle calls for financial reporting of **any financial facts significant enough to influence the judgment of an informed reader**. In some situations, the benefits of disclosure may be apparent but the costs uncertain. In other instances, the costs may be certain but the benefits of disclosure not as apparent.

ILLUSTRATION 24.1 **Types of Financial Information**

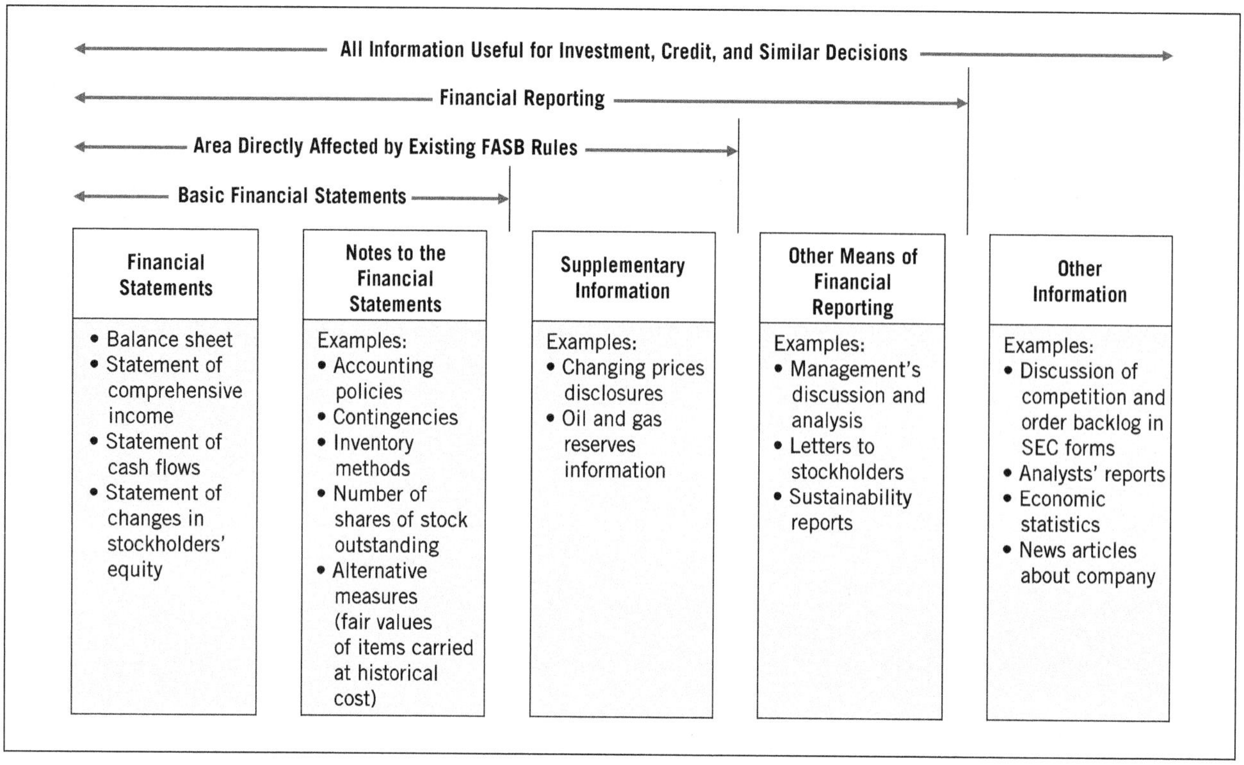

> **Underlying Concepts**
>
> Here is a good example of the trade-off between cost considerations and the benefits of full disclosure.

For example, the SEC required companies to provide expanded disclosures about their contractual obligations. In light of the off-balance-sheet accounting frauds at companies like **Enron**, the benefits of these expanded disclosures seem fairly obvious to the investing public. While no one has documented the exact costs of disclosure in these situations, they would appear to be relatively small.

On the other hand, the cost of disclosure can be substantial in some cases and the benefits difficult to assess. For example, at one time the *Wall Street Journal* reported that if segment reporting were adopted, a company like **Fruehauf** would have had to increase its accounting staff 50 percent, from 300 to 450 individuals. In this case, the cost of disclosure can be measured, but the benefits are less well defined (see **Underlying Concepts**).

Some even argue that the reporting requirements are so detailed and substantial that users have a difficult time absorbing the information. These critics charge the profession with engaging in **information overload**.

Financial disasters at **Microstrategy**, **PharMor**, **WorldCom**, and **Theranos** highlight the difficulty of implementing the full disclosure principle. They raise the issue of why investors were not aware of potential problems. Was the information these companies presented not comprehensible? Was it buried? Was it too technical? Was it properly presented and fully disclosed as of the financial statement date, but the situation later deteriorated? Or was it simply not there? In the following sections, we describe the elements of high-quality disclosure that will enable companies to avoid these disclosure pitfalls.

Increase in Reporting Requirements

Disclosure requirements have increased substantially. One survey showed that the size of many companies' annual reports is growing in response to demands for increased transparency. For example, annual report page counts ranged from 51 pages for **Tootsie Roll** to a much higher count of 166 for **The Coca Cola Company**'s annual report. One analysis from Moody's Investors Services documented "tremendous growth" in the volume of pages in company annual reports, with 75-page financial statements in the late 1990s, increasing to 120 pages in the early 2000s, and 400 pages in the most recent years. One analyst remarked, "that's very challenging for investors to get through. . . ."[1] This result is not surprising. As illustrated throughout this text, the FASB has issued many pronouncements in recent years that have substantial disclosure provisions.

The reasons for this increase in disclosure requirements are varied. Some of them are:

- ***Complexity of the business environment.*** The increasing complexity of business operations magnifies the difficulty of distilling economic events into summarized reports. Such areas as derivatives, leasing, business combinations, pensions, financing arrangements, revenue recognition, and deferred taxes are complex. As a result, companies extensively use **notes to the financial statements** to explain these transactions and their future effects.
- ***Necessity for timely information.*** Today, more than ever before, users are demanding information that is current and predictive. For example, users want more complete **interim data**. Also, the SEC recommends enhanced fair value and sustainability disclosures.
- ***Accounting as a control and monitoring device.*** The government has recently sought public disclosure of such phenomena as management compensation, off-balance-sheet financing arrangements, and related-party transactions. An "Enronitis" concern is expressed in many of these newer disclosure requirements, and the SEC has selected accountants and auditors as the agents to assist in controlling and monitoring these concerns.

Underlying Concepts

Surveys indicate that users differ in their needs for information and that not all companies should report all elements of information. Thus, some contend that companies should report only information that users and preparers agree is needed in the particular circumstances.

Differential Disclosure

A trend toward **differential disclosure** is also occurring. For example, the SEC requires that companies report to it certain substantive information that is not found in annual reports to stockholders. Likewise, the FASB, recognizing that certain disclosure requirements are costly and unnecessary for certain companies, has eliminated reporting requirements for private (nonpublic) companies in such areas as fair value of financial instruments and segment reporting (see Underlying Concepts).

Some still complain that the FASB has not gone far enough. They note that certain types of companies (small or private) should not have to follow complex GAAP requirements such as those for deferred income taxes, leases, or pensions. This issue, often referred to as "**big GAAP versus little GAAP**," continues to be controversial.[2]

The FASB has traditionally taken the position that there should be one set of GAAP. However, due to growing concern about differential costs and benefits of a "one size fits all" reporting package, the FASB has considered providing alternative accounting treatments for private companies in areas that include recognition and measurement, presentation and disclosure, effective dates, and transition methods for financial accounting standards. (see Global View). Since 2012, the FASB has worked with the Private Company Council (PCC) to improve the process of setting accounting standards for private companies. The PCC uses the recently developed Private Company Decision-Making Framework[3] to evaluate whether alternatives to existing GAAP are necessary to address the needs of users of private company financial statements. The PCC also provides input to the FASB on the appropriate treatment for private companies for items under active consideration on the FASB's technical agenda. We provide an expanded discussion of the PCC and private company alternatives in Appendix A.

Global View

IFRS allows different accounting for small- and medium-sized entities.

[1]"Kroeker: Disclosure Overhaul May Result in More Footnote Rules for U.S. GAAP," *https://tax.thomsonreuters.com/checkpoint-news* (September 28, 2016). Concern about disclosure overload is not confined to financial statements. A recent study of annual proxy statements, which supplement the accounting reports with information on company risks and executive compensation, indicates that the compensation section alone has grown dramatically in recent years. This growth is expected to continue as major new accounting standards are adopted and as companies implement rules to disclose the ratio of chief executive pay relative to the median compensation of employees. See T. Shumsky, "As Company Disclosures Balloon, It's Getting Easier to Bury Information," *Wall Street Journal* (February 26, 2016).

[2]In response to cost-benefit concerns, the SEC has exempted some small public companies from certain rules implemented in response to the Sarbanes-Oxley Act. For example, smaller companies have more time to comply with the internal control rules required by the Sarbanes-Oxley law and have more time to file annual and interim reports.

[3]FASB, *Private Company Decision-Making Framework: A Framework for Evaluating Financial Accounting and Reporting Guidance for Private Companies* (December 2013).

Evolving Issue Disclosure—Quantity and Quality

There is no better illustration of the adage that both quality and quantity are important than the issue of financial disclosure. While the full disclosure principle holds that more is better, how much more and of what form? An evaluation of this issue requires careful analysis of costs and benefits. Furthermore, as noted by one FASB member, the usefulness of expanded required disclosure also depends on users' ability to distinguish between the form of reporting (i.e., disclosed versus recognized items in financial statements). Research to date is inconclusive on this matter. So it is not just the amount but the quality.

The FASB has responded by initiating a Disclosure Framework project with the goal of improving the effectiveness of disclosures in notes to financial statements. This project has resulted in a new FASB concepts statement ["Conceptual Framework for Financial Reporting—Chapter 8, Notes to Financial Statements" (August 2018)], which addresses the Board's decision process in identifying disclosures to be considered when setting disclosure requirements for individual accounting standards and evaluating existing disclosure requirements.

The Disclosure Framework project has been well-received by a variety of stakeholders. Indeed some companies have taken up the charge to improve the readability of their financial statements, including the notes. For example, after revising and integrating its annual report package, **General Electric (GE)** saw downloads at its website go from 2,700 to over 9,000. The FASB observes that reducing the volume of the notes to financial statements is not the primary focus of the Disclosure Framework project. The Board hopes that a sharper focus on important information, as was done at GE, will result in higher quality and reduced volume in most cases.

Sources: K. Schipper, "Required Disclosures in Financial Reports," Presidential address to the American Accounting Association Annual Meeting (San Francisco, Calif., August 2005); B. Bratten, P. Choudhary, and K. Schipper, "Evidence that Market Participants Assess Recognized and Disclosed Items Similarly When Reliability Is Not an Issue," *The Accounting Review* (July 2013); *FASB News Release*, "FASB Improves the Effectiveness of Disclosures in Notes to Financial Statements," *www.fasb.org* (August 28, 2018); and C. Westfall, "Disclosure Doesn't Need to Be Difficult: GE's Bornstein," *FEI Daily* (September 28, 2016).

Notes to the Financial Statements

As you know from your study of this text, notes are an integral part of the financial statements of a business enterprise. However, readers of financial statements often overlook them because they are highly technical and often appear in small print. **Notes are the means of amplifying or explaining the items presented in the main body of the statements.** They can explain in qualitative terms information pertinent to specific financial statement items. In addition, they can provide supplementary data of a quantitative nature to expand the information in the financial statements. Notes also can explain restrictions imposed by financial arrangements or basic contractual agreements. Although notes may be technical and difficult to understand, they provide meaningful information for the user of the financial statements.[4]

Accounting Policies

Accounting policies are the specific accounting principles and methods a company currently uses and considers most appropriate to present fairly its financial statements. GAAP states that information about the accounting policies adopted by a reporting entity is essential for financial statement users in making economic decisions. It recommends that companies should present **as an integral part of the financial statements a statement identifying the accounting policies adopted and followed by the reporting entity**. Companies should present the disclosure as the first note or in a separate Summary of Significant Accounting Policies section preceding the notes to the financial statements.

The Summary of Significant Accounting Policies section answers such questions as: What method of depreciation is used on plant assets? What valuation method is employed on inventories? What amortization policy is followed in regard to intangible assets? How are marketing costs handled for financial reporting purposes?

Refer to the financial statements and notes to the financial statements for **The Procter & Gamble Company** (available online) for an illustration of note disclosure of accounting policies (Note 1) and other notes accompanying the audited financial statements.

[4]"Conceptual Framework for Financial Reporting—Chapter 8, Notes to Financial Statements," *Statement of Financial Accounting Concepts No. 8* (Norwalk, Conn.: FASB, August 2018).

Analysts examine carefully the summary of accounting policies to determine whether a company is using conservative or liberal accounting practices. For example, depreciating plant assets over an unusually long period of time is considered liberal. Using LIFO inventory valuation in a period of inflation is generally viewed as conservative.

Companies that fail to adopt high-quality reporting policies may be heavily penalized by the market. For example, as discussed in the opening story, when **Sunrun** disclosed its accounting problems, its share price dropped substantially. Investors viewed Sunrun's quality of earnings as low.

Common Notes

We have discussed many of the **notes to the financial statements** throughout this text and will discuss others more fully in this chapter. The more common notes are as follows.

Major Disclosures

Inventory. Companies should report the basis upon which inventory amounts are stated (e.g., lower-of-cost-or-net realizable value or lower-of-cost-or-market) and the method used in determining cost (LIFO, FIFO, average-cost, etc.). Manufacturers should report, either in the balance sheet or in a separate schedule in the notes, the inventory composition (finished goods, work in process, raw materials). Unusual or significant financing arrangements relating to inventories that may require disclosure include transactions with related parties, product financing arrangements, firm purchase commitments, involuntary liquidation of LIFO inventories, and pledging of inventories as collateral. Chapter 9 illustrates these disclosures.

Property, Plant, and Equipment. Companies should state the basis of valuation for property, plant, and equipment. It is usually historical cost. Companies also should disclose pledges, liens, and other commitments related to these assets. In the presentation of depreciation, companies should disclose the following in the financial statements or in the notes: (1) depreciation expense for the period; (2) balances of major classes of depreciable assets, by nature and function, at the balance sheet date; (3) accumulated depreciation, either by major classes of depreciable assets or in total, at the balance sheet date; and (4) a general description of the method or methods used in computing depreciation with respect to major classes of depreciable assets. Finally, companies should explain any major impairments. Chapter 11 illustrates property, plant, and equipment.

Creditor Claims. Investors normally find it extremely useful to understand the nature and cost of creditor claims. However, the liabilities section in the balance sheet can provide the major types of liabilities only in the aggregate. Note schedules regarding such obligations provide additional information about how a company is financing its operations, the costs that it will bear in future periods, and the timing of future cash outflows. Financial statements must disclose for each of the five years following the date of the statements the aggregate amount of maturities and sinking fund requirements for all long-term borrowings. Chapter 14 illustrates these disclosures.

Equityholders' Claims. Many companies present in the body of the balance sheet information about equity securities: the number of shares authorized, issued, and outstanding and the par value for each type of security. Or, companies may present such data in a note. Beyond that, a common equity note disclosure relates to contracts and senior securities outstanding that might affect the various claims of the residual equityholders. An example would be the existence of outstanding stock options, outstanding convertible debt, redeemable preferred stock, and convertible preferred stock. In addition, it is necessary to disclose certain types of restrictions currently in force. Generally, these types of restrictions involve the amount of earnings available for dividend distribution. Examples of these types of disclosures are illustrated in Chapter 15 and Chapter 16.

Contingencies and Commitments. A company may have gain or loss contingencies that are not disclosed in the body of the financial statements. These contingencies include litigation, debt and other guarantees, possible tax assessments, renegotiation of government contracts, and sales of receivables with recourse. In addition, companies should disclose in the notes commitments that relate to dividend restrictions, purchase agreements (through-put and take-or-pay), hedge contracts, and employment contracts. Disclosures of such items are illustrated in Chapter 7, Chapter 9, and Chapter 13.

Fair Values. Companies that have assets or liabilities measured at fair value must disclose both the cost and the fair value of all financial instruments in the notes to the financial statements. Fair value measurements may be used for many financial assets and liabilities, investments, impairments of long-lived assets, and some contingencies. Companies also provide disclosure of information that enables users to determine the extent of usage of fair value and the inputs used to implement fair value measurement. This fair value hierarchy identifies three broad levels related to the measurement of fair values (Levels 1, 2, and 3). The levels indicate the reliability of the measurement of fair value information. Appendix 17B discusses in detail fair value disclosures.

Revenue. Users carefully review revenue disclosures to understand the nature, amount, timing, and uncertainty of revenue and cash flows arising from contracts with customers. Companies disclose information about (1) contracts with customers, including significant information related to its performance obligations; (2) significant judgments and changes in these judgments that affect the determination of the transaction price, the allocation of the transaction price, and the determination of the timing of revenue; and (3) assets recognized from costs incurred to fulfill contracts, including the amount of amortization recognized and the method used for amortization. See Chapter 18.

Deferred Taxes, Pensions, and Leases. The FASB also requires extensive disclosure in the areas of deferred taxes, pensions, and leases. Chapter 19, Chapter 20, and Chapter 21 discuss in detail each of these disclosures. Users of financial statements should carefully read notes to the financial statements for information about off-balance-sheet commitments, future financing needs, and the quality of a company's earnings.

Changes in Accounting Principles. The profession defines various types of accounting changes and establishes guides for reporting each type. Companies discuss, either in the summary of significant accounting policies or in the other notes, changes in accounting principles (as well as material changes in estimates and corrections of errors). See Chapter 22.

In earlier chapters, we discussed the disclosures listed above. The following sections of this chapter illustrate four additional disclosures of significance—special transactions or events, subsequent events, segment reporting, and interim reporting.

What Do the Numbers Mean? Footnote Secrets

Often, note disclosures are needed to give a complete picture of a company's financial position. A good example of such disclosures is the required disclosure of debt triggers that may be buried in financing arrangements. These triggers can require a company to pay off a loan immediately if the debt rating collapses; they are one of the reasons **Enron** crumbled so quickly. But few Enron stockholders knew about the debt triggers until the gun had gone off. Companies are also disclosing more about their bank credit lines, liquidity, and any special-purpose entities. (The latter were major villains in the Enron drama.)

How can you get better informed about note disclosures that may contain important information related to your investments? Beyond your study in this class, a good resource for understanding the contents of note disclosures is the **footnoted.com** website. The site provides alerts on financial reporting practices, such as the growing trend of companies' filing financial statements late—a possible signal of accounting shenanigans. The footnoted.com site also highlights "the things companies bury in their SEC filings." It notes that company reports are more complete of late, but only the largest companies are preparing documents that are readable. As the editor of the site noted, "[some companies] are being dragged kicking and screaming into plain English."

Sources: Gretchen Morgenson, "Annual Reports: More Pages, but Better?" *The New York Times* (March 17, 2002); D. Stead, "The Secrets in SEC Filings," *BusinessWeek* (August 25, 2008), p. 12; and C. Grant and D. Reilly, "Valeant: Why Showing Up Late Matters," *Wall Street Journal* (March 18, 2016).

Disclosure Issues

LEARNING OBJECTIVE 2

Discuss the disclosure requirements for related-party transactions, post-balance-sheet events, major business segments, and interim reporting.

Related-party transactions, post-balance-sheet events, major business segments, and interim reporting can pose especially difficult problems. The accountant/auditor who has responsibility for reporting on these types of transactions must take care to properly balance the rights of the reporting company and the needs of users of the financial statements.

Related Parties

Related-party transactions arise when a company engages in transactions in which one of the parties has the ability to significantly influence the policies of the other. They may also occur when a nontransacting party has the ability to influence the policies of the two transacting parties.[5] Competitive, free-market dealings may not exist in related-party transactions, and so an "arm's-length" basis cannot be assumed. Transactions such as borrowing or lending money at abnormally low or high interest rates, real estate sales at amounts that differ significantly from appraised value, exchanges of nonmonetary assets, and transactions involving enterprises that have no economic substance ("shell corporations") suggest that related parties may be involved.

In order to make adequate disclosure, companies should report the economic substance, rather than the legal form, of these transactions. GAAP requires the following disclosures of material related-party transactions. [1] (See the FASB Codification References near the end of the chapter.)

1. The nature of the relationship(s) involved.
2. A description of the transactions (including transactions to which no amounts or nominal amounts were ascribed) for each of the periods for which income statements are presented.
3. The dollar amounts of transactions for each of the periods for which income statements are presented.
4. Amounts due from or to related parties as of the date of each balance sheet presented.

Illustration 24.2, from the annual report of **Harley-Davidson, Inc.**, shows disclosure of related-party transactions.

ILLUSTRATION 24.2

Disclosure of Related-Party Transactions

Harley-Davidson, Inc.

20. Related Party Transactions (in part)

A director of the Company is Chairman and Chief Executive Officer and an equity owner of Fred Deeley Imports Ltd. (Deeley Imports), the exclusive distributor of the Company's motorcycles in Canada. The Company recorded motorcycles and related products revenue and financial services revenue from Deeley Imports during current and prior years of $194.8 million and $204.8 million, respectively, and had finance receivables balances due from Deeley Imports of $7.4 million and $11.5 million, at December 31 of the current and prior years, respectively. All such products were provided in the ordinary course of business at prices and on terms and conditions that the Company believes are the same as those that would result from arm's-length negotiations between unrelated parties.

Post-Balance-Sheet Events (Subsequent Events)

Notes to the financial statements should explain any significant financial events that took place after the formal balance sheet date, but before the statement is issued. These events are referred to as **post-balance-sheet events** or **subsequent events**. **Illustration 24.3** shows a time diagram of the subsequent events period.

ILLUSTRATION 24.3

Time Periods for Subsequent Events

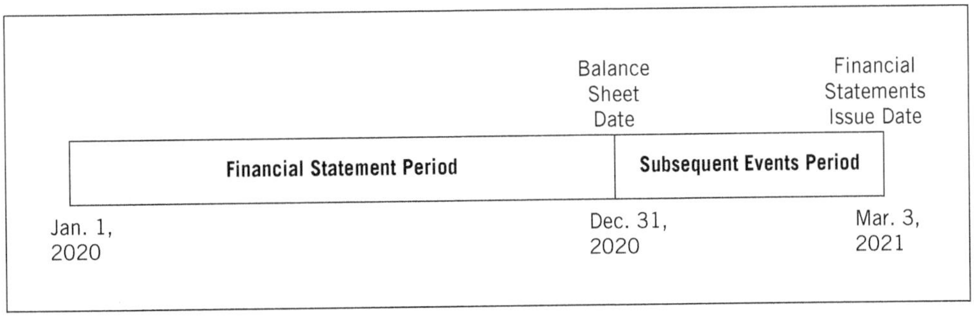

A period of several weeks, and sometimes months, may elapse after the end of the fiscal year but before the company issues financial statements. Various activities involved in closing

[5] Examples of related-party transactions include transactions between (a) a parent company and its subsidiaries, (b) subsidiaries of a common parent, (c) a company and trusts for the benefit of employees (controlled or managed by the enterprise), and (d) a company and its principal owners, management, or members of immediate families, and affiliates. Two classic cases of related-party transactions were **Enron**, with its misuse of special-purpose entities, and **Tyco International**, which forgave loans to its management team.

the books for the period and issuing the statements all take time: counting and pricing the inventory, reconciling subsidiary ledgers with controlling accounts, preparing necessary adjusting entries, ensuring that all transactions for the period have been entered, obtaining an audit of the financial statements by independent certified public accountants, and printing the annual report. During the period between the balance sheet date and its distribution to stockholders and creditors, important transactions or other events may occur that materially affect the company's financial position or operating situation.

Many who read a balance sheet believe the balance sheet condition is constant, and they project it into the future. However, readers must be told if the company has experienced a significant change—e.g., sold one of its plants, acquired a subsidiary, settled significant litigation, or experienced any other important event in the post-balance-sheet period. Without an explanation in a note, the reader might be misled and draw inappropriate conclusions.

Two types of events or transactions occurring after the balance sheet date may have a material effect on the financial statements or may need disclosure so that readers interpret these statements accurately:

1. Events that provide additional evidence about conditions **that existed** at the balance sheet date, including the estimates inherent in the process of preparing financial statements. These events are referred to as **recognized subsequent events** and require adjustments to the financial statements. All information available prior to the issuance of the financial statements helps investors and creditors evaluate estimates previously made. To ignore these subsequent events is to pass up an opportunity to improve the accuracy of the financial statements. This first type of event encompasses information that an accountant would have recorded in the accounts had the information been known at the balance sheet date.

Recognized Subsequent Events
Situation: A loss on an account receivable results from a customer's bankruptcy subsequent to the balance sheet date, but before the financial statements are issued. ***Solution:*** The company adjusts the financial statements before their issuance. The bankruptcy stems from the customer's poor financial health existing at the balance sheet date.
Other examples: The company must adjust the financial statements before their issuance for the following situations: (1) for settlements of litigation, if the events that gave rise to the litigation, such as personal injury or patent infringement, took place prior to the balance sheet date; (2) for warranty obligations, if defects arose on products sold prior to the balance sheet date; or (3) a tax dispute related to taxes payable at the balance sheet date is settled before issuance of the statements.

2. Events that provide evidence about conditions that **did not exist** at the balance sheet date but arise subsequent to that date. These events are referred to as **nonrecognized subsequent events** and do not require adjustment of the financial statements.

Nonrecognized Subsequent Events
Situation: A company has a loss from a fire or flood *after* the balance sheet. ***Solution:*** Adjustment of the financial statements is not necessary. A fire after the balance sheet date but before the financial statement date does not reflect conditions existing at the balance sheet date.
Other examples: A company should not recognize subsequent events that provide evidence about conditions that did not exist at the date of the balance sheet **but that arose after the balance sheet** for the following specific examples: (1) strikes, (2) sale of a bond or capital stock issued, (3) a business combination occurs, (4) settlement of litigation, (5) losses on receivables resulting from conditions (such as a customer's major casualty) arising, (6) changes in the quoted market prices of securities or foreign exchange rates, and (7) entering into significant commitments or contingent liabilities, for example, by issuing significant guarantees.[2]

As indicated, a company should not recognize subsequent events that provide evidence about conditions that did not exist at the date of the balance sheet but that arose after the balance sheet date.[6]

Some nonrecognized subsequent events may have to be disclosed to keep the financial statements from being misleading. For such events, a company discloses the nature of the event and an estimate of its financial effect (see Underlying Concepts).

Illustration 24.4 presents an example of subsequent events disclosure, excerpted from the annual report of Commercial Metals Company.

ILLUSTRATION 24.4

Disclosure of Subsequent Events

Commercial Metals Company

NOTE 24. SUBSEQUENT EVENTS

In September (following the August 31 fiscal year-end) the Company made the decision to exit its steel distribution business in Australia. Despite focused efforts and substantial progress to stabilize and improve the results of the Australian distribution business, the Company determined that achieving acceptable financial returns would take additional time and investment.

Underlying Concepts

A company also should consider supplementing the historical financial statements with pro forma financial data. Occasionally, a nonrecognized subsequent event may be so significant that disclosure can best be made by means of pro forma financial data.

Many subsequent events or developments do not require adjustment of or disclosure in the financial statements. Typically, these are nonaccounting events or conditions that management normally communicates by other means. These events include legislation, product changes, management changes, unionization, marketing agreements, and loss of important customers.

Reporting for Diversified (Conglomerate) Companies

In certain business climates, companies have a tendency to diversify their operations. Take the case of conglomerate General Electric (GE), whose products include locomotives, jet engines, and water purification systems. Or, consider cable giant Comcast; its NBC Universal subsidiary owns NBC TV, Telemundo, Universal Pictures, and Universal Parks and Resorts. When businesses are so diversified, investors and investment analysts want more information about the details behind conglomerate financial statements. Particularly, they want income statement, balance sheet, and cash flow information on the **individual segments** that compose the total income figure.

Illustration 24.5 shows **segmented** (disaggregated) financial information of an office equipment and auto parts company.

Much information is hidden in the aggregated totals. If the analyst has only the consolidated figures, he/she cannot tell the extent to which the differing product lines **contribute to the company's profitability, risk, and growth potential**. For example, in Illustration 24.5, the office equipment segment looks like a risky venture. Segmented reporting would provide useful information about the two business segments and would be useful for making an informed investment decision regarding the whole company.

[6]The effects from natural disasters, like hurricanes Katrina, Sandy, and Florence, which occurred after the year-end for companies with August fiscal years, require disclosure in order to keep the statements from being misleading. Some companies had to consider whether these disasters affected their ability to continue as going concerns. *Accounting Trends and Techniques* listed the following types of subsequent events and their frequency of occurrence among the 500 companies surveyed: acquisitions, 32; debt incurred, reduced, or refinanced, 31; business combinations pending or effected, 29; capital stock issued or purchased, 18; discontinued operations or asset disposals, 15; litigation, 14, and restructuring/bankruptcy, 13.

ILLUSTRATION 24.5

Segmented Income Statement

Office Equipment and Auto Parts Company
Income Statement Data
(in millions)

	Consolidated	Office Equipment	Auto Parts
Net sales	$78.8	$18.0	$60.8
Manufacturing costs			
Inventories, beginning	12.3	4.0	8.3
Materials and services	38.9	10.8	28.1
Wages	12.9	3.8	9.1
Inventories, ending	(13.3)	(3.9)	(9.4)
	50.8	14.7	36.1
Selling and administrative expenses	12.1	1.6	10.5
Total operating expenses	62.9	16.3	46.6
Income before taxes	15.9	1.7	14.2
Income taxes	(9.3)	(1.0)	(8.3)
Net income	$ 6.6	$ 0.7	$ 5.9

A classic situation that demonstrates the need for segmented data involved **Caterpillar, Inc.** The SEC cited Caterpillar because it failed to tell investors that nearly a quarter of its income in one year came from a Brazilian unit and was nonrecurring in nature. The company knew that different economic policies in the next year would probably greatly affect earnings of the Brazilian unit. But Caterpillar presented its financial results on a consolidated basis, not disclosing the Brazilian operations. The SEC found that Caterpillar's failure to include information about Brazil left investors with an incomplete picture of the company's financial results and denied investors the opportunity to see the company "through the eyes of management."

Companies have always been somewhat hesitant to disclose segmented data for various reasons, such as indicated below.

Arguments Opposing Segment Reporting
1. Without a thorough knowledge of the business and an understanding of such important factors as the competitive environment and capital investment requirements, the investor may find the segmented information meaningless or may even draw improper conclusions about the reported earnings of the segments.
2. Additional disclosure may be helpful to competitors, labor unions, suppliers, and certain government regulatory agencies, and thus harm the reporting company.
3. Additional disclosure may discourage management from taking intelligent business risks because segments reporting losses or unsatisfactory earnings may cause stockholder dissatisfaction with management.
4. The wide variation among companies in the choice of segments, cost allocation, and other accounting problems limits comparability, and hence the usefulness of segmented information.
5. The investor is investing in the company as a whole and not in the particular segments, and it should not matter how any single segment is performing if the overall performance is satisfactory.
6. Certain technical problems, such as classification of segments and allocation of segment revenues and costs (especially "common costs"), are formidable.

On the other hand, the advocates of segmented disclosures offer these following reasons in support of the practice.

Arguments Supporting Segment Reporting
1. Investors need segmented information to make an intelligent investment decision regarding a diversified company. **a.** Sales and earnings of individual segments enable investors to evaluate the differences between segments in growth rate, risk, and profitability, and to forecast consolidated profits. **b.** Segmented reports help investors evaluate the company's investment worth by disclosing the nature of a company's businesses and the relative size of the components.
2. The absence of segmented reporting by a diversified company may put its unsegmented, single product-line competitors at a competitive disadvantage because the conglomerate may obscure information that its competitors must disclose.

The advocates of segmented disclosures appear to have a much stronger case based on the usefulness of segment information to users of financial statements. The objective of reporting segmented financial data is to provide information about the **different types of business activities** in which an enterprise engages and the **different economic environments** in which it operates. Meeting this objective will help users of financial statements do the following.

a. Better understand the enterprise's performance.

b. Better assess its prospects for future net cash flows.

c. Make more informed judgments about the enterprise as a whole.

Implementing Segment Reporting

Financial statements can be disaggregated in several ways. For example, they can be disaggregated by products or services, by geography, by legal entity, or by type of customer. However, it is not feasible to provide all of that information in every set of financial statements. GAAP requires that general-purpose financial statements include selected information on a single basis of segmentation. Thus, a company can meet the segmented reporting objective by providing financial statements segmented based on how the company's operations are managed. The method chosen is referred to as the **management approach**. [3] **The management approach reflects how management segments the company for making operating decisions.** The segments are evident from the components of the company's organization structure. These components are called **operating segments.**

Identifying Operating Segments

An **operating segment** is a component of an enterprise:

a. That engages in business activities from which it earns revenues and incurs expenses.

b. Whose operating results are regularly reviewed by the company's chief operating decision-maker to assess segment performance and allocate resources to the segment.

c. For which discrete financial information is available that is generated by or based on the internal financial reporting system.

Companies may aggregate information about two or more operating segments only if the segments have the same basic characteristics in each of the following areas.

a. The nature of the products and services provided.

b. The nature of the production process.

c. The type or class of customer.

d. The methods of product or service distribution.

e. If applicable, the nature of the regulatory environment.

After the company decides on the possible segments for disclosure, it makes a quantitative materiality test. This test determines whether the segment is significant enough to warrant actual disclosure. An operating segment is deemed significant, and therefore a reportable segment, if it satisfies **one or more** of the following quantitative thresholds.

1. Its **revenue** (including both sales to external customers and intersegment sales or transfers) is 10 percent or more of the combined revenue of all the company's operating segments.
2. The absolute amount of its **profit or loss** is 10 percent or more of the greater, in absolute amount, of (a) the combined operating profit of all operating segments that did not incur a loss, or (b) the combined loss of all operating segments that did report a loss.
3. Its **identifiable assets** are 10 percent or more of the combined assets of all operating segments.

In applying these tests, the company must consider two additional factors. First, segment data must explain a significant portion of the company's business. Specifically, the segmented results must equal or exceed 75 percent of the combined sales to unaffiliated customers for the entire company. This test prevents a company from providing limited information on only a few segments and lumping all the rest into one category.

Second, the profession recognizes that reporting too many segments may overwhelm users with detailed information. The FASB decided that 10 is a reasonable upper limit for the number of segments that a company must disclose.[7]

To illustrate these requirements, assume a company has identified six possible reporting segments, as shown in Illustration 24.6 (000s omitted).

ILLUSTRATION 24.6

Data for Different Possible Reporting Segments

Segments	Total Revenue (Unaffiliated)	Operating Profit (Loss)	Identifiable Assets
A	$ 100	$10	$ 60
B	50	2	30
C	700	40	390
D	300	20	160
E	900	18	280
F	100	(5)	50
	$2,150	$85	$970

The company would apply the respective tests as follows.

Revenue test: .10 × $2,150 = $215; C, D, and E meet this test.

Operating profit (loss) test: .10 × $90 = $9 (note that the $5 loss is ignored because the test is based on non-loss segments); A, C, D, and E meet this test.

Identifiable assets tests: .10 × $970 = $97; C, D, and E meet this test.

The reporting segments are therefore A, C, D, and E, assuming that these four segments have enough sales to meet the 75 percent of combined sales test. The 75 percent test is computed as follows.

75% of combined sales test: .75 × $2,150 = $1,612.50. The sales of A, C, D, and E total $2,000 ($100 + $700 + $300 + $900); therefore, the 75 percent test is met.

Measurement Principles The accounting principles that companies use for segment disclosure need not be the same as the principles they use to prepare the consolidated statements. This flexibility may at first appear inconsistent. But, preparing segment information in accordance with generally accepted accounting principles would be difficult because some principles are not expected to apply at a segment level. Examples are accounting for the cost of company-wide employee benefit plans, accounting for income taxes in a company that files a consolidated tax return, and accounting for inventory on a LIFO basis if the pool includes items in more than one segment.

The FASB does not require allocations of joint, common, or company-wide costs solely for external reporting purposes. Common costs are those incurred for the benefit of more than one segment and whose interrelated nature prevents a completely objective division of costs among segments. For example, the company president's salary is difficult to allocate to various segments. Allocations of common costs are inherently arbitrary and may not be meaningful. There is a presumption that if companies allocate common costs to segments, these allocations are either directly attributable or reasonably allocable.

Segmented Information Reported The FASB requires that an enterprise report the following.

1. ***General information about its operating segments.*** This includes factors that management considers most significant in determining the company's operating segments,

[7]According to a recent study by Deloitte, segment reporting issues are one of the five top SEC comment letter topics. For example, PowerSecure received a $500,000 fine for failure to adequately identify reportable segments [S. Quinlivan, "SEC Charges Issuer with Inadequate Segment Reporting," *Dodd-Frank.com* (November 7, 2016)]. In response to these segment reporting challenges, the FASB is conducting a study of segment aggregation criteria and disclosures to provide users with more decision-useful information about the reportable segments, including new approaches to identifying reportable segments (see the FASB website; click on Projects and then Presentation and Disclosure).

and the types of products and services from which each operating segment derives its revenues.

2. ***Segment profit and loss and related information.*** Specifically, companies must report the following information about each operating segment **if the amounts are included in determining segment profit or loss.**
   - Commonly reported elements include:
     a. Revenues from transactions with external customers.
     b. Depreciation, depletion, and amortization expense.
   - Other information, which may be included in segment profit and loss and should be reported includes:
     a. Revenues from transactions with other operating segments of the same enterprise.
     b. Interest revenue and interest expense.
     c. Unusual and infrequent items.
     d. Equity in the net income of investees accounted for by the equity method.
     e. Income tax expense or benefit.
     f. Significant noncash items other than depreciation, depletion, and amortization expense.
3. ***Segment assets.*** A company must report each operating segment's total assets.
4. ***Reconciliations.*** A company must provide a reconciliation of the total of the segments' revenues to total revenues, a reconciliation of the total of the operating segments' profits and losses to its income before income taxes, and a reconciliation of the total of the operating segments' assets to total assets.
5. ***Information about products and services and geographic areas.*** For each operating segment not based on geography, the company must report (unless it is impracticable): (1) revenues from external customers, (2) long-lived assets, and (3) expenditures during the period for long-lived assets. This information, if material, must be reported (a) in the enterprise's country of domicile and (b) in each other country.
6. ***Major customers.*** If 10 percent or more of company revenue is derived from a single customer, the company must disclose the total amount of revenue from each such customer by segment.

Illustration of Disaggregated Information

Illustration 24.7 shows the segment disclosure for Johnson & Johnson.

Interim Reports

Another source of information for the investor is interim reports. As noted earlier, interim reports cover periods of less than one year. The stock exchanges, the SEC, and the accounting profession have an active interest in the presentation of interim information.

Interim reporting by public companies on a quarterly basis is a well-established and accepted practice. Analysts and investors want financial information as soon as possible, before it is old news (see Underlying Concepts). However, quarterly reporting is not without critics. Today, many contend that U.S. management is too oriented to the short-term. The truth of this statement is echoed by the words of the president of a large company who decided to retire early: "I wanted to look forward to a year made up of four seasons rather than four quarters." While some are calling for the SEC to eliminate all interim reporting requirements in response to the negative consequences of short-termism, others are calling for a common sense approach, encouraging standard-setters to consider both costs and benefits.

Presently, the SEC mandates that certain companies file a **Form 10-Q**, in which a company discloses quarterly data similar to that disclosed in the annual report. It also requires those companies to disclose selected quarterly information in notes to the annual financial statements. Illustration 24.8 presents the selected quarterly disclosure of Tootsie Roll Industries, Inc. In addition to Form 10-Q, GAAP narrows the reporting alternatives related to interim reports. [4]

Underlying Concepts

For information to be relevant, it must be available to decision-makers before it loses its capacity to influence their decisions (timeliness). Interim reporting is an excellent example of this concept.

ILLUSTRATION 24.7 **Segment Disclosure**

Johnson & Johnson
(notes excluded)

Segments of Business and Geographic Areas

(Dollars in Millions)	Sales to Customers 2017	Sales to Customers 2016
Consumer—United States	$ 5,565	$ 5,420
International	8,037	7,887
Total	13,602	13,307
Pharmaceutical—United States	21,474	20,125
International	14,7(82	13,339
Total	36,256	33,464
Medical Devices—United States	12,824	12,266
International	13,768	12,853
Total	26,592	25,119
Worldwide total	$76,450	$71,890

Segment revenues

(Dollars in Millions)	Pre-Tax Profit 2017	Pre-Tax Profit 2016	Identifiable Assets 2017	Identifiable Assets 2016
Consumer	$ 2,524	$ 2,441	$ 25,030	$ 23,971
Pharmaceutical	11,083	12,827	59,450	27,477
Medical Devices	5,392	5,578	45,413	39,773
Total	18,999	20,846	129,893	91,221
Less: Expense not allocated to segments (1)	1,326	1043		
General corporate (2)			27,410	49,987
Worldwide total	$17,673	$19,803	$157,303	$141,208

Segment profit, segment assets

(Dollars in Millions)	Additions to Property, Plant & Equipment 2017	Additions to Property, Plant & Equipment 2016	Depreciation and Amortization 2017	Depreciation and Amortization 2016
Consumer	$ 485	$ 486	$ 674	$ 608
Pharmaceutical	936	927	2,416	886
Medical Devices	1,566	1,472	2,216	1,928
Segments total	2,987	2,885	5,306	3,422
General corporate	292	341	336	332
Worldwide total	$3,279	$3,226	$5,642	$3,754

Information on property, plant, and equipment

(Dollars in Millions)	Sales to Customers 2017	Sales to Customers 2016	Long-Lived Assets 2017	Long-Lived Assets 2016
United States	$39,863	$37,811	$ 38,556	$ 36,934
Europe	17,126	15,770	56,677	21,996
Western Hemisphere excluding U.S.	6,041	5,734	2,990	2,961
Asia-Pacific, Africa	13,420	12,575	2,773	2,512
Segments total	76,450	71,890	100,996	64,403
General corporate			1,143	1,190
Other non long-lived assets			55,164	75,615
Worldwide total	$76,450	$71,890	$157,303	$141,208

Geographic information

Interim Reporting Requirements

Generally, companies should use the same accounting principles for interim reports and for annual reports. They should recognize revenues in interim periods on the same basis as they are for annual periods. For example, if Cedars Corp. uses the percentage-of-completion method as the basis for recognizing revenue on an annual basis, then it should use the percentage-of-completion basis for interim reports as well. Also, Cedars should treat costs

ILLUSTRATION 24.8
Disclosure of Selected Quarterly Data

Tootsie Roll Industries, Inc.
For the Year Ended December 31, 2017

(Thousands of dollars except per share data)

	First	Second	Third	Fourth	Total
Net product sales	$103,425	$104,897	$182,173	$125,179	$515,674
Product gross margin	38,009	39,638	67,325	44,778	189,750
Net earnings	10,051	11,895	26,933	31,985	80,864
Net earnings per share	0.16	0.19	0.43	0.51	1.29

	Stock Prices 2017		Dividends 2017
	High	Low	
1st Qtr	$40.55	$37.00	$0.09
2nd Qtr	38.90	34.45	0.09
3rd Qtr	38.00	34.95	0.09
4th Qtr	38.45	34.75	0.09

directly associated with revenues (product costs, such as materials, labor and related fringe benefits, and manufacturing overhead) in the same manner for interim reports as for annual reports.

Companies should use the same inventory pricing methods (FIFO, LIFO, etc.) for interim reports and for annual reports. However, the following exceptions are appropriate at interim reporting periods.

1. Companies may use the gross profit method for interim inventory pricing. But they must disclose the method and adjustments to reconcile with annual inventory.
2. When a company liquidates LIFO inventories at an interim date and expects to replace them by year-end, cost of goods sold should include the expected cost of replacing the liquidated LIFO base, rather than give effect to the interim liquidation.
3. Companies should not defer inventory market declines beyond the interim period unless they are temporary and no loss is expected for the fiscal year.
4. Companies ordinarily should defer planned variances under a standard cost system; such variances are expected to be absorbed by year-end.

Companies often charge to the interim period, as incurred, costs and expenses other than product costs (often referred to as **period costs**). But companies may allocate these costs among interim periods on the basis of an estimate of time expired, benefit received, or activity associated with the periods. Companies display considerable latitude in accounting for these costs in interim periods, and many believe more definitive guidelines are needed.

Regarding disclosure, companies should report the following interim data at a minimum.

1. Sales or gross revenues, provision for income taxes, and net income.
2. Basic and diluted earnings per share where appropriate.
3. Seasonal revenue, cost, or expenses.
4. Significant changes in estimates or provisions for income taxes.
5. Disposal of a component of a business, and unusual or infrequently occurring items.
6. Contingent items.
7. Changes in accounting principles or estimates.
8. Significant changes in financial position.

The FASB encourages, but does not require, companies to publish an interim balance sheet and statement of cash flows. If a company does not present this information, it should disclose significant changes in such items as liquid assets, net working capital, long-term liabilities, and stockholders' equity.

Unique Problems of Interim Reporting

Because of the short-term nature of the information in interim reports, there is considerable controversy as to the general approach companies should employ. One group, which favors the **discrete approach**, believes that companies should treat each interim period as a separate accounting period. Using that treatment, companies would follow the principles for deferrals and accruals used for annual reports. In this view, companies should report accounting transactions as they occur, and expense recognition should not change with the period of time covered.

Another group, which favors the **integral approach**, believes that the interim report is an integral part of the annual report and that deferrals and accruals should take into consideration what will happen for the entire year. In this approach, companies should assign estimated expenses to parts of a year on the basis of sales volume or some other activity base.

At present, many companies follow the discrete approach for certain types of expenses and the integral approach for others, given the standards currently employed in practice are vague and lead to differing interpretations.

Current GAAP reflects a preference for the integral approach. However, within this broad guideline, a number of unique reporting problems develop related to the following items.

Advertising and Similar Costs The general guidelines are that companies should defer in an interim period costs such as advertising if the benefits extend beyond that period; otherwise, the company should expense those costs as incurred. But such a determination is difficult, and even if the company defers the costs, how should it allocate them between quarters?

Because of the vague guidelines in this area, accounting for advertising varies widely. At one time, some companies in the food industry, such as RJR Nabisco and Pillsbury, charged advertising costs as a percentage of sales and adjusted to actual at year-end, whereas General Foods and Kellogg's expensed these costs as incurred.

The same type of problem relates to such items as Social Security taxes, research and development costs, and major repairs. For example, should the company expense Social Security costs (payroll taxes) on highly paid personnel early in the year, or allocate and spread them to subsequent quarters? Should a major repair that occurs later in the year be anticipated and allocated proportionately to earlier periods?

Expenses Subject to Year-End Adjustment Companies often do not know with a great deal of certainty amounts of bad debts, executive bonuses, pension costs, and inventory shrinkage until year-end. **They should estimate these costs and allocate them to interim periods as best they can.** Companies use a variety of allocation techniques to accomplish this objective.

Income Taxes Not every dollar of corporate taxable income is taxed at the same rate; the tax rate structure is progressive. This aspect of business income taxes poses a problem in preparing interim financial statements. Should the company use the **annualized approach**, which is to annualize income to date and accrue the proportionate income tax for the period to date? Or should it follow the **marginal principle approach**, which is to apply the lower rate of tax to the first amount of income earned? At one time, companies generally followed the latter approach and accrued the tax applicable to each additional dollar of income.

The profession now, however, uses the annualized approach. This requires that "at the end of each interim period the company should make its best estimate of the effective tax rate expected to be applicable for the full fiscal year. The rate so determined should be used in providing for income taxes on income for the quarter." [5][8]

[8]As discussed in Chapter 19, the Tax Cuts and Jobs Act (TCJA) of 2017 enacted a flat federal tax rate of 21 percent. However, state, local, and some foreign tax rates follow a graduated (progressive) schedule. The estimated annual effective tax rate should reflect anticipated tax credits, foreign tax rates, percentage depletion, capital gains rates, and other available tax-planning alternatives.

Because businesses did not uniformly apply this guideline in accounting for similar situations, the FASB issued authoritative guidance. GAAP now requires companies, when computing the year-to-date tax, to apply the **estimated annual effective tax rate** to the year-to-date "ordinary" income at the end of each interim period. Further, the **interim period tax** related to "ordinary" income shall be the difference between the amount so computed and the amounts reported for previous interim periods of the fiscal period. [6][9]

Earnings per Share Interim reporting of earnings per share has all the problems inherent in computing and presenting annual earnings per share, and then some. If a company issues shares in the third period, EPS for the first two periods will not reflect year-end EPS. For purposes of computing earnings per share and making the required disclosure determinations, each interim period should stand alone. That is, all applicable tests should be made for that single period.

Seasonality **Seasonality** occurs when most of a company's sales occur in one short period of the year while certain costs are fairly evenly spread throughout the year. For example, the natural gas industry has its heavy sales in the winter months. In contrast, the beverage industry has its heavy sales in the summer months.

The problem of seasonality is related to the expense recognition principle in accounting. Generally, expenses are associated with the revenues they create. In a seasonal business, wide fluctuations in profits occur because off-season sales do not absorb the company's fixed costs (for example, manufacturing, selling, and administrative costs that tend to remain fairly constant regardless of sales or production).

To illustrate why seasonality is a problem, assume the information shown in **Illustration 24.9**.

ILLUSTRATION 24.9

Data for Seasonality Example

Selling price per unit	$1
Annual sales for the period (projected and actual)	
100,000 units @ $1	$100,000
Manufacturing costs	
Variable	10¢ per unit
Fixed	20¢ per unit or $20,000 for the year
Nonmanufacturing costs	
Variable	10¢ per unit
Fixed	30¢ per unit or $30,000 for the year

Illustration 24.10 presents sales for four quarters and the year (projected and actual).

ILLUSTRATION 24.10

Sales Data for Seasonality Example

		Percent of Sales
1st Quarter	$ 20,000	20%
2nd Quarter	5,000	5
3rd Quarter	10,000	10
4th Quarter	65,000	65
Total for the year	$100,000	100%

Under the present accounting framework, the income statements for the quarters might be as shown in **Illustration 24.11**.

An investor who uses the first quarter's results might be misled. If the first quarter's earnings are $4,500, should this figure be multiplied by four to predict annual earnings of $18,000? Or, if first-quarter sales of $20,000 are 20 percent of the predicted sales for the year, would the net income for the year be $22,500 ($4,500 × 5)? Both figures are obviously wrong, and after the second quarter's results occur, the investor may become even more confused.

The problem with the conventional approach is that the fixed nonmanufacturing costs are not charged in proportion to sales. Some enterprises have adopted a way of avoiding this problem by making all fixed nonmanufacturing costs follow the sales pattern, as shown in **Illustration 24.12**.

[9]"Ordinary" income (or loss) refers to income (or loss) from operations or income (or loss) from continuing operations, when discontinued operations are involved.

ILLUSTRATION 24.11

Interim Net Income for Seasonal Business—Discrete Approach

	1st Qtr	2nd Qtr	3rd Qtr	4th Qtr	Year
Sales	$20,000	$ 5,000	$10,000	$65,000	$100,000
Manufacturing costs					
Variable	(2,000)	(500)	(1,000)	(6,500)	(10,000)
Fixed[a]	(4,000)	(1,000)	(2,000)	(13,000)	(20,000)
	14,000	3,500	7,000	45,500	70,000
Nonmanufacturing costs					
Variable	(2,000)	(500)	(1,000)	(6,500)	(10,000)
Fixed[b]	(7,500)	(7,500)	(7,500)	(7,500)	(30,000)
Net income	$ 4,500	$(4,500)	$ (1,500)	$31,500	$ 30,000

[a]The fixed manufacturing costs are inventoried, so that equal amounts of fixed costs do not appear during each quarter.
[b]The fixed nonmanufacturing costs are not inventoried, so equal amounts of fixed costs appear during each quarter.

ILLUSTRATION 24.12

Interim Net Income for Seasonal Business—Integral Approach

	1st Qtr	2nd Qtr	3rd Qtr	4th Qtr	Year
Sales	$20,000	$ 5,000	$10,000	$65,000	$100,000
Manufacturing costs					
Variable	(2,000)	(500)	(1,000)	(6,500)	(10,000)
Fixed	(4,000)	(1,000)	(2,000)	(13,000)	(20,000)
	14,000	3,500	7,000	45,500	70,000
Nonmanufacturing costs					
Variable	(2,000)	(500)	(1,000)	(6,500)	(10,000)
Fixed	(6,000)	(1,500)	(3,000)	(19,500)	(30,000)
Net income	$ 6,000	$ 1,500	$ 3,000	$19,500	$ 30,000

This approach solves some of the seasonality problems of interim reporting. Sales in the first quarter are 20 percent of total sales for the year, and net income in the first quarter is 20 percent of total income. In this case, as in the previous example, the investor cannot rely on multiplying any given quarter by four but can use comparative data or rely on some estimate of sales in relation to income for a given period.

The greater the degree of seasonality experienced by a company, the greater the possibility of distortion. Because there are no definitive guidelines for handling such items as the fixed nonmanufacturing costs, variability in income can be substantial. To alleviate this problem, the profession recommends that companies subject to material seasonal variations disclose the seasonal nature of their business and consider supplementing their interim reports with information for 12-month periods ended at the interim date for the current and preceding years.

The two illustrations highlight the difference between the **discrete** and **integral** approaches. Illustration 24.11 represents the discrete approach, in which the fixed nonmanufacturing expenses are expensed as incurred. Illustration 24.12 shows the integral approach, in which expenses are charged to expense on the basis of some measure of activity (see Global View).

Global View

IFRS requires that interim financial statements use the discrete method, except for tax expenses.

Evolving Issue It's Faster but Is It Better?

The profession has developed some rules for interim reporting, but much still has to be done. As yet, it is unclear whether the discrete or the integral method, or some combination of the two, will be settled on.

Discussion also persists about the independent auditor's involvement in interim reports. Many auditors are reluctant to express an opinion on interim financial information, arguing that the data are too tentative and subjective. On the other hand, more people are advocating some examination of interim reports. As a compromise, the SEC currently requires that auditors perform a review of interim financial information. Such a review, which is much more limited in its procedures than the annual audit, provides some assurance that the interim information appears to be in accord with GAAP. [See AU-C Section 930, "Interim Financial Information," *Statement on Auditing Standards No. 122*. Effective for audits of financial statements for periods ending on or after December 31, 2013. Predecessor literature: "Interim Financial Information," *Statement on Auditing Standards No. 101* (New York: AICPA, 2002).]

The SEC also believes that timeliness of information is of extreme importance. First, the SEC has said that large public companies will have only 60 days to complete their annual reports, down from 90 days. Quarterly reports must be done within 40 days of the close of the quarter, instead of 45. In addition, corporate executives and shareholders with more than 10 percent of a company's outstanding stock now have just two days to disclose their sale or purchase of stock.

In a bid to increase Internet disclosure, the SEC encourages companies to post current, quarterly, and annual reports on their websites—or explain why they don't. The Internet postings would have to be made by the day the company submits the information to the SEC, rather than within 24 hours as current rules allow. A steady stream of information from the company to the investor could be very positive because it might alleviate management's continual concern with short-run interim numbers.

As discussed, many contend that U.S. management is too oriented to the short-term, and some are calling for the SEC to eliminate all interim reporting requirements in response to the negative consequences of short-termism. For example, the Oracle of Omaha, Warren Buffett, has issued a call to move away from quarterly reporting. And President Trump tweeted that public companies should report their financial results only twice a year instead of quarterly, arguing it would reduce companies' costs of complying with bureaucratic red tape and help corporate executives focus on longer-term goals. The FASB is being judicious when establishing disclosures that are mandatory every reporting period and that the hurdle should be high for such requirements. The FASB is considering such advice in its Disclosure Framework project.

Sources: D. Benoit, "Time to End Quarterly Reports, Law Firm Says," *Wall Street Journal* (August 19, 2015); PricewaterhouseCoopers, "The Interim Reporting Model: Time to Get Back to Basics," *Point of View* (November 2014); M. Rapoport, "Buffett, Dimon Team Up to Curb 'Unhealthy Focus' on Quarterly Earnings," *Wall Street Journal* (June 7, 2018); and J. Zweig, "The End of Quarterly Reporting? Not Much to Cheer About," *Wall Street Journal* (August 17, 2018).

Auditor's and Management's Reports

LEARNING OBJECTIVE 3

Identify the major disclosures in the auditor's report and understand management's responsibilities for the financial statements.

Auditor's Report

Another important source of information, which is often overlooked, is the **auditor's report**. An **auditor** is an accounting professional who conducts an independent examination of a company's accounting data.

If satisfied that the financial statements present the financial position, results of operations, and cash flows fairly in accordance with generally accepted accounting principles, the auditor expresses an **unqualified opinion**. An example is shown in **Illustration 24.13**.[10]

In preparing the report, the auditor follows these reporting standards.

1. The report states whether the financial statements are in accordance with generally accepted accounting principles.
2. The report identifies those circumstances in which the company has not consistently observed such principles in the current period in relation to the preceding period.
3. Users are to regard the informative disclosures in the financial statements as reasonably adequate unless the report states otherwise.
4. The report contains either an expression of opinion regarding the financial statements taken as a whole or an assertion to the effect that an opinion cannot be expressed. When the auditor cannot express an overall opinion, the report should state the reasons. In all cases where an auditor's name is associated with financial statements, the report should contain a clear-cut indication of the character of the auditor's examination, if any, and the degree of responsibility being taken.

[10]This audit report conforms to the PCAOB standard on the audit report [*The Auditor's Report on an Audit of Financial Statements When the Auditor Expresses an Unqualified Opinion* (PCAOB Release No. 2017-001, June 1, 2017)]. The provisions are required for public companies beginning in 2018. The audit report for private companies is governed by auditing standards issued by the AICPA [See AU-C Section 700, "Forming an Opinion and Reporting on Financial Statements," *Statement on Auditing Standards No. 122*. Effective for audits of financial statements for periods ending on or after December 31, 2013. Predecessor literature: "Reports on Audited Financial Statements," *Statement on Auditing Standards No. 58* (New York: AICPA, 1988).] Notable differences for public companies under the PCAOB rules relate to (1) identification of the engagement partner; (2) auditor tenure (how long the auditor has served this client); (3) guidance on auditor reporting on supplemental information, interim financial information, and special reports; and (4) auditor communication of Critical Audit Matters (CAMs).

ILLUSTRATION 24.13

Auditor's Report

Report of Independent Registered Public Accounting Firm

To the shareholders and the board of directors of Raintree Company:

Opinion on the Financial Statements

We have audited the accompanying balance sheets of Raintree Company (the "Company") as of December 31, 2020 and 2019, the related statements of income, comprehensive income, stockholders' equity, and cash flows, for each of the three years in the period ended December 31, 2020, and the related notes [and schedules] (collectively referred to as the "financial statements"). In our opinion, the financial statements present fairly, in all material respects, the financial position of the Company as of December 31, 2020 and 2019, and the results of its operations and its cash flows for each of the three years in the period ended December 31, 2020, in conformity with U.S. GAAP.

Basis for Opinion

These financial statements are the responsibility of the Company's management. Our responsibility is to express an opinion on the Company's financial statements based on our audits. We are a public accounting firm registered with the Public Company Accounting Oversight Board (United States) ("PCAOB") and are required to be independent with respect to the Company in accordance with the U.S. federal securities laws and the applicable rules and regulations of the Securities and Exchange Commission and the PCAOB.

We conducted our audits in accordance with the standards of the PCAOB. Those standards require that we plan and perform the audit to obtain reasonable assurance about whether the financial statements are free of material misstatement, whether due to error or fraud. Our audits included performing procedures to assess the risks of material misstatement of the financial statements, whether due to error or fraud, and performing procedures that respond to those risks. Such procedures included examining, on a test basis, evidence regarding the amounts and disclosures in the financial statements.

Our audits also included evaluating the accounting principles used and significant estimates made by management, as well as evaluating the overall presentation of the financial statements. We believe that our audits provide a reasonable basis for our opinion.

Richardson & Associates LLP

The engagement partner on our audit for the year ended December 31, 2020, was William Richardson, CPA. We have served as the Company's auditor since 2011.

Minneapolis, MN
March 31, 2021

In most cases, the auditor issues a standard **unqualified (clean) opinion**. That is, the auditor expresses the opinion that the financial statements present fairly, in all material respects, the financial position, results of operations, and cash flows of the entity in conformity with generally accepted accounting principles.

Certain circumstances, although they do not affect the auditor's unqualified opinion, may require the auditor to add an explanatory paragraph to the audit report. Some of the more important circumstances are as follows.

1. ***Going concern.*** The auditor must evaluate whether there is substantial doubt about the entity's **ability to continue as a going concern** for a reasonable period of time, taking into consideration all available information about the future. (The future is at least, but not limited to, 12 months from the end of the reporting period.) If substantial doubt exists about the company continuing as a going concern, the auditor adds to the report an explanatory note describing the potential problem.[11]
2. ***Lack of consistency.*** If a company has changed accounting principles or the method of their application in a way that has a material effect on the comparability of its financial statements, the auditor should refer to the change in an explanatory paragraph of the report. Such an explanatory paragraph should identify the nature of the change and

[11]Although auditors are responsible for assessing going concern uncertainties, until recently there has been no guidance in GAAP for management disclosures in this area. The FASB now requires companies to evaluate conditions or events that raise substantial doubt about the company's ability to continue as a going concern (defined as when it is probable that the company will be unable to meet its obligations as they become due within one year after the date that the financial statements are issued). When management concludes there is substantial doubt about the going concern assumption, this must be disclosed along with information to explain that conclusion. Management should also consider and disclose actions that, if implemented, will mitigate the conditions that could lead to a going concern disclosure. [7]

refer readers to the note in the financial statements that discusses the change in detail. The auditor's concurrence with a change is implicit unless the auditor takes exception to the change in expressing an opinion as to fair presentation in conformity with generally accepted accounting principles.

3. ***Emphasis of a matter.*** The auditor may wish to emphasize a matter regarding the financial statements but nevertheless intends to express an unqualified opinion. For example, the auditor may wish to emphasize that the entity is a component of a larger business enterprise or that it has had significant transactions with related parties. The auditor presents such explanatory information in a separate paragraph of the report.[12]

In some situations, however, the auditor is required to express (1) a **qualified** opinion or (2) an **adverse** opinion, or (3) to **disclaim** an opinion.

A **qualified opinion** contains an exception to the standard opinion. Ordinarily, the exception is not of sufficient magnitude to invalidate the statements as a whole; if it were, an adverse opinion would be rendered. The usual circumstances in which the auditor may deviate from the standard unqualified short-form report on financial statements are as follows.

1. The scope of the examination is limited or affected by conditions or restrictions.
2. The statements do not fairly present financial position or results of operations because of:
   a. Lack of conformity with generally accepted accounting principles and standards.
   b. Inadequate disclosure.

If confronted with one of the situations noted above, the auditor must offer a qualified opinion. A qualified opinion states that, except for the effects of the matter to which the qualification relates, the financial statements present fairly, in all material respects, the financial position, results of operations, and cash flows in conformity with generally accepted accounting principles.

Illustration 24.14 shows an example of an auditor's report with a qualified opinion. The auditor qualified the opinion because the company used an accounting principle at variance with generally accepted accounting principles.

ILLUSTRATION 24.14
Qualified Auditor's Report

Helio Company

Independent Auditor's Report

(Same first and second paragraphs as the standard report)

Helio Company has excluded, from property and debt in the accompanying balance sheets, certain lease obligations that, in our opinion, should be capitalized in order to conform with generally accepted accounting principles. If these lease obligations were capitalized, property would be increased by $1,500,000 and $1,300,000, long-term debt by $1,400,000 and $1,200,000, and retained earnings by $100,000 and $50,000 as of December 31, in the current and prior year, respectively. Additionally, net income would be decreased by $40,000 and $30,000 and earnings per share would be decreased by $.06 and $.04, respectively, for the years then ended.

In our opinion, except for the effects of not capitalizing certain lease obligations as discussed in the preceding paragraph, the financial statements referred to above present fairly, in all material respects, the financial position of Helio Company, and the results of its operations and its cash flows for the years then ended in conformity with generally accepted accounting principles.

An **adverse opinion** is required in any report in which the exceptions to fair presentation are so material that in the independent auditor's judgment, a qualified opinion is not justified. In such a case, the financial statements taken as a whole are not presented in accordance with generally accepted accounting principles. Adverse opinions are rare, because most companies change their accounting to conform with GAAP. The SEC will not permit a company listed on an exchange to have an adverse opinion.

[12]Under the recent PCAOB standard (*op. cit.*), certain public companies are required to include in the auditor's report a communication regarding critical audit matters (CAMs). CAMs are defined as matters arising from the audit that have been communicated or were required to be communicated to the audit committee and that (1) relate to accounts or disclosures that are material to the financial statements and (2) involved especially challenging, subjective, or complex auditor judgment. The AICPA is considering a similar requirement for the audits of private companies. See *https://www.aicpa.org/research/exposuredrafts/accountingandauditing.html.*

A **disclaimer of an opinion** is appropriate when the auditor has gathered so little information on the financial statements that no opinion can be expressed.

The audit report should provide useful information to the investor. One investment banker noted, "Probably the first item to check is the auditor's opinion to see whether or not it is a clean one—'in conformity with generally accepted accounting principles'—or is qualified in regard to differences between the auditor and company management in the accounting treatment of some major item, or in the outcome of some major litigation."

What Do the Numbers Mean? Heart of the Matter

As we discussed in the opening story, financial disclosure is one of a number of institutional features that contribute to vibrant security markets. In fact, a recent study of disclosure and other mechanisms (such as civil lawsuits and criminal sanctions) found that good disclosure is the most important contributor to a vibrant market. The study, which compared disclosure and other legal and regulatory elements across 49 countries, found that countries with the best disclosure laws have the biggest stock markets.

Countries with more successful market environments also tend to have regulations that make it relatively easy for private investors to sue corporations that provide bad information. That is, while criminal sanctions can be effective in some circumstances, disclosure and other legal and regulatory elements encouraging good disclosure are the most important determinants of highly liquid and deep securities markets.

These findings hold for nations in all stages of economic development, with particular importance for nations that are in the early stages of securities regulation. In addition, countries with fewer market protections likely will benefit the most from adoption of international standards for market regulation and disclosure. The lesson: Disclosure is good for your market.

Sources: Rebecca Christie, "Study: Disclosure at Heart of Effective Securities Laws," *Wall Street Journal Online* (August 11, 2003); and L. Hail, C. Leuz, and P. Wysocki, "Global Accounting Convergence and the Potential Adoption of IFRS by the U.S. (Part I): Conceptual Underpinnings and Economic Analysis," *Accounting Horizons* (September 2010). See also N. Trentmann, "Financial Reports Could Be Better, Says U.K. Regulator," *Wall Street Journal* (October 23, 2017).

Management's Reports

Management's Discussion and Analysis

The SEC mandates inclusion of **management's discussion and analysis (MD&A)**. This section covers three financial aspects of an enterprise's business—liquidity, capital resources, and results of operations. In it, management highlights favorable or unfavorable trends and identifies significant events and uncertainties that affect these three factors. This approach obviously involves subjective estimates, opinions, and soft data. However, the SEC believes that the relevance of this information exceeds the potential lack of faithful representation.

Illustration 24.15 presents an excerpt from the MD&A section ("Business Risks" only) of **PepsiCo**'s annual report.

The MD&A section also must provide information about the effects of inflation and changing prices, if they are material to financial statement trends. The SEC has not required specific numerical computations, and companies have provided little analysis on changing prices.

An additional disclosure provided in the MD&A of many companies is discussion of the company's critical accounting policies. This disclosure identifies accounting policies that require management to make subjective judgments regarding uncertainties, resulting in potentially significant effects on the financial results.[13] For example, in its critical accounting policy disclosure, **PepsiCo** showed the impact on stock-based compensation expense in response to changes in estimated interest rates and stock return volatility. Through this voluntary disclosure, companies can expand on the information contained in the notes to the financial statements to indicate the sensitivity of the financial results to accounting policy judgments.

[13]See *Cautionary Advice Regarding Disclosure about Critical Accounting Policies,* Release Nos. 33-8040; 34-45149; FR-60 (Washington, D.C.: SEC); and *Proposed Rule: Disclosure in Management's Discussion and Analysis about the Application of Critical Accounting Policies,* Release Nos. 33-8098; 34-45907; International Series Release No. 1258; File No. S7-16-02 (Washington, D.C.: SEC).

ILLUSTRATION 24.15

Management's Discussion and Analysis

PepsiCo, Inc.

MD&A Our business risks (in part)

Risk Management Framework

The achievement of our strategic and operating objectives involves taking risks and that those risks may evolve over time. To identify, assess, prioritize, address, manage, monitor and communicate these risks across the Company's operations, we leverage an integrated risk management framework. This framework includes the following:

- PepsiCo's Board of Directors has oversight responsibility for PepsiCo's integrated risk management framework. One of the Board's primary responsibilities is overseeing and interacting with senior management with respect to key aspects of the Company's business, including risk assessment and risk mitigation of the Company's top risks.
- The Audit Committee of the Board reviews and assesses the guidelines and policies governing PepsiCo's risk management and oversight processes, and assists the Board's oversight of financial, compliance and employee safety risks facing PepsiCo;
- The Public Policy and Sustainability Committee of the Board assists the Board in its oversight of PepsiCo's policies, programs and related risks that concern key public policy and sustainability matters.
- The PepsiCo Risk Committee (PRC), which is comprised of a cross-functional, geographically diverse, senior management group, meets regularly to identify, assess, prioritize and address top strategic, financial, operating, compliance, safety, reputational and other risks. The PRC is also responsible for reporting progress on our risk mitigation efforts to the Board; and
- PepsiCo's Compliance & Ethics Department leads and coordinates our compliance policies and practices.

Market Risks

We are exposed to market risks arising from adverse changes in:

- commodity prices, affecting the cost of our raw materials and energy,
- foreign exchange rates, and
- interest rates.

In the normal course of business, we manage these risks through a variety of strategies, including productivity initiatives, global purchasing programs and hedging strategies. Ongoing productivity initiatives involve the identification and effective implementation of meaningful cost saving opportunities or efficiencies. Our global purchasing programs include fixed-price purchase orders and pricing agreements.

Management's Responsibilities for Financial Statements

The Sarbanes-Oxley Act requires the SEC to develop guidelines for *all* publicly traded companies to report on management's responsibilities for, and assessment of, the internal control system. An example of the type of disclosure that public companies are now making is shown in **Illustration 24.16**.[14]

ILLUSTRATION 24.16

Report on Management's Responsibilities

Home Depot

Item 9A. Controls and Procedures.

Disclosure Controls and Procedures

We maintain disclosure controls and procedures as defined in Rule 13a-15(e) under the Exchange Act that are designed to ensure that information required to be disclosed in our Exchange Act reports is recorded, processed, summarized, and reported within the time periods specified in the SEC's rules and forms, and that such information is accumulated and communicated to our management, including our Chief Executive Officer and Chief Financial Officer, as appropriate, to allow timely decisions regarding required disclosure.

Management, with the participation of our Chief Executive Officer and Chief Financial Officer, has evaluated the effectiveness of our disclosure controls and procedures as of the end of the period covered by this report. Based on that evaluation, our Chief Executive Officer and Chief Financial Officer have concluded that, as of the end of the period covered by this report, our disclosure controls and procedures were effective.

(continued)

[14]As indicated in this disclosure, management is responsible for preparing the financial statements and establishing and maintaining an effective system of internal controls. The auditor provides an independent assessment of whether the financial statements are prepared in accordance with GAAP, and for public companies, whether the internal controls are effective.

ILLUSTRATION 24.16
(continued)

Changes in Internal Control over Financial Reporting

There have not been any changes in our internal control over financial reporting during the fiscal quarter ended January 28, 2018 that have materially affected, or are reasonably likely to materially affect, our internal control over financial reporting.

Management's Report on Internal Control over Financial Reporting

Our management is responsible for establishing and maintaining adequate internal control over financial reporting, as such term is defined in Rule 13a-15(f) promulgated under the Exchange Act. Under the supervision and with the participation of our management, including our Chief Executive Officer and Chief Financial Officer, we conducted an evaluation of the effectiveness of our internal control over financial reporting as of January 28, 2018 based on the framework in Internal Control—Integrated Framework (2013) issued by the Committee of Sponsoring Organizations of the Treadway Commission. Based on our evaluation, our management concluded that our internal control over financial reporting was effective as of January 28, 2018 in providing reasonable assurance regarding the reliability of financial reporting and the preparation of financial statements for external purposes in accordance with GAAP. The effectiveness of our internal control over financial reporting as of January 28, 2018 has been audited by KPMG LLP, an independent registered public accounting firm, as stated in their report which is included herein.

Craig A. Menear
Chairman, Chief Executive Officer and President

Carol B. Tomé
Chief Financial Officer and
Executive Vice President—Corporate Services

Current Reporting Issues

LEARNING OBJECTIVE 4

Identify reporting issues related to fraudulent financial reporting and financial forecasts.

Fraudulent Financial Reporting

Fraudulent financial reporting is defined as "intentional or reckless conduct, whether act or omission, that results in materially misleading financial statements."[15] Fraudulent reporting can involve gross and deliberate distortion of corporate records (such as inventory count tags), or misapplication of accounting principles (failure to disclose material transactions). Although frauds are unusual, recent events involving such well-known companies as **Enron**, **WorldCom**, **Adelphia**, and **Theranos** indicate that more must be done to address this issue.

Causes of Fraudulent Financial Reporting

Fraudulent financial reporting usually occurs because of conditions in a company's internal or external environment. Influences in the **internal environment** relate to poor internal control systems, management's poor attitude toward ethics, or perhaps a company's liquidity or profitability. Those in the **external environment** may relate to industry conditions, overall business environment, or legal and regulatory considerations.

General incentives for fraudulent financial reporting vary. Common ones are the desire to obtain a higher stock price, to avoid default on a loan covenant, or to make a personal gain of some type (additional compensation, promotion). Situational pressures on the company or an individual manager also may lead to fraudulent financial reporting. Examples of these situational pressures include the following.

- ***Sudden decreases in revenue or market share*** for a single company or an entire industry.

[15] "Report of the National Commission on Fraudulent Financial Reporting" (Washington, D.C., 1987), page 2. Unintentional errors as well as corporate improprieties (such as tax fraud, employee embezzlements, and so on) which do not cause the financial statements to be misleading are excluded from the definition of fraudulent financial reporting.

- ***Unrealistic budget pressures*** may occur when headquarters arbitrarily determines profit objectives (particularly for short-term results) and budgets without taking actual conditions into account.
- ***Financial pressure resulting from bonus plans*** that depend on short-term economic performance. This pressure is particularly acute when the bonus is a significant component of the individual's total compensation.

Opportunities for fraudulent financial reporting are present in circumstances when the fraud is easy to commit and when detection is difficult. Frequently, these opportunities arise from:

1. ***The absence of a board of directors or audit committee*** that vigilantly oversees the financial reporting process.
2. ***Weak or nonexistent internal accounting controls.*** This situation can occur, for example, when a company's revenue system is overloaded as a result of a rapid expansion of sales, an acquisition of a new division, or the entry into a new, unfamiliar line of business.
3. ***Unusual or complex transactions*** such as the consolidation of two companies, the divestiture or closing of a specific operation, and the purchase and sale of derivative instruments.
4. ***Accounting estimates requiring significant subjective judgment*** by company management, such as the allowance for loan losses and the estimated liability for warranty expense.
5. ***Ineffective internal audit staffs*** resulting from inadequate staff size and severely limited audit scope.

A weak corporate ethical climate contributes to these situations. Opportunities for fraudulent financial reporting also increase dramatically when the accounting principles followed in reporting transactions are nonexistent, evolving, or subject to varying interpretations.[16]

Trends

While fraudulent financial reporting is the exception rather than the rule, economic crime is on the rise around the world. A recent global survey of over 7,200 executives from 123 countries documented the growth of economic crimes, as shown in Illustration 24.17.

ILLUSTRATION 24.17

Growth of Economic Crime

Q. Has your organisation experienced any fraud and/or economic crime within the last 24 months?

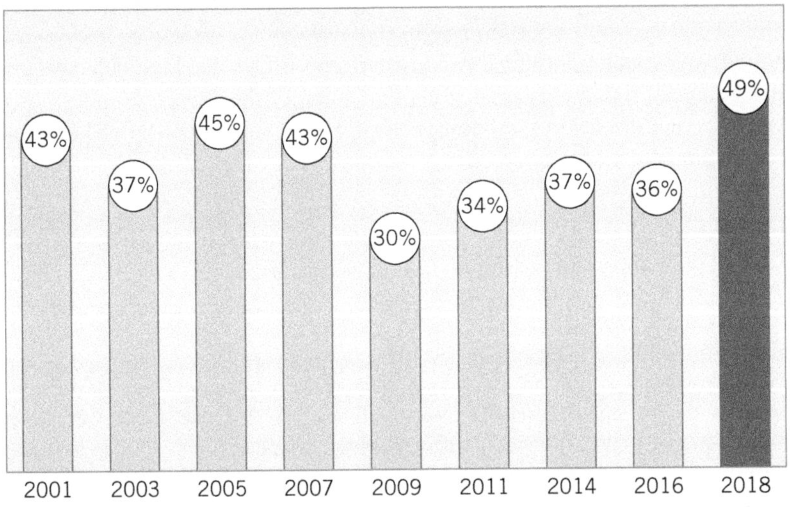

Source: PwC, *2018 Global Economic Crime and Fraud Survey.*

As indicated, economic crimes are on the rise. As shown in Illustration 24.18, asset misappropriation and cybercrime are generally the most common. Accounting fraud is another top source as identified in the professional services (auditors) industry.

[16]The discussion in this section is based on the Report of the National Commission on Fraudulent Financial Reporting, pp. 23–24 (2004). See also "2012 Report to the Nation on Occupational Fraud and Abuse, Association of Certified Fraud Examiners" (*http://www.acfe.com/uploadedFiles/ACFE_Website/Content/rttn/2012-report-to-nations.pdf*), for fraudulent financial reporting causes and consequences.

ILLUSTRATION 24.18

Trends in Reported Fraud

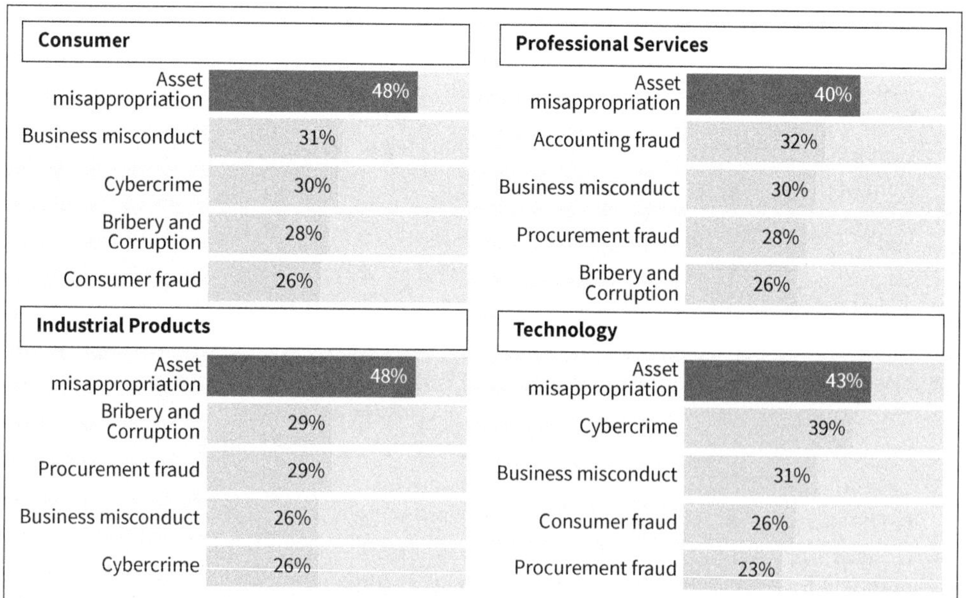

Source: PwC, *2018 Global Economic Crime and Fraud Survey.*

Accounting **errors** are **unintentional** mistakes, whereas **fraud** (misappropriation of assets and fraudulent financial reporting) involves **intentional** distortions of financial statements.[17] Companies should correct the financial statements when they discover errors. The same treatment should be given to fraud. The discovery of fraud, however, gives rise to a different set of procedures and responsibilities for the accountant/auditor.[18] **Illegal acts** encompass such items as illegal political contributions, bribes, kickbacks, and other violations of laws and regulations.[19] In these situations, the accountant/auditor must evaluate the adequacy of disclosure in the financial statements. For example, if a company derives revenue from an illegal act that is considered material in relation to the financial statements, this information should be disclosed. The Sarbanes-Oxley Act is intended to deter these illegal acts. This law adds significant fines and longer jail time for those who improperly sign off on the correctness of financial statements that include willing and knowing misstatements.

Disclosure plays a very important role in these types of transactions because the events are more qualitative than quantitative and involve more subjective than objective evaluation. Users of the financial statements need some indication of the existence and nature of these transactions, through disclosures, modifications in the auditor's report (as discussed above), or reports of changes in auditors.

Response by the Profession

The AICPA has issued numerous auditing standards in response to concerns of the accounting profession, the media, and the public.[20] For example, the standard on fraudulent financial

[17]See AU-C Section 240, "Consideration of Fraud in a Financial Statement Audit," *Statement of Auditing Standards No. 122.* Effective for audits of financial statements for periods ending on or after December 31, 2013. Predecessor literature: "Consideration of Fraud in a Financial Statement Audit," *Statement on Auditing Standards No. 99* (New York: AICPA, 2002). Since passage of the Sarbanes-Oxley Act, auditors of public companies are regulated by the Public Company Accounting Oversight Board (PCAOB). The PCAOB is now the audit standard-setter for auditors of public companies. It has adopted much of the prior auditing standards issued by the Auditing Standards Board of the AICPA.

[18]The profession became so concerned with certain management frauds that affect financial statements that it established a National Commission on Fraudulent Financial Reporting. The major purpose of this organization was to determine how fraudulent reporting practices could be constrained. Fraudulent financial reporting is discussed later in this chapter.

[19]See AU-C Section 250, "Consideration of Laws and Regulations in an Audit of Financial Statements," *Statement of Auditing Standards No. 122.* Effective for audits of financial statements for periods ending on or after December 31, 2013. Predecessor literature: "Illegal Acts by Clients," *Statement on Auditing Standards No. 54* (New York: AICPA, 1988).

[20]Because the profession believes that the role of the auditor is not well understood outside the profession, much attention has been focused on the expectation gap. The **expectation gap** is the gap between (1) the expectation of financial statement users concerning the level of assurance they believe the independent auditor provides, and (2) the assurance that the independent auditor actually does provide under generally accepted auditing standards.

reporting "raises the bar" on the performance of financial statement audits by explicitly requiring auditors to assess the risk of material financial misstatement due to fraud.[21] As indicated earlier, the Sarbanes-Oxley Act now raises the penalty substantially for executives who are involved in fraudulent financial reporting.

Internet Financial Reporting

Most companies now use the power and reach of the Internet to provide more useful information to financial statement readers. All large companies have Internet sites, and a large proportion of companies' websites contain links to their financial statements and other disclosures. The popularity of such reporting is not surprising since it reduces the companies' costs of printing and disseminating paper reports.

Does Internet financial reporting improve the usefulness of a company's financial reports? Yes, in several ways. First, dissemination of reports via the Web allows firms **to communicate more easily and quickly with users** than do traditional paper reports. In addition, **Internet reporting allows users to take advantage of tools** such as search engines and hyperlinks to quickly find information about the firm and to download the information for analysis. Finally, **Internet reporting can help make financial reports more relevant** by allowing companies to report expanded disaggregated data and more timely data than is possible through paper-based reporting. For example, some companies voluntarily report weekly sales data and segment operating data on their websites.

Given the widespread use of the Internet by investors and creditors, it is not surprising that organizations are developing new technologies and standards to further enable and enhance Internet financial reporting. An example is the established use of eXtensible Business Reporting Language (XBRL). **XBRL** is a computer language adapted from the code of the Internet. It "tags" accounting data to correspond to financial reporting items that are reported in the balance sheet, income statement, and the cash flow statement. Once tagged, any company's XBRL data can be easily processed using spreadsheets and other computer programs. In fact, the SEC is phasing in requirements for all companies and mutual funds to prepare their financial reports using XBRL, thereby allowing users to more easily search a company's reports, extract and analyze data, and perform financial comparisons within industries.[22]

To complement the implementation of XBRL use, the SEC has supplemented its EDGAR database with a system called IDEA (short for Interactive Data Electronic Applications). This enhancement of EDGAR marks the SEC's transition from collecting forms and documents to making the information itself freely available to investors in a timely form they can readily use. With IDEA, investors are able to quickly collate information from thousands of companies and forms and create reports and analyses on the fly, in any way they choose. IDEA has opened the door for both the SEC and investors to the new world of financial disclosure in interactive data (XBRL) format.[23]

---

[21]See AU-C Section 240, "Consideration of Fraud in a Financial Statement Audit," *Statement of Auditing Standards No. 122.* Effective for audits of financial statements for periods ending on or after December 31, 2013. Predecessor literature: "Consideration of Fraud in a Financial Statement Audit," *Statement on Auditing Standards No. 99* (New York: AICPA, 2002).

[22]See *SEC Interactive Data Rules for Operating Companies* (*http://www.sec.gov/rules/final/2009/33-9002.pdf*); and C. Twarowski, "Financial Data 'on Steroids'," *Washington Post* (August 19, 2008), p. D01. The FASB (and IASB) have collaborated to implement XBRL with their standards. See the FASB website; click on Taxonomy (XBRL).

[23]See *http://www.sec.gov/edgar/aboutedgar.htm*. The SEC has implemented other regulations to ensure that investors get high-quality disclosures. For example, as discussed in Chapter 4, the SEC was concerned that companies may use pro forma reporting to deflect investor attention from bad news. In response, the SEC issued Regulation G, which requires companies to reconcile non-GAAP financial measures to GAAP. This regulation provides investors with a roadmap to analyze adjustments companies make to their GAAP numbers to arrive at pro forma results. [See SEC Regulation G, "Conditions for Use of Non-GAAP Financial Measures," Release No. 33-8176 (March 28, 2003).] Regulation FD (Release Nos. 33-7881) was issued in 2000 to address the concern that some analysts were receiving information sooner than the general public (e.g., during conference calls with analysts when earnings releases were discussed). Regulation FD requires that when relevant information is released, all have equal access to it.

Reporting on Financial Forecasts and Projections

In recent years, the investing public's demand for more and better information has focused on disclosure of corporate expectations for the future.[24] These disclosures take one of two forms:[25]

- ***Financial forecasts.*** A **financial forecast** is a set of prospective financial statements that present, to the best of the responsible party's knowledge and belief, a company's expected financial position, results of operations, and cash flows. The responsible party bases a financial forecast on conditions it expects to exist and the course of action it expects to take.
- ***Financial projections.*** **Financial projections** are prospective financial statements that present, to the best of the responsible party's knowledge and belief, given one or more *hypothetical assumptions*, an entity's expected financial position, results of operations, and cash flows. The responsible party bases a financial projection on conditions it expects *would* exist and the course of action it expects *would* be taken, given one or more hypothetical assumptions.

The difference between a financial forecast and a financial projection is clear-cut. A forecast provides information on what is **expected** to happen, whereas a projection provides information on what **might** take place but is not necessarily expected to happen.

Whether companies should be required to provide financial forecasts is the subject of intensive discussion with journalists, corporate executives, the SEC, financial analysts, accountants, and others. Predictably, there are strong arguments on either side. Presented below are some of the arguments.

Underlying Concepts

The profession indicates that the legal environment discourages companies from disclosing forward-looking information. Companies should not have to expand reporting of forward-looking information unless there are more effective deterrents to unwarranted litigation.

Arguments for Requiring Published Forecasts
1. Investment decisions are based on future expectations. Therefore, information about the future facilitates better decisions.
2. Companies already circulate forecasts informally. This situation should be regulated to ensure that the forecasts are available to all investors.
3. Circumstances change so rapidly that historical information is no longer adequate for prediction.

Arguments Against Requiring Published Forecasts
1. No one can foretell the future. Therefore, forecasts will inevitably be wrong. Worse, they may mislead, if they convey an impression of precision about the future.
2. Companies may strive only to meet their published forecasts, thereby failing to produce results that are in the stockholders' best interest.
3. If forecasts prove inaccurate, there will be recriminations and probably legal actions (see **Underlying Concepts**).[26]
4. Disclosure of forecasts will be detrimental to organizations, because forecasts will inform competitors (foreign and domestic) as well as investors.

The AICPA has issued a statement on standards for accountants' services on prospective financial information. This statement establishes guidelines for the preparation and presentation of financial forecasts and projections.[27] It requires accountants to provide (1) a summary of significant assumptions used in the forecast or projection and (2) guidelines for minimum presentation.

[24]Some areas in which companies are using financial information about the future are equipment lease-versus-buy analysis, analysis of a company's ability to successfully enter new markets, and examination of merger and acquisition opportunities. In addition, companies also prepare forecasts and projections for use by third parties in public offering documents (requiring financial forecasts), tax-oriented investments, and financial feasibility studies. Use of forward-looking data has been enhanced by the increased capability of microcomputers to analyze, compare, and manipulate large quantities of data.

[25]See AT-C Section 305, "Prospective Financial Information," *Statement of Auditing Standards No. 18: Concepts Common to All Attestation Engagements.* Predecessor literature: "Financial Forecasts and Projections" and "Guide for Prospective Financial Information," *Codification of Statements on Standards for Attestation Engagements* (New York: AICPA 2006), paras. 3.04 and 3.05.

[26]The issue is serious. Over a recent three-year period, 8 percent of the companies on the NYSE were sued because of an alleged lack of financial disclosure. Companies complain that they are subject to lawsuits whenever the stock price drops. And as one executive noted, "You can even be sued if the stock price goes up—because you did not disclose the good news fast enough."

[27]*Op. cit.*

To encourage management to disclose prospective financial information, the SEC has a **safe harbor rule**. It provides protection to a company that presents an erroneous forecast, as long as the company prepared the forecast on a reasonable basis and disclosed it in good faith.[28] However, many companies note that the safe harbor rule does not work in practice, since it does not cover oral statements, nor has it kept them from investor lawsuits.

What Do the Numbers Mean? Global Forecasts

Great Britain permits financial forecasts, and the results have been fairly successful. Some significant differences do exist between the English and the U.S. business and legal environments. The British system, for example, does not permit litigation on forecasted information, and the solicitor (lawyer) is not permitted to work on a contingent-fee basis.

But such differences probably could be overcome if influential interests in this country cooperated to produce an atmosphere conducive to quality forecasting. A typical British forecast adapted from a construction company's report to support a public offering of stock is as follows.

> Profits have grown substantially over the past 10 years and directors are confident of being able to continue this expansion. . . . While the rate of expansion will be dependent on the level of economic activity in Ireland and England, the group is well structured to avail itself of opportunities as they arise, particularly in the field of property development, which is expected to play an increasingly important role in the group's future expansion.
>
> Profits before taxation for the half year ended 30th June were 402,000 pounds. On the basis of trading experiences since that date and the present level of sales and completions, the directors expect that in the absence of unforeseen circumstances, the group's profits before taxation for the year to 31st December will be not less than 960,000 pounds.
>
> No dividends will be paid in respect of the current year. In a full financial year, on the basis of above forecasts (not including full year profits) it would be the intention of the board, assuming current rates of tax, to recommend dividends totaling 40% (of after-tax profits), which will be payable in the next two years.

A general narrative-type forecast issued by a U.S. corporation might appear as follows.

> On the basis of promotions planned by the company for the second half of the fiscal year, net earnings for that period are expected to be approximately the same as those for the first half of the fiscal year, with net earnings for the third quarter expected to make the predominant contribution to net earnings for the second half of the year.

As indicated, the U.S. version is much less specific in its forecasted information.

Source: See "A Case for Forecasting—The British Have Tried It and Find That It Works," *World* (New York: Peat, Marwick, Mitchell & Co., Autumn 1978), pp. 10–13. In a recent survey, U.K. companies remain stubbornly backward-looking. Just 5 percent of FTSE 100 companies address the future of the business in their discussion and analysis. See PricewaterhouseCoopers, "Guide to Forward-looking Information: Don't Fear the Future" (2006).

Questions of Liability

What happens if a company does not meet its forecasts? Can the company and the auditor be sued? If a company, for example, projects an earnings increase of 15 percent and achieves only 5 percent, should stockholders be permitted to have some judicial recourse against the company?

One court case involving **Monsanto Chemical Corporation** set a precedent. In this case, Monsanto predicted that sales would increase 8 to 9 percent and that earnings would rise 4 to 5 percent. In the last part of the year, the demand for Monsanto's products dropped as a result of a business turndown. Instead of increasing, the company's earnings declined. Investors sued the company because the projected earnings figure was erroneous, but a judge dismissed the suit because the forecasts were the best estimates of qualified people whose intents were honest.

As indicated earlier, the SEC's safe harbor rules are intended to protect companies that provide good-faith projections. However, much concern exists as to how the SEC and the courts will interpret such terms as "good faith" and "reasonable assumptions" when erroneous forecasts mislead users of this information.

Criteria for Making Accounting and Reporting Choices

Throughout this text, we have stressed the need to provide information that is useful to predict the amounts, timing, and uncertainty of future cash flows. To achieve this objective,

[28]"Safe-Harbor Rule for Projections," *Release No. 5993* (Washington, D.C.: SEC, 1979). The Private Securities Litigation Reform Act of 1995 recognizes that some information that is useful to investors is inherently subject to less certainty or reliability than other information. By providing safe harbor for forward-looking statements, Congress has sought to facilitate access to this information by investors.

companies must make judicious choices between alternative accounting concepts, methods, and means of disclosure. You are probably surprised by the large number of choices that exist among acceptable alternatives.

You should recognize, however, as indicated in Chapter 1, that accounting is greatly influenced by its environment. It does not exist in a vacuum. Therefore, it is unrealistic to assume that the profession can entirely eliminate alternative presentations of certain transactions and events. Nevertheless, we are hopeful that the profession, by adhering to the conceptual framework, will be able to focus on the needs of financial statement users and eliminate diversity where appropriate. The SEC's and FASB's projects on principles-based standards and disclosure effectiveness are directed at these very issues. They seek to develop guidance that will result in accounting and financial reporting that reflects the economic substance of the transactions, not the desired financial result of management. The profession must continue its efforts to develop a sound foundation upon which to build financial standards and practice (see **Underlying Concepts**). As Aristotle said, "The correct beginning is more than half the whole."

Underlying Concepts

The FASB concept statements on the objective of financial reporting, elements of financial statements, qualitative characteristics of accounting information, and recognition and measurement are important steps in the right direction.

APPENDIX 24A Basic Financial Statement Analysis

LEARNING OBJECTIVE *5

Describe the approach to financial statement analysis.

What would be important to you in studying a company's financial statements? The answer depends on your particular interest—whether you are a creditor, stockholder, potential investor, manager, government agency, or labor leader. For example, **short-term creditors** such as banks are primarily interested in the ability of the firm to pay its currently maturing obligations. In that case, you would examine the current assets and their relation to short-term liabilities to evaluate the short-run solvency of the firm.

Bondholders, on the other hand, look more to long-term indicators, such as the enterprise's capital structure, past and projected earnings, and changes in financial position. **Stockholders**, present or prospective, also are interested in many of the features considered by a long-term creditor. As a stockholder, you would focus on the earnings picture, because changes in it greatly affect the market price of your investment. You also would be concerned with the financial position of the company, because it affects indirectly the stability of earnings.

The **managers** of a company are concerned about the composition of its capital structure and about the changes and trends in earnings. This financial information has a direct influence on the type, amount, and cost of external financing that the company can obtain. In addition, the company managers find financial information useful on a day-to-day operating basis in such areas as capital budgeting, break-even analysis, variance analysis, gross margin analysis, and for internal control purposes.

Perspective on Financial Statement Analysis

Readers of financial statements can gather information by examining relationships between items on the statements and identifying trends in these relationships. The relationships are expressed numerically in ratios and percentages, and trends are identified through comparative analysis (see **Underlying Concepts**).

A problem with learning how to analyze statements is that the means may become an end in itself. Analysts could identify and calculate thousands of possible relationships and trends. If one knows only how to calculate ratios and trends without understanding

Underlying Concepts

Because financial statements report on the past, they emphasize the *qualitative characteristic of feedback value*. This feedback value is useful because it can be used to better achieve the *qualitative characteristic of predictive value.*

how such information can be used, little is accomplished. Therefore, a logical approach to financial statement analysis is necessary, consisting of the following steps.

1. ***Know the questions for which you want to find answers.*** As indicated earlier, various groups have different types of interest in a company.
2. ***Know the questions that particular ratios and comparisons are able to help answer.*** These will be discussed in this appendix.
3. ***Match 1 and 2 above.*** By such a matching, the statement analysis will have a logical direction and purpose.

Several caveats must be mentioned. **Financial statements report on the past.** Thus, analysis of these data is an examination of the past. When using such information in a decision-making (future-oriented) process, analysts assume that the past is a reasonable basis for predicting the future. This is usually a reasonable approach, but its limitations should be recognized.

Also, ratio and trend analyses will help identify a company's present strengths and weaknesses. They may serve as "red flags" indicating problem areas. In many cases, however, such analyses will not reveal **why** things are as they are. Finding answers about "why" usually requires an in-depth analysis and an awareness of many factors about a company that are not reported in the financial statements.

Another caveat is that a **single ratio by itself is not likely to be very useful**. For example, analysts may generally view a current ratio of 2 to 1 (current assets are twice current liabilities) as satisfactory. However, if the industry average is 3 to 1, such a conclusion may be invalid. Even given this industry average, one may conclude that the particular company is doing well if one knows the previous year's ratio was 1.5 to 1. Consequently, to derive meaning from ratios, analysts need some standard against which to compare them. Such a standard may come from industry averages, past years' amounts, a particular competitor, or planned levels.

Finally, **awareness of the limitations of accounting numbers used in an analysis** is important (see Global View). We will discuss some of these limitations and their consequences later in this appendix.

Global View

Some companies outside the United States provide "convenience" financial statements for U.S. readers. These financial statements have been translated into English, and they may also translate the currency units into U.S. dollars. However, the statements are *not restated* using U.S. accounting principles; financial statement analysis needs to take this fact into account.

Ratio Analysis

LEARNING OBJECTIVE *6

Identify major analytic ratios and describe their calculation.

In analyzing financial statement data, analysts use various devices to bring out the comparative and relative significance of the financial information presented. These devices include ratio analysis, comparative analysis, percentage analysis, and examination of related data. No one device is more useful than another. Every situation is different, and analysts often obtain the needed answers only upon close examination of the interrelationships among all the data provided. Ratio analysis is the starting point. Ratios can be classified as follows.

Major Types of Ratios

Liquidity Ratios. Measures of the company's short-run ability to pay its maturing obligations.

Activity Ratios. Measures of how effectively the company is using the assets employed.

Profitability Ratios. Measures of the degree of success or failure of a given company or division for a given period of time.

Coverage Ratios. Measures of the degree of protection for long-term creditors and investors.[29]

[29] Some analysts use other terms to categorize these ratios. For example, liquidity ratios are sometimes referred to as *solvency* ratios; activity ratios as *turnover* or *efficiency* ratios; and coverage ratios as *leverage* or *capital structure* ratios.

We have integrated discussions and illustrations about the computation and use of these financial ratios throughout this text. Illustration 24A.1 summarizes all of the ratios presented in this text and identifies the specific chapters that present this material.

ILLUSTRATION 24A.1

Summary of Financial Ratios

Ratio	Formula for Computation	Reference
I. Liquidity		
1. Current ratio	Current assets / Current liabilities	Chapter 13
2. Quick or acid-test ratio	(Cash + Short-term investments + Accounts receivable (net)) / Current liabilities	Chapter 13
3. Current cash debt coverage	Net cash provided by operating activities / Average current liabilities	Chapter 5
II. Activity		
4. Accounts receivable turnover	Net sales / Average net accounts receivable	Chapter 7
5. Inventory turnover	Cost of goods sold / Average inventory	Chapter 9
6. Asset turnover	Net sales / Average total assets	Chapter 11
III. Profitability		
7. Profit margin on sales	Net income / Net sales	Chapter 11
8. Return on assets	Net income / Average total assets	Chapter 11
9. Return on common stockholders' equity	(Net income − Preferred dividends) / Average common stockholders' equity	Chapter 15
10. Earnings per share	(Net income − Preferred dividends) / Weighted-average common shares outstanding	Chapter 16
11. Payout ratio	Cash dividends / Net income	Chapter 15
IV. Coverage		
12. Debt to assets ratio	Total liabilities / Total assets	Chapter 14
13. Times interest earned	(Net income + Interest expense + Income tax expense) / Interest expense	Chapter 14
14. Cash debt coverage	Net cash provided by operating activities / Average total liabilities	Chapter 5
15. Book value per share	Common stockholders' equity / Outstanding shares	Chapter 15

Additional coverage of these ratios, accompanied by assignment material, is available online. This supplemental coverage takes the form of a comprehensive case adapted from the annual report of a large international chemical company that we have disguised under the name of Anetek Chemical Corporation.

Limitations of Ratio Analysis

LEARNING OBJECTIVE *7

Explain the limitations of ratio analysis.

The reader of financial statements must understand the basic limitations associated with ratio analysis. As analytical tools, ratios are attractive because they are simple and convenient. But too frequently, decision-makers base their decisions on only these simple computations. The ratios are only as good as the data upon which they are based and the information with which they are compared.

One important limitation of ratios is that they generally are **based on historical cost, which can lead to distortions in measuring performance**. Inaccurate assessments of the enterprise's financial condition and performance can result from failing to incorporate fair value information.

Also, investors must remember that **where estimated items (such as depreciation and amortization) are significant, income ratios lose some of their credibility**. For example, income recognized before the termination of a company's life is an approximation. In analyzing the income statement, users should be aware of the uncertainty surrounding the computation of net income.

As one writer aptly noted, "The physicist has long since conceded that the location of an electron is best expressed by a probability curve. Surely an abstraction like earnings per share is even more subject to the rules of probability and risk."[30]

Probably the greatest limitation of ratio analysis is the **difficult problem of achieving comparability among firms in a given industry**. Achieving comparability requires that the analyst (1) identify basic differences in companies' accounting principles and procedures, and (2) adjust the balances to achieve comparability (see **Underlying Concepts**). Basic differences in accounting usually involve one of the following areas.

Underlying Concepts

Consistency and comparability are important concepts for financial statement analysis. If the principles and assumptions used to prepare the financial statements are continually changing, accurate assessments of a company's progress become difficult.

1. Inventory valuation (FIFO, LIFO, average-cost).
2. Depreciation methods, particularly the use of straight-line versus accelerated depreciation.
3. Capitalization versus expensing of certain costs.
4. Investments in common stock carried at equity versus fair value.
5. Differing treatments of postretirement benefit costs.
6. Questionable practices of defining discontinued operations and impairments.

The use of these different alternatives can make a significant difference in the ratios computed. For example, at one time **Anheuser-Busch InBev** noted that if it had used average-cost for inventory valuation instead of LIFO, inventories would have increased approximately $33,000,000. Such an increase would have a substantive impact on the current ratio. Several studies have analyzed the impact of different accounting methods on financial statement analysis. The differences in income that can develop are staggering in some cases. Investors must be aware of the potential pitfalls if they are to be able to make the proper adjustments.

Finally, analysts should recognize that a **substantial amount of important information** is not included in a company's financial statements. Events involving such things as industry changes, management changes, competitors' actions, technological developments, government actions, and union activities are often critical to a company's successful operation. These events occur continuously, and information about them must come from careful analysis of financial reports in the media and other sources. Indeed many argue, in what is known as the **efficient-market hypothesis**, that financial statements contain "no surprises" to those engaged in market activities. They contend that the effect of these events is known in the marketplace—and the price of the company's stock adjusts accordingly—well before the issuance of such reports.

[30]Richard E. Cheney, "How Dependable Is the Bottom Line?" *The Financial Executive* (January 1971), p. 12.

Comparative Analysis

LEARNING OBJECTIVE *8

Describe techniques of comparative analysis.

Comparative analysis presents the same information for two or more different dates or periods, so that like items may be compared. Ratio analysis provides only a single snapshot, for one given point or period in time. In a comparative analysis, an investment analyst can concentrate on a given item and determine whether it appears to be growing or diminishing year by year and the proportion of such change to related items. Generally, companies present comparative financial statements. They typically include two years of balance sheet information and three years of income statement information.

In addition, many companies include in their annual reports five- or ten-year summaries of pertinent data that permit readers to examine and analyze trends. As indicated in GAAP, "the presentation of comparative financial statements in annual and other reports enhances the usefulness of such reports and brings out more clearly the nature and trends of current changes affecting the enterprise." **Illustration 24A.2** presents a five-year condensed statement, with additional supporting data, of Anetek Chemical Corporation.

ILLUSTRATION 24A.2 **Condensed Comparative Financial Information**

Anetek Chemical Corporation
Condensed Comparative Statements
(000,000 omitted)

	2020	2019	2018	2010	2011	10 Years Ago 2010	20 Years Ago 2000
Sales and other revenue:							
Net sales	$1,600.0	$1,350.0	$1,309.7	$1,176.2	$1,077.5	$636.2	$170.7
Other revenue	75.0	50.0	39.4	34.1	24.6	9.0	3.7
Total	1,675.0	1,400.0	1,349.1	1,210.3	1,102.1	645.2	174.4
Costs and other charges:							
Cost of sales	1,000.0	850.0	827.4	737.6	684.2	386.8	111.0
Depreciation and amortization	150.0	150.0	122.6	115.6	98.7	82.4	14.2
Selling and administrative expenses	225.0	150.0	144.2	133.7	126.7	66.7	10.7
Interest expense	50.0	25.0	28.5	20.7	9.4	8.9	1.8
Income taxes	100.0	75.0	79.5	73.5	68.3	42.4	12.4
Total	1,525.0	1,250.0	1,202.2	1,081.1	987.3	587.2	150.1
Net income for the year	$ 150.0	$ 150.0	$ 146.9	$ 129.2	$ 114.8	$ 58.0	$ 24.3
Other Statistics							
Earnings per share on common stock (in dollars)[a]	$ 5.00	$ 5.00	$ 4.90	$ 3.58	$ 3.11	$ 1.66	$ 1.06
Cash dividends per share on common stock (in dollars)[a]	2.25	2.15	1.95	1.79	1.71	1.11	0.25
Cash dividends declared on common stock	67.5	64.5	58.5	64.6	63.1	38.8	5.7
Stock dividend at approximate market value				46.8		27.3	
Taxes (major)	144.5	125.9	116.5	105.6	97.8	59.8	17.0
Wages paid	389.3	325.6	302.1	279.6	263.2	183.2	48.6
Cost of employee benefits	50.8	36.2	32.9	28.7	27.2	18.4	4.4
Number of employees at year end (thousands)	47.4	36.4	35.0	33.8	33.2	26.6	14.6
Additions to property	306.3	192.3	241.5	248.3	166.1	185.0	49.0

[a]Adjusted for stock splits and stock dividends.

Percentage (Common-Size) Analysis

LEARNING OBJECTIVE *9

Describe techniques of percentage analysis.

Analysts also use percentage analysis to help them evaluate and compare companies. **Percentage analysis** consists of reducing a series of related amounts to a series of percentages of a given base. For example, analysts frequently express all items in an income statement as a percentage of sales or sometimes as a percentage of cost of goods sold. They may analyze a balance sheet on the basis of total assets. Percentage analysis facilitates comparison and is helpful in evaluating the relative size of items or the relative change in items. A conversion of absolute dollar amounts to percentages may also facilitate comparison between companies of different size.

Illustration 24A.3 shows a comparative analysis of the expense section of Anetek for the last two years.

ILLUSTRATION 24A.3

Horizontal Percentage Analysis

Anetek Chemical Corporation
Horizontal Comparative Analysis
(000,000 omitted)

	2020	2019	Difference	% Change Inc. (Dec.)
Cost of sales	$1,000.0	$850.0	$150.0	17.6%
Depreciation and amortization	150.0	150.0	0	0
Selling and administrative expenses	225.0	150.0	75.0	50.0
Interest expense	50.0	25.0	25.0	100.0
Income taxes	100.0	75.0	25.0	33.3

This approach, normally called **horizontal analysis**, indicates the proportionate change over a period of time. It is especially useful in evaluating trends, because absolute changes are often deceiving.

Another comparative approach, called **vertical analysis**, is the proportional expression of each financial statement item in a given period to a base figure. For example, Anetek Chemical's 2020 income statement using the percentage analysis approach appears in Illustration 24A.4.

ILLUSTRATION 24A.4

Vertical Percentage Analysis

Anetek Chemical Corporation
Income Statement
(000,000 omitted)

	Amount	Percentage of Total Revenue
Net sales	$1,600.0	96%
Other revenue	75.0	4
Total revenue	1,675.0	100
Less:		
Cost of sales	1,000.0	60
Depreciation and amortization	150.0	9
Selling and administrative expenses	225.0	13
Interest expense	50.0	3
Income taxes	100.0	6
Total expenses	1,525.0	91
Net income	$ 150.0	9%

Vertical analysis is frequently called **common-size analysis** because it reduces all of the statement items to a "common size." That is, all of the elements within each statement are expressed in percentages of some common number and always add up to

100 percent. Common-size (percentage) analysis reveals the composition of each of the financial statements.

In the analysis of the balance sheet, common-size analysis answers such questions as: What percentage of the capital structure is stockholders' equity, current liabilities, and long-term debt? What is the mix of assets (percentage-wise) with which the company has chosen to conduct business? What percentage of current assets is in inventory, receivables, and so forth?

Common-size analysis of the income statement typically relates each item to sales. It is instructive to know what proportion of each sales dollar is absorbed by various costs and expenses incurred by the enterprise.

Analysts may use common-size statements to compare one company's statements from different years in order to detect trends not evident from comparing absolute amounts. Also, common-size statements provide intercompany comparisons regardless of size because they recast financial statements into a comparable common-size format.

Review and Practice

Key Terms Review

accounting policies 24-6
*accounts receivable turnover 24-34
*acid-test ratio 24-34
*activity ratios 24-33
adverse opinion 24-23
*asset turnover 24-34
auditor 24-21
auditor's report 24-21
*book value per share 24-34
*cash debt coverage 24-34
common costs 24-14
*common-size analysis 24-37
*comparative analysis 24-36
*coverage ratios 24-33
*current cash debt coverage 24-34
*current ratio 24-34
*debt to assets ratio 24-34
differential disclosure 24-5
disclaimer of an opinion 24-24
discrete approach 24-18
*earnings per share 24-34
errors 24-28
financial forecast 24-30
financial projection 24-30
fraud 24-28
fraudulent financial reporting 24-26
full disclosure principle 24-3
*horizontal analysis 24-37
illegal acts 24-28
integral approach 24-18
interim reports 24-15
*inventory turnover 24-34
*liquidity ratios 24-33
management approach 24-13
management's discussion and analysis (MD&A) 24-24
nonrecognized subsequent event 24-10
notes to the financial statements 24-7
operating segment 24-13
*payout ratio 24-34
*percentage analysis 24-37
post-balance-sheet events 24-9
*profitability ratios 24-33
*profit margin on sales 24-34
qualified opinion 24-23
*quick ratio 24-34
recognized subsequent event 24-10
related-party transactions 24-8
*return on assets 24-34
*return on common stockholders' equity 24-34
safe harbor rule 24-31
seasonality 24-19
subsequent events 24-9
*times interest earned 24-34
unqualified (clean) opinion 24-22
*vertical analysis 24-37
XBRL 24-29

Learning Objectives Review

1 Review the full disclosure principle and describe how it is implemented.

The **full disclosure principle** calls for financial reporting of any financial facts significant enough to influence the judgment of an informed reader. Implementing the full disclosure principle is difficult because the cost of disclosure can be substantial and the benefits difficult to assess. Disclosure requirements have increased because of (1) the growing complexity of the business environment, (2) the necessity for timely information, and (3) the use of accounting as a control and monitoring device.

Notes in financial statement preparation. Notes are the accountant's means of amplifying or explaining the items presented in the main body of the statements. Notes can explain in qualitative terms information pertinent to specific financial statement items, and can provide supplementary data of a quantitative nature. Common note disclosures relate to such items as accounting policies; inventories; property, plant, and equipment; creditor claims; contingencies and commitments; and subsequent events.

2 Discuss the disclosure requirements for related-party transactions, post-balance-sheet events, major business segments, and interim reporting.

In **related-party transactions,** one party has the ability to significantly influence the policies of the other. As a result, GAAP requires disclosure of the relationship(s) involved, a description and dollar amounts of the transactions, and amounts due from or to related parties. For **post-balance-sheet events**, companies should disclose recognized subsequent events as well as nonrecognized subsequent events. Finally, aggregated figures hide much information about the composition of these consolidated figures. There is no way to tell from the consolidated data the extent to which the differing product lines contribute to the company's profitability, risk, and growth potential. As a result, the profession requires **segment information** in certain situations.

Interim reports cover periods of less than one year. Two viewpoints exist regarding interim reports. The discrete approach holds that each interim period should be treated as a separate accounting period. The integral approach is that the interim report is an integral part of the annual report and that deferrals and accruals should take into consideration what will happen for the entire year.

Companies should use the same accounting principles for interim reports that they use for annual reports. A number of unique reporting problems develop related to the following items: (1) advertising and similar costs, (2) expenses subject to year-end adjustment, (3) income taxes, (4) earnings per share, and (5) seasonality.

3 Identify the major disclosures in the auditor's report and understand management's responsibilities for the financial statements.

In the **auditor's report,** the auditor expresses an unqualified opinion if satisfied that the financial statements present the financial position, results of operations, and cash flows fairly in accordance with generally accepted accounting principles. A qualified opinion contains an exception to the standard opinion; ordinarily, the exception is not of sufficient magnitude to invalidate the statements as a whole.

An adverse opinion is required when the exceptions to fair presentation are so material that a qualified opinion is not justified. A disclaimer of an opinion is appropriate when the auditor has so little information on the financial statements that no opinion can be expressed.

Management's responsibilities for financials. Management's discussion and analysis (MD&A) section covers three financial aspects of an enterprise's business: liquidity, capital resources, and results of operations. Management's responsibility for the financial statements is often indicated in a letter to stockholders in the annual report.

4 Identify reporting issues related to fraudulent financial reporting and financial forecasts.

The profession's response to fraudulent financial reporting. Fraudulent financial reporting is intentional or reckless conduct, whether through act or omission, that results in materially misleading financial statements. Fraudulent financial reporting usually occurs because of poor internal control, management's poor attitude toward ethics, poor performance, and so on. The Sarbanes-Oxley Act has numerous provisions intended to help prevent fraudulent financial reporting.

Financial forecasts. The SEC has indicated that companies are permitted (not required) to include profit forecasts in their reports. To encourage management to disclose such information, the SEC issued a safe harbor rule. The rule provides protection to a company that presents an erroneous forecast, as long as it prepared the projection on a reasonable basis and disclosed it in good faith. However, the safe harbor rule has not worked well in practice.

*5 Describe the approach to financial statement analysis.

Basic financial statement analysis involves examining relationships between items on the statements (ratio and percentage analysis) and identifying trends in these relationships (comparative analysis). Analysis is used to predict the future, but ratio analysis is limited because the data are from the past. Also, ratio analysis identifies present strengths and weaknesses of a company, but it may not reveal *why* they exist. Although single ratios are helpful, they are not conclusive. For maximum usefulness, analysts must compare them with industry averages, past years, planned amounts, and the like.

*6 Identify major analytic ratios and describe their calculation.

Ratios are classified as liquidity ratios, activity ratios, profitability ratios, and coverage ratios. (1) *Liquidity ratio analysis* measures the short-run ability of a company to pay its currently maturing obligations. (2) *Activity ratio analysis* measures how effectively a company is using its assets. (3) *Profitability ratio analysis* measures the degree of success or failure of a company to generate revenues adequate to cover its costs of operation and provide a return to the owners. (4) *Coverage ratio analysis* measures the degree of protection afforded long-term creditors and investors.

*7 Explain the limitations of ratio analysis.

Ratios are based on historical cost, which can lead to distortions in measuring performance. Also, where estimated items are significant, income ratios lose some of their credibility. In addition, comparability problems exist because companies use different accounting principles and procedures. Finally, analysts must recognize that a substantial amount of important information is not included in a company's financial statements.

*8 Describe techniques of comparative analysis.

Companies present comparative data, which generally includes two years of balance sheet information and three years of income statement information. In addition, many companies include in their annual reports five- to ten-year summaries of pertinent data that permit the reader to analyze trends.

*9 Describe techniques of percentage analysis.

Percentage analysis consists of reducing a series of related amounts to a series of percentages of a given base. Analysts use two approaches. *Horizontal analysis* indicates the proportionate change in financial statement items over a period of time; such analysis is most helpful in evaluating trends. *Vertical analysis* (common-size analysis) is a proportional expression of each item on the financial statements in a given period to a base amount. It analyzes the composition of each of the financial statements from different years (a) to detect trends not evident from the comparison of absolute amounts and (b) to make intercompany comparisons of different-sized enterprises.

Enhanced Review and Practice

Go online for multiple-choice questions with solutions, review exercises with solutions, and a full glossary of all key terms.

Practice Problem

Konetzke Corporation, a publicly traded company, is preparing the interim financial data which it will issue to its stockholders and the Securities and Exchange Commission (SEC) for the fiscal year ending December 31, 2020. Your job as a member of the accounting team is to help determine the appropriate disclosures and any other potential year-end adjustments. You have collected the following information.

1. Konetzke is involved in four separate industries. The following information is available for each of the four industries. Konetzke wonders which segments are reportable.

Operating Segment	Total Revenue	Operating Profit (Loss)	Identifiable Assets
Badger	$ 60,000	$15,000	$167,000
Spartan	10,000	1,500	83,000
Cornhusker	23,000	(2,000)	21,000
Hawkeye	9,000	1,000	19,000
	$102,000	$15,500	$290,000

2. On February 3, 2021, one of Konetzke's customers declared bankruptcy. At December 31, 2020, this company owed Konetzke $15,000, of which $3,000 was paid in January 2021.
3. On January 18, 2021, one of the three major plants of the client burned down.
4. On January 23, 2021, a strike was called at one of Konetzke's largest plants, which halted 30% of its production. As of today (February 13), the strike has not been settled.
5. On February 1, 2019, the board of directors adopted a resolution accepting the offer of an investment banker to guarantee the marketing of $1,200,000 of preferred stock.

Instructions

a. State in each case how the 2020 financial statements would be affected, if at all.

b. Moving ahead to the first quarter of 2021, your team has compiled the following summarized revenue and expense data for the first quarter of the year.

Sales revenue	$30,000
Cost of goods sold	18,000
Variable selling expenses	500
Fixed selling expenses	1,500

Included in the fixed selling expenses was the single lump-sum payment of $800 for Internet advertisements for the entire year. Address the following with respect to the first quarter report. (1) Explain whether Konetzke should report its operating results for the quarter as if the quarter were a separate reporting period in and of itself, or as if the quarter were an integral part of the annual reporting period. (2) State how the sales revenue, cost of goods sold, and fixed selling expenses would be reflected in Konetzke's quarterly report prepared for the first quarter of 2021.

Solution

a. 1. Konetzke first conducts the following three tests:

Revenue test: .10 × $102,000 = $10,200. The Badger ($60,000) and Cornhusker ($23,000) segments both meet this test.

Operating profit (loss) test: .10 × ($15,000 + $1,500 + $1,000) = $1,750. The Badger ($15,000) and Cornhusker ($2,000 absolute amount) segments both meet this test.

Identifiable assets test: .10 × $290,000 = $29,000. The Badger ($167,000) and Spartan ($83,000) segments both meet this test.

Thus, Konetzke has three reportable segments for which segment information should be disclosed.

Regarding the post-balance-sheet events:

2. The financial statements should be adjusted for the expected loss pertaining to the remaining receivable of $12,000. Such adjustment should reduce accounts receivable to their realizable value as of December 31, 2020.

3. Report the fire loss in a footnote to the balance sheet and refer to it in connection with the income statement, since earnings power is presumably affected.

4. Strikes are considered general knowledge and therefore disclosure is not required. Many auditors, however, would encourage disclosure in all cases.

5. Report the action of the new stock issue in a footnote to the balance sheet.

b. 1. The company should report its quarterly results as if each interim period is an integral part of the annual period.

2. The company's revenue and expenses would be reported as follows on its quarterly report prepared for the first quarter of 2021:

Sales revenue	$30,000
Cost of goods sold	18,000
Variable selling expenses	500
Fixed selling expenses	
Advertising ($800 ÷ 4)	200
Other ($1,500 – $800)	700

Sales revenue and cost of goods sold receive the same treatment as if this were an annual report. Costs and expenses other than product costs should be charged to expense in interim periods as incurred or allocated among interim periods. Consequently, the variable selling expenses and the portion of fixed selling expenses not related to Internet advertising should be reported in full. One-fourth of the Internet advertising is reported as an expense in the first quarter, assuming the advertising is constant throughout the year. These costs can be deferred within the fiscal period if the benefits of the expenditure clearly extend beyond the interim period in which the expenditure is made.

WileyPLUS

Exercises, Problems, Problem Solution Walkthrough Videos, and many more assessment tools and resources are available for practice in WileyPLUS.

Note: All asterisked Questions, Exercises, and Problems relate to material in the appendix to the chapter.

Questions

1. What are the major advantages of notes to the financial statements? What types of items are usually reported in notes?

2. What is the full disclosure principle in accounting? Why has disclosure increased substantially in the last 10 years?

3. The FASB requires a reconciliation between the effective tax rate and the federal government's statutory rate. Of what benefit is such a disclosure requirement?

4. What type of disclosure or accounting do you believe is necessary for the following items?

a. Because of a general increase in the number of labor disputes and strikes, both within and outside the industry, there is an increased likelihood that a company will suffer a costly strike in the near future.

b. A company reports a material unusual and infrequent loss on the income statement. No other mention is made of this item in the annual report.

c. A company expects to recover a substantial amount in connection with a pending refund claim for a prior year's taxes. Although the claim is being contested, counsel for the company has confirmed the client's expectation of recovery.

5. The following information was described in a note of Canon Packing Co.

"During August, Holland Products Corporation purchased 311,003 shares of the Company's common stock which constitutes approximately 35% of the stock outstanding. Holland has since obtained representation on the Board of Directors."

"An affiliate of Holland Products Corporation acts as a food broker for Canon Packing in the greater New York City marketing area. The commissions for such services after August amounted to approximately $20,000."

Why is this information disclosed?

6. What are the major types of subsequent events? Indicate how each of the following "subsequent events" would be reported.

a. Collection of a note written off in a prior period.

b. Issuance of a large preferred stock offering.

c. Acquisition of a company in a different industry.

d. Destruction of a major plant in a flood.

e. Death of the company's chief executive officer (CEO).

f. Additional wage costs associated with settlement of a four-week strike.

g. Settlement of a federal income tax case at considerably more tax than anticipated at year-end.

h. Change in the product mix from consumer goods to industrial goods.

7. What are diversified companies? What accounting problems are related to diversified companies?

8. What quantitative materiality tests are applied to determine whether a segment is significant enough to warrant separate disclosure?

9. Identify the segment information that is required to be disclosed by GAAP.

10. What is an operating segment, and when can information about two operating segments be aggregated?

11. The controller for Lafayette Inc. recently commented, "If I have to disclose our segments individually, the only people who will gain are our competitors and the only people that will lose are our present stockholders." Evaluate this comment.

12. An article in the financial press entitled "Important Information in Annual Reports This Year" noted that annual reports include a management's discussion and analysis section. What would this section contain?

13. "The financial statements of a company are management's, not the accountant's." Discuss the implications of this statement.

14. What are interim reports? Why are balance sheets often not provided with interim data?

15. What are the accounting problems related to the presentation of interim data?

16. Dierdorf Inc., a closely held corporation, has decided to go public. The controller, Ed Floyd, is concerned with presenting interim data when a LIFO inventory valuation is used. What problems are encountered with LIFO inventories when quarterly data are presented?

17. What approaches have been suggested to overcome the seasonality problem related to interim reporting?

18. What is the difference between a CPA's unqualified opinion or "clean" opinion and a qualified one?

19. Jane Ellerby and Sam Callison are discussing the recent fraud that occurred at LowRental Leasing, Inc. The fraud involved the improper reporting of revenue to ensure that the company would have income in excess of $1 million. What is fraudulent financial reporting, and how does it differ from an embezzlement of company funds?

20. Olga Conrad, a financial writer, noted recently, "There are substantial arguments for including earnings projections in annual reports and the like. The most compelling is that it would give anyone interested something now available to only a relatively select few—like large stockholders, creditors, and attentive bartenders." Identify some arguments against providing earnings projections.

21. The following comment appeared in the financial press: "Inadequate financial disclosure, particularly with respect to how management views the future and its role in the marketplace, has always been a stone in the shoe. After all, if you don't know how a company views the future, how can you judge the worth of its corporate strategy?" What are some arguments for reporting earnings forecasts?

*22. "The significance of financial statement data is not in the amount alone." Discuss the meaning of this statement.

*23. A close friend of yours, who is a history major and who has not had any college courses or any experience in business, is receiving the financial statements from companies in which he has minor investments (acquired for him by his now-deceased grandfather). He asks you what he needs to know to interpret and to evaluate the financial statement data that he is receiving. What would you tell him?

*24. Distinguish between ratio analysis and percentage analysis relative to the interpretation of financial statements. What is the value of these two types of analyses?

*25. In calculating inventory turnover, why is cost of goods sold used as the numerator? As the inventory turnover increases, what increasing risk does the business assume?

*26. What is the relationship of the asset turnover to the return on assets?

*27. Explain the meaning of the following terms: (a) common-size analysis, (b) vertical analysis, (c) horizontal analysis, and (d) percentage analysis.

*28. Presently, the profession requires that earnings per share be disclosed on the face of the income statement. What are some disadvantages of reporting ratios on the financial statements?

Brief Exercises

BE24.1 **(LO 1)** An annual report of Crestwood Industries states, "The company and its subsidiaries have long-term leases expiring on various dates after December 31, 2020. Amounts payable under such commitments, without reduction for related rental income, are expected to average approximately $5,711,000 annually for the next 3 years. Related rental income from certain subleases to others is estimated to average $3,094,000 annually for the next 3 years." What information is provided by this note?

BE24.2 **(LO 1)** An annual report of **Ford Motor Corporation** states, "Net income per share is computed based upon the average number of shares of capital stock of all classes outstanding. Additional shares of common stock may be issued or delivered in the future on conversion of outstanding convertible debentures, exercise of outstanding employee stock options, and for payment of defined supplemental compensation. Had such additional shares been outstanding, net income a share would have been reduced by 10¢ in the current year and 3¢ in the previous year. . . . As a result of capital stock transactions by the company during the current year (primarily the purchase of Class A Stock from Ford Foundation), net income a share was increased by 6¢." What information is provided by this note?

BE24.3 (LO 2) Morlan Corporation is preparing its December 31, 2020, financial statements. Two events that occurred between December 31, 2020, and March 10, 2021, when the statements were issued, are described below.

1. A liability, estimated at $160,000 at December 31, 2020, was settled on February 26, 2021, at $170,000.
2. A flood loss of $80,000 occurred on March 1, 2021.

What effect do these subsequent events have on 2020 net income?

BE24.4 (LO 2) Tina Bailey, a student of intermediate accounting, was heard to remark after a class discussion on segment reporting, "All this is very confusing to me. First, we are told that there is merit in presenting the consolidated results, and now we are told that it is better to show segmental results. I wish they would make up their minds." Evaluate this comment.

BE24.5 (LO 2) Foley Corporation has seven industry segments with total revenues as follows.

Penley	$600	Cheng	$225
Konami	650	Takuhi	200
KSC	250	Molina	700
Red Moon	275		

Based only on the revenues test, which industry segments are reportable?

BE24.6 (LO 2) Operating profits and losses for the seven industry segments of Foley Corporation are:

Penley	$ 90	Cheng	$ (20)
Konami	(40)	Takuhi	34
KSC	25	Molina	150
Red Moon	50		

Based only on the operating profit (loss) test, which industry segments are reportable?

BE24.7 (LO 2) Identifiable assets for the seven industry segments of Foley Corporation are:

Penley	$500	Cheng	$200
Konami	550	Takuhi	150
KSC	250	Molina	475
Red Moon	400		

Based only on the identifiable assets test, which industry segments are reportable?

***BE24.8 (LO 6)** Answer each of the questions in the following unrelated situations.

a. The current ratio of a company is 5:1 and its acid-test ratio is 1:1. If the inventories and prepaid items amount to $500,000, what is the amount of current liabilities?

b. A company had an average inventory last year of $200,000 and its inventory turnover was 5. If sales volume and unit cost remain the same this year as last and inventory turnover is 8 this year, what will average inventory have to be during the current year?

c. A company has current assets of $90,000 (of which $40,000 is inventory and prepaid items) and current liabilities of $40,000. What is the current ratio? What is the acid-test ratio? If the company borrows $15,000 cash from a bank on a 120-day loan, what will its current ratio be? What will the acid-test ratio be?

d. A company has current assets of $600,000 and current liabilities of $240,000. The board of directors declares a cash dividend of $180,000. What is the current ratio after the declaration but before payment? What is the current ratio after the payment of the dividend?

***BE24.9 (LO 6)** Heartland Company's budgeted sales and budgeted cost of goods sold for the coming year are $144,000,000 and $99,000,000, respectively. Short-term interest rates are expected to average 10%. If Heartland can increase inventory turnover from its present level of 9 times a year to a level of 12 times per year, compute its expected cost savings for the coming year.

Exercises

E24.1 (LO 2) (Post-Balance-Sheet Events) Madrasah Corporation issued its financial statements for the year ended December 31, 2020, on March 10, 2021. The following events took place early in 2021.

a. On January 10, 10,000 shares of $5 par value common stock were issued at $66 per share.

b. On March 1, Madrasah determined after negotiations with the Internal Revenue Service that income taxes payable for 2020 should be $1,270,000. At December 31, 2020, income taxes payable were recorded at $1,100,000.

Instructions

Discuss how the preceding post-balance-sheet events should be reflected in the 2020 financial statements.

E24.2 **(LO 2)** Excel **(Post-Balance-Sheet Events)** For each of the following subsequent (post-balance-sheet) events, indicate whether a company should (a) adjust the financial statements, (b) disclose in notes to the financial statements, or (c) neither adjust nor disclose.

_______ **1.** Settlement of federal tax case at a cost considerably in excess of the amount expected at year-end.

_______ **2.** Introduction of a new product line.

_______ **3.** Loss of assembly plant due to fire.

_______ **4.** Sale of a significant portion of the company's assets.

_______ **5.** Retirement of the company president.

_______ **6.** Prolonged employee strike.

_______ **7.** Loss of a significant customer.

_______ **8.** Issuance of a significant number of shares of common stock.

_______ **9.** Material loss on a year-end receivable because of a customer's bankruptcy.

_______ **10.** Hiring of a new president.

_______ **11.** Settlement of prior year's litigation against the company (no loss was accrued).

_______ **12.** Merger with another company of comparable size.

E24.3 **(LO 2)** Excel **(Segmented Reporting)** Carlton Company is involved in four separate industries. The following information is available for each of the four industries.

Operating Segment	Total Revenue	Operating Profit (Loss)	Identifiable Assets
W	$ 60,000	$15,000	$167,000
X	10,000	3,000	83,000
Y	23,000	(2,000)	21,000
Z	9,000	1,000	19,000
	$102,000	$17,000	$290,000

Instructions

Determine which of the operating segments are reportable based on the:

a. Revenue test.

b. Operating profit (loss) test.

c. Identifiable assets test.

*E24.4 **(LO 6)** **(Ratio Computation and Analysis; Liquidity)** As loan analyst for Utrillo Bank, you have been presented the following information.

	Toulouse Co.	Lautrec Co.
Assets		
Cash	$ 120,000	$ 320,000
Receivables	220,000	302,000
Inventories	570,000	518,000
Total current assets	910,000	1,140,000
Other assets	500,000	612,000
Total assets	$1,410,000	$1,752,000
Liabilities and Stockholders' Equity		
Current liabilities	$ 305,000	$ 350,000
Long-term liabilities	400,000	500,000
Capital stock and retained earnings	705,000	902,000
Total liabilities and stockholders' equity	$1,410,000	$1,752,000
Annual sales	$ 930,000	$1,500,000
Rate of gross profit on sales	30%	40%

Each of these companies has requested a loan of $50,000 for 6 months with no collateral offered. Because your bank has reached its quota for loans of this type, only one of these requests is to be granted.

Instructions

Which of the two companies, as judged by the information given above, would you recommend as the better risk and why? Assume that the ending account balances are representative of the entire year.

*E24.5 **(LO 6)** **(Analysis of Given Ratios)** Picasso Company is a wholesale distributor of packaging equipment and supplies. The company's sales have averaged about $900,000 annually for the 3-year period 2018–2020. The firm's total assets at the end of 2020 amounted to $850,000.

The president of Picasso Company has asked the controller to prepare a report that summarizes the financial aspects of the company's operations for the past 3 years. This report will be presented to the board of directors at their next meeting.

In addition to comparative financial statements, the controller has decided to present a number of relevant financial ratios which can assist in the identification and interpretation of trends. At the request of the controller, the accounting staff has calculated the following ratios for the 3-year period 2018–2020.

	2018	2019	2020
Current ratio	1.80	1.89	1.96
Acid-test (quick) ratio	1.04	0.99	0.87
Accounts receivable turnover	8.75	7.71	6.42
Inventory turnover	4.91	4.32	3.42
Debt to assets ratio	51.0%	46.0%	41.0%
Long-term debt to assets ratio	31.0%	27.0%	24.0%
Sales to fixed assets (fixed asset turnover)	1.58	1.69	1.79
Sales as a percent of 2018 sales	1.00	1.03	1.07
Gross margin percentage	36.0%	35.1%	34.6%
Net income to sales	6.9%	7.0%	7.2%
Return on assets	7.7%	7.7%	7.8%
Return on common stockholders' equity	13.6%	13.1%	12.7%

In preparation of the report, the controller has decided first to examine the financial ratios independent of any other data to determine if the ratios themselves reveal any significant trends over the 3-year period.

Instructions

a. The current ratio is increasing while the acid-test (quick) ratio is decreasing. Using the ratios provided, identify and explain the contributing factor(s) for this apparently divergent trend.

b. In terms of the ratios provided, what conclusion(s) can be drawn regarding the company's use of financial leverage during the 2018–2020 period?

c. Using the ratios provided, what conclusion(s) can be drawn regarding the company's net investment in plant and equipment?

*E24.6 **(LO 6)** **(Ratio Analysis)** Edna Millay Inc. is a manufacturer of electronic components and accessories with total assets of $20,000,000. Selected financial ratios for Millay and the industry averages for firms of similar size are presented below.

	Edna Millay			2020 Industry
	2018	2019	2020	Average
Current ratio	2.09	2.27	2.51	2.24
Quick ratio	1.15	1.12	1.19	1.22
Inventory turnover	2.40	2.18	2.02	3.50
Net sales to stockholders' equity	2.71	2.80	2.99	2.85
Return on common stockholders' equity	0.14	0.15	0.17	0.11
Total liabilities to stockholders' equity	1.41	1.37	1.44	0.95

Millay is being reviewed by several entities whose interests vary, and the company's financial ratios are a part of the data being considered. Each of the parties listed below must recommend an action based on its evaluation of Millay's financial position.

Archibald MacLeish Bank. The bank is processing Millay's application for a new 5-year term note. Archibald MacLeish has been Millay's banker for several years but must reevaluate the company's financial position for each major transaction.

Robert Lowell Company. Lowell is a new supplier to Millay and must decide on the appropriate credit terms to extend to the company.

Robert Penn Warren. A brokerage firm specializing in the stock of electronics firms that are sold over-the-counter, Robert Penn Warren must decide if it will include Millay in a new fund being established for sale to Robert Penn Warren's clients.

Working Capital Management Committee. This is a committee of Millay's management personnel chaired by the chief operating officer. The committee is charged with the responsibility of periodically reviewing the company's working capital position, comparing actual data against budgets, and recommending changes in strategy as needed.

Instructions

a. Describe the analytical use of each of the six ratios presented above.

b. For each of the four entities, identify two financial ratios, from the ratios presented above, that would be most valuable as a basis for its decision regarding Millay.

c. Discuss what the financial ratios presented in the question reveal about Millay. Support your answer by citing specific ratio levels and trends as well as the interrelationships between these ratios.

(CMA adapted)

Problems

P24.1 **(LO 2)** **(Subsequent Events)** Your firm has been engaged to examine the financial statements of Almaden Corporation for the year 2020. The bookkeeper who maintains the financial records has prepared all the unaudited financial statements for the corporation since its organization on January 2, 2015. The client provides you with the following information.

Almaden Corporation
Balance Sheet
December 31, 2020

Assets		Liabilities	
Current assets	$1,881,100	Current liabilities	$ 962,400
Other assets	5,171,400	Long-term liabilities	1,439,500
		Stockholders' equity	4,650,600
	$7,052,500		$7,052,500

An analysis of current assets discloses the following.

Cash (restricted in the amount of $300,000 for plant expansion)	$ 571,000
Investments in land	185,000
Accounts receivable less allowance of $30,000	480,000
Inventories (LIFO flow assumption)	645,100
	$1,881,100

Other assets include:

Prepaid expenses	$ 62,400
Plant and equipment less accumulated depreciation of $1,430,000	4,130,000
Cash surrender value of life insurance policy	84,000
Unamortized bond discount	34,500
Notes receivable (short-term)	162,300
Goodwill	252,000
Land	446,200
	$5,171,400

Current liabilities include:

Accounts payable	$ 510,000
Notes payable (due 2023)	157,400

Estimated income taxes payable	145,000
Premium on common stock	150,000
	$ 962,400

Long-term liabilities include:

Unearned revenue	$ 489,500
Dividends payable (cash)	200,000
8% bonds payable (due May 1, 2025)	750,000
	$1,439,500

Stockholders' equity includes:

Retained earnings	$2,810,600
Common stock, par value $10; authorized 200,000 shares, 184,000 shares issued	1,840,000
	$4,650,600

The supplementary information below is also provided.

1. On May 1, 2020, the corporation issued at 95.4, $750,000 of bonds to finance plant expansion. The long-term bond agreement provided for the annual payment of interest every May 1. The existing plant was pledged as security for the loan. Use the straight-line method for discount amortization.
2. The bookkeeper made the following mistakes.
   a. In 2018, the ending inventory was overstated by $183,000. The ending inventories for 2019 and 2020 were correctly computed.
   b. In 2020, accrued wages in the amount of $225,000 were omitted from the balance sheet, and these expenses were not charged on the income statement.
   c. In 2020, a gain of $175,000 (net of tax) on the sale of certain plant assets was credited directly to retained earnings.
3. A major competitor has introduced a line of products that will compete directly with Almaden's primary line, now being produced in a specially designed new plant. Because of manufacturing innovations, the competitor's line will be of comparable quality but priced 50% below Almaden's line. The competitor announced its new line on January 14, 2021. Almaden indicates that the company will meet the lower prices that are high enough to cover variable manufacturing and selling expenses, but permit recovery of only a portion of fixed costs.
4. You learned on January 28, 2021, prior to completion of the audit, of heavy damage because of a recent fire to one of Almaden's two plants; the loss will not be reimbursed by insurance. The newspapers described the event in detail.

Instructions

Analyze the above information to prepare a corrected balance sheet for Almaden in accordance with proper accounting and reporting principles. Prepare a description of any notes that might need to be prepared. The books are closed and adjustments to income are to be made through retained earnings.

P24.2 **(LO 2)** **(Segmented Reporting)** Cineplex Corporation is a diversified company that operates in five different industries: A, B, C, D, and E. The following information relating to each segment is available for 2021.

	A	B	C	D	E
Sales revenue	$40,000	$ 75,000	$580,000	$35,000	$55,000
Cost of goods sold	19,000	50,000	270,000	19,000	30,000
Operating expenses	10,000	40,000	235,000	12,000	18,000
Total expenses	29,000	90,000	505,000	31,000	48,000
Operating profit (loss)	$11,000	$(15,000)	$ 75,000	$ 4,000	$ 7,000
Identifiable assets	$35,000	$ 80,000	$500,000	$65,000	$50,000

Sales of segments B and C included intersegment sales of $20,000 and $100,000, respectively.

Instructions

a. Determine which of the segments are reportable based on the:

1. Revenue test.
2. Operating profit (loss) test.
3. Identifiable assets test.

b. Prepare the necessary disclosures required by GAAP.

*P24.3 **(LO 6,8)** **Excel** **Groupwork** **(Ratio Computations and Additional Analysis)** Bradburn Corporation was formed 5 years ago through a public subscription of common stock. Daniel Brown, who owns 15% of the common stock, was one of the organizers of Bradburn and is its current president. The company has been successful, but it currently is experiencing a shortage of funds. On June 10, 2021, Daniel Brown approached the Topeka National Bank, asking for a 24-month extension on two $35,000 notes, which are due on June 30, 2021, and September 30, 2021. Another note of $6,000 is due on March 31, 2022, but he expects no difficulty in paying this note on its due date. Brown explained that Bradburn's cash flow problems are due primarily to the company's desire to finance a $300,000 plant expansion over the next 2 fiscal years through internally generated funds.

The commercial loan officer of Topeka National Bank requested the following financial reports for the last 2 fiscal years.

Bradburn Corporation
Balance Sheet
March 31

Assets	2021	2020
Cash	$ 18,200	$ 12,500
Notes receivable	148,000	132,000
Accounts receivable (net)	131,800	125,500
Inventories (at cost)	105,000	50,000
Plant & equipment (net of depreciation)	1,449,000	1,420,500
Total assets	$1,852,000	$1,740,500
Liabilities and Stockholders' Equity		
Accounts payable	$ 79,000	$ 91,000
Notes payable	76,000	61,500
Accrued liabilities	9,000	6,000
Common stock (130,000 shares, $10 par)	1,300,000	1,300,000
Retained earnings[a]	388,000	282,000
Total liabilities and stockholders' equity	$1,852,000	$1,740,500

[a]Cash dividends were paid at the rate of $1 per share in fiscal year 2020 and $2 per share in fiscal year 2021.

Bradburn Corporation
Income Statement
For the Fiscal Years Ended March 31

	2021	2020
Sales revenue	$3,000,000	$2,700,000
Cost of goods sold[a]	1,530,000	1,425,000
Gross margin	1,470,000	1,275,000
Operating expenses	860,000	780,000
Income before income taxes	610,000	495,000
Income taxes (40%)	244,000	198,000
Net income	$ 366,000	$ 297,000

[a]Depreciation charges on the plant and equipment of $100,000 and $102,500 for fiscal years ended March 31, 2020 and 2021, respectively, are included in cost of goods sold.

Instructions

a. Compute the following items for Bradburn Corporation.

1. Current ratio for fiscal years 2020 and 2021.
2. Acid-test (quick) ratio for fiscal years 2020 and 2021.
3. Inventory turnover for fiscal year 2021.
4. Return on assets for fiscal years 2020 and 2021. (Assume total assets were $1,688,500 at 3/31/19.)
5. Percentage change in sales, cost of goods sold, gross margin, and net income after taxes from fiscal year 2020 to 2021.

b. Identify and explain what other financial reports and/or financial analyses might be helpful to the commercial loan officer of Topeka National Bank in evaluating Daniel Brown's request for a time extension on Bradburn's notes.

c. Assume that the percentage changes experienced in fiscal year 2021 as compared with fiscal year 2020 for sales, cost of goods sold, and operating expenses will be repeated in each of the next 2 years. Is Bradburn's desire to finance the plant expansion from internally generated funds realistic? Discuss.

d. Should Topeka National Bank grant the extension on Bradburn's notes considering Daniel Brown's statement about financing the plant expansion through internally generated funds? Discuss.

*P24.4 **(LO 9)** Excel **(Horizontal and Vertical Analysis)** Presented below is the comparative balance sheet for Gilmour Company.

Gilmour Company
Comparative Balance Sheet
As of December 31, 2021 and 2020

	December 31	
	2021	2020
Assets		
Cash	$ 180,000	$ 275,000
Accounts receivable (net)	220,000	155,000
Short-term investments	270,000	150,000
Inventories	1,060,000	980,000
Prepaid expenses	25,000	25,000
Plant & equipment	2,585,000	1,950,000
Accumulated depreciation	(1,000,000)	(750,000)
	$3,340,000	$2,785,000
Liabilities and Stockholders' Equity		
Accounts payable	$ 50,000	$ 75,000
Accrued expenses	170,000	200,000
Bonds payable	450,000	190,000
Common stock	2,100,000	1,770,000
Retained earnings	570,000	550,000
	$3,340,000	$2,785,000

Instructions

(Round to two decimal places.)

a. Prepare a comparative balance sheet of Gilmour Company showing the percent each item is of the total assets or total liabilities and stockholders' equity.

b. Prepare a comparative balance sheet of Gilmour Company showing the dollar change and the percent change for each item.

c. Of what value is the additional information provided in part (a)?

d. Of what value is the additional information provided in part (b)?

*P24.5 **(LO 6)** Writing **(Dividend Policy Analysis)** Matheny Inc. went public 3 years ago. The board of directors will be meeting shortly after the end of the year to decide on a dividend policy. In the past, growth has been financed primarily through the retention of earnings. A stock or a cash dividend has never been declared. Presented below is a brief financial summary of Matheny Inc. operations.

	($000 omitted)				
	2021	2020	2019	2018	2017
Sales revenue	$20,000	$16,000	$14,000	$6,000	$4,000
Net income	2,400	1,400	800	700	250
Average total assets	22,000	19,000	11,500	4,200	3,000
Current assets	8,000	6,000	3,000	1,200	1,000
Working capital	3,600	3,200	1,200	500	400
Common shares:					
Number of shares outstanding (000)	2,000	2,000	2,000	20	20
Average market price	$9	$6	$4	—	—

Instructions

a. Suggest factors to be considered by the board of directors in establishing a dividend policy.

b. Compute the return on assets, profit margin on sales, earnings per share, price-earnings ratio, and current ratio for each of the 5 years for Matheny Inc.

c. Comment on the appropriateness of declaring a cash dividend at this time, using the ratios computed in part (b) as a major factor in your analysis.

Concepts for Analysis

CA24.1 **(LO 1, 2)** **(General Disclosures; Inventories; Property, Plant, and Equipment)** Koch Corporation is in the process of preparing its annual financial statements for the fiscal year ended April 30, 2021. Because all of Koch's shares are traded intrastate, the company does not have to file any reports with the Securities and Exchange Commission. The company manufactures plastic, glass, and paper containers for sale to food and drink manufacturers and distributors.

Koch Corporation maintains separate control accounts for its raw materials, work in process, and finished goods inventories for each of the three types of containers. The inventories are valued at the lower-of-cost-or-market.

The company's property, plant, and equipment are classified in the following major categories: land, office buildings, furniture and fixtures, manufacturing facilities, manufacturing equipment, and leasehold improvements. All fixed assets are carried at cost. The depreciation methods employed depend on the type of asset (its classification) and when it was acquired.

Koch Corporation plans to present the inventory and fixed asset amounts in its April 30, 2021, balance sheet as shown below.

Inventories	$4,814,200
Property, plant, and equipment (net of depreciation)	6,310,000

Instructions

What information regarding inventories and property, plant, and equipment must be disclosed by Koch Corporation in the audited financial statements issued to stockholders, either in the body or the notes, for the 2020–2021 fiscal year?

(CMA adapted)

CA24.2 **(LO 1, 2)** **(Disclosures Required in Various Situations)** Ace Inc. produces electronic components for sale to manufacturers of radios, television sets, and digital sound systems. In connection with her examination of Ace's financial statements for the year ended December 31, 2021, Gloria Rodd, CPA, completed field work 2 weeks ago. Ms. Rodd now is evaluating the significance of the following items prior to preparing her auditor's report. Except as noted, none of these items have been disclosed in the financial statements or notes.

Item 1: A 10-year loan agreement, which the company entered into 3 years ago, provides that dividend payments may not exceed net income earned after taxes subsequent to the date of the agreement. The balance of retained earnings at the date of the loan agreement was $420,000. From that date through December 31, 2021, net income after taxes has totaled $570,000 and cash dividends have totaled $320,000. On the basis of these data, the staff auditor assigned to this review concluded that there was no retained earnings restriction at December 31, 2021.

Item 2: Recently Ace interrupted its policy of paying cash dividends quarterly to its stockholders. Dividends were paid regularly through 2020, discontinued for all of 2021 to finance purchase of equipment for the company's new plant, and resumed in the first quarter of 2022. In the annual report, dividend policy is to be discussed in the president's letter to stockholders.

Item 3: A major electronics firm has introduced a line of products that will compete directly with Ace's primary line, now being produced in the specially designed new plant. Because of manufacturing innovations, the competitor's line will be of comparable quality but priced 50% below Ace's line. The competitor announced its new line during the week following completion of field work. Ms. Rodd read the announcement in the newspaper and discussed the situation by telephone with Ace executives. Ace will meet the lower prices that are high enough to cover variable manufacturing and selling expenses but will permit recovery of only a portion of fixed costs.

Item 4: The company's new manufacturing plant building, which cost $2,400,000 and has an estimated life of 25 years, is leased from Wichita National Bank at an annual rental of $600,000. The company is obligated to pay property taxes, insurance, and maintenance. At the conclusion of its 10-year noncancelable lease, the company has the option of purchasing the property for $1. In Ace's income statement, the rental payment is reported on a separate line.

Instructions

For each of the above items, discuss any additional disclosures in the financial statements and notes that the auditor should recommend to her client. (The cumulative effect of the four items should not be considered.)

CA24.3 **(LO 1, 2)** **(Disclosures, Conditional and Contingent Liabilities)** Presented below are three independent situations.

Situation 1: A company offers a one-year warranty for the product that it manufactures. A history of warranty claims has been compiled, and the probable amounts of claims related to sales for a given period can be determined.

Situation 2: Subsequent to the date of a set of financial statements but prior to the issuance of the financial statements, a company enters into a contract that will probably result in a significant loss to the company. The amount of the loss can be reasonably estimated.

Situation 3: A company has adopted a policy of recording self-insurance for any possible losses resulting from injury to others by the company's vehicles. The premium for an insurance policy for the same risk from an independent insurance company would have an annual cost of $4,000. During the period covered by the financial statements, there were no accidents involving the company's vehicles that resulted in injury to others.

Instructions

Discuss the accrual or type of disclosure necessary (if any) and the reason(s) why such disclosure is appropriate for each of the three independent sets of facts above.

(AICPA adapted)

CA24.4 **(LO 2)** **Groupwork** **(Post-Balance-Sheet Events)** At December 31, 2020, Coburn Corp. has assets of $10,000,000, liabilities of $6,000,000, common stock of $2,000,000 (representing 2,000,000 shares of $1 par common stock), and retained earnings of $2,000,000. Net sales for the year 2020 were $18,000,000, and net income was $800,000. As auditors of this company, you are making a review of subsequent events on February 13, 2021, and you find the following.

1. On February 3, 2021, one of Coburn's customers declared bankruptcy. At December 31, 2020, this company owed Coburn $300,000, of which $60,000 was paid in January 2021.
2. On January 18, 2021, one of the three major plants of the client burned.
3. On January 23, 2021, a strike was called at one of Coburn's largest plants, which halted 30% of its production. As of today (February 13), the strike has not been settled.
4. A major electronics enterprise has introduced a line of products that would compete directly with Coburn's primary line, now being produced in a specially designed new plant. Because of manufacturing innovations, the competitor has been able to achieve quality similar to that of Coburn's products but at a price 50% lower. Coburn officials say they will meet the lower prices, which are high enough to cover variable manufacturing and selling costs but which permit recovery of only a portion of fixed costs.
5. Merchandise traded in the open market is recorded in the company's records at $1.40 per unit on December 31, 2020. This price had prevailed for 2 weeks, after release of an official market report

that predicted vastly enlarged supplies; however, no purchases were made at $1.40. The price throughout the preceding year had been about $2, which was the level experienced over several years. On January 18, 2021, the price returned to $2, after public disclosure of an error in the official calculations of the prior December, correction of which destroyed the expectations of excessive supplies. Inventory at December 31, 2020, was on a lower-of-LIFO-cost-or-market basis.

6. On February 1, 2021, the board of directors adopted a resolution accepting the offer of an investment banker to guarantee the marketing of $1,200,000 of preferred stock.

Instructions

State in each case how the 2020 financial statements would be affected, if at all.

CA24.5 **(LO 2)** Writing **(Segment Reporting)** You are compiling the consolidated financial statements for Winsor Corporation International. The corporation's accountant, Anthony Reese, has provided you with the following segment information.

Note 7: Major Segments of Business

WCI conducts funeral service and cemetery operations in the United States and Canada. Substantially all revenues of WCI's major segments of business are from unaffiliated customers. Segment information for fiscal 2021, 2020, and 2019 follows.

(thousands)

	Funeral	Floral	Cemetery	Real Estate	Dried Whey	Limousine	Consolidated
Revenues							
2021	$302,000	$10,000	$ 73,000	$ 2,000	$7,000	$12,000	$406,000
2020	245,000	6,000	61,000	4,000	4,000	4,000	324,000
2019	208,000	3,000	42,000	3,000	1,000	3,000	260,000
Operating Income							
2021	74,000	1,500	18,000	(36,000)	500	2,000	60,000
2020	64,000	200	12,000	(28,000)	200	400	48,800
2019	54,000	150	6,000	(21,000)	100	350	39,600
Capital Expenditures							
2021	26,000	1,000	9,000	400	300	1,000	37,700
2020	28,000	2,000	60,000	1,500	100	700	92,300
2019	14,000	25	8,000	600	25	50	22,700
Depreciation and Amortization							
2021	13,000	100	2,400	1,400	100	200	17,200
2020	10,000	50	1,400	700	50	100	12,300
2019	8,000	25	1,000	600	25	50	9,700
Identifiable Assets							
2021	334,000	1,500	162,000	114,000	500	8,000	620,000
2020	322,000	1,000	144,000	52,000	1,000	6,000	526,000
2019	223,000	500	78,000	34,000	500	3,500	339,500

Instructions

Determine which of the above segments must be reported separately and which can be combined under the category "Other." Then, write a one-page memo to the company's accountant, Anthony Reese, explaining the following.

a. What segments must be reported separately and what segments can be combined.

b. What criteria you used to determine reportable segments.

c. What major items for each must be disclosed.

CA24.6 **(LO 2)** **(Segment Reporting—Theory)** Presented below is an excerpt from the financial statements of **H. J. Heinz Company**.

Segment and Geographic Data

The company is engaged principally in one line of business—processed food products—which represents over 90% of consolidated sales. Information about the business of the company by geographic area is presented in the table below.

There were no material amounts of sales or transfers between geographic areas or between affiliates, and no material amounts of United States export sales.

(in thousands of U.S. dollars)	Domestic	Foreign: United Kingdom	Canada	Western Europe	Other	Total	Worldwide
Sales	$2,381,054	$547,527	$216,726	$383,784	$209,354	$1,357,391	$3,738,445
Operating income	246,780	61,282	34,146	29,146	25,111	149,685	396,465
Identifiable assets	1,362,152	265,218	112,620	294,732	143,971	816,541	2,178,693
Capital expenditures	72,712	12,262	13,790	8,253	4,368	38,673	111,385
Depreciation expense	42,279	8,364	3,592	6,355	3,606	21,917	64,196

Instructions

a. Why does H. J. Heinz not prepare segment information on its products or services?

b. What are export sales, and when should they be disclosed?

c. Why are sales by geographical area important to disclose?

CA24.7 **(LO 2)** Writing **(Segment Reporting—Theory)** The following article appeared in the *Wall Street Journal*.

WASHINGTON—The Securities and Exchange Commission staff issued guidelines for companies grappling with the problem of dividing up their business into industry segments for their annual reports.

An industry segment is defined by the Financial Accounting Standards Board as a part of an enterprise engaged in providing a product or service or a group of related products or services primarily to unaffiliated customers for a profit.

Although conceding that the process is a "subjective task" that "to a considerable extent, depends on the judgment of management," the SEC staff said companies should consider . . . various factors . . . to determine whether products and services should be grouped together or reported as segments.

Instructions

a. What does financial reporting for segments of a business enterprise involve?

b. Identify the reasons for requiring financial data to be reported by segments.

c. Identify the possible disadvantages of requiring financial data to be reported by segments.

d. Identify the accounting difficulties inherent in segment reporting.

CA24.8 **(LO 2)** **(Interim Reporting)** Snider Corporation, a publicly traded company, is preparing the interim financial data which it will issue to its stockholders and the Securities and Exchange Commission (SEC) at the end of the first quarter of the 2020–2021 fiscal year. Snider's financial accounting department has compiled the following summarized revenue and expense data for the first quarter of the year.

Sales revenue	$60,000,000
Cost of goods sold	36,000,000
Variable selling expenses	1,000,000
Fixed selling expenses	3,000,000

Included in the fixed selling expenses was the single lump-sum payment of $2,000,000 for television advertisements for the entire year.

Instructions

a. Snider Corporation must issue its quarterly financial statements in accordance with generally accepted accounting principles regarding interim financial reporting.

1. Explain whether Snider should report its operating results for the quarter as if the quarter were a separate reporting period in and of itself, or as if the quarter were an integral part of the annual reporting period.

2. State how the sales revenue, cost of goods sold, and fixed selling expenses would be reflected in Snider Corporation's quarterly report prepared for the first quarter of the 2020–2021 fiscal year. Briefly justify your presentation.

b. What financial information, as a minimum, must Snider Corporation disclose to its stockholders in its quarterly reports?

(CMA adapted)

CA24.9 **(LO 2)** **Groupwork** **(Treatment of Various Interim Reporting Situations)** The following statement is an excerpt from the FASB pronouncement related to interim reporting.

> Interim financial information is essential to provide investors and others with timely information as to the progress of the enterprise. The usefulness of such information rests on the relationship that it has to the annual results of operations. Accordingly, the Board has concluded that each interim period should be viewed primarily as an integral part of an annual period.
>
> In general, the results for each interim period should be based on the accounting principles and practices used by an enterprise in the preparation of its latest annual financial statements unless a change in an accounting practice or policy has been adopted in the current year. The Board has concluded, however, that certain accounting principles and practices followed for annual reporting purposes may require modification at interim reporting dates so that the reported results for the interim period may better relate to the results of operations for the annual period.

Instructions

The following six independent cases present how accounting facts might be reported on an individual company's interim financial reports. For each of these cases, state whether the method proposed to be used for interim reporting would be acceptable under generally accepted accounting principles applicable to interim financial data. Support each answer with a brief explanation.

a. J. D. Long Company takes a physical inventory at year-end for annual financial statement purposes. Inventory and cost of sales reported in the interim quarterly statements are based on estimated gross profit rates, because a physical inventory would result in a cessation of operations. Long Company does have reliable perpetual inventory records.

b. Rockford Company is planning to report one-fourth of its pension expense each quarter.

c. Republic Company wrote inventory down to reflect lower-of-cost-or-market in the first quarter. At year-end, the market exceeds the original acquisition cost of this inventory. Consequently, management plans to write the inventory back up to its original cost as a year-end adjustment.

d. Gansner Company realized a large gain on the sale of investments at the beginning of the second quarter. The company wants to report one-third of the gain in each of the remaining quarters.

e. Fredonia Company has estimated its annual audit fee. It plans to pro rate this expense equally over all four quarters.

f. LaBrava Company was reasonably certain it would have an employee strike in the third quarter. As a result, it shipped heavily during the second quarter but plans to defer the recognition of the sales in excess of the normal sales volume. The deferred sales will be recognized as sales in the third quarter when the strike is in progress. LaBrava Company management thinks this is more representative of normal second- and third-quarter operations.

CA24.10 **(LO 4)** **Writing** **(Financial Forecasts)** An article in *Barron's* noted the following.

> Okay. Last fall, someone with a long memory and an even longer arm reached into that bureau drawer and came out with a moldy cheese sandwich and the equally moldy notion of corporate forecasts. We tried to find out what happened to the cheese sandwich—but, rats!, even recourse to the Freedom of Information Act didn't help. However, the forecast proposal was dusted off, polished up and found quite serviceable. The SEC, indeed, lost no time in running it up the old flagpole—but no one was very eager to salute. Even after some of the more objectionable features—compulsory corrections and detailed explanations of why the estimates went awry—were peeled off the original proposal.
>
> Seemingly, despite the Commission's smiles and sweet talk, those craven corporations were still afraid that an honest mistake would lead them down the primrose path to consent decrees and class action suits. To lay to rest such qualms, the Commission last week approved a "Safe Harbor" rule that, providing the forecasts were made on a reasonable basis and in good faith, protected corporations from litigation should the projections prove wide of the mark (as only about 99% are apt to do).

Instructions

a. What are the arguments for preparing profit forecasts?

b. What is the purpose of the "safe harbor" rule?

c. Why are corporations concerned about presenting profit forecasts?

CA24.11 **(LO 4)** Ethics **(Disclosure of Estimates)** Nancy Tercek, the financial vice president, and Margaret Lilly, the controller, of Romine Manufacturing Company are reviewing the financial ratios of the company for the years 2020 and 2021. The financial vice president notes that the profit margin on sales ratio has increased from 6% to 12%, a hefty gain for the 2-year period. Tercek is in the process of issuing a media release that emphasizes the efficiency of Romine Manufacturing in controlling cost. Margaret Lilly knows that the difference in ratios is due primarily to an earlier company decision to reduce the estimates of warranty and bad debt expense for 2021. The controller, not sure of her supervisor's motives, hesitates to suggest to Tercek that the company's improvement is unrelated to efficiency in controlling cost. To complicate matters, the media release is scheduled in a few days.

Instructions

a. What, if any, is the ethical dilemma in this situation?
b. Should Lilly, the controller, remain silent? Give reasons.
c. What stakeholders might be affected by Tercek's media release?
d. Give your opinion on the following statement and cite reasons: "Because Tercek, the vice president, is most directly responsible for the media release, Lilly has no real responsibility in this matter."

CA24.12 **(LO 2)** Ethics **(Reporting of Subsequent Events)** In June 2020, the board of directors for McElroy Enterprises Inc. authorized the sale of $10,000,000 of corporate bonds. Jennifer Grayson, treasurer for McElroy Enterprises Inc., is concerned about the date when the bonds are issued. The company really needs the cash, but she is worried that if the bonds are issued before the company's year-end (December 31, 2020) the additional liability will have an adverse effect on a number of important ratios. In July, she explains to company president William McElroy that if they delay issuing the bonds until after December 31 the bonds will not affect the ratios until December 31, 2021. They will have to report the issuance as a subsequent event which requires only footnote disclosure. Grayson expects that with expected improved financial performance in 2021, ratios should be better.

Instructions

a. What are the ethical issues involved?
b. Should McElroy agree to the delay?

*CA24.13 **(LO 6)** Groupwork **(Effect of Transactions on Financial Statements and Ratios)** The transactions listed below relate to Wainwright Inc. You are to assume that on the date on which each of the transactions occurred, the corporation's accounts showed only common stock ($100 par) outstanding, a current ratio of 2.7:1, and a substantial net income for the year to date (before giving effect to the transaction concerned). On that date, the book value per share of stock was $151.53.

Each numbered transaction is to be considered completely independent of the others, and its related answer should be based on the effect(s) of that transaction alone. Assume that all numbered transactions occurred during 2021 and that the amount involved in each case is sufficiently material to distort reported net income if improperly included in the determination of net income. Assume further that each transaction was recorded in accordance with generally accepted accounting principles and, where applicable, in conformity with the all-inclusive concept of the income statement.

For each of the numbered transactions, you are to decide whether it:

a. Increased the corporation's 2021 net income.
b. Decreased the corporation's 2021 net income.
c. Increased the corporation's total retained earnings directly (i.e., not via net income).
d. Decreased the corporation's total retained earnings directly.
e. Increased the corporation's current ratio.
f. Decreased the corporation's current ratio.
g. Increased each stockholder's proportionate share of total stockholders' equity.
h. Decreased each stockholder's proportionate share of total stockholders' equity.
i. Increased each stockholder's equity per share of stock (book value).
j. Decreased each stockholder's equity per share of stock (book value).
k. Had none of the foregoing effects.

Instructions

List the numbers 1 through 9. Select as many letters as you deem appropriate to reflect the effect(s) of each transaction as of the date of the transaction by printing beside the transaction number the letter(s) that identifies that transaction's effect(s).

Transactions

______ **1.** In January, the board directed the write-off of certain patent rights that had suddenly and unexpectedly become worthless.

______ **2.** The corporation sold at a profit land and a building that had been idle for some time. Under the terms of the sale, the corporation received a portion of the sales price in cash immediately, the balance maturing at 6-month intervals.

______ **3.** Treasury stock originally repurchased and carried at $127 per share was sold for cash at $153 per share.

______ **4.** The corporation wrote off all of the unamortized discount applicable to bonds that it refinanced in 2021.

______ **5.** The corporation called in all its outstanding shares of stock and exchanged them for new shares on a 2-for-1 basis, reducing the par value at the same time to $50 per share.

______ **6.** The corporation paid a cash dividend that had been recorded in the accounts at time of declaration.

______ **7.** Litigation involving Wainwright Inc. as defendant was settled in the corporation's favor, with the plaintiff paying all court costs and legal fees. In 2018, the corporation had appropriately established a special contingency for this court action. (Indicate the effect of reversing the contingency only.)

______ **8.** The corporation received a check for the proceeds of an insurance policy from the company with which it is insured against theft of trucks. No entries concerning the theft had been made previously, and the proceeds reduce but do not cover completely the loss.

______ **9.** Treasury stock, which had been repurchased at and carried at $127 per share, was issued as a stock dividend. In connection with this distribution, the board of directors of Wainwright Inc. had authorized a transfer from retained earnings to permanent capital of an amount equal to the aggregate market value ($153 per share) of the shares issued. No entries relating to this dividend had been made previously.

(AICPA adapted)

Using Your Judgment

Financial Reporting Problem

The Procter & Gamble Company (P&G)

As stated in the chapter, notes to the financial statements are the means of explaining the items presented in the main body of the statements. Common note disclosures relate to such items as accounting policies, segmented information, and interim reporting. The financial statements of **P&G** are presented in Appendix B. The company's complete annual report, including the notes to the financial statements, is available online.

Instructions

Refer to P&G's financial statements and the accompanying notes to answer the following questions.

a. What specific items does P&G discuss in its Note 1—Summary of Significant Accounting Policies? (List the headings only.)

b. For what segments did P&G report segmented information? Which segment is the largest? Who is P&G's largest customer?

c. What interim information was reported by P&G?

Comparative Analysis Case

The Coca-Cola Company and PepsiCo, Inc.

The financial statements of **Coca-Cola** and **PepsiCo** are presented in Appendices C and D, respectively. The companies' complete annual reports, including the notes to the financial statements, are available online.

Instructions

Use the companies' financial information to answer the following questions.

a. 1. What specific items does Coca-Cola discuss in its Note 1—Accounting Policies? (Prepare a list of the headings only.)

2. What specific items does PepsiCo discuss in its Note 2—Our Summary of Significant Accounting Policies? (Prepare a list of the headings only.)

b. For what lines of business or segments do Coca-Cola and PepsiCo present segmented information?

c. Note and comment on the similarities and differences between the auditors' reports submitted by the independent auditors of Coca-Cola and PepsiCo for the year 2017.

*Financial Statement Analysis Case

RNA Inc. manufactures a variety of consumer products. The company's founders have run the company for 30 years and are now interested in retiring. Consequently, they are seeking a purchaser who will continue its operations, and a group of investors, Morgan Inc., is looking into the acquisition of RNA. To evaluate its financial stability and operating efficiency, RNA was requested to provide the latest financial statements and selected financial ratios. Summary information provided by RNA is as follows.

RNA Inc.
Income Statement
For the Year Ended November 30, 2021
(in thousands)

Sales (net)	$30,500
Interest income	500
Total revenue	31,000
Costs and expenses	
Cost of goods sold	17,600
Selling and administrative expenses	3,550
Depreciation and amortization expense	1,890
Interest expense	900
Total costs and expenses	23,940
Income before taxes	7,060
Income taxes	2,800
Net income	$ 4,260

RNA Inc.
Balance Sheet
As of November 30
(in thousands)

	2021	2020
Cash	$ 400	$ 500
Short-term investments (at cost)	300	200
Accounts receivable (net)	3,200	2,900
Inventory	6,000	5,400
Total current assets	9,900	9,000
Property, plant, & equipment (net)	7,100	7,000
Total assets	$17,000	$16,000
Accounts payable	$ 3,700	$ 3,400
Income taxes payable	900	800
Accrued expenses	1,700	1,400
Total current liabilities	6,300	5,600
Long-term debt	2,000	1,800
Total liabilities	8,300	7,400
Common stock ($1 par value)	2,700	2,700
Paid-in capital in excess of par	1,000	1,000
Retained earnings	5,000	4,900
Total stockholders' equity	8,700	8,600
Total liabilities and stockholders' equity	$17,000	$16,000

Selected Financial Ratios

	RNA Inc. 2020	RNA Inc. 2019	Current Industry Average
Current ratio	1.61	1.62	1.63
Acid-test ratio	.64	.63	.68
Times interest earned	8.55	8.50	8.45
Profit margin on sales	13.2%	12.1%	13.0%
Asset turnover	1.84	1.83	1.84
Inventory turnover	3.17	3.21	3.18

Instructions

a. Calculate a new set of ratios for the fiscal year 2021 for RNA based on the financial statements presented.

b. Explain the analytical use of each of the six ratios presented, describing what the investors can learn about RNA's financial stability and operating efficiency.

c. Identify two limitations of ratio analysis.

(CMA adapted)

Accounting, Analysis, and Principles

Savannah, Inc. is a company that manufactures and sells a single product. Unit sales for each of the four quarters of 2020 are projected as follows.

Quarter	Units
First	80,000
Second	150,000
Third	550,000
Fourth	120,000
Annual total	900,000

Savannah incurs variable manufacturing costs of $0.40 per unit and variable nonmanufacturing costs of $0.35 per unit. Savannah will incur fixed manufacturing costs of $720,000 and fixed nonmanufacturing costs of $1,080,000. Savannah will sell its product for $4.00 per unit.

Accounting

Determine the amount of net income Savannah will report in each of the four quarters of 2020, assuming actual sales are as projected and employing the integral approach to interim financial reporting. (Ignore income taxes.) Repeat the analysis under the discrete approach.

Analysis

Compute Savannah's profit margin on sales for each of the four quarters of 2020 under both the integral and discrete approaches. Discuss the effects of employing the integral and the discrete approaches on the degree to which Savannah's profit margin on sales varies from quarter to quarter.

Principles

Explain the conceptual rationale behind the integral approach to interim financial reporting.

Bridge to the Profession

FASB Codification References

[1] FASB ASC 850-10-05 [Predecessor literature: "Related Party Disclosures," *Statement of Financial Accounting Standards No. 57* (Stamford, Conn.: FASB, 1982).]

[2] FASB ASC 855-10-05 [Predecessor literature: "Subsequent Events," *Statement on Auditing Standards No. 1* (New York: AICPA, 1973), pp. 123–124.]

[3] FASB ASC 280-10-05-3. [Predecessor literature: "Disclosures about Segments of an Enterprise and Related Information," *Statement of Financial Accounting Standards No. 131* (Norwalk, Conn.: FASB, 1997).]

[4] FASB ASC 270-10. [Predecessor literature: "Interim Financial Reporting," *Opinions of the Accounting Principles Board No. 28* (New York: AICPA, 1973).]

[5] FASB ASC 740-270-30-2 through 3. [Predecessor literature: "Interim Financial Reporting," *Opinions of the Accounting Principles Board No. 28* (New York: AICPA, 1973), par. 19.]

[6] FASB ASC 740-270-35-4. [Predecessor literature: "Accounting for Income Taxes in Interim Periods," *FASB Interpretation No. 18* (Stamford, Conn.: FASB, March 1977), par. 9.]

[7] FASB ASC 205-40 [Predecessor literature: "The Auditor's Consideration of an Entity's Ability to Continue as a Going Concern," *Statement on Auditing Standards No. 59* (New York: AICPA, 1988).]

Codification Exercises

If your school has a subscription to the FASB Codification, log in and prepare responses to the following. Provide Codification references for your responses.

CE24.1 Access the glossary ("Master Glossary") to answer the following.

a. What is the definition of "ordinary income" (loss)?

b. What is an error in previously issued financial statements?

c. What is the definition of "earnings per share"?

d. What is a publicly traded company?

CE24.2 What are some examples of related parties?

CE24.3 What are the quantitative thresholds that would require a public company to report separately information about an operating segment?

CE24.4 If an SEC-registered company uses the gross profit method to determine cost of goods sold for interim periods, would it be acceptable for the company to state that it's not practicable to determine components of inventory at interim periods? Why or why not?

Codification Research Case

As part of the year-end audit, you are discussing the disclosure checklist with your client. The checklist identifies the items that must be disclosed in a set of GAAP financial statements. The client is surprised by the disclosure item related to accounting policies. Specifically, since the audit report will attest to the statements being prepared in accordance with GAAP, the client questions the accounting policy checklist item. The client has asked you to conduct some research to verify the accounting policy disclosures.

Instructions

If your school has a subscription to the FASB Codification, log in and prepare responses to the following. Provide Codification references for your responses.

a. In general, what should disclosures of accounting policies encompass?

b. List some examples of the most commonly required accounting policy disclosures.

Additional Professional Resources

Go to WileyPLUS for other career-readiness resources, such as career coaching, internship opportunities, and CPAexcel prep.

IFRS Insights

LEARNING OBJECTIVE 10

Compare the disclosure requirements under GAAP and IFRS.

IFRS and GAAP disclosure requirements are similar in many regards. The IFRS addressing various disclosure issues are *IAS 24* ("Related Party Disclosures"), disclosure and recognition of post-statement of financial position events in *IAS 10* ("Events after the Balance Sheet Date"), segment reporting IFRS provisions in *IFRS 8* ("Operating Segments"), and interim reporting requirements in *IAS 34* ("Interim Financial Reporting").

Relevant Facts

Following are the key similarities and differences between GAAP and IFRS related to disclosures.

Similarities

- GAAP and IFRS have similar standards on post-statement of financial position (subsequent) events. That is, under both sets of standards, events that occurred after the statement of financial position date, and which provide additional evidence of conditions that existed at the statement of financial position date, are recognized in the financial statements.
- Like GAAP, IFRS requires that for transactions with related parties, companies disclose the amounts involved in a transaction; the amount, terms, and nature of the outstanding balances; and any doubtful amounts related to those outstanding balances for each major category of related parties.
- Following the issuance of *IFRS 8*, "Operating Segments," the requirements under IFRS and GAAP are very similar. That is, both standards use the management approach to identify reportable segments, and similar segment disclosures are required.
- Neither GAAP nor IFRS require interim reports. Rather, the SEC and securities exchanges outside the United States establish the rules. In the United States, interim reports generally are provided on a quarterly basis; outside the United States, six-month interim reports are common.

Differences

- Due to the broader range of judgments allowed in more principles-based IFRS, note disclosures generally are more expansive under IFRS compared to GAAP.
- Subsequent (or post-statement of financial position) events under IFRS are evaluated through the date that financial instruments are "authorized for issue." GAAP uses the date when financial statements are "issued." Also, for share dividends and splits in the subsequent period, IFRS does not adjust but GAAP does.
- Under IFRS, there is no specific requirement to disclose the name of the related party, which is the case under GAAP.
- Under IFRS, interim reports are prepared on a discrete basis; GAAP generally follows the integral approach.

About the Numbers

Differential Disclosure

A trend toward **differential disclosure** is occurring. The IASB has developed IFRS for small- and medium-sized entities (SMEs). SMEs are entities that publish general-purpose financial statements for external users but do not issue shares or other securities in a public market. Many believe a simplified set of standards makes sense for these companies because they do not have the resources to implement full IFRS. Simplified IFRS for SMEs is a single standard of fewer than 230 pages. It is designed to meet the needs and capabilities of SMEs, which are estimated to account for over 95 percent of all companies around the world. Compared with full IFRS (and many national accounting standards), simplified IFRS for SMEs is less complex in a number of ways:

- Topics not relevant for SMEs are omitted. Examples are earnings per share, interim financial reporting, and segment reporting.
- Simplified IFRS for SMEs allows fewer accounting policy choices. Examples are no option to revalue property, equipment, or intangibles.
- Many principles for recognizing and measuring assets, liabilities, revenue, and expenses are simplified. For example, goodwill is amortized (as a result, there is no annual impairment test), and all borrowing and R&D costs are expensed.
- Significantly fewer disclosures are required (roughly 300 versus 3,000).
- To further reduce standard overload, revisions to the IFRS for SMEs will be limited to once every three years.

Thus, the option of using simplified IFRS helps SMEs meet the needs of their financial statement users while balancing the costs and benefits from a preparer perspective.[31]

Events after the Reporting Period (Subsequent Events)

Notes to the financial statements should explain any significant financial events that took place after the formal statement of financial position date, but before the statements are authorized for issuance (hereafter referred to as the authorization date). These events are referred to as **events after the reporting date**, or **subsequent events**. Illustration IFRS24.1 shows a time diagram of the subsequent events period.

ILLUSTRATION IFRS24.1

Time Periods for Subsequent Events

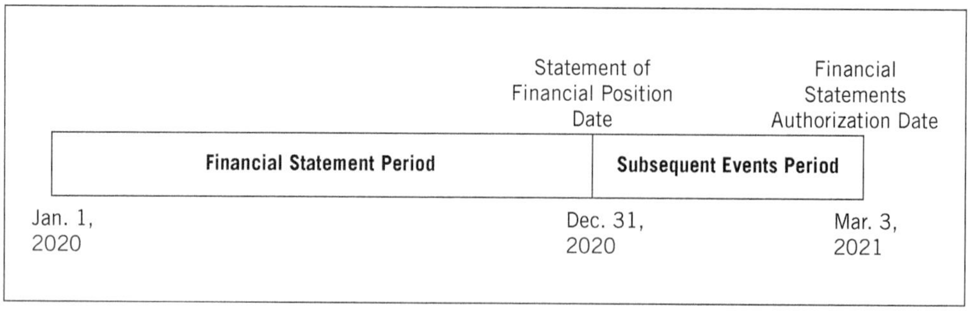

[31]In the United States, there has been a preference for one set of GAAP except in unusual situations. With the advent of simplified IFRS for SMEs, this position is under review. Both the FASB and the AICPA are studying the big GAAP/little GAAP issue to ensure that any kind of differential reporting is conceptually sound and meets the needs of users. As discussed in the chapter, the FASB has formed a Private Company Council, whose primary objectives are to provide recommendations on FASB standard-setting for privately held enterprises.

A period of several weeks, and sometimes several months, may elapse after the end of the fiscal year but before the management or the board of directors authorizes issuance of the financial statements. Various activities involved in closing the books for the period and issuing the statements all take time: taking and pricing the inventory, reconciling subsidiary ledgers with controlling accounts, preparing necessary adjusting entries, ensuring that all transactions for the period have been entered, obtaining an audit of the financial statements by independent certified public accountants, and printing the annual report. During the period between the statement of financial position date and its authorization date, important transactions or other events may occur that materially affect the company's financial position or operating situation.

Many who read a statement of financial position believe the financial condition is constant, and they project it into the future. However, readers must be told if the company has experienced a significant change—e.g., sold one of its plants, acquired a subsidiary, suffered unusual losses, settled significant litigation, or experienced any other important event in the post-statement of financial position period. Without an explanation in a note, the reader might be misled and draw inappropriate conclusions.

Two types of events or transactions occurring after the statement of financial position date may have a material effect on the financial statements or may need disclosure so that readers interpret these statements accurately:

1. Events that provide additional evidence about conditions **that existed** at the statement of financial position date, including the estimates inherent in the process of preparing financial statements. These events are referred to as **adjusted subsequent events** and require adjustments to the financial statements. All information available prior to the authorization date of the financial statements helps investors and creditors evaluate estimates previously made. To ignore these subsequent events is to pass up an opportunity to improve the accuracy of the financial statements. This first type of event encompasses information that an accountant would have recorded in the accounts had the information been known at the statement of financial position date.

   For example, if a loss on an account receivable results from a customer's bankruptcy subsequent to the statement of financial position date, the company adjusts the financial statements before their issuance. The bankruptcy stems from the customer's poor financial health existing at the statement of financial position date.

   The same criterion applies to settlements of litigation. The company must adjust the financial statements if the events that gave rise to the litigation, such as personal injury or patent infringement, took place prior to the statement of financial position date.

2. Events that provide evidence about conditions that **did not exist** at the statement of financial position date but arise subsequent to that date. These events are referred to as **non-adjusted subsequent events** and do not require adjustment of the financial statements. To illustrate, a loss resulting from a customer's fire or flood *after* the statement of financial position date does not reflect conditions existing at that date.

   Thus, adjustment of the financial statements is not necessary. A company should not recognize subsequent events that provide evidence about conditions that did not exist at the date of the statement of financial position but that arose after the statement of financial position date.

   The following are examples of non-adjusted subsequent events:

   - A major business combination after the reporting period or disposing of a major subsidiary.
   - Announcing a plan to discontinue an operation or commencing the implementation of a major restructuring.
   - Major purchases of assets, other disposals of assets, or expropriation of major assets by government.
   - The destruction of a major production plant or inventories by a fire or natural disaster after the reporting period.
   - Major ordinary share transactions and potential ordinary share transactions after the reporting period.[32]
   - Abnormally large changes after the reporting period in asset prices, foreign exchange rates, or taxes.
   - Entering into significant commitments or contingent liabilities, for example, by issuing significant guarantees after the statement date.

[32]The effects from natural disasters, like the recent eruption of the Icelandic volcano, which occurred after the year-end for companies with March fiscal years, require disclosure in order to keep the statements from being misleading. Some companies may have to consider whether these disasters affect their ability to continue as going concerns.

Some non-adjusted subsequent events may have to be disclosed to keep the financial statements from being misleading. For such events, a company discloses the nature of the event and an estimate of its financial effect. Illustration IFRS24.2 presents an example of subsequent events disclosure, excerpted from the annual report of Tieto Corporation.

ILLUSTRATION IFRS24.2

Disclosure of Subsequent Events

Tieto Corporation

Note 32. Events After the Balance Sheet Date

In February, Tieto agreed to sell the majority of its operations in Germany and Netherlands to the German Industrial Group Aurelius. Closing is expected to take place during the second quarter of 2013. Net sales of the divested business amounted to over EUR 110 million in 2012. German businesses were loss-making in 2012 and the divestment will improve Tieto's operating margin of underlying business by some 0.5 percentage points based on 2012 performance. Tieto booked about EUR 30 million in impairment in the fourth-quarter 2012. The divested business operations, including around 900 employees in total, will be transferred to the new owner at the time of closing. The divestment excludes Tieto's global businesses and customers, i.e. the forest industry business in Germany, the energy industry business in Netherlands, Product Engineering resources for global customers and selective other global roles.

Between 7 December and 31 December 2012, a total of 111,846 Tieto Corporation new shares have been subscribed for with the company's stock options 2006C, and a total of 3,500 shares with stock options 2009A. As a result of the subscriptions, the number of Tieto shares increased to 72,492,559 and the share capital to EUR 76,064,020.00. The shares subscribed for under the stock options were registered in the Trade Register on 18 January 2013.

Many subsequent events or developments do not require adjustment of or disclosure in the financial statements. Typically, these are non-accounting events or conditions that management normally communicates by other means. These events include legislation, product changes, management changes, strikes, unionization, marketing agreements, and loss of important customers.

Interim Reports

Another source of information for the investor is interim reports. As noted earlier, **interim reports** cover periods of less than one year. The securities exchanges, market regulators, and the accounting profession have an active interest in the presentation of interim information.

Because of the short-term nature of the information in these reports, there is considerable controversy as to the general approach companies should employ. One group, which favors the **discrete approach**, believes that companies should treat each interim period as a separate accounting period. Using that treatment, companies would follow the principles for deferrals and accruals used for annual reports. In this view, companies should report accounting transactions as they occur, and expense recognition should not change with the period of time covered.

Another group, which favors the **integral approach**, believes that the interim report is an integral part of the annual report and that deferrals and accruals should take into consideration what will happen for the entire year. In this approach, companies should assign estimated expenses to parts of a year on the basis of sales volume or some other activity base. In general, IFRS requires companies to follow the discrete approach.

Interim Reporting Requirements **Under IFRS, companies should use the same accounting policies for interim reports and for annual reports.** They should recognize revenues in interim periods on the same basis as they do for annual periods. For example, if Cedars Corp. uses the percentage-of-completion method as the basis for recognizing revenue on an annual basis, it should use the percentage-of-completion method for interim reports as well. Also, Cedars should treat costs directly associated with revenues (product costs, such as materials, labor and related fringe benefits, and manufacturing overhead) in the same manner for interim reports as for annual reports.

Companies should use the same inventory pricing methods (FIFO, average-cost, etc.) for interim reports and for annual reports. However, companies may use the gross profit method for interim inventory pricing. But, they must disclose the method and adjustments to reconcile with annual inventory.

Discrete Approach Following the discrete approach, companies record in interim reports revenues and expenses according to the revenue and expense recognition principles. This includes costs and expenses other than product costs (often referred to as period costs). No accruals or deferrals in anticipation of future events during the year should be reported. For example, the cost of a planned major periodic maintenance or overhaul for a company like Airbus or other seasonal expenditure that is expected to occur late in the year is not anticipated for interim reporting purposes. The mere intention or necessity to incur expenditure related to the future is not sufficient to give rise to an obligation.

Or, a company like **Carrefour** may budget certain costs expected to be incurred irregularly during the financial year, such as advertising and employee training costs. Those costs generally are discretionary even though they are planned and tend to recur from year to year. However, recognizing an obligation at the end of an interim financial reporting period for such costs that have not yet been incurred generally is not consistent with the definition of a liability.

While year-to-date measurements may involve changes in estimates of amounts reported in prior interim periods of the current financial year, the principles for recognizing assets, liabilities, income, and expenses for interim periods are the same as in annual financial statements. For example, **Wm Morrison Supermarkets plc** records losses from inventory write-downs, restructurings, or impairments in an interim period similar to how it would treat these items in the annual financial statements (when incurred). However, if an estimate from a prior interim period changes in a subsequent interim period of that year, the original estimate is adjusted in the subsequent interim period.

Interim Disclosures IFRS does not require a complete set of financial statements at the interim reporting date. Rather, companies may comply with the requirements by providing condensed financial statements and selected explanatory notes. Because users of interim financial reports also have access to the most recent annual financial report, companies only need provide explanation of significant events and transactions since the end of the last annual reporting period. Companies should report the following interim data at a minimum.

1. Statement that the same accounting policies and methods of computation are followed in the interim financial statements as compared with the most recent annual financial statements or, if those policies or methods have been changed, a description of the nature and effect of the change.
2. Explanatory comments about the seasonality or cyclicality of interim operations.
3. The nature and amount of items affecting assets, liabilities, equity, net income, or cash flows that are unusual because of their nature, size, or incidence.
4. The nature and amount of changes in accounting policies and estimates of amounts previously reported.
5. Issuances, repurchases, and repayments of debt and equity securities.
6. Dividends paid (aggregate or per share) separately for ordinary shares and other shares.
7. Segment information, as required by *IFRS 8*, "Operating Segments."
8. Changes in contingent liabilities or contingent assets since the end of the last annual reporting period.
9. Effect of changes in the composition of the company during the interim period, such as business combinations, obtaining or losing control of subsidiaries and long-term investments, restructurings, and discontinued operations.
10. Other material events subsequent to the end of the interim period that have not been reflected in the financial statements for the interim period.

If a complete set of financial statements is provided in the interim report, companies comply with the provisions of *IAS 1*, "Presentation of Financial Statements."

On the Horizon

Hans Hoogervorst, chairperson of the IASB, recently noted: "High quality financial information is the lifeblood of market-based economies. If the blood is of poor quality, then the body shuts down and the patient dies. It is the same with financial reporting. If investors cannot trust the numbers, then financial markets stop working. For market-based economies, that is really bad news. It is an essential public good for market-based economies. . . . And in the past 10 years, most of the world's economies—developed and emerging—have embraced IFRSs." While the United States has yet to adopt IFRS, there is no question that IFRS and GAAP are converging quickly. We have provided expanded discussion in the *Global Views* and *IFRS Insights* to help you understand the issues surrounding convergence as they relate to intermediate accounting. After reading these discussions, you should realize that IFRS and GAAP are very similar in many areas, with differences in those areas revolving around some minor technical points. In other situations, the differences are major; for example, IFRS does not permit LIFO inventory accounting. Our hope is that the FASB and IASB can continue to narrow differences in accounting standards for use by companies around the world.

What Do the Numbers Mean? Disclosure Overload

As we discussed in Chapter 1 and throughout the text, IFRS is gaining popularity around the world. The U.S. Securities and Exchange Commission is still studying whether and how to incorporate IFRS in the accounting rules used by publicly traded companies in the United States. There is some debate on U.S. readiness to make the switch. For example, there are several areas in which the FASB and the IASB must iron out a number of technical accounting issues before they reach a substantially converged set of accounting standards. Here is a list of important areas yet to be converged:

1. ***Error correction.*** According to *IAS 8*, it's not always necessary to retrospectively restate financial results when a company corrects errors, especially if the adjustment is impractical or too costly. GAAP, on the other hand, requires restatements in many error-correction cases.
2. ***Death of LIFO.*** Last-in, first-out (LIFO) inventory accounting is prohibited under *IAS 2*, so any U.S. company using the method will have to abandon it (and the tax benefits) and move to another methodology. Although LIFO is permitted under GAAP, the repeal of LIFO for tax purposes is an ongoing debate.
3. ***Reversal of impairments.*** *IAS 36* permits companies to reverse impairment losses up to the amount of the original impairment when the reason for the charge decreases or no longer exists. However, GAAP bans reversal.
4. ***PP&E revaluation.*** *IAS 16* allows for the revaluation of property, plant, and equipment, but the entire asset class must be revalued. That means a company can choose to use the revaluation model if the asset class's fair value can be measured reliably. But, it must choose to use one model or the other; both cannot be used at the same time. GAAP does not allow revaluation.
5. ***Component depreciation.*** Also under *IAS 16*, companies must recognize and depreciate equipment components separately if the components can be physically separated from the asset and have different useful life spans. In practical terms, that means controllers will have to rely on the operations side of the business to help assess equipment components. GAAP allows component depreciation, but it is not required.
6. ***Development costs.*** Based on *IAS 38*, companies are permitted to capitalize development costs as long as they meet six criteria. However, research costs are still expensed. GAAP requires that all R&D costs be charged to expense when incurred.
7. ***Sustainability reporting.*** Such reporting on environmental, social, and corporate governance (ESG) issues is not required by GAAP or IFRS. However, a growing number of companies (especially those who use IFRS) are voluntarily disclosing supplementary Information on ESG. While much of this information is nonfinancial, the effects of sustainability efforts do have financial consequences—about which investors want to know. As discussed in Chapter 12, ESG reporting standards are coming online and if companies continue to get on the sustainability reporting bandwagon, such reporting will add to the heft of the annual reporting package.

Some are already debating what will happen if and when U.S. companies adopt these new standards. It is almost certain that expanded disclosure will be needed to help users navigate accounting reports upon adoption of IFRS. As one accounting analyst remarked, "Get ready for an avalanche of footnotes." Since using IFRS requires more judgment than using GAAP, two to three times as many footnotes will be needed to explain the rationales for accounting approaches. So while principles-based standards should promote more comparability, they require investors to dig into the disclosures in the footnotes.

Sources: Marie Leone, "GAAP and IFRS: Six Degrees of Separation," *CFO.com* (June 30, 2010); E. Harrell, "How Accounting Can Help Build a Sustainable Economy," *Harvard Business Review* (December 14, 2015); and M. Cohn, "Companies Struggle to Go Beyond Boilerplate in Sustainability Disclosures," *Accounting Today* (June 15, 2017).

IFRS Self-Test Questions

1. Which of the following is **false**?
   - **a.** In general, IFRS note disclosures are more expansive compared to GAAP.
   - **b.** GAAP and IFRS have similar standards on subsequent events.
   - **c.** Both IFRS and GAAP require interim reports although the reporting frequency varies.
   - **d.** Segment reporting requirements are very similar under IFRS and GAAP.
2. Differential reporting for small- and medium-sized entities:
   - **a.** is required for all companies less than a certain size.
   - **b.** omits accounting topics not relevant for SMEs, such as earnings per share, and interim and segment reporting.
   - **c.** has different rules for topics such as earnings per share, and interim and segment reporting.
   - **d.** requires significantly more disclosures, since more items are not recognized in the financial statements.
3. Subsequent events are reviewed through which date under IFRS?
   - **a.** Statement of financial position date.
   - **b.** Sixty days after the year-end date.
   - **c.** Date of independent auditor's opinion.
   - **d.** Authorization date of the financial statements.
4. Under IFRS, share dividends declared after the statement of financial position date but before the end of the subsequent events period are:
   - **a.** accounted for similar to errors as a prior period adjustment.
   - **b.** adjusted subsequent events, because they are paid from prior year earnings.
   - **c.** not adjusted in the current year's financial statements.
   - **d.** recognized on a prospective basis from the date of declaration.
5. Interim reporting under IFRS:
   - **a.** is prepared using the discrete approach.
   - **b.** is prepared using a combination of the discrete and integral approach.
   - **c.** requires a complete set of financial statements for each interim period.
   - **d.** permits companies to omit disclosure of material events subsequent to the interim reporting date.

IFRS Concepts and Application

IFRS24.1 Where can authoritative IFRS be found related to the various disclosure issues discussed in the chapter?

IFRS24.2 What are the major types of subsequent events? Indicate how each of the following "subsequent events" would be reported.

- **a.** Collection of a note written off in a prior period.
- **b.** Issuance of a large preference share offering.
- **c.** Acquisition of a company in a different industry.
- **d.** Destruction of a major plant in a flood.
- **e.** Death of the company's chief executive officer (CEO).
- **f.** Additional wage costs associated with settlement of a four-week strike.
- **g.** Settlement of an income tax case at considerably more tax than anticipated at year-end.
- **h.** Change in the product mix from consumer goods to industrial goods.

IFRS24.3 Morlan Corporation is preparing its December 31, 2020, financial statements. Two events that occurred between December 31, 2020, and March 10, 2021, when the statements were authorized for issue, are described below.

1. A liability, estimated at $160,000 at December 31, 2020, was settled on February 26, 2021, at $170,000.
2. A flood loss of $80,000 occurred on March 1, 2021.

Instructions

What effect do these subsequent events have on 2020 net income?

IFRS24.4 Keystone Corporation's financial statements for the year ended December 31, 2020, were authorized for issue on March 10, 2021. The following events took place early in 2021.

- **a.** On January 10, 10,000 ordinary shares of $5 par value were issued at $66 per share.
- **b.** On March 1, Keystone determined after negotiations with the taxing authorities that income taxes payable for 2020 should be $1,320,000. At December 31, 2020, income taxes payable were recorded at $1,100,000.

Instructions

Discuss how the preceding subsequent events should be reflected in the 2020 financial statements.

IFRS24.5 For each of the following subsequent events, indicate whether a company should (a) adjust the financial statements, (b) disclose in notes to the financial statements, or (c) neither adjust nor disclose.

______ 1. Settlement of a tax case at a cost considerably in excess of the amount expected at year-end.
______ 2. Introduction of a new product line.
______ 3. Loss of assembly plant due to fire.
______ 4. Sale of a significant portion of the company's assets.
______ 5. Retirement of the company president.
______ 6. Issuance of a significant number of ordinary shares.
______ 7. Loss of a significant customer.
______ 8. Prolonged employee strike.
______ 9. Material loss on a year-end receivable because of a customer's bankruptcy.
______ 10. Hiring of a new president.
______ 11. Settlement of prior year's litigation against the company (no loss was accrued).
______ 12. Merger with another company of comparable size.

IFRS24.6 What are interim reports? Why is a complete set of financial statements often not provided with interim data? What are the accounting problems related to the presentation of interim data?

IFRS24.7 Dierdorf Inc., a closely held corporation, has decided to go public. The controller, Ed Floyd, is concerned with presenting interim data when an inventory write-down is recorded. What problems are encountered with inventories when quarterly data are presented?

IFRS24.8 Bill Novak is working on an audit of an IFRS client. In his review of the client's interim reports, he notes that the reports are prepared on a discrete basis. That is, each interim report is viewed as a distinct period. Is this acceptable under IFRS? If so, explain how that treatment could affect comparisons to a GAAP company.

IFRS24.9 Snider Corporation, a publicly traded company, is preparing the interim financial data which it will issue to its shareholders at the end of the first quarter of the 2020–2021 fiscal year. Snider's financial accounting department has compiled the following summarized revenue and expense data for the first quarter of the year.

Sales revenue	$60,000,000
Cost of goods sold	36,000,000
Variable selling expenses	1,000,000
Fixed selling expenses	3,000,000

Included in the fixed selling expenses was the single lump-sum payment of $2,000,000 for television advertisements for the entire year.

Instructions

a. Snider Corporation must issue its quarterly financial statements in accordance with IFRS regarding interim financial reporting.

1. Explain whether Snider should report its operating results for the quarter as if the quarter were a separate reporting period in and of itself, or as if the quarter were an integral part of the annual reporting period.

2. State how the sales revenue, cost of goods sold, and fixed selling expenses would be reflected in Snider Corporation's quarterly report prepared for the first quarter of the 2020–2021 fiscal year. Briefly justify your presentation.

b. What financial information, as a minimum, must Snider Corporation disclose to its shareholders in its quarterly reports?

Professional Research

IFRS24.10 As part of the year-end audit, you are discussing the disclosure checklist with your client. The checklist identifies the items that must be disclosed in a set of IFRS financial statements. The client is surprised by the disclosure item related to accounting policies. Specifically, since the audit report will attest to the statements being prepared in accordance with IFRS, the client questions the accounting policy checklist item. The client has asked you to conduct some research to verify the accounting policy disclosures.

Instructions

Access the IFRS authoritative literature at the IASB website. (Click on the IFRS tab and then register for free eIFRS access if necessary.) When you have accessed the documents, you can use the search tool in your Internet browser to respond to the following questions. (Provide paragraph citations.)

a. In general, what should disclosures of accounting policies encompass?

b. List some examples of the most commonly required disclosures.

International Financial Reporting Problem

Marks and Spencer plc (M&S)

IFRS24.11 The financial statements of **M&S** are presented in Appendix E. The company's complete annual report, including the notes to the financial statements, is available online.

Instructions

Refer to M&S's financial statements and the accompanying notes to answer the following questions.

a. What specific items does M&S discuss in its Note 1—Summary of Significant Accounting Policies? (List the headings only.)

b. For what segments did M&S report segmented information? Which segment is the largest? Who is M&S's largest customer?

c. What interim information was reported by M&S?

Answers to IFRS Self-Test Questions

1. c **2.** b **3.** d **4.** c **5.** a

Appendix A

Private Company Accounting

The FASB has traditionally taken the position that there should be one set of GAAP. However, due to growing concern about differential costs and benefits of a "one size fits all" reporting package, the FASB has considered providing alternative accounting treatments for private companies in areas that include (1) recognition and measurement, (2) presentation and disclosure, and (3) transition methods for financial accounting standards and effective dates. Since 2012, the FASB has worked with the Private Company Council (PCC) to improve the process of setting accounting standards for private companies.

The Private Company Council (PCC)

Background on the PCC

The PCC is comprised of 9–12 members with balanced representation from private company auditing, preparer, and user communities. The PCC has two principal responsibilities:

1. The PCC determines, using the Private Company Decision-Making Framework (PCC Framework), whether alternatives to existing GAAP are necessary to address the needs of users of private company financial statements.
2. The PCC serves as the primary advisory body to the FASB on the appropriate treatment for private companies for items under active consideration on the FASB's technical agenda.[1]

Following a FASB endorsement process, alternatives for private companies developed by the PCC are incorporated into GAAP.

Private Company Decision-Making Framework

One of the PCC's first responsibilities was to work with the FASB to develop mutually agreed-on criteria for private company alternatives. The result of that joint effort was the *Private Company Decision-Making Framework: A Guide for Evaluating Financial Accounting and Reporting for Private Companies* (the PCC Framework), issued in December 2013. This guide assists the Board and the PCC in determining whether and in what circumstances to provide alternative recognition, measurement, disclosure, display, effective date, and transition guidance for private companies reporting under GAAP.

In making these assessments, the Board and the PCC first should determine whether the alternative recognition or measurement guidance being evaluated provides **relevant information** to users of private company financial statements at a **reasonable cost**. That analysis

[1]The Financial Accounting Foundation (FAF) recently completed a three-year review of the PCC. In response to stakeholder input, the FAF trustees made targeted improvements to increase the PCC's effectiveness without significantly changing the PCC's roles and responsibilities. The changes to the PCC operating procedures will increase the PCC's focus on providing the FASB with private company perspectives on the FASB's active agenda projects. As a result, the PCC will operate in a fashion similar to FASB's other advisory groups [Investors Technical Advisory Committee (ITAC), the Not-for-Profit Advisor Committee (NAC), and the Valuation Resource Group (VRG)], which share their views and expertise with the Board on matters related to projects on the Board's agenda, from the perspectives of various constituencies.

should focus on (a) the relevance of the information in meeting the objective of financial reporting for typical users of private company financial statements, (b) the characteristics that differentiate users of private company financial statements from users of public company financial statements, and (c) the cost and complexity of applying the guidance.

The guide helps the Board and the PCC identify differential information needs of users of public company financial statements and users of private company financial statements, and to identify opportunities to reduce the complexity and costs of preparing financial statements in accordance with GAAP.

PCC Accomplishments

Since its first meeting in December 2012, the PCC has addressed a number of financial accounting and reporting issues that are important to private company stakeholders as well as the wider financial reporting community. In addition to developing the PCC Framework, the FASB also issued an Accounting Standards Update on the definition of a public business entity. The FASB and the PCC use that definition to identify the types of companies that are excluded from the scope of the PCC Framework. In general, a company is considered a public business entity if is required to file or furnish financial statements to the SEC or to file or furnish financial statements with a regulatory agency (domestic or foreign) other than the SEC in preparation for the sale of or for purposes of issuing securities.

The PCC also has become a springboard for efforts to reduce complexity in GAAP for all types of organizations, not just private companies. The FASB has adopted a practice of considering whether any GAAP alternative proposed by the PCC may make sense for public as well as private companies—along with not-for-profit organizations. For example, the FASB issued an Accounting Standards Update to address financial reporting complexity for both public and private development-stage companies.

Two issues addressed by the PCC relate to the accounting for intangible assets and the amortization of goodwill.

Private Company Alternatives for Intangible Assets and Goodwill

Accounting for Identifiable Intangible Assets

In December 2014, the FASB issued an Accounting Standards Update, developed with the PCC, that provides an alternative to exempt private companies from separately recognizing and measuring non-competition agreements and customer-related intangible assets (such as customer relationships) that are not capable of being sold or licensed independently in a business combination.[2]

Additional Background

As discussed in Chapter 12, in a business combination the acquirer separately recognizes all intangible assets that are **identifiable**, at their acquisition-date fair values. An intangible asset is identifiable if it meets either of the following criteria:

1. It arises from contractual or other legal rights, regardless of whether those rights are transferable or separable from the entity or from other rights and obligations.

[2]Accounting Standards Update No. 2014-18, *Business Combinations (Topic 805): Accounting for Identifiable Intangible Assets in a Business Combination* (a consensus of the Private Company Council).

2. It is separable, that is, capable of being separated from the company and sold, transferred, licensed, rented, or exchanged, either individually or together with a related contract, identifiable asset, or liability, regardless of whether the company intends to do so.

For example, in the Tractorling example presented in Chapter 12, Multi-Diversified included patents (which meet the identifiable definition) in its calculation of the net identifiable assets.

In its reexamination of this accounting for private companies, the PCC found that separate information on certain customer-related intangible assets is not decision-useful because the assets may not be transferable and estimates of their fair values are highly subjective. As a result, the PCC recommended, and the FASB endorsed, an alternative that, if elected, indicates that private company acquirers shall not recognize separately from goodwill the following intangible assets:

- Customer-related intangible assets *unless* they are capable of being sold or licensed independently from other assets of a business.
- Non-competition agreements.

Examples of customer-related intangible assets include (1) mortgage servicing rights, (2) commodity supply contracts, (3) core deposits, and (4) customer information (for example, names and contact information).

Alternative Accounting Example

To illustrate in the context of the Tractorling example in Chapter 12, recall that goodwill is recorded only when an entire business is purchased. To record goodwill, a company compares the fair value of the net tangible and **identifiable intangible assets** with the purchase price of the acquired business. The difference is considered goodwill. Goodwill is the residual—the excess of cost over fair value of the identifiable net assets acquired.

In its acquisition of Tractorling, Multi-Diversified determined the fair value of net assets to be $350,000, but it was willing to pay $400,000 due to Tractorling's established reputation, good credit rating, top management team, well-trained employees, and so on. These factors make the value of the business greater than $350,000. Multi-Diversified places a premium on the future earning power of these attributes as well as on the basic asset structure of the company today.

Multi-Diversified labels the difference between the purchase price of $400,000 and the fair value of net assets of $350,000 as goodwill. Goodwill is viewed as one or a group of unidentifiable values (intangible assets), the cost of which "is measured by the difference between the cost of the group of assets or enterprise acquired and the sum of the assigned costs of individual tangible and identifiable intangible assets acquired less liabilities assumed." This procedure assumes goodwill covers all the values that cannot be specifically identified with any identifiable tangible or intangible asset. **Illustration A.1** shows this approach.

ILLUSTRATION A.1

Determination of Goodwill—Master Valuation Approach

Assigned to purchase price of $400,000	Cash	$ 25,000
	Accounts receivable	35,000
	Inventory	122,000
	Property, plant, and equipment, net	205,000
	Patents	18,000
	Liabilities	(55,000)
	Fair value of net identifiable assets	350,000
	Purchase price	400,000
	Value assigned to goodwill	$ 50,000

Multi-Diversified records this transaction as follows.

Cash	25,000	
Accounts Receivable	35,000	
Inventory	122,000	
Property, Plant, and Equipment	205,000	
Patents	18,000	
Goodwill	50,000	
Liabilities		55,000
Cash		400,000

To illustrate the private company alternative, assume that **instead of patents**, Tractorling employees had a non-compete agreement with Tractorling management that would preclude them from working for any competing companies for one year following the acquisition (with an estimated fair value of $18,000) should they leave the company. Such agreements are common in business combinations to ensure a smooth transition period.

If Multi-Diversified was a public company, as with the patents, it would recognize this non-compete agreement separately from goodwill on the post-acquisition balance sheet. However, a private company that chooses the alternative accounting would not recognize a separate intangible asset for the non-compete agreement but instead include the $18,000 in the Goodwill balance. That is, rather than the entry recorded above, a private company would make the following entry.

Cash	25,000	
Accounts Receivable	35,000	
Inventory	122,000	
Property, Plant, and Equipment	205,000	
Goodwill	68,000	
Liabilities		55,000
Cash		400,000

Note that the Goodwill balance ($50,000 + $18,000) includes the amount attributed to the non-compete agreement. **Private companies that elect this accounting alternative must also elect the private company alternative to amortize goodwill (discussed in the next section).**

Accounting for Goodwill

The FASB also issued guidance developed with the PCC that provides an alternative for private companies in the accounting for goodwill.[3] Under the alternative, rather than considering goodwill to have an indefinite life, private companies can elect to amortize goodwill on a straight-line basis over a period not to exceed 10 years. In addition, goodwill under this alternative will be tested for impairment when a triggering event occurs and based on a comparison of the carrying value of the goodwill to the fair value of the company or reporting unit.

Additional Background

As discussed in Chapter 12, companies consider goodwill to have an indefinite life and therefore should not amortize it. Although goodwill may decrease in value over time, predicting the actual life of goodwill and an appropriate pattern of amortization is extremely difficult. In

[3]Accounting Standards Update No. 2014-02, *Intangibles—Goodwill and Other (Topic 350): Accounting for Goodwill* (a consensus of the Private Company Council).

addition, investors find the amortization charge of little use in evaluating financial performance. Furthermore, the investment community wants to know the amount invested in goodwill, which often is the largest intangible asset on a company's balance sheet. Therefore, companies adjust its carrying value only when goodwill is impaired.

As part of its research and outreach efforts on intangible assets and goodwill, the PCC obtained feedback from private company stakeholders that the benefits of the current accounting for goodwill after initial recognition do not justify the related costs. Feedback from users of private company financial statements indicated that the current goodwill impairment test provides limited decision-useful information because most users of private company financial statements generally disregard goodwill and goodwill impairment losses in their analysis of a private company's financial condition and operating performance. The PCC also received input from preparers and auditors of private company financial statements indicating concerns about the cost and complexity involved in performing the current goodwill impairment test. Even though the recent introduction of the optional qualitative assessment has provided some cost reduction in testing goodwill for impairment, many of those stakeholders stated that the level of cost reduction has not been significant.

Private Company Alternative

In response to this input, the PCC proposed (and the FASB endorsed) an alternative accounting for private companies. Under the alternative, private companies that elect the accounting alternative will:

1. Amortize goodwill on a straight-line basis over 10 years, or less than 10 years if a shorter useful life is more appropriate.
2. Test goodwill for impairment when a triggering event occurs that indicates that the fair value of a company (or a reporting unit) may be below its carrying amount.

When a triggering event occurs, a company has the option to first assess qualitative factors to determine whether the quantitative impairment test is necessary. If that qualitative assessment indicates that it is more likely than not that goodwill is impaired, the company must perform the quantitative test to compare the company's fair value with its carrying amount, including goodwill (or the fair value of the reporting unit with the carrying amount, including goodwill, of the reporting unit). If the qualitative assessment indicates that it is not more likely than not that goodwill is impaired, further testing is unnecessary. The goodwill impairment loss cannot exceed the company's (or the reporting unit's) carrying amount of goodwill.

Alternative Accounting Example

To illustrate the accounting under the private company alternative, refer to our Tractorling example in the prior section, in which Multi-Diversified recorded goodwill of $68,000 (including the value of the non-compete agreement for Tractorling management). Under the private company alternative, using the maximum life of 10 years, Multi-Diversified will amortize goodwill through the following entry each year following the acquisition.

Amortization Expense ($68,000 ÷ 10)	6,800	
Goodwill		6,800

Going forward, the recorded goodwill is evaluated for impairment only if there is a triggering event that indicates that the goodwill's fair value may be less than the carrying value. Thus, the alternative accounting is similar to the accounting for limited-life intangible assets.[4]

[4]As noted, if a private company makes the election to apply the identifiable intangible asset alternative discussed in the prior section, it must also elect the alternative for goodwill amortization and impairment.

Summary

As reflected in the feedback received in the three-year review, the PCC has generally been graded as a success in helping the FASB respond to private company concerns related to unique user needs and the cost and complexity of applying accounting guidance. In developing the private company alternatives for intangible assets and goodwill, the FASB and PCC was guided by the PCC Framework to assess whether the recognition or measurement guidance being evaluated provides relevant information to users of private company financial statements at a reasonable cost. While some users may not find the information resulting from applying these alternatives as relevant, the alternatives provide private companies relief from costs associated with estimating the fair value of some identifiable intangibles and annual goodwill impairment tests. That is, amortization will reduce the likelihood of impairments because private companies generally will test goodwill for impairment less frequently.[5]

While the work of the PCC is at an early stage, a recent survey indicates that 16 percent of approximately 2,900 surveyed private companies have adopted or intend to adopt the goodwill amortization alternatives. The jury is still out on other private company alternatives.[6] Although the PCC has not addressed all of the topics it originally identified as priorities, the topics that remain are generally encompassed by the FASB's simplification initiatives, which are aimed at reducing complexity for both public *and* private companies, or as part of its Disclosure Framework project.

[5]Based in part on its deliberation of this private company issue, the FASB recently added a project to its agenda on the subsequent accounting for goodwill for public business entities and not-for-profit entities. That is, some of the same benefits and reduction in cost and complexity associated with goodwill alternatives for private companies may also be relevant to public companies.

[6]PricewaterhouseCoopers, "Representing Private Companies at the FASB: The Next Phase for the PCC," *Point of View* (June 2015).

Appendix B

Specimen Financial Statements: The Procter & Gamble Company

Once each year, a corporation communicates to its stockholders and other interested parties by issuing a complete set of audited financial statements. The **annual report**, as this communication is called, summarizes the financial results of the company's operations for the year and its plans for the future. Many annual reports are attractive, multicolored, glossy public relations pieces, containing pictures of corporate officers and directors as well as photos and descriptions of new products and new buildings. Yet the basic function of every annual report is to report financial information, almost all of which is a product of the corporation's accounting system.

The content and organization of corporate annual reports have become fairly standardized. Excluding the public relations part of the report (pictures, products, etc.), the following are the traditional financial portions of the annual report:

- Financial Highlights
- Letter to the Stockholders
- Management's Discussion and Analysis
- Financial Statements
- Notes to the Financial Statements
- Management's Responsibility for Financial Reporting
- Management's Report on Internal Control over Financial Reporting
- Report of Independent Registered Public Accounting Firm
- Selected Financial Data

The official SEC filing of the annual report is called a **Form 10-K**, which often omits the public relations pieces found in most standard annual reports. On the following pages, we present **The Procter & Gamble Company (P&G)**'s financial statements taken from the company's 2017 Form 10-K.

Consolidated Statements of Earnings

Amounts in millions except per share amounts; Years ended June 30	2017	2016	2015
NET SALES	**$ 65,058**	$ 65,299	$ 70,749
Cost of products sold	**32,535**	32,909	37,056
Selling, general and administrative expense	**18,568**	18,949	20,616
Venezuela deconsolidation charge	**—**	—	2,028
OPERATING INCOME	**13,955**	13,441	11,049
Interest expense	**465**	579	626
Interest income	**171**	182	149
Other non-operating income/(expense), net	**(404)**	325	440
EARNINGS FROM CONTINUING OPERATIONS BEFORE INCOME TAXES	**13,257**	13,369	11,012
Income taxes on continuing operations	**3,063**	3,342	2,725
NET EARNINGS FROM CONTINUING OPERATIONS	**10,194**	10,027	8,287
NET EARNINGS/(LOSS) FROM DISCONTINUED OPERATIONS	**5,217**	577	(1,143)
NET EARNINGS	**15,411**	10,604	7,144
Less: Net earnings attributable to noncontrolling interests	**85**	96	108
NET EARNINGS ATTRIBUTABLE TO PROCTER & GAMBLE	**$ 15,326**	$ 10,508	$ 7,036
BASIC NET EARNINGS PER COMMON SHARE: (1)			
Earnings from continuing operations	**$ 3.79**	$ 3.59	$ 2.92
Earnings/(loss) from discontinued operations	**2.01**	0.21	(0.42)
BASIC NET EARNINGS PER COMMON SHARE	**$ 5.80**	$ 3.80	$ 2.50
DILUTED NET EARNINGS PER COMMON SHARE: (1)			
Earnings from continuing operations	**$ 3.69**	$ 3.49	$ 2.84
Earnings/(loss) from discontinued operations	**1.90**	0.20	(0.40)
DILUTED NET EARNINGS PER COMMON SHARE	**$ 5.59**	$ 3.69	$ 2.44
DIVIDENDS PER COMMON SHARE	**$ 2.70**	$ 2.66	$ 2.59

(1) Basic net earnings per common share and Diluted net earnings per common share are calculated on Net earnings attributable to Procter & Gamble.

Consolidated Statements of Comprehensive Income

Amounts in millions; Years ended June 30	2017	2016	2015
NET EARNINGS	**$ 15,411**	$ 10,604	$ 7,144
OTHER COMPREHENSIVE INCOME/(LOSS), NET OF TAX			
Financial statement translation	**239**	(1,679)	(7,220)
Unrealized gains/(losses) on hedges (net of $(186), $5 and $739 tax, respectively)	**(306)**	1	1,234
Unrealized gains/(losses) on investment securities (net of $(6), $7 and $0 tax, respectively)	**(59)**	28	24
Unrealized gains/(losses) on defined benefit retirement plans (net of $551, $(621) and $328 tax, respectively)	**1,401**	(1,477)	844
TOTAL OTHER COMPREHENSIVE INCOME/(LOSS), NET OF TAX	**1,275**	(3,127)	(5,118)
TOTAL COMPREHENSIVE INCOME	**16,686**	7,477	2,026
Less: Total comprehensive income attributable to noncontrolling interests	**85**	96	108
TOTAL COMPREHENSIVE INCOME ATTRIBUTABLE TO PROCTER & GAMBLE	**$ 16,601**	$ 7,381	$ 1,918

Consolidated Balance Sheets

Amounts in millions; As of June 30	2017	2016
Assets		
CURRENT ASSETS		
Cash and cash equivalents	$ 5,569	$ 7,102
Available-for-sale investment securities	9,568	6,246
Accounts receivable	4,594	4,373
INVENTORIES		
Materials and supplies	1,308	1,188
Work in process	529	563
Finished goods	2,787	2,965
Total inventories	4,624	4,716
Deferred income taxes	—	1,507
Prepaid expenses and other current assets	2,139	2,653
Current assets held for sale	—	7,185
TOTAL CURRENT ASSETS	26,494	33,782
PROPERTY, PLANT AND EQUIPMENT, NET	19,893	19,385
GOODWILL	44,699	44,350
TRADEMARKS AND OTHER INTANGIBLE ASSETS, NET	24,187	24,527
OTHER NONCURRENT ASSETS	5,133	5,092
TOTAL ASSETS	$ 120,406	$ 127,136
Liabilities and Shareholders' Equity		
CURRENT LIABILITIES		
Accounts payable	$ 9,632	$ 9,325
Accrued and other liabilities	7,024	7,449
Current liabilities held for sale	—	2,343
Debt due within one year	13,554	11,653
TOTAL CURRENT LIABILITIES	30,210	30,770
LONG-TERM DEBT	18,038	18,945
DEFERRED INCOME TAXES	8,126	9,113
OTHER NONCURRENT LIABILITIES	8,254	10,325
TOTAL LIABILITIES	64,628	69,153
SHAREHOLDERS' EQUITY		
Convertible Class A preferred stock, stated value $1 per share (600 shares authorized)	1,006	1,038
Non-Voting Class B preferred stock, stated value $1 per share (200 shares authorized)	—	—
Common stock, stated value $1 per share (10,000 shares authorized; shares issued: 2017 - 4,009.2, 2016 - 4,009.2)	4,009	4,009
Additional paid-in capital	63,641	63,714
Reserve for ESOP debt retirement	(1,249)	(1,290)
Accumulated other comprehensive income/(loss)	(14,632)	(15,907)
Treasury stock, at cost (shares held: 2017 - 1,455.9, 2016 - 1,341.2)	(93,715)	(82,176)
Retained earnings	96,124	87,953
Noncontrolling interest	594	642
TOTAL SHAREHOLDERS' EQUITY	55,778	57,983
TOTAL LIABILITIES AND SHAREHOLDERS' EQUITY	$ 120,406	$ 127,136

See accompanying Notes to Consolidated Financial Statements.

Consolidated Statements of Shareholders' Equity

Dollars in millions; Shares in thousands	Common Shares Outstanding	Common Stock	Preferred Stock	Additional Paid-In Capital	Reserve for ESOP Debt Retirement	Accumulated Other Comprehensive Income/ (Loss)	Treasury Stock	Retained Earnings	Non-controlling Interest	Total Share-holders' Equity
BALANCE JUNE 30, 2014	2,710,806	$4,009	$1,111	$63,911	($1,340)	($7,662)	($75,805)	$84,990	$762	$69,976
Net earnings								7,036	108	7,144
Other comprehensive loss						(5,118)				(5,118)
Dividends to shareholders:										
Common								(7,028)		(7,028)
Preferred, net of tax benefits								(259)		(259)
Treasury purchases	(54,670)						(4,604)			(4,604)
Employee plan issuances	54,100			156			3,153			3,309
Preferred stock conversions	4,335		(34)	4			30			—
ESOP debt impacts					20			68		88
Noncontrolling interest, net				(219)					(239)	(458)
BALANCE JUNE 30, 2015	2,714,571	$4,009	$1,077	$63,852	($1,320)	($12,780)	($77,226)	$84,807	$631	$63,050
Net earnings								10,508	96	10,604
Other comprehensive loss						(3,127)				(3,127)
Dividends to shareholders:										
Common								(7,181)		(7,181)
Preferred, net of tax benefits								(255)		(255)
Treasury purchases [(1)]	(103,449)						(8,217)			(8,217)
Employee plan issuances	52,089			(144)			3,234			3,090
Preferred stock conversions	4,863		(39)	6			33			—
ESOP debt impacts					30			74		104
Noncontrolling interest, net									(85)	(85)
BALANCE JUNE 30, 2016	2,668,074	$4,009	$1,038	$63,714	($1,290)	($15,907)	($82,176)	$87,953	$642	$57,983
Net earnings								**15,326**	**85**	**15,411**
Other comprehensive loss						**1,275**				**1,275**
Dividends to shareholders:										
Common								**(6,989)**		**(6,989)**
Preferred, net of tax benefits								**(247)**		**(247)**
Treasury purchases [(2)]	**(164,866)**						**(14,625)**			**(14,625)**
Employee plan issuances	**45,848**			**(77)**			**3,058**			**2,981**
Preferred stock conversions	**4,241**		**(32)**	**4**			**28**			**—**
ESOP debt impacts					**41**			**81**		**122**
Noncontrolling interest, net									**(133)**	**(133)**
BALANCE JUNE 30, 2017	**2,553,297**	**$4,009**	**$1,006**	**$63,641**	**($1,249)**	**($14,632)**	**($93,715)**	**$96,124**	**$594**	**$55,778**

(1) Includes $4,213 of treasury shares acquired in the divestiture of the Batteries business (see Note 13).
(2) Includes $9,421 of treasury shares received as part of the share exchange in the Beauty Brands transaction (see Note 13).

See accompanying Notes to Consolidated Financial Statements.

Consolidated Statements of Cash Flows

Amounts in millions; Years ended June 30	2017	2016	2015
CASH AND CASH EQUIVALENTS, BEGINNING OF YEAR	**$ 7,102**	$ 6,836	$ 8,548
OPERATING ACTIVITIES			
Net earnings	**15,411**	10,604	7,144
Depreciation and amortization	**2,820**	3,078	3,134
Loss on early extinguishment of debt	**543**	—	—
Share-based compensation expense	**351**	335	337
Deferred income taxes	**(601)**	(815)	(803)
Gain on sale of assets	**(5,490)**	(41)	(766)
Venezuela deconsolidation charge	**—**	—	2,028
Goodwill and intangible asset impairment charges	**—**	450	2,174
Change in accounts receivable	**(322)**	35	349
Change in inventories	**71**	116	313
Change in accounts payable, accrued and other liabilities	**(149)**	1,285	928
Change in other operating assets and liabilities	**(43)**	204	(976)
Other	**162**	184	746
TOTAL OPERATING ACTIVITIES	**12,753**	15,435	14,608
INVESTING ACTIVITIES			
Capital expenditures	**(3,384)**	(3,314)	(3,736)
Proceeds from asset sales	**571**	432	4,498
Cash related to deconsolidated Venezuela operations	**—**	—	(908)
Acquisitions, net of cash acquired	**(16)**	(186)	(137)
Purchases of short-term investments	**(4,843)**	(2,815)	(3,647)
Proceeds from sales and maturities of short-term investments	**1,488**	1,354	1,203
Pre-divestiture addition of restricted cash related to the Beauty Brands divestiture	**(874)**	(996)	—
Cash transferred at closing related to the Beauty Brands divestiture	**(475)**	—	—
Release of restricted cash upon closing of the Beauty Brands divestiture	**1,870**	—	—
Cash transferred in Batteries divestiture	**—**	(143)	—
Change in other investments	**(26)**	93	(163)
TOTAL INVESTING ACTIVITIES	**(5,689)**	(5,575)	(2,890)
FINANCING ACTIVITIES			
Dividends to shareholders	**(7,236)**	(7,436)	(7,287)
Change in short-term debt	**2,727**	(418)	(2,580)
Additions to long-term debt	**3,603**	3,916	2,138
Reductions of long-term debt	**(4,931)** [1]	(2,213)	(3,512)
Treasury stock purchases	**(5,204)**	(4,004)	(4,604)
Treasury stock from cash infused in Batteries divestiture	**—**	(1,730)	—
Impact of stock options and other	**2,473**	2,672	2,826
TOTAL FINANCING ACTIVITIES	**(8,568)**	(9,213)	(13,019)
EFFECT OF EXCHANGE RATE CHANGES ON CASH AND CASH EQUIVALENTS	**(29)**	(381)	(411)
CHANGE IN CASH AND CASH EQUIVALENTS	**(1,533)**	266	(1,712)
CASH AND CASH EQUIVALENTS, END OF YEAR	**$ 5,569**	$ 7,102	$ 6,836
SUPPLEMENTAL DISCLOSURE			
Cash payments for interest	**$ 518**	$ 569	$ 678
Cash payment for income taxes	**3,714**	3,730	4,558
Divestiture of Batteries business in exchange for shares of P&G stock [2]	**—**	4,213	—
Divestiture of Beauty business in exchange for shares of P&G stock and assumption of debt	**11,360**	—	—
Assets acquired through non-cash capital leases are immaterial for all periods.			

(1) Includes $543 of costs related to early extinguishment of debt.

(2) Includes $1,730 from cash infused into the Batteries business pursuant to the divestiture agreement (see Note 13).

See accompanying Notes to Consolidated Financial Statements.

Specimen Financial Statements: The Coca-Cola Company

The Coca-Cola Company is the world's largest beverage company. It owns or licenses and markets more than 500 nonalcoholic beverage brands, primarily sparkling beverages, but also a variety of still beverages such as waters, enhanced waters, juices and juice drinks, ready-to-drink teas and coffees, and energy and sports drinks. Finished beverage products bearing Coca-Cola trademarks, sold in the United States since 1886, are now available in more than 200 countries.

THE COCA-COLA COMPANY AND SUBSIDIARIES

CONSOLIDATED STATEMENTS OF INCOME

Year Ended December 31,	**2017**	2016	2015
(In millions except per share data)			
NET OPERATING REVENUES	**$ 35,410**	$ 41,863	$ 44,294
Cost of goods sold	**13,256**	16,465	17,482
GROSS PROFIT	**22,154**	25,398	26,812
Selling, general and administrative expenses	**12,496**	15,262	16,427
Other operating charges	**2,157**	1,510	1,657
OPERATING INCOME	**7,501**	8,626	8,728
Interest income	**677**	642	613
Interest expense	**841**	733	856
Equity income (loss) — net	**1,071**	835	489
Other income (loss) — net	**(1,666)**	(1,234)	631
INCOME FROM CONTINUING OPERATIONS BEFORE INCOME TAXES	**6,742**	8,136	9,605
Income taxes from continuing operations	**5,560**	1,586	2,239
NET INCOME FROM CONTINUING OPERATIONS	**1,182**	6,550	7,366
Income from discontinued operations (net of income taxes of $47, $0 and $0, respectively)	**101**	—	—
CONSOLIDATED NET INCOME	**1,283**	6,550	7,366
Less: Net income attributable to noncontrolling interests	**35**	23	15
NET INCOME ATTRIBUTABLE TO SHAREOWNERS OF THE COCA-COLA COMPANY	**$ 1,248**	$ 6,527	$ 7,351
Basic net income per share from continuing operations[1]	**$ 0.28**	$ 1.51	$ 1.69
Basic net income per share from discontinued operations[2]	**0.02**	—	—
BASIC NET INCOME PER SHARE	**$ 0.29[3]**	$ 1.51	$ 1.69
Diluted net income per share from continuing operations[1]	**$ 0.27**	$ 1.49	$ 1.67
Diluted net income per share from discontinued operations[2]	**0.02**	—	—
DILUTED NET INCOME PER SHARE	**$ 0.29**	$ 1.49	$ 1.67
AVERAGE SHARES OUTSTANDING — BASIC	**4,272**	4,317	4,352
Effect of dilutive securities	**52**	50	53
AVERAGE SHARES OUTSTANDING — DILUTED	**4,324**	4,367	4,405

[1] Calculated based on net income from continuing operations less net income from continuing operations attributable to noncontrolling interests.

[2] Calculated based on net income from discontinued operations less net income from discontinued operations attributable to noncontrolling interests.

[3] Per share amounts do not add due to rounding.

Refer to Notes to Consolidated Financial Statements.

THE COCA-COLA COMPANY AND SUBSIDIARIES

CONSOLIDATED STATEMENTS OF COMPREHENSIVE INCOME

Year Ended December 31,	2017	2016	2015
(In millions)			
CONSOLIDATED NET INCOME	**$ 1,283**	$ 6,550	$ 7,366
Other comprehensive income:			
Net foreign currency translation adjustment	**861**	(626)	(3,959)
Net gain (loss) on derivatives	**(433)**	(382)	142
Net unrealized gain (loss) on available-for-sale securities	**188**	17	(684)
Net change in pension and other benefit liabilities	**322**	(53)	86
TOTAL COMPREHENSIVE INCOME (LOSS)	**2,221**	5,506	2,951
Less: Comprehensive income (loss) attributable to noncontrolling interests	**73**	10	(3)
TOTAL COMPREHENSIVE INCOME (LOSS) ATTRIBUTABLE TO SHAREOWNERS OF THE COCA-COLA COMPANY	**$ 2,148**	$ 5,496	$ 2,954

THE COCA-COLA COMPANY AND SUBSIDIARIES

CONSOLIDATED BALANCE SHEETS

December 31,	2017	2016
(In millions except par value)		
ASSETS		
CURRENT ASSETS		
Cash and cash equivalents	**$ 6,006**	$ 8,555
Short-term investments	**9,352**	9,595
TOTAL CASH, CASH EQUIVALENTS AND SHORT-TERM INVESTMENTS	**15,358**	18,150
Marketable securities	**5,317**	4,051
Trade accounts receivable, less allowances of $477 and $466, respectively	**3,667**	3,856
Inventories	**2,655**	2,675
Prepaid expenses and other assets	**2,000**	2,481
Assets held for sale	**219**	2,797
Assets held for sale — discontinued operations	**7,329**	—
TOTAL CURRENT ASSETS	**36,545**	34,010
EQUITY METHOD INVESTMENTS	**20,856**	16,260
OTHER INVESTMENTS	**1,096**	989
OTHER ASSETS	**4,560**	4,248
PROPERTY, PLANT AND EQUIPMENT — net	**8,203**	10,635
TRADEMARKS WITH INDEFINITE LIVES	**6,729**	6,097
BOTTLERS' FRANCHISE RIGHTS WITH INDEFINITE LIVES	**138**	3,676
GOODWILL	**9,401**	10,629
OTHER INTANGIBLE ASSETS	**368**	726
TOTAL ASSETS	**$ 87,896**	$ 87,270
LIABILITIES AND EQUITY		
CURRENT LIABILITIES		
Accounts payable and accrued expenses	**$ 8,748**	$ 9,490
Loans and notes payable	**13,205**	12,498
Current maturities of long-term debt	**3,298**	3,527
Accrued income taxes	**410**	307
Liabilities held for sale	**37**	710
Liabilities held for sale — discontinued operations	**1,496**	—
TOTAL CURRENT LIABILITIES	**27,194**	26,532
LONG-TERM DEBT	**31,182**	29,684
OTHER LIABILITIES	**8,021**	4,081
DEFERRED INCOME TAXES	**2,522**	3,753
THE COCA-COLA COMPANY SHAREOWNERS' EQUITY		
Common stock, $0.25 par value; Authorized — 11,200 shares; Issued — 7,040 and 7,040 shares, respectively	**1,760**	1,760
Capital surplus	**15,864**	14,993
Reinvested earnings	**60,430**	65,502
Accumulated other comprehensive income (loss)	**(10,305)**	(11,205)
Treasury stock, at cost — 2,781 and 2,752 shares, respectively	**(50,677)**	(47,988)
EQUITY ATTRIBUTABLE TO SHAREOWNERS OF THE COCA-COLA COMPANY	**17,072**	23,062
EQUITY ATTRIBUTABLE TO NONCONTROLLING INTERESTS	**1,905**	158
TOTAL EQUITY	**18,977**	23,220
TOTAL LIABILITIES AND EQUITY	**$ 87,896**	$ 87,270

Refer to Notes to Consolidated Financial Statements.

THE COCA-COLA COMPANY AND SUBSIDIARIES

CONSOLIDATED STATEMENTS OF CASH FLOWS

Year Ended December 31,	2017	2016	2015
(In millions)			
OPERATING ACTIVITIES			
Consolidated net income	$ 1,283	$ 6,550	$ 7,366
(Income) loss from discontinued operations	(101)	—	—
Net income from continuing operations	1,182	6,550	7,366
Depreciation and amortization	1,260	1,787	1,970
Stock-based compensation expense	219	258	236
Deferred income taxes	(1,256)	(856)	73
Equity (income) loss — net of dividends	(628)	(449)	(122)
Foreign currency adjustments	281	158	(137)
Significant (gains) losses on sales of assets — net	1,459	1,146	(374)
Other operating charges	1,218	647	929
Other items	(269)	(224)	744
Net change in operating assets and liabilities	3,529	(221)	(157)
Net cash provided by operating activities	6,995	8,796	10,528
INVESTING ACTIVITIES			
Purchases of investments	(16,520)	(15,499)	(15,831)
Proceeds from disposals of investments	15,911	16,624	14,079
Acquisitions of businesses, equity method investments and nonmarketable securities	(3,900)	(838)	(2,491)
Proceeds from disposals of businesses, equity method investments and nonmarketable securities	3,821	1,035	565
Purchases of property, plant and equipment	(1,675)	(2,262)	(2,553)
Proceeds from disposals of property, plant and equipment	104	150	85
Other investing activities	(126)	(209)	(40)
Net cash provided by (used in) investing activities	(2,385)	(999)	(6,186)
FINANCING ACTIVITIES			
Issuances of debt	29,857	27,281	40,434
Payments of debt	(28,768)	(25,615)	(37,738)
Issuances of stock	1,595	1,434	1,245
Purchases of stock for treasury	(3,682)	(3,681)	(3,564)
Dividends	(6,320)	(6,043)	(5,741)
Other financing activities	(91)	79	251
Net cash provided by (used in) financing activities	(7,409)	(6,545)	(5,113)
CASH FLOWS FROM DISCONTINUED OPERATIONS			
Net cash provided by (used in) operating activities from discontinued operations	111	—	—
Net cash provided by (used in) investing activities from discontinued operations	(65)	—	—
Net cash provided by (used in) financing activities from discontinued operations	(38)	—	—
Net cash provided by (used in) discontinued operations	8	—	—
EFFECT OF EXCHANGE RATE CHANGES ON CASH AND CASH EQUIVALENTS	242	(6)	(878)
CASH AND CASH EQUIVALENTS			
Net increase (decrease) during the year	(2,549)	1,246	(1,649)
Balance at beginning of year	8,555	7,309	8,958
Balance at end of year	$ 6,006	$ 8,555	$ 7,309

Refer to Notes to Consolidated Financial Statements.

THE COCA-COLA COMPANY AND SUBSIDIARIES

CONSOLIDATED STATEMENTS OF SHAREOWNERS' EQUITY

Year Ended December 31,	2017	2016	2015
(In millions except per share data)			
EQUITY ATTRIBUTABLE TO SHAREOWNERS OF THE COCA-COLA COMPANY			
NUMBER OF COMMON SHARES OUTSTANDING			
Balance at beginning of year	**4,288**	4,324	4,366
Treasury stock issued to employees related to stock compensation plans	**53**	50	44
Purchases of stock for treasury	**(82)**	(86)	(86)
Balance at end of year	**4,259**	4,288	4,324
COMMON STOCK	**$ 1,760**	$ 1,760	$ 1,760
CAPITAL SURPLUS			
Balance at beginning of year	**14,993**	14,016	13,154
Stock issued to employees related to stock compensation plans	**655**	589	532
Tax benefit (charge) from stock compensation plans	**—**	130	94
Stock-based compensation expense	**219**	258	236
Other activities	**(3)**	—	—
Balance at end of year	**15,864**	14,993	14,016
REINVESTED EARNINGS			
Balance at beginning of year	**65,502**	65,018	63,408
Net income attributable to shareowners of The Coca-Cola Company	**1,248**	6,527	7,351
Dividends (per share — $1.48, $1.40 and $1.32 in 2017, 2016 and 2015, respectively)	**(6,320)**	(6,043)	(5,741)
Balance at end of year	**60,430**	65,502	65,018
ACCUMULATED OTHER COMPREHENSIVE INCOME (LOSS)			
Balance at beginning of year	**(11,205)**	(10,174)	(5,777)
Net other comprehensive income (loss)	**900**	(1,031)	(4,397)
Balance at end of year	**(10,305)**	(11,205)	(10,174)
TREASURY STOCK			
Balance at beginning of year	**(47,988)**	(45,066)	(42,225)
Treasury stock issued to employees related to stock compensation plans	**909**	811	696
Purchases of stock for treasury	**(3,598)**	(3,733)	(3,537)
Balance at end of year	**(50,677)**	(47,988)	(45,066)
TOTAL EQUITY ATTRIBUTABLE TO SHAREOWNERS OF THE COCA-COLA COMPANY	**$ 17,072**	$ 23,062	$ 25,554
EQUITY ATTRIBUTABLE TO NONCONTROLLING INTERESTS			
Balance at beginning of year	**$ 158**	$ 210	$ 241
Net income attributable to noncontrolling interests	**35**	23	15
Net foreign currency translation adjustment	**38**	(13)	(18)
Dividends paid to noncontrolling interests	**(15)**	(25)	(31)
Contributions by noncontrolling interests	**—**	1	—
Business combinations	**1,805**	—	(3)
Deconsolidation of certain entities	**(157)**	(34)	—
Other activities	**41**	(4)	6
TOTAL EQUITY ATTRIBUTABLE TO NONCONTROLLING INTERESTS	**$ 1,905**	$ 158	$ 210

Refer to Notes to Consolidated Financial Statements.

Specimen Financial Statements: PepsiCo, Inc.

Pepsico, Inc. is a leading global food and beverage company with a complementary portfolio of enjoyable brands, including Frito-Lay, Gatorade, Pepsi-Cola, Quaker, and Tropicana. Through its operations, authorized bottlers, contract manufacturers, and other third parties, PepsiCo makes, markets, distributes, and sells a wide variety of convenient and enjoyable beverages, foods, and snacks, serving customers and consumers in more than 200 countries and territories.

Consolidated Statement of Income
PepsiCo, Inc. and Subsidiaries
Fiscal years ended December 27, 2017, December 28, 2016 and December 29, 2015
(in millions except per share amounts)

	2017	2016	2015
Net Revenue	**$ 63,525**	$ 62,799	$ 63,056
Cost of sales	**28,785**	28,209	28,731
Gross profit	**34,740**	34,590	34,325
Selling, general and administrative expenses	**24,231**	24,805	24,613
Venezuela impairment charges	**—**	—	1,359
Operating Profit	**10,509**	9,785	8,353
Interest expense	**(1,151)**	(1,342)	(970)
Interest income and other	**244**	110	59
Income before income taxes	**9,602**	8,553	7,442
Provision for income taxes (See Note 5)	**4,694**	2,174	1,941
Net income	**4,908**	6,379	5,501
Less: Net income attributable to noncontrolling interests	**51**	50	49
Net Income Attributable to PepsiCo	**$ 4,857**	$ 6,329	$ 5,452
Net Income Attributable to PepsiCo per Common Share			
Basic	**$ 3.40**	$ 4.39	$ 3.71
Diluted	**$ 3.38**	$ 4.36	$ 3.67
Weighted-average common shares outstanding			
Basic	**1,425**	1,439	1,469
Diluted	**1,438**	1,452	1,485
Cash dividends declared per common share	**$ 3.1675**	$ 2.96	$ 2.7625

Consolidated Statement of Comprehensive Income
PepsiCo, Inc. and Subsidiaries
Fiscal years ended December 30, 2017, December 31, 2016 and December 26, 2015
(in millions)

	2017	2016	2015
Net income	**$ 4,908**	$ 6,379	$ 5,501
Other comprehensive income/(loss), net of taxes:			
Net currency translation adjustment	**1,109**	(302)	(2,827)
Net change on cash flow hedges	**(36)**	46	3
Net pension and retiree medical adjustments	**(159)**	(316)	171
Net change on securities	**(68)**	(24)	1
Other	**16**	—	—
	862	(596)	(2,652)
Comprehensive income	**5,770**	5,783	2,849
Comprehensive income attributable to noncontrolling interests	**(51)**	(54)	(47)
Comprehensive Income Attributable to PepsiCo	**$ 5,719**	$ 5,729	$ 2,802

See accompanying notes to the consolidated financial statements.

Consolidated Statement of Cash Flows
PepsiCo, Inc. and Subsidiaries
Fiscal years ended December 30, 2017, December 31, 2016 and December 26, 2015
(in millions)

	2017	2016	2015
Operating Activities			
Net income	$ 4,908	$ 6,379	$ 5,501
Depreciation and amortization	2,369	2,368	2,416
Share-based compensation expense	292	284	295
Restructuring and impairment charges	295	160	230
Cash payments for restructuring charges	(113)	(125)	(208)
Charges related to the transaction with Tingyi	—	373	73
Venezuela impairment charges	—	—	1,359
Pension and retiree medical plan expenses	221	501	467
Pension and retiree medical plan contributions	(220)	(695)	(205)
Deferred income taxes and other tax charges and credits	619	452	78
Provisional net tax expense related to the TCJ Act	2,451	—	—
Change in assets and liabilities:			
Accounts and notes receivable	(202)	(349)	(461)
Inventories	(168)	(75)	(244)
Prepaid expenses and other current assets	20	10	(50)
Accounts payable and other current liabilities	201	997	1,692
Income taxes payable	(338)	329	55
Other, net	(341)	64	(134)
Net Cash Provided by Operating Activities	9,994	10,673	10,864
Investing Activities			
Capital spending	(2,969)	(3,040)	(2,758)
Sales of property, plant and equipment	180	99	86
Acquisitions and investments in noncontrolled affiliates	(61)	(212)	(86)
Reduction of cash due to Venezuela deconsolidation	—	—	(568)
Divestitures	267	85	76
Short-term investments, by original maturity:			
More than three months - purchases	(18,385)	(12,504)	(4,428)
More than three months - maturities	15,744	8,399	4,111
More than three months - sales	790	—	—
Three months or less, net	2	16	3
Other investing, net	29	9	(5)
Net Cash Used for Investing Activities	(4,403)	(7,148)	(3,569)
Financing Activities			
Proceeds from issuances of long-term debt	7,509	7,818	8,702
Payments of long-term debt	(4,406)	(3,105)	(4,095)
Debt redemptions	—	(2,504)	—
Short-term borrowings, by original maturity:			
More than three months - proceeds	91	59	15
More than three months - payments	(128)	(27)	(43)
Three months or less, net	(1,016)	1,505	53
Cash dividends paid	(4,472)	(4,227)	(4,040)
Share repurchases - common	(2,000)	(3,000)	(5,000)
Share repurchases - preferred	(5)	(7)	(5)
Proceeds from exercises of stock options	462	465	504
Withholding tax payments on RSUs, PSUs and PEPunits converted	(145)	(130)	(151)
Other financing	(76)	(58)	(52)
Net Cash Used for Financing Activities	(4,186)	(3,211)	(4,112)
Effect of exchange rate changes on cash and cash equivalents	47	(252)	(221)
Net Increase in Cash and Cash Equivalents	1,452	62	2,962
Cash and Cash Equivalents, Beginning of Year	9,158	9,096	6,134
Cash and Cash Equivalents, End of Year	$ 10,610	$ 9,158	$ 9,096

See accompanying notes to the consolidated financial statements.

Consolidated Balance Sheet
PepsiCo, Inc. and Subsidiaries
December 30, 2017 and December 31, 2016
(in millions except per share amounts)

	2017	2016
ASSETS		
Current Assets		
Cash and cash equivalents	$ 10,610	$ 9,158
Short-term investments	8,900	6,967
Accounts and notes receivable, net	7,024	6,694
Inventories	2,947	2,723
Prepaid expenses and other current assets	1,546	908
Total Current Assets	31,027	26,450
Property, Plant and Equipment, net	17,240	16,591
Amortizable Intangible Assets, net	1,268	1,237
Goodwill	14,744	14,430
Other nonamortizable intangible assets	12,570	12,196
Nonamortizable Intangible Assets	27,314	26,626
Investments in Noncontrolled Affiliates	2,042	1,950
Other Assets	913	636
Total Assets	$ 79,804	$ 73,490
LIABILITIES AND EQUITY		
Current Liabilities		
Short-term debt obligations	$ 5,485	$ 6,892
Accounts payable and other current liabilities	15,017	14,243
Total Current Liabilities	20,502	21,135
Long-Term Debt Obligations	33,796	30,053
Other Liabilities	11,283	6,669
Deferred Income Taxes	3,242	4,434
Total Liabilities	68,823	62,291
Commitments and contingencies		
Preferred Stock, no par value	41	41
Repurchased Preferred Stock	(197)	(192)
PepsiCo Common Shareholders' Equity		
Common stock, par value $1^{2}/_{3}$¢ per share (authorized 3,600 shares, issued, net of repurchased common stock at par value: 1,420 and 1,428 shares, respectively)	24	24
Capital in excess of par value	3,996	4,091
Retained earnings	52,839	52,518
Accumulated other comprehensive loss	(13,057)	(13,919)
Repurchased common stock, in excess of par value (446 and 438 shares, respectively)	(32,757)	(31,468)
Total PepsiCo Common Shareholders' Equity	11,045	11,246
Noncontrolling interests	92	104
Total Equity	10,981	11,199
Total Liabilities and Equity	$ 79,804	$ 73,490

See accompanying notes to the consolidated financial statements.

Consolidated Statement of Equity

PepsiCo, Inc. and Subsidiaries
Fiscal years ended December 30, 2017, December 31, 2016 and December 26, 2015
(in millions)

	2017		2016		2015	
	Shares	Amount	Shares	Amount	Shares	Amount
Preferred Stock	0.8	$ 41	0.8	$ 41	0.8	$ 41
Balance, beginning of year	(0.7)	(192)	(0.7)	(186)	(0.7)	(181)
Redemptions	—	(5)	—	(6)	—	(5)
Balance, end of year	(0.7)	(197)	(0.7)	(192)	(0.7)	(186)
Common Stock						
Balance, beginning of year	1,428	24	1,448	24	1,488	25
Change in repurchased common stock	(8)	—	(20)	—	(40)	(1)
Balance, end of year	1,420	24	1,428	24	1,448	24
Capital in Excess of Par Value						
Balance, beginning of year		4,091		4,076		4,115
Share-based compensation expense		290		289		299
Stock option exercises, RSUs, PSUs and PEPunits converted [(a)]		(236)		(138)		(182)
Withholding tax on RSUs, PSUs and PEPunits converted		(145)		(130)		(151)
Other		(4)		(6)		(5)
Balance, end of year		3,996		4,091		4,076
Retained Earnings						
Balance, beginning of year		52,518		50,472		49,092
Net income attributable to PepsiCo		4,857		6,329		5,452
Cash dividends declared - common		(4,536)		(4,282)		(4,071)
Cash dividends declared - preferred		—		(1)		(1)
Balance, end of year		52,839		52,518		50,472
Accumulated Other Comprehensive Loss						
Balance, beginning of year		(13,919)		(13,319)		(10,669)
Other comprehensive income/(loss) attributable to PepsiCo		862		(600)		(2,650)
Balance, end of year		(13,057)		(13,919)		(13,319)
Repurchased Common Stock						
Balance, beginning of year	(438)	(31,468)	(418)	(29,185)	(378)	(24,985)
Share repurchases	(18)	(2,000)	(29)	(3,000)	(52)	(4,999)
Stock option exercises, RSUs, PSUs and PEPunits converted	10	708	9	712	12	794
Other	—	3	—	5	—	5
Balance, end of year	(446)	(32,757)	(438)	(31,468)	(418)	(29,185)
Total PepsiCo Common Shareholders' Equity		11,045		11,246		12,068
Noncontrolling Interests						
Balance, beginning of year		104		107		110
Net income attributable to noncontrolling interests		51		50		49
Distributions to noncontrolling interests		(62)		(55)		(48)
Currency translation adjustment		—		4		(2)
Other, net		(1)		(2)		(2)
Balance, end of year		92		104		107
Total Equity		$ 10,981		$ 11,199		$ 12,030

(a) Includes total tax benefits of $110 million in 2016 and $107 million in 2015.

See accompanying notes to the consolidated financial statements.

Specimen Financial Statements: Marks and Spencer plc

Marks and Spencer (M&S) plc is one of the United Kingdom's leading retailers, with over 1,330 stores worldwide. The company is committed to delivering sustainable, high-quality food, clothing, and home products.

CONSOLIDATED INCOME STATEMENT

		53 weeks ended 1 April 2017			53 weeks ended 2 April 2016		
	Notes	Underlying £m	Non-underlying £m	Total £m	Underlying £m	Non-underlying £m	Total £m
Revenue	2,3	**10,622.0**	**–**	**10,622.0**	10,555.4	–	10,555.4
Operating profit	2,3,5	**690.6**	**(437.4)**	**253.2**	784.9	(200.8)	584.1
Finance income	6	**36.2**	**–**	**36.2**	21.1	–	21.1
Finance costs	6	**(113.0)**	**–**	**(113.0)**	(116.4)	–	(116.4)
Profit before tax	4,5	**613.8**	**(437.4)**	**176.4**	689.6	(200.8)	488.8
Income tax expense	7	**(122.4)**	**61.7**	**(60.7)**	(118.8)	34.4	(84.4)
Profit for the year		**491.4**	**(375.7)**	**115.7**	570.8	(166.4)	404.4
Attributable to:							
Owners of the parent		**492.8**	**(375.7)**	**117.1**	573.3	(166.4)	406.9
Non-controlling interests		**(1.4)**	**–**	**(1.4)**	(2.5)	–	(2.5)
		491.4	**(375.7)**	**115.7**	570.8	(166.4)	404.4
Basic earnings per share	8	**30.4p**		**7.2p**	35.0p		24.9p
Diluted earnings per share	8	**30.2p**		**7.2p**	34.9p		24.8p

CONSOLIDATED STATEMENT OF COMPREHENSIVE INCOME

	Notes	53 weeks ended 1 April 2017 £m	53 weeks ended 2 April 2016 £m
Profit for the year		**115.7**	404.4
Other comprehensive income:			
Items that will not be reclassified to profit or loss			
Remeasurements of retirement benefit schemes	11	**(68.9)**	346.2
Tax charge/(credit) on items that will not be reclassified		**25.3**	(45.6)
		(43.6)	300.6
Items that will be reclassified subsequently to profit or loss			
Foreign currency translation differences		**31.0**	7.3
Cash flow hedges and net investment hedges			
– fair value movements recognised in other comprehensive income		**56.1**	(30.1)
– reclassified and reported in profit or loss		**(72.4)**	(22.1)
– amount recognised in inventories		**(20.1)**	5.9
Tax credit on cash flow hedges and net investment hedges		**4.1**	6.5
		(1.3)	(32.5)
Other comprehensive (expense)/income for the year, net of tax		**(44.9)**	268.1
Total comprehensive income for the year		**70.8**	672.5
Attributable to:			
Owners of the parent		**72.2**	675.0
Non-controlling interests		**(1.4)**	(2.5)
		70.8	672.5

CONSOLIDATED STATEMENT OF FINANCIAL POSITION

	Notes	As at 1 April 2017 £m	As at 2 April 2016 £m
Assets			
Non-current assets			
Intangible assets	14	**709.0**	802.8
Property, plant and equipment	15	**4,837.8**	5,027.1
Investment property		**15.5**	15.5
Investment in joint ventures		**7.0**	6.9
Other financial assets	16	**3.0**	3.0
Retirement benefit asset	11	**706.0**	851.0
Trade and other receivables	17	**234.1**	234.7
Derivative financial instruments	21	**56.8**	74.0
Deferred tax assets	23	**–**	–
		6,569.2	7,015.0
Current assets			
Inventories		**758.5**	799.9
Other financial assets	16	**14.5**	19.1
Trade and other receivables	17	**318.6**	321.1
Derivative financial instruments	21	**163.1**	72.1
Current tax assets		**–**	1.6
Cash and cash equivalents	18	**468.6**	247.6
		1,723.3	1,461.4
Total assets		**8,292.5**	8,476.4
Liabilities			
Current liabilities			
Trade and other payables	19	**1,553.8**	1,617.7
Partnership liability to the Marks & Spencer UK Pension Scheme	12	**71.9**	71.9
Borrowings and other financial liabilities	20	**518.0**	297.5
Derivative financial instruments	21	**10.5**	28.5
Provisions	22	**147.2**	14.0
Current tax liabilities		**66.6**	75.2
		2,368.0	2,104.8
Non-current liabilities			
Retirement benefit deficit	11	**13.2**	26.9
Trade and other payables	19	**328.5**	353.0
Partnership liability to the Marks & Spencer UK Pension Scheme	12	**324.6**	383.8
Borrowings and other financial liabilities	20	**1,711.7**	1,774.7
Derivative financial instruments	21	**0.8**	0.2
Provisions	22	**113.5**	52.0
Deferred tax liabilities	23	**281.8**	337.6
		2,774.1	2,928.2
Total liabilities		**5,142.1**	5,033.0
Net assets		**3,150.4**	3,443.4
Equity			
Issued share capital	24	**406.2**	405.8
Share premium account		**416.4**	411.3
Capital redemption reserve		**2,210.5**	2,210.5
Hedging reserve		**17.3**	32.3
Other reserve		**(6,542.2)**	(6,542.2)
Retained earnings		**6,648.1**	6,927.5
Total shareholders' equity		**3,156.3**	3,445.2
Non-controlling interests in equity		**(5.9)**	(1.8)
Total equity		**3,150.4**	3,443.4

CONSOLIDATED STATEMENT OF CHANGES IN EQUITY

	Ordinary share capital £m	Share premium account £m	Capital redemption reserve £m	Hedging reserve £m	Other reserve[1] £m	Foreign exchange reserve[3] £m	Retained earnings £m	Total £m	Non-controlling interest £m	Total £m
As at 29 March 2015	412.0	392.4	2,202.6	64.3	(6,542.2)	(12.6)	6,683.1	3,199.6	(0.8)	3,198.8
Profit/(loss) for the year	–	–	–	–	–	–	406.9	406.9	(2.5)	404.4
Other comprehensive (expense)/income:										
Foreign currency translation	–	–	–	(0.5)	–	7.8	–	7.3	–	7.3
Remeasurements of retirement benefit schemes	–	–	–	–	–	–	346.2	346.2	–	346.2
Tax charge on items that will not be reclassified		–	–	–	–	–	(45.6)	(45.6)	–	(45.6)
Cash flow hedges and net investment hedges										
– fair value movement recognised in other comprehensive income	–	–	–	(21.8)	–	–	(8.3)	(30.1)	–	(30.1)
– reclassified and reported in profit or loss[2]	–	–	–	(22.1)	–	–	–	(22.1)	–	(22.1)
– amount recognised in inventories	–	–	–	5.9	–	–	–	5.9	–	5.9
Tax on cash flow hedges and net investment hedges	–	–	–	6.5	–	–	–	6.5	–	6.5
Other comprehensive income/(expense)	–	–	–	(32.0)	–	7.8	292.3	268.1	–	268.1
Total comprehensive income/(expense)	–	–	–	(32.0)	–	7.8	699.2	675.0	(2.5)	672.5
Transactions with owners:										
Dividends	–	–	–	–	–	–	(301.7)	(301.7)	–	(301.7)
Transactions with non-controlling shareholders	–	–	–	–	–	–	–	–	1.5	1.5
Shares issued on exercise of employee share options	1.7	18.9	–	–	–	–	–	20.6	–	20.6
Purchase of own shares held by employee trusts	–	–	–	–	–	–	(10.9)	(10.9)	–	(10.9)
Shares purchased in buy back	(7.9)	–	7.9	–	–	–	(150.7)	(150.7)	–	(150.7)
Credit for share-based payments	–	–	–	–	–	–	17.2	17.2	–	17.2
Deferred tax on share schemes	–	–	–	–	–	–	(3.9)	(3.9)	–	(3.9)
As at 2 April 2016	405.8	411.3	2,210.5	32.3	(6,542.2)	(4.8)	6,932.3	3,445.2	(1.8)	3,443.4
As at 3 April 2016	**405.8**	**411.3**	**2,210.5**	**32.3**	**(6,542.2)**	**(4.8)**	**6,932.3**	**3,445.2**	**(1.8)**	**3,443.4**
Profit/(loss) for the year	–	–	–	–	–	–	**117.1**	**117.1**	**(1.4)**	**115.7**
Other comprehensive (expense)/income:										
Foreign currency translation	–	–	–	**(4.3)**	–	**35.3**	–	**31.0**	–	**31.0**
Remeasurements of retirement benefit schemes	–	–	–	–	–	–	**(68.9)**	**(68.9)**	–	**(68.9)**
Tax credit on items that will not be reclassified	–	–	–	–	–	–	**25.3**	**25.3**	–	**25.3**
Cash flow hedges and net investment hedges										
– fair value movement recognised in other comprehensive income	–	–	–	**77.7**	–	–	**(21.6)**	**56.1**	–	**56.1**
– reclassified and reported in profit or loss[2]	–	–	–	**(72.4)**	–	–	–	**(72.4)**	–	**(72.4)**
– amount recognised in inventories	–	–	–	**(20.1)**	–	–	–	**(20.1)**	–	**(20.1)**
Tax on cash flow hedges and net investment hedges	–	–	–	**4.1**	–	–	–	**4.1**	–	**4.1**
Other comprehensive income/(expense)	–	–	–	**(15.0)**	–	**35.3**	**(65.2)**	**(44.9)**	–	**(44.9)**
Total comprehensive income/(expense)	–	–	–	**(15.0)**	–	**35.3**	**51.9**	**72.2**	**(1.4)**	**70.8**
Transactions with owners:										
Dividends	–	–	–	–	–	–	**(377.5)**	**(377.5)**	–	**(377.5)**
Transactions with non-controlling shareholders	–	–	–	–	–	–	–	–	**(2.7)**	**(2.7)**
Shares issued on exercise of employee share options	**0.4**	**5.1**	–	–	–	–	–	**5.5**	–	**5.5**
Purchase of own shares held by employee trusts	–	–	–	–	–	–	–	–	–	–
Credit for share-based payments	–	–	–	–	–	–	**13.5**	**13.5**	–	**13.5**
Deferred tax on share schemes	–	–	–	–	–	–	**(2.6)**	**(2.6)**	–	**(2.6)**
As at 1 April 2017	**406.2**	**416.4**	**2,210.5**	**17.3**	**(6,542.2)**	**30.5**	**6,617.6**	**3,156.3**	**(5.9)**	**3,150.4**

1. The 'Other reserve' was originally created as part of the capital restructuring that took place in 2002. It represents the difference between the nominal value of the shares issued prior to the capital reduction by the Company (being the carrying value of the investment in Marks and Spencer plc) and the share capital, share premium and capital redemption reserve of Marks and Spencer plc at the date of the transaction.
2. Amounts 'reclassified and reported in profit or loss' includes the revaluation of the cross currency swaps, offsetting the revaluation of the US dollar hedged bonds within finance costs.
3. In the prior year financial statements, the foreign exchange reserve was presented within Retained earnings.

CONSOLIDATED STATEMENT OF CASH FLOWS

	Notes	53 weeks ended 1 April 2017 £m	53 weeks ended 2 April 2016 £m
Cash flows from operating activities			
Cash generated from operations	26	**1,165.7**	1,311.3
Income tax paid		**(98.0)**	(99.3)
Net cash inflow from operating activities		**1,067.7**	1,212.0
Cash flows from investing activities			
Proceeds on property disposals		**27.0**	30.6
Purchase of property, plant and equipment		**(309.1)**	(363.3)
Purchase of intangible assets		**(101.1)**	(186.8)
Reduction/(purchase) of current financial assets		**4.6**	(7.2)
Interest received		**6.6**	6.8
Acquisition of subsidiary		**–**	(56.2)
Net cash used in investing activities		**(372.0)**	(576.1)
Cash flows from financing activities			
Interest paid[1]		**(111.2)**	(113.5)
Cash (outflow)/inflow from borrowings		**(32.7)**	3.1
Repayment of syndicated loan notes		**(215.3)**	(19.9)
Issuance of medium-term notes		**300.0**	–
Decrease in obligations under finance leases		**(2.0)**	(2.4)
Payment of liability to the Marks & Spencer UK Pension Scheme		**(57.9)**	(56.0)
Equity dividends paid		**(377.5)**	(301.7)
Shares issued on exercise of employee share options		**5.5**	20.6
Purchase of own shares by employee trust		**–**	(10.9)
Share buy back		**–**	(150.7)
Net cash used in financing activities		**(491.1)**	(631.4)
Net cash inflow from activities		**204.6**	4.5
Effects of exchange rate changes		**5.6**	3.7
Opening net cash		**196.0**	187.8
Closing net cash	27	**406.2**	196.0

1. Includes interest on the partnership liability to the Marks & Spencer UK Pension Scheme.

	Notes	53 weeks ended 1 April 2017 £m	53 weeks ended 2 April 2016 £m
Reconciliation of net cash flow to movement in net debt			
Opening net debt		**(2,138.3)**	(2,223.2)
Net cash inflow from activities		**204.6**	4.5
(Decrease)/increase in current financial assets		**(4.6)**	7.2
Decrease in debt financing		**7.9**	75.2
Exchange and other non-cash movements		**(4.3)**	(2.0)
Movement in net debt		**203.6**	84.9
Closing net debt	27	**(1,934.7)**	(2,138.3)

Intermediate Accounting 17E: List of Accounts

A

Accounts Payable
Accounts Receivable
Accrued Liabilities
Accumulated Depreciation
Accumulated Depreciation—Buildings
Accumulated Depreciation—Equipment
Accumulation Depreciation—Machinery
Accumulated Depreciation—Plant Assets
Accumulated Depreciation—Trucks
Adjustment to Record Inventory at Cost
Administrative Expenses
Admissions Revenue
Advances to Employees
Advertising Expense
Allowance for Doubtful Accounts
Allowance for Expropriation
Allowance for Sales Returns and Allowances
Allowance to Reduce Deferred Tax Asset to Expected Realizable Value
Allowance to Reduce Inventory to LIFO
Allowance to Reduce Inventory to Market
Amortization Expense
Asset Retirement Obligation

B

Bad Debt Expense
Billings on Construction in Process
Bond Issue Expense
Bond Sinking Fund
Bonds Payable
Buildings

C

Call Option
Cash
Cash Over and Short
Cash Surrender Value of Life Insurance
Coal Mine
Commission Expense
Commission Payable
Commission Revenue
Common Stock
Common Stock Dividend Distributable
Compensation Expense
Computer Software Costs
Construction Expenses
Construction in Process
Contract Asset
Contract Liability
Contribution Expense
Contribution Revenue
Convertible Preferred Stock
Copyrights
Cost of Goods Sold
Cost of Installment Sales
Costs of Construction
Current Maturity of Long-Term Debt

D

Dealer's Fund Reserve
Debt Conversion Expense
Debt Investments
Deferred Gross Profit
Deferred Tax Asset
Deferred Tax Liability
Delivery Expense
Depreciation Expense
Direct Labor
Discount on Bonds Payable
Discount on Notes Payable
Discount on Notes Receivable
Dividend Receivable
Dividend Revenue
Dividends
Dividends Payable
Due from Factor
Due to Customer
Dues Revenue

E

Entertainment Expense
Equipment
Equity Investments
Estimated Inventory Returns
Estimated Liability on Purchase Commitments
Executory Costs
Executory Costs Payable

F

Factory Overhead
Fair Value Adjustment
FICA Taxes Payable
Finance Charge
Finance Expense
Finance Revenue
Finished Goods Inventory
Franchise Revenue
Franchises
Freight-In
Freight-Out
FUTA Taxes Payable
Futures Contract

G

Gain on Disposal of Equipment
Gain on Disposal of Land
Gain on Disposal of Machinery
Gain on Disposal of Plant Assets
Gain on Disposal of Trucks
Gain on Redemption of Bonds
Gain on Repossession
Gain on Restructuring of Debt
Gain on Sale of Investments
Gain on Sale of Land
Gain on Sale of Machinery
Gain on Sale of Plant Assets
Gain on Settlement of ARO
Goodwill
Green Fees Revenue

I

Income Summary
Income Tax Expense
Income Taxes Payable
Income Taxes Receivable
Income Tax Refund Receivable
Installment Accounts Receivable
Installment Sales Revenue
Insurance Expense
Insurance Premium Payable
Insurance Revenue
Intangible Assets
Interest Expense
Interest Payable
Interest Receivable
Interest Revenue
Inventory
Inventory on Consignment
Inventory Over and Short
Investment Revenue
Investments
Investments in Common Stock
Investments in Stocks and Bonds

L

Land
Land Improvements
Lawsuit Liability
Lawsuit Loss
Lease Liability
Lease Receivable
Leased Buildings
Leased Equipment
Liability under Stock-Appreciation Plan
Litigation Expense or Loss
Litigation Liability
Loss Due to Market Decline of Inventory
Loss from Expropriation
Loss from Long-Term Contracts
Loss on ARO Settlement
Loss on Capital Lease
Loss on Disposal of Equipment
Loss on Disposal of Land
Loss on Disposal of Machinery
Loss on Disposal of Plant Assets
Loss on Disposal of Trucks
Loss on Impairment
Loss on Investments
Loss on Redemption of Bonds
Loss on Repossession
Loss on Sale of Investments
Loss on Sale of Receivables

Loss on Settlement of Call Option
Loss on Settlement of Put Option

M

Machinery
Maintenance and Repairs Expense
Materials
Memo entry
Miscellaneous Expense
Mortgage Payable

N

No entry
Noncontrolling Interest
Notes Payable
Notes Receivable

O

Office Expense
Oil Platform
Operating Expenses
Organization Expense
Other Comprehensive Income (G/L)
Other Comprehensive Income (PSC)
Other Expense
Other Revenue
Owner's Capital
Owner's Drawings

P

Paid-in Capital from Treasury Stock
Paid-in Capital in Excess of Par—Common Stock
Paid-in Capital in Excess of Par—Preferred Stock
Paid-in Capital in Excess of Stated Value—Common Stock
Paid-in Capital—Expired Stock Options
Paid-in Capital—Stock Options
Paid-in Capital—Stock Warrants
Patents
Payroll Tax Expense
Payroll Taxes Payable
Pension Asset/Liability
Pension Expense
Pension Obligation
Petty Cash
Plant Assets
Postage Expense
Postretirement Asset/Liability
Postretirement Expense
Preferred Stock
Premium Expense
Premium Inventory
Premium Liability
Premium on Bonds Payable
Prepaid Advertising
Prepaid Expenses
Prepaid Insurance
Prepaid Lease Executory Costs
Prepaid Rent
Property Dividends Payable
Property Tax Expense
Property Taxes Payable
Purchase Discounts
Purchase Discounts Lost
Purchase Returns and Allowances
Purchases
Put Option

R

Raw Materials
Realized Gross Profit
Recourse Liability
Recovery of Loss from Impairment
Rent Expense
Rent Payable
Rent Receivable
Rent Revenue
Repossessed Merchandise
Research and Development Expense
Restricted Cash
Retained Earnings
Returnable Deposit
Returned Inventory
Revenue from Consignment Sales
Revenue from Franchise Fees
Revenue from Investment
Revenue from Long-Term Contracts

S

Salaries and Wages Expense
Salaries and Wages Payable
Sales Commission Expense
Sales Commissions Payable
Sales Discounts
Sales Discounts Forfeited
Sales Returns and Allowances
Sales Revenue
Sales Tax Expense
Sales Taxes Payable
Selling Expenses
Service Revenue
Shipping Expense
Supplies
Supplies Expense
SUTA Taxes Payable
Swap Contract

T

Telephone and Internet Expense
Timber
Timberland
Trademarks
Trade Names
Trading Securities
Travel Expense
Treasury Stock
Trucks

U

Unamortized Bond Issue Costs
Unearned Admissions Revenue
Unearned Advertising Revenue
Unearned Compensation
Unearned Dues Revenue
Unearned Franchise Revenue
Unearned Profit on Sale-Leaseback
Unearned Rent Revenue
Unearned Revenue
Unearned Sales Revenue
Unearned Service Revenue
Unearned Subscriptions Revenue
Unearned Warranty Revenue
Union Dues Payable
Unrealized Holding Gain or Loss—Equity
Unrealized Holding Gain or Loss—Income
Utilities Expenses

W

Warranty Expense
Warranty Liability
Warranty Payable
Warranty Revenue
Withholding Taxes Payable
Work-in-Process
Write-Off of Goodwill
Write-Off of Inventory

Index

D

E

T

U

V

W

X

Y

I-13